FINANCE

AN INTRODUCTION

FOURTH EDITION

FINANCE

AN INTRODUCTION

FOURTH EDITION

HERBERT B. MAYO

Trenton State College

The Dryden Press
A Harcourt Brace Jovanovich College Publisher
Fort Worth Philadelphia San Diego New York Orlando Austin San Antonio
Toronto Montreal London Sydney Tokyo

Acquisitions Editor: Ann Heath
Project Editor: Susan Jansen
Art and Design Supervisor: Annette Spadoni
Production Manager: Bob Lange
Director of Editing, Design, and Production: Jane Perkins

Copy Editor: Pamela Johnson
Compositor: G&S Typesetters
Text Type: 10/12 Baskerville

Library of Congress Cataloging-in-Publication Data
Mayo, Herbert B.
Finance : an introduction / Herbert B. Mayo. — 4th ed.
p. cm.
Includes index.
ISBN 0-03-055018-1
1. Finance. I. Title.
HG173.M395 1991
658.15—dc20 91-475
CIP

Printed in the United States of America
123-016-987654321

Address orders:
The Dryden Press
Orlando, Florida 32887

Address editorial correspondence:
The Dryden Press
301 Commerce Street, Suite 3700
Fort Worth, TX 76102

The Dryden Press
Harcourt Brace Jovanovich

In memory of Mildred

The Dryden Press Series in Finance

Berry and Young
Managing Investments: A Case Approach

Boyet
Security Analysis for Investment Decisions: Text and Software

Brigham
Fundamentals of Financial Management, *Sixth Edition*

Brigham and Gapenski
Cases in Financial Management

Brigham and Gapenski
Cases in Financial Management: Module A

Brigham and Gapenski
Cases in Financial Management: Module B

Brigham and Gapenski
Cases in Financial Management: Module C

Brigham and Gapenski
Financial Management: Theory and Practice, *Sixth Edition*

Brigham and Gapenski
Intermediate Financial Management, *Third Edition*

Brigham, Gapenski, and Aberwald
Finance with Lotus 1-2-3, *Second Edition*

Campsey and Brigham
Introduction to Financial Management, *Third Edition*

Chance
An Introduction to Options and Futures, *Second Edition*

Cooley
Advances in Business Financial Management: A Collection of Readings

Cooley and Roden
Business Financial Management, *Second Edition*

Curran
Principles of Corporate Finance

Evans
International Finance: A Markets Approach

Fama and Miller
The Theory of Finance

Gardner and Mills
Managing Financial Institutions: An Asset/Liability Approach, *Second Edition*

Gitman and Joehnk
Personal Financial Planning, *Fifth Edition*

Goldstein Software, Inc.
Joe Spreadsheet

Harrington
Case Studies in Financial Decision Making, *Second Edition*

Hayes and Meerschwam
Financial Institutions: Contemporary Cases in the Financial Services Industry

Johnson
Issues and Readings in Managerial Finance, *Third Edition*

Kidwell and Peterson
Financial Institutions, Markets, and Money, *Fourth Edition*

Koch
Bank Management, *Second Edition*

Lee and Finnerty
Corporate Finance: Theory, Method, and Application

Maisel
Real Estate Finance, *Second Edition*

Martin, Cox, and MacMinn
The Theory of Finance: Evidence and Applications

Mayo
Finance: An Introduction, *Fourth Edition*

Mayo
Investments: An Introduction, *Third Edition*

Pettijohn
PROFIT +

Reilly
Investment Analysis and Portfolio Management, *Third Edition*

Reilly
Investments, *Third Edition*

Seitz
Capital Budgeting and Long-Term Financing Decisions

Siegel and Siegel
Futures Markets

Smith and Spudeck
Interest Rates: Principles and Applications

Stickney
Financial Statement Analysis: A Strategic Perspective

Turnbull
Option Valuation

Weston and Brigham
Essentials of Managerial Finance, *Ninth Edition*

Weston and Copeland
Managerial Finance, *Ninth Edition*

Wood and Wood
Financial Markets

PREFACE

When I was an undergraduate, I had no real conception of how I would spend my life. I was even uncertain as to my major field of study. Like many students, I sampled a variety of subjects for any number of reasons. In retrospect, such sampling provided me with not only breadth (if not depth) of knowledge but also with a better definition of my likes and dislikes.

Many students have followed a similar pattern of taking a variety of courses, and no doubt many more will do so in the future. Introductory courses and textbooks thus can play an extremely important role in their development, exposing students to a discipline about which they may have virtually no awareness. Time constraints, of course, mean such courses cannot cover material in depth, but they can whet a student's appetite for further study in the area.

Even within a general area of study such as business administration or education, students may receive only a brief exposure to particular fields. Most business students receive only a sampling of the various functional areas of business administration. An accounting major, for example, may take just one course in marketing or management, and a marketing major may take only one course in finance. It is for these students that this text is written. Since many aspects of business and business administration involve finance, it is desirable for specialists in the various disciplines of business to have some knowledge of financial institutions, investments, and business finance. While many students may have only this one exposure to the subject, it should give them a working knowledge of the terms, environment, and mechanics of finance and financial decision making.

Besides introducing the finance student to the world of finance, a major purpose of the text is to entice the non-finance major to do more work in this field. Faculty members naturally want students to pursue their own area of specialty. I want students to take advanced courses in the field, for such advanced work is more stimulating for the instructor. But the fact remains that introductory courses are the bread and butter of teaching. Such courses have the largest enrollments and are a main source of demand for the faculty's services. These courses do offer the instructor an excellent opportunity to encourage and entice students to continue studying in the field, and a clearly written and stimulating text can be of considerable help in encouraging students to take additional courses.

CHANGES FROM THE PREVIOUS EDITION

While the previous edition was a complete restructuring of *Finance: An Introduction,* this edition is primarily a refining and development of that restructuring. The division of the text into the three areas of finance—financial institutions, investments, and business finance—has been retained. No chapters have been added or deleted, but virtually every chapter has been revised to introduce new material, to refine existing material and increase clarity, and to update where appropriate. Specific changes are as follows:

1. Chapter 2 now emphasizes the creation of financial assets and the transfer of funds from savers to users. Investment banking has been shifted to this chapter, and the role of interest rates and the term structure of yields has been expanded.
2. Chapter 3 is exclusively devoted to the variety of financial intermediaries, and a discussion of the savings and loan debacle has been added.
3. Chapter 4 combines the roles of fiscal and monetary policy. The creation of money and credit is integrated with the tools of monetary policy. This discussion has been streamlined, and the use of T-accounts has been deleted. A section on target growth in the money supply has been added.
4. Chapter 5 on international finance has been completely revised, especially the material on the balance of payments.
5. Chapter 6 is now exclusively devoted to secondary markets. Material on short selling, the use of margin, and efficient financial markets has been added.
6. Chapter 7 on the time value of money has additional illustrations, such as the determination of a mortgage repayment schedule.
7. Risk and its measurement (Chapter 8) are particularly hard topics to present in an introductory text. Material on expected return and correlation coefficients has been added. Discussions of the sources of risk and the use of standard deviations to measure risk have been rewritten.
8. The calculation of the yield to maturity in Chapter 9 has been expanded to further illustrate the mechanics of the calculation.
9. The material in Chapter 10 on dividend policy and the retention of earnings to finance growth has been increased.
10. Chapter 13, which introduces futures and options, now includes put options.
11. Part Three on business finance has been the most extensively revised of the three divisions of the text. The material in Chapter 15 on de-

preciation has been expanded to better explain the half-year convention for the application of depreciation, and the carry-back and carry-forward of losses for corporate tax purposes have been illustrated.

12. Chapter 16 on the analysis of financial statements has a new section on the statement of cash flows that replaces the material on the statement of changes in financial position. The section on the DuPont system has been rewritten to clarify and better illustrate the analysis.
13. Chapter 17 now combines operating and financial leverage. Leverage is also tied into stock valuation.
14. Chapter 19 on the management of short-term assets includes more material on the weakness in the EOQ; the calculation of maximum, minimum, and average inventory using the EOQ; and the calculation of true annualized yields on short-term money market securities. Analogous material on the calculation of the true annualized cost of short-term credit is presented in Chapter 20.
15. The material on lease versus buy in Chapter 21 has been recast in terms of cash flows. The conditions under which lease payments must be capitalized have been illustrated.
16. Chapter 22 on the cost of capital has been completely recast to include (1) more than one means to determine the cost of equity, (2) the difference between the cost of retained earnings and the cost of new equity, and (3) the marginal cost of capital.
17. The linkage between valuation and capital budgeting has been added to Chapter 23. The material on payback has been tightened, and the material on risk analysis in capital budgeting has been expanded. The refunding decision has been added as an illustration of capital budgeting.
18. Hostile takeovers, leveraged buyouts, and prepackaged bankruptcies have been added to Chapter 24.

In addition to the specific changes enumerated above, several modifications are applied throughout the text. Marginal definitions of terms are now provided when the term is introduced, and figures and exhibits contain brief textual descriptions. Several reviewers suggested adding harder problems or more realistic problems. To meet both suggestions, I have added several problems cast as cases. These are more involved and perceptibly harder than the problems associated with the chapters.

Several features from the previous edition have been retained, including the boxed inserts "Financial Facts" and "The Job Mart," which provides descriptions of careers. The study of finance can lead to an exciting career, but students may not be aware of many of the occupations that employ the material introduced in this text. The job descriptions are based on ads that were placed in *The Wall Street Journal* and the *New York Times*. While these positions are not entry-level jobs, they do give an indication of possible careers in finance and may encourage individuals to pursue advanced work in the discipline.

PEDAGOGICAL FEATURES

The text is constructed with the beginning student in mind. First, the chapters are compact and direct. No attempt is made to pad the text with theoretical subtleties and exceptions. Students will have plenty of opportunity to build on this base if they choose to do so in the future. Second, all the examples in the text are relatively simple, for complex examples are not needed to clarify the points being discussed. The numerical examples employ simple arithmetic, and small numbers are used in these examples. Of course, in the real world a firm will not have sales of $100 or expenses of $80, but this text is seeking not to illustrate the complexity of the real world but to clarify a point in finance. Third, there is a minimum of footnotes and few references in the text to the academic and professional literature. Students interested in doing further study may consult the reading lists at the end of each chapter.

Finance employs many tools and concepts taught in introductory courses in accounting and economics. Knowledge of certain aspects of economics and accounting is desirable if the student is to have a good grasp of basic finance. Even though the student may have had a course or courses in either or both subjects, this text will review material pertinent to finance. Thus, this text may also be used by the student who wants an introduction to the world of finance but who lacks any formal coursework in economics or accounting.

Besides the text material, each chapter has additional aids for the student. Each chapter begins with a set of **learning objectives,** which identify topics to look for and learn as the chapter develops. Each objective is stated using an action verb such as "differentiate" or "define" or "describe." The choice of the verb gives the student an indication as to how the material may be learned. For example, the objective "Differentiate systematic and unsystematic risk" directs the student to learn how these sources of risk differ. Without such knowledge, it is difficult to understand why systematic risk is more important from an aggregate view of risk management.

Each chapter includes **review questions** and, where appropriate, **problems.** The questions and problems are straightforward and are designed primarily to review the material. The instructor's manual includes points to consider when answering the questions, as well as solutions to the problems. Similar problems are also provided in the instructor's manual.

The chapters end with annotated **suggested readings** intended to give the student a brief description of selected bibliography. These readings are drawn from a wide cross-section of the literature on finance. However, the references are generally not technical, and while they may require serious reading, they should be accessible to the student using this text.

An *Instructor's Manual and Test Bank* is available to instructors who adopt the book. The manual contains teaching guides for questions and problems in the text, as well as true/false and multiple choice test questions and answers. A set of additional problems and questions can be used for homework assignments or as extra test items. The *Test Bank* is also available in computerized form for the IBM PC.

A *Study Guide and Workbook in Finance,* which includes chapter outlines and summaries, problem illustrations, and fill-in-the-blank, multiple choice, and true-false questions, is available for the student.

ACKNOWLEDGMENTS

A book like this evolves and develops over time. I owe considerable debt to the many students who endured classes and tests in which I experimented with the examples, questions, and techniques that are incorporated in this text. The students' criticisms (often implicit in the looks on their faces) helped me mold my writing style and develop the examples and questions needed to communicate the concepts and tools of financial analysis.

I owe considerable debt to reviewers who over the various editions offered extensive comments and suggestions, many of which I was able to incorporate into the final manuscript. For this edition, I would like to extend a special thank you to

Rahul Bishnoi, Hofstra University
Tom Geary, University of Phoenix
Tom Hamilton, University of Wyoming
John McGinnis, Penn State University
Mary Myles, Jackson State University
Knowles Parker, Wake Technical Community College
Anand Shetty, Hagan School of Business, Iona College
Marianne Westerman, University of Colorado–Denver
Elizabeth Yelland, North Hennepin Community College

POSSIBLE ORGANIZATIONS OF AN INTRODUCTORY FINANCE COURSE

Finance: An Introduction has 25 chapters. Few, if any, instructors will complete all of the chapters during one semester. One major advantage offered by this text is its adaptability to several different approaches. If the course is a true survey of the field, the instructor may select material from all three sections of the text. The most appropriate chapters for a general approach would include Chapters 2–6 on financial institutions; Chapter 7 (time value of money); Chapters 9–11 on stocks and bonds; Chapter 14 on investment companies; and the corporate finance chapters, especially Chapters 15–17, 19, 20, 22, and 23.

An alternative strategy is to approach the study of finance through investments. Because students often have a natural interest in investments, the course may be built around this topic. Additional work on corporate finance can come later in the students' academic careers and can build upon the foundation laid by the initial course. This approach would stress the chapters in Part Two; the chapters that cover the financial markets (Chapters 2–6); and those corporate finance chapters that aid in investment analysis (Chapters 15–16 on the analysis of financial statements). Coverage of the material on the management of cash, financial leverage, mergers, and bankruptcy may also be included in a course that stresses investments.

If the course is primarily a corporate finance course, the emphasis will be on Part Three of the text. However, the material in Chapters 2 and 5 (investment banking and international finance) should also be included, along with Chapters 7–11 (time value of money, analysis of risk, corporate bonds and stock, and security valuation). A possible course sequence might be Chapters 1 and 2, 7–12, and 15–25; this sequence covers the material usually taught in a traditional business finance course.

Over the years, the editorial staff at Dryden has been a joy to work with. The production crew for this book maintained that high quality of professionalism and gentle encouragement that facilitate the completion of a text. In particular, I would like to thank Ann Heath, who as my editor always encourages and prods me to put forth more effort; Jennifer Lloyd, Ann's assistant who secured reviews on time; Susan Jansen, who efficiently took the manuscript through production; and Pamela Johnson, who served as an exceptionally detailed copy editor.

I was once asked if I seriously consider comments from readers and reviewers. The answer is unequivocally "Yes!" Individuals reading the text know what is not clear, so I invite all readers to send me your comments, both complimentary or critical. Either will be appreciated. I may be reached at 85 Linvale Rd., Ringoes, NJ 08551.

Brief Contents

part three Corporate Finance 437

Contents

chapter

1

Introduction to Finance

Learning Objectives

1	Differentiate the areas of finance.
2	Illustrate why a source of finance to one economic unit, such as a firm, requires an investment by another economic unit.
3	Identify the sources of return and the sources of risk.
4	Isolate the criterion used in finance to judge performance.
5	Recognize the importance of finance to both your career and your personal life.

"Nothing endures but change."

"Times change and we change with them."

"Princes come and princes go."

These three quotes from Heraclitus, Lothair, and the musical *Kismet* are exceptionally apropos to finance. Yesterday's major success stories may be today's failures. Leading retailers like Federated Department Stores declared bankruptcy. Major financial personalities in the 1980s fell from grace as was illustrated by Michael Milken and Donald Trump. Other firms and their managers, however, achieved surprising success. Leslie Wexler led The Limited from a small operation to one of the most successful and largest retailers at the beginning of 1990. Warren Buffett of Berkshire Hathaway achieved star status for his ability to consistently identify superior stock investments. The result of his investment decisions was to convert a small investment in his company's stock into over $1,000,000.

The ability to innovate, to anticipate, to adapt, and to change is required for success in business. This is true for all the functional areas of business: marketing, management, and finance. You may not enjoy change; it may be very disruptive. But to be successful and to maintain that success, you must change. That is one of the prime reasons for education in business. While studying business administration will increase your capacity to work in a business environment, it should also increase your capacity to adjust to change.

Finance ▲
The study of money and its management

Finance, which is the study of money and its management, has been very fluid during the last twenty years. Money market mutual funds, interest-bearing checking accounts, organized exchanges for options, financial futures, and flexible exchange rates did not exist twenty years ago. Americans could not legally own gold bullion, and banks were limited as to the maximum rate of interest they could pay to depositors. Some aspects of the federal tax code are changed every year, and the Internal Revenue Service continually issues rulings on how the current tax code is to be interpreted.

Of course, the ever-fluid world of finance is a crucial component of any business. While business administration involves the study of business operations and their management, finance is the study of money and its management. Successful business administration requires successful financial management. No matter how large or small the operation, someone has to make financial plans and financial decisions. Constructing meaningful plans that will help achieve successful management requires knowledge of (1) financial institutions and how they function within the economy, (2) the alternative investments available for inclusion in a portfolio, and (3) the techniques used by portfolio managers and

FIGURE 1.1

The Composition of Finance

The components of finance are interdependent.

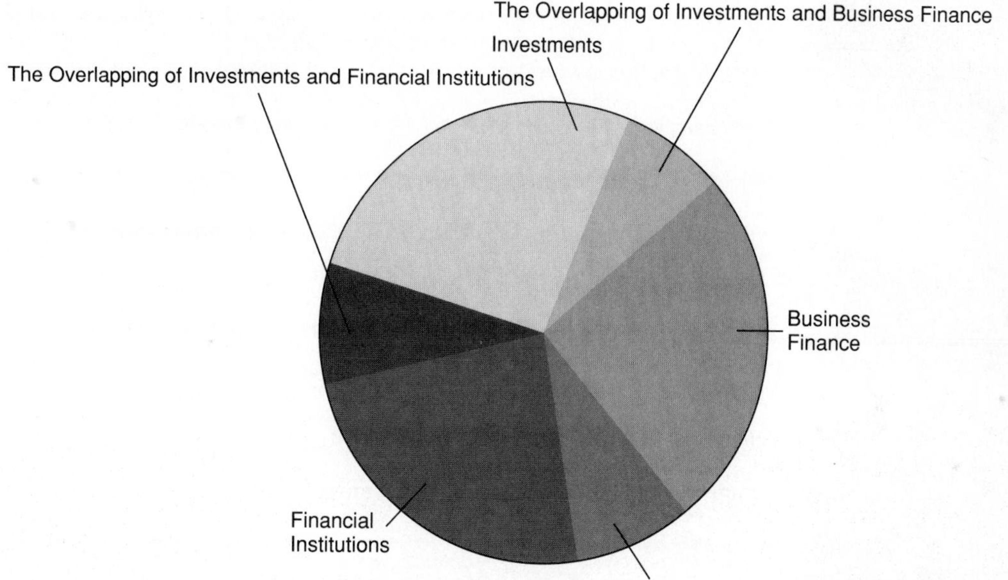

financial managers to reach financial decisions. This text will introduce you to all three aspects of finance.

Finance as a discipline is generally divided into these three areas: financial institutions, investments, and business finance. The divisions are somewhat arbitrary, and they certainly overlap. This is illustrated in Figure 1.1, which presents the areas of finance as three overlapping pieces of a pie. While any one of the three may be studied alone (and many colleges and universities offer courses devoted to each specific area), they should be viewed as interdependent. Investment decisions and corporate financing decisions are made within the current financial environment and its institutions. And business finance is not independent of investments. For a firm to be able to issue and sell new securities, there must be individuals who are willing to invest in and buy the new securities.

The study of financial institutions, as the name implies, is concerned with the institutional aspects of the discipline, which encompass the creation of financial assets, the markets for trading securities (e.g., the New York Stock Exchange), and the regulation of financial markets. Financial assets are created through investment bankers and financial intermediaries such as commercial banks, savings and loan associations, and life insurance companies. Each of these financial firms transfers the savings of individuals to firms needing funds, and this transfer produces financial assets. Once these financial assets are created, many may subsequently be bought and sold in the secondary markets. These security markets transfer billions of dollars of financial assets among investors ranging from individuals with small amounts to invest to large corporate giants.

The study of investments is primarily concerned with the analysis of individual assets and the construction of optimal portfolios. Such portfolios will earn the highest return for a given amount of risk. The study of investments encompasses financial planning, specifying the investor's financial goals, analyzing various securities that the individual may acquire, and constructing diversified portfolios. Of course, investment decisions are not made in a vacuum, and the financial environment can play a major role in the investment decision process. Certainly taxation, the monetary policy of the Federal Reserve, and the flow of information that publicly held firms are required to provide stockholders can and do affect the decision to buy or sell specific assets.

The study of corporate or business finance emphasizes the role of the financial manager. The financial manager must make certain that the firm can meet its obligations as they come due, determine which are the best sources of financing for the firm, and allocate the firm's resources among competing investment alternatives. The financial manager has a large and demanding job; in a large corporation, this job is usually performed by a staff that reports to a vice-president of finance. Of course, the management of a small business must also make many of the same decisions, but these individuals often have fewer resources to devote to financial management.

Corporate financial management decisions, like investment decisions, are made in the same economic and regulatory environment. In a sense, investments and business finance are the opposite sides of the same coin. The securities issued by firms are owned by investors. Both financial managers and investors, be they creditors or owners, want the firm to be successful. If the firm fails, its creditors such as its bondholders as well as its stockholders will sustain losses. Many of the concepts that apply to an individual's investment decisions apply to corporate financial management. The tools used to analyze a firm from an investor's perspective may also be used by the firm's financial managers. The measurement of risk and return, the construction of a diversified portfolio of assets, the valuation of assets, and the evaluation of performance apply both to investments and to corporate financial management.

While individual investors may work alone, a firm's financial manager must work within the framework of the business. Marketing and managing decisions can have important implications for the firm's financial well-being. Virtually every business decision has a financial implication, and financial resources are often a major constraint on the firm's non-financial personnel. It is certainly desirable for individuals in marketing, human resources, data processing, and planning to understand at least the basic concepts of finance and the role of the financial manager. Such understanding may lead to better communication, the creation of better data for decision making, and better integration of the various components of the business.

Finance is a relatively young and derivative discipline. It builds upon accounting and economic concepts and assumes that the student has had some background in these subjects. This background need not be extensive, but it is important. While this text does review some economic and accounting concepts, it is assumed that the student does bring some prior knowledge of these concepts to the study of finance.

KEY FINANCIAL CONCEPTS

Three crucial concepts appear throughout this text. While they cannot be fully developed in this introductory chapter, they should be introduced so the student is aware of them. The first is the source of finance used by a firm. Firms can acquire assets only if someone puts up the funds. For every dollar that the firm invests, someone must invest that dollar in the firm.

The second concept centers around risk and return. Individuals and firms make investments in order to earn a return, but that return is not certain. All financial decisions involve risk. The third concept is valuation, or what an asset is worth. Because the return earned by an asset occurs in the future, the anticipated cash flow to be generated by the asset must be expressed in the present. That is, the asset must be valued in today's dollars in order to determine whether or not to make the investment. Since the goal of financial management is usually specified as the maximization of the value of the firm, the valuation of assets is probably individually the most crucial concept covered in this text.

Sources of Finance

Finance is concerned with the management of assets, especially financial assets, and the sources of finance used to acquire the assets. These sources and the assets that a firm owns are often summarized in a financial statement called a **balance sheet.** A balance sheet enumerates at a moment in time what an economic unit, such as a firm, owns—its **assets;** what it owes, its **liabilities;** and the owners' contributions to the firm, the **equity.**

Balance sheet ▲
Financial statement that enumerates (as of a point in time) what an economic unit owns and owes and its net worth

Assets ▲
Item or property owned by a firm, household, or government and valued in monetary terms

Other economic units, such as a household or a government, may also have a balance sheet that lists what is owned (assets) and what is owed (liabilities). However, since there are no owners, the equity section may be given a different name. For example, the difference between the assets and the liabilities might be referred to as the person's "net worth" or "estate."

While the construction of financial statements is explained in Chapter 16, the following balance sheet can serve as a simple introduction:

ASSETS		LIABILITIES AND EQUITY	
Total assets	$100	Liabilities	$ 40
		Equity	60
	$100		$100

Liabilities ▲
What an economic unit owes expressed in monetary terms

Equity ▲
Assets minus liabilities; net worth; the investment in a firm by its stockholders

Notice that the economic unit, a firm, has $100 in assets. It could not have acquired these assets unless someone (or some other firm) put up the funds. In this example, $40 was lent to the firm, and the lenders have a legal claim on the firm. The equity ($60) represents the funds invested by the owners, who also have a claim on the firm. The nature of the owners' claim, however, is different because the firm does not owe them anything. Instead, the owners receive the benefits and bear the risks associated with controlling the firm.

Both the creditors who have lent funds to the firm and the individuals who own the firm are investors. Both groups are sources of the capital that will subsequently be invested in the firm's assets. It is important to realize that creditors as well as owners are investors; the difference lies in the nature of their respective claims. The creditors have a legal claim that the borrower must meet; the owners do not have such a claim. The creditors and the owners, however, are both willing to make their respective investments in anticipation of earning a return, and both bear the risk associated with their investments.

A large part of this text is devoted to the sources of finance and their subsequent investment by the firm's financial managers. For example, Chapters 19 and 23 are devoted to the management of current and long-term assets, while Chapters 9–12, 20, and 21 consider various sources of finance. It is important to understand the interdependence between the firm that uses the funds and the investors who supply the funds. Bonds, for example, are a major source of long-term funds for many firms, but it should be remembered that individuals buy the bonds that a firm (or government) issues. The sale of the bonds is a source of finance to the firm, while the purchase of the bonds is a use of investors' funds. The basic features of the bonds, however, are the same for both the issuer and the buyer.

Risk and Return

All investments are made because the individual or management anticipates earning a **return.** Without the expectation of a return, an asset would not be acquired. While assets may generate this return in different ways, the sources of return are the income generated and/or price appreciation. For example, one individual may buy stock in anticipation of dividend income and/or capital gains (price appreciation). Another individual may place funds in a savings account because he or she hopes to earn interest income. The financial manager of a firm may invest in a

Return ▲
What is earned on an investment; the sum of income and capital gains generated by an investment

particular piece of equipment in hopes that the equipment will generate cash flow and profits. A real estate investor may acquire land in order to develop it and sell the properties at an anticipated higher price. And the financial manager of a nonprofit institution may acquire short-term securities issued by the federal government in anticipation of the interest earned.

In each case, the investment is made in anticipation of a return in the future. However, the expected return may not be attained. That is the element of risk. **Risk** is the *uncertainty that an expected return may not be achieved.* All investments involve some element of risk. Even the funds deposited in a federally insured savings account are at risk if the rate of inflation exceeds the interest rate earned. In that case, the investor sustains a loss of purchasing power. The individual certainly would not have made that investment if such a loss had been anticipated; instead, an alternative course of action would have been selected.

Risk ▲
Possibility of loss; the uncertainty that the anticipated return will not be achieved

Although the word "risk" generally has a negative connotation, it should be noted that the uncertainty of achieving the expected return may be positive. The asset may earn a return that exceeds the expected return. For example, a person who purchased the stock of NCR in November 1990, when the stock was selling for less than $60 a share, earned a large return when the stock sold for over $90 a share in December in response to AT&T's merger offer. A price increase from $60 to $90 is a 50 percent increase ($30/$60), which occurred in less than a few days and must have exceeded most investors' anticipated return.

Since financial decisions are made in the present but the results occur in the future, risk permeates financial decision making. The future is not certain; it is only expected. However, possible sources of risk can be identified, and to some extent, risk can be managed. The sources of risk are

1. Diversifiable risk
   a. business risk
   b. financial risk
2. Non-diversifiable risk
   a. market risk
   b. interest rate risk
   c. purchasing power risk
   d. exchange rate risk

Diversifiable risks are related to specific assets, and as the name implies, may be reduced through the construction of a diversified portfolio of assets. Diversification is achieved through the construction of a portfolio consisting of a variety of assets. When the portfolio is diversified, events that reduce the return on a particular asset increase the return on another. For example, higher oil prices may benefit oil drilling operations but may hurt users of petroleum products. By combining both in the portfolio, the investor reduces the risk associated with investing in either the oil producer or the oil consumer.

Business risk refers to the nature of the business and how it is operated. Rapid changes in consumer taste leading to fluctuations in demand, the types of assets needed for operations, and the speed of technological change all affect business risk. Some firms operate in industries that are inherently more risky than others. For example, American and United airlines have a large amount of business risk. They operate in a very competitive business that requires substantial investments in equipment. Airlines face many uncertainties, such as possible changes in fuel prices, union contracts, government regulation, and the air traffic control system. Firms that face such uncertainties have large amounts of business risk—risk that is inherent in the industries in which they operate.

Business risk ▲
Risk associated with the nature of a business

Financial risk refers to the ways in which management chooses to finance the firm. As shown in the simple balance sheet presented earlier in the chapter, there are two basic sources of financing: creditors' funds and owners' funds. The management of American and United airlines, for example, must decide how to finance their airplanes. Should the airline issue debt to creditors or seek to sell additional stock? Should the aircraft be leased or purchased? Should the firm pay less dividends and retain more earnings to pay for the planes? These questions illustrate some of the financing decisions facing the management of an airline, or any firm. How management chooses to answer these questions affects the financial risk associated with the firm.

Financial risk ▲
Risk associated with the types of financing used to acquire assets

The use of debt financing, or borrowed funds, is called "financial leverage." Sometimes it is referred to as "trading on the equity." The prime advantage of borrowing funds instead of increasing equity is that the successful use of financial leverage may increase the return to the firm's owners. If the firm earns more with the funds than it must pay in interest, the additional return accrues to the equity (this concept is explained in detail in Chapter 17). By borrowing funds and successfully using financial leverage (for example, by borrowing funds at 10 percent and using them to earn 12 percent), management increases the return to the equity. However, if management unsuccessfully uses financial leverage (if it borrows at 10 percent but earns only 8 percent), the return to the equity is reduced.

The use of borrowed funds commits the firm to several legal obligations. These obligations vary with such factors as the amount of the loan; the length of time, or the "term," that the loan is outstanding; and the creditworthiness of the borrower. Each loan is an individual package, and individual loans may have subtle features that differentiate them from others. If a firm fails to meet the terms of the loan, its creditors can take the firm to court to enforce the obligations. Such legal obligations increase the element of risk. Thus, the financing decisions of management affect not only the potential return to the owners but also the risk to which they are exposed.

Business and financial risk are associated with the individual enterprise. They are micro sources of risk that can be reduced through the construction of a diversified portfolio. The non-diversifiable sources of risk discussed below are macro or aggregate in nature. These sources of risk cannot be reduced through the construction of a diversified portfolio.

Market risk ▲
Risk associated with fluctuations in security prices

Market risk is the risk associated with movements in security prices, especially stock prices. If an individual buys a stock and the market as a whole declines, the price of the specific stock will probably fall. Conversely, if the market increases, the price of the stock will probably also tend to increase.

Interest rate risk ▲
Risk associated with changes in interest rates

Interest rate risk is the risk associated with fluctuations in interest rates. Suppose that a financial manager borrows funds under one set of terms only to have interest rates subsequently fall. If the financial manager had waited, the cost of these borrowed funds would have been lower. Movements in interest rates also affect security prices, especially the prices of fixed income securities such as bonds and preferred stock. As explained in Chapter 9, there is an inverse relationship between changes in interest rates and security prices. Thus, a rise in interest rates will drive down security prices and inflict a loss on the investors who own the affected securities.

Purchasing power risk ▲
Uncertainty that future inflation will erode the purchasing power of assets and income

Purchasing power risk is the risk associated with inflation, which all investors and financial managers must bear. A conservative investor may deposit funds in a savings account that pays a modest rate of interest. If the rate of inflation exceeds the rate of interest, the investor sustains a loss.

Since the rate of inflation has varied perceptibly during the last decade, the importance of purchasing power risk has varied. During the early 1980s, the rate of inflation rose, and purchasing power risk became a major concern of financial managers and investors. These individuals were forced to take actions designed to reduce the impact of inflation. Variable interest rate bonds and variable rate mortgages are examples of two debt instruments that were developed in response to this inflation and to the risk associated with the loss of purchasing power. During the middle of the 1980s, the rate of inflation declined and the impact of purchasing power risk diminished. However, inflation has not disappeared; the risk still exists and must be taken into consideration when making financial decisions.

Exchange rate risk ▲
Risk of loss from changes in the value of foreign currencies

While the rate of inflation was declining, another source of risk was becoming more prominent: fluctuations in the value of the dollar relative to other currencies. This **exchange rate risk** is the risk associated with fluctuations in the prices of foreign moneys. Many firms make and receive payments in foreign countries, and Americans travel abroad, making payments in foreign currencies. In addition, many individuals and financial managers make foreign investments. Any investment in-

FIGURE 1.2

Relationship between Risk and Return

Higher expected return requires bearing additional risk.

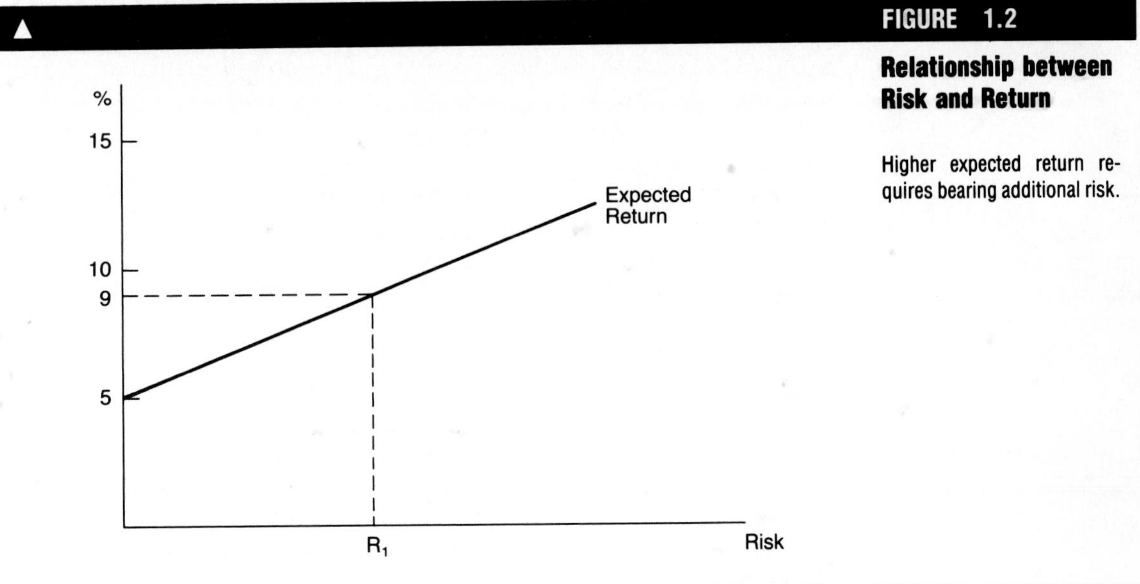

volving foreign money subjects the investor to risk from changes in the value of the foreign currency. The dollar value of a foreign currency can rise, thus increasing the return when the funds are converted back to dollars. The value of the foreign currency can also fall, however, reducing the return on the investment when converted back to dollars.

These various sources of risk appear repeatedly throughout this text, since risk is an integral part of financial decision making. Of course, all financial managers want to earn a return that is commensurate with the amount of risk borne. The relationship between risk and return is illustrated in Figure 1.2, which plots risk on the horizontal axis and return on the vertical axis. While return is measured as a percent, Figure 1.2 presents risk on an intuitive basis. Units for the measurement of risk are discussed in Chapter 8.

Figure 1.2 indicates that at very low levels of risk, the expected return is modest. An investor may even be able to achieve a modest return and bear no risk. A federally insured savings account that earns 5 percent annually during a period of stable prices would be an example of a risk-free investment. Such low risk, low return assets will be referred to in subsequent chapters as risk-free investments. To earn a higher return, the individual investor or the firm's management will have to bear additional risk, as indicated by the positively sloped curve showing the tradeoff between risk and return in Figure 1.2. Correspondingly, to induce financial managers to bear more risk, such as R_1 units of risk, a higher return must be expected (such as the 9 percent in Figure 1.2).

Valuation

Assets are acquired in the present, but their returns accrue in the future. No individual or firm would purchase an asset unless there was an expected return to compensate for the risk. Since the return is in the uncertain future, however, there has to be a way to express the future in terms of the present. The process of determining what an asset is currently worth is called **valuation.** An asset's value is the present value of the future benefits. For example, the current value of an AT&T bond is the sum of the present value of the expected interest payments and the expected repayment of the principal. The current value of a piece of equipment is the present value of the expected cash flows it will generate. And the current value of a stock is the present value of expected future dividends and the expected sale price.

Valuation ▲ Process of determining what an asset is currently worth

The determination of present value is one of the most important topics developed in this text. It requires estimates of future cash flows and measurements of what the funds invested in the asset could earn in alternative, competitive investments. The mechanics of determining present value (as well as determining future value) are covered in Chapter 7. Understanding this material is crucial to understanding much of the material covered in this text.

A firm is a combination of many assets, and therefore its value must be related to the value of the assets it owns. The value of these assets, in turn, depends on the returns they will generate in the future. In finance, the goal of the financial manager is to *maximize the value of the firm*. Many managers consider the maximization of value as their primary goal. Schering-Plough even titled its 1986 annual report, "Maximizing Shareholder Value." All financial decisions are judged by their impact on the value of the firm. These decisions are made in the present, but their results occur in the future. Because the future is uncertain, the financial manager's decisions affect both the profitability of and the risk associated with the firm. The ultimate judgment of those decisions is their impact on the value of the firm. Did the decision increase or reduce the present value of the firm?

This value may be readily measured if the firm has shares of ownership (stock) held by the general public. The market price of the stock is indicative of the value of the company. Since the value of the firm is the sum of the value of its shares, the market value of a share of stock times the number of shares gives the value of the company. For example, as of January 1991 CBS had 23,676,000 shares outstanding. At a price of $171.50 a share, that made the value of the firm's equity to be $4,060,434,000.

While security prices are subject to fluctuations, firms that have consistently grown and prospered have seen the price of the stock, and hence the value of the company, increase. At the beginning of 1986 CBS had 23,440,000 shares outstanding. At the then current price of

$115.875, the value of CBS was $2,716,110,000; the value of CBS thus rose over $1.3 billion from 1986 to 1991. This suggests that management made decisions that increased the value of the company. Over a period of time, the price of a company's stock is indicative of management performance.

Smaller firms or firms whose stock is not owned by the general public—by far the largest number of firms in existence—do not have market prices for their stock. Hence, owners and managers may not be able to ascertain the value of the firm. In these cases, the value is determined only when the firm is liquidated or sold (at that time, the value of the firm is the liquidation value or sale price). Since such liquidation or sale generally occurs only once, the owners and managers do not know what the true value of the firm is. They may use the value of the firm's equity as shown on the accounting statements as some indication of the firm's worth, but management cannot be certain of the firm's true value.

PLAN OF THE TEXT

This text is divided into three sections that encompass the three major divisions of finance: financial institutions, investments, and corporate (or business) finance. Part One is devoted to financial institutions and the environment in which financial decisions are made. Chapter 2 considers the transfer of funds from savers seeking to invest the money to firms in need of external financing. This chapter develops the direct transfer of these savings through investment bankers. Chapter 3 considers the indirect transfer of savings through financial intermediaries such as commercial banks. The chapter also covers the changing regulatory environment and the blurring of distinctions among the various financial intermediaries. Chapter 4 discusses the multiple expansion in the supply of money and credit with emphasis on the Federal Reserve and monetary and fiscal policy. Chapter 5 covers the international financial system. Part One ends with a discussion in Chapter 6 on secondary financial markets such as the New York Stock Exchange. These security markets transfer previously issued securities between investors seeking to liquidate their positions and other individuals seeking to add to their portfolios. This chapter also covers the mechanics of buying and selling securities and the role of brokerage firms.

Part Two is devoted to investments and is primarily concerned with the financial assets an individual may include in his or her portfolio. The first two chapters in this section cover two of the most important topics in finance—the time value of money (Chapter 7) and the sources and measurement of risk (Chapter 8).

Most financial decisions involve time. An investment is made today but the return is earned in the future. Standardizing for time is done by expressing the present in terms of the future or the future in terms of the present. This is one of the most difficult financial concepts to grasp, but it is also one of the most crucial. Each student using this text needs to read carefully and understand the material in Chapter 7. Without an understanding of the time value of money, much of what is subsequently covered will have little meaning.

Chapter 8 is devoted to risk and return. While risk can be understood on an intuitive basis, this chapter examines the sources of risk, the measurement of risk, and the means to manage it. As with the time value of money, the measurement of risk can be a difficult and involved topic. However, Chapter 8 is general and descriptive; there will be plenty of time for the student to develop this topic at more depth in advanced courses.

Chapters 9 through 14 are devoted to specific financial assets. Chapters 9 through 11 cover the traditional financial assets that individuals acquire—bonds and stock. Chapter 9 discusses the features and valuation of bonds. Chapter 10 covers equity: preferred stock and common stock. This chapter includes dividends, stock splits, and the rights of stockholders. Chapter 11 is devoted to another crucial concept in finance: the valuation of stock. Chapters 12 through 14 discuss several alternatives to investing in stocks and bonds. These alternatives include convertible bonds (Chapter 12), futures and options (Chapter 13), and shares in investment companies, including mutual funds (Chapter 14).

Part Three is devoted to corporate finance from the perspective of the financial manager. This section begins with a discussion of the corporate form of business, taxation, and depreciation (Chapter 15). Chapter 16 describes the analysis of financial statements, beginning with a review of financial statements. This chapter covers the basic components of financial statements to give students a working knowledge of their composition. Since many students who enroll in finance courses have had some exposure to financial statements, this section may be omitted. However, for those students who have not had such an introduction, this material is crucial for understanding the ratios that are used to analyze the financial statements presented in Chapter 16.

Chapters 17 and 18 consider corporate financial planning and control. Chapter 17 is devoted to break-even analysis and operating and financial leverage. Chapter 18 discusses techniques used to forecast a firm's financial needs (the percent of sales and regression analysis). This chapter also covers the cash budget, which indicates if and when a firm will need short-term funds and when it will have excess funds available for short-term investments.

Chapters 19 and 20 are devoted to the management of short-term assets and liabilities—the firm's "working capital." Chapter 19 discusses the management of a firm's short-term assets, while Chapter 20 considers the various sources of short-term funds.

The remaining chapters of the text are devoted to long-term investment and financing decisions. Chapter 21 covers two additional sources of funds: intermediate-term debt and leasing. Chapter 22 is devoted to financial leverage and the determination of the firm's best combination of debt and equity financing. The optimal combination, which determines the cost of funds, is used to help select long-term investments. This selection process, called capital budgeting, is discussed in Chapter 23. Chapter 24 briefly considers growth through mergers and business failure and bankruptcy. And the last chapter, Chapter 25, recapitulates the role of the firm's financial manager and the environment in which financial decisions are made.

The Job Mart

Although completing an introductory course in finance does not sufficiently prepare a person for a career in finance, it can indicate several career choices. Many of today's most successful businesspeople have a background in finance; even those who did not have formal training must certainly have learned many financial concepts as their careers developed.

A person may not be aware of the possible career choices available to those with a knowledge of finance. Many careers will require advanced study, such as an MBA (master's degree in business administration), and certainly all will require experience. No one will hire a new undergraduate to manage $100,000,000 in trust accounts or to be responsible for the decision to invest $75,000,000 in new plant and equipment. The student can, however, become aware of career possibilities and their requirements.

Throughout this text there are descriptions of career options available in finance. The descriptions briefly cover such facets of the career as what the individual does and what special education or certification may be required. While these career descriptions are not exhaustive, they may give an indication of how the study of finance can help prepare the student for a rewarding occupation.

Computer Applications

Finance lends itself to computer applications. Many of the problems illustrated in this text can be solved through the use of computers. There are two basic methods for using computers to solve financial problems. First, a person can become adept at using a computer program such as Lotus 1-2-3®. Lotus 1-2-3® is a spreadsheet that may be set up in a variety of ways to solve financial problems. This is probably the best method for integrating computers and finance. It offers the most flexibility because different assumptions may be built into the analysis, permitting the individual to analyze a variety of "what if" questions. This approach requires, however, that a person be able to use the spreadsheet.

The second method involves the use of software programs that have already been written and are available for use with existing programs. For example, a computer system called a template may be available for use with a spreadsheet. A person enters the appropriate data into the template, and the program solves the problem. Each template may be used to solve various problems, such as the cash budget problem explained in Chapter 18 or the capital budgeting problem in Chapter 23.

This approach does, however, have two serious drawbacks. First, the templates may have only limited applicability if they do not permit changes in the format of the program. For example, if a cash budget problem covers an entire year but the template is set up for only six months, the use of the program is obviously limited. Second, a person may enter the appropriate numbers without understanding the point of the problem. In this case, the computer facilitates the mechanics but hides the essence of problem solving.

To give students some computer exposure, many of the problems in this text may be solved by using James B. Pettijohn's *PROFIT+*, Dryden 1988. *PROFIT+* is a set of computer software programs for solving financial problems in a college setting. While the programs are simpler than real-world software packages, they do expose students to the use of computers in solving financial problems. Many of the problems in this text may be solved through the use of *PROFIT+*. However, not every problem in this text (or in real life) will fit into a single set of computer programs. There are problems that will have to be solved through a person's own efforts and initiative!

SUMMARY

Finance is the study of money and its management. The discipline may be divided into three overlapping areas: financial institutions, investments, and business finance. The subject matter of finance involves how an economic unit such as a firm raises funds (i.e., its sources of finance) and how these funds are invested. All investments are made with the anticipation of earning a return. However, since the future is uncertain, all investments involve risk.

The sources of risk include (1) the nature of the operation itself (business risk) and (2) the ways in which the operation is financed (financial risk). These sources of risk apply to the individual firm. Other sources of risk include the tendency for securities prices to move together (market risk); the inverse relationship between changes in interest rates and security prices (interest rate risk); the loss of purchasing power due to inflation (purchasing power risk); and fluctuations in the value of one currency relative to other currencies (exchange rate risk). These sources of risk apply to the aggregate economy. While investors and financial managers must bear all the sources of risk, they seek to maximize their returns for a given amount of risk. They will bear more risk only if the anticipated return is higher.

An asset has value because investors anticipate future income and/or capital appreciation. The valuation of an asset thus requires estimates of future cash flows and an expression of these cash flows in present value terms. Valuation is a crucial topic in finance because the goal of the financial manager is to maximize the present worth of the firm. Hence, all financial decisions are judged by their impact on the value of the firm. The financial manager should make only those investments that increase the value of the firm.

Review Questions

1. What is the primary criterion used in finance to judge performance?
2. What are the sources of risk and the sources of return?
3. What affects the value of an asset?

Suggested Readings

Each of the subsequent chapters has a list of selected readings. These bibliographies have been annotated to facilitate their use. The readings are not exhaustive and do not include extensive lists of material found in academic journals. Instead, these readings tend to be more pragmatic. They can be read in conjunction with the material covered in the chapter or as additional material that the individual student may choose to pursue on completion of this text.

part one

Financial Institutions

▲ My bank has assets in excess of $10,000,000,000. My checking account may have $1,000 in it. I account for about 0.0001 percent of my bank's sources of funds. Just think how many depositors my bank must have in order to generate the money it has lent.

I own 500 shares of Textron. At $26 a share, that is $13,000. While $13,000 is sufficient to buy any of a number of consumer goods, it is a very small fraction of the total value of all Textron shares. The firm has 85,323,000 shares outstanding for a total value of $2,218,398,000. My holdings are obviously a minute portion of the total.

Last year my family took a vacation in Canada. We spent over $1,500 outside the country, which added to the nation's deficit in its balance of trade. The amount we spent was very small, however, when compared to the federal government's foreign aid programs or military spending abroad, which also contributed to the deficit in the balance of trade.

Hardly a day goes by that I do not have contact with a financial institution. The same is true for most individuals. They write and receive checks, make deposits and withdrawals from depository institutions, buy and sell shares of stock in corporations and mutual funds, make contributions to pension plans, pay taxes, buy imported goods, and borrow funds from a variety of sources. Each of these acts involves contact with a financial institution.

The first part of this text discusses the financial environment and institutions with which we have so much contact. Some of these financial institutions facilitate the transfer of funds from lenders to borrowers (e.g., commercial banks), while others facilitate the exchange of securities from sellers to buyers (e.g., the stock exchanges). Other financial institutions affect the level of income and the stability of consumer prices (e.g., the Federal Reserve), and yet another financial institution, the market for foreign currency, makes possible the exchange of foreign goods and services. The participants in these markets for financial products and services range from the large corporate giants and the federal government to the small corner store and the individual saver. Everyone reading this text is touched by these financial institutions, and increasing your knowledge of them by learning the material in the next five chapters can only help you function in today's financial environment.

chapter

2

The Creation of Financial Assets

Learning Objectives

1. Define money, enumerate its functions, and identify the composition of the money supply.
2. Differentiate the roles of money and interest rates.
3. Illustrate the direct and indirect transfer of funds to business.
4. Distinguish between a financial intermediary and an investment banker.
5. Describe the components of a public sale of new securities.
6. Differentiate a venture capitalist from an investment banker.

Polonius, in Shakespeare's *Hamlet,* gives the advice, "neither a borrower nor a lender be." Fortunately, few individuals follow that advice, for borrowing and lending are crucial components of an advanced economy's financial system. Such an economy could not exist without them. Through borrowing and lending, resources are channeled into productive investments. Consider how firms would be constrained if they could not borrow funds to purchase plant or equipment, or how individuals would be prevented from purchasing homes without borrowing money to purchase the homes through mortgage loans.

A sophisticated financial system has evolved to facilitate the transfer for funds from those with money to invest to those in need of funds. Each of the components plays an important, and in some cases, an indispensable role. These components include a variety of financial intermediaries that stand between the suppliers and users of funds, a mechanism for issuing and selling new securities (i.e., stocks and bonds), and a market for the subsequent sales of existing securities.

Since the deregulation of the banking system and the increase in competition among the various depository institutions, the clear distinction among commercial banks, savings institutions, brokerage firms, insurance companies, and other firms providing customer financial services has diminished. Many firms now offer savers a wide spectrum of choices ranging from traditional saving vehicles to new and sophisticated financial instruments. What has emerged is a type of financial supermarket that offers the customer (both the saver and the borrower) a variety of financial services and instruments.

Deregulation, increased competition, and technological change are also altering the way in which individuals make contact with a bank. Currently some banks offer services to individuals with access to personal computers. For example, you may transfer money from your checking account to your savings account, apply for a loan, make your mortgage, car, and credit card payments, and shop for consumer goods that you view on TV, have the goods shipped, and immediately have the money debited from your bank account to pay for the goods. If this trend continues, you may never have to visit a bank again and many banks will have sold most of their branches and replaced them with automatic teller machines located in various retail establishments.

While differences among financial firms have diminished, some remain, and the primary role of financial intermediaries and financial markets remains the same. Financial markets transfer funds from individuals, firms, and governments with money to invest to individuals, firms, and governments in need of funds. Explaining this transfer and differentiating among the various firms is the primary thrust of this and the subsequent chapter. This chapter begins with a discussion of the roles of money and interest rates. Next is a discussion of the indirect transfer of funds to businesses through financial intermediaries. The balance of the chapter is devoted to the mechanics of the sale of new securities through investment bankers. The subsequent chapter considers the variety of financial intermediaries such as commercial banks and differentiates them from investment banking.

THE ROLE OF MONEY

Money ▲
Anything that is generally accepted as a means of payment

Money is anything that is generally accepted in payment for goods and services or for the retirement of debt. This definition has several important words, especially *anything* and *generally accepted.* Anything may perform the role of money, and many different items, including shells, stones, and metals, have served as money. During the history of this country, a variety of coins and paper moneys have been used. In the past, gold coins served as money in the United States, but today this is no longer the case.[1] Coins are presently made of cheaper metals, such as copper. The value of the metallic content of these coins is less than the value of the coin. For example, the value of copper contained in a penny is less than the value of the penny. If the copper in a penny were worth more in other uses than as money, people would melt pennies and remove the copper. Copper pennies would cease to exist as money, and the U.S. Treasury would have to alter the metallic content of the penny.

Since the value of the metal is less than the value of the coin, coins are only "token" money. The extreme case of such token money is paper money, which has virtually no physical value. Paper money is cheap for the government to print and is very convenient to use. Hence, it is often employed as a substitute for coins. Perhaps the most convenient form of money is demand deposits (i.e., checking accounts) in depository institutions. These deposits are readily transferred by check and are generally accepted as a means of payment. Actually, the form of money is not really important, for the role of money is not determined by its physical content. As long as an item is generally accepted as payment for goods, services, or the retirement of debt, it is money.

The other important words in this definition of money are *generally accepted.* What serves as money in one place may not be money else-

[1]The U.S. Treasury still mints limited-edition gold coins for sale to collectors.

where. This fact is readily understood by a person who travels abroad and must convert one currency to another. The paper that serves as money in Great Britain, called pounds, is not used as money in Paris, where French francs are used. Pounds must be converted into francs for the holder to buy goods in Paris. U.S. dollars must be converted into pounds, or francs, or other currencies in nations where they, the dollars, are not generally accepted.[2]

Money performs a variety of important roles. It is (1) a medium of exchange and (2) a store of value. It is also (3) a unit of account and (4) a standard of deferred payment. Without money, there would be considerably fewer transactions of goods and services, for such transactions would occur only if two parties could agree on terms for a mutual exchange. Such direct transfer of goods and services is called **barter.** Barter is an extremely inefficient means of transferring goods, and it should be no surprise to students of finance that money developed as a substitute for bartering. Instead of trading one good for another, individuals sell goods and services for money and then use the money to purchase other goods and services. Money thus facilitates the flow of goods and services by being a medium of exchange. An advanced economy could not exist without something functioning as a medium of exchange, and even less economically developed nations have a form of money to aid in the exchange of goods.

Barter ▲
Transfer of goods and services without the use of money; the trading of one good for another

Money may also be used to transfer purchasing power to the future. In this second role, money acts as a store of value from one time period to another. Money, however, is only one of many assets that may be used as a store of value. Stocks, bonds, savings accounts, savings bonds, real estate, gold, and collectibles are some of the various assets that savers may use to store value.

All of these nonmonetary assets must be converted into money for the saver to exercise the purchasing power that has been stored. The ease with which an asset may be converted into money with little loss of value is called **liquidity.** Money is, of course, the most liquid of all assets. Some assets may not be readily converted into cash, and investing in them may cause the saver to lose a substantial amount of liquidity. For example, antiques may inflate in value but converting them into money may be a time-consuming and costly process. Hence, this type of asset may be very illiquid.

Liquidity ▲
Ease of converting an asset into cash without loss

With the exception of interest-bearing checking accounts (called *NOW accounts,* for negotiable order of withdrawal), money earns noth-

---

[2]Many western European countries are moving toward one currency, which would be usable in each country. One currency will end the need to convert moneys and should facilitate economic trade among the nations in the trading bloc. As of this writing, the British have not agreed to join, so that the pound will remain the currency in Britain. Even if one currency evolves for use within a group of nations, that currency will still have to be exchanged for other currencies outside the trading bloc.

ing for its owner.[3] Other assets provide their owners a flow of income or services. Bonds and savings accounts pay interest; stocks may pay dividends and grow in value; and physical goods provide enjoyment and may appreciate. For money to be attractive as a store of value, its liquidity must offset the advantages offered by other assets.

During periods of high interest rates or rising prices, money is a poor store of value. The inflation experienced during the 1970s and 1980s taught many savers the need to minimize the amount of money held as a store of value. From 1978 to 1989, the price of consumer goods more than doubled. Anyone who held non-interest-earning money as a store of value during that era suffered a considerable loss in purchasing power.

Money also performs two other functions. It is a unit of account and a standard of deferred payment. The prices of goods are determined in terms of money instead of in terms of each other. For example, an apple costs $0.50 and a bottle of beer costs $1.00. The price of the apple is not expressed as the price of half a bottle of beer. Both the price of the apple and the price of the beer are expressed in terms of money. Money is also the standard for expressing payments over time. For example, loans which are repaid in the future are defined in terms of money. A mortgage loan may be repaid at the rate of $750 per month for twenty years.

The power to create money is given by the Constitution to the federal government. Congress established a central bank, the Federal Reserve System, and gave it power to control the supply of money and to oversee the commercial banking system. Initially it was not the intent of Congress to create a central bank, for in the Federal Reserve Act of 1913 twelve district banks were established. The Federal Reserve was reorganized by the Banking Acts of 1933 and 1935 to become the central bank known today. The organization of the Federal Reserve and how it controls the supply of money are discussed in Chapter 4. While the Federal Reserve has control over the supply of money, most of the money supply is created through the process of loan creation by the banking system. (This process of loan creation is explained in Chapter 4.)

Measures of the Supply of Money

There are several measures of the composition of the **money supply.** The traditional measure (commonly referred to as **M-1**) is the sum of coins and currency in circulation plus demand deposits (including NOW accounts and travelers' checks) held by the general public in all deposi-

Money supply ▲
Total amount of money in circulation

M-1 ▲
Sum of coins, currency, and demand deposits

[3] There is an exception to this general statement. If prices were to fall, money would purchase more goods in which case holding money generates a positive return, but interest-bearing savings accounts would earn a higher return.

M-2 ▲
Sum of coins, currency, demand deposits, and savings accounts and small-denomination time deposits

tory institutions. A broader definition of the supply of money (commonly referred to as **M-2**) includes not only demand deposits, coins, and currency but also regular savings accounts and small-denomination time deposits (i.e., certificates of deposit of less than $100,000).[4] The actual amount of money outstanding depends on which definition is used. As of September 1990, the Federal Reserve reported that M-1 and M-2 were as follows:

The large amount invested in savings accounts and time deposits results in M-2 being four times the size of M-1.

	M-1	M-2
Coin and currency	$241.5	$ 241.5
Demand deposits	279.9	279.9
Other checkable deposits (i.e., NOW accounts)	293.1	293.1
Travelers' checks	8.3	8.3
Savings accounts and time deposits	—	2,495.0
	$822.8	$3,317.8

Derived from the Federal Reserve Bulletin, *December 1990, p. A13.*

As may be seen in the above data, savings accounts constitute more than 75 percent of the money supply when the broader definition (i.e., M-2) is used. This broader definition of the money supply is preferred by those economists and financial analysts who stress the ease with which individuals may transfer funds among the components of M-2. There is virtually no monetary cost or effort for the individual to transfer funds from a savings account or time deposit into a checking account. Such a movement will increase M-1, because demand deposits have risen, but the transaction has no impact on M-2, because the increase in demand deposits is offset by the decline in the other account.

Actually, the best definition of the money supply may depend in part on the anticipated use for the information. If the analyst is primarily concerned with the actual transactions, M-1 may be preferred, since funds in other accounts must be transferred into an account that can be used for transactions (e.g., a checking account or a NOW account). If the analyst is primarily concerned with liquidity within the economy, the emphasis will be placed on M-2.[5] The difference in liquidity among these accounts is so small, and the distinction between savings and checking

[4]Certificates of deposit are discussed in more detail in Chapter 3.

[5]There is also an even broader definition of the money supply, M-3, which adds large certificates of deposit in excess of $100,000 and selected money market instruments to M-2.

accounts has been so blurred, that financial analysts who study liquidity have adopted the broader definition of the money supply, M-2.

Economists study the supply of money because of its impact on the economy. These studies seek to forecast economic activity, such as the level of national income or employment. Unfortunately, there is an empirical argument among economists as to which definition, M-1 or M-2, is the better predictor of economic activity. Currently, there is no consensus as to which definition leads to better forecasts.

While money is obviously important as a medium of exchange, one group of economists places special emphasis on changes in the supply of money and the level of national income, employment, and inflation. These **monetarists** believe that changes in the supply of money should reflect and accommodate economic growth. However, if the money supply were to be increased too quickly, it would create inflationary pressure and prices would rise. The goal of economic policy as prescribed by the monetarists is to increase the money supply sufficiently to sustain income, employment, and economic growth, but not to create inflation.

Monetarists ▲
Economists who stress the direct linkage between change in the money supply and economic activity

In summary, money is crucial to an advanced economy, for it facilitates the transfer of goods and resources. An advanced economy could not exist without something to perform the role of money. Since a large proportion of the money supply consists of deposits in various depository institutions, the student of finance should understand the banking system and its regulation. This is a large topic and is covered in detail in the next two chapters. The remainder of this chapter is devoted to a discussion of interest rates and the transfer of funds to business with special emphasis on investment banking.

THE ROLE OF INTEREST RATES

The words "money" and "interest" are often used together, but their meanings differ, and money and interest perform different roles. Money is used as a medium of exchange; its value is related to what it will purchase. If money is not acceptable for the payment for the purchases of goods and services, it is worthless. The more dollars necessary to purchase something, the less each dollar is worth.

While the value or price of money depends on what it will purchase, an interest rate is the price of credit. Interest is not the price of money; it is the price paid for the use of someone else's money, that is, the cost of credit. The use of credit permits the borrower to defer payment until the loan is repaid.

The role of interest rates is to allocate scarce credit. Higher interest rates make borrowing more expensive and should discouarge the use of credit. Only those willing and able to pay the higher rate will obtain the

EXHIBIT 2.1

The Variety of Debt Instruments

Discussion of the various debt instruments is located throughout the text.

Debt Instrument	Where Covered
Certificates of deposit	Chapters 3, 19
Commercial bank loans	Chapter 20
Commercial paper	Chapter 20
Convertible bonds	Chapter 12
Debentures	Chapter 9
Eurobonds	Chapter 5
Intermediate-term loans	Chapter 21
Leases	Chapter 21
Mortgage loans	Chapter 7
Repurchase agreement	Chapter 19
Revolving credit agreement	Chapter 20
Series EE bonds	Chapter 9
Tax-exempt (municipal) bonds	Chapters 3, 9
Trade credit	Chapter 20
Treasury bills	Chapter 19
Variable rate bonds	Chapter 9
Zero coupon bonds	Chapter 9

funds. Thus, higher interest rates allocate the existing supply of credit among the competing users seeking to borrow the funds.

As is discussed throughout this text, there are many types of loans (e.g., mortgage loans, consumer credit, bonds). A list of various types of debt instruments and where they are covered in this text is presented in Exhibit 2.1. In addition to many debt instruments, there are also many interest rates that reflect the amount borrowed, the length of time the borrower will have the use of the funds, and the creditworthiness of the borrower. Generally, the longer the term of the debt and the riskier (i.e., less creditworthy) the debt instrument the higher will be the rate of interest.

Debt, and hence interest rates, is often referred to as short- or long-term. The time period is arbitrarily established at one year. Short-term refers to a year or less. Long-term refers to greater than a year. (Debt that matures in one to ten years is sometimes referred to as intermediate-term.) Of course, with the passage of time long-term debt instruments become short-term when they mature within a year.[6]

Financial markets have an analogous classification. The "money market" refers to the market for debt instruments that will mature within a

[6] Firms with bonds approaching maturity classify debt maturing within a year as a current liability and separate this debt on their balance sheets from bonds that mature after a year. The latter are classified as long-term liabilities.

year. The "capital market" refers to securities with a longer term horizon. In the case of a bond or mortgage loan, the term may be ten, twenty, or more years. In some cases such as common stock, the time dimension is indefinite. A corporation may exist for centuries. Many of the nation's banks such as Chemical Bank or Citicorp were started in the 1700s or early 1800s. Industrial firms such as AT&T, Coca-Cola, and Exxon commenced operations in the 1800s. These three corporations have been paying cash dividends for over 100 years.

The Term Structure of Interest Rates

The relationship between interest rates (i.e., the cost of credit) and the length of time to maturity (i.e., the term) for debt in a given risk class is referred to as the **term structure of interest rates.** This structure is illustrated by a **yield curve,** which relates the yield on debt instruments with different terms to maturity. Such a yield curve is illustrated in Figure 2.1 which plots the yield on various United States government securities as of January 1985. This figure shows that the bonds with the longest term to maturity have the highest interest rates. For example, short-term securities with three months to maturity had yields of 10.3 percent, one-year bonds paid 11.4 percent, and bonds that matured after ten years paid in excess of 12 percent.

Term structure of interest rates ▲
Relationship between yields and the time to maturity for debt with a given level of risk

Yield curve ▲
Graph relating interest rates and the term to maturity

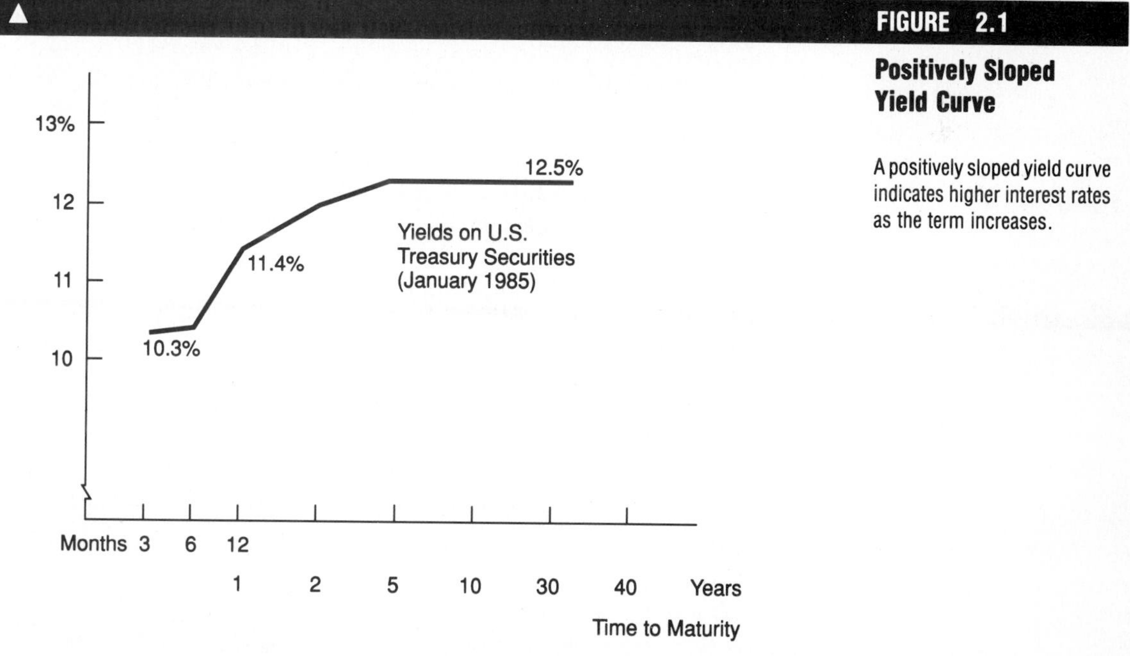

FIGURE 2.1

Positively Sloped Yield Curve

A positively sloped yield curve indicates higher interest rates as the term increases.

FIGURE 2.2

Yield Curves (Yields on Federal Government Securities)

A negative yield curve indicates lower interest rates as the term increases. With a flat yield curve the rate of interest is virtually unchanged as the term increases.

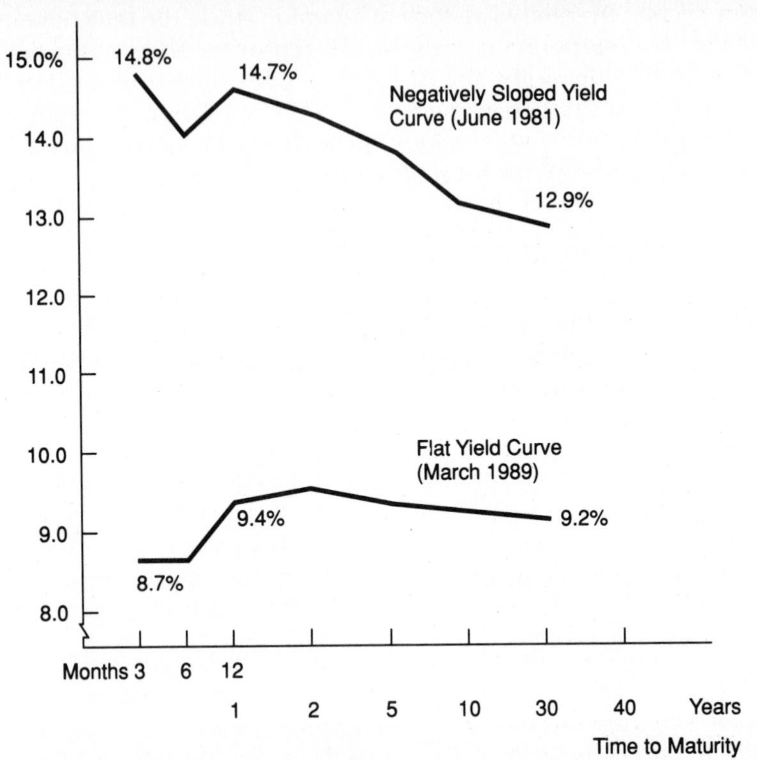

One would expect such a relationship between interest rates and the term to maturity. To induce investors to lend their money for lengthier periods, it is usually necessary to pay them more interest. In addition, the fortunes of the issuer are more difficult to assess for longer time periods. This suggests that long-term investments are riskier, and investors will ordinarily require additional compensation for bearing the additional risk associated with long-term debt instruments.

Although the positive relationship between time and interest rates illustrated in Figure 2.1 does usually exist, there have been periods when the opposite occurred. During 1981, short-term rates exceeded long-term rates; the yield curve becomes inverted and has a negative slope. This is illustrated in Figure 2.2. Securities maturing in less than a year had yields exceeding 14 percent, while long-term debt that matured after 10 years yielded 13 percent.

Such a yield curve can be explained by inflation and the action of the Federal Reserve to curb rising prices. As is explained in Chapter 4, the Federal Reserve fights inflation by selling short-term securities. Such sales absorb credit by reducing the supply of money and the capacity of banks to lend because paying the Federal Reserve for the securities pulls money out of the banking system.

The sales depress security prices and increase their yields. While the yields on all debt instruments are responsive to the changes in the supply of credit, the Federal Reserve's selling of short-term securities has the most impact on short-term rates. In the illustration in Figure 2.2, short-term yields rose above long-term rates resulting in an inverted yield curve. When the rate of inflation abated, the yield curve returned to the positive slope that it has maintained during most periods.

There have also been periods when the yield curve was relatively flat. Such a structure is also illustrated in Figure 2.2 by the yield curve for March 1989. The yield on short-term debt with three to six months to maturity was approximately 8.7 percent, and the rate on thirty-year bonds was 9.2 percent. While the long-term rate did exceed the short-term rate, the small difference produced a gently rising, almost flat, yield curve.

THE TRANSFER OF FUNDS TO BUSINESS

The role of money is to serve as a medium of exchange to simplify the purchases and sales of goods and services. Interest rates help allocate credit among the different potential users of the credit. The role of financial markets is to facilitate the transfer for funds from lenders to borrowers and to ease the exchange of securities among investors. In the process of transferring funds from lenders to borrowers, a spectrum of financial assets is created. These securities expedite the transfer of savings from those with funds to those who need funds. Savers may include individuals, firms, or governments. Savings represent a command of resources that are currently not being used. Thus a government that has collected tax receipts but has not spent the funds has, in effect, savings. So has a firm that has earned profits from the sale of goods but has not distributed the earnings. Until the earnings are distributed, the firm has savings.

Those in need of funds may include individuals, firms, and governments. For example, an individual may need funds to purchase a house. The local school board may need funds to build a school, or AT&T may require funds to purchase new equipment. The individual cannot obtain a mortgage to purchase a house, the school board cannot build the school, or AT&T cannot purchase the equipment if some individual, firm, or government does not put up the funds.

All financial assets (e.g., stocks, bonds, bank deposits, and government bonds) are created to facilitate this transfer. The creation of financial assets and the transfer of funds are crucial for the well-being of every economy. The individual could not obtain the resources to acquire the house, the local government could not build the school, and AT&T could not obtain the new equipment without the transfer of resources. And this transfer could not occur without the creation of financial assets.

All financial assets represent claims, and these claims may be divided into two types: debt obligations and equity obligations. Debt obligations, such as bonds or certificates of deposit with a commercial bank, are loans. The borrower pays interest for the use of the funds and agrees to repay the principal after some specified period of time. These debt obligations represent legal obligations on the part of the borrower that are enforceable in a court of law.

An equity claim represents ownership. Owners of common stock are the owners of the corporation that issued the stock. The individual who owns a home has equity in the home. Equity claims are paid after all debt obligations are met. This residual status means that owners reap the rewards when a business is successful but may sustain substantial losses when the operation is unsuccessful. This does not mean that lenders (creditors) may not sustain losses. It means that the owner has the riskier position than the creditor. Correspondingly the owner may earn a greater return for bearing more risk.

While all financial assets represent a debt or an equity claim, the individual assets come in a variety of forms with differing features. One of the purposes of this text is to explain this variety and to clarify the advantages and risks associated with each asset from the perspectives of both the issuer and the investor. Nor are all financial assets clearly debt or equity instruments. Some have elements of both such as the convertible bond, which is a debt instrument that may be converted into equity. Such bonds have to be analyzed from two perspectives: as a debt instrument and as an equity instrument.

The Direct and Indirect Transfers of Funds

There are bascially two methods of transferring funds to businesses. One is the direct investment of money into businesses by the general public. This occurs when firms issue new securities that are purchased by investors or when individuals invest in partnerships or sole proprietorships. This initial market for securities is referred to as the **primary market** to differentiate it from the **secondary market.** The secondary market refers to subsequent sales of the securities in which one investor transfers the security to another. As is explained in detail later in this chapter and in Chapter 6, the role of the secondary market is to permit investors to buy and sell existing securities. None of the funds transferred by these sales and purchases go to the firm that issued the securities. The firm receives funds only once when the securities are initially issued and sold in the primary market.

Primary market ▲
Market for the initial sale of securities

Secondary market ▲
Market for buying and selling previously issued securities

When a corporation issues a new security (e.g., a bond) in the primary market and sells it to the general public, the following transaction occurs:

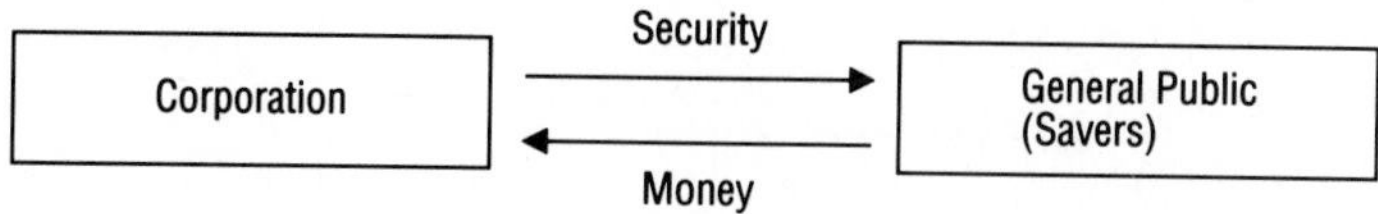

The saver purchases the security with money, thereby trading one asset for another. The firm acquires the funds by issuing the security; there is a direct transfer of money from the saver to the firm.

The second method for transferring savings to businesses is the indirect transfer through a **financial intermediary.** A financial intermediary transfers funds to firms and other borrowers from individuals such as savers or firms that currently are not using the money. The intermediary acquires the funds from savers by *issuing a claim on itself,* such as a savings account. The intermediary then lends the funds or buys new securities issued by the economic unit in need of the money. Since the financial intermediary stands between the ultimate supplier and the ultimate user of the funds, it facilitates the flow of money and credit between the suppliers and the users.

Financial intermediary ▲
Firm that transfers savings to borrowers by creating claims on itself

The flow of funds to the financial intermediary is illustrated by the following chart:

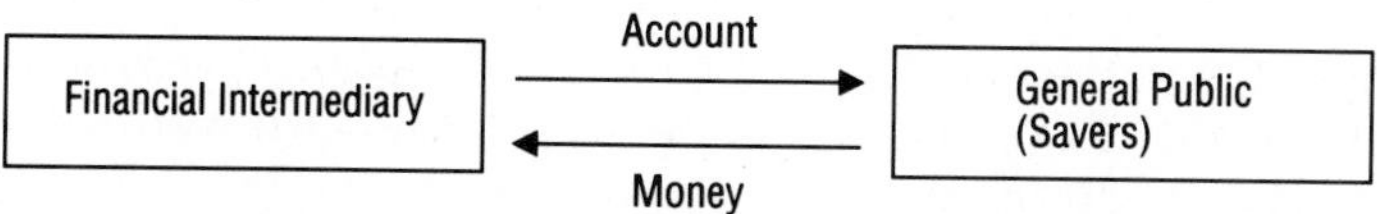

The saver trades one asset (the money) for another (the claim on the financial intermediary), and the financial intermediary acquires the funds by issuing a claim on itself.

The financial intermediary then lends the funds to an entity such as a firm, government, or household in need of the funds. That is, the financial intermediary buys a security such as a bond or makes a new loan, at which time the following transaction occurs:

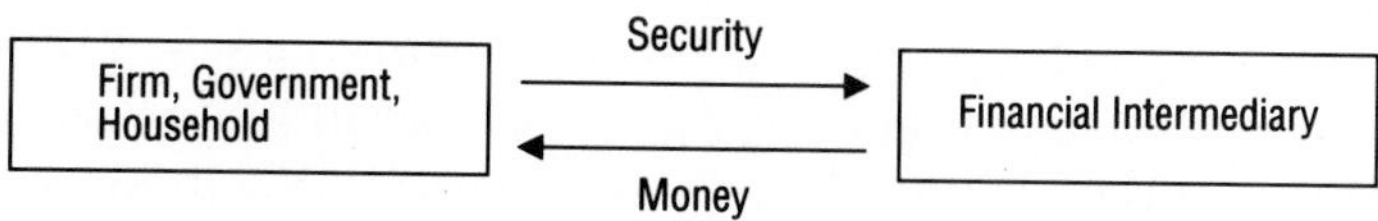

The financial intermediary gives up one asset, the money, to acquire another asset, the claim on the borrower. The borrower acquires the funds by promising to return them in the future and to pay interest while the loan is outstanding.

The preceding charts may be combined to illustrate the process of transferring funds from the ultimate lender (the saver) to the ultimate borrower.

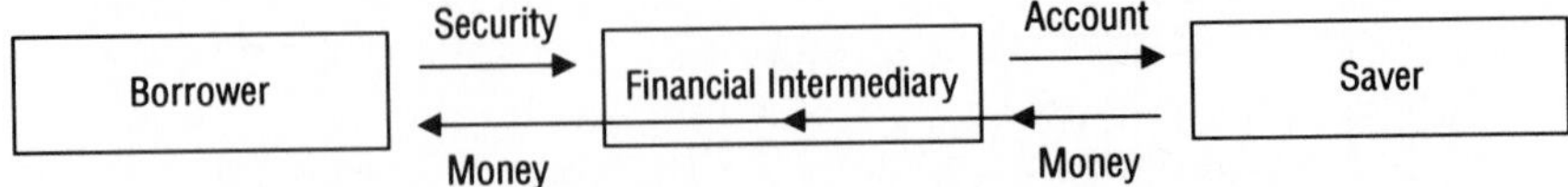

The saver's funds are transferred to the borrower through the financial intermediary. Through this process the borrower is able to acquire the funds because the financial intermediary was able to issue a claim on itself (i.e., the account) that the saver would accept.

THE ISSUING AND SELLING OF NEW SECURITIES

As was previously discussed, users of capital obtain funds directly by selling securities to the suppliers of the money or indirectly through the use of financial intermediaries. From the viewpoint of the aggregate economy, the indirect transfer of money from savers to firms through financial intermediaries is more important than the sale of new securities. Most individual households do not invest their savings directly in business. In addition, many firms sell new securities only on an intermittent basis, and many years may elapse between issues. Instead, funds are transferred through the system of financial intermediaries.

There is a large variety of financial intermediaries ranging from local commercial banks to insurance companies to money market mutual funds. The variety of financial intermediaries and their relative importance will be discussed in the next chapter. The remainder of this chapter will be devoted to the direct transfer of funds through the issuing and sale of new securities. While the total amount raised by the sale of securities to the general public may be small when compared to the funds raised through financial intermediaries, this direct transfer of funds is important since the securities traded on the stock exchanges came into existence through this process.

It is important to realize that most purchases of securities by households do not transfer savings to businesses. Such transfers occur only once, in the primary market when the securities are issued. Any ensuing sales are between investors (i.e., from the seller to the buyer) and not between investors and the issuing firm. These sales are made in secondary markets like the New York Stock Exchange. Secondary markets are an important component of the financial structure and their primary purpose is to transfer securities among investors. Secondary markets permit investors to hold securities for varying amounts of time. An investor does not have to hold the stock of IBM until the firm is liquidated in order to obtain the funds invested in the stock. Instead, the owner of IBM stock sells the stock and transfers the ownership to the buyer. Without secondary markets, individuals would be less willing to purchase securities and it would be exceedingly difficult for firms to sell new securities when their financial managers wanted to raise funds directly from investors instead of through financial intermediaries.

Secondary markets, like financial intermediaries, are obviously important to the financial health of the economy. However, the discussion of these markets and how individuals buy and sell securities is deferred until Chapter 6, after the coverage of the material on the initial security sales, the material on financial intermediaries, and factors that affect these financial markets such as the Federal Reserve System and the flow of funds to and from foreign countries.

The Role of the Investment Banker

A firm could market securities directly to the public in several ways: by contacting its current stockholders and creditors and asking them to purchase the new securities; by advertising the securities; or even by peddling them from door to door. Although this last scenario is exaggerated, it illustrates that there is a cost to selling new securities, which may be considerable if the firm itself undertakes the task. For this reason, firms employ help in marketing new securities; they use the services of **investment bankers,** who sell new securities to the general public. In effect, an investment banker serves as a middleman to channel money from investors to the firm that needs the capital.

Investment banker ▲
Middleman who brings together investors and firms (and governments) issuing new securities

Investment banking is an important financial institution, but confusion exists concerning it, part of which may be attributable to the misnomer *investment banker.* An investment banker is rarely a banker and does not generally invest. Instead, the investment banker is usually a division of a brokerage firm like Merrill Lynch, Pierce, Fenner and Smith or First Boston Corporation. Although these brokerage firms own securities, they do not necessarily buy and hold the newly issued securities for investment purposes.

Investment bankers perform a middleman function that brings together individuals who have money to invest and firms that need financing. Since brokerage firms have many customers, they are able to sell new securities without the costly search that the individual firm may have to make to sell its own securities. Thus, although the firm in need of financing must pay for the services, it is able to raise external capital at less expense through the investment banker than it could by selling the securities itself.

THE MECHANICS OF UNDERWRITING If a firm needs funds from an external source, it can approach an investment banker to discuss an **underwriting.** The term *underwriting* refers to the process of selling new securities. In an underwriting the firm that is selling the securities, and not the firm that is issuing the shares, bears the risk associated with the sale. When an investment banker agrees to underwrite a sale of securities, it is agreeing to buy the securities and thus supply the firm with a specified amount of money (i.e., it guarantees the sale). If the investment banker is subsequently unable to sell the securities to the general public, it must still pay the agreed-on sum to the firm. Failure to sell the securities imposes significant losses on the underwriter, who must remit funds for securities that have not been sold to the general public.

Underwriting ▲
Purchase of an issue of new securities for subsequent sale by investment bankers; the guaranteeing of the sale of a new issue of securities

The firm that is in need of financing and the investment banker discuss the amount of funds needed, the type of security to be issued, the price and any special features of the security, and the cost to the firm of issuing the securities. All of these factors are negotiated by the firm that is seeking capital and the investment banker. If mutually acceptable terms are reached, the investment banker will be the middleman through which the securities are sold by the firm to the general public.

Because an underwriting starts with a particular brokerage firm, which manages the underwriting, that firm is called the **originating house.** The originating house need not be a single firm if the negotiation involves several investment bankers. In this case, several firms can join together to manage the underwriting and the selling of securities to the general public.

Originating house ▲
Investment banker who makes an agreement to sell a new issue and forms a syndicate to sell the securities

The originating house does not usually try to sell all of the securities by itself but forms a **syndicate** to market them. The syndicate is a group of brokerage houses that have joined together to underwrite a specific sale of securities. Each member of the syndicate is then allotted a specified number of the securities and is responsible for their sale.

Syndicate ▲
Selling group formed to market a new issue of securities

The use of a syndicate has several advantages. The syndicate has access to many potential buyers for the securities. Also, by using a syndicate the number of securities that each brokerage firm must sell is reduced. This increase in the number of potential customers and the decrease in the amount that each broker must sell increase the probability that the entire issue of securities will be sold. Thus, syndication makes possible both the sale of a large offering of securities and a reduction in the risk borne by each member of the selling group.

TYPES OF AGREEMENTS The agreement between the investment bankers and the firm may be one of two types. The investment bankers may agree to purchase (i.e., to underwrite) the entire issue of securities and to sell them to the general public. This guarantees a specified amount of money to the firm that is issuing the securities. The alternative is a **best efforts agreement,** in which the investment bankers make the best ef-

Best efforts agreement ▲
Contract with an investment banker for the sale of securities in which the investment banker does not guarantee the sale but does agree to make the best effort to sell the securities

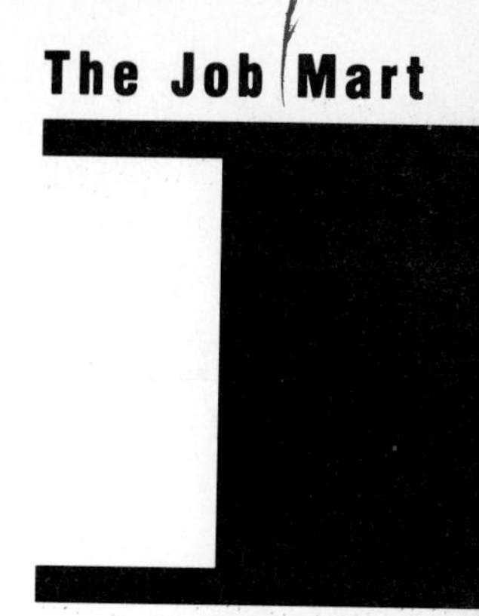

Investment Banker

■ Job Description: Raise funds for firms and governments through the initial sale of securities to the general public and financial institutions. May specialize in (1) a specific type of financing, such as the leasing of capital equipment, (2) a particular type of security, such as junk bonds or municipal securities, or (3) special situations, such as bankruptcy and corporate reorganizations. ■ Job Requirements: Knowledge of security markets, financial accounting, taxation, regulation of security markets, and federal security laws. Ability to use spreadsheets and other computer-driven programs. ■ Characteristics: Position demands excellent communication and negotiation skills in addition to the analytical and technical knowledge required for the particular area of specialization.

---

forts to sell the securities but do not guarantee that a specified amount of money will be raised. The risk of the sale is borne by the issuing firm because if the sale fails, the firm does not receive the funds. In an underwriting the risk of selling the securities is borne by the investment bankers, and most sales of new securities are of this type. The underwriters purchase all of the securities, pay the expenses, and bear the risk of selling the securities, with the anticipation of recouping the expenses through the sale. Since they have agreed to purchase the entire issue, the underwriters must pay the firm for all of the securities even if the syndicate is unable to sell them.

It is for this reason that the pricing of securities is crucial. If the initial offer price is too high, the syndicate will be unable to sell the securities. When this occurs, the investment bankers have two choices: (1) to maintain the offer price and to hold the securities in inventory until they are sold or (2) to let the market find a lower price level that will induce investors to purchase the securities. Neither choice benefits the investment bankers. If the underwriters purchase the securities and hold them in inventory, they either must tie up their own funds, which could be earning a return elsewhere, or must borrow funds to pay for the securities. Like any other firm the investment bankers must pay interest on these borrowed funds. Thus, the decision to support the offer price of the securities prevents the investment bankers from investing their own capital elsewhere or (and this case is the more likely) requires that they borrow substantial amounts of capital. In either case, the profit margin on the underwriting is substantially decreased, and the investment bankers may even experience a loss on the underwriting.

Instead of supporting the price, the underwriters may choose to let the price of the securities fall. The inventory of unsold securities can then be sold, and the underwriters will not tie up capital or have to borrow money from their sources of credit. If the underwriters make this choice, they force losses on themselves when the securities are sold at less than cost. But they also cause the customers who bought the securities at the initial offer price to lose. The underwriters certainly do not want to inflict losses on these customers, because if they experience losses continually, the underwriters' market for future security issues will vanish. Therefore, the investment bankers try not to overprice a new issue of securities, for overpricing will ultimately result in their suffering losses.

There is also an incentive to avoid underpricing new securities. If the issue is underpriced, all of the securities will readily be sold, and their price will rise because demand will have exceeded supply. The buyers of the securities will be satisfied, for the price of the securities will have increased as a result of the underpricing. The initial purchasers of the securities reap windfall profits, but these profits are really at the expense of the company whose securities were underpriced. If the underwriters had assigned a higher price to the securities, the company would have raised more capital. Underwriting is a very competitive business, and each security issue is individually negotiated; hence, if one investment banker consistently underprices securities, firms will employ competitors to underwrite their securities.

Preliminary prospectus ▲
First document filed with the SEC describing a proposed new issue of securities to be sold to the general public

Securities and Exchange Commission (SEC) ▲
Federal agency that enforces the federal security laws

Registration ▲
Process by which information concerning an issue of securities to be sold to the public is filed with the SEC

Flotation costs ▲
Costs associated with an issue of securities

MARKETING NEW SECURITIES Once the terms of the sale have been agreed on, the managing house may issue a **preliminary prospectus.** This is often referred to as a "red herring" because of the red lettering on the title page. This lettering informs the prospective buyer that the securities are being registered with the **Securities and Exchange Commission (SEC)** and may subsequently be offered for sale. As is explained in more detail in Chapter 6, the SEC is the agency that enforces the federal security laws. **Registration** refers to the disclosure of information concerning the firm, the securities being offered for sale, and the use of the proceeds from the sale.

The cost of printing the red herring is borne by the underwriters, who recoup this cost through the underwriting fees (i.e., **flotation costs**). This preliminary prospectus describes the company and the securities to be issued; it includes the firm's income statement and balance sheets, its current activities (such as a pending merger or labor negotiation), the regulatory bodies to which it is subject, and the nature of its competition. The preliminary prospectus is thus a detailed document concerning the company and is, unfortunately, usually tedious reading.

The preliminary prospectus does not include the price of the securities. That will be determined on the day that the securities are issued. If security prices decline or rise, the price of the new securities may be adjusted for the change in market conditions. In fact, if prices decline sufficiently, the firm has the option of postponing or even canceling the underwriting.

EXHIBIT 2.2

Title Page of a Prospectus

The title page of a prospectus gives the number of securities being issued, their price, the flotation costs, and the underwriters.

Company →

1,984,730 Shares

JAMES RIVER CORPORATION

OF VIRGINIA

Common Stock, $.10 Par Value

All of the shares offered hereby will be offered for the accounts of the selling stockholders named herein under "Selling Stockholders".

The Common Stock is listed on the New York Stock Exchange. The last reported sale price of the Common Stock on such exchange on June 25, 1984 was $27 1/4 per share.

THESE SECURITIES HAVE NOT BEEN APPROVED OR DISAPPROVED BY THE SECURITIES AND EXCHANGE COMMISSION NOR HAS THE COMMISSION PASSED UPON THE ACCURACY OR ADEQUACY OF THIS PROSPECTUS. ANY REPRESENTATION TO THE CONTRARY IS A CRIMINAL OFFENSE.

Price Data →

	Price to Public	Underwriting Discount	Proceeds to Selling Stockholders(1)
Per Share	$27.250	$1.125	$26.125
Total	$54,083,892.50	$2,232,821.25	$51,851,071.25

(1) James River estimates its expenses in connection with this offering to be $130,000.

Flotation Costs

The above shares of Common Stock are offered by the several Underwriters when, as and if issued and accepted by the Underwriters and subject to their right to reject orders in whole or in part, and certain other conditions. It is expected that delivery of the shares will be made on or about July 3, 1984.

Underwriters →

Kidder, Peabody & Co.
Incorporated

Scott & Stringfellow, Inc.

Wheat, First Securities, Inc.

Source: Reprinted with permission from Scott & Stringfellow, Inc.

After the shares have been approved for issue by the SEC, a final **prospectus** is published. Except for changes that are required by the SEC, it is virtually identical to the preliminary prospectus. The red lettering is removed, and information regarding the price of the security, the underwriting discount, and the proceeds to the company, along with any more recent financial data, is added. Exhibit 2.2 illustrates the title page for the final prospectus for an issue of 1,984,730 shares of James River Corporation. The names of the managing underwriters are in large print at the bottom of the page. These managing underwriters formed the syndicate that sold the shares to the general public. In this example, more than 80 firms participated in the selling group.[7]

Prospectus Document filed with the SEC that describes a new issue of securities and that is sent to each investor who purchases the securities

[7] How this stock has performed is illustrated in the next section.

The cost of underwriting, which is the difference between the price of the securities to the public and the proceeds to the firm, is also given in the prospectus shown in Exhibit 2.2. In this example, the cost is $1.125 per share, which is 4.31 percent of the proceeds received by the firm for each share. The total cost is $2,232,821.25 for the sale of these shares. Underwriting fees tend to vary with the dollar value of the securities being underwritten and the type of securities being sold. Since some of the expenses are fixed (e.g., preparation of the prospectus), the unit cost for a large underwriting is smaller. Also, it may be more difficult to sell speculative securities than quality securities. Thus, underwriting fees for speculative issues tend to be higher.

In addition to the fee, the underwriter may receive indirect compensation, which may be in the form of the right (or option) to buy additional securities or membership on the firm's board of directors. Such indirect compensation may be as important as the monetary fee because it unites the underwriter and the firm. After the initial sale, the underwriter often becomes a market maker for the securities, which is particularly important to the investing public. Without a secondary market in which to sell the security, investors would be less interested in buying the securities initially. By maintaining a market in the security, the brokerage firm eases the task of selling the securities originally.

VOLATILITY OF THE NEW ISSUE MARKET The new issue market (especially for common stock) can be extremely volatile. There have been periods when the investing public seemed willing to purchase virtually any security that was being sold on the market. There have also been periods during which new companies were simply unable to raise money, and large companies did so only under onerous terms.

The new issue market is not only volatile regarding the number of securities that are offered but also regarding the price changes of the new issues. When the new issue market is "hot," it is not unusual for the prices to rise dramatically. In many cases, however, prices subsequently decline even more remarkably. The dramatic decline of Activision is illustrated in Figure 2.3. Activision, a manufacturer of video games and cassettes, went public near the end of the initial video game fad. The sales and profits of the firm rapidly slumped, and the price of the stock fell about 90 percent from its initial offer price. Obviously, investors who purchased those shares when they were initially offered to the general public suffered losses.[8]

Not all new issues perform like that of Activision. Despite the fact that some firms do not grow and prosper, others succeed and steadily grow. For example, James River Corporation went public on March 16, 1973, and has done quite well. This performance is illustrated in Fig-

[8]The stock closed 1990 at 15/32 and the firm's name had been changed to Mediagenic.

FIGURE 2.3

Price of Activision, Inc. (June 1983–January 1991)

The prices of some new issues decline dramatically in the secondary markets.

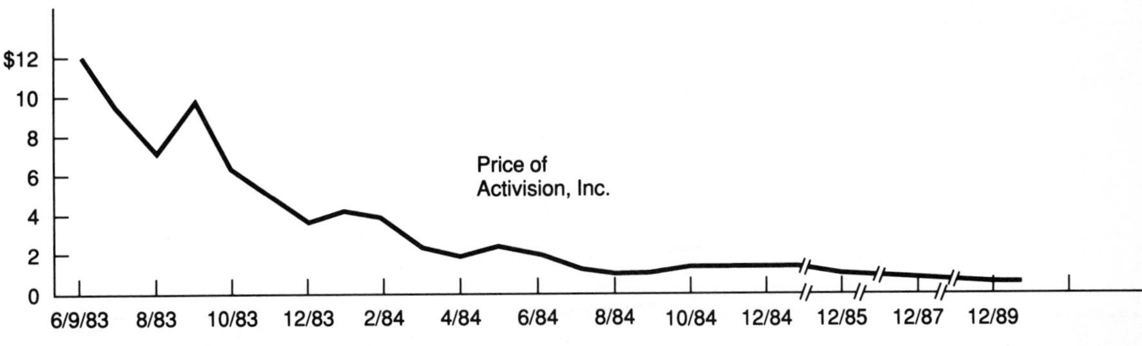

ure 2.4, which plots the annual range of the stock's price and the firm's earnings per share through 1989. As may be seen from the graph, there has been a steady increase in the firm's earnings and in the price of its stock.

All firms, of course, were small at one time, and each one had to go public to have a market for its shares. Someone bought the shares of IBM, Xerox, and Johnson & Johnson when these firms initially sold shares to the general public. The new issue market has offered and continues to offer the opportunity to invest in emerging firms, some of which may achieve substantial returns for those investors or speculators who are willing to accept the risk. It is the possibility of such large rewards that makes the new issue market so exciting. However, if the past is an indicator of the future, many firms that go public will fail and will inflict significant losses on those investors who have accepted this risk by purchasing securities issued by the small, emerging firms.

SHELF-REGISTRATIONS The previous discussion was cast in terms of firms initially selling their stock to the general public (i.e., the "initial public offering" or "going public"). Firms that have previously issued securities and are currently public may also raise funds by selling new securities. If the sales are to the general public, the same basic procedure applies. The new securities must be registered with and approved by the SEC before they may be sold to the public, and the firm often must use the services of an investment banker to facilitate the sale.

There are, however, differences between an initial public offering and the sale of additional securities by a publicly-held firm. The first major difference concerns the price of the securities. Because a market

FIGURE 2.4

Annual Price Range and Earnings per Share of James River Corporation (Prices Adjusted for Stock Splits)

The per share earnings and stock price have risen since the firm went public.

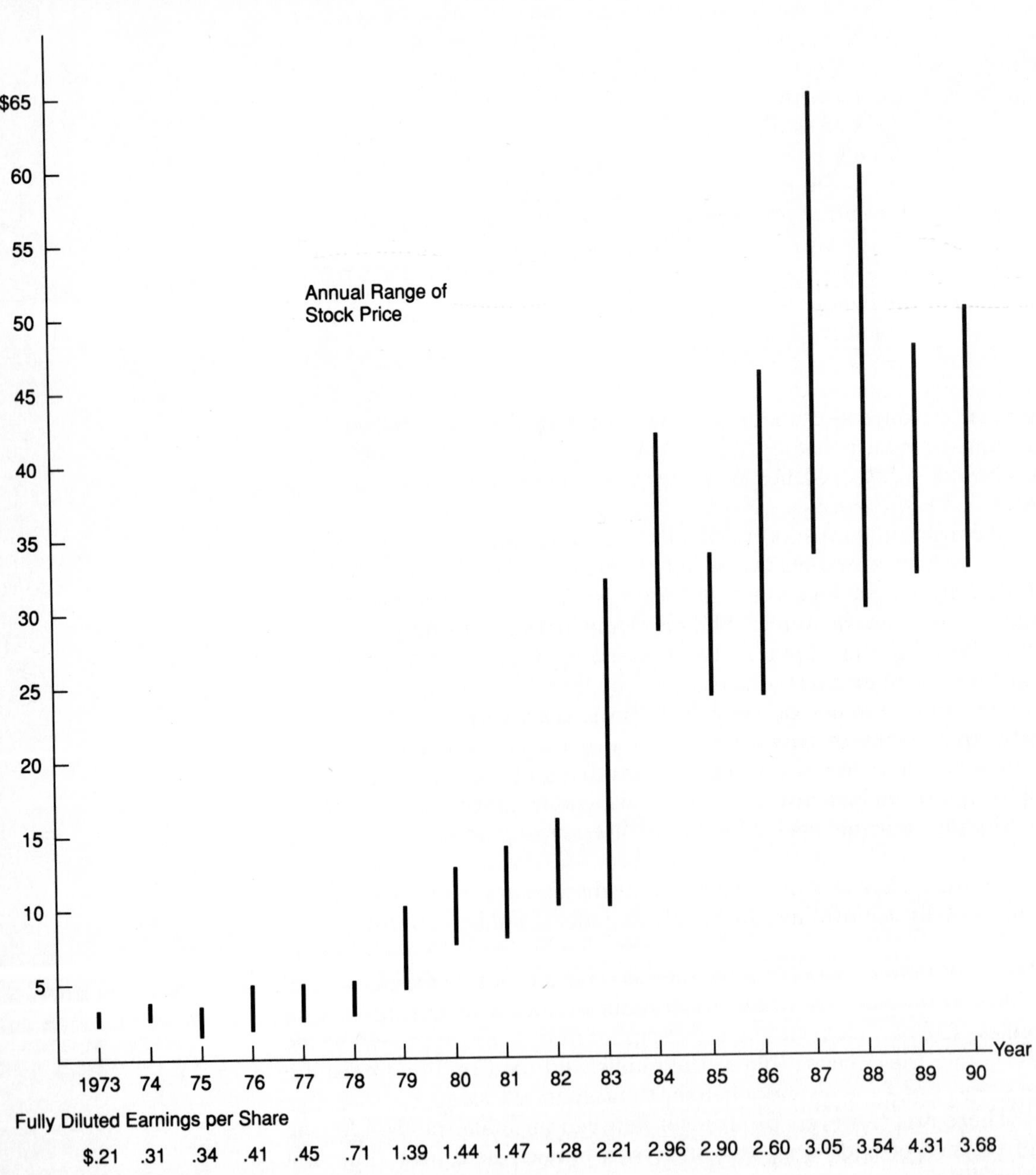

Source: James River annual reports, various issues.

already exists for the firm's stock, the problem of an appropriate price for the additional shares is virtually eliminated. This price will approximate the going market price on the date of issue. Second, because the firm must periodically publish information (e.g., the annual report) and file documents with the SEC, there is less need for a detailed prospectus. Many publicly-held firms construct a prospectus describing a proposed issue of new securities and file it with the SEC. This document is called a "shelf-registration." After the shelf-registration has been approved, the firm may sell the securities whenever the need for the funds arises. Such shelf-registrations offer the issuing firm considerable flexibility because the securities do not have to be issued but can be quickly sold if the firm deems that the conditions are optimal for the sale.

Some **private placements** are made with venture capital firms or mutual funds that specialize in emerging firms. Small firms are often unable to raise capital through traditional sources. The size of the issue may be too small or the firm perceived as too risky for an underwriting through an investment banker. Venture capitalists thus fill a void by acquiring securities issued by small firms with exceptional growth potential.

Private placement ▲
Nonpublic sale of securities to a financial institution

Of course, not all small firms with exceptional growth potential realize that potential. Venture capitalists often sustain large losses on these investments, but their successes can generate very large returns. If a venture capitalist invests $1,000,000 in five firms and four fail but one grows into a successful business, the one large gain can more than offset the investments in the four losers.

The venture capitalist's success depends on the ability to identify quality management and new products with market potential. While venture capitalists must negotiate terms that will reward their risk taking, they must not stifle the entrepreneurial spirit necessary to successfully manage an emerging business.

Once the firm does grow and achieve success, the securities purchased by the venture capitalist may be sold to the general public through a public offering. Many initial public offerings of securities combine a sale of new securities to raise funds for the firm and a sale of existing securities by existing stockholders. These holdings are often composed of shares originally purchased by the venture capitalists who are using the initial public sale as a means to realize their profits on their investments in the successful firm.

SUMMARY

Money is anything that is generally accepted for the exchange of goods and services. The supply of money depends on the amount of coins and currency in circulation and the demand deposits in banks. The value of money depends on what it may purchase. This value is different from an interest rate which is the price of credit. While the role of money is to facilitate transactions, the role of interest rates is to allocate the nation's scarce supply of credit.

The flow of capital to business is exceedingly important to an advanced economy, as the nation's supply of goods and services would be reduced if the funds available for investment were not transferred to firms, individuals, and governments in need of the funds. This transfer has led to the development of a sophisticated financial system which includes the issuing of new securities, the creation of financial intermediaries, and the development of secondary markets for the transferring of existing securities among investors.

The transfer of funds from individuals, firms, or governments with excess funds to those economic units needing the funds may occur either directly or indirectly. The direct transfer occurs when individuals invest in their own businesses or buy newly issued securities. The indirect transfer occurs through financial intermediaries that stand between the ultimate suppliers and ultimate users of the funds. A financial intermediary creates a claim on itself, such as a savings account, when it obtains the money from savers. When the intermediary lends the money, it creates a claim on the borrower. Thus, a financial intermediary in effect takes on the claim against the borrower and converts it into a claim on itself that the saver is willing to accept.

Firms may also obtain capital directly by selling new securities to savers. These sales are facilitated by investment bankers who act as middlemen between the issuing firm and the savers. In many cases the investment bankers guarantee the issuing firm a specified amount of money. That is, the investment bankers underwrite the securities and bear the risk of the sale. Investment bankers, however, do not create claims on themselves such as the savings account issued by financial intermediaries. The savers who purchase new securities own claims on the firms that issued the securities. These savers do not own claims on the investment bankers.

Firms may also sell a block of securities to one buyer such as an insurance company. Such a sale is a private placement, and it avoids the costs associated with an underwriting. There are also specialized venture capital firms that provide funds to small, emerging firms that offer exceptional potential for growth.

Review Questions

1. What is the role of money? How is the supply of money measured? How does the role of money differ from the role of interest rates?
2. What is a yield curve? Generally, what is the relationship between the term of a loan and the rate of interest?
3. How do financial intermediaries differ from investment bankers? What role

does the creation of claims have on the transfer of funds from savers to firms and governments?

4. What role does each of the following play in an underwriting?
   a. the originating house
   b. the syndicate
   c. the prospectus
   d. the underwriting discount
5. If a company went public at $30 a share and the price of the stock immediately rose to $35, who receives the windfall gain? From the viewpoint of the underwriter, was this a successful underwriting? Why would an underwriter not want to overprice a new issue?
6. Risk is an unavoidable part of selling a new issue of securities. Who bears the risk in a best efforts sale, and how does such a sale differ from an underwriting? How does the sale of securities to a venture capitalist differ from a sale through an investment banker?

Suggested Readings

For a discussion of the evolving financial services industry, see:

Gart, Alan. *The Insider's Guide to the Financial Services Revolution.* New York: McGraw-Hill, 1984.

Textbooks for courses in financial institutions include:

Henning, Charles N., William Pigott, and Robert Haney Scott. *Financial Markets and the Economy.* 5th ed. Englewood Cliffs, N.J.: Prentice Hall, Inc., 1988.

Kidwell, David S., and Richard L. Peterson, *Financial Institutions, Markets, and Money.* 4th ed. Hinsdale, Ill.: The Dryden Press, 1989.

Rose, Peter S. *Money and Capital Markets.* 3rd ed. Homewood, Ill.: Richard D. Irwin, Inc., 1989.

van Horne, James C. *Financial Markets Rates & Flows.* 3rd ed. Englewood Cliffs, N.J.: Prentice Hall, Inc., 1990.

For a book of readings covering such topics as interest rates, financial institutions, and financial markets, consult:

Havrilesky, Thomas M., and Robert Schweitzer, eds. *Contemporary Developments in Financial Institutions and Markets.* 2d ed. Arlington Heights, Ill.: Harlan Davidson, Inc., 1987.

For a discussion of selling new securities to the general public, see:

Bloch, Ernest. *Inside Investment Banking.* Homewood, Ill.: Dow Jones-Irwin, 1986.

This book explains the process of issuing new securities and the subsequent making of markets in these securities and discusses recent financial innovations and public policy regarding investment banking.

Hayes, Samuel L. III. "The Transformation of Investment Banking." *Harvard Business Review,* January–February 1979, pp. 153–170.

This article details changes in investment banking that occurred in response to negotiated commissions and the decline in stock prices that occurred during the 1970s.

Hayes, Samuel L. III, and Philip M. Hubbard. *Investment Banking—A Tale of Three Cities.* Boston, Mass.: Harvard Business School Press, 1990.

This book traces the evolution of international investment banking with emphasis on London, New York, and Tokyo.

Financial Intermediaries

Learning Objectives

1. Explain the advantages associated with financial intermediaries.
2. Enumerate the assets and liabilities of a commercial bank.
3. Explain the source of a commercial bank's profits and the role played by differences in yields.
4. Differentiate the portfolios of the various financial intermediaries.
5. Explain the popularity and pattern of growth in money market mutual funds.
6. Enumerate causes of the savings and loan debacle.
7. Explain the role of the Office of Trust Supervision and the Resolution Trust Corporation.

Robert Frost noted that "a bank is a place where they lend you an umbrella in fine weather and ask for it back when it begins to rain." Banks and their managers are often viewed with more than a bit of cynicism. Perhaps this cynicism is the result of the visibility of commercial banks and other depository institutions. Virtually everyone has contact with a bank. The public is bombarded with advertisements ranging from types of deposits being offered to a variety of loans available to potential borrowers. In addition, the failure of many thrift institutions, especially savings and loan associations, and the resulting large, even staggering, losses inflicted upon taxpayers are frequently part of the daily news.

Of course, a bank or any financial intermediary can only lend what is lent to it. All depository institutions and the various financial intermediaries intensely compete for those funds. The loans that are made by banks also compete with other sources of credit available to borrowers. Thus, an individual financial intermediary competes with other intermediaries for both funds and loans. To be successful, a financial intermediary must attract money and subsequently lend it for a profit. Profit margins are usually small, and a few bad loans can significantly reduce the intermediary's earnings.

This chapter is concerned with financial intermediaries—the assets they own, the liabilities they owe, the differences among them, and the recent failures by a large number of savings institutions. Since commercial banks constitute such an important intermediary, special emphasis is devoted to their assets, liabilities, and earnings. After this coverage of commercial banks, other depository institutions such as savings and loan associations, life insurance companies, and money market mutual funds are discussed. The chapter ends with coverage of the causes of the large losses sustained during the late 1980s by savings and loan associations and discussion of the Office of Thrift Supervision and the Resolution Trust Corporation, which is responsible for the sale and liquidation of bankrupt thrift institutions.

THE VARIETY OF FINANCIAL INTERMEDIARIES

As was explained in the previous chapter, a financial intermediary transfers command over resources (i.e., savings) from those with funds to lend to those who need funds. This process is achieved through the intermediary's creating a claim on itself. This process of creation of claims is crucial to the definition of a financial intermediary. A brokerage firm that buys and sells stock for its clients does not create a claim on itself; thus, it is not a financial intermediary but a middleman that facilitates the buying and selling of securities.

When a saver deposits funds in a financial intermediary, that individual has a claim on the intermediary, not on the person to whom the intermediary lends the funds. If the saver had directly lent the money to the ultimate user and the user subsequently failed, the saver would have sustained a loss. This may not happen if the saver lends the money to a financial intermediary. For example, if a financial intermediary makes a bad loan and sustains a loss, the saver does not sustain the loss unless the financial intermediary fails. Even then the saver may not sustain a loss if the deposits are insured. The combination of a claim on the intermediary (and not on the ultimate user of the funds) and the insuring of deposits have made depository institutions a primary haven for the savings of many risk-averse investors.

To tap these sources of savings, a variety of institutions have evolved that perform the role of a financial intermediary. Commercial banks, savings and loan associations, credit unions, and life insurance companies are all financial intermediaries that channel the funds of savers to borrowers. During the 1980s, the differentiation among these various financial institutions was blurred by changes in the regulation of the banking system.

Today it is probably safe to assert that many savers and potential borrowers are not aware of differences among commercial banks, savings and loan associations, and mutual savings banks. These institutions offer similar services and pay virtually the same rate of interest on deposits. In addition, the portfolio of assets acquired by each depository institution is more similar than in the past. While previously the savings banks made primarily mortgage loans, their portfolios have been broadened to include a more varied mix of assets.

This blurring of the distinctions among the various financial intermediaries is the result of changes in the regulatory environment. Under the Depository Institutions Deregulation and Monetary Control Act of 1980 (referred to hereafter as the Monetary Control Act of 1980), all depository institutions (i.e., commercial banks, savings and loan associations, mutual savings banks, and credit unions) became subject to the regulation of the Federal Reserve. The Federal Reserve's powers extend to the types of accounts these institutions may offer and the amount that the various depository institutions must hold in reserve against their deposits.

While the Federal Reserve has supervisory power over depository institutions' portfolios, the Monetary Control Act of 1980 gave the managements of various financial institutions more flexibility to vary their loan portfolios. In addition, each depository institution was granted the right to borrow funds from the Federal Reserve. This reform legislation also provided for the phasing out of Regulation Q, which placed ceilings on the interest rates banks could pay depositors. Banks may now offer whatever yields they deem desirable to attract deposits. The net effect of these reforms has been to reduce the differentiation among the various types of financial intermediaries. Thus, for most individuals the difference between the local bank and the local savings and loan association is slight.

Advantages of Financial Intermediaries

What are the advantages of a system of financial intermediaries? Obviously, for such a system to exist there have to be advantages to all concerned—borrower, lender, and the financial intermediary. One of the major advantages to the borrower is that the intermediary is able to pool the funds of many people and thus make loans of substantial size. A corporation like General Motors would have a major problem if it continually had to approach individual savers to borrow money. Commercial banks, however, can lend General Motors a significant amount of money, and thus the commercial banks save General Motors the cost of the search for funds. A bank is able to do this because it pools the deposits of many savers and so has larger amounts available to lend.

For the saver, financial intermediaries offer the advantages of income, convenience, and risk reduction. Savings accounts and NOW accounts pay interest, and checking accounts are a convenient means to make payments. These accounts also permit the savers to deposit and withdraw small amounts of money. Other securities, like stocks and bonds, may not be divisible into such small quantities, and if small quantities are available, there is a substantial commission cost for dealing with such small amounts of securities. Hence, these securities may not be as convenient as savings and checking accounts.

In addition, these accounts provide ways to earn modest returns with very little risk of loss. If an individual with a modest sum to invest (e.g., \$5,000–\$10,000) were to lend the funds directly to a firm or individual, the entire amount could be lost. Even if the borrower were not to default on the loan, the saver may be unable to sell the debt instrument in case the funds were needed before the loan matured. A secondary market for many types of individual loans simply does not exist. Even if a secondary market does exist, there still is no assurance the seller will receive the initial amount invested in the debt instruments.

One of the most important advantages offered individual savers by banking institutions is the virtual elimination of these sources of risk. Such safety of principal cannot be achieved by savers who directly lend to other individuals and firms. However, there is virtually no risk of loss of funds deposited in a savings or a checking account. This is particularly true since the advent of federal deposit insurance. If a saver places \$1,000 in a federally insured savings account, the \$1,000 principal is safe and may be withdrawn at the saver's option.

While federal insurance ensures this safety of principal, the very nature of the intermediary's portfolio itself reduces the risk of loss to the saver. The financial intermediary pools the funds of many savers and acquires a diversified portfolio of loans, which spreads the risk.[1] Even if

[1] Risk reduction through the construction of diversified portfolios is discussed in Chapter 8.

the value of some of the intermediary's assets were to decline, such declines may not endanger the financial position of the intermediary. In the case in which the financial intermediary does experience financial difficulty, federal deposit insurance protects the depositors.

While many financial intermediaries do offer federal deposit insurance, it is important to realize that *not all offer such insurance.* For example, there is no federal insurance program for life insurance companies. A saver's policy is only as strong as the company and the assets it owns. If the company were to fail, the saver would stand to lose the funds that have been invested in the life insurance. Hence, it is incorrect to assume that savings invested in a financial intermediary are necessarily free from the risk of loss.

Besides advantages to borrowers and lenders, there must also be an advantage to the financial intermediary. It must receive compensation for the service it is providing the lenders and the borrowers. This compensation is the potential for profit. The source of this profit is the difference between what the intermediaries pay depositors and what they charge borrowers. Of course, the lenders and the borrowers could deal directly with each other and share these profits (which they do when stocks and bonds are issued and sold to households). But the advantages offered by financial intermediaries, such as convenience and reduced risk to savers and the continuous availability of large sources of funds for large corporate borrowers, may not exist when the borrowers and lenders deal directly with each other.

Financial intermediaries also offer an important advantage to the aggregate economy. Since they facilitate the transfer of funds from savers to firms and households that need funds, financial intermediaries increase the aggregate level of income and employment. Because firms are able to acquire funds through the intermediaries, they are able to employ additional labor. These workers would not have been employed if firms had been unable to acquire the necessary funds from the financial intermediaries. Thus, all members of the society benefit from the existence of the financial intermediaries. The nation's level of output would be considerably lower if financial intermediaries did not make possible the transfer of funds from savers to borrowers.

COMMERCIAL BANKS

In terms of size, commercial banks are the most important depository institution. The total amount of deposits and loans made by commercial banks is given in Exhibit 3.1. Commercial banks' importance to business is evident, as loans to firms exceeded $646.7 billion and accounted for 19.5 percent of commercial banks' total assets. Commercial banks are also a prime source of funds to consumers, with consumer loans ac-

EXHIBIT 3.1

Assets and Liabilities of Commercial Banks as of September 1990 (in Billions)

Loans constitute over 68 percent of commercial banks' assets, and deposits constitute over 69 percent of their sources of finance.

Assets			
Cash (currency and coins)		$ 29.2	0.9%
Reserves with the Federal Reserve		33.9	1.0
U.S. government securities		432.2	13.0
Other securities		168.2	5.1
Loans			
Commercial and industrial	$ 646.7		19.5
Real estate	817.4		24.6
Loans to individuals	383.9		11.6
Interbank loans	188.8		5.7
Other loans	227.1		6.8
		$2,263.9	
Other assets		392.7	11.8
		$3,320.1	100.0%
Liabilities			
Demand deposits	$ 596.3		18.0%
Savings accounts	563.5		17.0
Time deposits	1,138.3		34.3
		$2,298.1	
Other borrowings and liabilities		801.5	24.1
Equity (net worth)		220.5	6.6
		$3,320.1	100.0%

Derived from the Federal Reserve Bulletin, *December 1990, p. A18.*

counting for 11.6 percent of banks' total assets. Most of the loans to firms and households are for a relatively short term (i.e., less than one to five years to maturity). Commercial banks tend to stress loans that mature quickly. This emphasis on short maturities is the result of the rapid turnover of bank deposits (especially demand deposits) and the need for banks to coordinate their portfolios with changes in the economic environment and the level of interest rates.

A Commercial Bank's Balance Sheet

An individual commercial bank's balance sheet is given in Exhibit 3.2. It is similar to the balance sheet of the aggregation of all commercial banks given in Exhibit 3.1. The largest asset is the bank's loan portfolio, which constitutes over 70 percent of its total assets.

Besides the loan portfolio, commercial banks hold a variety of investment debt securities. While the loans are individually negotiated between the bank and the borrower, these securities are bought (and sold)

EXHIBIT 3.2

A Simple Balance Sheet for a Commercial Bank as of 12/31/XX (in Millions)

Loans constitute a large proportion of a commercial bank's assets, and deposits constitute a large proportion of its sources of finance.

Assets		
Cash and reserves	$ 140.0	9.2%
U.S. government securities	70.0	4.6
State and local government securities	180.0	11.8
Loans	1,080.0	71.0
Miscellaneous assets	50.0	3.4
	$1,520.0	100.0%
Liabilities		
Demand deposits	$ 400.0	26.3%
Savings accounts	310.0	20.4
Corporate and government savings accounts	250.0	16.4
Savings certificates (time deposits)	230.0	15.1
Loans from other banks	80.0	5.3
Short-term borrowing	140.0	9.2
Stockholders' Equity	110.0	7.3
	$1,520.0	100.0%

in the securities markets. The assets of the bank include the debt of state and local governments ($180 million and 11.8 percent of the total assets) and U.S. government securities ($70 million and 4.6 percent). The remaining assets are cash and reserves ($140 million and 9.2 percent) and various miscellaneous assets ($50 million and 3.4 percent).

The debts of state and local governments are called **municipal bonds** or **tax-exempt bonds,** because the interest is exempt from federal income tax. These tax-exempt bonds are purchased by the bank in order for the bank to receive tax-free income. For a particular bank these bonds will frequently include the issues of local governments served by the bank. Many local governments have excellent working relationships with local banks; they keep their accounts in these banks and borrow from them. Such working relationships between local governments and local banks are often important for small communities, for these communities may have difficulty borrowing outside their geographical region.

Municipal (tax-exempt) bonds
Bonds issued by a state or local government whose interest is not subject to federal income taxation

Cash and reserves are assets that the bank is required to hold against its deposit liabilities. These assets do not earn interest for the bank, and hence it seeks to minimize the amount of funds tied up in these assets. (The reserve requirement is set by the Federal Reserve and is discussed in more detail in the subsequent chapter.) The miscellaneous assets include such items as the building, plant, and equipment.

The primary liabilities of the commercial bank are its deposits: checking accounts (demand deposits) and various types of savings and time deposits. These deposits constitute 26.3 percent and 51.9 percent, respectively, of the bank's sources of finance. Demand deposits are payable

Financial Facts

Variable Term Certificates of Deposit

Most commercial banks and savings banks offer savers certificates of deposit for a specified term with a specific interest rate. A few banks permit the saver to specify the term and then assign a rate of interest. Such variable term certificates give savers a very convenient means for managing short-term funds. • Suppose a person's parents have accumulated $10,000 for his or her education, but the tuition and room/board bills fall due 35 days and 76 days in the future, respectively. Variable term CDs permit an individual to invest the funds for exactly the number of days that the funds aren't needed. In this case, two certificates could be acquired; one would mature after 34 days, and the other after 75 days. If the bank had only offered three-month certificates, the person would have had to invest the funds in some other alternative, such as a money market mutual fund. The variable term CD permits individuals to invest their funds for exactly the time period desired, while still having the safety associated with FDIC, since the certificates would be insured up to the legal limit. •

---

on demand, for the owner of a checking account may demand immediate cash, and funds in the account may be readily transferred by check.

Savings accounts and savings certificates are interest-bearing accounts. Funds deposited in a regular savings account may be withdrawn at will. Time deposits, which are also referred to as **certificates of deposit** (or **CDs,** as they are commonly called), are issued for a fixed term such as six months or two years. The saver may redeem the CD prior to maturity, but early redemption results in a penalty, such as the loss of interest for one quarter. For CDs issued in denominations greater than $100,000, the terms (i.e., the rate of interest and the length of time to maturity) are mutually agreed upon by the bank and the saver with the funds. These "jumbo CDs" may be subsequently sold, as there is a secondary market in CDs with denominations exceeding $100,000. Since large denomination CDs may be bought and sold, they are often referred to as **negotiable CDs** to differentiate them from smaller denomination CDs for which no secondary market exists.

Certificate of deposit (CD) ▲
Time deposit issued by a bank with a specified interest rate and maturity

Negotiable CD ▲
Certificate of deposit issued in amounts of $100,000 or more whose terms are individually negotiated between the bank and the lender and for which there exists a secondary market

For denominations of less than $100,000, the bank establishes the terms and offers the CD to the general public. If the public finds the terms unattractive (e.g., the rate of interest is less than that offered by competing banks), the bank does not receive any deposits. Thus, it is not surprising that the terms offered by one bank are very similar to the terms offered by competing banks; differences tend to be small or very subtle, such as the frequency with which interest is added to the principal. (The more frequently the interest is added, or compounded, the more interest the depositor earns, as interest earns additional interest.)[2]

---

[2]Compounding and the earning of interest on previously earned interest are discussed in Chapter 7 on the time value of money.

The remaining liabilities of the commercial bank include other borrowings from a variety of sources. For example, commercial banks borrow from each other in a special market referred to as "federal funds," and they borrow from the Federal Reserve. The last entry on the commercial bank's balance sheet is stockholders' equity, which represents the stockholders' investment in the firm.

While this balance sheet shows the various sources of funds available to the bank, it also illustrates that the various types of deposits are the most important. For this bank, checking and savings accounts constitute 78.2 percent of the firm's sources of finance. The balance sheet also indicates that total deposits greatly exceed stockholders' equity. The bank has a large amount of debt outstanding when it is realized that the deposits are really loans to the bank by households, firms, and governments.

Since the bank has only a small amount of equity and a large amount of debt, a small decrease in the value of the assets could eliminate the bank's equity. In this case, a 7.3 percent decline in the value of the assets, from $1,520 million to $1,410 million, will erase the equity. Bankers are aware of this potential risk, and it is one reason why they tend to be conservative. A bank must be cautious when making loans and investments, because a small amount of loss may cause the bank to fail.

A Commercial Bank's Earnings

A commercial bank's earnings are generated by the assets that it owns relative to the liabilities that it owes. The assets generate revenues that cover the bank's costs. If the bank generates sufficient revenues, it will operate profitably. Exhibit 3.3, a simple income statement, lists a bank's revenues and expenses. As may be seen from the exhibit, the prime source of the commercial bank's revenues is the interest earned by its loans. Interest charges on the bank's loan portfolio accounted for 86.7 percent of the bank's total revenues. The tax-exempt bonds produced 5.3 percent, and the U.S. government securities generated 2.6 percent of the bank's revenues. Service charges and income produced by the other assets contributed 5.4 percent. The cash in the vault and the reserves produced no revenue for the commercial bank, and hence it is no surprise that banks seek to minimize the amount of cash and reserves they hold.

The commercial bank's expenses include everyday running expenses, such as wages, salaries, and various employee benefits. These accounted for 23.4 percent of its expenses. The bank pays interest to its creditors, who include the holders of time and savings deposits and the various other sources from which the bank has borrowed funds. These interest expenses accounted for 55.5 percent of the bank's total costs. Miscellaneous expenses include insurance, maintenance, and advertising. These accounted for 21.0 percent of the total cost of operations.

EXHIBIT 3.3

Simplified Income Statement for a Commercial Bank for the Period 1/1/XX–12/31/XX (in Millions)

A bank's earnings primarily depend on its interest income relative to its interest expense.

Revenues		
Interest on loans	\$144.4	86.7%
Interest on U.S. government securities	4.4	2.6
Interest on state and local securities	8.8	5.3
Service charges and other income	9.0	5.4
	\$166.6	100.0%
Expenses		
Salaries and employee benefits	36.0	23.4%
Interest on deposits	51.7	33.7
Interest on other borrowings	33.5	21.8
Other expenses	32.2	21.0
	\$153.4	99.9%
Earnings	\$ 13.2	

Operations for this bank were profitable, for it earned \$13.2 million in profits. While the bank's operations were profitable, it took the bank \$1,520 million in assets to earn the \$13.2 million. Thus, the bank's return on its total assets was only 0.86 percent (\$13.2/\$1,520), which appears to be a meager return.[3] Unless it were able to increase the return on its assets, this return implies that the bank would have to increase its assets by \$1,162 to earn an additional \$10.00 (\$1,162 × 0.0086 = \$10). While this profit margin is small, such a small profit margin on total assets is typical of the banking industry. A bank must have a large amount of assets (and, correspondingly, a large amount of deposits) to generate any significant amount of profit.

While the profit margin on total assets is quite modest, the profits earned for the stockholders can be substantial. As may be seen from the balance sheet in Exhibit 3.2, equity is \$110 million, which is only 7.3 percent of the firm's sources of funds. Debt obligations, such as deposits, account for the remaining 92.7 percent. The use of debt financing to acquire assets is called "financial leverage." Financial leverage is one of the most important concepts covered in this text and is discussed in detail in Chapter 17.

The successful use of financial leverage will increase the return earned for the owners (i.e., the stockholders) of the bank. When earnings are expressed as a percent of the equity, the resulting quotient gives the return the bank earned on its stockholders' investment in the firm. For this bank the return on equity is 12 percent (\$13.2/\$110), which is

[3] For a discussion of profit margin and return on equity, see Chapter 16.

considerably higher than the 0.86 percent the bank earned on its total assets.

Why are these percentages so different? How is the bank able to earn only 0.86 percent on its assets but earn 12 percent on its equity? The answer lies in the fact that the bank pays less interest for the funds it borrows and earns more interest on its portfolio of assets. It has borrowed $1,410 million and paid interest of $85.2 million ($51.7 million on deposits and $33.5 million on other borrowings). The average interest cost was 6.04 percent ($85.2/$1,410). The bank loaned these borrowed funds and constructed a portfolio of investments consisting of U.S. government securities ($70 million), state and local securities ($180 million), and loans ($1,080 million). This portfolio earned interest of $157.6 million ($4.4 million on U.S. government securities, $8.8 million on state and local government securities, and $144.4 million on loans). The average return on the portfolio was 11.85 percent ($157.6/$1,330). By borrowing at 6.04 percent and lending at 11.85 percent, the bank successfully generated profits and magnified the return on its stockholders' investment. Thus, even though the bank nets only $0.86 on every $100 in assets, the stockholders earn 12 percent on their funds invested in the firm.

Regulation of Commercial Banks

Commercial banks and other savings banks are subject to a considerable amount of government regulation. The purpose of this regulation is to protect the banks' creditors, especially their depositors. The very nature of banking, with its high use of financial leverage, implies that when a commercial bank fails, substantial losses could be sustained by the bank's depositors. This is exactly what occurred during the Great Depression of the 1930s, when the failure of many commercial banks imposed substantial losses on depositors. These losses led to increased regulation of commercial banks and the establishment of federal deposit insurance, both of which are designed to protect depositors. Such protection should in turn promote a viable banking system and ease the flow of savings into investment.

The regulation of banks comes from both state and federal banking authorities and the Federal Deposit Insurance Corporation. Banks that have national charters must join the Federal Reserve and are subjected to its regulation as well as examination by the Comptroller of the Currency, which is the federal agency that grants national bank charters. Banks with state charters are regulated by the individual state banking commissions and, under the Monetary Control Act of 1980, are subject to regulation by the Federal Reserve. These various authorities regulate and supervise such facets of a bank's operations as its geographic location, the number of banks and branches in an area, and the types of loans and investments the banks may make.

Financial Facts

The Consumer's Bank—Citicorp

A bank earns profits by charging interest on its loans and fees for its services. Many banks specialize in wholesale loans, which are loans to firms and governments. Citibank, a division of Citicorp, is carving a niche for itself by stressing consumer banking. (See Robert E. Norton, "Citibank Wows the Consumer," *Fortune,* June 8, 1987, 48–54). Consumer banking stresses the mass merchandising of financial services, such as automatic teller machines (ATMs), loans to individuals, and bank cards such as Visa and MasterCard. In addition to these cards, Citibank also operates the Diner's Club card and has 9 percent of the total U.S. market for bank credit cards. • In its effort to build up its operations, Citibank has acquired failing savings and loan associations in various geographic areas throughout the country. These purchases will also position the firm for expansion if complete interstate banking becomes a reality. (Currently, limited interstate banking is permitted.) In addition to expansion through acquisitions, Citibank has been willing to grant credit cards to poor credit risks. While the bank has had to take initial losses on some bad debts, the remaining card users are of good quality. The rate of interest on credit card loans tends to be relatively high, so there is a large spread between what the bank earns and what it has to pay for funds. Generally, cardholders are more concerned with convenience and less with the rate of interest being charged, so these loans tend to be very profitable. • Cardholders are also a large pool of potential buyers. Citicorp sells insurance and conducts direct mail merchandising to its cardholders. By selling products directly to customers, the firm avoids the need for retail outlets. The direct sales also help inventory control, because the manufacturer does not have to carry the inventory for as long a period, a fact which should also increase the profitability of the sales. •

Required reserves ▲
Funds that banks must hold against deposit liabilities

Federal Deposit Insurance Corporation (FDIC) ▲
Agency of the federal government that supervises banks and insures deposits

RESERVES Commercial banks and all other depository institutions (i.e., savings and loan associations, mutual savings banks, and credit unions) must keep funds in reserve against their deposit liabilities (i.e., **required reserves**). Under the Depository Institutions Deregulation and Monetary Control Act of 1980, the minimum amount that all banks must maintain as a reserve is determined by the Federal Reserve. This reserve requirement does offer the depositor some degree of safety for deposits, but the prime source of safety for funds deposited in a commercial bank is the deposit insurance obtained from the **Federal Deposit Insurance Corporation (FDIC).** While holding reserves against deposit liabilities may increase the safety of the deposits, such safety is not the prime reason for having reserve requirements. As will be explained in Chapter 4, the reserve requirement is one of the major tools of monetary control. It is this element of control, not safety, that is the reason for having a reserve requirement against the deposit liabilities of banks.

The amount of the reserve requirement varies with the type of account. For example, as of January 1, 1991, checking accounts have a reserve requirement of 12 percent. (The first $40.4 million in checking accounts, NOW accounts, and automatic transfer accounts have a reserve requirement of 3 percent.) Time deposits have reserve requirements

EXHIBIT 3.4

Reserve Requirements as of December 1990

The reserve requirement is primarily against checking accounts.

Checking accounts, NOW accounts, and automatic transfer accounts	
First $40.4 million in deposits	3%
Total deposits exceeding $40.4 million	12%
Time deposit	
Maturity of less than 1½ years	3%
Maturity of 1½ years or more	0%

Source: Federal Reserve Bulletin, *December 1990, p. A8.*

of 0 to 3 percent. These various reserve requirements are given in Exhibit 3.4.

Commercial banks may hold their reserves in two forms: (1) cash in the vault or (2) deposits with another bank, especially the Federal Reserve. If the banks' reserve requirement is 12 percent for demand deposits and the bank receives $100 cash in a checking account, it must hold $12 in reserve against the new demand deposit. The entire $100 in cash is considered part of the bank's total reserves, but the bank must hold only $12 against the deposit liability. The bank may choose to hold $1 of the required reserves in cash in the vault (to meet cash withdrawals) and $11 in the Federal Reserve. The remaining $88 are funds that the bank does not have to hold in reserve, and this amount is called **excess reserves.** Excess reserves are the difference between the bank's total reserves and its required reserves. In this example the difference is $100 − $12 = $88. It is a commercial bank's excess reserves that may be lent to borrowers or used for some other purpose, such as purchasing government securities. If a commercial bank does not have any excess reserves, it is said to be "fully loaned up." To acquire additional income-earning assets such as a government security or a business loan, the bank would have to acquire additional excess reserves.

Excess reserves Reserves held by a bank in excess of those it must hold to meet its reserve requirement

Commercial banks (and other depository institutions) may deposit their reserves in a Federal Reserve bank, or they may deposit their reserves in other banks called **correspondent banks.** Correspondent banks in many cases are large, metropolitan commercial banks. These large correspondent banks frequently provide additional services. For example, they have efficient mechanisms for the clearing of checks and can facilitate check clearing for the smaller banks. The correspondent banks also have research staffs and give management advice and investment counsel. Thus, they are extremely important to the well-being of the small, local banks. Of course, the reason that the correspondent banks are willing to provide these services is that a small bank's deposits are like any other deposits: they are a source of funds that the larger banks may use. Thus, the large commercial banks receive compensation for the ser-

Correspondent bank Major bank with which a smaller bank has a relationship to facilitate check clearing and to serve as a depository for reserves

vices provided to the small banks by being able to use the funds deposited in them by small banks to purchase income-earning assets.

Secondary reserves ▲ Short-term securities, especially treasury bills, held by banks to increase their liquidity

In addition to the required reserves, commercial banks also hold **secondary reserves.** These are high-quality, short-term marketable securities. While regular reserves on deposit at the Federal Reserve do not earn interest, the marketable securities do earn interest. These assets, such as U.S. government securities (Treasury bills), are also very liquid. If the banks were to need funds to meet their reserve requirements, the secondary reserves could be readily liquidated to meet the need. Thus, such securities offer banks both liquidity and a source of interest income.

The importance of reserves and reserve requirements cannot be exaggerated. As is explained in the next chapter, the commercial banking system, through the process of loan creation, can expand or contract the nation's supply of money. The ability of commercial banks and other depository institutions to lend depends on their excess reserves. Thus anything that affects their reserves alters their ability to lend and create money and credit. There are many financial transactions that affect commercial banks' reserves, including the federal government's methods of financing a deficit or the open market operations of the Federal Reserve. The next chapter will discuss several of these financial transactions and their potential impact on commercial bank reserves.

DEPOSIT INSURANCE Federal government deposit insurance is one of the positive results of the Great Depression of the 1930s. The large losses sustained by commercial banks' depositors led to the establishment of the Federal Deposit Insurance Corporation. The establishment of FDIC has significantly increased the general public's confidence in commercial banks. As of this writing, FDIC insures deposits to $100,000. Thus, if a commercial bank should fail, FDIC will reimburse depositors up to the $100,000 limit. Since most individuals do not have that much on deposit, these individuals know that their funds are safe. (If an individual has more than $100,000, the same degree of safety can be achieved by placing amounts up to $100,000 in different banks.) The $100,000 limits does mean that large depositors, including many corporations, are not fully insured and do stand to take losses should a bank fail.

All commercial banks that are members of the Federal Reserve System must be insured by FDIC, and many state banking authorities also require that FDIC insurance be carried by their state nonmember banks. However, some state banking authorities do not require federal deposit insurance. Also foreign banks, such as Bank Leumi (Israel's largest commercial bank), that are licensed to operate in the United States do not have to carry FDIC insurance.

FDIC insurance is not free, for the commercial banks purchase it from FDIC. Even when the insurance is not required, the majority of commercial banks do carry it. This indicates that the managers as well as the regulators of most state banks recognize the importance of the insur-

The Job Mart

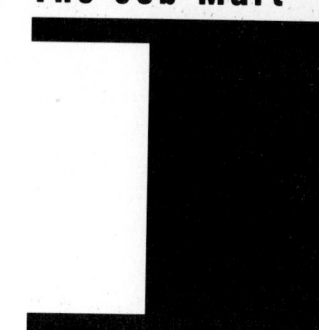

Bank Examiner

■ Job Description: Examine and audit financial statements and loan portfolios of commercial banks and other financial institutions. Determine risk exposure to depositors and identify poor portfolio management and/or poor internal controls. Potential employers include the Federal Reserve or the Comptroller of the Currency. ■ Job Requirements: Background in finance, accounting, and management of loan portfolios. Knowledge of federal or state bank regulations and laws. Experience in banking and/or bank accounting. ■ Characteristics: Since banks and other depository institutions are subject to substantial federal and state legislation, both the banks and the regulatory bodies need individuals to examine the loans and internal procedures of banks. For examiners working for regulatory bodies, substantial travel may be required to cover the banks in a specific geographic area.

---

ance to their depositors and realize that the potential benefits more than justify the cost.

Besides offering deposit insurance, FDIC has further increased public confidence in the banking system through its powers of bank examination. By exercising this power to examine banks, FDIC, along with other regulatory agencies, has improved bank practices. The improved bank practices plus the deposit insurance have significantly improved the quality of banking. However, the establishment of FDIC and other regulatory agencies has not eliminated bank failures, for banks do fail. Most of these are small banks, and losses are not sustained by the many individuals who deposit modest sums with these commercial banks. If necessary, such deposits are reimbursed in full by FDIC up to the $100,000 legal limit. Thus, for most individuals, depositing funds in a commercial bank does not subject the funds to risk of loss.[4]

When a commercial bank does fail, FDIC generally seeks to merge that bank into a stronger bank. This transfer of the deposits to the strong bank saves FDIC from having to reimburse the depositors. If such a merger cannot be arranged, the failed bank may be liquidated, in which case the depositors are reimbursed up to the legal limit, or the failed bank may be reorganized. Perhaps the most famous reorganizations occurred when FDIC assumed control of Continental Illinois National Bank and Trust Company and the Bank of New England in an effort to

---

[4]When the privately owned Exchange Bank of Bloomfield, Iowa, failed, the bank did not have FDIC insurance. Thus, the failure meant the depositors stood to lose a substantial proportion of their funds unless the bank's assets were sufficient to reimburse the depositors.

stop the banks from failing. Since both were among the nation's largest banks, failure to bail them out probably would have reduced the public's confidence in the banking system.

TRENDS IN COMMERCIAL BANK REGULATION Since the passage of deregulation legislation (i.e., the Monetary Control Act of 1980), the banking industry has been undergoing swift and significant change. The industry is very fluid as banking practices and strategies are altered to meet the current legal and competitive environment. Certainly the blurring of the distinctions among various financial intermediaries is a direct result of the deregulation of the banking system. This trend will continue until it may be impossible for the depositor to differentiate between what used to be referred to as a commercial bank and what was referred to as a savings bank.

Even within the group referred to as commercial banks, there will continue to be important changes. One big issue is interstate banking (i.e., permitting commercial banks to cross state lines). While the Monetary Control Act of 1980 precipitated increased competition among banks, it is still uncertain whether commercial banks will also be permitted to expand their banking operations beyond their home state. Currently, bank holding companies can have non-banking operations across state lines. Thus, a bank holding company such as Citicorp, which is the parent of New York's Citibank, has national credit card operations (Diner's Club and Carte Blanche) and an international investment banking operation (Capital Markets Group) that operates in twenty-five countries.

If commercial banks are allowed to operate across state borders, many smaller banks will combine into one larger bank to compete with larger banks. Other small banks may choose to sell out or merge with larger banks. In either case, the number of banks in existence will decline, and the size of the remaining banks will increase.

Many banks are already positioning themselves for these anticipated changes. Moderate-size regional banks have been purchasing smaller banks or merging with each other to be better able to compete with the large banks located in financial centers. For example, Virginia National Bankshares and First and Merchants merged to form Sovran Financial Corporation, which became the largest banking operation in the state of Virginia.

To make the regulatory environment even more complex, some states (e.g., Georgia) have passed enabling legislation that permits interstate banking across their borders with states that pass reciprocal legislation. This resulted in the merger of Citizens and Southern, a large Georgia bank, and the previously mentioned Sovran to form C & S Sovran Corporation, one of the region's largest banking operations. Unless the federal government passes laws banning such regional interstate

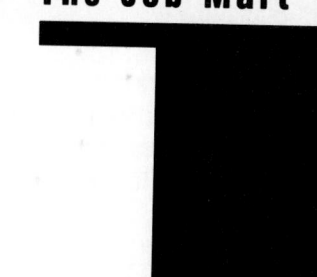

Personal Financial Services Representative

■ Job Description: Develop and implement financial plans for individuals. Explain services and products offered by banks and by brokerage, insurance, and financial planning firms. Review existing financial plans and recommend changes required by changes in client's financial position or obligations. ■ Job Requirements: Broad knowledge of finance, including taxation, financial institutions, business communications, and report writing. Understand financial decision making, budgeting, insurance, real estate, retirement and estate planning, and financial counseling. ■ Characteristics: Position involves initial and frequent contact with clients and the general public. Excellent interpersonal skills and an ability to listen and work well with people are necessary for success. ■

banking, this state legislation will open the door for limited interstate banking even if enabling legislation is not passed by Congress.

SAVINGS AND LOAN ASSOCIATIONS[5]

Savings and loan associations (S&Ls) are just what the name implies: a place for savers to deposit funds that are subsequently loaned by the association. Funds deposited in savings and loan associations may be withdrawn with ease, so savers may consider these accounts to be very liquid. Even after the large losses sustained by some savings and loans during the 1980s, savers' deposits in S&Ls remain safe, because the deposits are now insured by the Savings Association Insurance Fund (SAIF). SAIF, a subsidiary of the FDIC, replaced the Federal Savings and Loan Insurance Corporation (FSLIC), the agency of the federal government that previously had insured deposits in S&Ls. This replacement was necessitated by the failure of so many S&Ls during the late 1980s, since the amount of the losses exceeded the FSLIC's capacity to cover them. The agency became insolvent and collapsed, which led to the creation of the SAIF.[6]

To attract deposits, S&Ls tend to pay a rate of interest that is slightly higher than the rate paid by commercial banks (e.g., ¼ to ½ percent

[5]Savings and loans and mutual savings banks are often referred to as "thrift institutions."

[6]The causes of the failure of S&Ls and the creation of the Office of Thrift Supervision and the Resolution Trust Corporation are discussed later in this chapter.

EXHIBIT 3.5

Assets, Liabilities, and Equity for Savings and Loan Associations as of May 1990 (in Millions)

Equity constitutes a small percentage of S&Ls' sources of finance.

Assets		
Mortgages and mortgage backed securities	$ 874,287	73.0%
Investments in securities and cash	152,393	12.7
Other assets	171,144	14.3
Total assets	$1,197,824	100.0%
Liabilities		
Savings accounts	$ 902,634	75.4%
Other borrowings	270,833	22.6
Equity (net worth)	24,357	2.0
Total liability and equity	$1,197,824	100.0%

Derived from the Federal Reserve Bulletin, *December 1990, p. A26.*

higher). Like commercial banks, S&Ls must hold reserves against their deposit liabilities. Since the amount of required reserves is the same for all depository institutions, the capacity of S&Ls to grant loans is no different than that of the commercial banks.

While commercial banks grant a variety of loans, savings and loans have historically invested most of their funds in mortgage loans, especially loans to finance personal homes. The importance of savings and loan associations to the mortgage market is illustrated by the aggregate balance sheet in Exhibit 3.5, which shows the amount of mortgage loans S&Ls were financing as of May 1990. As may be seen from the balance sheet, savings and loans owned $874.3 billion in mortgage loans and mortgage backed securities, which accounted for 73.0 percent of their assets. They also had $902.6 billion in savings accounts outstanding, which accounted for 75.4 percent of their total liabilities and equity. Hence, savings and loan associations are obviously borrowing funds from savers and passing the funds to households and firms in need of mortgage money.

Intermediation ▲ Process of lending funds to a financial intermediary which in turn lends the funds to the ultimate user of the money

Disintermediation ▲ Process of withdrawing funds from financial intermediaries and investing the funds in other securities

If additional savings were deposited into savings and loans (a process called **intermediation**), their ability to make additional mortgage loans would be increased. If funds were to flow out of these savings accounts (a process called **disintermediation**), the ability of savings and loans to grant mortgage loans would be reduced. Since they hold such a large proportion of their funds in mortgages, flows of savings into or out of savings and loan associations have considerable impact on the building sector of the economy. The ability to obtain mortage money influences the demand for construction (especially residential housing). Since the flow of savings into savings and loans alters the ability of potential homeowners to obtain mortgage money, this flow of savings has an important influence on the construction industry.

EXHIBIT 3.6

Assets of Mutual Savings Banks as of April 1990 (in Millions)

As with S&Ls, the primary assets of federal savings banks are mortgage loans.

Assets		
Mortgages and mortgage backed securities	$414,330	69.8%
Commercial loans	20,324	3.4
Consumer loans	20,324	3.4
Cash and investments	72,618	12.2
Other assets	65,749	11.1
Total assets	$593,345	99.9%

Source: Federal Reserve Bulletin, *December 1990, p. A26.*

start here next class

MUTUAL SAVINGS BANKS (Federal Savings Banks)

Mutual savings banks, which are also referred to as federal savings banks, are very similar to savings and loan associations. They act as a depository for the funds of savers and, in turn, these savings are lent to households and firms seeking financing. The depositors are the owners of mutual savings banks, but the banks are managed by a board of trustees. While a mutual savings bank may legally view its depositors as owners and not creditors, the owners may readily withdraw their funds. Thus, the mutual savings banks are similar to other banks, including savings and loan associations and commercial banks, for they must have sufficient liquidity to meet withdrawals.

Exhibit 3.6 presents the assets for all mutual savings banks as of April 1990. While mutual savings banks do perform the role of a financial intermediary, the total dollar value of their assets indicates that they are a relatively small component of the financial system. The assets of all savings and loan associations are more than twice the assets of mutual savings banks. This difference in size is partially explained by the fact that less than half of the states permit mutual savings banks. Most of these banks were started in the northeast during the previous century to encourage saving by working people such as sailors. These origins are often indicated by some of the banks' colorful names (e.g., Merchant Seaman's Bank or Bowery Savings Bank.)

Mortgages and mortgage backed securities, by far, constitute the most important asset of mutual savings banks and make up 69.8 percent of their total assets.[7] Mutual banks also own a substantial amount of

[7]Since mutual savings banks hold a substantial proportion of their assets in the form of mortgages, they suffered the same problems that faced the savings and loan associations. However, many mutual savings banks were insured by the FDIC, so their depositors did not sustain losses.

cash and investments (12.2 percent). The cash would be the banks' reserves, while the securities would primarily be obligations of the federal government.

LIFE INSURANCE COMPANIES

Life insurance companies also perform the role of a financial intermediary because they receive the funds of savers, create a claim on themselves, and lend the funds to borrowers. Since other types of insurance companies do not perform this financial intermediary role, a distinction has to be made between them and life insurance companies. Other types of insurance, such as property and liability insurance, are exclusively services that the individual buys. The price of the insurance is related to the cost of the product, just as the cost of any service, such as a hotel reservation or an electrician, is related to the cost of producing the service. Of course, the property and liability insurance companies invest the funds they receive from policyholders. However, suppliers of other services will also use the funds they receive. In neither case is there a transfer of savings to borrowers.

The feature that differentiates life insurance from other forms of insurance and makes life insurance companies financial intermediaries is that life insurance may provide more than insurance against premature death. Ordinary and universal life insurance policies and endowments contain two elements, the insurance and a savings plan. The policy's premiums cover both the cost of the insurance and the savings program. As long as the policy is in force, the policy accumulates cash value, which is the savings component of the policy. Many savers find such policies attractive because the periodic payments assure them of insurance plus a savings program. Others find them unattractive because the interest rate paid on the savings may be less than can be earned on alternative investments.

Life insurance companies use the proceeds of the policies to acquire income-earning assets. Exhibit 3.7, which presents the total assets of all life insurance companies as of December 1989, indicates that these companies purchase a varied mix of financial assets. Holdings of corporate debt and stock account for 49.2 percent and 9.7 percent, respectively, of the total assets, while mortgages account for 19.6 percent. The remaining assets include government securities, real estate, loans to policyholders, and various miscellaneous assets. As the table indicates, life insurance companies are a major source of financing for corporations, for many companies are able to sell a substantial amount of stock and debt to life insurance companies. Therefore, life insurance companies are a major alternative to commercial banks for corporations.

EXHIBIT 3.7

Assets of Life Insurance Companies as of December 1989 (in Millions)

Corporate bonds and stock constitute the largest portion of life insurance companies' assets.

Assets		
U.S. government securities	$ 77,297	5.9%
State and local government securities	52,517	4.0
Foreign government securities	9,028	0.7
Corporate bonds	638,907	49.2
Corporate stock	125,614	9.7
Mortgage loans	254,215	19.6
Real estate	39,908	3.1
Policy loans	57,439	4.4
Other assets	44,831	3.4
Total assets	$1,299,756	100.0%

Source: Federal Reserve Bulletin, *December 1990, p. A27.*

While life insurance companies do compete with commercial banks for corporate loans, they serve somewhat different financial markets. First, commercial banks stress liquidity and, hence, are a primary source of short-term finance. Life insurance companies, however, do not need to stress liquidity. Mortality tables are scientifically constructed and can predict with accuracy the volume of death benefits the life insurance company will have to pay. The company can forecast with a high degree of accuracy the amount of benefits it will have to pay during the year. Thus, it is able to construct a portfolio of assets that permits the company to have not only sufficient liquidity but also long-term investments. Since the long-term investments tend to have higher interest rates, a life insurance company will seek to have a substantial amount of its funds in these more profitable assets. The very nature of its financial obligations permits a life insurance company to own more long-term debt than a commercial bank would find prudent to hold.

Second, life insurance companies may hold the stock of corporations, while commercial banks may not. Thus, life insurance companies participate in a market that is closed to commercial banks. (Commercial banks do manage other people's money in trust accounts and can purchase stock for these accounts.) There are also special tax laws that encourage corporations, including life insurance companies, to make investments in the stock of other corporations. For corporations, 70 percent of the dividends received from these investments is exempt from federal income taxation. Therefore, life insurance companies have an added incentive to purchase the stock of corporations and supply corporations with additional equity financing.

PENSION PLANS

The role of a pension plan is to accumulate assets for workers so that they will have funds to live on after retirement. Funds are periodically put in the pension plan by the saver, the employer, or both. The money deposited with the fund then is used to purchase an income-earning asset. The saver's funds grow over time as additional funds are paid into the pension plan, and the funds already in the plan earn income.

There are many pension plans in existence, but not all of them really perform the function of financial intermediaries. Not all pension plans in turn invest or lend the money directly to borrowers. Instead they may purchase *existing* securities, such as the stock of General Motors. That is, the pension plan participates in the secondary, and not the primary, market for securities. For a pension plan to serve as a financial intermediary, it must pass the funds directly to a borrower or invest them directly in a firm.

This distinction between pension plans may be illustrated by the pension plans used by many colleges and universities for their employees. Funds may be contributed by both the employer and the employee to the Teachers Insurance and Annuity Association (TIAA) or to the College Retirement Equity Fund (CREF). The actual dollar amount of the contribution varies with the school and the employee's salary. The funds may be contributed to either plan or may be split between the two plans.

CREF primarily purchases existing corporate stock. Money that flows into CREF does not go to the companies that issued the stock. Instead, the money goes to the seller of the stock, who may have purchased the shares many years ago. As was explained in Chapter 2, the only time a company receives the proceeds of a stock sale occurs when the shares are first issued in the primary market. All subsequent sales are secondhand transactions, with the proceeds flowing from the individual buying the security to the individual selling the security. Funds are not being transferred to the firm. By purchasing the secondhand security, CREF is not performing the role of a financial intermediary.

TIAA purchases an entirely different type of portfolio that stresses debt, especially mortgages. In this case funds are transferred from savers to borrowers, and the pension plan is acting as a financial intermediary. It creates a claim on itself when it receives the savers' funds, and it receives a claim from borrowers when the funds are lent to finance purchases. The transfer of purchasing power from saver to borrower by an intermediary that creates claims on itself is the role of a financial intermediary. Hence, TIAA is an example of a pension plan that does serve the role of a financial intermediary.

INVESTMENT COMPANIES: MONEY MARKET MUTUAL FUNDS

One of the most important financial institutions is the mutual fund that invests on behalf of individuals.[8] However, the majority of these funds are not financial intermediaries in the sense that they borrow from savers and lend the funds to the ultimate users. It is true that they do create claims on themselves, since investors own shares in the funds (i.e., the investors own equity claims). Whether the fund is a financial intermediary depends on what it does with the money raised by selling the shares: Does it acquire newly issued securities or buy previously issued securities?

If the fund buys securities in the secondary markets, it is not serving as a financial intermediary. No money is transferred to a firm, government, or individual seeking to borrow funds. Instead, the money is transferred to another investor who is seeking to liquidate a position in the particular security.

Of course, a mutual fund could buy newly issued securities. Some funds specialize in purchasing shares of emerging and new firms, and to the extent that these funds participate in the primary market, they are operating as financial intermediaries. Other mutual funds specialize in government securities, which are purchased when the bonds are issued. Such funds also serve as financial intermediaries, transferring the money of savers to the ultimate users of the money. Most mutual funds, however, do not serve as financial intermediaries, as they primarily buy and sell existing securities.

Even though most mutual funds are not financial intermediaries, there is one major exception, the **money market mutual fund** that acquires short-term securities. While there are secondary markets in some money market instruments, money market mutual funds tend to acquire newly issued short-term debt instruments. These securities are then held until they are redeemed at maturity, at which time the process is repeated.

Money market mutual fund ▲
Investment company that invests solely in short-term money market instruments

The development of these funds and their explosive growth was one of the most important developments in the financial markets during the late 1970s and early 1980s. This growth is illustrated in Figure 3.1, which presents the value of money market mutual fund assets from their inception in 1975 through 1989.

The initial growth was nothing short of phenomenal, as total assets rose from less than $10 billion in 1977 to an amazing $185 billion in 1981. This immediate popularity may be explained by three factors: safety of principal, liquidity, and high interest rates. The shares are safe

---

[8]This section considers mutual funds only as financial intermediaries. The general discussion of these investment companies is deferred until Chapter 14.

FIGURE 3.1

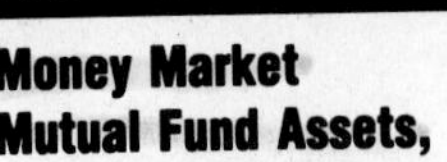

Money Market Mutual Fund Assets, 1975–89 (in Billions)

The shares of money market mutual funds have grown rapidly since their inception in the mid-1970s.

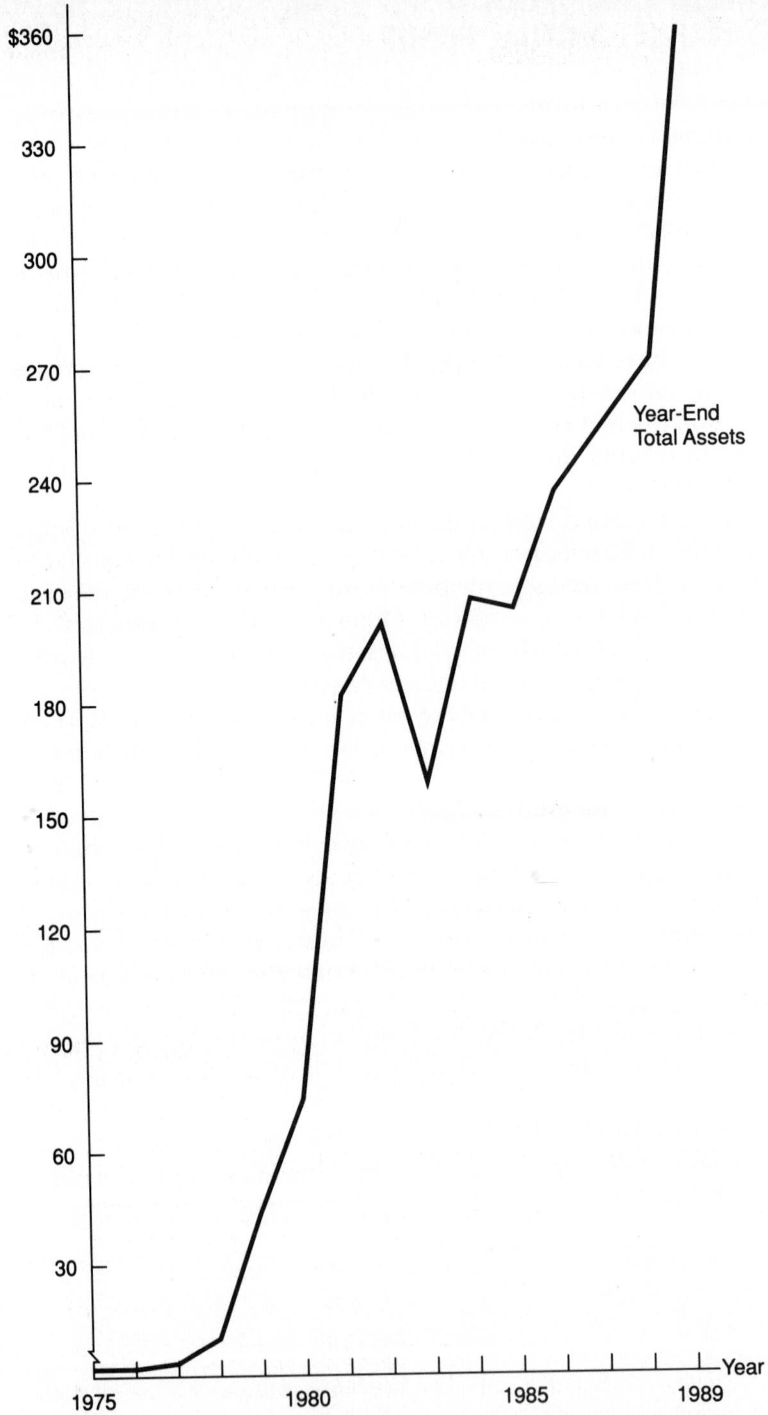

Source: Derived from 1990 Mutual Fund Fact Book, *p. 24.*

since the money funds acquire short-term debt obligations whose values are subject to minimal price fluctuations. In addition, these debt obligations tend to have high credit ratings, so there is minimal risk of default.

Investors may withdraw money invested in the money funds (i.e., redeem shares) at will. This ease of converting to cash with minimal chance of loss of principal means these shares are among the most liquid assets available to savers. The shares of money market mutual funds also offer savers competitive short-term yields. In many cases, these yields are higher than those offered by commercial banks and other financial intermediaries.

The initial growth in the money funds was primarily caused by the regulation of commercial banks and other depository institutions. Prior to the Monetary Control Act of 1980, commercial banks and other depository institutions were constrained as to the maximum rate of interest they could offer depositors. When interest rates rose, banks could not pay their depositors the higher rates. The money market mutual funds, however, were not subject to this constraint, so funds flowed from the various depository institutions into the money market funds. The rapid growth in the funds was one of the reasons for the deregulation of the banking system, which was unable to compete with the money market funds.

Under deregulation, depository institutions are no longer constrained as to the rate of interest they may pay. Thus, the yields they pay are now competitive with the yields offered savers by the money market mutual funds. As of 1984, depository institutions could issue money market accounts that offered limited checking privileges and paid a rate of interest that was comparable to the yield paid by the money funds. In addition, these institutions were permitted to offer super-NOW accounts. These accounts pay money market rates of interest and have unlimited checking privileges. However, the banks may require large minimum balances in order for the depositor to receive these services free of charge.

The deregulation of interest rates paid depositors has reduced the growth of the money market mutual funds. This decline in growth may be seen in Figure 3.1. From 1982 through 1985, there was virtually no increase in their assets. However, after 1985, growth was resumed. Since the money market funds hold over $358 billion in financial assets, they are important financial intermediaries. While the holdings of each individual fund vary, in the aggregate they are a major source of short-term credit for many corporations and the federal government.

The fact that the funds' portfolios cover a broad spectrum of money market instruments is illustrated in Exhibit 3.8, which presents the distribution of the money market funds' assets. As may be seen in the exhibit, their portfolios include a variety of short-term securities that range from U.S. government securities (i.e., Treasury bills) to short-term for-

EXHIBIT 3.8

Distribution of Money Market Mutual Funds' Assets (in Millions)

While money market mutual funds hold a variety of assets, short-term corporate debt (commercial paper) is their primary asset.

Commercial paper	$179,138.9	49.9%
U.S. government securities	35,827.9	10.0
Repurchase agreements	54,867.7	15.3
Eurodollar certificates of deposit	26,378.2	7.4
Negotiable certificates of deposit	33,593.4	9.4
Bankers' acceptances	7,468.3	2.1
Other	21,444.8	6.0
	$358,719.2	100.1%

Source: Derived from Investment Company Institute 1989 Mutual Fund Fact Book, *p. 106.*

eign securities (i.e., Eurodollar CDs).[9] However, while the group as a whole owns a broad spectrum of money market instruments, the portfolios of individual funds can be very specialized. For example, First Variable Rate Fund invests only in federal government securities or securities backed by the federal government. Its portfolio differs significantly from Merrill Lynch's Ready Assets' portfolio, which includes a broad spectrum of short-term money market securities.

COMPETITION FOR FUNDS

A commercial bank or any financial intermediary can only lend what has been lent to it. Unless the bank is able to induce individuals, firms, and governments to make deposits, that bank will be unable to grant loans and make investments. This general statement, of course, holds for all financial intermediaries. None can make investments without a source of funds. Whether these claims on the intermediaries are called life insurance policies or savings accounts or shares in money market mutual funds, the essential point remains the same. No financial intermediary can exist without its sources of funds.

Conversely, if funds flow out of financial intermediaries (i.e., if disintermediation occurs), all intermediaries will be able to hold fewer assets (i.e., make fewer loans). Unless the outflow is reversed, it will tend to increase the cost of credit as the intermediaries raise the rates of interest they charge in order to ration their remaining lending capacity.

[9] See Chapter 19 for descriptions of these various money market instruments.

In addition to the aggregate flows in and out of all financial intermediaries, credit markets may feel the impact of flows among financial intermediaries. Funds deposited in one particular bank are not deposited in another competitive bank. If an individual saver has funds to invest and chooses a money market mutual fund instead of the local savings and loan association, it is the mutual fund that can lend the funds and not the savings and loan association. From the standpoint of the borrowers, it would not matter which intermediary makes the loans if all financial intermediaries had similar portfolios. But the portfolios of various financial intermediaries vary, as was illustrated in Exhibits 3.1, and 3.5 through 3.8. As these exhibits showed, the holdings of the various intermediaries do differ.

These differences can have an important implication. A transfer of funds from one intermediary (e.g., a savings and loan association) to another (e.g., a money market mutual fund) can have an important impact on the supply of credit available to a particular sector of the economy. While the total supply of credit is unaffected (because the money market fund can lend only what the savings and loan association loses), there will be a redistribution of credit from those who borrow from savings and loan associations to those who borrow from the money funds. The money market mutual fund now has more funds to acquire income-earning assets such as short-term securities. Simultaneously, the flow of funds out of the savings and loan association reduces its capacity to grant mortgage loans. Such a redistribution of funds from savings and loan associations to money market mutual funds will certainly be felt by the construction industry and home buyers as the supply of mortgage money declines.

As this discussion implies, financial intermediaries compete with each other for funds. This competition occurs through yields and services offered. With the deregulation of interest rates, virtually all financial intermediaries offer competitive yields. If a particular intermediary did not offer competitive rates, funds would flow from it to those intermediaries offering higher yields. Thus, differentiation among the intermediaries on the basis of yields tends to be small.

Historically, financial intermediaries have been categorized on the basis of services or products offered. Today, however, this is only partially true. The financial services industry is currently going through a period of rapid change as the various intermediaries compete for funds. In the past, savers bought life insurance through insurance agents, bought stocks through securities brokers, and invested funds in a savings account in a bank. Those days of specialization are rapidly disappearing. Insurance agents, stockbrokers, and bankers today offer a wide spectrum of services and financial products. For example, many commercial banks offer savers not only the traditional services of savings and checking accounts but other products as well, such as discount brokerage services (to compete with stockbrokers), money market accounts (to compete with money market mutual funds), and pension plans (to compete with insurance companies and mutual funds). Such product competition also applies to savings banks. Savings and loan associations offer a variety of savings accounts as well as checking accounts (NOW accounts that compete with commercial banks). Some S&Ls even sell savings and loan life insurance and offer discount brokerage services.

The reduction in regulation and lifting of interest rate ceilings has resulted in (and will continue to result in) a blurring of the distinctions among commercial banks, savings and loan associations, and mutual savings banks. In addition, these banks are experiencing increased competition from other financial intermediaries. Money market mutual funds and insurance companies (along with securities brokerage firms) will increasingly seek to divert savers' funds from the various types of banks.

A type of financial supermarket that encompasses a variety of financial services is evolving. For example, Sears owns Dean Witter Reynolds, Inc., the brokerage firm; Allstate Insurance Companies; and Coldwell, Banker and Company, real estate. Prudential, the insurance company, acquired a brokerage firm, Bache Halsey Stuart Shields Inc. American Express also owns a brokerage firm, Shearson Loeb Rhoades Inc. All of these firms are illustrations of evolving financial supermarkets that offer the individual a variety of financial products and services.

Of course, some distinctions among the various intermediaries will continue to exist. Commercial banks should remain the primary depository for checking accounts and will continue to be a major source of short-term funds for corporations. Savings and loan associations will probably continue to be an important source of mortgage money for individuals buying homes. Insurance companies will remain the primary source of their products: life, health, and casuality insurance. However, unless there is a movement back toward regulation of the banking system, financial intermediaries will continue to encroach on the domain of their competitors as each offers savers and depositors increasingly similar financial services and products.

THE SAVINGS AND LOAN DEBACLE

The 1980s were an exceptionally momentous decade for financial intermediaries. It began with the deregulation of commercial banks and the placing of all depository institutions under the control of the Federal Reserve. It ended with the failure of many savings and loan associations, the collapse of the FSLIC, which insured S&L deposits, and the creation of the Office of Thrift Supervision and the Resolution Trust Corporation (RTC) to oversee the assets of the failed thrifts and to provide the orderly liquidation of their assets.

In 1990, *The Wall Street Journal* reported that savings and loan associations lost $200 billion in the preceding fifteen years and that the losses were continuing to mount.[10] Depositors in federally insured S&Ls, however, did not sustain losses (up to the legal limit).[11] While stockholders and uninsured creditors experienced losses, most of the losses were sustained by the insuring agent, the federal government. Hence, it was the nation's taxpayers that ultimately sustained the losses, as tax money had to be used to pay the interest and redeem the deposits.

Where did the lost money go? It did not vanish into thin air; someone had to receive the benefits. What were the causes of the massive losses sustained by some thrifts, and why did some thrifts manage to avoid the losses? These are hard questions to answer because the money did not go to one beneficiary nor is there a single cause of the failures.

The S&L business itself is inherently risky. As was previously explained in the section on a commercial bank's earnings, depository institutions, especially savings and loan associations, use a large amount of financial leverage. The small equity relative to the large amount of deposits means that a small decline in the value of an S&L's assets wipes out its equity. Thus, only a few problem loans destroy the profitability and solvency of a savings and loan association.

In addition, S&Ls tend to violate a major financial principle. They borrow relatively short-term and lend long-term. The term of their deposits may be for one, two, or three years. In some cases such as a savings account, the depositor may withdraw the money on demand. While an S&L's source of money is short- to intermediate-term, its primary assets tend to have a longer term (e.g., 25-year mortgages). This can be a major problem if interest rates rise. The S&Ls have to pay higher interest on their deposits but have made long-term loans with lower rates of interest. A 25-year mortgage loan made in 1976 at 8.25 percent may generate a profit if the interest rate paid depositors is 6.0 percent. That situation rapidly changes when interest rates rise, and depositors must be paid the higher rates, unless the S&L takes some action to hedge its loan portfolio or to better balance its sources of deposits with its loans. This situation is exacerbated if the depositors withdraw funds in an effort to earn higher yields on alternative investments. In that case the S&L could sustain large losses if forced to liquidate assets to meet substantial withdrawals by depositors.

While S&Ls are risky enterprises, that risk does not explain the large losses sustained during the late 1980s. For example, not all S&Ls sustained large losses, and even though other financial intermediaries such

---

[10] Paulette Thomas and Thomas E. Ricks, "Tracing What Happened to All That Money the Savings & Loans Lost?" *The Wall Street Journal,* November 5, 1990, p. A1.

[11] The same cannot be said of deposits in state insured S&Ls. Some state deposit insurance funds were insufficient to cover the losses, so depositors covered by this insurance did sustain losses.

as commercial banks did sustain losses, the amount of the losses were not comparable to those the S&Ls experienced.

Several reasons account for some of the high S&L losses: (1) the high interest rates that thrifts paid to attract deposits after the deregulation of the banking system and especially the brokering of deposits; (2) excessive risk taking, in particular some real estate loans; and (3) mismanagement, which in some cases was possible fraud. In addition, part of the losses can be laid on the regulation itself and on Congress for increasing deposit insurance, which transferred risk from the S&Ls' managements to the federal government and ultimately to taxpayers.

A savings and loan could operate as a corner store and attract deposits from local savers and make loans to finance local home purchases. This essentially was their role prior to the deregulation of the banking system. After deregulation, many S&Ls sought to expand and to attract deposits throughout the nation. To facilitate raising these funds, brokerage firms (e.g., Merrill Lynch) would raise money for the S&Ls (i.e., Merrill would "broker" deposits). A saver in New Jersey with $100,000 to invest would not have to deposit the money in Centennial Savings and Loan, an S&L in Trenton. Instead, that individual could deposit the money with Merrill Lynch and have Merrill purchase a certificate issued by a savings and loan in Texas or California or Florida.

This process certainly contributed to S&Ls' losses. To attract these deposits, the S&Ls offered high yields and paid Merrill Lynch a fee for brokering the deposits. The New Jersey saver would earn a higher rate of interest, and since the money was invested in a federally insured S&L, the individual still had safety of principal. From the saver's perspective, this certificate was a superior investment: a higher return for no additional risk. The financial condition of the S&L was irrelevant. Obviously, part of the losses sustained by the S&Ls went to the brokerage firms in fees and into the pockets of investors with sufficient funds to participate in this market for brokered deposits.

Since these S&Ls were paying higher rates of interest to attract deposits, they, in turn, had to collect higher rates in order to cover their costs and still earn a profit. To obtain higher yields, these S&Ls made riskier loans, especially real estate loans. A large portion of the S&L losses went to developers, real estate agents, lawyers, and title insurance companies who participated in the development of real estate. To earn a higher return, a savings and loan would lend funds to develop an office building. Higher interest rates were charged than would be possible from conventional mortgages, and in some cases, the S&L would take an equity position in the property in anticipation of earning an even higher return.

The equity position may be granted by the developers in return for reduced interest payments. The reduced interest eases the debt burden while the property is developed but increases the S&L's risk exposure. A lower interest rate reduces the S&L's current receipt of cash, which reduces its ability to service (i.e., pay interest on) its own obligations. In addition, the equity position generates a higher return only when, and if, the completed properties are sold. If many S&Ls are following the same strategy, more properties are developed than the local real estate markets can absorb. This leads to defaults by the developers and foreclosures by the S&Ls. While foreclosure results in the S&Ls' owning the properties, these foreclosed properties generate no income, but the deposits necessary to obtain the money to develop the properties continue to require interest payments. In effect, the S&L is caught on both sides of its balance sheet: a nonearning asset that can only be sold at a loss (if sold at all) and the requirement to pay the higher interest it agreed to pay depositors. Obviously losses continue to grow as long as the situation continues.

Some S&Ls also acquired high-yield but high-risk debt obligations, the so-called "junk bonds." The mid-1980s saw a large increase in the number of these securities resulting from mergers and leveraged buyouts in which high-yield securities were issued to buy out the firm's shares held by the general public. Southland (Seven-Eleven) and Interco (Florsheim Shoes) are only two of many firms that issued substantial amounts of high-yield securities and subsequently defaulted. While S&Ls were not the only investors to purchase high-yield debt, their losses on these investments contributed to the losses that taxpayers ultimately had to bear.

In addition, the managements of some S&Ls were less cost conscious and ran up operating expenses. Wasteful expenditures, such as owning jet airplanes or contracting for corporate jet services and spending on lavish interior design for offices, reduce earnings. While extravagance cannot account for the large total losses, they certainly contributed to those losses.

The line between mismanagement and fraud is probably impossible to determine, but the managements of some S&Ls did make questionable loans. Large loans to managers, family members, and close business associates may be legal but may not be prudent. Contributions to political figures, especially members of Congress with connections to banking regulators, may be legal but perhaps not ethical. Certainly such practices reinforced, if not caused, the S&L failures.

It has even been suggested that the insuring of deposits played a role in the failure of thrifts. Deposit insurance may have helped to shift the risk associated with servicing deposits from the S&L managements to the taxpayer, who is the ultimate insurer of the deposits. Without deposit insurance, management may have made more prudent investments, since the losses would have been sustained by the S&L's depositors. Savers may also have scrutinized the banks more closely and not lent funds, especially the brokered deposits, if the deposits were not insured. Under this line of reasoning, the increase in deposit insurance from $40,000 to $100,000 in 1980 reduced savers' need to be concerned with the safety of the banks in which funds were deposited and reduced managements' concerns for losses. Instead, the burden was transferred to the regulatory authorities and, ultimately, to the taxpayers.

The S&L debacle led to a restructuring of deposit insurance and regulation. The changes are the result of the Financial Reform, Recovery, and Enforcement Act (FIRRE) of 1989, which transferred regulatory power from the Federal Home Loan Bank Board to the newly created Office of Thrift Supervision. This office was made part of the Treasury Department and thus was placed under the control of the administration.

The FIRRE Act sought to strengthen S&Ls by increasing their required capital base (i.e., increased their required equity or net worth) by mandating that a savings and loan's equity be equal to at least 3 percent of its assets. The act also reestablished deposit insurance through the Resolution Funding Corporation and financed that operation through an initial issue of $50 billion of federally guaranteed bonds. However, losses have proven to exceed that amount, so the Office of Thrift Supervision has had to seek additional funding from Congress.

The FIRRE Act also created the Resolution Trust Corporation (RTC) and gave it the power to seize failing thrifts. Obviously the Resolution Trust Corporation could not immediately seize all financially weak thrifts. Initially, the weakest thrifts were closed, and their assets transferred to the RTC. Insured depositors were paid off in full from the newly created insurance fund. Thus, insured depositors did not sustain losses. (Losses were sustained by the owners of the thrifts and the uninsured creditors of the thrifts.) Many financially weak thrifts, however, were permitted to continue to operate. These savings and loans were given a period of time to improve their financial condition or face the threat of seizure.

After taking title to a failed S&L's assets, the RTC sought to sell the assets. Unfortunately, many of the assets were foreclosed properties and loans that were in default. The defaulted loans led to additional foreclosures by the RTC. While some of the assets were sold to profitable savings and loans and other banking firms, many of the assets were virtually worthless, and others had to be sold at fire-sale prices.[12] These lower than anticipated prices further contributed to the losses sustained by taxpayers. It has even been suggested that the RTC's desire to sell seized assets produced sales that will further cost taxpayers, because tax breaks were granted to buyers to take the properties. Such tax benefits will reduce future tax revenues.

---

[12] Some of the assets acquired by the RTC seemed ludicrous. For example, one failed Colorado S&L had a community swimming pool that was not serviced by the community water supply.

SUMMARY

The flow of funds to those in need of funds is exceedingly important for an advanced economy. The benefits accrue to savers, who have a place to invest their funds, borrowers in need of funds, the financial intermediaries themselves through the opportunity to earn a profit, and the economy as a whole, since the level of economic activity would be lower without financial intermediaries.

The types of financial intermediaries include commercial banks, savings banks (savings and loan associations and mutual savings banks), life insurance companies, pension plans, and money market mutual funds. All of these financial institutions compete for funds, since an individual intermediary can only acquire a portfolio of assets if it can obtain funds. The deregulation of the banking system has increased competition among the various intermediaries and blurred the distinctions among them, allowing them to offer products and services that previously were the exclusive domain of a particular intermediary.

In terms of size, commercial banks are the most important financial intermediary. These banks make a variety of loans but tend to stress loans that are quickly repaid. Other financial intermediaries such as savings and loan associations and life insurance companies make longer-term loans.

The profit margins of a commercial bank are the result of the difference between what it pays depositors and what it charges borrowers. These margins tend to be very small. Also, commercial banks and other financial intermediaries must raise a substantial amount of money through the creation of claims on themselves. They are highly financially leveraged, which increases the risk associated with the operation.

Recent developments in financial intermediaries include the large growth in money market mutual funds and the large losses sustained by savings and loan associations. Money market mutual funds compete directly with banks; they offer the advantages of somewhat higher yields and almost comparable safety. While the shares are not federally insured as are the deposits in banks, the short-term nature of their portfolios affords the saver safety of principal.

Such safety exists for individuals making deposits in most commercial banks, mutual savings banks, and savings and loan associations because the deposits are federally insured. During the late 1980s, many S&Ls sustained large losses as the result of making excessively risky loans, paying too high rates of interest to attract deposits, and mismanaging their portfolios. Since deposits were federally insured, the savers in S&Ls did not sustain losses. Instead, the bailout of the thrift institutions cost taxpayers, who had to redeem the deposits at face value through the newly created Resolution Funding Corporation. Congress also created the Office of Thrift Management and the Resolution Trust

Corporation, which seized the assets of failed thrifts. Unfortunately, these assets could not be readily sold, and those that were brought fire-sale prices, which further contributed to the losses sustained by the taxpayer.

Review Questions

1. What are a commercial bank's sources of funds and profits? What effect will a change in interest rates have on a bank's earnings?
2. What are the differences among a bank's total reserves, excess reserves, and required reserves?
3. What are the primary assets of a savings and loan association? If an individual deposits money in a savings account with a savings and loan, is that deposit safe? What are the roles of the FDIC and SAIF?
4. What differentiates the portfolios of a savings and loan association and a life insurance company?
5. What explained the initial growth in money market mutual funds? Are the shares of these funds insured by the federal government? Are investments in the shares of these funds more risky than an investment in a commercial bank's certificate of deposit?
6. What proportion of a financial intermediary's assets are financed by debt and by equity? What effect does this financing have on the risk associated with a financial intermediary?
7. What are possible causes of the large losses sustained by financial intermediaries during the late 1980s? Who sustained the losses?

Suggested Readings

Bowden, Elbert V., and Judith L. Holbert. *Revolution in Banking.* 2d ed. Reston, Va.: Reston Publishing Company, Inc., 1984.

This clear and concise book discusses the changes (e.g., the erosion of differences among financial institutions, increased competition, and the electronic transfer of funds) that have occurred since the passage of the Monetary Control Act of 1980.

Brick, John R., ed. *Bank Management: Concepts and Issues.* Richmond, Va.: Robert F. Dame, 1983.

This is an extensive book of readings that covers the management of a bank's assets and liabilities, regulation, international banking, and profitability.

Haslem, John A. *Bank Funds Management.* Reston, Va.: Reston Publishing Company, Inc., 1984.

This unique book combines traditional textual material with readings that cover a broad area of banking. Topics include the management of banks' sources of funds, investment policies, and the reduction of risk.

Hempel, George H., et al. *Bank Management, Text and Cases.* 3d ed. New York: Wiley, 1990.

This text includes discussions of auditing, personnel management, marketing, and community relations of commercial banks.

Reed, Edward W., and Edward K. Gill. *Commercial Banking.* 4th ed. Englewood Cliffs, N.J.: Prentice-Hall, 1989.

This comprehensive text covers the structure and regulation of banks, portfolio management, and international banking.

Textbooks described for courses in financial institutions include:

Henning, Charles N., William Pigott, and Robert Haney Scott. *Financial Markets and the Economy.* 5th ed. Englewood Cliffs, N.J.: Prentice-Hall, 1988.

Kidwell, David S., and Richard L. Peterson. *Financial Institutions, Markets, and Money.* 4th ed. Hinsdale, Ill.: The Dryden Press, 1989.

Rose, Peter S. *Money and Capital Markets.* 3d ed. Homewood, Ill.: Irwin, 1989.

For a book of readings covering such topics as interest rates, financial institutions, and financial markets, consult:

Havrilesky, Thomas M., and Robert Schweitzer, eds. *Contemporary Developments in Financial Institutions and Markets.* 2d ed. Arlington Heights, Ill.: Harlan Davidson, Inc., 1987.

chapter

4

The Federal Reserve and the Supply and Cost of Credit

Learning Objectives

1. List the goals of fiscal and monetary policy.
2. Enumerate the assets and liabilities of the Federal Reserve and describe its structure.
3. Explain how cash deposits may lead to a multiple expansion in the money supply.
4. Illustrate how the tools of monetary policy affect the supply of money and credit.
5. Identify who may finance the federal government's deficit and the potential impact this financing may have on the supply of credit.
6. Explain how inflation may affect the cost of credit, and differentiate between the nominal and real rates of interest.

According to Will Rogers, "There have been three great inventions since the beginning of time: fire, the wheel, and central banking." While greatness may be disputed, there can be no denying the potential impact the nation's central bank, the Federal Reserve, can have on credit markets and the supply of money. By using its tools of monetary policy, the Federal Reserve may expand or contract the supply of money and credit and thereby have significant impact on the financial health of the economy as a whole and firms in particular.

In addition to the potential impact of the Federal Reserve, the fiscal policy of the federal government can also affect credit markets and the well-being of firms. When the federal government runs a deficit, that deficit must be financed. In 1989, the annual deficit had grown to $151,989,000,000, up from a surplus of $3,236,000,000 in 1969.[1] Someone had to put up in 1989 over $150 billion to cover the deficit. When the federal government borrows from the general public or the banking system, it competes with firms and individuals for the existing supply of credit. This competition can have an impact on interest rates and the capacity of the banking system to lend to firms.

Deficit spending, if financed through excessive creation of money by the Federal Reserve, results in higher prices. Such inflation also affects financial decision making as financial managers and individuals take actions designed to protect themselves from price increases. The higher cost of goods and services is also felt in the financial markets as interest rates rise in conjunction with price increases.

This chapter is concerned with the Federal Reserve and its impact on the supply of money and the cost of credit. Initially, the roles and composition of the Federal Reserve are described. The second section discusses how changes in banks' reserves lead to a multiple expansion or contraction of the money supply. The third section considers the Federal Reserve's tools of monetary policy and their impact on the reserves of banks. The next section is devoted to the federal government's fiscal policy and the way financing its deficit may have an impact on the supply of money and credit. The last sections consider inflation, its effect on credit markets and interest rates, and the impact of monetary and fiscal policy on the individual firm.

---

[1] *Survey of Current Business,* December 1990, S-4.

THE ROLE OF THE FEDERAL RESERVE SYSTEM

The purpose of the Federal Reserve System is to help achieve stable prices, full employment, and economic growth through the regulation of the supply of credit and money in the economy. Changing the supply of money and credit to achieve these three goals is called **monetary policy.**

Monetary policy ▲
Management of the money supply for the purpose of maintaining stable prices, full employment, and economic growth

The Federal Reserve (the "Fed") has several tools of effectuate monetary policy. The primary tool is open market operations, while secondary tools are the discount rate and reserve requirements. The Federal Reserve uses these monetary tools to expand or contract the supply of money to pursue the economic goals of prosperity with full employment and stable prices. When the Federal Reserve seeks to increase the supply of money and credit to help expand the level of income and employment, that is called an "easy" monetary policy. When it seeks to contract the supply of money and credit to help fight inflation, that is referred to as a "tight" monetary policy.

While controlling the supply of money and credit is the primary role of the Federal Reserve, it also serves a variety of other functions. The many roles that the Federal Reserve System plays are mirrored by the assets and liabilities on its balance sheet. A simplified balance sheet for the Federal Reserve is shown in Exhibit 4.1. The majority of the Federal

EXHIBIT 4.1

Simplified Federal Reserve Balance Sheet as of September 26, 1990 (in Millions)

U.S. securities and Federal Reserve notes are the primary assets and liabilities of the Federal Reserve banks.

Assets		
Gold certificates	$ 11,063	3.6%
U.S. government securities	236,575	76.2
Loans to member banks	501	0.1
Cash items in process of collection	5,209	1.7
Other assets	57,103	18.4
Total assets	$310,451	100.0%
Liabilities		
Federal Reserve notes	$252,681	81.4%
Deposits:		
Member bank reserves	37,766	12.2
U.S. Treasury	5,402	1.7
Foreign	198	0.0
Other liabilities	9,202	3.0
Capital	5,202	1.7
Total liabilities and capital	$310,451	100.0%

Source: Federal Reserve Bulletin, *December 1990, p. A10.*

Reserve's assets are gold certificates and the debt of the United States government.

The Federal Reserve's Assets and Liabilities

Gold certificates ▲
Warehouse receipts issued by the United States Treasury for gold it holds.

The **gold certificates** are warehouse receipts for gold held by the Treasury. Until the Gold Reserve Act of 1934, there had to be a dollar's worth of gold for every dollar in Federal Reserve Notes. The gold was held in vaults (e.g., Fort Knox) for safekeeping, and paper money, which could be converted into gold, was used as a substitute for gold. In 1934 the nation changed its monetary system so that only a fraction of its paper money was backed by gold. The fraction of gold necessary to cover the money supply was established by the federal government. Eventually this gold requirement was completely eliminated, and today gold in no way supports the nation's currency. It is the faith of the public in the purchasing power of the money supply that "backs" the currency.

While the Treasury does not have to own gold to support the money supply, it still owns gold, and the Treasury can issue gold certificates and sell them to the Federal Reserve to acquire funds. Instead of issuing gold certificates and selling them to the Federal Reserve, the Treasury could sell the gold to the general public, for as of January 1, 1975, the general public can legally hold gold. In either case—by issuing gold certificates or selling the gold to the general public—the Treasury is able to obtain funds.

The other major asset of the Federal Reserve is the debt of the federal government. As is explained later, this debt is bought and sold by the Federal Reserve through open market operations. These purchases and sales alter the money supply and the ability of banks to create credit and are the most important tool of monetary policy. The Federal Reserve balance sheet mirrors the importance of this element of monetary policy by the large amount of Treasury debt owned by the central bank. This debt is also a source of revenues to operate the Federal Reserve System, for the debt pays interest. In fact, the Federal Reserve collects sufficient interest to meet its expenses and have a profit. It pays banks a modest dividend of 6 percent on the amount these banks are required to invest in the Federal Reserve. If there is a residual profit after these dividends, the funds are returned to the Treasury.

Cash items in process ▲
Checks that have not cleared; the float

The remaining assets of the Federal Reserve include **cash items in process** and loans to banks. The term "cash items" is misleading because it does not involve cash but is concerned with the clearing of checks. This clearing of checks is one of the most important services provided to banks by the Federal Reserve. At a given moment there are always checks being cleared, and they appear on the Federal Reserve's balance sheet as cash items in process.

This process of check clearing is illustrated by the flow chart in Exhibit 4.2. When a $100 check is drawn on an account (e.g., a deposit in

EXHIBIT 4.2

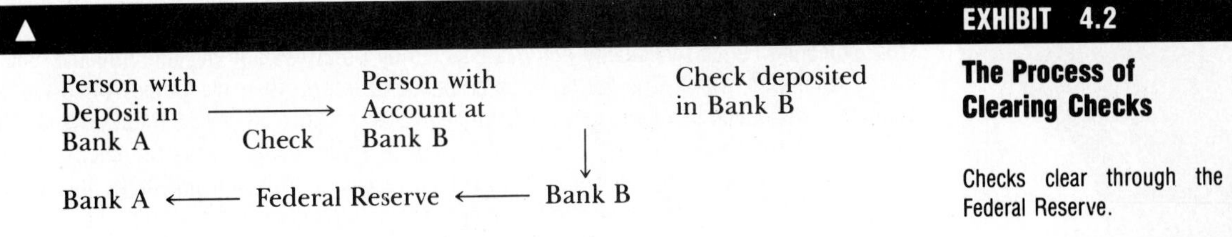

The Process of Clearing Checks

Checks clear through the Federal Reserve.

Bank A), the funds remain in that bank until the check clears. The bank that receives the check (Bank B) credits $100 to the account in which the check was deposited (i.e., its demand deposits increase). The second bank then processes the check by sending it to the Federal Reserve for clearing. The Federal Reserve subsequently sends the check to Bank A, but for a few days that deposit exists in two banks. Both banks may have the reserves because after two days the Federal Reserve credits the second bank with $100 in reserves. In effect the reserves and the deposits are being double-counted.

Float
Checks in the process of clearing that are simultaneously counted as deposits in two banks

This double-counting is called the **float.** If checks take longer to clear, the float increases. This is expansionary because the money is in two places at the same time. For example, if checks take six days instead of four days to clear, both banks have the use of the reserves for two additional days. Thus, changes in the float are important because they affect the reserves of commercial banks and alter the ability of these banks to lend and create credit. Of course, once the entire check-clearing process is completed, the float disappears, and the reserves are transferred from one bank to the other (i.e., from Bank A to Bank B).

The Federal Reserve may lend reserves to depository institutions; thus, the promises of banks to repay these loans constitute additional assets. As is discussed later in this chapter, banks borrow reserves from the Federal Reserve to meet their reserve requirements. These reserves are not free, and the discount rate, which is the interest rate charged for borrowing from the Federal Reserve, is one of the major tools of monetary policy.

The miscellaneous assets of the Federal Reserve include foreign currencies. In recent years there has been a large increase in the volume of foreign trade, and such transactions involve foreign currencies. For example, American dollars will flow abroad when Americans travel in foreign countries, when American firms invest abroad, or when the U.S. government spends money in or gives aid to a foreign country. These dollars must be exchanged for the local currency, and central banks are the mechanisms through which foreign currencies are converted into domestic currencies. Thus, the Federal Reserve has holdings of foreign currencies, just as the banks in other countries have holdings of dollars.

Federal Reserve Notes
Paper currency of the U.S. issued by the Federal Reserve

The largest liability of the Federal Reserve is the paper currency held by the general public (i.e., **Federal Reserve Notes**). The Federal

Financial Facts

The Expedited Funds Availability Act

The Expedited Funds Availability Act was enacted by Congress and became effective September 1, 1990. The act requires all banks to inform their customers when funds deposited in an account will become available. Since all checks must go through the check clearing process (i.e., the receiving bank returns the check to the bank on which it was drawn), the receiving bank will not make the funds immediately available to the depositor. This time lapse or "float" varies with the type of deposit and the location of the bank on which the check is drawn. • Generally, funds from cash transfers, checks drawn on the same bank, wire and electronic transfers, U.S. Treasury checks, Federal Reserve Checks, and U.S. Postal money orders are available the next business day. Funds transferred by checks drawn on local banks may be available in two business days, while funds transferred by checks drawn on non-local banks may require five business days to clear. Even though the depositor may not be able to withdraw the money, the funds may earn interest from the date of deposit. • The bank receiving the deposit may permit the depositor to withdraw up to a specified amount (e.g., $2,500) of the deposit on the next business day. However, this amount is subject to the check's clearing, and if the check should fail to clear, the depositor is responsible for any withdrawals. • The bank may also establish longer delays under specific circumstances. For example, the bank may not permit withdrawals if (1) the amount of the check exceeds $5,000, (2) the depositor is a new customer and is opening an account, (3) the depositor has a record of repeatedly overdrawing the account, or (4) the deposit is a redeposit of a check that was previously returned for insufficient funds. In any event, the bank must inform its depositors of these exceptions to its general policy concerning the availability of money deposited in an account in the bank. •

Reserve also serves as a depository for banks, the Treasury, and foreign financial institutions.[2] Banks deposit their reserves in the Federal Reserve, and the Treasury may deposit its funds, such as tax receipts, in the Federal Reserve banks. The foreign deposits arise as the result of international monetary transactions. Of all the different deposits, the most important are the reserves of depository institutions. By altering these reserves and the amount of Federal Reserve Notes outstanding, the Federal Reserve is able to alter the supply of money and the ability of these institutions to create loans. It is through the power of the Federal Reserve to create and destroy these liabilities that credit is eased or tightened. Presently there are no constraints on the Federal Reserve's power to create or destroy these liabilities. Only the goals of public policy, such as price stability or full employment, constrain the central bank, for it is assumed that the Federal Reserve will act to help achieve these economic goals.

---

[2] Commercial banks, savings and loan associations, mutual savings banks, and credit unions may deposit reserves with the Federal Reserve.

Under the Monetary Control Act of 1980, Congress has also given the Federal Reserve vast supervisory power over depository institutions. The purpose of this power is not only to control the supply of money and credit but also to protect the depositors from poor financial management by individual banks. The supervisory power of the Federal Reserve includes the enforcement of bank regulations and periodic examination of banks. Periodic reports to the Federal Reserve concerning an individual bank's loans, expenses, and earnings are also required. If the examinations and reports indicate that a bank is following unsound financial policies, the Federal Reserve can require the bank's management to correct these policies. This ability to force a bank's management to change policy gives the Federal Reserve's supervisory powers real force. The mere existence of this force is sufficient to keep the majority of banks pursuing sound financial policies.

Structure of the Federal Reserve

The power in the Federal Reserve System is concentrated in a **Board of Governors,** consisting of seven people appointed by the president of the United States with the confirmation of the Senate. The appointments are for fourteen years, and the terms are staggered so that one new appointment is made every two years. The long terms and the staggering of these terms reduce political pressures and thus contribute to the federal system of checks and balances. The chairman of the Board of Governors is usually the major spokesperson for monetary policy and frequently acts as an advisor to the president on economic policy. The power of the Board of Governors manifests itself in several ways through its power of appointment and control of open market operations.

Board of Governors ▲
Controlling body of the Federal Reserve whose members are appointed by the president of the United States

The country is divided into twelve districts, with a Federal Reserve bank in each district. Each **district bank** is managed by nine directors, three of whom are appointed by the Board of Governors. The remaining six directors are elected by member banks and represent the member banks, industry, commerce, and agriculture. By dividing the nation into districts, it is possible to have an individual reserve bank perform specialized financial services pertaining to its region. For example, the financial problems of rural regions may differ from those of urban areas. Decentralizing the central bank into districts permits a more flexible approach to regional financial problems. Since the city of New York is the financial center of the nation, the district bank in New York is the largest and most important individual reserve bank.

District bank ▲
Twelve banks that comprise the Federal Reserve

Member banks constitute the next component of the Federal Reserve System. Commercial banks have either state or national charters. All banks with national charters must join the Federal Reserve. State banks have the option to join, but many do not choose to join. Since the Federal Reserve permits non-member banks to use its check-clearing

FIGURE 4.1

Structure of the Federal Reserve

The power within the Federal Reserve rests with the Board of Governors.

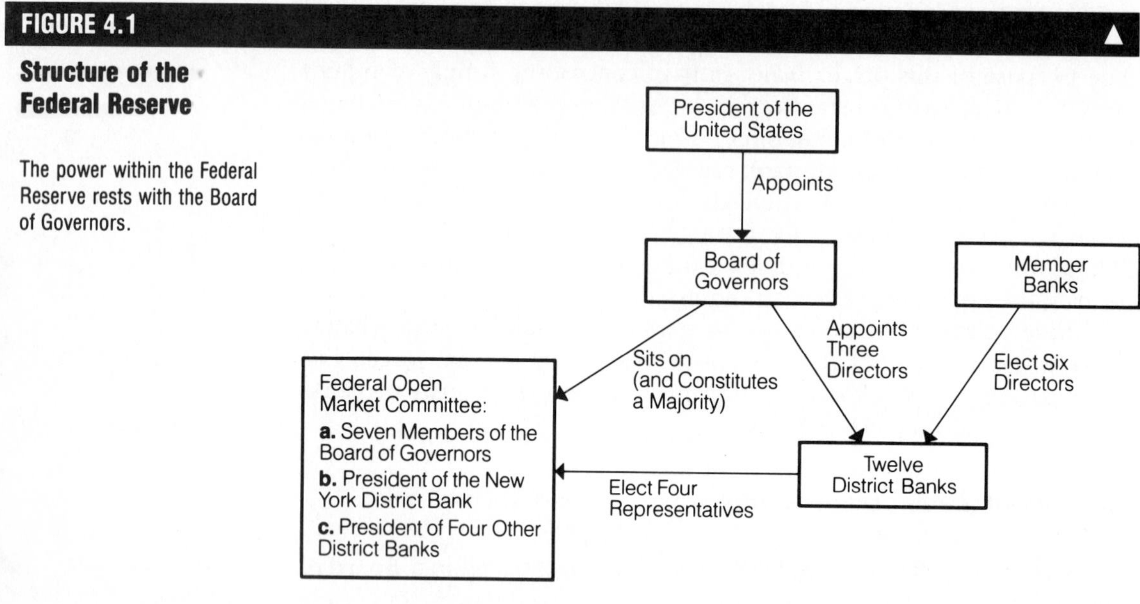

facilities and to borrow reserves at the discount window, these services are available to all banks without their joining the system.

The member banks are required to invest capital in their district's Federal Reserve bank. The members are the owners of the Federal Reserve banks, and for this investment they receive a modest return on their capital from the earnings of the Federal Reserve. As was explained previously, the source of these earnings is the interest earned on the U.S. government debt owned by the Federal Reserve. If the Federal Reserve earns profits that exceed its required dividends to member banks, the excess profits are returned to the Treasury.

Federal Open Market Committee ▲
Part of the Federal Reserve that establishes and executes monetary policy

The last component of the Federal Reserve is the **Federal Open Market Committee,** which has control over open market operations. Since open market operations are the most important tool of monetary policy, this committee is a powerful component of the system. The committee consists of the seven members of the Board of Governors and five presidents of the district banks. The president of the New York district bank is a permanent member of the committee, while the four remaining positions rotate among the district bank presidents. Since by voting as a bloc the Board of Governors has a majority on the committee, the Board has power over open market operations.

In summary, the important components of the Federal Reserve System are (1) the Board of Governors, (2) the district reserve banks, (3) the member banks, and (4) the Federal Open Market Committee. This structure is summarized by Figure 4.1. While the president of the United States appoints the Board of Governors, and the member banks own the

Federal Reserve, the real power rests with the Board of Governors. It has this power because it (1) appoints three of the nine directors of the district reserve banks, (2) composes a majority of the Federal Open Market Committee, and (3) has regulatory authority over the commercial banks. Thus, the Board of Governors is individually the most important part of the Federal Reserve System.

THE EXPANSION OF MONEY AND CREDIT

The Federal Reserve affects the supply of money and credit through its impact on the reserves of banks, which alters their lending capacity. A small change in banks' reserves can have a much larger change in the money supply because of the fractional reserve system. Understanding the potential impact of monetary policy requires understanding how the banking system expands and contracts the supply of money and credit; that is, understanding how a fractional reserve banking system alters the supply of money.

Banks' ability to lend comes from investors: the depositors, general creditors, and owners who invest in various types of instruments (e.g., certificates of deposit or the bank's stock) issued by each bank. An individual bank can only lend what it obtains from its sources of finance, but, as is subsequently explained, the aggregate banking system can expand the supply of money. As this money flows among banks, the aggregate supply is increased. This increase is the result of the fractional reserve requirements established by the Federal Reserve.

This section is concerned with the banking system's ability to expand and contract the supply of money and credit. The next section will consider how the Federal Reserve affects the capacity of banks to lend and thus affects the supply of money and credit. Although the following discussion could become quite involved as different scenarios are considered, only one simple case is given, since the purpose of the discussion is to illustrate the expansion of money and credit and not to illustrate how differing assumptions may alter the amount of change in the money supply.[3]

The process of loan creation will be illustrated under the following assumptions: (1) Cash is always deposited in a demand deposit, and none is held in the form of cash. (2) Banks hold no excess reserves; all excess

---

[3] For a discussion of different scenarios under different assumptions, consult a money and banking text such as Lawrence Ritter and William Silber, *Principles of Money, Banking, and Financial Markets,* 6th ed. (New York: Basic Books, 1988); or Colin Campbell and Rosemary Campbell, *An Introduction to Money and Banking,* 5th ed. (Hinsdale, Ill.: The Dryden Press, 1984).

reserves are loaned. (3) There are sufficient borrowers to consume the excess reserves of the banks. If these assumptions are violated, there are leakages within the system that decrease the potential expansion. For example, if individuals hold cash, that money is not deposited in a bank and hence cannot be lent by a bank. Such a holding of cash reduces the assets of banks and reduces their capacity to expand the supply of money and credit.

What is the potential effect of cash deposited in a checking account? As was explained in Chapter 2, the money supply (M-1) is the sum of demand deposits plus coins and currency in circulation. Cash deposited into checking accounts does not change the money supply. All that is changed is the form of the money from cash to demand deposits. Such transactions, however, are extremely important, for they increase the banks' ability to lend. When the banks use this ability and make loans, they expand the supply of money.

Consider what happens when $100 is deposited in a checking account. The $100 has been removed from circulation and replaced by the demand deposit. After the bank receives the $100 cash deposit, the $100 becomes part of the reserves of the bank. This $100 reserve is divided into two categories: (1) those reserves that must be held against the demand deposit, the required reserves; and (2) those reserves in excess of the reserve requirement, which are called excess reserves. If the reserve requirement is 20 percent, then $20 of the $100 cash reserve is required and $80 is excess reserves.[4] These excess reserves are very important because commercial banks use their excess reserves to acquire income-earning assets such as loans and securities. Depositing cash in a commercial bank thus gives it the ability to create loans, because the bank obtains a resource that it may lend—excess reserves. Banks do not lend and cannot lend their deposit liabilities.

If a borrower enters the bank and the bank grants a loan of $80, what effect will this transaction have on (1) the depositor, (2) the bank, and (3) the borrower? Since this transaction does not concern the depositor, it has no effect on the depositor. As far as the depositor is concerned, the bank still owes on demand $100. The borrower receives an asset—a demand deposit at the bank—and also incurs a liability, the IOU to the bank. The bank acquires an asset, the $80 loan, and the bank incurs a new liability, the $80 demand deposit. This deposit is the money that the borrower receives for the loan.

Why does the commercial bank create a new demand deposit instead of just lending the person the cash? The answer is that the bank does not want the borrower to remove the cash from the bank. The bank wants to keep that cash as long as possible, for it is part of the bank's reserves. The

---

[4]As of January 1, 1991, the reserve requirement was 12 percent. Twenty percent is easier to work with and is used for explanatory purposes.

bank does realize that the borrower will spend the money and the reserves will probably be transferred to another bank, but the bank still wants the use of the reserves as long as possible.

Why does the borrower take out the loan? Obviously, the borrower does not want to leave the money in the bank and pay interest on the loan but intends to spend it. When the borrower does spend the money, the recipient of the check will either cash it or deposit it in a commercial bank. When the check is deposited, the probability of this bank and the borrower's bank being the same is quite small, since there are thousands of commercial banks in the country. When the check is deposited in the second bank, that bank sends the check to the first bank for payment. The first bank transfers $80 worth of reserves (i.e., the cash) to the second bank. This flow of deposits and reserves may be summarized by the following figure:

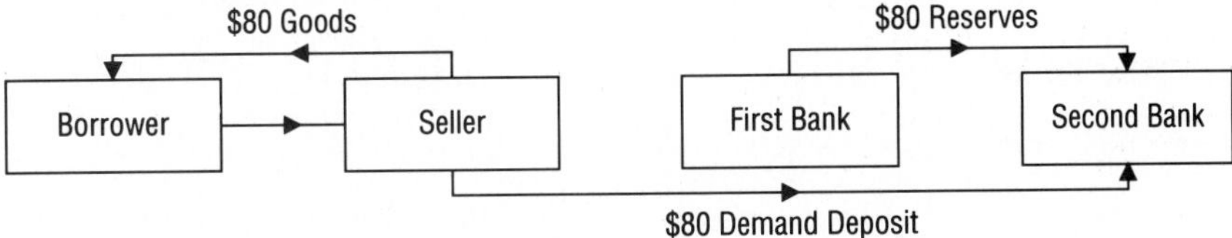

In summary, the loan made possible a purchase by the borrower, and thus a seller has made a sale that may not have occurred without the creation of the loan. Goods have flowed from the seller to the buyer. When the seller deposited the payment in a commercial bank, this caused reserves to flow between the seller's bank and the borrower's bank.

What is the net effect of this transaction on the money supply and amount of credit? Both have increased. There are $180 in demand deposits, the initial $100 deposit in the first bank and the new $80 deposit in the second bank. There has been a net increase in the money supply of $80. This $80 increase came through the process of loan creation, for there is now $80 in new credit. The act of depositing cash in a checking account led to a net increase in the supply of money through the process of loan creation.

The process of loan creation is not limited to the initial expansion of $80, for the second bank now has a new deposit. It must hold reserves against the new checking account. Since the reserve requirement is 20 percent, the bank must hold in reserve $16 ($80 × 0.20). It received $80 in reserves from the first bank when the check cleared. Thus, $64 of these reserves are excess reserves that the second bank may use to purchase an income-earning asset or grant a new loan. If the second bank grants a loan for $64, it creates a new demand deposit of $64. The borrower then purchases goods and services and pays for them with a check drawn on the new demand deposit. The $64 check then is deposited in a third bank and is cleared. This creates for the third bank a new deposit

EXHIBIT 4.3

Multiple Expansion of the Supply of Money

The creation of new excess reserves leads to a multiple expansion in the supply of new credit.

	Initial Deposit = $100		Reserve Requirement = 20%	
	New Demand Deposits	Cumulative New Credit Created	Cumulative Required Reserves	Excess Reserves
1st bank	$100.00	$ 0	$ 20.00	$80.00
2nd bank	80.00	80.00	36.00	64.00
3rd bank	64.00	144.00	48.80	51.20
4th bank	51.20	195.20	59.04	40.96
5th bank	40.96	236.16	67.23	32.77
6th bank	32.77	268.93	73.79	26.21
7th bank	26.21	295.14	79.03	20.97
8th bank	20.97	316.11	83.22	16.78
.	.	.	.	.
.	.	.	.	.
.	.	.	.	.
Final round	0	$400.00	$100.00	0

and transfers to it $64 in reserves from the second bank. The third bank divides these reserves into required reserves ($\$64 \times 0.20 = \$12.80$) and excess reserves of $51.20. The third bank now has the capacity to acquire income-earning assets and create new loans.

This process of lending and passing reserves among commercial banks may continue until there are no more excess reserves. With each new loan there is expansion in the money supply. The net increase in new credit and in demand deposits is many times the initial deposit. This expansion is illustrated in Exhibit 4.3, which continues the multiple expansion for the first eight rounds. As may be seen in the table, each additional loan and new demand deposit (column 1) is smaller, but the sum of the new loans increases (column 2). As the total of demand deposits rises, required reserves also rise (column 3), so excess reserves must decline (column 4). Of course, it is this decline in excess reserves that causes each new loan to be smaller. Eventually, if the expansion continues indefinitely, the excess reserves will become zero and the total $100 in reserves will be required reserves.

If the expansion continues until there are no excess reserves, how much will the money supply increase? What is the increase in new loans? These questions may be answered by the following simple equation.

4.1 $$\frac{\text{Change in excess reserves}}{\text{Reserve requirement}} = \text{Change in the money supply.}$$

Equation 4.1 gives the increase in *both* new credit and the money supply. In the previous example, the cash deposit of $100 increased excess reserves by $80. Since the reserve requirement was 20 percent, the maximum possible expansion in the money supply and new credit is

$$\$80/0.2 = \$400.$$

Depositing $100 in a demand deposit permits an expansion of $400 of new money. Since the new money came through the creation of new credit, $400 is also the maximum possible increase in new credit. The change in the money supply and the change in credit thus is five times the initial change in the excess reserves.

Cash Withdrawals and the Reduction in Reserves

In the previous example, cash was deposited in an account, which created new excess reserves and led to the expansion in the supply of money and credit. A cash withdrawal from a bank reverses the process and reduces the bank's reserves. If the bank has excess reserves, the withdrawal creates no problems for the bank, because it takes the funds out of its excess reserves. After the withdrawal, the bank's lending capacity is reduced because the bank has lost excess reserves.

The situation is considerably different if the bank has no excess reserves. While the bank may be able to meet the withdrawal from its existing (and required) reserves, it now has a major problem: its reserves are insufficient to meet its reserve requirements against its deposit liabilities. Thus, the bank must take some action to restore its reserves.

One possibility is to borrow the reserves from another bank. If bank A borrows reserves from bank B, bank A will now meet its reserve requirement. Will bank B meet its reserve requirement? The answer should be obvious. Bank B can only make this loan if it has excess reserves! The borrowing of reserves transfers reserves from one bank to another; it does not alter the total supply of reserves in the banking system. All that changes is a change in the location of the reserves from bank B to bank A.

The market for these reserves is called the **federal funds market.** Federal funds is one of the most well-developed of all short-term credit markets. If a commercial bank lacks sufficient reserves against its deposit liabilities, it is able to borrow reserves from a commercial bank that has excess reserves. If a bank has excess reserves, it can put these funds to work by lending them in the federal funds market. Thus, the bank converts a sterile asset, the excess reserves, into an income-earning asset, for it charges the borrowing bank interest for the use of the reserves.

Federal funds market ▲
Market in which banks borrow and lend excess reserves

Since the reserves may be needed for only a very short time, the loans made in the federal funds market are usually for extremely short periods of time (e.g., a day). Thus, any commercial bank that has a temporary surplus of loanable funds may briefly lend them in the federal funds market and earn interest on the funds. Any commercial bank that is temporarily deficient in reserves is able to borrow them for as short a period of time as necessary.

The federal funds market illustrates the importance of good management of short-term assets. Since the loans may be for as short a period *as a day,* a bank with excess reserves may put this asset to work for this brief period. Since these loans are of such short duration, the interest rate on federal funds can fluctuate significantly and quickly. When excess reserves exist in the banking system, the interest rate may fall to nothing, for the quantity of the excess reserves supplied exceeds the quantity demanded. But during periods of excess demand, commercial banks may pay a substantial rate of interest for these loans in order to meet their reserve requirement.

If the banking system lacks excess reserves, the bank that experienced the cash withdrawal could borrow the reserves from the Federal Reserve. Unlike the banking system, the Federal Reserve has the power to create reserves. If bank A is short and all other banks lack excess reserves, then borrowing from the Federal Reserve creates the reserves needed by bank A. Of course, the Federal Reserve charges interest on this loan, just as bank B would charge bank A interest for the use of its reserves. This interest rate, called the **discount rate,** is a major tool of monetary policy and is discussed in detail in the next section on the tools of monetary policy.

Discount rate ▲
Interest rate charged banks for borrowing reserves from the Federal Reserve

Suppose, however, that the banking system has no excess reserves and bank A does not want to borrow reserves from the Federal Reserve. What will happen? The bank will have to liquidate some of its assets, and since there are no excess reserves in the banking system, the multiple expansion illustrated previously works in reverse. The reduction in reserves will cause the supply of money and credit to contract. Just as the cash deposit leads to a multiple expansion, the withdrawal of cash when the banking system is fully loaned up will cause a multiple contraction in the money supply and in the supply of credit.

This process of a multiple contraction is illustrated in Exhibit 4.4, which essentially reverses the procedure illustrated in Exhibit 4.3. The initial cash withdrawal of $100 reduces demand deposits by $100 (column 1). Total reserves also decline by $100, but since required reserves decline by only $20 (column 3), the decline in total reserves of $100 means the bank is now short reserves by $80. The bank liquidates an asset worth $80 to replace its lost reserves and the shortage is transferred to the second bank. The second bank now loses $80 in deposits and reserves and the process is repeated. Unless the cash is returned to the banking system, the system must contract. The cumulative decline in demand deposits is given in the second column, and the fourth column presents the cumulative change in required reserves with each subsequent contraction. As in the cash of the expansion in demand deposits,

EXHIBIT 4.4

Multiple Contraction in the Supply of Money

If the banking system has no excess reserves, a cash withdrawal will result in a multiple contraction in the supply of money unless the cash is returned to the banking system.

	Initial Withdrawal = $100		Reserve Requirement = 20%	
	Change in Demand Deposits	**Cumulative Change in Demand Deposits**	**Reduction in Required Reserves**	**Cumulative Change in Required Reserves**
1st bank	−$100.00	−$100.00	−$20.00	−$20.00
2nd bank	−80.00	−180.00	−16.00	−36.00
3rd bank	−64.00	−244.00	−12.80	−48.80
4th bank	−51.20	−295.20	−10.24	−59.04
.	.	.	.	.
.	.	.	.	.
.	.	.	.	.
Final round	0	−$400.00	0	−$100.00

the maximum decrease in demand deposits is −$400 (− $100/.2) and the cumulative change in required reserves is −$100, which is the amount of the initial cash withdrawal.

This contraction is precisely what happened during the Great Depression, when there were large withdrawals from commercial banks. Banks had insufficient liquidity to meet these withdrawals. Since the Federal Reserve did not put reserves into the system, many commercial banks were unable to meet the withdrawals and had to close their doors. Thus, a major role of the central bank should be to act as a source of reserves and liquidity to commercial banks when all other sources have been drained. The Federal Reserve, by its ability to create bank reserves, is able to create liquidity for banks when such liquidity is needed to meet withdrawals.

The previous discussion suggests that a flow of funds out of a bank can create a significant liquidity problem. Cash withdrawals or an outflow of deposits reduces the individual bank's reserves. (Such cash withdrawals need not affect the reserves of the banking system if the funds are deposited in another bank.) The management staff of banks are very conscious of the impact of a flow of funds from the bank and thus take steps to reduce the impact by seeking to match their loan portfolio and anticipated cash drains. Such matching would be very simple if all deposits were 30-day certificates of deposit. The bank could assure having the funds to meet the CDs by only making 30-day loans. The maturing loans would cover the maturing CDs. If the CDs were renewed, then the banks could make new loans for an additional thirty days.

Of course, portfolio management of banks is not that simple because the bank issues a variety of instruments to induce deposits. These range from very short-term deposits (e.g., demand deposits) to instruments that may not mature for many years (e.g., a five-year CD). In addition, as is explained in Chapter 20, commercial banks grant lines of credit that permit the creditor to borrow varying amounts over a period of time. Such loans mean that bankers do not know from day to day exactly how much will be loaned, nor do they know exactly when the loans will be paid off.

Management will have had experience with the rate at which deposits flow into and out of the bank, how many loans will be granted, and when they will be repaid. This knowledge permits the bank to construct a portfolio consistent with management's anticipated need for funds to meet withdrawals. However, there have been periods when a bank's managers have found themselves in precarious situations. This is especially true during periods when interest rates rise rapidly. Depositors may withdraw more funds than had been anticipated by the bank's management. Presumably these withdrawals are being made by savers seeking to earn a higher return in an alternative institution that competes with the accounts offered by the bank. Meeting these withdrawals can hurt the individual bank, especially if it must pay higher interest rates to raise the funds to meet the withdrawals. Unless the bank is also able to raise the rates it charges on its loans, the profitability of the bank is hurt, since its cost of funds is increased.

THE TOOLS OF MONETARY POLICY

As the previous discussion indicates, the reserves of commercial banks are an exceedingly important component of the financial system. Anything that affects these reserves affects the ability of commercial banks to create money and credit. Ultimately, the control of the supply of money rests with the Federal Reserve. It is through the impact on banks' reserves that the Fed is able to alter the supply of money.

The Federal Reserve has three primary tools for affecting the reserves of depository institutions: the discount rate, the reserve requirements, and open market operations. Each is important through its ability to change excess reserves and hence affect banks' lending capacity. In addition to these primary tools of monetary policy, the Federal Reserve has selective credit controls concerning real estate and consumer loans and purchase of securities with borrowed funds (i.e., the margin requirement discussed in Chapter 6). However, the primary tools of monetary policy give the Federal Reserve its power to affect the economy. The ensuing discussion explains how each is used to alter the reserves of banks and thus affect the supply of money and credit in the economy.

Discount Rate

As was previously explained, the discount rate is the interest rate that the Federal Reserve charges banks when they borrow reserves to meet temporary shortages in their required reserves. A change in the cost of borrowing reserves will alter banks' willingness to borrow from the Federal Reserve. Thus, a decrease in the discount rate may stimulate increased borrowing, while an increase in the discount rate should discourage further borrowing and may cause banks to retire debt owed the Federal Reserve.

Although the discount rate may induce banks' behavior, it is a passive tool of monetary policy. The initiative for changes in the level of borrowing rests with the banks. The Federal Reserve may alter the discount rate, but it cannot force banks to borrow or to cease borrowing. An increase in the discount rate does not mean that the banks will cease borrowing and retire existing debt owed the Federal Reserve. If the banks are able to pass on to their customers the higher cost of borrowing, there may be little contraction in the level of credit. Furthermore, not all banks borrow from the Federal Reserve. Some banks prefer to remain free of this obligation. Thus, an increase in the discount rate will not affect the lending behavior of these banks.

During the 1960s, the Federal Reserve changed the discount rate infrequently. From 1960 to 1968 the rate was changed only seven times. In the 1970s the Federal Reserve altered the discount rate more frequently in response to changing economic conditions. These fluctuations in the discount rate are illustrated in Figure 4.2. For example, there was a rapid increase in the rate from 6½ percent in 1978 to a high of 13 percent in 1980. This doubling of the discount rate occurred during a period of inflation and high interest rates, when the Federal Reserve sought to restore more stable prices. As inflation and interest rates subsided from 1983 to 1984, the Federal Reserve lowered the discount rate to encourage economic growth and higher levels of employment.

Changes in the discount rate often occur in response to changes in other short-term interest rates. Instead of initiating the change in the price of credit, the discount rate reflects fluctuations in other short-term interest rates. For example, when commercial banks increase the rates they charge on loans, this increases the difference between these rates and the discount rate. This increased differential makes borrowing from the Federal Reserve potentially more profitable. Unless the Federal Reserve wants to encourage such expansion, it will increase the discount rate to decrease the difference between the discount rate and other interest rates. The increase will then discourage the use of borrowed reserves to finance the loans. Thus, changes in the discount rate often follow changes in interest rates and do not initiate the change. While the Federal Reserve can seek to tighten the supply of credit by increasing the

FIGURE 4.2

Discount Rate (1974–1990)

The discount rate dramatically rose during the early 1980s but was relatively stable during the late 1980s.

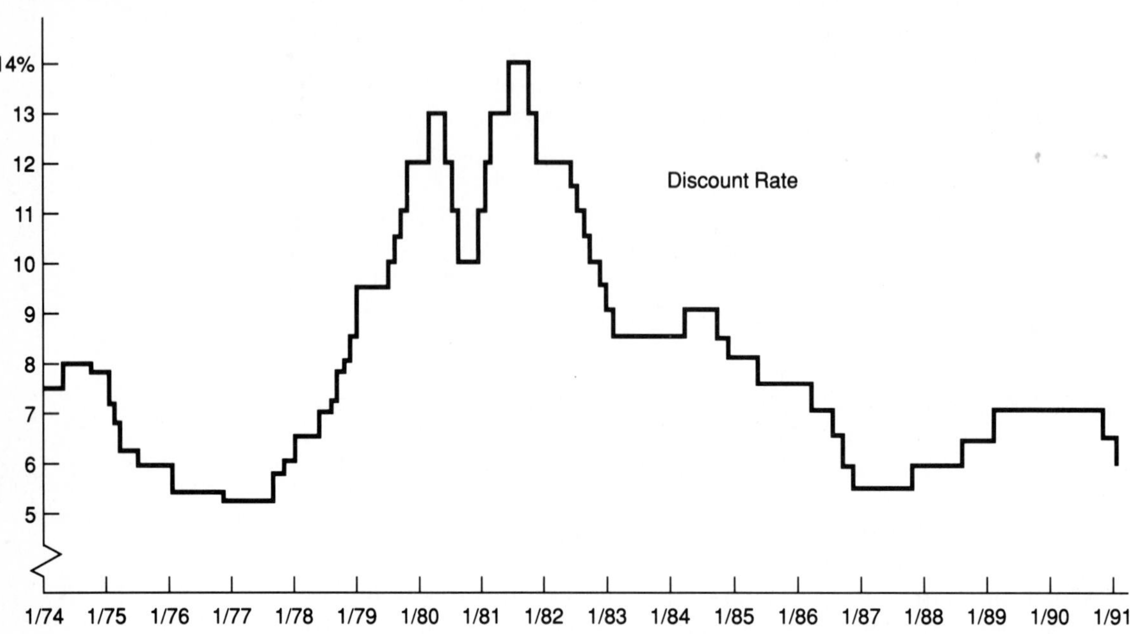

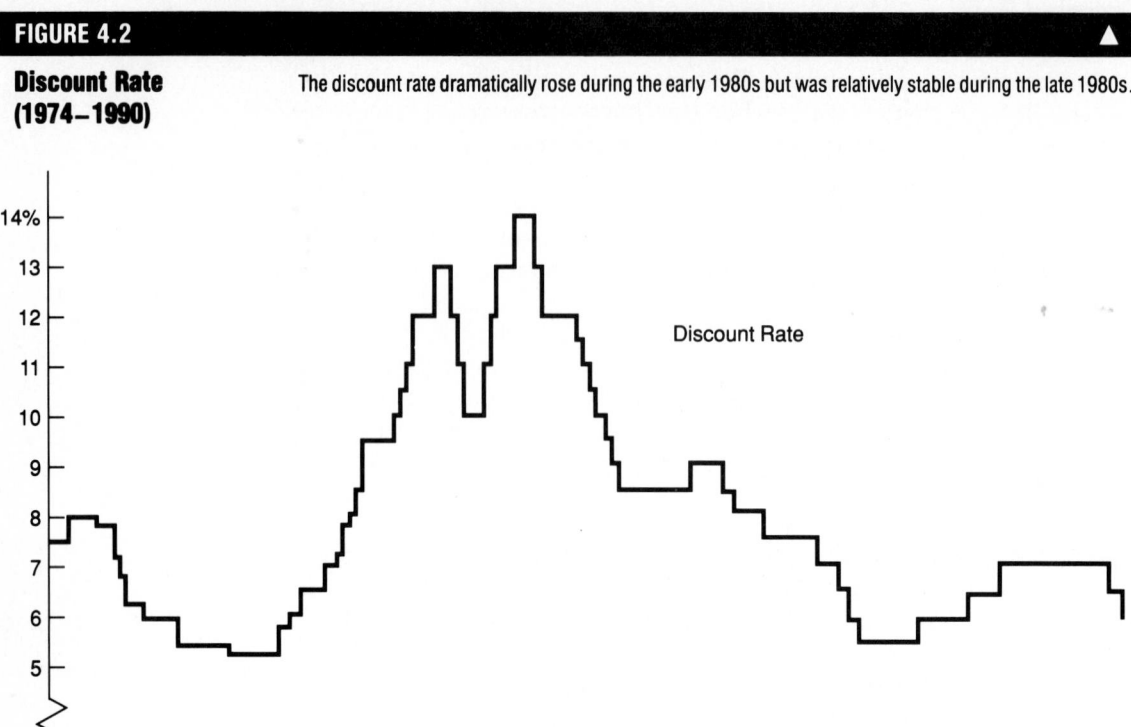

Source: Federal Reserve Bulletin, *various issues.*

discount rate and thereby induce banks to increase their interest rates, the Federal Reserve rarely uses the discount rate as an active tool of monetary policy. Instead it employs open market operations to achieve its objectives more efficiently.

Reserve Requirement

Changing the reserve requirement against bank deposits constitutes the second major tool of monetary policy. Like the discount rate, it is infrequently used as an active tool of monetary policy. Since all depository institutions must maintain reserves against their deposit liabilities, any change in these required reserves alters all banks' ability to lend. For example, if the reserve requirement for demand deposits is 12 percent and is raised to 15 percent, every depository institution will need to increase its required reserves. While they previously had to hold $12 in reserves against every $100 in demand deposits, these banks will now have to hold $15 in reserves. Therefore, by simply increasing the reserve requirement, the Federal Reserve immediately decreases banks' capacity to grant loans. A decrease in the reserve requirement has the opposite effect, for it immediately increases banks' ability to lend.

Obviously this tool of monetary policy cannot be used to fine-tune the money supply to changing liquidity needs. For example, how could this tool be used to put liquidity into the system for seasonal changes in the demand for money? Since changing the reserve requirement is unable to produce subtle changes in the money supply, it is rarely used as a tool of monetary policy. During the period 1963 to 1991, the reserve requirement against demand deposits was changed on only seven occasions. The major advantage of changing the reserve requirement is to release or absorb a large amount of excess reserves in one act. In addition, a change in the reserve requirement has an "announcement effect" that serves to indicate the seriousness of particular policy of the Federal Reserve.

Open Market Operations

Of the three tools of monetary policy, by far the most important is **open market operations.** Open market operations refer to the purchase and sale of government securities by the Federal Reserve. By buying and selling these securities, the Federal Reserve is able to alter the supply of money in circulation and the reserves of the banking system. The Federal Reserve may buy and sell securities at any time and in any volume. Open market operations, then, are not only a means of significantly changing the money supply and the availability of credit but also of fine-tuning the supply of money on a day-by-day basis.

Open market operations ▲
Buying and selling of U.S. Treasury securities by the Federal Reserve

The Federal Reserve does not directly buy and sell securities to the general public or banks. The transactions are negotiated through private U.S. government security dealers who make markets in these securities. The dealers in turn sell the government securities to the general public and to banks. Since the sales and purchases are in many millions of dollars, the security dealers must have substantial capital and borrowing capacity to make these markets.

If the Federal Reserve seeks to expand the supply of money, it purchases securities. After the transactions are negotiated, payments must be made, and the act of paying for the securities alters the money supply and the reserves of banks. Ownership of the securities is transferred to the Federal Reserve, and the Federal Reserve pays for the securities by writing a check drawn on itself, which the sellers deposit in banks. The banks clear the checks and receive payment in the form of reserves from the Federal Reserve. The total effect of these transactions is (1) to increase the supply of money because demand deposits are increased and (2) to increase the reserves of the banking system. The required reserves of the banks rise, for the bank's deposit liabilities have risen. However,

Financial Facts

Chairman of the Federal Reserve—Alan Greenspan

The Federal Reserve is controlled by the seven individuals who comprise the Board of Governors. While each member has an equal vote, the Chairman of the Board of Governors has special powers as the leader of the Federal Reserve. Since he or she acts as a spokesperson for monetary policy, the monetary philosophy of the chairman is considered by the financial community to be exceedingly important. • During 1987, the Chairman of the Federal Reserve, Paul Volcker, retired. Volcker was considered to have been responsible for the decline in the rate of inflation that the nation experienced during the early 1980s. According to *The Wall Street Journal* (June 3, 1987, p. 21), he was a "symbol of steady, credible U.S. monetary policy." • His successor was Alan Greenspan, an economist who served as head of the Council of Economic Advisors to President Ford. Greenspan is an economic conservative who continued to follow the general philosophy and policies of his predecessor. That is, the Federal Reserve has tended to follow a moderately expansionary monetary policy with a primary emphasis on the stabilization of prices. • Greenspan is also a firm believer in free markets. This suggests that he tends to support less regulation of banks and to let the dollar trade freely against foreign currencies. If the value of the dollar were to fall relative to the value of other currencies, Greenspan's belief in free markets suggests that he would not take action to support the dollar and stop the decline in its value. However, belief in free markets and a desire to retard inflation do not mean that Chairman Greenspan and the Federal Reserve will not take action to stimulate economic growth. As the economy appeared to decline into recession in late 1990, the Federal Reserve did put reserves into the banking system and lowered the discount rate, actions which are designed to stimulate economic expansion. •

---

only a fraction of the increase in reserves will be required reserves. Thus, the excess reserves of the banks also rise.

When the Federal Reserve seeks to contract the money supply, it sells government securities. Once again, it is the payment for the purchased securities that alters the money supply and the capacity of banks to lend. If the public buys the securities, it draws down demand deposits, and the money supply and reserves of banks are decreased. The total effect of these transactions is (1) to decrease the money supply, because demand deposits are decreased, and (2) to decrease the total reserves of the banking system, because banks have fewer reserves on deposit in the Federal Reserve. Since only a percentage of these reserves was required against the deposit liabilities, the excess reserves of the bank were also decreased. Thus, by selling securities, the Federal Reserve decreases the supply of money and decreases the excess reserves of the banks, which reduces their ability to lend and create credit.

Target Monetary Growth

The prior discussion suggests that the Federal Reserve and its monetary policy can have a major impact on the supply of money and credit. While the Federal Reserve will alter the supply of money and credit to effectu-

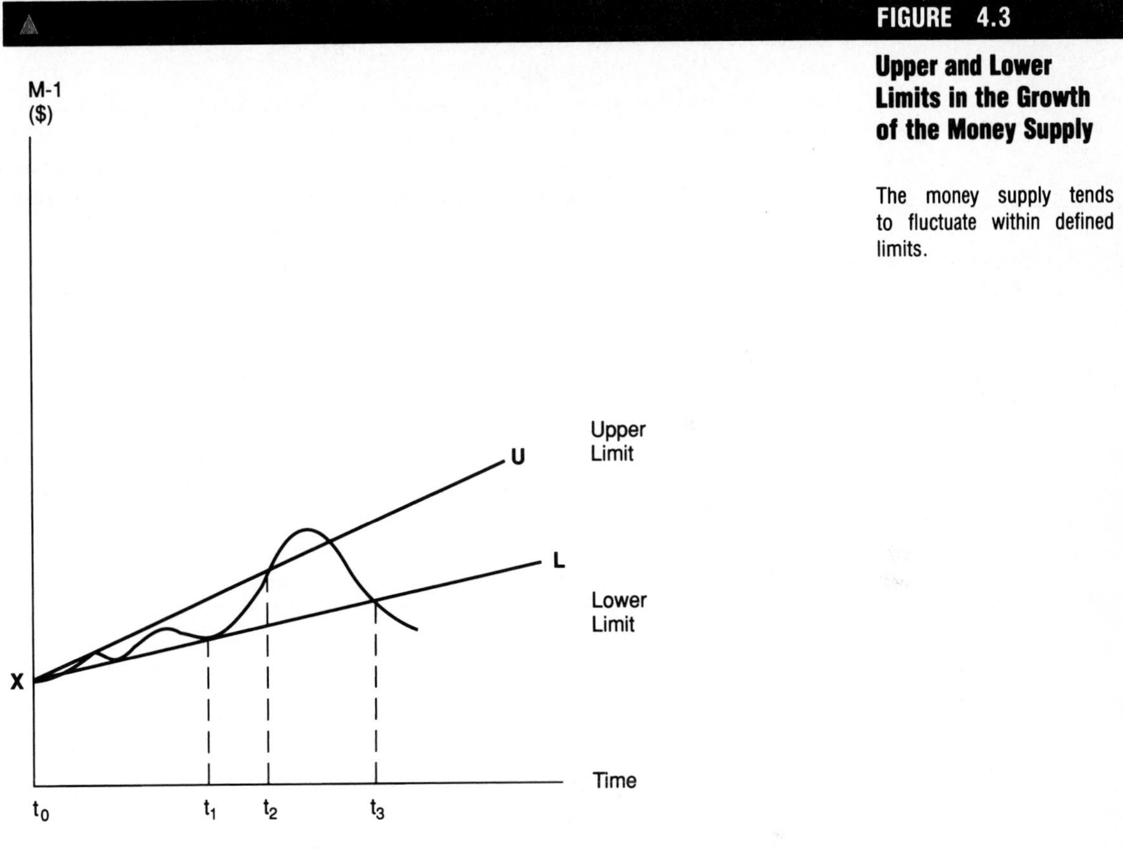

FIGURE 4.3

Upper and Lower Limits in the Growth of the Money Supply

The money supply tends to fluctuate within defined limits.

ate a particular monetary policy, it will also over a period of time sustain monetary growth. That is, the Federal Reserve systematically expands the money supply over time to accommodate economic growth. While the Federal Reserve cannot exactly control the week-to-week changes in the supply of money, it can maintain growth within defined targets. These targets are established within the bounds the Fed believes will maintain economic growth without increasing inflationary pressure.

For illustrative purposes, consider Figure 4.3, in which the vertical axis measures the money supply while the horizontal axis measures time. At the present (t_0), the money supply is some amount X. If this amount grows at the upper limit, it will follow line XU. If, however, the growth in the money supply is the lower limit, it will follow XL. The actual money supply may fluctuate between the two targets, as illustrated during the time period t_0t_1.

If the rate of growth were to increase and the money supply break the upper limit (e.g., at t_2), the Federal Reserve would take steps to reduce the rate of growth in the supply of money. Financial managers and investors could expect monetary policy to tighten to decrease the rate of growth in the money supply. Conversely, if the rate of growth were to decrease and the money supply break the lower limit (e.g., at t_3), the Federal Reserve would probably take steps to increase the rate of growth in the supply of money. Financial managers and investors could expect monetary policy to loosen, and the rate of growth in the money supply may increase.

Notice that the individual financial manager or investor is not necessarily concerned with the absolute level of the money supply but the trend and changes in the trend. Emphasis is placed on anticipating changes in the Federal Reserve's policy in order to anticipate changes in the cost of credit and possible changes in security prices. Correctly anticipating changes in interest rates can lead to avoiding costly errors that result from borrowing before a decline in interest rates or that result from purchasing securities prior to a price decline. Unfortunately, anticipating what the Federal Reserve will do is similar to anticipating changes in the tax laws or changes in the political climate. Anticipating change is not the same as knowing when the change will occur or what impact it will have.

FISCAL POLICY AND FINANCING THE FEDERAL GOVERNMENT'S DEFICITS

Even though the Federal Reserve can affect the supply of money and credit in the economy, it does not have complete control over them. There are forces beyond its control that can affect the supply of money and credit. One of these forces is the fiscal policy of the federal government.

Fiscal policy ▲
Taxation, expenditures, and debt management of the federal government

Fiscal policy is taxation, expenditures, and debt management by the federal government. Like monetary policy, fiscal policy may be used to pursue the economic goals of full employment, price stability, and economic growth. Like monetary policy, fiscal policy can affect the supply of money and the capacity of the banking system to lend.

Deficit ▲
Disbursements exceeding receipts

Surplus ▲
Receipts exceeding disbursements

Taxation or government expenditures by themselves do not alter the money supply. However, when government expenditures exceed revenues, this **deficit** must be financed. When government revenues exceed expenditures, the government must do something with this **surplus.** It is the financing of the deficit or disposing of the surplus that may affect the supply of money and the capacity of banks to lend. This section is concerned with the effect that fiscal policy may have on the money supply and bank reserves. Emphasis is placed on deficit spending and how the federal government may finance the deficit.

The federal government may obtain funds to finance a deficit from three sources: (1) the general public, (2) banks, and (3) the Federal Reserve. The effect on banks' reserves varies with each of these three sources of finance. An example in which the federal government runs a $100 deficit will be used to illustrate the different impact on banks' capacity to lend using each of the sources of funds to finance the deficit.

Borrowing from the General Public

Since the government is running a deficit of $100, it issues securities to raise the money to finance the deficit. The securities are purchased by the general public, which pays for the securities by check. This payment transfers $100 from the general public's account to the Treasury's account. Then the Treasury purchases domestic goods and services from the general public for $100. When the Treasury pays for these goods and services, the public's deposits are restored as the money is transferred from the Treasury's account to the general public's accounts.

What is the change in the money supply and the reserves of the banking system as a result of these transactions? The answer is none. There is no change in the money supply because there is no change in total demand deposits, currency, or coins. There is also no change in the reserves of the banking system; thus, there is no change in banks' ability to lend. All that occurs is that the government obtains $100 worth of resources by borrowing from the public. In doing so, the Treasury does not affect the supply of money or the ability of the banks to lend.

Borrowing from Banks

Suppose the Treasury issues $100 of securities and sells them to banks. The banks pay for the securities by crediting funds to the Treasury's account. In effect, the Treasury has obtained $100 by borrowing from the banks. Of course, for the banks to make this loan, they must have excess reserves. At this stage the only difference between borrowing from banks or from the public is that the purchaser of the government securities is different. In either case, the Treasury acquires $100 by issuing new debt.

The Treasury now spends the $100 to purchase domestic goods and services and pays for them by drawing on its accounts in the banks. The money flows to the general public, which increases its accounts at the banks. As in the previous case, the Treasury still acquires $100 worth of goods and services. The question becomes, What happens to the money supply and the ability of the banks to lend as a result of the banks' buying the securities to finance the deficit?

The answer is the money supply is increased because total demand deposits are increased by $100. The total reserves of the banking system, however, have not been affected. Since demand deposits increase, the required reserves of the banks must rise. Since total reserves do not increase, the excess reserves of banks decline. That is exactly what happens because the banks use excess reserves to purchase the securities. There is no difference between banks' granting loans to business and banks' purchasing securities that finance a deficit. In either case the banks use their excess reserves to purchase income-earning assets. When banks lend to the government by purchasing securities, the money supply is expanded in the same way it is expanded through lending to individuals and firms. Of course, if the banks use their excess reserves to lend to the federal government, then the banks cannot create loans for the general public.

Borrowing from the Federal Reserve

The Treasury may also finance its deficit by borrowing from the Federal Reserve. In this case the $100 of securities are purchased by the Federal Reserve, which credits $100 to the Treasury's account with the Fed. The Treasury now spends the funds, buying $100 worth of domestic goods and services by using the funds in its account at the Federal Reserve. The general public sells $100 worth of goods and services to the government and deposits the checks in its checking accounts. The banks request payment from the Federal Reserve, and the Federal Reserve makes payment by increasing the reserves of the banks and decreasing the Treasury account by $100.

Now comes the crucial question: what happens to the money supply and the ability of banks to lend as a result of the Treasury's running a deficit and financing it by borrowing from the Federal Reserve? Total demand deposits of the public increase; thus, the money supply is increased. That is no different from the instance in which the Treasury borrowed from the banks. The important difference in this third case is that the *reserves* of banks also increase. While required reserves rise to cover the increase in demand deposits, there is also an increase in total reserves of the banking system. With a fractional reserve system of banking, there is an increase in the excess reserves of the banks. That is, the ability of banks to create further loans and expand the money supply is increased. Thus, when the Treasury finances the deficit by selling securities to the Federal Reserve, the money supply and the ability of the banks to lend and further expand the supply of money are both increased. These three cases for financing a government deficit are summarized in Exhibit 4.5.

Of these three possibilities, the most inflationary is the third, because both the money supply and the ability of banks to lend rise. There is no increase in the money supply or the ability of banks to lend when the Treasury borrows from the general public. There is an increase in the supply of money when the Treasury borrows from the banks, but this increase uses the excess reserves of banks. While there is a net increase in the money supply, the banks' ability to lend to businesses and

The Job Mart

Financial Economist

■ Job Description: Work for financial institutions, the federal or state governments, or the Federal Reserve conducting research that combines economics and finance. Analyze demand and supply of commodities, construct indicators of business activity, forecast economic and employment trends, analyze competition among financial institutions, and determine the impact of changes in monetary or fiscal policy on financial markets and the economy. ■ Job Requirements: Strong background in economics (microeconomic and macroeconomic theory), and statistical techniques used to test economic and financial theory. Advanced degree in economics or finance required for advancement. ■ Characteristics: Position involves data manipulation, computer applications of statistical methods, and use of spreadsheets, data bases, and computer-driven programs. Reports and presentations to legislative bodies require writing skills and the capacity to communicate with individuals who do not have specialized training.

EXHIBIT 4.5

Summary of the Impact of Deficit Spending on the Money Supply and the Reserves of Commercial Banks

Borrowing from the Federal Reserve to finance the deficit increases the money supply and the capacity of banks to lend.

	Change in Money Supply	Change in Total Reserves of Banks*	Change in Excess Reserves of Banks
Case I			
Borrowing from General Public	None	None	None
Case II			
Borrowing from Banks	Increase	None	Decrease
Case III			
Borrowing from the Federal Reserve	Increase	Increase	Increase

**Excess reserves plus required reserves.*

individuals is reduced. Only when the Treasury borrows from the Federal Reserve is there an expansion in both the money supply and the banks' ability to lend.

As this discussion indicates, a federal government deficit may have an impact on the supply of money and credit. If the Federal Reserve deems this impact to be undesirable, it may take actions to offset the impact. For example, if the deficit is financed by banks and this results in fewer loans to businesses and households, the Federal Reserve could create more reserves. This would be accomplished through open market operations. The Federal Reserve would buy securities, which would restore reserves to the banking system. Thus, while the Federal Reserve cannot control the federal government's deficit, it can take action to reduce the impact on the supply of credit caused by financing the deficit.

IMPACT OF AN INFLATIONARY ECONOMIC ENVIRONMENT ON CREDIT MARKETS

Inflation ▲
General increase in prices with special emphasis on increases in consumer prices

Inflation is a general increase in prices. That is a very simple definition with two crucial words: *prices* and *general.* The first important word is *prices,* indicating what consumers pay to obtain goods and services. *Prices* could also mean what producers must pay for plant and equipment, but when the word *inflation* is used, the implication is that the prices of consumer goods and services are rising. The second important word is *general.* Inflation does not mean that all prices are rising but that the prices of most goods and services are increasing. The prices of some specific goods could be falling while most prices were rising.

Inflation is frequently expressed as a rate of increase in an index. The index that is most often used is the Consumer Price Index, or CPI. The CPI is compiled monthly by the Bureau of Labor Statistics and is an aggregation of the prices of goods and services paid by consumers. Changes in the CPI are usually expressed in percentages. For example, newspapers may report that the rate of inflation is 10 percent. This usually means that prices as measured by the CPI are rising annually at a rate of 10 percent.

That inflation has occurred is obvious from Figure 4.4, which shows the Consumer Price Index from 1960 to 1989 in the top half of the graph and the annual percentage change in the index in the bottom half. While the top half of Figure 4.4 shows a steady climb in consumer prices, the bottom half indicates considerable change from year to year in the rate of inflation. While consumer prices rose over 12 percent in 1980, they rose less than 2 percent in 1986.

While several explanations of inflation have been put forth, the most frequently offered is excessive spending. This spending could come from consumers, firms, or governments, but the effect on prices is the same no matter what the source of the spending. Generally this excess spending is financed by or results from *excessive creation of money* and credit by the Federal Reserve. This cause of inflation is often summarized by the expression "too much money chasing too few goods."

The traditional tools for fighting inflation created by excessive demand are fiscal policy and monetary policy. With fiscal policy, government spending is reduced or taxes are increased. The reduction in

FIGURE 4.4

Consumer Price Index and Annual Percentage Change in the CPI (1960–1989)

After the large increases in consumer prices during the late 1970s and early 1980s, the rate of inflation has declined.

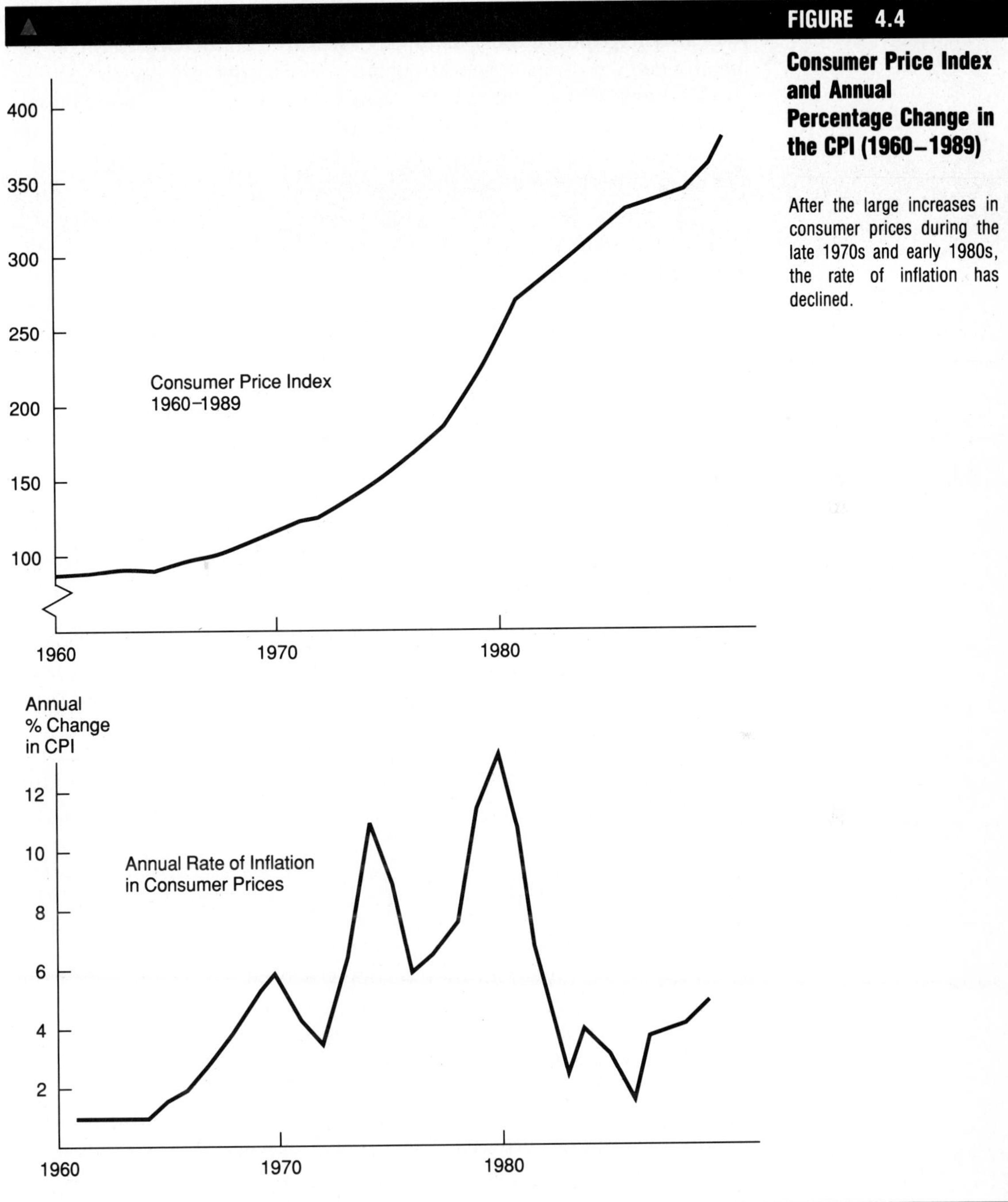

government spending should decrease the demand for goods and services and help reduce the inflationary pressure. An increase in corporate income taxes reduces corporate profits, which cuts into the capacity of corporations to pay dividends and reinvest earnings. An increase in personal taxes reduces individuals' disposable income. All these tax increases reduce aggregate demand for goods and services and, therefore, should reduce the tendency for prices to rise.

If monetary policy is used to fight inflation, the Federal Reserve sells securities, raises the reserve requirement, and raises the discount rate. These actions reduce the supply of money, reduce banks' excess reserves, and increase the cost of credit (i.e., interest rates). The reduction in the supply of money and the higher interest rates should reduce aggregate demand, which is causing prices to rise.

These increases in interest rates may be insufficient to stop inflation. Firms may be willing to pay higher interest costs because they usually are able to pass on the cost of credit through higher prices. Also, as is explained in Chapter 17, the deductibility of the interest expense reduces the effective cost of the loan. As a result of these two factors (the ability to pass on the interest cost and the deductibility of the interest expense), many firms do not find higher interest rates sufficiently costly to induce them to stop borrowing.

During the early 1980s, many individuals also came to the same conclusion. Inflation pushes up the prices of goods, so many individuals reasoned that they were better off borrowing funds and buying than postponing spending. Higher prices tomorrow would more than compensate for the interest expense necessary to buy the goods today. The expectation of future price increases strongly argues for buying during an inflationary period, even if that means borrowing at extremely high interest rates.

Inflation will also have an impact on interest rates. Inflation may redistribute resources from creditors to debtors (from lenders to borrowers), since the debtors will repay the creditors in the future with funds that purchase less. However, for such a redistribution to occur, the lenders would have to lack an awareness of inflation. If the lenders do anticipate the inflation, they certainly will take steps to protect the purchasing power of their funds. Such protection is achieved by charging more interest so their return equals or exceeds the rate of inflation.

If lenders do not fully anticipate inflation and do not earn a sufficient rate of interest, there will be a transfer of resources to borrowers from the lenders. The belief that savers will not correctly anticipate the severity of inflation has encouraged some individuals and firms to finance purchases through issuing debt. Thus, inflation (or at least the expectation of it) alters economic decision making and affects credit markets. Inflation encourages the use of debt financing to make current purchases.

FIGURE 4.5

Rate of Inflation and the Real Rate of Interest (1973–1989)

After a period of virtually no real return followed by a period of abnormally high real returns, the real return has levelled off at about 5 percent.

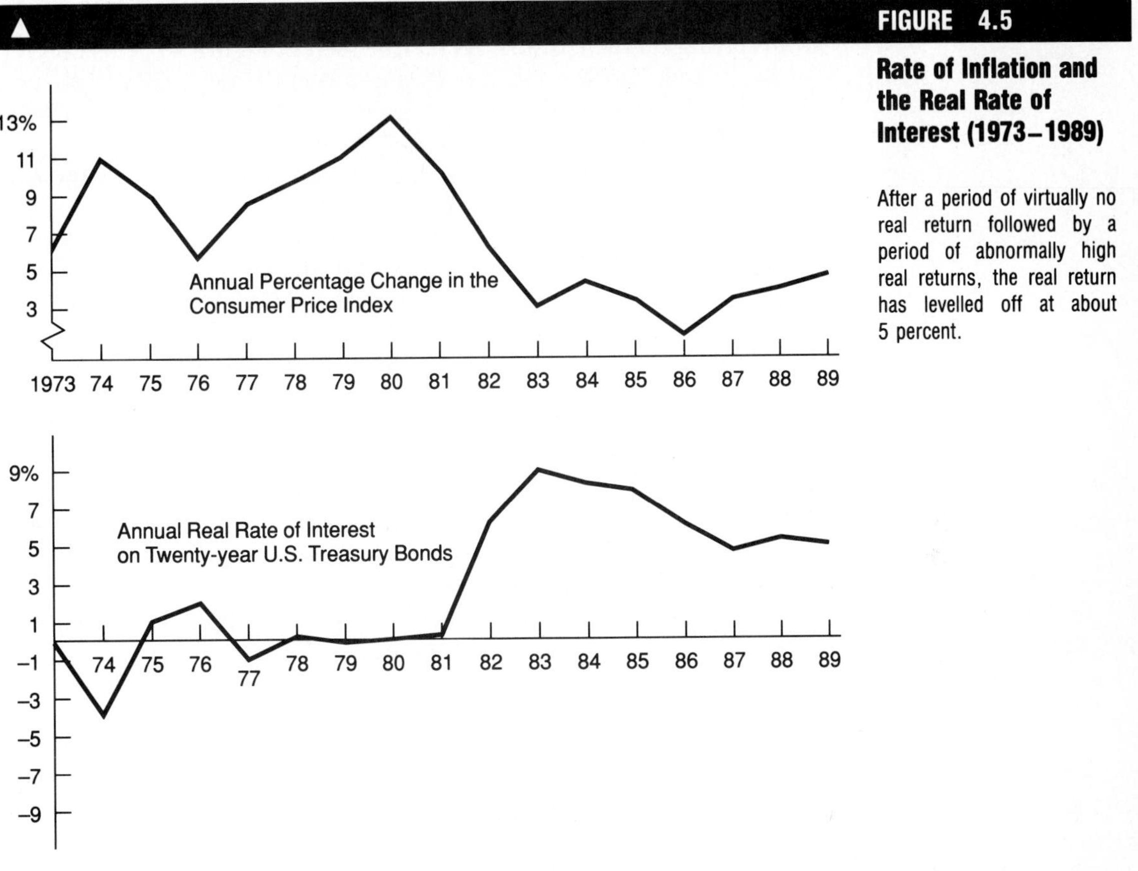

Lenders, however, may certainly anticipate inflation just as borrowers may anticipate it. Expectations of inflation, then, should tend to drive up interest rates as (1) borrowers seek to obtain funds to purchase goods before their prices rise, (2) lenders seek to protect the purchasing power of their funds by requiring higher rates to compensate them for lending, and (3) the Federal Reserve tightens credit in an effort to retard the inflationary pressure.

Certainly the high interest rates of the late 1970s and early 1980s confirm that inflation is associated with higher rates and that inflation can transfer resources from lenders to borrowers. The top half of Figure 4.5 presents the annual rate of inflation. The bottom half of the figure shows the difference between the rate of inflation and the nominal interest rate and indicates the purchasing power of the interest. Thus, in 1976 the rate of inflation was about 6 percent but the nominal interest rate was 8 percent, so the difference was 2 percent. This 2 percent is sometimes referred to as the **real rate of interest** that lenders are earning.

Real rate of interest Purchasing power of the rate of interest; interest rate minus the rate of inflation

The real rate is a measure of the purchasing power that the lenders are receiving on their funds. As may be seen in Figure 4.5, this real rate has fluctuated. Lenders lost purchasing power during 1977 to 1980, but the real rate subsequently rose dramatically in the mid-1980s as inflation abated and interest rates declined only modestly.

In addition to raising the cost of credit, inflation also makes financial decision making more difficult. Forecasts of sales and earnings will have to account for the anticipated inflation. Financial analysts who use financial statements will have to be more careful when comparing a firm's performance over a period of years, as the data may not be comparable. As plant and equipment wear out, the firm will have to raise even larger sums of money just to maintain its operations. These are just a few of many possible examples of the broad impact that inflation may have on financial analysis and decision making.

The problem of inflation can be severe. It hurts individuals who are on fixed incomes or whose income does not keep up with rising prices. Unfortunately, there may be a necessary trade-off for successfully reducing inflation. At least initially, reducing inflation may contribute to unemployment and lead to recession.

Deflation ▲
Period of declining prices

Recession ▲
Period (e.g., for at least six months) of increased unemployment and negative economic growth

Recession is not the opposite of inflation. The opposite of inflation is **deflation,** which is a general decline in prices.[5] Prices, however, tend to be sticky and may not fall. If prices were more volatile, a reduction in demand would result in lower prices. Since the prices of many goods and services are not responsive to a decline in demand, such reductions result in a decline in the quantity of goods and services produced. Instead of prices declining, workers are laid off. The result is a **recession:** an increase in unemployment and a reduction in the nation's output for a period of time (e.g., six months).[6]

During the mid-1980s some firms began to experience the problems of deflation. After the extended period of inflation during the 1970s and early 1980s, the prices of some goods, especially commodities such as metals, started to fall. These price declines, along with the high real interest rates illustrated in Figure 4.5, suggest that for some firms deflation could become a major problem. Firms with outstanding long-term debt (issued when interest rates were high and prices were expected to rise) may have difficulty paying the interest and retiring the principal if the prices of their products weaken. For example, Global Marine, a major owner of oil rigs, was forced into bankruptcy when lower oil prices re-

---

[5]Deflation should not be confused with "disinflation," a term that is sometimes used to indicate a decline in the rate of inflation.

[6]Higher unemployment and a stagnating economy can also coexist with continued inflation. Such a scenario has been dubbed "stagflation" and is the result of the inertia associated with the inflationary process. If production costs continue to rise even in the face of increased unemployment, price increases will persist, thus creating higher unemployment and inflation.

sulted in less drilling for oil. Even if firms are able to retire or refund this debt, the higher real rates will reduce the profitability of their operations. Managements accustomed to rising prices may have difficulty adjusting to deflation and the financial problems that lower prices will generate.

While some firms and individuals may be hurt by falling prices, others may benefit. Lower prices will mean lower cost of goods sold, which should increase profits for some firms. Lower oil prices may have caused the bankruptcy of Global Marine, but lower oil prices benefit any firms or individuals that use oil. Electric utilities that burn oil to generate electricity and individuals who heat their homes with oil furnaces obviously benefit from lower prices.

Lower prices also benefit retired individuals who live on a fixed income. The real purchasing power of their income is increased by lower prices. Creditors benefit as the purchasing power of the interest they earn is increased. Banks may benefit from lower interest rates that tend to accompany lower prices of goods and services. While banks may pay their depositors a lower rate of interest, they may also charge borrowers a lower rate of interest. Individuals may then be able to purchase homes since the cost of mortgage loans is reduced. Obviously, contractors and those in the building trades benefit from increased demand for housing that is stimulated by the lower cost of credit.

Lower prices, just like higher prices, tend to benefit some individuals and firms but hurt others. Higher prices are not necessarily "good" nor are lower prices necessarily "bad." Just as expected inflation induces certain types of behavior such as increased borrowing in anticipation of higher interest rates, expectations of lower prices encourage certain types of behavior. Individuals may postpone purchases in anticipation of lower prices. Investors may seek to lock in yields and thus make long-term investments before interest rates decline. To the extent that individuals or managers correctly anticipate changes in prices in either direction, they may take steps that are beneficial.

IMPACT OF MONETARY AND FISCAL POLICY ON THE FIRM

To financial managers, the importance of monetary and fiscal policy is their impact on money and credit and the firm's earnings. As the previous discussion suggests, the actions of the Federal Reserve can have an exceedingly important impact on the supply and hence on the cost of credit. A tight monetary policy designed to fight inflation will increase interest rates. A monetary policy that is expansionary will initially decrease interest rates. As is explained in Chapter 22, the cost of credit is an important component of the firm's cost of capital. Increases in interest rates, caused by the Federal Reserve's tightening of credit or by increased demand for funds resulting from larger deficit spending by the federal government, will make financing a firm's operations more expensive. Unless this cost can be passed on through price increases, the effect will be to reduce the firm's earnings.

While monetary policy and the federal government's deficits affect the cost of a firm's sources of finance, fiscal policy can affect a firm in other ways. Taxation and spending by the federal government can have a very powerful and direct impact on individual firms. Taxation of earnings obviously affects all profitable firms, since it lowers their net earnings, thus reducing the firms' capacity to pay dividends or to expand through investing retained earnings. Other tax policies such as the speed with which the firm is permitted to depreciate investments in plant and equipment also affect the earnings and cash flow of a firm's operations.

In addition, spending by the federal government can strongly affect the well-being of selected firms. A large proportion of the federal government's expenditures is directed to firms (e.g., defense contractors or road construction). Other disbursements (e.g., social security payments) are directed to individuals, who in turn buy goods and services from firms. Thus, many firms may experience increased demand and increased earnings as a result of the federal government's spending.

Firms and their financial managers do not live in a vacuum. They cannot be oblivious to the impact of monetary and fiscal policy on the firm's cost of funds or demand for its products. The ability to anticipate changes in monetary and fiscal policy can help the financial manager plan the firm's financial strategy. For example, if higher interest rates are anticipated, long-term funds should be borrowed before the rates increase. If interest rates are expected to decline, the financial manager should postpone long-term borrowing until the rates have fallen. Of course, the expected changes may not occur, and the financial manager may make a costly error (e.g., postpone borrowing in anticipation of lower rates only to have interest rates rise). However, the financial manager cannot ignore the potential impact of monetary and fiscal policy and take no actions based on expected future changes in these policies.

SUMMARY

The Federal Reserve is the nation's central bank. Its purpose is to control the supply of money and credit in the nation. Through this control the Federal Reserve pursues the goals of monetary policy: higher levels of employment, stable prices, and economic growth.

Monetary policy works through its impact on banks' reserves. Since banking is organized under a system of fractional reserves, any transaction that puts reserves into the system will lead to expansion in the supply of money and credit. Transactions that take reserves out of the system will cause the supply of money and credit to contract unless there are excess reserves in the system to meet the reduction in the reserves.

The tools of monetary policy include open market operations, the reserve requirement, and the discount rate. Open market operations, the buying and selling of government securities by the Federal Reserve, are individually the most important tool of monetary policy. When the Federal Reserve seeks to expand the money supply, it buys securities. When it seeks to contract the money supply, it sells securities. Such purchases and sales affect the reserves of banks and thus alter their ability to lend. By altering banks' reserves, the Federal Reserve pursues its economic goals.

The fiscal policy of the federal government, like monetary policy, may have an impact on the money supply and the reserves of banks. When the federal government spends more than it receives in tax revenues, the resulting deficit must be financed. When the Federal Reserve supplies the funds to cover the deficit, the effect is the same as the Federal Reserve's purchasing securities. In both cases the money supply and the reserves of banks are increased.

Inflation is a general increase in prices. The anticipation of inflation affects financial decision making as individuals, financial managers, and creditors take actions designed to protect their purchasing power. Inflation encourages spending to acquire goods before prices rise further and to finance the purchases with borrowed funds. Such loans will then be retired in the future with money that buys fewer goods. Lenders, however, also seek to protect themselves from inflation by charging a higher rate of interest to compensate for the inflation. During a period of inflation, the Federal Reserve will pursue a tight monetary policy and sell securities to reduce inflationary pressures. The net effect of these forces will be to increase interest rates during the inflationary period.

Both monetary and fiscal policy may affect the operations and profits of a firm. Monetary policy primarily affects the cost of finance required by the firm's operations. Fiscal policy may directly affect the firm through taxation, which alters the firm's earnings, or through government expenditures, which may alter the demand for the firm's products. Fiscal policy may also indirectly affect the firm's cost of credit because the federal government's securities compete with the securities issued by firms to obtain the funds of savers. Funds that flow to the federal government do not flow to firms, thus increasing the cost of their sources of financing.

Review Questions

1. Why is it correct to suggest that the power within the Federal Reserve rests with the Board of Governors? Is the Federal Reserve owned by the U.S. Treasury? What happens to the earnings generated by the Federal Reserve?

2. If there are no excess reserves in the banking system and $1 billion in new reserves are created by the Federal Reserve, what should happen to the supply of money? Would your answer be different if the reserve requirement were 10 percent instead of 15 percent?
3. If there were cash withdrawals when the banking system had excess reserves, would the money supply necessarily contract?
4. How could the Federal Reserve use open market operations to contract the supply of money?
5. The discount rate is a passive tool of monetary policy. Does that mean the rate never changes? Do changes in the discount rate tend to precede or follow changes in other interest rates?
6. If the federal government runs a deficit during a period of inflation, is it more desirable for the deficit to be financed by commercial banks or by the general public? Why may a U.S. Treasury surplus produce a restraint on the economy?
7. What is inflation, and how is it measured? How are monetary and fiscal policy used to combat inflation? What impact will inflation have on the level of interest rates?
8. From a creditor's viewpoint, why is the expectation of inflation important? If you noticed that interest rates were declining, what may that imply about inflation in the future?
9. What impact does each of the following have on the capacity of commercial banks to lend?
   a. The Federal Reserve sells bonds that are purchased by the general public.
   b. The Federal Reserve lowers the discount rate, and commercial banks increase their borrowings from the Federal Reserve.
   c. The Federal Reserve raises the reserve requirement on savings accounts.
   d. The federal government sells a new issue of bonds that are purchased by the Federal Reserve. The Treasury deposits the proceeds in its accounts at commercial banks.
   e. The Treasury borrows from commercial banks and uses the funds to buy defense goods (e.g., airplanes).
10. Who may benefit and who may lose from lower prices?

Suggested Readings

There are several excellent texts for courses in money and banking that devote considerable coverage to the Federal Reserve and monetary policy. See, for example:

Campbell, Colin; Rosemary Campbell; and Edwin G. Dolan. *Money, Banking, and Monetary Policy.* Hinsdale, Ill.: The Dryden Press, 1988.

Ritter, Lawrence S., and William L. Silber. *Principles of Money, Banking, and Financial Markets.* 6th ed. New York: Basic Books, 1988.

Other readings for this chapter include:

Friedman, Milton, and Rose Friedman. *Free to Choose: A Personal Statement.* New York: Harcourt Brace Jovanovich, 1980.

This book is must reading for conservatives and believers in free markets. See in particular Chapters 2 and 9 for the effect of economic controls and the causes of and cures for inflation.

U.S. President's Council of Economic Advisors, *Economic Report of the President.*

This annual publication, which is available through the Government Printing Office, Washington, D.C., reports the fiscal policy of the federal government.

The Board of Governors of the Federal Reserve and the various reserve banks issue a variety of publications, some of which are available free of charge. See in particular:

The Federal Reserve System: Purposes and Functions. 6th ed. Washington, D.C.: Board of Governors, 1974.

This is a concise introduction to the structure and role of the Federal Reserve.

Federal Reserve Bulletin, monthly.

Monetary statistics (e.g., M-1, consumer prices, unemployment) are published each month in the Federal Reserve Bulletin.

chapter

5

International Finance

Learning Objectives

1 Define foreign exchange and foreign exchange rates.

2 Differentiate devaluations and revaluations, their causes, and their impact on the demand for a nation's exports.

3 Explain how international currency flows may affect a nation's money supply and the reserves of its commercial banks.

4 Describe the components of a nation's balance of payments and the role of the IMF.

5 Define "multinational firm," and explain why such firms developed and how they may be financed.

6 Identify the sources of risk from foreign investments, and explain how these risks may be reduced.

More than 200 years ago, Benjamin Franklin stated, "No nation was ever ruined by trade." Supporters of free, competitive markets believe that maxim today. Even though international markets are not completely competitive and some barriers still exist, many goods and services flow across national borders. Nations do not live in a vacuum. A nation such as the United States exports and imports goods, services, and capital to and from many nations.

Firms also do not operate in a vacuum. Virtually every American firm of any substantial size must have some contact with foreign trade. Many have operations abroad, and others import raw materials or export to foreign markets goods made in the United States. Large American firms may have a substantial part of their operations abroad. Reynolds Metals, for example, reported in its *1989 Annual Report* that it was a partner in a new aluminum can plant in Brazil, was expanding its foil capacity in Spain, was building a recycling plant in Italy, and had acquired an interest in Fata European Group of Italy, which has strong experience in the U.S.S.R. and other eastern European nations. Even if a firm has no foreign operations, buys no raw material abroad, or sells no products in foreign countries, it may still face foreign competition for its domestic markets. A textile firm such as Tultex, a manufacturer of fleeced knit apparel and spun yarns, may have no foreign operations but must face stiff foreign competition for its products.

The importing and exporting of goods and services and the making of foreign investments in plant and equipment and financial assets lead to international currency flows. This chapter begins with a discussion of these flows and the rate of exchange. Next follows the impact that currency flows may have on a nation's supply of money and on the capacity of its banks to lend. The third section presents a discussion of the balance of payments and the way a deficit on a nation's merchandise trade balance must be covered either by foreigners' holding the country's debt obligations or by the nation's borrowing from the International Monetary Fund. The final sections of the chapter discuss the multinational firm and international financial management: foreign investments and their sources of risk. The chapter ends with a discussion of risk management and the use of futures contracts to reduce the risk of loss associated with fluctuations in exchange rates.

FOREIGN CURRENCIES AND THE RATE OF EXCHANGE

Demand for foreign goods is also a demand for foreign money. Foreign merchants want payment in their nation's currency, and the buyers must acquire that currency. To acquire this money, the buyers use their nation's currency, which they offer in exchange for the foreign currency. For example, if Americans want British goods, they must convert U.S. dollars into pounds. They offer (i.e., supply) American dollars in exchange for British pounds. The opposite is true when British citizens seek to buy American goods. To acquire the goods, they must have American dollars, and to obtain these dollars they supply British pounds in exchange for American dollars. Thus, demand for foreign goods, and demand for foreign currency, implies supplying the domestic currency.

The market for foreign currencies is called the **foreign exchange market.** Billions of dollars worth of currencies are traded daily in the financial centers: New York, London, Tokyo, and Zurich. The price of one currency in terms of another is referred to as the **exchange rate,** and the prices of major currencies are reported in the financial press. While prices change frequently, a person needing British pounds or French francs (or any other reported currency) has a reasonable idea of their current prices.

Foreign exchange market ▲
Market for the purchase and sale of currencies

Exchange rate ▲
Price of a foreign currency; the value of one currency in terms of another

Exhibit 5.1, a clipping from *The Wall Street Journal,* gives selected currency prices as of January 3, 1991. At that time the price of a British pound was \$1.9495 and a French franc was \$0.19716. The exhibit also expresses the value of each currency in terms of a dollar. Thus, \$1 purchased 0.513 British pounds or 5.072 French francs. These amounts may be derived by dividing \$1 by the dollar price of the foreign currency. For example, \$1/\$1.9495 = 0.513 units of the British pound.

The demand for foreign money arises in many ways that are not limited to the importing of foreign goods and services. Travel abroad requires foreign currency and in effect is no different from importing goods and services. Investing in foreign securities or in plant and equipment in foreign nations also requires foreign funds, as does federal government foreign aid or military spending in foreign countries. If one thinks about all the transactions that Americans have with foreign firms, individuals, and governments, it is quite obvious that there is a substantial demand for foreign moneys by Americans. Of course, this large demand may be balanced by foreigners seeking American goods and securities and foreign firms investing in plant and equipment in the United States.

The price of a currency depends on the supply of and the demand for that currency. An imbalance in the demand for or the supply of a currency causes its price to change. Excess demand generates a higher price, while excess supply depresses the price. Such price changes are

EXHIBIT 5.1

Major Foreign Exchange Rates

Exhibit gives the values of the major currencies expressed in terms of each other.

Price of the British Pound in Dollars

Price of One Dollar in British Pounds

Price of the French Franc in Dollars

Price of One Dollar in French Francs

EXCHANGE RATES

Thursday, January 3, 1991

The New York foreign exchange selling rates below apply to trading among banks in amounts of $1 million and more, as quoted at 3 p.m. Eastern time by Bankers Trust Co. Retail transactions provide fewer units of foreign currency per dollar.

	U.S. $ equiv.		Currency per U.S. $	
Country	**Thurs.**	**Wed.**	**Thurs.**	**Wed.**
Argentina (Austral) ...	.0001925	.0001925	5194.00	5194.00
Australia (Dollar)	.7787	.7743	1.2842	1.2915
Austria (Schilling)	.09528	.09542	10.49	10.48
Bahrain (Dinar)	2.6525	2.6525	.3770	.3770
Belgium (Franc)				
Commercial rate	.03245	.03253	30.82	30.74
Brazil (Cruzeiro)	.00621	.00621	161.02	161.02
Britain (Pound)	1.9495	1.9435	.5130	.5145
30-Day Forward	1.9386	1.9326	.5158	.5174
90-Day Forward	1.9191	1.9138	.5211	.5225
180-Day Forward	1.8948	1.8887	.5278	.5295
Canada (Dollar)	.8669	.8651	1.1535	1.1560
30-Day Forward	.8641	.8622	1.1573	1.1598
90-Day Forward	.8590	.8643	1.1641	1.1571
180-Day Forward	.8514	.8494	1.1745	1.1773
Chile (Official rate)	.003058	.003060	326.98	326.75
China (Renmimbi)	.191205	.191205	5.2300	5.2300
Colombia (Peso)	.001912	.001912	523.00	523.00
Denmark (Krone)	.1741	.1744	5.7442	5.7340
Ecuador (Sucre)				
Floating rate	.001142	.001142	876.00	876.00
Finland (Markka)	.27793	.27785	3.5980	3.5990
France (Franc)	.19716	.19740	5.0720	5.0658
30-Day Forward	.19686	.19710	5.0798	5.0736
90-Day Forward	.19596	.19620	5.1030	5.0968
180-Day Forward	.19448	.19471	5.1420	5.1358
Germany (Mark)	.6702	.6720	1.4920	1.4880
30-Day Forward	.6693	.6712	1.4941	1.4899
90-Day Forward	.6669	.6690	1.4994	1.4947
180-Day Forward	.6630	.6652	1.5083	1.5032
Greece (Drachma)	.006378	.006402	156.80	15[illegible].20
Hong Kong (Dollar) ...	.12832	.12830	7.7930	7.7945
India (Rupee)	.05528	.05528	18.09	18.09
Indonesia (Rupiah)	.0005376	.0005376	1860.02	1860.02
Ireland (Punt)	1.7890	1.7870	.5590	.559[illegible]
Israel (Shekel)	.5035	.4999	1.9862	2.0003
Italy (Lira)	.0008901	.0008921	1123.51	1121.00
Japan (Yen)	.007524	.007438	132.90	134.45
30-Day Forward	.007520	.007434	132.98	134.52
90-Day Forward	.007511	.007426	133.14	134.67
180-Day Forward	.007508	.007424	133.19	134.69
Jordan (Dinar)	1.4995	1.4995	.6669	.6669
Kuwait (Dinar)	z	z	z	z
Lebanon (Pound)	.001153	.001153	867.50	867.50
Malaysia (Ringgit)	.3696	.3697	2.7055	2.7050
Malta (Lira)	3.3445	3.3445	.2990	.2990
Mexico (Peso)				
Floating rate	.0003390	.0003390	2950.00	2950.00
Netherland (Guilder) .	.5944	.5956	1.6825	1.6790
New Zealand (Dollar)	.5940	.5925	1.6835	1.6878
Norway (Krone)	.1712	.1712	5.8395	5.8404
Pakistan (Rupee)	.0459	.0459	21.80	21.80
Peru (Inti)	.00000190	.00000190	524934.38	524934.38
Philippines (Peso)	.03676	.03677	27.20	27.20
Portugal (Escudo)	.007519	.007519	133.00	133.00
Saudi Arabia (Riyal) ..	.26667	.26667	3.7500	3.7500
Singapore (Dollar)	.5737	.5754	1.7430	1.7380
South Africa (Rand)				
Commercial rate	.3933	.3926	2.5425	2.5468
Financial rate	.2937	.2941	3.4050	3.4000
South Korea (Won)	.0013996	.0013996	714.50	714.50
Spain (Peseta)	.010554	.010521	94.75	95.05
Sweden (Krona)	.1784	.1787	5.6050	5.5960
Switzerland (Franc) ..	.7910	.7921	1.2642	1.2625
30-Day Forward	.7900	.7913	1.2658	1.2637
90-Day Forward	.7880	.7894	1.2690	1.2668
180-Day Forward	.7854	.7870	1.2732	1.2707
Taiwan (Dollar)	.037558	.037558	26.63	26.63
Thailand (Baht)	.03976	.03976	25.15	25.15
Turkey (Lira)	.0003455	.0003451	2894.00	2898.00
United Arab (Dirham)	.2723	.2723	3.6725	3.6725
Uruguay (New Peso)				
Financial	.000623	.000623	1605.01	1605.01
Venezuela (Bolivar)				
Floating rate	.02010	.02010	49.74	49.74
SDR	1.42995	1.42586	.69933	.70133
ECU	1.36857	1.37006	....	....

Special Drawing Rights (SDR) are based on exchange rates for the U.S., German, British, French and Japanese currencies. Source: International Monetary Fund.

European Currency Unit (ECU) is based on a basket of community currencies. Source: European Community Commission.

z-Not quoted.

Source: The Wall Street Journal, *January 4, 1991, p. C10.*

often referred to as devaluations and revaluations. A **devaluation** implies that one currency's value declines ("depreciates") relative to all other currencies. A **revaluation** implies that one currency's value rises ("appreciates") relative to all other currencies.

Devaluation ▲
Decrease in the price of one currency relative to other currencies

Revaluation ▲
Increase in the price of one currency relative to other currencies

How devaluation changes the price of one currency relative to all other currencies may be explained by a simple example. Let it be assumed that the British pound costs $2.20 in American dollars. If a good is priced at 2.5 pounds, it costs $5.50 in American money (2.5 times $2.20). If the British were to devalue the pound, it would take fewer dollars to buy a pound. Thus, if the pound were devalued by 5 percent, it would take 5 percent fewer dollars to buy a pound. The pound's price in terms of dollars would fall from $2.20 to $2.09. The good would now cost $5.23, because Americans could buy pounds at a lower price. The price of the good in terms of pounds would not be reduced. It would still cost 2.5 pounds, and hence its price to anyone holding pounds would be unaltered. However, anyone holding a different currency could purchase pounds at the lower, devalued price. Thus devaluation does not lower prices to the domestic population but lowers the price of domestic goods to foreigners.

Conversely, devaluation also raises all foreign prices to the domestic population. The British now would have to pay more pounds for foreign goods. Before the devaluation, a British pound could purchase $2.20 worth of American goods. If a good cost $3.30, it cost 1.5 pounds ($3.30/$2.2). After the devaluation, the number of pounds necessary to purchase the good would increase to 1.57 ($3.30/$2.09) because the value of the pound in terms of dollars has been lowered. Thus, all foreign goods would be more expensive to holders of British pounds because the pound would buy smaller amounts of foreign currencies.

Since prices of goods and services have been altered by the devaluation, the quantity demanded will also be altered. Holders of British pounds would demand fewer foreign goods because their prices are higher. Simultaneously, since all other currencies can purchase more pounds, the quantity demanded of British goods will increase. British citizens will import fewer foreign goods, and the rest of the world will buy more British goods.

The opposite is true for revaluations, which increase the value of one currency relative to another. A revaluation has the effect of raising the price of domestic goods to foreigners and lowering the price of all foreign goods to the domestic population. For example, if the British revalued the pound by 10 percent, the price of a pound in terms of dollars would rise from $2.20 to $2.42. To foreigners, the prices of all British goods would increase. Simultaneously, the British pound would now buy more foreign money, for a pound would purchase $2.42 worth of American goods. The increased prices of British goods should reduce the quantity demanded, while the reduced price of imports would increase the quantity demanded. Thus, the revaluation would reduce the demand for domestically produced goods and increase the demand for imports.

FIGURE 5.1

Price of the British Pound in Dollars (1975–1990)

While the value of the pound in dollars declined from 1980–1985, it rose to approximately $2.00 at the end of 1990.

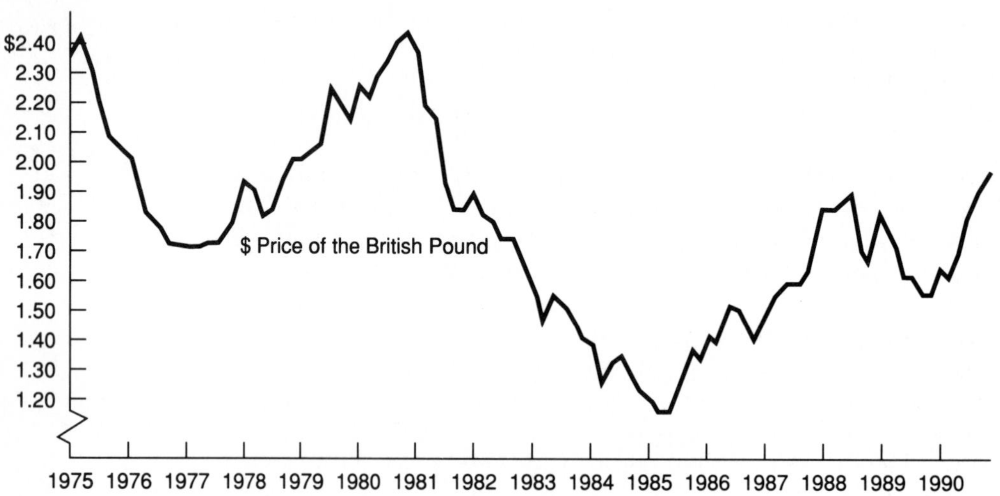

Under the current international monetary system such devaluations and revaluations occur daily, for the prices of currencies are permitted to fluctuate. If the demand for a particular currency rises so that demand exceeds supply, the price of that currency rises relative to other currencies. If the supply of the currency exceeds the demand, the price falls. Since prices are permitted to fluctuate every day, there are continual devaluations and revaluations as the prices of currencies vary in accordance with supply and demand. These fluctuations are illustrated by Figure 5.1, which plots the price of a pound in dollars from 1975 through 1990. As may be seen in this chart, the pound's price literally varied day by day and experienced a considerable decline in terms of dollars from a high of more than $2.40 in March 1975 to less than $1.20 in 1985. However, since 1985 the pound has steadily risen against the dollar and reached $1.87 at the end of 1987.

EFFECT ON BANKS' RESERVES AND THE DOMESTIC MONEY SUPPLY

As was explained in the first section of this chapter, when purchases are made, a set of international currency flows is established. The effect of these flows may be to alter the ability of domestic and foreign banks to create credit. This effect on banks' ability to create credit may be illustrated by the following example in which United States citizens buy goods in England. When the purchases are made, the Americans acquire goods and pay for them with a check drawn on an American bank. The British merchant deposits the check in a bank and thus obtains a new demand deposit.

The British bank has a new demand deposit and a check drawn on an American bank. The British bank cannot present the check to another British bank for payment, because the check is drawn on an American bank. Thus the check is sent to the British central bank, the Bank of England.

Since the check is drawn on an American bank, the Bank of England sends the check to the Federal Reserve, which is the institution through which foreign banking transactions are cleared for payment. This payment from the Federal Reserve can take a variety of forms. For example, the British central bank can request payment in British pounds or American dollars. The British need not take physical delivery of the dollars but can accept an account at the Federal Reserve. Foreign banks may maintain accounts at the Federal Reserve just as the United States Federal Government may keep an account with the Federal Reserve. Such accounts can supply funds to British citizens when they make purchases in the United States. The British bank could request payment in another currency, such as German marks. Thus if the Bank of England needs a currency other than American dollars, payment could be made in a third currency.

If the Bank of England accepts an account at the Federal Reserve, the following transactions occur. The check is sent to the Federal Reserve for payment. The Bank of England receives the account, and the Federal Reserve issues a new claim on itself in payment for the check.

This entire transaction may be illustrated by the flow chart presented below. The check goes from the American citizen to the British citizen to pay for goods and services. For the check to clear, it passes through a British bank to the Bank of England to the Federal Reserve to the bank on which it was drawn.

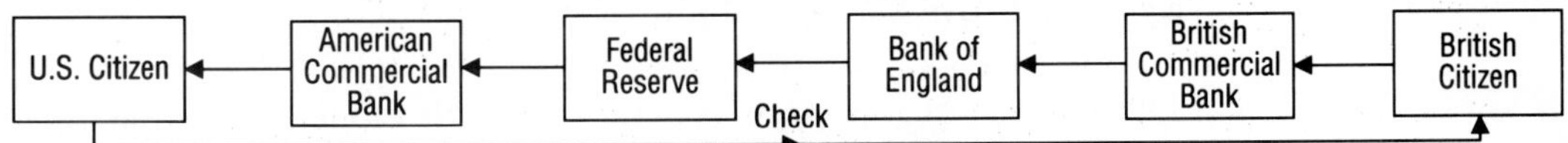

There has been a flow of funds abroad that are lodged in the British banking system and have increased demand deposits and the reserves of the British banks. Since the funds are abroad, they are no longer part of the United States money supply. Demand deposits and reserves of banks in the United States are reduced. In effect, Americans now have British goods and services, and the British have a claim (represented by the account of the Bank of England at the Federal Reserve) on American goods and services.

If the British purchase American goods, they may use the American dollars that were used to purchase British goods. The money that flowed to Great Britain when the Americans purchased British goods is returned to the United States. Hence, if British people are purchasing American goods and services at approximately the same time and at the same value at which Americans are buying British goods and services, the currency flows cancel each other. The dollars that go abroad are returned when the British purchase American goods, and there will be no net effect on the banking system. The same conclusion holds if the British use the American dollars to buy goods in another country, such as Germany, and if the Germans use the dollars to buy American goods. The only difference is that this is a three-way transaction. Americans sell goods to Britain; the British use the dollars to buy German goods; and the Germans use the dollars to buy American goods. The dollars that flowed out to purchase English goods are returned to America. There is a balance in the flow of currencies, and the foreign transactions of all three nations are in balance.

If, however, the British do not exercise the claim on American goods or do not pass the claim to a third party who exercises the claim, the value of purchases of goods and services among nations is not equal, and one nation's currency is lodging itself in another nation. As is explained in the next section, the country doing the purchasing has a deficit in its balance of trade, while the other country has a surplus. The deficit nation is losing currency and receiving goods while the surplus nation is losing goods and receiving money. The importance of these transactions on the banking system in each nation is the effect the currency flows have on reserves of banks and on each nation's money supply. The reserves of banks and the money supply of the deficit nation are reduced, while the reserves of banks and the money supply of the surplus nation are increased. The potential for banks to expand and create credit is reduced in the deficit nation. But the converse is true in the surplus nation, for the ability of its banks to expand the money supply is increased.

BALANCE OF PAYMENTS

The balance of payments is a record of all monetary transactions between a country and the rest of the world during a period of time.[1] While the general time period is a year, many countries compile and report the data quarterly. The balance of payments records transactions by double-entry bookkeeping. Each transaction is recorded as both a debit

[1] Some transactions do avoid being counted. The value of goods smuggled because they are illegal or because the smugglers wish to avoid tariffs is obviously excluded. In addition, the flight of capital from politically unstable countries may also evade being counted.

and a credit, so the total of all debits must equal credits. However, individual parts or subsets of the balance of payments statement may have a surplus or deficit.

While an elaborate discussion of all the parts of the balance of payments is beyond the scope of this text, the essential parts are (1) the current account, (2) the capital account, and (3) the official reserve account. The **current account** enumerates the value of goods and services imported and exported, government spending abroad, and foreign investment income for the time period. It is the broadest measure of a country's international trade in goods and services.

Current account ▲
Part of the balance of payments that enumerates the importing and exporting of goods and services by a nation over a period of time

The difference between the value of imports and exports is often referred to as a country's "balance of trade." If a country imports more goods than it exports, it is running a deficit in its "merchandise trade" account. If a country is exporting more goods than it imports, it is running a surplus. As is illustrated later, a country can run a surplus or a deficit in its balance of trade but not in its balance of payments. For every credit in the balance of payments, there is a corresponding and offsetting debit, so the balance of payments must balance even though the current account may have a surplus or deficit.

The **capital account** consists of investment flows and measures capital investments made between the domestic country and all other countries. Capital investments include direct investments in plant and equipment in a foreign country and the purchases of foreign securities. Security transactions may be long or short term. Long-term transactions are purchases and sales of foreign bonds and stocks. Short-term capital transactions primarily take the form of changes in bank balances held abroad and in foreign money market instruments.

Capital account ▲
Part of the balance of payments that enumerates the importing and exporting of investments and long-term securities

The third account, the **official reserve account,** is a balancing account and reflects the change in a country's international reserves. If a country imports more than it exports or makes more foreign investments, its foreign reserves will decline. If a country exports more than it imports and experiences foreign investments, its holding of foreign reserves will rise. These changes in its reserves may also affect its drawing rights on its account with the International Monetary Fund (IMF).[2]

Official reserve account ▲
Part of the balance of payments that enumerates changes in a country's international reserves

An illustration of a balance of payments is presented in Exhibit 5.2. The exhibit is divided into the current account, the capital account, and the official reserve account. The vertical columns give the credits (+) and the debits (−). Credits represent currency inflows while debits are currency outflows, and the sum of the debits and credits must be equal.

The current account starts with merchandise exports, a credit of \$224.4, and merchandise imports, a debit of \$368.7. The difference (\$224.40 − \$368.70 = −\$144.3) is the merchandise balance of trade, and since the amount is a negative number, that indicates a net currency out-

[2]The rule of the IMF is discussed in the next section.

EXHIBIT 5.2

Simplified Balance of Payments for the Time Period 12/31/X0 through 12/31/X1

A balance of payments enumerates currency flows between a nation and the world economic community.

Current Account	Credit (+)	Debit (−)	Balance
Exports	$224.40		
Imports		$368.70	
Balance of trade			$(144.30)
Government spending abroad		15.30	
Net income from investment abroad	20.80		
Balance on current account			$(138.80)
Capital Account			
Long-term			
Direct investment abroad		130.10	
Foreign investments in the country	117.60		
Purchases of foreign securities		27.40	
Foreign purchases of domestic securities	41.00		
Short-term			
Purchases of short-term foreign investments		9.30	
Foreign purchases of short-term investments	95.70		
Balance on capital account			87.50
Official Reserves			
Statistical adjustment	3.90		
Net change in foreign reserves	47.40		
	$550.80	$550.80	

flow. The next entry is government spending abroad, a debit of $15.3. If a government spends abroad, that has the same impact on currency flows as individuals' spending abroad. It does not matter whether the government buys goods and services abroad or the nation's citizens buy foreign goods and services. Both are currency outflows (i.e., both are debits).

Net income from investments abroad, a credit of $20.8, is a currency inflow. It should be noted that this currency inflow is the result of previous currency outflows. Current foreign investments in plant and equipment or in foreign securities require currency outflows that are reported in the capital account. These investments may generate future income that will produce a currency inflow in the current account. Of course, foreign investors will also be earning income on their investments in the domestic country. For the country to experience a net currency inflow, the income received from the foreign investments must exceed the income paid foreign investors. In this illustration, the net investment income is a currency inflow of $20.80, which is reported in the credit column. A currency outflow would have been reported in the debit column.

The sum of all these transactions (−$138.80) is the balance on the current account. In this illustration, the net income from previous investments helped offset some of the currency outflow from the merchandise trade balance, but the total on the current account indicates a currency outflow.

The capital account represents currency flows resulting from investments in physical assets such as plant and equipment and financial assets such as stocks and bonds. It also includes investments in short-term financial assets. If a country has a net currency outflow in the current account, that outflow may be offset by an inflow in the capital account. If the foreigners use the currency to make investments in that country, the money is returned. Correspondingly, if a country is running a surplus in its current account, it is receiving money it may use to invest in the foreign country. Such investments, of course, may be in actual physical assets or in financial assets. If the receiving country just holds the other country's cash, it is investing in a financial asset. However, as is discussed later, the currency is usually invested in an income-earning asset, since holding the money itself earns nothing.

In this illustration, direct investments generate an outflow (a debit of $130.10), while direct foreign investments in the country generate an inflow (a credit of $117.60). Purchases of long-term foreign securities were $27.40, and foreign purchases were $41.00. Purchases of short-term foreign securities were $9.30, while foreign purchases were $95.70. The total credits on the capital account exceeded the debits by $87.50, indicating a cash inflow. If there had been a currency outflow (i.e., debits exceeded credits), the balance would be negative.

The sum of the currency inflows and outflows on the current and capital accounts still may not balance. The official reserve account is the final balancing item that equates the currency inflows and outflows. If there is a net credit balance on the current and capital accounts, there has to be a debit on the official reserve account. A net credit balance on the official reserve account indicates the opposite, a net debit on the current and capital accounts.

Transactions involving the reserve account can result when the country borrows or repays credit granted by the International Monetary Fund and when it uses or adds to its international reserves created by the IMF. Also, there is a statistical discrepancy account for errors and omissions. Such errors can occur when transactions are not recorded (e.g., illegal transactions). For example, if individuals in a politically unstable country smuggle out money to invest in a safe haven, the transaction may not be recorded on the country's current or capital accounts.

Of all the three accounts in the balance of payments, the merchandise trade balance receives the most publicity. A debit on the merchandise trade account indicates that the country is importing more goods than it is exporting. Money is flowing out of the country into other countries. That money does not disappear, so the question becomes, What

FIGURE 5.2

U.S. Merchandise Trade Balance, 1970–1989) (in billions)

The U.S. trade deficit rose dramatically during the 1980s.

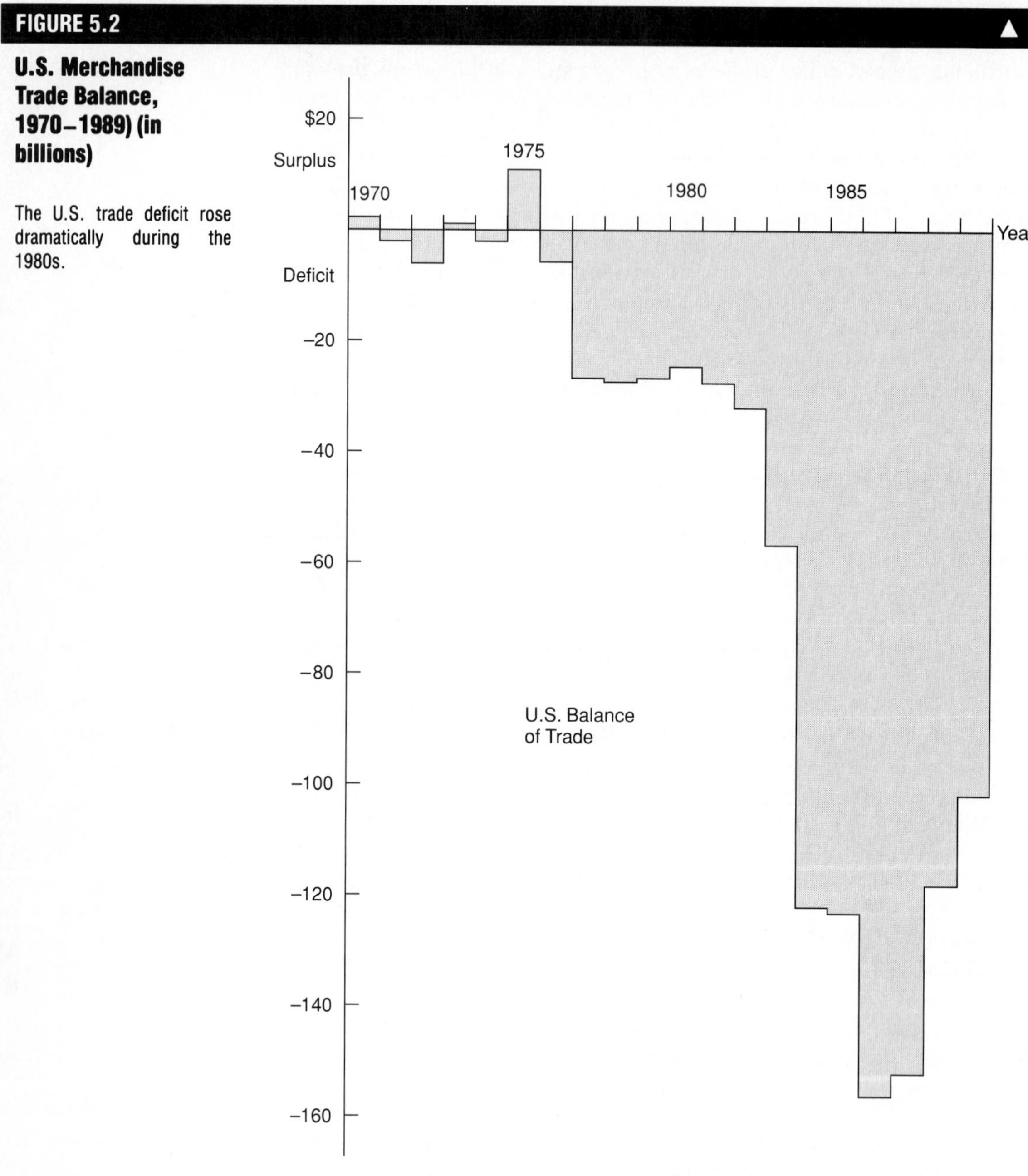

happens to this money and what are the implications of the cash outflow? These are not easy questions to answer but are obviously important from the perspective of the country, its commercial banks, and financial managers. The merchandise trade balance for the United States from 1970 through 1989 is presented in Figure 5.2. In recent years the United States has imported a large amount of goods relative to its exports, so dollars have been flowing out of the country.

Until August 15, 1971, foreigners could demand payment for dollars in gold. When they bought the gold, the currency would be returned in the United States. Today the dollar is not convertible into gold, so foreigners must take another course of action. They may simply hold the dollars. However, since dollars do not earn anything, they will be used to acquire something such as short-term federal government securities (i.e., Treasury bills). Thus, the willingness of foreigners to hold U.S. financial assets absorbs a large amount of the dollars that flow abroad as a result of the merchandise trade deficit. The purchase of these securities, of course, returns the dollars to the United States.

Even if the foreigners do not return the dollars by purchasing financial assets issued in the United States, they do not retain dollars as such. Instead, the holders deposit the dollars in foreign commercial banks. These deposits may be denominated in dollars instead of the local currency (i.e., the dollars are not converted into the local currency). Such dollar-denominated deposits placed in banks in Europe are referred to as **Eurodollars.** A Eurodollar, then, is a deposit in any foreign bank that is denominated in dollars. (The bank need not necessarily be located in Europe; a dollar-denominated deposit located in a Hong Kong bank is still called a Eurodollar.)

Eurodollars ▲
Deposit in a foreign bank denominated in dollars

The creation of Eurodollar deposits led large European banks to accept deposits in other currencies. For example, a bank in London could have deposits denominated in francs, marks, dollars, and yen, as well as British pounds. Such deposits resulted in the creation of the term "Eurocurrency." Eurocurrency deposits, like any deposits, are a source of funds that the bank can lend. Thus, foreign banks may create loans that are denominated in many currencies, as well as loans denominated in their local currency.

The Role of the International Monetary Fund

If a country consistently has a deficit on the current account, the potential for a disequilibrium exists. If foreigners become unwilling to accept the additional currency and to hold additional financial assets, a disequilibrium will occur. Such a situation cannot exist indefinitely. One country cannot continually experience a currency outflow. Eventually the other countries will cease to hold the currency or financial assets denominated in that currency.

One temporary solution to a currency outflow is for a country to draw on its reserves at the International Monetary Fund (IMF). The IMF, which was created by the Bretton Woods agreements of 1944, oversees the international monetary order. It is a sort of central bank for the world's central banks. The initial agreement created the IMF as a pool of currencies contributed by the countries that joined the IMF. These funds are made available to countries with temporary balance of payment difficulties. The primary contributors to this fund are the major economic powers: the United States, the United Kingdom, Germany, France, and Japan.

If a country experiences a currency outflow, it may draw from the pool of currencies. The drawings are, in effect, a purchase of foreign currencies that is paid for by the country's currency. Each drawing increases the amount of the deficit country's currency held by the IMF. The drawings are to be reversed in three to five years by the country's repurchasing its currency with foreign exchange. Of course, to acquire the foreign exchange, the country must cease experiencing currency outflows and start experiencing currency inflows.

As the country draws currencies from the IMF, it is required to take corrective action to stop the currency outflow. Responsibility for this action generally falls on the country experiencing the currency outflow and not on the countries receiving the currency inflow. Under a system of flexible exchange rates, the adjustment primarily comes through changes in the value of currencies. As was explained earlier, an excess supply of one currency relative to other currencies causes its price to decline, which increases the quantity demanded of its products and hence of its currency. An excessive currency inflow would have the opposite effect. The increased demand for its currency (i.e., the currency inflow) will cause the value of the currency to rise, making goods more expensive to foreigners and reducing the quantity demanded.

While the major free-world economic powers operate under a system of fluctuating rates, some countries do not permit the value of their currency to freely fluctuate. Instead they "peg" the value of their currency to a particular currency (e.g., the dollar) or to an index or "basket" of currencies. Since the value of a basket of currencies may be more stable than the value of an individual currency, the value of the currency pegged to the basket may be more stable than if the currency were tied to the dollar or the franc. If a country that pegs its currency to another currency or basket of currencies experiences a consistent outflow, it will still have to adjust the value of its currency relative to the pegged currency or basket of currencies. A large devaluation (e.g., 10 percent) may occur overnight as the deficit nation's government lowers the value of its currency to discourage imports and encourage exports in an effort to stop the currency outflow. For example, in December 1990, Yugoslavia reduced the value of its dinar by 22.2 percent against the German mark.

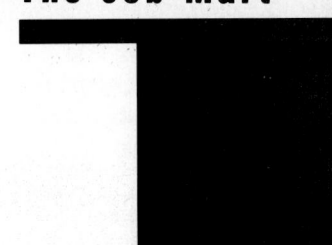

International Trader or Operations Specialist

■ Job Description: Manage operations located abroad; have responsibility for obtaining international sources of funds and making international investment decisions. ■ Job Requirements: Knowledge of foreign security markets, foreign customs, mores, and laws; ability to use futures and options to reduce risk of loss from fluctuations in exchange rates. Fluency in a foreign language, especially French, Spanish, or an Oriental language, may also be required. ■ Characteristics: Many American firms have foreign investments that require Americans to work abroad, and many foreign firms have operations in the United States that require Americans to go abroad to meet the foreign managers and owners. The global interrelationships of economies and the rapid changes in technology necessitate corporate managers to have a global perspective of investments and financial markets.

The devaluation of the dinar against the mark, of course, is a devaluation against all currencies.

FOREIGN TRADE AND MULTINATIONAL FIRMS

The ending of World War II, the rebuilding of Europe and Japan, the reduction in trade barriers, and the development of international trade agreements to facilitate trade led to a large number of American firms expanding their operations by investing abroad. This expansion of firms beyond their home borders has resulted in the development of large multinational firms with operations in many countries. Exxon typifies a multinational corporate giant. Its 1989 annual report discusses operations in many geographical areas, such as the North Sea (with the cooperation of Great Britain and Norway), and in many countries (e.g., Venezuela, Suriname, French Guiana, the Netherlands, Germany, Japan, Saudi Arabia, and Egypt). Exxon's products, which include chemicals, coal, and nuclear fuel, as well as petroleum products, are sold throughout the world, and its fleet of tankers plow the world's major bodies of water.

The initial pattern was for American firms to invest abroad; however, with the increase in foreign income, many foreign firms now invest in the United States. Since World War II, firms from many countries (e.g., Great Britain, Germany, and Japan) have invested in both plant and equipment in the United States and in American securities. Ex-

EXHIBIT 5.3

Foreign Firms with Substantial Exports to or Investments in the United States

Many large foreign firms have substantial operations in the United States.

Firm	Country	Industry
ICI Chemical	Great Britain	Chemicals
Matsushita Electric	Japan	Electronics (Panasonic and Quasar)
Plessy	Great Britain	Telecommunications equipment
Seagrams	Canada	Distillery
SONY	Japan	Electronics
Hoffman-La Roche	Switzerland	Drugs
BASF	Germany	Electronics
Unilever	Netherlands	Consumer products (Lever Brothers, Lipton)
Royal Dutch/Shell	Netherlands/ Great Britain	Petroleum
Alcan	Canada	Aluminum
Saint-Gobain-Pont-a-Mousson	France	Building supplies (Certain-Teed)

amples of firms with large investments in the United States are given in Exhibit 5.3.

Growth through international investments has special risks and rewards. Conceptually, the decision to invest in a foreign country is no different from the decision to expand domestic production. In each case management is seeking those investments that maximize the value of the firm. Management must identify and quantify the factors that affect the cash flow from the foreign investment and then determine which investments are the most profitable. But management also needs to be aware that while foreign investments may offer the firm excellent opportunities for growth, they may also subject the firm to special risks. These risk factors, which are discussed later in this chapter, must be considered when the decision is made to invest abroad.

The potential returns are very obvious. Foreign countries offer the firm new markets for existing products (e.g., Exxon's petroleum products). The firm has already acquired the technology and usually can readily transfer that technology from one country to another. Also, operating a plant abroad may be considerably less expensive than expanding a domestic plant, for foreign labor costs may be cheaper. Hence, a new foreign plant that combines a new market with less expensive labor and the latest in equipment and technology can result in considerable profit. Even if a new plant is not built, exporting domestically produced goods to the new market may substantially increase profits if the old plant can operate at a higher level of efficiency.

Financing Foreign Investments

When an American firm invests abroad, it may use its traditional sources of capital to finance investments. The firm may use internally generated funds, such as retained earnings, or it may borrow from American banks or use other sources, such as commercial paper. The firm then takes the funds abroad and converts them into the foreign currency or deposits them in foreign banks. It may, however, borrow funds or sell securities abroad. These funds may be denominated in the local currency or, if the firm borrows in the Eurodollar market, be denominated in dollars.

Funds borrowed in the local currency must be retired with the local currency, while funds borrowed in the Eurodollar market must be retired with dollars. Of course, the firm may always buy and sell currencies to obtain the funds needed to retire the debt. If a firm has an outstanding loan denominated in German marks, it could sell dollars to obtain marks. Of course, if the value of the mark rose, the number of dollars necessary to repay the loan would increase. The converse would be true if the price of the mark fell; then the firm would have to expend fewer dollars to obtain the marks necessary to retire the debt.

Many large multinational firms with investments in several foreign countries finance their operations by borrowing short- and intermediate-term funds in the Eurodollar market. Such loans are usually unsecured, with maturities from 30 days to several years. The interest rates vary with the creditworthiness of the borrowers and tend to fluctuate with the "London interbank offer rate" (LIBOR). The safest (prime) borrowers generally receive a rate that is ¾ to 1 percent above the LIBOR rate.

Firms may also issue long-term debt called **Eurobonds.** Eurobonds may be denominated in dollars or another strong currency, such as the German mark. Part of an issue of Eurobonds may be denominated in one currency while the remainder is denominated in a second currency. Many American firms issue substantial amounts of Eurobonds and other securities outside the United States. For example, Exxon reported in its 1989 annual report that $1.6 billion of its $7.6 billion long-term debt (i.e., 21.0 percent of its total long-term debt) was payable in foreign currencies. Public sales of securities by American companies in foreign countries are not subject to the Securities and Exchange Commission's disclosure requirements. Foreign security issues thus avoid the costs associated with the disclosure rules. In addition, the terms of Eurobonds and other foreign securities may be more advantageous to the issuing firm than if the funds were borrowed in the U.S. and invested abroad. This is particularly true if the host country seeks to promote economic development and growth by offering generous terms for investments within the country.

Eurobonds ▲
Bonds issued abroad denominated in dollars or a strong currency

The Eurodollar and Eurobond markets have grown rapidly during the last decade. The large increase in international trade and continued deficits in the U.S. balance of trade have resulted in a substantial increase in Eurodollars. Since foreign banks have fewer restrictions on dollar deposits than on domestic deposits, they readily grant Eurodollar loans with terms that are appealing to borrowers. In addition, increased foreign demand for American securities has resulted in a worldwide market for the stocks of large American companies. Firms such as IBM or Ford have had their securities listed on foreign exchanges in major foreign financial centers such as London or Paris. The stocks of these companies trade abroad in much the same way that they trade in the United States. The active secondary markets increase foreign interest in the companies, and their investors become potential sources of funds for future sales of securities.

Risk and Foreign Investments

While offering potentially acceptable returns, foreign investments may significantly alter the firm's risk position. The firm may become less risky as the result of foreign investments. If a firm is in a cyclical industry, foreign investments may reduce the impact of the cycle on its earnings. While economic conditions may be similar in many countries, foreign investments may lessen the effect of a domestic recession or economic stagnation. If the domestic market is weak and foreign markets continue to be strong, the effects of the weak domestic market on the firm's earnings are reduced. Besides reducing the impact of the economic cycle, foreign investments may reduce risk by assuring the firm a supply of raw materials. For example, a smelter and fabricator of metal needs a supply of ore and hence invests in foreign mining operations. By assuring itself of a source of supply, the firm reduces the riskiness of its operations.

International investment, however, may subject the firm to substantial increases in risk. Such risks are the result of local politics, fluctuations in the local economy, and exchange rate fluctuations. While the political climate in the United States does change, it is quite stable. Such stability may not exist in foreign countries, or if it does exist, the political climate can change dramatically. For example, Great Britain's attitude toward business seems to change as the government changes. When the Labour Party is in power, the chance of nationalization is considerably greater than when the Conservatives have control of Parliament.

Even when the Labour Party is in power, Great Britain is still politically very stable when compared with other countries. Many American firms with investments abroad have experienced the nationalization and expropriation of their investments. These firms may or may not receive compensation for the seized assets. For example, Cuba did not offer compensation when Fidel Castro came to power and nationalized the facilities of American firms. Venezuela, however, nationalized Exxon's oil investments in that country and agreed to compensate Exxon by paying

$72 million in cash and $435 million in interest-bearing bonds. The amount of compensation and the means of payment are frequently political questions that are negotiated between governments, as well as between a government and the firm whose facilities are being expropriated. Such power plays and political maneuverings are beyond the world of finance, but if a firm makes foreign investments that subject it to these problems, the element of risk can be significantly increased for the firm.

One method to reduce political risk is for the firm to join with the foreign government in a joint venture. For example, Exxon and other oil companies have had working relationships with the Arab countries that produce oil. Only in the 1970s have these countries sought complete control and ownership of the production facilities in their countries. The exact relationship between the firm and the host country varies with each agreement, but the effect is to give the foreign government remuneration from the profits of the investment. This may reduce friction and increase cooperation between the firm and the foreign government. It may also result in lower taxes and reduced chances of nationalization. Such agreements, however, usually have time durations, after which they must be renegotiated. And if there is a change in the government, the new politicians may repudiate old agreements. Hence, while joint ventures may reduce political risks, they cannot erase them.

Foreign governments can also burden the investing firm with a variety of legal constraints. For example, the country can require the firm to hire domestic labor, thus limiting the ability of the firm to import specialized labor to operate foreign plants. The foreign government may also have special laws limiting the ability of the firm to convert currencies. In this case if a firm invests capital in the country, it may be unable to take the funds out of the country. Any profits earned are effectively locked into the country and cannot be returned to the parent company. Certainly one of the most important constraints is the local government's tax laws. Foreign governments may tax income, the property, or the value added by the production process. The latter tax, the so-called value added tax, is particularly popular in European countries. The foreign government, however, may use tax laws to encourage investment by granting special tax concessions, such as no income or property tax for a specified time period. Such concessions are specifically designed to encourage foreign investment and are used primarily by underdeveloped nations to attract capital.

In addition to political and legal problems, local economic conditions may increase the firm's risk exposure. While it is hoped that foreign investments may expand the firm's markets or permit it to produce goods more cheaply, these goals may not be achieved. Anticipated markets may not materialize. Labor unrest or raw material shortages may develop. The foreign country may experience economic problems such as recession or inflation. While the financial manager will seek to anticipate

Financial Facts

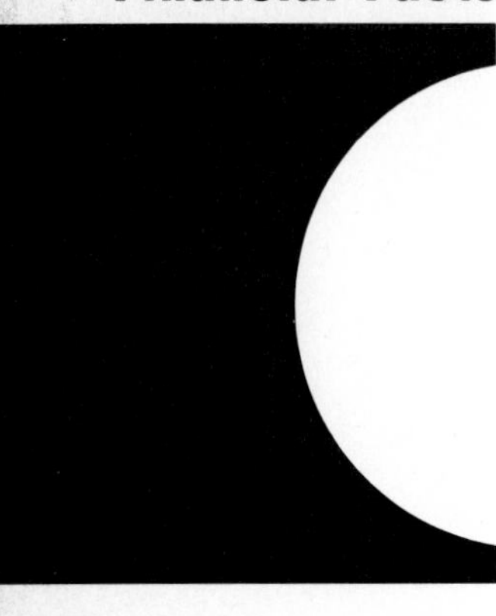

Latin American Loans and Reserves for Losses

When a bank grants loans, it establishes a reserve for losses. For example, if a bank makes loans of $10,000,000, it may establish a reserve of $50,000 (0.5% of the total). Such a reserve is prudent since not every loan will be repaid. The effect of this reserve is to reduce income, because the amount of the reserve is charged against income. Thus, if the above bank earned 10 percent on its loans, its income before other expenses would be $1,000,000 – $50,000 = $950,000. Since the reserve reduces income, it also reduces taxes. • Generally the reserve is a very small percentage of the bank's loan portfolio (i.e., less than 1.0 percent of the loan portfolio). However, the suspension of interest payments in 1987 by several Latin American countries forced several large money center banks to increase dramatically their reserves. These increases by Citibank ($3 billion), Chase Manhattan ($1.6 billion), Chemical Bank ($1.1 billion), and other large banks were sufficient to offset their entire earnings, so the banks reported losses instead of profits. The smaller regional banks, however, such as Citizens & Southern, Corestates Financial, and United Jersey Banks did not have to increase their loss reserves because they had virtually no loans to Latin America. • This increase in reserves and the resulting losses is one case in which losses, instead of earnings, received a favorable review on Wall Street. Since the loan defaults occurred before the reserves were established, the increased reserves only acknowledged what Wall Street already knew: the banks were carrying poor quality assets on their balance sheets. By establishing the reserves, which in effect took these assets off the balance sheet, the banks improved the quality of their financial statements and reduced their taxes (since the losses reduced their taxable income). Both of these results were supported by Wall Street, and the prices of the banks' stocks rose in response to the reported losses! •

---

these problems and their solutions before making foreign investments, uncertainties concerning the foreign economy may expose the firm to increased risk.

There is also the risk associated with fluctuations in exchange rates. As was explained earlier, the prices of foreign moneys change daily in relation to the demand for and supply of each currency. Such exchange rate fluctuations can have a severe impact on a firm that invests abroad. Some of the largest American firms (e.g., Dow Chemical, Xerox) have lost millions of dollars through exchange rate fluctuations.

How such fluctuations may produce losses can be demonstrated by the following examples. If a firm accepts a bid for plant and equipment in Germany and the German mark subsequently rises by 10 percent, the cost of the facility will increase by 10 percent. Such an increase in cost may convert a profitable investment into a losing operation. Another example of a potential loss from an increase in exchange rates occurs when a firm borrows in another country and must repay in the country's own currency. If the value of that currency appreciates, it will take more American dollars to retire the loan.

Exchange rate variations may also benefit the firm. For example, if a country's currency rises in price, previous investments are worth more.

If the firm in the above example already had a plant in Germany, any cash flow generated by the operation would convert into 10 percent more dollars. Such a 10 percent increase in the price of the mark would increase the firm's profitability when it converted the marks to dollars. Thus, exchange rate fluctuations may help as well as hurt the firm's financial position.

Since exchange rates vary daily, the firm continuously runs the risk of loss through a decline in a currency's value. Management needs to be very skilled at reducing this risk by constantly trading currencies. The financial manager seeks to sell currencies whose price may decline and to purchase currencies appreciating in value. If he or she anticipates a deterioration in the value of French francs and an increase in the value of the German mark, francs should be sold for marks. If the price of the franc does decline, the marks will buy more francs in the future. Of course, if the financial manager is wrong and the franc rises in value, this transaction will produce a loss because the German marks will purchase fewer French francs.

Risk Reduction through Hedging

One means to reduce the risk of loss from exchange rate fluctuations is hedging with currency futures.[3] For example, a firm contracts to buy a plant in Germany for 40,000,000 marks in six months (line 1 in Exhibit 5.4). If the current price of the mark is \$0.40, the cost of the plant is \$16,000,000 (\$0.40 × 40,000,000 in line 2). If the price of the mark were to fall to \$0.35, the cost of the plant would decline to \$14,000,000 and the cost saving is \$2,000,000 (line 4). However, if the price of the mark were to rise to \$0.45, the cost would increase to \$18,000,000 for a net increase of \$2,000,000 (line 6).

Since the payment will be made in the future, the cost of the German marks necessary to make the future payment may rise or fall depending on fluctuations in the demand for and supply of marks. To avoid the possibility of loss through an increase in the price of the mark, the financial manager enters into a futures contract to purchase marks (i.e., to sell dollars) for a specified price. If the six-month futures price of the mark is \$0.405, the financial manager can purchase marks for delivery in six months at that price. The total cost of the marks necessary to pay for the plant will then be \$16,200,000 (line 7). If the firm does enter the futures contract, it has a hedged position. In effect, the firm has agreed to purchase 40,000,000 marks for \$16,200,000; the firm then can use these marks to pay for the plant. The net effect is to increase the cost of the plant by \$200,000 (line 8).

---

[3] Futures are explained in Chapter 13. The student may defer this section until after completing that discussion.

EXHIBIT 5.4

Gains or Losses from Changes in the Value of the Mark Relative to the U.S. Dollar

Hedging locks in the future cost of the mark, thus protecting against an appreciation in the currency but forgoing any gain that would occur if the currency depreciated.

Current Cost of the Plant		
1.	Cost of the plant in marks	40,000,000
2.	Cost of the plant in dollars (based on the spot price of marks)	$16,000,000
Possible Gain from Decrease in the Cost of the Mark		
3.	Cost of the plant in dollars (if the price of the mark declines to $0.35)	$14,000,000
4.	Decrease in cost from the depreciation in the mark (line 2 minus line 3)	$2,000,000
Possible Loss from Increase in the Cost of the Mark		
5.	Cost of the plant in dollars (if the price of the mark rises to $0.45)	$18,000,000
6.	Increase in cost from the appreciation in the mark (line 5 minus line 2)	$2,000,000
Impact of Hedging		
7.	Cost of the plant in dollars (based on the futures price of marks)	$16,200,000
8.	Cost of hedging (line 7 minus line 2)	$200,000

By constructing a hedge, the financial manager has protected the firm against an increase in the price of the mark, because the firm now has a contract to receive marks for $0.405. If the value of the mark did increase to $0.45, the contract for future delivery at $0.405 would appreciate in value, offsetting the increased cost of marks. The price of the German currency, and thus the price of the plant, cannot exceed $16,200,000. By hedging, the financial manager has locked in the price of the currency. However, while the firm is protected if the price of the mark were to increase, the firm would not gain from a decline in the value of the mark. If the price of the mark declined to $0.35, the value of the contract to receive marks in the future would also decline, thus offsetting the firm's gain from the mark's price decline.

A firm expecting to receive payment in the future would use the opposite procedure. For example, if a firm anticipates a payment in British pounds after three months, it would enter a futures contract to deliver (i.e., to sell) pounds. If the pound is currently selling for $1.95 and the futures price is $1.94, the firm is assured of receiving $1.94 for a pound. Thus, for the cost of 1 cent a pound, the firm is protected from an exchange rate fluctuation. If the pound were to decline to $1.75, the firm would still receive $1.94. Conversely, the possibility of gain is lost. If the pound were to rise to $2.18, the firm would receive only $1.94. Of course, the purpose of entering into the contract is to reduce the risk of loss from changes in exchange rates. To achieve this reduction in risk, the firm must give up the potential for profit through speculating in exchange rate fluctuations.

While hedging may reduce the risk of loss from fluctuations in currency values, it may not entirely erase it. If a price change in a currency is widely anticipated, the futures price will indicate that expectation. In the above example, the current price of the British pound was $1.95, and the futures price was $1.94. If there was widespread belief that the pound would decline in value, the futures price would be lower. No one would want to enter into a contract to buy the pounds for $1.94 if they expected the value of the pounds to be $1.80 after three months. Such speculators would bid a lower price for the futures contract. If a substantial price decline were anticipated, there might be no buyers for future delivery of pounds, or the futures price might be so low that sellers would prefer to hold the currency and bear the risk.

SUMMARY

This chapter has presented a brief introduction to multinational finance and the international monetary system. The demand for a nation's products is also a demand for its currency. Currencies (i.e., foreign exchange) are traded daily in the foreign exchange market. The price of a currency varies daily with the demand for and supply of that currency.

If a country imports more than it exports, it is experiencing a deficit in its merchandise trade balance, and currency flows out of the country. If a country exports more than it imports, it has a surplus in its merchandise balance of trade, and foreign currencies flow into the country. Imbalances in the demand and supply of a currency result in changes in its value relative to other currencies. Deficits result in a devaluation, while a surplus leads to a revaluation.

Currency flows arising from foreign trade and foreign investments are recorded on a nation's balance of payments, which is a system of double entry bookkeeping for the recording of international monetary transactions. While a nation may have a deficit or surplus in its current account or capital accounts, the balance of payments must balance. If a country has a short-term problem, especially a deficit, in its balance of trade, it may purchase foreign exchange from the International Monetary Fund. The nation is then required to take corrective action to stop the outflow of currency and to repurchase its currency with foreign exchange within three to five years.

The reduction in trade barriers, the development of an international monetary system, and expanding economies after World War II have led to a large expansion in international trade. Initially, many U.S.

corporations expanded their foreign operations to take advantage of potentially profitable investment opportunities, but during the 1970s and 1980s, foreign corporations made substantial investments in the United States. The results of these investments have been the development of large multinational firms that are global in scope.

Foreign investments may be financed by internally generated funds or by borrowing and selling securities abroad. Funds borrowed abroad may be denominated in the local currency or in dollars. Eurobonds and short-term Eurodollar loans are a major source of capital to finance foreign investments.

Foreign investments involve special risks, including political risks, local legal constraints, problems with local economic conditions, and the risk associated with fluctuations in exchange rates. Management may reduce the latter risk by hedging in the foreign exchange futures markets. By taking positions to buy or sell currencies in the future, the financial manager locks in the value of the currency and reduces the risk of loss from changes in the value of one currency relative to the other.

Review Questions

1. If the value of the Canadian dollar rises, what does that imply about demand for its products in the United States? What may have caused the value of the Canadian dollar to rise? Since the Canadian dollar rose, could you conclude that the country was running a deficit on its merchandise trade balance?
2. If a country has a consistent surplus in its balance of trade, what impact may that have on its commercial banks? Why may the surplus in the balance of trade make it easier for this nation to finance long-term investments in other countries?
3. If the IMF is supplying a country with foreign exchange, what does that action imply? What would you expect to happen to the value of that nation's currency?
4. Why may a domestic firm seek to make investments abroad, and why may foreign firms seek to make investments in the United States? If the value of the American dollar rises, what does that imply about the profitability of these investments?
5. Why do American firms issue dollar-denominated Eurobonds instead of bonds denominated in the local currency? Could the firm borrow the funds in another currency? What risk is associated with such borrowing?
6. All business ventures involve risk. Foreign investments have additional risks. How do joint ventures and hedging with futures contracts reduce risk?
7. If you expect the value of the dollar to rise against the British pound and anticipate receiving a future payment denominated in pounds, do you enter into a contract to deliver pounds or into a contract to deliver dollars?

Problems

1. If the price of a British pound is $1.25, how many pounds are necessary to purchase $1.00? If the value of a French franc is $0.23, how many francs are necessary to purchase $1.00?
2. Given the following information, construct the balance on the United States' current account and capital accounts:

imports	$211.5
net income from foreign investments	32.3
foreign investments in U.S.	7.7
government spending abroad	4.6
exports	182.1
U.S. investments abroad	24.7
foreign securities bought by U.S.	4.9
U.S. securities bought by foreigners	2.8
purchase of short-term foreign securities	6.5
foreign purchases of U.S. short-term securities	9.1

Is there a net inflow or outflow of currency into the U.S.?

3. An American firm expects to make a $10 million payment in German marks in six months. Management believes the value of the mark will rise in the near future. What course of action should it take? The spot price of the mark is $0.50 and the futures price is $0.504. What would be the cost to the firm of the course of action you recommend?
4. You expect to receive a payment of 1 million British pounds after six months. The pound is currently worth $1.60 (i.e., £1 = $1.60), but the six-month futures price is $1.56 (i.e., £1 = $1.56). You expect the price of the pound to decline (i.e., the value of the dollar to rise). If this expectation is fulfilled, you will suffer a loss when the pounds are converted into dollars when you receive them six months in the future.
   a. Given the current exchange rate, what is the expected payment in dollars?
   b. Given the future exchange rate, how much would you receive in dollars?
   c. If, after six months, the pound is worth $1.35, what is your loss from the decline in the value of the pound?
   d. To avoid this potential loss, you decide to hedge and enter a contract for the future delivery of pounds at the going futures price of $1.56. What is the cost to you of this protection from the possible decline in the value of the pound?
   e. If, after hedging, the price of the pound falls to $1.35, what is the maximum amount that you lose? (Why is your answer different than your answer to (c) above?)
   f. If, after hedging, the price of the pound rises to $1.80, how much do you gain from your position?

g. How would your answer be different to (f) if you had not hedged and the price of the pound had risen to $1.80?

Suggested Readings

For texts on international financial management and international investments, obtain:

Shapiro, Alan C. *Multinational Financial Management,* 3rd ed. Boston: Allyn and Bacon, 1989.

Solnik, Bruno. *International Investments.* Reading, Mass.: Addison-Wesley Publishing Company, 1987.

Descriptions of the major foreign security markets are given in:

Directory of World Stock Exchanges. Compiled by The Economist Publications. Baltimore, Maryland: Johns Hopkins University Press, 1988.

Nix, William E. *The Dow Jones-Irwin Guide to International Securities, Futures, and Options Markets.* Homewood, Ill.: Dow Jones-Irwin, 1988.

Books devoted to the Japanese securities markets include:

Matsumoto, Toru. *Japanese Stocks: A Basic Guide for the Intelligent Investor.* Tokyo: Kodansha International, 1989.

Tamashita, Takeji. *Japan's Securities Markets.* Singapore: Butterworths, 1989.

The explosive growth in new foreign security issues, the development of dual-tranche offerings (offering of securities in two countries), and the regulation of foreign securities issued in the United States and domestic securities issued abroad are covered in:

Clements, Jonathan, ed. *Stock Answers—A Guide to the International Equities Market.* New York: Nichols Publishing, 1988.

In addition to the above named books, the student may consult:

Eaker, Mark R. "Denomination Decision for Multinational Transactions." *Financial Management* (Autumn 1980), pp. 23–29.

Severn, Alan K., and David R. Meinster. "The Use of Multicurrency Financing by the Financial Manager." *Financial Management* (Winter 1978), pp. 45–53.

Both of these articles discuss the use of financing denominated in foreign currencies. (The student should be forewarned that both of these articles are technical and require considerable effort on the part of the reader.)

Loosigian, Allan M. *Foreign Exchange Futures.* Homewood, Ill.: Dow Jones-Irwin, 1982.

Westerfield, Janice M. "How U.S. Multinationals Manage Currency Risk." Federal Reserve Bank of Philadelphia, *Business Review* (March 1980), pp. 19–27.

The Westerfield article is exceptionally clear and easy to read. Loosigian's book traces the development of foreign exchange markets from the gold standard through freely fluctuating exchange rates. A considerable proportion of the book is devoted to the futures market, its participants, sources of risk, and risk management.

chapter 6

The Role of Security Markets

Learning Objectives

1. Differentiate (1) organized exchanges from the over-the-counter markets, (2) brokers from dealers, (3) market orders from limit orders.
2. Trace the mechanics of a security purchase.
3. Explain the advantage and risk associated with buying stock on margin.
4. Contrast a short sale from a purchase of a stock.
5. Distinguish among various aggregate measures of the stock market.
6. Identify the regulatory body that enforces the federal security laws and state its objectives.
7. Determine how American Depository Receipts facilitate purchasing foreign securities.
8. Explain why an investor should not expect to outperform the market consistently.

An anonymous sage once suggested, "A fool and his money are soon parted." The stock market is definitely one place where such separation may occur. On Monday, October 19, 1987, the Dow Jones Industrial Average plummeted 508 points, a 22.6 percent decline in the market in one day. That decline exceeded the decline that occurred October 28, 1929. On that fateful day the value of the market only declined 12.8 percent!

The stock market may also generate large increases in wealth. While excess speculation may lead to financial ruin, prudent investing in stocks and bonds can be a means to store wealth from the present to the future. The individual who purchased 100 shares of Paramount Communications at the end of 1970 for $1,800 had stock worth $29,500 at the end of 1990. Certainly such an investment is an important alternative to the savings and time deposits offered by depository institutions.

The stock market is probably the most fascinating and well-known financial institution. The Dow Jones averages and the happenings on Wall Street are newsworthy events that are reported here and abroad. But even with all the publicity, the role of security markets is rarely understood. A security market is *not* a financial intermediary, for it does not transfer funds from lenders to borrowers. Instead, it is a *secondary* market that transfers securities from sellers to buyers. Firms do not receive the proceeds of the sales. The one and only time that a firm receives proceeds from the sale of securities occurs when the securities are issued and sold for the first time in the *primary* market.

Security markets transfer existing securities from owners who no longer desire to maintain their investments to buyers who wish to increase those specific investments. There is no net change in the number of securities in existence, for there is only a transfer of ownership. The role of security markets is to facilitate this transfer of ownership. The marketability of securities is extremely important, for security holders know that there exists a secondary market in which they may sell their security holdings. The ease with which securities may be sold and converted into cash increases the willingness of people to hold securities and thus increases the ability of firms to issue securities.

Initially this chapter considers many of the basic elements of investing. The mechanics of investing, measures of stock prices, the regulation of security markets, and the mechanics of buying foreign stock are covered. The chapter ends with a discussion of the efficient market hypothesis, which suggests that over a period of years few investors will outperform the market.

SECURITY TRANSACTIONS

Market Makers

After stocks and bonds are issued, they may subsequently be sold in the secondary markets. Securities are bought and sold every day by investors who never meet each other. The market impersonally transfers the securities from the sellers to the buyers. This transfer may occur on an **organized exchange,** such as the New York Stock Exchange, or an unorganized, informal market, called an **over-the-counter (OTC) market.** In both cases there exists a professional security dealer who makes a market in the security. This **market maker** offers to buy the securities from any seller and to sell the securities to any purchaser. Market makers set a specified price at which they will buy and sell the security. For example, a market maker may be willing to purchase stock at $20 a share and sell at $21; the security is then quoted 20–21, which is the **bid and ask price.** The market maker is willing to purchase (bid) the stock at $20 and to sell (ask) the stock for $21.

The difference between the bid and the ask is the **spread,** and this spread, like brokerage commissions, is part of the cost of investing. When an investor buys a security, the value of the security is the bid price, but the investor pays the ask price. Thus, the difference between the bid and the ask is a cost to the investor. If there are several market makers in a particular security, this spread will be small. If, however, there are only one or two market makers, the spread may be quite large (at least as a percentage of the bid price). The spread is also affected by the volume of transactions in the security and the number of shares the firm has outstanding. If there is a large volume of transactions or the number of outstanding shares is large, then there is usually a larger number of market makers. This increased competition reduces the spread between the bid and ask. If the number of outstanding shares is small, the spread is usually larger.

Transactions are either **round lots** or **odd lots.** A round lot is the basic unit for a transaction and for stock is usually 100 shares. Smaller transactions, like 37 shares, are odd lots. For some stocks the round lot is different from 100 shares. For example, for very inexpensive stocks a round lot may be 500 or 1,000 shares. For bonds a round lot may be five

Organized exchange ▲
Organized secondary market for the buying and selling of securities

Over-the-counter (OTC) market ▲
Informal, unorganized secondary market for the buying and selling of securities

Market maker ▲
Security dealer who offers to buy and sell securities from his or her own account

Bid and ask prices ▲
Security prices quoted by market makers at which they are willing to buy and sell securities

Spread ▲
Difference between the bid and ask prices

Round lot ▲
Normal unit of trading in a security

Odd lot ▲
Unit of trading that is less than a round lot

$1,000 bonds (i.e., $5,000), or $10,000, or even $100,000 face value of the bonds. Since odd lots are not profitable business for brokerage firms and market makers, the effective cost charged the purchaser is usually higher than the cost of a round lot. This cost may not be explicitly stated but hidden in a higher asking price for the security.

Specialist ▲
Market maker on an organized exchange

Dealer ▲
Market maker in unlisted, OTC securities

Market makers for securities listed on the New York and American stock exchanges are called **specialists.**[1] Market makers for over-the-counter securities are called **dealers.** Both specialists and dealers quote prices on a bid and ask basis and buy at one price and sell at the other. This spread is one source of their profits as they turn over the securities in their portfolios. Market makers profit as well when the prices of the securities rise, for the value of their inventory of securities rises. (They also bear the risk if the value of any securities they hold were to fall.) The profits are a necessary facet of security markets, for the profits induce the market makers to serve the crucial function of buying and selling securities. These market makers guarantee to buy and sell at the prices they announce. Thus an investor knows (1) what the securities are worth at a point in time and (2) that there is a place to sell current security holdings or to purchase additional securities. For this service the market makers must be compensated, and this compensation is generated through the spread between the bid and ask, dividends and interest earned, and profits on the inventory of securities (if their prices rise).

While the bid and ask prices are set by the market makers, the level of these security prices is set by investors. The market maker only guarantees to make a transaction at the bid-ask prices. If the market maker sets too low a price for a stock, there will be a large quantity of shares demanded by investors. If the market maker is unable or does not want to satisfy this demand for the stock, this dealer (or specialist) will sell one round lot and increase the bid-ask prices. The increase in the price of the stock will (1) induce some holders of the stock to sell their shares and thereby replenish the market maker's inventory and (2) induce some investors seeking the stock to drop out of the market.

If the market maker sets too high a price for the stock, there will be a large quantity of shares offered for sale. If the market maker is unable or does not want to absorb all these shares, the dealer may purchase a round lot and lower the bid-ask prices. The decline in the price of the stock will (1) induce some potential sellers to hold their stock and (2) induce some investors to enter the market and purchase the shares, thereby reducing any excess buildup of inventory by the market maker. Thus, while market makers may set the bid and ask prices for a security, they cannot set the general level of security prices.

---

[1] As of December 31, 1988, 446 individuals operated as specialists. New York Stock Exchange, *1989 Annual Report,* 2.

The Job Mart

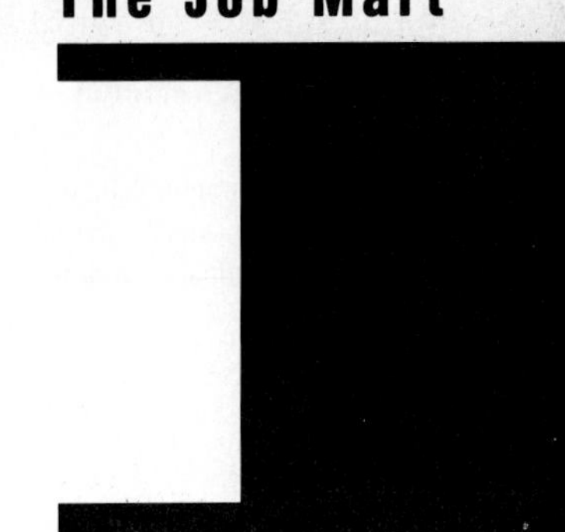

Security Trader and Market Maker

■ Job Description: Buy and sell securities for one's own account. Execute orders for a security firm either for its customers or as a buyer or seller for the firm's accounts. May specialize in type of security, such as bonds or options, or in an industry's securities, such as stocks issued by airlines or utilities. ■ Job Requirements: Knowledge of security markets; ability to make quick decisions concerning changes in the supply or demand for securities and changes in conditions in the financial markets. ■ Characteristics: In today's global financial markets, security transactions occur virtually continuously. Prices can change rapidly and dramatically. A security trader must be able to concentrate and work well under pressure. Ability to manage risk and think clearly under stress are crucial to success.

To set the general price level, market makers must be able to absorb excess securities into their inventory when there exists excess supply and to sell securities from their inventory when there exists excess demand. The buying of these excess securities will require that they pay for them, and the selling of securities will require that they deliver the securities sold. No market maker has an infinite source of money or securities. While they may build up or decrease their inventory, they cannot indefinitely support the price by buying, nor can they stop a price increase by selling. The market maker's function is not to set the level of security prices; all investors do that through buying and selling. The market maker's function is to facilitate the orderly process by which buyers and sellers of securities are brought together.

Security Exchanges

When a company first sells its securities to the public, the securities are traded in the over-the-counter market. However, the firm may subsequently desire to have its securities listed on one of the major organized exchanges: the New York Stock Exchange (NYSE, or "the big board") or the American Stock Exchange (AMEX, or "the curb"). (Although the inclusion of the word *stock* in the names implies a market that deals solely in stock, some bond issues are also traded on these exchanges.) The listing of a firm's securities on a major exchange has an element of prestige, for it indicates that the company has grown above local importance and has attained a specified level of size and profitability. Listing may also facilitate selling additional securities in the future, for investors may be more willing to purchase the securities of companies whose stocks or bonds are publicly traded on an exchange.

EXHIBIT 6.1

Listing Requirements

To be listed on an exchange, the company must meet minimum listing requirements.

Requirements	New York Stock Exchange	American Stock Exchange
Number of shares held by the general public	1,100,000	400,000
Number of stockholders owning 100 or more shares	2,000	1,200, of which 500 must own 100 to 500 shares
Pretax income for latest fiscal year	$ 2,500,000	$ 750,000
Pretax income for preceding two years	$ 2,000,000	
Minimum aggregate value of shares publicly held	$18,000,000	$ 300,000
Tangible assets*	$18,000,000	$4,000,000

**An asset with bodily substance (e.g., plant, equipment, land, inventory).*

In addition to these national exchanges, there are several regional stock exchanges, including the Philadelphia Exchange, the Midwest Exchange, and the Pacific Exchange. These regional exchanges list companies of particular interest to their geographic areas. For example, Canadian Southern Petroleum is primarily a regional company and is appropriately listed on the Pacific Exchange. Other firms in the region, such as Georgia Pacific, are listed on several exchanges (i.e., have dual listing). This company has a national market for its stock but is also of particular interest to investors living on the West Coast, since it has large timber holdings there. Its securities are actively traded on *both* the New York and the Pacific stock exchanges. The trading of such dual-listed securities accounts for most transactions on the regional exchanges.

The NYSE is the largest exchange and lists the securities of companies of national interest that are expected to maintain their relative positions in their respective industries. The AMEX is smaller than the NYSE. Many of the firms listed on the NYSE were originally listed on the AMEX. After achieving larger earnings and size, these firms transferred their securities from the AMEX to the NYSE.

The listing requirements for both exchanges are presented in Exhibit 6.1. As may be seen in the exhibit, the criteria that must be fulfilled in order to be listed are essentially the same for both exchanges, but the required sums are larger for the NYSE. In addition to the conditions stated in Exhibit 6.1, listing requires the firm to conform to certain procedures, including publishing quarterly reports, soliciting proxies, and announcing publicly any developments that may affect the value of the securities.

Once the securities are accepted for trading on an exchange, the firm must continue to meet the listing requirements. The exchange may delist the securities if the firm is unable to continue to meet the criteria for listing. Such delistings do occur, but over a period of years the number of listed securities has increased. Whereas 1,253 stocks were traded on the NYSE in 1965, the number had grown to 2,234 issues of 1,681 companies in 1988.[2]

Reporting of Transactions

Trading in listed and over-the-counter securities is reported in the financial press and other daily newspapers. The amount of information reported depends on the space that the publication chooses to give to the transactions. Exhibit 6.2 reproduces part of the trades in stocks listed on the New York Stock Exchange and OTC transactions. These illustrations are typical of financial reporting of security transactions.

The information is fairly obvious. Consider the entries for Aetna Life:

52 Weeks High	Low	Stock	Dividend	Yield	P-E	Sales 100s	High	Low	Close	Net Change
58⅜	29	AetnaLife	2.76	7.5	9	1588	37⅝	36¾	36¾	−⅞

The high and the low (58⅜, which is $58.375, and 29, which is $29.00, respectively) represent the highest and lowest prices achieved by the security during the past 12 months. After the abbreviated name of the firm comes the annual dividend currently being paid ($2.76) and the current yield on the stock. This is the annual dividend divided by the closing price ($2.76/$36¾ = 7.5%). Next is the ratio of the stock's price to per share earnings (9 for Aetna). This price/earnings (P/E) ratio is a measure of what the market is willing to pay for the firm's earnings. Firms that are expected to grow rapidly tend to have higher P/E ratios. After the P/E ratio comes information concerning the day's trading. First is the volume (1588) expressed in hundreds of shares. Thus, 1588 means 158,800 shares were traded. The high, low, and closing prices were 37⅝, 36¾, and 36¾, respectively. The net change for the day was −⅞.[3]

Securities of companies with shares issued to the general public that are not traded on an exchange are traded over-the-counter. The prices of many of these securities are also reported daily in the financial sections of newspapers. In *The Wall Street Journal* these entries are subdivided into the NASDAQ over-the-counter national market, NASDAQ bid and asked quotations, and additional OTC quotes. **NASDAQ** is an acronym for National Association of Security Dealers Automated Quota-

NASDAQ ▲
National Association of Security Dealers Automated Quotation system; quotation system for over-the-counter securities

[2] New York Stock Exchange. *Fact Book 1989*, p. 25.

[3] Dividends and stock valuation are covered in more detail in Chapters 10 and 11.

EXHIBIT 6.2

Reporting of Security Transactions

Security transactions and prices are reported daily in the financial press and encompass listed and unlisted securities.

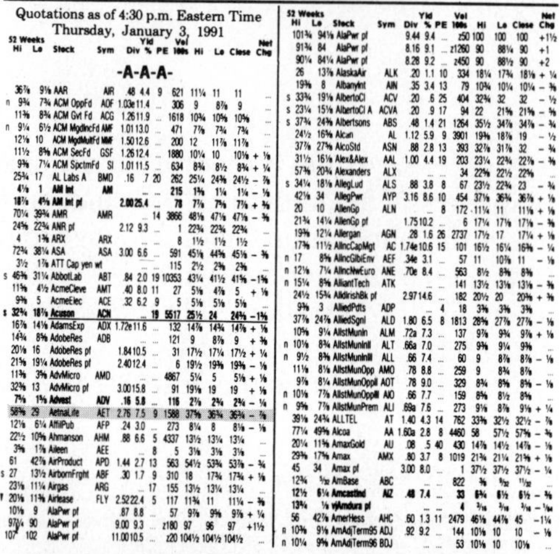

NEW YORK COMPOSITE

Quotations as of 4:30 p.m. Eastern Time
Thursday, January 3, 1991

NASDAQ NATIONAL MARKET ISSUES

Quotations as of 4:00 p.m. Eastern Time
Thursday, January 3, 1991

NASDAQ BID & ASKED QUOTATIONS

Source: The Wall Street Journal, *January 4, 1991, pp. C3 and C6.*

tion system, which is the impressive system of communication for over-the-counter price quotations. All major unlisted stocks are included in this system. A broker may thereby readily obtain the bid and ask prices for many stocks and bonds by simply entering the firm's code into the NASDAQ system.

As may be seen in Exhibit 6.2, the reporting of the NASDAQ national market issues is virtually the same as the reporting of listed securities. The information given includes the 52-week high and low prices, the firm's dividend, the volume of transactions, the high, low, and closing prices, and the net change from the previous day. Some papers even include the yield and the P/E ratio.

In addition to the NASDAQ national market issues, *The Wall Street Journal* and other papers that give thorough coverage of security prices report the NASDAQ over-the-counter bid and ask price quotations (the last part of Exhibit 6.2). These are generally limited to the company, the dividend (if any), the volume of transactions, the closing bid and ask prices, and the net change in the bid price from the previous day. A typical NASDAQ over-the-counter entry would read as follows:

Stock and Dividend	Sales 100s	Bid	Asked	Net Change
Santa Monica Bank .60	22	46	51	−2

This tells the investor that the bank pays an annual dividend of $0.60, that 2,200 shares were traded, and that the net change in the bid price was −2 (i.e., $2) from the previous day.

Some regional papers also report additional OTC quotes. These are generally limited to the bid and ask prices, and, in many cases, these quotations are limited to small firms traded in the geographical area served by the paper. The volume of transactions in these regional issues and in NASDAQ-OTC stocks is generally small. If they were actively traded, these stocks would be reported with the NASDAQ national market issues.

THE MECHANICS OF INVESTING IN SECURITIES

An investor, after deciding to purchase a security, places a purchase order with a broker whose role is to buy and sell securities for customers. The broker and the market maker (i.e., the specialist or security dealer) should not be confused since they perform different, but crucial, roles in the mechanics of purchasing and selling securities. Brokers are agents who execute orders for customers. Security dealers act as principals who, in the process of making a market, buy and sell securities for their own accounts. Dealers bear the risk associated with their purchases and sales. Since brokers do not buy and sell for their own accounts, they do not bear the risk associated with fluctuations in security prices. These risks are borne by the investors.

The investor may ask the broker to buy the security at the best price currently available, which is the asking price set by the market maker. Such a request is a **market order.** The investor is not assured of receiving the security at the currently quoted price, since that price may change by the time the order is executed. However, the order is generally executed at or very near the asking price.

Market order ▲
Order to buy or sell a security at the best current price

The investor may enter a *limit order* and specify a price below the current asking price and wait until the price declines to the specified level. Such an order may be placed for one day (i.e., a **day order**), or the order may remain in effect indefinitely (i.e., a **good-till-canceled order**). Such an order remains on the books of the broker until it is either executed or canceled. If the price of the security does not decline to the specified level, the purchase is never made. Such an order may then become a nuisance for the broker, who must periodically inform the customer that the order is still in effect.

Day order ▲
Order to buy or sell at a specified price that is canceled at the end of the day if it is not executed

Good-till-canceled order ▲
Order to buy or sell at a specified price that remains in effect until it is executed by the broker or canceled by the investor

Once the purchase has been made, the broker sends the investor a confirmation statement (Exhibit 6.3). This confirmation statement gives the number of shares and type of security purchased (100 shares of Clevepak Corporation), the per unit price (12⅛ or $12.125), and the total amount due ($1,244.26). The amount due includes the price of the security and the transaction fees. The major transaction fee is the brokerage firm's **commission,** but there may also be state transfer taxes and other miscellaneous fees. The investor has five business days after the date of purchase (8/16/XX) to pay the amount due and must make payment by the **settlement date** (8/23/XX).

Commission ▲
Payment to broker for executing an investor's buy and sell orders

Settlement date ▲
Date by which payment for the purchase of securities must be made; date by which delivery of securities sold must be made

Brokerage firms establish their own commission schedules, and it may pay the small investor to shop around for the best rates. Large investors are able to negotiate commissions, so that the brokerage costs are less than 1 percent of the value of the securities. Some brokerage firms offer investors discount rates that may reduce brokerage fees. However, these firms rarely offer other services such as research and investment advice.

For investors who do not need the services offered by a full service broker, the potential savings offered by the discount broker can be substantial. Both the discount and full service brokers charge a minimum fee (e.g., $35 to $40) per transaction, so the cost of buying, for example, 100 shares at $10 a share (i.e., $1,000) will be approximately the same for all brokers. However, if the investor buys 500 shares at $10 a share for a total of $5,000, the savings on commissions are considerable. A full service brokerage firm will charge approximately $120 (i.e., about 2½

EXHIBIT 6.3

Confirmation Statement of a Security Purchase

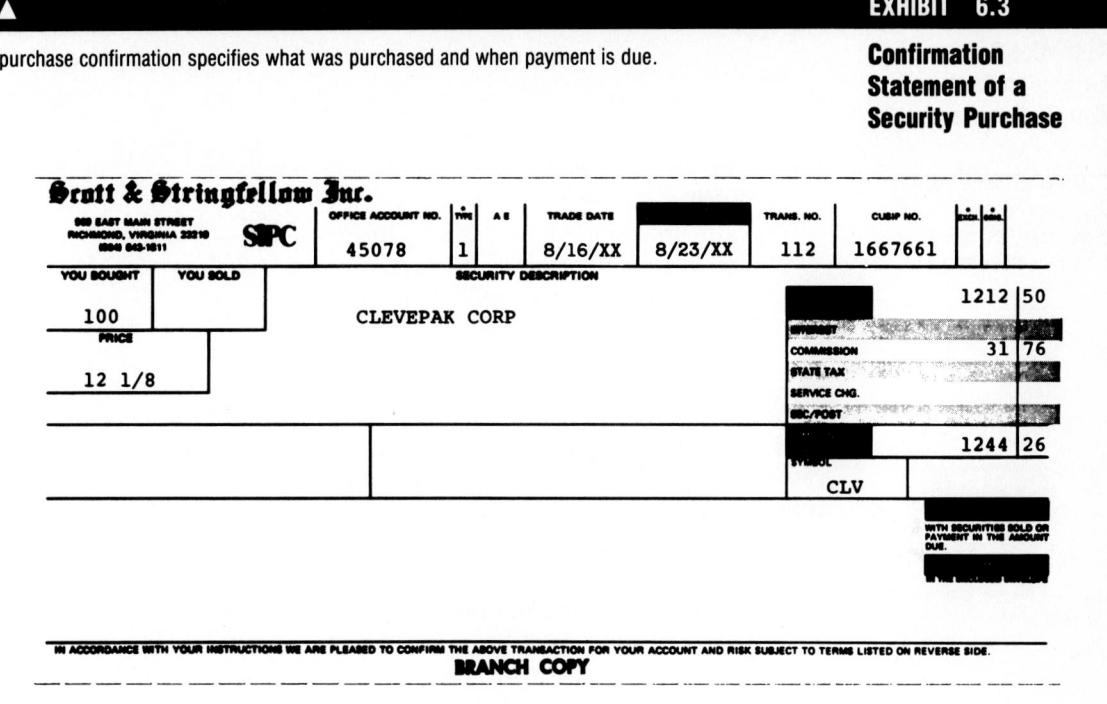

A purchase confirmation specifies what was purchased and when payment is due.

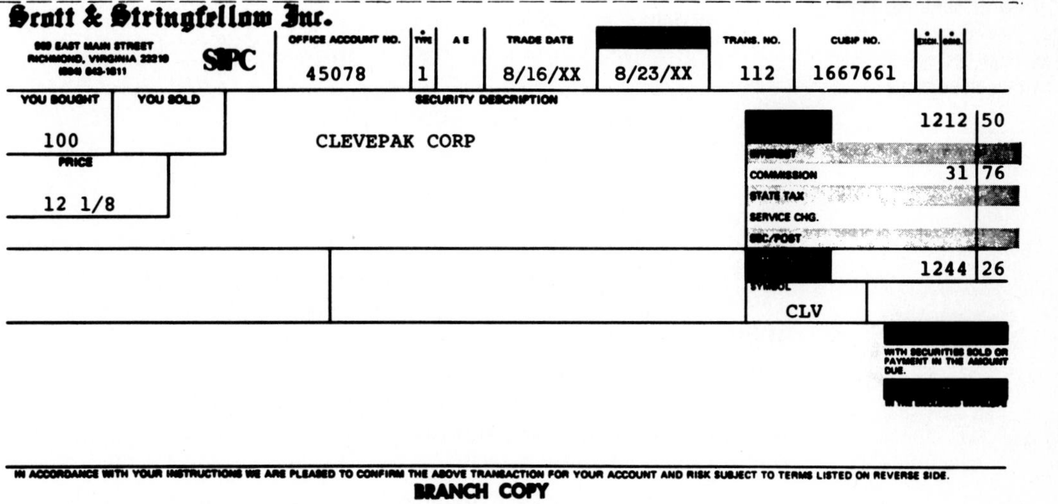

Scott & Stringfellow Inc.
EAST MAIN STREET
RICHMOND, VIRGINIA
SIPC

OFFICE ACCOUNT NO.	TYPE	A E	TRADE DATE	[illegible]	TRANS. NO.	CUSIP NO.	EXCH.	ORIG.
45078	1		8/16/XX	8/23/XX	112	1667661		

YOU BOUGHT	YOU SOLD	SECURITY DESCRIPTION
100		CLEVEPAK CORP

PRICE: 12 1/8

[illegible]	1212 50
INTEREST	
COMMISSION	31 76
STATE TAX	
SERVICE CHG.	
SEC/POST	
[illegible]	1244 26

SYMBOL: CLV

WITH SECURITIES SOLD OR PAYMENT IN THE AMOUNT DUE.

IN ACCORDANCE WITH YOUR INSTRUCTIONS WE ARE PLEASED TO CONFIRM THE ABOVE TRANSACTION FOR YOUR ACCOUNT AND RISK SUBJECT TO TERMS LISTED ON REVERSE SIDE.

BRANCH COPY

Source: Reprinted with permission from Scott & Stringfellow, Inc.

percent of the value of the trade), while a discount brokerage firm may charge $60 to $70.

The investor may purchase the security on **margin,** which is buying the stock with a combination of the investor's cash and credit supplied by the broker. The phrase "on margin" can be confusing since it is similar to buying "on credit." Margin is not the amount borrowed but is the investor's equity in the security. This amount is often expressed as a percentage:

Margin
Investor's equity in a security position

$$\text{Margin} = \text{Equity/Total value of the portfolio},$$

so if the investor owns stock worth $10,000 but owes $2,000, the individual's margin is 80 percent ($8,000/$10,000).

The **margin requirement** is the minimum percentage of the total price that the investor must pay and is set by the Federal Reserve Board. Individual brokers, however, may require more margin. The minimum payment required of the investor is the value of the securities times the margin requirement. Thus, if the margin requirement is 60 percent and the price plus the commission on 100 shares of Clevepak Corporation is

Margin requirement
Minimum percentage set by the Federal Reserve of the total price that must be put up to buy securities

EXHIBIT 6.4

Potential Return Earned on Cash and Margin Purchases

The use of borrowed funds (i.e., buying stock on margin) magnifies the possible *return* on an investment.

	Cash Purchase	Margin Purchase
Purchase price	\$1,244.26	\$1,244.26 cash—\$746.56 debt—\$497.70
Sale price	\$1,500.00	\$1,500.00
Profit on sale	\$ 255.74	\$ 255.74
Percent earned	$\frac{\$255.74}{\$1,244.26} \times 100\% = 20.6\%$	$\frac{\$255.74}{\$746.56} \times 100\% = 34.3\%$

\$1,244.26, the investor must supply \$746.56 in cash and borrow \$497.70 from the broker, who in turn borrows the funds from a commercial bank. The investor pays interest to the broker on \$497.70. The interest rate will depend on the rate that the broker must pay to the lending institution. The investor, of course, may avoid the interest charges by paying the entire \$1,244.26 and not using borrowed funds.

Investors use margin to increase the potential return on the investment. When they expect the price of the security to rise, some investors pay for part of their purchases with borrowed funds. How the use of borrowed funds increases the potential return is illustrated in Exhibit 6.4. If the price of shares of Clevepak Corporation rises from 12⅛ to 15, the profit is \$255.74 (excluding commissions on the sale). If the investor pays the entire \$1,244.26, the percentage return is 20.6 percent. However, if the investor uses margin and pays for the stock with \$746.56 in equity and \$497.70 in borrowed funds, the investor's percentage return is increased (before the interest expense) to 34.3 percent. In this case, the use of margin is favorable because it increases the investor's return on the invested funds.

Of course, if *the price of the stock falls,* the reverse occurs—that is, *the percentage loss is greater,* as is illustrated in Exhibit 6.5. If the price falls to \$10, the investor loses \$244.26 before commissions on the sale. The percentage loss is 19.6 percent. However, if the investor uses margin, the percentage loss is increased to 32.7 percent. Since the investor has borrowed money and thus reduced the amount of funds that he or she has committed to the investment, the percentage loss is greater. The use of margin magnifies not only the potential gain but also the potential loss. Because the potential loss is increased, buying securities on credit increases the element of risk that must be borne by the investor.

An individual's use of margin could increase the broker's risk exposure. If the price of the stock declined sufficiently, it would wipe out the investor's margin, but the investor would still owe the broker the funds borrowed to purchase the securities. If the investor then defaulted (i.e., did not pay off the loan), the broker would lose. Obviously brokers do not want to be at risk, so as the security's price and the investor's mar-

EXHIBIT 6.5

Potential Loss from Cash and Margin Purchases

Purchasing a stock on margin also increases the possible risk of an investment.

	Cash Purchase	Margin Purchase
Purchase price	$1,244.26	$1,244.26 cash—$746.56 debt—$497.70
Sale price	$1,000.00	$1,000.00
Loss on sale	$-244.26	$-244.26
Percent lost	$\frac{\$-244.26}{\$1,244.26} \times 100\% = -19.6\%$	$\frac{\$-244.26}{\$\ 746.56} \times 100\% = -32.7\%$

gin decline, the broker will request additional collateral. This request may be met by having the investor deposit cash or additional securities in the account. The request for additional assets is referred to as a "margin call." Once the cash and/or securities are placed in the account, the investor's margin is increased. The restoration of the margin means that, once again, it is the investor, and not the broker, who is at risk.

Delivery of Securities

Once the shares have been purchased and paid for, the investor must decide whether to leave the securities with the broker or to take delivery. (In the case of a margin account, the investor *must* leave the securities with the broker.) If the shares are left with the broker, they will be registered in the broker's name (i.e., in the **street name**). The broker then becomes custodian of the securities, is responsible for them, and sends a monthly statement of the securities that are being held in the street name to the investor. The monthly statement also includes any transactions that have taken place during the month and any dividends and interest that have been received. The investor may either leave the dividends and interest payments to accumulate with the broker or receive payment from the broker.

Street name
Registation of securities in a broker's name instead of in the buyer's name

An example of the general form used for monthly statements is given in Exhibit 6.6. The statement has three parts. The first gives summary data such as the beginning and closing cash balances and interest and dividends received to date. The summary of dividend and interest income received so far during the year may help the investor plan for income tax purposes. The statement may also include the value of securities for which prices are available. If, for example, a stock is inactively traded (e.g., CFW Communications), price data may not be available.

The second part of the statement gives the activity during the month. In this case, 100 shares of Chesapeake Corp. were purchased and 58 shares of IBM were sold. The investor deposited 220 shares of

EXHIBIT 6.6

Adapted Brokerage Firm Monthly Statement

Monthly statements enumerate cash disbursements and receipts and summarize the investor's positions.

Statement of Security Account

Account #876 55352
SS# or ID #223 54 4321
Account Executive A. B. Broker, III

Statement Period	Financial Summary	
Beginning 06-29-XX	Opening Money Balance	$.00
Ending 07-30-XX	Closing Money Balance	$120.00
	Price Portfolio Balance	$54,075.88

Year-to-Date	
Dividends	$1200.00
Interest	.00
Municipal Bond Interest	150.00

Activity for This Period

Date	Bought/ Received	Sold/ Delivered	Description	Price	Amount Charged	Amount Credited
06-30			CFW Communications	Div		100.00
07-01			GT&E	Div		60.00
07-01			NJ Housing Auth.	Int		150.00
07-03			Funds received			2000.00
07-04	100		Chesapeake Corp.	19	1950.00	
07-10		58	IBM	100		5710.10
07-13			Check balance		6070.10	
07-25	220		Conquest Exp.	Rec		
07-25			James River	Div		120.00

Positions

Long	Short		Ticker Symbol	Price	Value
200		CFW Communications	NA	NA	NA
250		Chesapeake Corp.	CSK	20	5000.00
220		Conquest Exp.	CQX	2	440.00
300		GT&E	GTE	58⅜	17512.50
400		James River	JR	27½	11000.00
259		Kerr-McGee Corp.	KMG	49⅛	12723.38
100		Salomon Incorp.	SB	24	2400.00
5000		NJ Housing Auth. 6.00% 07-01-99	NA	100	5000.00

Certified Financial Planner

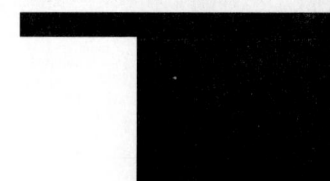

■ Job Description: Develop financial goals and strategies and, in some cases, execute the plans for individual clients and small businesses. Develop (1) pension and retirement plans for small firms and self-employed individuals, (2) estate plans for wealthy individuals, and (3) insurance programs. ■ Job Requirements: Generalist with broad knowledge of personal finance. Ability to communicate and work with people, to write clearly, and to listen well to the financial concerns of individuals in order to establish the rapport necessary for the development and execution of successful financial plans. ■ Characteristics: The Certified Financial Planner (CFP) designation is awarded by the International Board of Standards and Practices for Certified Financial Planners (IBCFP) to individuals who have completed specified educational and work experience requirements. The educational requirements may be satisfied by completing a series of examinations given through the College For Financial Planning, 4695 South Monaco Street, Denver, Colorado 80237.

Conquest Exploration in the account, and no securities were delivered. Dividends were received from three companies, and the $5,000 NJ Housing Authority bond paid $150 in interest. Also during the month, the investor deposited $2,000 in the account but later withdrew $6,070.10.

The last part of the statement enumerates the various securities (i.e., positions) held in street name by the brokerage firm for the investor. This information may include the number of shares or principal amount of debt, the ticker symbol (if available), prices of the securities on the statement's closing day, and the value of each holding. In this case the investor owns stock in seven companies and $5,000 face amount of bonds.

The main advantage of leaving the securities with the broker is convenience. The investor does not have to worry about storing the securities and can readily sell them, since they are in the broker's possession. The accrued interest and dividends may be viewed as a kind of forced savings program, for they may be immediately reinvested before the investor has an opportunity to spend the money elsewhere. The monthly statements are a readily accessible source of information for tax purposes.

There are, however, a few important disadvantages of leaving the securities in the broker's name. If the brokerage firm fails or becomes insolvent, investors may have difficulty having the securities transferred into their name and collecting any dividends or interest owed them by the brokerage firm.[4] Second, since the securities are registered in the brokerage firm's name, interim financial statements, annual reports, and other announcements sent by the firm to its security holders are sent to the brokerage firm and not to the investors. The brokerage firm should forward each investor this material but may not. To overcome this, an investor may write the firm and ask to be placed on the firm's mailing list. The firm, however, may choose not to oblige, for it has sent the material to the brokerage firm and may view the additional mailing as an unnecessary expense.

Whether the investor ultimately decides to leave the securities with the broker or take delivery depends on the individual investor. If the securities are purchased on margin, the investor must leave the securities with the broker. If the investor frequently buys and sells securities (i.e., is a trader), then the securities should be left with the broker in order to facilitate the transactions. If the investor is satisfied with the services of the broker and is convinced that the firm is financially secure, then he or she may also decide to have the securities registered in the street name of the broker for reasons of convenience.

Stock certificates ▲ Document evidencing a share of ownership in a corporation

If the investor chooses to take delivery of the securities, the investor receives the **stock certificates,** such as the Clean Harbors, Inc. certificate illustrated in Exhibit 6.7. The front of the stock certificate identifies the name of the owner, the number of shares, and the name of the transfer agent who transferred the certificates from the seller to the buyer. To transfer ownership the investor must endorse the certificate on the back, just like endorsing a check before depositing or cashing it. Since the certificates may become negotiable if stolen, the investor should take caution to store them in a safe place (e.g., a lockbox in a bank). If the certificates are lost or destroyed, they can be replaced, but only at a considerable expense in terms of money and lost time.

The Short Sale

The previous discussion was limited to what is called a "long" position in which the investor purchases a stock and profits when its price rises. Of course, this individual will sustain a loss if the price of the stock declines. Can the investor earn a profit from a decline in the price of a stock? The answer is "Yes" if the individual establishes a "short" position. In a short sale the investor *borrows* stock and sells it. If the price declines, the individual buys back the stock and pays off the loan (i.e., returns the borrowed stock). The investor earns a profit because the stock is bought for less than it was sold.

---

[4] As is discussed later under the regulation of security markets, most accounts with brokers are insured by the Securities Investor Protection Corporation (SIPC).

EXHIBIT 6.7

Example of Stock Certificate

Certificate specifies the type of security, number of shares, and the registered owner.

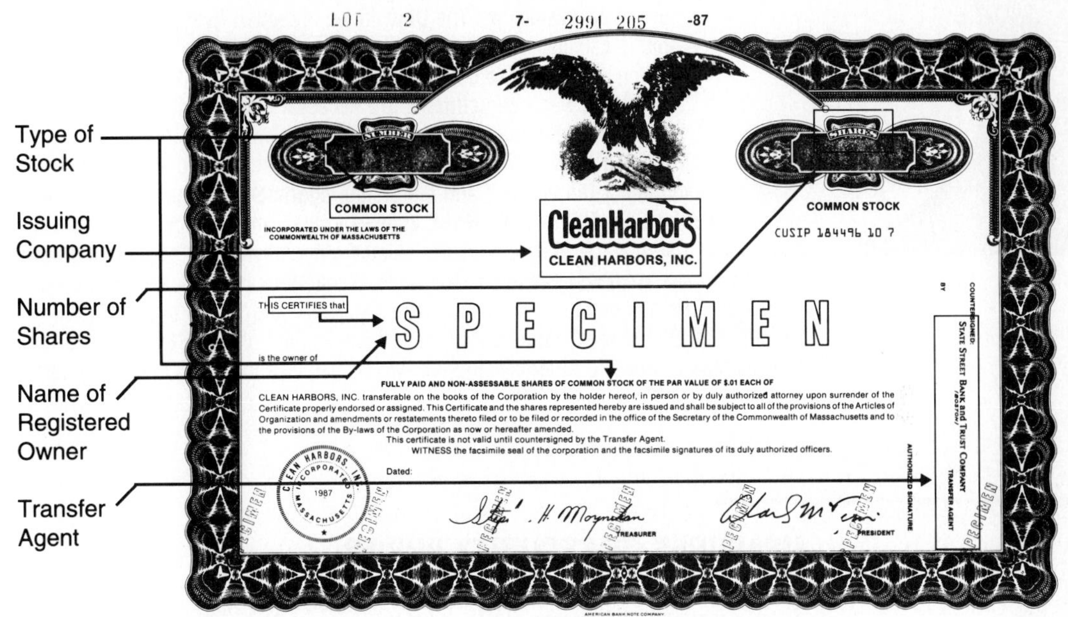

Source: Reproduced with the permission of Clean Harbors, Inc.

Perhaps this process is best seen by a simple illustration. A stock is selling for $39. The investor believes that the stock is overvalued and that the price will decline. The investor then borrows the stock through a broker and sells it for $39. Several weeks later the stock is selling for $25. The individual buys the stock for $25 and returns it to whomever the stock was borrowed from. That person made $14 a share because he or she purchased the stock for $25 and sold it for $39. Of course, if the price rises to $46, the individual loses because the stock would have to be bought at the higher price. In that case, the stock would be sold for $39 but would be bought at $46.

Short sales are very common in business since a short sale is simply a contract for future delivery. When a school takes a student's tuition money before the semester begins, it enters into a contract for the future delivery of services (i.e., courses). This is a short position because if the price of providing the services falls, the school profits. If, however, the price of providing the services rises, the school loses. Entering into contracts for the future delivery of goods and services is common practice in business. In each case, the firm has executed a short sale.

Financial Facts

The Calculation of Aggregate Measures of the Stock Market

As this chapter has indicated, there are several measures of security prices. These include the Dow Jones Industrial Average, the Standard and Poor's 500 (S&P 500) index, and the New York Stock Exchange (NYSE) index. These measures differ in two important ways: (1) in which securities are included and (2) in how the measure is calculated • The Dow Jones Industrial Average is a simple average that is calculated by summing the prices of 30 industrial stocks and then dividing. However, adjustments have been made over time so that the divisor is not 30. Such adjustments are necessary when a firm splits the stock or when one company is removed from the average and another is substituted. Without the adjustment, the split or the substitution of one firm for another would affect the average and distort the aggregate measure of stock prices. • While the S&P 500 and the NYSE indexes employ more stock prices than the Dow Jones Industrial Average, they are also calculated differently. These aggregate measures of stock prices are weighted averages. The price of the stock is multiplied by the number of shares the firm has outstanding. Thus, firms like AT&T and IBM with over 1,000,000,000 and 600,000,000 shares, respectively, have more impact on the S&P 500 and the NYSE indexes than a firm like American Brands, which has less than 125,000,000 shares. •

MEASURES OF SECURITY PRICES

Dow Jones Industrial Average ▲
Average of the stock prices of thirty industrial firms

Security prices fluctuate daily, and several indexes have been developed to measure the price performance of securities. The best known and most widely quoted is the **Dow Jones Industrial Average** of 30 industrial stocks. Dow Jones and Company also computes averages for 15 utility stocks and 20 transportation stocks as well as a composite index of all 65 stocks. As may be seen in Exhibit 6.8, the companies that comprise the Dow Jones averages are among the largest, most well-established firms in the nation. Small firms and many firms that have grown into prominence since World War II (e.g., Johnson and Johnson) are excluded from this average. This has led to criticism of the Dow Jones averages on the basis that they are too narrow and not representative of the stock market. This criticism has led to the development of other indexes such as the Standard and Poor's 500 Stock Index and the New York Stock Exchange Index. The Standard and Poor's 500 includes 425 industrials, 25 railroads, and 50 utility stocks. The New York Stock Exchange Common Stock Index includes all listed common stocks. The American Stock Exchange also publishes an index that includes all securities traded on that exchange. These three indexes encompass more securities than the Dow Jones Industrials and, therefore, may be better indicators of general price movements in the stock market.

How have stock prices performed? The answer in part depends on the time period selected. Figure 6-1 is based on the high and low values

EXHIBIT 6.8

Stocks Included in the Dow Jones Averages as of May 1991

Sixty-five of the nation's largest corporations comprise the Dow Jones averages.

The Dow Jones Industrial Stocks

Allied-Signal Corp.
Aluminum Co. of America
American Express
American Telephone and Telegraph
Bethlehem Steel Corp.
Boeing Corp.
Caterpillar Inc.
Chevron Corp.
Coca Cola Co.
Walt Disney Co.
E. I. duPont de Nemours Co.
Eastman Kodak Co.
Exxon Corp.
General Electric Co.
General Motors Corp.
Goodyear Tire & Rubber Co.
International Business Machines Corp.
International Paper
J. P. Morgan & Co.
McDonald's Corp.
Merck & Co.
Minnesota Mining & Manufacturing
Phillip Morris Inc.
Procter & Gamble Co.
Sears Roebuck & Co.
Texaco Inc.
Union Carbide Corp.
United Technologies Corp.
Westinghouse Electric Corp.
F. W. Woolworth Co.

The Dow Jones Transportation Stocks

AMR Corp. (American Airlines)
Airborn Freight
Alaska Air
American President Lines, Ltd.
Burlington Northern Inc.
Carolina Freight Corp.
Consolidated Freightways Inc.
Consolidated Rail
CSX Corp.
Delta Air Lines Inc.
Federal Express Corp.
Norfolk Southern Corp.
Pan American Corp.
Ryder Systems
Santa Fe Southern Pacific Corp.
Southwest Airlines Co.
UAL Corp.
Union Pacific Corp.
USAir Group, Inc.
XTRA Corp.

The Dow Jones Public Utility Stocks

American Electric Power Co.
Centerior Energy Corp.
Columbia Gas System, Inc.
Commonwealth Edison Co.
Consolidated Edison Company of New York, Inc.
Consolidated Natural Gas Co.
Detroit Edison Company
Houston Industries Inc.
Niagara Mohawk Power Corp.
Pacific Gas & Electric Co.
Panhandle Eastern Corp.
Peoples Energy Corp.
Philadelphia Electric Co.
Public Service Enterprise Group
Southern California Edison Co.

of the Dow Jones Industrial Average from 1960 through 1990. As may be seen in this graph, security prices rose during several periods (e.g., 1962 to 1965, 1981 to 1983, and 1985 to 1987). However, there were also periods when security prices fell. The decline experienced from 1972 to 1974 was particularly severe, for the Dow Jones Industrial Aver-

FIGURE 6.1

High and Low Values of the Dow Jones Industrial Average, 1960–1990

Security prices rose dramatically during the mid-1980s.

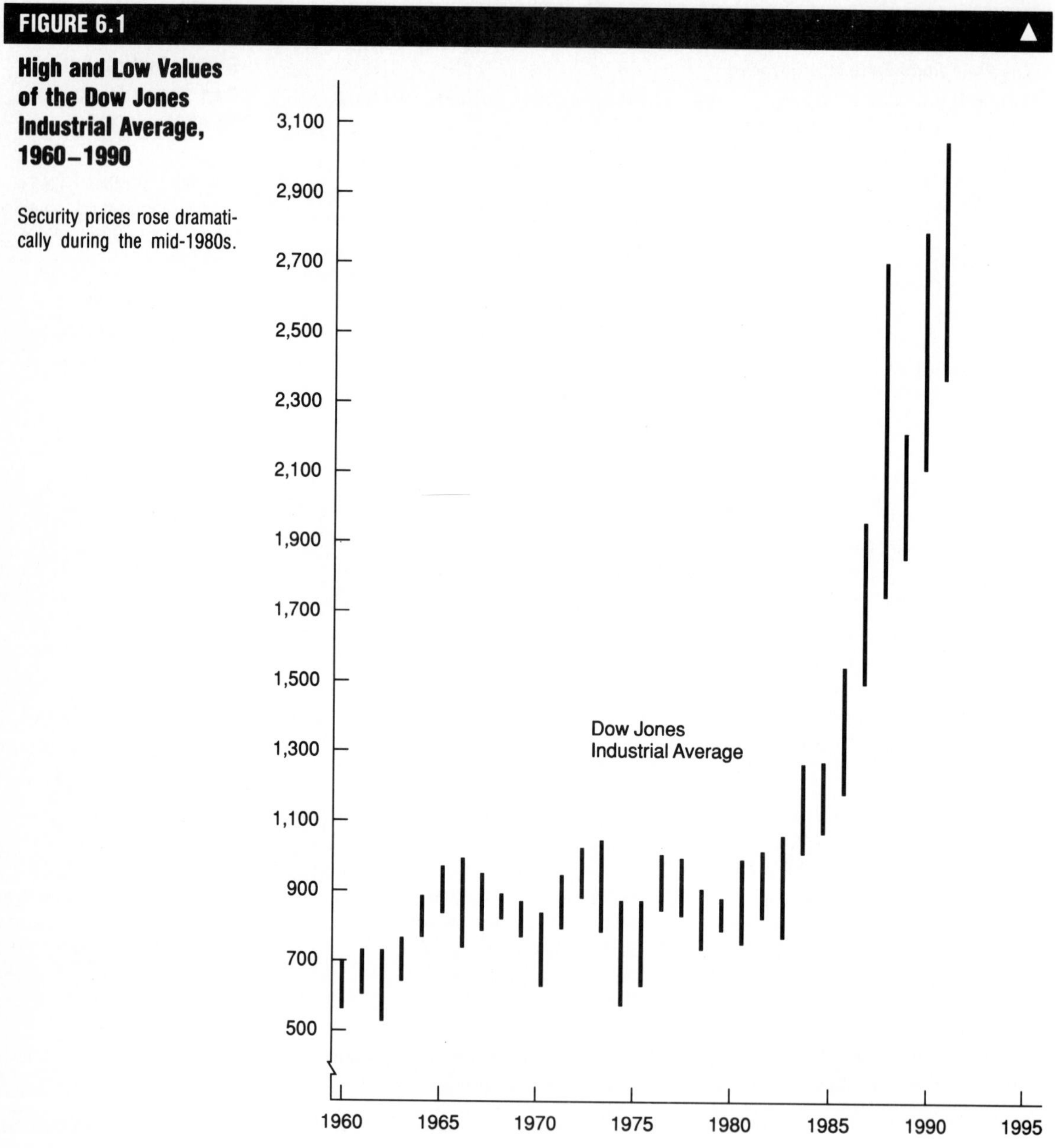

age declined from 1020 at the end of 1972 to 607 in September 1974. That is a 40 percent decline in the average and was the worst setback the market experienced since the great stock market crash in 1929. (The Dow Jones fell from 2709 to 1738 in 1987, but that is *only* a 35.8 percent decline.)

Investors who purchased stock in 1973 and held through 1976 or purchased it in 1980 and held through 1986 probably experienced profits on the investments. However, just because security prices rose, it does not follow that an individual investor experienced profits. An individual's securities may decline in price even though the majority of stock prices rise, but in general the price performance of a diversified portfolio should tend to follow the market.

Many security profits are only **paper profits** because the investors do not sell the securities and realize the profits. The tax laws encourage such retention of securities, for the gains are taxed only when realized. Realized profits are taxed as **capital gains.** Prior to 1988, long-term capital gains were taxed at a lower rate than ordinary income. Under tax reform, however, capital gains no longer receive preferential tax treatment; as of January 1988, the tax rate on capital gains is the same as the rate on other sources of income. However, the gain must be realized for the tax to apply, and the capital gains tax may be avoided if an individual holds a security until death (at which time the value of the asset is taxed as part of the individual's estate). These tax considerations encourage the retention of securities that have risen in price. Unfortunately, security prices that have risen may not continue to rise, and many investors who retained securities have watched their paper profits melt away when security prices subsequently declined.

Paper profits ▲
Unrealized profits

Capital gains ▲
Increase in the value of a capital asset such as a stock

REGULATION

Like many industries, the securities industry is subject to a large amount of regulation. Since the majority of securities cross state borders, the primary regulation is at the federal level. The purpose of this regulation is to protect the investing public by providing investors with information to help prevent fraud and the manipulation of security prices. The regulation in no way assures investors that they will make profits on their investments. It is not the purpose of the regulation to protect investors from their own mistakes.

Federal regulation developed as a direct result of the debacle in the security markets during the early 1930s. The first major pieces of legislation were the Securities Act of 1933 and the Securities Exchange Act of 1934. These are concerned with issuing and trading securities. The 1933 act is concerned with new issues of securities, and the 1934 act is concerned with the trading of existing securities. To administer these acts, the Securities and Exchange Commission (commonly called the SEC) was established.

These acts are also referred to as the **full-disclosure laws,** for their intent is to require companies with publicly held securities to inform the public of facts relating to the companies. As was explained in Chapter 2,

Full-disclosure laws ▲
Federal security laws requiring the timely disclosure of information that may affect the value of a firm's securities

Financial Facts

The Objectives of the SEC

To ensure that individuals have sufficient information to make informed investment decisions. • To provide the public with information by the registration of corporate securities prior to their sale to the general public, and to require timely and regular disclosure of corporate information and financial statements. • To prevent manipulation of security prices by regulating trading in the securities markets; by requiring insiders to register the buying and selling of securities; and by regulating the activities of corporate officers and directors. • To regulate investment companies (e.g., mutual funds) and investment advisors. • To work in conjunction with the Federal Reserve to limit the use of credit to acquire securities. • To work with the National Association of Security Dealers, the self-regulatory association of brokers and dealers, to supervise the regulation of member firms, brokers, and security dealers. •

---

a firm can issue new securities only after filing a registration statement with the SEC. The SEC will not clear the securities for sale until it appears that all material facts that may affect the value of the securities have been disclosed. The SEC does not comment on the worthiness of the securities as an investment. It is assumed that the investor who has received the required information will be able to make his or her own determination of the quality of the securities as an investment.

Once the securities are in the hands of the general public, the companies are required to keep current the information on file with the SEC. This is achieved by having the firm file a report (called the **10-K report**) with the SEC annually. The 10-K report has a substantial amount of factual information concerning the firm, and this information is usually sent in summary form to the stockholders in the company's annual report. (Companies will, on request, also send stockholders a copy of the 10-K report without charge.)

10-K report ▲
Required annual report filed with the SEC by publicly held firms

Firms are also required to release during the year any information that may materially affect the value of their securities. Information concerning new discoveries or lawsuits or strikes is disseminated to the general public. The SEC has the power to suspend trading in a firm's securities if the firm does not release this information. This is a drastic act and is seldom used, for most firms continually have news releases that inform the investing public of significant changes affecting the firm. Sometimes the firm itself will ask to have trading in its securities stopped until a news release can be prepared and disseminated.

The disclosure requirements do not insist that the firm tell everything about its operations. The firm, of course, has trade secrets that it does not want known by its competitors. The purpose of full disclosure is not to stifle the corporation but (1) to inform the investors so they can make informed decisions and (2) to prevent the firm's employees from using privileged information for personal gain. It should be obvious that employees may have access to information before it reaches the general public. Such inside information may significantly enhance their ability to make profits by buying or selling the company's securities before the announcement is made. Such profiteering from inside information is illegal. Officers and directors of the company must report their holdings and any changes in their holdings of the firm's securities with the SEC. Thus, it is possible for the SEC to determine if transactions are made prior to public announcements.

Inside information, however, is not limited to individuals who work for a firm. The concept applies to people who work for another firm that has access to privileged information. For example, accountants, lawyers, advertising agency employees, and creditors, such as commercial bankers, have access to inside information also. Certainly a firm's investment bankers will know if a firm is anticipating a merger, seeking to take over another company, or intending to issue new securities. These investment bankers are, in effect, insiders. Neither they, nor anyone they give this information to, may legally use the information for personal gain.

The illegal use of inside information created a major scandal on Wall Street in 1986–1987 when it was learned that some insiders, especially selected individuals working for some of the country's most prestigious investment banking firms, used or passed on inside information. There were admissions of guilt and plea bargaining arrangements with federal prosecutors by such individuals as as Dennis Levine of Drexel, Burnham, Lambert, and Ivan Boesky, a Wall Street arbitrageur. These events shook the financial markets and raised serious questions concerning the extent to which insiders have abused their access to privileged information.

One change in the regulation of security markets was the establishment in 1970 of the **Securities Investor Protection Corporation (SIPC).** This agency is similar in purpose to FDIC, for SIPC is designed to protect investors from failure by brokerage firms. SIPC insurance applies to those investors who leave securities and cash with brokerage firms. If the firm were to fail, these investors might lose part of their funds and investments. SIPC insurance is designed to protect investors from this type of loss. The insurance, however, is limited to $500,000 per customer, of which only $100,000 applies to cash balances. Hence, if an investor leaves a substantial amount of securities and cash with a brokerage firm that fails, the investor is not fully protected by the insurance. To increase coverage, some brokerage firms carry additional insurance with private companies to protect their customers.

Securities Investor Protection Corporation (SIPC) ▲
Federal agency that insures investors against failure by brokerage firms

FOREIGN SECURITIES

In addition to domestic securities, Americans may purchase foreign stocks and bonds. Foreign companies, like American companies, issue a variety of securities as a means to acquire funds. These securities subse-

Financial Facts

Illegal Use of Inside Information

The use of inside (privileged) information for personal gain is illegal. Management cannot buy a stock, make an announcement that causes the value of the stock to rise, and then sell the stock for a profit. If insiders do this, the corporation or its stockholders may sue, and if the defendants are found guilty, any profits must be returned to the corporation. • The law does not forbid insiders from buying and subsequently selling the stock. However, the Securities Exchange Act of 1934 requires that each officer, director, and major stockholder (i.e., any individual who owns more than 5 percent of the stock) of a publicly held corporation must file a report with the SEC disclosing the amount of stock held. These individuals must also file a monthly report if there are any changes in the holdings. This information is subsequently published by the SEC. If these insiders make a profit on a transaction that is completed (i.e., the stock is bought and sold) within six months, it is assumed the profit is the result of illegally using confidential corporate information. • Individuals who may be considered insiders are not limited to the corporation's officers and directors. An insider is any individual with "material information" not yet disclosed to the public. Material information implies information that could reasonably be expected to affect the value of the firm's securities. The individual need not necessarily be employed by the firm but could have access to inside information through business relationships, family ties, or being informed (tipped off) by insiders. Use of such privileged information even by nonemployees is also illegal. In one of the most famous cases concerning the illegal use of inside information, several officers and directors of Texas Gulf Sulfur became aware of new mineral discoveries. Not only were their purchases ruled illegal, but purchases made by individuals they had informed were also ruled illegal. Thus, an insider who may not directly profit through the use of inside information cannot pass that information to another party who profits from using that knowledge. •

---

quently trade on foreign exchanges or foreign over-the-counter markets. There are stock exchanges in London, Paris, Tokyo, and other foreign financial centers. Unless Americans and other foreigners are forbidden to acquire these securities, Americans can buy and sell stocks through these exchanges in much the same way that they purchase domestic American stocks and bonds. Thus, foreign securities may be purchased through the use of American brokers who have access to trading on these exchanges. In many cases this access is obtained through a correspondent relationship with foreign security brokers.

By far the easiest way to buy foreign stocks is to purchase the shares of firms that are traded on American exchanges or through American over-the-counter markets (i.e., through NASDAQ). To be eligible for such trading, the foreign securities must be registered with the SEC. About 100 foreign stocks are listed on the New York and American stock exchanges and more than 250 trade through NASDAQ.

Exhibit 6.9 enumerates several foreign firms whose shares are traded in the United States. The exhibit gives the company, its country of origin, its primary industry, and where the shares are traded. As may be seen in the exhibit, many foreign stocks, such as SONY and KLM

EXHIBIT 6.9

Selected Foreign Securities Traded on the New York Stock Exchange, on the American Stock Exchange, and through NASDAQ

The ADRs of some foreign corporations actively trade in the U.S. security markets.

Firm	Country of Origin	Primary Industry	Where Traded in the United States
Alcan Aluminum	Canada	Aluminum	NYSE
Campbell Red Lakes	Canada	Gold mining	NYSE
Dunlop Holdings	Britain	Tires, sporting goods	AMEX
Hitachi	Japan	Electronics	NYSE
Imperial Group	Britain	Tobacco, food	AMEX
Japan Airlines	Japan	Airline	NASDAQ
KLM Royal Dutch Airlines	Netherlands	Airline	NYSE
Kloof Gold Mines	South Africa	Gold mining	NASDAQ
Plessey	Britain	Electronics equipment	NYSE
SONY	Japan	Electronics	NYSE
TDK	Japan	Electronics	NYSE
Volkswagenwerk	Germany	Automobiles	NASDAQ

Royal Dutch Airlines, are traded on the New York Stock Exchange. Others, such as Dunlop Holdings, trade on the American Stock Exchange, and many others trade through NASDAQ.[5] The majority of the firms whose securities are actively traded in the United States are either Japanese or Canadian.

These domestic markets do not actually trade the foreign shares but trade receipts for the stock called **American Depository Receipts** or **ADRs.** Such recepits are created by large financial institutions such as commercial banks. The ADRs are then sold to the American public and continue to trade in the United States.

American Depository Receipts (ADRs)
Receipts issued for foreign securities held by a trustee

The creation of ADRs greatly facilitates trading in foreign securities. First, ADRs reduce the risk of fraud. If the investor purchased a foreign stock issued by a Japanese firm, the stock certificate would be written in Japanese. It is highly unlikely that the American investor could read the language, and thus he or she could become prey to bogus certificates. ADRs erase that risk, since the certificates are in English and their authenticity is certified by the issuing agent. The investor is assured that the receipt is genuine even though it is an obligation of the issuing agent. The ADR represents only the underlying securities held by the agent and is not an obligation of the firm that issued the stock.

[5] Foreign stock exchanges may also list American securities. The London Stock Exchange is the most liberal and actually encourages foreign listings.

EXHIBIT 6.10

Selected Closing Prices for Foreign Securities

Reporting of foreign stocks is limited to their closing prices in their currencies.

OVERSEAS MARKETS

Friday, January 4, 1991

TOKYO
(in yen)

	Close	Prev. Close
ANA	1340	1280
Aiwa	1140	1140
Ajinomoto	1550	1570
Alps Elec	1290	1280
Amada Co	1040	1050
Ando Elec	1470	1490
Anritsu	1650	1700
Asahi Chem	740	744
Asahi Glass	1260	1230
Bank of Tokyo	1070	1080
Bk of Yokohama	1020	1060
Banyu Pharm	1020	1040
Bridgestone	989	990
Brother Ind	577	580
C. Itoh	697	645
CSK	4040	4040
Canon Inc	1270	1280
Canon Sales	3410	3410
Casio Computer	970	963
Chubu Pwr	2850	2770
Chugai Pharm	1050	1050
Citizen Watch	841	846
Dai Nippon Print	1470	1450
Dai-ichi Kangyo	1990	1950
Daiei	1190	1220
Daiichi Seiyaku	2200	2230
Dainippon Pharm	1870	1850
Daiwa Danchi	1000	1000
Daiwa House	1800	1820
Daiwa Securities	1170	1140
Eisai	1800	1830
Ezaki Glico	970	990
Fanuc	4350	4450
Fuji Bank	2440	2440
Fuji HI	442	446
Fuji Photo Film	3160	3190
Fujisawa Pharm	1520	1470
Fujitsu	988	980
Furukawa Elec	670	656
Green Cross	1050	1030
Haseko	801	800
Hirose Elec	4950	5030
Hitachi Cable	930	940
Hitachi Credit	1300	1330
Hitachi Ltd	1100	1130
Hitachi Maxell	1840	1810
Hitachi Metals	1260	1240
Hitachi Sales	696	696
Honda Motor	1250	1290
Hosiden Elec	1600	1610
Hoya	1830	1900
IHI	675	670
Ind Bank Japan	3270	3300
Intec	2810	2850
Isetan	2220	2210
Isuzu	505	506
Ito-yokado	3650	3550
Iwatsu Elec	705	695
JAL	1090	1080
JEOL	900	904
Mitsubishi Elec	619	637
Mitsubishi Real	1400	1400
Mitsubishi HI	685	668
Mitsubishi Kasei	555	555
Mitsubishi Matl	574	575
Mitsubishi Trust	1820	1800
Mitsubishi Whse	1500	1450
Mitsui Real	1250	1250
Mitsui TaiyoKobe	1950	1900
Mitsui Trust	1490	1460
Mitsui & Co	792	768
Mitsukoshi	1150	1160
Mochida Pharm	2380	2360
NCR Japan	1300	1320
NEC	1290	1290
NGK Spark	776	793
NIFCO	1390	1370
NKK	404	402
NTN	715	715
NTT	999000	980000
Nihon Unisys Ltd	2760	2700
Nikko Securities	960	929
Nikon Corp	1050	1030
Nintendo	18700	18900
Nippon Chemi-con	775	784
Nippon Columbia	900	879
Nippon El Glass	1300	1340
Nippon Express	755	755
Nippon Hodo	2510	2540
Nippon Meat	1350	1350
Nippon Mining	484	470
Nippon Oil	911	915
Nippon Sanso	609	609
Nippon Seiko	695	705
Nippon Shinpan	839	840
Nippon Steel	459	448
Nissan Motor	696	700
Nissin Food	2060	2080
Nitsuko	877	900
Nomura Securities	1820	1770
Odakyu Railway	1170	1130
Ohbayashi Corp	834	864
Oji Paper	840	810
Oki Elec Ind	708	695
Okuma Mach	1240	1250
Olympus Optical	998	998
Ono Pharm	4340	4400
Onoda Cement	619	625
Onward	1700	1690
Orient Corp	944	974
Osaka Kiko	700	700
Pioneer Electron	3990	3910
Renown	717	737
Ricoh Co	710	715
Royal Co	1810	1800
Ryobi	595	601
Secom	4140	4140
SMK	661	669
Sankyo Co	2430	2420
Sanrio	3500	3620
Sanwa Bank	1930	1930
Sanyo Elec	567	598
Sapporo Brewery	1340	1390
Toto	1590	1590
Toyo Seikan	4600	4520
Toyobo	530	550
Toyoda Mach	1020	1070
Toyota Motor	1750	1750
Tsugami	630	615
Uny	1450	1420
Ushio	815	820
Wacoal	970	995
Yamaha	1720	1690
Yamaichi Sec	959	945
Yamanouchi Phm	2730	2700
Yamatake-Hnywl	1530	1520
Yamato Transport	1150	1180
Yamazaki Baking	1350	1360
Yasuda Fire	910	890
Yokogawa Elec	1150	1140

LONDON
(in pence)

	Close	Prev. Close
Albert Fisher	116	115
Allied-Lyons	490	484
Argyll Group	250	245
Assoc Brit Fds	437	434
BAA plc	405	403
Barclays	356	350
Bass	1036	1034
BAT Indus	589	579
Blue Circle	219	216
BOC Group	487	480
Boots	314	312
Borland	n.a.	1508
Bowater Indus	467	477
BPB Indus	180	176
British Aero	525	526
British Airwys	143	140
British Gas	227	225
British Pete	323	328
British Steel	116.5	116.5
British Telcom	282	281.5
BTR	319	318
Burmah Castrol	498	507
Cable&Wireless	460	449
Cadbury Schwp	322	317
Charter Cons	415	415
Coats Viyella	104	103
Commercial Un	459	455
Courtaulds	322	319
Dixons	134	132
Dowty Group	166	164
Eng Ch Clay	348	343
Fisons	373	369
GEC	171.5	169
Genrl Accidnt	470	469
GKN	323	324
Glaxo Hldgs	811	825
Sears	85	85
Sedgwick Grp	230	228
Shell Trnspt	446	453
Siebe plc	319	324
Smithkln Bchm	609	617
Smith&Nephew	103	102.5
Std Chartrd	249	247
STC	324	324
Storehouse	103	110
Sun Alliance	335	330
Tarmac	236	235
Tate & Lyle	266	265
Tesco	231	227
Thorn EMI	679	672
Trafalgar Hse	199	195
Trusthse Forte	246	245
TSB Group	133	131
Ultramar	327	327
Utd Biscuits	323	319
Unilever	680	678
Warburg	334	334
Wellcome	435	434
WPP Group	70	67

South African Mines
(in U.S. dollars)

	Close	Prev. Close
Bracken	0.65	0.65
Deelkraal	2.58	2.68
Doornfontein	0.75	0.75
Durban Deep	5.50	5.50
E. Rand Gold	2.44	2.44
E. Rand Prop	4.62	4.62
Elandsrand	7.25	7.00
Elsburg	0.73	0.68
Grootvlei	1.25	1.25
Harmony	7.37	7.37
Hartebstftn	5.55	5.55
Impala Pltm	13.12	13.12
Kinross	15.88	15.87
Leslie	1.38	1.38
Libanon	0.65	0.65
Loraine	2.43	2.48
Randfontein	4.50	4.50
Rustenburg	17.12	17.12
Southvaal	26.25	26.25
Stilfontein	2.63	2.63
Unisel	4.50	4.50
West Areas	1.25	1.15
Winkelhaak	18.00	18.00

MILAN
(in lire)

	Close	Prev. Close
Banca Com	4149	4080
Benetton	8511	8499
Ciga	2975	2979

PARIS
(in French francs)

	Close	Prev. Close
Accor	672	668
Air Liquide	629	625
Alcatel Alstm	549	540
BSN-Gervais	737	735
Carrefour	3331	3340
Club Med	448.10	452
Dassault Avitn	428	428
Elf Aquitaine	279.30	285.50
Euro Disneyld	94.60	93.80
Generale Eaux	2182	2160
Hachette	157	158
Havas	436	442
Imetal	208	205
Lafarge Coppe	316.50	313.30
LVMH	3489	3465
Machines Bull	30	32
Matra	225.50	228
Michelin	66.70	66.50
L'Oreal	498.50	488
Paribas	430.90	426.80
Pernod Ricard	948	940
Peugeot	507	500
Saint Gobain	370.50	359
Sanofi	754	739
Source Perrier	1154	1140
Suez	278	278.20
Thomson CSF	119	117.60
Total Francais	601	623

AMSTERDAM
(in guilders)

	Close	Prev. Close
ABN Amro	32.20	31.90
Aegon	104.80	104.70
Ahold	67.20	66.10
Akzo	75.20	75.20
AMEV	46.80	46.30
Buhrmn-Tett	45	44.90
DSM	86.70	85.50
Elsevier	76.10	76.20
Fokker	29.70	29.30
Gist-Brocades	28.50	28.30
Heineken	137.80	137.30
Hoogovens	50.50	50.80
KLM	21	19.90
Nat-Ndrlndn	50.60	49.30
Nedlloyd	35.90	35.80
Oce-van Grntn	35.30	34.50
Pakhoed Hldg	197.50	196.90
Philips	20.60	20.40
Robeco	86.10	86.20
Rodamco	55.60	55.90
Rolinco	80.10	80.30
Rorento	60.20	60.20
Royal Dutch	130	130.60
Unilever	151.50	152
VOC	43.40	43

FRANKFURT
(in marks)

	Close	Prev. Close
AEG	211	207.5
Allianz	2065	2022
Asko	989	971
BASF	202	198
Bayer	219.5	214.8
Byr Vereinsbk	327	320.5
BMW	384	378
Commerzbank	229.5	222.5
Continental	204	199.5
Daimler Benz	549	536.2
Degussa	295	289.5
Deutsche Bank	595.5	584
Dresdner Bank	344.5	338
Henkel	497	494.8
Hochtief	1066	1066
Hoechst	206.5	203.7
Karstadt	580	580
Kaufhof	458.5	451
Linde	770	771.5
Lufthansa	111	109.2
Mannesmann	259.5	254.5
MAN	353	349
Metallges	432	426.5
Munchen Ruck	2220	2230
Nixdorf	305.5	302
Porsche	n.a.	715
RWE	378	366.5
SEL	310.5	309
Schering	698.5	695
Siemens	587.9	574.2
Thyssen	187	181
Veba	300	288.7
VEW	204.3	204
Volkswagen	339	329

SYDNEY
(in Australian dollars)

	Close	Prev. Close
Amcor	3.90	3.97
ANZ Group	3.07	3.23
Ashton	1.25	1.28
Bell Group	0.04	0.04
Boral	3.21	3.26
Bougainville	0.71	0.71
Brambles Inds	14.10	14.45
Brokn Hill Prp	9.60	9.96
Burns Philp	2.45	2.46
Coles Myer	7.84	7.94
Comalco	3.40	3.55
Centrl Norsemn	0.22	0.23
CRA	9.04	9.30
CSR	4.58	4.62
Foster's	1.28	1.38
Gld Mns Kalgo	0.65	0.70
Goodman	1.35	1.35

Source: The Wall Street Journal, *January 4, 1991, p. C14.*

Besides reducing the risk of fraud, ADRs are convenient. Securities do not have to be delivered through international mail; prices are quoted in dollars; and dividend payments are received in dollars. The ADR can represent any number of foreign shares. For example, Japanese stocks traditionally trade for low prices; such stocks would be considered penny stocks in the United States. To make the prices comparable to U.S. security prices, an ADR may represent ten or fifteen Japanese shares. Thus, if a Japanese share is worth $2.00, that will translate into $20 if the ADR represents ten shares.

The prices of a number of foreign stocks are given daily in the American financial press. For example, *The Wall Street Journal* gives prices for selected securities traded on several exchanges. Exhibit 6.10 reproduces a sample of the prices reported in *The Wall Street Journal.* As may be seen in the exhibit, the information is limited to prices—there is no reporting of volume of transactions, dividends, or P/E ratios. However, the number of foreign stock prices reported in the American press is small. If the investor seeks to track the prices of many foreign stocks, that will require access to a foreign publication such as the *Financial Times,* a British newspaper that is comparable to *The Wall Street Journal.*

In addition to stocks, Americans may also acquire bonds sold in foreign countries. There are basically three general types: (1) bonds issued by foreign firms; (2) bonds issued by foreign governments; and (3) bonds issued in foreign countries by American firms.

Bonds issued abroad by American firms are basically of two types, depending on the currency in which they are denominated. The American firm can sell bonds denominated in the local currency (e.g., British pounds or French francs), or the firm can sell abroad bonds denominated in American dollars, called Eurobonds. This term applies even though the bonds may be issued in, say, Asia instead of Europe. When a firm issues a Eurobond, the American firm promises to make payments in dollars. In this case the American investor will not have to convert the payments from the local currency (e.g., British pounds) back into dollars.

COMPETITION IN THE SECURITY MARKETS

Economics teaches that the market will be very competitive if there are many informed participants who may readily enter and exit. Both the stock and bond markets meet these conditions. Individuals may readily buy and sell securities; information is rapidly disseminated, and prices quickly change in reaction to changes in the economic and financial environment. The securities markets are among the most competitive markets in existence.

Financial Facts

Investing in Third World Countries and the Eastern Bloc

Foreign investments by U.S. investors generally imply the acquisition of assets in advanced economies, but emerging economies such as Chile, Korea, or Thailand could offer superior opportunities. Emerging economies may grow more rapidly and be less responsive to global economic changes than firms in advanced economies. More rapid economic growth suggests higher potential returns, and less sensitivity to recession experienced by advanced economies suggests more opportunities for diversification. • In addition to emerging economies, the sudden change in the political environment in eastern Europe and the Soviet Union may also offer opportunities for the adventurous investor. While it is premature to determine if security markets will develop in formerly communist countries, certainly American, Japanese, and western European firms will seek to enter these potential markets. Even though it is not possible for investors to participate directly in these economies through equity investments, individuals may purchase the shares of firms seeking to expand operations into eastern Europe and the Soviet Union. Of course, for that strategy to generate a positive return, the firm's earnings must increase as a result of these foreign investments. Since most of the firms capable of making these investments will tend to be large, global firms, it may be impossible to isolate the impact that eastern European investments have on these firms' bottom lines (i.e., their earnings). •

Efficient market hypothesis ▲
Theory that securities prices correctly measure the current value of a firm's future earnings and dividends

This competition among investors has led to the **efficient market hypothesis,** which asserts that security markets are so competitive that the current price of a stock properly values the firm's future prospects—that is, the firm's future earnings and its dividends. Today's price then is a true measure of the security's worth. For the individual investor, therefore, a security analysis designed to determine if a stock is overpriced or underpriced is futile, because the stock is neither.

An important implication of this theory of efficient markets is that the individual investor cannot consistently beat the market; rather, he or she will earn a return consistent with the market return and the amount of risk borne by the investor. The efficient market hypothesis suggests that the individual investor should realize that the probability of outperforming the market over any extended period is very small. That does not mean an investor cannot outperform (or underperform) the market during a short period of time. During a brief period, such as a year, some investors will earn a return that is better than the return earned by the market. However, there is little chance that those individuals will be able to achieve superior results for an extended period of time (i.e., to outperform the market consistently).

One of the primary reasons for the efficient market hypothesis is the speed with which security prices adjust to new information. The hypothesis requires that prices adjust extremely rapidly as new information is disseminated. In the modern world of advanced communication, information is rapidly dispersed in the investment community. The market then adjusts security prices in accordance with the impact of the news on the firm's future earnings and dividends. By the time that the individ-

FIGURE 6.2

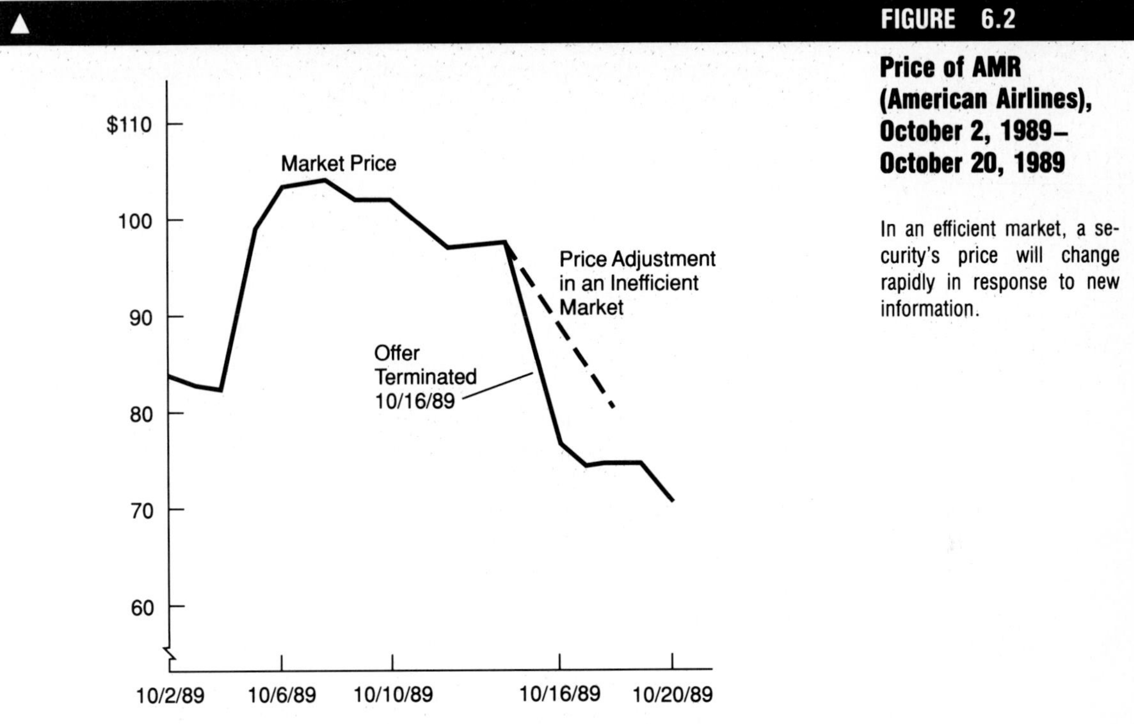

Price of AMR (American Airlines), October 2, 1989– October 20, 1989

In an efficient market, a security's price will change rapidly in response to new information.

ual investor has learned the information, security prices probably will have already changed. Thus, the investor will not be able to profit from acting on the information.

This adjustment process is illustrated in Figure 6.2, which plots the price of AMR (American Airlines) stock during October 1989. In early October, AMR received a buyout offer at $120, and the stock rose quickly and dramatically. However, the offer was terminated on October 16, and the price of the stock fell 22⅛ points from $98⅝ to $76½ in one day. Such price behavior is exactly what the efficient market hypothesis suggests: The market adjusts very rapidly to new information. By the time the announcement was reported in the financial press on October 17, it was too late for the individual investor to react, as the price change had already occurred.

If the market were not so efficient and prices did not adjust rapidly, some investors would be able to adjust their holdings and take advantage of differences in investors' knowledge. Consider the broken line in Figure 6.2. If some investors knew that the agreement had been terminated but others did not, the former could sell their holdings to those who were not informed. The price then may fall over a period of time as the knowledgeable sellers accepted progressively lower prices in order to unload their stock. Of course, if a sufficient number of investors had learned quickly of the termination, the price decline would be rapid as these investors adjusted their valuations of the stock in accordance with the new information. That is exactly what happened, because a sufficient number of investors were rapidly informed and the efficient market quickly adjusted the stock's price.

If an investor were able to anticipate the termination of the merger before it was announced, that individual could avoid the price decline. Obviously some investors did sell their shares just prior to the announcement, but it is also evident that some individuals bought those shares. Certainly one of the reasons for learning the material and performing the various types of analysis throughout this text is to increase one's ability to anticipate events before they occur. However, the investor should realize that considerable evidence supports the efficient market hypothesis and strongly suggests few investors will over a period of time outperform the market consistently.[6]

SUMMARY

This chapter has covered security markets and the mechanics of buying securities. Securities are traded on organized exchanges, such as the NYSE, or in the informal over-the-counter markets. Securities are primarily bought through brokers, who buy and sell for their customers' accounts. The brokers obtain the securities from dealers, who make markets in them. These dealers offer to buy and sell at specified prices (quotes), which are called the bid and the ask. Brokers and investors obtain these prices through a sophisticated electronic system that transmits the quotes from the various dealers (NASDAQ).

After securities are purchased, the investor must pay for them with either cash or a combination of cash and borrowed funds. When the investor uses borrowed funds, that individual is buying on margin. Buying on margin increases both the potential return and the potential risk of loss for the investor.

Investors may take delivery of their securities or leave them with the broker. Leaving securities registered in the street name offers the advantage of convenience because the broker becomes the custodian of the certificates. Since the advent of the SIPC and its insurance protection, there is little risk of loss to the investor from leaving securities with the broker.

[6] For a summary of this evidence consult: Russell J. Fuller and James L. Farrell, Jr., *Modern Investments and Security Analysis* (New York: McGraw-Hill Book Company, 1987), Chs. 5 and 21.

Investors establish long or short positions. With a long position, the investor purchases stock in anticipation of its price rising. If the price of the stock rises, the individual may sell it for a profit. With a short position, the individual sells borrowed stock in anticipation of its price declining. If the price of the stock falls, the individual may repurchase it at the lower price and return it to the lender. The position generates a profit because the selling price exceeds the purchase price.

Both the long and short positions are the logical outcomes of security analysis. If the investor thinks a stock is underpriced, a long position (i.e., purchase of the stock) should be established. If the investor thinks a stock is overvalued, a short position should be established. In either case if the investor is correct, the position will generate a profit. Either position may, however, generate a loss if prices move against the investor's prediction.

The issuing and subsequent trading of securities is regulated by the federal government, and the laws are enforced by the Securities and Exchange Commission. The primary purpose of the security laws is to provide individuals with information so they may make informed investment decisions. The laws prohibit the use of privileged information ("inside information") for personal gain. Federal security legislation also created SIPC, the Securities Investor Protection Corporation, which insures investors from failure by brokerage firms.

American investors may purchase securities issued by foreign firms. This is usually accomplished through the purchase of American Depository Receipts, ADRs, which are issued by financial institutions and represent the foreign securities. Americans may also acquire securities such as Eurobonds—debt instruments issued abroad by American firms that are denominated in dollars instead of the foreign currency.

Security markets are very competitive and efficient. New information is disseminated rapidly, and prices adjust quickly in response to the new information. The efficient market hypothesis suggests that few investors will be able to outperform the market. While an individual may outperform (or underperform) the market for a given time period, consistently superior returns may be impossible to achieve.

Review Questions

1. Why are organized exchanges examples of secondary markets? Do these exchanges transfer funds from savers to firms (i.e., are they financial intermediaries)?
2. Securities are purchased through brokers from dealers who "make a market." What does it mean to make a market? How does the market maker earn a profit? What is the essential difference between a broker and market maker?

3. If a stock is quoted 45–45½, does that mean the investor can buy the stock for a price between $45 and $45.50? If you owned the stock and wanted to sell, how much could you expect to receive before commissions on the sale?
4. What does it mean to buy a stock on margin? If a stock sold for $36 and the margin requirement was 60 percent, how much would the individual have to commit (excluding commissions) of his or her own funds? If the stock's price subsequently declined to $27, what is (1) the percentage decline in the value of the stock, and (2) the percentage loss the investor would realize? Why are these two percentages different?
5. If a stock is selling for $26 but you anticipate its price declining, what strategy might you follow?
6. How may Americans purchase foreign securities? Are foreign stocks traded on the organized American stock exchanges? How do ADRs facilitate the purchasing of foreign stocks?
7. The security industry, like the banking industry, is regulated. What is the purpose of this regulation? How is this purpose different from the purpose of the regulation of commercial banks?
8. What are the roles of the SEC and SIPC? How is SIPC similar to the FDIC?
9. Can an investor expect to outperform the market over an extended period of time? How rapidly do changes in stock prices occur when a firm makes a new announcement such as a merger agreement?

Problems

1. A stock sells for $40 per share. You purchase one hundred shares for $40 a share (i.e., $4,000), and after a year the price rises to $50. What will be the percentage return on your investment if you bought the stock on margin and the margin requirement was (a) 25 percent, (b) 50 percent, and (c) 75 percent? (Ignore commissions, dividends, and interest expense).
2. Repeat Problem 1 to determine the percentage return on your investment but in this case suppose the price of the stock falls to $30 per share. What generalization can be inferred from your answers to Problems 1 and 2?
3. An investor sells a stock short for $53. The price subsequently rises to $62. What was the investor's profit or loss on the short position?
4. Barbara B. buys 100 shares of DC at $25 a share and 200 shares of GOP at $31½ a share. She buys on margin and the broker charges interest of 10 percent on the loan.
   a. If the margin requirement is 55 percent, what is the maximum amount she can borrow?
   b. If she buys the stocks using the borrowed money and holds the securities for a year, how much interest must she pay?
   c. If after a year she sells DC for $29 a share and GOP for $22 a share, how much did she lose on her investment?
   d. What is the percentage loss on the funds she invested if the interest payment is included in the calculation?

5. After an analysis of Lion/Bear, Inc., Hamilton H. has concluded that the firm will face financial difficulty within a year. The stock is currently selling for $5¼, and Mr. H wants to sell it short. His broker is willing to execute the transaction but only if Mr. H puts up cash as collateral equal to the amount of the short sale. If Mr. H does sell the stock short, what is the percentage return he earns if the price of the stock rises to $7⅝? What would be the percentage return if the firm went bankrupt and folded?

Suggested Readings

A large quantity of material has been written on security markets. Some is as fascinating as fiction (which it may also be). Other material can be very technical as the authors seek to explain various models for selecting securities. The following readings are just a brief sample of the many possibilities available to the student of the stock market.

For a history of the organized exchanges and the SEC, consult:

Skousen, K. Fred. *An Introduction to the SEC.* Cincinnati, Ohio: South-Western Publishing Co., 1983.

Sobel, Robert. *The Big Board: A History of the New York Stock Market.* New York: The Free Press, 1965.

Sobel, Robert. *The Curbstone Brokers: The Origins of the American Stock Exchange.* New York: Macmillan, 1970.

For a history of financial disasters on Wall Street including the sharp decline in October 1987 read:

Sobel, Robert. *Panic on Wall Street.* New York: E. P. Dutton, 1988.

The sharp decline in securities prices that occurred in October 1987 is chronicled in:

Barro, Robert J. *Black Monday and the Future of Financial Markets.* Homewood, Ill.: Dow Jones-Irwin, 1989.

For explanations of portfolio theories and evidence of returns earned from investments in securities, see:

Lorie, James H., et al. *The Stock Market: Theories and Evidence.* 2d ed. Homewood, Ill.: Richard D. Irwin, 1985.

Malkiel, Burton G. *A Random Walk Down Wall Street.* 4th ed. New York: W. W. Norton & Co., 1985.

part two

Investments

● Virtually everyone makes investment decisions. My 14-year-old daughter has a savings account. My father owned stock in Ford at the age of 90. In between these extremes, every member of my family has made an investment in some type of asset.

The same is true for most families. Individuals purchase homes, make contributions to tax deferred pension plans, acquire shares in mutual funds, and purchase precious metals such as gold. Some individuals actively manage their portfolios and make their own investment decisions, such as which specific stocks or bonds to buy and sell. Other individuals delegate this decision making. They may purchase the shares in an investment company and let its management decide which specific assets to acquire.

Part Two is concerned with the financial assets the individual or portfolio manager may acquire. These assets range from relatively safe debt obligations, such as the bonds issued by the federal government, to extremely risky investments, such as futures contracts. Of course, a person should first decide why he or she is investing (i.e., the financial goals of the portfolio) before making investment decisions. Six of the next eight chapters discuss the alternative investments available to an individual once the investment goals have been specified.

chapter

7

The Time Value of Money

Learning Objectives

1. Explain why a dollar received tomorrow is not equal in value to a dollar received today.
2. Differentiate between compounding and discounting.
3. Distinguish between the present value of a dollar to be received in the future and the present value of an annuity.
4. Determine the future value of a dollar and the present value of a dollar to be received in the future.
5. Solve problems concerning the time value of money.

As Benjamin Franklin so aptly expressed it: "Money makes money. And the money that money makes makes more money." That is the essence of the time value of money: a dollar received in the future is not equivalent in value to a dollar received in the present. The concept of the time value of money answers such questions as: If $100 is deposited in a savings account in a commercial bank today, how much will be in the account ten years from now if the funds earn 6 percent annually? Should a firm whose cost of funds is 12 percent acquire equipment that costs $12 million and offers a return of $1.5 million a year for twelve years? If an investor buys a stock for $50 and sells it after two years for $60, what was the rate of return on the investment?

The time value of money is one of the most crucial concepts in finance. An investment decision is made at a given time. For example, an investor buys stock or a firm decides to establish a pension plan today. The returns on these investment decisions will be received in the future. There has to be a means to compare the future results of these investments with their present cost. Such comparisons require an understanding of the time value of money.

The chapter considers four concepts: (1) the future value of a dollar, (2) the present value of a dollar, (3) the future value of an annuity, and (4) the present value of an annuity. After each has been explained, several examples will illustrate how they are applied.

THE FUTURE VALUE OF A DOLLAR

If \$100 is deposited in a savings account that pays 5 percent annually, how much money will be in the account at the end of the year? The answer is easy to determine: \$100 plus \$5 interest, for a total of \$105. This answer is derived by multiplying \$100 by 5 percent, which gives the interest earned during the year, and by adding this interest to the initial principal. That is,

$$\text{Initial principal} + (\text{Interest rate} \times \text{Initial principal}) = \text{Principal after one year}.$$

This simple calculation is expressed in algebraic form in Equation 7.1, in which P represents the principal and i is the rate of interest. This equation employs subscripts to represent time. The subscript 0 indicates the present, and 1 means the end of the first year. (The second year, third year, and so on to any number of years will be represented by 2, 3, . . . n, respectively.)

7.1 $$P_0 + iP_0 = P_1.$$

If P_0 is the initial principal (\$100) and i is the interest rate (5%), the principal after one year (P_1) will be

$$\$100 + 0.05(\$100) = \$105.$$

How much will be in the account after two years? This answer is obtained in the same manner by adding the interest earned during the second year to the principal at the beginning of the second year; i.e., \$105 plus 0.05 times \$105 equals \$110.25, which may be expressed as:

7.2 $$P_1 + iP_1 = P_2.$$

After two years the initial deposit of \$100 will have grown to \$110.25; the savings account will have earned \$10.25 in interest. This total interest is composed of \$10, representing interest on the initial principal, and \$0.25, representing interest that has accrued during the second year on the \$5 in interest earned during the first year. This earning of interest on interest is called **compounding.** Money that is deposited in savings accounts is frequently referred to as being compounded, for interest is earned on both the principal and the previously earned interest.

Compounding ▲
Process by which interest is paid on interest that was previously earned

The words *interest* and *compounded* are frequently used together. For example, banks may advertise that interest is compounded daily for savings accounts, or the cost of a loan may be expressed as 18 percent compounded annually. In the previous example, interest was earned only once during the year, i.e., compounded annually. In many cases interest is not compounded annually but quarterly, semiannually, or even daily. The more frequently it is compounded (i.e., the more frequently the interest is added to the principal), the more rapidly the interest is put to work to earn even more interest.

How much will be in the account at the end of three years? This answer can be determined by the same general formula that was previously used. The amount in the account at the end of the second year (\$110.25) is added to the interest that is earned during the third year (0.05 × \$110.25). That is,

$$\$110.25 + \$5.5125 = \$115.76.$$

or the formula may be expressed as:

7.3 $$P_2 + iP_2 = P_3.$$

By continuing with this method, it is possible to determine the amount that will be in the account at the end of 20 or more years, but doing so is obviously a lot of work. Fortunately, there is a simpler way to ascertain how much will be in the account after any given number of years. This is done by the use of an interest table.

Appendix A at the end of the text is an interest table that gives the interest factor for the **future value of a dollar.** The interest rates at which a dollar is compounded annually are read horizontally at the top of the table. The number of years is read vertically along the left-hand

Future value of a dollar ▲
Amount to which a single payment will grow at some rate of interest

Financial Facts

Simple versus Compound Interest

"Simple interest" does not consider the earning of interest on interest; "compound interest" does take into consideration the earning of interest on interest. The calculation of compound interest uses the equations and tables presented in the body of this chapter. To calculate simple interest, multiply the principal by the interest rate by the number of years. For example, the amount of simple interest earned for three years on $1,000 at 5 percent would be $1,000 × .05 × 3 = $150. • By the same reasoning, the interest earned over 20 years would be $1,000 × .05 × 20 = $1,000. • On first impression it might appear that the difference between simple interest (and its simple calculation) and compound interest (and the more complicated use of interest tables) is so small that the calculation of simple interest is sufficient. (Your banker might agree as far as deposits are concerned but certainly not in regard to borrowings.) A compound interest table will show, however, that $1,000 compounded annually at 5 percent for 20 years will grow to $2,653 ($1,000 × 2.653). The amount of interest is $1,653, and the difference is $653. • The difference between simple and compound interest is even larger if the number of years or the rate of interest is increased. For example, $1,000 invested for 25 years at 10 percent yields simple interest of $1,000 × .1 × 25 = $2,500. Compound interest, however, yields interest of $9,835 [($1,000 × 10.835) − $1,000]. The difference in the calculations is $7,335. So borrow from your younger brother using simple interest, but lend to him using compound interest. •

---

margin. To determine the amount to which $100 will grow in three years at 5 percent interest, find the interest factor (1.158) and multiply it by $100. That calculation yields $115.80, which is the answer that was derived previously by working out the equations (except for rounding off). To ascertain the amount to which $100 will grow in 25 years at 5 percent interest compounded annually, multiply $100 by the interest factor, 3.386, to obtain the answer, $338.60. Thus, if $100 were placed in a savings account that paid 5 percent interest annually, there would be $338.60 in the account after 25 years.

Tables for the interest factor for the future value of a dollar are based on a general formulation of the simple equations that were used above. To determine the amount in the savings account at the end of year 1, the following equation was used:

$$P_0 + iP_0 = P_1,$$

which may be written as:

$$P_0(1 + i) = P_1.$$

To calculate the amount after two years, the following equation was used:

$$P_1 + iP_1 = P_2,$$

which may be written as:

$$P_1(1 + i) = P_2.$$

Since P_1 equals $P_0(1 + i)$, the amount in the account at the end of year 2 may be expressed as:

$$P_0(1 + i)(1 + i) = P_2.$$

This equation uses the term $1 + i$ twice, for P_0 is being multiplied by $1 + i$ twice. Thus, it is possible to write this equation as:

$$P_0(1 + i)^2 = P_2.$$

The amount to which a dollar will grow may always be expressed in terms of the initial dollar (i.e., P_0). The general formula for finding the amount to which a dollar will grow in n number of years, if it is compounded annually, is

7.4 $$P_0(1 + i)^n = P_n.$$

The general formula (Equation 7.4) for finding the future value of a dollar (P_n) is actually a simple equation in the following general form:

$$A \times B = C.$$

A is the present amount, B is the interest factor, and C is the future amount. Thus, the equation states:

Present amount × Interest factor = Future amount

The *future value* of $1 *interest factor* (FVIF) is

7.5 $$\text{FVIF} = (1 + i)^n,$$

so the future value of a dollar is

$$P_0 \times \text{FVIF}(i,n) = P_n$$

in which FVIF (i,n) represents the interest factor *for* i *interest rate and* n *time periods*. For example, the future value of a given amount at the end of twenty years when the interest rate is 8 percent is the present amount times the interest factor for the future value of $1 at 8 percent for twenty years:

$$P_0 \times \text{FVIF}(8\%,20\text{Y}) = P_n.$$

If the present amount is $100, the future value is $100(4.661) = $466.10.

FIGURE 7.1

Future Value of One Dollar

The future value of $1 increases as the interest rate rises and time increases.

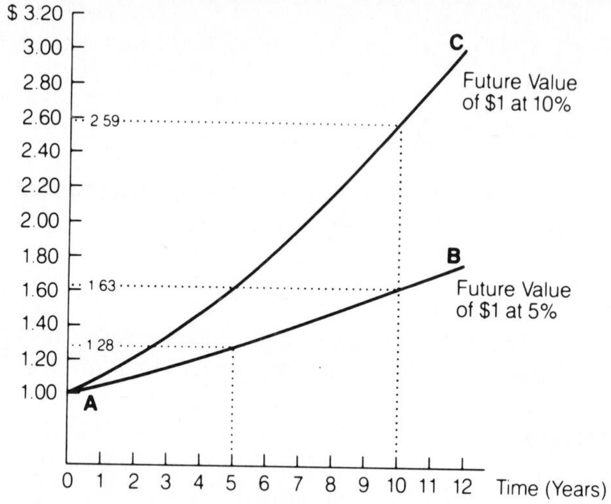

The actual calculation of a future value can be very tedious if you must manually perform the task. For example, determining the value of the interest factor $(1 + 0.08)^{20}$ will be very time-consuming. The interest tables eliminate this calculation. By finding the value in the table of 8 percent compounded for 20 years, you find the value of interest factor $(1 + 0.08)^{20}$, which is 4.661.

As may be seen in Appendix A, the value of a dollar grows with increases in the length of time and in the rate of interest. These relationships are illustrated in Figure 7.1. If $1 is compounded at 5 percent interest (AB on the graph), it will grow to $1.28 after five years and to $1.63 after ten years. However, if $1 is compounded at 10 percent interest (AC on the graph), it will grow to $2.59 in ten years. These cases illustrate the basic nature of compounding: The longer the funds continue to grow and the higher the interest rate, the higher will be the final value.

It should be noted that doubling the interest rate more than doubles the amount of interest that is earned. In the example just given, when the interest rate was doubled from 5 percent to 10 percent, the amount of interest that was accumulated in ten years rose from $0.63 at 5 percent to $1.59 at 10 percent. The same conclusion applies to doubling the number of years. In the above example, when the dollar was compounded annually for five years at 5 percent, the interest earned was $0.28 but rose to $0.63 after ten years. These conclusions are the result of the fact that compounding involves a geometric progression. The interest factor $(1 + i)$ has been raised to some power (n).

THE PRESENT VALUE OF A DOLLAR

In the preceding section, we examined the way in which a dollar was compounded over time. In this section we will consider the reverse situation. How much is a dollar that will be received in the future worth today? For example, how much will a payment of $1,000 20 years hence be worth today if the funds earn 5 percent annually? This question incorporates the time value of money, but instead of asking how much a dollar will be worth at some future date, it asks how much that future dollar is worth today. This is a question of **present value.** The process by which this question is answered is called **discounting.** Discounting determines the worth of funds that are to be received in the future in terms of their present value.

Present value ▲
Current value of a dollar to be received in the future

Discounting ▲
Process of determining present value

In the earlier section, the future value of a dollar was calculated by Equation 7.4:

$$P_0(1 + i)^n = P_n.$$

Discounting reverses this equation. The present value (P_0) is ascertained by dividing the future value (P_n) by the interest factor $(1 + i)^n$. This is expressed in Equation 7.6.

7.6
$$P_0 = \frac{P_n}{(1 + i)^n}.$$

The future amount is discounted by the appropriate interest factor to determine the present value. For example, if the interest rate is 6 percent, the present value of $100 to be received five years from today is

$$P_0 = \frac{\$100}{(1 + 0.06)^5},$$

$$P_0 = \frac{\$100}{1.338},$$

$$P_0 = \$74.73.$$

Equation 7.6, like the equation for the future value of $1, breaks down into three simple components: the amount in the future, the amount in the present, and the interest factor that links the present and future values. Thus, the future amount times the interest factor for the present value of $1 is

$$P_n \times \text{PVIF}(i,n) = P_0.$$

PVIF (i,n) represents the interest factor:

7.7
$$\text{PVIF} = \frac{1}{(1 + i)^n}.$$

FIGURE 7.2

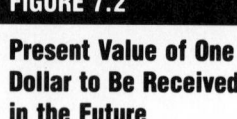

Present Value of One Dollar to Be Received in the Future

The present value of $1 decreases as the interest rate and time decrease.

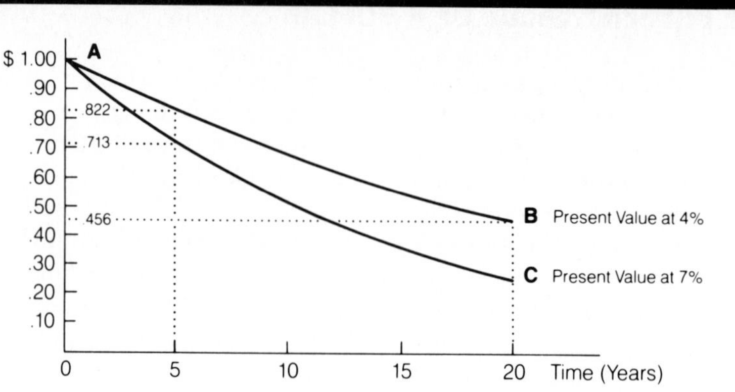

For example, if the interest rate is 6 percent, the present value of $100 to be received five years from today is

$$P_0 = \$100 \times \text{PVIF}(6\%,5\text{Y}).$$

To answer the problem use the interest table for the present value of $1 (Appendix B). This table presents the interest factors for selected interest rates and years. The interest rates are read horizontally at the top, and the number of years is read vertically along the left-hand side. To determine the present value of $1 that will be received in five years if the current interest rate is 6 percent, multiply $1 by the interest factor, which is found in the table under the vertical column for 6 percent and in the horizontal column for five years. The present value of $1 is

$$\$1 \times .747 = \$0.747.$$

Thus, $100 that will be received after five years is currently worth only $74.70 if the interest rate is 6 percent. This is the same answer that was determined with Equation 7.6 (except for rounding off).[1]

As may be seen in Equation 7.6, the present value of a dollar depends on the length of time before it will be received and the interest rate. The further into the future the dollar will be received and the higher the interest rate, the lower is the present value of the dollar. This is illustrated by Figure 7.2, which gives the relationship between the present value of a dollar and the length of time at various interest rates.

[1]Notice that the table is constructed so you multiply even though according to the equation you are dividing. Thus, $\$100/(1 + 0.06)^5$ equals $\$100 \times .747$ because $1/(1 + 0.06)^5 = .747$.

Lines AB and AC give the present value of a dollar at 4 percent and 7 percent, respectively. As may be seen in this graph, a dollar to be received after 20 years is worth considerably less than a dollar to be received after five years when both are discounted at the same percentage. At 4 percent (line AB) the current value of $1 to be received after 20 years is only $0.456, whereas $1 to be received after five years is worth $0.822. Also, the higher the interest rate (i.e., discount factor), the lower is the present value of a dollar. For example, the present value of $1 to be received after five years is $0.822 at 4 percent, but it is only $0.713 at 7 percent.

THE FUTURE VALUE OF AN ANNUITY

How much will be in a savings account after three years if $100 is deposited annually and the account pays 5 percent interest? This is similar to the future value of a dollar except that the payment is not received as one lump sum but as a series. If the payments are equal (e.g., rent or a loan repayment schedule), the series is called an **annuity.** The above question is then an illustration of the **future value of an annuity.**

Annuity ▲
Series of equal, annual payments

Future value of an annuity ▲
Amount to which a series of equal payments will grow at some rate of interest

Annuity due ▲
Annuity in which the payments are made at the beginning of the time period

Ordinary annuity ▲
Annuity in which the payments are made at the end of the time period

To determine how much will be in the account we must consider not only the interest rate earned but also whether deposits are made at the beginning of the year or the end of the year. If each deposit is made at the beginning of the year, the series is called an **annuity due.** If the deposits are made at the end of the year, the series is an **ordinary annuity.** What is the future value of an annuity if $100 is deposited in an account for three years starting right now? What is the future value of an annuity if $100 is placed in an account for three years starting at the end of the first year? The first question concerns an annuity due, while the second question illustrates an ordinary annuity.

The flow of deposits for these two types of annuities is illustrated in Exhibit 7.1. In both cases the $100 is deposited for three years in a savings account that pays 5 percent interest. The top half of the figure shows the annuity due, while the bottom half illustrates the ordinary annuity. In both cases, three years elapse from the present to when the final amount is determined. The difference in the timing of the deposits results in a difference in the interest earned. For example, the initial $100 deposit for the annuity due earns three interest payments ($5.00, $5.25, and $5.51 for a total of $15.76 in interest). The initial $100 deposit for the ordinary annuity earns only two interest payments ($5.00 and $5.25 for a total of $10.25 in interest). Since in an annuity due the deposits are made at the beginning of each year, the annuity due earns more interest ($31.01 versus $15.25) and thus has the higher terminal

EXHIBIT 7.1

Flow of Deposits and Interest for the Future Value of an Annuity Due and an Ordinary Annuity

The future value of an annuity is higher if payments are made at the beginning of the year.

Annuity Due

	1/1/x0	1/1/x1	1/1/x2	1/1/x3	Sum
Interest earned	—	5.00	5.25	5.51	115.76
The deposits			5.00	5.25	110.25
	$100.00	100.00	100.00	5.00	105.00
Amount in the Account	$100.00	205.00	315.25	331.01	$331.01

Ordinary Annuity

	1/1/x0	1/1/x1	1/1/x2	1/1/x3	Sum
Interest earned	—	—	5.00	5.25	$110.25
The deposits				5.00	105.00
	—	$100.00	100.00	100.00	100.00
Amount in the Account	—	100.00	205.00	315.25	$315.25

value ($331.01 versus $315.25). As will be illustrated later in the chapter, the greater the interest rate and the longer the time period, the greater will be this difference in terminal values.

The procedures for determining the future value of an annuity due (*FVAD*) and the future value of an ordinary annuity (*FVOA*) are stated formally in Equations 7.8 and 7.9, respectively. In each equation, A represents the equal, periodic payment, i represents the rate of interest, and n represents the number of years that elapse from the present until the end of the time period. For the annuity due, the equation is

7.8 $$FVAD = A(1 + i)^1 + A(1 + i)^2 + \ldots + A(1 + i)^n.$$

When this equation is applied to the previous example in which $i = 0.05$, $n = 3$, and the annual payment $A = \$100$, the accumulated sum is

$$\begin{aligned} FVAD &= \$100(1 + 0.05)^1 + 100(1 + 0.05)^2 + 10(1 + 0.05)^3 \\ &= \$105 + 110.25 + 115.76 \\ &= 331.01. \end{aligned}$$

For the ordinary annuity the equation is

7.9 $$FVOA = A(1 + i)^0 + A(1 + i)^1 + \ldots + A(1 + i)^{n-1}.$$

When this equation is applied to the above example, the accumulated sum is

$$\begin{aligned} FVOA &= \$100(1 + 0.05)^0 + 100(1 + 0.05)^1 + 100(1 + 0.05)^{3-1} \\ &= \$100 + 105 + 110.25 \\ &= \$315.25. \end{aligned}$$

As with the future value of \$1 and the present value of \$1, the future value of an annuity (*FVA*) is determined by a simple equation:

$$A \times \text{FVAIF}(i,n) = FVA$$

in which *A* represents the annual payment, the annuity, and FVAIF(i,n) is the interest factor for an annuity at i percent for n time periods. This interest factor is given in Equation 7.10.

7.10
$$\text{FVAIF}(i,n) = \frac{(1 + i)^n - 1}{i}$$

An interest table (Appendix C) has been developed for the future value of an *ordinary* annuity. (Interest tables are usually given only for ordinary annuities. How these interest factors may be converted into the interest factor for an annuity due is illustrated in the appendix to this chapter.) The number of periods is read vertically at the left, and the interest rates are read horizontally at the top. To ascertain the future value of the ordinary annuity in the previous example, find the interest factor for the future value of an annuity at 5 percent for 3 years (3.152). So the future value of the annuity is

$$\$100 \times 3.152 = \$315.20.$$

This is the same answer that was derived by determining the future values of each \$100 deposit and totaling them. The slight difference in the two answers is the result of rounding off.

The future value of an annuity of a dollar compounded annually depends on the number of payments (i.e., the number of years over which deposits are made) and the interest rate. The longer the time period and the higher the interest rate, the greater will be the sum that will have accumulated in the future. This is illustrated by Figure 7.3. Lines AB and AC show the value of the annuity at 4 and 8 percent, respectively. After five years the value of the \$1 annuity will grow to \$5.87 at 8 percent but to only \$5.42 at 4 percent. If these annuities are continued for another five years for a total duration of ten years, they will be worth \$14.49 and \$12.01, respectively. Thus, both the rate at which the annuity compounds and the length of time affect the annuity's value.

FIGURE 7.3

Future Sum (i.e., Value) of an Annuity of One Dollar

The future sum of an annuity of $1 increases as the number of periods and payments increase and as the interest rate increases.

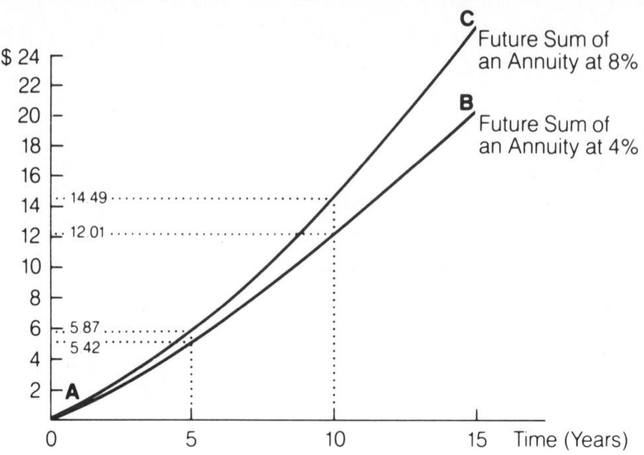

THE PRESENT VALUE OF AN ANNUITY

Present value of an annuity
Current value of a series of equal payments to be received in the future

In financial analysis the individual is often concerned not with the future value but with the **present value of an annuity.** The investor or the financial manager who will receive periodic payments often wishes to know the current value of these payments. Of course, the present value of these future payments could be determined by obtaining the present value of each payment and summing these values. This approach is illustrated by the following simple example. The recipient expects to receive $100 at the end of each year for three years and wants to know how much this series of annual payments is currently worth if 6 percent can be earned on invested funds. Notice the payments are made at the end of the year, so this is an illustration of an ordinary annuity. If the payments had been made at the beginning of the year, the series of payments would be an annuity due.

One method for determining the current worth of this ordinary annuity is to calculate the present value of each $100 payment (find the appropriate interest factors in Appendix B and multiply them by $100) and to sum these individual present values, which in this case yields $267.30, as may be seen in Exhibit 7.2.

This process is expressed in more general terms by Equation 7.11. The present value (PV) of the equal, annual payments (A) is found by discounting these payments at the appropriate interest rate (i) and summing (Σ) them from the first payment through the last (n) payment.

EXHIBIT 7.2

Present Value of a $100 Ordinary Annuity at Six Percent for Three Years

Payment	Year	Interest Factor	Present Value
$100	1	.943	$ 94.30
100	2	.890	89.00
100	3	.840	84.00
			$267.30

The present value of an annuity is the sum of the present values of the individual payments.

7.11

$$PV = \frac{A}{(1+i)^1} + \ldots + \frac{A}{(1+i)^n}$$

$$PV = \sum_{t=1}^{n} \frac{A}{(1+i)^t}.$$

When the values from the previous example are inserted into the equation, it reads:

$$\begin{aligned} PV &= \frac{\$100}{(1+0.06)} + \frac{\$100}{(1+0.06)^2} + \frac{\$100}{(1+0.06)^3} \\ &= \frac{\$100}{1.060} + \frac{\$100}{1.123} + \frac{\$100}{1.191} \\ &= \$267.35. \end{aligned}$$

Equation 7.11 may be rewritten as follows:

$$PV = (A)\left(\sum_{t=1}^{n} \frac{1}{(1+i)^t}\right).$$

This can be written as a simple equation in the general form of

$$AB = C.$$

The annual annuity payment is multiplied by an interest factor to determine the present value, which implies that the interest factor for the present value of an annuity (PVAIF) is[2]

7.12

$$\text{PVAIF} = \sum_{t=1}^{n} \frac{1}{(1+i)^t}.$$

[2] Equation 7.12 may also be written as follows:

$$\text{PVAIF} = \frac{1 - \frac{1}{(1+i)^n}}{i}.$$

The interest factor in this form is easier to apply when interest tables are not available.

FIGURE 7.4

Present Value of an Annuity of One Dollar

The present value of an annuity of $1 increases as the number of periods and payments increase but decreases as the interest rate rises.

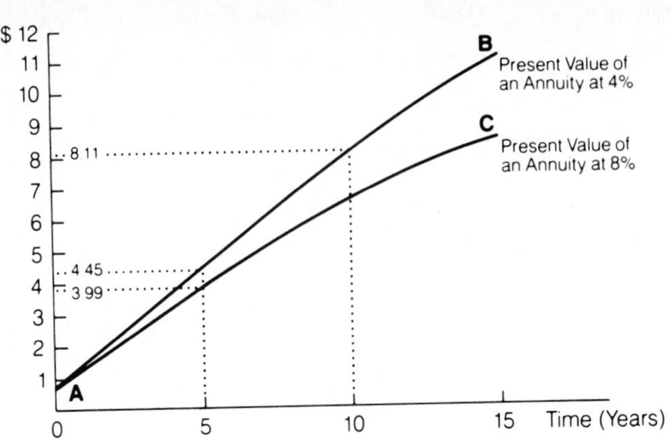

Thus, the determination of present value of an ordinary annuity is

$$A \times \text{PVAIF}(i,n) = PV$$

in which A is the annuity payment, PVAIF(i,n) is the interest factor for the present value of an ordinary annuity at i percent for n time periods, and PV is the present value of the annuity. The interest factors for the present value of an ordinary annuity are given in Appendix D. (How these interest factors may be converted into interest factors for an annuity due is explained in the appendix to this chapter.) The selected interest rates are read horizontally along the top, and the number of years is read vertically at the left. To determine the present value of an annuity of $100 that is to be received for three years when interest rates are 6 percent, find the interest factor for three years at 6 percent (2.673) and then multiply $100 by this interest factor. The present value of this annuity is $267.30, which is the same value (except for rounding off) that was derived by obtaining each of the individual present values and summing them. The price that one would be willing to pay at the present time in exchange for three future annual payments of $100, when the rate of return on alternative investments is 6 percent, is $267.30.

As with the present value of a dollar, the present value of an annuity is related to the interest rate and the length of time over which the annuity payments are made. The lower the interest rate and the longer the duration of the annuity, the greater is the current value of the annuity. Figure 7.4 illustrates the relationship between the duration of the annuity and the present value of the annuity at various interest rates. As may be seen by comparing lines AB and AC, the lower the interest rate, the higher is the present dollar value. For example, if payments are to be

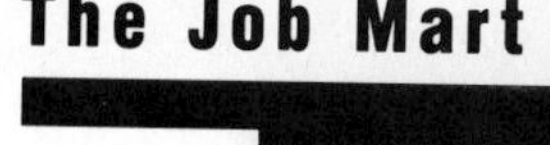

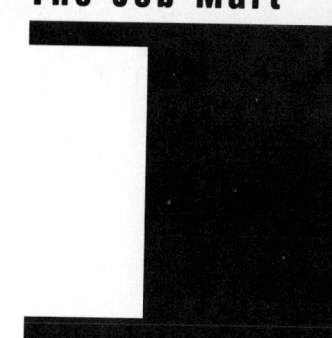

Actuary

■ Job Description: Develop estimates of future payments and their present value. Estimate future pension costs and the amount necessary to fund the benefits. Develop life insurance policies by constructing mortality tables and determining the policies' prices, or "premiums." Establish reserves to cover death claims and provide for annual increments in the cash values of life insurance policies. ■ Job Requirements: Mathematical and computer skills, combined with a thorough knowledge of the time value of money. Advanced knowledge concerning insurance, pensions, and benefit packages required for specializations. ■ Characteristics: Primary employers of actuaries are insurance companies, but any corporation (e.g., a commercial bank or a large firm such as IBM) may employ actuaries for estimating the present costs of future benefit packages. The occupation may become more in demand if federal legislation is enacted to require that firms establish funds to cover the costs of future medical benefits promised to retirees.

---

made over five years, the present value of an annuity of $1 is $4.45 at 4 percent but only $3.99 at 8 percent. The longer the duration of the annuity, the higher is the present value; hence, the present value of an annuity of $1 at 4 percent is $4.45 for five years, whereas the present value is $8.11 for ten years.

ILLUSTRATIONS OF COMPOUNDING AND DISCOUNTING

The previous sections have explained the various computations involving time value, and this section will illustrate them in a series of problems that the investor or financial manager may encounter. These illustrations are similar to examples that are used throughout the text. If one understands these examples, comprehending the rest of the text material should be much easier, because the emphasis can then be placed on the analysis of the value of specific assets instead of on the mechanics of the calculations.

Answering the time value of money problems requires determining which of the four tables to use. The following decision tree may aid in this selection process. First, determine if the problem involves a lump-sum payment or a set of equal payments (i.e., an annuity). Then determine if the problem concerns going from the present to the future (i.e., future value) or from the future to the present (present value).

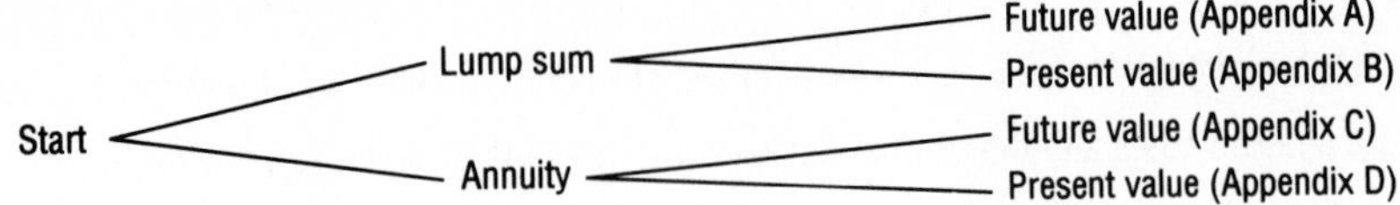

For example, if the current tuition cost of a four-year college education is $20,000, what will be the cost after ten years if prices rise annually by 6 percent? First, determine if the problem is concerned with an annuity or a lump sum. Since the question asks about total tuition costs, it is an illustration of a lump sum and not an annuity. Second, determine the time dimension. Since the problem is not concerned with the current cost of an education but with future costs, it is an example of future value and not present value. Thus, from the decision tree presented below, the appropriate table is determined to be the future value of a dollar table (Appendix A).

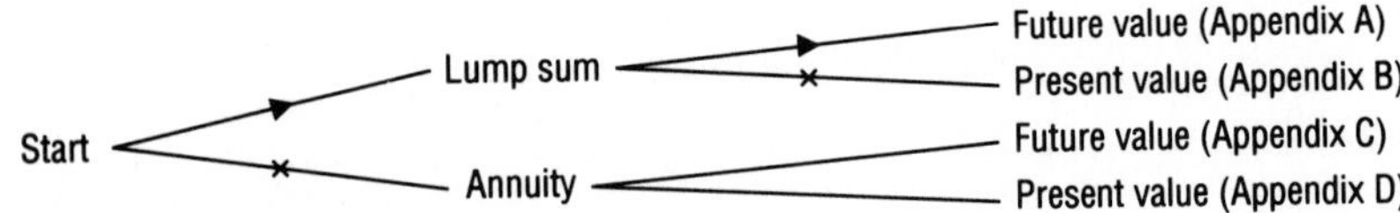

In addition to determining which interest table to use, the student needs to determine what is known and what is asked for. All time value problems involve four variables: the present amount, the future amount, the interest rate, and the number of time periods. Since there is only one equation, three of the four variables must be given. That is, three of the variables are independent, and one is dependent.

Consider, for example, that an investor buys a stock for $10 per share and expects the value of the stock to rise annually at 9 percent. After ten years this investor plans to sell the stock. What is the anticipated sale price? The three known variables (the independent variables) are the present amount ($10), the rate of growth which is analogous to the interest rate (9 percent), and the number of years (10). The unknown variable (i.e., the dependent variable) is the sale price. The problem illustrates the future value of a dollar since the unknown is the future amount, that is, the sale price. That future value is

$$\begin{aligned} P_n &= P_0(1 + i)^n \\ P_{10} &= \$10(1 + .09)^{10} \\ P_{10} &= \$10(\text{FVIF}9\%,10\text{Y}) \\ P_{10} &= \$10(2.367) = \$23.67 \end{aligned}$$

where 2.367 is the interest factor for the future value of a dollar at 9 percent for ten years (Appendix A). The investor anticipates selling the stock for $23.67.

Next, consider that an investor sells a stock for $23.67 that was held for ten years. A return of 9 percent was earned. What was the original cost of the investment? This is an example of the present value of a dollar discounted back at 9 percent for ten years. The purchase price was

$$P_0 = \frac{P_n}{(1 + i)^n}$$
$$P_0 = \frac{\$23.67}{(1 + 0.09)^{10}}$$
$$P_0 = \$23.67(\text{PVIF}9\%,10\text{Y})$$
$$P_0 = \$23.67(.422) = \$9.98 \approx \$10,$$

where .422 is the interest factor for the present value of a dollar discounted at 9 percent for ten years (Appendix B). The investment cost $10 when it was purchased.

The student should know that the examples just given are two views of the same investment. In the first example the $10 investment grew to $23.67. In the second example the value at the time the stock was sold was brought back to the value of the initial investment. Another variation of this question would be as follows. If an investor brought stock for $10, held it for ten years, and then sold it for $23.67, what was the return on the investment? In this case the values of the stock at the time it was bought and sold are known, but the rate of growth is unknown. The answer can be found by using *either* the future value of a dollar table or the present value of a dollar table. By solving for either interest factor, the rate of growth may be determined.

If the future value table (Appendix A) is used, the question is: At what rate (x) will $10 grow in ten years to equal $23.67? The answer is

$$P_0(1 + x)^n = P_n$$
$$\$10(1 + x)^{10} = \$23.67,$$
$$\$10(\text{FVIF}) = \$23.67$$
$$\text{FVIF} = 2.367$$

The interest factor is 2.367, which, according to the future value of a dollar table for ten years, makes the interest rate 9 percent because this interest factor is located under the vertical column for 9 percent and in the horizontal column for ten years.

If the present value table (Appendix B) is used, the question asks what discount rate (x) at ten years will bring $23.67 back to $10. The answer is found as follows:

$$P_0 = \frac{P_n}{(1 + x)^n}$$
$$\$10 = \frac{\$23.67}{(1 + x)^{10}}$$
$$\$10 = \$23.67(\text{PVIF})$$
$$\text{PVIF} = \frac{\$10}{\$23.67} = .422.$$

Financial Facts

The Annual Increase in the Cost of a College Education

In 1890, tuition to attend a major, private university cost $60. One hundred years later, the tuition was $10,000. In absolute dollars, that is a substantial increase in tuition, but is the increase so astonishing when expressed as an annual rate of growth? • That question may be answered by the use of time value of money. The question is "In 100 years, $60 grows into $10,000 at what rate?" That is $\$60(1 + g)^{100} = \$10,000$, $(1 + g)^{100} = 10,000/60 = 166.67$, and $g = \sqrt[100]{166.67} - 1 = 1.0525 - 1 = 5.25\%$. • $60 invested at only 5.25 percent grows into $10,000 after 100 years! From that perspective, the increase in the tuition cost does not seem so astonishing. However, if the 5.25 percent annual rate of growth is maintained, tuition in year 2090 will be $1,590,648! •

The interest factor is .422, which may be found in the present value of a dollar table for ten years in the 9 percent column. Thus, this problem may be solved by the proper application of either the compound value or present value tables.

Now consider a third example. An employer offers to start a pension plan for a 45-year-old employee. The plan is to place $1,000 at the end of each year in a savings account that earns 6 percent annually. The employee wants to know how much will have accumulated by retirement at age 65.

This is an example of the future value of an ordinary annuity. The payment is $1,000 annually, and it will grow at 6 percent for 20 years. The fund will thus grow to

$$
\begin{aligned}
FVA &= A(1 + i)^0 + \ldots + A(1 + i)^{n-1} \\
&= \$1,000(1 + 0.06)^0 + \ldots + \$1,000(1 + 0.06)^{19} \\
&= \$1,000(\text{FVAIF}) \\
&= \$1,000(36.786) = \$36,786
\end{aligned}
$$

where 36.786 is the interest factor for the future value of an annuity of one dollar compounded annually at 6 percent for 20 years (Appendix C).

In a fourth example, the same employer decides to place a lump sum in an account that earns 6 percent and to draw on the account to make the annual payments of $1,000. After 20 years all of the funds in the account will be depleted. How much must be deposited initially in the account?

This is an example of the present value of an ordinary annuity. The annuity of $1,000 per year at 6 percent for 20 years is worth how much today? The present value (i.e., the amount of the initial deposit necessary to fund the annuity) is

$$
\begin{aligned}
PVA &= \sum_{1}^{n} \frac{A}{(1+i)} + \ldots + \frac{A}{(1+i)^n} \\
&= \frac{\$1{,}000}{1+0.06} + \ldots + \frac{\$1{,}000}{(1+0.06)^{20}} \\
&= \$1{,}000(\text{PVAIF}) \\
&= \$1{,}000(11.470) = \$11{,}470,
\end{aligned}
$$

where 11.470 is the interest factor for the present value of the sum (Σ) of an annuity of a dollar at 6 percent for 20 years (Appendix D). Thus, the employer need deposit only $11,470 in an account that earns 6 percent to meet the $1,000 pension payment for 20 years.

The student should notice the difference between the answers in the last two examples. In the third example a set of payments earns interest, and thus the future value is larger than just the sum of the 20 payments of $1,000. In the fourth example a future set of payments is valued in present terms. Since future payments are worth less today, the current value is less than the sum of the 20 payments of $1,000.

As a final example, consider that an investment pays $50 per year for ten years, after which $1,000 is returned to the investor. If the investor can earn 6 percent, how much should this investment cost? This question really contains two questions: What is the present value of the sum (Σ) of an annuity of $50 at 6 percent for ten years, and what is the present value of $1,000 after ten years at 6 percent? The answer is

$$
\begin{aligned}
PV &= \sum_{1}^{n} \frac{A}{(1+i)^1} + \ldots + \frac{A}{(1+i)^n} + \frac{P_n}{(1+i)^n} \\
&= \frac{\$50}{(1+0.06)} + \ldots + \frac{\$50}{(1+0.06)^{10}} + \frac{\$1{,}000}{(1+0.06)^{10}} \\
&= \$50(\text{PVAIF}) + \$1{,}000(\text{PVIF}) \\
&= \$50(7.360) + \$1{,}000(.558) = \$926,
\end{aligned}
$$

where 7.360 and .558 are the interest factors for the present value of an annuity of a dollar and the present value of a dollar, respectively, both at 6 percent for ten years (Appendixes D and B, respectively).

This example illustrates that many investments may involve both a series of payments (the annuity component) and a lump sum payment. This particular investment is similar to a bond, the valuation of which is discussed in Chapter 9.

The previous examples illustrate the use of interest tables. These problems could be done without such tables, but the amount of calculation would be substantial. The use of interest tables obviously expedites work on any problems that are somewhat involved. Students with access to computer programs or pocket calculators will find these to be excellent substitutes for interest tables. Some electronic calculators have been programmed to include interest tables. Other calculators may be used to determine the appropriate interest factor.

APPLICATIONS OF THE TIME VALUE OF MONEY

Throughout the remainder of this text there will be numerous applications of the concept of the time value of money. This concept plays an exceedingly crucial role in finance because so many decisions must be made today while the returns occur many years into the future. For example, understanding the time value of money and the processes of discounting and compounding are prerequisites to understanding the process of selecting long-term investments (i.e., capital budgeting). Suppose the financial manager is faced with the following investments and must choose among them:

A: Generates $275 a year for five years.
B: Generates $300 a year for two years and $250 for three years.
C: Generates $1,600 at the end of the fifth year.

While each investment has a life of five years, the timing of the cash flows generated by each investment differs. How will the financial manager compare the three investments in order to choose among them?

The time value of money is one means to facilitate the necessary comparison. If the financial manager computes the present value of each cash flow, the investments may be compared. If, for example, the cost of funds is 10 percent annually, the present value of each investment is

A: $275(3.791) = $1,042.53.
B: $300(.909) + 300(.826) + 250(.751) + 250(.683) + 250(.621)
= $1,034.25.
C: $1,600(.621) = $993.50.

Having determined the present value of each cash flow, the financial manager now knows that Investment A has the highest present value and should be preferred.[3]

Time value also has numerous illustrations for individuals. Suppose you purchase a home for $100,000, making a down payment of 20 percent ($20,000) and borrowing the balance ($80,000). The mortgage loan is for 25 years and the bank charges 10 percent. What is your annual payment required by this loan? (Mortgage payments are usually made monthly, but to keep this illustration simple, assume the payment is made at the end of each year.) This is a common application of the time value of money, and even if the lender makes the calculation, the individual can perform the following calculation to determine approximately what the mortgage payment will be prior to asking for the loan.

[3]The same ranking could be made by comparing the future values of the cash flows at the end of the fifth year.

In some way this problem is harder than those previously used to illustrate the time value of money. In the previous examples used to illustrate the present value of an annuity, the amount of the annuity was given, and the example asked for the present value of the annuity. In this case, the present value of the annuity is given and the annual amount is the unknown. As with all time value problems, identify the known variables. They are the amount borrowed in the present (\$80,000), the rate of interest (10 percent), and the term of the loan (25 years). The unknown is the annual payment required to pay the interest and retire the loan. Since the payments will be made at the end of each year, the mortgage is an illustration of an ordinary annuity. Since the loan is being made in the present, the problem requires the use of the present value interest table. That is

$$\$80{,}000 = A(\text{PVAIF}10\%{,}25\text{Y})$$
$$\$80{,}000 = A(9.077)$$
$$A = \frac{\$80{,}000}{9.077} = \$8{,}813.48.$$

Thus, the annual mortgage payment is \$8,813.48.

Ask yourself, "Does this answer make sense?" If you make twenty-five payments of \$8,813.48, the total amount paid is

$$25 \times \$8{,}813.48 = \$220{,}337.$$

That's a lot of money, but remember you are paying interest for twenty-five years and are retiring a loan of \$80,000, so the answer is reasonable. It still may be wrong if you selected the wrong interest factor (e.g., the present value of an annuity at 10 percent for twenty years).

If you had set up the problem incorrectly, the answer would make no sense. For example, suppose you thought the problem concerned the future value of an annuity since the payments are made in the future. While that is incorrect, it is easy to fall into that trap. However, when you divide \$80,000 by the interest factor for the future value of an annuity (98.347), the answer is \$813.45. This answer makes no sense, because after making twenty-five payments of \$813.45, your total payments would only be \$20,336, which obviously does not retire the \$80,000 loan. You should always ask yourself upon completing the problem, "Does the answer make sense?" If it does, your reasoning should be correct even if your eyes selected the wrong interest factor or you made an arithmetic error.

Now that we know your annual payment required to make the loan is \$8,813.48, you may wish to split the payment into the interest payment and the principal repayment. This division may be important, since you may be able to deduct the interest payment on the mortgage for federal income taxation. Since the interest rate is 10 percent and the initial amount of the loan is \$80,000, the interest during the first year is \$8,000.

The balance of the payment ($813.48) reduces the amount owed to $79,186.52.

Since the amount owed is reduced, the interest paid during the second year declines to $7,918.65 (.1 × $79,186.52). Since the annual payment remains $8,813.48, the balance owed is reduced by $894.83 ($8,813.48 − 7,918.65), so the balance owed after the second year is $78,291.69. This type of calculation is used to generate a repayment schedule, which is referred to as a loan amortization schedule.

Such a schedule is illustrated in Exhibit 7.3. The first column gives the number of the payment, and the second and third columns break the payment into the payments for interest and principal repayment. The last column gives the balance due on the loan. As may be seen from the table, as payments are made (1) the amount of the outstanding principal declines, (2) the amount of interest paid each month declines, and (3) the rate at which the principal is repaid increases. In the early years of a mortgage, most of the payment covers the interest charges, but during the later life of the mortgage most of the payment retires the principal.

In the first application illustrated in this section, the financial manager used time value to compare three investments. In the second application a potential homeowner used the concept to determine the repayment of a mortgage loan. Many more applications are given in the problems at the end of this chapter. However, before leaving this section, let's consider one final application. Suppose your 85-year-old Auntie Bea has to enter a nursing home that charges $2,000 a month (i.e., $24,000 a year). You have power of attorney and sell her home for $115,000. Excluding any other sources of income (e.g., social security payments) and any other expenses (e.g., doctors), how long will her money last if you are able to earn 8 percent annually? This may strike you as a morbid situation, but it is a very real problem facing many elderly individuals and their families. Actually your Auntie Bea is better off than many elderly. She had a house and was able to live in it until the age 85.

Once again this problem is an illustration of an annuity. The known variables are (1) the amount of money she has in the present ($115,000), (2) the rate of interest she will earn on the funds (8 percent), and (3) the amount of the annuity payment ($24,000). The unknown is the number of years that the funds will last. Since she has the money now, this is another illustration of the present value of an annuity. Auntie Bea's problem is set up as follows:

$$\$115{,}000 = \$24{,}000(\text{PVAIF}8\%,n)$$

$$\text{PVAIF} = \frac{\$115{,}000}{\$24{,}000} = 4.792.$$

Looking up this factor in the table for the present value of an annuity at 8 percent derives an answer of six to seven years. Auntie Bea's assets will

EXHIBIT 7.3

Selections from a Loan Amortization Schedule for an $80,000 Mortgage at 10 Percent for 25 Years (Annual Payment = $8,813.48)

Number of Payment	Interest Payment	Principal Repayment	Balance of Loan
1	$8,000.00	$813.48	$79,186.52
2	7,918.65	894.83	78,291.69
3	7,829.17	984.31	77,307.38
—			
—			
12	6,492.59	2,320.89	62,605.01
13	6,260.50	2,552.98	60,052.03
—			
—			
24	1,529.64	7,283.84	8,012.60
25	801.26	8,012.22	.00

With a conventional mortgage, the monthly payments do not change. The amount of interest diminishes and the principal repayment increases with each additional payment.

cover the nursing home until after she reaches the age of 91. Since life expectancy for a female age 85 is about 6.5 to 7.0 years, Auntie Bea is in relatively good shape financially. Of course, if she lives longer than her life expectancy, there may be a financial problem unless a greater rate of return can be earned on her funds or she has other sources of income.

NONANNUAL COMPOUNDING

The student should have noticed that in the previous examples compounding occurred only once a year. Compounding can and often does occur more frequently, such as twice a year (or semiannually). **Nonannual compounding** requires that the equations presented earlier be adjusted. This section extends the discussion of the compound value of a dollar to include compounding for time periods other than a year.

Nonannual compounding
Payment of interest more frequently than once a year

This discussion, however, is limited to the future value of a dollar. Similar adjustments must be made in the future value of an annuity, the present value of a dollar, or present value of an annuity when the funds are compounded more frequently than annually. These adjustments are not explained here but may be found in specialized texts concerning the time value of money.[4]

[4] See, for instance, Gary Clayton and Christopher B. Spivey, *The Time Value of Money* (Philadelphia: W. B. Saunders Co., 1978), or Robert Cissell, Helen Cissell, and David Flaspohler, *The Mathematics of Finance*, 7th ed. (Boston: Houghton Mifflin Co., 1986).

Converting annual compounding to other time periods necessitates two adjustments in Equation 7.1. These adjustments are not particularly difficult. First, a year is divided into the same number of time periods as the funds that are being compounded. For semiannual compounding a year consists of two time periods, whereas for quarterly compounding the year comprises four time periods.

After adjusting for the number of time periods, the individual adjusts the interest rate to find the rate per time period. This is done by dividing the stated interest rate by the number of time periods per year. If the interest rate is 8 percent compounded semiannually, 8 percent is divided by 2, giving an interest rate of 4 percent earned in *each* time period. If the annual rate of interest is 8 percent compounded quarterly, the interest rate is 2 percent (0.08 ÷ 4) in each of the four time periods.

These adjustments may be expressed in more formal terms by modifying Equation 7.4 as follows:

7.13
$$P_0\left(1 + \frac{i}{c}\right)^{n\times c} = P_n.$$

The only new symbol is c, which represents the frequency of compounding. The interest rate (i) is divided by the frequency of compounding (c) to determine the interest rate in each period. The number of years (n) is multiplied by the frequency of compounding to determine the number of time periods.

The application of this equation may be illustrated by a simple example. An individual invests \$100 in an asset that pays 8 percent compounded quarterly. What will the future value of this asset be after five years? In other words, \$100 will grow to what amount after five years if it is compounded quarterly at 8 percent? Algebraically, that is

$$\begin{aligned} P_5 &= P_0\left(1 + \frac{i}{c}\right)^{n\times c} \\ &= \$100\left(1 + \frac{0.08}{4}\right)^{5\times 4} \\ &= \$100(1 + 0.02)^{20}. \end{aligned}$$

In this formulation the investor is earning 2 percent for 20 time periods. To solve this equation, the interest factor for the compound value of a dollar at 2 percent for 20 periods (1.486) is multiplied by \$100. Thus, the future value is

$$P_5 = \$100(1.486) = \$148.60.$$

The difference between compounding annually and compounding more frequently can be seen by comparing this problem with a problem in which the values are identical except that the interest is compounded annually. The question is then, \$100 will grow to what amount after five years at 8 percent compounded annually? The answer is

$$\begin{aligned} P_5 &= \$100(1 + 0.08)^5 \\ &= \$100(1.469) \\ &= \$146.90. \end{aligned}$$

This sum, \$146.90, is less than the amount that was earned when the funds were compounded quarterly. We may conclude that the more frequently interest is compounded, the greater will be the future amount.

ELECTRONIC CALCULATORS

Once a student has mastered the concepts of future value and present value and understands how the amounts are determined, the tedium associated with the actual calculations may be reduced through the use of electronic calculators programmed to solve time value problems. Even if your electronic calculator is not preprogrammed to perform these types of problems, you may still be able to derive the interest factors for the future value of a dollar and the present value of a dollar. This derivation requires that the calculator have the exponent key (y^x).

The equation for the interest factor for the future value of a dollar (FVIF) is

7.5 $$\text{FVIF} = (1 + i)^n.$$

To find the interest factor for 6 percent for three years [i.e., $(1 + .06)^3$], first enter 1 plus the interest rate: 1.06. The display should read 1.06. Next, raise this amount to the third power, which is achieved by striking the y^x key and the number 3. Press "equal," and the display should read 1.1910, which is the interest factor that may be found in Appendix A under the column for 6 percent and three years.

The equation for the interest factor for the present value of a dollar (PVIF) is

7.7 $$\text{PVIF} = \frac{1}{(1 + i)^n}.$$

The interest factor for the present value is the reciprocal of the interest factor for the future value of \$1. To derive the interest factor for the present value of a dollar at 6 percent for three years, do the above steps used to determine the future value of a dollar and then take the reciprocal. If the calculator has the $1/x$ key, press this key, and the reciprocal is automatically determined. If the calculator lacks this key, the reciprocal is found by dividing 1 by the number derived above. In the above illustration, the reciprocal for 1.191 is .8396 (1/1.191), which is the interest factor for the present value of a dollar at 6 percent for three years. You may verify this number by looking under the column for the present value of a dollar at 6 percent for three years in Appendix B, which gives the interest factor as .840. The difference is, of course, the result of rounding.

The above discussion indicates that the interest factors for the future value of a dollar and the present value of a dollar may be derived using an electronic calculator. However, the derivation of the interest factors for the future value of an annuity and the present value of an annuity can be quite tedious. These calculations require adding individual interest factors for each year. For example, the interest factor for the present value of an ordinary annuity for 20 years requires summing 20 different interest factors for the present value of $1. In such a case, even if the electronic calculator is used to derive the interest factors, adding the individual interest factors may be impractical.

Fortunately, there is a simpler method. The equation for the interest factor for the future value of an annuity (FVAIF) is

7.10

$$\text{FVAIF} = \frac{(1 + i)^n - 1}{i}.$$

Thus if the interest rate is 5 percent and the number of years is four, then the interest factor is

$$\text{FVAIF} = \frac{(1 + 0.05)^4 - 1}{0.05} = \frac{1.2155 - 1}{0.05} = 4.310,$$

which is the same number found in the table for the future value of an annuity for four years at 5 percent.

The equation for the interest factor for the present value of an annuity (PVAIF) is

7.12n

$$\text{PVAIF} = \frac{1 - \dfrac{1}{(1 + i)^n}}{i}.$$

If the interest rate is 6 percent and the number of years is three, then the interest factor is

$$\text{PVAIF} = \frac{1 - \dfrac{1}{(1 + 0.06)^3}}{0.06} = \frac{1 - .8396}{0.06} = 2.673,$$

which is the interest factor found in the table for the present value of an annuity at 6 percent for three years.

In addition to facilitating the calculation of interest factors, the electronic calculator also offers a major advantage over the use of interest tables. While more detailed tables may be available, most interest tables are limited to exact rates (e.g., 5 percent) and whole years (e.g., 6 years). Unless the individual interpolates between the given interest factors, the tables cannot provide the interest factor for 6.7 percent for 5 years and 3 months. However, this interest factor can be determined by using the electronic calculator. The interest factor for the future value of $1 at 6.7 percent for 5 years and 3 months may be found as follows:

1) Enter 1.067.
2) Raise 1.067 by 5.25 (i.e., $y^x = 1.067^{5.25}$).
3) Press "equal" to derive the interest factor: 1.4056.

Thus if $100 is invested at 6.7 percent, compounded annually for 5 years and 3 months, the future value is $140.56.

While electronic calculators may ease the burden of the arithmetic, they cannot set up the problems to be solved. You must still determine if the problem concerns future value or present value and whether the problem deals with a lump sum or an annuity. Since failure to set up the problem correctly will only lead to incorrect results, it is imperative that the student be able to determine what is being used and which of the various cases apply to the individual problem.

SUMMARY

Money has time value. A dollar to be received in the future is worth less than a dollar received today. People will forgo current consumption only if future growth in their funds is possible. Such appreciation is called compounding. The longer the funds compound and the higher the rate at which they compound, the greater will be the amount of funds in the future.

The opposite of compounding is discounting, which determines the present value of funds that are to be received in the future. The present value of a future sum depends both on how far in the future the funds are to be received and on the discount rate.

Compounding and discounting are applied both to single payments and to series of payments. If the payments in a series are equal and are made annually, the series is called an annuity.

The ability to compare future dollars with present dollars is crucial to financial decision making. Many financial decisions involve the current outlay of funds, for investments are made in the present. The returns on these investments occur in the future. The concepts presented in this chapter are basic to an understanding of both capital budgeting (Chapter 23) and the valuation of securities (Chapters 9–12).

Review Questions

1. What is the difference between a lump-sum payment and an annuity? Are all series of payments annuities?
2. What is the difference between compounding (i.e., the determination of future value) and discounting (i.e., the determination of present value)?
3. For a given interest rate, what happens to the numerical value of the interest factor as time increases for the
   a. future value of a dollar;
   b. future value of an annuity;
   c. present value of a dollar;
   d. present value of an annuity?
4. For a given time period, what happens to the numerical value of the interest factor as the interest rate increases for the
   a. future value of a dollar;
   b. future value of an annuity;
   c. present value of a dollar;
   d. present value of an annuity?
5. What does the phrase "discounting the future at a high rate" imply?
6. As is explained in subsequent chapters, increases in interest rates cause the value of assets to decline. Why would you expect this relationship?

Problems

Solving time value of money problems may be facilitated by the use of computer programs. The *Profit+* programs will certainly ease the calculations necessary to answer the following problems. However, you must realize that the computer may not answer the specific question being asked. For example, consider the following problem: "How much interest is earned if $1 is invested at 5 percent for ten years?" The computer program will give you the amount to which $1 will grow at 5 percent for ten years. You will have to determine how much of the total is interest earned.

While using the computer will ease the calculations, you should not lose sight of the concept being illustrated by the problem. If all you are doing is plugging in numbers and having the computer crank out answers, then you are not learning the mechanics or the concepts. Perhaps the best way to use the computer in a principles or foundation course is first to do the problems (to make certain that you understand the mechanics and concepts) and then repeat the problems using the computer to check your calculations and answers. This strategy, of course, requires more effort on your part, but you learn more (i.e., you learn the mechanics, the concepts, and the computer applications).

You should also realize that computer programs may have specific names for particular calculations. It may appear that no program applies to the particular question being asked. For example, a problem may ask for a rate of interest (i.e., "$1 grew to $2.50 in seven years. What was the rate of interest?"). To answer this problem, you may have to use the program that computes rates of return. In effect the problem becomes: "You invested $1 and after seven years received

$2.50. What was the rate of return on the investment?" Thus, using the computer may require some ingenuity or willingness to experiment to determine which of the programs applies to a specific problem. (Another possible difficulty you may have is the distinction between an ordinary annuity and an annuity due. The following annuity problems are ordinary annuities.)

1. A saver places $1,000 in a certificate of deposit that matures after ten years and pays 7 percent interest, which is compounded annually until the certificate matures.
   a. How much interest will the saver earn if the interest is left to accumulate?
   b. How much interest will the saver earn if the interest is withdrawn each year?
2. A self-employed person deposits $1,500 annually in a retirement account that earns 8 percent.
   a. How much will be in the account when the individual retires at the age of 65 if the savings program starts when the person is age 45?
   b. How much additional money will be in the account if the saver defers retirement until age 70 and continues the annual contributions?
   c. How much additional money will be in the account if the saver discontinues the contributions but does not retire until age 70?
3. A 40-year-old man decides to put funds into a retirement plan. He can save $2,000 a year and earn 7 percent on this savings. How much will he have accumulated when he retires at age 65? At retirement how much can he withdraw each year for 20 years from his accumulated savings if his savings continue to earn 7 percent?

(Problems 2 and 3 illustrate the basic elements of pension plans. A sum of money is systematically set aside. It earns interest so that by retirement a considerable amount has been accumulated. Then the retired person draws on the fund until it is exhausted (or until death occurs, in which case the remainder of the fund becomes part of the estate). Of course, while the retired person draws on the fund, the remaining principal continues to earn interest. Federal income tax laws permit workers who are not covered by pension plans to set up their own plans through a financial institution such as a commercial bank. These plans not only permit the building of retirement funds but also defer federal income taxes.)

4. If a father wants to have $50,000 to send a child to college, how much must he invest annually for 18 years if he earns 9 percent on his funds?
   (Any current student who subsequently becomes a parent and wants to send a child to college should make this calculation early in the child's life.)
5. An investment offers $10,000 per year for 20 years. If an investor can earn 6 percent on other investments, what is the current value of this investment? If its current price is $120,000, should the investor buy it?
6. A company has two investment possibilities, with the following flows of cash:

	Year 1	Year 2	Year 3
A	$1,400	$1,700	$1,800
B	1,500	1,500	1,500

If the firm can earn 7 percent in other investments, what is the present value of investments A and B? If each investment costs $4,000, is the present value of each investment greater than the cost of the investment? (This question is a very simple example of one method of capital budgeting [Chapter 23]. This technique permits the firm to rank alternative investments and help select the potentially most profitable investment.)

7. a. If a person currently earns $10,000 and inflation continues at 8 percent for ten years, how much must the person make to maintain purchasing power?

   b. If a person bought a $50,000 home in 1970 and sold it in 2000, what would be the value of the house if the annual rate of inflation were 8 percent during the 30 years?

(These questions show the potential impact of inflation. Annual price increases may not be substantial. However, when they are compounded over a period of years, the effect can be astounding.)

8. You purchase a stock for $20 and expect its price to grow annually at a rate of 6 percent.
   a. What price are you expecting after five years?
   b. If the rate of increase in the price doubled from 6 percent to 12 percent, would that double the *increase* in the price? Why?

9. A person has an individual retirement account (IRA) and deposits $2,000 in the account annually for 20 years.
   a. If the funds earn 10 percent annually, how much will be in the account in 20 years?
   b. If an alternative IRA account offers 12 percent annually, how much additional interest would be earned in this alternative account?

10. An investment offers to pay you $10,000 a year for five years. If it costs $33,520, what will be your rate of return on the investment?

11. An investment costs $36,875 and offers a return of 10 percent annually for ten years. What are the annual cash flows (i.e., profits plus the repayment of the initial investment) anticipated from this investment?

12. You are offered $900 after five years or $150 a year for five years. If you can earn 6 percent on your funds, which offer will you accept? If you can earn 14 percent on your funds, which offer will you accept? Why are your answers different?

13. The Phillies currently have 30,000 spectators per game and anticipate annual growth in attendance of 9%. If Veteran's Stadium holds 55,000 people, how long will it take to fill up the stadium?

14. You are offered an annuity that will pay $10,000 a year for ten years, starting after five years have elapsed. If you seek an annual return of 12 percent, what is the maximum amount you should pay for this annuity?

15. You want your salary to double in six years. At what annual rate of growth must your salary increase to achieve your goal?

16. Each year you invest $2,000 in an account that earns 10 percent annually. How long will it take for you to accumulate $40,000?

17. Auntie Bea sells her house for $100,000, which is then invested to earn 10 percent annually. If her life expectancy is ten years, what is the maximum amount she can annually spend on a nursing home, doctors, and taxes?
18. You bought a house for $50,000 and sold it after five years for $88,000. What was the annual rate of growth in the value of the house?
19. You win a judgment in an auto accident for $100,000. You immediately receive $25,000 but must pay your lawyer's fee of $15,000. In addition, you will receive $2,500 a year for 20 years for a total of $50,000, after which the balance owed ($25,000) will be paid. If the interest rate is 12 percent, what is the current value of your settlement?
20. A firm must choose between two investment alternatives each costing $100,000. The first alternative generates $35,000 a year for four years. The second pays one large lump sum of $157,400 at the end of the fourth year. If the firm can raise the required funds to make the investment at an annual cost of 10 percent, which alternative should be preferred?

Funding a Pension Plan

Erin MacDowell was recently employed in the benefits division of a moderate size engineering firm. The firm has adopted a pension plan in which it promises to pay a maximum of 75 percent of an individual's last year salary if the employee has worked for the firm for twenty-five years. The amount of the pension is to be reduced by 3 percent for every year less than twenty-five, so that an individual who has been employed for fifteen years will receive a pension of 45 percent of the last year's salary [i.e., 75 percent − 10(3 percent)]. Pension payments will start at age sixty-five, provided the individual retired. There is no provision for early retirement. Continuing to work after age sixty-five may increase the individual's pension if he or she has worked for less than twenty-five years or if his or her salary were to increase.

One of the first tasks given Ms. MacDowell is to estimate the amount that the firm must set aside today to fund pensions. While management plans to hire actuaries to make the final determination, the managers believe the exercise may highlight some problems that they will want to be able to discuss with the actuaries. Ms. MacDowell was instructed to select two representative employees, estimate their annual pensions, and the annual contributions necessary to fund the pensions.

Ms. MacDowell decided to select Arnold Berg and Vanessa Barber. Berg is 58 years old, has been with the firm for twenty-seven years, and is earning $34,000. Ms. Barber is 47, has been with the firm for three years, and earns $42,000 annually. Ms. MacDowell believes that Berg will be with the firm until he retires; he is a competent worker whose salary will not increase by more than 4 percent annually, and it is anticipated he will retire at age 65. Ms. Barber is considerably different. A rising star, Ms. MacDowell expects Ms. Barber's salary to rise at least 7 percent annually in order to retain her until retirement at age 65.

To determine the amount that must be invested annually to fund the pension, Ms. MacDowell needs (in addition to an estimate of the amount of the pension) an estimate of how long the pension will be distributed (i.e., life expectancy) and how much the invested funds will earn. Since the firm must pay an interest rate of 8 percent to borrow money, she decides that the invested funds should be able to earn at least that amount.

Case Problems

1. If each individual retires at age 65, how much will be their estimated pensions if life expectancy is fifteen years?
2. If the firm buys an annuity from an insurance company to fund each pension and the insurance company asserts it is able to earn 9 percent on the funds invested in the annuity, what is the amount required to purchase the annuity contracts?
3. If the firm can earn 8 percent on the money it must invest annually to fund the pension, how much will the firm have to invest annually to have the money necessary to purchase the annuities?
4. What would be the impact of each of the following on the amount that the firm must invest annually to fund the pension?
   a. life expectancy is increased to twenty years
   b. the rate of interest on the annuity contract with the insurance company is reduced to 7 percent
   c. Ms. Barber retires at age 62 instead of 65

Suggested Readings

Cissell, Robert, Helen Cissell, and David Flaspohler. *Mathematics of Finance.* 7th ed. Boston: Houghton Mifflin Co., 1986.

This is a basic text that explains many of the variations on the time value of money.

Clayton, Gary, and Christopher B. Spivey. *The Time Value of Money.* Philadelphia: W. B. Saunders Co., 1978.

This is a primer illustrating many problems that can be solved by the basic time value of money tables.

Access to pocket calculators has greatly facilitated time value calculations. To increase your ability to use these calculators, consult:

Smith, Jon M. *Financial Analysis and Business Decisions on the Pocket Calculator.* New York: John Wiley and Sons, 1976.

For a reference book on time value of money calculations that includes loan amortization tables and mortgage balance tables, acquire:

Charles J. Woelfel. *The Desktop Guide to Money, Time, Interest and Yields.* Chicago: Probus Publishing, 1986.

Ordinary Annuities and Annuities Due

Annuity payments may be made at the beginning or at the end of the year. If the payments are made at the end of the year, such annuities are called ordinary annuities. These annuities should be differentiated from annuities due, in which the payments are made at the beginning of the year. This difference in the timing of payments may be seen in the following time lines for an annuity of $100 for three years.

Time	1/1/x1	12/31/x1	1/1/x2	12/31/x2	1/1/x3	12/31/x3
Payments:						
Ordinary Annuity	—	$100	—	$100	—	$100
Annuity Due	$100	—	$100	—	$100	—

In each annuity, three $100 payments are made; however, in the ordinary annuity, the payments occur at the end of the year while the annuity due payments occur at the beginning of the year.

THE FUTURE VALUE OF AN ANNUITY DUE

The impact of the difference in the timing of payments (deposits) was illustrated in Exhibit 7.1. In both cases $100 is deposited for three years in a savings account that pays 5 percent annually. The top half of the exhibit illustrated the annuity due, while the bottom half illustrated the ordinary annuity. In both cases, three years elapse from the present to the time when the final amount is determined, and in each case three payments are made. The difference in the timing of the payments results in a difference in the interest earned. Since payments for an annuity due are made at the beginning of each year, the annuity earns more interest ($31.01 versus $15.25) and thus has the higher terminal value ($331.01 versus $315.25).

The equations for the determination of the future values of an ordinary annuity and an annuity due were given in the body of the chapter. When applied to the previous example in which i = 5 percent = .05, n = 3 years, and A = $100, the accumulated sum for the future value of the ordinary annuity was

$$\$100(1 + 0.05)^0 + 100(1 + 0.05)^1 + 100(1 + 0.05)^2 =$$
$$\$100 + 105 + 110.25 = \$315.25.$$

The accumulated sum for the future value of the annuity due was

$$\$100(1 + 0.05)^1 + 100(1 + 0.05)^2 + 100(1 + 0.05)^3 =$$
$$\$105 + 110.25 + 115.76 = \$331.01$$

While it is possible to calculate the future sum of an ordinary annuity or an annuity due by performing each calculation and summing them, that technique is obviously tedious. This chapter used an interest table presented in Appendix C to facilitate the calculation of the future sum for an ordinary annuity, but the interest factors presented in that table presented in Appendix C to facilitate the calculation of the future value for an ordinary annuity, but the interest factors presented in that table may be converted into the interest factors for an annuity due. That deposited annually in the savings account for three years, the interest factor for the ordinary annuity was 3.152. This interest factor may be converted for an annuity due at 5 percent for three years by multiplying 3.152 by 1 + 0.05. That is,

$$3.152(1 + 0.05) = 3.3096$$

When this interest factor is applied to the example of \$100 deposited in the bank at 5 percent for three years with the deposits starting immediately, the resulting terminal value is

$$\$100(3.3096) = \$330.96$$

This is the same answer as derived by making each calculation individually and summing them. (Once again the small difference in the two answers is the result of rounding off.)

The difference between the terminal value of the two kinds of annuity payments can be quite substantial as the number of years increases or the interest rate rises. Consider an individual retirement account (IRA) in which the saver places \$2,000 annually for 20 years. If the deposits are made at the end of the year (an ordinary annuity) and the rate of interest is 7 percent, the terminal amount will be

$$\$2,000(40.995) = \$81,990.$$

However, if the deposits had been made at the beginning of each year (an annuity due), the terminal amount would be

$$\$2,000(40.995)(1 + 0.07) = \$87,729.30.$$

The difference is \$5,739.30! Almost \$6,000 in additional interest is earned if the deposits are made at the beginning, not at the end, of each year.

The difference between the ordinary annuity and the annuity due becomes even more dramatic if the interest rate rises. Suppose the above

IRA offered 12 percent instead of 7 percent. If the deposits are made at the end of each year, the terminal value is

$$\$2{,}000(72.052) = \$144{,}104.$$

If the deposits are made at the beginning of the year, the terminal value will be

$$\$2{,}000(72.052)(1 + 0.12) = \$161{,}396.48$$

The difference is now $17,292.48.

THE PRESENT VALUE OF AN ANNUITY DUE

The present value of an annuity, like the future value of an annuity, is affected by the timing of the payments. Many payments in finance are received at the end of the time period and thus are ordinary annuities. There are, however, payments that may occur at the beginning of the time period, such as the distributions from a pension plan; these would be examples of annuities due.

The difference in the flow of payments and the determination of the present values of an ordinary annuity and an annuity due are illustrated in Exhibit 7A.1. In each case the annuity is for $2,000 a year for three years and the interest rate is 10 percent. In the top half of the exhibit, the payments are made at the end of the year (an ordinary annuity),

EXHIBIT 7A.1

Flow of Payments and Determination of the Present Value of an Ordinary Annuity and an Annuity Due at 10 Percent for Three Years

The present value of an annuity is larger if the payments are made at the beginning of the year.

Ordinary Annuity

1/1/x0	1/1/x1	1/1/x2	1/1/x3
$1,818 ←	(0.909) 2,000		
1,652 ←		(0.826) 2,000	
1,502 ←			(0.751) 2,000
$4,972			

Annuity Due

1/1/x0	1/1/x1	1/1/x2	1/1/x3
$2,000			
1,818 ←	(0.909) 2,000		
1,652 ←		(0.826) 2,000	
$5,470			

while in the bottom half of the exhibit, the payments are made at the beginning of the year (an annuity due). As may be seen by the totals, the present value of the annuity due is higher ($5,470 versus $4,972). This is because the payments are received sooner and, hence, are more valuable. As may also be seen in the illustration, since the first payment of the annuity due is made immediately, its present value is the actual amount received. Because the first payment of the ordinary annuity is made at the end of the first year, that amount is discounted, and, hence, its present value is less than the actual amount received.

The interest tables for the present value of an annuity presented in this text (and in other finance and investment texts) apply to ordinary annuities. These interest factors may be converted into annuity due factors by multiplying them by $(1 + i)$. Thus the interest factor for the present value of an ordinary annuity for $1 at 10 percent for three years (2.487) may be converted into the interest factor for an annuity due of $1 at 10 percent for three years as follows:

$$2.487(1 + i) = 2.487(1 + 0.1) = 2.736.$$

When this interest factor is used to determine the present value of an annuity due of $2,000 for three years at 10 percent, the present value is

$$\$2{,}000(2.736) = \$5{,}472.$$

The present value of an ordinary annuity of $2,000 at 10 percent for three years is

$$\$2{,}000(2.487) = \$4{,}974.$$

These are essentially the same answers given in Exhibit 7A.1 with the small differences being the result of rounding.

Problems

1. Bob places $2,000 in his retirement account at the end of each year, while Betty places $2,000 in her account at the beginning of each year. If they both earn 8 percent annually on their funds and make contributions for 20 years, how much will each have in his or her account?
2. Investment A offers to pay you $1,000 a year for ten years with the payments occurring at the end of each year. Investment B pays $925 a year for ten years, but the payments commence at the beginning of each year. If you can earn 10 percent on your funds, which investment should be preferred?
3. A parent decides to put aside $1,000 annually toward a child's education. If the investment is made for ten years and earns 9 percent annually, what is the difference in the final amount if the contribution is made at the beginning of the year instead of at the end of the year?

4. A firm is facing two possible financing alternatives. The first requires the payment of $1,000 a year at the end of the year for ten years. The second requires an annual payment of $940 for ten years, but the payments must be made at the beginning of each year. Which alternative is preferred if the firm earns 5 percent on its funds? Would your answer be different if the firm could earn 10 percent? Explain.

Risk and Its Measurement

Learning Objectives

1. Be able to compute the expected return on an investment.
2. Contrast the sources of risk.
3. Explain the impact that diversification has on the different sources of risk.
4. Differentiate the standard deviation and the beta coefficient as measures of risk.
5. Illustrate how beta coefficients are used to determine the required return on an investment.

In *War As I Knew It,* George Patton said, "Take calculated risks; that is quite different from being rash." Investors and financial managers should realize that since the future is uncertain, they too must take calculated risks. Purchasing the bonds of Trump Taj Mahal when the potential return exceeded 25 percent annually may have been rash because in 1991 the firm declared bankruptcy. Purchasing the bonds of AT&T, however, which offered less than 10 percent annually—a yield almost double what was available in a savings account, may have been a calculated but prudent risk.

The reward for bearing risk is the anticipated return. Until the 1950s, investors and financial analysts dealt with risk and return on an intuitive basis; there were no theoretical models to indicate the interrelationships between risk and return. However, a theory of portfolio behavior and measures of risk and return developed because of the work of several financial analysts.

This chapter gives a brief introduction to the sources and analysis of risk and its use in modern portfolio construction. Risk may be measured by a standard deviation, which measures the dispersion around a central tendency, such as an average return. Risk may also be measured by a beta coefficient, which is an index of the volatility of a security's return relative to the return on the market. Much of this chapter is devoted to these measures of risk and the reduction of risk through diversification. The chapter ends with a discussion of the use of beta coefficients in the capital asset pricing model to help determine the required return that is necessary to justify the purchase of a common stock.

THE EXPECTED RETURN ON AN INVESTMENT

All investments are made in anticipation of a return. This applies not only to individuals but also to the financial managers of firms. An investment may offer a return from either of two sources. The first is the flow of income. A savings account yields the holder a flow of interest income while the account is held. The second source of return is capital appreciation. If an investor buys stock and its price subsequently increases, the investor will receive a capital gain. All investments offer the investor either potential income and/or capital appreciation. Some investments, like the savings account, offer only income, whereas other investments such as an investment in land, may offer only capital appreciation. In fact, some investments may require expenditures (e.g., property tax) on the part of the investor.

When the individual or financial manager makes an investment, a return is anticipated. The yield that is achieved on the investment is not known until after the investment is sold and converted to cash. It is important to differentiate between *the expected return* and *the realized return.* The expected return is the incentive for accepting risk, and it must be compared with the **required return,** which is the return necessary to induce that investor to bear the risk associated with a particular investment. The required return includes (1) what the investor may earn on alternative investments, such as the risk-free return available on Trea-

equired return ▲
eturn necessary to induce
individual to make an
vestment

sury bills,[1] and (2) a premium for bearing risk that includes compensation for the expected inflation rate and for fluctuations in security prices. A detailed description of this required return, however, requires a measurement of risk. Thus, specification of the required return will be deferred until after the discussion of the measures of risk.

Expected return depends on individual expected outcomes and the probability of their occurrence. For example, an investor may say, "Under normal economic conditions, which occur 60 percent of the time, I expect to earn a return of 10 percent on an investment in this stock. However, there is a 20 percent chance the economy will grow more rapidly and the company will do exceptionally well, in which case I will earn 15 percent. Conversely, there is a 20 percent chance the economy will enter a recession and the company will do poorly, in which case I will earn only 5 percent." Given the possible outcomes and their probabilities, what is the return this investor can anticipate?

The answer to this question depends on the outcomes and the probability of their occurring (i.e., the probability of the economy growing more rapidly, growing at a normal rate, or entering into a recession). Since the investor believes these probabilities are 20 percent, 60 percent, and 20 percent, respectively, the expected return on the investment is

$$.2(15\%) + .6(10\%) + .2(5\%) = 10\%.$$

Notice that the expected return is a weighted average of the individual expected outcomes and the probability of occurrence. If the individual expected outcomes had been different, the expected return would differ. For example, if the investor had expected the returns to be 19 percent, 9 percent, and 2 percent, the expected return on the investment would be

$$.2(19\%) + .6(9\%) + .2(2\%) = 9.6\%$$

If the probabilities had been different, the expected return would also differ. If, in the first illustration, the probabilities had been 15 percent, 50 percent, and 35 percent, the expected return would be

$$.15(15\%) + .5(10\%) + .35(5\%) = 9\%$$

Thus, a change in either the expected returns of the individual outcomes or their probability of occurrence causes the expected return on the investment to change.

---

[1]The features of Treasury bills are discussed in Chapter 19 on the management of short-term assets.

RISK AND ITS SOURCES

Risk is the uncertainty that the realized return will not equal the expected return. If there were no uncertainty, there would be no risk. In the real world, there is uncertainty which requires the financial manager or investor to analyze possible outcomes and assess the investment's risk. Of course, the realized outcome may be better than expected, but the emphasis in the analysis of risk is on the negative: the outcome will be worse than expected.

As was explained in Chapter 1, there are several sources of risk. These are frequently classified into "diversifiable" risk and "nondiversifiable" risk or "unsystematic risk" and "systematic risk." (Both sets of terms are used to differentiate the sources of risk.) A diversifiable risk refers to the risk associated with the individual asset. Since the investor buys specific assets, such as the stock of IBM or the bonds of AT&T, that individual must bear the risk associated with each specific investment.

Unsystematic risk ▲
Risk associated with individual events that affect a particular asset; firm-specific risk that is reduced through the construction of diversified portfolios

The sources of diversifiable risk (i.e., **unsystematic risk**) are the business and financial risks associated with the individual firm. Business risk refers to the nature of the firm's operations, and financial risk refers to how the firm finances its assets (i.e., whether the firm uses a substantial or modest amount of debt financing). For example, the business risk associated with USAir is affected by such factors as the cost of fuel, the capacity of planes, and seasonal changes in demand. The financial risk associated with USAir depends on how it finances its planes. Were the assets acquired by leasing, by retaining earnings, or by issuing bonds, preferred stock, or common stock? The use of debt obligations and lease obligations increases financial risk while the use of equity financing reduces financial risk.

As is illustrated later in this chapter, the construction of a diversified portfolio significantly reduces diversifiable risk. This reduction occurs because the events that decrease the return on one asset may increase the return on another. Notice there is little relationship between the returns on the individual assets; hence the name "unsystematic risk."

The possible beneficial effect of combining different assets in a portfolio may be intuitively grasped by considering the purchase of the stocks of an airline and an oil driller (e.g., USAir and Schlumberger). Higher oil prices may reduce the earnings of the airline but increase the profits of the drilling operation. Lower oil prices may have the opposite impact; thus, combining the stocks of these two firms will reduce the risk associated with the portfolio. Of course, the risk associated with each individual asset remains the same, but from the investor's perspective, it is the risk associated with the portfolio that matters and not the risk associated with the individual asset.

While the previous illustration applies to an individual's portfolio, the same concept applies to a firm. The financial managers of firms also bear the risk associated with specific assets. A firm invests in particular pieces of inventory, acquires specialized plant and equipment, and extends credit to specific buyers which results in investments in accounts receivable. Inventory may not sell, equipment may become obsolete, and debtors may default. The financial manager thus bears the unsystematic risk associated with each individual asset acquired by the firm in much the same way that the individual bears the unsystematic risk associated with individual stocks and bonds.

Since firms face unsystematic risk, the advantages associated with diversification may also apply. For example, Chesapeake Corporation stated in its 1990 fourth-quarter report to stockholders that "our corporate strategy to move the company into more profitable and less volatile niche markets will be beneficial." Such a strategy reduces the unsystematic risk associated with the individual "niche" markets. Many mergers have been justified (perhaps rationalized) on the grounds that combining two firms with similar, but different, product lines will create a stronger firm with a better and more diversified assortment of goods and services for sale.

Even though a firm may seek a broader mix of products, diversification primarily remains the responsibility of investors. Firms cannot achieve as diversified a mix of assets that is possible in an individual's portfolio which can include real estate, savings accounts, collectibles, and shares in mutual funds as well as the stocks and bonds issued by a variety of firms and governments.

Nondiversifiable, **systematic risk** refers to those sources that are not reduced through the construction of a diversified portfolio. These include fluctuations in security prices, changes in interest rates, inflation, and fluctuations in exchange rates. Asset prices and returns tend to move together. If stock prices rise in general, the price of a specific security tends to rise in sympathy with the market. Conversely, if the market were to decline, the value of an individual security would also tend to fall. Thus there is a systematic relationship between the price of a specific common stock and the market as a whole. As long as the investor buys securities, that individual cannot avoid bearing this market risk.

Systematic risk ▲
Risk associated with fluctuations in security prices and other non-firm-specific factors; market risk that is not reduced through the construction of diversified portfolios

Asset values are also affected by changes in interest rates. As is explained in Chapter 9, rising interest rates depress the prices of fixed income securities, such as long-term bonds and preferred stock. Conversely, if interest rates fall, the value of these assets rises. There is a systematic negative relationship between the prices of fixed income securities and changes in interest rates. As long as the investor acquires fixed income securities, that individual must bear the risk associated with fluctuations in interest rates.

Investors and financial managers must also endure a third source of nondiversifiable systematic risk: the loss of purchasing power through inflation. It is obvious that rising prices of goods and services erode the purchasing power of both the investor's income and assets. Like fluctuat-

Financial Facts

Risk and Foreign Debt

The federal government obviously issues a large amount of debt to finance its deficits. Foreign governments also issue debt, especially the third world nations who use the funds for economic development. Prior to 1987, large American banks such as Citibank and Chase Manhattan purchased a substantial amount of these foreign obligations. During 1987, several Latin American countries suspended interest and principal repayments on their obligations. These defaults caused the value of the debt obligations to decline dramatically. In the late 1980s, the bonds issued by Argentina, Mexico, and Brazil could be purchased for about \$0.55 for \$1 worth of debt. Bonds issued by other countries, such as Nigeria, were selling for only \$0.30 to \$0.35 for \$1 worth of debt. • Obviously these debt obligations are very risky. There is no certainty that the nations will resume interest payments or that they will ever repay the debt. The social and political climate in these countries is unstable. A change in governments can lead to a repudiation of foreign obligations. In 1959, Fidel Castro nationalized assets held by American firms and repudiated Cuba's foreign debt. Cuban bonds remain outstanding and *still trade,* even though they were due over a decade ago. • Many Latin American countries, such as Mexico, have natural resources such as oil. Political stability and an increase in oil prices may result in a resumption of interest and principal repayments; such actions would certainly increase the value of these debt obligations and handsomely reward those individuals willing to accept the risk of owning debt obligations that are currently in default. •

---

ing security prices or changes in interest rates, there is nothing the individual can do to stop inflation, so the goal should be to earn a return that exceeds the rate of inflation. If the investor cannot earn such a return, he or she may benefit more from spending the funds and consuming goods now.

Some investors and the financial managers of most companies also must bear the risk associated with fluctuations in exchange rates. Any foreign investment, such as the purchase of a stock issued in Germany (e.g., the stock of Volkswagenwerk AG) or plant and equipment located in a foreign country, exposes the individual (or firm) to foreign exchange rate risk. Since these assets require swapping dollars for the foreign currency, the individual runs the risk that the value of foreign currency will change relative to the dollar. Of course, the change may be beneficial if the value of the foreign currency subsequently rises and thus purchases more dollars when the individual repatriates the funds.

There is little the individual can do to stop fluctuations in stock prices, interest rates, or inflation. Correspondingly, the individual cannot stop fluctuations in the value of foreign currencies. If the investor or financial manager acquires foreign assets (or if a firm issues abroad securities such as bonds), that individual or firm is exposed to foreign exchange rate risk. Individual investors may avoid this risk by limiting investments to domestic assets. However, many firms engage in foreign trade and thus must bear the risk associated with changes in the value of currencies.

While investors and financial managers cannot stop the forces that cause nondiversifiable, systematic risk (i.e., they cannot control fluctuations in the stock market, changes in interest rates, inflation, or fluctuating exchange rates), they may be able to manage these risks. Such management comes through the use of beta coefficients, which are explained later in this chapter, and futures contracts and option contracts, which are explained in Chapter 13.

The Standard Deviation as a Measure of Risk

As was stated earlier, risk is concerned with the uncertainty that the realized return the investor earns will not equal the expected return. One measure of risk, the **standard deviation,** places emphasis on the extent to which the return differs from the average or expected return. An alternative measure of risk, a **beta coefficient,** is an index of the return on an asset relative to the return on a portfolio of assets (e.g., the return on a stock relative to the return on the Standard and Poor's 500 stock index). This section considers the standard deviation as it is used to measure risk while beta coefficients are explained later in the chapter.

Standard deviation ▲
Measure of dispersion around an average value; a measure of risk

Beta coefficient ▲
Index of systematic risk; measure of the volatility of a stock's return relative to the market return

The standard deviation measures the dispersion around an average value. As applied to investments, it considers an average return and the extent to which individual returns deviate from the average. If there is very little difference between the average return and the individual returns, the dispersion will be small. If there is a large difference between the average return and the individual returns, the dispersion will be large. The larger this dispersion, the greater the risk associated with the investment.

This measurement is perhaps best illustrated by a simple example. Consider the returns on two mutual funds over a period of nine years:

Year	Return Fund A	Return Fund B
1	13.5%	11%
2	14	11.5
3	14.25	12
4	14.5	12.5
5	15	15
6	15.5	17.5
7	15.75	18
8	16	18.5
9	16.5	19
average return	15.0%	15.0%

The average return over the nine years is the same for both mutual funds, 15 percent, but annual returns differ. Mutual fund A's individual returns were close to the average return. The worst year generated a 13.5 percent return while the best year generated a 16.5 percent return. None of the individual returns deviated from the average by more than 1.5 percent. Mutual fund B's returns are considerably different from the average return, ranging from a low of 11 percent to a high of 19 percent. With the exception of year 5, all the returns deviate from the average by more than 1.5 percent.

Even though both mutual funds achieved the same average return, common sense suggests that B was riskier than A. The individual returns are more dispersed around the average return and this implies greater risk. The larger dispersion means there were periods with smaller returns (or larger losses, if applicable) from the investment. Of course, there were periods when the returns were greater which, of course, would be expected if the risk were greater, but even so, the average return from B only matched the average return from A.

How may this dispersion be measured? One possible answer is the standard deviation. Since the standard deviation measures the tendency of the individual returns to cluster around the average return, it may be used as a measure of risk. The larger the dispersion, the greater the standard deviation and the larger the risk associated with the particular investment.

The standard deviation is calculated as follows:

1. Subtract the individual observations from the average return.
2. Square this difference.
3. Add these squared differences.
4. Divide this sum by the number of observations less 1.
5. Take the square root.

For stock A the standard deviation is determined as follows:

Average Return	Individual Return	Difference	Difference Squared
15	13.50	1.5	2.2500
15	14	1	1.0000
15	14.25	0.75	0.5625
15	14.50	0.5	0.25
15	15	0	0
15	15.50	−0.5	0.25
15	15.75	−0.75	0.5625
15	16	−1	1.000
15	16.50	−1.5	2.2500
The sum of the squared differences:			8.1250

The sum of the squared differences divided by the number of observations less 1:

FIGURE 8.1

Distribution of the Returns of Two Mutual Funds

The more dispersed the returns, the larger is the standard deviation.

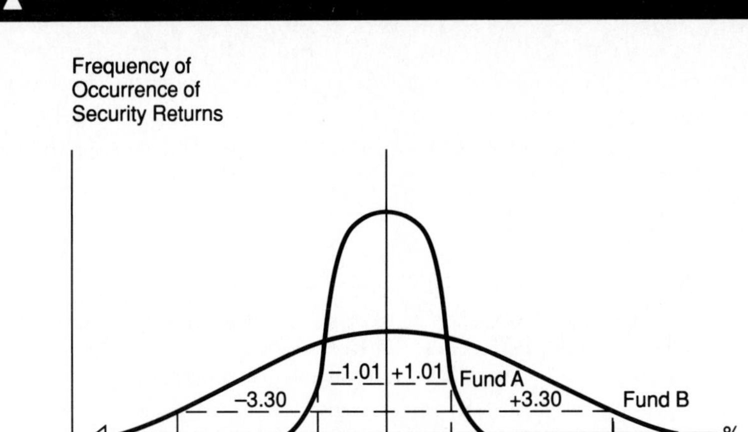

$$\frac{8.1250}{8} = 1.0156.$$

The square root: $\sqrt{1.0156} = \pm 1.01$.
Thus, the standard deviation is ± 1.01.

The investor must then interpret this result. Plus and minus one standard deviation has been shown for normal distributions to encompass approximately 68 percent of all observations (in this case, that is 68 percent of the returns). The standard deviation for stock A is ± 1.01, which means that approximately two-thirds of the returns fall between 13.99 and 16.01 percent. These returns are simply the average return (15 percent) plus 1.01 and minus 1.01 percent (i.e., plus and minus the standard deviation).

For stock B the standard deviation is ± 3.30, which means that approximately 68 percent of the returns fall between 11.7 percent and 18.3 percent. Fund B's returns have a wider dispersion from the average return, and this fact is indicated by a greater standard deviation.

These differences in the standard deviations are illustrated in Figure 8.1, which plots the various returns on the horizontal axis and the frequency of their occurrence on the vertical axis. While the example used only nine years, Figure 8.1 is drawn as if there were a large number of observations. Most of fund A's returns are close to the average return, so the frequency distribution is narrower and taller. The frequency distribution for B's returns is lower and wider, which indicates the greater dispersion in that fund's returns (i.e., the standard deviation for fund B is ± 3.30 versus ± 1.01 for A).

In the previous example historical returns were used to illustrate the standard deviation as a measure of risk. The same concept may be used to measure the risk associated with expected returns. Consider stock A; an investor believes there is a 20 percent chance of a 15 percent return, a 60 percent chance of a 10 percent return, and a 20 percent chance of a 5 percent return. The expected average return is 10 percent. However, there is dispersion around that expected return, and once again this dispersion may be measured by the standard deviation. In this case the calculation is as follows:

(1) Expected Average Return	(2) Expected Individual Return	(3) Difference (1) − (2)	(4) Difference Squared	(5) Probability of Occurrence	(6) Difference Squared Times the Probability (4) × (5)
10	15	−5	25	0.2	5.0
10	10	0	0	0.6	0.0
10	5	5	25	0.2	5.0
		Sum of the weighted squared differences:			10.0
		Square root of 10 (the standard deviation): ±3.162			

The standard deviation is ±3.162.

If the individual expected returns or the probabilities of occurrence were different, the standard deviation would be different. For example, if the individual expected returns for stock B were 20 percent, 10 percent, and 0 percent and the probabilities were the same, the expected return would be 10 percent (.2(20%) + .1(60%) + .0(20%) = 10%). The standard deviation around stock B's expected return is ±6.325. Since ±6.325 is larger than ±3.162, this indicates a larger dispersion in the expected return for stock B.

The larger dispersion around the expected return implies that the investment is riskier. The investor can be less certain of the return. The larger the dispersion, the greater is the chance of a smaller gain (or larger loss). Correspondingly, there is a greater chance of a larger return. However, this potential for increased gain is concomitant with bearing additional risk. Stock A involves less risk; it has the smaller dispersion. Since the expected returns on both stocks are the same, obviously stock A is to be preferred since it has less risk.

While the above discussion was limited to the return on an individual security and the dispersion around that return, the concepts can be applied to an entire portfolio. A portfolio also has an average return and dispersion around that return. The investor is concerned not only with the return and the risk associated with each investment, but also with the return and risk associated with the portfolio as a whole. This aggregate is, of course, the result of the individual investments and of each one's weight in the portfolio (i.e., the value of each asset, expressed in percentages, in proportion to the total value of the portfolio).

Consider a portfolio consisting of the following three stocks:

Stock	Return
1	8.3%
2	10.6
3	12.3

If 25 percent of the total value of the portfolio is invested in stocks 1 and 2 and 50 percent is invested in stock 3, the return is more heavily weighted in favor of stock 3. The return is a weighted average of each return times its proportion in the portfolio.

Return	×	Weight (percentage value of stock in proportion to total value of portfolio)	=	Weighted average
8.3%	×	0.25	=	2.075%.
10.6	×	0.25	=	2.650.
12.3	×	0.50	=	6.150.

The return is the sum of these weighted averages.

$$\begin{array}{r} 2.075\% \\ 2.650 \\ 6.150 \\ \hline 10.875\% \end{array}$$

The previous example is generalized in Equation 8.1, which states that the return on a portfolio r_p is a weighted average of the returns of the individual assets $[(r_1) \ldots (r_n)]$, each weighted by its proportion in the portfolio $(w_1 \ldots w_n)$:

8.1 $$r_p = w_1(r_1) + w_2(r_2) + \ldots + w_n(r_n).$$

Thus, if a portfolio has 20 securities, each plays a role in the determination of the portfolio's return. The extent of that role depends on the weight that each asset has in the portfolio. Obviously those securities that compose the largest part of the individual's portfolio have the largest impact on the portfolio's return.[2]

Unfortunately, an aggregate measure of the portfolio's risk (i.e., the portfolio's standard deviation) is more difficult to construct than the

[2]The same general equation may be applied to expected returns, in which case the expected return on a portfolio, $E(r_p)$, is a weighted average of the expected returns of the individual assets $[E(r_1) \ldots E(r_n)]$ each weighted by its proportion in the portfolio $(w_1 \ldots w_n)$:

$$E(r_p) = w_1E(r_1) + w_2E(r_2) + \ldots + w_nE(r_n).$$

weighted average of the returns. This is because security prices are not independent of each other. However, while security prices do move together, there can be considerable difference in these price movements. For example, prices of stocks of firms in homebuilding may be more sensitive to recession than stock prices of utilities, whose prices may decline only moderately. These relationships among the assets in the portfolio must be considered in the construction of a measure of risk associated with the entire portfolio. In more advanced texts, these inner relationships among stocks are called covariation.

Risk Reduction Through Diversification—An Illustration

The development of a measure of covariation and the calculation of a portfolio's standard deviation go beyond the scope of this text.[3] The concept, however, may be illustrated by considering the returns earned on two specific stocks, Public Service Enterprise Group and Mobil Corporation. Public Service Enterprise Group is primarily an electric and gas utility whose stock price fell with higher interest rates and inflation. Mobil is a resource company whose stock price rose during inflation in response to higher oil prices but fell during the 1980s as oil prices weakened and inflation receded.

The annual returns (dividends plus price change) on investments in these two stocks are given in Figure 8.2 for the period 1971 through 1990. As may be seen in the graph, there were several periods when the returns on the two stocks moved in opposite directions. For example, during 1971 and 1978, an investment in Public Service Enterprise Group generated a loss while an investment in Mobil produced profits. However, the converse occurred during 1981 as the trend in Public Service Enterprise Group's stock price started to improve. From 1980 to 1985 the price of Public Service Enterprise Group doubled, but the price of Mobil's stock declined so that most of the return earned on Mobil's stock during the mid-1980s was its dividend.

Figure 8.3 presents a scatter diagram of the returns on these two stocks. The horizontal axis presents the average annual return on Public Service Enterprise Group, while the vertical axis presents the average annual return on Mobil Corporation. As may be seen in the graph, the individual points lie throughout the plane representing the returns. For example, point A represents a positive return on Mobil but a negative return on Public Service Enterprise Group, and point B represents a positive return on Public Service Enterprise Group but a negative return on Mobil.

---

[3]See, for instance, Zri Bodie, Alex Kane, and Alan J. Marcus, *Investments,* Homewood, Ill.: Richard D. Irwin, Inc., 1989, pp. 138–144.

FIGURE 8.2

Annual Returns

The composite return is a weighted average of the individual returns.

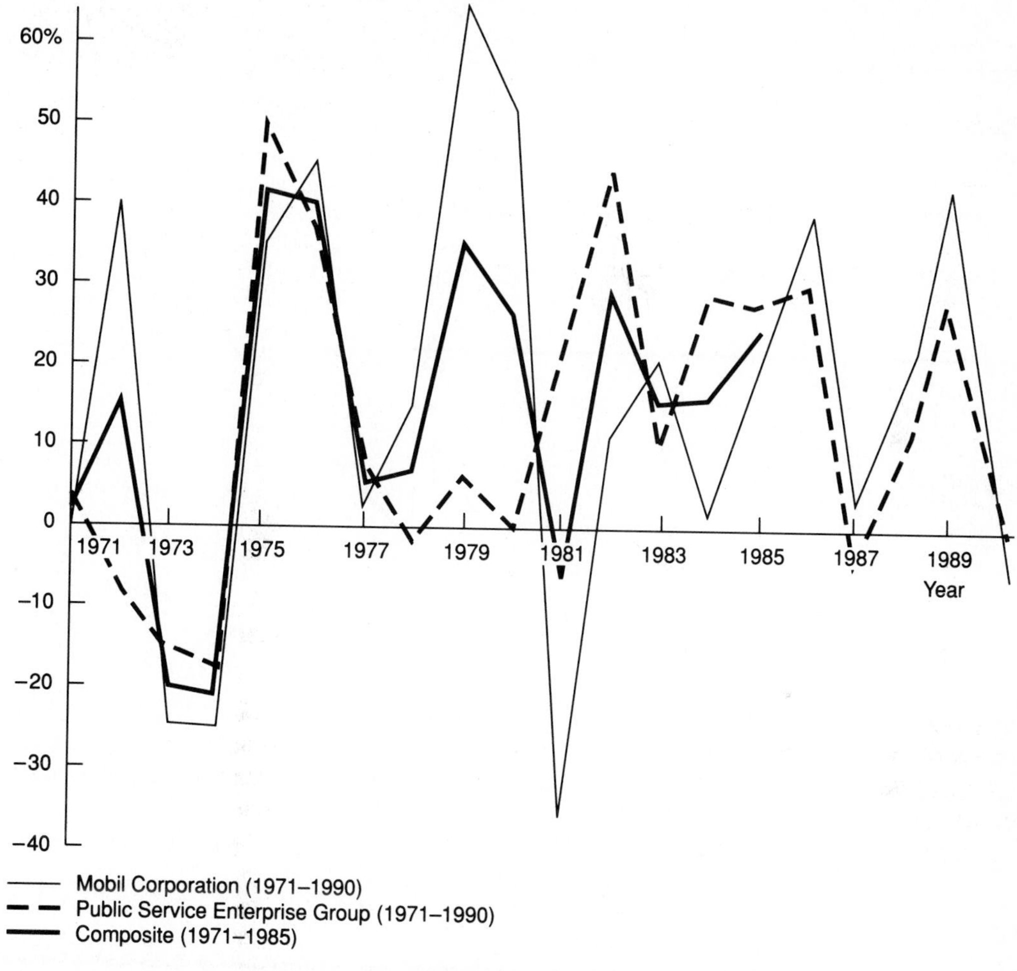

Combining these securities in a portfolio reduces the individual's risk exposure, as is also shown in Figure 8.2 for the years 1971 through 1985. The line representing the composite return runs between the lines representing the returns on the individual securities. Over the entire time period, the average annual returns on Mobil and Public Service Enterprise Group were 15.7 and 14.7 percent, respectively. The average annual return on the composite was 15.2 percent. The risk reduction (i.e., the reduction in the dispersion of the returns) can be seen by comparing the standard deviations of the returns. For the individual stocks

FIGURE 8.3

Scatter Diagram of Returns

This scatter diagram plots the individual, annual returns.

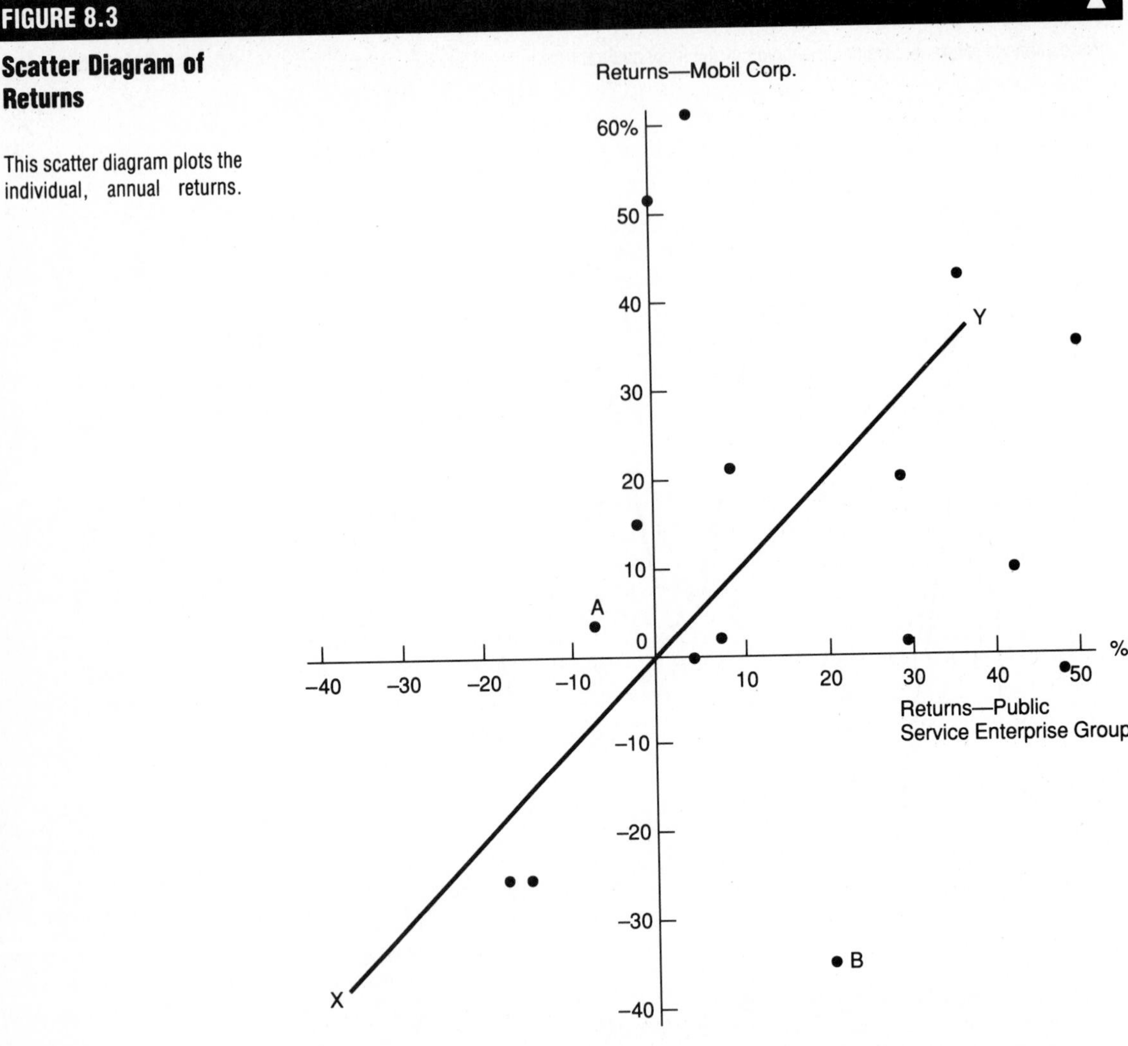

the standard deviations were ±27.8 percent and ±21.5 percent, respectively, for Mobil and Public Service Enterprise Group. However, the standard deviation for the composite return was ±19.4 percent, so the dispersion of the returns associated with the portfolio is less than the dispersion of the returns on either stock by itself.

Why is there less dispersion for the portfolio than for the individual stocks? The answer is that the returns are not highly correlated. Correlation may be measured by a statistical concept: the "correlation coefficient." The numerical value of the correlation coefficient ranges from

+1.0 to −1.0.[4] If the two variables move exactly together (i.e., if there is a perfect positive correlation between the two variables), the numerical value of the correlation coefficient is 1.0. If the two variables move exactly opposite of each other, the correlation coefficient equals −1.0. All other possible values lie between these two extremes. Low numerical values such as −0.12 or +0.19 indicate little relationship between the two variables.

The correlation coefficient relating the returns on Mobil and Public Service Enterprise Group stocks is 0.148, so there was little relationship between the returns on the two stocks. This lack of correlation is visible in Figure 8.3. If there were a high positive correlation between the two returns, the points would lie close to the line XY. Instead, the points are scattered throughout the figure. Thus, there is little correlation between the two returns, which is why combining the two securities reduces the individual's risk exposure.

Combining Mobil and Public Service Enterprise Group reduced risk because it decreased the dispersion of the portfolio, and this lower dispersion was the result of the low correlation between the returns. However, two additional points should be made. First, just because diversification was achieved in the past does not imply it will be achieved in the future. If the returns become positively correlated, combining the two stocks will not achieve diversification. This positive correlation appears to have occurred since 1985 because the returns appear to have moved together during that period. (The composite return has been omitted from 1985 through 1990 to better illustrate the close movement between the returns on the two stocks.) This suggests that investing in Mobil and Public Service Enterprise Group during 1985–1990 may have had little impact on diversification. Second, to the extent that diversification reduces risk, it only affects the risk associated with specific assets. Other sources of risk remain. Diversification does not reduce the risk associated with fluctuations in security prices, inflation, changes in interest rates, or fluctuations in exchange rates.

In effect, a diversified portfolio reduces the element of unsystematic risk. The risk associated with each individual investment is reduced by accumulating a diversified portfolio of assets. Even if one company fails (or does extremely well), the impact on the portfolio as a whole is re-

---

[4] The computation of the correlation coefficient is explained in statistics textbooks. See, for instance, Morris Hamburg, *Statistical Analysis for Decision Making*, 4th ed. (San Diego, California: Harcourt Brace Jovanovich, Publishers, 1987), pp. 401–403. Many computer programs developed for finance include the computation of the correlation coefficient. See, for instance, the section on descriptive statistics in James B. Pettijohn, PROFIT+, Hinsdale, Ill.: The Dryden Press, 1988. However, for the purpose of this discussion all that is necessary is that low values (i.e., 0.2 to −0.2) indicate, at best, a weak relationship between the two variables.

FIGURE 8.4

Portfolio Risk Consisting of Systematic and Unsystematic Risk

Diversification reduces portfolio risk by reducing unsystematic risk, but systematic risk is unaffected by the construction of a diversified portfolio.

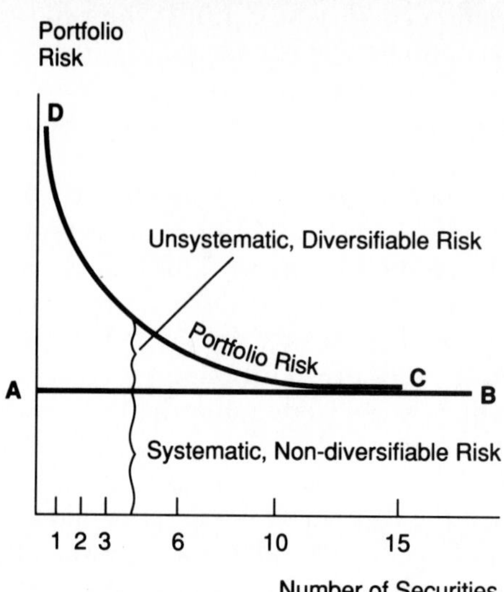

duced through diversification. Distributing investments among different industries, however, does not eliminate the other sources of risk. For example, the value of a group of securities will tend to follow the market values in general. The price movements of securities will be mirrored by the diversified portfolio; hence the investor cannot eliminate this source of systematic risk.

How many securities are necessary to achieve a diversified portfolio that reduces and almost eliminates unsystematic risk? The answer may be "surprisingly few." Several studies have found that risk has been significantly reduced in portfolios consisting of from 10 to 15 securities.[5]

This reduction in unsystematic risk is illustrated in Figure 8.4. The vertical axis measures units of risk, and the horizontal axis gives the number of securities. Since market risk is independent of the number of securities in the portfolio, this element of risk is illustrated by a line, AB,

[5]For further discussion, see the following: John Evans and Stephen Archer, "Diversification and the Reduction of Dispersion: An Empirical Analysis," *Journal of Finance* (December 1968), pp. 761–767; Bruce D. Fielitz, "Indirect Versus Direct Diversification," *Financial Management* (Winter 1974), pp. 54–62; H. Latané and W. Young, "Tests of Portfolio Building Rules," *Journal of Finance* (September 1969), pp. 595–612; and William Sharpe, "Risk, Market Sensitivity and Diversification," *Financial Analysts Journal* (January–February 1972), pp. 74–79. However, George Frankfurter suggests that even well-diversified portfolios have a substantial amount of nonsystematic risk. See his "Efficient Portfolios and Non-Systematic Risk," *The Financial Review* (Fall 1981), pp. 1–11.

that runs parallel to the horizontal axis. Regardless of the number of securities that an individual owns, the amount of market risk remains the same.

Portfolio risk (i.e., the sum of systematic and unsystematic risk), is indicated by line CD. The difference between line AB and line CD is the unsystematic risk associated with the specific securities in the portfolio. The amount of unsystematic risk depends on the number of securities held. As this number increases, unsystematic risk diminishes; this reduction in risk is illustrated in Figure 8.4 where line CD approaches line AB. For portfolios consisting of ten or more securities, the risk involved is primarily systematic.

Portfolio risk ▲
Total risk associated with owning a portfolio; sum of systematic and unsystematic risk

Such diversified portfolios, of course, do not consist of ten public utilities but of a cross section of American businesses. Investing $20,000 in ten stocks (i.e., $2,000 for each) may achieve a reasonably well-diversified portfolio. While such a portfolio may cost somewhat more in commissions than two $10,000 purchases, the small investor achieves a diversified mixture of securities, which should reduce the risk of loss associated with investment in a specific security. Unfortunately, the investor must still bear the systematic risk associated with investing.

BETA COEFFICIENTS

The computation of a standard deviation for a portfolio of any size is virtually impractical for the individual investor, since it requires the correlation among the individual stock returns. For a portfolio of three stocks (A, B, and C), the investor needs to know the correlation among stocks A and B, A and C, and B and C. If the portfolio has four stocks (A, B, C, and D), then you need the correlation between A and B, A and C, A and D, B and C, B and D, and C and D. Consider the number of correlations that would be necessary for a portfolio of 20 stocks! To make matters worse, data relating returns between stocks is not generally available. The investor would have to compute the individual correlation coefficients before computing the portfolio's standard deviation.

Fortunately there is an alternative. The previous discussion of diversification suggested that if a portfolio were sufficiently diversified, unsystematic risk is virtually erased. The remaining risk is the result of nondiversifiable, systematic risk. Is there a measure of systematic risk and may it be used instead of a standard deviation to indicate the risk associated with an asset or with a well-diversified portfolio?

The answer is "Yes." This measure of the systematic risk associated with an asset is called a *beta coefficient*. While the concept may be applied to any asset, the usual explanation is given using common stock. A beta coefficient is an index of risk that quantifies the responsiveness of a stock's return to changes in the return on the market. Since a beta coefficient measures a stock's return relative to the return on the market, it measures the systematic risk associated with the stock.

Beta coefficients have become widely used by financial analysts to measure the risk associated with individual stocks. The concept is also applied to portfolios, as they are computed for mutual funds in which case they compare the return on the fund with the return on the market. Portfolio betas are simply weighted averages of the individual betas in the portfolio. While the use of betas permeates finance, it is important to realize that these coefficients are only a *relative measure of risk.* They tell you nothing about how the market itself will fluctuate!

A beta coefficient of 1 means that the stock's return moves exactly with an index of the market as a whole. A 10 percent increase in the market produces a 10 percent increase in the return on the specific stock. Correspondingly, a 10 percent decline in the market results in a 10 percent decline in the return on the stock. A beta coefficient of less than 1 implies that the return on the stock tends to fluctuate less than the market as a whole. A coefficient of 0.7 indicates that the stock's return will rise only 7 percent as a result of a 10 percent increase in the market but will fall by only 7 percent when the market declines by 10 percent. A coefficient of 1.2 means that the return on the stock will rise by 12 percent if the market increases by 10 percent, but the return on the stock will decline by 12 percent when the market declines by 10 percent.

The greater the beta coefficient, the more risk is associated with the individual stock. High beta coefficients may indicate exceptional profits during rising markets, but they also indicate greater losses during declining markets. Stocks with high beta coefficients are referred to as aggressive. The converse is true for stocks with low beta coefficients, which should underperform the market during periods of rising stock prices but outperform the market as a whole during periods of declining prices. Such stocks are referred to as defensive.

This relationship between the return on a specific security and the market index as a whole is illustrated in Figures 8.5 and 8.6. In each graph, the horizontal axis represents the percentage return on the market index, and the vertical axis represents the percentage return on the individual stock. The line AB, which represents the market, is the same in both graphs. It is a positively-sloped line that runs through the point of origin and is equidistant from both axes (i.e., it makes a 45° angle with each axis).

Figure 8.5 illustrates a stock with a beta coefficient greater than 1. Line CD represents a stock whose return rises and declines more than the market's return. In this case the beta coefficient is 1.2, so when the market index is 10 percent, this stock's return is 12 percent.

Figure 8.6 illustrates a stock with a beta coefficient of less than 1. Line EF represents a stock whose return rises (and declines) more slowly

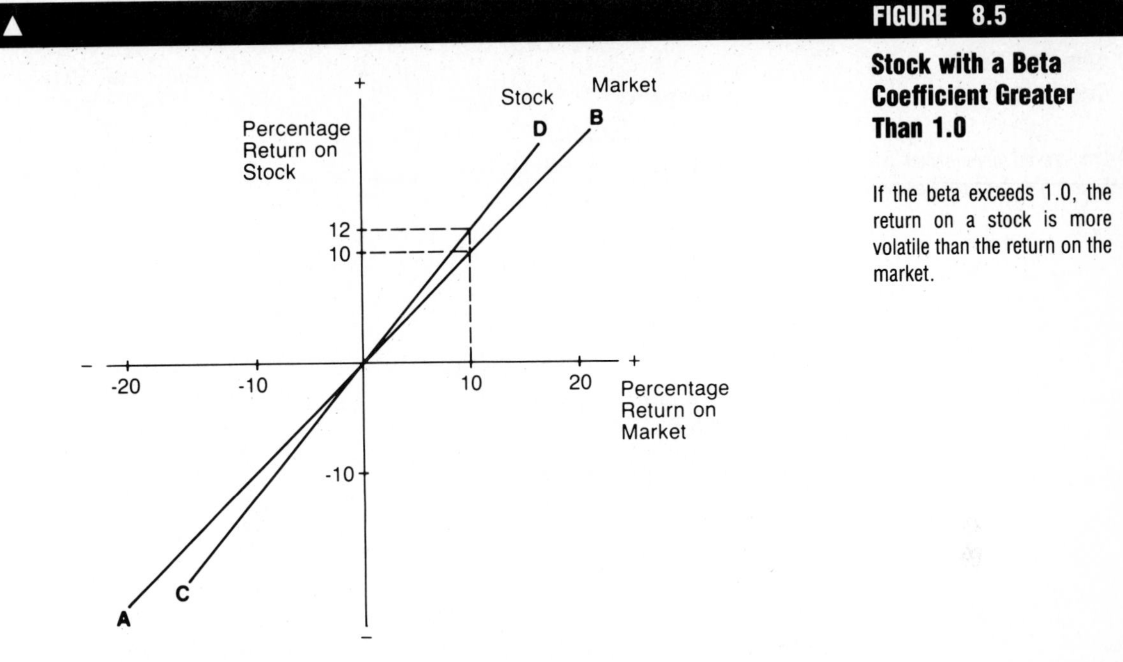

FIGURE 8.5

Stock with a Beta Coefficient Greater Than 1.0

If the beta exceeds 1.0, the return on a stock is more volatile than the return on the market.

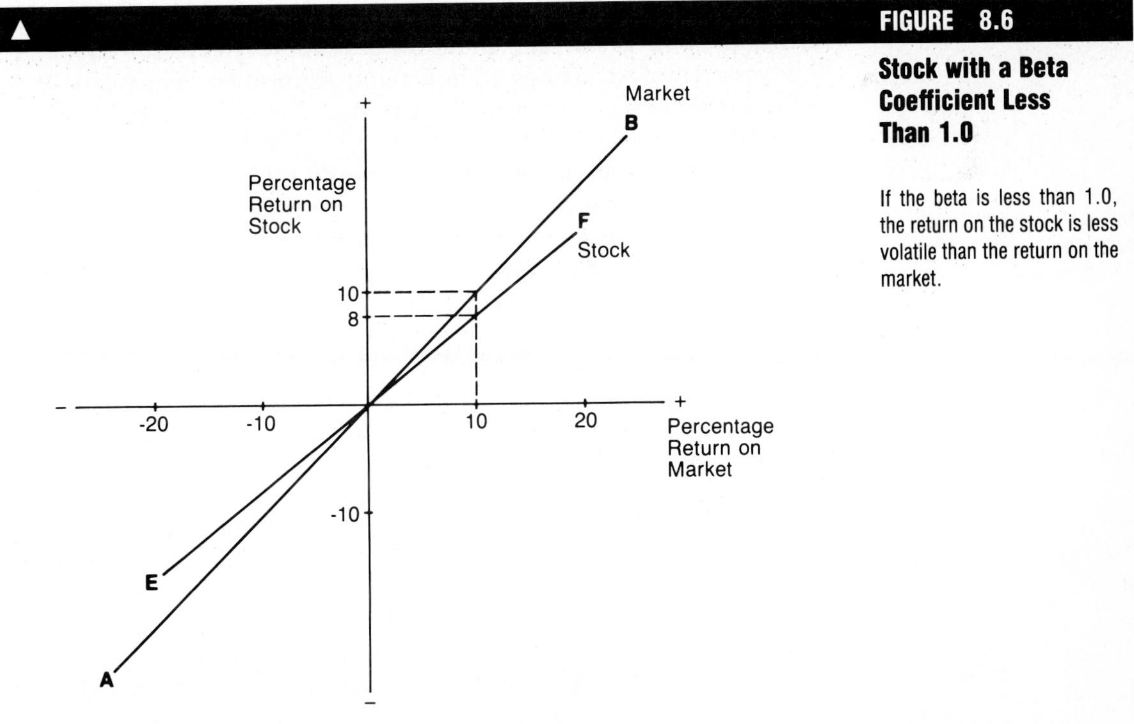

FIGURE 8.6

Stock with a Beta Coefficient Less Than 1.0

If the beta is less than 1.0, the return on the stock is less volatile than the return on the market.

EXHIBIT 8.1

Selected Beta Coefficients

Stocks with more market risk have higher beta coefficients.

Company	*Value Line* Beta Coefficient
Sunshine Mining	0.65
Piedmont Natural Gas	0.70
Boston Edison	0.70
Exxon	0.80
IBM Corp.	0.95
Boeing	1.00
CBS Inc.	1.05
General Electric Co.	1.10
E.I. duPont de Nemours Co.	1.15
Aluminum Company of America (ALCOA)	1.20
Deb Shops	1.30
Compaq Computer	1.35
Chrysler	1.40

Source: Value Line Investment Survey, January 18, 1991.

than that of the market. In this case the beta coefficient is 0.8, so when the market's return is 10 percent, this stock's return is 8 percent.

Since a beta coefficient indicates the systematic risk associated with a particular stock, it can be used in security selection and portfolio construction. Some assets offer the investor modest returns for taking very little risk. Insured savings accounts and short-term obligations of the federal government are virtually risk-free. To induce investors to purchase risky securities, such as common stock, the anticipated return must be sufficient to compensate the investor for the additional risk. Since unsystematic risk is reduced by diversification, systematic risk becomes very important in the selection of an asset. The investor must anticipate a sufficient return for bearing systematic risk, and increases in systematic risk will require larger expected returns. (How beta coefficients may be used in the valuation of a stock is explained in Chapter 11.)

Beta coefficients do vary among firms. This is illustrated in Exhibit 8.1, which presents the beta coefficients for selected firms as computed by *Value Line.* As may be seen in the table, some firms (e.g., Exxon) have relatively low beta coefficients, while the coefficients for other firms (e.g., Compaq Computer) are much higher. Investors who are willing to bear more risk may be attracted to those stocks with the higher beta coefficients, because when stock market prices rise, these stocks tend to outperform the market. Investors who are less inclined to bear risk may prefer the stocks with low beta coefficients. Although these investors may forgo some potential return during rising market prices, they should suffer milder losses during periods of declining stock prices.

To be useful, beta coefficients must be reliable predictors of future stock price behavior. For example, a conservative investor who desires stocks that will be stable will probably purchase stocks with a low beta coefficient. An investor selecting a stock with a beta coefficient of 0.6 will certainly be upset if the market prices decline by 10 percent and this stock's price falls by 15 percent, since a beta coefficient of 0.6 indicates that the stock price should decline by only 6 percent when market prices decline by 10 percent.

Unfortunately, beta coefficients are constructed with historical price data. Although such data may be accumulated and tabulated for many years, it still does not mean that the coefficients will be accurate predictors of future price movements in individual stocks. Beta coefficients can and do change over time. Empirical studies have shown that beta coefficients for individual securities tend to be very unstable.[6] Therefore, the investor should not rely solely on these coefficients in selecting a particular security. However, beta coefficients do give the investor some indication of the systematic risk associated with specific stocks and thus can play an important role in the selection of a security.

Unlike the beta coefficients for individual securities, the beta coefficient for a portfolio composed of several securities is fairly stable over time. Changes in the different beta coefficients tend to average out; while one stock's beta coefficient is increasing, the beta coefficient of another stock is declining. A portfolio's historical beta coefficients, then, can be used as a tool to forecast its future beta coefficient, and this projection should be more accurate than forecasts of an individual security's beta coefficient.

Since a portfolio's beta coefficient is stable, the investor can construct a portfolio that responds in a desired way to market changes. For example, the average beta coefficient of the portfolio illustrated in Exhibit 8.1 is approximately 1.03. If an equal dollar amount were invested in each security, the value of the portfolio should follow the market values fairly closely, even though individual beta coefficients are greater or less than 1. This tendency of the portfolio to mirror the performance of the market should hold true, even though selected securities may achieve a return that is superior (or inferior) to that of the market as a whole. Hence, the beta coefficient for the portfolio may be a more useful tool than the beta coefficients for individual securities.

Beta coefficients may also be used in portfolio construction if the investor believes that the market prices will move in a particular direction. For example, the investor who anticipates an increase in prices may construct an aggressive portfolio consisting solely of securities with high

---

[6]See Robert A. Levy, "Stationarity of Beta Coefficients," *Financial Analysts Journal* (November–December 1971), pp. 55–62.

beta coefficients. However, if the anticipated price increases do not occur and the market prices decline, such a strategy may result in a considerable loss.

Regression Analysis and the Estimation of Beta Coefficients*

A statistical technique, regression analysis, is used to estimate a stock's beta coefficient. As was previously explained, a beta coefficient is a measure of the responsiveness of a stock's return to movements in security prices in general. While it is not known exactly how a stock's return will react to changes in the market in the future, it is possible to measure this responsiveness in the past. For example, observations of the past relationship between the return on the market (r_m) and the return on stock A (r_s) are as follows:

Return on the Market (r_m)	Return on Stock A (r_s)
14%	13%
12	13
10	12
10	9
5	4
2	−1
−1	2
−5	−7
−7	−8
−12	−10

Each observation represents the return on the stock and the return on the market for a period of time (e.g., a week). These data are plotted in Figure 8.7 with each point representing one set of observations. For example, point A represents a 4 percent increase in the price of the stock in response to a 5 percent increase in the market. Point B represents a 7 percent decrease in the return on the stock in response to a 5 percent decline in the return on the market.

Individual observations like points A and B tell very little about the systematic risk of the stock, but all the observations, taken as a whole, may. The individual observations are summarized by linear regression analysis which is used to compute an equation relating the return on the stock (r_s, the dependent variable) to the return on the market (r_m, the

*This section may be omitted without loss of continuity.

FIGURE 8.7

Observations Relating the Return on a Stock to the Market

In this scatter diagram, the individual returns appear to lie close to a line relating the return on the stock to the return on the market.

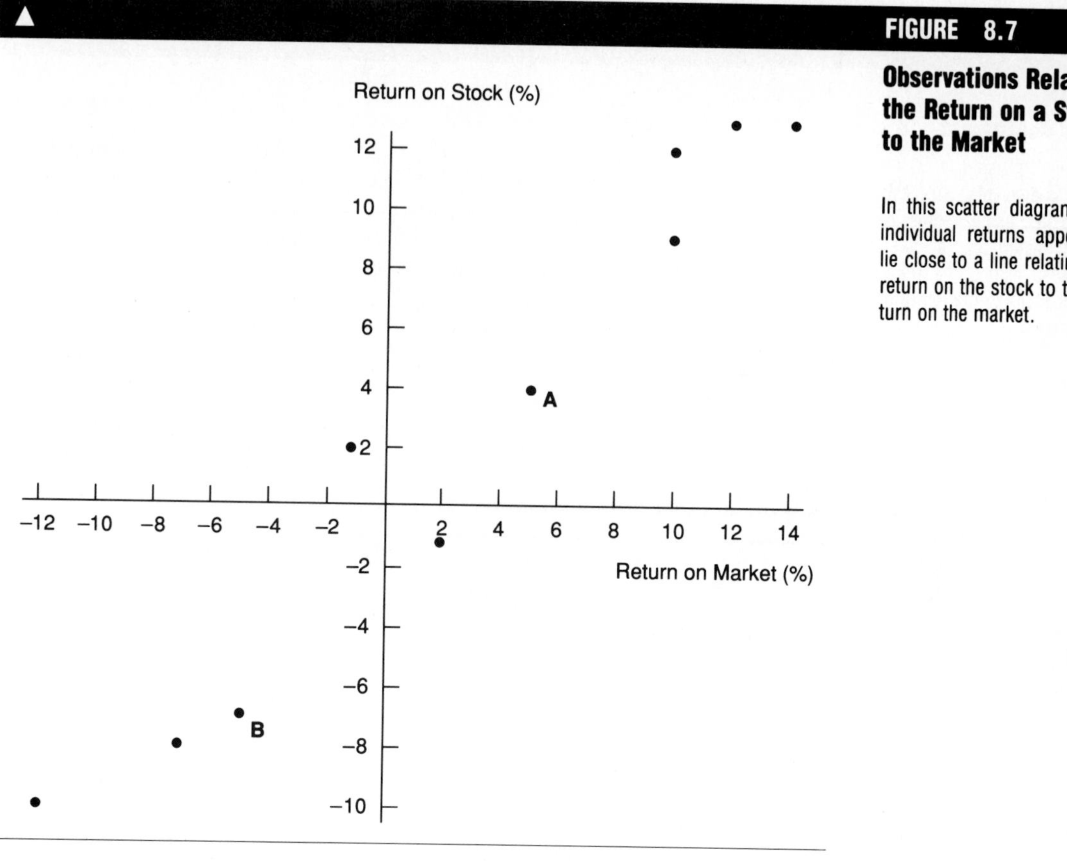

independent variable). The regression analysis computes the y-intercept (a) and the slope (b) for the following equation:

$$r_s = a + br_m.$$

This slope is the beta coefficient.

Like the correlation coefficient presented earlier in this chapter, regression analysis is a statistical concept. The actual computations of the intercept and the slope are generally performed by a computer program. A manual demonstration of the process is presented in Exhibit 8.2, in which the following equation is derived:

$$r_s = -0.000597 + 0.9856r_m.$$

This equation is given as line XY in Figure 8.8, which reproduces Figure 8.7 and adds the regression line. As may be seen from the graph, line XY runs through the individual points. Some of the observations are

EXHIBIT 8.2

The Computation of a Beta Coefficient

Beta coefficients are estimated by using regression which estimates a linear equation relating the return on the stock to the return on the market.

X (r_m)	Y (r_s)	X^2	Y^2	XY
0.14	0.13	0.0196	0.0169	0.0182
0.12	0.13	0.0144	0.0169	0.0156
0.10	0.12	0.0100	0.0144	0.0120
0.10	0.09	0.0100	0.0081	0.0090
0.05	0.04	0.0025	0.0016	0.0020
0.02	−0.01	0.0004	0.0001	−0.0002
−0.01	0.02	0.0001	0.0004	−0.0002
−0.05	−0.07	0.0025	0.0049	0.0035
−0.07	−0.08	0.0049	0.0064	0.0056
−0.12	−0.10	0.0144	0.0100	0.0120
$\Sigma X = 0.28$	$\Sigma Y = 0.27$	$\Sigma X^2 = 0.0788$	$\Sigma Y^2 = 0.0797$	$\Sigma XY = 0.0775$

n = the number of observations (10).

$$b = \frac{n\Sigma XY - (\Sigma X)(\Sigma Y)}{n\Sigma X^2 - (\Sigma X)^2}$$

$$= \frac{(10)(0.0775) - (0.28)(0.27)}{(10)(0.0788) - (0.28)(0.28)}$$

$$= \frac{0.7750 - 0.0756}{0.7880 - 0.0784} = 0.9856.$$

The a is computed as follows:

$$a = \frac{\Sigma Y}{n} - b\frac{\Sigma X}{n}$$

$$= \frac{0.27}{10} - (0.9856)\frac{0.28}{10} = -0.000597.$$

The estimated equation is $r_s = -0.000597 + 0.9856\, r_m$.

above the line while others are below it. However, all of the points are close to the line.

This regression equation can be used to forecast the expected return on the stock. If the individual anticipates that the market return will be 20 percent, the stock should yield a return of

$$r_s = -0.000597 + 0.9856(20\%) = 19.7\%$$

As with any forecast, this result may not be realized, because factors other than the increase in the market may affect the stock's return. However, for this particular beta, the predictive power may be excellent.

FIGURE 8.8

Regression Equation Relating the Return on a Stock to the Market

The regression line summarizes the individual observations.

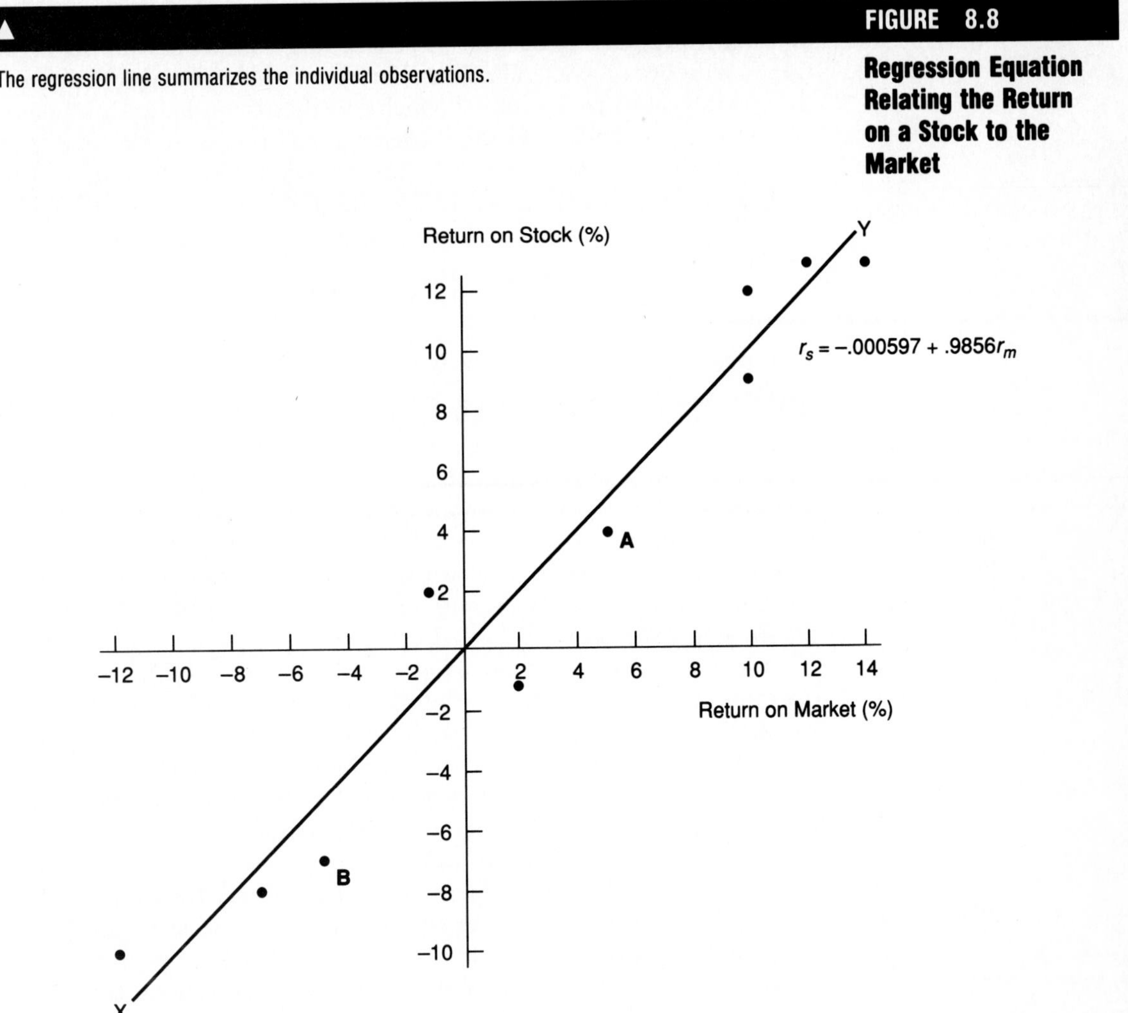

Since the individual observations lie close to the estimated regression line, that indicates a high correlation between the two variables. The actual correlation coefficient is 0.976, which indicates a very strong relationship between the return on the stock and the return on the market. (1.0 indicates a perfect, positive relationship.) Most of the fluctuations in the individual returns on the stock were caused by fluctuations in the return on the market. Of course, this high correlation may not continue in the future, but unless some fundamental change in the firm were to occur, the beta coefficient may be an excellent forecaster of the future responsiveness of the stock to changes in the market.

The development of beta coefficients and a theory of the reduction of risk through diversification was exceedingly important to the formation of a theory of asset valuation. This theory led to the development of the capital asset pricing model which specifies the relationship between risk and return and determines the required return for an asset. This required return is discussed in the next section and will be used subsequently to value investments such as the purchase of common stock by individuals or plant and equipment by a firm's management.

THE CAPITAL ASSET PRICING MODEL AND AN INVESTMENT'S REQUIRED RETURN

One of the most important decisions facing a financial manager or an investor is whether to acquire an asset. This decision requires a determination of either (1) an asset's value which is then compared to its cost or (2) an asset's expected return which is compared to the investor's required return. It is not necessary to do both, since either technique uses the same information.

When valuation is employed, the analyst uses the required return to discount future cash flows to determine what the asset is worth. This valuation is then compared to the asset's current price. If the value exceeds the cost, the asset should not be acquired. This technique will subsequently be used in the dividend-growth model for selecting stocks in Chapter 11 and in the net present value technique for selecting investments in plant and equipment in Chapter 23.

While valuation expresses an asset in monetary units (i.e., dollars), the required return and the expected return use percentages. The asset's cash flows are compared to its cost to determine an expected return which is compared to the investor's required rate of return. If the anticipated return exceeds the required return, the asset is acquired. The primary use for this technique is the computation of an investment's internal rate of return in Chapter 23, but it may also be used for the selection of stock in Chapter 11.

Capital asset pricing model (CAPM) ▲
Model used in the valuation of an asset which specifies the required return for different levels of risk

Both techniques need a required return, which has led to a general framework for the analyzing of risk and return called the **capital asset pricing model** or **CAPM.** The CAPM specifies the relationship between risk and return that is used either to value an asset or to judge an asset's expected return. While the model may be applied to any type of investment, it is generally explained in terms of acquiring common stock, so the following explanation is presented from the perspective of the individual investor.

The CAPM builds on the proposition that additional risk will require a higher return. This return has two components: (1) what may be

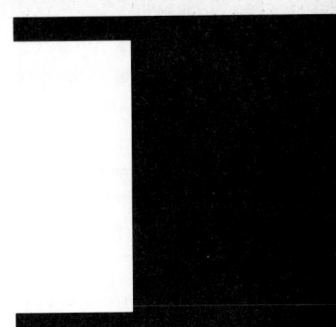

Director of Financial Research

■ Job Description: Manage staff of financial analysts who select long-term investments. Administer and direct staff necessary to support the financial analysts. ■ Job Requirements: Managerial experience and skills combined with analytical and statistical techniques. Specializations (e.g., equity investments or fixed income securities) require knowledge of security analysis and accounting concepts, and the ability to measure a creditor's capacity to meet its debt obligations. Advanced degree (MBA, PhD) desirable. ■ Characteristics: High-level position that builds on a successful career in financial analysis and reports directly to a firm's highest levels of management (e.g., Vice-President of Finance). Individual needs ability to motivate individuals, to communicate the firm's goals, and to identify superior talent for advancement.

---

earned on a risk-free asset such as a federally insured savings account or a U.S. Treasury bill plus (2) a premium for bearing risk. Since unsystematic risk is significantly reduced through diversification, a stock's risk premium is the additional return required to bear the systematic risk associated with the stock.

This risk-adjusted required return (k) is expressed in Equation 8.2:

8.2 $$k = \text{risk-free rate} + \text{risk premium}.$$

The risk premium is composed of two components: (1) the additional return that investing in securities in general offers above the risk-free rate and (2) the volatility of the particular security relative to the market as a whole. The volatility of the individual stock is measured by the beta coefficient (β), and the additional return is measured by the difference between the expected return on the market (r_m) and the risk-free rate (r_f). This differential ($r_m - r_f$) is the risk premium that is required to induce the individual to purchase risky assets. In more advanced literature on investments, it is called the "market price of risk."

To induce the investor to purchase a particular stock, the risk premium associated with the market must be adjusted by the market risk associated with the individual security. This risk adjustment uses the stock's beta coefficient, which indicates the stock's volatility relative to the market. The total risk adjustment is achieved by multiplying the security's beta coefficient by the difference between the expected return on the market and the risk-free rate. Thus the risk premium for the individual stock is

$$\text{risk premium} = (r_m - r_f)\ \text{beta coefficient}.$$

FIGURE 8.9

Relationship between Risk and the Required Return

The capital asset model specifies the required return on an investment at each level of risk.

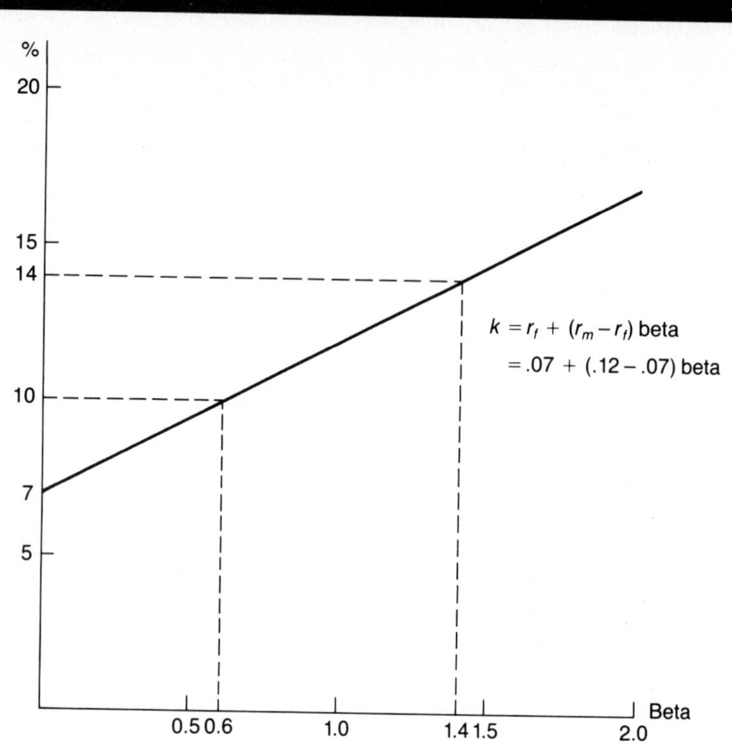

The total return required for investing in a particular stock is found by substituting this risk premium into Equation 8.2. Thus the required return is

8.3 $$\text{required return} = r_f + (r_m - r_f) \text{ beta coefficient.}$$

The relationship between various levels of risk and the required return indicated by Equation 8.3 is illustrated in Figure 8.9. Risk, as measured by the beta coefficient, is given on the horizontal axis while the required return, measured as a percentage, is on the vertical axis. If the risk-free rate is 7 percent and the expected return on the market is 12 percent, then the required rate of return on a stock with a beta coefficient of 0.6 is

$$k_A = .07 + (.12 - .07).6 = .10 = 10\%.$$

If a stock has a beta coefficient equal to 1.4, the required return is

$$k_B = .07 + (.12 - .07)\ 1.4 = .14 = 14\%.$$

The stock with the higher beta coefficient has the higher required return because it is riskier.

The above specification of the required rate of return will reappear several times in this text. It is used to value common stock in Chapter 11 and is part of the firm's cost of capital in Chapter 22. Since the cost of capital is part of the capital budgeting models covered in Chapter 23, the required return has an impact on the financial manager's decision to invest in plant and equipment.

SUMMARY

Investments are made in anticipation of a return which may be a flow of income and/or price appreciation. Individuals and financial managers make investments in anticipation of a return, but the realized return may differ from the expected return. That is the element of risk. The future is uncertain.

There are several sources of risk. These include the risk associated with the specific asset (diversifiable, unsystematic risk) and the nondiversifiable, systematic risk from fluctuations in security prices, changes in interest rates, inflation, and fluctuations in exchange rates.

The construction of a diversified portfolio reduces the risk associated with the particular asset. By owning a variety of assets whose returns are not highly positively correlated, the investor reduces unsystematic risk without necessarily reducing the potential return on the portfolio as a whole. Unfortunately, the construction of a diversified portfolio does not reduce the other sources of risk.

Risk may be measured by an asset's (or portfolio's) standard deviation, which measures the dispersion around the realized return (in the case of historical returns) or the expected return (in the case of anticipated returns). The larger the dispersion of the returns, the greater is the risk.

An alternative measure of risk determines the responsiveness of an asset's return relative to the market as a whole. This measure, called a beta coefficient, is an index of the systematic risk associated with the asset. The larger the beta coefficient, the greater the systematic risk associated with the security since its return has risen or fallen more rapidly than the return on the market as a whole.

Beta coefficients may be used to help determine an investor's required rate of return. This capital asset pricing model specifies the required return and includes (1) the risk-free rate that may be earned on very safe investments plus (2) a risk premium. The risk premium includes a premium for purchasing risky assets instead of the risk-free asset, plus an adjustment for the systematic risk associated with the particular investment.

Review Questions

1. What are the sources of return on an investment? What are the differences among the expected return, the required return, and the realized return?
2. Why does a diversified portfolio reduce unsystematic risk but have no impact on systematic risk? What condition must be met for a portfolio to be diversified? How many securities are necessary to achieve diversification?
3. What is a beta coefficient? What do beta coefficients of 0.5, 1.0, and 1.5 imply?
4. How may beta coefficients be used to help determine the required return on an investment?
5. What impact would each of the following have on a diversified portfolio?
   a. the stock market declines by 10 percent
   b. one of the stocks in the portfolio suspends its dividend
   c. the rate of inflation decreases
6. You compute the following expected returns and standard deviations of three portfolios.

Portfolio	Expected Return	Standard Deviation
1	18%	±5%
2	9	±2
3	12	±6

   Would you prefer portfolio 1 to 2? Would you prefer portfolio 1 to 3?
7. If stock A's beta coefficient is 1.5 while stock B's beta coefficient is 1.2, what does that suggest about their relative risks? Is this information sufficient to prefer either stock A or B?
8. When beta coefficients are computed, the correlation coefficient is also determined. If the correlation coefficient relating the return on a stock to the return on the market is 0.4 instead of 0.8, would that reduce or increase your confidence in the usefulness of the beta?

Problems

1. You are considering buying stock A. If the economy grows rapidly, you may earn 35 percent on the investment while a recession could result in a 17 percent loss. Sluggish economic growth may generate a return of 6 percent. If the probability of rapid growth is 15 percent and 20 percent for recession, what is the expected return on this investment?

2. You are considering investing in three stocks with the following expected returns:

Stock A	10%
Stock B	18
Stock C	23

What is the expected return on the portfolio if an equal amount is invested in each stock? What would be the expected return if 50 percent of your funds is invested in stock A and the remaining funds are split evenly between stocks B and C?

3. A portfolio consists of assets with the following expected returns:

Antiques	20%
Silver	15
AT&T stock	12
Savings account	5

a. What is the expected return on the portfolio if the investor spends an equal amount on each asset?
b. What is the expected return on the portfolio if the investor puts 50 percent of available funds in antiques, 10 percent in silver, 24 percent in AT&T stock, and 16 percent in the savings account?

4. Two investments generate the following returns:

	Investment X	**Investment Y**
19X0	10%	16%
19X1	20	18
19X2	30	15
19X3	20	20
19X4	10	21

a. What is the average annual rate of return on each investment?
b. What is the standard deviation of each return?
c. Which investment was riskier?

5. You expect to invest 25 percent of your funds in four stocks with the following expected returns:

Stock	**Expected Return**
A	16%
B	14
C	10
D	8

At the end of the year, each stock had the following realized returns:

Stock	Realized Return
A	−6%
B	18
C	3
D	−2

Compare the portfolio's expected and realized returns.

Suggested Readings

Bluestein, Paul. "What's the Big Fuss About Modern Portfolio Theory?" *Forbes,* June 12, 1978, pp. 41–51.

Wallace, Anise. "Is Beta Dead?" *Institutional Investor* (July 1980), pp. 23–29.

These two articles describe in layman's terms modern portfolio theory and attempts to verify it.

Other articles that discuss beta include:

Blume, Marshall E. "Betas and Their Regression Tendencies." *Journal of Finance* (June 1975), pp. 785–795.

Levy, Robert A. "Stationarity of Beta Coefficients." *Financial Analysts Journal* (November–December 1971), pp. 55–62.

Rosenberg, Barr, and James Guy. "Predication of Beta from Investment Fundamentals." *Financial Analysts Journal* (May–June 1976), pp. 60–73, and *Financial Analysts Journal* (July–August 1976), pp. 62–71.

Sharpe, William. "Risk, Market Sensitivity, and Diversification." *Financial Analysts Journal* (January–February 1972), pp. 74–79.

The Sharpe article discusses beta in general terms and explains how it is computed. The Levy article shows that beta for individual stocks may not be stable but that betas for a portfolio are stable and can be used as predictors. The Rosenberg and Guy article discusses the estimation of beta with historical data and explains why betas may change, thus reducing their usefulness as predictors. The Blume article suggests that the numerical value of a beta tends toward 1.0 over time.

The following includes discussions of risk, security selection, and returns earned by investors in layman's terms:

Malkiel, Burton G. *A Random Walk Down Wall Street.* 4th ed. New York: W. W. Norton and Co., 1985.

Portfolio diversification also applies to nonfinancial assets. See:

Grissom, Terry V., James L. Kuhle, and Carl H. Walther. "Diversification Works in Real Estate, Too." *The Journal of Portfolio Management* (Winter 1987), pp. 66–71.

For an extensive bibliography on the determination of beta and its estimation, see:

Callahan, Carolyn M., and Rosanne M. Mohr. "The Determinants of Systematic Risk: A Synthesis." *Financial Review* (May 1989), pp. 157–181.

chapter

9

Investing in Long-Term Debt (Bonds)

29 pages in chapter

Learning Objectives

1. Identify the general characteristics of all long-term debt instruments.
2. Isolate the feature(s) that distinguish each type of bond.
3. State the role of bond ratings.
4. Calculate the price of a bond.
5. Explain the inverse relationship between interest rates and the price of a bond.
6. Explain the difference between sinking funds and call features.

In *The Merchant of Venice,* Antonio sealed his debt to Shylock with a "pound of flesh." Today the terms of a bond are not so severe—creditors cannot require borrowers to offer their flesh as collateral. However, the terms of a debt can still kill a firm. When Eastern filed for bankruptcy, the secured creditors with liens on the airline's planes had the right to take possession of the aircraft. Without its planes, Eastern was dead; it would never fly again.

Many corporations issue long-term debt (bonds) to finance expansion of plant and equipment when the firm's internally generated funds are insufficient to finance the expansion. For example, as of 1991, AT&T had over $8 billion in bonds outstanding. Financing fixed assets with long-term debt offers the firm the advantage of financial leverage, and the debt may be retired by the cash flow generated by the plant and equipment.

This chapter is concerned with the long-term debt, especially the bonds, issued by corporations. It covers the characteristics common to all long-term debt and the different types of corporate debt. Bonds may be purchased by institutions in a private placement or by individuals through a public offering. Once the bonds have been issued, they may be bought and sold on organized security exchanges or in the over-the-counter market. Thus, bonds must have a market price, and this chapter considers how that price is determined. The debt must be paid off; the last section on corporate debt considers the retirement of bonds. The chapter closes with a brief discussion of the bonds issued by various levels of government and how the government forms corporate debt.

CHARACTERISTICS OF ALL DEBT INSTRUMENTS

Bond ▲
Long-term debt instrument which specifies 1) the *principal* (amount owed), 2) the *interest* (payment for the use of the principal), and 3) the *maturity date* (the day on which the debt must be repaid)

Yield ▲
Return on a bond expressed as 1) a *current yield* (interest divided by the current price of the bond) or 2) the *yield to maturity* (return earned from holding the bond until it matures)

Indenture ▲
Document specifying the terms of a debt issue

All **bonds** (i.e., long-term debt instruments) share a number of characteristics. They are liabilities of their issuers for a specified amount, called the **principal.** Virtually all debt has a **maturity date;** it must be paid off by a specified date. If maturity occurs after a year, it is long-term debt. When this debt is issued, the length of time to maturity can range from a few years to 20 or 30 years. The owners of debt instruments receive payments **(interest).** Interest should not be confused with other forms of income, such as cash dividends paid by common and preferred stock. Dividends come from the firm's earnings, while interest is an expense. Sometimes interest is called **yield** and may be expressed in two ways: **current yield** and **yield to maturity.** The difference between the two is discussed subsequently in the section on yields.

Each debt agreement has terms that the debtor must meet, and these are stated in a legal document called the **indenture.** One of the most frequent requirements is the pledging of collateral that the borrower must put up to secure the loan. For example, the collateral for a mortgage loan is the building and land. Other assets, such as securities or inventory owned by the borrower, may also be pledged to secure the loan. If the borrower defaults on the loan (i.e., if the borrower fails to pay the interest or fails to meet other terms of the indenture), the creditor may seize the collateral and sell it to recoup the principal.

Other examples of common loan restrictions are (1) limits on dividend payments, (2) limits on the issue of additional debt, and (3) the requirement to periodically retire a proportion of the debt. These examples do not exhaust all the possible conditions of a given loan. Since each loan is separately negotiated, there is ample opportunity for subtle differences among loan agreements. The important point, however, is that if any part of the loan agreement is violated, the creditor may declare that the debt is in default and the entire loan is due. **Default** is not just the failure to pay the interest. Failure to meet any of the indenture provisions places the loan in default, even though the interest is still being paid.

Default ▲
Failure to meet the terms specified in the indenture of a debt issue

Many debt instruments are purchased by investors who may be unaware of the terms of the indenture. Even if they are aware of the terms, the investors may be too geographically dispersed to take concerted action in case of default. To protect their interests, a **trustee** is appointed for each publicly held bond issue. It is the trustee's job to see that the terms of the indenture are upheld and to take remedial action if the company should default on the terms of the indenture. If the firm should default on the interest payments or other terms of the indenture, the trustee may take the firm to court on behalf of all the bondholders in order to protect their principal.

Trustee ▲
Representative of the rights of bondholders who enforces the terms of the indenture

Another characteristic of all debt is risk—risk that the interest will not be paid, risk that the principal will not be repaid, risk that the price of the debt instrument may decline, and risk that inflation will continue. Risk of default on interest and principal payments varies significantly with different types of debt. The debt of the federal government has no risk of default on its interest payments and principal repayments. The reason for this absolute safety is that the government has the power to print money. The government can always issue the money necessary to pay the interest and repay the principal.

The debt of firms and individuals is not so riskless, for both may default on their obligations. To aid potential buyers of debt instruments, there have developed **credit rating** services (Moody's, Dun & Bradstreet, and Standard & Poor's). These services rate the degree of risk of a debt instrument. Exhibit 9.1 illustrates the risk classifications offered by Moody's and Standard & Poor's. High-quality debt receives a rating of triple A, while poorer quality debt receives progressively lower ratings. While not all debt instruments are rated, the services do cover a significant number of debt obligations.

Credit ratings ▲
Classification schemes designed to indicate the risks associated with a particular debt instrument

Ratings play an important role in the marketing of debt obligations. Since the risk of default may be substantial for poor quality debt, some financial institutions and investors will not purchase debt with a low credit rating. If a firm's or municipality's debt rating falls, it may have difficulty selling its debt. Corporations and municipal governments thus seek to maintain good credit, for good credit ratings reduce the cost of borrowing and increase the marketability of the debt.

Financial Facts

A 14 Percent Return from a Quality Firm's Bonds?

Would you like to earn 14 percent on your money by lending to General Mills, a large manufacturer of consumer goods, apparel, and toys—whose bonds have an A+ rating from Standard & Poor's? At the same time, debt issued by IBM and AT&T is yielding less than 10 percent. Of course, you would prefer 14 percent. So what is the catch? • The catch is that these debt obligations are issued in Australia and are payable in Australian dollars. This catch does not mean that you can't purchase them; it means that General Mills will pay you in Australian dollars. This payment could work to your advantage or disadvantage. If the value of the American dollar falls relative to the Australian dollar, you win. The return will even exceed 14 percent. But if the value of the American dollar rises vis-à-vis the Australian dollar, the return will be less than 14 percent when the funds are converted back into American dollars. Just a modest deterioration in the Australian dollar, such as 5 percent a year, will wipe out the yield advantage. Obviously, the financial markets are expecting such a movement in the currency values, or General Mills wouldn't have to pay the 14 percent to raise the funds. So unless you are planning a vacation Down Under, you may prefer 9 percent from IBM to 14 percent from General Mills, if the latter is paying 14 percent in Australian dollars. •

Debt is also subject to the risk of price fluctuations. Once it has been issued, the market price of the debt will rise or fall depending on market conditions. If interest rates rise, the price of debt must fall so that its fixed interest payment is competitive. The opposite is true if interest rates decline. The price of debt will rise, for the fixed interest payment makes it more attractive, and buyers bid up the debt's price. Why these fluctuations in the price of debt instruments occur is explained in more detail in the subsequent section on the pricing of debt instruments.

There is, however, one feature of debt that partially compensates for the risk of price fluctuations. The holder knows that the debt ultimately matures; the principal must be repaid. Thus, if the price falls and the debt instrument sells for a discount (i.e., less than the face value), the value of the debt must appreciate as it approaches maturity. For on the day it matures, the full amount of the principal must be repaid.

The final risk that all creditors must endure is inflation, which reduces the value of money. During inflation the debtor repays the loan in money that purchases less. If the lenders anticipate inflation, they will demand a higher rate of interest to help protect their purchasing power. For example, if the rate of inflation is 8 percent, the creditors may demand 10 percent, which nets them 2 percent in real terms. While the inflation causes the real value of the capital to deteriorate, the high interest rate partially offsets the effects of inflation. Thus creditors must demand a rate of interest at least equal to the rate of inflation to maintain purchasing power.

EXHIBIT 9.1

Bond Ratings

Bond ratings indicate the risk associated with an issue of debt.

Moody's Bond Ratings

Grade	Rating	Description	Rating	Description	Grade
Investment Grade	Aaa	Bonds of highest quality	Ba	Bonds of speculative quality whose future cannot be considered well assured	Speculative Grade
	Aa	Bonds of high quality	B	Bonds that lack characteristics of a desirable investment	
	A	Bonds whose security of principal and interest is considered adequate but may be impaired in the future	Caa	Bonds in poor standing that may be defaulted	
	Baa	Bonds of medium grade that are neither highly protected nor poorly secured	Ca	Speculative bonds that are often in default	
			C	Bonds with little probability of any investment value (lowest rating)	

For ratings Aa through B, 1, 2, and 3 represent the high, middle, and low ratings within the class.

Standard & Poor's Ratings

Grade	Rating	Description	Rating	Description	Grade
Investment Grade	AAA	Bonds of highest quality	BB	Bonds of lower medium grade with few desirable investment characteristics	Speculative Grade
	AA	High-quality debt obligations	B, CCC	Primarily speculative bonds with great uncertainties and major risk if exposed to adverse conditions.	
	A	Bonds that have a strong capacity to pay interest and principal but may be susceptible to adverse effects	C	Income bonds on which no interest is being paid	
	BBB	Bonds that have an adequate capacity to pay interest and principal but are more vulnerable to adverse economic conditions or changing circumstances	D	Bonds in default	

Plus (+) and minus (−) are used to show relative strength within a rating category.

Source: Adapted from Moody's Bond Record *and Standard and Poor's* Bond Guide.

TYPES OF CORPORATE BONDS

There are many types of bonds that are issued by corporations. These bonds may be issued in this country or abroad, in which case they are called Eurobonds. The following list indicates the categories of corporate bonds:

- mortgage bonds
- equipment trust certificates
- debentures

- subordinated debentures
- income bonds; revenue bonds
- convertible bonds
- variable interest rate bonds
- zero coupon bonds

Each type of bond has characteristics that differentiate it from the others. Purchasers should be aware of the differences, for some types of bonds are decidedly more risky.

Mortgage Bonds

Mortgage bonds ▲
Bonds secured by a claim on real estate

Collateral ▲
Assets used to secure a loan or debt instrument

Mortgage bonds are issued to purchase specified real estate assets, and the acquired assets serve as **collateral.** That means the assets are pledged to secure the debt. If the firm should default on the interest or principal repayment, the creditors may take title to the pledged property. They may then choose to operate the fixed asset or to sell it. While the pledging of property may decrease the lender's risk of loss, the lender is not interested in taking possession and operating the property. Lenders earn their income through interest payments, not by the operation of the fixed assets. Such lenders are rarely qualified to operate the assets if they were to take possession of them. If they were forced to sell the assets, they might find few buyers and have to sell at distress prices. For example, if a school defaults on interest on the mortgage payments for its dormitories, what can the creditors do with the buildings if they take possession of them? While the pledging of the assets increases the safety of the principal, the lenders prefer the prompt payment of interest and principal.

Equipment Trust Certificates

Equipment trust certificates ▲
Serial bonds issued by transportation companies that are secured by the equipment purchased with the proceeds of the loan

Equipment trust certificates are issued to finance specified equipment, and the assets are pledged as collateral. These certificates are primarily issued by railroads and airlines to finance rolling stock and airplanes, and this equipment is the collateral. This collateral is considered to be of excellent quality, for unlike fixed assets this equipment can be readily *moved* and sold to other railroads and airlines should the firm default on the certificates.

Debentures

Debentures ▲
Unsecured bonds

Debentures are unsecured promissory notes of a company supported by the general credit of the firm. This type of debt is more risky, for in case of default or bankruptcy, the secured debt is redeemed before the debentures. Some debentures are **subordinated debentures,** and these are even riskier because they are subordinate to other debts of the firm. Even unsecured debt has a superior position to the subordinated debenture. These bonds are among the riskiest types of debt issued and usually have significantly higher interest rates or other features, such as convertibility into the stock of the company, to compensate the lenders for the increased risk.

Subordinated debentures ▲
Bonds with a lower (i.e., subordinate) claim on the firm's assets than the claims of other debt instruments

Financial institutions often prefer a firm to sell debentures to the general public. Since the debentures are general obligations of the company, they do not tie up its assets. If the firm needs additional money, it can use these assets as collateral. The financial institutions will be more willing to lend the firm the additional funds because of the collateral. If the assets had been previously pledged, the firm would lack this flexibility in its financing.

While the use of debentures may not decrease the ability of the firm to issue additional debt, default on the debentures usually means that all superior debt is in default. A frequent indenture clause stipulates that if any of the firm's debt is in default, all debt issues are in default, in which case the creditor may declare the entire debt to be due. Thus, a firm should not overextend itself through excessive use of unsecured debt any more than it should use excessive amounts of secured debt.

Income Bonds and Revenue Bonds

Income bonds require that the interest be paid only if the firm earns it. If the firm is unable to cover its other expenses, it is not legally obligated to pay the interest on these bonds. These are the riskiest of all types of bonds and are rarely issued today by corporations. There is, however, a type of bond frequently issued by state and local governments that is similar to income bonds. These are **revenue bonds,** which pay the interest only if the revenue is earned. Examples of this type are the bonds issued to finance toll roads. The interest on the debt is paid if the tolls generate sufficient revenue (after operating expenses) to cover the interest payments.

Income bonds ▲
Bonds whose interest is paid only if it is earned by the firm

Revenue bonds ▲
Bonds supported by the assets the bonds financed; income bonds

Convertible Bonds

Convertible bonds are a hybrid type of security. Technically they are debt: the bonds pay interest that is a fixed obligation of the firm, and the bonds have a maturity date. But these bonds have a special feature—they may be converted into a specified number of shares of common stock. For example, the Xerox convertible bonds may be exchanged for 10.87 shares of Xerox common stock. The value or market price of these bonds depends on both the value of the stock and the interest that the bonds pay.

Convertible bonds ▲
Bonds that may be converted into (exchanged for) stock at the option of the bondholder

This type of bond offers the investor the advantages of both debt and equity. If the price of the common stock rises, the value of the bond must rise. The investor has the opportunity for capital gain should the price of the common stock rise. If, however, the price of the common stock does not appreciate, the investor still owns a debt obligation of the company. The company must pay interest on this debt and must retire it at maturity. Thus, the investor has the safety of an investment in a debt instrument.

The convertible bond also offers the firm several advantages. First, if the firm gives investors the conversion feature, it is able to issue the bond with a lower rate of interest. Second, the conversion price is set above the market price of the stock when the bond is issued. If the bond is converted, the firm issues fewer shares than would have been issued if the firm had sold common stock. Therefore, the current stockholders' position is diluted less by the issuing of convertible bonds. Third, when the convertible bond is issued, the management of the firm does not anticipate having to retire the bond. Instead, management anticipates that the bond will be converted into stock, and this conversion ends the necessity to retire the debt. Fourth, when the bond is converted, the transfer of debt to common stock increases the equity base of the firm. Since the firm will then be less financially leveraged, it may be able to issue additional debt.

Convertible bonds appear to offer advantages to both investors and firms. They have been a popular financing vehicle for firms ranging from large established firms like IBM to small firms. However, since convertible bonds are a hybrid security that mixes elements of debt and equity, they are difficult to analyze. For this reason, a detailed discussion is deferred to Chapter 12, which follows the material on common stock.

Variable Interest Rate Bonds

Prior to the mid-1970s, once bonds were issued the amount of interest was fixed. With the advent of increased inflation in the 1970s, corporations started issuing bonds with variable interest rates. Citicorp was the first major American firm to offer **variable interest rate bonds** to the general public. These bonds were not the first examples of variable interest rate bonds, however, for there had been prior issues in the United States, and variable interest rate mortgages have existed in other countries for years.

Variable interest rate bonds ▲
Long-term debt instruments whose interest payments vary with changes in short-term interest rates

Two features of the Citicorp bond are unique: (1) a variable interest rate tied to the interest rate on Treasury bills, and (2) the right of the holder of the bond to redeem it at its face value. The interest rate of the Citicorp bond is 1 percent above the average Treasury bill rate during a specified time period. When the bonds were issued, the initial interest rate paid by the bonds was 9.7 percent. This variability of the interest rate means that if short-term interest rates rise, the interest rate paid by this bond will increase. The bond's owner participates in any increase in short-term interest rates. Of course, if the short-term interest rates decline, the holder of the bond will earn a lower rate of interest.

The second unique feature of the Citicorp bond is that the holder of the bond has the option to redeem the bond for its face value two years after it was issued. This option will subsequently recur every six months. The holder knows that the principal can be obtained twice a year. If the holder needs the money quicker, the bond may be sold, for there exists an active secondary market in these debt instruments. Thus, Citicorp bonds are very liquid debt instruments that also offer the holder an opportunity to participate in higher short-term interest rates (if they occur).

These bonds were issued in small denominations, initially in units of $5,000, but they are traded in units as small as $1,000. Many short-term debt instruments (e.g., commercial paper) are issued in large denominations, such as $100,000, and that excludes the small investor. The Citicorp bonds were especially designed to attract the small investor by offering an opportunity to participate, through variable interest, in the high yields that were commonly experienced in the short-term money market at the time the bonds were issued.

The Citicorp bond was very competitive with other short-term investments available to small investors. If an investor owned a two-year certificate of deposit that earned 6 percent, the Citicorp bond was an attractive alternative investment. A certificate of deposit earns more than a savings account, but, if the investor needs the money before two years elapse, a penalty is paid if the certificate of deposit is cashed. If this investor purchased the Citicorp bond, 9.7 percent is earned during the first year and an undetermined amount in the second year. After two years the investor may redeem the bond (just as the certificate of deposit matures). If the investor needs the money earlier, the bond may be sold on the exchange at the current market price. In this case the investor may lose some of the principal through the sale (just as interest would be lost if the certificate of deposit were to be cashed prematurely). Thus the Citicorp bond compared favorably with the certificate of deposit except that the interest in the second year was not known. However, it was very doubtful when the bonds were issued that this interest would be less than the amount paid by the certificate of deposit.

These bonds were severely criticized by savings and loan associations and other savings institutions, for the bonds initially offered investors higher yields than the savings institutions were allowed (by law) to pay. These institutions feared that deposits would be withdrawn and the money used to purchase the new bonds. Why would savers continue to place money in savings accounts if they could earn more interest and have virtually the same liquidity by investing in bonds? The initial demand for the Citicorp bond was great; the company was able to sell $600 million of the bonds. The success of the Citicorp issue led to imitators such as the Chase Manhattan, and there now exist several issues of similar variable interest rate bonds.

After these variable interest rate bonds were issued, short-term interest rates did, in fact, decline. The Citicorp bond paid only 6.6 percent during the second year, though that still exceeded the 6 percent paid by the two-year certificate of deposit. The decline in short-term interest rates resulted in a decline in investor fascination with variable interest rate bonds. This trend was reversed in the early 1980s, when short-term interest rates once again rose to historic highs.

Variable interest rate debt instruments demonstrate an essential point in finance: money will flow from one investment to a more attractive alternative. This flow of funds among alternative investments may alter the funds available to finance certain types of purchases. Since savings institutions primarily finance mortgages, any flow of deposits from these savings institutions reduces the credit available to finance homes. If funds were removed from savings accounts to purchase variable rate bonds, they diverted credit from the mortgage market.

Zero Coupon Bonds

In 1981 a new type of bond was sold to the general public. These bonds pay no interest and are sold at large discounts. The path-breaking issue was the J. C. Penney **zero coupon bond** of 1989. This bond was initially sold for a discount ($330) but paid $1,000 at maturity in 1989. The investor's funds grew from $330 to $1,000 after eight years. The rate of growth (i.e., the yield on the bond) was 14.86 percent.

Zero coupon bonds ▲ Bonds which are initially sold at a discount and on which interest accrues and is paid at maturity

After the initial success of this issue, several other firms including IBM Credit Corporation (the financing arm of IBM) and ITT Financial issued similar bonds. In each case the firm pays no interest. The bond sells for a large discount, and the investor's return accrues from the appreciation of the bond's value as it approaches maturity.

There is, however, a tax feature that reduces the attractiveness of zero coupon bonds. The IRS taxes the accrued interest as if it were received. The investor must pay federal income tax on the earned interest even though the investor receives the funds only when the bond matures. Thus, zero coupon bonds are of little interest to investors except as part of pension plans. Zero coupon bonds may be included in an individual's Keogh account or IRA because the tax on the accrued interest in the account is deferred until the funds are withdrawn. So the primary reason for acquiring a zero coupon bond is to use it in conjunction with a tax-deferred pension plan.

High-Yield Securities—Junk Bonds

Junk bonds ▲ Poor quality debt with high yields and high probability of default

High-yield securities (i.e., **junk bonds**) are not a particular type of bond but a name given to debt of low quality (i.e., bonds rated below triple B). Junk bonds are usually debentures and may be subordinated to the firm's other debt obligations. The poor quality of this debt requires that junk bonds offer high yields, which may be three to four percentage points greater than the yield available on high-quality bonds. Junk bonds are often issued to finance takeovers and mergers, and they may be bought by financial institutions and individuals who are accustomed to investing in poor-quality bonds and who are willing to accept the larger risk in order to earn the higher yields.

While some high-yield securities have existed for many years, the volume of new bonds with differing features virtually exploded during the 1980s. Many of these bonds may be treated as if they were equity instruments that will generate their potential return if the firm generates cash flow and survives.

Eurobonds

U.S. firms may also issue bonds in foreign countries to raise funds for foreign investments (e.g., plant and equipment). For example, Exxon reported in its 1990 annual report that it had long-term debt of $7,687 billion of which $1,422 billion (18.5 percent) was payable in foreign countries. These bonds fall into two basic types, depending on the currency in which they are denominated. U.S. firms can sell bonds denominated in the local currency (e.g., British pounds or French francs), or the firm can sell abroad bonds denominated in U.S. dollars, called **Eurobonds.** This term applies even though the bonds may be issued in, say, Asia instead of Europe.

Eurobonds ▲ Bonds denominated in U.S. dollars but issued abroad

When a firm issues a Eurobond, the U.S. firm promises to make payments in dollars. This means that the U.S. investor does not have to convert the payments from the local currency (e.g., British pounds) into dollars. Fluctuations in the value of one currency relative to another is a major source of risk that every individual who acquires foreign securities must bear. By acquiring Eurobonds, the U.S. investor avoids this currency risk. However, foreign investors do bear this risk. They have to convert the dollars into their currency, so the yields on Eurobonds tend to be higher than on comparable domestic securities. The higher yield is a major reason why investors find Eurobonds attractive.

REGISTERED AND COUPON BONDS

Registered bonds ▲ Bonds whose ownership is recorded with the commercial bank that distributes the interest and principal payments

In the past bonds were issued in two forms: (1) registered bonds and (2) coupon bonds. **Registered bonds** are registered as to principal and interest. They are similar in appearance to stock certificates, as is illustrated by the 8¾ percent AT&T bond in Exhibit 9.2. The interest payments (in this case $43.75 semiannually per $1,000) are sent to the

EXHIBIT 9.2

Example of a Registered Bond

A registered bond indicates the name of the owner as well as the important features of the debt instrument.

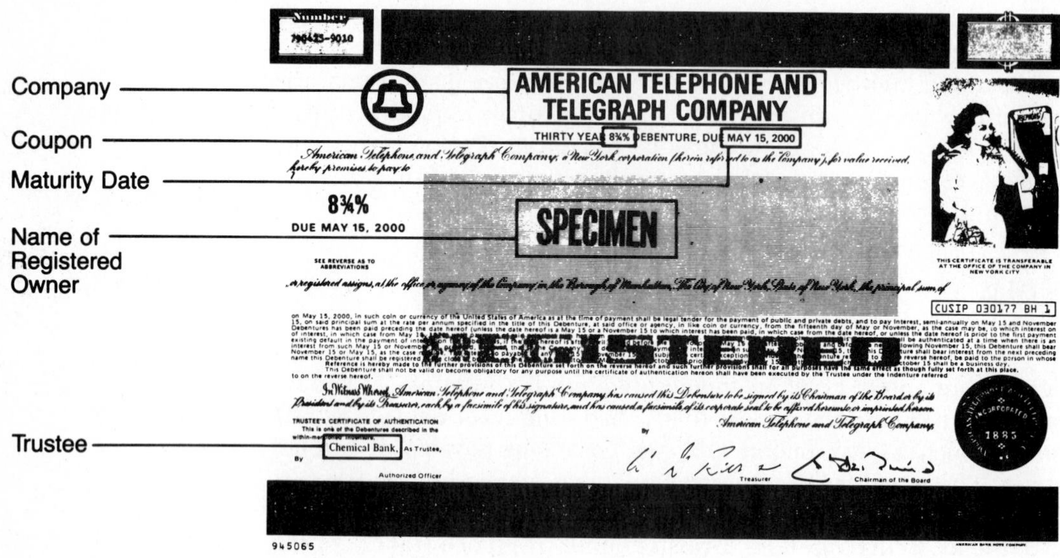

Source: Reprinted with permission from the American Telephone and Telegraph Company.

Coupon bonds ▲
Bonds with coupons attached that are removed and presented for payment of interest when due

registered owner. **Coupon bonds** are bearer bonds with coupons attached. The owner of the bond has to detach the coupons and send them to the paying agent to collect the interest. Under current tax laws, new issues of coupon bonds are no longer permitted.

An example of a coupon bond is given in Exhibit 9.3. The coupons are numbered from 1 to 50, and each represents a six-month interest payment. This Georgia & Florida Railroad 6 percent income nonmortgage debenture certainly was not a good investment. It still has all the coupons attached. This means that not one interest payment was made. While bonds are debt obligations, this particular bond is a debenture (i.e., not secured) and an income bond. As was previously explained, the debtor is obligated to pay the interest on an income bond only if the interest is earned. This railroad did not earn sufficient revenues to meet even the first interest payment.

In the past, most bonds were issued in coupon form, and people who lived on a fixed income were frequently referred to as "coupon clippers." The current trend is to issue bonds in "book form." No actual bonds are issued; instead a record of owners is maintained by the issuer and brokerage firms. A firm such as AT&T may have a $1 billion issue of bonds held by ten brokerage firms. The brokerage firms maintain records of the individual investors who purchased the bonds and make a market in the securities. Such a system is obviously more cost efficient than issuing actual physical certificates, but the brokerage firm may charge custodial fees, which either the issuer or the investor will have to pay.

DETERMINATION OF THE PRICE OF A BOND

Many bonds are sold to the general public and are traded daily like stocks. Some bonds are listed on the exchanges, and trades in these bonds are reported by the financial press. For example, *The Wall Street Journal* reports trades in hundreds of bonds daily. On January 7, 1991, for example, it reported transactions in 10 different bond issues of AT&T (whereas AT&T, of course, has only one issue of common stock).

The general form for reporting transactions in a bond issue is illustrated in Exhibit 9.4, which reproduces the prices for the AT&T bond illustrated in Exhibit 9.2. The entries in the exhibit are read as follows. The first entries describe the bond, which in this case is the AT&T 8¾00. The listing is for a $1,000 AT&T bond with a coupon of 8¾ percent that matures in the year 2000 (i.e., the 00 in Exhibit 9.4). On January 3, 1991, the current yield was 8.7 percent and 351 of these $1,000 bonds were traded during the day. The closing price was 100⅜ ($1,003.75), which was ⅝ ($6.25) higher than the close on the previous day.

While bond prices fluctuate daily, the price of a bond (in a given risk class) is primarily related to (1) the interest paid by the bond, (2) the interest rate investors may earn on competitive bonds, and (3) the maturity date of the bond. A bond is a debt instrument that makes periodic interest payments (usually semiannually) that are similar to annuity payments. Part of the bond's value is in the present value of these interest payments. At maturity the principal is repaid. The rest of the bond's value is in the present value of this principal repayment. Thus, the price of a bond today is determined by the present value of the interest payments and the present value of the principal repayment.

The value of a bond is expressed algebraically in Equation 9.1 in terms of the present value formulas discussed in Chapter 7. A bond's value is

9.1 $$P_B = \frac{I_1}{(1+i)^1} + \frac{I_2}{(1+i)^2} + \cdots + \frac{I_n}{(1+i)^n} + \frac{P}{(1+i)^n},$$

where P_B indicates the current price of the bond; I, the annual interest payment (with the subscripts indicating the year); n, the number of years to maturity; P, the principal; and i, the current interest rate.

The calculation of a bond's price using Equation 9.1 may be illustrated by a simple example. A firm has a $1,000 bond outstanding that matures in three years with a 6 percent coupon rate ($60 annually). All that is needed to determine the price of the bond is the current interest

EXHIBIT 9.3

Example of a Coupon Bond

A coupon bond does not indicate the owner. Possession of the bond is considered proof of ownership.

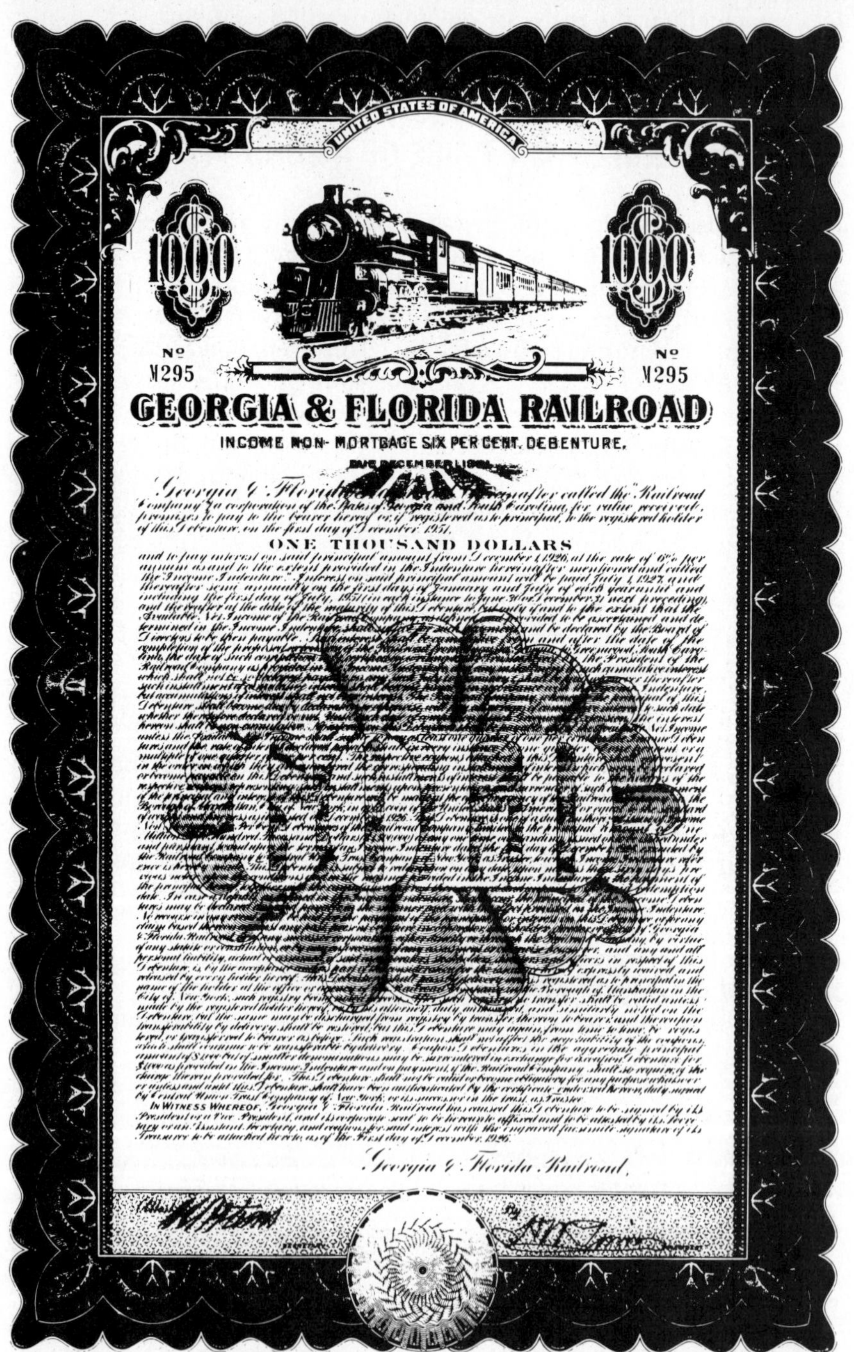

UNITED STATES OF AMERICA

1000 1000

Nº M295 Nº M295

GEORGIA & FLORIDA RAILROAD

INCOME NON-MORTGAGE SIX PER CENT. DEBENTURE.

ONE THOUSAND DOLLARS

VOID

Georgia & Florida Railroad,

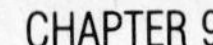

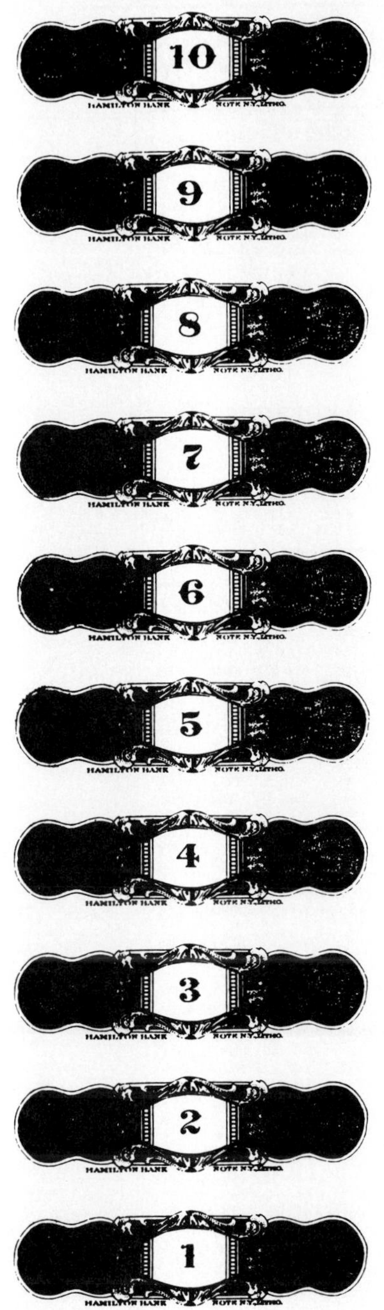
10
9
8
7
6
5
4
3
2
1

GEORGIA & FLORIDA RAILROAD,
IF AND WHEN SUCH INTEREST SHALL BECOME PAYABLE IN ACCORDANCE WITH THE PROVISIONS OF ITS INCOME INDENTURE TO CENTRAL UNION TRUST COMPANY OF NEW YORK, AS TRUSTEE, DATED DECEMBER 1, 1926, WILL PAY TO BEARER IN UNITED STATES GOLD COIN AT THE OFFICE OR AGENCY OF THE RAILROAD COMPANY IN THE BOROUGH OF MANHATTAN IN THE CITY OF NEW YORK, ON PRESENTATION AND SURRENDER OF THIS COUPON, THE
EST ON ITS INCOME NON-MORTGAGE SIX PER CENT
UNLESS SAID DEBENTURE SHALL HAVE BEEN CALLED FOR PREVIOUS REDEMPTION
TREASURER
295
HAMILTON BANK NOTE N.Y. LITHO
Tenth 10
Ninth 9
Eighth 8
Seventh 7
Sixth 6
Fifth 5
Fourth 4
Third 3
Second 2
First 1

EXHIBIT 9.4

Reporting of Bond Transactions

Bond reporting is limited to current yield, volume of transactions, closing price, and net change in price from the previous day.

NEW YORK EXCHANGE BONDS

Quotations as of 4 p.m. Eastern Time
Thursday, January 3, 1991

Volume $41,090,000

SALES SINCE JANUARY 1
(000 omitted)

1991	1990	1989
$74,500	$72,381	$47,965

	Domestic Thu.	Domestic Wed.	All Issues Thu.	All Issues Wed.
Issues traded	591	550	594	556
Advances	292	289	294	293
Declines	165	148	165	150
Unchanged	134	113	135	113
New highs	39	28	40	29
New lows	10	7	10	8

Dow Jones Bond Averages

–1990– High	–1990– Low	–1991– High	–1991– Low		–1991– Close	–1991– Chg.	–1991– %Yld	–1990– Close	–1990– Chg.
93.04	88.44	92.01	91.63	20 Bonds	92.01	+0.38	9.46	93.01	– 0.03
94.48	89.23	94.33	93.73	10 Utilities	94.33	+0.60	9.30	94.45	– 0.03
91.60	86.43	89.70	89.54	10 Industrials	89.70	+0.16	9.62	91.58	– 0.02

CORPORATION BONDS
Volume, $40,790,000

Bonds	Cur Yld	Vol	Close	Net Chg.
AL Lb 7¾14	cv	20	123	+ ½
Advst 9s08	cv	17	53½	– 1
AetnLf 8⅛07	8.9	24	91⅛	+ ⅝
AlaP 8½s01	8.9	3	95⅛	+ ¼
AlaP 8⅞s03	9.1	5	97¼	+ ⅜
AlaP 9¾s04	9.5	6	103	+ 1½
AlaP 10⅞05	10.6	11	102⅛	– 1¼
AlaP 9¼07	9.3	5	99	...
AlaP 9⅝08	9.5	2	101	...
AlaP 10s18	9.8	103	102	– 1
AlldC zr92	...	10	87	+ 1
AlldC zr2000	...	55	41	+ 2¼
AlldC zr9	...	5	80½	...
AlldC zr01	...	25	36¾	+ ⅛
AlldC zr03	...	5	28⅜	– ¼
AlldC zr07	...	30	19	– 1
AldSig 9⅞02	9.7	5	101⅝	+ 1¼
Alcoa 6s92	6.2	10	96⅜	– ⅝
Alcoa 9s95	9.0	10	100½	– ¼
Alcoa 7.45s96	7.9	5	94½	...
AMAX 9⅜00	9.9	21	95	...
AMAX 8⅝01	10.0	12	86½	+ 1¼
AmBas 14⅞98	42.7	2710	34⅞	+ 4⅜
AForP 5s30	10.0	18	50	+ 1½
AAirl 4¼92	4.5	60	93⅝	+ ⅝
ABrnd 9⅛16	9.6	22	95⅜	– ⅛
ATT 5⅝95	6.3	20	88⅞	– ⅞
ATT 5½97	6.4	92	85⅞	...
ATT 6s00	7.4	35	81½	+ ½
ATT 5⅛01	6.8	21	75⅝	+ ⅞
ATT 8¾00	8.7	351	100⅜	+ ⅝
ATT 7s01	8.0	65	87⅞	+ 1⅜
ATT 7⅛03	8.3	96	85½	– ⅛
ATT 8.80s05	8.9	189	99⅜	+ ⅞
ATT 8⅝s07	9.0	80	96	...
ATT 8⅝26	9.2	22	93⅜	+ ⅜
viAmes 7½14f	cv	95	4½	...
Amoco 6s91	6.1	35	98 9/16	...
Amoco 6s98	6.9	5	87¼	+ ⅝
ARch 10⅜95	9.6	22	108	– ½
ARch 10½95	10.0	50	104¾	...
ARch 9½96	9.2	515	102¾	– 1¼
Avnet 8s13	cv	3	89½	– 1
Avnet 6s12	cv	5	82¼	– 1¾
BRE 9½08	cv	29	88	+ ½
BakrHgh 9½06	cv	12	101	...
Ballys 6s98f	cv	120	13½	+ 2¼
Bally 10s06f	cv	59	19	...
BalGE 9⅜08	9.4	50	100	...
BalGE 9⅛16	9.3	18	98⅛	+ 1¼
Banka 8⅞05	9.5	43	93	– ¾
Banka 8¾01	9.4	10	93½	– 1½
Bkam zr92	...	8	85	– ⅛
Bkam zr91	...	4	99⅛	+ ¼
Bkam zr93	...	20	81⅜	...
Barnt 8½99	10.1	17	84½	– ¼
BellPa 8⅝06	8.8	25	98½	+ ½
BellPa 7½13	8.8	9	85½	+ ½
BellPa 9⅝14	9.4	27	102⅞	+ ⅛
BethSt 8.45s05	11.7	3	72⅛	+ 1⅛
Bevrly 7⅝03	cv	52	67	...
BlkBst zr04	...	12	38¾	– 1¼
Boeing 8⅜96	8.3	2	101	– ⅞
BoisC 7s16	cv	88	77½	...
BwnFer 6¼12	cv	31	80¼	+ ½
CBS 10⅞95	10.5	10	103¾	+ ¼
CIGNA 8.2s10	cv	7	87	– ¾
CPc4s perp	8.9	88	45	+ 3
CPC 4sr	9.4	28	42½	...
CapHd 12¾06	12.1	10	105¼	– 1¼
Carolco 14s93	20.3	20	69⅛	– ⅞
CaroFrt 6¼11	cv	25	63	+ 1½
CarPL 7¾02	8.6	20	90	+ ⅜
CaroT 7¾01	8.4	10	92½	+ 2½
CaroT 9s08	9.4	3	96	...
CartHaw 12¼96	25.1	125	48¾	+ ¾
CartHaw 12½02	31.6	6	39½	– ⅛
Caterp 8¾99	9.3	1	94	...
Cenco 4¾97	cv	10	58¼	...
CATS zr05-97	...	6	56	– 1¾
Champ 6½11	cv	27	88½	...

Source: The Wall Street Journal, *January 4, 1991, p. C14.*

rate, which is the interest rate that is being paid by newly issued, competitive bonds with the same length of time to maturity and the same degree of risk. If the competitive bonds yield 6 percent, then the price of this bond will be par ($1,000), for:

$$\begin{aligned} P_B &= \frac{\$60}{(1+0.06)^1} + \frac{\$60}{(1+0.06)^2} + \frac{\$60}{(1+0.06)^3} + \frac{\$1{,}000}{(1+0.06)^3} \\ &= \$56.60 + \$53.40 + \$50.38 + \$839.62 \\ &= \$1{,}000.00. \end{aligned}$$

If competitive bonds are selling to yield 8 percent, this bond will be unattractive to investors. They will not be willing to pay $1,000 for a bond yielding 6 percent when they could buy competing bonds at the same price that yield 8 percent. In order for this bond to compete with the others, its price must decline sufficiently to yield 8 percent. In terms of Equation 9.1, the price must be

$$\begin{aligned} P_B &= \frac{\$60}{(1+0.08)^1} + \frac{\$60}{(1+0.08)^2} + \frac{\$60}{(1+0.08)^3} + \frac{\$1{,}000}{(1+0.08)^3} \\ &= \$60(.926) + \$60(.857) + \$60(.794) + \$1{,}000(.794) \\ &= \$55.56 + \$51.42 + \$47.64 + \$794 \\ &= \$948.62. \end{aligned}$$

The price of the bond must decline to approximately $950, which means it must sell for a discount (i.e., a price less than the stated principal) to be competitive with comparable bonds. At that price, investors will earn $60 per year in interest and approximately $50 in capital gains over the three years, for a total annual return of 8 percent on their investment. The capital gain occurs because the bond is purchased for $948.62, but when it matures, the holder will receive $1,000.

If comparable debt were to yield 4 percent, the price of the bond in the previous example would rise. In this case the price of the bond would be

$$\begin{aligned} P_B &= \frac{\$60}{(1+0.04)^1} + \frac{\$60}{(1+0.04)^2} + \frac{\$60}{(1+0.04)^3} + \frac{\$1{,}000}{(1+0.04)^3} \\ &= \$60(.962) + \$60(.925) + \$60(.889) + \$1{,}000(.889) \\ &= \$1{,}055.56. \end{aligned}$$

The bond, therefore, would sell at a premium (i.e., a price greater than the stated principal). Although it may seem implausible for the bond to sell at a premium, this would occur if the market interest rate were to fall below the coupon rate of interest stated on the bond.

These price calculations are lengthy, but the number of computations can be reduced when one realizes that the valuation of a bond has two components: a flow of interest payments and a final repayment of principal. Since interest payments are fixed and are paid every year, they may be treated as an annuity. The principal repayment may be treated as a simple lump-sum payment. Thus the price of a bond is

$$\begin{aligned}\text{Price of bond} &= \text{coupon} \times \text{interest factor for the present value of an annuity} + \text{principal} \times \text{interest factor for the present value of \$1.00.}\\ &= \text{coupon} \times \text{PVAIF} + \text{principal} \times \text{PVIF}\end{aligned}$$

If a $1,000 bond pays $60 per year in interest and matures after three years, its current value is the present value of the $60 annuity for three years and the present value of the $1,000 that will be received after three years. If the interest rate is 8 percent, the current value of the bond is

$$P_B = \$60(\text{PVAIF } 8\%, 3\text{Y}) + \$1{,}000(\text{PVIF } 8\%, 3\text{Y})$$
$$P_B = \$60(2.577) + \$1{,}000(.794) = \$948.62,$$

where 2.577 is the interest factor for the present value of a $1 annuity at 8 percent for three years and .794 is the interest factor for the present value of $1 at 8 percent after three years. This is the same answer that was derived earlier, but the amount of arithmetic has been reduced.[1]

These examples illustrate the general conclusion that bond prices and changes in market interest are inversely related. *When market interest rates rise, bond prices decline. When market interest rates fall, bond prices rise.* Higher interest rates depressed the bond's current value. This general conclusion is illustrated in Figure 9.1. The bond's price declined from $1,000 to $948.62 when interest rates rose from 6 to 8 percent, but the price rose to $1,055.56 when interest rates declined to 4 percent.

This negative relationship between the price of a bond and changes in current interest rates is, of course, the interest rate risk discussed in the previous chapter. While all bonds exhibit this price volatility, the price fluctuations of bonds with longer terms to maturity tend to be greater than the price fluctuations of bonds with shorter terms to maturity. In the previous example, the price of the three-year bond declined

---

[1]Since most bonds pay interest semiannually, the above illustration may be adjusted for semiannual interest payments. First, divide the coupon by 2 to determine the six-month payment ($60/2 = $30); second, divide the rate of interest by 2 to determine the semiannual interest rate (8%/2 = 4%); and third, multiply the number of years by 2 to determine the number of time periods, denoted by the letter n when other than one year (3 × 2 = 6). After these adjustments, the value of the bond is

$$\begin{aligned}P_B &= \$30(\text{PVAIF } 4\%, 6n) + \$1{,}000(\text{PVIF } 4\%, 6n)\\ &= \$30(5.242) + \$1{,}000(.790) = \$947.26.\end{aligned}$$

This valuation is marginally smaller than when annual compounding was used since the bond's price must decline slightly more to compensate for the more frequent compounding. If interest rates rise and bond prices fall, the decline will be greater when the price is calculated using semiannual payments, because the investor forgos more lost interest from the higher rates when interest is paid semiannually. The lower price compensates the buyer for the lost interest.

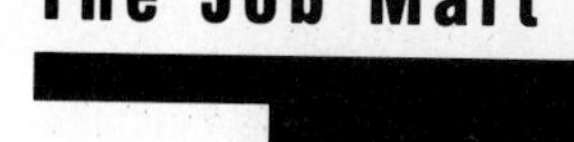

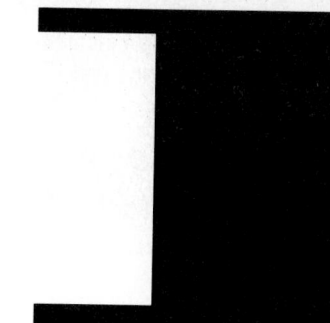

Investment Officer—Fixed Income Securities

■ Job Description: Responsible for portfolio of fixed income securities. Recommend purchases and sales of bonds and preferred stocks. Monitor performance of portfolio, analyze market conditions and the direction of change in interest rates, analyze yield differentials among types of securities, and determine the tax implications of portfolio strategies. ■ Job Requirements: Thorough knowledge of monetary policy, fixed income securities, and the measures of risk and its management. Skill in the application of mathematical tools to evaluate investments; ability to use data bases and spreadsheets. ■ Characteristics: Financial institutions (insurance companies, bond funds, and pension plans and trust accounts managed by commercial banks) have large holdings of fixed income securities. Individuals managing these funds are in visible positions; superior portfolio performance can lead to advancement to the position of portfolio manager.

---

from $1,000 to $948.62 when interest rates rose from 6 to 8 percent. If the bond had had a 20-year term to maturity, its price would have fallen to $803.59. The increased price volatility also applies if interest rates fall. Thus the price of a 20-year bond that pays $60 annually would rise to $1,271.82 if interest rates were to fall from 6 to 4 percent.

The inverse relationship between the price of a bond and the interest rate suggests a means to profit in the bond market. All that the investor needs to know is the direction of future changes in interest rates. If investors anticipate that interest rates will decline, they are expecting the price of previously issued bonds to rise. This price increase must occur for previously issued bonds to have the same yield as bonds being currently issued. The converse is also true, for if investors anticipate that interest rates will rise, they are also anticipating that the price of currently available bonds will decline. This decline must occur for previously issued bonds to offer the same yield as currently issued bonds. Therefore, if investors can anticipate the direction of change in interest rates, they can also anticipate the direction of change in the price of bonds.

Investors, however, may anticipate incorrectly and thus suffer losses in the bond market. If they buy bonds and interest rates rise, the market value of their bonds must decline and the investors suffer capital losses. These individuals, however, have something in their favor: The bonds must ultimately be retired. Since the principal must be redeemed, an investment error in the bond market may be corrected when the bond's price rises as the bond approaches maturity. The capital losses will eventually be erased. The correction of the error, however, may take years,

FIGURE 9.1

Relationship between a Bond's Price and Interest Rates

Higher interest rates are associated with lower bond prices.

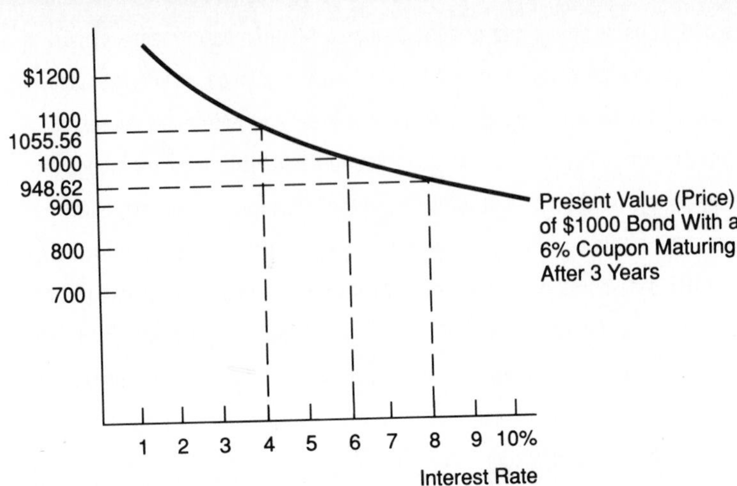

during which time the investors have lost the higher yields that were available on bonds issued after their initial investments.

YIELDS

The word *yield* is frequently used with regard to investing in bonds. There are two important types of yield: the current yield and the yield to maturity. This section will differentiate between these two yields.

The Current Yield

The current yield (CY) is the percentage that the investor earns annually. It is simply

9.2 $$CY = \frac{\text{Annual interest payment}}{\text{Price of the bond}}.$$

The bond used in the previous example has a coupon rate of 6 percent. Thus, when the price of the bond is $948.62, the current yield is

$$\frac{\$60}{\$948.62} = 6.3\%.$$

The current yield is important because it gives the investor an indication of the current return that will be earned on the investment. Investors who seek high current income prefer bonds that offer a high current yield.

The current yield, however, can be very misleading, for it fails to consider any change in the price of the bond that may occur if the bond is held to maturity. Obviously, if a bond is bought at a discount, its value must rise as it approaches maturity. The opposite occurs if the bond is purchased for a premium, for its price will decline as maturity approaches. For this reason it is desirable to know the bond's yield to maturity.

The Yield to Maturity

The yield to maturity considers not only the current income that is generated by the bond but also any change in its value when it is held to maturity. If the bond referred to earlier is purchased for $948.62 and is held to maturity, after three years the investor will receive a return of 8 percent. This is the yield to maturity, because this return considers not only the current interest return of 6.3 percent but also the price appreciation of the bond from $948.62 at the time of purchase to $1,000 at maturity. Since the yield to maturity considers both the flow of interest income and the price change, it is a more accurate measure of the return offered to investors by a particular bond issue than the current yield.

The yield to maturity may be determined by using Equation 9.1. That equation reads:

9.1
$$P_B = \frac{I_1}{(1+i)^1} + \frac{I_2}{(1+i)^2} + \cdots + \frac{I_n}{(1+i)^n} + \frac{P}{(1+i)^n}.$$

The i, which was defined as the rate of interest paid by newly issued bonds, is also the yield to maturity. It is that rate which equates the present value of the interest payments plus the present value of the principal repayment with the cost of the bond when the bond is held to maturity. If the investor buys a bond and holds it until maturity, the return is the yield to maturity, and that rate has to be the current rate of interest being paid by comparable bonds with the same term and credit ratings.

Determining the yield to maturity when the coupon rate of interest, the bond's price, and the maturity date are known is not easy, even with the use of an electronic calculator. For example, if a $1,000 bond that matures in three years and pays $100 annually were selling for $952 and the investor wanted to know the yield to maturity, the calculation would be

$$\$952 = \frac{\$100}{(1+i)^1} + \frac{\$100}{(1+i)^2} + \frac{\$100}{(1+i)^3} + \frac{\$1{,}000}{(1+i)^3}.$$

Solving this equation can be a formidable task because there is no simple arithmetical computation to determine the value of i. Instead, the investor selects a value for i and plugs it into the equation. If this value equates the left-hand and right-hand sides of the equation, then that value of i is the yield to maturity.

If the value does not equate the two sides of the equation, another value must be selected. This process is repeated until a value for i is found that equates both sides of the equation. Obviously, that can be a long process. For example, suppose the investor selects 14 percent and substitutes it into the right-hand side of the equation:

$$P_B = \frac{\$100}{(1 + 0.14)^1} + \frac{\$100}{(1 + 0.14)^2} + \frac{\$100}{(1 + 0.14)^3} + \frac{\$1{,}000}{(1 + 0.14)^3}$$

Since the individual has both an interest rate (0.14 percent) and the number of years (3 years), the interest factors for the present value of an annuity and of a dollar may be obtained from the appropriate interest tables and used to determine the value of the bond at that rate for that term to maturity. That is,

$$\begin{aligned} P_B &= \$100(\text{PVAIF } 14\%, 3\text{Y}) + \$1{,}000(\text{PVIF } 14\%, 3\text{Y}) \\ &= \$100(2.322) + \$1{,}000(0.675) \\ &= \$907.20 \end{aligned}$$

If the yield to maturity were 14 percent, the bond would sell for \$907.20; however, the bond is selling for \$952, so 14 percent cannot be its yield to maturity. The selected yield was too high, which caused the present value (the price of the bond) to be too low. The investor must select another, lower rate and repeat the process. (If the investor had obtained a value greater than the current price, the selected rate was too low, and the investor should select a higher rate.) If the investor had selected 12 percent, then

$$\begin{aligned} P_B &= \$100(\text{PVAIF } 12\%, 3\text{Y}) + \$1{,}000(\text{PVIF } 12\%, 3\text{Y}) \\ &= \$100(2.402) + \$1{,}000(0.712) \\ &= \$952.20. \end{aligned}$$

Thus, the yield to maturity, compounded annually, is approximately 12 percent. (If the individual needs a more exact yield to maturity—for example, 12.23 percent—a computer program such as *PROFIT +* or an electronic calculator programmed to compute yields to maturity is required for the calculation.)

The above process to determine the yield to maturity is quite tedious. However, the yield to maturity can be approximated by Equation 9.3.

9.3 $$i = \frac{I + \dfrac{P - P_B}{n}}{\dfrac{P + P_B}{2}}.$$

The symbols are the same that were used in Equation 9.1. If the current price of a \$1,000 bond (P = \$1,000) with a 10 percent coupon (I = \$100) is \$952 (P_B = \$952) and the bond matures in three years (n = 3), then the approximate yield to maturity is

$$i = \frac{\$100 + \frac{\$1{,}000 - 952}{3}}{\frac{\$1{,}000 + 952}{2}}$$

$$= \frac{100 + 48/3}{976}$$

$$= 11.88\%.$$

This answer, 11.88 percent, is approximately the 12 percent derived above by the more tedious, but technically correct, method.

A Comparison of the Current Yield and the Yield to Maturity

The current yield and the yield to maturity are equal only if the bond sells for its principal amount or par. If the bond sells at a discount, the yield to maturity exceeds the current yield. This may be illustrated by the bond in the previous example. When it sells at a discount (e.g., $952), the current yield is only 10.5 percent. However, the yield to maturity is 12 percent. Thus, the yield to maturity exceeds the current yield.

If the bond sells at a premium, the current yield exceeds the yield to maturity. For example, if the bond sells for $1,052, the current yield is 9.5 percent ($100 ÷ $1,052) and the yield to maturity is 8 percent. The yield to maturity is less in this case because the loss that the investor must suffer when the price of the bond declines from $1,052 to $1,000 at maturity has been incorporated.

Exhibit 9.5 presents the current yield and the yield to maturity at different prices for a bond with an 8 percent coupon that matures in ten years. As may be seen in the table, the larger the discount (or the smaller the premium), the greater are both the current yield and the yield to maturity. For example, when the bond sells for $881.50, the yield to maturity is 9.9 percent, but it rises to 11.5 percent when the price declines to $795.10.

EXHIBIT 9.5

Current Yields and Yields to Maturity for a Ten-Year Bond with an 8 Percent Coupon

Price of Bond	Coupon	Current Yield	Yield to Maturity
$1,109.00	8.0%	7.2%	6.5%
1,049.10	8.0	7.6	7.3
1,000.00	8.0	8.0	8.0
966.80	8.0	8.3	8.5
910.50	8.0	8.8	9.4
881.50	8.0	9.1	9.9
831.30	8.0	9.6	10.8
795.10	8.0	10.1	11.5

If a bond sells for a premium, the current yield exceeds the yield to maturity. If a bond sells for a discount, the yield to maturity exceeds the current yield.

EXHIBIT 9.6

A Serial Bond Issue: $26,025,000 Seaboard System Railroad

An equal amount of the debt is retired each year commencing one year after the issue date and extending for fifteen years.

Maturity	Yield	Amount Retired
1985	10.10%	$1,735,000
1986	11.05	1,735,000
1987	11.45	1,735,000
—	—	—
—	—	—
1991	11.95	1,735,000
1992	12.00	1,735,000
—	—	—
—	—	—
1997	12.00	1,735,000
1998	12.00	1,735,000
1999	12.00	1,735,000

RETIRING DEBT

Debt must ultimately be retired, and this retirement may occur on or before the maturity date of the debt. When the bond is issued, a method for periodic retirement is usually specified, for very few debt issues are retired in one lump payment at the final maturity date. Instead, part of the issue is systematically retired each year. This systematic retirement may be achieved by issuing the bond in series or by having a sinking fund. In addition, dramatic changes in interest rates may cause a corporation to retire bonds before maturity by repurchasing or by calling the debt.

Serial Bonds

Serial bonds Debt issued in a series so that some of the bonds periodically mature

In an issue of **serial bonds,** some bonds mature each year. This type of bond is usually issued by a corporation to finance specific equipment (e.g., railroad cars), and the equipment is pledged as collateral. As the equipment is depreciated, the cash flow generated by the profits and depreciation expense is used to retire the bonds in series as they mature.

Exhibits 9.6 and 9.7 present an issue of equipment trust certificates, which are illustrative of a serial bond issue. The entire issue of debt is for $26,025,000, but one-fifteenth of the certificates mature each year. The company retires $1,735,000 of the certificates each year as each series within the entire issue matures. Thus, at the end of the fifteenth year, the entire issue of certificates will have been retired.

While the Seaboard System Railroad equipment trust certificates are an example of a serial bond issue, few corporations issue serial bonds. They are primarily issued by state and local governments for capital im-

EXHIBIT 9.7

Example of a Serial Bond

This serial cannot be called prior to maturity and the longer term bonds within the issue have a higher rate of interest.

New Issue / October 26, 1984

$26,025,000

Seaboard System Railroad

Equipment Trust, No. 2

11¾% Equipment Trust Certificates
Non-Callable

Dividends to accrue from date of issuance. To mature in 15 equal annual installments of $1,735,000, commencing March 15, 1985.

Issued under the Philadelphia Plan with 20% original cash equity.

MATURITIES AND YIELDS

1985	10.10%	1989	11.70%	1993	12.00%	1997	12.00%
1986	11.05	1990	11.80	1994	12.00	1998	12.00
1987	11.45	1991	11.95	1995	12.00	1999	12.00
1988	11.60	1992	12.00	1996	12.00		

These certificates are offered subject to prior sale, when, as and if issued and received by us.

Salomon Brothers Inc

Drexel Burnham Lambert
Incorporated

L. F. Rothschild, Unterberg, Towbin

Source: Reprinted with permission from Salomon Brothers Inc.

provements (e.g., new school buildings). The series are then retired over a period of years by the tax revenues of the governmental unit.

Sinking Funds

Sinking fund ▲
Series of periodic payments to retire a bond issue

Sinking funds are generally employed to ease the retirement of long-term corporate debt. A **sinking fund** is a periodic payment for the purpose of retiring the debt issue. The payment may be made to a trustee, who invests the money to earn interest. The periodic payments plus the accumulated interest retire the debt when it matures.

In another type of sinking fund, the firm is required to retire a specified amount of the principal each year. The firm may randomly call the bonds to be retired. Once the sinking fund has selected the individual bonds to be retired, the holders must surrender the bonds to receive the principal. There is no reason for the bondholders to continue to hold the bonds, for interest payments cease.

A variation on this type of sinking fund permits the firm to buy back the bonds on the open market instead of randomly selecting and retiring them at par. If the bonds are currently selling at a discount, the firm does not have to expend $1,000 to retire the bonds. For example, if the current price of a bond is $800 for a $1,000 face amount of debt, the firm can retire the bond with an outlay of only $800. Such a repurchase meets the sinking fund requirement and obviously is advantageous for the firm.

Repurchasing Debt

If interest rates have risen and bond prices have therefore declined, a firm may seek to retire debt by purchasing it on the open market. The purchases may be made from time to time, and sellers of the bonds need not know that the company is purchasing and retiring the bonds. The company may also announce the intention to purchase and retire the bonds at a specified price. The bondholders then may tender their bonds at the specified price.

The advantage of retiring debt that is selling at a discount is the savings to the firm. If the firm issued $1,000 bonds that are currently selling for $600, it may reduce its debt by $1,000 with only a $600 outlay in cash. There is a $400 saving (i.e., extraordinary gain) from purchasing and retiring the debt at a discount. This gain generates income for the firm's stockholders. For example, Guilford Mills reported to its stockholders in 1991 that the firm earned over $2.3 million ($.27 a share) from repurchasing its long-term debt at a discount.

On the surface, this method may appear to be a desirable means to retire debt, but such appearances may be deceiving. Using money to repurchase debt is an investment decision just like buying plant and equipment. If the firm repurchases the debt, it cannot use the money for other purposes. The question is, which is the better use of the money: purchasing other income-earning assets, or retiring the debt? Unlike a sinking fund requirement (which management must meet), purchasing and retiring debt is a voluntary act by the firm's management. The lower the price of the debt, the greater the potential benefit from the purchase, but the firm's management must determine if it is the best use of the firm's scarce resource—cash. For most firms the discount is not sufficient to justify purchasing the bonds. They have better alternative uses for the funds.

Calling the Debt

Some bonds have a **call feature,** which permits the issuer to redeem the bond prior to maturity. If interest rates fall after a bond has been issued, it may be advantageous for the company to issue a new bond at the lower interest rates. The proceeds then can be used to retire the older bond with the higher interest rates. The company "calls" the older bond and retires it.

Call feature ▲
Right of a debtor to retire (i.e., call) a bond issued prior to maturity

Of course, such a refunding hurts the bondholders, who lose the higher yielding instruments. To protect these creditors, a call feature usually has a call penalty, such as a year's interest. If the initial issue had a 9 percent interest rate, the company would have to pay $1,090 to retire $1,000 worth of debt. While such a call penalty does protect bondholders, a company can still refinance if interest rates decline enough to justify paying the call penalty.

Such refinancing frequently occurred during 1986 and 1987, when interest rates fell significantly below the levels of the early 1980s. Utilities in particular, which had previously issued debt with high interest rates, issued new bonds with lower interest coupons, called the old debt, and paid any applicable penalties. For example, in 1986, Public Service of New Mexico redeemed mortgage bonds issued in 1981 and due in 2011, which paid *17½* percent. Such refinancing sufficiently reduced interest expense to justify paying the call penalty.

GOVERNMENT SECURITIES

In addition to corporate bonds, governments ranging from the federal government to the local school board issue bonds. The general features of these debt obligations are the same as corporate bonds. Government bonds pay interest, must be retired at their maturity date, may have a call feature, and generally provide for periodic retirement. There is an active secondary market for these bonds, so the investor may buy and sell these securities in much the same manner that corporate bonds are bought and sold. The risks associated with investing in government

EXHIBIT 9.8

Price Quotes and Yields on Federal Government Securities as of January 3, 1991

Reporting of Federal Government securities prices and yields.

TREASURY BONDS, NOTES & BILLS

Thursday, January 3, 1991

Representative Over-the-Counter quotations based on transactions of $1 million or more.

Treasury bond, note and bill quotes are as of mid-afternoon. Colons in bid-and-asked quotes represent 32nds; 101:01 means 101 1/32. Net changes in 32nds. n-Treasury note. Treasury bill quotes in hundredths, quoted on terms of a rate of discount. Days to maturity calculated from settlement date. All yields are to maturity and based on the asked quote. For bonds callable prior to maturity, yields are computed to the earliest call date for issues quoted above par and to the maturity date for issues below par. *-When issued.

Source: Federal Reserve Bank of New York.

U.S. Treasury strips as of 3 p.m. Eastern time, also based on transactions of $1 million or more. Colons in bid-and-asked quotes represent 32nds; 101:01 means 101 1/32. Net changes in 32nds. Yields calculated on the bid quotation. ci-stripped coupon interest. bp-Treasury bond, stripped principal. np-Treasury note, stripped principal.

Source: Bear, Stearns & Co. via Street Software Technology Inc.

GOVT. BONDS & NOTES

Rate	Maturity Mo/Yr	Bid	Asked	Chg.	Ask Yld.
$11\frac{3}{4}$	Jan 91n	100:05	100:07	− 1	1.59
9	Jan 91n	100:07	100:09	....	4.50
$7\frac{3}{8}$	Feb 91n	100:02	100:04	− 1	6.01
$9\frac{1}{8}$	Feb 91n	100:08	100:10	− 1	5.94
$9\frac{3}{8}$	Feb 91n	100:12	100:14	− 1	6.10
$6\frac{3}{4}$	Mar 91n	99:31	100:01	− 1	6.49
$9\frac{3}{4}$	Mar 91n	100:21	100:23	− 1	6.38
$12\frac{3}{8}$	Apr 91n	101:15	101:17	− 1	6.41
$9\frac{1}{4}$	Apr 91n	100:25	100:27	....	6.38
$8\frac{1}{8}$	May 91n	100:15	100:17	....	6.51
$14\frac{1}{2}$	May 91n	102:22	102:26	− 1	6.24
$8\frac{3}{4}$	May 91n	100:25	100:27	....	6.50
$7\frac{7}{8}$	Jun 91n	100:18	100:20	....	6.52
$8\frac{1}{4}$	Jun 91n	100:23	100:25	....	6.56
$13\frac{3}{4}$	Jul 91n	103:18	103:20	....	6.57
$7\frac{3}{4}$	Jul 91n	100:17	100:19	....	6.66
$7\frac{1}{2}$	Aug 91n	100:13	100:15	+ 1	6.70
$8\frac{3}{4}$	Aug 91n	101:04	101:06	....	6.72
$14\frac{7}{8}$	Aug 91n	104:25	104:29	− 1	6.51
$8\frac{1}{4}$	Aug 91n	100:27	100:29	+ 1	6.79
$8\frac{3}{8}$	Sep 91n	101:03	101:05	+ 1	6.73
$9\frac{1}{8}$	Sep 91n	101:20	101:22	....	6.72
$12\frac{1}{4}$	Oct 91n	104:01	104:03	+ 1	6.72
$7\frac{5}{8}$	Oct 91n	100:20	100:22	+ 1	6.74
$6\frac{1}{2}$	Nov 91n	99:24	99:26	+ 1	6.73
$8\frac{1}{2}$	Nov 91n	101:11	101:13	....	6.78
$14\frac{1}{4}$	Nov 91n	106:03	106:07	− 1	6.65
$7\frac{3}{4}$	Nov 91n	100:24	100:26	+ 1	6.80
$7\frac{5}{8}$	Dec 91n	100:23	100:25	+ 1	6.79
$8\frac{1}{4}$	Dec 91n	101:09	101:11	....	6.81
$11\frac{5}{8}$	Jan 92n	104:19	104:21	+ 1	6.83
$8\frac{1}{8}$	Jan 92n	101:07	101:09	....	6.86
$6\frac{5}{8}$	Feb 92n	99:19	99:21	+ 1	6.95
$9\frac{1}{8}$	Feb 92n	102:07	102:09	+ 1	6.95
$14\frac{5}{8}$	Feb 92n	107:31	108:03	....	6.91
$8\frac{1}{2}$	Feb 92n	101:20	101:22	+ 1	6.94
$7\frac{7}{8}$	Mar 92n	101:00	101:02	+ 1	6.96
$8\frac{1}{2}$	Mar 92n	101:23	101:25	....	6.96
$11\frac{3}{4}$	Apr 92n	105:20	105:22	+ 1	7.00
$8\frac{7}{8}$	Apr 92n	102:08	102:10	+ 1	7.00
$6\frac{5}{8}$	May 92n	99:15	99:17	+ 1	6.99
$7\frac{3}{8}$	May 96n	98:23	98:27	+ 3	7.64
$7\frac{7}{8}$	Jul 96n	100:26	100:30	+ 3	7.66
8	Oct 96n	101:08	101:12	+ 4	7.70
$7\frac{1}{4}$	Nov 96n	97:23	97:27	+ 4	7.71
8	Jan 97n	101:03	101:07	+ 6	7.74
$8\frac{1}{2}$	Apr 97n	103:12	103:16	+ 8	7.78
$8\frac{1}{2}$	May 97n	103:12	103:16	+ 8	7.79
$8\frac{1}{2}$	Jul 97n	103:12	103:14	+ 8	7.82
$8\frac{5}{8}$	Aug 97n	104:00	104:04	+ 9	7.81
$8\frac{3}{4}$	Oct 97n	104:22	104:24	+ 7	7.83
$8\frac{7}{8}$	Nov 97n	105:08	105:12	+ 6	7.85
$8\frac{1}{8}$	Feb 98n	101:13	101:17	+ 7	7.84
7	May 93-98	95:03	95:11	+ 10	7.85
9	May 98n	106:00	106:04	+ 7	7.89
$9\frac{1}{4}$	Aug 98n	107:15	107:19	+ 9	7.90
$3\frac{1}{2}$	Nov 98	94:10	95:10	− 2	4.21
$8\frac{7}{8}$	Nov 98n	105:11	105:15	+ 7	7.93
$8\frac{7}{8}$	Feb 99n	105:13	105:17	+ 8	7.94
$8\frac{1}{2}$	May 94-99	102:09	102:17	+ 6	7.63
$9\frac{1}{8}$	May 99n	106:28	107:00	+ 7	7.96
8	Aug 99n	100:09	100:13	+ 7	7.93
$7\frac{7}{8}$	Nov 99n	99:12	99:16	+ 8	7.95
$7\frac{7}{8}$	Feb 95-00	99:12	99:16	+ 6	7.95
$8\frac{1}{2}$	Feb 00n	103:10	103:14	+ 8	7.96
$8\frac{7}{8}$	May 00n	105:24	105:28	+ 8	7.97
$8\frac{3}{8}$	Aug 95-00	102:02	102:06	− 4	7.80
$8\frac{3}{4}$	Aug 00n	105:02	105:04	+ 7	7.98
$8\frac{1}{2}$	Nov 00n	103:27	103:29	+ 8	7.92
$11\frac{3}{4}$	Feb 01	125:20	125:28	+ 8	7.97
$13\frac{1}{8}$	May 01	135:20	135:28	+ 10	7.97
8	Aug 96-01	100:15	100:23	+ 6	7.84
$13\frac{3}{8}$	Aug 01	137:29	138:05	+ 10	7.98
$15\frac{3}{4}$	Nov 01	154:28	155:04	+ 8	8.04
$14\frac{1}{4}$	Feb 02	144:25	145:01	+ 14	8.04
$11\frac{5}{8}$	Nov 02	126:18	126:26	+ 9	8.07
$10\frac{3}{4}$	Feb 03	120:00	120:08	+ 9	8.09
$10\frac{3}{4}$	May 03	120:04	120:12	+ 10	8.11
$11\frac{1}{8}$	Aug 03	123:08	123:16	+ 10	8.11
$11\frac{7}{8}$	Nov 03	129:09	129:17	+ 8	8.13
$12\frac{3}{8}$	May 04	133:30	134:06	+ 11	8.13
$13\frac{3}{4}$	Aug 04	145:12	145:20	+ 13	8.14
$11\frac{5}{8}$	Nov 04	128:06	128:10	+ 12	8.17

TREASURY BILLS

Maturity	Days to Mat.	Bid	Asked	Chg.	Ask Yld.
Jan 10 '91	3	6.80	6.70	+0.19	6.80
Jan 17 '91	10	6.61	6.53	+0.13	6.63
Jan 24 '91	17	6.57	6.51	+0.23	6.62
Jan 31 '91	24	5.75	5.73	−0.07	5.83
Feb 07 '91	31	5.93	5.91	−0.02	6.02
Feb 14 '91	38	6.19	6.17	....	6.30
Feb 21 '91	45	6.28	6.26	+0.02	6.40
Feb 28 '91	52	6.29	6.27	+0.01	6.42
Mar 07 '91	59	6.40	6.38	+0.02	6.54
Mar 14 '91	66	6.44	6.42	−0.01	6.59
Mar 21 '91	73	6.41	6.39	−0.02	6.56
Mar 28 '91	80	6.40	6.38	−0.02	6.56
Apr 04 '91	87	6.44	6.42	−0.02	6.61
Apr 11 '91	94	6.41	6.39	−0.01	6.59
Apr 18 '91	101	6.36	6.34	−0.02	6.54
Apr 25 '91	108	6.47	6.45	−0.03	6.67
May 02 '91	115	6.43	6.41	−0.02	6.63
May 09 '91	122	6.42	6.40	−0.03	6.63
May 16 '91	129	6.42	6.40	−0.03	6.64
May 23 '91	136	6.41	6.39	−0.03	6.64
May 30 '91	143	6.39	6.37	−0.02	6.63
Jun 06 '91	150	6.31	6.29	−0.03	6.55
Jun 13 '91	157	6.36	6.34	−0.03	6.61
Jun 20 '91	164	6.36	6.34	−0.03	6.62
Jun 27 '91	171	6.33	6.31	−0.05	6.60
Jul 05 '91	179	6.40	6.38	−0.02	6.68
Aug 01 '91	206	6.39	6.37	−0.03	6.68
Aug 29 '91	234	6.38	6.36	−0.04	6.68
Sep 26 '91	262	6.31	6.29	−0.03	6.62
Oct 24 '91	290	6.39	6.37	−0.03	6.72
Nov 21 '91	318	6.38	6.36	−0.03	6.74
Dec 19 '91	346	6.32	6.30	−0.02	6.69

Source: The Wall Street Journal, *January 4, 1991, p. C14.*

bonds are the same as corporate bonds: the possibility of default,[2] an increase in interest rates driving down the market value of previously issued bonds, and inflation eroding the purchasing power of the interest payments and the principal repayment.

Federal Government Securities

The federal government issues a wide variety of securities from EE bonds that are sold in small denominations to bonds sold in units of $1,000,000. The maturities of the various debt instruments can range from a few months for Treasury bills to 40 years for long-term bonds. This variety of debt instruments is illustrated in Exhibit 9.8, which gives the price quotes and yields for selected federal government securities. As may be seen in the exhibit, the securities range from debt instruments that mature within a year to bonds that mature in the next century.

The trading and subsequent reporting of treasury bond prices is similar to that of corporate debt. However, there is an important difference that makes the prices in Exhibit 9.8 not comparable to the price quotes given for corporate bonds in Exhibit 9.4. Treasury bonds are quoted in 32nds, so a price such as 90.26 means $\$90^{26}/_{32}$ per $100 face amount of debt. Thus the 8¾ of August 2000, which was quoted 105:02–105:04, had a bid price of $\$105^{2}/_{32}$ and an asking price of $\$105^{4}/_{32}$ (i.e., $1,050.63 and $1,051.25, respectively, per $1,000 bond).

Municipal Bonds

Like the federal government, state and local governments issue a variety of bonds that range from short-term debt obligations to bonds that mature 25, 30, or more years into the future. There is, however, one important feature of these debt obligations that differentiates them from all other bonds—their tax implications. The interest earned on state and municipal government debt is exempt from federal income taxation; hence, these bonds are often referred to as **tax-exempt bonds.** (Conversely, the interest earned on federal government debt is exempt from local and state government taxation.) Since some states do not tax income, the primary emphasis is on the exemption of state and local debt from federal income taxation. However, in states and cities that do levy income taxes (e.g., both New York State and New York City tax income),

Tax-exempt bonds ▲
Bonds issued by a state or local government whose interest is exempt from federal income taxation

[2] The debt of the federal government is free of default risk, since the federal government has the power to tax and to create money. State and local governments, of course, lack the power to create money, so the possibility of default does exist. Since obtaining information on many state and local governments may be tedious, if not impossible, most investors rely on credit ratings of municipal debt as an indicator of possible default.

the exemption of the interest earned on federal government debt can lead to considerable savings in taxes.

Investors are willing to accept a lower return on state and local government debt because the after-tax return is equivalent to higher yields on corporate debt. For example, if an investor is in the 28 percent income tax bracket, the return after taxes is the same for a corporate bond paying 10 percent as a state bond that pays 7.2 percent. The after-tax return is 7.2 percent in either case.[3] The willingness of investors to acquire the debt of state and local governments is related to their tax brackets. Higher federal tax rates increase the appeal of tax-exempt bonds and increase their attractiveness relative to taxable bonds, such as those issued by corporations.

SUMMARY

This chapter has discussed the general features of long-term debt. While a corporation may issue a variety of bonds, ranging from secured mortgage bonds to unsecured subordinated debentures and income bonds, the general terms of each issue include the coupon rate of interest and the maturity date. A trustee is appointed for each bond issue to protect the rights of the individual investors. The risks associated with investing in bonds include default on interest and principal repayment, increased interest rates that decrease the current market value of the bond, and loss of purchasing power through inflation.

The current price of a bond depends on the bond's coupon, its term to maturity, and the current interest rates being paid on comparable debt. When interest rates rise, the market price of previously issued bonds declines, but the price of a bond rises when interest rates fall. These price fluctuations are the result of bonds paying a fixed amount of interest each year.

Bonds may be retired through the use of a sinking fund, which requires the issuer to retire a specified amount of the bonds each year or make a periodic payment to retire the debt issue. Some bonds are issued in series; each year one of the series within the issue is retired. Bonds may also be callable, which permits the issuer to pay off the entire issue prior to maturity. A bond will be called only if interest rates have fallen. If interest rates rise and cause a bond's price to fall, it would be more advantageous for the issuer to repurchase the bonds than to call and retire them at par.

[3] The individual may determine the equivalent yields on tax-exempt bonds (i_m) and taxable bonds (i_c) for a given tax rate (t) by the following equation:

$$i_c(1 - t) = i_m.$$

Governments as well as corporations issue bonds. The general features and risks associated with investing in government bonds are the same as with corporate bonds. The big difference between government bonds and corporate bonds is the taxation of the interest income. The interest on state and local government bonds is exempt from federal income taxation, while the interest on federal government debt is exempt from state taxation. The interest earned on an investment in corporate debt may be taxed by the federal, state, or local government. The tax exemption of interest earned on state and local government debt increases the appeal of government bonds, as investors seek to reduce their tax obligations.

Review Questions

1. Given:

Issuer of Bond	Maturity Date	Credit Rating	Yield to Maturity
ABC, Inc.	10 years	AAA	8%
DEF, Inc.	20 years	A	11
GHI, Inc.	20 years	B	13
JKL, Inc.	10 years	B	12

   How would you explain the differences in the rates of interest? What do these yields imply about (1) the effect of time and (2) the effect of risk?

2. What is the difference between the current yield and the yield to maturity? When would these two yields be equal? When would the yield to maturity exceed the current yield? If you thought that interest rates were going to decline, should you buy or sell bonds?
3. Debt must eventually be repaid. What is the difference between a serial bond issue and a bond issue with a sinking fund? If a bond issue lacks a call feature, how may a company retire the bonds prior to maturity?
4. Why may equipment trust certificates be safer than debentures? Why may debentures be safer from the investor's perspective than income bonds?
5. If you expected interest rates to rise, should you buy bonds or sell those you already own?
6. If interest rates fall after a bond is issued, why might you expect the firm to call the bond?
7. How is a call feature different from a sinking fund? From the firm's perspective, which is preferable?
8. Which is more important to the determination of the price of a twenty-year bond: the interest payments or the principal repayment? Would your answer be different if the bond matured in five years?
9. If municipal bonds were not tax-exempt, what would happen to the cost of borrowing for state and local governments?

Problems

1. A $1,000 bond has the following terms:
   - Coupon rate of interest: 12%
   - Interest paid annually: $120
   - Maturity: 20 years

   a. What would be the bond's price if comparable debt yields 10%?

   b. What would be the price if comparable debt yields 10% and the bond matures after five years?

   c. Why are the prices different in (a) and (b)?

   d. What proportion of the bonds' prices in (a) and (b) is attributable to the interest payments and to the principal repayment?

   e. What are the current yields and the yields to maturity in (a) and (b)?

2. Determine the current value (market price) of the following $1,000 bonds if today's interest rate on AAA rated bonds is 10% and answer the following questions.

XY, Inc.	Coupon	5-1/4%
	Maturity	20 years
	Rating	AAA
AB, Inc.	Coupon	14%
	Maturity	20 years
	Rating	AAA

   a. Which bond has a current yield that exceeds its yield to maturity? Explain.

   b. Which bond may you expect to be called? Why?

   c. If CD, Inc. had a bond with a 5¼ percent coupon and a maturity date of 20 years but which was rated BBB, what would be its price relative to the XY, Inc. bond? Explain.

3. A $1,000 bond that matures in ten years and has a coupon of 5 percent ($50 a year) is selling for $692.

   a. What is the current yield?

   b. What is the yield to maturity?

   c. If five years later the yield to maturity is 10 percent, what will be the price of the bond?

4. a. A $1,000 bond pays $75 a year (i.e., 7½ percent coupon) and matures after 12 years. If current interest rates are 9 percent, what should be the price of the bond?

   b. If after six years interest rates are still 9 percent, what should be the price of the bond?

   c. Even though interest rates have not changed in (a) and (b), why did the price of the bond change?

   d. Change the interest rate in (a) and (b) to 6 percent and rework your answers. Even though the interest rate is 6 percent in both calculations, why are the bond prices different?

5. Bond A has the following terms:
   - Coupon rate of interest: 14%
   - Principal: $1,000
   - Term to maturity: 8 years

   Bond B has the following terms:
   - Coupon rate of interest: 6%
   - Principal: $1,000
   - Term to maturity: 8 years

   a. What should be the price of each bond if interest rates are 14 percent?
   b. What will be the price of each bond if, after five years have elapsed, interest rates are 14 percent?
   c. What will be the price of each bond if, after eight years have elapsed, interest rates are 10 percent?

6. An investor buys a 20-year 7 percent $1,000 bond at par. After five years have passed, interest rates are 10 percent? How much has the investor lost on this investment?

7. A bond has the following features:
   - Coupon rate of interest: 9¼%
   - Principal: $1,000
   - Term to maturity: 12 years

   a. What will the holder receive when the bond matures?
   b. If the current rate of interest on comparable debt is 12 percent, what should be the price of this bond?
   c. Would you expect the firm to call this bond? Why?
   d. If the bond has a sinking fund that requires the firm to set aside annually with a trustee sufficient funds to retire the entire issue at maturity, how much must the firm remit each year if the funds earn 10 percent annually and there is $10 million outstanding?

8. You are given the following information concerning a noncallable, sinking fund debenture:
   - Principal: $1,000
   - Coupon rate of interest: 7%
   - Term to maturity: 15 years
   - Sinking fund: 5 percent of outstanding bonds retired annually; the balance at maturity

   a. If you buy the bond today at its face amount and interest rates rise to 9 percent after three years have passed, what is your capital gain (loss)?
   b. If you hold the bond 15 years, what do you receive at maturity?
   c. What is the bond's current yield as of right now?
   d. Given your price in (a), what is the yield to maturity?
   e. Is there any reason to believe that the bond will be called after three years have elapsed if interest rates decline?
   f. What proportion of the total debt issue is retired by the sinking fund?
   g. What assets secure this bond?
   h. If the final payment to retire this bond is $1,000,000, how much must the firm invest annually to accumulate this sum if the firm is able to earn 8 percent on the invested funds?

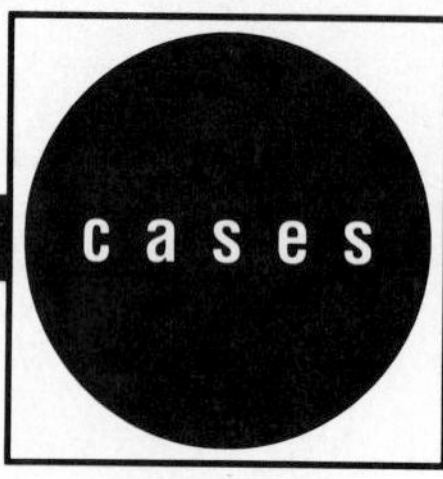

Building a Bond Portfolio

Antonin Gottshalk, a very conservative individual seeking financial advice, recently had an initial consultation with Robert Frederick Strauss (old "RF"), a personable financial planner. Gottshalk has $700,000 invested in certificates of deposit with maturities of one to three years and interest rates of 5.75 to 7.00 percent. Old RF thought this amount tied up in one type of asset is a decidedly inferior investment strategy, but he immediately realized that Gottshalk would not be willing to alter the portfolio if the change would have a large impact on risk.

Since Gottshalk is primarily concerned with income and safety of principal, RF decided that initially the best strategy would be to alter the portfolio by substituting quality bonds for a substantial proportion of the certificates of deposit. He suggested to Gottshalk that $500,000 be invested in bonds and the remaining $200,000 be held in three CDs in three different banks. $50,000 would be invested in triple A or double A rated bonds with one year to maturity; $50,000 with two years to maturity, and so on until the last $50,000 would be invested in bonds with ten years to maturity. Thus, none of the bonds would have a maturity exceeding ten years, none of the bonds would have a rating of less than double A, and $50,000 face amount of the bonds would mature each year.

Gottshalk agreed to the basic strategy but required that all the bonds be federal government obligations. Currently the structure of interest rates is as follows:

Term to Maturity	Coupon Rate of Interest
1	6.0%
2	6.0
3	6.0
4	7.0
5	7.0
6	7.0
7	8.0
8	8.0
9	9.0
10	9.0

All bonds are currently selling at par (i.e., $1,000 per $1,000 face amount). Gottshalk still had doubts concerning risk of loss of principal, but he liked the additional income that would be generated by the bonds with the higher coupons. He asked RF what the advantage was of placing $50,000 in bonds maturing each year versus investing the entire $500,000 in ten year federal government bonds.

Case Problems

1. How should RF respond to this question?
2. How much could Gottshalk lose of the $500,000 if he follows the recommended strategy and, after one year, interest rates rise one percentage point (100 basis points)?
3. Would the interest earned offset the loss?
4. How much additional loss would be incurred compared to the loss in Question 2 if Gottshalk invests the entire $500,000 in ten year bonds and one year later the rate rises to 10 percent?

Suggested Readings

There are several easy-to-read books that describe various debt instruments. Four possibilities are

Lamb, Robert. *How to Invest in Municipal Bonds.* New York: Franklin Watts, 1984.

Rosen, Lawrence R. *Investing in Zero Coupon Bonds.* New York: John Wiley & Sons, 1986.

Sherwood, Hugh C. *How to Invest in Bonds,* revised ed. New York: McGraw-Hill Book Company, 1983.

Stigum, Marcia, and Frank J. Fabozzi. *The Dow Jones-Irwin Guide to Bond and Money Market Instruments.* Homewood, Ill.: Dow Jones-Irwin, 1987.

Other readings on corporate debt include:

Johnson, Rodney, and Richard Klein. "Corporate Motives in Repurchases of Discounted Bonds." *Financial Management* (Autumn 1974), pp. 44–49.

This article suggests that the temporary increase in earnings from retiring debt at a discount is the primary motive for such refundings.

Sherwood, Hugh C. *How Corporate and Municipal Debt Is Rated.* New York: John Wiley & Sons, 1976.

This book describes the objective and subjective techniques used to rate debt by Standard & Poor's rating service.

Standard & Poor's Corp. *Corporation Records.* New York. Published annually.

This reference service provides complete information on the features of bonds held by the general public.

chapter

10

Equity: Preferred and Common Stock

29 pages in chapter

Learning Objectives

1 Differentiate preferred stock from bonds.

2 Analyze the firm's capacity to pay preferred stock dividends.

3 Enumerate cash dividend policies.

4 Illustrate the effect that income taxes have on cash dividends and the retention of earnings.

5 Explain recapitalizations: stock dividends and stock splits.

6 Determine the impact of cash dividends, stock dividends, and stock splits on the firm's earnings, assets, equity, and stock price.

7 Describe dividend reinvestment plans and their advantages.

The seventeenth century English poet George Herbert wrote, "By no means run in debt: take thine own measure." While a few firms are able to operate without some debt financing, equity is a major and necessary source of funds for business. The single proprietor invests money and other assets in the business and thus has equity in the firm. Partners invest funds into the partnership and have an equity claim on the firm.

Corporations raise funds by selling preferred and common stock to individuals who become the owners (shareholders) of the firm. While the features of preferred stock are similar to the features of debt, it is still a form of equity.

Many corporations do not issue preferred stock, but all issue common stock. These stockholders are the ultimate owners of the firm and bear the risk associated with that ownership. For bearing that risk, these investors anticipate a return on their funds, either through dividends or through price appreciation.

Companies that experience consistent growth in earnings tend to increase their dividends periodically. United Telecommunications annually increased its dividend over twenty-five years from $0.31 in 1958 to $1.88 in 1984, an annual compounded increase of 5.2 percent. However, when this firm experienced a decline in earnings, the dividend increments ceased. Many firms have paid dividends for over a century. The First National Bank of Boston and the Bank of New York started distributing dividends in 1784 and 1785, respectively. Of course, some firms are forced to suspend dividends (e.g., Northern Indiana Public Service and Consumers Power) when their financial condition deteriorates sufficiently so that continuing the dividend may be detrimental to the firm's continued existence.

This chapter and the subsequent one are devoted to stock. Chapter 10 is descriptive and covers the features of stock, the voting right of stockholders, dividend payments, stock splits, dividend reinvestment plans, and corporate repurchases of stock. Chapter 11 is more theoretical and is devoted to the valuation of stock. It covers models that are used to determine if a particular stock is undervalued and should be purchased or if it is overvalued and should be avoided.

EQUITY

A firm's sources of finance are either debt obligations or equity obligations. As was discussed in the previous chapter, there are a variety of debt instruments that are issued to tap the funds of savers seeking to invest in debt obligations, especially fixed income securities. Each debt instrument is differentiated by its terms, so that a debenture differs from a mortgage since the former is unsecured while the latter is secured by property. However, in both cases, the issuing firm must meet the terms of the debenture and the terms of the mortgage. Both are legal obligations of the firm.

Equity represents ownership in a firm. Like creditors, the holders of equity instruments such as common stock have a claim on the firm. Since the firm's debt obligations have a prior claim, equity represents a residual claim. Interest on debt must be paid before there are any earnings available to the owners. If the firm is dissolved, debts must be paid, and then any remaining assets are distributed to the owners.

Being the residual claim is one of the reasons why equity is riskier than debt. If the firm performs poorly, there may be little or nothing available to the equity. However, a profitable firm can generate a large return for its owners, since after the debt obligations are met, the residual accrues solely to the equity. Higher earnings, thus, accrue solely to the owners.

Stock represents equity in a corporation. While there may be many different types of debt instruments, there are only two types of stock: preferred stock and common stock.[1] As the name implies, preferred stock has a preferred or superior position. Common stock thus represents the final claim on a corporation's earnings and assets. While equity (ownership) represents the residual claim on a firm's earnings and assets, it still is a claim. The managers and employees of the firm work for and are responsible to the owners.

For the vast majority of firms, the owners, managers, and employees are one and the same. The owner of a small store must perform all the roles required to operate and manage the business. While the owner may employ individuals with special skills (e.g., an accountant or a lawyer) to perform specific tasks, management, marketing, and financing decisions all fall on the owner/manager. Since the owner and manager are one and the same, it seems reasonable to assume that management decisions are made with the welfare of the owner as a primary consideration.

In large corporations, the owners, managers, and employees differ. As is explained later in this chapter, the owners are represented by an elected board of directors who employ management who, in turn, hire the various individuals that staff the operation. It could be assumed that the goals of management are consistent with the owners' goals, since the managers have a fiduciary responsibility to the corporate owners. However, such an assumption may be at odds with reality. For example, higher salaries may be a goal of individual managers, but higher salaries will reduce earnings and come at the expense of the owners.

---

[1]Some corporations have also issued a "preference" stock. This stock is subordinated to preferred stock but has preference over common stock with regard to the payment of dividends. Such stock is another level of preferred stock, and in this text no distinction is made between the two.

Owners, therefore, must monitor managerial decisions and take steps to reduce the potential conflict between managers and owners. These actions may include (1) developing a structure in which the chain of command and responsibility starts with the owners and flows to the employees, (2) forming a system for the removal of employees who act in a way that is harmful to owners, or (3) instituting a system of rewards that is tied to performance so that the welfare of the owners, managers, and employees are interrelated. For example, higher earnings may result in larger bonuses as well as increased dividends for the owners.

Linking the welfare of owners, management, and employees will involve expenses. These expenditures are sometimes referred to as the "agency costs" that owners must bear to insure that management acts in the best interests of the owners and not solely on its own behalf. Creditors also may have similar costs since owners and managers can take actions that reduce the safety of debt instruments. For example, the paying of bonuses and extra dividends may reward management and owners, but such payments reduce the money available to pay interest and repay principal.

THE FEATURES OF PREFERRED STOCK

Preferred stock ▲
Class of stock (i.e., equity) that has a claim prior to common stock on the firm's earnings and assets

Arrears ▲
Dividends on a cumulative preferred stock that have not been paid and have accumulated

Cumulative preferred stock ▲
Preferred stock whose dividends accumulate (accrue) if not paid

Noncumulative preferred stock ▲
Preferred stock whose dividends do not accumulate if the firm misses a dividend payment

Preferred stock is an equity instrument that pays a fixed dividend. While most firms have only one issue of common stock, they may have several issues of preferred stock. As may be seen in Exhibit 10.1, Virginia Electric and Power has twenty-two issues of preferred stock. In each case the dividend rate is fixed. Thus for the series $8.60 preferred, the annual dividend is $8.60, which is distributed at the rate of $2.15 per share quarterly.

This fixed dividend is paid from the firm's earnings. If the firm does not have the earnings, it may not declare and pay the preferred stock dividends. If the firm should omit the preferred stock's dividend, the dividend is said to be in **arrears.** The firm does not have to remove this arrearage. In most cases, however, any omitted dividends have to be paid in the future before any dividends may be paid to the holders of the common stock. Such cases, in which the preferred stock's dividends accumulate, are called **cumulative preferred.** Most preferred stock is cumulative, but there are examples of **noncumulative preferred** stocks whose dividends do not have to be made up if missed (e.g., the Ruddick Corp. $0.56 Convertible Preferred stock is noncumulative). For investors holding preferred stock in firms having financial difficulty, the difference between cumulative and noncumulative may be immaterial. Forcing the firm to pay dividends to erase the arrearage may further weaken the firm and hurt the owner of the preferred stock more than

EXHIBIT 10.1

The Preferred Stocks of Virginia Electric and Power

Virginia Electric and Power has over twenty issues of preferred stock, each with distinctive features.

Preferred Stock Not Subject to Mandatory Retirement

	Annual Dividend per Share	Outstanding Shares
	$4.04	12,926
	4.20	14,797
	4.12	32,534
	4.80	73,206
	5.00	106,677
	7.72	350,000
	7.45	400,000
	7.20	450,000
	7.72	500,000
1987–1	Money market preferred	500,000
1987–2	Money market preferred	750,000
1988	Money market preferred	750,000
1989	Money market preferred	750,000

Preferred Stock Subject to Mandatory Retirement

Annual Dividend per Share	Outstanding Shares 12/31/81	12/31/89
$ 7.30	—	500,000
7.325	—	484,419
8.925	280,000	196,000
8.60	**347,000**	**252,432**
8.625	370,000	240,500
8.20	600,000	390,000
7.58	700,000	600,000
8.40	800,000	576,000
10.25	—	200,000

Source: 1982 and 1989 Annual Reports.

would forgoing the dividends. Once the firm has regained its profitability, erasing the arrearage may become important not only to holders of the stock but also to the company as a demonstration of its improved financial condition.

An example of a firm clearing the arrearage on its preferred stock is Chrysler. In December 1979, Chrysler suspended payments on its $2.75 preferred stock. The dividends accumulated for four years, by which time the arrearage had reached $11 per share. In December 1983, Chrysler paid sufficient dividends to the preferred stockholders to erase the arrearage, and less than a year later (October 31, 1984), the firm redeemed each share of the preferred stock.

Once the preferred stock is issued, the firm may never have to concern itself with the retirement of the preferred stock if it is perpetual. This may be both an advantage and a disadvantage. Since the firm may never have to retire the preferred stock, it does not have to generate the money to retire it. The firm may instead use its funds elsewhere (e.g., to purchase plant and equipment). However, should the firm ever want to change its capital structure and substitute debt financing for the preferred stock, the firm may have difficulty in retiring the preferred stock. The firm may have to purchase the preferred stock on the open market, and in order to induce the holders to sell the preferred shares, the firm will probably have to bid up the price of the preferred stock.

To maintain some control over the preferred stock, the firm may seek to add to the preferred issue a call feature. This gives the firm the option to call and redeem the issue. For example, the James River $3.50 preferred stock may be redeemed after October 1, 1989. While the actual terms of a call feature will vary with each preferred stock issue, the general features are similar. First, the call is at the option of the firm. Second, the call price is specified. Third, the firm may pay a call penalty (e.g., a year's dividends). Fourth, after the issue is called, future dividend payments will cease; this, of course, forces any recalcitrant holders to surrender their certificates.

In addition to a call feature, some preferred stocks have mandatory sinking fund requirements. These sinking funds require that the firm periodically retire some of the issue. For example, the $8.60 preferred stock in Exhibit 10.1 has a mandatory sinking fund that started in 1985. It requires Virginia Electric and Power to redeem annually at $100 per share 4 percent of the shares originally issued. Thus by 2010 all the shares will have been retired. Such issues of preferred stock with mandatory sinking funds are very similar to bonds, which also are not perpetual and must be retired.[2]

PREFERRED STOCK AND BONDS CONTRASTED

Since preferred stock pays a fixed dividend, it is purchased primarily by investors seeking a fixed flow of income. Since preferred stock pays a fixed dividend, it is analyzed and valued like any other fixed income se-

[2]In 1979 a change in how property and casualty insurance companies account for investments in preferred stock shifted their preference for sinking fund preferred stock vis-à-vis perpetual preferred stock. Utilities, which are the primary issuers of preferred stock, responded to this change by starting to issue preferred stock with mandatory retirement features (i.e., sinking funds). See M. J. C. Roth, "New Look at Preferred Stock Financing," *Public Utilities Fortnightly* (March 27, 1980), pp. 26–28.

curity (i.e., long-term bonds). But preferred stock differs from long-term debt, as the subsequent discussion will demonstrate, and these differences are significant.

First, for investors preferred stock is riskier than debt. The terms of a bond are legal obligations of the firm. If the corporation fails to pay the interest or meet any of the terms of the indenture, the bondholders may take the firm to court to force payment of the interest or to seek liquidation of the firm in order to protect the bondholders' principal. Preferred stockholders do not have that power, for the firm is not legally obligated to pay the preferred stock dividends.

In addition, debt must be retired, while preferred stock is often perpetual. If the security is perpetual, the only means to recoup the amount invested is to sell the preferred stock in the secondary market. The investor cannot expect the firm to redeem the security. Market price fluctuations tend to be greater for preferred stock than for long-term bonds. Price fluctuations for long-term bonds are greater than price fluctuations experienced by short-term debt. This principle holds when comparing long-term bonds and preferred stock. The price of a perpetual preferred stock will fluctuate more than the price of a long-term bond with a finite life.

Second, the yield differential between preferred stock and bonds is smaller than would be expected on the basis of risk differentials. This small differential between the yields on bonds and preferred stock may be explained by the corporate income tax laws. Dividends paid by one corporation to another receive favorable tax treatment. Only 30 percent of the dividends are taxed as income of the corporation receiving the dividends. Thus for a firm such as an insurance company in the 34 percent corporate income tax bracket, this shelter is very important. If the company receives $100 in interest, it nets only $66 as $34 is taxed away. However, if this company were to receive $100 in preferred stock dividends, only $30 would be subject to federal income tax. Thus the firm pays only $10.20 ($30 × 0.34) in taxes and gets to keep the remaining $89.80 of the dividends.

For this reason, a corporation may choose to purchase preferred stocks instead of long-term bonds. The impact of this preference is to drive up the price of preferred stocks, which reduces their yields. Since individual investors do not enjoy this tax break, they may prefer bonds that offer comparable yields to preferred stock but are less risky. To induce these investors to purchase preferred stock, the firm often offers other features such as the convertibility of the preferred stock into the firm's common stock.

A third important difference (at least from the viewpoint of the firm) between debt and preferred stock is that the interest on debt is a tax-deductible expense while the dividend on preferred stock is not. Preferred dividends are paid out of earnings. This difference in the tax treatment of interest expense and preferred stock dividends affects the firm's earnings available to its common stockholders. The use of debt instead of preferred stock as a source of funds will result in higher earnings per common share.

Consider a firm with operating income of $1,000,000 (i.e., earnings before interest and taxes). The firm has 100,000 common shares outstanding and is in the 40 percent corporate income tax bracket. If the firm issues $2,000,000 of *debt* with a 10 percent rate of interest, its earnings per common share are

Earnings before interest and taxes	$1,000,000
Interest	200,000
Earnings before taxes	800,000
Taxes	320,000
Net income	$ 480,000

Earnings per common share: $480,000/100,000 = $4.80

If the firm had issued $2,000,000 in *preferred stock* that also paid 10 percent, the earnings per common share would be

Earnings before interest and taxes	$1,000,000
Interest	00
Earnings before taxes	1,000,000
Taxes	400,000
Earnings before preferred stock dividends	600,000
Preferred stock dividends	200,000
Earnings available to common stock	$ 400,000

Earnings per common share: 400,000/100,000 = $4.00

The use of preferred stock has resulted in lower earnings per common share. This reduction in earnings is the result of the different tax treatment of interest, which is a tax-deductible expense, and the preferred stock dividends, which are not deductible.

ANALYSIS OF PREFERRED STOCK

Because preferred stock is an income-producing investment, the analysis is primarily concerned with the capacity of the firm to meet the dividend payments. Although dividends must ultimately be related to current earnings and the firm's future earning capacity, preferred dividends are paid from cash. Even if the firm is temporarily running a deficit (i.e., experiencing an accounting loss), it may still be able to pay dividends to the preferred stockholders if it has sufficient cash. In fact, cash dividends might be paid despite the deficit to indicate that the losses are expected to be temporary and that the firm is financially strong.

An analysis of the firm's financial statements (such as the ratios used to analyze a firm's financial condition in Chapter 16) may reveal the liquidity position and profitability of the firm. The more liquid and profitable the firm, the safer should be the dividend payment. The investor may also analyze how well the firm covers its preferred dividend. This analysis is achieved by computing the **times-dividend-earned** ratio which is

Times-dividend-earned ▲
Ratio of earnings divided by preferred dividend requirements

$$\frac{\text{Earnings after taxes}}{\text{Dividends on preferred stock}}.$$

The larger this ratio, the safer should be the preferred stock's dividend. Notice that the numerator consists of *total* earnings. Although the preferred stock dividends are subtracted from the total earnings to derive the earnings that are available to the common stockholders, all of the firm's earnings are available to pay the preferred stock dividend.

A variation on this ratio is **earnings per preferred share.** This ratio is

Earnings per preferred share ▲
Total earnings divided by the number of preferred shares outstanding

$$\frac{\text{Earnings after taxes}}{\text{Number of preferred shares outstanding}}.$$

The larger the earnings per preferred share, the safer is the dividend payment. However, neither of these ratios indicates whether the firm has sufficient cash to pay the dividends. They can only indicate the extent to which earnings cover the dividend requirements of the preferred stock.

How each ratio is computed can be illustrated by the following simple example. A firm has earnings of $6 million and is in the 40 percent tax bracket. It has 100,000 shares of preferred stock outstanding, and each share pays a dividend of $5. The times-dividend-earned ratio is

$$\frac{\$6{,}000{,}000 - \$2{,}400{,}000}{\$500{,}000} = 7.2,$$

and the earnings per preferred share are

$$\frac{\$6{,}000{,}000 - \$2{,}400{,}000}{100{,}000} = \$36.$$

Both ratios, in effect, show the same thing. In the first, the preferred dividend is covered by a multiple of 7.2 : 1. The second ratio shows an earnings per preferred share of $36, which is 7.2 times the $5 dividend paid for each share.

DISADVANTAGES OF PREFERRED STOCK

While most preferred stock does offer the investor the advantage of a fixed flow of income, this advantage may be more than offset by several disadvantages. Like any fixed income security, preferred stock offers no protection from inflation. If the rate of inflation increases, the real purchasing power of the dividend is diminished. In addition, increased inflation will probably lead to higher interest rates, which (as is explained in the next chapter) will drive down the market value of the preferred stock. Thus, higher rates of inflation doubly curse preferred stock as the purchasing power of the dividend and the market value of the stock will both be diminished.[3]

Preferred stock also tends to be less marketable than other securities. Marketability of a particular preferred stock depends on the size of the issue. However, most preferred stock is bought by insurance companies and pension plans. The market for the remaining shares may be quite small, so the spread between the bid and ask prices can be substantial. While this may not be a disadvantage if the investor intends to hold the security, it will reduce the attractiveness of the preferred stock in cases in which investors desire marketability.

The impact of inflation and reduced marketability are not the only disadvantages associated with preferred stock. Other disadvantages were alluded to earlier in the chapter but were not explicitly stated as disadvantages. The first of these is the inferior position of preferred stock to debt obligations. The investor must realize that preferred stock is perceptibly riskier than bonds. For example, in May 1986, Zapata Corporation omitted dividends on its two issues of preferred stock but continued to make the interest payments on its debentures. One of these issues is noncumulative, so those dividend payments are lost forever.[4]

The second disadvantage that was previously alluded to is that the yields offered by preferred stock are probably insufficient to justify the additional risk. The yields on preferred stock are not necessarily higher than those available on bonds because of the tax advantages that preferred stock offers corporate investors. Only 30 percent of the dividends paid by one corporation and received by a second corporation are subject to corporate income tax. This tax advantage artificially drives up the price of preferred stock and drives down the yield. Since individual investors are unable to take advantage of the tax break, they may earn an inferior yield after adjusting for the additional risk associated with investing in a security that is subordinated to the firm's bonds.

---

[3]This disadvantage, of course, applies to all fixed income, long-term securities.

[4]Zapata defaulted on the bonds in 1989. The interest continued to accrue and was paid in 1991.

COMMON STOCK

While preferred stock legally is equity and hence represents ownership, common stock represents the bottom line. **Common stock** represents the residual claim on the assets and earnings of a corporation. In case of liquidation, the holder of common stock receives whatever is left after all other claims have been satisfied; he or she receives earnings that have accrued after the payment of expenses, interest, and preferred stock dividends. In effect, it is this group of investors who bear the risk and reap the rewards associated with the ownership of a corporation.

Common stock ▲
Security representing ownership in a corporation; common stock owners have a final claim on the firm's assets and earnings after the firm has met its obligations to creditors and preferred stockholders

The investors who purchase common stock receive all the rights of ownership. These rights include the option to vote the shares. The stockholders elect a **board of directors** that selects the firm's management. Management is then responsible to the board of directors, which, in turn, is responsible to the firm's stockholders. If the stockholders do not think that the board is doing a competent job, they may elect another board to represent them.

Board of directors ▲
Body elected by and responsible to stockholders to set policy and hire management to run a corporation

For publicly held corporations, such democracy rarely works. Stockholders are usually widely dispersed, while the firm's management and board of directors generally form a cohesive unit. Rarely does the individual investor's vote mean much.[5] However, there is always the possibility that if the firm does poorly, another firm may offer to buy the outstanding stock held by the public. Once such purchases are made, the new owners of the stock may remove the board of directors and establish new management. To some extent this possibility encourages a corporation's board of directors and management to pursue the goal of increasing the value of the firm's stock.

A stockholder generally has one vote for each share owned, but there are two ways to distribute this vote. The difference between these two methods is best explained by an example. Suppose a firm has 1,000 shares outstanding and a board of directors composed of five members. With the traditional method of voting, each share gives the stockholder the right to vote for one individual for each seat on the board. Under this system, if a majority group voted as a block, a minority group could not elect a representative. For example, a majority group of 70 percent of the stockholders could give each of its candidates 70 percent of the vote, thus denying representation to a minority group of 30 percent of the stockholders.

There is another system, called **cumulative voting,** which gives minority stockholders a means to obtain representation, but not a majority,

Cumulative voting ▲
Voting system that encourages minority representation by permitting stockholders to cast all of their shares (votes) for one candidate for the firm's board of directors

[5]One notable exception occurred in 1981 when Penn Central stockholders voted down a merger with Colt Industries. Management supported the merger but lost the vote: 10,245,440 shares against versus 10,104,220 shares in favor.

Financial Facts

Voting by Proxy

A corporation's board of directors holds at least one stockholders meeting a year. At the meeting stockholders vote on a variety of issues including the election of the members of the board, the approval of the firm's auditors, the authority to issue additional shares, and any other matters that may arise. The board may also call a special meeting to vote upon a specific topic such as the approval of a merger. • Stockholders of a publicly held corporation are dispersed throughout the country and, in the case of large firms like AT&T, throughout the world. Obviously, most stockholders are not going to make the trip to the meeting to vote their shares. Instead they vote by proxy, which is a document giving the power to vote the shares to the holder of the proxy. Management solicits proxies to vote on stockholders' behalf. Even if the investor signs and submits the proxy, he or she can later rescind the authorization to vote the shares. If a dissident group wants to gain control of the company, it also may solicit proxies in which case a "proxy fight" could erupt. However, such solicitations are expensive, so the number of proxy fights is minuscule. • Even if the individual signs the proxy, he or she may attend the stockholders meeting. Besides conducting the formal voting, management often reviews the firm's accomplishments and future goals. Good news such as a dividend increase may be announced at the meeting and samples of the firm's products, especially if the corporation makes consumer products, may be distributed to stockholders. •

---

on the firm's board of directors. Under cumulative voting, the stockholder in the previous example who owns one share has a total of five votes (one vote for each seat on the board of directors). That stockholder may cast up to five votes for one candidate. (Of course, then the stockholder could not vote for anyone else running for the remaining seats.) The 70 percent majority would have a total of 3,500 votes (700 shares × 5). The 30 percent minority would have 1,500 votes (300 shares × 5), and by voting as a block for specific candidates could assure itself of representation on the board of directors.

For example, if the 30 percent minority ran two candidates against the five candidates of the majority, the following voting could occur:

Majority Candidates	Votes
A	700
B	700
C	700
D	700
E	700
Minority Candidates	**Votes**
F	750
G	750

The majority has cast its 3,500 votes evenly among its candidates, and the minority has also cast its 1,500 votes evenly between its two candi-

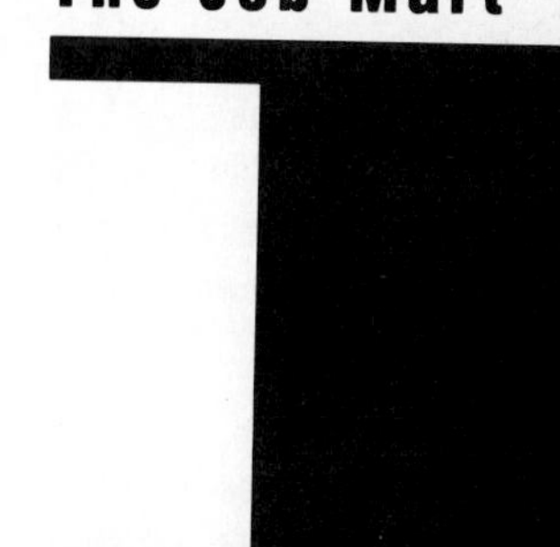

Investor Relations

■ Job Description: Responsible for the distribution of annual reports and the preparation of news releases. Handle stockholder inquiries, prepare for annual stockholders meeting, and arrange for management presentations to professional and civic organizations. ■ Job Requirements: General background in finance and the ability to work well with people, especially those with little background in finance. Excellent communication skills coupled with knowledge of a special area, such as SEC reporting requirements. ■ Characteristics: Positions in investor relations may be open to nonfinance majors or even nonbusiness majors who possess writing skills and the ability to work well within a corporate environment. Strong interpersonal skills are necessary to coordinate the many facets of the job.

---

dates. In this election the minority wins two seats. Even if the majority were to cast more votes for candidates A through D, these votes would be at the expense of candidate E. For example, if the majority cast 800 votes for each of candidates A through D, it would have only 300 votes available for candidate E. These 300 votes are not enough to gain election, and the minority would still win one seat on the board of directors.[6]

While cumulative voting can help a minority group obtain representation, it cannot assure representation if the minority is too small. If the minority in this example had been 15 percent, it would have had 750 votes and the 85 percent majority would have had 4,250 votes. Each of the five majority candidates would have received 850 votes (4,250/5) and would have beaten any single minority candidate with 750 votes. For the minority to win representation, the total of its combined votes must be large enough to exceed the majority's per-seat voting capacity.

---

[6]The number of shares (S) required to elect a specific number of seats can be determined by the following equation:

$$S = \frac{V \times P}{D + 1} + 1$$

The definition of each symbol is
V: number of voting shares,
P: number of positions desired on the board of directors,
D: total number of directors to be elected.
Thus, in the above example, if the minority wanted to elect two seats, it would have to control 334 shares. That is,

$$S = \frac{1{,}000 \times 2}{5 + 1} + 1 = 334.33$$

Since it controls only 300 shares, the minority can be assured of electing only one director.

Preemptive Rights

Preemptive rights ▲ Right of current stockholders to maintain their proportionate ownership in the firm

Rights offering ▲ Sale of new securities to stockholders by offering them the option (i.e., right) to purchase new shares

Some stockholders have **preemptive rights,** which is their prerogative to maintain their proportionate ownership in the firm. If the firm wants to sell additional shares to the general public, these new shares must be offered initially to the existing stockholders in a sale called a **rights offering.** If the stockholders wish to maintain their proportionate ownership in the firm, they can exercise their rights by purchasing the new shares. However, if they do not want to take advantage of this offering, they may sell their privilege to whomever wants to purchase the new shares.

Preemptive rights may be illustrated by a simple example. If a firm has 1,000 shares outstanding and an individual has 100 shares, that individual owns 10 percent of the firm's stock. If the firm wants to sell 400 new shares and the stockholders have preemptive rights, these new shares must be offered to the existing stockholders before they are sold to the general public. The individual who owns 100 shares would have the right to purchase 40, or 10 percent, of the new shares. If the purchase is made, then that stockholder's relative position is maintained, for the stockholder owns 10 percent of the firm both before and after the sale of the new stock.

Although preemptive rights are required in some states for incorporation, their importance has diminished and the number of rights offerings has declined. In 1969 there were 118 public rights offerings, but the number declined to only 26 in 1988 involving NYSE and AMEX companies.[7] Some firms have tried to have their by-laws changed in order to eliminate preemptive rights. For example, AT&T asked its stockholders to relinquish these rights. The rationale for this request was that issuing new shares through rights offerings was more expensive than selling the shares to the general public through an underwriting. Investors who desired to maintain their relative position could still purchase the new shares, and all stockholders would benefit through the cost savings and the flexibility given to the firm's management. Most stockholders accepted the management's request and voted to relinquish their preemptive rights. Now AT&T does not have to offer any new shares to its current stockholders before it offers them publicly.

DIVIDEND POLICY

Cash dividends ▲ Distribution from earnings paid in the form of cash

After a corporation has earned profits, management must decide what to do with these earnings: retain them and increase each stockholder's investment in the firm, or distribute them in **cash dividends.** If the earn-

[7]Moody's Dividend Record, 1988, pp. 481–484.

ings are distributed, the cash flows out of the firm. If the earnings are retained, management will put the funds to work by purchasing income-earning assets or retiring outstanding debt.

Suppose a firm begins the year with the following balance sheet:

ASSETS		LIABILITIES AND EQUITY	
Assets	$10,000	Debt	$3,000
		Equity	7,000
	$10,000		$10,000

During the year the firm earns $1,000. The impact of the dividend policy on the firm's balance sheet depends on whether it (1) distributes the earnings, (2) retains the earnings and acquires more assets, or (3) retains the earnings and retires debt. The impact on the balance sheet of these alternatives is as follows:

The firm's balance sheet after earning $1,000 and

1. distributing the earnings:

ASSETS		LIABILITIES AND EQUITY	
Assets	$10,000	Debt	$ 3,000
		Equity	7,000
	$10,000		$10,000

2. retaining the earnings and investing the funds in income-earning assets

ASSETS		LIABILITIES AND EQUITY	
Assets	$11,000	Debt	$ 3,000
		Equity	8,000
	$11,000		$11,000

3. retaining the earnings and using the funds to retire outstanding debt:

ASSETS		LIABILITIES AND EQUITY	
Assets	$10,000	Debt	$ 2,000
		Equity	8,000
	$10,000		$10,000

The firm that retains earnings and uses the funds to reinvest in income-earning assets may be able to achieve future earnings growth. If this growth is achieved, presumably the value of the firm will also grow. The tendency of earnings growth to increase the value of the stock may

EXHIBIT 10.2

Per Share Earnings, Average Price of Stock, and Compound Growth Rates for The Limited, 1980 and 1989

The rapid growth in The Limited's per share earnings is mirrored in the rapid growth in the value of its stock.

	The Limited	
Year	Per Share Earnings	Average Price of the Stock
1980	$0.03	$ 0.40
1989	1.42	16.28
Annual growth rate	47%	45%

be illustrated by numerous examples. Exhibit 10.2 presents the per share earnings of The Limited for 1980 and 1989. The exhibit also includes the average price of the stock (average of the annual high and low prices) and the compound rate of growth in the earnings and in the average stock price during the time period. Obviously, this illustration vividly shows the growth in the value of the stock associated with the growth in earnings. Earnings compounded at 47 percent annually, and the average stock price grew at 45 percent. While other examples may not show such rapid growth, the general pattern holds. Even though there may be fluctuations in stock prices, over a period of time higher retained earnings generally produce higher earnings, which lead to higher stock prices.

If earnings are distributed as cash dividends, the firm's equity is not increased, and if management wants to invest in additional assets it will have to use an alternative source of funds. This money may be borrowed which may increase the financial risk of the firm. Or the funds may be obtained by issuing additional stock, but it may not make sense to distribute earnings and then issue new shares to raise equity. The retention of the earnings would achieve the same effect and not involve the costs associated with selling new stock.

Since the stockholders are the owners of the firm and thus are entitled to the earnings, the question becomes, What do the stockholders want? What is best for them, additional investment in the firm or cash dividends? This would seem to be an easy question to answer but, in reality, is not. Usually, many different stockholders own shares, and some may seek income through dividends while others may seek capital gains.

The decision concerning the distribution of earnings is sometimes viewed as that of management serving various clients. The intent is to identify what the clients (i.e., the stockholders) want and to satisfy that want. Retirees, individuals seeking supplementary income, managers of pension plans and trust funds, and corporate stockholders may prefer dividends to capital gains. Other investors with current income may prefer capital gains that may be realized in the future when the funds are needed. If management can identify which of these groups are the primary stockholders, then dividend policy may be designed to meet the needs of those stockholders.

Actually, the decision to retain versus distribute may be irrelevant. Suppose that at the beginning of the year a stock is selling for $100 and the individual buys 100 shares ($10,000). During the year, the firm earns $10 per share. As a result of the earnings growth, the value of a share rises to $110, and the stockholder's shares are now worth $11,000.

If the firm distributes the earnings, the stockholder receives $1,000 ($10 × 100 shares). However, the value of the share will fall by the amount of the dividend, so the price returns to the original $100.[8] The investor experiences neither a capital gain nor a loss and will have earned 10 percent on the investment (the $1,000 in dividends divided by the $10,000 cost of the investment).

Suppose the firm does not distribute the earnings, and the investor needs the cash. The individual could sell 9 shares to obtain $990 (9 shares × $110 a share). Of course, the investor still has 91 shares worth $10,010. Except for the $10 difference resulting from the inability to sell fractional shares, the investor's position is the same as before when earnings were distributed. In either case, the investor has $1,000 in cash and $10,000 worth of stock.

This discussion suggests that the stockholder's position is unaffected by the dividend policy of the firm; thus, dividend policy is irrelevant.[9] There are, however, considerations that may affect dividend policy and hence suggest that in the real world where management and investors make decisions, dividend policy is not irrelevant. Transaction costs such as commissions on the purchase and sales of securities or investment banking fees from the sale of new securities, taxation, and the firm's cash needs affect the dividend policy of the individual firm.

Impact of Transaction Costs

A situation where an investor must sell part of his or her holdings in order to generate cash argues for a cash dividend policy. In the previous illustration it would not be cost effective to sell 9 shares of stock. Com-

---

[8] That the price of a stock declines by the amount of the dividend is explained in the next section on cash dividends.

[9] For a discussion of the irrelevancy of dividends, see an advanced text on financial management such as Stephen A. Ross, Randolph W. Westerfield, and Jeffrey F. Jaffe, *Corporate Finance,* 2nd ed. (Homewood, Ill.: Richard D. Irwin, Inc., 1990), chapter 17.

missions would consume a large proportion of the proceeds of the sale; obviously, this expense is avoided by the receipt of dividends. Of course, if the firm paid dividends and then had to float additional shares to raise the funds necessary for operations or to make desirable investment opportunities, the firm would incur investment banking fees that would have been avoided if earnings had been retained and not distributed.

It should be noted that these transaction costs conclusively argue neither for nor against the distribution of dividends. If the corporation's primary stockholders desire dividends, then there may be a net cost saving from the distribution of earnings and flotation of new shares. Those stockholders who want the additional shares could purchase them, in which case they bear the expense. If the corporation's primary stockholders seek capital gains, then there may be a net cost saving from retaining the earnings. Those stockholders who want cash could sell part of their holdings, in which case they bear the expense.

Impact of Taxation

Taxation always plays a major role in financial decision making, and dividend policy is no exception. Consider the earlier example in which the stockholder received either a cash dividend or sold some of the stock. Dividends are subject to federal income taxes, while profits from security sales are subject to federal capital gains taxes. If these taxes are the same, then taxation does not matter. As of 1990, the federal income tax rates on dividend income and capital gains were the same, but that has not always been the case. Prior to tax reform in 1986, long-term capital gains (defined as gains realized after holding the security for longer than six months) were taxed at a lower rate. Such taxation argues for capital gains in favor of dividend income. While it is not possible to know what future tax policy will be, the re-institution of tax rates that favor capital gains is often offered as a means to stimulate economic growth and the creation of new jobs.

Even if dividends and capital gains are taxed at the same rate, there is still an argument in favor of capital gains. Dividends are taxed as received; the tax on capital gains is deferred until the gains are realized (i.e., when the shares are sold). If the corporation retains earnings and is able to grow, and the value of the shares rises in response to the growth, stockholders will not have to pay any tax as long as they hold their shares and do not realize the gains.

Even if the gains are realized after a number of years and taxed at the same rate as dividends, the ability to defer the tax permits the investor to take advantage of compounding. The following example illustrates how federal income taxes favor the retention of earnings through compounding. The example assumes that the stockholder is in the 28 percent income tax bracket and invests $1,000 in a firm. The firm earns 10 percent on the individual's equity in the firm. Case A illustrates the retention of earnings and the growth in the individual's investment in the firm.

Case A Initial Funds $1,000

	Earnings	Earnings Retained	Stockholder's Investment
Year 1	$100.00	$100.00	$1,100.00
Year 2	110.00	110.00	1,210.00
Year 3	121.00	121.00	1,331.00
Year 4	133.10	133.10	1,464.10

During the first year, the firm earns $100 for the investor (i.e., .1 × $1,000) and retains the earnings so the investor's equity rises to $1,100 ($1,000 + $100). After four years, the investor's equity in the firm grows to $1,464. If the shares are sold for $1,464, the investor has a capital gain of $464 ($1,464 − $1,000), which is taxed at 28 percent. The investor thus pays $130 (.28 × $464) in taxes and nets $334 after taxes.

In Case B the firm distributes the annual earnings in cash dividends. Since there is no retention of earnings, the firm earns and distributes $100 each year. The investor then pays personal income tax of $28 and nets $72 after tax.

Case B Initial Funds $1,000

	Earnings	Earnings Distributed	Income Tax	After-Tax Income	Stockholder's Investment
Year 1	$100	$100	$28	$72	$1,000
Year 2	100	100	28	72	1,000
Year 3	100	100	28	72	1,000
Year 4	100	100	28	72	1,000

After four years, the stockholder will have received $400 in cash dividends, paid $112 in taxes, and netted $288. The $288 is less than the $334 netted in Case A, in which the earnings were allowed to grow and the tax was deferred.

As may be seen from the example, federal tax laws favor the retention of earnings rather than the distribution of earnings in the form of cash dividends. The difference in the after-tax return, however, would be smaller if the investor had invested the dividends elsewhere and earned more than the firm earned on the retained earnings. Thus, an investor would be better off receiving the earnings if there were a use for

Financial Facts

Classes of Common Stock

Suppose some stockholders want management to distribute cash dividends while others want management to retain earnings to finance future growth. Can management distribute earnings to one group and retain earnings for the other stockholders? Essentially, the answer is no; some owners of a class of stock cannot receive cash dividends while others have their earnings reinvested. What applies to one applies to all. Of course, some stockholders may opt to have their cash dividends reinvested in additional shares through dividend reinvestment plans. This choice to have cash dividends reinvested is made by the individual and not by management. • Although the preceding paragraph states that all stockholders in a class are treated the same, there is a very important qualifying phrase: "in a class." Some companies have more than one class of common stock. For example, Oshkosh B'Gosh has two classes of common stock. Class A shares have limited voting rights and receive 15 percent higher dividends than the Class B shares. Other publicly held corporations with two classes of common stock include Food Lion and Media General. • While the stockholders of the different classes of common stock may receive different cash dividends, the purpose of two classes is not the distribution of dividends but the distribution of voting power. Often one of the classes has no or only limited voting rights. Thus, voting power can be concentrated in the hands of a few stockholders who own the class of stock with voting power, which virtually assures them control over the firm. •

---

the money that overcame the deferral of the tax. Many investors, however, may not have such investment opportunities, so the retention of earnings is often viewed as being in the best interests of the firm and its stockholders who are seeking growth in capital.

Impact of the Firm's Need for Cash

The previous discussion suggested that transaction costs and taxation may affect a firm's dividend policy. The firm's need for cash may also have an impact. For example, in Chapter 18 a cash budget will illustrate a case in which the firm's needs for cash fluctuate during the year. Such variations in cash requirements affect the firm's capacity to pay dividends. If management must pay dividends during a period when the firm has insufficient cash, such payments will require the firm to borrow money. Management may be reluctant to borrow funds just to pay the dividend, since such borrowings will require interest payments and the financial community may not approve of such a policy. Thus, the fluctuation in the firm's cash needs can have an impact on the desirability and the firm's capacity to distribute cash dividends.

Firms in cyclical industries have a similar problem except that it is spread over a longer period of time. These firms are primarily in industries that produce capital goods (manufacturers of machinery and machine tools) or durable goods (automobiles and housing). Firms in cyclical industries experience large fluctuations in earnings that affect both their capacity to pay dividends and their need to retain earnings. During periods of economic prosperity their earnings tend to expand, which would permit higher dividends. However, management may prefer to retain the earnings to help finance the firm's operations during periods of economic slowdown and stagnation. During recessions the firm's earnings may decline severely, or the firm may even operate at a loss. If the firm had previously retained earnings, its capacity to endure economic stagnation would be increased.

Inflation also has an impact on dividends. Since the cost of plant and equipment rises during a period of inflation, the firm will need more sources of funds to finance the replacement of worn-out assets. Notice that this replacement of plant and equipment is not the same as expansion of the firm's operations; inflation means that the firm will have to spend more just to maintain its current size of operations. Such expenditures require financing, and the retention of earnings is potentially a major source of those funds. Of course, if the firm distributes its earnings, it will have to find other sources of funds to replace the obsolete plant and equipment.

Inflation is really a two-edged sword because stockholders also are affected by higher prices. Stockholders may want the firm to maintain and even increase its cash dividends so that they may retain their purchasing power. No doubt management is aware of the stockholders' position and is caught between the need to increase spending to maintain the viability of the firm and the stockholders' need for additional income to offset the impact of inflation.

The prior discussion has indicated that there is no unique dividend policy that all firms follow. Reasons such as saving brokerage commission explain why the individual investor may prefer cash to capital gains. And reasons such as deferring capital gains taxes explain why the individual investor may prefer the retention of earnings. There are also reasons such as the availability of investment opportunities or the need for cash that explain why management may prefer to retain earnings.

If management seeks to maximize the wealth of the stockholders, the dividend decision basically depends on who has the better use for the money—the stockholders or the firm. Management, however, may not know the stockholders' alternative uses for the money, or may choose to ignore the stockholders' alleged uses, and decide to retain the earnings. Stockholders who do not like the firm's dividend policy may then seek to sell their shares. If stockholders like the dividend policy, they may seek to purchase more shares. If the sellers exceed the buyers, the value of the shares will fall, and management will be made aware of the stockholders' preference for the cash dividends instead of the retention of earnings.

CASH DIVIDENDS

Companies that pay cash dividends usually have a policy that is either stated or implicitly known by the investment community. Most American companies that pay cash dividends distribute a regular cash dividend on a quarterly basis. A few companies make monthly distributions (e.g., Winn-Dixie), and some make the distribution semiannually or annually. Frequently, in the case of semiannual and annual payments, the dollar amount is small. Instead of paying 2½ cents a share quarterly, the company pays 10 cents annually, which reduces the expense of distributing the dividend.

While most companies with cash dividend policies pay regular quarterly dividends, there are other types of dividend policies. Some companies pay quarterly dividends plus extras. Maytag pays a quarterly dividend but distributes an extra dividend at year end if the company has a good year. Such a policy is appropriate for a firm in a cyclical industry because earnings fluctuate over time, and the firm may be hard pressed to maintain a higher level of regular quarterly dividends. By having a set cash payment supplemented with extras in good years, the firm is able not only to maintain a fixed payment that is relatively assured but also to supplement the dividend when appropriate.

Payout ratio ▲ Ratio of cash dividends to earnings

Management may view the dividend policy as a distribution of a certain proportion of the earnings. The ratio of dividends to earnings is the **payout ratio,** which gives the proportion of the earnings the firm is distributing. For some firms this ratio has remained rather stable. For example, from 1985 to 1990, Coca-Cola paid out an annual average of 45 percent of its earnings.

Some firms pay cash dividends that are irregular; there is no set dividend payment. For example, to maintain favorable tax treatment, real estate investment trusts are required by law to distribute their earnings. These earnings fluctuate, causing the cash dividends to fluctuate. For example, BRT Realty Trust paid $2.43 in 1988 but only $1.46 in 1990, when its earnings fell. The special tax laws pertaining to these trusts cause BRT Realty Trust and other real estate investment trusts to have irregular dividend payments.

As the earnings of the company grow, the firm is able to increase its cash dividends. There is, however, a reluctance to increase the cash dividend immediately with an increase in earnings. The reason for this lag is management's reluctance to reduce cash dividends if earnings decline. Management apparently fears that the reduction will be interpreted as a sign of financial weakness. The unwillingness to cut dividends has resulted in a tendency for management to raise dividends only when it is certain that the higher level of earnings will be maintained.

Most companies announce their dividend policy. There are many areas of a firm's operation about which investors know little and which perhaps they would not understand even if they were kept informed. The dividend policy of the firm is readily understood and may have an important effect on the investors' attitude toward the firm. Some stockholders seek a flow of income from their investments and prefer stocks that pay generous cash dividends. These investors will purchase stock in companies that pay out a large proportion of the firm's earnings. Other investors prefer capital gains and purchase stocks of companies that retain earnings to finance growth. Thus, investors need to know the firm's dividend policy. It is advisable that the firm announce its dividend policy, and most firms do.

The process by which dividends are distributed takes time. The first step is the dividend meeting by the firm's directors. If they decide to distribute a cash dividend, two important dates are established. The first date determines who is to receive the dividend. On a particular day the ownership books of the corporation are closed, and everyone owning stock in the company at the end of that day receives the dividend. This is called the **date of record.** If the stock is purchased after the date of record, the purchaser does not receive the dividend. The stock is purchased excluding the dividend; this is referred to as **ex dividend,** for the price of the stock does not include the dividend payment. The ex dividend day is four working days before the date of record, because the settlement date is five working days after the transaction. In the financial papers, purchases of the stock on the ex dividend day are indicated by an X next to sales volume. The following entry indicates that the stock of Sun Company traded on that day was purchased exclusive of the dividend.

Date of record ▲
Day on which an investor must own stock in order to receive the dividend payment

Ex dividend ▲
Stock purchases exclusive of any dividend payment

Stock	Dividend	Sales	High	Low	Close	Net Change
Sun Co.	2	**X** 135	47⅜	47	47⅜	+ ¼

The $0.50 (i.e., $2.00/4) quarterly dividend will be paid to the owners of record of the previous day and not to the investors who purchased the stock on the ex dividend day. In this example there was a net change of ¼ in the price of the stock for the ex dividend day. This indicates that the closing price on the previous day was $47⅝ and not $47⅛ as might be expected from the increase of ¼ for the day. Since the current buyers will not receive the $0.50 dividend, the price of the stock is reduced for the dividend. The net change in the stock's price from the previous day's trading is figured from the adjusted price (i.e., $47⅝ minus the $0.50 dividend).

Distribution date ▲ Day on which a dividend is paid to stockholders

The second important date is the day that the dividend is distributed, or the **distribution date.** The distribution date may be several weeks after the record date, as the company must determine the owners on the record date and process the checks. The company may not perform this task itself; instead it uses its commercial bank, for which service the bank charges a fee. The day that the dividend is received by the stockholder is thus likely to be many weeks after the board of directors announced the dividend payment.

STOCK DIVIDENDS

Stock dividends ▲ Distribution from earnings paid in additional shares of stock

Some firms make a practice of paying **stock dividends** in addition to or in lieu of cash dividends. Unfortunately the recipients frequently misunderstand what they are receiving. Stock dividends are a form of *recapitalization* and do *not* increase the assets of the firm. Since the assets and their management produce income for the firm, a stock dividend does not by itself increase the potential earning power of the firm. Investors, however, may believe that stock dividends will enhance the earning capacity of the firm and the value of the stock. They mistakenly believe that the stock dividend increases the firm's assets.

To facilitate the demonstration of stock dividends, the following equity section of a balance sheet will be used:

Equity	
Equity: $2 par common stock (2,000,000 shares authorized; 1,000,000 outstanding)	$2,000,000
Additional paid-in capital	500,000
Retained earnings	5,000,000
	$7,500,000

Since a stock dividend is only a recapitalization, the assets and liabilities are not affected by declaring and paying the stock dividend. Only the entries in the equity section of the balance sheet are affected by a stock dividend. The stock dividend transfers amounts from retained earnings to common stock and additional paid-in capital. The amount transferred depends on (1) the number of new shares issued through the stock dividend and (2) the market price of the stock. If the above company issued a 10 percent stock dividend when the price of the common stock was $20 a share, this would cause the issuing of 100,000 shares with a value of $2,000,000. This amount is subtracted from the retained earnings and transferred to the common stock and additional paid-in capital. The amount transferred to common stock will be 100,000 times the par value of the stock ($2 × 100,000 = $200,000). The remaining amount ($1,800,000) is transferred to additional paid-in capital. The equity section then becomes:

Equity	
Equity: $2 par common stock (2,000,000 shares authorized; 1,100,000 outstanding)	$2,200,000
Additional paid-in capital	2,300,000
Retained earnings	3,000,000
	$7,500,000

The stock dividend is said to have transferred funds from retained earnings to the "permanent capital" of the firm. This statement is misleading, for no funds have been transferred.[10] There has been an increase in the number of shares outstanding, but there has been no increase in cash and no increase in assets that may be used to earn profits. All that has happened is a recapitalization: the equity entries have been altered.

The stock dividend does not increase the wealth of the stockholder but does increase the number of shares owned. In the above example, a stockholder who owned 100 shares before the stock dividend had stock worth $2,000. After the stock dividend this stockholder owns 110 shares, and the 110 shares are also worth $2,000, for the price per share falls from $20 to $18.18 ($2,000/110 = $18.18). Why does the price of the stock fall? The answer is that there are 10 percent more shares outstanding, but there has been no increase in the firm's assets and earning power. The old shares have been *diluted* and hence the price of the stock must decline to indicate this **dilution.** If the price of the stock did not fall, all companies could make their stockholders wealthier by declaring stock dividends. But investors would soon realize that the stock dividend does not increase the assets and earning power of the firm, and they would not be willing to pay the old price for a larger number of shares. The market price would fall to adjust to the dilution of the old shares, and that is exactly what happens.

Dilution ▲
Reduction in earnings per share as the result of issuing additional shares

The major misconception concerning the stock dividend is that it increases the ability of the firm to grow. If the stock dividend were a substitute for a cash dividend, the statement would be partially true, because

[10] Since cash dividends are paid from earnings, this transfer of capital from retained earnings to common stock and paid-in capital will reduce the firm's ability to pay cash dividends.

the firm still has the asset cash that would have been paid to stockholders if a cash dividend had been declared. The firm, however, would still have the cash if it did not pay the stock dividend, for a firm may retain its cash and not pay a stock dividend. Hence, the decision to pay the stock dividend does not increase the firm's cash; it is the decision not to pay the cash dividend that conserves the cash. When a stock dividend is paid in lieu of cash, it may even be interpreted as a screen; the stock dividend is hiding the failure to pay cash dividends.

Perhaps the primary advantage of the stock dividend is to bring to the current stockholders' attention the fact that the firm is retaining its cash in order to grow and to indicate that the stockholders will be rewarded through the retention of assets. By retaining the assets, the firm may be able to earn more than the stockholders are able to earn, which will increase the price of the stock in the future. However, this same result may be achieved without the expense of the stock dividend.

STOCK SPLITS

Stock split ▲
Recapitalization achieved by changing the number of shares outstanding

After the price of a stock has risen substantially, management may choose to split the stock. This **stock split** will lower the price of the stock and make it more accessible to investors. Implicit in this statement is the belief that investors prefer lower priced shares and that reducing the price of the stock will benefit the current stockholders by widening the market for their stock.

Like the stock dividend, the stock split is a recapitalization.[11] It does not affect the assets or liabilities of the firm. It does not increase the earning power of the firm, and the wealth of the stockholder is not increased unless other investors prefer lower priced stocks and increase the demand for this stock.

The equity section of a balance sheet used previously for illustrating the stock dividend will now be employed to demonstrate a two-for-one stock split. In a two-for-one stock split, one old share becomes two new shares, and the par value of the stock is halved. There are no changes in the additional paid-in capital or retained earnings. All that has happened is that there are now twice as many shares outstanding and each share is worth half as much as an old share.

---

[11] A stock split may be differentiated from a stock dividend by the number of shares issued. If the number of shares is increased by 25 percent or more, the recapitalization is considered a stock split. If the number of shares increases by less than 25 percent, the recapitalization is a stock dividend. An eleven for ten stock split would, in effect, be a 10 percent stock dividend.

EXHIBIT 10.3

Selected Stock Splits Distributed in 1991

Stock splits have various terms, with 2 for 1 being the most common.

Firm	Terms of Split
Multimedia	3 for 1
Tambrands	2 for 1
Honeywell	2 for 1
Pfizer	2 for 1
Biomet	2 for 1
AST Research	2 for 1
Merry-Go-Round	3 for 2
Fabri-Centers of America	3 for 2
Wassau Papers	5 for 4

Equity	
Equity: $1 par common stock (2,000,000 shares authorized; 2,000,000 outstanding)	$2,000,000
Additional paid-in capital	500,000
Retained earnings	5,000,000
	$7,500,000

Stock splits may be in any combination of terms, as can be seen in Exhibit 10.3, which gives the terms of nine stock splits. The most common splits are two for one or three for two. Occasionally there is a reverse split, which reduces the number of shares and raises the price of the stock. For example, Wickes split its stock one for five. Thus, 100 shares became 20 shares after the split.

All stock splits affect the price of the stock. With a two-for-one split the stock's price is cut in half. A one-for-ten split raises the price by a factor of ten. An easy method for finding the price of the stock after the split is to multiply the stock's price before the split by the reciprocal of the terms of the split. For example, if a stock is selling for $54 a share and is split 3 for 2, then the price of the stock after the split will be $\$54 \times \frac{2}{3} = \$36$.

Stock splits, like stock dividends, do not by themselves increase the wealth of the stockholder, for the stock split does not increase the assets and earning power of the firm. All that changes is the number of shares and their price. A stock split is like a pie that is cut into eight instead of four pieces. The size of the pie remains the same, but the size of each piece is altered.

The usual rationale given by management for splitting a stock is that a lower selling price increases the marketability of the shares. That is, the split produces a wider distribution of ownership and increases investor interest in the company. This increased interest and marketability may ultimately cause the value of the stock to appreciate. For example, if Ford splits its stock (as it did in 1988), the wider distribution may lead to an increase in sales. Larger sales then produce higher earnings and an increase in the price of the shares. If such a scenario were to occur (and there is no evidence that it will), the current stockholders would benefit; however, the source of a subsequent price increase in the stock's value would still be the increase in earnings and not the stock split.

DIVIDEND REINVESTMENT PLANS

Dividend reinvestment plans ▲
Plans that permit stockholders to have cash dividends reinvested in additional shares instead of receiving the cash

Many corporations that pay cash dividends also have **dividend reinvestment plans.** These permit stockholders to have cash dividends used to purchase additional shares of stock. Dividend reinvestment plans started in the 1960s, but the growth in the plans occurred in the 1970s.

There are two types of dividend reinvestment plans. In most plans a bank acts on behalf of the corporation and its stockholders. The bank collects the cash dividends for the stockholders and in some plans offers the stockholders the option of making additional cash contributions. The bank pools all of the funds and purchases the stock on the open market. Since the bank is able to purchase a larger block of shares, it receives a substantial reduction in the per-share commission cost of the purchase. This reduced brokerage fee is spread over all the shares purchased by the bank, so even the smallest investor receives the advantage of the reduced brokerage fees. The bank does charge a fee for its service, but this fee is usually modest and does not offset the potential savings in brokerage fees.

In the second type of reinvestment plan, the company issues new shares of stock, and the money is directly rechanneled to the company. The investor may also have the option of making additional cash contributions. This type of plan offers the investor a further advantage in that the brokerage fees are entirely circumvented. The entire amount of the cash dividend is used to purchase shares, with the issuing cost paid by the company.

Besides the potential savings in brokerage fees, the major advantage to investors of dividend reinvestment plans is the "forced savings." Such forced saving may be desirable for investors who wish to save but have a tendency to spend money once it is received. The plans also offer advantages to the firm. They create goodwill and may result in some cost savings (e.g., lower costs of preparing and mailing dividend checks). The shares accumulated by stockholders are more likely to be retained by these stockholders and may produce support for the price of the company's stock. The reinvestment plans that result in the new issue of stock also increase the company's equity base.

REPURCHASE OF STOCK

A firm with excess cash may choose to repurchase some of its outstanding shares of stock. The effect of such an act is to decrease the number of shares outstanding. This will increase the earnings per share and increase the use of financial leverage employed by the firm.

The repurchasing of shares is another example of the question of selecting among alternatives. The company may repurchase shares because management may believe that it is the best use of the money. The shares may then be used in the future in merger agreements or for exercising stock options. Repurchases also occur because firms believe that the price of their shares is too low and the shares are undervalued. Repurchasing the shares, then, is viewed as the best investment currently available to the firm.

The repurchasing of shares may be viewed as an alternative to paying cash dividends. Instead of distributing the money as cash dividends, the firm offers to purchase the shares from the stockholders. This offers the stockholders a major advantage. They have the option to sell or retain their shares. If the stockholders believe that the firm's potential is sufficient to warrant retention of the shares, they do not have to sell them. The option to sell the shares rests with the stockholder.

Perhaps the most spectacular repurchase occurred when Teledyne repurchased 8.7 million of its shares at $200 each for a total outlay of $1.74 billion. Teledyne initially offered to repurchase 5 million shares at $200. At that time the stock was selling for $156, so the offer represented a 28 percent premium over the current price. The large premium probably caused more shares to be tendered than 5 million. While Teledyne could have prorated its purchases, it instead chose to accept all the shares. The result was to reduce the amount of outstanding stock from 20.4 million to 11.7 million shares—a reduction of 40 percent. The reduction in the number of shares outstanding increased Teledyne's earnings per share by more than $7. After the repurchase had been completed, the stock's price continued to increase and sold for more than $240 a share within a few weeks. Obviously the security market believed that the repurchase was in the best interests of the remaining stockholders.

If a company does repurchase its stock, the number of outstanding shares is reduced. Thus the firm's earnings will be spread over fewer shares, and its earnings per share should increase. The higher earnings then may lead to a higher stock price in the future.

SUMMARY

Corporations issue and sell stock to individuals as a means to raise equity funds. The stockholders are the owners of the corporation. Although preferred stock is legally considered to be equity, its features make it similar to debt. Preferred stock pays a fixed dividend. If the firm misses a payment, the amount of the dividend usually accumulates and must be paid before dividends can be paid to the common stockholders. While some preferred stock is perpetual, other preferred issues have a sinking fund or call feature. The investor can expect these issues of preferred stock to have a finite life.

Although preferred stock is similar to debt, in some ways it is also different. From the investor's perspective, it is riskier than bonds because the terms of preferred stock are not legal obligations of the firm. From the firm's viewpoint, preferred stock is less attractive than debt because the dividends are paid from earnings and are not tax deductible. Interest on bonds is a tax-deductible expense.

Common stock represents the residual claim on the corporation's earnings and assets. The owners of common stock generally have the right to vote their shares. Once a corporation has achieved earnings, the earnings are either distributed or retained. Retained earnings, which are an important source of funds for corporations, increase the stockholders' investment in the firm and permit the firm to retire debt or increase its assets. Thus, retained earnings finance further growth, which, if achieved, should tend to increase the value of the shares.

Some corporations also pay stock dividends, which increase the number of shares outstanding. Stock dividends are perceptibly different from cash dividends, which require the firm to distribute funds. Stock dividends (and stock splits) do not change the firm's assets, liabilities, or total equity. Thus, they do not affect the firm's earning capacity. They do, however, lower the stock's price in proportion to the number of new shares issued.

Many firms offer dividend reinvestment plans that permit stockholders to accumulate additional shares at little or no brokerage cost. Occasionally, a firm will elect to repurchase shares instead of making a cash distribution. Such repurchases generally occur if management believes that the shares are undervalued.

Review Questions

1. What are the features common to most preferred stock?
2. Must a firm pay preferred stock dividends? What does being in arrears mean? What is the advantage offered by having a cumulative preferred stock?

3. From the viewpoint of the corporation, preferred stock is less risky than bonds. From the viewpoint of the investor preferred stock is riskier. Why are these statements concerning risk true?
4. Why is earnings per preferred share a measure of the safety of preferred stock?
5. If you were a minority stockholder, why may you support cumulative voting?
6. What impact may federal income taxes have on the retention of earnings?
7. Which dividend policy, a constant payout or a stable dollar, would you prefer a firm to follow? Which policy would a retired individual prefer?
8. Why does the price of a stock decline after a 10 percent stock dividend?
9. If you purchase a stock on the ex dividend day, do you receive the dividend?
10. What is a dividend reinvestment plan, and what advantage does it offer investors?

Problems

1. Firm A had the following items on its balance sheet:

Cash	$ 28,000,000
Common stock (2,000,000 shares; $50 par)	100,000,000
Paid-in capital	10,000,000
Retained earnings	62,000,000

How would each of these accounts appear after:

a. a cash dividend of $1 per share?
b. a 5 percent stock dividend (fair market value is $60 per share)?
c. a 1-for-2 reverse split?

2. A firm's balance sheet has the following entries:

Cash	$10,000,000
Total liabilities	30,000,000
Common stock (2,000,000 shares outstanding; $5 par)	10,000,000
Paid-in capital	3,000,000
Retained earnings	42,000,000

What will be each of these balance sheet entries after:

a. a 3-for-1 stock split?
b. a $1.25 per share cash dividend?
c. a 10 percent stock dividend (current price of the stock is $15 per share)?

3. What effect will a 2-for-1 stock split have on the following items found on a firm's financial statements?

a. Earnings per share $4.20

b. Total equity $10,000,000
c. Long-term debt $ 4,300,000
d. Paid-in capital $ 1,534,000
e. Number of shares outstanding 1,000,000
f. Earnings $ 4,200,000

4. You are considering purchasing the preferred stock of a firm but are concerned with its capacity to pay the dividend. To help allay that fear, you compute the times-dividend-earned ratio for the past three years from the following data taken from the firm's financial statements:

Year	19X1	19X2	19X3
Operating income	$12,000,000	$15,000,000	$17,000,000
Interest	3,000,000	5,900,000	11,000,000
Taxes	4,000,000	5,400,000	4,000,000
Preferred dividends	1,000,000	1,000,000	1,500,000
Common dividends	3,000,000	2,000,000	—

What does your analysis indicate concerning the firm's capacity to pay the preferred stock dividends?

5. A firm has the following balance sheet:

ASSETS		LIABILITIES AND EQUITY	
Cash	$ 20,000	Accounts payable	$ 20,000
Accounts receivable	110,000	Long-term debt	100,000
Inventory	120,000	Common stock ($8 par; 4,000 shares outstanding)	32,000
Plant and equipment	250,000		
		Paid-in capital	148,000
		Retained earnings	200,000
	$500,000		$500,000

a. Construct a new balance sheet showing the impact of a 3-for-1 split. If the current market price of the stock is $54, what is the price after the split?

ASSETS		LIABILITIES AND EQUITY	
Cash	$_____	Accounts payable	$_____
Accounts Receivable	_____	Long-term debt	_____
Inventory	_____	Common stock ($__ par; _____ shares outstanding)	_____
Plant and equipment	_____		
		Paid-in capital	_____
		Retained earnings	_____
	$_____		$_____

b. Construct a new balance sheet showing the impact of a 10 percent stock dividend. After the stock dividend, what is the new price of the common stock?

ASSETS		LIABILITIES AND EQUITY	
Cash	$______	Accounts payable	$______
Accounts Receivable	______	Long-term debt	______
Inventory	______	Common stock ($__ par; ______ shares outstanding)	______
Plant and equipment	______	Paid-in capital	______
		Retained earnings	______
	$		$

cases

Strategies to Increase Equity

Theresa Anderson is preparing for a meeting of the board of directors of Chesapeake Bay Corporation, a developer of moderate priced homes and vacation homes in the Chesapeake Bay area. The combination of the location near major metropolitan areas with the recreational facilities associated with the Chesapeake Bay has made the firm one of the most successful homebuilders in the nation. During the last five years, the firm's cash dividend has risen from $2.10 to $3.74, and the price of its stock has risen from $36 to $75. Since the firm has 1,200,000 shares outstanding, the market value of the stock is $90,000,000. Given the volatile nature of its industry, the increases in the price of the stock and in the dividend were substantial achievements.

Management, however, is considering entering into non-building areas in an effort to diversify the firm. These new investments will require more financing. Although additional debt financing is a possibility, management believes that it is unwise to issue only new debt and not increase the firm's equity base. New equity could be obtained by issuing additional stock or reducing the dividend, and thus retaining a larger proportion of the firm's earnings. Two major points had previously been raised against these strategies: Issuing additional shares may dilute the existing stockholders' position, and reducing the dividend could cause the value of the stock to decline.

Even though it is possible that no change will be made and that the firm will continue its present course, the board believes that a thorough discussion of all possibilities is desirable. Ms. Anderson has been instructed to develop alternatives to the two strategies for the next meeting of the board in two weeks.

The short period for preparation means that a thorough analysis may be impossible, especially of the possible impact of a dividend cut on the value of the stock, but Ms. Anderson presumes that some additional alternatives do exist. One of her assistants suggested that the firm institute a dividend reinvestment plan, in which additional shares would be sold to stockholders to raise additional equity capital. Her other assistant suggested that the company substitute a 5 percent stock dividend for the cash dividend. Before making either (or both) suggestions to the board, Ms. Anderson decided to answer several questions:

Case Problems

1. Would implementing the suggestions dilute the existing stockholders' position?
2. How much new equity would be raised by each action?
3. What may happen to the price of the stock?
4. What are the costs associated with each strategy?
5. Would a stock split combined with either strategy help raise additional equity financing?
6. Would an increase in the cash dividend coupled with the dividend reinvestment plan help raise additional equity financing?
7. Is there any reason to prefer or exclude any one of the four strategies (i.e., issuing new shares, reducing the dividend, instituting a dividend reinvestment plan, or substituting a stock dividend for the cash dividend)?

Suggested Readings

Whether or not the distribution of cash dividends increases stockholder wealth is subject to debate. See, for instance:

Black, Fisher. "The Dividend Puzzle." *Journal of Portfolio Management* (Winter 1976), pp. 5–8.

Hayes, Linda. "Fresh Evidence That Dividends Don't Matter." *Fortune,* May 4, 1981.

A survey of corporate financial managers suggests that management is concerned with dividend continuity as an indicator of the future prospects of the firm. The results are reported in:

Baker, W. Kent, Gail E. Farrelly, and Richard B. Edelman. "A Survey of Management Views on Dividend Policy." *Financial Management* (Autumn 1985), pp. 78–84.

Even though the finance literature attributes no value to stock dividends and stock splits, managements still declare them. For an explanation consult:

Baker, W. Kent, and Patricia L. Gallagher. "Management's View of Stock Splits." *Financial Management* (Summer 1980), pp. 73–77.

Eisemann, Peter C., and Edward A. Moses. "Stock Dividends: Management's View." *Financial Analysts Journal* (July–August 1979), pp. 77–80.

Stock repurchases have become common. For the characteristics of firms that repurchase their own stock, consult:

Finnerty, Joseph E. "Corporate Stock Issue and Repurchase." *Financial Management* (October 1975), pp. 62–66.

Houston, John L. "Common Stock Repurchases: A Bane or Boon to Shareholders." *AAII Journal* (February 1984), pp. 7–10.

chapter

11

Valuation of Stock

15 pages in chapter

Learning Objectives

1. Illustrate the pricing of preferred stock.
2. Show the relationship between changes in interest rates and the value of preferred stock.
3. Calculate the value of a common stock using the dividend-growth model.
4. Identify the components of an investor's required return.
5. Adjust the dividend-growth model for differences in risk.
6. Determine if a stock is undervalued or overvalued.
7. Illustrate the impact of changes in the expected return on the market or in the risk-free rate on the value of a common stock.
8. Use price/earnings (P/E) ratios as a means to value common stock.

In *Lady Windermere's Fan,* Oscar Wilde defines a cynic as "a man who knows the price of everything, and the value of nothing." This quote could be paraphrased as "an uninformed investor is a person who knows the price of every stock, and the value of none." Anybody can find the price of a stock. Yesterday's prices are reported in the financial press, and current quotes may be obtained from brokers. But the current price does not tell an investor if the stock is a good purchase. To answer that question, the investor needs to know what the stock is worth: its value.

One individual who certainly did learn how to determine the value of a stock was Warren Buffett. A $10,000 investment in 1956 in a partnership he started grew into $1,500,000 worth of Berkshire Hathaway stock in 1990. Buffett's success resulted from his capacity to identify excellent management and to find undervalued stocks by using security analysis and valuation techniques.[1]

This chapter is devoted to the valuation of stock. The first section describes the valuation of preferred stock. Since preferred stock is similar to bonds (i.e., they both are fixed income securities), the valuation of preferred stock is essentially the same as the valuation of bonds.

The next section, which forms the bulk of the chapter, centers around the valuation of common stock. Although this can be an elusive topic, the individual needs to know what a stock is worth in order to determine if it is a good purchase. If a stock is selling for $15 and the individual determines it is only worth $13, the stock certainly is not a good investment.

The valuation of common stock revolves around the firm's earnings, its dividend, the future growth in dividends, and the amount that investors can earn on alternative investments. The standard dividend-growth model used in finance is explained and illustrated, and an adjustment for risk is introduced into the dividend-growth model. The chapter ends with a description of the use of P/E ratios to select stocks.

VALUATION OF PREFERRED STOCK

The process of valuing (i.e., pricing) preferred stock is essentially the same as that used to price debt. The payments in the future are brought back to the present at the appropriate discount rate. If the preferred stock does not have a required sinking fund or call feature, it may be

[1] Warren Buffett's success is chronicled in John Train, *The Midas Touch* (New York: Harper and Row, Inc., 1987).

viewed as a perpetual debt instrument. The fixed dividend (D_p) will continue indefinitely. These dividends must be discounted by the yield being earned on newly issued preferred stock (k_p). The process for determining the present value of the preferred stock (P_p) is given in Equation 11.1:

11.1 $$P_p = \frac{D_p}{(1 + k_p)^1} + \frac{D_p}{(1 + k_p)^2} + \frac{D_p}{(1 + k_p)^3} + \cdots$$

This equation reduces to

11.2 $$P_p = \frac{D_p}{k_p}.$$

Thus, if a preferred stock pays an annual dividend of \$4 and the appropriate discount rate is 8 percent, the present value of the stock is

$$P_p = \frac{\$4}{(1 + 0.08)^1} + \frac{\$4}{(1 + 0.08)^2} + \frac{\$4}{(1 + 0.08)^3} + \cdots$$
$$P_p = \frac{\$4}{0.08} = \$50.$$

If an investor buys this preferred stock for \$50, he or she can expect to earn 8 percent (i.e., \$50 × 0.08 = \$4) on the investment. Of course, the realized rate of return on the investment will not be known until the investor sells the stock and adjusts this 8 percent return for any capital gain or loss. However, at the current price, the preferred stock is selling for an 8 percent dividend yield.

If the preferred stock has a finite life, this fact must be considered in determining its value. As with the valuation of long-term debt, the amount that is repaid when the preferred stock is retired must be discounted back to the present value. Thus, when preferred stock has a finite life, the valuation equation becomes

11.3 $$P_p = \frac{D_p}{(1 + k_p)^1} + \frac{D_p}{(1 + k_p)^2} + \cdots + \frac{D_p}{(1 + k_p)^n} + \frac{S}{(1 + k_p)^n},$$

where S represents the amount that is returned to the stockholder when the preferred stock is retired after n number of years. If the preferred stock in the previous example is retired after 30 years for \$100 per share, its current value would be

$$\begin{aligned} P_p &= \frac{\$4}{(1 + 0.08)^1} + \cdots + \frac{\$4}{(1 + 0.08)^{30}} + \frac{\$100}{(1 + 0.08)^{30}} \\ &= \$4(\text{PVAIF } 8\%, 30\text{Y}) + \$100(\text{PVIF } 8\%, 30\text{Y}) \\ &= \$4(11.258) + \$100(.099) \\ &= \$54.93, \end{aligned}$$

where 11.258 is the interest factor for the present value of an annuity of $1 for 30 years at 8 percent (Appendix D), and .099 is the interest factor for the present value of $1 to be received after 30 years when yields are 8 percent (Appendix B). Instead of being valued at $50, the preferred stock would be valued at $54.93. The yield is still 8 percent, but the return in this case consists of a current dividend yield of 7.28 percent ($4 ÷ $54.93) and a capital gain as the price of the stock rises from $54.93 to $100 when it is retired 30 years hence.

Since preferred stock pays a fixed dividend and is priced like a debt instrument, its price rises and declines with changes in interest rates. If interest rates rise, the rate at which preferred stock is discounted also rises, causing the price of preferred stock to decline. Conversely, when interest rates fall, the rate at which preferred stock is discounted falls, causing its price to rise. Like bond prices, the price of preferred stock moves inversely with changes in interest rates. Any investor who knows the direction of change of future interest rates knows the direction of price changes in preferred stock.

Individuals who desire income from their investments may find preferred stock attractive. However, these investors should realize that the firm is not bound to pay dividends on preferred stock. Unlike debt, which imposes legal obligations on the firm, preferred stock imposes only moral obligations. Therefore, from the investor's point of view, preferred stock is riskier than debt. Income-seeking investors would probably do better buying long-term debt than owning preferred stock, unless the stock has certain features that make it more attractive. For this reason, some preferred stock that is issued by industrial firms is convertible into the firm's common stock. As is explained in Chapter 12, convertible preferred stock is perceptibly different from nonconvertible preferred stock because its price rises and declines with the price of the stock into which it may be converted. Whereas nonconvertible stock is analyzed as if it were debt, convertible preferred stock is analyzed as both debt and equity.

VALUATION OF COMMON STOCK: THE PRESENT VALUE AND THE GROWTH OF DIVIDENDS

As with the valuation of debt and preferred stock, the valuation of common stock involves bringing future payments back to the present at the appropriate discount factor. For the individual investor, the discount factor is the required rate of return for an investment in common stock. Thus, the valuation involves discounting future cash flows (i.e., dividends) back to the present at the investor's required rate of return. The present value is then compared with the current price to determine if the stock is a good purchase.

The process of valuation and security selection is readily illustrated by the simple case in which the stock pays a fixed dividend of \$1 that is not expected to change. That is, the anticipated flow of dividend payments is

Year	1	2	3	4	...
	\$1	\$1	\$1	\$1	...

The current value of this indefinite flow of payments (i.e., the dividend) depends on the discount rate (i.e., the investor's required rate of return). If this rate is 12 percent, the stock's value (V) is

$$V = \frac{\$1}{(1 + .12)^1} + \frac{\$1}{(1 + .12)^2} + \frac{\$1}{(1 + .12)^3} + \frac{\$1}{(1 + .12)^4} + \cdots$$
$$V = \$8.33.$$

This process is expressed in the following equation in which the new variables are the dividend (D) and the required rate of return (k):

11.4 $$V = \frac{D}{(1 + k)^1} + \frac{D}{(1 + k)^2} + \cdots + \frac{D}{(1 + k)^n},$$

which simplifies to

11.5 $$V = \frac{D}{k}.$$

Thus, if a stock pays a dividend of \$1 and the investor's required rate of return is 12 percent, then the valuation is

$$V = \frac{D}{k} = \frac{\$1}{0.12} = \$8.33.$$

If the stock pays a fixed annual dividend of \$1 and the required return is 12 percent, the stock is worth \$8.33. Conversely, if the investor buys this stock for \$8.33, the return is 12 percent (\$1/\$8.33). Any price greater than \$8.33 will result in a return that is less than 12 percent. Therefore, for this investor to achieve the required rate of return of 12 percent, the price of the stock must not exceed \$8.33.

There is, however, no reason to anticipate that common stock dividends will be fixed indefinitely into the future. Common stocks offer the potential for growth, both in value and in dividends. For example, if the investor expects the \$1 dividend to grow annually at 6 percent, the anticipated flow of dividend payments is

Year	1	2	3	4	...
	\$1	\$1.06	\$1.124	\$1.191	...

The current value of this indefinite flow of growing payments (i.e., the growing dividend) also depends on the discount rate (i.e., the investor's required rate of return). If this rate is 12 percent, the stock's value is

$$V = \frac{\$1}{(1 + .12)^1} + \frac{1.06}{(1 + .12)^2} + \frac{1.124}{(1 + .12)^3} + \frac{1.191}{(1 + .12)^4} + \cdots$$

In this form, the value cannot be determined, but Equation 11.1 may be modified for the growth in the dividend. The only new variable is the rate of growth in the dividend (g), and it is assumed that this growth rate is *fixed and will continue indefinitely into the future*. Given this assumption, the **dividend-growth model** is

Dividend-growth model ▲
Valuation model for common stock that discounts future dividends

$$V = \frac{D(1 + g)^1}{(1 + k)^1} + \frac{D(1 + g)^2}{(1 + k)^2} + \frac{D(1 + g)^3}{(1 + k)^3} + \cdots + \frac{D(1 + g)^n}{(1 + k)^n},$$

which simplifies to

11.6
$$V = \frac{D_0(1 + g)}{k - g}.$$

The stock's intrinsic value is thus related to (1) the current dividend, (2) the growth in earnings and dividends, and (3) the required rate of return. The application of this model may be illustrated by a simple example. If the investor's required return is 12 percent and the stock is currently paying a \$1 per share dividend and is growing indefinitely into the future at 6 percent annually, its value is

$$V = \frac{\$1(1 + 0.06)}{0.12 - 0.06} = \$17.67.$$

Any price greater than \$17.67 will result in a total yield of less than 12 percent. Conversely, a price less than \$17.67 will produce a return in excess of 12 percent. These **rates of return** can be determined by rearranging the equation and substituting the current price for the value of the stock. Thus the rate of return (r) on an investment in stock is

Rate of return ▲
Percentage earned on an investment

11.7
$$r = \frac{D_0(1 + g)}{P} + g.$$

The $D_0(1 + g)/P$ is the dividend yield, and g is the expected rate of growth in the dividend. If the price were \$20, the rate of return would be

$$r = \frac{\$1(1 + 0.06)}{\$20} + 0.06$$
$$= 11.3\%.$$

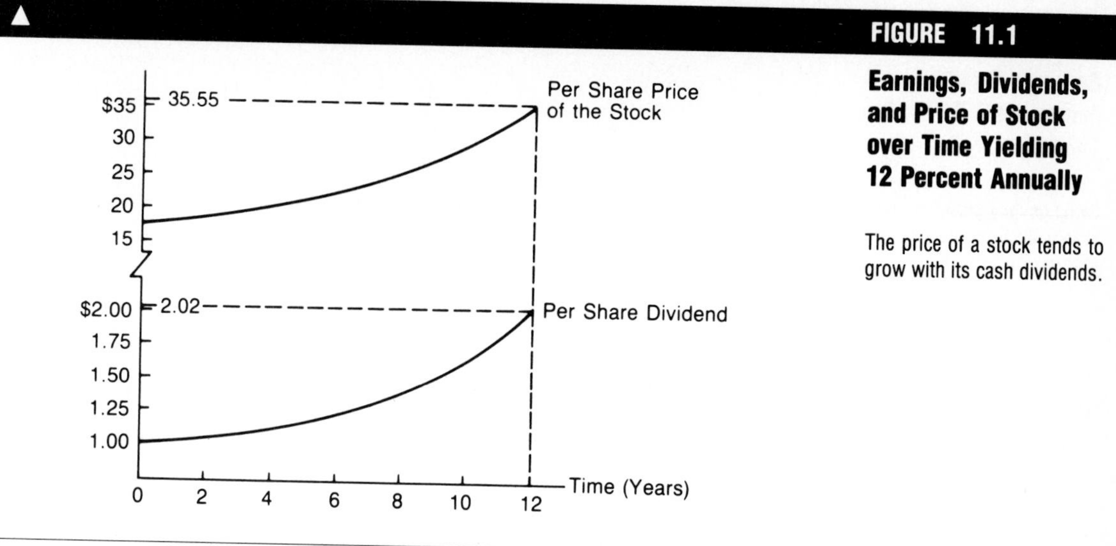

FIGURE 11.1

Earnings, Dividends, and Price of Stock over Time Yielding 12 Percent Annually

The price of a stock tends to grow with its cash dividends.

Since 11.3 percent is less than the required 12 percent, investors will not purchase the stock. If the price is $15, the return is

$$\begin{aligned} r &= \frac{\$1(1 + 0.06)}{\$15} + 0.06 \\ &= 13.1\%. \end{aligned}$$

This return is greater than the 12 percent required by the investor. Since the security offers a superior return, it is undervalued. This investor, then, would try to buy it.

Only at a price of $17.67 does the stock offer a return of 12 percent. At that price the stock's rate of return equals the required return, which is the return available on alternative investments of the same risk (i.e., $r = k$). The investment will yield 12 percent because the dividend yield during the year is 6 percent and the earnings and dividends are growing annually at the rate of 6 percent. These relationships are illustrated in Figure 11.1, which shows the growth in dividends and the price of the stock that will produce a constant yield of 12 percent. After 12 years the dividend will have grown to $2.02, and the price of the stock will be $35.55. The total return on this investment will still be 12 percent. During the year the dividend will grow to $2.14, giving a 6 percent dividend yield, and the price will continue to appreciate annually at the 6 percent growth rate in earnings and dividends.

The student should note that in Figure 11.1 the lines representing the dividend and the price of the stock are curved. The earnings and the price of the stock are growing at the same rate, but they are not growing

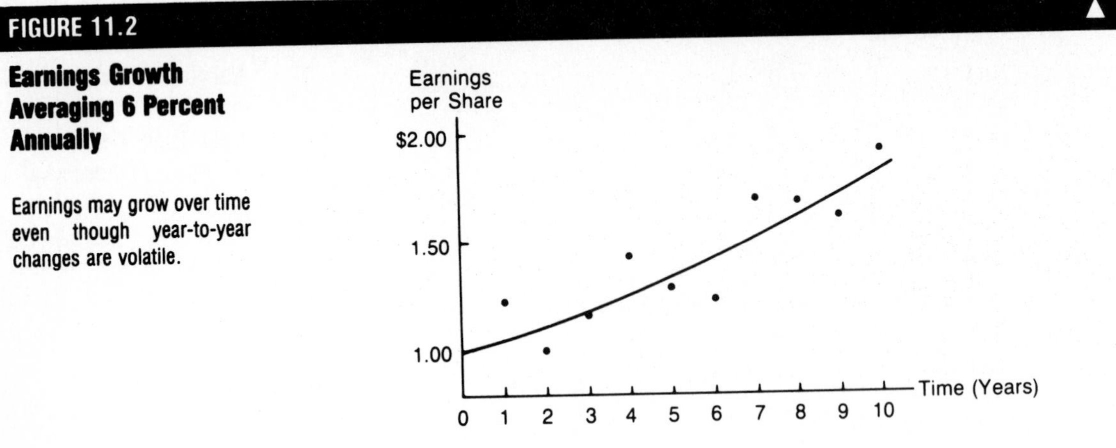

FIGURE 11.2

Earnings Growth Averaging 6 Percent Annually

Earnings may grow over time even though year-to-year changes are volatile.

by the same amount each year. This is another illustration of the time value of money, as the earnings, dividends, and price of the stock are all compounding annually at 6 percent.

A firm's earnings need not grow steadily at this rate. Figure 11.2 illustrates a case in which the firm's earnings grow annually at an average of 6 percent, but the year-to-year changes stray considerably from 6 percent. These fluctuations are not in themselves necessarily reason for concern. The firm exists within the economic environment, which fluctuates over time. Exogenous factors, such as a strike or an energy curtailment, may affect earnings during a particular year. If these factors continue to plague the firm, they will obviously play an important role in the valuation of the shares. However, the emphasis in valuation is on the flow of dividends and the growth in earnings over a period of years. This longer time dimension smooths out temporary fluctuations in earnings and dividends.

The common stock valuation model presented thus far assumes that (1) the firm's earnings will grow indefinitely at a certain rate and (2) the firm's dividend policy is unchanged so the dividend also grows at that rate. These assumptions, however, need not apply; the model may be modified so that different growth patterns can be built into the valuation.

Dividends can increase (or decrease), and these increments need not be at a constant rate. For example, an emerging firm may not pay any dividends initially but may retain all earnings to finance expansion. After achieving a certain level of growth, management may start to pay cash dividends. The initial rate of growth in the dividend may be very large, if for no other reason than that an increment from $0.02 to $0.04 is a 100 percent increase. As the firm matures and the rate of growth in earnings declines, the rate of growth in the dividend will also decline.

The firm's dividend will then increase at a stable rate. This pattern of dividends is illustrated in the table below, which represents the cash dividend and the percentage change from the preceding year:

Year	Cash Dividend	Percentage Change in the Dividend
1	—	—
2	—	—
3	$0.10	—
4	0.20	100.0%
5	0.35	75.0
6	0.50	42.9
7	0.60	20.0
8	0.66	10.0
9	0.726	10.0
10	0.80	10.0
.	.	.
.	.	.

Initially (years 1 and 2), the firm did not distribute a cash dividend. Years 3 through 7 represent a period during which the dividend rose rapidly. From year 8 into the indefinite future, the dividend grows at a constant rate of 10 percent.

The dividend-growth model may still be used to value this stock. Each of the individual dividend payments for years 1 through 7 are discounted back to the present at the required rate (e.g., 12 percent) and are summed:

$$\begin{aligned} V &= \frac{\$0.00}{(1.12)^1} + \frac{0.00}{(1.12)^2} + \frac{0.10}{(1.12)^3} + \frac{0.20}{(1.12)^4} + \frac{0.35}{(1.12)^5} + \frac{0.50}{(1.12)^6} + \frac{0.60}{(1.12)^7} \\ &= \$0.00 + 0.00 + 0.10(.712) + 0.20(.636) + 0.35(.567) + 0.50(.507) + \\ &\quad 0.60(.452) \\ &= \$0.92. \end{aligned}$$

Thus the flow of dividends during years 1 through 7 is currently worth $0.92.

For year 8 and all subsequent years, the dividend grows annually at 10 percent, so the constant dividend-growth model may be applied. The value of future dividends is

$$V = \frac{\$0.60(1 + .1)}{.12 - .10} = \$33.$$

This value, however, is as of the end of year 7, so the $33 must be discounted back to the present at 12 percent to determine its current value:

$$\frac{\$33}{(1.12)^7} = \$33(.452) = \$14.92.$$

(The .452 is the interest factor for the present value of $1 at 12 percent for seven years.)

The value of the stock is the sum of the two pieces: the present value of the dividends during the period of variable growth ($0.92) plus the present value of the dividends during the period of stable growth ($14.92). Thus the value of the stock is

$$V = \$0.92 + \$14.92 = \$15.84$$

Although the above illustration appears long and complicated, the valuation process is not. Valuation remains the present value of future dividend payments. Each anticipated future payment is discounted back to the present at the required rate of return, and the present value of each payment is summed to determine the current value of the stock. Thus, the valuation of a common stock and the valuations of preferred stocks and bonds all involve the same basic process. Each asset is worth the present value of the expected cash payments that the asset will generate.

RISK AND STOCK VALUATION

The previous discussion presented models for the valuation of stock. However, no statement was made concerning the risk associated with each security. Obviously, not all firms are equally risky, so presumably the investor would require a higher return for riskier stocks.

Actually, such a risk adjustment is part of the valuation process, for the investor's required return (k) adjusts for risk. In Chapter 8, the required return was divided into two components: (1) the risk-free return that an investor can earn on a risk-free security such as a Treasury bill and (2) a risk premium. The risk premium is also composed of two components: (1) the additional return that investing in securities offers above the risk-free rate and (2) the volatility of the particular stock relative to the market as a whole. The volatility of the individual stock is measured by beta (β), and the additional return is measured by the difference between the expected return on the market (r_m) and the risk-free rate (r_f). This differential ($r_m - r_f$) is the risk premium that is required to induce individuals to purchase stocks.

To induce the investor to purchase a particular security, the risk premium associated with the market must be adjusted by the risk associated with the individual security. This adjustment is achieved by using the

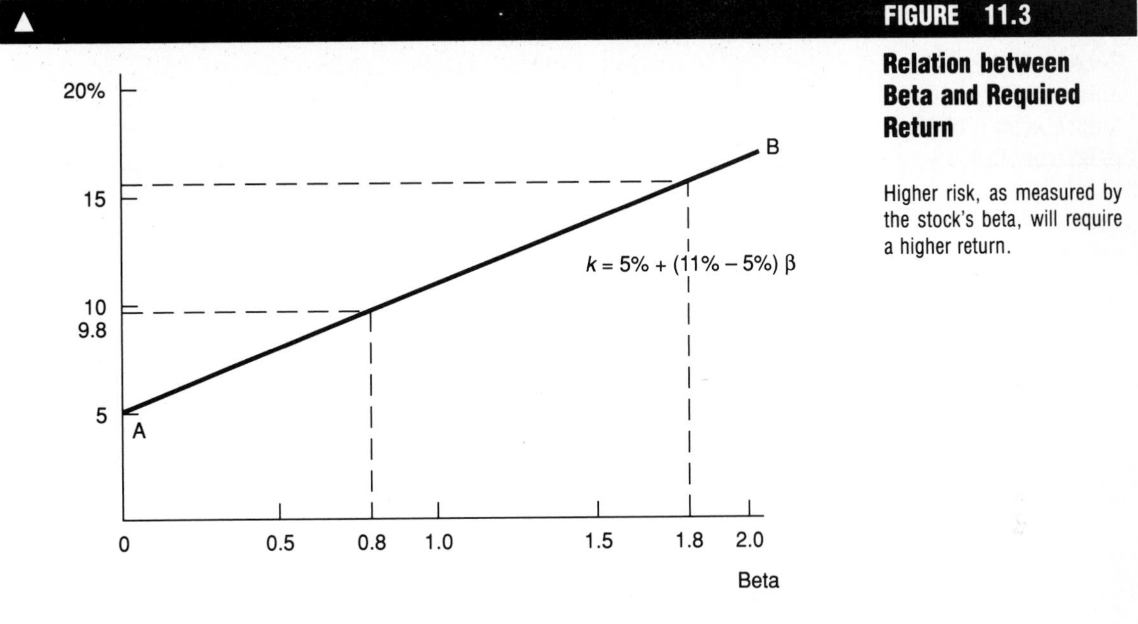

FIGURE 11.3

Relation between Beta and Required Return

Higher risk, as measured by the stock's beta, will require a higher return.

stock's beta, so the required return for investing in a particular stock, as specified in Equation 8.3, is

$$k = r_f + (r_m - r_f)\beta.$$

The relationship between the required rate of return and beta is illustrated in Figure 11.3. The **security market line** (AB) represents all the required rates of return associated with each level of risk. In this figure, the risk-free rate is 5 percent and the expected return on the market is 11 percent. Thus for a beta of .8, the required rate of return is 9.8 percent [.05 + (.11 − .05).8 = 9.8 percent], and for a beta of 1.8 the required rate of return is 15.8 percent [.05 + (.11 − .05)1.8 = 15.8 percent].

Security market line ▲
Line specifying the required return for different levels of risk

Line AB crosses the vertical axis at the current risk-free rate (5 percent). The slope of the line is the difference between the market return and the risk-free rate (.11 − .05). Movements along the line represent changes in risk as measured by beta (i.e., the increase in beta from 0.8 to 1.8 and the corresponding increase in the required return from 9.8 percent to 15.8 percent). The line shifts if either the risk-free rate or the expected return on the market changes. Such a shift is illustrated in Figure 11.4, in which the risk-free rate rises from 5 to 6 percent and the expected return on the market rises from 11 to 12 percent. The security market line shifts from AB to A′B′. Thus, the required return at each level of risk (i.e., at each beta) correspondingly increases. The required

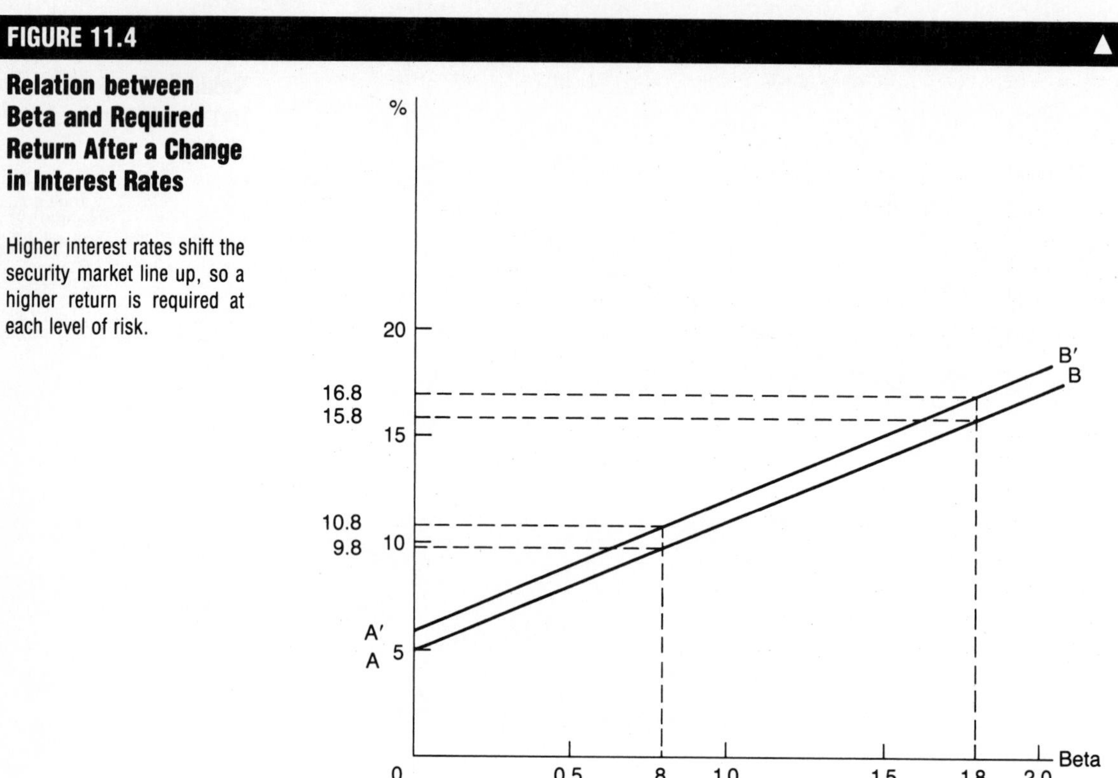

FIGURE 11.4

Relation between Beta and Required Return After a Change in Interest Rates

Higher interest rates shift the security market line up, so a higher return is required at each level of risk.

return for a stock with a beta of 0.8 now becomes 10.8 percent, while the required return for a stock with a beta of 1.8 rises to 16.8 percent.

How this risk-adjusted discount rate may be applied to the valuation of a specific stock is illustrated by the following example. From 1981 through 1990, Exxon's dividend rose from \$1.50 to \$2.68. This yields an annual compound growth rate of approximately 6 percent. According to the *Value Line Investment Survey,* the stock has a beta of 0.8. As of January 3, 1991, U.S. Treasury bills of six-month duration offered a risk-free return of 6.5 percent. If an investor anticipated that the market would rise annually at a compound rate of 12.5 percent (i.e., about 6 percentage points more than the risk-free rate) and that the Exxon dividend growth would continue indefinitely at 6 percent, what would be the maximum price this investor should pay for the stock?

The first step in answering the question is to determine the risk-adjusted required rate of return for Exxon:

$$\begin{aligned} k &= r_f + (r_m - r_f)\beta \\ &= 0.065 + (0.125 - 0.065)0.8 \\ &= 0.113 = 11.3\% \end{aligned}$$

The Job Mart

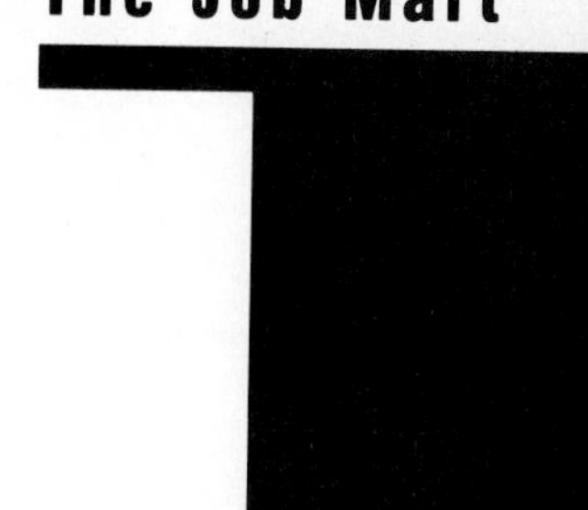

Chartered Financial Analyst (CFA)

■ Job Description: Conduct security research and analysis; perform valuations of individual companies. Identify and execute investments and risk management strategies. Provide fundamental analysis for stockholders, financial planners, and trust managers. ■ Job Requirements: Strong background in finance and economics, including knowledge of monetary and fiscal policy, structure of yields, and market strategies. ■ Characteristics: The CFA designation is awarded by the Institute of Chartered Financial Analysts to individuals who pass a series of examinations and who meet work experience requirements. Information may be obtained from the Financial Analysts Federation, P.O. Box 3726, Charlottesville, Virginia 22903.

Next, this risk-adjusted required rate of return is used in the dividend-growth model presented earlier:

$$
\begin{aligned}
V &= \frac{D_0(1 + g)}{k - g} \\
&= \frac{2.68(1 + 0.06)}{.113 - .06} \\
&= \$53.59
\end{aligned}
$$

As of January 3, 1991, the price of Exxon stock was $51. Thus, according to the dividend-growth model, the stock was slightly underpriced and should be bought.

While this procedure does bring a risk adjustment into the valuation model, it should be remembered that the results or conclusions can only be as good as the data employed. While this model and others presented in this text (e.g., the net present value of an investment presented in Chapter 23) are theoretically sound, their accuracy depends on the data used. The possibility of inaccurate data should be obvious in the above valuation model. Any of the estimates (i.e., the growth rate, the expected return on the market, the beta coefficient) may be incorrect, in which case the resulting valuation is incorrect. For example, if Exxon's expected growth rate were decreased from 6 percent to 3 percent, the effect would be to lower the valuation from $53.59 to $33.26. At a valuation of $33.26, the stock is overvalued and would not be a good purchase.

The problem of inaccurate data does not mean that the use of models in financial decision making is undesirable. Without such models there would be no means to value an asset. Hunches, intuition, or just plain guessing would then be used to value and select assets. By using theoretical models investors and financial managers are forced to identify real economic forces (e.g., earnings and growth rates) and alternatives (e.g., the risk-free rate and the return earned by the market as a whole). Even if the analysis may sometimes be inaccurate, it is still fundamentally sound and should prove better than random guessing or intuitive feelings.

VALUATION OF COMMON STOCK: P/E RATIOS

Applying the dividend-growth model requires estimates of the future growth in dividends. In addition, not all common stocks currently pay a cash dividend. Estimating future growth may be difficult, and the lack of a current dividend may render the dividend-growth model inapplicable since the numerator employs dividends. If there are no dividends, the model determines the value of the stock to be zero. However, a firm that is not currently paying dividends may distribute cash dividends in the future. As was previously illustrated, if the investor anticipates that the firm will start paying cash dividends, the dividend-growth model may be modified for these future dividends. This adjustment, of course, still requires an estimate of when the distributions will begin and how much they will be.

P/E ratio ▲
Ratio of the price of a stock divided by per share earnings

As an alternative to the dividend-growth model, the financial analyst may use **P/E ratios** (i.e., the ratio of the price of a stock to its per share earnings) as an earnings multiple to value a stock. This is a relatively simple technique that lacks the theoretical background of the dividend-growth model. This method suggests that the value of a stock may be determined by using Equation 11.8:

11.8 $$\text{Value of the stock} = \text{Earnings} \times \text{Earnings multiple.}$$

To use this technique, the individual needs an estimate of the earnings and the appropriate multiple. For example, if the earnings are expected to be \$2.45 and the appropriate multiple is 13 (i.e., the appropriate P/E ratio), then the value of the stock is

$$\$2.45 \times 13 = \$31.85.$$

If the current price of the stock is less than \$31.85, the stock is undervalued and should be purchased. If the price of the stock is greater than \$31.85, the stock is overvalued and should not be purchased.

As with the dividend-growth model, the use of P/E ratios to value a common stock requires two important estimates. The first is the estimate of earnings. If the individual does not have (or cannot perform) the required forecasts, estimates of earnings may be obtained from the brokerage firms or from such financial publications as *Forbes* and *The Wall*

Street Transcript, which report estimated earnings. Having obtained these estimates, the next consideration is the appropriate multiple.

One way to determine the multiple is to use the historic P/E ratios that the firm has achieved. Most stocks tend to trade within a range of P/E ratios. For example, the historic low P/E ratio for Bristol-Myers Squibb has averaged 10.4 while the historic high P/E ratio has averaged 14.3. Thus, if the estimated earnings are $3.50, the price of the stock should tend to trade between $36.40 ($3.50 × 10.4) and $50.05 ($3.50 × 14.3). If the stock is trading outside this range, that would suggest it may be currently undervalued or overvalued.

The use of P/E ratios provides a range of values but not necessarily a unique value. To obtain a unique value, the individual would have to determine a unique earnings multiple. If the average P/E ratio of all firms in an industry is 13.2, then that earnings multiple may be applied to a specific firm within the industry. For example, if the average P/E ratio for household products and toiletries is 13.2 and Bristol-Myers Squibb is expected to earn $3.50, then the value of the stock is $46.20 (13.2 × $3.50).

Such application of P/E ratios for valuation suggests that there is a unique P/E ratio for all firms within an industry. This is, of course, an oversimplification since there can be significant differences among firms within an industry. Differences in factors such as size, product lines, sources of finance, and domestic versus foreign operations can affect the risk associated with a particular firm. Thus, using a unique average P/E ratio to value all firms may be inappropriate.

An alternative to the use of P/E ratios to obtain an earnings multiple is to use the reciprocal of the risk-adjusted required return employed in the dividend-growth model. Thus, if the risk-adjusted required return is 12.5 percent, the earnings multiple is 8 (1/.125). If the estimated earnings are $4, then the value of the stock is $32 ($4.00 × 8).

The simplicity of using earnings multiples and P/E ratios as a basis of stock selection is very appealing. In addition, there is some evidence that limiting purchases to stocks with low P/E ratios produces superior investment results.[2] Such results run counter to the efficient market hypothesis discussed in Chapter 6, which asserts that few investors will outperform the market on a risk-adjusted basis over a period of time. However, the empirical evidence supports a strategy of investing in low P/E stocks, and that conclusion is inconsistent with the general empirical support for the efficient market hypothesis.

[2]See, for example, S. Basu, "Investment Performance of Common Stocks in Relation to Their Price-Earnings Ratios: A Test of the Efficient Market Hypothesis," *Journal of Finance* (June 1977), pp. 663–694; and David Dreman, *The New Contarian Strategy* (New York: Random House, 1980).

SUMMARY

Although preferred stock is legally equity, its valuation is identical to that of a long-term bond. Both bonds and preferred stock are fixed income securities whose value is the present value of their future payments (interest or dividends and the repayment of the principal). The value of all fixed income securities moves inversely with changes in interest rates. Thus, if interest rates rise, the price of preferred stock falls; if interest rates fall, the price of preferred stock rises.

Common stock is more difficult to value than preferred stock because it is not a fixed income security. The dividend-growth model is often used to value common stock. In its simplest form, the model assumes that the current dividend will grow indefinitely into the future at a constant rate. This growing dividend is discounted back to the present using the investors' required rate of return. The required rate of return is specified by the capital asset pricing model in which the return depends on the risk-free rate plus a risk premium. The risk premium depends on the return on the market and the systematic risk associated with the stock as measured by its beta coefficient.

Once the value of the stock has been determined, this value is compared to the current market price of the stock. If the current price exceeds the valuation, the stock is overpriced and should not be purchased. If the current price is less than the valuation, the stock is undervalued and should be purchased.

An alternate to the dividend-growth model is the use of P/E ratios and forecasted earnings to determine the value of a stock. In this technique an estimate of the firm's future earnings is multiplied by the appropriate factor to determine the value of the stock. This value is then compared to the current market price of the stock to determine if the stock should be bought or sold.

Review Questions

1. Why is the valuation of preferred stock more similar to the valuation of bonds than to the valuation of common stock?
2. According to the dividend-growth model, what variables affect the value of common stock? If the required rate of return increases, what should happen to the value of the stock?
3. Is it necessary to assume that the rate of growth in a firm's cash dividend is fixed in order to value the firm's common stock?
4. How can the analysis of risk be integrated into the valuation of common stock? What should happen to the value of a common stock if its beta increases?

5. Why should the value of both preferred stock and common stock fall when interest rates rise?
6. What impact does each of the following have on the value of a common stock:
   a. an increase in earnings and dividends
   b. an increase in the P/E ratio
   c. an increase in the expected return on the market
   d. a decrease in the risk-free rate and the return on the market

Problems

1. What should be the prices of the following preferred stocks if comparable securities yield 10 percent? Why are the valuations different?
   a. MN Inc., $4 preferred ($100 par)
   b. CH Inc., $4 preferred ($100 par) with mandatory retirement after 20 years
2. Repeat the previous problem but assume that comparable yields are 12 percent.
3. What will be the capital losses if an investor purchases the following securities when yields on comparable securities are 10 percent but subsequently rise to 12 percent?
   a. 100 shares of $10 par, preferred stock with a $1 dividend (i.e., an investment of $1,000)
   b. $1,000 face amount, 10 percent debenture that matures after ten years

   Why are the losses different?
4. The dividend-growth model may be used to value a stock.

$$V = \frac{D_0(1 + g)}{k - g}.$$

   a. What is the value of a stock if:

$$D_0 = \$2,$$
$$k = 14\%,$$
$$g = 6\%.$$

   b. What is the value of this stock if the dividend is increased to $3 and the other variables remain constant?
   c. What is the value of this stock if the required rate of return declines to 13 percent and the other variables remain constant?
   d. What is the value of this stock if the growth rate declines to 5 percent and the other variables remain constant?
   e. What is the value of this stock if the dividend is increased to $2.30 but the growth rate declines to 4 percent?
5. An investor with a required rate of return of 14 percent for investments in common stock has analyzed three firms and must decide which, if any, to purchase. The information is as follows:

Firm	A	B	C
Current earnings	\$2.00	\$3.20	\$7.00
Current dividend	\$1.00	\$3.00	\$7.50
Expected annual growth rate in dividends and earnings	7%	2%	−1%
Current market price	\$23	\$47	\$60

a. What is the maximum price that the investor should pay for each stock based on the dividend-growth model.
b. If the investor does buy Stock A, what is the implied rate of return?
c. If the appropriate P/E ratio is 7, what is the maximum price the investor should pay for each stock?
d. What does Stock C's negative growth rate imply?

6. The risk-free rate of return is 8 percent, and the expected rate of return on the market is 12 percent. Stock A has a beta coefficient of 1.4, an earnings and dividend growth rate of 5 percent, and a current dividend of \$2.60 a share.
   a. What should be the market price of the stock?
   b. If the current market price of the stock is \$27, what should you do?
   c. If the risk-free return falls to 6 percent and the other variables remain constant, what will be the value of the stock?
   d. If the expected return on the market rises to 14 percent and the other variables remain constant, what will be the value of the stock?
   e. If the beta coefficient falls to 1.1 and the other variables remain constant, what will be the value of the stock?
   f. Explain why the stock's value changes in (c) through (e).
7. The security market line is estimated to be

$$k = 7\% + (14\% - 7\%)\beta.$$

   You are considering two stocks. The beta of A is 1.4. The firm offers a dividend yield during the year of 5 percent and a growth rate of 10 percent. The beta of B is 0.8. The firm offers a dividend yield during the year of 7 percent and a growth rate of 5 percent.
   a. Graph the security market line.
   b. What is the required rate of return for each security?
   c. If the required rates of return are different, why (or why not)?
   d. Since A offers higher potential growth, should it be purchased?
   e. Since B offers higher dividend yield, should it be purchased?
8. You are considering two stocks with the following information:

	A	B
Dividend payout	20%	60%
Earnings per share	\$1.00	\$1.00
Rate of return earned on capital	10%	10%
Beta coefficient	1.2	0.8
Price	\$10	\$10

If Treasury bills yield 5 percent and the expected rate of return for the market is 12 percent, which stock(s) should you purchase? (Verify your answer by applying a mathematical stock price valuation model.)

9. Two stocks each currently pay a dividend of $2.50 per share. It is anticipated that both firms' earnings and dividends will grow annually at the rate of 9 percent. Firm A has a beta coefficient of .88 while the beta coefficient of Firm B is 1.35.
   a. If U.S. Treasury bills currently yield 8.4 percent and you expect the market to increase at an annual rate of 14.1 percent, what are the valuations of these two stocks using the dividend-growth model?
   b. Why are your valuations different?
   c. If Stock A's price were $51 and Stock B's price were $42, what would you do?

10. The dividend-growth model,

$$V = \frac{D_0(1 + g)}{k - g},$$

suggests that an increase in the growth rate will increase the value of a stock. However, if the increase in the growth rate causes the dividend to diminish, the value of the stock may fall. Thus, management may be faced with a dilemma: dividends versus growth. As of now, it appears that the investors' required return is 13 percent. The current dividend is $1 a share and is expected to grow annually by 7 percent, so the current market price of the stock is $17.80. Management may make an investment that will increase the firm's growth rate to 10 percent, but the investment will require an increase in retained earnings, so the firm's dividend must be cut to $.60 a share. Should management make the investment and cut the dividend?

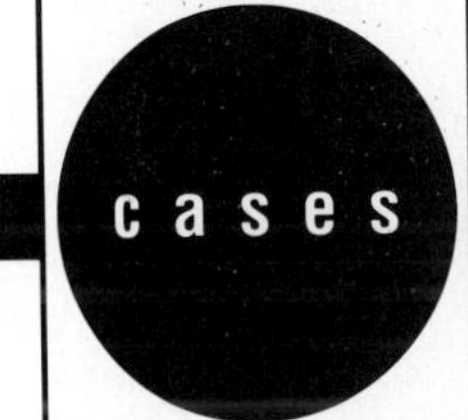

Determining the Value of a Business

Erik Satie has just inherited his father's company. Prior to his death, Mr. Satie was the sole stockholder, and he left the entire company to his only son. Although Erik has worked for the firm for many years as a commercial artist, he does not feel qualified to manage the operation. He has considered selling the firm while it is still a viable operation and before his father's absence causes the value of the firm to deteriorate. Erik realizes that selling the firm will result in his losing control, but his father granted him a long-term contract that guarantees employment or a generous severance package. Furthermore, if Erik were to sell for cash, he should receive a substantial amount of money, so his financial position would be secure.

Even though Erik would like to sell out, he has enough business sense to realize that he does not know how to place an asking price (i.e., a value) on the firm. The IRS had established a value on his father's stock of $100 a share, and since he owned 100,000 shares, the value of the company for estate tax purposes was $10,000,000. Erik thought that was a reasonable amount but decided to consult with Sophie Wagner, a CPA who completed the estate tax return.

Ms. Wagner suggested that the firm could be valued using a discounted cash flow method in which the current and future dividends are discounted back to the present to determine the value of the firm. She explained to Erik that this technique, the dividend-growth model, is an important theoretical model used for the valuation of companies. In addition, she suggested that the price/earnings ratio of similar firms may be used as a guide to the value of the firm. Erik asked Ms. Wagner to prepare a valuation of the stock based on P/E ratios and the dividend-growth model. While Erik realized that he could get only one price, he requested a range of values from an optimistic price to a minimum, rock-bottom value below which he should not accept.

To aid in the valuation process, Ms. Wagner assembled the following information. The firm earned $8.50 a share and distributed 60 percent in cash dividends during its last fiscal year. This payout ratio had been maintained for several years, with 40 percent of the earnings being retained to finance future growth. The per share earnings for the past five years were

Year	Per Share Earnings
1	$6.70
2	7.40
3	7.85
4	8.20
5	8.50

Publicly held firms in the industry have an average P/E ratio of 12 with the highest being 17 and the lowest, 9. The betas of these firms tend to be less than 1.0 with 0.85 being typical. While the firm is not publicly held, it is similar in structure to other firms in the industry. It is, however, perceptibly smaller than the publicly held firms. The Treasury bill rate is currently 5.2 percent, and most financial analysts anticipate that the market as a whole will average a return of 6 to 6.5 percent greater than the Treasury bill rate.

Case Problems

1. What are the lowest and highest values based on P/E ratios and the dividend-growth model?
2. What assumptions must be made to determine these values?

Suggested Readings

The dividend-growth model was developed by Myron Gordon. See:

Gordon, Myron. *The Investment, Financing and Valuation of the Corporation.* Homewood, Ill.: Richard D. Irwin, 1962.

For a practitioner's explanation of the dividend-growth model and other techniques used to value securities, see:

Crowell, Richard A. *Stock Market Strategy.* New York: McGraw-Hill, 1977.

Valuation is a major topic covered in depth in more advanced texts. See:

Bodie, Zvi; Alex Kane; and Alan J. Marcus. *Investments.* Homewood, Ill.: Richard D. Irwin, 1989, Chapter 17.

Radcliffe, Robert C. *Investment Concepts, Analysis, and Strategy.* 3d ed. Glenview, Ill.: Scott, Foresman and Company, 1990, Chapter 13.

Sharpe, William F. *Investments.* 3d ed. Englewood Cliffs, N.J.: Prentice-Hall, Inc., 1985, Chapters 4–8.

chapter

12

Convertible Bonds and Convertible Preferred Stock

Learning Objectives

1. Describe the features common to all convertible bonds.
2. Determine the "floor" or minimum price of a convertible bond.
3. List the factors that affect the price of a convertible bond.
4. Identify the two premiums paid for a convertible bond.
5. Explain why the two premiums are inversely related.
6. Compare convertible preferred stock with convertible bonds.

The Gospel according to John suggests that you should "judge not according to appearances," and the Greek Stoic philosopher Epictetus suggested during the first century A.D. that things may "not be what they appear to be." According to *The Wall Street Journal,* on January 7, 1991, a $1,000 bond issued by Clayton Homes sold for $1,480. Another $1,000 bond issued by Union Pacific sold for $4,500. If an investor purchased the Union Pacific bond and redeemed it at maturity, he or she would collect $427.50 in interest and $1,000 in principal for a total of $1,427.50. Yet someone bought this bond for $4,500! Are appearances deceiving? Did *The Wall Street Journal* incorrectly report the price that was paid?

In this case the appearance is correct. The Union Pacific bond did trade for $4,500. This bond may be converted into $4,500 worth of the firm's stock; thus the bond also must be worth $4,500. If *The Wall Street Journal* had reported that the bond traded for $1,000, that would have been deceiving. Unlike other bonds, convertible bonds (and convertible preferred stock) include a built-in option: The owner may exchange the bond for the issuing firm's stock. However, the bonds still offer investors the features of debt. The firm must pay interest and retire the principal. Since the bonds may be converted into stock, however, they also offer the potential for capital gains if the price of the common stock rises.

This chapter discusses convertible bonds and convertible preferred stocks. First the features and terms of convertible bonds are described, followed by a discussion of their pricing. This includes the premiums paid for convertible bonds and the relationship between their price and the price of the stock into which they may be converted. The next section is devoted to convertible preferred stock, which is similar to convertible bonds but lacks the safety associated with debt. The chapter ends with brief histories of two convertible bonds that illustrate the potential profits and risks associated with convertible securities.

FEATURES OF CONVERTIBLE BONDS

Convertible bond ▲
Bond that may be converted into (exchanged for) stock at the option of the holder

Convertible bonds are debentures (i.e., unsecured debt instruments) that may be converted at the holder's option into the stock of the issuing company. As was seen in Chapter 9, firms issue a variety of debt instruments to tap funds in the capital markets. Convertible bonds are one means to do so; the conversion feature is granted to bondholders to induce them to buy the debt. Since the firm has granted the holder the right to convert the bonds, these bonds are usually subordinated to the firm's other debt. They also tend to offer a lower rate of interest (i.e., coupon rate) than is available on nonconvertible debt. Thus, the conversion feature means that the firm can issue lower quality debt at a lower interest cost. Investors are willing to accept this reduced quality and interest income because the market value of the bond will appreciate *if* the price of the stock rises. These investors are thus trading quality and interest for possible capital gains.

Convertible bonds have been a popular means for firms to raise funds in the capital markets. A sample of firms and their convertible

EXHIBIT 12.1

Selected Convertible Bonds

Convertible bonds are issued by financially strong as well as by financially weak firms. Coupon rates vary both with the quality of the debt and with competitive rates when the bond was issued.

Corporation	Coupon Rate of Interest	Month and Year in Which Bond Was Issued	Year of Maturity	Moody's Rating
Ashland Oil	6¾%	7/89	2014	Baa
Control Data	8½	6/86	2011	B3
IBM	7⅞	11/84	2004	Aa1
Midway Airlines	8½	12/82	2002	Caa
Pfizer	4	2/72	1997	Aa1

bonds is presented in Exhibit 12.1. As may be seen in the exhibit, the bonds are not issued just by lower quality firms with poor credit ratings. Some of the country's most prestigious firms (e.g., IBM and Pfizer) have convertible bonds outstanding.

Since convertible bonds are long-term debt instruments, they have features that are common to all bonds. They are usually issued in $1,000 denominations, pay interest semiannually, and have a fixed maturity date. However, if the bonds are converted into stock, the maturity date is irrelevant because the bonds are retired when they are converted. Convertible bonds frequently have a sinking fund requirement, which, like the maturity date, is meaningless once the bonds are converted.

A noteworthy feature of convertible bonds is that they are always callable. The firm uses the call to force the holders to convert the bonds. Once the bond is called, the owner must convert, or any appreciation in price that has resulted from an increase in the stock's value will be lost. Such forced conversion is extremely important to the issuing firm, because it no longer has to repay the debt.

Convertible bonds are attractive to some investors because they offer the safety features of debt. The firm must meet the terms of the indenture, and the bonds must be retired if they are not converted. The flow of interest income usually exceeds the dividend yield that may be earned on the firm's stock. In addition, since the bonds may be converted into stock, the holder will share in the growth of the company. If the price of the stock rises in response to the firm's growth, the value of the convertible bond must also rise. It is this combination of the safety of debt and the potential for capital gain that makes convertible bonds an attractive investment, particularly to investors who desire income and some capital appreciation.

Like all investments, convertible bonds subject the holder to risk. If the company fails, the holder of a bond stands to lose the funds invested in the debt. This is particularly true with regard to convertible bonds,

EXHIBIT 12.2

1978 Year-End Prices for Four Convertible Bonds and What Subsequently Happened to Each Bond

Convertible bonds will either (1) be called and converted, (2) be redeemed at face value, or (3) go into default.

Bond	Prices as of December 31,			
	1978	**1981**	**1985**	**1988**
Ampex 5½ 1994	61	74½	Called and converted	NA
Gulf and Western 5½ 1993	78	Called and converted	NA	NA
Pan Am 4½ 1986	59	46¼	96	Redeemed in 1986 at face
Seatrain 6 1995	56	16	No price quote	NA

because they are usually subordinated to the firm's other debt. Thus, convertible bonds are considerably less safe than senior debt or debt that is secured by specific collateral. In case of a default or bankruptcy, holders of convertible bonds may at best realize only a fraction of the principal amount invested. However, their position is still superior to that of the stockholders.

Default is not the only potential source of risk to investors. Convertible bonds are actively traded, and their prices can and do fluctuate. As is explained in detail in the next section, their price is partially related to the value of the stock into which they may be converted. Fluctuations in the value of the stock produce fluctuations in the price of the bond. These price changes are *in addition* to price movements caused by variations in interest rates.

During periods of higher interest rates and lower stock prices, convertible bonds are doubly cursed. Their lower coupon rates of interest cause their prices to decline more than those of nonconvertible debt. This, in addition to the decline in the value of the stock into which they may be converted, results in considerable price declines for convertible bonds. Such declines are illustrated in Exhibit 12.2, which gives the year-end prices for four convertible bonds for four selected years. Each bond had initially been issued for $1,000 but at the end of 1978, each was selling for a discount. The last three columns of the exhibit show the variety of possible outcomes for convertible bonds. The Ampex and Gulf and Western bonds were called and converted. Obviously, the prices of the underlying stock rose sufficiently that the bondholders converted the bonds into stock. Seatrain defaulted and declared bankruptcy, and the market for its bonds ceased to exist (i.e., there were no price quotes). The Pan Am bond was redeemed for its face value but was not converted.

THE VALUATION OF CONVERTIBLE BONDS

The value of a convertible bond is related to (1) the value of the stock into which it may be converted and (2) the value of the bond as a debt instrument. Although each of these factors affects the market price of the bond, the importance of each element varies with changing conditions in the security markets. In the final analysis, the valuation of a convertible bond is extremely difficult, because it is a hybrid security that combines debt and equity.

This section has three subdivisions. The first considers the value of the bond solely as stock. The second covers the bond's value only as a debt instrument, and the last section combines these values to show the hybrid nature of convertible bonds. In order to differentiate the value of the bond as stock from its value as debt, subscripts are added to the symbols used. S will represent stock, and D will represent debt. Although this may make the equations appear more complex, it will clearly distinguish the value of the bond as stock from the value as debt.

The Convertible Bond as Stock

The value of a convertible bond in terms of the stock into which it may be converted (C_s) depends upon (1) the principal amount of the bond (P), (2) the conversion (or exercise) price per share of the bond (P_e), and (3) the market price of the common stock (P_s). The principal divided by the conversion price of the bond gives the number of shares into which the bond may be converted. For example, if a \$1,000 bond may be converted at \$20 per share, the bond may be converted into 50 shares (\$1,000 ÷ \$20). The number of shares times the market price of a share gives the value of the bond in terms of stock. If the bond is convertible into 50 shares and the stock sells for \$15 per share, the bond is worth \$750 in terms of stock.

This conversion value of the bond as stock is expressed in Equation 12.1

12.1
$$C_s = \frac{P}{P_e} \times P_s$$

and is illustrated in Exhibit 12.3. In this example a \$1,000 bond is convertible into 50 shares (i.e., a conversion price of \$20 per share). The first column gives various prices of the stock. The second column presents the number of shares into which the bond is convertible (i.e., 50 shares). The third column gives the value of the bond in terms of stock (i.e., the product of the values in the first two columns). Thus, if the

EXHIBIT 12.3

Relationship between the Price of a Stock and the Value of a Convertible Bond

The value of a convertible bond rises as the price of the stock rises.

Price of the Stock	Shares into which the Bond Is Convertible	Value of the Bond in Terms of Stock
$ 0	50	$ 0
5	50	250
10	50	500
15	50	750
20	50	1,000
25	50	1,250
30	50	1,500

price of the stock is $15, the conversion value of the bond is $1,000/$20 × $15 = $750. As may be seen in the exhibit, the value of the bond in terms of stock rises as the price of the stock increases.

This relationship between the price of the stock and the conversion value of the bond is illustrated in Figure 12.1. The price of the stock (P_s) is given on the horizontal axis, and the conversion value of the bond (C_s) is shown on the vertical axis. As the price of the stock rises, the conversion value of the bond increases. This is shown in the graph by line C_s, which represents the value of the bond in terms of stock. Line C_s is a straight line running through the origin. If the stock has no value, the value of the bond in terms of stock is also worthless. If the exercise price of the bond and the market price of the stock are equal (i.e., $P_s = P_e$, which in this case is $20), the bond's value as stock is equal to the principal amount. As the price of the stock rises above the exercise price of the bond, the value of the bond in terms of stock increases to more than the principal amount of the debt.

The market price of a convertible bond cannot be less than the bond's conversion value as stock. If the price of the bond were less than its value as stock, an opportunity for profit would exist. Investors would purchase the convertible bond, exercise the conversion feature, and sell the shares acquired through the conversion. The investors would then make a profit equal to the difference between the price of the convertible bond and the conversion value of the bond. For example, if in the preceding example the bond were selling for $800 when the stock sold for $20, the bond would be worth $1,000 in terms of the stock (i.e., $20 × 50). Investors would buy the bond for $800 and exercise it. Then they would sell the 20 shares for $1,000 and earn $200 profit (before commissions).

As investors sought to purchase the bonds, they would drive up their price. The price increase would continue until there was no opportunity for profit. This would occur when the price of the bond was equal to or

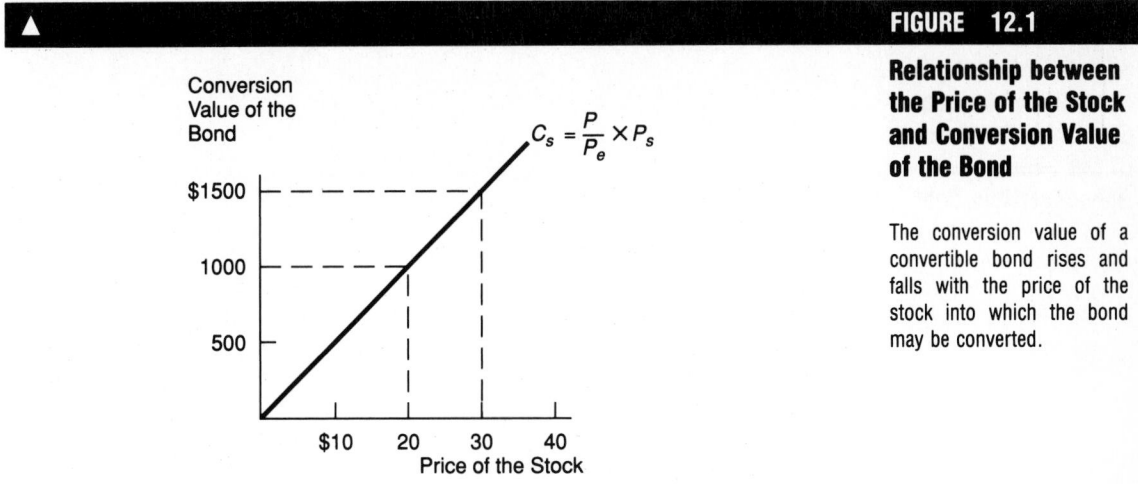

FIGURE 12.1

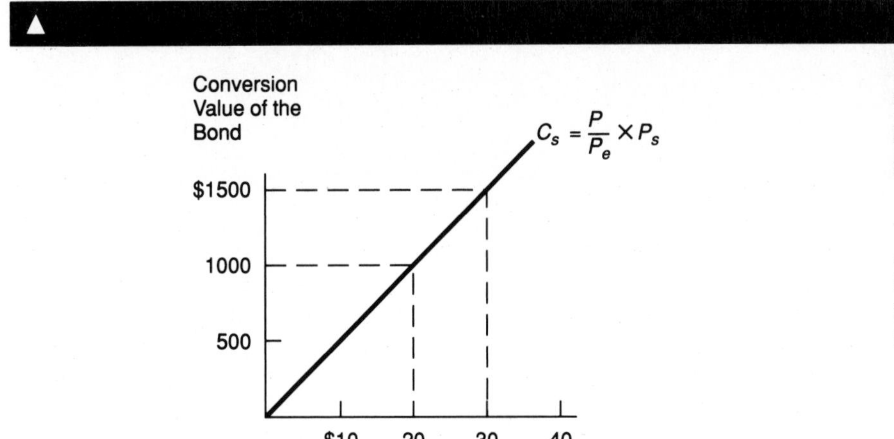

Relationship between the Price of the Stock and Conversion Value of the Bond

The conversion value of a convertible bond rises and falls with the price of the stock into which the bond may be converted.

greater than the bond's value as stock. Thus the value of the bond in terms of stock sets the minimum price of the bond. The market price of a convertible bond will be at least equal to its conversion value.

However, the market price of the convertible bond is rarely equal to the conversion value of the bond. The bond frequently sells for a premium over its conversion value, because the convertible bond may also have value as a debt instrument. As a pure (i.e., nonconvertible) bond, it competes with other nonconvertible debt. Like the conversion feature, this element of debt may affect the bond's price. Its impact is important, for it has the effect of putting a minimum price on the convertible bond, giving investors in convertible bonds an element of safety that stock lacks.

The Convertible Bond as Debt

The value of a convertible bond as debt (C_D) is related to (1) the annual interest or coupon rate that the bond pays (I), (2) the current interest rate being paid on comparable nonconvertible debt (i), and (3) the requirement that the principal or face value (P) be retired at maturity (after n years) if the bond is not converted. In terms of present value calculations, the value of a convertible bond as nonconvertible debt is given in Equation 12.2:

12.2 $$C_D = \frac{I}{(1+i)^1} + \frac{I}{(1+i)^2} + \cdots + \frac{I}{(1+i)^n} + \frac{P}{(1+i)^n}.$$

FIGURE 12.2

Relationship between the Price of Common Stock and the Value of the Bond as Nonconvertible Debt

The value of a convertible bond as debt is independent of the price of the stock. This value places a floor on the price of the convertible bond.

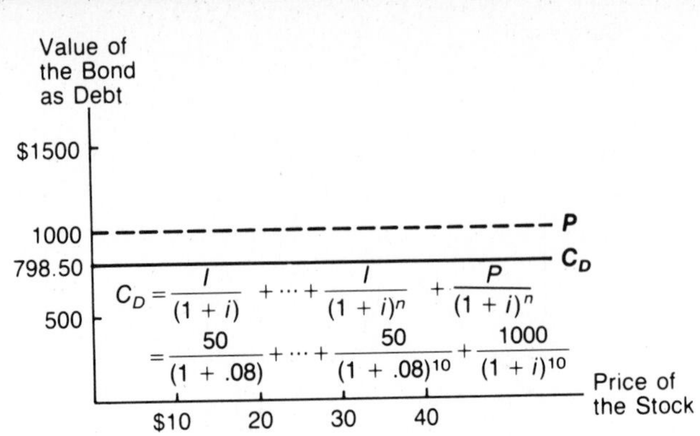

Equation 12.2 is simply the present value of any bond (i.e., Equation 9.1 given in Chapter 9). Thus, the equation used to determine the present value of a nonconvertible bond is used to determine the convertible bond's value as debt.

Equation 12.2 may be illustrated by the following example. Assume that the convertible bond in Exhibit 12.3 matures in ten years and pays 5 percent annually. Nonconvertible debt of the same risk class currently yields 8 percent. When these values are inserted into Equation 12.2, the value of the bond as nonconvertible debt is $798.50.

$$C_D = \frac{\$50}{(1+0.08)^1} + \frac{\$50}{(1+0.08)^2} + \cdots + \frac{\$50}{(1+0.08)^9} + \frac{\$50}{(1+0.08)^{10}} + \frac{\$1{,}000}{(1+0.08)^{10}},$$
$$= \$50(\text{PVAIF } 8\%, 10\text{Y}) + \$1{,}000(\text{PVIF } 8\%, 10\text{Y})$$
$$= \$50(6.710) + \$1{,}000(.463) = \$798.50.$$

This equation is solved by the use of present value tables. The 6.710 is the interest factor for the present value of an annuity of $1 for ten years at 8 percent, and .463 is the interest factor for the present value of $1 to be received ten years in the future when it is discounted at 8 percent. To be competitive with nonconvertible debt, this bond would have to sell for $798.50.

The relationship between the price of the common stock and the value of this bond as nonconvertible debt is illustrated in Figure 12.2. This figure consists of a horizontal line (C_D) that shows what the price ($798.50) of the bond would be if it were not convertible into stock, in which case the price is independent of the value of the stock. The principal amount of the bond is also shown in Figure 12.2 by the broken line

EXHIBIT 12.4

Relationship between Interest Rates and the Value of a Bond

Higher interest rates reduce the value of the bond as debt.

Interest Rate	Coupon Rate	Value of a Ten-Year Bond
3%	5%	$1,170.50
4	5	1,081.55
5	5	1,000.0
6	5	926.00
7	5	864.20
8	5	798.50
10	5	692.25
12	5	631.70

P, which is above the line C_D. The principal amount exceeds the value of the bond as pure debt because this bond must sell at a discount to be competitive with nonconvertible debt.

The value of the convertible bond as debt varies with market interest rates. Since the interest paid by the bond is fixed, the value of the bond as debt varies inversely with interest rates. An increase in interest rates causes this value to fall; a decline in interest rates causes the value to rise.

The relationship between the value of the preceding convertible bond as debt and various interest rates is presented in Exhibit 12.4. The first column gives various interest rates; the second column gives the nominal (i.e., coupon) rate of interest, and the last column gives the value of the bond as nonconvertible debt. The inverse relationship is readily apparent, for as the interest rate rises from 3 percent to 12 percent, the value of the bond declines from $1,170.50 to $631.70.

The value of the bond as nonconvertible debt is important because it sets another minimum value that the bond will command in the market. At that price the convertible bond is competitive with nonconvertible debt of the same maturity and degree of risk. If the bond were to sell below this price, it would offer a yield that is more attractive (i.e., higher) than that of nonconvertible debt. Investors would seek to buy the bond to attain this higher yield. They would bid up the bond's price until its yield was comparable to that of nonconvertible debt. Thus, the bond's value as nonconvertible debt becomes a floor on the price of the convertible bond. Even if the value of the stock into which the bond may be converted were to fall, this floor would halt the decline in the price of the convertible bond.

The actual minimum price of a convertible bond combines its value as stock and its value as debt. This is illustrated in Figure 12.3, which combines the preceding figures for the value of the bond in terms of stock and the value of the bond as nonconvertible debt. The bond's price is always greater than or equal to the higher of the two valuations. If the

FIGURE 12.3

Actual Minimum Price of a Convertible Bond

The price of a bond will not be less than its value as stock or its value as debt.

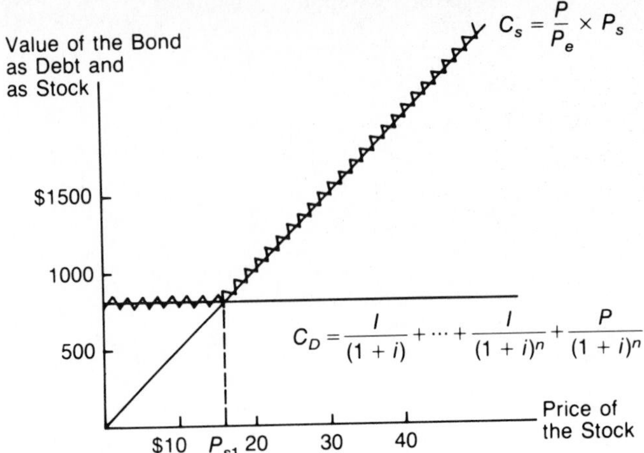

price of the convertible bond were below its value as common stock, investors would bid up its price. If the bond sold for a price below its value as debt, investors in debt instruments would bid up the price.

The minimum price of the convertible bond is either its value in terms of stock or its value as nonconvertible debt, but the importance of these determinants varies. For low stock prices (i.e., stock prices less than P_{s1} in Figure 12.3), the minimum price is set by the bond's value as debt. However, for stock prices greater than P_{s1}, it is the bond's value as stock that determines the minimum price.

The Bond's Value as a Hybrid Security

The market price (P_m) of the convertible bond combines both the conversion value of the bond and its value as nonconvertible debt. If the price of the stock were to decline significantly below the exercise price of the bond, the market price of the convertible bond would be influenced primarily by the bond's value as nonconvertible debt. In effect, the bond would be priced as if it were a pure debt instrument. As the price of the stock rises, the conversion value of the bond rises and plays an increasingly important role in the determination of the market price of the convertible bond. At sufficiently high stock prices, the market price of the bond is identical with its conversion value.

These relationships are illustrated in Figure 12.4, which reproduces Figure 12.3 and adds to it the market price of the convertible bond (P_m). For prices of the common stock below P_{s1}, the market price is identical to

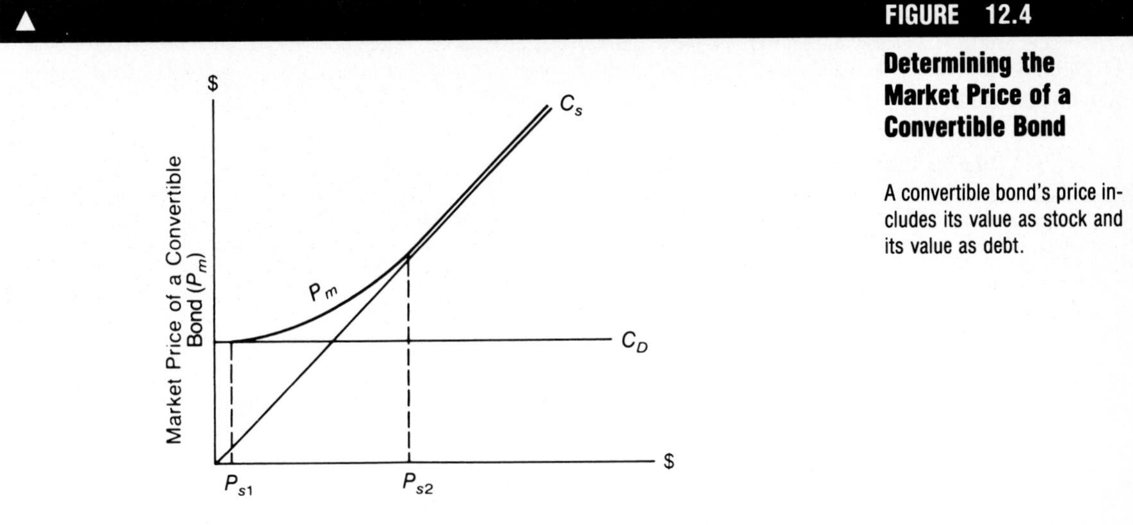

FIGURE 12.4

Determining the Market Price of a Convertible Bond

A convertible bond's price includes its value as stock and its value as debt.

the bond's value as nonconvertible debt. For prices of the common stock above P_{s2}, the price of the bond is identical to its value as common stock. At these extreme stock prices, the bond may be analyzed as if it were either pure debt or stock. For all prices between these two extremes, the market price of the convertible bond is influenced by the bond's value both as nonconvertible debt and as stock. This dual influence makes the analysis of convertible bonds difficult, since the investor pays a premium over the bond's value as stock and as debt.

PREMIUMS PAID FOR CONVERTIBLE DEBT

One way to analyze a convertible bond is to measure the premium over the bond's value as debt or as stock. For example, if a particular convertible bond is commanding a higher premium than is paid for similar convertible securities, perhaps this bond should be sold. Conversely, if the premium is relatively low, the bond may be a good investment. Of course, the lower premium may indicate financial weakness, in which case the bond would not be a good investment. Thus, a lower premium is not sufficient reason to acquire a convertible bond, but it may suggest that the bond be considered for purchase after further analysis.

The premiums paid for a convertible bond are illustrated in Exhibit 12.5, which reproduces Exhibit 12.3 and adds the value of the bond as nonconvertible debt (column 4) along with hypothetical market prices for the bond (column 5). The premium that an investor pays for a con-

EXHIBIT 12.5

Premiums Paid for Convertible Debt

Convertible bonds tend to sell for premiums over their value as stock and over their value as debt.

Price of the Stock	Shares into which the Bond May Be Converted	Value of the Bond in Terms of Stock	Value of the Bond as Nonconvertible Debt	Hypothetical Price of the Convertible Bond	Premium in Terms of Stock*	Premium in Terms of Nonconvertible Debt†
$ 0	50	$ 0	$798.50	$ 798.50	$798.50	$ 0.00
5	50	250	798.50	798.50	548.50	0.00
10	50	500	798.50	798.50	298.50	0.00
15	50	750	798.50	900.00	150.00	101.50
20	50	1,000	798.50	1,100.00	100.00	301.50
25	50	1,250	798.50	1,300.00	50.00	501.50
30	50	1,500	798.50	1,500.00	0.00	701.50

** The premium in terms of stock is equal to the hypothetical price of the convertible bond minus the value of the bond in terms of stock.*

† The premium in terms of nonconvertible debt is equal to the hypothetical price of the convertible bond minus the value of the bond as nonconvertible debt.

vertible bond may be viewed in either of two ways: the premium over the bond's value as stock or the premium over the bond's value as debt. Column 6 gives the premium in terms of stock. This is the difference between the bond's market price and its value as stock (i.e., the value in column 5 minus the value in column 3). This premium declines as the price of the stock rises and plays a more important role in the determination of the bond's price. Column 7 gives the premium in terms of nonconvertible debt. This is the difference between the bond's market price and its value as debt (i.e., the value in column 5 minus the value in column 4). This premium rises as the price of the stock rises, because the debt element of the bond is less important.

The inverse relationship between the two premiums is also illustrated in Figure 12.5. The premiums are shown by the differences between the line representing the market price (P_m) and the lines representing the value of the bond in terms of stock (C_s) and the value of the bond as nonconvertible debt (C_D).

When the price of the stock is low and the bond is selling close to its value as debt, the premium above the bond's value as stock is substantial, but the premium above the bond's value as debt is small. For example, at P_{s1} the price of the stock is $10, the bond's value in terms of stock is $500 (Line AB in Figure 12.5), and the premium is $298.50 (Line BC). However, the bond is selling for its value as nonconvertible debt ($798.50), and there is no premium over its value as debt. When the price of the stock is $25 and the bond is selling for $1,300, the premium in terms

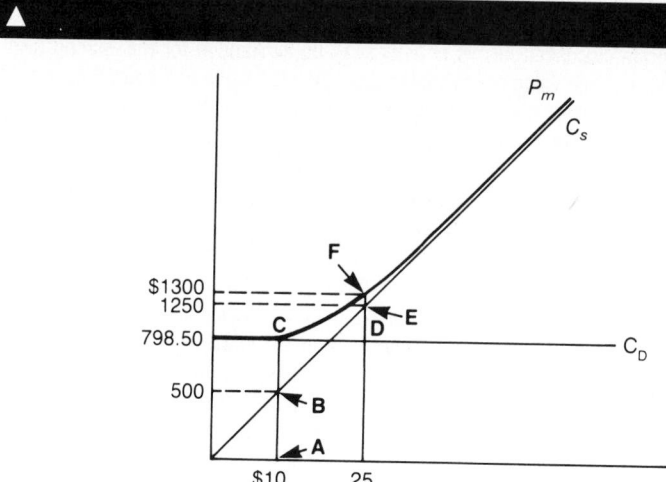

FIGURE 12.5

Premiums Paid for a Convertible Bond

The premiums paid for a convertible bond are the differences between the price of the bond and its value as stock and its value as debt.

of stock is only $50 (Line EF). However, the bond's premium over its value as nonconvertible debt is $501.50 (Line DF).

As these examples illustrate, the premium paid for the bond over its value as stock declines as the price of the stock rises. This decline in the premium is the result of the increasing importance of the conversion value on the bond's market price and the decreasing importance of the debt element on the bond's price.

As the price of the stock rises, the safety feature of the debt diminishes. If the price of the common stock ceased to rise and started to fall, then the price of the convertible bond could decline considerably before it reached the floor price set by the nonconvertible debt. For example, if the price of the stock declined from $30 to $15 (a 50 percent decline), the price of the convertible bond could fall from $1,500 to $798.50 (a 46.8 percent decline). Such a price decline would indicate that the floor value of $798.50 had little impact on the decline in the price of the bond.

In addition, as the price of the stock (and hence the price of the convertible bond) rises, the probability that the bond will be called rises. When the bond is called, it can be worth only its value as stock. The call forces the holder to convert the bond into stock. For example, when the price of the stock is $30, the bond is worth $1,500 in terms of stock. Should the company call the bond and offer to retire it for its face value ($1,000), no one would accept the offer. Instead they would convert the bond into $1,500 worth of stock. If the investor paid a premium over this conversion value (such as $1,600) and the bond were called, the investor would suffer a loss. Thus, as the probability of a call increases, the

Financial Facts

Funny Bonds

The convertible bonds discussed in this chapter may be exchanged for the issuing firm's common stock. If the value of the stock rises, then the value of the bond also rises. There are, however, bonds with differing conversion features, such as the conversion feature of a bond that is issued by one firm but that is convertible into the stock of another firm. For example, the Heritage Communications 7% convertible bond may be exchanged for shares of Telecommunications Corp. This unusual feature is the result of the takeover of Heritage by Telecommunications. • Bonds with other unusual features include the Oak Industries bond, whose coupon the firm may pay in stock in lieu of cash; the Cenco convertible bond, which may be exchanged for debentures issued by Manor Care; and the Heldor Industries convertible bond, which has a variable interest coupon. With this last bond, interest is distributed every three months instead of every six months, and the rate is changed every quarter in response to fluctuations in interest rates. The Unisys Eurodollar convertible bond also has an unusual conversion feature; it may be exchanged for Series A preferred stock and $510 in cash. • The Ito-Yokado Co. LTD. and Canon Inc. convertible bonds, which are denominated in dollars, may be exchanged for a specified number of Japanese companies' shares at a specified exchange rate. Thus both the value of the yen and the value of the firm's stock affect the value of these bonds. Such bonds offer Americans a way to speculate on a rise in the value of the yen. Since the bonds are convertible at a specified number of yen, an increase in the value of the yen increases the value of the bond. The increase in the value of the underlying stock and the decline in the value of the dollar vis-a-vis the yen during 1986–87 caused the value of these bonds to rise dramatically. For example, a $1,000 Ito-Yokado bond was worth over $7,900 when it was called in July 1987. •

---

willingness to pay a premium over the bond's value as stock declines, and the price of the convertible bond ultimately converges with its value as stock.

This decline in the premium also means that the price of the stock will rise more rapidly than the price of the bond. As may be seen in both Exhibit 12.5 and Figure 12.5, the market price of the convertible bond rises and falls with the price of the stock, because the conversion value of the bond rises and falls. However, the market price of the convertible bond does not rise as rapidly as the conversion value of the bond. For example, when the stock's price increased from $20 to $25 (a 25 percent increase), the convertible bond's price rose from $1,100 to $1,300 (an 18.2 percent increase). The reason for this difference in the rate of increase is the declining premium paid for the convertible bond. Since the premium declines as the price of the stock rises, the rate of increase in the price of the stock must exceed the rate of increase in the price of the bond. In summary, convertible bonds offer investors the opportunity for some capital growth with less risk.

EXHIBIT 12.6

Terms of Selected Convertible Preferred Stocks (as of December 1, 1990)

Convertible preferred stock tends to sell for a premium over its value as common stock.

Corporation	Preferred Dividend (per Share)	Number of Shares into which Preferred May Be Converted	Price of Common Stock	Value of Preferred Stock as Common Stock	Price of Preferred Stock
Arkla Inc.	$3.00	1.7467	$20⅞	$36.46	$41
Household International	6.25	2.327	27	62.83	69
James River	3.50	1.25	22⅞	28.59	38⅜
Paine Webber Group	1.37	0.5666	13¼	7.51	11⅞

Source: Standard & Poor's Stock Guide, *December 1990.*

CONVERTIBLE PREFERRED STOCK

Convertible preferred stock
Preferred stock that may be converted into common stock at the option of the holder

In addition to convertible bonds, many firms have issued **convertible preferred stock.** As its name implies, this stock may be converted into the common stock of the issuing corporation. A sampling of convertible preferred stock is presented in Exhibit 12.6. This exhibit illustrates the diversity of companies that have this security outstanding, including energy, financial, and consumer products. Thus, while nonconvertible preferred stock is primarily issued by utilities, the entire spectrum of firms issues convertible preferred stock.

Several of these issues of convertible preferred stock came into existence through mergers. As will be explained in Chapter 24, the tax laws permit firms to combine through an exchange of stock, which is not taxable (i.e., it is a tax-free exchange). If one firm purchases another firm for cash, the stockholders who sell their shares have an obvious realized sale. Profits and losses from the sale are then subject to capital gains taxation. However, the Internal Revenue Service has ruled that an exchange of "like securities" is not a realized sale and thus is not subject to capital gains taxation until the investor sells the new shares.

This tax ruling has encouraged mergers through the exchange of stock. In many cases the firm that is taking over (the surviving firm) offers to the stockholders of the firm that is being taken over an opportunity to trade their shares for a new convertible preferred stock. Since the stock is convertible into the common stock of the surviving firm, it is a "like security." Thus, the transaction is not subject to capital gains taxation. To encourage the stockholders to tender their shares, the surviving firm may offer a generous dividend yield on the convertible preferred stock. For this reason many convertible preferred stocks have considerably more generous dividend yields than that which is available through investing in the firm's common stock.

Convertible preferred stock is similar to convertible debt; however, there are some important differences. The differences are primarily the same as those between nonconvertible preferred stock and nonconvertible debt. Preferred stock is treated as an equity instrument. Thus, the firm is not under any legal obligation to pay the dividends. In addition, the preferred stock may be a perpetual security and may not have to be retired as debt must be. However, many convertible preferred stocks do have a required sinking fund, which forces the firm to retire the preferred stock over a period of years.

The value of convertible preferred stock (like convertible bonds) is related to the price of the stock into which it may be converted and to the value of competitive nonconvertible preferred stock. As with convertible bonds, these values set floors on the price of the convertible preferred stock. It cannot sell for any significant length of time below its value as stock. If it did, investors would enter the market and buy the preferred stock, which would increase its price. Thus, the minimum value of the convertible preferred stock (like the minimum value of the convertible bond) must be equal to the conversion value of the stock (P_c). In equation form that is

12.3 $$P_c = P_s \times N,$$

where P_s is the market price of the stock into which the convertible preferred stock may be converted, and N is the number of shares an investor obtains through conversion. Equation 12.3 is similar to Equation 12.1, which gave the value of the convertible bond as stock.

The convertible preferred stock's value as nonconvertible preferred stock (P) is related to the dividend it pays (D) and to the appropriate discount factor (k), which is the yield earned on competitive nonconvertible preferred stock. In equation form that is

12.4 $$P = \frac{D}{k},$$

which is essentially the same as the convertible bond's value as debt, except that the preferred stock has no definite maturity date. However, this value does set a floor on the price of a convertible preferred stock because at that price it is competitive with nonconvertible preferred stock.

As with convertible bonds, the convertible preferred stock is a hybrid security whose value combines its worth both as stock and as nonconvertible preferred stock. Convertible preferred stock tends to sell for a premium over both its value as stock and its value as straight preferred stock. Figures 12.4 and 12.5, which illustrated the value of the convertible bond at various prices of the stock into which it may be converted, also apply to convertible preferred stock. The only difference is the premium that the preferred stock commands over the value as common stock. This premium tends to be smaller. The reason for this reduced premium is that the preferred stock does not have the safety associated with debt. Its features are more similar to common stock than are the features of the convertible bond. Thus, its price usually commands less of a premium over its value as stock. This smaller premium is illustrated in Exhibit 12.6, as most of these convertible preferreds are selling near their value as common stock.

THE HISTORY OF TWO CONVERTIBLE BONDS

Perhaps the best way to understand convertible bonds is to examine the history of two such bonds. The first is a success story in that the price of the common stock rose, and, therefore, the value of the bond also rose. The second is a not-so-successful story, for the price of the stock declined and so did the value of the bond. However, the bond was retired at maturity; its value did not appreciate over the face amount because the price of the stock did not rise.

The American Quasar Convertible Bond

American Quasar is a firm devoted to exploring and drilling for oil and gas. It not only develops known reserves but also drills wells in search of new discoveries. Such wells (called wildcats) can prove to be highly lucrative; however, the majority of such drilling leads only to dry holes (i.e., no oil or gas is found). Because of the nature of its operations, American Quasar is a speculative firm at best. Speculative firms, however, need funds to operate, so the firm issued $17,500,000 in face value of convertible bonds. The coupon rate was set at 7¼ percent, and the exercise price of the bond was $21 (i.e., it was convertible into 47.6 shares), which was a premium of 17 percent over the approximate price of the stock ($18) at the date of issue.

After the bond was issued, American Quasar's stock did particularly well. Perhaps the discovery of some sizable wells in the Midwest and the problems associated with energy in general helped bolster the firm's stock. Of course, the value of the convertible bond rose as the price of the stock rose. The prices of the bond and the stock moved closely together until the bond was called, which forced conversion of the bond into the stock. The bond's life was short, as it was called less than two years after it was issued.

The Pan American World Airways Convertible Bond

While the previous example illustrated how the price of a convertible bond may rise as the price of the stock rises, the Pan American World Airways 5¼ 89 demonstrates the opposite. When the price of the stock declined, the price of the convertible bond followed it. This bond was issued in 1969, when Pan Am was riding the crest of popularity (which may partially explain why the coupon rate of interest was low on the bond).

Unfortunately for investors purchasing either the stock or the bond, Pan Am's popularity vanished, and with years of continued deficits the price of the stock declined drastically. The decline and its effect on the price of the convertible bond are illustrated in Figure 12.6, which plots the high and low stock and bond prices for 1969 through its redemption in 1989. Both the stock and the bond fell to "bargain basement" prices in 1974. The market seemed to think that the firm would certainly default on its debt and enter bankruptcy. At that time the bond reached a low of $137.50 for a $1,000 bond!

After this nadir, the price of both the bond and the stock recovered somewhat, so that in 1978 the stock was selling for more than $10 per share and the bond sold as high as $730. However, both prices were still below the 1969 prices, when the bond was initially issued, and after 1978 both the bond's and the stock's prices fell once again.

This example certainly illustrates the risk associated with investing in convertible bonds. If the firm becomes financially weak, the price of the convertible bond can fall drastically. The price of the stock fell from a high of $31¾ in 1969 to a low of $1¾ in 1974, and the price of the bond fell from $1,000 to $137.50. However, the bond was still an obligation of Pan Am that had to be retired by 1989. Thus, when Pan Am did redeem the bond, investors who purchased it initially for $1,000 received their principal. However, during the many years that the bond had been outstanding, there were certainly many periods when it appeared that the bond might have become worthless.[1]

---

[1] Unfortunately for bondholders who purchased bonds that mature after 1990, Pan Am declared bankruptcy in 1991.

FIGURE 12.6

Annual Price Range for Pan Am's Common Stock and 5¼% of 1989 Convertible Bond

The Pan Am 5¼ of 1989 was never converted but was redeemed for its face value at maturity.

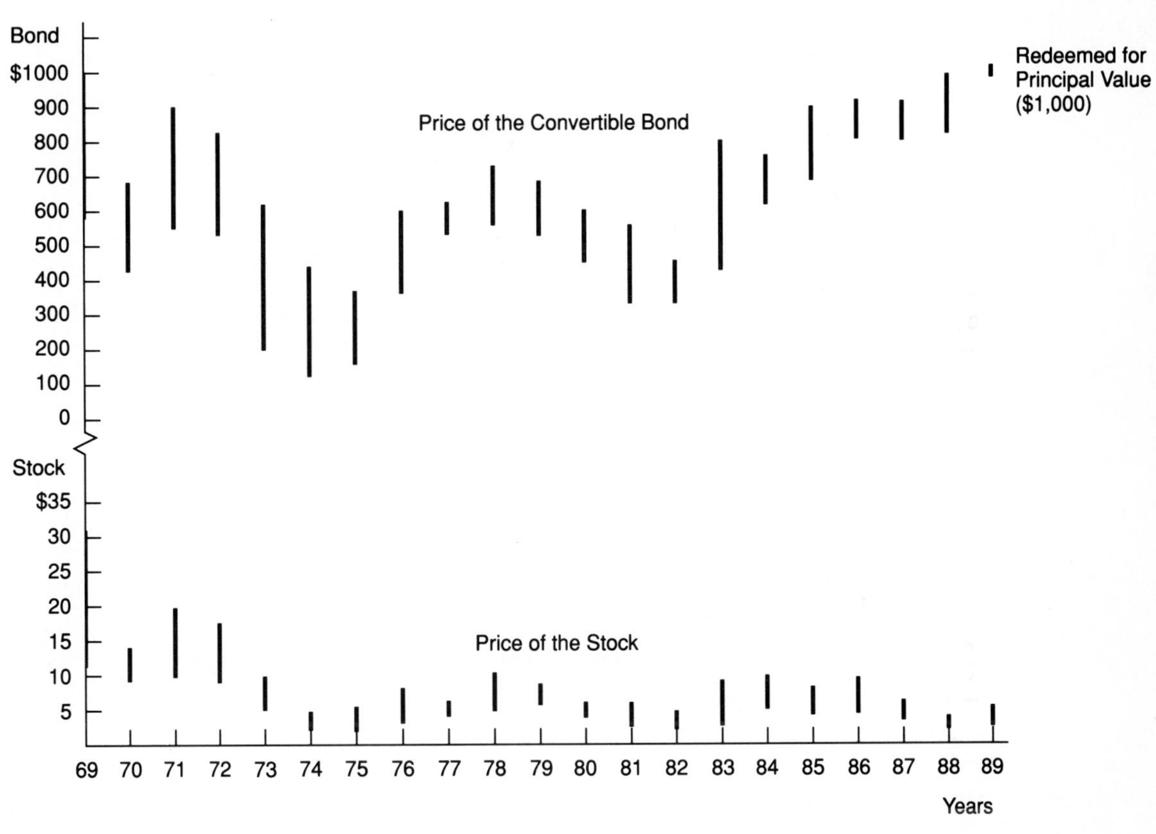

SUMMARY

A convertible bond is a debt instrument that may be converted into stock. The value of this bond depends on the value of the stock into which the bond may be converted and on the value of the bond as a debt instrument.

As the value of the stock rises, so does the value of the convertible bond. If the price of the stock declines, the value of the bond will also fall. However, the stock's price will decline faster, because the convertible bond's value as debt will halt the fall in the bond's price.

Since a convertible bond's price rises with the price of the stock, the bond offers the investor an opportunity for appreciation as the value of the firm increases. In addition, the bond's value as a debt sets a floor on the bond's price, which reduces the risk of loss to the investor. Should the stock decline in value, the debt element reduces the risk of loss to the bondholder.

Convertible preferred stock is similar to convertible debt, except that it lacks the safety implied by a debt instrument. Its price is related to its conversion value, the flow of dividend income, and the rate that investors may earn on nonconvertible preferred stock.

Review Questions

1. What differentiates convertible bonds from other bonds?
2. How is the value of a convertible bond in terms of stock determined? What effect does this value have on the price of the bond?
3. How is the value of a convertible bond in terms of debt determined? What effect does this value have on the price of the bond?
4. Why may convertible bonds be called by the firm? When are these bonds most likely to be called?
5. Why are convertible bonds less risky than stock but usually more risky than nonconvertible bonds?
6. Why does the premium over the bond's value as stock decline as the value of the stock rises?
7. How are convertible preferred stocks different from convertible bonds?
8. What advantages do convertible securities offer? What are the risks associated with these investments?

Problems

1. Given the following information concerning a convertible bond,

Principal	$1,000
Coupon	5%
Maturity	15 years
Call price	$1,050
Conversion price	$37 (i.e., 27 shares)
Market price of the common stock	$32
Market price of the bond	$1,040

answer the following questions:

a. What is the current yield of this bond?
b. What is the value of the bond based on the market price of the common stock?
c. What is the value of the common stock based on the market price of the bond?
d. What is the premium in terms of stock that the investor pays when he or she purchases the convertible bond instead of the stock?
e. Nonconvertible bonds are selling with a yield to maturity of 7 percent. If this bond lacked the conversion feature, what would the approximate price of the bond be?
f. What is the premium in terms of debt that the investor pays when he or she purchases the convertible bond instead of a nonconvertible bond?
g. What is the probability that the corporation will call this bond?
h. Why are investors willing to pay the premiums mentioned in Problems d and f?

2. Given the following information concerning a convertible bond:
   - Coupon 6% ($60 per $1,000 bond)
   - Exercise price: $25
   - Maturity date: 20 years
   - Call price: $1,040
   - Price of the common stock: $30

   a. If this bond were nonconvertible, what would be its approximate value if comparable interest rates were 12 percent?
   b. How many shares can the bond be converted into?
   c. What is the value of the bond in terms of stock?
   d. What is the current minimum price that the bond will command?
   e. Is there any reason to anticipate that the firm will call the bond?
   f. What do investors receive if they do not convert the bond when it is called?
   g. If the bond were called, would it be advantageous to convert?

3. Given the following information:
   - Corporation X $2.00 Convertible Preferred Stock
   - One share of preferred is convertible into 0.33 share of common stock
   - Price of common stock: $34
   - Price of convertible preferred stock: $17

   a. What is the value of the preferred stock in terms of common stock?
   b. What is the premium over the preferred stock's value as common stock?
   c. If the preferred stock is perpetual and comparable preferred stock offers a dividend yield of 15 percent, what would be the minimum price of this stock if it were not convertible?
   d. If the price of the common stock rose to $60, what would be the minimum increase in the value of the preferred stock that you would expect?

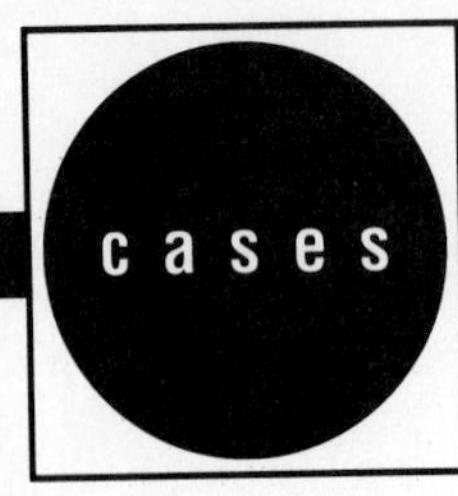

Calculating the Investment Value of Convertible Bonds

Arthur Bax is a CPA whose primary clients are small- to medium-sized private businesses. One of his clients, Alban Schoenberg, is considering how to finance the education of his two children, ages 10 and 12. Currently, neither child has any assets, so Schoenberg is considering investing a modest amount in convertible bonds in their names with his wife, Alma, as custodian. Alma Schoenberg has doubts because she does not believe that it is wise to risk their hard-earned money on risky investments. Mr. Schoenberg believes that the amount to be transferred is small enough to risk. Besides, he is fascinated with the convertible bonds issued by UT&T, a large company with a good, if not superior, credit rating.

Currently the bonds trade for par ($1,000), have a coupon of 8 percent, mature in ten years, and are convertible into the stock at $10 a share (100 shares per $1,000 bond). Other bonds issued by the company pay 10 percent interest; its stock sells for $8.50 and pays no cash dividends. While Mr. Schoenberg believes that the bonds are a fine investment, Mrs. Schoenberg has doubts and raises several questions for Bax to answer.

Case Problems

1. If the bonds were not convertible, what would they be worth?
2. Since the bonds are convertible, what is their stock value?
3. If the value of the stock rose to $15, what would happen to the value of the bonds?
4. If the price of the stock declined to $5, what would happen to the value of the bonds?
5. If the money were invested in the nonconvertible bonds and the price of the stock changed, what would happen to the bonds?
6. If the price of the stock rose, would Mrs. Schoenberg have to exchange the bonds for the stock?
7. If she changed her mind and wanted to get the principal back, could she?
8. If the company were to fail, what would happen to the bonds?

9. Would buying the bonds be preferable to putting the money in the firm's stock?
10. Would buying the bonds be preferable to putting the money in a certificate of deposit in a federally insured commercial bank?
11. Given the nature of Mrs. Schoenberg's questions, do you believe that the money should be invested in these convertible bonds?

Suggested Readings

For an elementary discussion of convertible bonds consult:

Noddings, Thomas. *Investor's Guide to Convertible Bonds.* Homewood, Ill.: Dow Jones-Irwin, 1982.

Techniques used to analyze convertible bonds are discussed in:

Liebowitz, Martin L. "Understanding Convertible Securities." *Financial Analysts Journal* (November–December 1974), pp. 57–67.

Tennican, Michael L. *Convertible Debentures and Related Securities.* Boston, Mass.: Harvard University Press, 1975.

The reader should be warned that some of this material requires some understanding of mathematics.

While convertibles have higher default risk than nonconvertible debt, from 1978 to 1987 their returns almost doubled the returns on nonconvertible debt. These returns were highly correlated with returns from common stock, which suggests combining convertibles with common stock does not help achieve diversification. See:

Altman, Edward I. "The Convertible Debt Market: Are Returns Worth the Risk?" *Financial Analysts Journal* (July–August 1989), pp. 23–31.

More advanced books on convertibles include:

Calamos, John P. *Investing in Convertible Securities.* Chicago, Ill.: Longman Financial Services Publishing, 1988.

Gepts, Stefaan J. *Valuation and Selection of Convertible Bonds.* Westport, Conn.: Greenwood Press, 1987.

Calamos is president of a firm that specializes in research and management of portfolios of convertible securities for financial institutions. Both his and Gepts' books are reference guides primarily written for financial professionals and cover risk, returns, and hedging with convertibles. Gepts' book integrates option valuation theory and the valuation of convertible bonds and includes material on convertible Eurobonds.

chapter 13

Futures and Options

Learning Objectives

1. Define futures contract, warrant, call option, and put option.
2. Differentiate between a long and a short position in a futures contract.
3. Contrast the use of margin in the stock market, its role in the futures market, and the use of options as an alternative to the use of margin.
4. Identify the source of leverage in a futures contract and in an option.
5. Distinguish speculators from hedgers and describe the role played by each.
6. Define an option's intrinsic value and its time premium.
7. Explain how speculators and investors earn profits and sustain losses in the markets for futures and options.
8. Explain how financial managers and portfolio managers may use stock index futures or stock index options to reduce the risk from fluctuations in security prices and changes in interest rates.

Bernard Baruch pointed out a fundamental fact concerning free markets: "Markets will fluctuate." On Friday, November 30, 1990, a call option to buy the stock of NCR sold for $375; on Monday it sold for $2,687.50. That's an increase in excess of 500 percent over the weekend! Yes, free markets can fluctuate. If you own something that appreciates, you make money. But "fortune is like the market . . . if you can stay a little, the price will fall." Francis Bacon obviously understood that prices can decline. If you own the asset, you will suffer a loss, but for those with cash, your misfortune may be their good fortune.

This chapter is concerned with two types of financial assets whose values can and do fluctuate dramatically: futures contracts and options. The first half of the chapter is devoted to futures contracts to buy and sell commodities or financial assets. These contracts are made by speculators who anticipate price changes and by hedgers who employ the contracts to reduce risk. The hedgers are the growers, producers, and financial managers who seek to protect themselves from price fluctuations. By hedging, they pass the risk of loss to the speculators.

The second half of the chapter is devoted to options: warrants, calls, and puts. These securities are purchased by individuals seeking to increase the returns on their investments. However, unlike other securities, options permit the individual to create securities and thus to take positions that are not possible with traditional securities. Options may also be used by investors and portfolio managers to hedge and reduce risk.

Chapter 13 is an elementary introduction to futures contracts and options. Because these are extremely sophisticated investments, only the barest fundamentals can be covered. The chapter describes these securities, the mechanics of establishing positions, the role of margin and financial leverage, speculators' long and short positions, and the ways in which these securities are used to reduce risk.

WHAT IS INVESTING IN COMMODITY FUTURES?

Futures contract ▲
Agreement for the future delivery or receipt of a commodity at a specified price and time

Speculators ▲
Individuals who are willing to accept substantial risk for the possibility of a large return

A commodity such as wheat or a financial asset such as a Treasury bond may be purchased for current delivery or for future delivery. A **futures contract** is a formal agreement executed through a commodity exchange for the delivery of goods in the future. One party agrees to accept a specific commodity that meets a specified quality in a specified month. The other party agrees to deliver the specified commodity during the designated month.

Individuals who enter futures contracts but do not deal in the actual commodities are generally called **speculators.** This distinguishes them from the growers, processors, warehousers, and other participants who enter contracts but who also deal in the actual commodity. Such participants are the **hedgers,** who use the contracts to reduce the risk of loss from fluctuating prices. (Hedging is explained later in the chapter.)

Hedgers ▲
Individuals or firms that enter into offsetting contracts to reduce risk

The primary appeal of futures contracts to speculators is the potential for a large return on the investment. The large return is the result of the leverage that exists because (1) a futures contract controls a substantial amount of the commodity and (2) the investor must make only a small payment to enter into a contract to buy or sell a commodity (i.e., there is small margin requirement). These two points are discussed in some detail later in this chapter.

The Mechanics of Purchasing Futures

Like stocks and bonds, futures contracts are traded in several markets. The most important is the Chicago Board of Trade, which executes contracts in agricultural commodities such as wheat, soybeans, and livestock. More than 50 commodities are traded on 10 exchanges in the United States and Canada. These markets developed close to the regions in which the commodity is produced. Thus, the markets for wheat are located not only in Chicago but also in Kansas City and Minneapolis.

Futures contracts are entered into through brokers, just as stocks and bonds are bought and sold. The broker (or a member of a brokerage firm) owns a seat on the commodity exchange. Membership on each exchange is limited, and only members are allowed to execute contracts. If the investor's broker lacks a seat, that broker must have a correspondent relationship with another broker who does own a seat. The brokers will charge a commission fee for executing orders. This fee tends to be modest and covers both the purchase and subsequent sale of the contract.

Commodity Positions

An individual may acquire a contract to accept future delivery (i.e., to buy). This is the **long position,** in which the buyer will profit if the price of the commodity, and hence the value of the contract, rises. The individual may also enter into a contract to make future delivery (i.e., to sell). This is the **short position,** in which the seller agrees to make good the contract (i.e., to deliver the goods) sometime in the future. This investor will profit if the price of the commodity, and hence the value of the contract, declines.

Long position ▲
Contract to accept delivery, to buy

Short position ▲
Contract to make delivery, to sell

The way in which each position generates a profit can be seen in a simple example. Assume that the **futures price** of wheat is \$3.50 per bushel. If a contract is made to accept delivery in six months at \$3.50 per bushel, the buyer will profit from this long position if the price of wheat *rises.* If the price increases to \$4.00 per bushel, the buyer can exercise the

Futures price ▲
Price for the future delivery of a commodity or financial asset

contract by taking delivery and paying $3.50 per bushel. The speculator then sells the wheat for $4 per bushel, which produces a profit of $0.50 per bushel.[1]

The opposite occurs when the price of wheat declines. If the price of wheat falls to $3.00 per bushel, the individual who made the contract to accept delivery at $3.50 suffers a loss. But the speculator who made the contract to deliver wheat (i.e., who took the short position) earns a profit from the price decline. The speculator can then buy wheat at the market price (which is referred to as the **spot price**) of $3.00, deliver it for the contract price of $3.50, and earn a $0.50 profit per bushel.

Spot price ▲
Current price of a commodity or financial asset

If the price rises, the short position will produce a loss. If the price increases from $3.50 to $4.00 per bushel, the speculator who made the contract to deliver suffers a loss of $0.50 per bushel, because he or she must pay $4.00 to obtain the wheat that will be delivered for $3.50 per bushel.

Actually, these losses and profits are generated without the goods being delivered. Of course, when a speculator makes a contract to accept future delivery, there is always the possibility that this individual will receive the goods and have to buy them. Conversely, if the speculator enters into a contract to make future delivery, there is the possibility that the goods will have to be supplied. Such deliveries occur infrequently, however, because the speculator can offset the contract before the delivery date.

This process of offsetting existing contracts is illustrated in the following example. Suppose a speculator has a contract to buy wheat in January. If the individual wants to close the position, he or she can make a contract to sell wheat in January. The two contracts cancel each other, as one is a purchase and the other is a sale. If the speculator actually received the wheat by executing the purchase agreement, he or she could pass on the wheat by executing the sell agreement. However, since the two contracts offset each other, the actual delivery and subsequent sale are not necessary. Instead, the speculator's position in wheat is closed, and the actual physical transfers do not occur.

Correspondingly, if the speculator has a contract for the sale of wheat in January, he or she can cancel it by making a contract for the purchase of wheat in January. If the speculator were called upon to deliver wheat as the result of the contract to sell, the individual would exercise the contract to purchase wheat. The buy and sell contracts cancel each other, and no physical transfers of wheat occur. Once again the speculator has closed the initial position by taking the opposite position (i.e., the sales contract is canceled by a purchase contract).

---

[1] As is explained in the section on margin, profits and losses are settled on a daily basis.

Because these contracts are canceled and actual deliveries do not take place, it should not be assumed that profits or losses do not occur. The two contracts need not be executed at the same price. For example, the speculator may have entered into a contract for the future sale of wheat at $3.50 per bushel. Any contract for the future purchase of comparable wheat can cancel the contract for the sale. But the cost of the wheat for future delivery could be $3.60 or $3.40 (or any conceivable price). If the price of wheat rises (e.g., from $3.50 to $3.60 per bushel), the speculator with a long position earns a profit, but the short position suffers a loss. If the price declines (e.g., from $3.50 to $3.40 per bushel), the short seller earns a profit, but the long position sustains a loss.

The Units of Commodity Contracts

To facilitate trading, contracts must be uniform. For a particular commodity the contracts must be identical. Besides identifying the delivery month, the contract must specify the grade and type of the commodity (e.g., a particular type of wheat) and the units of the commodity (e.g., 5,000 bushels). Thus, when an individual makes a contract, there can be no doubt as to the nature of the obligation. For example, if the investor enters into a contract to buy wheat for January delivery, there can be no confusion with a contract for the purchase of wheat for February delivery. These are two different commodities in the same way that AT&T common stock, AT&T preferred stock, and AT&T bonds are all different securities. Without such standardization of contracts, there would be chaos in the commodity (or any) markets.

The units of trading vary with each commodity. For example, if the investor buys a contract for corn, the unit of trading is 5,000 bushels. If the investor buys a contract for eggs, the unit of trading is 22,500 dozen. A list of selected commodities, the exchange on which they are traded, and the units of each contract are given in Exhibit 13.1.

Reporting on Futures Trading

Futures prices and the number of contracts are reported in the financial press in much the same way as stock and bond transactions are. This is illustrated in Exhibit 13.2, which was taken from *The Wall Street Journal.* As may be seen in the exhibit, corn is traded on the Chicago Board of Trade (CBT). The unit for trading is 5,000 bushels, and prices are quoted in cents per bushel. The opening price for December delivery was 248¾¢ ($2.49) per bushel, while the high, low, and closing (i.e., the "settle") prices were 249¾¢, 248½¢, and 248¾¢, respectively. This closing price was +¼¢ from the closing price on the previous day. The high and low prices (prior to the previous day of trading) for the lifetime

EXHIBIT 13.1

Selected Futures: Their Exchanges and Units of Trading

A variety of futures contracts exist and are traded on several commodity exchanges.

Commodity	Exchange	Unit of One Contract
Corn	Chicago Board of Trade	5,000 bushels
Soybeans	Chicago Board of Trade	5,000 bushels
Barley	Winnipeg Commodity Exchange	20 metric tons
Cattle	Chicago Mercantile Exchange	30,000 tons
Coffee	New York Coffee and Sugar Exchange	37,500 pounds
Copper	Commodity Exchange Inc. of New York	25,000 pounds
Platinum	New York Mercantile Exchange	50 troy ounces
Silver	Commodity Exchange Inc. of New York	5,000 troy ounces
Lumber	Chicago Mercantile Exchange	100,000 board feet
Cotton	New York Cotton Exchange	50,000 pounds
British pound	International Monetary Market	25,000 pounds
Japanese yen	International Monetary Market	12.5 million yen
Treasury bonds	Chicago Board of Trade	$100,000
Treasury bills	International Monetary Market	$1,000,000
Standard & Poor's 500 futures index	Chicago Mercantile Exchange	500 times S&P 500 index

Open interest ▲
Number of futures contracts for a particular commodity or financial asset in existence

of the contract were 275¢ and 242½¢, respectively. The **open interest,** which is the number of contracts in existence, was 19,832.

This open interest varies over the life of the contract. Initially, the open interest rises as buyers and sellers establish positions. Then it declines as the delivery date approaches and the positions are closed. This changing number of contracts is illustrated in Figure 13.1, which plots the spot and futures prices and the open interest for a September contract to buy Kansas City wheat. When the contracts were initially traded in late 19X1, there were only a few contracts in existence. By June 19X2 the open interest had risen to more than 10,000 contracts. As the remaining life of the contracts declined, the number of contracts fell as the various participants closed their positions. By late September only a few contracts were still outstanding.

Figure 13.1 also shows the spot price (i.e., the current price) and the futures price for Kansas City wheat. In this case the futures price was generally less than the spot price. This relationship between the two prices occurs when investors believe that the price of the commodity will decline in the future. These investors seek to sell contracts now to lock in the higher prices so they may buy back the contracts at a lower price in the future. This selling of the futures drives the futures price down below the spot price.

EXHIBIT 13.2

Selected Futures Prices

The reporting of futures contracts includes prices, net change in price, and the number of contracts in existence.

COMMODITY FUTURES PRICES

Thursday, January 3, 1991

Open Interest Reflects Previous Trading Day.

–GRAINS AND OILSEEDS–

	Open	High	Low	Settle	Change	Lifetime High	Lifetime Low	Open Interest
CORN (CBT) 5,000 bu.; cents per bu.								
Mar	232¼	233	231¾	232¼	+ ½	302½	227¼	90,398
May	239¾	240½	239¼	240	+ ¾	306½	235	37,212
July	245½	246¾	245½	246¼	+ 1	308¼	241½	52,220
Sept	247¾	248¾	247¼	247¼	+ 1	287½	240¼	7,066
Dec	248¾	249¾	248½	248¾	+ ¼	275	242½	19,832
Mr92	256	256	255¼	255¾	+ ¼	262	249	1,292
Est vol 33,000; vol Wed 26,963; open int 208,040, +2,520.								
OATS (CBT) 5,000 bu.; cents per bu.								
Mar	108¾	110½	108¾	109¼	– ¼	201	107	7,164
May	114¾	116	114½	115¼	....	183¾	113	2,604
July	121	121¾	120½	121	– ½	164¾	118½	1,652
Est vol 1,250; vol Wed 795; open int 11,566, –10.								
SOYBEANS (CBT) 5,000 bu.; cents per bu.								
Jan	554	559	554	558½	+ 4¾	692	549¾	8,263
Mar	568	571¾	567	570¼	+ 3	703	563½	48,846
May	582½	585½	581½	584	+ 2½	711	578	22,472
July	595½	599¼	595	597	+ 2¼	718	592	20,790
Aug	600	601½	599¾	600¼	+ 1¾	695	596	3,583
Sept	599½	601	598½	598¾	– ¼	670	597	2,983
Nov	603½	606	601½	601¾	– 1	674	601	8,988
Ja92	616	616	613½	613½	– 1½	642½	613	355
Mar	628	629	625	625	– 1½	654	625	107
Est vol 44,000; vol Wed 48,793; open int 116,387, –138.								
SOYBEAN MEAL (CBT) 100 tons; $ per ton.								
Jan	163.20	165.50	163.00	165.30	+ 2.50	204.00	160.80	3,407
Mar	168.40	170.10	167.90	169.90	+ 2.20	212.00	165.80	32,274
May	172.80	174.50	172.50	173.80	+ 1.70	208.00	170.50	12,920
July	176.70	178.50	176.70	177.90	+ 1.50	209.00	175.00	7,611
Aug	178.50	180.00	178.50	179.20	+ 1.50	199.00	176.50	2,442
Sept	180.50	180.50	179.50	179.50	+ 1.00	193.50	175.50	2,489
Oct	179.50	180.50	179.00	179.00	+ .50	190.00	177.00	838
Dec	181.00	182.00	181.00	181.20	+ .20	191.50	179.00	2,223
Ja92	....	....	....	179.20	– .50	190.50	180.00	145
Est vol 19,000; vol Wed 15,218; open int 64,349, +507.								
SOYBEAN OIL (CBT) 60,000 lbs.; cents per lb.								
Jan	20.45	20.48	20.30	20.39	– .05	25.55	19.81	5,575
Mar	20.77	20.80	20.60	20.71	– .02	25.61	19.85	34,215
May	21.10	21.15	21.00	21.09	– .04	25.65	20.25	16,882
July	21.45	21.45	21.26	21.37	– .07	25.70	20.90	10,472
Aug	21.40	21.42	21.30	21.31	– .09	25.50	21.25	2,392
Sept	21.46	21.46	21.30	21.30	– .16	25.10	21.25	1,617
Oct	21.45	21.47	21.30	21.30	– .15	24.90	21.30	1,238
Dec	21.55	21.60	21.35	21.36	– .19	24.75	21.30	1,923
Ja92	....	....	....	20.95	– .27	22.95	21.31	297
Est vol 16,000; vol Wed 15,025; open int 74,611, +1,769.								
WHEAT (CBT) 5,000 bu.; cents per bu.								
Mar	262½	262¾	258½	259½	– 4	382½	256	25,731
May	268½	269¼	265½	266¾	– 3	373	263½	9,215
July	272½	273¼	270¼	270½	– 2¾	355	267½	11,869
Sept	279¼	279¾	277	277	– 2¾	326	274½	1,096
Dec	291½	291½	288¾	288¾	– 3¾	318	286	690
Est vol 12,000; vol Wed 10,062; open int 48,621, +1,649.								
WHEAT (KC) 5,000 bu.; cents per bu.								
Mar	262½	263¾	261¾	261¾	– 2	430	257¾	16,415
May	268½	269	266½	266¾	– 2¼	362¾	262	5,155
July	270½	271¾	270	270¼	– ¾	320½	265½	4,529
Sept	277½	277½	276½	276½	– ½	302½	274	423
Est vol 4,219; vol Wed 4,657; open int 26,547, –81.								
WHEAT (MPLS) 5,000 bu.; cents per bu.								
Mar	259¼	260	258	258¼	– 1¾	379¼	257	7,926
May	266¼	266¾	265¼	265¼	– 1¾	361	263½	1,370
July	273	273	271½	271¾	– 1½	306	269½	1,030
Sept	278	278	278	277½	– 1¾	299	277¾	140
Est vol 4,960; vol Wed 1,483; open int 10,466, +485.								
BARLEY (WPG) 20 metric tons; Can. $ per ton								
Mar	87.40	89.20	87.40	89.20	+ 1.90	116.50	85.50	3,045
May	93.00	93.00	93.00	93.00	+ 1.20	101.50	90.40	3,680
July	94.30	95.70	94.30	95.70	+ 1.90	102.00	92.50	262
Oct	....	....	....	91.70	+ 1.90	93.50	88.50	188
Est vol 420; vol Wed 100; open int 7,175, +17.								
FLAXSEED (WPG) 20 metric tons; Can. $ per ton								
Mar	251.00	253.40	250.80	251.20	+ 1.50	329.00	249.00	2,516
May	258.50	259.70	257.30	257.50	+ 1.40	307.40	255.80	1,060
July	265.50	266.00	264.20	264.20	+ 1.20	296.00	262.80	107
Oct	270.50	272.00	270.20	270.20	+ 1.40	292.00	268.30	378
Est vol 475; vol Wed 342; open int 4,061, –20.								
CANOLA (WPG) 20 metric tons; Can. $ per ton								
Jan	283.30	285.00	282.70	283.70	+ 1.40	357.00	281.10	6,545
Mar	286.80	288.80	286.20	287.20	+ 1.40	363.00	284.40	7,917
June	295.60	297.30	295.00	296.10	+ 1.00	351.30	293.80	3,834
Sept	301.00	303.50	301.00	301.70	+ 1.40	339.00	299.20	2,678
Nov	305.50	308.10	304.50	306.30	+ 1.50	326.50	303.70	2,100
Est vol 2,500; vol Wed 3,693; open int 23,074, –626.								
WHEAT (WPG) 20 metric tons; Can. $ per ton								
Mar	107.00	108.20	107.00	108.20	+ 1.60	119.70	106.00	4,046
May	109.60	110.20	109.60	110.20	+ 1.00	127.00	108.50	5,150
July	111.00	111.30	111.00	111.20	+ .60	118.50	110.00	205
Oct	106.50	107.20	106.50	107.20	+ 1.00	111.60	106.00	458
Est vol 340; vol Wed 344; open int 9,859, +17.								

–LIVESTOCK & MEAT–

	Open	High	Low	Settle	Change	Lifetime High	Lifetime Low	Open Interest
CATTLE–FEEDER (CME) 44,000 lbs.; cents per lb.								
Jan	88.95	89.25	88.95	89.15	+ .05	89.62	79.50	3,664
Mar	86.10	86.47	86.02	86.32	+ .05	87.00	80.90	3,612
Apr	84.65	85.05	84.65	84.95	+ .10	85.50	81.20	1,447
May	83.55	83.75	83.40	83.55	– .05	84.25	80.20	2,448
Aug	83.05	83.32	83.05	83.17	....	83.85	80.20	863
Est vol 920; vol Wed 619; open int 12,182, +59.								
CATTLE–LIVE (CME) 40,000 lbs.; cents per lb.								
Feb	77.00	77.70	76.95	77.45	+ .37	77.80	72.50	29,674
Apr	76.02	76.50	76.00	76.35	+ .25	78.05	74.00	18,768
June	74.40	74.80	74.30	74.65	+ .22	75.45	72.15	14,249
Aug	72.85	73.25	72.80	73.17	+ .22	73.85	70.35	4,616
Oct	72.95	73.40	72.90	73.05	+ .20	73.40	70.70	3,266
Dec	73.50	73.75	73.45	73.55	+ .30	74.30	71.75	1,161
Est vol 11,870; vol Wed 7,944; open int 71,739, +321.								
HOGS (CME) 30,000 lbs.; cents per lb.								
Feb	48.05	48.62	48.00	48.55	+ .47	53.15	46.20	12,636
Apr	45.90	46.55	45.90	46.47	+ .32	49.90	43.60	6,257
June	50.80	51.40	50.75	51.32	+ .45	53.75	47.70	2,428
July	50.80	51.25	50.80	51.25	+ .25	53.65	48.30	790
Aug	49.10	49.20	48.75	49.12	– .12	51.75	46.90	421
Est vol 6,669; vol Wed 5,103; open int 22,633, –267.								
PORK BELLIES (CME) 40,000 lbs.; cents per lb.								
Feb	61.50	63.00	60.77	62.90	+ 1.77	73.80	49.40	7,859
Mar	61.12	62.10	60.00	62.02	+ 1.40	73.45	49.20	1,720
May	61.90	62.70	61.10	62.65	+ 1.05	73.12	49.50	1,932
July	62.00	62.70	61.15	62.65	+ .97	72.80	50.15	584
Aug	60.40	60.80	59.75	60.25	+ .25	70.05	51.60	210
Est vol 5,092; vol Wed 3,092; open int 12,305, +258.								

–FOOD & FIBER–

	Open	High	Low	Settle	Change	Lifetime High	Lifetime Low	Open Interest
COCOA (CSCE)–10 metric tons; $ per ton.								
Mar	1,155	1,160	1,140	1,141	– 5	1,581	985	15,642
May	1,196	1,196	1,183	1,185	– 1	1,572	1,000	7,703
July	1,235	1,235	1,228	1,228	– 2	1,590	1,060	7,572
Sept	1,270	1,270	1,270	1,267	– 1	1,515	1,262	4,353
Dec	1,320	1,320	1,313	1,313	– 2	1,535	1,310	5,828
Mr92	1,360	1,360	1,360	1,360	+ 3	1,538	1,356	591
Est vol 2,840; vol Wed 2,396; open int 41,689, +3.								
COFFEE (CSCE)–37,500 lbs.; cents per lb.								
Mar	87.80	90.10	87.75	89.25	+ 1.20	112.00	84.35	26,965
May	90.25	92.30	90.20	91.70	+ 1.20	113.00	87.00	8,652
July	92.50	94.25	92.50	94.15	+ 1.40	111.50	89.25	2,781
Sept	94.90	96.50	94.90	96.50	+ 1.60	113.50	91.80	1,727
Dec	....	....	....	98.75	+ 1.25	116.00	95.35	701
Est vol 6,815; vol Wed 4,025; open int 40,888, +650.								
SUGAR–WORLD (CSCE)–112,000 lbs.; cents per lb.								
Mar	9.17	9.25	9.05	9.11	– .01	15.22	9.02	53,886
May	9.25	9.33	9.15	9.23	+ .01	15.05	9.09	27,949
July	9.32	9.36	9.20	9.29	+ .01	14.90	9.15	15,389
Oct	9.34	9.42	9.23	9.29	– .05	14.40	9.19	17,340
Mr92	9.37	9.38	9.34	9.42	– .04	10.14	9.34	900
Est vol 19,601; vol Wed 34,104; open int 115,509, –6,766.								
SUGAR–DOMESTIC (CSCE)–112,000 lbs.; cents per lb.								
Mar	22.34	22.34	22.32	22.34	– .01	23.35	22.30	2,077
May	22.43	22.46	22.43	22.45	– .01	23.41	22.43	3,270
July	22.56	22.56	22.55	22.56	– .01	23.41	22.55	2,941
Sept	22.56	22.56	22.56	22.56	– .01	23.35	22.56	2,060
Nov	....	....	....	22.59	+ .03	23.14	22.51	1,606
Mr92	....	....	....	22.60	– .03	22.80	22.45	101
Est vol 529; vol Wed 86; open int 12,118, +5.								
COTTON (CTN)–50,000 lbs.; cents per lb.								
Mar	75.50	77.00	75.05	76.80	+ 1.00	77.80	63.82	18,779
May	74.12	75.15	73.80	75.05	+ .86	77.40	64.40	11,858
July	73.48	74.50	73.31	74.50	+ .92	78.38	65.67	5,749
Oct	67.45	67.66	67.25	67.63	+ .05	72.85	66.75	1,433
Dec	64.35	64.60	64.12	64.60	+ .11	69.10	64.12	3,882
Mr92	65.30	65.30	65.20	65.35	– .05	68.50	65.20	438
Est vol 7,500; vol Wed 8,370; open int 42,165, +221.								
ORANGE JUICE (CTN)–15,000 lbs.; cents per lb.								
Jan	103.50	106.25	103.50	106.15	+ .80	196.75	99.00	1,194
Mar	106.15	109.00	106.15	108.15	– 3.00	190.50	101.20	5,004
May	109.00	110.75	109.00	110.65	– 3.35	190.00	101.50	1,283
July	110.85	112.50	110.85	112.00	– 3.85	180.00	102.50	383
Est vol 2,800; vol Wed 1,383; open int 7,892, –255.								

–METALS & PETROLEUM–

	Open	High	Low	Settle	Change	Lifetime High	Lifetime Low	Open Interest
COPPER-HIGH (CMX)–25,000 lbs.; cents per lb.								
Jan	118.40	118.50	117.10	117.15	– 2.90	126.40	94.00	1,970
Fb91	118.70	118.70	117.10	117.15	– 3.15	120.00	99.50	1,075
Mar	117.50	117.80	115.90	116.30	– 3.00	122.60	92.30	19,851
Apr	....	114.70	114.70	114.65	– 2.40	117.90	99.85	330
May	114.10	114.50	112.90	113.10	– 2.70	117.80	97.00	3,632
June	....	....	....	111.90	– 2.90	115.00	102.30	230
July	111.85	111.85	110.90	110.70	– 2.60	113.50	96.50	3,156
Aug	....	....	....	109.80	– 2.55	107.00	103.30	160
Sept	110.00	110.00	109.30	108.90	– 2.50	110.50	95.50	2,197
Oct	....	....	....	108.15	– 2.35	106.00	102.50	176
Nov	....	....	....	107.35	– 2.30	103.25	102.00	101
Dec	106.90	106.90	106.30	106.50	– 2.40	108.50	94.50	3,136
Mr92	105.50	105.50	105.00	105.00	– 2.00	106.80	96.00	125
Est vol 9,000; vol wed 14,296; open int 36,257, +474.								
GOLD (CMX)–100 troy oz.; $ per troy oz.								
Ja91	....	....	....	386.50	– 2.60	393.00	374.00	7
Fb91	388.00	390.00	385.00	388.90	– 2.20	457.50	362.00	48,725
Apr	391.00	392.70	388.00	392.10	– 2.30	526.00	366.20	18,501
June	395.30	396.30	393.00	395.60	– 2.40	466.20	372.00	14,345
Aug	....	....	....	398.90	– 2.50	468.00	375.00	5,731
Oct	402.50	402.50	401.80	402.20	– 2.50	476.00	385.00	1,605
Dec	404.30	405.50	404.30	405.60	– 2.50	483.00	384.00	8,272
Fb92	409.00	409.00	409.00	409.30	– 2.60	456.50	391.90	3,317
Apr	....	....	....	412.80	– 2.60	446.00	394.00	2,043
June	....	....	....	416.60	– 2.60	467.00	398.50	4,105
Aug	....	....	....	420.50	– 2.60	423.50	412.50	282
Est vol 40,000; vol Wed 36,530; open int 106,943, –667.								
PLATINUM (NYM)–50 troy oz.; $ per troy oz.								
Jan	405.00	412.60	405.00	411.40	+ 2.20	551.00	388.10	1,424
Apr	410.50	417.50	410.20	415.90	+ 2.40	554.50	394.50	11,958
July	414.50	419.30	414.50	419.90	+ 2.80	528.50	400.00	2,367
Oct	418.50	425.00	418.50	423.90	+ 2.70	513.00	415.00	897
Est vol 3,020; vol Wed 3,476; open int 16,689, +600.								
PALLADIUM (NYM) 100 troy oz.; $ per troy oz.								
Mar	81.50	83.40	81.50	82.70	+ .95	142.00	80.55	3,167
June	84.00	84.00	84.00	83.70	+ .95	125.25	82.60	1,140
Sept	85.50	85.50	85.50	84.95	+ .95	119.40	84.00	189
Est vol 105; vol Wed 106; open int 4,553, –24.								
SILVER (CMX)–5,000 troy oz.; cents per troy oz.								
Jan	406.5	420.0	406.5	421.4	+ 10.0	688.0	400.0	377
Mr91	412.0	428.5	412.0	426.7	+ 10.0	665.0	398.5	59,589
May	419.5	434.0	419.5	432.5	+ 10.2	647.0	404.0	10,425
July	424.0	439.0	424.0	438.0	+ 10.3	667.5	410.0	6,546
Sept	441.5	443.0	441.5	443.6	+ 10.4	654.0	415.0	2,172
Dec	449.5	452.0	449.0	451.4	+ 10.5	623.5	423.0	3,676
Mr92	447.0	447.0	447.0	459.8	+ 10.6	613.0	432.0	1,275
May	....	....	....	465.7	+ 10.7	589.0	451.5	865
July	....	....	....	471.5	+ 10.8	557.0	441.5	430
Est vol 19,000; vol Wed 13,968; open int 85,386, +1,043.								

EXCHANGE ABBREVIATIONS
(for commodity futures and futures options)

CBT-Chicago Board of Trade; CME-Chicago Mercantile Exchange; CMX-Commodity Exchange, New York; CRCE-Chicago Rice & Cotton Exchange; CTN-New York Cotton Exchange; CSCE-Coffee, Sugar & Cocoa Exchange, New York; IPE-International Petroleum Exchange; KC-Kansas City Board of Trade; MCE-MidAmerica Commodity Exchange; MPLS-Minneapolis Grain Exchange; NYM-New York Mercantile Exchange; PBOT-Philadelphia Board of Trade; WPG-Winnipeg Commodity Exchange.

	Open	High	Low	Settle	Change	Lifetime High	Lifetime Low	Open Interest
SILVER (CBT)–1,000 troy oz.; cents per troy oz.								
Jan	415.0	420.0	415.0	420.0	+ 11.0	420.0	400.0	7
Feb	410.0	425.0	410.0	423.0	+ 9.5	647.0	394.0	1,039
Apr	416.0	431.0	416.0	429.0	+ 10.0	603.0	399.0	725
June	421.0	437.0	421.0	436.0	+ 11.0	579.0	405.0	8,060
Dec	454.0	454.0	454.0	454.0	+ 11.0	575.0	420.0	411
Est vol 300; vol Wed 135; open int 10,336, +47.								
CRUDE OIL, Light Sweet (NYM) 1,000 bbls.; $ per bbl.								
Feb	25.61	26.20	24.90	25.48	– 1.01	36.80	18.15	48,993
Mar	25.00	25.50	24.40	24.87	– 1.03	35.40	18.40	34,939
Apr	24.20	24.65	23.85	24.26	– .95	33.90	18.03	24,560
May	23.40	23.85	23.20	23.56	– .74	32.70	18.03	17,410
June	22.80	23.25	22.70	22.96	– .56	31.50	18.30	13,066
July	22.50	22.50	22.10	22.45	– .45	30.40	18.31	9,490
Aug	22.00	22.10	21.90	22.07	– .40	29.50	18.70	9,282
Sept	21.82	21.82	21.51	21.80	– .37	28.72	19.10	6,255
Oct	21.35	21.65	21.35	21.63	– .34	28.40	19.60	7,067
Nov	21.40	21.45	21.25	21.51	– .31	28.10	19.10	6,090
Dec	21.50	21.50	21.10	21.41	– .30	27.70	19.45	15,538
Ja92	21.35	21.35	21.05	21.34	– .29	27.60	20.20	5,584
Feb	20.90	20.90	20.90	21.28	– .28	27.00	20.90	3,526
Mar	....	....	....	21.24	– .27	26.75	21.10	4,346
Apr	21.25	21.25	20.80	21.21	– .26	26.50	20.75	10,832
May	....	....	....	21.18	– .25	24.57	21.25	1,520
June	20.62	20.62	20.62	21.15	– .24	24.50	21.40	3,949
July	20.60	2069	20.60	21.13	– .22	22.11	20.60	1,912
Sept	....	....	....	21.07	– .18	24.00	23.00	725
Dec	21.25	21.25	21.25	21.00	– .10	24.00	21.25	1,383
Ju93	....	....	....	20.94	– .04	23.00	23.00	300
Est vol 101,657; vol Wed 72,369; open int 226,817, +7,344.								
HEATING OIL NO. 2 (NYM) 42,000 gal.; $ per gal.								
Feb	.7170	.7255	.6950	.7024	–.0306	1.0200	.5260	28,534
Mar	.6900	.6980	.6715	.6766	–.0302	.9650	.5070	11,503
Apr	.6575	.6630	.6450	.6513	–.0237	.9200	.4930	5,833
May	.6330	.6400	.6220	.6288	–.0172	.8850	.4840	2,555
June	.6140	.6175	.6050	.6113	–.0152	.8575	.4800	5,195
July	.6050	.6100	.5970	.6033	–.0147	.8500	.4855	4,823
Aug	.6110	.6110	.6000	.6063	–.0147	.8507	.524	963
Sept	.6200	.6200	.6095	.6163	–.0147	.8428	.609	358
Oct	.6290	.6290	.6240	.6243	–.0147	.8500	.6240	585
Nov	.6325	.6325	.6325	.6323	–.0147	.7800	.6325	412
Dec	.6405	.6405	.6405	.6403	–.0147	.8262	.6350	6,444
Ja92	.6430	.6430	.6430	.6430	–.0147	.8200	.6430	140
Est vol 29,773; vol Wed 22,882; open int 73,745, +1,301.								
GASOLINE, Unleaded (NYM) 42,000 gal.; $ per gal.								
Feb	.6600	.6715	.6490	.6592	–.0218	.9500	.4985	20,159
Mar	.6700	.6790	.6570	.6675	–.0214	.9500	.5065	11,454
Apr	.7105	.7170	.6980	.7070	–.0260	.9825	.5490	9,248
May	.6970	.7010	.6945	.7015	–.0245	.9700	.5545	4,451
June	.6915	.6915	.6825	.6850	–.0235	.9550	.5490	2,885
July	.6730	.6750	.6670	.6670	–.0225	.8270	.6670	1,188
Aug	.6500	.6530	.6500	.6510	–.0220	.9050	.5350	1,243
Sept	....	....	....	.6360	–.0220	.9025	.6480	1,371
Oct	....	....	....	.6120	–.0220	.8625	.6070	1,228
Dec	....	....	....	.5890	–.0220	.7525	.5950	153
Est vol 15,680; vol Wed 16,004; open int 53,928, +600.								
NATURAL GAS, (NYM) 10,000 MMBtu.; $ per MMBtu's								
Feb	1.770	1.800	1.750	1.782	– .050	2.755	1.750	1,565
Mar	1.550	1.600	1.550	1.597	+ .007	2.000	1.550	1,646
Apr	1.465	1.500	1.465	1.497	– .003	1.800	1.465	763
May	1.495	1.510	1.485	1.507	+ .002	1.780	1.485	932
June	1.510	1.535	1.505	1.540	– .010	1.800	1.505	950
July	1.545	1.560	1.545	1.570	– .015	1.810	1.545	546
Aug	1.570	1.585	1.570	1.600	+ .005	1.840	1.570	619
Sept	1.585	1.610	1.585	1.620	....	1.860	1.585	1,056
Oct	1.640	1.640	1.640	1.660	....	1.840	1.640	536
Nov	....	....	....	1.880	– .015	2.040	1.840	323
Dec	....	....	....	2.220	– .020	2.360	2.180	173
Est vol 796; vol Wed 966; open int 9,140, +76.								
BRENT CRUDE (IPE) 1,000 net bbls.; $ per bbl.								
Feb	26.50	26.60	24.60	24.89	– 1.55	36.62	19.38	35,767
Mar	25.70	25.80	23.40	24.17	– 1.15	33.15	19.35	11,500
Apr	24.60	24.65	23.35	23.50	– .90	32.66	21.00	2,931
May	22.76	22.76	22.76	22.60	– .70	27.00	22.00	1,743
June	....	....	....	22.10	– 1.15	24.60	23.00	180
Est vol 30,100; vol Wed 16,475; open int 52,146, +4,120.								
GAS OIL (IPE) 100 metric tons; $ per ton								
Jan	253.00	256.50	235.00	236.75	–21.75	325.00	150.75	16,388
Feb	241.00	244.00	235.00	225.75	–21.00	310.00	147.25	13,632
Mar	230.50	231.75	214.00	214.25	–19.25	298.50	140.00	4,647
Apr	218.50	219.00	204.00	204.00	–16.50	280.50	160.00	7,914
May	213.00	213.00	200.00	200.00	–15.00	278.50	190.00	1,982
June	212.00	212.00	198.00	198.00	–14.00	268.50	190.00	970
July	195.00	196.00	195.00	196.00	–15.00	237.00	194.00	1,198
Est vol 10,700; vol Wed 8,095; open int 46,861, +2,147.								

–WOOD–

	Open	High	Low	Settle	Change	Lifetime High	Lifetime Low	Open Interest
LUMBER (CME)–150,000 bd. ft.; $ per 1,000 bd. ft.								
Jan	171.50	171.50	169.00	169.60	– 2.60	207.00	151.60	691
Mar	169.50	170.60	168.10	169.20	– 1.00	207.00	156.50	853
May	171.00	172.70	169.80	171.70	– .40	207.90	159.10	349
Est vol 792; vol Wed 596; open int 1,937, –30.								

–OTHER COMMODITY FUTURES–

Settlement prices of selected contracts. Volume and open interest of all contract months.

Cattle-Live (MCE) 20,000 lb.; ¢ per lb.
Feb 77.45 +.37; Est. vol. 75; Open Int. 215
Corn (MCE) 1,000 bu.; cents per bu.
Mar 232¼ +½; Est. vol. 700; Open Int. 4,431
Gold-Kilo (CBT) 32.15 troy oz.; $ per troy oz.
Feb 388.90 –2.10; Est. vol. 100; Open Int. 511
Hogs-Live (MCE) 15,000 lb.; ¢ per lb.
Feb 48.55 +.47; Est. vol. 100; Open Int. 173
Propane (NYM) 42,000 gal.; ¢ per gal.
Feb 34.92 –2.01; Est. vol. 267; Open Int. 2,513
Rice-Rough (CRCE) 2000 cwt; $ per cwt
Mar 7.14 –.07; Est. vol. 125; Open Int. 2,570
Silver (MCE) 1,000 troy oz.; cents per troy oz.
Mar 426.7 +10.0; Est. vol. 5; Open Int. 551
Sorghum (KC) 5,000 bu.; cents per bu.
Mar 222¼ +1¼; Est. vol. 20; Open Int. 160
Soybeans (MCE) 1,000 bu.; cents per bu.
Mar 570¼ +3; Est. vol. 5,250; Open Int. 15,539
Soybean Meal (MCE) 20 tons; $ per ton
Mar 169.90 +2.20; Est. vol. 25; Open Int. 470
Wheat (MCE) 1,000 bu.; cents per bu.
Mar 259½ –4; Est. vol. 200; Open Int. 3,099

Source: The Wall Street Journal, *January 4, 1991, p. C12.*

FIGURE 13.1

Spot and Futures Prices and Open Interest for a September 19X2 Contract for Kansas City Wheat

During the time period when these contracts were in existence, the futures and spot prices of wheat fell. The figure also shows the initial rise and subsequent decline in the number of contracts.

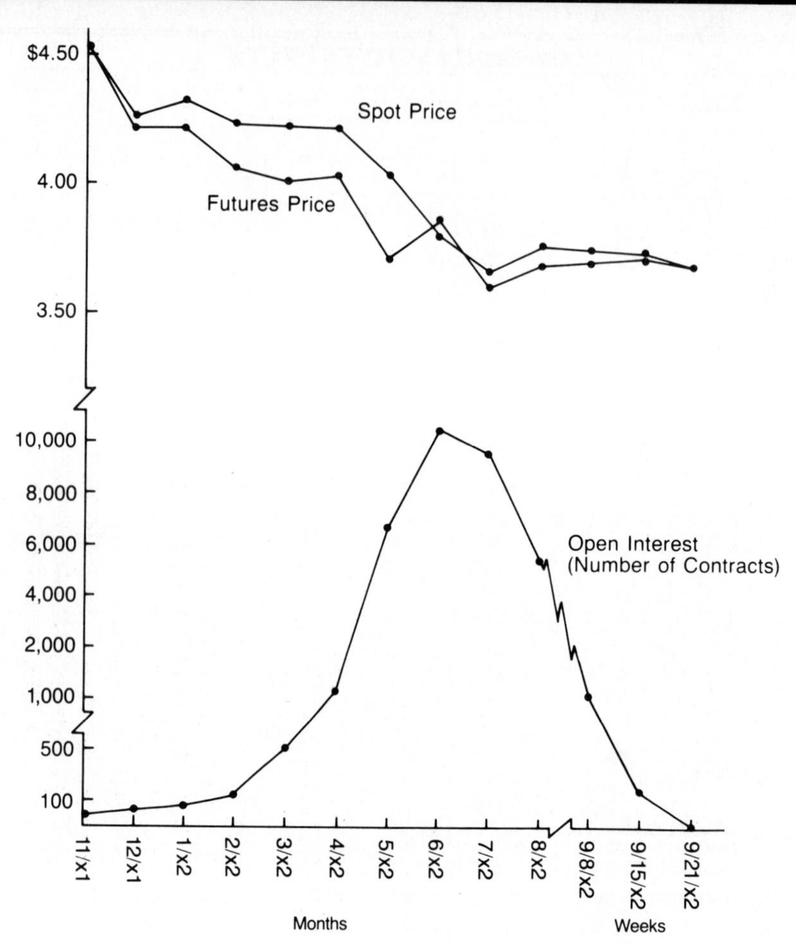

If investors had anticipated higher prices for wheat in the future, they would seek to enter contracts to buy (i.e., to accept the future delivery of wheat). This would drive up the futures price relative to the spot price. The value of the futures would then exceed the current price of the commodity.

The value of the futures contract can be worth only the value of the underlying commodity at the expiration date. Hence the spot and futures prices must converge with the approach of the expiration date. This pattern of price behavior is also illustrated in Figure 13.1. In March, April, and May there was a considerable differential between the two prices. However, in late September the futures and spot prices converged and erased the differential.

Leverage

Commodities are paid for on delivery. Thus, when an individual enters into a contract for future delivery, he or she does not pay for the commodity unless actual delivery is made. When the contract is made, the investor provides an amount of money, which is called **margin,** to guarantee the contract and protect the broker. This margin is not to be confused with the margin that is used in the purchase of stocks and bonds. In the trading of stocks and bonds, margin represents the investor's equity in the position, whereas margin for a commodity contract is a deposit to show the investor's good faith and to protect the broker against an adverse change in the price of the commodity.

Margin ▲
Good faith deposit used to secure a futures contract

In the stock market, the amount of margin that is required varies with the price of the security, but in the commodity markets the amount of margin does not vary with the dollar value of the transaction. Instead, each contract has a fixed minimum margin requirement. For example, the investor who makes a contract to buy cocoa must put up $1,000. These margin requirements are established by the commodity exchanges, but individual brokers may require more.

The margin requirements are only a small percentage of the value of the contract. For example, the $1,000 margin requirement for cocoa gives the owner of the contract to buy a claim on 10 metric tons of cocoa. If cocoa is selling for $1,400 a metric ton, the total value of the contract is $14,000. The margin requirement as a percent of the value of the contract is only 7.14 percent ($1,000/$14,000). This small amount of margin is one reason why a commodity contract offers so much potential leverage.

The potential leverage from speculating in commodity futures may be illustrated in a simple example. Consider a contract to buy wheat at $3.50 per bushel. Such a contract controls 5,000 bushels of wheat worth a total of $17,500 (5,000 × $3.50). If the investor owns this contract to buy and the margin requirement is $1,000, the investor must remit $1,000. An increase of only $0.20 per bushel in the price of the commodity produces an increase of $1,000 in the value of the contract. This $1,000 is simply the product of the price change ($0.20) and the number of units in the contract (5,000). The profit on the contract is $1,000.

What is the rate of return on the investment? With a margin of $1,000 the return is 100 percent, because the investor put up $1,000 and then earned an additional $1,000. An increase of less than 6 percent in the price of wheat produced a return on the speculator's money of 100 percent. Such a return is the result of leverage that comes from the small margin requirement and the large amount of the commodity controlled by the contract.

Leverage, of course, works both ways. In the previous example, if the price of the commodity declines by $0.10, the contract will be worth $17,000. A decline of only 2.9 percent in the price reduces the investor's margin from $1,000 to $500. To maintain the position, the investor must deposit additional margin with the broker. The broker's request for additional funds is referred to as a **margin call.** Failure to meet the margin call will result in the broker's closing the position. Should the investor default on the contract, the broker becomes responsible for the execution of the contract. The margin call thus protects the broker.

Margin call ▲
Request by the broker for an investor to place additional funds to restore the good faith deposit

Actually, there are two margin requirements. The first is the minimum initial deposit, and the second is the maintenance margin. The **maintenance margin** specifies when the investor must deposit additional funds with the broker to cover a decline in the value of a commodity contract. For example, the margin requirement for wheat is $1,000 and the maintenance margin is $750. If the investor owns a contract for the purchase of wheat and the value of the contract declines by $250 to the level of the maintenance margin ($750), the broker makes a margin call. This requires the investor to deposit an additional $250 into the account, which restores the initial $1,000 margin. This additional deposit protects the broker, since the value of the contract has declined and the investor has sustained a loss.

Maintenance margin ▲
Minimum level of funds in a margin account that triggers a margin call

Maintenance margin applies to both buyers and sellers. If, in the previous example, the price of wheat were to rise by $250, the speculators who had entered the contract to deliver wheat would see their margin decline from the initial deposit of $1,000 to $750. The broker would then make a margin call, which would require the short sellers to restore the $1,000 margin. Once again this protects the broker, since the value of the contract has risen and the short seller has sustained the loss.

These margin adjustments occur *daily.* After the market closes, the value of each account is totaled. In the jargon of futures trading, each account is *"marked to the market."* If the account does not meet the margin requirement, the broker issues a margin call that the individual must meet or the broker will close the position.

HEDGING

One of the prime reasons for the development of futures markets was the desire of producers to reduce the risk of loss through price fluctuations. The procedure for this reduction in risk is called **hedging,** which consists of taking opposite positions at the same time.[2] In effect, a hedger

Hedging ▲
Simultaneous purchase and sale designed to reduce risk of loss from price fluctuations

[2] Hedging cannot erase risk and may even increase it. For a discussion of how such an increase may occur, see Richard J. Teweles, Charles V. Harlow, and Herbert L. Stone, *The Commodity Futures Game—Who Wins? Who Loses? Why?* (New York: McGraw-Hill, 1974), pp. 35–43.

simultaneously takes the long and the short positions in a particular commodity.

Hedging is best explained by illustrations. In the first example, a wheat farmer expects to harvest a crop at a specified time. Since the costs of production are determined, the farmer knows the price that is necessary to earn a profit. Although the price that will be paid for wheat at harvest time is unknown, the current price of a contract for the future delivery of wheat is known. The farmer can then enter a contract to sell (i.e., to make future delivery). Such a contract is a hedged position, because the farmer takes a long position (the wheat in the ground) and a short position (the contract for future delivery).

Such a position reduces the farmer's risk of loss from a price decline. Suppose the cost to produce the wheat is $2.50 per bushel and September wheat is selling in June for $2.75. If the farmer sells wheat for September delivery, a $0.25 per bushel profit is assured, because the buyer of the contract agrees to pay $2.75 per bushel upon delivery in September. If the price of wheat declines to $2.50, the farmer is still assured $2.75. However, if the price of wheat rises to $3.10 in September, the farmer still gets only $2.75. The additional $0.35 gain goes to the owner of the contract for delivery who buys the wheat for $2.75 but can now sell it for $3.10.

Is this transaction unfair? Remember that the farmer wanted protection against a decline in the price of wheat. If the price had declined to $2.40 and the farmer had not hedged, the farmer would have suffered a loss of $0.10 (the $2.40 price minus the $2.50 cost) per bushel. To obtain protection from this risk of loss, the farmer accepted the modest profit of $0.25 per bushel and relinquished the possibility of a larger profit. The speculator who entered the contract to buy the wheat bore the risk of loss from a price decline and received the reward from a price increase.

Users of wheat hedge in the opposite direction. A flour producer desires to know the future cost of wheat in order to plan production levels and the prices that will be charged to distributors. However, the spot price of wheat need not hold into the future. This producer then enters a contract to accept future delivery and thereby hedges the position. This is hedging because the producer has a long position (the contract to accept the future delivery of wheat) and a short position (the future production of flour, which requires the future delivery of wheat).

If the flour producer enters a contract in June for the delivery of wheat in September at $2.75 per bushel, the future cost of the grain becomes known. The producer cannot be hurt by a price increase in wheat from $2.75 to $3.10, because the contract is for delivery at $2.75. However, the producer has forgone the chance of profit from a decline in the price of wheat from $2.75 to $2.40 per bushel.

Instead, the possibility of profit from a decline in the price of wheat rests with the speculator who entered the contract to deliver wheat. If the price of wheat were to decline, the speculator could buy the wheat in September at the lower price, deliver it, and collect the $2.75 that is specified in the contract. However, this speculator would suffer a loss if the price of September wheat rose over $2.75. Then the cost would exceed the delivery price specified in the contract.

These two examples illustrate why growers and producers hedge. They often take the opposite side of hedge positions. If all growers and producers were to agree on prices for future delivery, there would be no need for speculators; but this is not the case. Speculators enter contracts when there is an excess or an insufficient supply. If the farmer in the preceding example could not find a producer to enter into the contract to accept the future delivery of wheat, a speculator would make the contract and accept the risk of a price decline. If the producer could not find a farmer to supply a contract for the future delivery of wheat, the speculator would make the contract to sell (i.e., to deliver) and accept the risk of a price increase.

Of course, farmers, producers, and speculators are simultaneously entering contracts. No one knows who buys and who sells at a specific moment. However, if there is an excess or a shortage of one type of contract, the futures price of the commodity changes, which induces a certain behavior. For example, if September wheat is quoted at $2.75 per bushel, but no one is willing to buy at that price, the price declines. This induces some potential sellers to withdraw from the market and some potential buyers to enter the market. By this process, an imbalance of supply and demand for contracts for a particular delivery date is erased. It is the interaction of the hedgers and the speculators that establishes the price of each contract.

FINANCIAL FUTURES

Financial futures ▲
Contract for the future delivery of a financial asset

Currency futures ▲
Contract for the future delivery of a currency

In the previous discussion, futures contracts meant commodity contracts for the delivery of physical goods. However, there are also **financial futures,** which are contracts for the future delivery of a security such as a Treasury bill, and **currency futures,** which are contracts for the future delivery of currencies (e.g., the British pound or the German mark). The market for financial futures, like the market for commodity futures, has two participants: the speculators and the hedgers. It is the interaction of their demands for and supplies of these contracts that determines the price of a given financial futures contract.

While any speculator may participate in any of the financial or currency futures markets, the hedgers differ from the speculators because they also deal in the security or the currency itself. The hedgers in currency futures are primarily multinational firms that make and receive payments in foreign moneys. Since the value of these currencies can change, the value of payments that the firms must make or receive can change. Firms thus establish hedge positions in order to lock in the price of the currency and thereby avoid the risk associated with fluctuations in the value of one currency relative to another.

Financial futures are used in hedge positions by financial institutions and borrowers to lock in yields. As interest rates and bond prices change, the yields from lending and the cost of borrowing are altered. To reduce the risk of loss from fluctuations in interest rates, borrowers and lenders may establish hedge positions to lock in a particular interest rate.

Speculators, of course, are not seeking to reduce risk but to reap large returns for taking risks. The speculators are bearing the risk that the hedgers are seeking to avoid. The speculators seek to anticipate correctly changes in the value of currencies and the direction of changes in interest rates and security prices and to take positions that will yield profits. The return the speculators earn (if successful) is magnified because of the leverage offered by the small margin requirements necessary to establish the positions.

How financial futures may produce profits for speculators may be illustrated with an example that employs the futures contract for the delivery of U.S. Treasury bonds. Suppose a speculator expects interest rates to fall and bond prices to rise. This individual would enter into a contract to accept (i.e., to buy) and take delivery of Treasury bonds in the future (i.e., the *long* position). If interest rates do fall and bond prices rise, the value of this contract increases, because the speculator has the contract for the delivery of bonds at a lower price (i.e., higher yield). If, however, interest rates rise, bond prices fall, and the value of this contract declines. The decline in the value of the contract inflicts a loss on the speculator who accepted the contract when yields were lower.

If the speculator expects interest rates to rise, that individual enters into a contract to sell and to make future delivery of Treasury bonds (i.e., establishes a *short* position). If interest rates do rise and the value of the bond declines, the value of this contract must decline, but the speculator earns a profit. This short seller can buy the bonds at a lower price and deliver them at the price specified in the contract. Of course, if this speculator is wrong and interest rates fall, the value of the bonds increases, which inflicts a loss on the speculator who must now pay more to buy the bonds to cover the contract.

While speculators use financial futures as a means to take advantage of fluctuations in interest rates and security prices, financial managers or portfolio managers may use these futures to reduce the risk of loss from the same price fluctuations. For example, suppose a firm has decided to invest in plant and equipment. The decision to make this investment used the capital budgeting techniques that will be presented in Chapter 23. However, consummating the investment may take time, during which the cost of capital may change as interest rates and security prices fluctuate.

If the cost of capital falls, the investment may become even more profitable. However, if interest rates rise and security prices fall (i.e., the cost of capital rises), an investment that was previously judged to be profitable may now be unprofitable.

It is the risk associated with fluctuations in interest rates and security prices that the financial manager seeks to reduce. One means to avoid this risk is to acquire the funds to finance the investment when the investment decision is made. But this may not be possible, since raising funds may require time. The financial manager then may use financial futures as a means to reduce the risk of loss from an increase in the cost of capital. Of course, hedging reduces the possibility of gain should the cost of capital fall. However, the emphasis is on risk reduction and not on increased profitability through speculating on changes in the cost of funds.

The reduction in risk is achieved by the financial manager entering a contract to make future delivery (i.e., taking a short position). The impact of this hedge may be seen in the following illustration. In six months a firm plans to issue $1 million of 20-year bonds. If interest rates increase, the firm will have to pay an additional $10,000 annually for every 1 percent increase in the rate of interest. To hedge against the potential loss if interest rates rise, the financial manager enters a contract to deliver Treasury bonds.[3] If interest rates do rise, the value of these contracts declines. The financial manager may then close out the position in these contracts at a profit, which will help offset the loss resulting from the increased cost of funds.

The previous illustration considered the borrower's reduction of loss through hedging. Lenders also bear risk associated with fluctuations in interest rates, but the risk is from lower, not higher, interest rates. For example, suppose a financial institution agrees to make a loan in six months at the then current rate of interest. That rate could be higher or lower than the now current rate. If interest rates rise, the lender will earn a higher return on the loan; if interest rates fall, the yield will be lower. Lenders can protect themselves from a decline in interest rates by hedging through the use of financial futures.

Unlike borrowers, who enter futures contracts to sell (i.e., to deliver) to hedge their positions, lenders enter futures contracts to buy (i.e., to accept delivery). If interest rates do fall, the value of the contracts will increase. This increase in the value of the contract will partially offset the interest lost as a result of lower rates. Of course, the lender will have forgone the possibility of earning a higher yield if interest rates were to in-

---

[3] To determine the exact number of contracts that should be sold to offset the potential loss, see Nancy H. Rothstein, *The Handbook of Financial Futures* (New York: McGraw-Hill, 1984), pp. 262–264.

The Job Mart

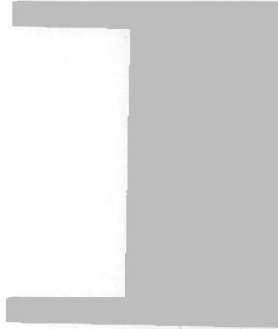

Risk Manager—Hedger

■ Job Description: Reduce the risk exposure that results from fluctuating commodity prices, exchange rates, and interest rates by constructing hedge positions with options or futures contracts. ■ Job Requirements: Thorough knowledge of options, futures markets, and hedging techniques. The required background in financial theory includes portfolio management, option valuation, and pricing models. ■ Characteristics: This is a high-pressure position, as the hedger must continually be aware of events affecting the demand and supply of commodities. The individual must work well under stress and be able to make rapid decisions as dictated by changes in market conditions.

---

crease. Higher interest rates would reduce the value of the contract and thus offset the higher rate earned on the loan.

STOCK MARKET INDEX FUTURES

Stock index futures ▲ Contract based on an index of security prices

During 1982, a new type of futures contract based on an index of the stock market (e.g., the Value Line stock index, the Standard & Poor's 500 stock index, or the New York Stock Exchange Composite Index) started trading. These **stock index futures** contracts offer speculators and hedgers opportunities for profit or risk reduction that are not possible through the purchase of individual securities. For example, the NYSE Composite Index futures contracts have a value that is $500 times the value of the NYSE Index. Thus, if the NYSE Index is 70, the contract is worth $35,000. By entering a contract to buy (i.e., by establishing a long position), the holder profits if the market rises. If the NYSE Index rose to 75, the value of the contract would increase to $37,500. The investor would then earn a profit of $2,500. Of course, if the NYSE Index declined, the buyer would experience a loss.

The sellers of these contracts also participate in the fluctuations of the market, but their positions are the opposite of the buyers (i.e., they are short). If the value of the NYSE Index fell from 70 to 65, the value of the contract would decline from $35,000 to $32,500, and the short seller would earn a $2,500 profit. Of course, if the market rose, the short seller would suffer a loss. Obviously, if the individual anticipates a rising market, that investor should take a long position in a futures contract. Conversely, if the investor expects the market to fall, he or she should take a short position.

These contracts may also be used by professional money managers who are not speculating on price movements but who seek to hedge against adverse price movements. For example, suppose a portfolio manager has a well-diversified portfolio of stocks as part of a firm's pension plan. If the market rises, the value of this portfolio appreciates. However, there would be the risk of loss if the market were to decline. The portfolio manager can reduce this risk by entering a NYSE Index futures contract to sell at the specified price (i.e., taking a short position). If the market declines, the losses experienced by the portfolio will at least be partially offset by the appreciation in the value of the short position in the futures contract.

NYSE Index futures contracts are similar to other futures contracts. The buyers and sellers must make good faith deposits (i.e., margin payments). Since the amount of this margin is modest (only $3,500 per contract), these contracts offer considerable leverage. If stock prices move against the investor and the investor's equity in the position declines, the individual will have to place additional funds in the account to support the contract. Since there is an active market in the contracts, the investor may close a position at any time by taking the opposite position. Thus if the investor has a contract to buy, that long position is closed by a contract to sell. If the investor has a contract to sell (i.e., to deliver), that short position is closed by a contract to buy (i.e., to accept delivery).

There is one important difference between stock market futures and other futures contracts. Settlement at the expiration or maturity of the contract occurs in cash. There is no physical delivery of securities as could occur with a commodity futures contract to buy or sell wheat or corn. Instead, gains and losses are totaled and are added to or subtracted from the participants' accounts. The long and the short positions are then closed.

OPTIONS

An option is the right to do something. When the term "option" is used with regard to securities, it means the right to buy or sell stock. The word "right" is extremely important; the owner of an option is *not obligated* to do anything. The holder of an option to buy stock does not have to buy the stock, nor does the holder of a right to sell stock have to sell the stock. This makes options considerably different from futures contracts. The individual who acquires a futures contract to buy must either close the position or meet the obligation.

The rights to buy and sell stock are not the only options in finance. For example, many bonds are callable. A call feature is an example of an option because the firm that issued the bonds has the right to call the bonds and retire them prior to maturity. Many business transactions involve options. For example, a landowner may sell to a developer an option to buy the land. The developer does not have to buy the land but has the right to purchase it.

Options to buy stock are called **warrants** if they are issued by firms and **calls** if they are issued by individuals.[4] A warrant or a call may be defined as the right to buy stock at a specified price within a specified time period. In the jargon of option trading, the market price of the option is often referred to as the **premium.** The price at which the holder may buy the shares is called the **strike price** or "**exercise price,**" and the day on which the option expires is called the **expiration date.** Options to sell stock are called **puts.** A put may be defined as the right to sell stock at a specified price within a specified time period.

Options are an extremely involved topic, and the discussion of them in this chapter can only skim the surface. Emphasis will be placed on the potential leverage they offer to investors. Since the volume of transactions is greatest for warrants and calls, the discussion emphasizes them.

Warrant ▲
Option (issued by a corporation) to buy stock at a specified price within a specified time period

Call ▲
Option (issued by an individual) to buy stock at a specified price within a specified time period

Premium ▲
Market price of an option

Strike price (Exercise price) ▲
Price at which the option holder may buy the underlying stock

Expiration date ▲
Date by which an option must be exercised

Put ▲
Option to sell stock at a specified price within a specified time period

Intrinsic value ▲
Value of an option as stock

THE INTRINSIC VALUE OF A WARRANT OR CALL

What a warrant or call is worth in terms of the underlying stock (i.e., the stock that the investor has the option to buy) is called the **intrinsic value** of the option. For an option to buy stock, this intrinsic value is the difference between the price of the stock and the per share exercise price (strike price) of the option. If an option is the right to buy stock at $30 a share and the stock is selling for $40, then the intrinsic value is $10 ($40 − $30 = $10).

If the stock is selling for a price greater than the per share exercise price, the option has positive intrinsic value. This may be referred to as the option's being "in the money." If the common stock is selling for a price that equals the strike price, the option is "at the money." And if the price of the stock is less than the strike price, the option has no intrinsic value. The option is "out of the money." No one would purchase and exercise an option to buy stock when the stock could be purchased for a price that is less than the strike price of the option. However, as is explained subsequently, such options may still trade.

The relationships among the price of a stock, the strike price (i.e., the exercise price of an option), and the option's intrinsic value are illus-

---

[4] A firm may also issue an option called a "right." Rights are issued to current stockholders when the firm is offering them the privilege of subscribing to a new issue of stock. By exercising the right and buying the new shares, current stockholders maintain their proportionate ownership in the corporation. Rights have a very short duration, such as four weeks, while a warrant may exist for many years.

EXHIBIT 13.3

The Price of a Stock and the Intrinsic Value of an Option to Buy the Stock at $50 per Share

The intrinsic value of an option to buy rises as the price of the underlying stock rises.

Price of the Stock	Per Share Strike Price of the Option	Intrinsic Value of the Option
$ 0	$50	$ 0
10	50	0
20	50	0
30	50	0
40	50	0
50	50	0
60	50	10
70	50	20
80	50	30
90	50	40

trated in Exhibit 13.3 and Figure 13.2. In these examples, the option is the right to buy the stock at $50 per share. The first column of the exhibit (the horizontal axis on the graph) gives various prices of the stock. The second column presents the strike price of the option ($50), and the last column gives the intrinsic value of the option (i.e., the difference between the values in the first and second columns). The values in this third column are illustrated in the figure by line ABC, which shows the relationship between the price of the stock and the option's intrinsic value. It is evident from both the exhibit and the figure that as the price of the stock rises, the intrinsic value of the option also rises. However, for all stock prices below $50, the intrinsic value is zero, since security prices are never negative. Only after the stock's price has risen above $50 does the option's intrinsic value become positive.

The intrinsic value is one of the most important aspects of analyzing options. First, the market price of an option must approach its intrinsic value as the option approaches its expiration date. On the day that the option is to expire, the market price can be only what the option is worth as stock. It can be worth only the difference between the market price of the stock and the exercise price of the option. This fact means that the investor may use the intrinsic value of an option as an indication of the option's future price, for the investor knows that the market price of the option must approach its intrinsic value as the option approaches expiration.

Second, the intrinsic value of an option sets the minimum price that the security will command. Suppose the price of a stock is $60 and the strike price of the option is $50. The option's intrinsic value is $10 ($60 − $50). If the current market price of the option were $6, an investor could buy the option and exercise it to acquire stock worth $60. The investor could then sell the stock and make a $4 profit.

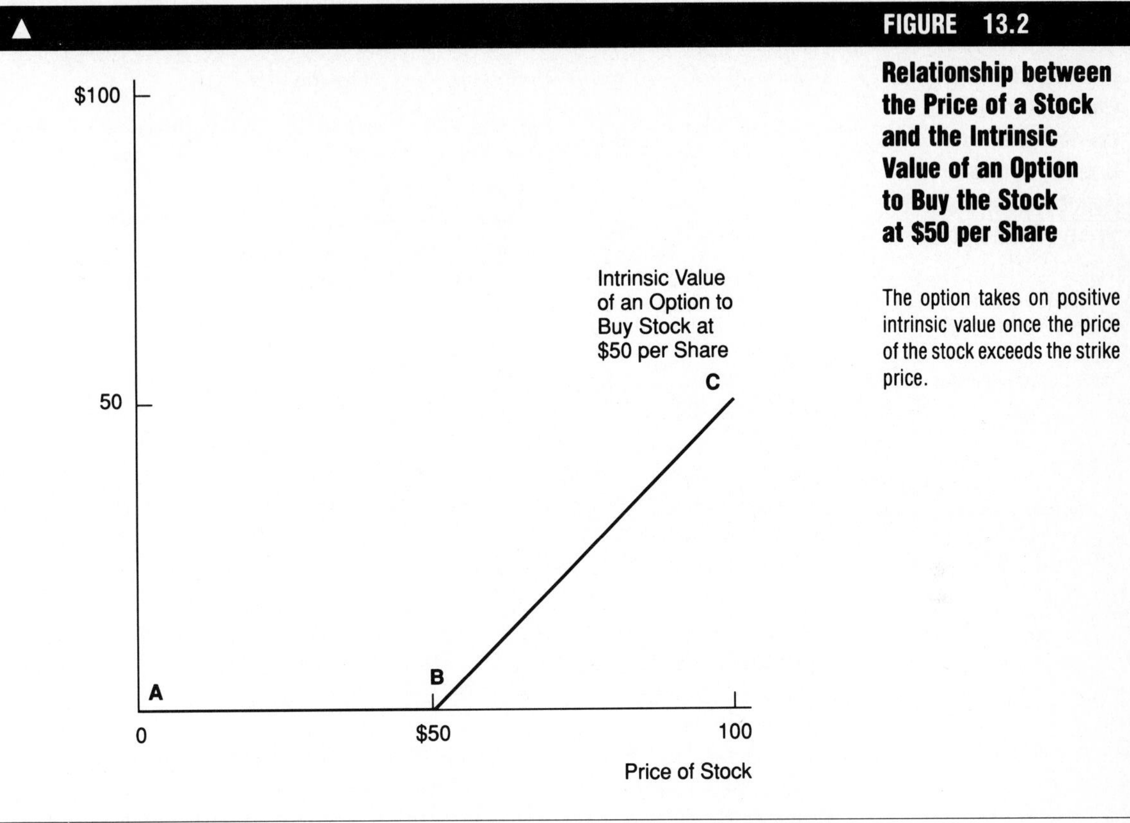

FIGURE 13.2

Relationship between the Price of a Stock and the Intrinsic Value of an Option to Buy the Stock at $50 per Share

The option takes on positive intrinsic value once the price of the stock exceeds the strike price.

The act of buying the option and selling the stock will tend to increase the price of the option and decrease the price of the stock. However, as long as the option sells for less than its intrinsic value, investors will continue to buy the option and sell the stock; thus the price of the former will continue to rise while the price of the latter will fall. Such price changes will continue until the option sells for at least its intrinsic value. The intrinsic value thus sets the minimum price that an option will command, for as soon as an option sells for less than its intrinsic value, forces will be set in motion to assure that the option's market price returns to the option's intrinsic value.

LEVERAGE

While an option is a "right," it represents none of the legal rights of ownership. An option does, however, offer investors one very important advantage: leverage. The potential return on an investment in an option

EXHIBIT 13.4

Relationship between the Price of Stock, the Value of an Option, and the Hypothetical Market Price of the Option

The market price of an option exceeds the intrinsic value because the option commands a time premium.

	Option		
Price of the Common Stock	Per Share Strike Price	Intrinsic Value	Hypothetical Market Price
$ 10	$50	$ 0	$ 1
20	50	0	5
30	50	0	9
40	50	0	13
50	50	0	18
60	50	10	22
70	50	20	27
80	50	30	34
90	50	40	42
100	50	50	51

may exceed the potential return on an investment in the underlying stock. Like the use of margin, this magnification of the potential return is an example of financial leverage. If options did not offer such leverage, there would be no reason for investors to purchase them in preference to the stock.

Exhibit 13.4, which illustrates the relationship between the price of a stock and an option's intrinsic value, also demonstrates the potential leverage that options offer. For example, if the price of the stock rose from $60 to $70, the intrinsic value of the option would rise from $10 to $20. The percentage increase in the price of the stock is 16.67 percent ([$70 − $60] ÷ $60), whereas the percentage increase in the intrinsic value of the option is 100 percent ([$20 − $10] ÷ $10). The percentage increase in the intrinsic value of the option exceeds the percentage increase in the price of the stock. If the investor purchased the option for its intrinsic value and the price of the stock then rose, the return on the investment in the option would exceed the return on the investment in the stock.

Leverage, however, works in both directions. Although it may increase the investor's potential return, it may also increase the potential loss if the price of the stock declines. For example, if the price of the stock in Exhibit 13.4 fell from $70 to $60 for a 14.3 percent decline, the intrinsic value of the option would fall from $20 to $10 for a 50 percent decline. As with any investment, the investor must decide if the increase in the potential return offered by leverage is worth the increased risk.

If an option offers a greater potential return than does the stock, investors may prefer to buy the option. In an effort to purchase the option, investors will bid up its price, so the market price will exceed the option's intrinsic value. Since the market price of an option is frequently

FIGURE 13.3

Relationships among the Price of the Stock, the Intrinsic Value of the Option, and the Hypothetical Price of the Option

The option's time premium is the difference between the option's price and its intrinsic value.

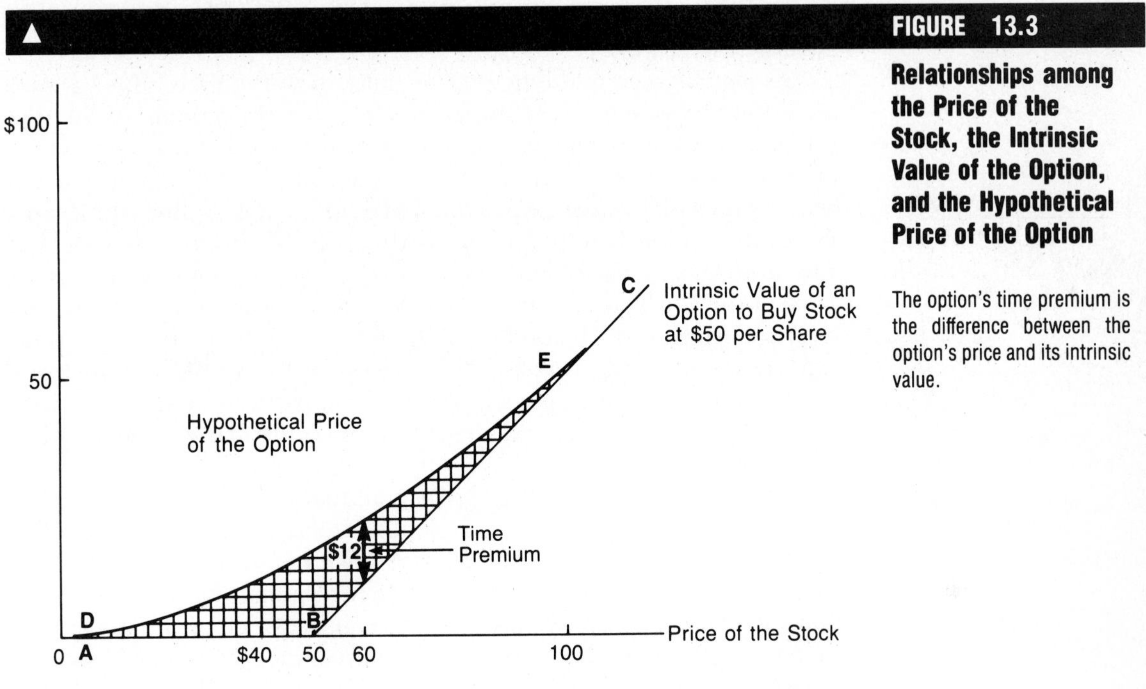

referred to as the "premium," the extent to which this price exceeds the option's intrinsic value is referred to as the **time premium** or time value. Investors are willing to pay this time premium for the potential leverage the option offers. This time premium, however, reduces the potential return and increases the potential loss.

Time premium Amount by which an option's price exceeds its intrinsic value

The time premium is also illustrated in Exhibit 13.4, which adds to Exhibit 13.3 a hypothetical set of option prices in column 4. The hypothetical market prices are greater than the intrinsic values of the option because investors have bid up the prices. To purchase the option, an investor must pay the market price and not the intrinsic value. Thus, in this example when the market price of the stock is $60 and the intrinsic value of the option is $10, the market price of the option is $22. The investor must pay $22 to purchase the option, which is $12 more than the option's intrinsic value.

The relationships in Exhibit 13.4 among the price of the stock, the intrinsic value of the option, and the hypothetical price of the option are illustrated in Figure 13.3. The time premium paid for the option over its intrinsic value is easily seen in the graph, for it is the shaded area that is the difference between the line representing the market price of the option (line DE) and the line representing its intrinsic value (line ABC). Thus, when the prices of the stock and option are $60 and $22, respectively, the time premium is $12 (the price of the option, $22, minus its intrinsic value, $10).

As may be seen in the figure, the amount of the time value varies at the different price levels of the stock. However, the amount of the time premium declines as the price of the stock rises above the option's strike price. Once the price of the stock has risen considerably, the option may command virtually no time premium over its intrinsic value. At $100 per share, the option is selling at approximately its intrinsic value of $50. The primary reason for this decline in the time premium is that as the price of the stock and the intrinsic value of the option rise, the potential leverage is reduced. In addition, at higher prices the potential price decline in the option is greater if the price of the stock falls. For these reasons investors become less willing to bid up the price of the option as the price of the stock rises, and hence the amount of the time premium diminishes.

The time premium decreases the potential leverage and return from investing in options. If, for example, this stock's price rose from $60 to $70 for a 16.7 percent gain, the option's price would rise from $22 to $27 for a 22.7 percent gain. The percentage increase in the price of the option still exceeds the percentage increase in the price of the stock; however, the difference between the two percentage increases is smaller, since the option sells for more than its intrinsic value. The time premium has substantially reduced the potential leverage that the option offers investors.

Investors who are considering purchasing options should ask themselves what price increase they can expect in the option if the price of the underlying stock should rise. For the option to be attractive, its anticipated percentage increase in price must exceed the anticipated percentage increase in the price of the stock. The option must offer the investor leverage to justify the additional risk. Obviously, an investor should not purchase the option if the stock's price is expected to appreciate in value more rapidly than the option's price. The previous example illustrates that the time premium paid for an option may substantially decrease the potential leverage. Thus, recognition of the time premium that an option commands over its intrinsic value is one of the most important considerations in the selection of an option for investment.

WARRANTS

While the preceding discussion covered options in general, the next two sections are devoted to specific options. The following section will discuss call options; this section briefly covers warrants.

Earlier a warrant was defined as an option issued by a firm to buy its stock at a specified price within a specified time period. This definition encompasses the essentials that apply to all warrants, but there can be subtle differences among warrants. For example, the specified exercise price of some warrants rises at predetermined intervals (e.g., $5 every five years), or the firm may have the right to extend the expiration date of the warrant. A warrant issued by Navistar, for example, offers the right to purchase one share of Navistar stock at $5 per share through December 15, 1993. If this warrant is not exercised by December 15, 1993, it will expire and become worthless. Thus, unlike the firm's common stock, which is perpetual (i.e., continues in existence until the company is liquidated or merged into another company), a warrant has a finite life.

Warrants are usually issued by firms in conjunction with other financing. They are attached to other securities, such as debentures or preferred stock, and are a sweetener to induce investors to purchase the securities. For example, in July 1978, Chrysler Corporation issued preferred stock with warrants attached. The warrants were an added inducement to purchase the stock.

When a warrant is exercised, the firm issues new stock and receives the proceeds. For this reason, most warrants usually have a finite life. The expiration date ultimately forces the holder to exercise the option if the strike price is less than the current market price of the stock. However, if the strike price exceeds the stock's price at expiration (i.e., if the warrant has no intrinsic value), the warrant will not be exercised and will expire. After the expiration date, the warrant is worthless. This was the case with the Gulf & Western warrant. The warrant was not exercised because it had no intrinsic value as an option. On the day it expired the price of the stock was $11, but the exercise price of the warrant was $19.37. No one would exercise the warrant to buy stock at $19.37 when the stock could be purchased for $11 on the New York Stock Exchange.

Exhibit 13.5 presents selected warrants and their strike price, market price, and intrinsic value, along with the market price of the stock, the expiration date of the warrants, and the time premium paid for each warrant. As may be seen in the exhibit, all of the warrants sell for a time premium (i.e., the market price exceeds the intrinsic value). Four of these warrants have strike prices that exceed the price of the stock. These warrants have no intrinsic value.

As is evident in the last column, there is variation in the time premiums, which range from only $5/16 for the Hasbro warrant to $9 1/4 for the British Petroleum warrant. What accounts for this variation? Obviously, as the warrant approaches expiration, its market price will approach the option's intrinsic value. On the expiration date, the warrant cannot command a price greater than its true value. Thus, as the warrant nears expiration, it will sell for a lower time premium. While the

EXHIBIT 13.5

Terms and Time Premiums Paid for Selected Warrants as of December 1, 1990

Many options have no intrinsic value. Unless the prices of the stocks rise, these options will become worthless.

Company	Price of the Stock	Per Share Strike Price	Expiration Date	Market Price	Intrinsic Value	Time Premium
British Petroleum	\$80¼	\$80.00	1-31-93	\$9½	\$¼	\$9¼
Hasbro	15⅜	28.38	7-12-94	5/16	0	5/16
Manville Corp.	5	9.40	6-05-96	¾	0	¾
Nabors Industries	5⅜	5.50	8-28-93	2	0	2
Safeway Inc.	12½	13.51	11-24-96	2½	0	2½

Source: Standard and Poor's Stock Guide, *December 1990.*

time to the expiration date of the option is an important determinant of the observed differences in time premiums, cash dividends and the volatility of the common stock also affect the amount of the time premium.

Warrants of companies that pay cash dividends tend to sell for lower time premiums. There may be two explanations for this relationship. Companies that do not distribute earnings but retain them will have more funds available for investments. By retaining and reinvesting their earnings, the companies may grow more rapidly. This growth may be reflected in the price of their stock, and hence the potential gain in the price of the warrant may be greater if the firm retains its earnings and does not pay a dividend. A second explanation is that if the company pays a cash dividend, the holder of the warrant does not receive the cash payment. The warrant will be less attractive relative to the common stock, for the owner of the warrant must forgo the dividend. Therefore, investors will not be as willing to pay as much for the warrant, and it will sell for a lower time premium.

A third factor that influences the time premium paid for a warrant is the volatility of the price of the common stock. If the stock's price fluctuates substantially, the warrant may be more attractive and hence may command a higher time premium. Since the price of the warrant follows the price of the common stock, fluctuations in the price of the stock will be reflected in the warrant's price. The more volatile the price of the stock, the more opportunity the warrant offers speculators. Thus, the warrants of volatile common stocks may be more attractive (especially to speculators), and hence the time premium commanded by these warrants will tend to be greater than that commanded by warrants of less volatile stocks.

CALL OPTIONS

Although warrants were a popular speculative option during the 1970s, their popularity has declined with the development of organized markets in call options. As was explained earlier, a call option is the right to buy a specified number of shares (usually 100) at a specified price (the strike price) within a specified time period. Calls are similar to warrants, but they have several distinguishing features. While warrants are issued by firms, individuals may issue call options. The process of creating and issuing a call is often referred to as "writing." The ability of the individual investor to write call options is very important, for it means the investor can be either a buyer *or* a writer. Because calls enable individuals to write options, they offer opportunities for profit that are not available with warrants.

A second distinction between warrants and calls is the duration of the option. When warrants are issued, their expiration is fixed, but the expiration date is generally several years into the future. Call options have a relatively short duration—three, six, or nine months. (In 1990, call options with lives up to two years on selected companies came into being and started to trade.)

The third distinguishing feature of calls occurs when they are exercised. When a warrant is exercised, the firm issues new stock. The writer of a call, however, cannot create the stock but must either purchase it on the open market or surrender the stock from personal holdings. When the stock is supplied to the investor who is exercising the call, the option writer, and not the firm, receives the proceeds. The development of the **Chicago Board Options Exchange (CBOE)** has been the primary reason why calls have replaced warrants in popularity. The CBOE is an organized secondary market in put and call options. An investor who purchases a call through the CBOE knows that there is a ready market in which the option may be sold. This ability to buy and sell options in a secondary market has increased investor interest in put and call options. For the first time, an investor can readily open and close positions in these options.

Chicago Board Options Exchange (CBOE) ▲
First organized secondary market in options

There are several features of the CBOE that are conducive to the development of secondary markets for the calls. First, transactions are continuously reported, and daily summaries of transactions appear in leading newspapers. Exhibit 13.6 presents a clipping of selected calls and puts traded on the CBOE on January 4, 1991, as reported in *The Wall Street Journal.* As may be seen from the exhibit, there are several options traded on each of the securities. The company and its closing stock price are given on the left. Then the "strike" price (exercise price) is given. For Dow Chemical the strike prices of the options are 40, 45, 50, and 55. The next three columns are devoted to call options and the last three col-

EXHIBIT 13.6

Listing of Selected Options Traded on the CBOE

The closing prices of puts and calls are reported daily in the financial press.

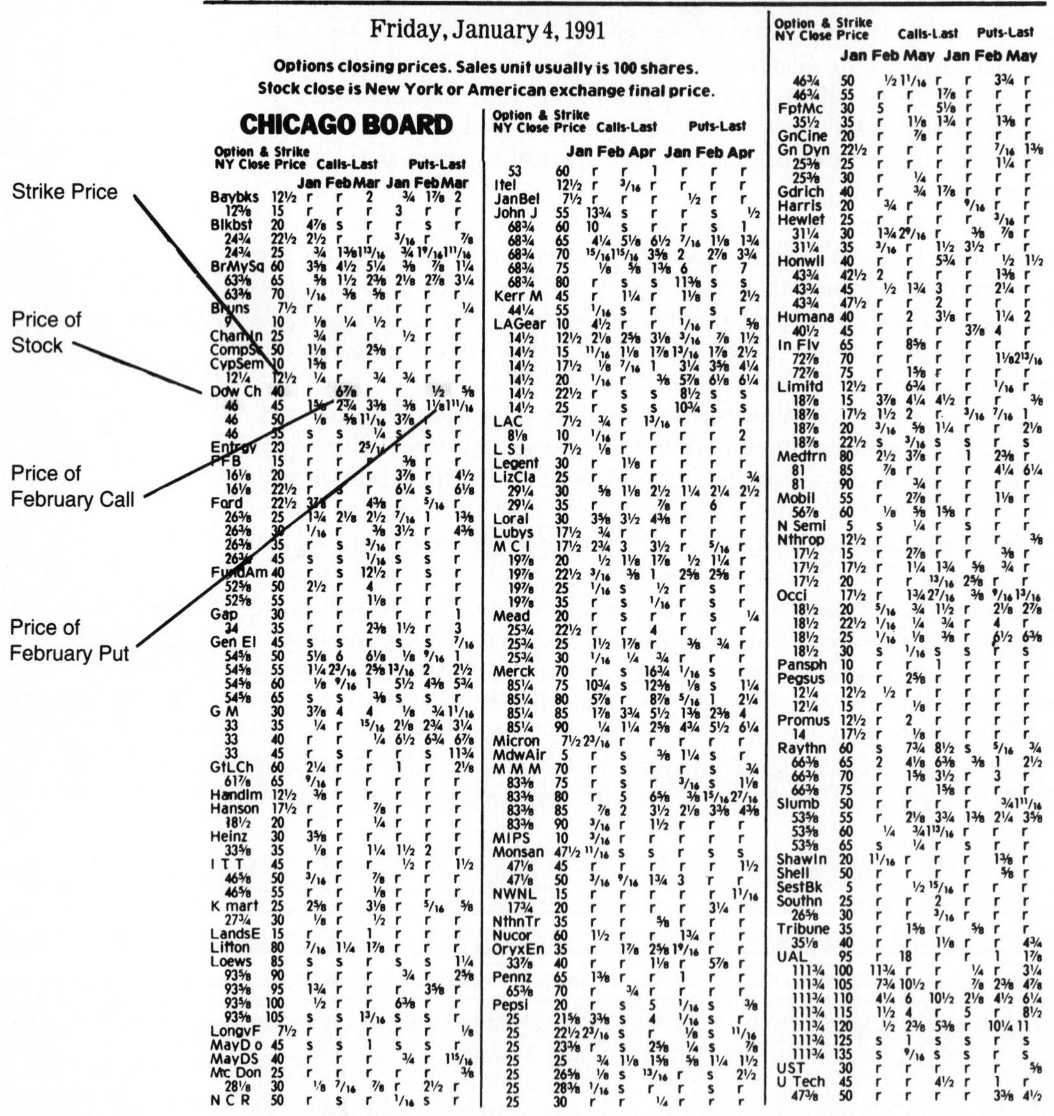

LISTED OPTIONS QUOTATIONS

Friday, January 4, 1991

Options closing prices. Sales unit usually is 100 shares.
Stock close is New York or American exchange final price.

CHICAGO BOARD

Option & NY Close	Strike Price	Calls-Last Jan	Calls-Last Feb	Calls-Last Mar	Puts-Last Jan	Puts-Last Feb	Puts-Last Mar
Baybks	12 1/2	r	r	2	3/4	1 7/8	2
12 3/8	15	r	r	r	3	r	r
Blkbst	20	4 7/8	s	r	r	s	r
24 3/4	22 1/2	2 1/2	r	r	3/16	r	7/8
24 3/4	25	3/4	1 3/8	1 13/16	3/4	1 9/16	1 11/16
BrMySq	60	3 5/8	4 1/2	5 1/4	3/8	7/8	1 1/4
63 3/8	65	5/8	1 1/2	2 3/8	2 1/8	2 7/8	3 1/4
63 3/8	70	1/16	3/8	5/8	r	r	r
Bruns	7 1/2	r	r	r	r	r	1/4
9	10	1/8	1/4	1/2	r	r	r
ChamIn	25	3/4	r	r	1/2	r	r
CompSc	50	1 1/8	r	2 5/8	r	r	r
CypSem	10	1 5/8	r	r	r	r	r
12 1/4	12 1/2	1/4	r	3/4	3/4	r	r
Dow Ch	40	r	6 7/8	r	r	1/2	5/8
46	45	1 5/8	2 3/4	3 3/8	3/8	1 1/8	1 11/16
46	50	1/8	5/8	1 1/16	3 7/8	r	r
46	55	s	s	1/4	s	s	r
Entrgy	20	r	r	2 5/16	r	r	r
FFB	15	r	r	r	3/8	r	r
16 1/8	20	r	r	r	3 7/8	r	4 1/2
16 1/8	22 1/2	r	s	r	6 1/4	s	6 1/8
Ford	22 1/2	3 7/8	r	4 3/8	r	5/16	r
26 3/8	25	1 3/4	2 1/8	2 1/2	7/16	1	1 3/8
26 3/8	30	1/16	r	3/8	3 1/2	r	4 3/8
26 3/8	35	r	s	3/16	r	s	r
26 3/8	45	s	s	1/16	s	s	r
FundAm	40	r	s	12 1/2	r	s	r
52 5/8	50	2 1/2	r	4	r	r	r
52 5/8	55	r	r	1 1/8	r	r	r
Gap	30	r	r	r	r	r	1
34	35	r	r	2 3/8	1 1/2	r	3
Gen El	45	s	s	r	s	s	7/16
54 5/8	50	5 1/8	6	6 1/8	1/8	9/16	1
54 5/8	55	1 1/4	2 3/16	2 5/8	1 3/16	2	2 1/2
54 5/8	60	1/8	9/16	1	5 1/2	4 3/8	5 3/4
54 5/8	65	s	s	3/8	s	s	r
G M	30	3 7/8	4	4	1/8	3/4	1 1/16
33	35	1/4	r	15/16	2 1/8	2 3/4	3 1/4
33	40	r	r	1/4	6 1/2	6 3/4	6 7/8
33	45	r	s	r	r	s	11 3/4
GtLCh	60	2 1/4	r	r	1	r	2 1/8
61 7/8	65	9/16	r	r	r	r	r
Handlm	12 1/2	3/8	r	r	r	r	r
Hanson	17 1/2	r	r	7/8	r	r	r
18 1/2	20	r	r	1/4	r	r	r
Heinz	30	3 5/8	r	r	r	r	r
33 5/8	35	1/8	r	1 1/4	1 1/2	2	r
I T T	45	r	r	r	1/2	r	1 1/2
46 5/8	50	3/16	r	7/8	r	r	r
46 5/8	55	r	r	1/8	r	r	r
K mart	25	2 5/8	r	3 1/8	r	5/16	5/8
27 3/4	30	1/8	r	1/2	r	r	r
LandsE	15	r	r	1	r	r	r
Litton	80	7/16	1 1/4	1 7/8	r	r	r
Loews	85	s	s	r	s	s	1 1/4
93 5/8	90	r	r	r	3/4	r	2 5/8
93 5/8	95	1 3/4	r	r	r	3 5/8	r
93 5/8	100	1/2	r	r	6 3/8	r	r
93 5/8	105	s	s	1 3/16	s	s	r
LongvF	7 1/2	r	r	r	r	r	1/8
MayD o	45	s	s	1	s	s	r
MayDS	40	r	r	r	3/4	r	1 15/16
Mc Don	25	r	r	r	r	r	3/8
28 1/8	30	1/8	7/16	7/8	r	2 1/2	r
N C R	50	r	s	r	1/16	s	r

Option & NY Close	Strike Price	Calls-Last Jan	Calls-Last Feb	Calls-Last Apr	Puts-Last Jan	Puts-Last Feb	Puts-Last Apr
53	60	r	r	1	r	r	r
Itel	12 1/2	r	3/16	r	r	r	r
JanBel	7 1/2	r	r	r	1/2	r	r
John J	55	13 3/4	s	r	r	s	1/2
68 3/4	60	10	s	r	r	s	1
68 3/4	65	4 1/4	5 1/8	6 1/2	7/16	1 1/8	1 3/4
68 3/4	70	15/16	1 15/16	3 5/8	2	2 7/8	3 3/4
68 3/4	75	1/8	5/8	1 3/8	6	r	7
68 3/4	80	r	s	s	11 3/8	s	s
Kerr M	45	r	1 1/4	r	1 1/8	r	2 1/2
44 1/4	55	1/16	s	r	r	s	r
LAGear	10	4 1/2	r	r	1/16	r	5/8
14 1/2	12 1/2	2 1/8	2 5/8	3 1/8	3/16	7/8	1 1/2
14 1/2	15	11/16	1 1/8	1 7/8	1 3/16	1 7/8	2 1/2
14 1/2	17 1/2	1/8	7/16	1	3 1/4	3 5/8	4 1/4
14 1/2	20	1/16	r	3/8	5 7/8	6 1/8	6 1/4
14 1/2	22 1/2	r	s	s	8 1/2	s	s
14 1/2	25	r	s	s	10 3/4	s	s
LAC	7 1/2	3/4	r	1 3/16	r	r	r
8 1/8	10	1/16	r	r	r	r	2
L S I	7 1/2	1/8	r	r	r	r	r
Legent	30	r	1 1/8	r	r	r	r
LizCla	25	r	r	r	r	r	3/4
29 1/4	30	5/8	1 1/8	2 1/2	1 1/4	2 1/4	2 1/2
29 1/4	35	r	r	7/8	r	6	r
Loral	30	3 5/8	3 1/2	4 3/8	r	r	r
Lubys	17 1/2	3/4	r	r	r	r	r
M C I	17 1/2	2 3/4	3	3 1/2	r	5/16	r
19 7/8	20	1/2	1 1/8	1 7/8	1/2	1 1/4	r
19 7/8	22 1/2	3/16	3/8	1	2 5/8	2 5/8	r
19 7/8	25	1/16	s	1/2	r	s	r
19 7/8	35	r	s	1/16	r	s	r
Mead	20	r	s	r	r	s	1/4
25 3/4	22 1/2	r	r	4	r	r	r
25 3/4	25	1 1/2	1 7/8	r	3/8	3/4	r
25 3/4	30	1/16	1/4	3/4	r	r	r
Merck	70	r	s	16 3/4	1/16	s	r
85 1/4	75	10 3/4	s	12 3/8	1/8	s	1 1/4
85 1/4	80	5 7/8	r	8 7/8	5/16	1	2 1/4
85 1/4	85	1 7/8	3 3/4	5 1/2	1 3/8	2 3/8	4
85 1/4	90	1/4	1 1/4	2 5/8	4 3/4	5 1/2	6 1/4
Micron	7 1/2	2 3/16	r	r	r	r	r
MdwAir	5	r	s	3/8	1 1/4	s	r
M M M	70	r	s	r	r	s	3/4
83 3/8	75	r	s	r	3/16	s	1 1/8
83 3/8	80	r	5	6 5/8	3/8	1 5/16	2 7/16
83 3/8	85	7/8	2	3 1/2	2 1/8	3 3/8	4 3/8
83 3/8	90	3/16	r	1 1/2	r	r	r
MIPS	10	3/16	r	r	r	r	r
Monsan	47 1/2	11/16	s	s	r	s	s
47 1/8	45	r	r	r	r	r	1 1/2
47 1/8	50	3/16	9/16	1 3/4	3	r	r
NWNL	15	r	r	r	r	r	1 1/16
17 3/4	20	r	r	r	r	3 1/4	r
NthnTr	35	r	r	5/8	r	r	r
Nucor	60	1 1/2	r	r	1 3/4	r	r
OryxEn	35	r	1 7/8	2 5/8	1 9/16	r	r
33 7/8	40	r	r	1 1/8	r	5 7/8	r
Pennz	65	1 3/8	r	r	1	r	r
65 3/8	70	r	3/4	r	r	r	r
Pepsi	20	r	s	5	1/16	s	3/8
25	21 5/8	3 3/8	s	4	1/16	s	r
25	22 1/2	2 3/16	s	r	1/8	s	11/16
25	23 3/8	r	s	2 5/8	1/4	s	7/8
25	25	3/4	1 1/8	1 5/8	5/8	1 1/4	1 1/2
25	26 5/8	1/8	s	13/16	r	s	2 1/2
25	28 3/8	1/16	s	r	r	s	r
25	30	r	r	1/4	r	r	r

Option & NY Close	Strike Price	Calls-Last Jan	Calls-Last Feb	Calls-Last May	Puts-Last Jan	Puts-Last Feb	Puts-Last May
46 3/4	50	1/2	1 1/16	r	r	3 3/4	r
46 3/4	55	r	r	1 7/8	r	r	r
FptMc	30	5	r	5 1/8	r	r	r
35 1/2	35	r	1 1/8	1 3/4	r	1 3/8	r
GnCine	20	r	7/8	r	r	r	r
Gn Dyn	22 1/2	r	r	r	r	7/16	1 3/8
25 3/8	25	r	r	r	r	1 1/4	r
25 3/8	30	r	1/4	r	r	r	r
Gdrich	40	r	3/4	1 7/8	r	r	r
Harris	20	3/4	r	r	9/16	r	r
Hewlet	25	r	r	r	r	3/16	r
31 1/4	30	1 3/4	2 9/16	r	3/8	7/8	r
31 1/4	35	3/16	r	1 1/2	3 1/2	r	r
Honwll	40	r	r	5 3/4	r	1/2	1 1/2
43 3/4	42 1/2	2	r	r	r	1 3/8	r
43 3/4	45	1/2	1 3/4	3	r	2 1/4	r
43 3/4	47 1/2	r	r	2	r	r	r
Humana	40	r	2	3 1/8	r	1 1/4	2
40 1/2	45	r	r	r	3 7/8	4	r
In Flv	65	r	8 5/8	r	r	r	r
72 7/8	70	r	r	r	r	1 1/8	2 13/16
72 7/8	75	r	1 5/8	r	r	r	r
Limitd	12 1/2	r	6 3/4	r	r	1/16	r
18 7/8	15	3 7/8	4 1/4	4 1/2	r	r	3/8
18 7/8	17 1/2	1 1/2	2	r	3/16	7/16	1
18 7/8	20	3/16	5/8	1 1/4	r	r	2 1/8
18 7/8	22 1/2	s	3/16	s	s	r	s
Medtrn	80	2 1/2	3 7/8	r	1	2 3/8	r
81	85	7/8	r	r	r	4 1/4	6 1/4
81	90	r	3/4	r	r	r	r
Mobil	55	r	2 7/8	r	r	1 1/8	r
56 7/8	60	1/8	5/8	1 5/8	r	r	r
N Semi	5	s	1/4	r	s	r	r
Nthrop	12 1/2	r	r	r	r	r	3/8
17 1/2	15	r	2 7/8	r	r	3/8	r
17 1/2	17 1/2	r	1 1/4	1 3/4	5/8	3/4	r
17 1/2	20	r	r	13/16	2 5/8	r	r
Occi	17 1/2	r	1 3/4	2 7/16	3/8	9/16	1 13/16
18 1/2	20	5/16	3/4	1 1/2	r	2 1/8	2 7/8
18 1/2	22 1/2	1/16	1/4	3/4	r	4	r
18 1/2	25	1/16	1/8	3/8	r	6 1/2	6 3/8
18 1/2	30	s	1/16	s	s	r	s
Pansph	10	r	r	1	r	r	r
Pegsus	10	r	2 5/8	r	r	r	r
12 1/4	12 1/2	1/2	r	r	r	r	r
12 1/4	15	r	1/8	r	r	r	r
Promus	12 1/2	r	2	r	r	r	r
14	17 1/2	r	1/8	r	r	r	r
Raythn	60	s	7 3/4	8 1/2	s	5/16	3/4
66 3/8	65	2	4 1/8	6 3/8	3/8	1	2 1/2
66 3/8	70	r	1 5/8	3 1/2	r	3	r
66 3/8	75	r	r	1 5/8	r	r	r
Slumb	50	r	r	r	r	3/4	1 11/16
53 5/8	55	r	2 1/8	3 3/4	1 3/8	2 1/4	3 5/8
53 5/8	60	1/4	3/4	1 13/16	r	r	r
53 5/8	65	s	1/4	r	s	r	r
Shawln	20	1 1/16	r	r	r	1 3/8	r
Shell	50	r	r	r	r	5/8	r
SestBk	5	r	1/2	15/16	r	r	r
Southn	25	r	r	2	r	r	r
26 5/8	30	r	r	3/16	r	r	r
Tribune	35	r	1 5/8	r	5/8	r	r
35 1/8	40	r	r	1 1/8	r	r	4 3/4
UAL	95	r	18	r	r	1	1 7/8
111 3/4	100	11 3/4	r	r	1/4	r	3 1/4
111 3/4	105	7 3/4	10 1/2	r	7/8	2 3/8	4 7/8
111 3/4	110	4 1/4	6	10 1/2	2 1/8	4 1/2	6 1/4
111 3/4	115	1 1/2	4	r	5	r	8 1/2
111 3/4	120	1/2	2 3/8	5 3/8	r	10 1/4	11
111 3/4	125	s	1	s	s	r	s
111 3/4	135	s	9/16	s	s	r	s
UST	30	r	r	r	r	r	5/8
U Tech	45	r	r	4 1/2	r	1	r
47 3/8	50	r	r	r	r	3 3/8	4 1/2

Source: The Wall Street Journal, *January 7, 1991, p. C15.*

umns are devoted to put options. These six columns report the closing prices of the options. If no options were traded during the day, an *r* is listed. If no options were offered, an *s* is listed. The month that each of the options expires is given at the top of the columns. Thus from these listings an investor learns that the closing price of Dow was 46 and that the February call and put options with a strike price of $40 closed at 6⅞ and ½, respectively.

Second, a clearinghouse was established for the CBOE that maintains a daily record of options issued in the accounts of its members. The members are required to keep a continuous record of their respective customers' positions in options. No actual options certificates are issued; only the bookkeeping is maintained by the clearinghouse. A centralized clearinghouse greatly facilitates trading in the options, for it serves as the intermediary through which purchases and sales of the calls are recorded.

Third, the CBOE is self-regulated. It has the power to impose requirements that must be met before calls may be traded on the exchange, and options on only a selected number of securities have been accepted for trading on the exchange. Investors must be approved before they can purchase and sell through the CBOE, and there is a limit to the number of options on a single stock that an investor may own. Brokers on the floor of the exchange must have a minimum amount of capital. Although such self-regulation does not guarantee the absence of illegal transactions, it is conducive to the development of organized security markets.

The initial success of the CBOE exceeded expectations. Soon after its formation, other exchanges started to list call options. Currently, call options are traded not only on the CBOE but also on the New York, American, Pacific, and Philadelphia exchanges. While not all companies meet the criteria for having options listed, over a thousand firms are eligible to have options on their stock listed and traded.

The Advantage of Purchasing Calls: Leverage

Warrants and calls are similar in many ways. Both represent the right to buy stock at a specified price within a specified time period. The reason for purchasing either warrants or calls is the potential leverage that they offer the investor. Calls, however, tend to offer greater leverage than warrants, since they sell for a smaller time premium above their intrinsic value. Because of the short duration of the call option, the time premium paid is less than that paid for a warrant, which is of longer duration.

The considerable potential leverage offered by a call to buy XYZ stock at $60 is shown in Exhibit 13.7. This exhibit presents the price of the XYZ stock (column 1); the strike price of the call (column 2); the intrinsic value of the call, that is, the difference between the price of the

EXHIBIT 13.7

Potential Leverage Offered by CBOE Call to Buy XYZ Stock at $60

A small change in the price of the underlying stock may generate a large percentage change in the price of a call option.

Price of XYZ Stock	Strike Price of the Call	Intrinsic Value of the Call	Hypothetical Price of the Call	Percentage Change in the Price of the Stock	Percentage Change in the Price of the Call
$50	$60	$ 0	$ ¼	...	...
55	60	0	1	10.0%	300%
60	60	0	3	9.1	200
65	60	5	6	8.3	100
70	60	10	10½	7.7	75

common stock and the per share strike price of the call (column 3); and some hypothetical market prices of the call (column 4). The exhibit also includes the percentage change in the price of the common stock for successive increments of $5 (column 5) and the percentage change in the hypothetical price of the call (column 6). As may be seen in the exhibit, if the price of XYZ's common stock rose from $60 to $65 (an 8.3 percent increase), the hypothetical price of this call would rise from $3 to $6 (a 100 percent increase). If equal amounts were invested in the common stock and the call, the call would have the potential to yield much more profit.

Although the potential leverage that calls offer is the primary reason for purchasing them, the investor does accept substantial risk. On its expiration date the call can be worth only its intrinsic value. The call will be worthless if the price of XYZ stock is less than the strike price (i.e., below $60). This call will prove to be a profitable investment only if the price of the common stock rises. Thus, for a call to be profitable, the price of the common stock must increase during the call's relatively short life span.

The Advantage of Writing Calls: Income

The preceding section considered the reason for purchasing calls; this section will consider the advantages of writing them. (The process of issuing and selling an option is referred to as "writing.") While buying calls gives the investor an opportunity to profit from the leverage that call options offer, issuing calls produces revenue from their sale. The selling of options may also offer the investor an opportunity to earn a respectable return when the option is used in conjunction with stock already owned.

Covered option writing
Selling an option when an individual has a position in the underlying stock

There are two ways to write options. The first is the more conservative method, which is called **covered option writing.** The investor buys the stock and then sells an option to buy that stock. If the option is

EXHIBIT 13.8

Profit on a Hedge Position Consisting of the Purchase of 100 Shares of XYZ Stock and the Sale of One Call to Buy 100 Shares of XYZ at $50 a Share

Covered call writing limits the possible profit but reduces risk.

Price of XYZ Stock at Expiration of the Call	Net Profit on the Stock	Value of the Call at Expiration	Net Profit on the Sale of the Call	Net Profit on the Position
$40	−$1,000	$0	$500	−$500
42	−800	0	500	−300
44	−600	0	500	−100
46	−400	0	500	100
48	−200	0	500	300
50	0	0	500	500
52	200	200	300	500
54	400	400	100	500
56	600	600	−100	500
58	800	800	−300	500
60	1,000	1,000	−500	500

exercised, the investor supplies the stock that was previously purchased (i.e., "covers" the option with the stock). The second method entails selling the call without owning the stock. This is referred to as **naked option writing,** for the investor is exposed to considerable risk. If the price of the stock rises and the call is exercised, the option writer must buy the stock at the higher market price in order to supply it to the buyer. With naked option writing the potential for loss is considerably greater than with covered option writing.

Naked option writing Selling an option when an individual does not have a position in the underlying stock

The reason for writing options is the income to be gained from their sale. The potential profit from writing a *covered call* option may be seen in Exhibit 13.8. In this example the investor purchases 100 shares of XYZ stock at the current market price of $50 per share and simultaneously sells for $5 a call to buy the shares at the strike price of $50. Thus, the investor sells the call for $500 (i.e., $5 × 100 shares). The possible future prices for XYZ stock at the expiration of the call are given in column 1. Column 2 presents the net profit to the investor from the purchase of the stock. Column 3 gives the value of the call at expiration, and column 4 presents the profit to the investor from the sale of the call. As may be seen in column 4, the sale of the call is profitable to the investor as long as the price of the common stock remains below $55 per share. The last column gives the net profit on the entire position. As long as the price of the common stock stays *above $45 per share,* the entire position will yield a profit before commission fees. The maximum amount of this profit, however, is limited to $500. Thus, by selling the covered call the investor forgoes the possibility of large gains. For example, if the price of the stock were to rise to $70 per share, the holder of the call would exer-

FIGURE 13.4

Profit or Loss on Selling a Covered Call

As long as the price of the stock exceeds $45, the covered call generates a profit.

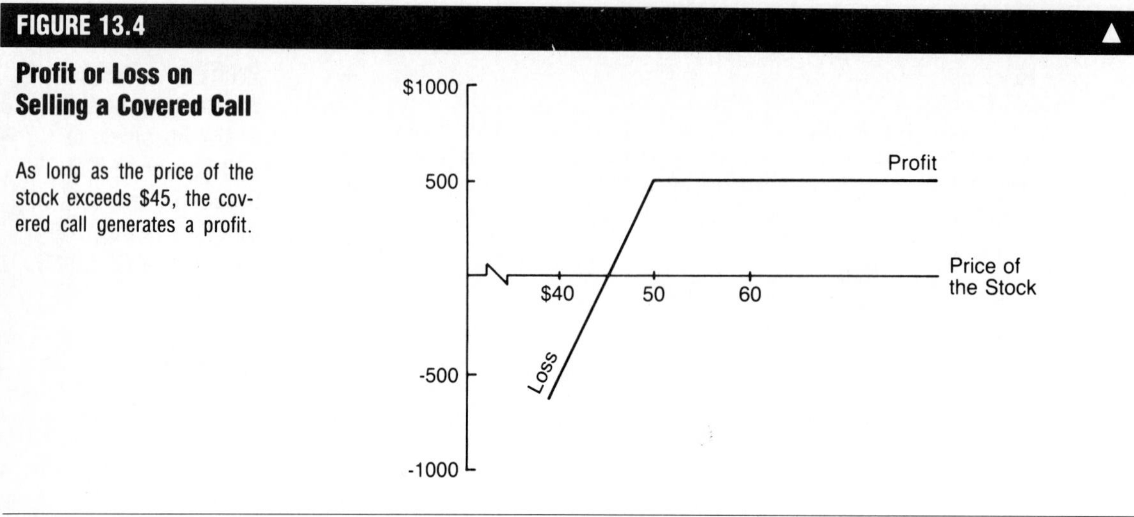

cise it and purchase the 100 shares from the seller at $50 per share. The seller would then make only the $500 that was received from the sale of the call.

If the price of the stock were to fall below $45, the entire position would result in a loss to the seller. For example, if the price of the common stock fell to $40, the investor would lose $1,000 on the purchase of the stock. However, $500 has been received from the sale of the call. Thus, the net loss is only $500. The investor still owns the stock and may now write another call on that stock. As long as the investor owns the stock, the same 100 shares may be used over and over to cover the writing of options. Thus, even if the price of the stock does fall, the investor may continue to use it to write more options. The more options that can be written, the more profitable the shares become. For individuals who write options, the best possible situation would be for the stock's price to remain stable. In that case the investors would receive the income from writing the options and never suffer a capital loss from a decline in the price of the stock on which the option is being written.

The relationship between the price of the stock and the profit or loss on writing a covered call is illustrated in Figure 13.4, which plots the first and fifth columns of Exhibit 13.8. As may be seen from the figure, the sale of the covered option produces a profit (before commissions) for all prices of the stock above $45. However, the maximum profit (before commissions) is only $500.

Option writers do not have to own the common stock on which they write calls. Although such naked or uncovered option writing exposes the investor to a large amount of risk, the returns may be considerable.

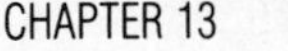

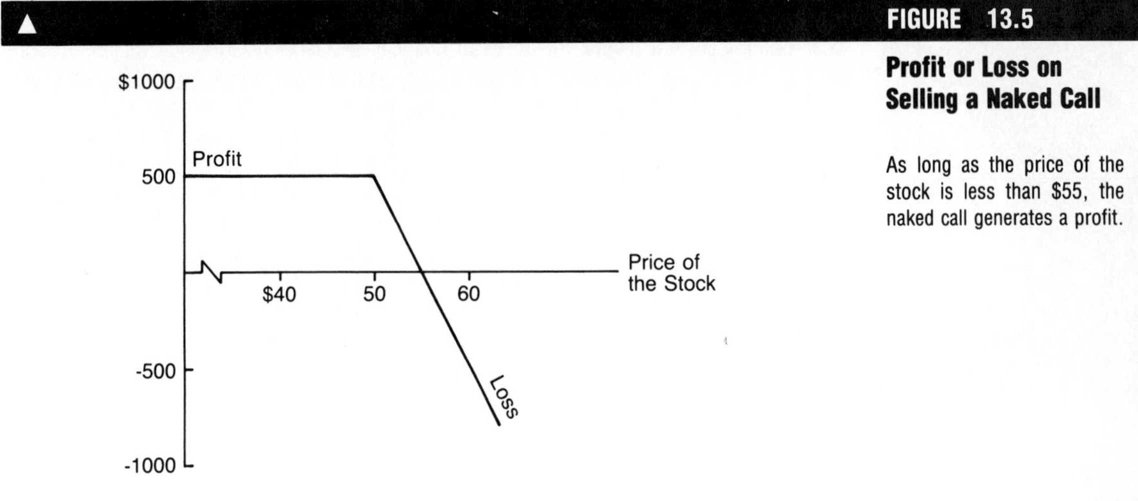

FIGURE 13.5

Profit or Loss on Selling a Naked Call

As long as the price of the stock is less than $55, the naked call generates a profit.

If the writer of the XYZ option given in Exhibit 13.8 had not owned the stock and had sold the option for $500, the position would have been profitable as long as the price of the common stock remained below $55 per share at the expiration of the call. The potential loss, however, is theoretically infinite, for the naked option loses $100 for every $1 increase in the price of the stock above the call's exercise price. For example, if the price of the stock were to rise to $70 per share, the call would be worth $2,000. The owner of the call would exercise it and purchase the 100 shares for $5,000. The writer of the call would then have to purchase the shares on the open market for $7,000. Since the writer received only $500 when the call was sold and $5,000 when the call was exercised, the loss would be $1,500. Therefore, uncovered option writing exposes the writer to considerable risk if the price of the stock rises.

The relationship between the price of the stock and the profit or loss on writing a naked call option is illustrated in Figure 13.5. In this case the option writer earns a profit (before commissions) as long as the price of the stock does not exceed $55 at the expiration of the call. Notice that the investor earns the entire $500 if the stock's price falls below $50. However, the potential for loss is considerable if the price of the stock increases.

Investors should write naked call options only if they anticipate a decline (or at least no increase) in the price of the stock. These investors may write covered call options if they believe the price of the stock may rise but are not certain of the price increase. And they may purchase the stock (or the option) and not write calls if they believe there is substantial potential for a price increase.

Financial Facts

Foreign Options

Call options are not unique to American financial markets but are also available in some foreign security markets. These foreign call options, however, differ significantly from American call options. Specific differences vary from country to country but revolve around the term of the option and the existence of secondary markets. For example, the typical British option expires within three months; six- and nine-month options are not available. • In addition, many foreign call options do not have secondary markets. For example, there is no secondary market for the three-month British call. Once purchased, the option cannot be sold. The investor must either exercise the option at the specified time or let the option expire. This is the most important difference between an American call option and the so-called European call: The investor must exercise the European call to realize any gain achieved through appreciation in its value. •

PUTS

At first, only call options were traded on the CBOE and other exchanges, but as of May 31, 1977, put options were admitted for trading. A put option is an option to *sell* stock (usually 100 shares) at a specified price within a specified time period. As with calls, the time period is short—three, six, or nine months. Like all options, a put has an intrinsic value, which is the difference between the strike price of the put and the price of the stock.[5] The relationship between the price of a stock and the intrinsic value of a put is illustrated in Exhibit 13.9. This put is an option to sell 100 shares at $30 per share. The first column gives the strike price of the put, the second column presents the hypothetical prices of the stock, and the third column gives the intrinsic value of the put (i.e., the strike price minus the price of the stock).

If the price of the stock is less than the strike price, the put has a positive intrinsic value and is said to be "in the money." If the price of the stock is greater than the strike price, the put has no intrinsic value and is said to be "out of the money." If the price of the stock equals the strike price, the put is "at the money." As with call options, the market price of a put is called "the premium."

As may be seen in Exhibit 13.9, when the price of the stock declines the intrinsic value of the put rises. Since the owner of the put may sell the stock at the price specified in the option agreement, the value of the option rises as the price of the stock falls. Thus, if the price of the stock is

[5] Note that the intrinsic value of a put is the reverse of the intrinsic value of an option to buy (i.e., a call). Compare Exhibits 13.3 and 13.9.

EXHIBIT 13.9

Relationship between the Strike Price of the Put, the Price of the Stock, and the Hypothetical Price of the Put

Strike Price of the Put	Price of the Stock	Intrinsic Value of the Put	Hypothetical Price of the Put
$30	$15	$15	$15¼
30	20	10	12
30	25	5	8
30	30	0	6
30	35	0	3½
30	40	0	1
30	50	0	—

The intrinsic value of a put rises as the price of the stock declines.

$15 and the exercise price of the put is $30, the put's intrinsic value as an option must be $1,500 (for 100 shares). The investor can purchase the 100 shares of stock for $1,500 on the stock market and sell them for $3,000 to the person who issued the put. The put, then, must be worth the $1,500 difference between the purchase and sale prices.

Why should an investor purchase a put? The reason is the same for puts as it is for other speculative options: The put offers potential leverage to the investor. Such leverage may be seen in the example presented in Exhibit 13.9. When the price of the stock declines from $25 to $20 (a 20 percent decrease), the intrinsic value of the put rises from $5 to $10 (a 100 percent increase). In this example a 20 percent decline in the price of the stock produces a larger percentage increase in the intrinsic value of the put. It is this potential leverage that makes put options attractive to investors.

As with other options, investors are willing to pay a price that is greater than the put's intrinsic value: The put commands a time premium above its intrinsic value as an option. As with warrants and calls, the amount of this time premium depends on such factors as the volatility of the stock's price, the duration of the put, and the potential for *decline* in the price of the stock.

The relationship between the price of the stock and hypothetical prices of the put are also illustrated in Exhibit 13.9, in which the fourth column presents prices of the put. As may be seen, the price of the put exceeds the intrinsic value, for the put commands a time premium over its intrinsic value as an option.

Figure 13.6 illustrates the relationships among the price of the common stock, the intrinsic value of the put, and the hypothetical market value of the put that were presented in Exhibit 13.9. This figure shows the inverse relationship between the price of the stock and the put's intrinsic value. As the price of the stock declines, the intrinsic value of the

FIGURE 13.6

Relationships among the Price of the Stock, the Intrinsic Value of a Put Option, and the Hypothetical Price of the Option

The put option's time premium is the difference between the price of the option and its intrinsic value.

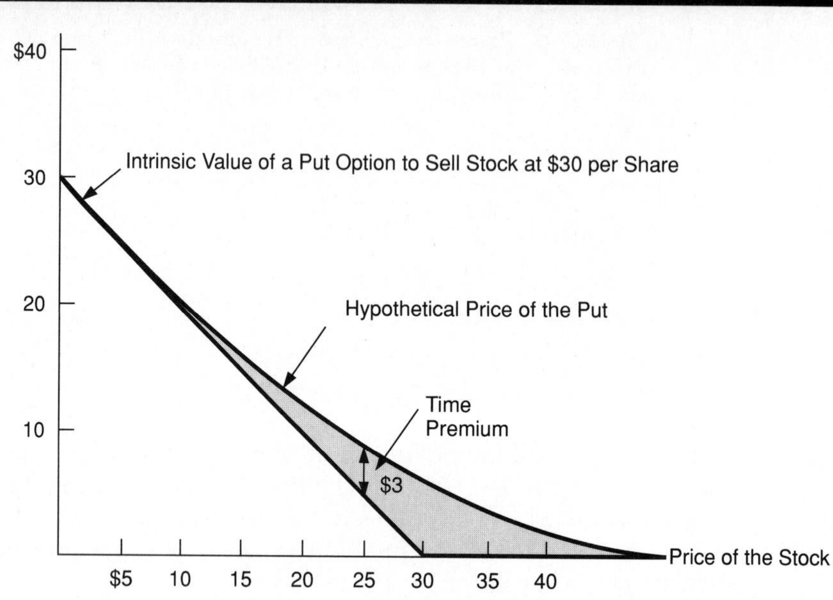

put increases (e.g., from $5 to $10 when the stock's price declines from $25 to $20). The figure also readily shows the time premium paid for the option, which is the difference between the price of the put and the option's intrinsic value. If the price of the put is $8 and the intrinsic value is $5, the time premium is $3.

As may be seen in both Exhibit 13.9 and Figure 13.6, the hypothetical market price of the put converges with the put's intrinsic value as the price of the stock declines. If the price of the stock is sufficiently high (e.g., $50), the put will not have any market value because the price of the stock must decline substantially for the put to have any intrinsic value. At the other extreme, when the price of the stock is low (e.g., $15), the price of the put is equal to the put's intrinsic value as an option. Once again, there are two reasons for this convergence. First, as the price of the stock declines below the strike price of the put, the potential risk to the investor if the price of the stock should start to rise becomes greater. Thus, put buyers are less willing to pay a time premium above the put's intrinsic value. Second, as the intrinsic value of a put rises when the price of the stock declines, the investor must spend more to buy the put; therefore, the potential return on the investment is less. As the potential return declines, the willingness to pay a time premium diminishes.

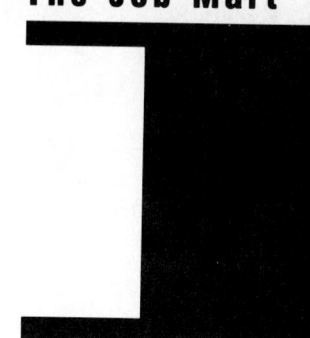

Arbitrageur

■ Job Description: Simultaneously buy and sell commodities or securities to take advantage of price differentials in the two markets. Take positions in companies involved with mergers and takeovers. Buy options and simultaneously sell the underlying stock when the option sells for less than its intrinsic value. ■ Job Requirements: Thorough knowledge of security markets, especially the option and commodity markets. Ability to identify mispriced securities that create arbitrage opportunities and to make and execute decisions rapidly. ■ Characteristics: An arbitrageur works in an extremely high-pressure environment in which individuals buy and sell large quantities of securities. Individuals must be able to work under stress and to bear the risk associated with taking positions in volatile markets. Since many arbitrage strategies are built into computer programs, the arbitrageur needs computer literacy.

STOCK INDEX OPTIONS

Stock index option ▲ Right to buy or sell stock based on an index of stock prices

While put and call options were initially created for individual stocks, **stock index options** have developed. These stock index options are similar to options based on individual stocks, but the index option is based on an aggregate measure of the market, such as the Standard & Poor's 500 stock index. In addition, there are also options based on subsets of the market, such as computer technology stocks or oil stocks. A listing of these index options and where they are traded is given in Exhibit 13.10. Stock index options have proved to be particularly popular and account for a substantial proportion of the daily transactions in options.

These options are popular because they permit the investor to take a position in the market or in a group of companies without having to select specific securities. For example, suppose an investor anticipates that the stock market will rise. What does this individual do? He or she cannot buy every stock but must select individual stocks.[6] Remember from the discussion of risk in Chapter 8 that there are two sources of risk associated with the individual stock: systematic risk and unsystematic risk. Systematic risk refers to the tendency of a stock's price to move with the market. Unsystematic risk refers to price movements generated by the

[6] As is explained in Chapter 14, the investor could buy an index mutual fund. Such funds construct portfolios that mirror aggregate measures of the stock market.

EXHIBIT 13.10

Index Options and Where They Are Traded

Put and call options are not limited to individual securities.

The Option	Where Traded
S&P 100 Index	Chicago Board Options Exchange
S&P 500 Index	Chicago Board Options Exchange
Major Market Index	American Stock Exchange
AMEX Market Value Index	American Stock Exchange
Computer Technology Index	American Stock Exchange
Oil Index	American Stock Exchange
Airline Index	American Stock Exchange
Value Line Index	Philadelphia Exchange
National O-T-C Index	Philadelphia Exchange
Technology Index	Pacific Exchange
NYSE Options Index	New York Stock Exchange

security that are independent of the market (e.g., a takeover announcement, dividend cut, or large increase in earnings).

If the investor buys a particular stock on the expectation of a rising market, it does not necessarily follow that the individual stock's price will increase when the market rises. Investors construct diversified portfolios to reduce the unsystematic risk associated with the individual asset. As the portfolio becomes more diversified, unsystematic risk is reduced further and the return on the portfolio mirrors the return on the market. (Whether or not the return on the portfolio exceeds the market depends on the portfolio's beta. If the individual selects stocks with high betas, the return on the portfolio should be greater than the return on the market as a whole during rising markets, but the losses should be greater during declining markets.)

Index options offer the investor an alternative to creating diversified portfolios as a means to earn the return associated with movements in the market. For example, if the investor anticipates that the market will rise in the near future, he or she may purchase a call option based on an index of the market as a whole (such as the Standard & Poor's 500 stock index). If the market does rise, the value of the call option also increases. The investor has avoided the unsystematic risk associated with the individual stock. In addition, the investor has avoided the large commission costs necessary to construct a diversified portfolio.

Stock index options also give investors a means to hedge their existing portfolios. This is particularly important for portfolio managers with large holdings and for individuals who want to improve the tax management of these holdings. Consider a substantial stock portfolio that has appreciated in value. If the investor anticipates declining stock prices and sells the shares, this transaction is taxable. Instead of selling the stocks, the investor may sell stock index calls. Then if the market declines, the value of the calls declines, so the profits in the position in the call will help offset the losses on the individual stocks.

There is one major difference between stock index options and call options on specific stocks. With a call option to buy shares of IBM, for example, the owner may exercise the option and buy the stock. Such purchases are not possible with a stock index option. The owner of the call cannot exercise it and receive the index. Instead stock index options are settled in cash. For example, suppose the owner of a call based on the Standard & Poor's 500 index does not sell the option prior to expiration (and thereby closes the position). At expiration the intrinsic value of the option is determined and that amount is paid by the seller of the option to the owner. Of course, if the option has no intrinsic value at expiration, it is worthless and expires. The seller of the option then has no further obligation to the option's owner. In that case the premium paid for the option (i.e., its price) becomes profit for the seller.

In addition to stock index options, there are options on debt instruments (e.g., Treasury bonds) and foreign currencies. Each of these options permits the investor (1) to take positions on the underlying assets without actually acquiring them or (2) to establish hedge positions that reduce the risk of loss from price fluctuations. For example, if an investor anticipates declining interest rates, he or she will buy a call option to purchase bonds. If interest rates do fall, the value of bonds will rise, increasing the value of the call option. The call option's price will rise more rapidly than the bond's price because the call offers leverage. However, if the investor were to purchase the call option and interest rates rose, the investor's maximum possible loss would be limited to the cost of the option.

The same concepts apply to options on foreign currencies. If the investor expects the value of the British pound to rise, that individual buys a call option on the pound. Of course, if the investor anticipates a price decline in the pound, he or she would acquire a put option on the pound. If the anticipated price change were to occur, then the investor would earn a profit. However, if the price were to move in the opposite direction (e.g., rise after the purchase of the put), the maximum the investor would lose is the cost of the option.

SUMMARY

Investing in commodity futures involves entering contracts for future delivery of a commodity such as wheat or corn. An individual takes a long position by entering into a contract to buy and accept future delivery. The opposite, or short, position occurs when the individual enters into a contract to sell and make future delivery. The long position profits if the price of the commodity rises, since the individual has a contract to buy at a lower price. The short position profits if the price of the commodity falls, since the individual has a contract to sell at a higher price.

Futures contracts are made through brokers who own seats or who have correspondent relationships with firms that own seats on the commodity exchanges. Futures contracts are supported by deposits, called margin, that signify the individual's good faith to honor the contract. The margin requirement is only a small fraction of the value of the contract, and this produces considerable potential for leverage. A small change in the price of the commodity produces a large profit or loss relative to the small amount of margin.

Hedging plays an important role in futures markets. Growers, miners, and other users of commodities often desire to reduce their risk of loss from price fluctuations and thus hedge their positions. Growers enter contracts to make future delivery, and producers enter contracts to accept future delivery. It is frequently the speculators who are offering the contracts sought by the hedgers. In this way, the risks that the hedgers seek to reduce are passed on to the speculators.

Besides commodity futures there are also financial futures, currency futures, and stock market futures. Financial futures are contracts for the delivery of financial assets such as U.S. Treasury bills and bonds. Currency futures are contracts for the future delivery of foreign moneys such as German marks or British pounds. Stock market futures are based on a broad measure of the market (e.g., the New York Stock Exchange Composite Index). Speculators who anticipate movements in interest rates, foreign currencies, or the stock market can speculate on these anticipated price changes by taking appropriate positions in futures contracts. Financial managers may use these contracts as a means to reduce the risk associated with fluctuations in interest rates, security prices, or currency values.

Options are the right to buy or sell stock at specified prices within specified time periods. A warrant is an option to buy stock issued by a corporation. When the option is exercised, the firm issues the new stock and receives the proceeds. A call is an option to buy stock issued by an individual. When the option is exercised, the seller (called the "writer") of the option must supply the stock, and he or she receives the proceeds of the sale. A put is an option to sell stock.

Options may have an intrinsic value, which for an option to buy stock is the difference between the market price of the stock and the option's exercise price (called the "strike price"). For a put option, the intrinsic value is the strike price minus the market price of the stock. While an option tends to sell for a time premium over its intrinsic value, the option's price (called the "premium") must equal the option's intrinsic value at the option's expiration.

Individuals buy options as a way to lever their positions. In general, the price of an option experiences larger percentage changes than does the price of the underlying stock. Individuals sell options to hedge their positions or to speculate on an anticipated price change. The existence of stock index options permits individuals to take a position without having to select individual securities; these individuals thus avoid the risk associated with the specific securities.

Review Questions

1. What is a futures contract? What are the spot and futures prices of a commodity? What role does margin play in establishing a position in a futures contract? Why is margin a source of financial leverage?
2. What is the difference between a long and a short position in a futures contract? Who profits if the commodity's price declines? What position should be established if you expect a commodity's price to rise?
3. What is a financial futures contract? If an investor expects interest rates to fall, should he or she enter a contract to make future delivery of U.S. Treasury bonds?
4. What is hedging? How does the financial manager of a firm that uses copper hedge against a price increase in copper?
5. What is the difference between the long and short positions in a contract for Treasury bills?
6. The loan officer of a commercial bank has made a loan commitment three months in the future at the current rate of interest. How can the loan officer hedge against a rise in interest rates?
7. What are warrants and calls? How are these options' minimum prices determined?
8. What advantages do options offer investors? Why may options be considered to be speculative investments?
9. What impact does the time premium have on the potential leverage offered by an option? What happens to the time premium as the option approaches its expiration date?
10. Why were secondary markets crucial to the development of the popularity of put and call options?
11. What is the difference between covered and naked call writing?
12. If an investor "writes" a call option, how is the position closed?
13. What is a put option and how does it differ from a call option? Contrast the possible profits and losses from buying a put and selling a naked call.
14. If an investor anticipates that stock prices may rise, why may that individual buy a stock index call option instead of buying the stock of AT&T?

Problems

1. You expect the stock market to increase, but instead of acquiring stock, you decide to acquire a stock index futures contract based on the New York Stock Exchange Composite Index. That index is currently 58.8, and the contract has a value that is $500 times the amount of the index. The margin requirement is $2,500.
   a. When you make the contract, how much must you put up?
   b. What is the value of the contract based on the index?
   c. If the value of the index rises 1 percent to 59.39, what is the profit on the investment? What is the percentage earned on the funds you put up?
   d. If the value of the index declines 1 percent to 58.2, what percentage of your funds will you lose?
   e. What is the percentage you earn (or lose) if the index falls to 53.8?
2. What are the intrinsic values and time premiums of the following call options if the price of the underlying stock is $35?

Option Strike Price	Price of the Option
$30	$7½
$35	$3

   If the stock sells for $31 at the expiration of each option, what is the profit (or loss) to the buyer of each option?
3. A certain warrant is the option to buy stock at $25. It expires after one year and currently sells for $4. The underlying stock is selling for $26.
   a. What is the intrinsic value and the time premium paid for the warrant?
   b. What will be the value of this warrant if the price of the stock at the warrant's expiration is $20? $25? $30? $40?
   c. If the price of the stock sells for $45 at the expiration of the warrant, what is the percentage return that is earned by an investor in the stock and an investor in the warrant? Why does the warrant in this problem illustrate the successful use of financial leverage?
4. The price of a stock is $61, and a six-month call with a strike price of $60 sells for $5.
   a. What is the option's intrinsic value?
   b. What is the option's time premium?
   c. If the price of the stock falls, what happens to the price of the call?
   d. If the price of the stock falls to $45, what is the maximum you could lose from buying the call?
   e. What is the maximum profit you could earn by selling the call uncovered (i.e., naked)?

f. If, at the expiration of the call, the price of the stock is $66, what is the profit (or loss) from buying the call?

g. If, at the expiration of the call, the price of the stock is $66, what is the profit (or loss) from selling the call naked?

h. If, at the expiration of the call, the price of the stock is $46, what is the profit (or loss) from buying the call?

i. If, at the expiration of the call, the price of the stock is $46, what is the profit (or loss) from selling the call naked?

5. The price of a stock is $39, and a six-month call with a strike price of $35 sells for $8.

   a. What is the option's intrinsic value?

   b. What is the option's time premium?

   c. If the price of the stock rises, what happens to the price of the call?

   d. If the price of the stock falls to $36, what is the maximum you could lose from buying the call?

   e. What is the maximum profit you could earn by selling the call uncovered (i.e., naked)?

   f. If, at the expiration of the call, the price of the stock is $35, what is the profit (or loss) from buying the call?

   g. If, at the expiration of the call, the price of the stock is $35, what is the profit (or loss) from selling the call naked?

   h. If, at the expiration of the call, the price of the stock is $46, what is the profit (or loss) from buying the call?

   i. If, at the expiration of the call, the price of the stock is $46, what is the profit (or loss) from selling the call naked?

6. A certain six-month call is the right to buy stock at $20. Currently, the stock is selling for $22, and the call is selling for $5. You buy 100 shares ($2,200) and sell one call (i.e., you receive $500).

   a. Does this position illustrate covered or naked call writing?

   b. If, at the expiration date of the call, the price of the stock is $29, what is your profit on the combined position?

   c. If, at the expiration date of the call, the price of the stock is $19, what is your profit on the combined position?

7. A particular put is the option to sell stock at $40. It expires after three months and currently sells for $3 when the price of the stock is $42.

   a. If an investor buys this put, what will the profit be after three months if the price of the stock is $45? $40? $35?

   b. What will the profit from selling this put be after three months if the price of the stock is $45? $40? $35?

Profits and Losses from Straddles

Brian Ailey, a sophisticated investor who is both willing and able to take risk, has just noticed that Mid-West Airlines has become the target of a hostile takeover. Prior to the announcement of the offer to purchase the stock for $72 a share, the stock had been selling for $59. Immediately after the offer, the stock rose to $75, a premium over the offer price. Such premiums are often indicative that investors, in the aggregate, expect a higher price to be forthcoming. Such a higher price could occur if a bidding war erupts for the company or if management leads an employee or management buyout of the firm. Of course, if neither of these scenarios occurs, the price of the stock could fall back to the $72 offer price. In addition, if the offer were to be withdrawn or defeated by management, the price of the stock could fall below the original stock price.

Ailey has no reason to anticipate that any of these possibilities will be the final outcome, but he realizes that the price of the stock will not remain at $75. If a bidding war erupts, the price could easily exceed $100. Conversely, if the takeover fails, he expects the price to decline below $55 a share, since he previously believed that the price of the stock was overvalued at $59. With such uncertainty, Ailey does not want to own the stock but is intrigued with the possibility of earning a profit from a price movement which he is certain must occur.

Currently there are several three-month options traded on the stock. Their strike and market prices are as follows:

Strike Price	Market Price of Call	Market Price of Put
$50	$26.00	$0.125
55	21.50	0.50
60	17.00	1.00
65	13.25	1.75
70	8.00	3.50
75	4.25	6.00
80	1.00	9.75

Ailey decides the best strategy is to purchase both a put and a call option (i.e., to establish a straddle). Deciding on a strategy is one thing; determining the best way to execute it is quite another. For example, he could buy the options with the extreme strike prices (e.g., the call at $80 and the put at $50). Or he could buy the options with the strike price closest to the original $72 offer price (i.e., buy the put and the call at $70).

To help determine the potential profits and losses from various positions, Ailey developed profit profiles at various stock prices. That is, he filled in the following chart for each position:

Price of the Stock	Intrinsic Value of the Call	Profit on the Call	Intrinsic Value of the Put	Profit on the Put	Total Profit
$50					
55					
60					
65					
70					
75					
80					
85					

To limit the number of calculations, he decided to make three comparisons: (1) the purchase of two inexpensive options (i.e., buy the call with the $80 strike price and the put with the $60 strike price), (2) the purchase of the options with the $70 strike price, and (3) the purchase of the options with the price closest to the original stock price (i.e., the options with the $60 strike price).

Construct Ailey's profit profiles and answer the following questions.

Case Problems

1. Which strategy works best if a bidding war erupts?
2. Which strategy works best if the hostile takeover is defeated?
3. Which strategy works best if the original offer price becomes the final price?
4. Which of the three positions produces the worst result and under what condition does it occur?
5. If you were in Ailey's place, which strategy would you adopt?

Suggested Readings

For general but detailed descriptions of commodity futures trading and hedging, consult:

Commodity Trading Manual. Chicago, Ill.: Chicago Board of Trade, 1985.

Teweles, Richard J.; Charles V. Harlow; and Herbert L. Stone. *The Commodity Futures Game—Who Wins? Who Loses? Why?* 2d ed. New York: McGraw-Hill, 1986.

Financial futures and currency futures are covered in:

Loosigian, Allan M. *Foreign Exchange Futures.* Homewood, Ill.: Dow Jones-Irwin, 1981.

Loosigian, Allan M. *Interest Rate Futures.* Homewood, Ill.: Dow Jones-Irwin, 1980.

Nix, William E., and Susan W. Nix. *The Dow Jones-Irwin Guide to Stock Index Futures and Options.* Homewood, Ill.: Dow Jones-Irwin, 1984.

Strategies using various put and call options are discussed in:

Angell, George. *Sure-Thing Options Trading.* Garden City, N.Y.: Doubleday, 1983.

Bookstaber, Richard M. *Option Pricing and Strategies in Investing.* Reading, Mass.: Addison-Wesley, 1981.

McMillan, Lawrence G. *Options as a Strategic Investment.* 2d ed. New York: New York Institute of Finance, 1986.

The development of a body of research has led to courses in options, and several textbooks have recently been published directed at this market. These include:

The development of a body of research has led to courses in options, and several textbooks have recently been published directed at this market. These include:

Chance, Don. *An Introduction to Options and Futures.* Hinsdale, Ill.: The Dryden Press, 1989.

Hull, John. *Options, Futures, and Other Derivative Securities.* Englewood Cliffs, N.J.: Prentice-Hall, 1989.

Ritchken, Peter. *Options: Theory, Strategy, and Applications.* Glenview, Ill.: Scott, Foresman and Company, 1987.

For a VCR tape on futures, write to request:

Where the World's Market Forces Converge. Modern Talking Pictures Services, 5000 Park Street North, St. Petersburg, Florida 33709.

chapter

14

Investment Companies

20 pages in chapter

Learning Objectives

1 Differentiate between closed-end and open-end investment companies.

2 Define net asset value.

3 Identify the costs of investing in mutual funds and in closed-end investment companies.

4 List the advantages offered by investment companies.

5 Distinguish among the types of investment companies.

6 Explain the tax implications of purchasing shares in investment companies.

7 Determine if investment companies consistently outperform the market.

Herodotus suggested in the fifth century B.C. that "great deeds are usually wrought at great risks." Large investment returns usually also require great risks, but most investors do not want to bear these risks. They seek diversified portfolios that reduce the risk of loss but also reduce the chance of a large return. The construction and management of a diversified portfolio can be difficult and time consuming, so many investors purchase shares in investment companies. The managements of these companies construct diversified portfolios and manage them for the benefit of the investment companies' shareholders.

Many investment companies are started by money managers who have developed celebrity status in the investment community. During 1986, the Allmon Growth Stock Outlook Trust, the Gabelli Equity Trust, and the Zweig Fund were all started by individuals with superstar status. Unfortunately for the initial investors, the value of these investment companies' shares soon sold for a discount from the initial offer prices. The efficient market can be hard on everyone, even superstars.

This chapter is concerned with investment companies, especially mutual funds. It covers the mechanics of buying and selling the shares, the taxation of investment companies, the costs associated with these investments, and the potential sources of profit. Also included in the chapter are the specialized investment companies, such as stock index funds and global funds, which have recently developed. These offer individuals a broad spectrum of investment alternatives to the direct purchase of stocks and bonds through brokers.

INVESTMENT COMPANIES: ORIGINS AND TERMINOLOGY

Closed-end investment company ▲
Investment company with a fixed number of outstanding shares

Open-end investment company ▲
Mutual fund that issues new shares and agrees to redeem the shares on the demand of the shareholder

Mutual fund ▲
Open-end investment company that stands to issue and redeem its shares on demand.

Investment companies are not a recent development but were established in Britain during the 1860s. Initially, these investment companies were referred to as trusts because the securities were held in trust for the firm's stockholders. These firms issued a specified number of shares and used the funds that were obtained through the sale of the stock certificates to acquire shares of other firms. Today the descendants of these companies are referred to as **closed-end investment companies** because the number of shares is fixed.

While the first trusts offered a specified number of shares, the most common type of investment company today does not. Instead, the number of shares varies as investors buy more shares from the trust or sell them back to the trust. This **open-end investment company** is commonly called a **mutual fund.** Such funds started in 1924 when Massachusetts Investor Trust offered new shares and redeemed (i.e., bought) existing shares on demand by stockholders.

The rationale for investment companies is very simple and appealing. The firms receive the funds from many investors, pool them, and purchase securities. The individual investors receive (1) the advantage of

FIGURE 14.1

Mutual Funds Total Assets and Net Sales, 1971–1989 (in Billions)

The assets and sales of mutual fund shares grew rapidly during the 1980s.

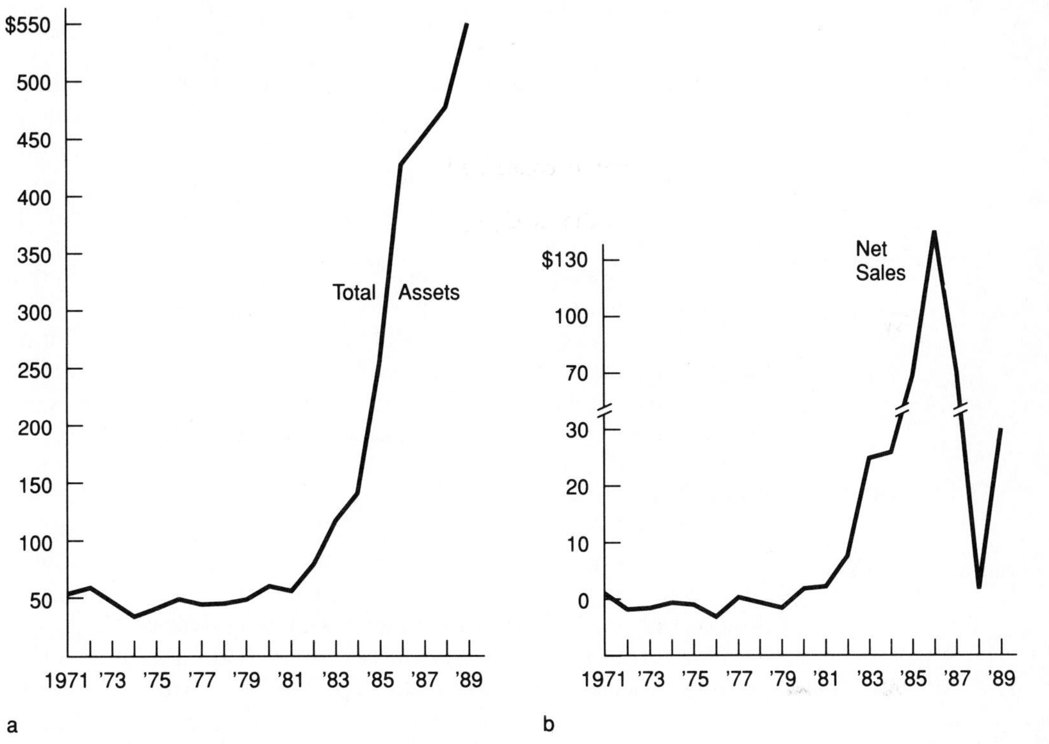

Source: Derived from Investment Company 1990 Mutual Fund Fact Book, *pp. 80 and 86.*

professional management of their money, (2) the benefit of ownership in a diversified portfolio, (3) the potential savings in commissions, as the investment company buys and sells in large blocks, and (4) custodial services (e.g., the storing of certificates and the collecting and disbursing of funds).

The advantages and services help to explain why both the number of mutual funds and the dollar value of their shares have grown since the 1940s. This growth is illustrated in Figure 14.1, which presents mutual funds' net sales and total assets from 1971 through 1989.[1] Net sales

[1]The assets of money market mutual funds are excluded.

are gross sales minus redemptions, which are shares sold back to the mutual fund. Thus, net sales indicate the flow of money into mutual funds.

During the 1970s, the growth in mutual funds stopped as redemptions exceeded sales for several years. The redemptions, plus the general decline in the market, produced a 23 percent decline in mutual funds' total assets during 1974. However, during the 1980s sales of shares plus the general increase in security prices have dramatically increased mutual funds' total assets from $137.1 billion in 1984 to $553.9 billion in 1989.[2]

Investment companies receive special tax treatment. Their earnings (i.e., dividend and interest income) and capital gains are exempt from taxation at the corporate level. Instead, these profits are taxed through their stockholders' income tax returns. Dividends, interest income, and capital gains realized (whether they are distributed or not) by the investment companies must be reported by their shareholders, who pay the appropriate income taxes.

For this reason, income that is received by investment companies and capital gains that are realized are usually distributed. The companies, however, offer their stockholders the option of having the firm retain and reinvest these distributions. While such reinvestments do not erase the stockholders' tax liabilities, they are an easy, convenient means to accumulate shares. The advantages offered by the dividend reinvestment plans of individual firms that were discussed in Chapter 10 also apply to the dividend reinvestment plans offered by investment companies. Certainly the most important of these advantages is the element of forced savings. Since the stockholder does not receive the money, there is no temptation to spend it. Rather, the funds are immediately channeled back into additional income-earning assets.

Net asset value ▲
Asset value of a share in an investment company; investment company's assets minus liabilities divided by the number of shares outstanding

One term frequently encountered in a discussion of an investment company is its per share **net asset value.** The per share net asset value of an investment company is the total value of its stocks, bonds, cash, and other assets minus any liabilities (e.g., accrued fees) divided by the number of shares outstanding. Thus, net asset value may be obtained as follows:

Value of stock owned	$ 1,000,000
Value of debt owned	+1,500,000
Value of total assets	$ 2,500,000
Liabilities	− 100,000
Net worth	$ 2,400,000
Number of shares outstanding	1,000,000
Net asset value per share	$2.40

[2]The value of closed-end investment companies has also grown, but the total value of their assets is less than one-tenth the value of mutual funds' assets.

The net asset value is extremely important for the valuation of an investment company, for it gives the value of the shares should the company be liquidated. Changes in the net asset value, then, alter the value of the investment company's shares. Thus, if the value of the firm's assets appreciates, the net asset value will increase, which may also cause the price of the investment company's stock to increase.

CLOSED-END INVESTMENT COMPANIES

As was explained in the previous section, the difference between open-end and closed-end investment companies is the nature of their capital structure. The closed-end investment company has a set capital structure that may be composed of all stock or a combination of stock and debt. The number of shares and the dollar amount of debts that the company may issue are specified. In an open-end investment company (i.e., a mutual fund), the number of shares outstanding varies as investors purchase and redeem them. Since the closed-end investment company has a specified number of shares, an individual who wants to invest in a particular company must purchase existing shares from current stockholders. Conversely, any investor who owns shares and wishes to liquidate the position must sell the shares. Thus, the shares in closed-end investment companies are bought and sold in the open market, just as the stock of IBM is traded. Shares of these companies are traded on the New York Stock Exchange (e.g., Adams Express), on the American Stock Exchange (e.g., Washington Real Estate Investment Trust), and in the over-the-counter markets (e.g., VMS Mortgage Investors).[3] Sales and prices of these shares are reported in the financial press along with the shares of other firms.

The market value of these shares is related to the potential return on the investment. The market price of stock in a closed-end company, however, need not be the net asset value per share; it may be above or below this value, depending on the demand and the supply of stock in the secondary market. If the market price is below the net asset value of the shares, the shares are selling for a **discount.** If the market price is above the net asset value, the shares are selling for a **premium.**

Discount ▲
Extent to which the price of a closed-end investment company's stock is less than the share's net asset value

Premium ▲
Extent to which the price of a closed-end investment company's stock exceeds the share's net asset value

These differences between the investment company's net asset value per share and the stock price are illustrated in Exhibit 14.1, which gives the price, the net asset value, and the discount or the premium as of the beginning of 1991 for closed-end investment companies. All of the

[3]Many AMEX and OTC closed-end investment companies are real estate investment trusts.

Financial Facts

Real Estate Investment Trusts

One means to invest in real estate is to acquire shares in a real estate investment trust, commonly referred to as a REIT. REITs are specialized, closed-end investment companies that invest in mortgages (a mortgage trust), real properties (an equity trust), or a combination of mortgages and properties. As long as the trust derives 75 percent of its income from real estate and distributes 95 percent of its income as cash dividends, the trust is exempt from federal income taxation. Shares in REITs actively trade on the NYSE and other security exchanges, so the individual may readily add to or liquidate positions in the trusts, which is unlike the often lengthy process of buying or selling properties. • Some REITs specialize in types of properties (e.g., United Dominion REIT invests primarily in apartments), while others specialize in types of mortgages (e.g., Realty ReFund invests primarily in refinanced, wrap-around mortgages). While REITs offer a real estate investment vehicle to individuals with only modest amounts to invest, these securities should be considered risky. Even though the shares of REITs permit the investor to obtain more diversification than is possible through directly acquiring properties, fluctuations in interest rates, occupancy rates, and property values mean that the shares of REITs tend to be riskier than the shares of investment companies with more broadly based portfolios. •

---

shares sold for a discount (i.e., below their net asset values). The cause of this discount is not really known, but it is believed to be the result of taxation. The potential impact of capital gains taxation on the price of the shares is illustrated in the following example.

A closed-end investment company initially sells stock for $10 per share and uses the proceeds to buy the stock of other companies. If transaction costs are ignored, the net asset value of a share is $10, and the shares may trade in the secondary market for $10. The value of the firm's portfolio subsequently rises to $16 (i.e., the net asset value is $16). The firm has a potential capital gain of $6 per share. If it is realized and these profits are distributed, the net asset value will return to $10 and each stockholder will receive $6 in capital gains, for which he or she will pay the appropriate capital gains tax.

Suppose, however, that the capital gains are not realized (i.e., the net asset value remains $16). What will the market price of the stock be? This is difficult to determine, but it will probably be below $16. Why? Suppose an investor bought a share for $16 and the firm then realized and distributed the $6 capital gain. After the distribution of the $6, the investor would be responsible for any capital gains tax, but the net asset value of the share would decrease to $10.

Obviously this is not advantageous to the buyer. Individuals may only be willing to purchase the shares at a discount that reduces the potential impact of realized capital gains and the subsequent capital gains taxes. Suppose the share had cost $14 (i.e., it sold for a discount of $2 from the net asset value), and the firm realized and distributed the gain. The buyer who paid $14 now owns a share with a net asset value of $10

EXHIBIT 14.1

Net Asset Value and Market Prices of Selected Closed-End Investment Companies as of January 26, 1991

The shares of most closed-end investment companies sell for a discount from their net asset value.

Company	Price	Net Asset Value	Discount or (Premium) as a Percentage of Net Asset Value
Adams Express	$14⅞	$17.14	13.2%
Baker, Fentress & Co.	15	19.01	21.0
General American Investors	18⅞	21.56	12.4
Tri-Continental	21⅞	24.90	12.1

Source: The New York Times, *January 26, 1991, p. 42.*

and receives a capital gain of $6. Although this investor will have to pay the appropriate capital gains tax, the impact is reduced because the investor paid only $14 to purchase the share whose total value is $16 (the $10 net asset value plus the $6 capital gain).

Since the shares may sell for a discount or a premium relative to their net asset value, it is possible for the market price of a closed-end investment company to fluctuate more or less than the net asset value. For example, during 1990 the net asset value of Adams Express declined from $18.35 to $16.15 (a 12 percent decrease), but the stock decreased only 5 percent (15⅜ to 14⅝) as the discount fell from 16.2 to 9.4 percent. Since the market price can change relative to the net asset value, an investor is subject to an additional source of risk. The value of the investment may decline not only because the net asset value may decrease but also because the shares may sell for a larger discount from their net asset value.

Some investors view the market price relative to the net asset value as a guide to buying and selling the shares of a closed-end investment company. If the shares are selling for a sufficient discount, they are considered for purchase. If the shares are selling for a small discount or at a premium, they are considered for sale. Of course, determining the premium that will justify the sale or the discount that will justify the purchase is not simple.

Sources of Profit from Investing in Closed-End Investment Companies

Profits are the difference between costs and revenues. Investing in closed-end investment companies involves several costs. First, since the shares are purchased on the open market, there is the brokerage commission

EXHIBIT 14.2

Annual Returns on an Investment in Salomon Brothers Fund, a Closed-End Investment Company

Total return varies from year to year, ranging from a high of 35.1 percent to a low of −10.9 percent.

Distributions and Price Changes	1989	1988	1987
Per-share income distributions	$ 0.70	0.501	0.49
Per-share capital gains distributions	$ 1.37	0.49	1.88
Year-end net asset value	$15.43	14.37	13.26
Year-end market price	$13.00	11.63	11.00
Annual return based on prior year's market price			
a. Dividend yield	6.0%	4.6	3.3
b. Capital gains yield	11.8%	4.4	12.5
c. Change in price	11.8%	5.7	(25.7)
Total return	29.6%	14.7	(10.9)

Source: The Lehman Corporation Annual Reports.

for the purchase and for any subsequent sale. Second, the investment company charges a fee to manage the assets. This fee is subtracted from any income that the firm's assets earn. These management fees range from 1 to 2 percent of the net asset value. Third, when the investment company purchases or sells securities, it also has to pay brokerage fees, which are passed on to the investor.

The purchase of shares in closed-end investment companies thus involves three costs that the investor must bear. Some alternative investments, such as savings accounts in commercial banks, do not involve these costs. Although commission fees are incurred when stock is purchased through a broker, the other expenses associated with a closed-end investment company are avoided. However, the investment company does relieve the individual of some of the cost of storing securities and keeping the records necessary for the preparation of tax papers.

Investors in closed-end investment companies may earn profits in a variety of ways. If the investment company collects dividends and interest on its portfolio of assets, this income is distributed to the stockholders in the form of dividends. Second, if the value of the firm's assets increases, the company may sell the assets and realize profits. These profits are then distributed as capital gains to the stockholders. Third, the net asset value of the portfolio may increase, which will cause the market price of the company's stock to rise. In this case the investor may sell the shares in the market and realize a capital gain. Fourth, the market price of the shares may rise relative to the net asset value (i.e., the premium may increase or the discount may decrease); the investor may then earn a profit through the sale of the shares.

These sources of profit are illustrated in Exhibit 14.2, which presents the distributions and price changes for Salomon Brothers Fund from December 31, 1981, through December 31, 1989. As may be seen from this exhibit, the firm distributed cash dividends of $0.495 and capi-

1986	1985	1984	1983	1982	1981
0.515	**0.495**	0.545	0.625	0.71	0.72
3.085	**1.085**	2.44	1.365	2.01	2.04
15.42	**16.78**	14.67	18.25	16.64	15.56
15.00	**16.00**	15.00	18.625	17.375	14.875
3.2	**3.3**	2.9	3.6	4.8	4.5
19.3	**7.2**	13.1	7.9	13.5	16.8
(6.3)	**6.7**	(19.5)	7.2	16.8	(7.0)
16.2	**17.2**	(3.5)	18.7	35.1	10.3

tal gains of $1.085 in 1985. The net asset value rose from $14.67 to $16.78 and the price of the stock likewise rose (from $15 to $16 at 12/31/85). An investor who bought these shares in December 1984 and sold them in December 1985 earned a return of 17.2 percent on the investment (before commissions on the purchase and subsequent sale).[4]

The potential for loss is also illustrated in Exhibit 14.2. If an investor bought the shares on December 31, 1983, he or she suffered a loss during 1984. While Salomon Brothers distributed $0.545 per share in income and $2.44 in capital gains, the net asset value and the price of the stock declined sufficiently to more than offset the income and capital gains distributions.

UNIT TRUSTS

A variation on the closed-end investment company is the fixed-unit investment trust, commonly referred to as a **unit trust.** These trusts, which are formed by brokerage firms and sold to investors in units of $1,000, hold a fixed portfolio of securities such as federal government or corporate bonds, municipal bonds, or mortgage loans. An example of such a trust is Merrill Lynch's Government Securities Income Fund, which invested solely in U.S. Treasury securities and other obligations backed by the full faith and credit of the federal government.

Unit trust ▲
Passive investment company with a fixed portfolio of assets that are self-liquidating

[4]The calculation of the annual return is

$$\frac{\$16.00 + \$0.495 + \$1.085 - \$15.00}{\$15.00} = 17.2\%.$$

A unit trust is a passive investment, as its assets are not traded but are frozen. The trust collects income (e.g., interest on its portfolio) and, eventually, the repayment of principal. The trust is also self-liquidating because as the funds are received, they are not reinvested but are distributed to stockholders. Since the trust's portfolio is fixed and not altered, operating expenses are low. Such trusts are primarily attractive to investors such as retirees who seek a steady, periodic flow of payments. If the investor needs the funds earlier, the shares may be sold back to the trust at their current net asset value.

MUTUAL FUNDS

Open-end investment companies, which are commonly called mutual funds, are similar to closed-end investment companies. However, there are some important differences. The first concerns their capital structure. Shares in mutual funds are not traded like other stocks and bonds. Instead, an investor who wants a position in a particular mutual fund purchases shares directly from the company. After receiving the money, the mutual fund issues new shares and purchases assets with these newly acquired funds. If an investor owns shares in the fund and wants to liquidate the position, the shares are sold back to the company. The shares are redeemed, and the fund pays the investor from its cash holdings. If the fund lacks sufficient cash, it will sell some of the securities it owns to obtain the money to redeem the shares. The fund cannot suspend this redemption feature except in an emergency, and then it may be done only with the permission of the Securities and Exchange Commission (SEC).

A second important difference between open-end and closed-end investment companies pertains to the cost of investing. Mutual funds continuously offer to sell new shares, and these shares are sold at their net asset value plus a sales fee, which is commonly called a *loading charge.* When the investor liquidates the position, the shares are redeemed at their net asset value. Most funds do not charge for the redemption, but some funds do assess an exit fee (i.e., a "back-end load") if the investor redeems the shares soon after they were purchased (e.g., six months later). Such fees are designed to discourage quick redemption of the shares.

No-load fund ▲
Investment company that does not charge a sales commission when individuals purchase shares from the fund

Load fund ▲
Investment company that charges commissions when individuals purchase shares from the fund

The loading fee may range from zero for **no-load mutual funds** to between 5 and 9.3 percent for **load funds.** Exhibit 14.3 presents the loading fees for six mutual funds. If the individual makes a substantial investment, the loading fee is usually reduced. For example, the American Balanced Fund offers the following schedule of fees:

EXHIBIT 14.3

Loading Charges for Selected Mutual Funds

Many mutual funds charge a sales commission, commonly called a loading charge or loading fee.

	Net Asset Value	Price	Loading Charge (as a Percentage of Net Asset Value)
American Balanced Fund	$11.41	$12.11	6.1%
American Growth Fund	20.17	21.40	6.1
Dean Witter High-Yield Fund	8.56	9.06	5.8
Franklin Group Gold Fund	14.88	15.50	4.2
Lord Abbott Government Securities	2.91	3.06	5.2
Merrill Lynch Basic Value Fund	19.94	21.33	7.0

Source: The Wall Street Journal, *January 2, 1990, C18.*

Investment	Fee
$ 25,000	6.0%
50,000	4.5
100,000	3.5
250,000	2.5

The investor should be warned that mutual funds state the loading charge as a percentage of the *offer* price. The effect of the fee being a percentage of the offer price and not a percentage of the net asset value is an increase in the effective percentage charged. If the loading charge is 8 percent and the offer price is $10, then the loading fee is $0.80. However, the net asset value is $9.20 ($10 minus $0.80). In this example, the loading charge as a percentage of the net asset value is 8.7 percent (8.0%/[1 − 0.08] = 8.0/0.92 = 8.7%), which is higher than the stated 8 percent loading charge.

It is immediately apparent which funds are no-load funds by the way in which mutual fund prices are quoted. Exhibit 14.4, which reproduces a quotation of mutual fund prices from *The Wall Street Journal,* illustrates this difference. The publication reports the net asset value (NAV), the offer price, and any change in the asset value from the previous day. If the offer price and the net asset value are the same (i.e., if the fund has no loading charge), "N.L." is printed in the offer price column. For example, the AARP Capital Growth fund has a net asset value of $23.04, and "N.L." appears in the offer column. Thus, these shares may be bought and sold from the company at their net asset value.

The quotation of funds with loading fees includes the net asset value and the offer price. For example, The Alliance Capital Balanced Fund has a net asset value of $11.09 per share and an offer price of $11.74. It

EXHIBIT 14.4

Offer Price and Net Asset Value (NAV) for Selected Mutual Funds

The reporting of mutual fund prices includes the fund's net asset value.

MUTUAL FUND QUOTATIONS

Friday, January 4, 1991

Price ranges for investment companies, as quoted by the National Association of Securities Dealers. NAV stands for net asset value per share; the offering includes net asset value plus maximum sales charge, if any.

	NAV	Offer Price	NAV Chg.
AAL Mutual:			
CaGr p	10.75	11.29	− .02
Inco p	9.71	10.20	− .02
MuBd p	9.97	10.47	− .01
AARP Invst:			
CaGr	23.04	NL	− .03
GinlM	15.35	NL	− .03
GthInc	23.15	NL	− .02
HQ Bd	15.21	NL	− .04
TxFBd	16.74	NL	− .01
TxFSh	15.22	NL	+ .01
ABT Funds:			
Emrg p	7.54	7.92	− .05
FL TF	10.29	10.80	.....
GthIn p	8.26	8.67	− .01
SecIn p	9.14	9.60	.....
UtilIn p	11.39	11.96	− .03
AHA Bal	9.82	NL	− .04
AdsnCa p	16.15	16.65	− .10
ADTEK	9.03	9.03	− .05
AEGON USA:			
CapApp	3.02	3.17	.....
HiYld	9.26	9.72	.....
Gwth	4.94	5.19	.....
AFA NAv	8.78	9.22	+ .01
AFA Tele	12.43	13.05	+ .09
AIM Funds:			
Chart p	6.38	6.75	− .02
Const p	7.38	7.81	− .04
CvYld p	9.28	9.74	− .03
HiYld p	4.96	5.21	+ .01
LimM p	9.90	10.08	− .01
Sumit	7.27	.....	− .04
Weing p	11.74	12.42	− .06
A M A Family:			
ClaGt p	7.28	NL	− .02
GlbGt p	19.39	NL	.....
GlbIn p	19.39	NL	− .02
GIST p		unavail	
USGv p	8.62	NL	.....
AMEV Funds:			
AstAl p	11.07	11.59	− .02
Capitl p	12.46	13.08	− .03
CaAp p	12.58	13.17	− .09
Fidcr p	19.92	20.86	− .05
Grwth p	16.95	17.80	− .13
HiYld p	5.61	5.87	+ .01
TF MN	9.70	10.16	.....
TF Nat	9.86	10.32	− .01
US Gvt	9.79	10.25	− .03
AMF Funds:			
Cp Bd	9.21	NL	− .02
IntlLiq	10.52	NL	− .02
MtgSc	10.92	NL	− .03
AcornF	32.14	32.14	− .09
Afuture	8.77	NL	− .05
Advance America:			
EqInc	9.00	9.45	− .04
TF In p	9.73	10.22	− .01
US Gv p	9.27	9.73	− .03
Advest Advant:			
Govt p	8.52	8.52	− .02
Gwth p	12.20	12.20	− .02
HY Bd p	6.26	6.26	− .01
Inco p	10.02	10.02	− .05
Spcl p	10.43	10.43	− .03
AlgrSCp t	14.52	14.52	− .06
AlgerG t	12.80	12.80	− .05
Alliance Cap:			
Allan p	5.07	5.37	− .02
Balan p	11.09	11.74	− .02
Canad p	5.61	5.94	+ .02
Conv p	6.73	7.12	.....
Count p	15.49	16.39	− .06
GlbSA p	8.29	8.77	− .02
Govt p	8.21	8.69	− .03
GrInc p	2.12	2.24	.....
HiYld p	4.57	4.84	− .04
IntlA p	13.76	14.56	− .04
ICalT p	12.46	13.05	.....
InsMu	9.56	10.01	.....

	NAV	Offer Price	NAV Chg.
Bernstein Fds:			
GvSh	12.68	NL	− .01
ShtDur	12.54	NL	.....
IntDur	12.70	NL	− .04
Ca Mu	12.72	NL	− .01
DivMu	12.78	NL	.....
NYMu	12.80	NL	− .01
BlanPr p	5.79	5.79	− .15
BlnSGr p	9.13	9.13	− .07
Boston Co:			
CaAp p	22.62	NL	− .10
Intl	10.84	NL	+ .02
IntGv p	12.04	NL	− .02
Mgdl p	10.60	NL	− .02
SpGth p	13.18	NL	− .07
Brndyw	14.87	NL	− .06
Bruce	91.58	NL	− .91
Bull & Bear Gp:			
CaGr p	6.05	NL	+ .01
EqInc p	10.60	NL	− .03
FNCI p	12.57	NL	− .03
Gold p	12.06	NL	− .11
HiYld p	7.74	NL	− .04
SpEq p	13.54	NL	− .11
TxFr p	16.97	NL	.....
USGv p	13.99	NL	− .05
Burnhm	19.45	20.47	− .04
CGM Funds:			
CapDv	17.55	NL	− .17
Mutl	21.09	NL	− .17
CJL Trst x	10.13	10.60	− .15
Calmos f	9.77	NL	− .02
CalMun p	8.64	8.64	− .01
CalTrst	11.55	NL	− .01
CalUS	9,68	NL	− .04
Calvert Group:			
Ariel	22.25	23.30	− .10
ArielA	14.10	14.76	− .08
Capitl p	18.13	18.98	− .02
GvLtd	14.81	15.11	− .01
Inco	15.97	16.72	− .04
Social p	25.75	26.96	− .10
SocBd	15.99	16.74	− .04
SocEq	16.43	17.20	− .08
TxF Lt	10.63	10.85	+ .01
TxF Lg	15.44	16.17	.....
US Gov	14.84	15.54	.....
WshA p	9.18	9.61	− .08
Capstone Group:			
CshFar	8.28	8.69	− .02
Fd SW	12.08	12.68	− .09
Incom	4.55	4.78	− .01
MedRs	13.59	14.27	− .03
PBHG	8.47	8.89	− .03
Ray EI	6.13	6.44	− .02
Trend	11.66	12.24	− .04
CarilCa	10.44	10.99	− .01
Carneg Cappielo:			
EmGr p	7.85	8.22	− .07
Grow p	14.51	15.19	− .03
TRetn p	9.65	10.10	+ .04
Carnegie Funds:			
Govt p	9.34	9.78	− .03
TEOhG	9.12	9.55	.....
TENHi	9.59	10.04	− .01
Cardnl	9.76	10.67	− .01
CrdnlGv	8.87	9.31	− .01
Cnt Shs	16.45	NL	− .02
ChanFI p	10.11	10.61	− .01
Chestnt	90.80	NL	− .01
CIGNA Funds:			
Agrsv p	11.48	12.05	− .03
GvSc p	9.99	10.52	− .01
Grth p	12.00	12.63	− .06
HiYld p	7.08	7.45	.....
Inco p	7.47	7.86	− .02
MunB p	7.69	8.09	− .01
Util p	12.38	13.03	+ .01
Value p	13.44	14.15	.....
Citibank IRA-CIT:			
Balan f	2.24	NL	− .02

Source: The Wall Street Journal, *June 7, 1991, p. C20.*

is a load fund. The buyer pays a load charge of $0.65 ($11.74 – $11.09) to purchase a share worth $11.09. Such a charge is 5.5 percent of the asking price and 5.9 percent of the net asset value.

In addition to loading charges, investors in mutual funds have to pay management fees, which are deducted from the income earned by the fund's portfolio. The fund also pays brokerage commissions when it buys and sells securities. The total cost of investing in mutual funds may be substantial when all of the costs (the loading charge and management and brokerage fees) are considered. Of course, the cost of investing is substantially reduced when the individual buys shares in no-load funds. The investor, however, must still pay the management fees and commission costs.

The third difference between closed-end and open-end investment companies is the source of profits to the investor. As with closed-end investment companies, individuals may profit from investments in mutual funds from several sources. Any income that is earned from the fund's assets in excess of expenses is distributed as dividends. If the fund's assets appreciate in value and the fund realizes these profits, the gains are distributed as capital gains. If the net asset value of the shares appreciates, the investor may redeem them at the appreciated price. Thus, in general, the open-end mutual fund offers investors the same means of earning profits as the closed-end investment company does, with one exception. In the case of closed-end investment companies, the price of the stock may rise relative to the net asset value of the shares. The possibility of a decreased discount or an increased premium is a potential source of profit that is available only through closed-end investment companies. It does not exist for mutual funds because their shares never sell at a discount.[5] Hence, changes in the discount or premium are a source of profit or loss to investors in closed-end but not in open-end investment companies.

While purchases of shares in investment companies may generate profits, they also subject the investor to risk. In Chapters 1 and 8 several sources of risk were discussed. These included the risk associated with investments in the securities of a particular firm (e.g., the stocks and bonds issued by AT&T). Since investment companies construct diversified portfolios, the impact of a particular investment on the outcome of the portfolio as a whole is reduced. Thus, the risk associated with an individual firm's securities is small (if not nonexistent).[6]

Other sources of risk, however, cannot be eliminated through the purchases of shares of investment companies. If security prices in gen-

[5] Load funds are actually sold at a premium (i.e., the loading fee).

[6] The investor still must bear the unsystematic risk associated with the individual investment company. This source of risk is reduced by investing in several investment companies.

Financial Facts

12b-1 Fees

While no-load mutual funds do not have a sales charge for the purchase of their shares, the funds may levy a fee charged against their income or assets to pay for marketing expenses. These funds have adopted a 12b-1 fee, which is named for the SEC rule that enables the funds to charge this fee. Unlike the loading fee, which is levied only once when the shares are purchased, 12b-1 fees are assessed every year. The fee is levied when the fund does well, and it is levied in years in which the fund experiences losses. These fees obviously reduce the return that the stockholder earns. In addition, since the fee is levied each year, the total amount paid over a period of time may exceed the one-time sales fee charged by the load mutual funds. • One way to determine if a no-load mutual fund has a 12b-1 fee is to read the fund's prospectus. This method, however, requires reading the prospectus of every fund that a person is considering for purchase. An alternate method is to consult *The Individual Investor's Guide to No-Load Mutual Funds,* which is published annually by the American Association of Individual Investors, 625 North Michigan Avenue, Chicago, Illinois 60611. This publication not only tells you if the fund has a 12b-1 fee but also reports the fund's performance, what services it offers, and other pertinent information that may help determine if this fund should be considered for inclusion in your portfolio. •

---

eral rise (or fall), the value of the investment company's portfolio will probably also rise (or fall). The managements of investment companies cannot consistently predict changes in the market and adjust their portfolios accordingly. The value of investment companies' portfolios and the value of their shares tend to move systematically with the market as a whole. Thus the risk associated with movements in the market is not eliminated through the purchase of shares in investment companies.

Inflation is also another source of risk that cannot be eliminated by acquiring shares in investment companies. If the return these firms earn is insufficient (i.e., below the rate of inflation), their stockholders experience a loss of purchasing power. It is even possible that the value of the investment company's stock may decline while inflation continues, in which case the investors are worse off than if they had held a regular savings account with a commercial bank.

The Portfolios of Mutual Funds

The portfolios of investment companies may be diversified or very specialized, but most may be classified into one of four types: income, growth, special situations, and balanced. Income funds stress assets that produce income; they buy stocks and bonds that pay generous dividends or interest income. The Value Line Income Fund is an example of a fund whose objective is income. Virtually all of its assets are income stocks, such as those of utilities, which pay generous dividends and periodically increase them as their earnings grow.

Growth funds stress appreciation in the value of the assets, and little emphasis is given to current income. The portfolio of the Value Line Fund is an example of a growth fund. The majority of the assets are the common stocks of companies with potential for growth. These **growth stocks** include the shares of very well known firms as well as those of smaller firms that may offer superior growth potential.

Growth stock ▲
Common stock whose earnings and stock price are expected to grow at an above average rate

Even within the class of growth funds there can be many differences. Some stress riskier securities in order to achieve larger returns and faster appreciation in their investors' funds. For example, the 44 Wall Street Fund seeks capital appreciation by investing in riskier securities including new issues, over-the-counter stocks, and warrants. Other growth funds, however, are more conservative. The Delaware Fund is a growth fund emphasizing larger companies that still are considered to offer capital appreciation.

Special situation investment companies specialize in more speculative securities that, given the "special situation," may yield large returns. These investment companies are perhaps the riskiest of all the mutual funds. The portfolio of Value Line Special Situation Funds illustrates this element of risk. The stocks in this portfolio tend to be in small companies or companies that have fallen on bad times but whose course may be changing. Investments in special situation securities can be very rewarding but some do not fulfill their potential return.

Balanced funds own a mixture of securities that sample the attributes of the assets of other mutual funds. A balanced fund, such as the Sentinel Group Balanced Fund, owns a variety of stocks, some of which offer potential growth while others are primarily income producers. A balanced portfolio may include short-term debt (such as U.S. Treasury bills), long-term debt, and preferred stock. Such a portfolio seeks a balance of income from dividends and interest and capital appreciation.

Many investment companies manage a wide spectrum of mutual funds. Each fund has a separate goal and hence has a different portfolio designed to achieve the fund's purpose. As may be seen in Exhibit 14.4, portfolio management firms offer investors the choice among numerous different mutual funds covering a wide spectrum of investment alternatives. For example, AIM offers seven funds, and the Calvert Group offers twelve. The individual may choose any combination of these funds. Therefore, an investor who seeks income may acquire shares in an equity income fund, a government securities fund, and a bond fund. Such investments would give that individual a diversified portfolio of income-earning assets.

In addition to offering a variety of funds from which to choose, companies that manage several mutual funds may permit the investor to shift investments from one fund to another fund without paying any fees. For example, an individual who is currently employed may seek capital appreciation and invest in a growth-oriented fund but on retirement may shift the proceeds to a bond fund to collect a flow of interest

Financial Facts

Families of Funds

Mutual funds are often managed by firms that specialize in money management. These firms establish diverse mutual funds with varying objectives to tap the savings of investors with different portfolio goals. For example, Vanguard offers the following funds with their objectives: • Vanguard Equity-Income: stocks that generate dividends; Vanguard Explorer: small company stocks for growth; Vanguard High-Yield Stock: poor quality, potential high income; Vanguard Index 500: index fund; Vanguard Quantitative: small company stocks for growth; Vanguard Small Capitalization Stock: small company stocks for growth; Vanguard Special Energy: natural resource companies; Vanguard Special Gold & Precious Metal: precious metals; Vanguard Special Health Care: health, pharmaceutical; Vanguard Star: balanced portfolio; and Vanguard World International: growth Global, growth fund. • How have the various Vanguard funds performed? During 1990, their annual returns ranged from 16.8 percent for the health care fund to −29.5 percent for the high-yield fund. These returns and how the funds performed relative to competitive funds are reported annually in the "Mutual Fund Scoreboard" in *Business Week*. For example, the −29.5 percent loss resulted in a rank of 30th out of the 30 high-yield funds covered by the *Business Week* scorecard. (*Business Week*, February 18, 1991, p. 105.) The *BW* scorecard includes the fund's load charge (if applicable), the historic return over 3, 5, and 10 years, the turnover of the fund's portfolio, the fund's largest holding, the P/E ratio, and the risk associated with the fund. •

---

income. Such a shift could be achieved by converting the shares in the growth fund into shares of the bond fund. In many cases this switch may be made without the investor paying any commissions on the transaction.

The Portfolios of Specialized Mutual Funds

Investment trusts initially sought to pool the funds of many savers and to invest these funds in a diversified portfolio of assets. Such diversification spread the risk of investing and reduced the risk of loss to the individual investor. While a particular investment company had a specified goal, such as growth or income, the portfolio was still sufficiently diversified so that the element of unsystematic risk was reduced.

Today, however, a variety of funds have developed that have moved away from this concept of diversification and the reduction of risk. Instead of offering investors a cross section of American business, many funds have been created to offer investors specialized investments. For example, an investment company may be limited to investments in the securities of a particular sector of the economy or particular industry, such as gold (e.g., ASA, Limited). There are also funds that specialize in a particular type of security, such as bonds (e.g., American General Bond Fund).

During the 1970s the scope of some investment companies became even narrower. For example, the Dreyfus Merger and Acquisition Fund seeks to identify firms that are potential candidates for merger with or takeover by other firms. Such mergers and takeovers often result in substantial profits for the stockholders of the target firms. These profits can be even larger if two firms seek to take over a third company and a bidding war erupts. The management of the Dreyfus Merger and Acquisition Fund tries to identify the stocks of companies that appear to be underpriced and that may be bought out at substantial premiums over their current prices. Obviously, this is a very specialized fund, and its investors bear two considerable risks not borne by investors in the traditional mutual fund. These risks involve (1) the ability of the fund's management to identify takeover candidates and (2) the possibility that the mergers and takeovers will not actually occur. If a stock is underpriced but no one seeks to take over the firm, then the stock may remain underpriced for a long period of time.[7]

In addition to these speculative funds, several specialized investment companies have been established that offer real alternatives to traditional types of mutual funds. For example, money market mutual funds, which were discussed in Chapter 2, provide the individual with a means to invest indirectly in money market instruments such as Treasury bills and negotiable certificates of deposit. Funds that acquire foreign securities offer the individual a means to invest in stocks of companies located in Europe and Asia. Other specialized funds include index funds and tax-exempt funds.

Index fund ▲ Mutual fund whose portfolio seeks to duplicate an index of stock prices

The purpose of an **index fund** is almost diametrically opposed to the traditional purpose of a mutual fund. Instead of identifying specific securities for purchase, the managements of these funds seek to duplicate the composition of an index, such as Standard & Poor's 500 stock index. Such funds should then perform in tandem with the market as a whole. Although they cannot generally outperform the market, neither can they underperform the market. Part of the popularity of such funds has been attributed to the poor performance of mutual funds in general in the past. (The returns earned by mutual funds will be discussed later in this chapter.) While these funds cannot overcome any risk associated with price fluctuations in the market as a whole, they do eliminate the risk associated with the selection of specific securities (i.e., unsystematic risk).

In addition to erasing asset-specific risk, index funds help investors manage systematic risk. Index funds permit different individuals to tailor their portfolios in accordance with the level of systematic risk they are willing to accept. By altering the proportion of risk-free assets in a diversified portfolio, the individual may establish different levels of risk and return. Thus, conservative investors may invest a large proportion

---

[7] The efficient market hypothesis suggests that such undervaluations will quickly disappear. If a firm were a takeover candidate, its price should already discount that information.

of their wealth in risk-free assets (e.g., federally insured savings accounts, shares in money market mutual funds, and U.S. Treasury bills) and a small proportion in an index fund. Such portfolios would have a modest expected return but would involve nominal risk. More aggressive investors may commit a larger proportion of their wealth to the index fund. These individuals would expect a higher return because they are bearing more risk. This, of course, is the relationship between risk and return that was presented on an intuitive basis in Figure 1.2 and stated more formally in the presentation of the capital asset pricing model illustrated in Figure 8.9.

Another recently introduced specialized mutual fund is the investment company whose portfolio is devoted to tax-exempt bonds. Until 1976, open-end mutual funds were legally barred from this market. However, with the passage of enabling legislation, mutual funds were permitted to own tax-exempt bonds, and several funds were immediately started that specialize in tax-exempt securities. These funds offer investors, especially those with modest funds to invest, an opportunity to earn tax-free income and maintain a diversified portfolio. Since municipal bonds are sold in minimum units of $5,000, a sizable sum is required for an individual investor to obtain a diversified portfolio. Ten bonds of ten different state and local governments would cost about $50,000. The advantages of tax-free income and a reduction in risk were virtually impossible for most investors.

However, mutual funds that specialize in tax-exempt bonds offer small investors both of these advantages. The funds are sold in smaller denominations. For example, $1,000 may be the minimum initial investment, and additional investments may be made for as little as $100. The ability to buy in small denominations means that modest investors may buy shares in these funds. Since the firms pool the funds of many investors, small investors also obtain the advantage of diversification.

MUTUAL FUNDS WITH FOREIGN INVESTMENTS

Global fund ▲
Mutual fund whose portfolio includes foreign and U.S. firms, especially those with international operations

From an American perspective, there are basically three types of mutual funds with international investments. **Global funds** invest in foreign and American securities. Many American mutual funds are global, as they maintain some part of their portfolios in foreign investments. While these funds do not specialize in foreign securities, they do offer the individual investor the advantages associated with foreign investments: returns through global economic growth, diversification from assets whose returns are not positively correlated, and possible excess returns from inefficient foreign financial markets.

In addition to global funds, there are **international funds,** which invest solely in foreign securities and hold no American securities, and **regional funds,** which specialize in a particular geographic area, such as Asia. (There are also mutual funds that specialize in a particular geographic area within the United States.) While the regional funds obviously specialize, the international funds may also specialize during particular time periods. (The objectives and types of more than 900 funds may be obtained from *Barron's/Lipper Gauge,* published quarterly.)

International fund ▲
Mutual fund whose portfolio is limited to non-U.S. securities

Regional fund ▲
Mutual fund that specializes in the firms in a particular geographical area

American investors may also acquire shares in foreign investment companies, such as the British mutual funds called "unit trusts." Thus, if an American investor cannot find an acceptable domestic fund, the search may be extended to a foreign fund. However, since these securities are not registered with the SEC, some foreign funds will not sell shares directly to Americans, as these funds believe such sales are illegal. In other cases purchases may be made for a fee through foreign banks with branches in the United States. However, the individual should probably ask himself or herself if the potential return is worth the additional expense required to acquire the shares.

THE RETURNS EARNED ON INVESTMENTS IN MUTUAL FUNDS

As was previously explained, the securities of investment companies offer individuals several advantages. First, the investor receives the advantages of a diversified portfolio, which reduces risk. Some investors may lack the resources to construct a diversified portfolio, and the purchase of shares in an investment company permits these investors to own a portion of a diversified portfolio. Second, the portfolio is professionally managed and under continuous supervision. Many investors may not have the time and expertise to manage their own portfolios and, except in the case of large portfolios, may lack the funds to obtain professional management. By purchasing shares in an investment company, individuals buy the services of professional management, which may increase the investor's return. Third, the administrative detail and custodial aspects of the portfolio (e.g., the physical handling of securities) are taken care of by the management of the company.

Although investment companies offer advantages, there are also disadvantages. The services offered by an investment company are not unique but may be obtained elsewhere. For example, the trust department of a commercial bank offers custodial services, and leaving the securities with the broker and registering them in the broker's name relieves the investor of storing the securities and keeping some of the records. In addition, the investor may acquire a diversified portfolio with only a modest amount of capital. Diversification does not require 100 different stocks. If the investor has $20,000, a reasonably diversified portfolio may be produced by investing in the stock of eight to ten companies in different industries. One does not have to purchase shares in an investment company to obtain the advantage of diversification.

Investment companies do offer the advantage of professional management, but this management cannot guarantee to outperform the market. A particular firm may do well in any given year, but it may do very poorly in subsequent years. Several studies have been undertaken to determine if professional management results in superior performance for mutual funds.

The first study, conducted for the SEC, covered the period from 1952 through 1958.[8] This study found that the performance of mutual funds was not significantly different from that of an unmanaged portfolio of similar assets. About half the funds outperformed Standard & Poor's indices, but the other half underperformed these aggregate measures of the market. In addition, there was no evidence of superior performance by a particular fund over a number of years.

These initial results were confirmed by later studies.[9] When the loading charges are included in the analysis, the return earned by investors tends to be less than that which would be achieved through a random selection of securities.

These results are easy to misinterpret. They do not imply that the managements of mutual funds are incompetent. Efficient financial markets suggest that the managers of mutual funds will not consistently outperform the market, and the findings give strong support for the efficient market hypothesis that was discussed in Chapter 6.

What these results do imply is that mutual funds and other investment companies may offer investors a means to match the performance of the market and still obtain the advantages of diversification and custodial services. For some, these are sufficient reasons to invest in the shares of investment companies instead of directly in stocks and bonds. These investors do not have to concern themselves with the selection of individual securities.

---

[8]See Irwin Friend et al., *A Study of Mutual Funds* (Washington, D.C.: U.S. Government Printing Office, 1962).

[9]See, for instance, William F. Sharpe, "Mutual Fund Performance," *Journal of Business*, special supplement, 39 (January 1966), pp. 119–138; Michael C. Jensen, "The Performance of Mutual Funds in the Period 1945–64," *Journal of Finance*, 23 (May 1968), pp. 389–416; Patricia Dunn and Rolf D. Theisen, "How Consistently Do Active Managers Win?" *Journal of Portfolio Management*, 9 (Summer 1983), pp. 47–50; and Frank J. Fabozzi, Jack C. Francis, and Cheng F. Lee, "Generalized Functional Form for Mutual Fund Performance," *Journal of Financial and Quantitative Analysis*, 15 (December 1980), pp. 1107–1120.

The Job Mart

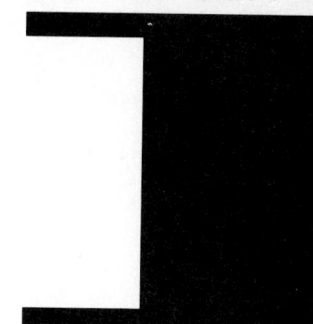

Bank Trust Officer

■ Job Description: Responsible for the management of individuals' funds. Serve as trustee for the elderly, the incompetent, the infirm, or children who are unable to manage their own funds. Allocate trust funds among various investments, time and execute portfolio changes, and develop long-term investment goals and strategies. ■ Job Requirements: Strong background in investment techniques and portfolio management, especially the ability to identify investments that offer good returns for moderate amounts of risk. A law degree or additional background or specialized work in taxation with emphasis on personal and estate taxation is desirable. ■ Characteristics: Since taxation plays a crucial role in the management of trust funds, a trust officer must keep abreast of changes in the tax laws. Strong interpersonal skills are desirable, including the ability to communicate with customers who establish trusts and with their beneficiaries.

SUMMARY

Instead of directly investing in securities, individuals may buy shares in investment companies. These firms, in turn, invest the funds in various assets, such as stocks and bonds.

There are two types of investment companies. A closed-end investment company has a specified number of shares that are bought and sold in the same manner as the stock of firms such as AT&T. An open-end investment company (i.e., a mutual fund) has a variable number of shares sold directly to investors. Investors who desire to liquidate their holdings sell them back to the company.

Investment companies offer several advantages, including professional management, diversification, and custodial services. Dividends and the interest earned on the firm's assets are distributed to stockholders. In addition, if the value of the company's assets rises, the stockholders profit as capital gains are realized and distributed.

Mutual funds may be classified by the types of assets they own. Some stress income-producing assets, such as bonds, preferred stock, and common stock of firms that distribute a large proportion of their income. Other mutual funds stress growth in their net asset values through investments in firms with the potential to grow and generate capital gains. There are also investment companies that specialize in special situations, particular sectors of the economy, and tax-exempt securities. There are even mutual funds that seek to duplicate an index of the stock market.

To select an investment company, the individual should match his or her objectives with those of the particular fund. The past performance of the fund may also be used to select funds; however, the historical returns may not indicate future returns. The managements of few mutual funds have outperformed the market over a number of years. Instead, mutual funds tend to achieve about the same results as the market as a whole. This performance is consistent with the efficient market hypothesis, which suggests that few, if any, investors will outperform the market over an extended period of time.

Review Questions

1. What is the difference between a closed-end and an open-end investment company?
2. Are mutual funds subject to federal income taxation?
3. What custodial services do investment companies provide?
4. What is a loading charge? Do all investment companies charge this fee?
5. Why may the small investor prefer mutual funds to other investments?
6. What is a specialized mutual fund? How is it different from a special situation fund?
7. Should an investor expect a mutual fund to outperform the market? If not, why should the investor buy the shares?

Problems

1. What is the net asset value of an investment company with $10,000,000 in assets, $790,000 in current liabilities, and 1,200,000 shares outstanding?
2. If a mutual fund's net asset value is $23.40 and the fund sells its shares for $25, what is the load fee as a percentage of the net asset value?
3. If an investor buys shares in a no-load mutual fund for $31.40 and after two years the shares appreciate to $44.60, what is (1) the percentage return and (2) the annual rate of return?
4. An investor buys shares in a mutual fund for $20. At the end of the year the fund distributes a dividend of $0.58, and after the distribution the net asset value of a share is $23.41. What would be the investor's return on the investment?

Suggested Readings

For essential information on investment companies (e.g., address, purpose, dividend distributions, price performance, and so on), consult:

Investment Companies. New York: Wiesenberger Services, Inc. Published annually.

For similar information that is limited to no-load funds, consult:

The Individual Investors' Guide to No-Load Mutual Funds. Chicago: American Association of Individual Investors. Published annually.

Quarterly data concerning the performance of mutual funds is reported in* Barron's *in a section entitled "Barron's/Lipper Gauge—A Quarterly Survey of Mutual Fund Performance."

General books that discuss the merits of investing in mutual funds include:

Anderson, Carl E. *Anderson on Mutual Funds.* Glenview, Ill.: Scott, Foresman, 1984.

Rugg, Donald D., and Norman B. Hale. *The Dow Jones-Irwin Guide to Mutual Funds.* 3d ed. Homewood, Ill.: Dow Jones-Irwin, 1986.

For discussion of mutual funds whose portfolios seek to match broad indices of the market (i.e., the so-called "index" funds), consult:

Calderwood, Stanford. "The Truth About Index Funds." *Financial Analysts Journal* (July–August 1977), pp. 36–47.

A guide to a mutual fund's prospectus is given in:

Perritt, Gerald W. "Fund Literature: A Guide to the Essentials," *AAII Journal* (March 1986), pp. 22–24.

Corporate Finance

■ In 1990, Exxon had assets of $74,000,000,000. Imagine managing that many assets! Sanmark-Stardust, a much smaller firm that once concluded a licensing agreement with actress Joan Collins for a line of lingerie to bear her name, has assets of $80,000,000. Someone also has to be responsible for the management of Sanmark-Stardust's assets, and the financial managers of both Exxon and Sanmark-Stardust must find financing to carry their respective firm's assets.

Although managing these firms' assets is important, it may have little impact on you or me (unless we work for either firm). Financing these assets, however, may have considerable impact on us. It is the savings of individuals, other firms, and governments that form the source of finance that permits Exxon and Sanmark-Stardust to acquire their assets. The well-being of our investments may very much be affected by the management of these firms' assets. Even if we don't directly invest in either firm, we may own shares in mutual funds or pension plans that do invest in Exxon or Sanmark-Stardust.

Parts One and Two of this text covered areas in finance that touch the lives of everyone: financial institutions and the individual's investments. This last section is devoted to financial management from the business perspective. While few individuals may become financial managers, they may have contact with specific components of corporate finance (e.g., how Exxon chooses to finance its assets). And, of course, an individual who chooses to become an entrepreneur and operate his or her own business will be facing many of the same decisions required of the corporate financial manager.

The remaining 11 chapters cover a variety of corporate financial decisions: the management of short- and long-term assets, how these assets should be financed, which combination of debt and equity funds is optimal, how to plan when the firm will need finance, how to analyze the firm's performance, and whether the firm should grow through mergers. Financial decisions permeate virtually all business decisions since most business decisions have financial implications. Thus, it is particularly desirable for nonfinance students to be aware of the components of financial decision making. Such knowledge can help individuals to communicate and advance within the business community.

chapter 15

The Forms of Business and Federal Income Taxation

20 pages in chapter

Learning Objectives

1. Enumerate the differences and similarities among types of businesses.
2. Differentiate among progressive, proportional, and regressive taxes.
3. Explain how the taxation of corporate earnings, dividends, and personal income affect the decision to incorporate.
4. Distinguish between straight-line and accelerated cost recovery systems of depreciation.
5. Explain why accelerated depreciation stimulates investment spending.

The former prime minister of Canada, W. L. MacKenzie King, said, "Labor can do nothing without capital, capital can do nothing without labor, and neither labor nor capital can do anything without the guiding genius of management." The preceding chapters have considered (1) how the economy generates and allocates capital through a sophisticated system of financial institutions and (2) the securities available to the individual investor. The remainder of this text will be devoted to the financial manager's tasks. Successful business administration requires the genius of a successful financial manager.

All firms employ someone who performs the role of the financial manager. As the subsequent chapters of this text will discuss, the role of the financial manager is broad, covering financial planning and analysis, management of current assets and liabilities, and long-term investments and financing decisions. This chapter sets the stage for the subsequent discussion by considering the forms of business, the impact of federal taxation, and depreciation. The chapter begins with a discussion of the differences among sole proprietorships, partnerships, and corporations.

A major reason for preferring the corporate form of business over sole proprietorships and partnerships is federal income taxation. One of the important tasks of financial management is to reduce the tax liability of the firm. This chapter discusses differences in personal and corporate income taxes. Special consideration is given to the methods of depreciation that affect both the firm's taxes and the cash flow that are generated by an investment. The chapter ends with a discussion of the carry back and carry forward of corporate tax losses.

FORMS OF BUSINESS

Most businesses can be classified into one of three forms: sole proprietorships, partnerships, and corporations. Other forms include syndications, trusts, and joint stock companies. By far the largest number is sole proprietorships. As of 1986, there were 12,394,000 sole proprietorships to only 1,703,000 partnerships and 3,429,000 corporations. However, corporations generated revenues of $8,281.9 billion and profits of $269.4 billion, while sole proprietorships had revenues and profits of $559.4 billion and $90.4 billion, respectively.[1] Obviously, corporations own the majority of the nation's productive capacity, generate most of the sales, and earn most of the profits. Sole proprietorships are primarily "ma and pa" operations that are limited to small operations like the corner store. However, many large corporations had such modest beginnings, and American business is filled with stories of a talented person building a small business into an industrial leader.

Sole proprietorship Firm with one owner ▲

A **sole proprietorship,** as the name implies, has one owner. The firm may employ other people and may borrow money, but the sole pro-

[1] *The 1990 Statistical Abstract of the United States* (Washington, D.C.: U.S. Department of Commerce), p. 521.

prietor bears the risk of ownership and reaps the profits if they are earned. These are important elements of a sole proprietorship, for the firm has no existence without its proprietor. The firm is not a legal entity that can be held responsible for its actions. The sole proprietor is responsible for the firm's actions and thus is legally liable for the firm's debts. Sole proprietors bear the risk of ownership, and this risk is not limited to their personal investments. They can lose more than the money invested in their businesses, because the sole proprietor can be held liable for the debts incurred to operate the business. However, since the sole proprietorship is not a legal entity, the firm pays no income taxes. Any profits are considered to be income for the sole proprietor and thus are subject only to personal income taxation.

A **partnership** is very similar to a proprietorship except that there are at least two owners (i.e., partners) of the business. While a partnership may have as few as two owners, there is no limit to the number of partners. A partnership has no life without its partners. The partners are the owners, and they reap the rewards and bear the risks of ownership. Each of the partners contributes something to the firm, and this contribution need not be money. For example, several partners may contribute money while others contribute expertise.

Partnership ▲
Firm formed by two or more individuals, each of whom is liable for the firm's debts

When a partnership is formed, the rights and obligations of the partners are established. The most important of these are the partners' shares of profits and the extent of their liability. In the simplest case, each partner contributes some percentage of the money necessary to run the business and receives this percentage of the profits. However, not all partnership agreements are this simple. For example, if one partner contributes cash and the other contributes expertise, the division of profits may not be 50–50. Instead, the distribution will be mutually established by the partners.

In general, all the partners bear the risk of enterprise. Each partner is liable for the total debt of the firm. Thus, the individual partner's liability is not limited to his or her contribution to the firm. While creditors initially seek settlement of claims from the firm, they can sue the partners for payment if the firm fails to meet the claims. If one partner is unable to pay the prorated share of these obligations, the other partners are liable for these debts. In addition, a partner's share in the firm may be seized to settle *personal* debts. While the creditors must initially sue the individual for personal obligations, if these cannot be met the creditors then have a claim on the partnership. These claims and counterclaims may be complex, but the general order is that personal creditors have an initial claim on the partners' personal assets, and the firm's creditors have the initial claim on the partnership's assets. If personal assets are insufficient to meet the individual's obligations, creditors may make a claim against that partner's share of the partnership. If the firm's assets are insufficient, the partnership's creditors may make claims against the individual partners.

Financial Facts

Financial Ethics

Finance courses are generally taught from a positive, rather than a normative, viewpoint. The emphasis is on market forces and the belief that quantitative techniques and the rational application of financial and economic theory lead to correct financial decision making. Phrases such as "the financial manager should take a particular action" suggest that the best financial strategy is the one that will increase both the value of the firm and the decision maker's power or income. • Financial decisions, however, may not be independent of moral decisions. For example, should a firm invest in South Africa? The analysis may suggest that such an investment will be profitable and therefore will increase the value of the firm. From a positive perspective, therefore, the investment "should" be made. A normative perspective, however, may interject that such an investment suggests implicit support for the segregation policies followed by the South African government. Even though the logic itself may not be correct (i.e., the investment need not imply support for segregation), the financial decision maker is still faced with a normative question: "Should the investment not be made because it appears to support segregation?" • Many corporate managers have in fact decided to withdraw from South Africa, but it is impossible to determine whether they left on moral grounds or whether they came to the conclusion that remaining would reduce the value of the firm and decrease their power and income. (This unanswerable question is not limited to financial decisions. The legislature of New Jersey passed a law requiring the state's pension plans to divest themselves of investments in firms with operations in South Africa. Was this law passed on moral grounds or because failure to pass it may have lost votes?) • Since finance is concerned with the management of money and resources, moral questions frequently lie under the surface. Some are more obvious than others. The use of inside information for personal profit is, of course, both morally and legally wrong. The decision to relocate a plant is neither morally nor legally wrong but will certainly inflict pain on the individuals affected. How that pain may be alleviated may be both a moral and a financial problem that management will have to face. •

Limited partnership ▲ Partnership in which some of the partners have limited liability and are not liable for the partnership's debts

Limited liability ▲ Individual's personal liability extending only to his or her investment in the firm

Corporation ▲ Economic unit created by a state, having the power to own assets, incur liabilities, and engage in specific activities

There is a type of partnership that grants limited liability to certain partners. These partnerships are called **limited partnerships;** in these, the limited partners are liable for only their contributions. While these partners have **limited liability,** they have no control over the operation of the firm. Such control rests with the remaining (or general) partners, who are subject to unlimited liability. This form of partnership is popular for risky types of enterprises, such as oil and gas drilling operations, prospecting and mining, and real estate.

A **corporation** is an artificial, legal economic unit established by a state. Every corporation must be incorporated in a state. There is much variation in the individual state laws that establish corporations, and this variation has caused some states to become more popular than others in which to form a corporation. Under the state laws, the firm is issued a certificate of incorporation that gives the name of the corporation, the location of the corporation's principal office, the purpose of the corpora-

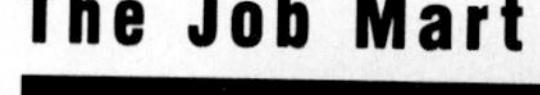

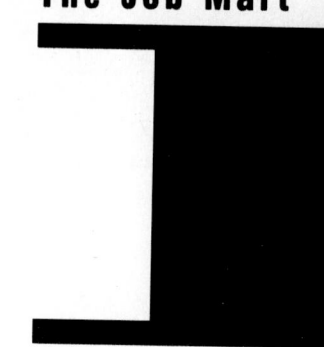

Financial Journalist and Writer

■ Job Description: Report on current events in finance and investments. Prepare quarterly and annual reports, news bulletins, and press releases. Write speeches for management or sales/marketing copy for advertising. ■ Job Requirements: Knowledge of economics, finance, financial institutions, and technical writing. Strong interpersonal skills are necessary as authors specializing in business writing have contact with people ranging from editors and production staff to individuals from many facets of a firm's operations. ■ Characteristics: Individual must work well under pressure to meet deadlines. Ability to use word processing, wire service reports, data bases, and library searches are assumed, in addition to writing skills.

---

tion, and the number of shares of stock (shares of ownership) that are authorized (i.e., the number of shares that the firm may issue). In addition to the certificate of incorporation, the firm receives a **charter** that specifies the relationship between the corporation and the state. At the initial meeting of stockholders, **bylaws** are established that set the rules by which the firm is governed (e.g., the voting rights of the stockholders).

Charter ▲ Document specifying the relationship between a firm and the state in which the firm is incorporated

Bylaws ▲ Document specifying the relationship between a corporation and its stockholders

In the eyes of the law a corporation is a legal entity that is separate from its owners. It may enter contracts and is legally responsible for its obligations. This significantly differentiates corporations from sole proprietorships and partnerships. Once a firm incorporates, the owners of the corporation are liable only for the amount of their investment in the company. Owners of corporations have "limited liability," and this limited liability is a major advantage of incorporating. Creditors may sue the corporation for payment if the corporation defaults on its obligations, but the creditors cannot sue the stockholders.

For many small corporations, however, limited liability may not exist. Creditors may ask that the stockholders pledge their personal assets to secure a small corporation's loans. Thus, if the corporation defaults, the creditors may seize assets that the shareholders have pledged. If this occurs, the liability of the shareholders is not limited to their initial investment. Limited liability does apply in substance to large corporations that have assets to pledge or sufficient credit ratings to receive unsecured loans. Thus, an investor knows that on purchasing the stock in a company such as General Motors, the maximum amount that can be lost is the amount of the investment. If the firm goes bankrupt, the creditors cannot seize the assets of the stockholders. Such limited liability is a major advantage of incorporating a firm, for large corporations (e.g., Continental Airlines, Federated Department Stores, and Interco) do go bankrupt.

A second potential advantage of incorporation is the ease with which title of ownership may be transferred from one investor to another. All that is necessary for such transfer is for the investor to sell the shares of stock (which are evidence of ownership) and have the name of the new owner recorded on the corporation's record of stockholders. Such transfers occur daily through organized security exchanges like the New York Stock Exchange. This transfer of ownership, however, may be considerably more difficult for small corporations or corporations that are owned by just a few stockholders. For the ease of transfer to occur, there must exist a ready market for the stock. Since there is no ready market for small corporations' stock, the owners may have difficulty transferring the title to their shares. Finding a buyer for stock in a small corporation may be a very difficult task. Thus, while the ease of transferring ownership is an advantage of incorporating, this advantage does not apply to all corporations.

A third advantage of incorporating is permanence. Since the corporation is established by the laws of the state, it is permanent until dissolved by the state. Proprietorships and partnerships cease when one of the owners dies or goes bankrupt and must be re-formed in order to continue to operate. Corporations, however, continue to exist when one of the owners dies. The stock becomes part of the deceased owner's estate and is transferred to the heirs. The company continues to operate, and a new corporation is not formed. Permanence offers a major advantage for incorporating if the owners envision the firm's growing in size and operating for many years, since the expense of re-forming the relationship among the owners is avoided.

Incorporating may also offer the firm the advantage of being able to raise large amounts of money by issuing bonds and stock. Limited liability for stockholders, the potential for capital gains, and the existence of secondary markets in which the securities can be bought and sold are advantages associated with incorporating that do not exist for unincorporated firms. For example, firms such as IBM can readily issue new bonds or new stock to raise capital. Even corporations with credit ratings that are inferior to IBM's may be able to raise substantial amounts of money through new issues of stocks and/or bonds. Although these corporations may have to offer higher yields on their securities to induce investors to bear the additional risk, they still may use this source of funds.

This ability of corporations to obtain substantial amounts of money by issuing new securities usually applies only to large firms. The managers of small, privately held corporations may not be able to raise outside financing by selling stocks and bonds. Thus, the advantage of incorporating as a means to raise external funds is limited to a small proportion of the total number of corporations in existence. The remaining corporations encounter the same difficulties obtaining outside funding that the owners of sole proprietorships and partnerships face.

TAXES

Taxes play an extremely important role in financial decision making. Most of the decisions involving taxes stress minimizing the amount of taxes that the firm or individual has to pay. The diversity and complexities of tax laws that affect financial decision making are staggering and require tax expertise. Unfortunately, few individual business executives can obtain this expertise and still perform their other roles. Hence, some lawyers and accountants have become tax experts and sell their services to individuals and managers of firms.

Taxes are levied by governments at all levels. The financial manager, from the sole proprietor through the manager of the largest corporation, will find a variety of tax laws that affect the business. These taxes include corporate income taxes, capital gains taxes, and state and local taxes on property such as real estate, plant and equipment, and inventory. Within this country there are thousands of governmental units ranging from small localities to the federal government.

Progressivity of Taxes

The federal government's personal and corporate income taxes are progressive. Other taxes, such as a municipality's property taxes or a state's sales taxes, are not progressive but are regressive or proportional. What do the terms progressive, regressive, or proportional imply?

Progressivity and regressivity are determined by the taxes paid relative to some tax base, such as an individual's income or a corporation's profits. An income tax is **progressive** if, as the individual's income rises, the tax *rate* increases. It is not sufficient for the absolute amount of taxes paid to increase with the increases in income. For a tax to be **regressive,** the tax rate declines as the tax base increases. If the tax rate remains constant as income increases, then the tax is **proportionate.**

Progressive tax ▲
Tax in which the tax rate increases as the tax base increases

Regressive tax ▲
Tax in which the tax rate decreases as the tax base increases

Proportionate tax ▲
Tax in which the rate remains unchanged as the tax base increases

The differences in progressive, regressive, and proportionate taxes are illustrated in Exhibit 15.1. The first column gives an individual's income. The second and third columns illustrate a progressive tax, for the tax rate increases with the increases in income. The fourth and fifth columns illustrate a regressive tax, for the tax rate declines as incomes rise. The last two columns illustrate a proportionate tax, for the rate remains constant as income changes. As may be seen in this table, the absolute amount of tax paid increases in each case. However, the effect of the higher tax rates on the total amount of taxes is considerable as the income rises from $10,000 to $50,000. With the regressive tax structure, the tax rises from $1,000 to $3,000. With the progressive tax, the amount paid in taxes rises to $15,000.

EXHIBIT 15.1

Differences in Taxes Paid under Hypothetical Progressive, Regressive, and Proportional Tax Rates

Income	Progressive Tax Rate	Total Tax Paid	Regressive Tax Rate	Total Tax Paid	Proportional Tax Rate	Total Tax Paid
$10,000	10%	$ 1,000	10%	$1,000	20%	$ 2,000
20,000	15	3,000	9	1,800	20	4,000
30,000	20	6,000	8	2,400	20	6,000
40,000	25	10,000	7	2,800	20	8,000
50,000	30	15,000	6	3,000	20	10,000

For a tax to be progressive, the tax rate must increase with the tax base.

EXHIBIT 15.2

Income Levels and Marginal Tax Rates for a Married Couple Filing a Joint Return for 1991

Taxable Income	Marginal Tax Rate
$0–34,000	15%
$34,001–82,150	28
$82,150	31

The federal personal income tax is progressive as the tax rate rises with income.

Many people believe that taxes should be progressive because individuals with higher income are better able to pay and should bear a larger proportion of the cost of the government. It is on this basis that many regressive and proportional taxes (especially the property tax) are criticized. Regressive taxes place a larger share of the cost of government on those individuals who are the least able to afford the burden. Arguments for progressive taxes, however, are primarily based on ethical or normative beliefs. It is a moral judgment that people with higher income should pay a proportionately higher amount of tax.

The federal personal income tax is progressive, for as the individual's taxable income rises, the tax rate increases. As the individual reaches higher income tax brackets, the rate at which additional income is taxed rises. The tax rate on this marginal income is referred to as the individual's **marginal tax rate.** Exhibit 15.2 gives the federal income tax rates for a married couple filing a joint return in 1992 for income earned during 1991. As may be seen in the exhibit, the marginal tax rates increase with income, indicating that federal income tax is progressive.

Marginal tax rate Tax rate paid on the last (marginal) dollar of income or earnings

EXHIBIT 15.3

Income Levels and Marginal Tax Rates for a Corporation Filing for 1991

Taxable Income	Marginal Tax Rate
$0–50,000	15%
$50,001–75,000	25
Over $75,000	34

The federal corporate income tax is progressive as the tax rate increases with income.

The federal corporate income tax is also progressive, as is illustrated in Exhibit 15.3. The left-hand column gives the corporation's taxable income; the column on the right gives the marginal tax rate. Since the tax rate rises with increases in corporate income, the federal corporate income tax is progressive.

Differences in Tax Rates and the Decision to Incorporate

The effect of taxes on the decision to incorporate is illustrated in Exhibit 15.4. This table shows the disposable income that an individual will have with a sole proprietorship and with a corporation under two sets of assumptions concerning the retention of earnings. In the first case, there is no reinvestment of funds in the business. In the second example, an equal amount for the proprietorship and the corporation is reinvested in the firm. In both cases, taxes paid reflect the individual's filing a joint return in 1991 for income earned during 1990.[2]

Both cases in Exhibit 15.4 start with $50,000 of earnings. Taxes are then subtracted from these earnings to determine the individual's disposable income. Since the proprietorship pays no taxes, the entire $50,000 becomes income of the owner in both cases. In the first case the corporation pays $7,500 in corporate income tax, and the net earnings ($42,500) are distributed as dividends to the owner. The owner then pays personal income tax ($9,782 on the proprietorship's income or $7,689 on the corporation's dividends). The residual is disposable income. As may be seen in the last line of the first case, disposable income is greater for the proprietorship ($40,218 versus $34,811). Why is it larger? The answer lies in the fact that for the corporation the $50,000 was taxed twice, once at the corporate level ($7,500) and once at the personal level ($7,689), for total taxes of $15,189.

[2]To ease the calculations, personal exemptions and deductions are not included in the determination of personal taxable income.

EXHIBIT 15.4

Comparison of Total Federal Income Tax for a Sole Proprietorship and a Corporation

The need to reinvest earnings in the firm and differences in corporate and personal income tax rates lead to differences in spendable income.

	Proprietorship	Corporation
Case 1: No Retention of Earnings		
Profits	$50,000	$50,000
Corporate income tax	—	7,500
Net profits	50,000	42,500
Earnings distributed	50,000	42,500
Personal income tax (married, filing a joint return)	9,782	7,689
Disposable income	40,218	34,811
Case 2: Retention of Earnings		
Profits (before salary)	50,000	50,000
Salary	—	20,000
Corporate taxable income	—	30,000
Corporate income taxes	—	4,500
Net available for reinvestment	—	25,500
Personal income	50,000	20,000
Personal income tax (married, filing a joint return)	9,782	3,004
Spendable income	40,218	16,996
Personal reinvestment in firm	25,500	—
Disposable income	14,718	16,996

The second example in Exhibit 15.4 illustrates a different situation, in which funds are reinvested in the company. Once again, both the sole proprietorship and the corporation earn $50,000. However, in this illustration the corporation pays the owner (and manager) a $20,000 salary and has a net profit of $30,000. It then pays $4,500 in corporate income tax and retains $25,500 in earnings, which will be reinvested in the firm. The proprietorship, however, cannot retain earnings but must distribute its earnings to the owner. Thus, in the case of the proprietorship, the owner receives $50,000, compared with only $20,000 in salary from the corporation. The owner pays personal income tax of $9,782 for the proprietorship and $3,004 for the corporation, leaving net income of $40,218 and $16,996, respectively. If the proprietor now invests $25,500 in the firm (as was done in the case of the corporation), the individual's disposable income is reduced to $14,718, which is smaller than the $16,996 the owner obtained through the corporate form of business. In this example, the corporate form of enterprise resulted in total taxes of $7,504, while the proprietorship resulted in taxes totaling $9,782. Thus, the corporate form saved the individual (and owner of the business) $2,278.

This tax saving is the result of the way in which the corporation's funds were distributed. Corporations may pay salaries to managers who are also stockholders and treat these payments as expenses. Salaries to the sole proprietor are not permitted, and all profits are income to the owner. It is the splitting of funds between the corporation and the owners that permits the corporate structure to take advantage of the lower tax rates. If the firm needs additional funds, the ability to pay salaries and retain earnings strongly argues for the corporate form of enterprise.

However, if the firm pays low salaries and distributes earnings as cash dividends, the argument is reversed. Cash dividends are subject to "double taxation" because they are taxed as earnings to the corporation and again as part of the individual recipient's personal income.[3] Such double taxation argues against incorporation. Thus, the decision to incorporate is strongly influenced by (1) the amount of profits earned, (2) the tax rates on the firm's earnings and the owners' income tax bracket, (3) the firm's need to retain earnings, and (4) the owners' need for income. These variables will, of course, differ for various cases; hence, there is no clear-cut answer to the question of whether or not to incorporate. However, if the sole proprietor intends to reinvest earnings and have the firm grow, it will probably be advantageous to incorporate.

S CORPORATIONS

There is one option stockholders of small corporations may elect that permits them to have the advantages associated with corporations (e.g., permanence, limited liability, and ease of transfer) without the disadvantage of double taxation (i.e., the taxation of corporate income and the subsequent taxation of dividends received by the stockholders). Under 1982 legislation, if a corporation has 35 or fewer stockholders, the firm may elect to be taxed as an **S corporation.** If the firm does elect to be taxed as an S corporation, its income is not subject to federal corporate income taxation. Instead, the firm's earnings are taxed as income to its stockholders. Thus, the tax treatment is the same as for partnership or sole proprietorship income.

S corporation ▲
Corporation that is taxed as if it were a partnership

While electing S corporate status circumvents the problem of double taxation, it also means that the individual stockholders are responsible

[3]The possibility of "triple taxation" exists when corporation A buys shares in corporation B. If B generates earnings, it pays federal income taxes. If B then distributes the earnings, A must pay income tax on the dividends (providing that A has taxable income). If A then distributes its earnings, which would include the dividends it received from B, A's stockholders would pay income tax on the distribution. In such a case, there is triple taxation. The earnings are taxed twice at the corporate level and again at the individual level.

However, the impact of triple taxation is reduced by the corporate dividend exclusion, which was discussed in Chapter 10. This exclusion permits A to exclude 70 percent of the dividends it receives from B, so only 30 percent of the dividends received by A from B may be subject to triple taxation.

for the appropriate income taxes. This taxation applies even if the corporation does not distribute its earnings as dividends. Thus, if the firm retains earnings for reinvestment, the stockholders will still have to pay taxes on the undistributed earnings. If management desires to retain earnings to finance future growth, the election to be taxed as an S corporation would be the incorrect decision. The firm would be better off having its earnings taxed at the corporate level and retaining (not distributing) its earnings.

OTHER TAX CONSIDERATIONS: FRINGE BENEFITS

Besides differences in the tax treatment given personal and corporate incomes, there are a variety of tax laws that affect financial management. Three areas are particularly important: deductible expenses, depreciation, and losses that generate tax savings.

Business expenses affect taxation because they reduce taxable income. Workers' fringe benefits constitute a particularly important expense. Fringe benefits are expenses to the firm but are not taxed as income. Income tax is levied when income is received, but by using fringe benefits, firms may increase employees' compensation without increasing their taxes. For example, if medical insurance costs $1,000 annually, an individual in the 28 percent federal income tax bracket would have to earn $1,389 before taxes [$1,389 − .28($1,389) = $1,000] in order to have $1,000 after taxes to purchase the insurance. However, an employer may participate in a group insurance plan that covers the employees. The employees do not receive monetary income but instead receive free medical insurance. The receipt of the insurance is not treated as taxable income, but the firm still has the expense that reduces its taxable income. (There are periodic proposals before Congress to tax fringe benefits or at least limit the amount of untaxed benefits.)

Fringe benefits have become a popular means to increase employees' wages and salaries. Many large corporations have been willing to grant generous fringes instead of increased wages, because the cost of the fringes to the employer is less than the increase in wages that would be necessary for the workers to purchase the goods or services themselves. Employees realize the potential tax savings of fringe benefits, so these benefits become an important reason for working for specific employers. Medical insurance, paid sick leave, life insurance, and pension plans are all illustrative of possible fringe benefits that either escape or defer taxation.

In addition to the deductibility of fringe benefits, the firm may deduct any cost of doing business. Employee wages and salaries, the cost of goods sold, insurance, local property taxes, interest paid, and advertising are examples of expenses that are paid and deducted before a business determines its taxable income. Each one of these expenses also requires the payment of cash. There is, however, one important expense that does not involve the payment of cash. This expense, depreciation, is exceedingly important. Like any expense it reduces taxes, but since it is a non-cash expense, it is added back to earnings to help determine cash flow from operations.[4]

DEPRECIATION

Depreciation is the allocation of the cost of fixed assets, such as plant and equipment, over a period of time. Part of the cost of these assets is written off against the firm's revenues each year. If this allocation of costs is for the same dollar amount each year, the firm is using **straight-line depreciation.** The allocation, however, may be in larger dollar amounts during the initial years and smaller amounts during the later years of the investment's life. This allocation system is called **accelerated depreciation.** As will be illustrated below, the advantage of accelerated depreciation is that since it allocates the cost of the asset faster, it recoups most of the cost of the investment quicker *and* initially reduces the firm's income taxes.

Depreciation ▲
Allocation of the cost of plant and equipment over a period of time

Straight-line depreciation ▲
Allocation of the cost of plant and equipment by equal annual amounts over a period of time

Accelerated depreciation ▲
Allocating the cost of plant and equipment in such a way that a larger proportion of an asset's cost is recovered during the earlier years of the asset's life

Depreciation expense arises in the following way. A firm has the following balance sheet:

Firm X
Balance Sheet
as of 12/31/X0

ASSETS		LIABILITIES AND EQUITY	
Cash	$1,000	Debt	$500
		Equity	$500

It currently has only cash that it acquired from investors (the equity) and from creditors (the debt). In order to produce some product, the firm uses $400 of the cash to acquire equipment. After the purchase, the balance sheet becomes as follows:

ASSETS		LIABILITIES AND EQUITY	
Cash	$600	Debt	$500
Equipment	$400	Equity	$500

[4] See the Statement of Cash Flows in Chapter 16.

The $400 cash was spent when the equipment was acquired; thus the firm no longer has these funds.

When the firm purchases equipment to produce output to sell, it anticipates that the equipment will operate for several years. For example, the firm may anticipate that the equipment may last four years, after which time it will have to be junked and replaced. If the firm anticipates that the $400 machine will have a useful life of four years, the firm may depreciate the machine on a straight-line basis for $100 a year. This is determined by using the following formula:

15.1 $$\text{Annual depreciation} = \frac{\text{Cost}}{\text{Anticipated useful life in years}}.$$

In this case annual depreciation is

$$\frac{\$400}{4} = \$100.$$

In effect the firm is saying that $100 worth of the machine is depreciated or consumed each year and that at the end of four years the machine is totally consumed and valueless.

Depreciation is important for two reasons. First, since it is an expense, it alters the firm's earnings and taxes. Second, since depreciation is a non-cash expense, it is treated in finance as a source of cash for the firm. Both these points are discussed below and are illustrated by the depreciation expense on the firm's $400 piece of equipment. To simplify the illustration, straight-line depreciation is used. The annual depreciation expense is thus $100.

The importance of depreciation expense on profit and corporate income tax is illustrated as follows. If the output produced by the firm's machine is sold for $800, and if, after operating and administrative expenses of $500, the firm has earnings of $300, is the $300 a true statement of the earnings? The answer is no, because no allowance has been made for the $100 of the machine's value that has been consumed to produce the output. The true profit is not $300 but $200, which is $300 gross earnings minus the $100 depreciation expense. The firm now pays corporate income tax on its earnings of $200 and not on the earnings before the depreciation expense. If the corporate income tax rate is 25%, the firm pays $50 (0.25 × $200) in taxes instead of the $75 (0.25 × $300) it would have to pay if the depreciation expense were omitted. Since the depreciation expense reduces the firm's earnings, it also reduces its income taxes.

Since the firm bought the equipment in the first year, it might seem reasonable to add the entire cost of the equipment to the firm's expenses for that year. In that case would the firm have a true statement of its earnings? It would not, because the firm's costs are incorrectly stated.

The firm's expenses would be $900, which includes the $500 operating expense and the $400 cost of the equipment. The firm would be operating at a loss of $100 ($800 revenues minus $900 expenses). This understates the earnings because the equipment's entire value was not consumed during the year. Only one-fourth of its value was consumed during the first year. Hence, only one-fourth of the equipment's value should be charged (i.e., "expensed") against the firm's annual revenues. Overstating depreciation, like understating depreciation, alters the firm's earnings.

The second important feature of depreciation is its impact on cash flow. In the above example, the $100 depreciation expense did not involve an outlay of cash. The operating and administrative expenses required that the firm make an outlay of money, but the depreciation expense did not involve the expenditure of money. The outlay of cash occurred when the machine was initially purchased and not while it was being used. Depreciation is a non-cash expense item that allocates the initial cash outlay (i.e., the purchase price of the equipment plus the cost of putting the equipment in place) over a period of time. Since no cash is expended by the firm as a result of the depreciation expense, depreciation is said to be a source of cash flow because it is recouping the original outlay for the machine. Hence, depreciation increases the flow of cash in the firm.

This seemingly contradictory statement (that an expense will increase the firm's cash flow) may be illustrated by further considering the previous example. A simple income statement for the firm is as follows:

Sales	$800
Operating expenses	500
Income before depreciation	300
Depreciation	100
Taxable income	200
Taxes	50
Net income	$150

Only the operating expenses ($500) and the tax ($50) required a disbursement of cash. The firm has $250 ($800 − $550) left. This is the $150 profit and the $100 depreciation expense that is added back to the profits to obtain the cash flow generated by operations. Thus, cash flow is the earnings (after taxes) plus depreciation expense. The firm has $250 that it may use and $100 of the cash is the result of the depreciation expense. The firm must now decide what to do with the $100 generated by the depreciated asset. For example, it may restore the depreciated asset, purchase a different asset, retire outstanding debt, or make payments to stockholders. Each of these acts is a possible use for the cash generated by the non-cash expenditure, depreciation.

Accelerated Depreciation

Conceptually, accelerated depreciation is no different from straight-line depreciation except that a greater proportion of the asset's purchase price is depreciated in the early years of the asset's life. Depreciation charges are larger when the plant and equipment are new and smaller when the plant and equipment are old. This variation in the expense, of course, alters the firm's earnings. When the depreciation charge is larger, the firm's profits and corporate income taxes are smaller. By using accelerated depreciation the firm initially is able to decrease its profits and taxes but increase its cash flow (i.e., accelerated depreciation initially increases the sum of earnings plus depreciation expense).

Modified accelerated cost recovery system (MACRS) ▲
Type of accelerated depreciation that became law under the tax revision of 1981 and that was revised under the 1986 Tax Reform Act

Under the Tax Reform Act of 1986, most plant and equipment may be depreciated under the **modified accelerated cost recovery system (MACRS),** which uses the schedules given in Exhibit 15.5. The first column presents the year, and the other columns present (for the given classes of depreciable assets) the proportion of the asset's cost that may be depreciated in that year. For example, if an asset is to be depreciated over five years, 32.0 percent of the cost of that asset is written off in the second year.

The number of years that may be used for depreciating a particular asset is similar to the asset's economic life. For example, cars and light trucks are depreciated over five years, and office equipment is depreciated over seven years. An asset, however, may be used for longer than the period allowed to write off its cost. Prior to the establishment of the accelerated cost recovery system (ACRS) and its subsequent modification (MACRS), depreciation was determined by the asset's useful life. Thus, a piece of equipment that had an expected useful life of ten years would be depreciated over ten years. Under current law, that equipment would be classified as a seven-year asset, and the seven-year schedule would be applied.

Two additional observations should be made. First, a close look at the schedules presented in Exhibit 15.5 reveals that the depreciation schedules are one year longer than the stated number of years. For example, the depreciation of a five-year asset occurs over six years. This is because depreciation *does not start until the asset has been owned for six months.* Thus, a five-year asset is depreciated over 5½ years. Second, the depreciation schedules do not consider any residual value that the asset may have. Thus, an asset classified as depreciable under the seven-year schedule will have no value at the end of the eighth year according to the depreciation schedule, even though in reality it may have some residual value.

EXHIBIT 15.5

Depreciation Schedules Under the Modified Accelerated Cost Recovery System

Depreciation schedules vary with the number of years over which the asset is depreciated.

Recovery Year	Percentage of Cost Depreciated Over: 3 Years	5 Years	7 Years	10 Years	15 Years	20 Years
1	33.00%	20.00%	14.28%	10.00%	5.00%	3.79%
2	45.00	32.00	24.49	18.00	9.50	7.22
3	15.00	19.20	17.49	14.40	8.55	6.68
4	7.00	11.52	12.49	11.52	7.69	6.18
5		11.52	8.93	9.22	6.93	5.71
6		5.76	8.93	7.37	6.23	5.28
7			8.93	6.55	5.90	4.89
8			4.46	6.55	5.90	4.52
9				6.55	5.90	4.46
10				6.55	5.90	4.46
11				3.29	5.90	4.46
12					5.90	4.46
13					5.90	4.46
14					5.90	4.46
15					5.90	4.46
16					3.00	4.46
17						4.46
18						4.46
19						4.46
20						4.46
21						2.25

Methods of Depreciation Compared

All methods of depreciation allocate the cost of plant and equipment over a period of time. The differences relate to their effects on the firm's earnings and thus to their effects on the firm's taxes and the cash flow from the firm's investments. Straight-line depreciation and the accelerated cost recovery system are compared in Exhibit 15.6 for an asset that costs $1,000 and is depreciated over ten years. The first section of this table illustrates straight-line depreciation over the asset's economic life. Notice the half-year convention also applies to straight-line depreciation. Since depreciation does not start until the asset has been owned for six months, only half of the annual depreciation expense is deducted the first year. To fully depreciate the asset, the final deduction occurs in the 11th year in the exhibit.

The second section illustrates the accelerated cost recovery system, which classifies the asset as a seven-year asset. The first column gives the year and the second column gives the firm's operating revenues after all expenses except depreciation. The third column gives the depreciation

EXHIBIT 15.6

Comparison of Straight-Line and Accelerated Cost Recovery Methods of Depreciation

While total depreciation is the same under both methods, the timing of the cash flows differs.

Year	Income before Depreciation	Depreciation Expense	Income before Taxes	Income Taxes	Net Income after Taxes	Cash Flow
Straight-line Depreciation						
1	$300	$ 50	$250	$ 62.50	$ 187.50	$ 237.50
2	300	100	200	50.00	150.00	250.00
3	300	100	200	50.00	150.00	250.00
4	300	100	200	50.00	150.00	250.00
5	300	100	200	50.00	150.00	250.00
6	300	100	200	50.00	150.00	250.00
7	300	100	200	50.00	150.00	250.00
8	300	100	200	50.00	150.00	250.00
9	300	100	200	50.00	150.00	250.00
10	300	100	200	50.00	150.00	250.00
11	300	50	250	62.50	187.50	237.50
Totals		$1,000		$575.00	$1,725.00	$2,725.00
Accelerated Cost Recovery						
1	$300	$ 142.80	$157.20	$ 39.30	$ 117.90	$ 260.70
2	300	244.90	55.10	13.78	41.32	286.22
3	300	174.90	125.10	31.28	93.82	268.72
4	300	124.90	175.10	43.78	131.32	256.22
5	300	89.30	210.70	52.67	158.03	247.33
6	300	89.30	210.70	52.67	158.03	247.33
7	300	89.30	210.70	52.67	158.03	247.33
8	300	44.60	255.40	63.85	191.55	236.15
9	300	—	300.00	75.00	225.00	225.00
10	300	—	300.00	75.00	225.00	225.00
11	300	—	300.00	75.00	225.00	225.00
Totals		$1,000.00		$575.00	$1,725.00	$2,725.00

expense for each of the years. The remaining four columns illustrate the effects of depreciation expense. The fourth column presents the firm's taxable income; the fifth column gives the income taxes (assuming a tax rate of 25 percent), and the sixth column gives the net income or profit after the taxes. The seventh column gives the firm's cash flow, which is the sum of its earnings after taxes and its depreciation expense. As may be seen in the table, the accelerated method of depreciation initially (1) reduces the firm's taxable income, which reduces its taxes, and (2) increases the firm's cash flow.

The table, however, also illustrates that the accelerated method of depreciation increases the firm's income and taxes and reduces its cash flow in the later years of the asset's life. Actually, the total depreciation expense, net income after taxes, taxes, and cash flow over the asset's life are the same for both methods of depreciation. This can be seen by adding the depreciation expense, taxes, net income, and cash flow columns. The sums are equal for both methods.

If accelerated depreciation does not ultimately reduce the firm's taxes and increase its cash flow over the life of the asset, what is its advantage? The answer to this question is the timing of the taxes and the cash flows. Accelerated depreciation increases the firm's cash flow during the early years of the asset's life and delays the payment of taxes to the later years of the asset's life. Accelerated depreciation increases the cash flow now, and thus the firm has the cash to invest and increase earnings. By deferring taxes, the firm is receiving a current loan in the form of deferred taxes from the federal government. And equally important, this loan has no interest cost.

In effect, the federal government, by permitting accelerated depreciation, is granting firms interest-free loans that may be used to earn more profits. Accelerated depreciation is another of those devices that the federal government uses to influence behavior. By granting accelerated depreciation, the federal government encourages investment in plant and equipment, for firms want to take advantage of the delayed taxes and the initial increased cash flow. By encouraging such investment, the federal government is encouraging firms to increase the productive capacity of the nation and to increase the level of employment, for workers must build the plant and equipment and operate it after it has been installed.

LOSSES AND TAX SAVINGS

Not all corporations are profitable. Some operate at a loss, and this loss, like earnings, has tax consequences. All firms must report earnings annually and pay appropriate income taxes. Taxes are paid each fiscal year, but a firm operates for many years, during which the firm may operate at a loss some years and for a profit other years. Firms in cyclical industries especially may have profitable years followed by years of losses. Fortunately, the federal government permits losses from one year to be used to offset income from profitable years, so that over a number of years it is the firm's net earnings after losses that are taxed and not just the earnings in profitable years.

If a corporation operates at a loss in the current fiscal year, the loss is carried back to offset income earned in the previous three years. In effect, the corporation receives a refund for previously paid taxes. If any loss remains because the total loss exceeded the earnings of the previous three years, the remaining loss is carried forward for up to fifteen years to offset future earnings. In this case, the carry forward of the loss erases future taxes.

The impact of the carry back and carry forward of losses may be seen by considering the following illustrations. In each case the corporation has a loss in the current year (i.e., year 4). The corporate income tax rate is assumed to be 30 percent.

	Year					
	1	2	3	4	5	6
Case A						
Earnings	$400	400	400	(1,000)	400	400
Taxes	$120	120	120	0	120	120
(Tax refund)				($300)		
Net taxes paid (after refund)	0	0	$60	0	120	120

The loss in year 4 of $1,000 is used to offset the total earnings in years 1 and 2, and $200 of the earnings in year 3. Thus, the $120 in taxes paid in each of years 1 and 2 and $60 of the taxes paid for year 3 are refunded in year 4. The $1,000 loss in year 4 recaptures the taxes paid in years 1 and 2 and part of year 3's taxes.

Two important points need to be made. First, notice that the loss is initially used against year 1's income. If that income does not exhaust the loss, the residual is carried to year 2 to offset that year's income. Once again if the earnings do not exhaust the loss, the residual is carried to year 3. The loss is carried forward to years 5, 6, and so on only if it exceeds the sum of the earnings in years 1, 2, and 3. Second, notice that the loss is used first against year 1's and not against year 3's income. The loss is carried back three years and then any remaining loss is moved forward.

	Year							
	1	2	3	4	5	6	7	8
Case B								
Earnings	$400	400	400	(1,500)	-	-	-	-
Taxes	$120	120	120	0	-	-	-	-
(Tax refund)				($360)				
Net taxes paid (after refund)	0	0	0	0				

In case B, the loss in year 4 exceeds the combined earnings of years 1 through 3 (the $1,500 loss versus the $1,200 combined earnings), so the remaining $300 loss will be carried forward to offset income earnings in subsequent years. The entire $360 previously paid in taxes will be refunded, and the corporation will not have to pay corporate federal income tax on the next $300 of earnings. Of course, this future tax savings depends on the firm's generating future earnings, and in this illustration there are, as of now, no future earnings, so this potential tax saving may be lost.

	Year							
	1	2	3	4	5	6	7	8
Case C								
Earnings	-	-	-	($1,500)	400	600	800	1,000
Taxes	-	-	-	0	120	180	240	300
(Tax refund)	-	-	-	-	($120)	(180)	(200)	-
Net taxes paid (after refund)	-	-	-	0	0	0	$40	300

In case C the firm had no earnings or losses in the first three years, so the entire $1,500 loss is carried forward. The order of carry forward is chronological, so the entire $400 profit in year 5 is offset as are the earnings of $600 in year 6. The earnings in years 5 and 6 are offset by only $1,000 of year 4's $1,500 loss. The remaining $500 is used to partially offset the $800 earned in year 7. After year 7, however, the entire loss has been used to offset income, so any income earned in year 8 ($1,000) will be subject to federal corporate income tax.

SUMMARY

Most firms are either sole proprietorships, partnerships, or corporations. The decision to use a particular form of business is often influenced by tax considerations. While both personal and corporate federal income taxes are somewhat progressive, the tax rates differ. Hence, individuals may be able to reduce the total taxes paid by using a particular form of business. The tax laws particularly encourage incorporation if the owners desire the firm to grow. The retention and reinvestment of earnings result in lower taxes than the distribution of earnings and their subsequent reinvestment in the firm.

After a firm acquires fixed assets, they are depreciated, which is the allocation of the cost of investment in plant and equipment over a period of time. Under straight-line depreciation, the same dollar amount is subtracted from revenues each year. Under accelerated depreciation, the initial cost of the investment is reduced more rapidly, for larger dollar amounts are subtracted during the early years of an investment's life. Thus, accelerated depreciation permits the cost of the investment to be written off faster, which initially reduces the firm's earnings and taxes. Since depreciation is a non-cash expense, accelerated depreciation initially increases the cash flow from the investment. This increased cash flow may be reinvested to increase the profitability of the firm.

Rules for depreciation are established by Congress and the Internal Revenue Service. Since accelerated depreciation writes off an investment more rapidly and increases the cash flow generated by the investment, it encourages capital spending. By altering depreciation schedules, the federal government induces behavior consistent with the economic goals of full employment, stable prices, and economic growth.

If a corporation operates at a loss, the loss is carried back three years to offset earnings that were previously taxed. This carry back may result in the corporation receiving a tax refund. If the previous three years' earnings are offset by the loss, any remaining loss is carried forward and used to offset future earnings. This carry forward may be extended up to fifteen years; however, for the loss carry forward to produce tax savings, the corporation must generate earnings in the future.

Review Questions

1. If you purchase the stock of IBM, do you have limited liability? What does limited liability mean, and what is the maximum amount that you can lose on your investment in IBM? If you start your own corporation, why may you not have limited liability?
2. One of the advantages of incorporating is the ease of transferring ownership in the corporation. Why is this more true for large, publicly held corporations than for small, privately held corporations?
3. If you saw the following information, what would you conclude about the progressivity of the tax system?

Individual	Income Earned	Taxes Paid
A	$10,000	$ 500
B	20,000	900
C	40,000	1,400

4. It is sometimes suggested that stockholders pay double taxation. What does that mean? Does it apply if a corporation retains all of its earnings? Does double taxation apply to S corporations?
5. What is the difference between a general and a limited partner? Which has unlimited liability?

6. If a firm uses accelerated instead of straight-line depreciation, can the firm depreciate an asset by a larger amount? What impact will the use of accelerated depreciation have on the cash flow from an investment in plant and equipment?
7. The right to use accelerated depreciation for tax purposes is granted by the federal government. Why does the federal government permit the use of accelerated depreciation?
8. Can all assets be depreciated? If the value of a piece of equipment appreciates in value, does that mean the firm cannot depreciate the equipment?
9. What are the implications if a corporation operates at a loss? How may the potential savings in taxes be lost?

Problems

1. What is the tax owed on the following additions to income if the individual is in the 28 percent income tax bracket?
   a. $1,000 of interest income
   b. $1,000 overtime pay
   c. $1,000 capital gain
2. If a corporation earns $100,000 in pretax income, what is the amount of federal income tax owed?
3. An asset costs $100,000 and is classified as a ten-year asset. What is the annual depreciation expense for the first three years under the straight-line and the modified accelerated cost recovery systems of depreciation?
4. A firm has earnings of $12,000 before interest, depreciation, and taxes. A new piece of equipment is installed at a cost of $10,000. The equipment will be depreciated over five years, and the firm pays 25 percent of its earnings in taxes. What are the earnings and cash flows for the firm in years two and five, using the two methods of depreciation discussed in the chapter? What is the source of the difference in earnings and cash flow?
5. A firm had earnings of $100,000 in the prior year and paid taxes of $30,000 (30 percent tax rate). This year it operated at a loss of $120,000. What are the taxes owed or refund it will receive? Is there any tax-loss carry forward? What would be the implication if the firm had lost $100,000 in the prior year instead of earning a profit?
6. Over the last five years, firm A has been consistently profitable. Its earnings before taxes were as follows:

Year	1	2	3	4	5
Earnings	$1,000	3,000	4,300	5,200	4,400

   a. If the corporate tax rate was 25 percent, what were its income taxes for each year?
   b. Unfortunately, in year 6 the firm experienced a major decline in sales, which resulted in a loss of $10,800. What impact will the loss have on the firm's taxes for each of the six years?

Suggested Readings

Virtually some aspect of the federal tax laws is changed every year. In addition, the IRS often issues interpretations and regulations concerning existing laws. Staying current with these laws and regulations is exceedingly time consuming. These two publications are updated annually, so they are one means by which individuals may obtain recent information on current tax laws.

Federal Tax Course. Englewood Cliffs, N.J.: Prentice-Hall.

Lasser Institute. *J. K. Lasser's Your Income Tax.* New York: Simon & Schuster.

Specialized books and pamphlets on specific tax topics are published by Commerce Clearing House, Inc. and by The National Underwriter Co. A catalogue of their current publications may be obtained by writing them at 4025 W. Peterson Ave., Chicago, Illinois 60646, and 450 East Fourth Street, Cincinnati, Ohio 45202–9960, respectively.

chapter 16

Analysis of Financial Statements

Learning Objectives

1. Define assets, liabilities, equity, book value, and net worth.
2. Differentiate among receipts, income, cash, and retained earnings.
3. Differentiate the accounting statements covered in the text.
4. Illustrate the difference between cross sectional analysis and time series analysis.
5. Be able to compute and interpret the ratios covered in the text.
6. Understand the limitations of accounting data and of the analysis that employs this data.

"Annual income twenty pounds, annual expenditure nineteen nineteen six, result happiness. Annual income twenty pounds, annual expenditure twenty pounds ought and six, result misery." As Charles Dickens so aptly expressed it in *David Copperfield,* the difference between operating at a profit or at a loss may be just a few pennies. This bottom line, however, plays a very important role both in the financial decisions made by management and in how management's performance is perceived by the public. Management wants to make those decisions that increase the value of the firm, which certainly include decisions affecting the firm's profitability.

By enumerating revenues and expenses in a firm's income statement (or statement of profit or loss, as it is sometimes called), accountants determine if a firm's operations are profitable. Profits are not, however, synonymous with cash. Revenues and expenses are not the same as receipts and disbursements. Not all sales are for cash; some are for credit. Not all expenses require the disbursement of cash; depreciation is a non-cash expense against the firm's revenues. This chapter is initially concerned with the construction of the firm's financial statements, such as the balance sheet or the income statement.

If the student is already familiar with the basic content of financial statements, the first half of the chapter may be omitted, and he or she can progress to the second half: the study of a firm's financial statements through ratio analysis. Ratio analysis is a popular tool because the ratios may be easily computed and readily interpreted. They are used by a firm's creditors, investors, and management. Creditors and investors employ ratio analysis to establish the ability of the firm to service its debt and earn profits for the owners. Management may use the analysis as (1) a planning device, (2) a tool for control, or (3) a means to identify weaknesses in the firm. After identifying the weaknesses, corrective action may be taken.

Although there are many ratios that the financial manager may use, they can all be classified into five groups. These include (1) liquidity ratios, which seek to determine if a firm can meet its current obligations as they come due; (2) activity ratios, which tell how rapidly assets flow through the firm; (3) profitability ratios, which measure performance; (4) leverage ratios, which measure the extent to which the firm uses debt financing; and (5) coverage ratios, which measure the ability to make (i.e., cover) specific payments.

GENERAL ACCOUNTING PRINCIPLES

Accounting statements seek to provide financial information concerning an enterprise. While the emphasis in this text is the statements' applications to firms, financial statements may be constructed for governments (e.g., the local municipality), nonprofit organizations (e.g., the Metropolitan Opera), or individuals. In all cases these statements seek to show the financial condition of the entity and its assets and how they were financed. This information can then be used to aid in financial decision making.

To be useful in decision making, financial statements must be reliable, understandable, and comparable. Reliability requires the statements to be objective and unbiased. The data included on the statements should be verifiable by independent experts. This does not mean that two accountants working with the same information will construct identical financial statements. Individual opinions and judgments may lead to different financial statements. For example, as is illustrated in Chapter 19, the decision to use last-in-first-out (LIFO) instead of first-in-first-out (FIFO) inventory valuation may affect the cost of goods sold and thus affect earnings. Another example that involves the accountant's judgment is the allowance for doubtful accounts receivable. Two accountants may establish differing amounts that will affect the firm's financial statements. However, it should not be concluded that two accountants will construct widely different statements. While the financial statements may differ, the amount of differentiation will probably be modest.

Accountants' second goal is that financial statements be understandable. The statement should be presented in an orderly manner and be readable by laypersons as well as professionals. Investors and other individuals who may use financial statements need not know all the principles used to construct a financial statement. However, a reasonably intelligent individual should be able to read a firm's financial statements and have some idea of the firm's profitability, its assets and liabilities, and its cash flow.

Comparability requires that one set of financial statements can be compared with other sets of the same financial statements constructed over different accounting periods. The principles used to construct one year's statements should be used for subsequent years. If the principles being applied are changed, the previous years' statements should be restated. If the firm's operations change, the financial statements should also reflect these changes. If, for example, the firm discontinues part of its operations, its sales, expenses, and profits for previous years should be restated. If this adjustment is not made, the users of the financial statements will be unable to compare the firm's financial condition and performance over a period of time for its continuing operations.

To increase the objectivity of financial statements, a general framework for accounting and financial reports has been established by the Financial Accounting Standards Board (FASB). Accounting principles that are "generally accepted" also receive the support of the American Institute of Certified Public Accountants and the Securities and Exchange Commission. While these bodies establish the principles under which financial statements are constructed, it should not be concluded that the principles are static. Their conceptual framework changes over time with changes in the business environment and the needs of the statements' users. For example, increases in foreign investments and fluctuations in the value of foreign currencies have generated a need for better methods of accounting for these foreign investments. This problem, plus others such as inflation, have resulted in changes in accounting principles as the profession seeks to improve the informational content of financial statements.

THE BALANCE SHEET

Balance sheet ▲
Financial statement that enumerates (as of a point in time) what an economic unit owns and owes and its net worth

Assets ▲
Item or property owned by a firm, household, or government and valued in monetary terms

Liabilities ▲
What an economic unit owes

Stockholders' equity ▲
Firm's net worth; stockholders' investment in the firm; the sum of stock, paid-in capital, and retained earnings

Consolidated balance sheet ▲
Parent company's balance sheet, which summarizes and combines the balance sheets of the firm's various subsidiaries

Current assets ▲
Short-term assets that are expected to be converted into cash during the fiscal year

What have the owners invested in a firm? One method of answering this question is to construct a **balance sheet** that enumerates what a business owns (i.e., its **assets**) and what it owes (i.e., its **liabilities**) and to calculate the difference. This difference is called the net worth or the **stockholders' equity** in the firm.

Exhibit 16.1 presents a simplified balance sheet for a hypothetical firm, EEM, Inc. For a publicly held firm, this balance sheet (and the other financial statements presented later in this chapter) would be published in the firm's annual report. This example combines the financial information for all the firm's subsidiaries and hence is called a **consolidated balance sheet.** The assets are divided into three groups: (1) **current assets,** which are expected to be used and converted into cash within a relatively short period of time, (2) **long-term assets,** which are those assets with a life span exceeding a year, and (3) **investments.** The liabilities and stockholders' equity are presented next, frequently on the righthand side of the balance sheet across from the assets. While it is not necessary for a balance sheet to be arranged in this manner, many firms use this general form because it clearly enumerates the assets, liabilities, and equity of the firm.

While current assets are listed in order of liquidity (cash, accounts receivable, and inventory), the following discussion considers each asset in reverse order. Raw materials are first acquired and converted into finished goods. This inventory is then sold, at which time the firm receives either an account receivable or cash.

Firms must have goods or services (or both) to sell. These are the firm's **inventory.** Not all inventory is ready for sale. Some of the goods may be unfinished ("goods-in-process"), and there also may be inventories of raw materials. According to the EEM balance sheet, total inventory amounted to $315,000 in 19X1. The balance sheet does not subdivide the inventory into finished goods, work in process, and raw materials. The financial analyst should remember that only finished items are available for sale. Considerable time and cost may be involved in processing

EXHIBIT 16.1

EEM Consolidated Balance Sheet (as of December 31, 19X1 and 19X0)

The balance sheet enumerates what the firm owns, what it owes, and the owners' equity.

	December 31, 19X1	December 31, 19X0
Assets		
Current assets		
Cash and cash equivalents	$ 200,000	$ 335,000
Accounts receivable, less allowance for doubtful accounts (19X1, $30,000; 19X0, $20,000)	510,000	380,000
Inventory	315,000	180,000
Total current assets	$1,025,000	$ 895,000
Property, plant, and equipment		
Land	130,000	130,000
Buildings	320,000	300,000
Machinery and equipment	735,000	682,000
	$1,185,000	$1,112,000
Less accumulated depreciation	371,000	258,000
Net property, plant, and equipment	$ 814,000	$ 854,000
Investments (stock)	21,000	95,000
	$1,860,000	$1,844,000
Liabilities		
Current liabilities		
Current maturities of long-term debt	$ 10,000	$ 10,000
Accounts payable and accrued liabilities	342,000	210,000
Notes payable to bank	38,000	17,000
Taxes due	33,000	28,000
Total current liabilities	$ 423,000	$ 265,000
Long-term debt	220,000	274,000
Total liabilities	$ 643,000	$ 539,000
Deferred taxes	54,000	44,000
Stockholders' equity		
Common stock ($0.25 par value; 150,000 shares authorized; shares outstanding: 100,000 in 19X1 and 90,000 in 19X0)	$ 25,000	$ 22,500
Additional paid-in capital	75,000	72,500
Retained earnings	1,183,000	1,166,000
Treasury stock (15,000 shares; at cost)	(120,000)	0
Total stockholders' equity	$1,163,000	$1,261,000
	$1,860,000	$1,844,000

Long-term assets ▲
Assets that are expected to be held for more than a year, such as plant and equipment

Investments ▲
(on balance sheet) Corporate securities (e.g., stock of another company) held by a firm

Inventory ▲
Raw materials, goods-in-process, and finished goods; what a firm has available to sell

Account receivable ▲
Account arising from a credit sale that has not been collected

raw materials into finished goods. Therefore, much of a firm's inventory may not be salable and cannot readily be converted into cash.[1]

When goods or services are sold, the firm receives either cash or a promise of payment in the future. A credit sale generates an **account receivable,** which represents money that is due to the firm. EEM, Inc. has $510,000 in receivables; this is a net figure obtained by subtracting the doubtful accounts ($30,000) from the total amount of receivables. Since a firm does not always obtain payment from all of its accounts receivable, it is necessary to make an allowance for these "doubtful accounts." Thus, only the net realizable figure is included in the tabulation of the firm's assets.

A cash sale generates the asset "cash" for the firm. Since holding cash will earn nothing, some of it may be invested in short-term money instruments, such as U.S. Treasury bills. Cash and short-term money instruments may be combined under a classification called cash and cash equivalents. For EEM cash and marketable securities total $200,000. This money is available to meet the firm's immediate financial obligations.

Cash and cash equivalents, accounts receivable, and inventory are the major short-term assets. In 19X1, EEM's total current assets amount to $1,025,000. These short-term assets will flow through the firm during its fiscal year and will be used to meet its financial obligations that must be paid during the year. The total value and the nature of these assets are very important in determining the firm's ability to meet its current obligations.

Long-term assets include the firm's property, plant, and equipment, which are used for many years. The firm's employees utilize these long-term assets in conjunction with the current assets to create the products or services that the company offers for sale. The type and quantity of long-term assets that a company uses vary with the industry. Some industries, such as utilities and transportation, require numerous plants and extensive equipment. Firms in these industries must have substantial investments in long-term assets in order to operate. Not all companies choose to own these assets; instead, they may rent them, which is called leasing. Regardless of whether the firm leases or owns these assets, it must have the use of the long-term assets to produce the company's output.

In 19X1, EEM, Inc. has $814,000 invested in long-term assets. The balance sheet indicates that the firm initially invested $320,000 in buildings and $735,000 in equipment. These assets have depreciated by $371,000 and are currently being carried on the books at $684,000

[1]Many balance sheets sent to stockholders present only aggregate numbers. Presumably management would have access to disaggregated figures and thus would know the amount of inventory that is finished goods and the amount that is raw materials.

($814,000 minus the value of the land). Depreciation is important because it is the process of allocating the cost of the plant and equipment over a period of time. Thus, the value of long-term assets on the balance sheet is reduced with time as the assets are used by the firm.

EEM owns land that is worth $130,000. Land does not depreciate with use, and hence the book value of the land is usually the purchase price. However, the value of the land may rise as a result of inflation, in which case the accountants could increase the land's value on the books. Such revaluations rarely occur, so many firms have **hidden assets,** such as land whose market value is understated.[2]

Hidden assets ▲ Assets that have appreciated in value but are carried on the balance sheet at a lower value, such as their original cost

The remaining entry on the asset side of the balance sheet is investments ($21,000 in 19X1 and $95,000 in 19X0). These include securities such as stock in other companies. Even though such stock can be sold and converted into cash, it may be considered separately from the firm's current assets. For example, if the securities were purchased with the intention of holding them for several years as an investment, they would be placed in a separate category on the balance sheet.

The total assets owned by EEM, Inc. are the sum of the short-term assets ($1,025,000), the long-term assets ($814,000), and the investments ($21,000). These assets are financed by the claims of creditors and stockholders—the firm's liabilities and equity—which are presented on the other half of the balance sheet.

The firm's liabilities are divided into two groups: **current liabilities,** which must be paid during the fiscal year, and **long-term liabilities,** which are due after the fiscal year. Current liabilities are primarily accounts payable and short-term loans. Just as the firm may sell goods on credit, it may also purchase goods and raw materials on credit. This trade credit is short-term and is retired as goods are produced and sold. In the balance sheet for EEM, Inc., accounts payable ($342,000 in 19X1) also include wages and salaries that have been earned but not paid out. (Many balance sheets have a separate entry called accrued liabilities to cover these current liabilities.) In addition to accounts payable, the firm has other short-term debt that must be paid during the fiscal year. This includes short-term notes for funds that the company has borrowed from commercial banks or other lending institutions ($38,000 in 19X1) and that portion of its long-term debt that must be retired this year ($10,000). The taxes that must be paid during the year ($33,000) constitute the remaining current obligation.

Current liability ▲ Debt that must be paid during the fiscal year

Long-term liability ▲ Debt that becomes due after one year

Long-term debt obligations must be retired at some time after the current fiscal year. Such obligations may include bonds that are out-

[2] The revaluation of an asset would create taxable income, so there is little reason to appreciate the value of the asset on the firm's balance sheet.

standing and mortgages on real property. These long-term debts represent part of the permanent financing of the firm because these funds are committed to financing the business for a long time. Short-term liabilities are usually not considered part of the firm's permanent financing because these liabilities must be paid within a relatively short period.[3] For EEM, Inc., the long-term liabilities consist solely of long-term debt ($220,000 in 19X1). On other financial statements, a breakdown of the various debt issues (if the debt consists of more than one issue) may be given in a footnote that appears after the body of the financial statement.

EEM also has deferred taxes of $54,000. Such taxes arise from the differences in the timing of when the taxes are incurred and when they are paid. For example, a firm may make a profitable installment sale and report the earnings in its current fiscal year. Even though the tax liability is incurred during the present year, the firm does not make the tax payment until it receives the installments. Thus, the tax payments are deferred. These deferred taxes appear on the balance sheet in a separate account from the current taxes due, which must be paid within the fiscal year and hence are a current liability.

On most balance sheets, the stockholders' equity is listed after the liabilities and deferred taxes. There are three essential entries: the stock outstanding, additional paid-in capital, and the earnings that have been retained. A fourth entry, treasury stock, may appear if the firm has repurchased some of its common stock. The stock outstanding shows the various types of stock that have been issued and their quantities. EEM, Inc. has only one issue—common stock. Many firms, however, not only have common stock but also have preferred stock.

Additional paid-in capital represents the funds paid for the common stock in excess of the stock's par value. For example, if a stock's par value is $0.25 and the shares are sold for $1.00, then $0.25 is credited to common stock and the balance ($0.75) is considered additional paid-in capital. EEM, Inc. in 19X1 had 100,000 shares of $0.25 par-value common stock outstanding. Thus, the common stock entry would be $25,000 (100,000 × $0.25). If the stock initially had been sold for $100,000, this $25,000 would not account for the entire amount of funds raised. The balance ($75,000) would be considered additional paid-in capital.

Retained earnings ▲
The sum of a firm's income earned over a period of time that has not been distributed

The third entry under common stock is **retained earnings,** which represent the accumulated earnings of the firm that have not been distributed. (This entry could be negative if the firm has operated at a loss.) In 19X1, EEM's retained earnings were $1,183,000. This represents the firm's undistributed earnings since its inception. Retained earnings, like

[3] Since some short-term liabilities (e.g., accrued wages) are always carried by the firm, these may be treated as part of the firm's permanent financing.

the common stock and additional paid-in capital, represent an investment in the firm by common stockholders. Since these stockholders would receive the earnings if they were distributed, retained earnings are part of the stockholders' contribution to the financing of the firm.

Some firms repurchase their stock and hold these shares "in their treasury." These shares could be retired, but if the firm desired to resell them to the general public, the shares would have to be reregistered with the SEC. Since treasury stock is held for future purposes, it is not retired, which avoids the cost associated with registering the shares. EEM holds 15,000 shares of treasury stock for which it paid $120,000. This reduces the total equity of the firm from $1,283,000 to $1,163,000. Notice that the reduction in equity is the cost to repurchase the shares (i.e., $120,000) and not what the shares initially sold for (i.e., the par value plus the paid-in capital).

Such repurchases have become common after periods of falling stock prices, such as occurred during October 1987 and after the invasion of Kuwait in 1990. Repurchases occur when management believes the shares to be undervalued and uses the firm's cash to reduce the number of shares outstanding instead of using the cash for other purposes. The purchases may be made on the open market or through privately negotiated sales. The latter may occur when one stockholder seeks to sell a large block, in which case the seller may approach management concerning the possible sale of the shares back to the firm.

Firms may also repurchase their stock as a defense tactic against an attempted takeover. The repurchase of shares owned by public stockholders increases management's proportionate ownership in the firm. The repurchased shares may be resold to "friendly hands," an investor who will support current management. For example, the shares may be repurchased by the employee pension plan. If the trustees of the pension plan support current management, the sale strengthens management's position against a hostile takeover.

Book value ▲
Firm's total assets minus total liabilities; equity; net worth

Book value per share ▲
Book value divided by number of shares outstanding

The **book value** of the firm is the equity that the investors have in the firm—the sum of common stock, additional paid-in capital, and retained earnings. For EEM, Inc., the book value is $1,163,000 in 19X1. This sum represents the common stockholders' investment in the firm. Individual investors are primarily concerned with the value of a share of stock and not with the value of all the shares. To obtain the **book value per share,** the total equity available to common stock is divided by the number of shares outstanding. For EEM, Inc., the per-share book value in 19X1 is $13.68 ($1,163,000/85,000). This amount is the accounting value of each of the 85,000 shares held by the firm's stockholders. The 85,000 shares are the 100,000 shares issued minus the 15,000 shares held in treasury.

If EEM were to cease operations, sell its assets, and pay off its liabilities, the owners would receive the remainder. If the assets and liabilities are accurately measured by their dollar values on the balance sheet, the book value equals the amount that stockholders would receive in the liquidation. However, as is discussed subsequently, the book value may not be an accurate measure of the market value of the firm or its assets.

Since a balance sheet presents a firm's assets, liabilities, and equity, it is in effect a summary of the firm's financial condition at a particular point in time. It shows how funds were raised and how they were allocated. The balance sheet for EEM indicates that in 19X1 the firm owns total assets valued at $1,860,000. These are the resources that the firm has to use, and (excluding the investment in the common stock of other firms) these resources are almost evenly allocated between short-term and long-term assets (i.e., 55 percent are short-term).

EEM has liabilities of $643,000, deferred taxes of $54,000, and equity of $1,163,000 in 19X1. The sum of the liabilities, deferred taxes, and equity must equal the sum of the assets, for it is the liabilities, deferred taxes, and equity that finance the acquisition of the assets. The assets could not have been acquired if creditors and owners had not provided the funds. For EEM, Inc., the balance sheet indicates that liabilities finance 34.6 percent ($643,000/$1,860,000 and that equity finances 62.5 percent ($1,163,000/$1,860,000) of the total assets. Thus, the balance sheet indicates the proportion of the assets financed with debt and the proportion financed with equity. (The remaining 2.9 percent is financed by deferred taxes.)

Two additional points need to be made about balance sheets. First, a balance sheet is constructed at the end of a fiscal period (e.g., a year). It indicates the value of the assets and liabilities and the net worth at that particular time. Since financial transactions occur continuously, the information contained in a balance sheet may become outdated rapidly. Second, the values assigned to the assets need not mirror their market value. Instead, the values of the assets may be overstated or understated. For example, the firm owns accounts receivable, not all of which will be paid. As was explained earlier, the firm does allow for these potential losses in an effort to make the balance sheet entries more accurate. However, the allowances may be insufficient, and the value of the assets may be overstated. Conversely, the value of other assets may be understated. For example, the land on which the plant is built may have increased in value but may continue to be carried on the company's books at its cost.

For the book value of the firm to be a true indication of its worth, all of the assets on the balance sheet should be valued at their market prices; however, this practice is not necessarily followed. Accountants suggest that assets be valued conservatively: (1) at the cost of the asset, or (2) at its market value, depending on which is less. Such conservatism is prudent but may result in assets having hidden or understated value if their appreciation is not recognized. Because of these accounting methods, the equity or net worth of a firm may not be a good measure of its value.

EXHIBIT 16.2

Consolidated Income Statement for EEM, Inc. and Subsidiaries (for the Years Ending December 31, 19X1 and 19X0)

The income statement enumerates the firm's revenues and expenses and determines the firm's earnings or loss.

	19X1	19X0
Net sales	$2,075,000	$1,974,400
Cost of goods sold	1,846,800	1,789,600
Gross profit	$ 228,200	$ 184,800
Selling and administrative expense	85,600	62,200
Operating earnings	$ 142,600	$ 122,600
Other income	6,600	5,000
Earnings before interest and taxes	$ 149,200	$ 127,600
Interest expense	20,200	9,600
Taxes	62,000	55,000
Net earnings	$ 67,000	$ 63,000
Earnings per share	$ 0.79	$ 0.74

THE INCOME STATEMENT

Income statement Financial statement that summarizes revenues and expenses for a period of time to determine profit or loss

The **income statement** tells investors how much accounting income or profits the company has earned during a period of time (e.g., its fiscal year). It is a summary of revenues and expenses and hence indicates the firm's accounting profits or losses. It is not, however, a summary of cash receipts and disbursements.[4]

Exhibit 16.2 is the 19X1 income statement for EEM, Inc. It gives earnings for both 19X1 and 19X0 to facilitate a year-to-year comparison. The statement starts with a summary of the firm's sources of revenues: net sales of $2,075,000.[5] Next follows a summary of the cost of goods sold ($1,846,800). The difference between the sales and the cost of goods sold is the gross profit ($228,200). Then the selling and administrative expenses are subtracted to determine the operating earnings ($142,600). If the firm has other sources of income (e.g., interest or dividends received), they are added to the operating earnings to determine the company's total earnings before interest and taxes. EEM, Inc. has $6,600 in other income, so this is added to the operating earnings to give earnings before interest expense and taxes (EBIT) of $149,200. To determine net earnings, interest expense ($20,200) and taxes ($62,000) must be sub-

[4]Receipts and disbursements are considered in the cash budget, which is discussed in Chapter 18.

[5]Net sales are total sales minus returns.

tracted from the $149,200, which in this case yields net earnings of $67,000.

Earnings per share ▲ Earnings divided by number of outstanding common shares

Stockholders are generally not concerned with total earnings but with **earnings per share.** The bottom line of the income statement shows the earnings per share (EPS = $0.79), which is net earnings divided by the number of shares outstanding ($67,000/85,000). This $0.79 is the amount of earnings available to each share of common stock.

When the firm earns profits, management must decide what to do with these earnings. There are two choices: (1) to pay out some or all of these profits to stockholders in the form of cash dividends, or (2) to retain the earnings. The retained earnings on the balance sheet are the sum of all of the firm's undistributed profits that have accumulated but that have not been paid out in dividends during the company's life. These retained earnings are used to finance the purchase of assets or to retire debt. How this year's earnings were used does not appear on the income statement. The income statement merely summarizes corporate revenues and expenses during the fiscal year and indicates whether the firm produced a net profit or loss.

STATEMENT OF CASH FLOWS

Accountants, financial managers, and investors have increased their emphasis on analyzing a firm's ability to generate cash. This emphasis has led to the creation of a new reporting requirement, a "statement of cash flows," which determines the changes in the firm's holdings of cash and cash equivalents (i.e., short-term liquid assets). Previously, a publicly held firm had to provide investors with the "statement of changes in financial position," which focused on the firm's liquidity position and highlighted the firm's sources and uses of funds. The statement served as a linkage between the income statement (which determines if the firm operated at a loss or at a profit) and the balance sheet (which enumerates the firm's assets, liabilities, and equity). Now a firm is required to provide a statement of cash flows. Although the new statement is similar to the statement of changes in financial position, it shifts the emphasis to inflows and outflows of cash from the firm's operations, investments, and financing decisions instead of the firm's sources and uses of funds.

Statement of cash flows ▲ Financial statement summarizing cash inflows and cash outflows

The **statement of cash flows** is divided into three sections: (1) operating activities, (2) investment activities, and (3) financing activities. In each section it enumerates the inflow and outflow of cash. The cash inflows for each section are

1. a decrease in an asset,
2. an increase in a liability, and
3. an increase in equity.

EXHIBIT 16.3

Statement of Cash Flows for EEM (for the Period Ending December 31, 19X1)

The statement of cash flows enumerates the firm's cash inflows and outflows and determines the change in the firm's cash position.

Operating activities	
Net income	$ 67,000
Adjustments	
Depreciation	113,000
Amortization	—
Non-cash revenues	—
Deferred taxes	15,000
Cash sources from operations	$195,000
Changes in operating assets and liabilities	
Accounts receivable	($130,000)
Inventory	(135,000)
Trade accounts and accrued wages payable	132,000
Net cash provided by operating activities	$ 62,000
Investment activities	
Purchases of plant	($ 78,000)
Proceeds from sale of plant	5,000
Net cash used in investment activities	($ 73,000)
Financing activities	
Net borrowings of short-term bank debt	$ 21,000
Payments of long-term debt	(76,000)
Proceeds from sale of long-term debt	22,000
Proceeds from sale of investments	74,000
Proceeds from sale of common stock	5,000
Stock repurchases	(120,000)
Dividends paid	(50,000)
Net cash used in financing activities	($124,000)
Decrease in cash	($135,000)
Cash at beginning of year	335,000
Cash at end of year	$200,000

The cash outflows for each section are

1. an increase in an asset,
2. a decrease in a liability, and
3. a decrease in equity.

The statement of cash flows starts with a firm's earnings and works through various entries to determine the change in the firm's cash and cash equivalents. This process is illustrated in Exhibit 16.3. The firm starts with earnings of $67,000. Since earnings are not synonymous with cash, adjustments must be made to put earnings on a cash basis. The first adjustment is to add back all non-cash expenses and deduct non-cash revenues.[6] The most important of these adjustments is usually depreciation, the non-cash expense that allocates the cost of plant and equipment over a period of time. Other non-cash expenses may include depletion of raw materials and amortization of intangible assets such as goodwill. In this illustration the firm has depreciation expense of $113,000 but no amortization and no non-cash revenues, so only the $113,000 is added to the firm's earnings.

Next, deferred taxes ($15,000) are added to earnings plus non-cash expenses. Earnings are determined after subtracting taxes owed for the time period but not necessarily paid. The firm may be able to defer paying some taxes until the future, so these deferred taxes do not result in an outflow of cash during the current accounting period. Although taxes actually paid are a cash outflow, deferred taxes recognized during the time period are not a cash outflow and are added back to earnings to determine the cash generated by operations. In Exhibit 16.3 the total of all these cash inflows from operations (i.e., earnings + non-cash expenses − non-cash earnings + deferred taxes) is

$$\$67{,}000 + \$113{,}000 - 0 + \$15{,}000 = \$195{,}000.$$

The next set of entries refers to changes in the firm's current assets and liabilities resulting from operations. Some of these changes will generate cash while others will consume it. If accounts receivable increase, that means during the accounting period the firm has experienced a net increase in credit sales. These credit sales do not generate cash until the receivables are collected, so an increase in accounts receivable is a cash outflow. In the illustration in Exhibit 16.3, receivables increased by $130,000, so there was a cash outflow of $130,000. The outflow is represented by the parentheses around the amount. Conversely, if accounts receivable had declined, it would mean the firm collected more receivables than it granted. Such a positive collection would result in a cash inflow. Since a decline in accounts receivable produces a positive inflow, the dollar amount of the decline would not be presented in parentheses on the statement. A decrease in accounts receivable increases, not decreases, cash.

An increase in inventory, like an increase in accounts receivable, is an outflow of cash. If the firm ends the time period with more inventory than when it began the period, it has experienced a cash outflow. Its cash has diminished. In Exhibit 16.3, inventory rose by $135,000, so this amount, like the increase in accounts receivable, is subtracted to deter-

---

[6] A firm's income may include earnings from an affiliate even though it receives no cash. These earnings must be subtracted to express the income on a cash basis.

mine cash generated by operations. Once again, the cash outflow is indicated by the dollar amount being in parentheses. If inventory had declined, that would indicate the firm sold more inventory than it acquired. This change would be an inflow of cash, and the amount would not be in parentheses.

These effects on cash by changes in accounts receivable and inventory also apply to other current assets. An increase in a current asset, other than cash or cash equivalents, is a cash outflow, while a decrease is a cash inflow. For example, if the firm prepays an insurance policy or makes a lease or rent payment at the beginning of the month, these payments are cash outflows. However, they are also increases in the asset pre-paid expense; thus, the increase in the asset represents a cash outflow. In the illustrated statement of cash flows for EEM, no other assets (e.g., prepaid expenses) were changed.

In addition to changes in current assets, normal day-to-day operations will alter the firm's current liabilities. Wages will accrue and other trade accounts may rise. An increase in the firm's payables is a cash inflow because the cash has not yet been paid out. In Exhibit 16.3, creditors have lent the firm an additional \$132,000 as part of the normal operations of both supplier (the creditor) and user (the borrower or debtor). This \$132,000 is an inflow, so the amount is not presented in parentheses. If payables decline, that means the firm experiences a cash outflow as the payables are retired. Such a reduction in a current liability is an outflow.

The sum of the changes in current assets and current liabilities from operations is

$$(\$130{,}000) + (\$135{,}000) + \$132{,}000 = (\$133{,}000).$$

The resulting amount is a negative number (i.e., it is in parentheses) and is subtracted from the \$195,000 of earnings after non-cash adjustments to determine the net cash provided by operations: \$195,000 − \$133,000 = \$62,000.

After the adjustments for changes in operating activities' current assets and current liabilities, the next part of the statement of cash flows analyzes the firm's investments in long-term assets. The acquisition of plant and equipment requires a cash outflow while the sale of plant and equipment generates cash (i.e., is an inflow). Expanding firms will need additional investment in plant and equipment, which consumes cash. A firm with excess capacity may sell plant and equipment, which generates cash. In the example in Exhibit 16.3, the firm acquired \$78,000 in new plant. This acquisition is a cash outflow, so the amount is in parentheses. The firm also sold plant for \$5,000, which is an inflow. The net amount of these investment activities is a negative \$73,000. The negative number indicates net investments in plant and equipment required a cash outlay.

The third part of the statement of changes in cash flows covers the financing decisions of the firm. Issuing new debt or new stock produces a cash inflow. Retiring debt, redeeming stock, or paying cash dividends are cash outflows. Financing decisions can be either long- or short-term. An increase in a short-term liability such as a bank loan or a long-term liability such as a bond outstanding is a source of cash. A reduction in these accounts, however, requires a cash outflow. An increase in equity is also an inflow of cash while a reduction in equity is a cash outflow.

In Exhibit 16.3, net payments of short-term bank loans after considering all new loans and loans repaid (i.e., net borrowings) are a positive $21,000, which is a cash inflow of $21,000. Payments of long-term debt of $76,000 exceeded proceeds of sales of long-term debt of $22,000. The sale is, of course, an inflow of cash, but the retirement is an outflow and hence is listed in parentheses on the statement.

Some firms make investments in the stock of other firms. Such investments are a cash outflow. Subsequent sale of this stock is a cash inflow. EEM reduced its stock investments and the proceeds of the sales were $74,000, which is a cash inflow.

EEM also sold and repurchased its own stock. The sale of $5,000 worth of stock is a cash inflow, while the repurchase cost of $120,000 is a cash outflow. The payment of cash dividends in the amount of $50,000 is also a cash outflow. The sum of all these financing activities is

$$\$21{,}000 + (\$76{,}000) + \$22{,}000 + \$74{,}000 +$$
$$\$5{,}000 + (\$120{,}000) + (\$50{,}000) = (\$124{,}000).$$

This net amount gives the cash generated or used by financing activities. In this case, the firm used more cash than it generated in its financing activities, so the final amount is a negative $124,000. The negative number indicates that $124,000 flowed out of the firm during the accounting period as a result of the firm's financing decisions.

The final part of the statement presents the firm's cash position at the end of the time period. Cash at the end of the accounting period is determined by the amount of initial cash and by the change in cash. In the illustration in Exhibit 16.3, the firm's cash inflow from operations was $62,000 but its investment activities resulted in a cash outflow of $73,000. The net change in cash from operations and investments in plant and equipment was $62,000 − $73,000 = ($11,000). This is a negative number which indicates a flow of cash out of the firm. Financing activities resulted in a cash outflow of $124,000, so after combining the cash flows from operations, investments, and financing, cash outflows exceeded inflows by $135,000. Since the firm began the year with $335,000, it ends the year with $200,000.

The bottom line of the statement of cash flows is the firm's cash position at the end of the accounting period. If the firm uses more cash than it generated, its cash holdings (or cash equivalents) will decline. Conversely, if the firm's cash inflows exceed the outflows, its cash and cash equivalents will rise.

What does the statement add to the financial analyst's knowledge? By placing the emphasis on cash, the statement permits the analyst to see where the firm generated cash and how this money was used. In the example in Exhibit 16.3, the firm generated cash from earnings and depreciation. Since these are part of operating activities, they are "internally" generated funds. How was this cash used? The answer is primarily to purchase plant. Since the internally generated cash was sufficient to cover the acquisition of plant, EEM did not need "external" sources to cover operations and its investments in plant and equipment. Some financing decisions were made (e.g., concerning the payment of dividends and a major change in the firm's capital structure); however, these decisions were not forced upon the firm by its operating with a cash drain. Instead, operations generated sufficient cash to cover the expansion in accounts receivable, inventory, and plant without necessitating an influx of cash from an outside source.

The statement also indicates a major change in EEM's capital structure. A large amount of cash was used to reduce long-term debt and equity. Cash declined by $135,000 partly as a result of a large repurchase of stock ($120,000) and a net reduction in long-term debt of $54,000 (i.e., the repayment of $76,000 less the proceeds of $22,000 from new debt). While the statement of cash flows cannot explain why management made these decisions, the decisions' impact (i.e., the decline in the firm's cash position) is immediately apparent from studying the statement.

Differences between statements of cash flows can be seen by comparing Exhibit 16.3 with Exhibit 16.4. The latter presents the statement of cash flows provided to stockholders by Georgia-Pacific after its acquisition of Great Northern Nekoosa. As may be readily seen from the statement, the acquisition was a large investment that required a substantial outflow of cash ($3,456 million). Where did the cash come from? Was it internally generated by operations? Were the funds borrowed, or did the firm issue new stock to raise the cash to pay for the acquisition?

Studying the statement of cash flows immediately answers these questions. Cash generated by operations, $214 million, was sufficient to cover the increases in inventory and receivables (i.e., cash provided by operations was positive) but was certainly insufficient to pay for the acquisition. Instead, Georgia-Pacific issued a substantial amount of long-term debt, $3,640 million, to pay for the investment. The large amount of cash used by investment activities was covered by external financing activities. Whether such actions have a positive or negative impact on the firm are, of course, for the financial analyst or investor to determine. The statement of cash flows, however, highlights the inflows and outflows of cash and facilitates determining the firm's financial condition.

EXHIBIT 16.4

Georgia-Pacific Statement of Cash Flows (in Millions; for the Three Months Ending March 31, 1990)

The Georgia-Pacific statement of cash flows shows the large cash inflow necessary to acquire Great Northern Nekoosa.

Operating activities	
Net income	$ 101
Adjustments	
Depreciation	131
Depletion	15
Deferred taxes	25
Cash sources from operations	$ 272
Changes in operating assets and liabilities	
Accounts receivable	($ 35)
Inventory	(27)
Other assets	3
Trade accounts payable and accruals	1
Net cash provided by operating activities	$ 214
Investment activities	
Purchases of plant	($ 118)
Timberlands purchased	(31)
Proceeds from sale of assets	30
Other	15
Acquisition	(3,456)
Net cash used in investment activities	($3,560)
Financing activities	
Net increase in short-term notes	$ 7
Payments of long-term debt	(226)
Proceeds from sale of long-term debt (after fees)	3,640
Proceeds from sale of common stock	—
Stock repurchases	—
Dividends paid	(35)
Net cash provided by financing activities	$3,386
Increase in cash	$ 40
Cash at beginning of year	23
Cash at end of year	$ 63

LIMITATIONS OF ACCOUNTING DATA

There are several weaknesses inherent in accounting statements, but this does not mean that financial analysis employing accounting data should be discounted. The financial analyst, however, needs to be aware of the limitations so that accounting statements may be interpreted in light of these weaknesses.

First, accounting data do not take into account nonmeasurable items, such as the quality of the research department or the marketing performance of the firm. Performance is measured solely in terms of money, and the implication of accounting data is that if the firm consistently leads its industry (or is at least above average), its management and divisions are qualitatively superior to its competitors. There probably does exist a relationship between performance and superior financial statements. The strong financial statements of IBM mirror the quality of its management and of its research and marketing staffs. However, many firms may be able to improve their financial position temporarily and achieve short-term superior performance that cannot be maintained.

Second, accounting data may not be sufficiently challenged by auditors. Although accounting records are examined for reasonableness and conformity with accounting principles, the auditors may lack knowledge in specific areas pertinent to the firm's accounting statements. For example, the auditors may accept the estimates of the firm's engineers because the auditors lack the specialized knowledge necessary to challenge the estimates. This is not meant to suggest that the auditors are incompetent; they may, however, lack specific knowledge that is necessary to verify the authenticity of some of the data used by the corporation's accountants.

Third, accounting statements that are available to the public give aggregate data. Although the company's management has access to itemized data, individual investors or security analysts may not receive sufficiently detailed information to guide investment decisions. For example, a company may not give its sales figures according to product lines. Aggregate sales data do not inform the public as to which of the company's products are its primary sources of revenue. The use of aggregate numbers in the firm's income statements and balance sheets may hide important information that the investor or security analyst could use in the study of the company.

Fourth, accounting data may be biased. For example, the valuation of assets by the lower of either cost or market value may result in biased information if the dollar value of the assets has significantly risen (as may occur during periods of inflation). Such increases in value are hidden by the use of the historical cost, and thus the accounting statements do not give a true indication of the value of the firm's assets. If the value of the assets has risen and this is not recognized by the accounting data, the rate of return earned by the company on its assets is slanted upward. If the true value of the assets were used to determine the rate of return that the firm earns on its assets, the rate would be lower. In this case the use of historical cost instead of market value results in inaccurate measures of the company's performance.

Fifth, during the 1970s and 1980s inflation caused a problem in interpreting accounting data. Items that had been purchased a number of

Financial Facts

The Role of the Auditor

The accounting statements of publicly held firms must be audited by an independent certified public accountant (CPA). These audits, which are an official examination of accounts, must be held annually. After conducting an audit, the CPA issues an auditor's opinion that attests to the "fairness" of the financial statements and their conformity with generally accepted accounting principles. By fairness accountants mean that the statements are not misleading. • The auditor's opinion must be included in the firm's annual report for publicly held firms. It is a brief document that usually consists of two paragraphs. The first covers the scope of the examination, and the second gives the opinion. On occasion, the opinion may include a discussion of specific factors that affect specific details in the financial statements. In this case the opinion is said to be "qualified." • Since audits are held by independent accountants, investors can have confidence in the financial statements. Accountants' objectivity enhances the statement's credibility. However, an auditor's opinion does not guarantee the accuracy of the statements. Responsibility for accuracy rests with management. •

years before could not be replaced at the same prices. As the firm's plant and equipment wore out, these assets had to be replaced at higher prices. For the firm to maintain its current capacity, additional financing was required to cover the higher costs. This decline in the purchasing power of money is not indicated by accounting data and poses one of the biggest problems that must be dealt with by accountants.

The preceding discussion illustrates some limitations in accounting data. Despite the problems that exist, financial analysis employing accounting data is a useful tool in evaluating a company's financial position. As long as the analyst is aware of the limitations of accounting data, financial statements may be interpreted in light of them.

RATIO ANALYSIS

Accounting data are often used to analyze the financial position of a firm. Such analysis may be conducted by creditors seeking to measure the safety of their loans. Investors also analyze financial statements to learn how well management is performing. The profitability of the firm and hence the return the firm's owners are achieving may be perceived in the financial statements. In addition, management also analyzes the data in financial statements. Such analysis may indicate weaknesses in the firm, which, if corrected, may increase the firm's profitability and value.

There are many ratios that may be computed by the financial analyst. These various ratios can be classified into the following groups: (1) liquidity, (2) activity, (3) profitability, (4) leverage, and (5) coverage. Liquidity ratios give an indication of the ability of the firm to meet its short-term obligations as they come due. Activity ratios are concerned with the amount of assets a firm needs to support its sales. The more rapidly assets turn over, the fewer assets the firm needs to generate sales. High turnover of inventory and accounts receivable also indicates how quickly the firm is able to convert these current assets into cash. Profitability ratios are a measure of performance; they indicate what the firm earns on its sales, assets, and equity. Leverage ratios are concerned with the firm's capital structure, or the extent to which debt is used to finance the firm's assets. Coverage ratios indicate the extent to which the firm generates operating income to cover an expense.

These ratios may be computed and interpreted from two viewpoints. They may be compiled for a period of years to perceive trends; this is **time series or trend analysis.** The ratios may be computed at the same time for several firms within an industry; this is **cross sectional analysis.** Time series and cross sectional analysis may be used together. Rarely will all the ratios indicate the same general tendency. When they are taken as a group, the ratios should give the investigator an indication of the direction in which the firm is moving and how it compares with other firms in its industry.

Time series analysis ▲
Analysis of a firm over a period of time

Cross sectional analysis ▲
Analysis of several firms in the same industry at a point in time

The analysis of financial statements through ratios can be a very useful tool for financial managers, investors, and creditors, who may use this type of analysis to ascertain how the firm is performing over time and relative to its competition. The ratios will tend to indicate trends, such as a deterioration in the firm's profitability. Such time series analyses of financial statements may indicate future difficulties while there is still time to take remedial action.

Even if the firm is not experiencing a deteriorating financial position, its performance may be inferior to other firms within its industry. A cross sectional analysis of firms will indicate if the particular firm is performing up to the norms of the industry. To make such comparisons, the financial analysts must have access to industry averages. The most widely known industry averages are the ratios compiled by Dun & Bradstreet and published annually in *Dun's Review.* Firms are classified by their SIC (Standard Industrial Classification) numbers, and the ratios are subdivided by the size of the firm.

Robert Morris Associates, a national association of bank loan officers, also publishes industry averages in its annual publication *Statement Studies.* The sources of its data are financial statements acquired by commercial banks from firms receiving loans. Sixteen ratios are given, and firms are classified by their SIC numbers.

Individual firms may also find calculating their own ratios to be useful, since they may stress the ratios most applicable to the intended use of the analysis. For example, commercial banks and other lending institutions are particularly concerned with the capacity of the borrower to service the loan (i.e., pay the interest and repay the principal). Thus, ratios concerning the borrower's use of debt or the coverage of interest payments are particularly important. Loan officers will use such ratios in credit reviews and in decisions to grant new loans, and often the individual bank may establish its own criteria that the loan applicant must meet, since these data may not be available from other sources.

Even if the financial analyst uses public sources of industry averages, there may be problems with the data. Published industry averages are based on last year's financial statements, reducing the comparability of the data with current-year financial ratios. Second, the individual firm may not fit neatly into one of the industry categories. Large firms such as CBS have operations in a variety of related fields (e.g., broadcasting and publishing), which reduces the comparability of ratios computed for similar, but not identical, firms (e.g., ABC and GE, owner of NBC). Third, even if industry averages are presented for firms in comparable industries, there is still the problem of comparing firms of different sizes. This problem is obvious for large size differentials (e.g., the local "ma and pa" grocery store with a large supermarket chain), but the problem may still apply when comparing larger firms in an industry. For example, are the ratios for a regional grocery firm comparable with the ratios for a national operation such as Safeway or ACME?

Although there may be problems with the application of ratio analysis, it is still a convenient means by which to analyze a firm's financial condition. The financial manager (or other analyst) certainly should not discard the analysis because there may be difficulties with its application or interpretation. Used with other tools of financial analysis, ratio analysis of financial statements can give a clear indication of the firm's performance and its direction. The analysis can be a harbinger of things to come and as such may indicate that action should be taken now to correct a small problem before it grows into a major source of financial embarrassment.

In the sections that follow, several ratios are discussed and illustrated. These ratios do not exhaust all the possible ratios, and certainly the analyst may find that in a specific occupation additional ratios or more sophisticated versions of some of the ratios presented below are needed. The purpose of this chapter is only to serve as an introduction to ratio analysis and to indicate how ratios are compiled, interpreted, and used. To illustrate the ratios, the balance sheet as of December 31, 19X1 (Exhibit 16.1), and income statement for the period ending December 31, 19X1 (Exhibit 16.2), of EEM, Inc. will be used.

LIQUIDITY RATIOS

Liquidity is the ease with which assets may be converted into cash without loss. If a firm is liquid, it will be able to meet its bills as they come due. Thus, liquidity ratios are useful not only to short-term creditors of the firm, who are concerned with being paid, but also to the firm's management, who must make the payments.

The Current Ratio

The **current ratio** is the ratio of current assets to current liabilities.

Current ratio ▲
Ratio of current assets to current liabilities; measure of liquidity

$$\text{Current ratio} = \text{Current assets/Current liabilities.}$$

It indicates how well the current liabilities, which must be paid within a year, are "covered." For the hypothetical firm the current assets are $1,025,000 and the current liabilities are $423,000; thus, the current ratio is

$$\frac{\$1{,}025{,}000}{\$423{,}000} = 2.42,$$

which indicates that for every dollar that the firm must pay within the year, there is $2.42 in an asset that is either cash or should become cash during the year.[7]

For most industries it is desirable to have more current assets than current liabilities. It is sometimes asserted that it is desirable to have at least $2 in current assets for every dollar in current liabilities (i.e., a current ratio of at least 2 : 1). If the current ratio is 2 : 1, then the firm's current assets could deteriorate in value by 50 percent and the firm still would be able to meet its short-term liabilities. While such rules of thumb are convenient, they need not apply to all industries. For example, electric utilities usually have current liabilities that exceed their current assets. Does this worry short-term creditors? No, because the short-term assets are of high quality (accounts receivable from electric users). Should a person fail to pay an electric bill, the company will cut off service, and this threat is usually sufficient to induce payment. The higher the quality of the current assets (i.e., the higher the probability that these assets can be converted to cash at their stated value), the smaller the need for the current ratio to exceed 1 : 1. The reason for selecting a current ratio such as 2 : 1 as a rule of thumb is that creditors frequently believe that not all current assets will in fact be converted into cash, and to protect themselves the creditors want a current ratio of at least 2 : 1.

While management also wants to know if the firm has sufficient liquid assets to meet its bills, the current ratio may have an additional use to management. A low current ratio is undesirable because it indicates

[7]The use of a year is arbitrary, as the life of current assets and current liabilities varies among industries.

financial weakness. A high current ratio may also be undesirable, for it may imply that the firm is not using funds economically. For example, the firm may have issued long-term debt and used it to finance too much inventory or accounts receivable. The high current ratio may also indicate that the firm is not taking advantage of available short-term financing. As was illustrated in Figure 2.1 short-term debt tends to be cheaper than long-term debt; failure to use short-term debt may reduce profitability. Thus, a high or low numerical value for the current ratio may be a signal that the management of short-term assets and liabilities needs changing.

Limitations of the Current Ratio

While the current ratio gives an indication of the ability of the firm to meet its current liabilities as they come due, the ratio does have limitations. The current ratio may be readily changed, and it is an aggregate measure of liquidity that does not differentiate the degree of liquidity of the different current assets. This section considers these disadvantages and suggests alternative measures of liquidity that give a better picture of the liquidity position of the firm.

The fact that the current ratio may be affected with ease is shown by the following examples. First, management may sell plant and equipment for cash, which will increase the current assets while holding constant the current liabilities, and thus the current ratio rises. While this does increase the degree of liquidity, it may be detrimental to the firm, for the firm may need plant and equipment in order to produce. Thus, liquidity has been bought at the expense of productive capacity.

Management may also sell plant and equipment for cash and use the cash to retire current liabilities (such as short-term notes or accounts payable). This certainly increases the current ratio, because the firm is reducing the denominator (current liabilities) in the ratio. For example, if the firm in Exhibit 16.1 sold $50,000 in equipment and retired $50,000 of the accounts payable, the current ratio for the firm would rise from 2.42 to 2.88. While the degree of liquidity has been increased, it may have again been bought at the expense of productive capacity. From the viewpoint of the current ratio, however, the firm is more liquid and therefore is better able to meet its current bills as they come due.

Management may issue more long-term debt and use the acquired cash to increase the current assets or to pay off short-term liabilities. This will increase the current ratio, but the increase is achieved by obligating the firm to pay interest over several years and to generate enough money to retire this long-term debt at some future date. Thus, while the firm may be increasing its liquidity now, it may be doing so at the expense of future liquidity.

The management of the firm may issue more stock and increase the equity base of the firm. The money acquired by issuing the stock may be used to increase current assets or to pay off current liabilities. Either of these will increase the current ratio, and the firm will be more liquid. However, the increased liquidity has been purchased by issuing more shares, which may reduce the return to the current stockholders (i.e., dilute the current stock) or may decrease management's ability to control the company, since there are now more shares in existence.

Management may retire current liabilities by paying them off with cash. This also will increase the current ratio (as long as the ratio exceeds one), but a firm needs cash to work with. Paying off short-term liabilities solely to improve the current ratio may be detrimental, for the firm has less cash, even though by the current ratio the firm appears to be more liquid.

The second type of problem with the current ratio is that it is an aggregation of all current assets and does not differentiate among current assets with regard to their degrees of liquidity. The ratio considers inventory that may be sold after three months on credit (payment for which in turn may not be collected for several additional months) as no different from cash or a short-term government security. This failure to distinguish among the degrees of liquidity has led to the development of ratios that explicitly consider the relative liquidity of the current assets.

The Quick Ratio (Acid Test)

It may take many months before inventory is sold and turned into cash. Inventory is not a very liquid current asset, so a variation on the current ratio is the ratio of all current assets except inventory divided by current liabilities. This ratio is called the **acid test** or **quick ratio** (both terms are used for this ratio) and is expressed as follows:[8]

Quick ratio ▲
(acid test) Current assets excluding inventory divided by current liabilities; measure of liquidity

$$\text{Quick ratio} = \frac{\text{Current liabilities} - \text{Inventory}}{\text{Current liabilities}}.$$

[8]The quick ratio is sometimes defined as

$$\text{Quick ratio} = \frac{\text{Cash} + \text{Marketable securities} + \text{Accounts receivable}}{\text{Current liabilities}}.$$

The two definitions will give the same answer if the firm's current assets are limited to cash, marketable securities, accounts receivable, and inventory. Some firms, however, do have other current assets, such as prepaid expenses, in which case the choice of definition will affect the quick ratio.

For EEM the quick ratio is

$$\frac{\$1{,}025{,}000 - \$315{,}000}{\$423{,}000} = 1.68,$$

which is perceptibly lower than the current ratio of 2.42 determined previously. The difference is, of course, the result of inventory that the company is carrying. A low acid test or quick ratio (especially less than 1 : 1) indicates that the firm may have difficulty meeting its obligations as they come due if it must rely on converting its inventory into cash to meet these current liabilities. The quick ratio, however, does not indicate that the firm will fail to pay. The ability to meet the obligations will be influenced by such factors as (1) how quickly cash flows into the firm, (2) the firm's ability to raise additional capital, (3) how rapidly obligations come due, and (4) the relationship the company has with its suppliers and their willingness to extend credit. The quick ratio simply indicates how well the current liabilities are covered by cash and assets that may be converted into cash relatively quickly. In effect, the quick ratio considers that not all current assets are equally liquid, and hence this test is a more stringent measure of liquidity.

The Components of the Current Assets

Another approach to this problem is to rank the current assets with regard to their degree of liquidity and determine each one's proportion of total current assets. The most liquid current asset is cash. Next is marketable securities such as Treasury bills or certificates of deposit. Then comes accounts receivable, and, finally, inventory. For the hypothetical firm the proportion of each amount to total current assets is as follows:

Current Asset	Proportion of Total Current Assets
Cash and short-term investments	19.5%
Accounts receivable	49.8
Inventory	30.7

This indicates that less than 20 percent of the firm's assets are cash and short-term securities but 50 percent are accounts receivable.

Since this technique ranks the current assets from the most liquid to the least liquid, it gives an indication of the degree of liquidity of the firm's total current assets. If a large proportion of the total current assets is inventory, the firm is not very liquid. This ranking takes into consideration that the degree of liquidity varies with the type of asset, and it recognizes that not all current assets are readily convertible into cash. The decomposition of the current assets according to their degree of liquidity, along with the quick ratio, gives management, creditors, and investors a better measure of the ability of the firm to meet its current liabilities as they come due than the current ratio provides. These ratios, then, are a basic supplement to the current ratio and should be used to analyze the liquidity of any firm that carries a significant amount of inventory in its operations.

ACTIVITY RATIOS

Activity ratios indicate how rapidly the firm is turning its assets (e.g., inventory and accounts receivable) into cash. Two activity ratios that are frequently encountered are inventory turnover and receivables turnover. The more rapidly the firm turns over its inventory and receivables, the more rapidly it is acquiring cash. Hence, high turnover indicates that the firm is rapidly receiving cash and is more able to pay its liabilities as they come due. Such high turnover, however, need not imply that the firm is maximizing profits. For example, high inventory turnover may indicate that the firm is selling items for too low a price in order to induce quicker sales. Or the firm may be carrying only rapidly moving items and possibly may be losing sales to competitors who offer a wider choice. A high receivables turnover may be an indication that the firm is too stringent in extending credit to buyers, and this may reduce total sales and result in lower profits. A high turnover rate is not desirable by itself. Comparisons must be made with industry averages in order to have some basis for making assertions that the turnover is too slow or too rapid.

Inventory Turnover

Inventory turnover may be defined as annual sales divided by average inventory. Thus, inventory turnover is as follows:

Inventory turnover ▲
Speed with which inventory is sold

$$\text{Inventory turnover} = \frac{\text{Sales}}{\text{Average inventory}}.$$

Since all assets must be financed, the more rapidly the inventory turns over, the less are the financing needs of the firm. If EEM's previous year-end inventory was $180,000, the inventory turnover for 19X1 is

$$\frac{\text{Sales}}{\text{Average inventory}} = \frac{\$2{,}075{,}000}{(\$315{,}000 + \$180{,}000)/2} = 8.4.$$

This indicates that annual sales are 8.4 times the level of inventory. Inventory turns over 8.4 times a year or about every 1.4 months (12/8.4 = 1.4). The turnover may be expressed in days by dividing the number of days in a year by the inventory turnover. Thus, in this illustration the firm holds an average item of inventory for 43 days (365/8.4 = 43). Since management can anticipate that on the average inventory will be held for 43 days, management will need to find financing for that period of time to carry the inventory.

Inventory turnover may also be defined as cost of goods sold divided by average inventory. Accountants in particular may prefer to use cost of goods sold, because accounting places much emphasis on the determination of cost. Financial managers may prefer to use sales in order to stress how rapidly the inventory flows into sales. In addition, Dun and Bradstreet uses sales instead of costs in its "Key Business Ratios." Hence, analysts must use sales to inventory if they are comparing a specific firm with the Dun and Bradstreet industry averages.

Either definition, however, may be acceptable provided that the user is consistent. If the cost of goods sold is used instead of annual sales, all inventory turnover ratios used as a basis of comparison must also use cost of goods sold instead of annual sales. This points out the need for the person doing ratio analysis to be aware of the definitions being used and to apply the definitions consistently. Otherwise, the analysis may be biased.

Receivables Turnover

Receivables turnover ▲ Speed with which accounts receivable are collected

Receivables turnover is defined as annual credit sales divided by receivables. Thus, the receivables turnover ratio is expressed as follows:

$$\text{Receivables turnover} = \frac{\text{Annual credit sales}}{\text{Accounts receivable}}.$$

An alternative definition substitutes annual sales for annual credit sales. That is,

$$\text{Receivables turnover} = \frac{\text{Annual sales}}{\text{Accounts receivable}}.$$

Either definition is acceptable as long as it is applied consistently. (The analyst may also use average accounts receivable instead of year-end accounts receivable.) While management may use either definition, investors may be limited to the data provided by the firm. If annual credit sales are not reported by the firm, the investor will have no choice but to use annual sales instead of annual credit sales.

The income statement of EEM indicates annual sales of $2,075,000; credit sales are not given. Thus, the first definition cannot be used, so the receivables turnover is

$$\text{Receivables turnover} = \frac{\$2{,}075{,}000}{\$510{,}000} = 4.07$$

This indicates that annual sales are four times receivables, which means that they are paid off about every three months (i.e., four times a year).

An alternative means to measure receivables turnover is the **average collection period,** which is also referred to as "days sales outstanding." The average collection period is

Average collection period (days sales outstanding) ▲
Number of days required on the average to collect an account receivable

$$\text{Average collection period} = \frac{\text{Receivables}}{\text{Sales per day}}.$$

For EEM sales per day are $5,685 ($2,075,000/365).[9] Thus, the average collection period is

$$\$510{,}000/\$5{,}685 = 90 \text{ days.}$$

This implies that when the firm makes a credit sale instead of a cash sale, it can expect payment in 90 days. This is essentially the same information derived by the receivables turnover rate. If it takes the firm 90 days to collect its receivables, they are turning over about four times a year.[10] This is the same answer given by the ratio of annual sales to accounts receivable. However, by stressing the number of days necessary to collect the receivables, the average collection period may be easier to interpret and may be preferred by some analysts.

Turnover ratios employing current assets need to be interpreted very cautiously. These ratios are dealing with dynamic measurements, since they are concerned with how long it takes for an event to occur. This problem of time implies that these turnover ratios may be significantly biased if the firm has (1) seasonal sales, (2) sales that do not occur evenly during the fiscal year, or (3) growth in inventory, accounts receivable, or sales during the fiscal year. Under these circumstances the use of year-end figures may produce ratios that are significantly biased.

The potential bias may be seen in the following example, which presents the monthly inventory of a firm that has a seasonal type of busi-

[9] A 360-day year is often used as a convenience. As stated previously, any definition is acceptable as long as it is applied consistently.

[10] The average collection period may also be calculated by dividing 365 by the receivables turnover. For EEM that is 365/4.07 = 90, which is the same average collection period derived in the body of the text.

ness. During the year, inventory is accumulated in anticipation of large sales during the season, which in this case is the Christmas season.

Month	Inventory at End of Month	Sales during the Month
January	$ 100	$ 50
February	100	50
March	200	50
April	200	50
May	300	50
June	400	50
July	500	50
August	700	50
September	1,000	400
October	1,000	1,300
November	1,200	2,000
December	300	1,200
		$6,300

If year-end figures for inventory and yearly sales figures are employed, the inventory turnover is 32 ($6,300/$200),[11] which indicates that inventory is turning over almost every twelve days (365/32). This, however, is very misleading because it fails to consider the large buildup of inventory that occurred during the middle of the year. In this case the use of year-end inventory figures significantly increases the inventory turnover. The inventory turnover appears to be more rapid than it actually was.

There are several means to help alleviate this problem. For example, the average of the monthly inventories may be used instead of the year-end inventory. The monthly average inventory is $500 (total inventory acquired during the year divided by 12). When this figure is used with the annual sales, the turnover is 12.6, or about once a month. This is much lower than the turnover indicated when the year-end inventory figures were used.

Other methods for removing the potential bias may be to construct monthly turnover averages or use moving averages. The point is that turnover ratios may be subject to bias and, hence, may be misleading. In order for these ratios to be helpful, users of these ratios need to recognize the potential bias and take steps to remove it. This increases the reliability of the ratios and makes them more useful financial tools.

[11] Average inventory is ($300 + $100)/2 = $200.

Fixed Asset Turnover

In addition to the turnover ratios that analyze the speed with which the firm turns over its current assets, there are also turnover ratios that employ the firm's long-term assets. The **fixed asset turnover** ratio is defined as:

Fixed asset turnover ▲ Ratio of sales to fixed assets; measure of fixed assets necessary to generate sales

$$\text{Fixed asset turnover} = \frac{\text{Sales}}{\text{Fixed assets}}.$$

For EEM the fixed asset turnover is

$$\frac{\$2{,}075{,}000}{\$814{,}000} = 2.55.$$

This indicates that sales are about 2.6 times the firm's fixed assets (i.e., its land, plant, and equipment). Many firms, such as utilities, must have substantial investment in plant and equipment to produce the output they sell. Other firms, especially those providing services, may need only modest amounts of fixed assets. The more rapidly fixed assets turn over, the smaller the amount of plant and equipment the firm is employing.

Total Asset Turnover

In addition to fixed asset turnover, the financial analyst may compute **total asset turnover,** which measures how many assets are used to generate sales. The definition of total asset turnover is

Total asset turnover ▲ Ratio of sales to total assets; measure of total assets required to generate sales

$$\text{Total asset turnover} = \frac{\text{Sales}}{\text{Total assets}}.$$

For EEM the total asset turnover is

$$\frac{\$2{,}075{,}000}{\$1{,}860{,}000} = 1.116.$$

This indicates the firm needs $1.00 in assets for every $1.12 generated in revenues.

By computing all the turnover ratios (i.e., the average collection period, inventory turnover, fixed asset turnover, and total asset turnover), the financial manager may be able to identify weak areas. For example, if the firm's accounts receivable and inventory turnover ratios are comparable to the industry but its total asset turnover is low, then the problem has to be the management of the firm's fixed assets. Once problems are identified, further analysis and remedial action can be directed toward the source of the problem.

PROFITABILITY RATIOS

Operating profit margin ▲ Ratio of operating income to sales; percentage earned on sales before deducting interest expense and taxes

Net profit margin ▲ Ratio of earnings after interest and taxes to sales; percentage earned on sales

Profitability ratios are measures of performance that indicate what the firm is earning on its sales or assets or equity. The **operating profit margin** is earnings before interest and taxes divided by sales, and the **net profit margin** is the ratio of earnings after interest and taxes to sales.[12]

$$\text{Operating profit margin} = \frac{\text{Earnings before interest and taxes}}{\text{Sales}}.$$

$$\text{Net profit margin} = \frac{\text{Earnings after interest and taxes}}{\text{Sales}}.$$

Computing both of these ratios may appear unnecessary, but it is best to compute them both. Management then can see the effect of changes in interest expense and taxes on profitability. If management computed only the net profit margin, an increase in tax rates or interest rates would decrease the profit margin even though there had been no internal deterioration in the profitability of the firm's operations.

For EEM the operating profit margin is

$$\text{Operating profit margin} = \frac{\$149{,}200}{\$2{,}075{,}000} = 7.2\%,$$

and the net profit margin is

$$\text{Net profit margin} = \frac{\$67{,}000}{\$2{,}075{,}000} = 3.23\%$$

These indicate that the company earns $0.072 before interest and taxes for every dollar of sales and $0.032 after interest and taxes for every dollar of sales.

Gross profit margin ▲ Ratio of revenues minus cost of goods sold to sales; percentage earnings on sales before considering operating expenses, interest, and taxes

In addition to the operating profit margin and the net profit margin, some financial analysts compute the **gross profit margin,** which is

$$\text{Gross profit margin} = \frac{\text{Revenues} - \text{Cost of goods sold}}{\text{Sales}}.$$

For EEM the gross profit margin is

$$\text{Gross profit margin} = \frac{\$228{,}200}{\$2{,}075{,}000} = 11.0\%.$$

[12]The words "profit," "income," and "earnings" are often synonymous.

This ratio indicates that the firm earns $0.11 on every dollar of sales before considering administrative, advertising, depreciation, and financing expenses. The gross profit margin is sensitive only to changes in the cost of goods sold but is not affected by other operating expenses. The operating profit margin, however, is affected by all operating expenses. By analyzing both the gross profit margin and the operating profit margin, the analyst can determine whether changes in the cost of goods sold or changes in other operating expenses are affecting the firm's earnings before interest and taxes (i.e., its operating income).

Other profitability ratios measure the **return on total assets** and the **return on equity.** The return on total assets is earnings divided by assets and measures what a firm earns on its resources.

Return on total assets ▲
Ratio of earnings to total assets; percentage earned on assets

$$\text{Return on total assets} = \frac{\text{Earnings after interest and taxes}}{\text{Total assets}}.$$

The return on equity is earnings divided by the equity or the net worth of the firm.

Return on equity ▲
Ratio of earnings to owners' equity; percentage earned on equity

$$\text{Return on equity} = \frac{\text{Earnings after interest and taxes}}{\text{Equity}}.$$

Equity is defined as the sum of the common stock, the additional paid-in capital (if any), and the retained earnings (if any). Return on equity measures the return the firm is earning on its stockholders' investment. (If the company has any preferred stock, the ratio must be adjusted by subtracting the dividends paid the preferred stockholders from the earnings and subtracting the par value of the preferred stock from the equity. Since the common stockholders are interested in the return on their investment, the preferred stock should not be included in determining the return on the common stock equity.) For EEM the return on total assets is

$$\text{Return on total assets} = \frac{\$67{,}000}{\$1{,}860{,}000} = 3.6\%.$$

The return on the equity is

$$\text{Return on equity} = \frac{\$67{,}000}{\$1{,}163{,}000} = 5.8\%.$$

This indicates that the firm returns $0.036 for every dollar invested in assets and $0.058 for every dollar invested by the common stockholders.

In addition to the return on total assets and return on equity, some financial analysts compute the return generated by operating income (earnings before interest and taxes, abbreviated as EBIT). This ratio, which may be referred to as the **basic earning power,** is

Basic earning power ▲
Ratio of operating income to total assets; measure of the firm's ability to generate income before considering interest and taxes

$$\text{Basic earning power} = \frac{\text{EBIT}}{\text{Total assets}},$$

and it measures what the firm earns on its assets independently of (1) how the assets were financed and (2) the taxes the firm has to pay. For EEM, its basic earning power is

$$\text{Basic earning power} = \frac{\$149{,}200}{\$1{,}860{,}000} = 8.0\%,$$

which indicates that $1 of the firm's assets generates $0.08 in operating income (i.e., income before paying interest and taxes).

This ratio may be particularly important to long-term creditors who are concerned with the capacity of management to generate earnings after meeting operating expenses. Since operating expenses are paid prior to debt service, the greater the basic earning power, the safer should be the creditors' interest payments.

LEVERAGE RATIOS

Debt/net worth ratio ▲ Ratio of debt to equity; debt divided by equity

Debt ratio ▲ Total debt divided by total assets; proportion of assets financed by debt; a measure of financial leverage

One of the more frequently computed types of ratios is the leverage ratio, which measures the firm's use of financial leverage (i.e., debt). The two most commonly used ratios to measure financial leverage are (1) debt to equity, which is often referred to as the **debt/net worth ratio,** and (2) debt to total assets, which is commonly referred to as the **debt ratio.** These ratios are as follows:

$$\text{Debt/net worth ratio} = \frac{\text{Debt}}{\text{Equity}}.$$

$$\text{Debt ratio} = \frac{\text{Debt}}{\text{Total assets}}.$$

For EEM total debt is $643,000 (i.e., the sum of current liabilities and long-term debt); thus the values of these ratios are, respectively,

$$\frac{\text{Debt}}{\text{Equity}} = \frac{\$643{,}000}{\$1{,}163{,}000} = 55.3\%,$$

$$\frac{\text{Debt}}{\text{Total assets}} = \frac{\$643{,}000}{\$1{,}860{,}000} = 34.6\%.$$

The debt-to-equity ratio indicates that there is $0.553 debt for every dollar of equity. The debt-to-assets ratio indicates that debt is financing 34.6 percent of the firm's assets.

Leverage ratios are aggregate ratios. They use total debt and hence do not differentiate between short-term and long-term debt. The debt-to-equity ratio uses total equity and does not differentiate between preferred and common stock financing.[13] The debt-to-total-assets ratio uses total assets and does not differentiate between current and long-term assets.

The financial manager may want to disaggregate the data. For example, if the emphasis is on long-term debt financing, current liabilities may be removed so that the debt ratio becomes

$$\frac{\text{Long-term debt}}{\text{Total assets}}.$$

This ratio indicates the extent to which long-term debt is financing the firm's assets. If the financial manager is primarily concerned with senior or subordinated long-term debt, similar adjustments can be made in the ratio (i.e., senior debt/total assets or subordinated debt/total assets).[14]

For most purposes the use of aggregate numbers does not pose a problem, for the debt ratio is measuring the proportion of the total assets that creditors (both short- and long-term) are financing. The smaller the proportion of total assets that creditors are financing, the larger the decline in value of the assets that may occur without threatening the creditors' position. Leverage ratios thus give an indication of risk. Firms that have high leverage ratios are considered riskier, because there is less cushion to protect creditors if the value of the assets deteriorates. For example, the debt ratio for EEM is 34.6 percent. This indicates that the value of the assets may decline by 65.4 percent (100% − 34.6%) before the equity is destroyed, leaving only enough assets to pay off the debt. If the debt ratio had been 70%, then only a 30% decline in the value of the assets would endanger the creditors' position.

Leverage ratios are not only an indication of risk to creditors but also a measure of risk to investors, for firms that are highly financially leveraged are riskier investments. If the value of the assets declines or if the firm should experience declining sales and losses, the equity is wiped out more quickly for financially leveraged firms than for unleveraged firms. Hence, leverage ratios are important measures of risk for investors as well as for creditors.

Leverage ratios differ significantly among firms. In Exhibit 16.5 the debt ratios (debt to total assets) for several large industrial firms are pre-

---

[13] If the firm has both preferred and common stock outstanding, the analyst may define the debt-to-net-worth ratio as debt/common equity.

[14] Some analysts add the deferred taxes to debt. Others define the debt ratio as permanent current liabilities plus long-term debt divided by total assets. Since there is no absolute, correct definition, any is acceptable provided it is applied consistently.

EXHIBIT 16.5

Debt Ratios (Total Debt/Total Assets) for Selected Industrial–Manufacturing Firms

Different managements decide to use varying amounts of debt to finance their firms' assets.

The Dial Corp.	79.4%
Coca-Cola	57.9
Exxon	57.2
Kerr-McGee	55.7
Schering-Plough	46.9
Louisiana-Pacific	42.1

Source: 1989 Annual Reports.

EXHIBIT 16.6

Debt Ratios (Total Debt/Total Assets) for Selected Telephone Companies

More than one half of the phone companies' assets are financed by debt.

Bell Atlantic	67.2%
Pacific Telesis	62.4
BellSouth	56.4

Source: 1989 Annual Reports.

sented. Exhibit 16.6 presents the debt ratios for selected telephone companies. The tables have been arranged in descending order from the highest debt ratio to the lowest. As may be seen from both tables, the proportion of a firm's total assets financed by debt varies not only across industries but also within an industry. The telephone companies' debt ratios do have less variation than the debt ratios of the industrial firms. While the range for the industrial firms is from 79.4 to 42.1 percent, the range for the phone companies is 67.2 to 56.4 percent.

Within an industry there is an optimal proportion of debt to total assets. Finding this optimal capital structure of debt and equity financing is important to maximizing the value of a firm, and Chapter 22 presents methods for determining the optimal capital structure of a firm. It is sufficient for now to suggest that finding the optimal use of financial leverage may significantly benefit the common stockholder by increasing the per share earnings of the company and permitting faster growth and larger dividends. If, however, the firm is too financially leveraged or *undercapitalized,* potential investors may be less willing to invest, and creditors may require a higher interest rate to compensate them for the increased risk. Thus, leverage ratios, which measure the use of financial leverage by the firm, may be among the most important ratios that managers, creditors, and investors may calculate.

Several of the ratios may be combined to analyze a firm. One such technique is the **DuPont system,** which was designed by that firm's management to measure a firm's earning power. The system combines net profit margin, total asset turnover, and leverage to determine the return on the firm's equity. Essentially, the DuPont system determines the return on equity by multiplying three things: (1) the net profit margin, (2) total asset turnover, and (3) an equity multiplier (used to indicate the amount of leverage).

DuPont system ▲ Measure of earning capacity that combines asset turnover, profitability, and financial leverage

The product of the net profit margin and total asset turnover determines the return on assets. That is

$$\text{Return on assets} = \frac{\text{Net profits}}{\text{Sales}} \times \frac{\text{Sales}}{\text{Assets}} = \frac{\text{Net profits}}{\text{Assets}}.$$

The product of the return on assets and the ratio of assets to equity (the equity multiplier) determines the return on equity. That is

$$\text{Return on equity} = \frac{\text{Net profits}}{\text{Assets}} \times \frac{\text{Assets}}{\text{Equity}}.$$

Thus, the DuPont system is

$$\text{Return on equity} = \frac{\text{Net profits}}{\text{Sales}} \times \frac{\text{Sales}}{\text{Assets}} \times \frac{\text{Assets}}{\text{Equity}} = \frac{\text{Net profits}}{\text{Equity}}$$

In the DuPont system, financial leverage is measured by the ratio of assets to equity (the equity multiplier mentioned earlier). This ratio is the reciprocal of the ratio of equity to total assets. Since the ratio of equity to total assets indicates the proportion of assets financed by equity, it is a measure of financial leverage. The smaller the proportion of assets financed by equity (i.e., the larger the proportion of the assets financed by debt), the larger will be the ratio of assets to equity, and, for a given return on assets, the greater will be the return on equity.

The DuPont system is illustrated in Exhibits 16.7 and 16.8. Exhibit 16.7 presents the general layout of the system and Exhibit 16.8 applies the system to the financial statements of EEM. While the end product of the system (i.e., the return on equity) is no different than the simple ratio of earnings to equity, the layout of the analysis facilitates locating internal sources of a firm's problems.

In addition to combining profitability, turnover, and leverage in one analysis, the system facilitates comparisons of firms in one industry with

EXHIBIT 16.7

The DuPont System of Financial Analysis

The DuPont system systematically lays out the determination of a firm's return on equity.

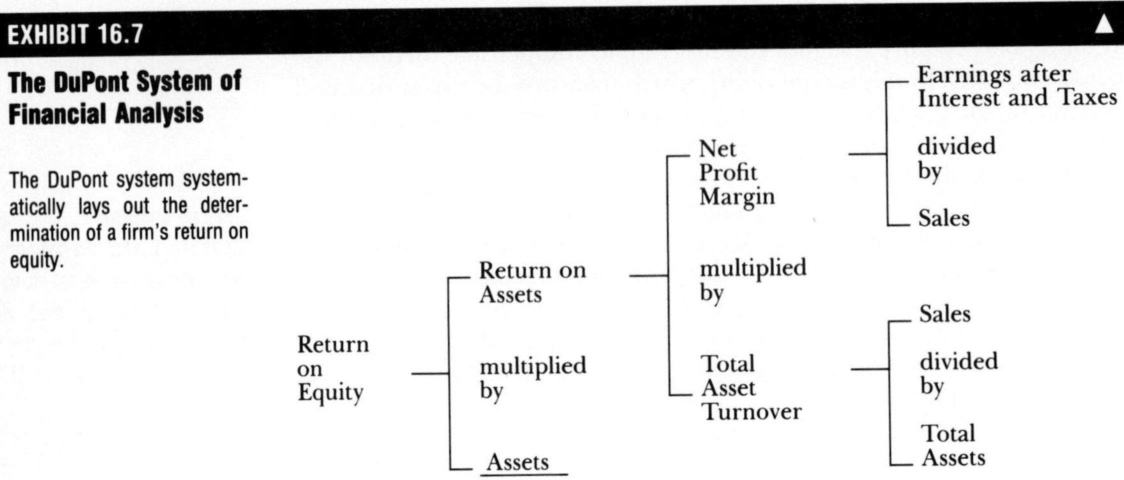

EXHIBIT 16.8

The DuPont System Applied to EEM's Financial Statements

This illustration shows how the DuPont system traces the return on equity to the firm's profitability and use of financial leverage.

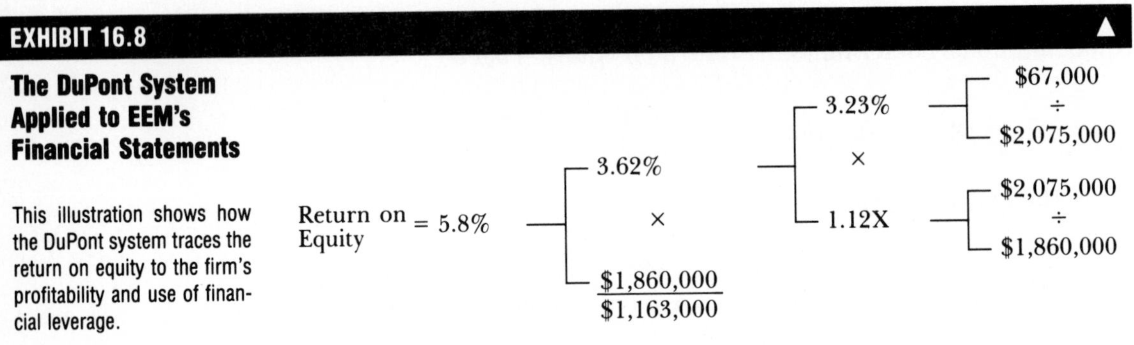

firms in different industries. Some firms, such as grocery stores, have rapid turnover but small profit margins. These low profit margins may appear to indicate that the firms are not very profitable. Other firms, such as furniture stores, may have large profit margins but slow turnover. If profit margins are considered in a vacuum, such firms appear to be very profitable. If these conclusions were true, owners of grocery stores would convert to furniture stores. This does not occur, however, because the return on equity may be similar for both firms when profitability, turnover, and leverage are considered together. A furniture store may turn over its inventory only twice a year; thus, it has to have large profit margins to compensate for its low turnover. Both firms may earn the same return for their stockholders when profitability, turnover, and leverage are taken together, and the DuPont system does just that by integrating them in one analysis.

COVERAGE RATIOS

In addition to the ratios previously covered in this chapter, the financial analyst may compute coverage ratios, which indicate the ability of the firm to service (i.e., "cover") some payment such as interest. All coverage ratios consider the funds available to meet a particular expense relative to that expense. The most common coverage ratio is **times-interest-earned,** which measures the ability of the firm to meet its interest obligations. That ratio is

Times-interest-earned Ratio of operating income (EBIT) to interest expense; measure of the safety of a debt instrument

$$\text{Times-interest-earned} = \frac{\text{Earnings before interest and taxes}}{\text{Annual interest charges}}.$$

A ratio of 2 indicates that the firm has \$2 for every \$1 in interest charges. Notice that the numerator uses operating income (i.e., earnings before interest and taxes, or EBIT), since interest is paid after other expenses but before taxes. The higher the ratio, the safer should be the interest payment. For EEM, the times-interest-earned ratio is

$$\text{Times-interest-earned} = \frac{\$149{,}000}{\$20{,}200} = 7.39.$$

This indicates that the firm is more than earning its interest expense: For every dollar of interest expense, the firm has operating income of \$7.39.

Ability to cover interest expense is important, for failure to meet interest payments as they come due may throw the firm into bankruptcy. Deterioration in the times-interest-earned ratio may give an early warning to creditors and investors, as well as to management, of a deteriorating financial position and an increased probability of default on interest payments.

In the above form, the times-interest-earned ratio is an aggregate ratio that lumps together all interest payments. Some debt issues may be subordinate to the other debt issues and may therefore be paid only after the senior debt is paid. Thus, it is possible that the senior debt may be paid in full but that nothing remains to pay the interest on the subordinated debt. When this subordination exists, the times-interest-earned ratio may be altered to acknowledge it. For example, consider a firm with \$1,000 in earnings before interest and taxes and with \$10,000 in debt consisting of two issues. Issue A is \$8,000 and carries an interest rate of 5 percent. Issue B is \$2,000, carries an interest rate of 7 percent, and is subordinate to issue A. The subordination may explain why the second issue has the higher interest rate, for the creditor demands the higher rate in return for accepting the riskier debt issue.

The times-interest-earned ratio for each debt issue is computed as follows. The interest on issue A is \$400 and on issue B is \$140. For issue

A there is $1,000 available to pay the $400 interest, and thus the coverage ratio is

$$\frac{\$1{,}000}{\$400} = 2.50.$$

For issue B there is $1,000 to cover the interest on A and B. Thus, for issue B the coverage ratio is

$$\frac{\$1{,}000}{\$400 + \$140} = 1.85.$$

It would be misleading to suggest that the coverage for issue B is the amount available *after* issue A was paid. In such a case, that would indicate coverage of

$$\frac{\$600}{\$140} = 4.29.$$

This is clearly misleading. Issue B would have the higher coverage ratio and thus would appear to be safer than the senior debt. The proper way to adjust for subordination is to add the interest charges to the denominator and not subtract the interest paid the senior issue from the numerator. Interest payments for successive issues of subordinated debt would be added to the denominator. Since the total amount of earnings available before taxes to pay the interest is spread over ever-increasing interest payments, the coverage ratio declines and hence gives a truer indication of the actual coverage of the subordinated debt.

The times-interest-earned ratio is limited to the coverage of interest payments. Creditors, especially bondholders, will also be concerned with the firm's capacity to generate earnings to retire the principal, as well as to pay the interest.[15] The capacity of the firm to meet both the interest and the principal repayment may be measured by the following expanded coverage ratio, which includes interest, principal repayment, operating income, and depreciation:

$$\frac{\text{Earnings before interest and taxes} + \text{Depreciation}}{\text{Interest expense} + \dfrac{\text{Principal repayment}}{(1 - \text{Firm's income tax rate})}}.$$

If EEM must retire $20,000 of its long-term debt each year, this ratio is

$$\frac{\$149{,}200 + \$113{,}000}{\$20{,}200 + \dfrac{\$20{,}000}{(1 - .35)}} = 5.1.$$

[15] Coverage ratios may also be used to analyze the safety of lease payments. See Chapter 21.

Notice that this expanded coverage ratio adds depreciation to operating income to determine the cash available to meet the interest and principal repayment. (The amount of depreciation, $113,000, is found on the statement of cash flows. Other applicable non-cash expenses, such as depletion and amortization, should also be added to operating income.) The principal repayment is added to the interest expense in the denominator. Since principal repayment is not a tax deductible expense, the amount of the payment must be expressed before tax. This adjustment is achieved by dividing the principal repayment by 1 minus the firm's tax rate. In this example, the tax rate is assumed to be 35 percent. The interpretation of this ratio is essentially the same as for the simpler times-interest-earned ratio. The larger the ratio, the greater is the firm's capacity to pay the interest and repay the principal.

AN APPLICATION OF RATIO ANALYSIS

Now that the various ratios have been defined and illustrated, the question becomes: What is the value of this information? Exhibit 16.9 summarizes the ratios and definitions and their application to EEM's financial statements. The last two columns of the table present a hypothetical industry average (for comparison with the firm's ratios) and an evaluation. A plus (+) means that the firm's ratio appears better than the industry average, while a minus (−) means that the firm's ratio is lower than the industry average. Whether the firm's ratios are significantly different from the industry averages, of course, depends on the interpretation of the analyst. There is no automatic rule or criterion that determines if a particular difference is important.

What do the results in Exhibit 16.9 suggest? As is often the case, the ratios present a mixed picture: some are better than the industry average while others are comparable or below the industry average. The leverage ratios are below the industry averages. This indicates that the firm uses less debt financing than the average firm in the industry. The firm's receivables turnover is comparable to the industry, so there is no obvious problem with the use of debt financing or the collection of receivables.

The firm's inventory is turning over less frequently than the industry average (i.e., 8.4 times versus 12.0). This indicates that the firm is excessively tying up funds in inventory, which may also explain why the current and quick ratios are slightly below the industry averages.

Excessive inventory may also reduce the firm's profitability. The return on assets is slightly less than the industry average (3.6 percent versus 4.0 percent), and the operating profit margin is less than the operating profit margin of the industry (7.2 percent versus 8.8 percent). However, since the firm uses less debt financing (and thus probably has less interest expense), the net profit margin seems comparable to the industry aver-

EXHIBIT 16.9

Summary of Ratios and Their Application to the Hypothetical Firm

While individual ratios may not tell much about a firm, the analysis of several ratios may give a clear indication of the firm's strengths and weaknesses.

Ratio		Calculation for the Hypothetical Firm		Industry Average	Evaluation
I. Liquidity Ratios					
a. Current Ratio					
(1)	$\frac{\text{Current assets}}{\text{Current liabilities}}$	$\frac{\$1{,}025{,}000}{\$423{,}000}$	= 2.42	2.5	OK
b. Quick Ratio					
(2)	$\frac{\text{Current assets} - \text{Inventory}}{\text{Current liabilities}}$	$\frac{\$1{,}025{,}000 - \$315{,}000}{\$423{,}000}$	= 1.68	1.8	OK
II. Activity Ratios					
a. Inventory Turnover					
(3)	$\frac{\text{Sales}}{\text{Average inventory}}$	$\frac{\$2{,}075{,}000}{(\$315{,}000 + \$180{,}000)/2}$	= 8.4	12.0	–
or					
(4)	$\frac{\text{Cost of goods sold}}{\text{Average inventory}}$	$\frac{\$1{,}846{,}800}{(\$315{,}000 + \$180{,}000)/2}$	= 7.5	N.A.	N.A.
b. Receivables Turnover					
(5)	$\frac{\text{Annual credit sales}}{\text{Accounts receivable}}$	$\frac{\text{Not given}}{\$510{,}000}$	= N.A.	N.A.	N.A.
or					
(6)	$\frac{\text{Annual sales}}{\text{Accounts receivable}}$	$\frac{\$2{,}075{,}000}{\$510{,}000}$	= 4.07	4.2	OK
c. Average Collection Period (Days Sales Outstanding)					
(7)	$\frac{\text{Receivables}}{\text{Sales per day}}$	$\frac{\$510{,}000}{\$2{,}075{,}000/365}$	= 90 days	88 days	OK
d. Fixed Asset Turnover					
(8)	$\frac{\text{Sales}}{\text{Fixed assets}}$	$\frac{\$2{,}075{,}000}{\$814{,}000}$	= 2.55	2.4	OK
e. Total Asset Turnover					
(9)	$\frac{\text{Sales}}{\text{Total assets}}$	$\frac{\$2{,}075{,}000}{\$1{,}860{,}000}$	= 1.12	1.2	OK
III. Profitability Ratios					
a. Gross Profit Margin					
(10)	$\frac{\text{Revenues} - \text{Cost of goods sold}}{\text{Sales}}$	$\frac{\$228{,}200}{\$2{,}075{,}000}$	= 11.0%	9.1%	+

Ratio		Calculation for the Hypothetical Firm	Industry Average	Evaluation
b. Operating Profit Margin				
(11)	$\frac{\text{Earnings before interest and taxes}}{\text{Sales}}$	$\frac{\$149,200}{\$2,075,000} = 7.2\%$	8.8%	OK
c. Net Profit Margin				
(12)	$\frac{\text{Earnings after interest and taxes}}{\text{Sales}}$	$\frac{\$67,000}{\$2,075,000} = 3.2\%$	3.0%	OK
d. Return on Total Assets				
(13)	$\frac{\text{Earnings after interest and taxes}}{\text{Total assets}}$	$\frac{\$67,000}{\$1,860,000} = 3.6\%$	4.0%	OK
e. Return on Equity				
(14)	$\frac{\text{Earnings after interest and taxes}}{\text{Equity}}$	$\frac{\$67,000}{\$1,163,000} = 5.8\%$	6.3%	OK
f. Basic Earning Power				
(15)	$\frac{\text{Earnings before interest and taxes}}{\text{Total assets}}$	$\frac{\$149,200}{\$1,860,000} = 8.0\%$	7.8%	OK
IV. Leverage Ratios				
a. Debt/Net Worth Ratio				
(16)	$\frac{\text{Debt}}{\text{Equity}}$	$\frac{\$643,000}{\$1,163,000} = 55.3\%$	100%	+
b. Debt Ratio				
(17)	$\frac{\text{Debt}}{\text{Total assets}}$	$\frac{\$643,000}{1,860,000} = 34.6\%$	50%	+
V. Coverage Ratios				
a. Coverage Ratio: Times-Interest-Earned				
(18)	$\frac{\text{Earnings before interest and taxes}}{\text{Annual interest expense}}$	$\frac{\$149,200}{\$20,200} = 7.39$	4.3X	+
b. Expanded Coverage Ratio				
(19)	$\frac{\text{Earnings before interest and taxes + Depreciation}}{\text{Interest expense} + \frac{\text{Principal repayment}}{(1 - \text{Firm's income tax rate})}}$	$\frac{\$149,200 + \$113,000}{\$20,200 + \frac{\$20,000}{(1 - .35)}} = 5.1$	N.A.	N.A.

age. The firm's use of less financial leverage may also explain why the return on equity is less than the industry average.

This ratio analysis does not imply that the firm is in trouble. It is operating profitably and has sufficient liquidity to meet current liabilities as they come due. However, the analysis does reveal that there may be some mismanagement of inventory. Perhaps the firm is holding obsolete inventory, or possibly its goods are priced above those of its competitors. Now that it appears that the firm's primary problem is inventory turnover, management may seek to identify the specific causes of the problem. After isolating the causes, corrective action may be taken.

SUMMARY

This chapter covered three essential financial statements. A balance sheet enumerates at a point in time what a firm owns (its assets), what it owes (its liabilities), and what owners have invested in a firm (its equity). An income statement enumerates a firm's revenues and expenses over a period of time and determines if a firm operated at a profit or for a loss. The statement of cash flows enumerates the flow of cash into and out of a firm over a period of time.

Ratio analysis provides a convenient method by which to analyze a firm's financial statements, for the ratios are easily computed and readily permit comparisons. Since publicly held corporations must give pertinent financial information to stockholders, ratio analysis may be employed not only by management and creditors but also by stockholders.

Of the many ratios that may be computed, only a selected few were presented in this chapter. Definitions of some of the ratios vary, as different analysts refine specific ratios to meet specific needs. Thus, it is very important that the analyst be aware of the definitions being used so that the application is consistent. Without such consistency, ratio analysis can be very misleading.

Liquidity ratios measure the capacity of the firm to meet its current obligations as they come due. Activity ratios indicate how rapidly assets flow through the firm and how many assets are used to generate sales. Profitability ratios measure performance; leverage ratios indicate the use of debt financing; coverage ratios measure the capacity of the firm to make certain payments such as interest. Once the pertinent ratios have been computed, the results may be compared over a series of years or compared with other firms within the industry. Such comparisons should help the analyst perceive the firm's position within the industry, as well as trends that are developing.

Review Questions

1. Specify which of the following are assets and which are liabilities:
   a. cash
   b. accrued interest owed
   c. equipment
   d. accounts payable
   e. taxes owed
   f. goods-in-process
   g. additional paid-in capital
2. Why may the market value of an asset be different from its book value?
3. Specify the time period covered by a balance sheet, by an income statement, and by a statement of cash flows.
4. Are a firm's profits equal to its cash? What may a corporation do with its earnings?
5. Which of the following generate a cash inflow and which a cash outflow?
   a. an increase in inventory
   b. an increase in accounts payable
   c. a decrease in accounts receivable
   d. a reduction in long-term debt
   e. an increase in equipment
   f. an increase in depreciation
6. Company A sells furniture, and its current ratio recently rose. Can you conclude that the firm's liquidity also rose? What other test of liquidity would you suggest? If this firm increased its inventory near the end of its fiscal year, why may the inventory turnover be a poor measure of activity?
7. If a firm has a current ratio of 2 : 1, what is the impact on the current ratio and quick ratio if:
   a. it buys inventory for cash?
   b. it buys inventory on credit?

   In which case does the firm appear to be more liquid? What is the source of funds used in (a) and (b) to finance the acquisition of the inventory?
8. Why would you expect different numerical values for the debt ratios of firms in different industries? Why may there be considerable differences in debt ratios for firms within the same industry?
9. Why is the times-interest-earned ratio important for an investor in bonds?
10. What are the differences among the gross profit margin, the operating profit margin, and the net profit margin? Why may it be desirable to compute all three ratios?
11. If a firm's liquidity improves, does that imply that its profitability also improved?

Problems

1. From the following information, construct a simple income statement and a balance sheet:

Sales	$1,000,000
Finished goods	200,000
Long-term debt	300,000
Raw materials	100,000
Cash	50,000
Cost of goods sold	600,000
Accounts receivable	250,000
Plant and equipment	400,000
Interest expense	80,000
Number of shares outstanding	100,000
Earnings before taxes	220,000
Taxes	100,000
Accounts payable	200,000
Other current liabilities	50,000
Other expenses	100,000
Equity	450,000

2. Given the following information, determine the per-share earnings of the common stock:

Earnings before interest and taxes	$100,000
Debt outstanding	$300,000
Income tax rate	30%
Interest rate on debt	12%
Preferred stock dividends	$20,000
Number of common shares outstanding	10,000

3. Given the following information, construct the firm's balance sheet:

Cash and cash equivalents	$ 300,000
Accumulated depreciation on plant and equipment	800,000
Plant and equipment	5,800,000
Accrued wages	400,000
Long-term debt	4,200,000
Inventory	6,400,000
Accounts receivable	4,100,000
Preferred stock	500,000
Retained earnings	7,700,000
Land	1,000,000
Accounts payable	2,100,000
Taxes due	100,000
Common stock	$10 par
Common shares outstanding	150,000
Current portion of long-term debt	$300,000

4. Fill in the blanks (______) with the correct entries.

ASSETS		LIABILITIES AND STOCKHOLDERS' EQUITY	
Current assets		Current liabilities	
Cash	$ 250,000	Accounts payable	$ 620,000
Accounts receivable (______ less allowance for doubtful accounts of $20,000)	1,320,000	Notes payable to banks	130,000
		Accrued wages	______
		Taxes owed	100,000
Inventory	1,410,000	Total current liabilities	$1,250,000
Total current assets	______	Long-term debt	______
Land	______	Stockholders' equity	
Plant and equipment ($2,800,000 less accumulated depreciation ______)	2,110,000	Preferred stock	1,000,000
		Common stock ($1 par, 750,000 shares authorized, 700,000 outstanding)	______
Total assets	$5,390,000	Retained earnings	______
		Total common stockholders' equity	$3,140,000
		Total liabilities and equity	______

5. Given the following information, compute the current and quick ratios:

Cash	$100,000
Accounts receivable	357,000
Inventory	458,000
Current liabilities	498,000
Long-term debt	610,000
Equity	598,000

6. If a firm has sales of $1,034,550 and accounts receivable of $268,700, what is the average collection period?
7. What is the debt/net worth ratio and the debt ratio for a firm with total debt of $600,000 and equity of $400,000?
8. A firm with sales of $500,000 has average inventory of $200,000. The industry average for inventory turnover is four times a year. What would be the reduction in inventory if this firm were to achieve a turnover comparable to the industry average?
9. Company A has three debt issues of $3,000 each. The interest rate of issue A is 4 percent, on B the rate is 6 percent, and on C the rate is 8 percent. Issue

B is subordinate to A, and issue C is subordinate to both A and B. The firm sold 150 units of output at $6 each and has variable costs of $3 per unit and fixed costs of $50. Compute the times-interest-earned for issue C. What does the answer imply? Does the answer mean that the interest will not be paid?

10. If a firm has sales of $25,689,000 a year, and the average collection period for the industry is 45 days, what should this firm's accounts receivable be if the firm is comparable to the industry?

11. Two firms have sales of $1 million each. Other financial information is as follows:

Firm	A	B
EBIT	$150,000	$150,000
Interest expense	10,000	75,000
Income tax	50,000	30,000
Debt	100,000	400,000
Equity	400,000	100,000

What are the operating profit margins and the net profit margins for these two firms? What are their returns on assets and on equity? Why are they different?

12. If a firm has the following sources of finance,

Current liabilities	$100,000
Long-term debt	350,000
Preferred stock	75,000
Common stock	225,000

earns a profit of $35,000 after taxes, and pays $7,500 in preferred stock dividends, what is the return on assets, the return on total equity, and the return on common equity?

13. If a firm has revenues of $1,220,000 in 19X1, what is the difference in its inventory turnover ratio if the financial analyst uses 19X1 year-end data instead of using average inventory? The firm's inventory was $300,000 in 19X0 and $450,000 in 19X1.

14. Perform a ratio analysis for the years 19X1 and 19X0 using the following financial statements, and answer the subsequent questions.

Firm X Balance Sheet as of 12/31/XX

Assets	**19X1**	**19X0**
Current assets		
Cash and cash equivalents	$ 953	$ 631
Accounts receivable	201	59
Inventory	5,824	4,655
Total current assets	$ 6,978	$5,345
Property and equipment	4,635	1,114
Total assets	$11,613	$6,459

Liabilities	**19X1**	**19X0**
Current liabilities		
Accounts payable	$ 783	$ 685
Accrued expenses	490	496
Rentals owed	241	97
Taxes due	86	84
Total current liabilities	$ 1,600	$1,362
Long-term debt	3,054	564
Total liabilities	$ 4,654	$1,926
Equity	6,959	4,533
Total liabilities and equity	$11,613	$6,459

Income Statement for the Fiscal Year Ended:

	12/31/X1	**12/31/X0**
Sales	$23,117	$18,428
Cost of goods sold	13,174	10,630
Gross profit	9,943	7,798
Selling and administrative expenses	7,460	5,976
Earnings before interest and taxes	2,483	1,822
Interest	317	177
Taxes	1,029	698
Net income	$ 1,137	$ 947

a. Given the following industry averages, are any weaknesses revealed in the ratio analysis?

Current ratio	4:1
Quick ratio	0.4:1
Average collection period	3 days
Inventory turnover	5×
Operating profit margin	11%
Net profit margin	3.5%
Return on assets	10%
Return on equity	22%
Debt ratio	50%
Times-interest-earned	5×

b. What kind of operation would have this firm's average collection period?

c. Why might the firm's operating profit margin be comparable to the industry but the net profit margin exceed the industry average?

d. What is the amount of annual change in the firm's equity from 19X0 to 19X1? Do the firm's earnings account for this change? What must have occurred during the fiscal year?

e. What general operating and financial decisions does management appear to have made and executed during the fiscal year?

Using Ratio Analysis to Determine the Safety of a Loan

Joseph Berio is a loan officer with the First Bank of Tennessee. Red Brick, Incorporated, a major producer of masonry products, has applied for a short-term loan. Red Brick supplies building material throughout the southern states, with brick plants located in Tennessee, Alabama, Georgia, and Indiana.

Mr. Berio knows that the brick production is affected by two factors: the cost of energy and the state of the building industry. First, manufacturing bricks uses a significant amount of energy. Red Brick, Inc. has recently converted many oil-fired kilns to coal. To finance these conversions, the company has recently issued a substantial amount of long-term debt that must be retired over the next 25 years.

Second, brick sales are very sensitive to activity in the building industry, especially new housing starts. The industry frequently follows a pattern of boom and bust, with sales and earnings responding to changes in the demand for building products.

Currently the economy is experiencing a severe recession, and housing starts have fallen more than 40 percent from the previous year. While the south and southwest have not experienced such a severe decline, housing starts there have declined 25 percent.

Red Brick, Inc. has not been immune to the economic environment. Sales have declined, and although the firm has reduced production, inventory has increased. The firm needs the short-term loan to finance its inventory. Mr. Berio must decide whether to grant or deny the loan. Such loans have been made to Red Brick in the past and have always been repaid when the economic picture improved.

The firm's income statement and balance sheet are given in Exhibit 1. Exhibit 2 presents both a ratio analysis of Red Brick's previous year's financial statements and the industry averages of the ratios.

To help decide whether to grant the loan, Mr. Berio computes several ratios and compares the results with the ratios given in Exhibit 2.

EXHIBIT 1

Income Statement for Red Brick (for the Time Period Ending December 31, 19X0)

Sales	$210,000,000
Cost of goods sold	170,000,000
Administrative expenses	26,000,000
Operating income	$ 14,000,000
Interest expense	13,000,000
Taxes	400,000
Net income	$ 600,000

Red Brick Balance Sheet as of 12/31/X0

ASSETS		LIABILITIES AND STOCKHOLDERS' EQUITY	
Cash	$ 600,000	Accounts payable	$ 39,000,000
Accounts receivable	33,000,000*	Notes payable	11,000,000
Inventory	75,400,000†	Long-term debt	45,000,000
Plant and equipment	132,000,000	Stockholders' equity	146,000,000
	$241,000,000		$241,000,000

*90% of sales are on credit.
†Previous year's inventory was $52,000,000.

EXHIBIT 2

	Company's Ratios (Previous Year)	Industry Average
Current ratio	4:1	2.2:1
Quick ratio	2:1	0.8:1
Inventory turnover	4.7×	4.6×
Average collection period	39 days	49 days
Debt ratio (debt/total assets)	39%	30%
Times-interest-earned	4.1	3.7
Return on equity	13.8%	14.1%
Return on assets	8.2%	10.2%
Operating profit margin	14.1%	15.2%
Net profit margin	8.8%	8.8%

Case Problems

1. What strengths and weaknesses are indicated by this analysis?
2. What may explain why the debt ratio exceeds the industry average? Is that necessarily a weakness in this case?

3. As a banker, is Mr. Berio more concerned with the firm's liquidity or its return on equity?
4. Based on the above analysis, should Mr. Berio grant the loan? Justify your position.

Suggested Readings

The father of conservative financial analysis is Benjamin Graham. His text is a classic that employs many of the ratios described in this chapter.

Graham, Benjamin; David L. Dodd; Sidney Cottle; and Charles Tatham. *Security Analysis: Principles and Techniques*. 4th ed. New York: McGraw-Hill, 1962.

See especially Part 4, "The Valuation of Common Stock," for the conservative financial approach to the analysis of common stock.

The analysis of financial statements and the interpretation of the analysis are covered in a variety of books written for courses in financial analysis or for individuals who use financial statements. See, for example:

Bernstein, Leopold. *Analysis of Financial Statements*. 3d ed. Homewood, Ill.: Richard D. Irwin, Inc. 1990.

Foster, George. *Financial Statement Analysis*. 2d ed. Englewood Cliffs, New Jersey: Prentice-Hall, Inc., 1986.

Fraser, Lyn M. *Understanding Financial Statements*. 2d ed. Englewood Cliffs, New Jersey: Prentice-Hall, Inc., 1988.

Helfert, Eric. *Techniques of Financial Analysis*. 7th ed. Homewood, Ill.: Richard D. Irwin, Inc. 1991.

For similar information in a simpler presentation, see:

O'glove, Thorton L. *Quality of Earnings*. New York: The Free Press, 1987.

Ratio analysis has been employed as a tool to help predict corporate bankruptcy. See, for instance:

Altman, Edward E. "Financial Ratios, Discriminant Analysis, and the Prediction of Corporate Bankruptcy." *Journal of Finance* (September 1968), pp. 589–610.

Gentry, James A.; Paul Newbold; and David T. Whitford. "Predicting Bankruptcy: If Cash Flow's Not the Bottom Line, What Is?" *Financial Analysts Journal* (September–October 1985), pp. 47–58.

A survey of more than 100 firms found that ratio analysis is an important tool used by management and that profitability ratios are the most important for judging performance. See:

Gibson, Charles H. "How Industry Perceives Financial Ratios." *Management Accounting* (April 1982), pp. 13–19.

A survey of 2,000 members of the Financial Analysts Federation found that analysts emphasize expected changes in return on equity, expected changes in earnings per share, prospects for the industry, and the general economic conditions. Importance is also given to qualitative factors such as quality of management and strategic planning, but the former is hard to measure and it is difficult to obtain good information on the latter. See:

Chugh, Lal C., and Joseph W. Meador. "The Stock Valuation Process: The Analyst's View." *Financial Analysts Journal* (November–December 1984), pp. 41–48.

chapter 17

Break-Even Analysis and Leverage

Learning Objectives

1. Calculate the break-even level of output and illustrate several of its uses.
2. State the sources of operating leverage and financial leverage and explain their impact on operating and net income.
3. Determine the impact of shifting variable costs to fixed costs.
4. Determine the impact of substituting debt financing for equity financing.
5. Explain why operating leverage and financial leverage increase risk.
6. Compute the degree of operating leverage, the degree of financial leverage, and the degree of total leverage.
7. Show how preferred stock is a source of financial leverage.

Disraeli suggested that "what we anticipate seldom occurs; what we least expect generally happens." Perhaps that explains why UAL's (United Airlines) per share earnings declined from $14.96 a share in 1989 to $4.33 in 1990. This large decline in earnings occurred even though revenues rose more than 12.7 percent.

One possible explanation is management's use of leverage. Operating leverage refers to the use of fixed inputs, such as plant and equipment, relative to variable factors, such as labor. A substitution of machinery for labor, for example, may produce the same level of output but may alter the firm's operating income (EBIT) and risk. Financial leverage refers to the use of debt financing relative to equity financing. A substitution of debt financing for equity financing may alter net income, the return on equity, and risk.

The degree of operating leverage measures how operating income changes with different levels of sales when fixed factors of production are used instead of variable factors (i.e., using fixed costs instead of variable costs). The degree of financial leverage measures the volatility of changes in net income to changes in operating income and indicates the risk associated with the use of debt financing. The degree of total leverage measures the change in net income to changes in revenues and indicates the risk associated with combining operating and financial leverage.

This chapter begins with a discussion of break-even analysis, which determines the level of output necessary to avoid losses. While this analysis cannot determine whether a decision will generate profits, it does help management decide what new products should be developed and what markets should be entered. Break-even analysis can also be used to show the impact of substituting fixed costs for variable costs, that is, the use of operating leverage.

The bulk of this chapter is devoted to leverage: the use of fixed costs relative to variable costs and the use of debt financing relative to equity financing. In the minds of some businesspeople, the concept of leverage is the most important concept in finance. For these individuals, the successful use of leverage to increase the return to stockholders is the "name of the game." Of course, the use of leverage may increase risk, so even if management is able to increase the return on equity, the value of the shares could still fall. Thus, one of management's goals is to successfully use leverage without unduly increasing the risk associated with the firm.

BREAK-EVEN ANALYSIS

Break-even analysis is a frequently used tool in financial planning. It seeks to determine the level of sales that generates neither profits nor losses and hence causes the firm to "break even." Break-even analysis also permits management to see the effects on the level of profits of (1) fluctuations in sales, (2) fluctuations in costs, and (3) changes in fixed costs relative to variable costs. Break-even analysis is based on the following three mathematical relationships: the relationship between (1) output and total revenues (i.e., sales), (2) output and variable costs of production, and (3) output and fixed costs of production.

Break-even analysis ▲ Technique used to determine that level of output at which total expenses equal total revenues (resulting in neither profits nor losses)

The relationship between output and total revenues (TR) is the number of units sold (Q) times the price (P) for each unit. This may be expressed as a simple equation: Total revenue equals price times quantity sold. In symbolic form this equation is expressed as follows:

17.1 $$TR = P \times Q.$$

The larger the number of units that are sold at a given price, the larger the firm's total revenue. This relationship is illustrated in the first three columns of Exhibit 17.1, which presents the costs and revenues of a firm used in break-even analysis. The first column gives the price of the product and the second column the quantity sold. By multiplying these together, the total revenue in the third column is obtained. For example, since the per unit price is $2.00, the total revenue for a level of sales of 1,000 units is $2,000.

In Figure 17.1, total revenue is illustrated as a straight line that runs through the origin, for at zero units of output there can be no revenues. As output is increased, total revenue increases. The rate at which total revenue increases (i.e., the slope of the line) is the price of the output. This rate is constant, for each additional unit of output is assumed to be sold at the given price.

Costs of production are divided into two classes: (1) costs that vary with production, such as labor expense; and (2) costs that do not vary with output, such as administrative expense or interest charges. This classification of costs is somewhat arbitrary, for fixed costs may become variable, and variable costs may become fixed. For example, a company may refinance its debt and change its *fixed* interest expense or may change its management personnel and change its *fixed* administrative expense. Union contracts may convert some variable costs into fixed costs. For example, a union contract may require severance pay. The firm may then be reluctant to lay off workers, and thus the labor cost becomes fixed and independent of the level of output. These qualifications make the actual classification of costs into fixed and variable more difficult, but they do

EXHIBIT 17.1

Relationships between Output and Revenues, Output and Costs, and Output and Profits

This table presents the relationship among revenues, costs, and profits for different levels of output.

1 P	2 Q	3 TR	4 FC	5 V	6 VC	7 TC	8 Profits
$2	0	$ 0	$1,000	$1	$ 0	$1,000	($1,000)
2	200	400	1,000	1	200	1,200	(800)
2	400	800	1,000	1	400	1,400	(600)
2	600	1,200	1,000	1	600	1,600	(400)
2	800	1,600	1,000	1	800	1,800	(200)
2	1,000	2,000	1,000	1	1,000	2,000	0
2	1,200	2,400	1,000	1	1,200	2,200	200
2	1,400	2,800	1,000	1	1,400	2,400	400
2	1,600	3,200	1,000	1	1,600	2,600	600

FIGURE 17.1

Relationship between Output and Fixed, Variable, and Total Costs

For a given price, total revenues rise with more output. Increased revenues eventually cover costs, and the firm breaks even.

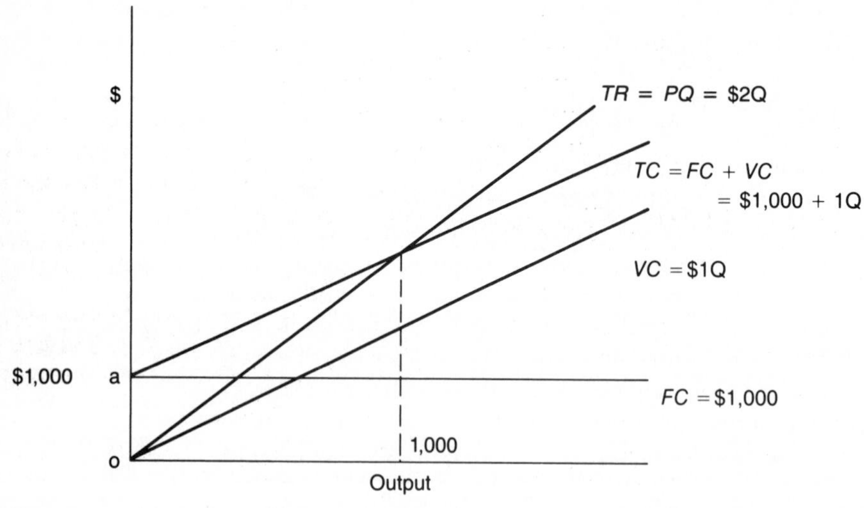

not invalidate the concept that some costs are fixed and independent of the level of output, while other costs vary with the level of output.

Fixed costs
Those costs that do not vary with the level of output

Fixed costs (*FC*) do not vary with the level of output, which may be expressed by the following simple equation:

17.2

$$\text{Fixed costs} = \text{Constant}.$$

In Exhibit 17.1, the fourth column gives the fixed costs of operation. These fixed costs are \$1,000 whether the firm produces 10 or 100 units of output. The relationship between output and fixed costs is shown in Figure 17.1 as a horizontal line (*FC*) that crosses the y-axis at *a*, the fixed dollar amount (\$1,000). The line *FC* has no slope, because fixed costs neither rise nor fall with the level of output. They are independent of the level of output.

Variable costs (*VC*) change with the level of output: the more output the firm produces, the larger the total variable costs of production. This relationship may also be expressed by a simple equation:

Variable costs ▲
Those costs that vary with the level of output

17.3 $$VC = \text{Per-unit variable cost} \times \text{Quantity} = VQ$$

The equation states that variable costs are per-unit variable costs time quantity of output, where *V* is the per-unit variable cost of production. As the level of output rises, variable costs rise in proportion to the increase in output. This relationship is shown in the fifth and sixth columns in Exhibit 17.1, which give the per-unit variable cost (\$1) and total variable costs of production. At zero level of output there are no variable costs. Each additional unit of output then adds \$1 to the firm's variable costs. Thus, at 200 units of output these costs are \$200, and at 1,000 units of output these costs have risen to \$1,000.

The total variable costs are represented in Figure 17.1 by the line *VC*. The variable costs line passes through the origin, which indicates that if operations were to cease, the firm would have no variable costs of operation. This is different from fixed costs, which still exist even if the firm ceases production. For example, during a strike variable labor costs cease, but certain costs (i.e., interest expense) do not disappear just because the firm stops production. A plant that is not operating because of a strike will not be generating output and sales, which puts pressure on management to settle the strike before the fixed costs become an intolerable burden.

Total costs (*TC*) of production are the sum of fixed costs and variable costs (i.e., $TC = FC + VC$). In Exhibit 17.1, total costs of operation are shown in the seventh column, which is the sum of columns four and six. In Figure 17.1, the total costs are illustrated by *TC*, which is the vertical summation of *FC* and *VC*.

Total costs ▲
Sum of fixed and variable costs

When a firm breaks even, its total costs of production are equal to its **total revenues,** which equal output times sales price. At the break-even level of output, the firm is neither making profits nor experiencing losses. If the firm were to produce less, it would experience losses. Management knows that it must maintain at least that level of output in order to cover all of its costs. If management does not believe that the break-even level of output can be produced and sold, it must make some changes. For example, it may decide to produce the output but also seek to find a means to reduce the per-unit costs of production.

Total revenues ▲
Price times quantity sold

The break-even level of output may be found by a simple formula. At the break-even point, total costs must equal total revenue. In equation form that is

17.4
$$TR = TC.$$

By substituting Equations 17.1, 17.2, and 17.3 into Equation 17.4 and solving for the break-even level of output (Q_B), this level of output is as follows:

17.5
$$\begin{aligned} PQ_B &= FC + VQ_B \\ PQ_B - VQ_B &= FC \\ Q_B(P - V) &= FC \\ Q_B &= \frac{FC}{P - V} \end{aligned}$$

(Equation 17.5 employs a subscript. In this case a particular level of output is being discussed. The Q represents any level of output. By adding the subscript B, one particular level of output is being denoted.) Since FC is the fixed cost of production and V is the per-unit variable cost of output, the formula for the break-even level of output (Q_B) expressed in words is as follows:

17.5
$$Q_B = \frac{\text{Fixed costs}}{\text{Price of product} - \text{Per-unit variable cost}}.$$

If this formula is applied to the numerical example in Exhibit 17.1, the break-even level of output is the following:

$$Q_B = \frac{\$1{,}000}{\$2 - \$1},$$
$$Q_B = 1{,}000.$$

This answer is the same that is obtained in the eighth column of Exhibit 17.1, which gives the profits of the firm. These profits are determined by subtracting column seven (total costs) from column three (total revenues). The break-even point is also illustrated in Figure 17.1. As may be seen in Figure 17.1 and Exhibit 17.1, the firm's total cost exceeds its total revenue for all levels of output below 1,000, and the firm makes a profit at all levels of output greater than 1,000. It breaks even when it produces and sells 1,000 units of output.

Uses for Break-Even Analysis

Besides indicating the level of output that must be achieved to avoid losses, break-even analysis is a means for management to analyze the effects of changes in prices and costs. For example, what would be the effect of a decline in the price of the product? If, as the result of increased competition, the price of the product were to fall from $2.00 to $1.50, break-even analysis indicates that the firm would now have to produce at least 2,000 units of output [$1,000/($1.50 – $1.00) = 2,000] to meet its total costs. While the decrease in price may produce an increase in sales, can management anticipate an increase sufficient to absorb 2,000 units of output? An example of a change in costs may be the suggestion of the advertising department for a stepped-up campaign to increase sales. Management may use break-even analysis to ascertain by how much the level of output must be expanded to cover the increased advertising expense. If the advertising campaign adds $0.25 per unit to the cost of the item, the break-even point becomes

$$\frac{\$1,000}{\$2 - \$1.25} = 1,333.$$

The advertising campaign will result in losses to the firm unless a level of sales of 1,333 units can be anticipated.

Break-even analysis may also be used to analyze the substitution of fixed costs for variable costs. This substitution is an important decision often faced by a firm's management. For example, the firm may be able to purchase a piece of equipment that reduces the per-unit variable cost of production but increases the fixed costs of operation. This substitution may also increase the level of output necessary to break even. If, in the above example, the fixed cost were to rise to $1,500 and the per-unit variable cost were to drop from $1.00 to $0.80, then the break-even level of output would rise from 1,000 to 1,250 [$1,500/($2 – $0.80)]. Thus, while the equipment may be cost-effective if management anticipates a larger level of output, it may also turn the firm into a losing operation should the level of sales decline.

These examples illustrate the types of situations and problems to which management may apply break-even analysis. They do not exhaust all the possible situations, however. When a firm is considering introducing a new product, the analysis may be used to determine the level of sales necessary to produce a profit. By determining this minimum level of sales, the analysis aids in managerial planning and decision making.

Limitations of Break-Even Analysis

Break-even analysis requires data, and the analysis can only be as good as the data that are used. Accurately estimating the data, such as the variable cost of production or the response of buyers to changes in price, may be difficult. While the collection of data and the computing of statistics may be done by a firm's engineers and technicians, management must be aware of the degree of accuracy of the data. The results of break-even analysis should be interpreted in light of the accuracy of the data.

Financial Facts

Breaking Even and Broadway's Angels

Shows are brought to Broadway by producers (general partners) and individual investors (limited partners called "angels"). The angels earn a return only after the show breaks even (i.e., meets its operating expenses and recoups the initial financing costs). The financing costs are fixed costs that are spent ("sunk") before the show opens. Once the show premiers, it only has to meet its variable cash costs to continue running. When ticket sales cover the cash operating expenses (when the show breaks even on a cash basis and not on a total cost basis), the producers can continue to run the show. While the angels do not recoup their investment, the producers do continue to collect their management fees. • The majority of Broadway shows open and rapidly close. Even those that have extended runs may cover only the cash operating expenses. Only a handful of shows ever recoup the funds invested in them, and few earn profits. So why invest? There are two obvious answers. Suppose the show is a success. Wouldn't you like to have put money in *Fiddler on the Roof* or *South Pacific?* The backers of those shows will reap the rewards of the investments indefinitely. And, of course, wouldn't you like to attend the cast party and meet ______? Well, you fill in that blank. •

Management also needs an awareness of the limitations and assumptions of break-even analysis. Break-even analysis is limited to identifying the level of output at which the firm ceases to operate at a loss and begins to make a profit. The analysis offers little insight as to the best level or profit-maximizing level of output that management should seek to obtain. Reliance on break-even analysis may then direct management's attention away from profits and value maximization.

Another weakness of simple break-even analysis is that it is built on linear functions. These functions assume (1) that the price of the product is constant, and (2) that the per-unit variable costs are constant. The analysis also assumes that no matter how many units are produced, the firm will be able to sell the output at that given price. Economics, however, teaches that in order to sell additional units of output, the firm may have to *lower its price.* The assumption of constant per-unit variable costs may also be invalid, for it implies that the firm produces the first unit of output and the ten-thousandth unit at the same per-unit variable cost. Economics, however, teaches that firms will experience diminishing returns and thus *per-unit variable costs will rise.*[1]

These factors may significantly reduce the reliability of simple break-even analysis. Failure on management's part to be aware of these limita-

---

[1]The expansion in output may initially reduce per-unit variable costs, but eventually unit costs must rise (i.e., diminishing returns must set in).

tions may result in the misuse of the analysis or in inaccurate interpretation of the results. Break-even analysis only indicates the minimum level of output that must be achieved in order to avoid losses. It should be used in conjunction with other tools to determine which courses of action are in the best interest of the firm and its owners.

DEGREE OF OPERATING LEVERAGE

Any given level of output may be produced with different combinations of the factors of production. One farmer and one tractor may plow a field, but the same result could be achieved by using several farmers and hoes. Of course, the latter may seem ludicrous given today's technology, but if the goal is a plowed field, the same results may be achieved in both cases.

If the firm uses more fixed factors of production (i.e., fixed costs) instead of variable factors (i.e., variable costs), it is employing operating leverage. Plowing the field with one farmer plus a tractor instead of several farmers with hoes illustrates using more fixed costs (the cost of the tractor) instead of variable costs (the costs of each farmer). In the previous section, fixed and variable costs were compared to revenues to determine the break-even level of output. This section will consider how the substitution of fixed for variable costs affects a firm's operating income (i.e., earnings before interest and taxes, or EBIT). Use of fixed instead of variable costs to produce a given level of output is referred to as **operating leverage.** As will be subsequently discussed, operating leverage may increase both the profitability and risk exposure of the firm.

Operating leverage ▲ Use of fixed factors of production (fixed costs) instead of variable factors of production (variable costs) to produce a level of output

The **degree of operating leverage** quantifies the responsiveness of operating income to changes in the level of output or sales. This measure gives management an indication of the response in profits that it can expect if the level of sales is altered. Specifically, the degree of operating leverage is defined as the percentage change in operating income divided by the percentage change in the level of output (if expressed in physical units) or sales (if expressed in dollars).[2] In symbolic terms this ratio is

Degree of operating leverage ▲ Measure of the responsiveness of operating income (EBIT) to changes in output or sales

17.6 $$DOL = \frac{\%\Delta EBIT}{\%\Delta S}.$$

[2] Since the degree of operating leverage is the ratio of two percentage changes, it makes no difference if the change in the denominator is in units of output or in dollars.

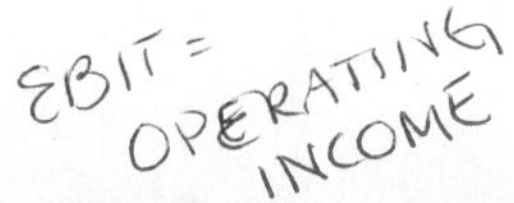

The symbols are defined as follows:

DOL = the degree of operating leverage.
Δ = change.
$EBIT$ = operating income.
S = sales.

This ratio answers the following type of question: If sales are increased by 10 percent, by what percentage will operating income increase? If the degree of operating leverage for a given level of sales is 2, then a 10 percent increase in sales will increase the level of operating income by 20 percent. A large degree of operating leverage indicates that small fluctuations in revenues will produce large fluctuations in the level of operating income.

The degree of operating leverage is not related to the way in which the firm's assets are financed. Operating leverage is independent of the firm's financing decisions. The firm's net income will depend not only on its operating leverage but also on its use of financial leverage. Operating leverage is a source of business risk because it relates to the nature of the firm's operations. The use of financial leverage (financial risk) and the degree of financial leverage are discussed later in this chapter.

An Alternative Method of Determining the Degree of Operating Leverage

The following equation is an alternative way to express the degree of operating leverage:

$$DOL = \frac{\text{Sales} - \text{Variable costs}}{\text{Sales} - \text{Total operating costs}}.$$

In symbols this is

17.7
$$DOL = \frac{Q(P - V)}{Q(P - V) - FC}.$$

The symbols are as follows:

Q = the initial level of output.
P = the price of the product.
V = the per-unit variable cost.
FC = the fixed operating costs.

In this form the degree of operating leverage is easier to compute, but it is also easy to forget that the degree of operating leverage is the ratio of two percentage changes and that it is a measure of the responsiveness of operating income to changes from one level of sales (or output) to another level of sales.[3] This alternative form masks the definition of the degree of operating leverage and thus may lead to an incorrect interpretation.

How equation 17.7 may be applied is illustrated by the following example. A firm is able to sell a unit of output for $5.00. Each unit has a variable cost of $3.00, and the fixed costs of operation are $1,000. What is the degree of operating leverage at 1,000 units? (Notice that the degree of operating leverage is computed at a *given level of sales or output.*) By substituting the numbers into Equation 17.7, the degree of operating leverage is

$$DOL = \frac{1{,}000(\$5 - \$3)}{1{,}000(\$5 - \$3) - \$1{,}000} = 2.$$

The number 2, then, indicates that if the firm increases output by 10 percent, operating income will rise by 20 percent. This increase is easily verified, for at 1,000 units the level of operating income is $1,000.

---

[3]Equations 17.6 and 17.7 are mathematically equivalent. Operating income is sales ($S = P \times Q$) minus variable costs ($V \times Q$) and fixed operating costs (FC). That is

$$EBIT = P \times Q - V \times Q - FC.$$

The change in operating income is

$$\Delta EBIT = P \times \Delta Q - V \times \Delta Q$$

Notice that price per unit sold and the variable cost per unit do not change. Only the level of output changes. Also, notice that FC do not change with sales and, hence, are excluded from the second equation.

The degree of operating leverage was defined in Equation 17.6 as

$$DOL = \frac{\%\Delta EBIT}{\%\Delta S}$$

The definitions of $EBIT$ and change in $EBIT$ are substituted into 17.6 and the variables rearranged:

$$DOL = \frac{\%\Delta EBIT}{\%\Delta S} = \frac{\dfrac{\Delta EBIT}{EBIT}}{\dfrac{P \times \Delta Q}{P \times Q}}$$

$$= \frac{\dfrac{P \times \Delta Q - V \times \Delta Q}{P \times Q - V \times Q - FC}}{\dfrac{P \times \Delta Q}{P \times Q}}$$

$$= \left(\frac{P \times \Delta Q - V \times \Delta Q}{P \times Q - V \times Q - FC}\right)\left(\frac{P \times Q}{P \times \Delta Q}\right).$$

Both ΔQ and P are in the numerator and denominator and so can be cancelled as shown, which leaves the DOL as:

$$DOL = \left(\frac{\cancel{\Delta Q}(P - V)}{Q(P - V) - FC}\right)\left(\frac{\cancel{P} \times Q}{\cancel{P} \times \cancel{\Delta Q}}\right) = \frac{Q(P - V)}{Q(P - V) - FC}.$$

$$\begin{array}{r l} TR = & \$5{,}000 \\ -\ TC = & \$3{,}000 + \$1{,}000 \\ \hline \text{Income} = & \$1{,}000 \end{array}$$

If output is increased by 10 percent to 1,100 units, operating income becomes $1,200, which is 20 percent higher.

$$\begin{array}{r l} TR = & \$5{,}500 \\ -\ TC = & \$3{,}300 + \$1{,}000 \\ \hline \text{Income} = & \$1{,}200 \end{array}$$

This alternative method to determine the degree of operating leverage points out the importance of fixed costs. The greater the fixed costs, the smaller the denominator in the ratio, and hence the larger the degree of operating leverage. Firms with small fixed costs will not have large amounts of operating leverage. For such firms the level of sales necessary to generate profits is small, and fluctuations in earnings with changes in level of sales are modest. Firms with larger amounts of fixed costs have to produce a larger level of output and sales in order to spread out these costs, but once the firms break even, operating income rises more rapidly with further increases in sales. Such firms have higher degrees of operating leverage.

Substitution of Fixed for Variable Costs

Operating leverage is affected when the firm substitutes fixed costs for variable costs (e.g., substitutes equipment for labor). There are two implications of such a change: Both the break-even level of output and the degree of operating leverage may be increased.[4]

These conclusions may be seen by using the simple example presented earlier. The firm's output sold for $5, and fixed and variable costs were $1,000 and $3 per unit, respectively. Suppose the firm increases fixed costs to $1,500 but is able to reduce variable costs to $2.50 per unit. The break-even level of output is changed from

$$Q_B = \frac{\$1{,}000}{\$5 - \$3} = 500 \text{ units}$$

to

$$Q_B = \frac{\$1{,}500}{\$5 - \$2.5} = 600 \text{ units.}$$

[4] If variable costs decline sufficiently, the break-even level of output will decline. See Problem 5 at the end of this chapter.

The degree of operating leverage is also increased at the given level of output. At 1,000 units the degree of operating leverage was

$$DOL = \frac{1{,}000(\$5 - \$3)}{1{,}000(\$5 - \$3) - \$1{,}000} = 2$$

and now it is

$$DOL = \frac{1{,}000(\$5 - \$2.5)}{1{,}000(\$5 - \$2.5) - \$1{,}500} = 2.5.$$

The higher degree of operating leverage means that if the firm were to increase output by 10 percent, operating income would increase by 25 percent, while previously operating income would have risen by only 20 percent.

These percentage responses in operating income are verified by the following income statements. Case A gives operating income at 1,000 units sold, while B and C present operating income after a 10 percent increase in sales from $5,000 to $5,500. Case B assumes no change in operating leverage, but Case C assumes fixed costs have been substituted for variable costs.

	A	B	C
Total revenue	$5,000	$5,500	$5,500
Variable costs	3,000	3,300	2,750
Fixed costs	1,000	1,000	1,500
Operating income	$1,000	$1,200	$1,250

Case C shows the effect of substituting fixed for variable costs. When sales rose 10 percent, operating income rose 25 percent from $1,000 to $1,250. The firm used more operating leverage (DOL = 2.5 in C versus 2.0 in B), which produced a larger increase in operating income.

It should be noted that if sales had fallen, the use of more operating leverage would have produced a larger decline in operating income. If sales were to decline to $4,500 (a 10 percent decline), operating income would have fallen to $800 in B but to $750 in C. This indicates that operating leverage magnifies the swings in earnings in both directions, as sales either rise or fall.

Operating Leverage and Risk

The previous discussion suggests that operating income will rise and fall more rapidly for a firm with a high degree of operating leverage. This section compares the degree of operating leverage for two industries, airlines and retailing, and shows how operating leverage affects the level of risk associated with each industry.

The airlines industry is an excellent example of an industry that has a large amount of operating leverage. A large proportion of airlines' costs are relatively fixed (e.g., depreciation on the planes and equipment). Equally important is that, once the plane is in the air, the cost of the flight is basically the same whether the plane carries one person or a full load. The difference between break-even and a profitable flight is often a matter of just a few passengers. Once this break-even number of passengers is reached, the profitability of the flight rises rapidly, because the fixed costs are being spread over an increasing number of passengers. Thus, once a profitable level of operation is reached, the level of profits rises very rapidly with further increases in the level of output (passengers carried). Airlines, then, have a large degree of operating leverage, for a small percentage change in the number of passengers carried will produce a much larger percentage change in profits.

Retailing is an entirely different type of operation. A firm may have few fixed costs (e.g., rent for the building) and many variable costs. As the firm expands output, these variable costs (e.g., wages) also expand. Such operations do not have a large degree of operating leverage, for as sales expand there is not a large expansion in profits.

Figure 17.2 compares an airline with a retailer to illustrate how changes in sales have more of an impact on the earnings of the firm with the higher degree of operating leverage. The top half of the figure is a break-even chart for an airline; the bottom half is a break-even chart for a retailer. For ease of comparison, both the break-even level of output (Q_B) and the total revenue curve (TR) are identical for both firms. The difference between the two firms rests entirely upon the nature of their cost curves. The retailer has lower fixed costs (0R versus 0S), but the total cost curve for the retailer rises more rapidly.

The effect of these differences in costs (i.e., the difference in operating leverage) can be seen by moving along the horizontal axis. If output increases from Q_B to Q_1, the earnings are greater for the airline than for the retailer (AB versus CD). If output decreases from Q_B to Q_2, the losses are greater for the airline than for the retailer (EF versus GH). The airline experiences greater fluctuations in earnings and losses for the same change in revenues because it has the higher degree of operating leverage.

These fluctuations in earnings imply that the airline is the riskier firm. In periods of declining sales, it will experience greater losses than the retailer. Firms with a higher degree of operating leverage are generally riskier than firms with a lower degree of operating leverage. While firms with the small degree of operating leverage may not achieve a rapid increase in profits as sales expand, they will not experience rapid declines in the level of earnings when sales decline, since most of their

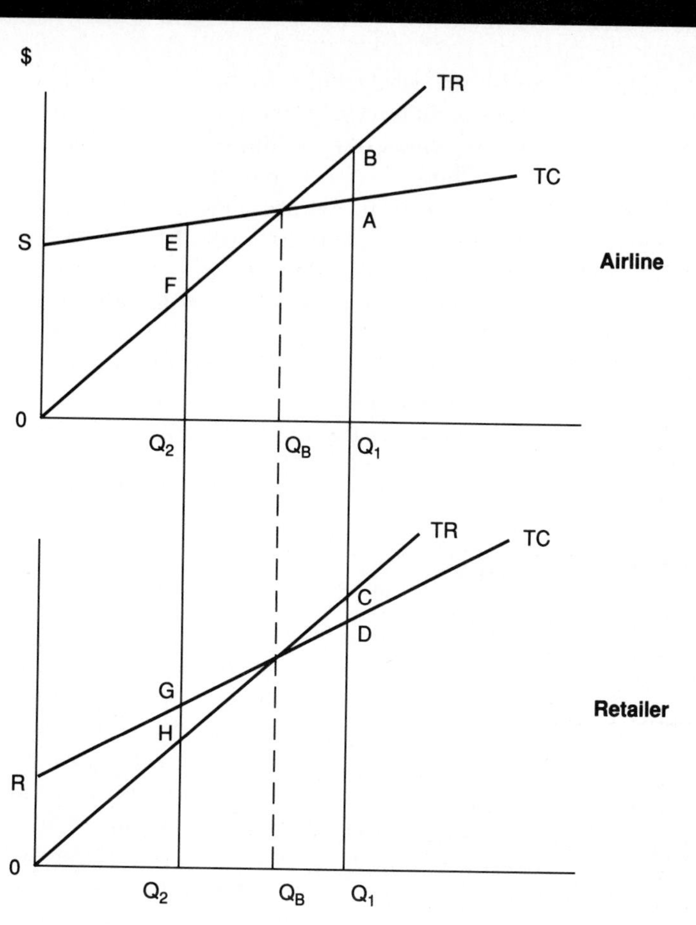

FIGURE 17.2

Break-Even Analysis and Fluctuations in Earnings for an Airline and a Retailer

The airline has more fixed costs (i.e., operating leverage), but the total costs of the retailer rise more rapidly.

costs are variable costs that also decrease with the decline in output and sales.

These differences in operating leverage indicate that some businesses are inherently more risky than others. For the individual firm, risk emanates from two sources: the nature of the business and how the business is financed (i.e., *business risk* and *financial risk*). Airlines, then, have a high degree of business risk, while retailers, especially those selling staples such as food and clothing, may not have this high degree of business risk.

Excessive risk diminishes the worth of a firm. While risk cannot be avoided by business, management can follow actions that reduce its impact. For example, if a firm has a high degree of operating leverage (i.e., a high degree of business risk), management may avoid using an excessive amount of debt financing. This would reduce financial risk so that the combined elements of business risk and financial risk are not excessive.

In summary, operating leverage, like the break-even level of output, is another tool that management may use in planning the level of operations. Operating leverage points out the importance of fixed costs and increases management's ability to perceive how fluctuations in sales will produce fluctuations in the level of operating income. The degree of operating leverage shows how increasing the level of fixed costs will affect the firm's earnings. Management needs to be aware that an increase in fixed costs may increase (1) fluctuations in profits as sales fluctuate and (2) the level of output necessary for the firm to be profitable. These, in turn, increase the element of risk and may reduce the value of the firm. Hence, an excessive amount of operating leverage will be detrimental to the firm's owners, for it decreases the value of their investment.

FINANCIAL LEVERAGE

Financial leverage ▲ Use of another person's or firm's funds in return for agreeing to pay a fixed return for the funds; the use of debt or preferred stock financing

The previous section demonstrated how the use of fixed costs instead of variable costs (operating leverage) increases the firm's operating income as sales expand but also increases the volatility of operating income. This section considers how the use of debt financing instead of equity financing (**financial leverage**) may increase the rate of return earned by the firm's owners; however, it also increases the volatility of the firm's net income. Financial leverage occurs when the firm uses debt financing such as bonds or a fixed income security such as preferred stock to obtain cash. Once the firm has acquired the funds, it may earn more than it has agreed to pay the sources of the funds. In the simplest terms, a firm may borrow money at 10 percent and earn 12 percent. The additional 2 percent accrues to the owners (i.e., the equity) of the firm and increases the return earned by the firm's stockholders.

How financial leverage works may be shown by a very simple example. Firm A needs $100 capital to operate and may acquire the money from the owners of the firm. Alternatively, it may acquire part of the money from stockholders and part from creditors. If the management acquires the $100 from stockholders, the firm uses no debt financing and is not financially leveraged. The firm would have the following simple balance sheet:

ASSETS		LIABILITIES AND EQUITY	
Cash	$100		
		Equity	$100

Once in business the firm generates the following simplified income statement:

Sales	$100
Expenses	80
Earnings before interest and taxes	$ 20
Taxes (40%)	8
Net earnings	$ 12

What is the return that the firm has earned on the owner's investment? The answer is 12 percent, for the investors contributed $100 and the firm earned $12 after taxes. The firm may pay the $12 to the investors in cash dividends or may retain the $12 to help finance future growth. Either way, however, the owners' rate of return on their investment is 12 percent.

By using financial leverage, management may be able to increase the owners' rate of return on their investment. What happens to their rate of return if management is able to borrow part of the capital needed to operate the firm? The answer to this question depends on (1) what proportion of the total capital is borrowed, and (2) the interest rate that must be paid to the creditors. If management is able to borrow 40 percent ($40) of the firm's capital needs at an interest cost of 5 percent, the balance sheet becomes:

ASSETS		LIABILITIES AND EQUITY	
Cash	$100	Debt	$40
		Equity	$60

Since the firm borrowed $40, it is now obligated to pay interest. Thus, the firm has a new expense that must be paid before it has any earnings for the common stockholder. The simple income statement now becomes:

Sales	$100.00
Expenses	80.00
Earnings before interest and taxes	$ 20.00
Interest expense	2.00
Taxable income	$ 18.00
Taxes	7.20
Net earnings	$ 10.80

EXHIBIT 17.2

Relationship between Debt Ratio and the Date of Return on Equity

The return on equity rises as the firm finances a larger proportion of its assets with debt financing.

Debt Ratio	0%	20	50	70	90
Amount of debt outstanding	$ 0	20	50	70	90
Equity	$100	80	50	30	10
Sales	$100	100	100	100	100
Expenses	$ 80	80	80	80	80
Earnings before interest and taxes	$ 20	20	20	20	20
Interest expense (5% interest rate)	$ 0	1	2.50	3.50	4.50
Taxable income	$ 20	19	17.50	16.50	15.50
Income taxes (50% tax rate)	$ 10	9.50	8.75	8.25	7.75
Net earnings	$ 10	9.50	8.75	8.25	7.75
Rate of return on equity	10%	11.87	17.50	27.50	77.50

FIGURE 17.3

Use of Financial Leverage and the Return on Equity

The successful use of financial leverage increases the return on the owners' equity.

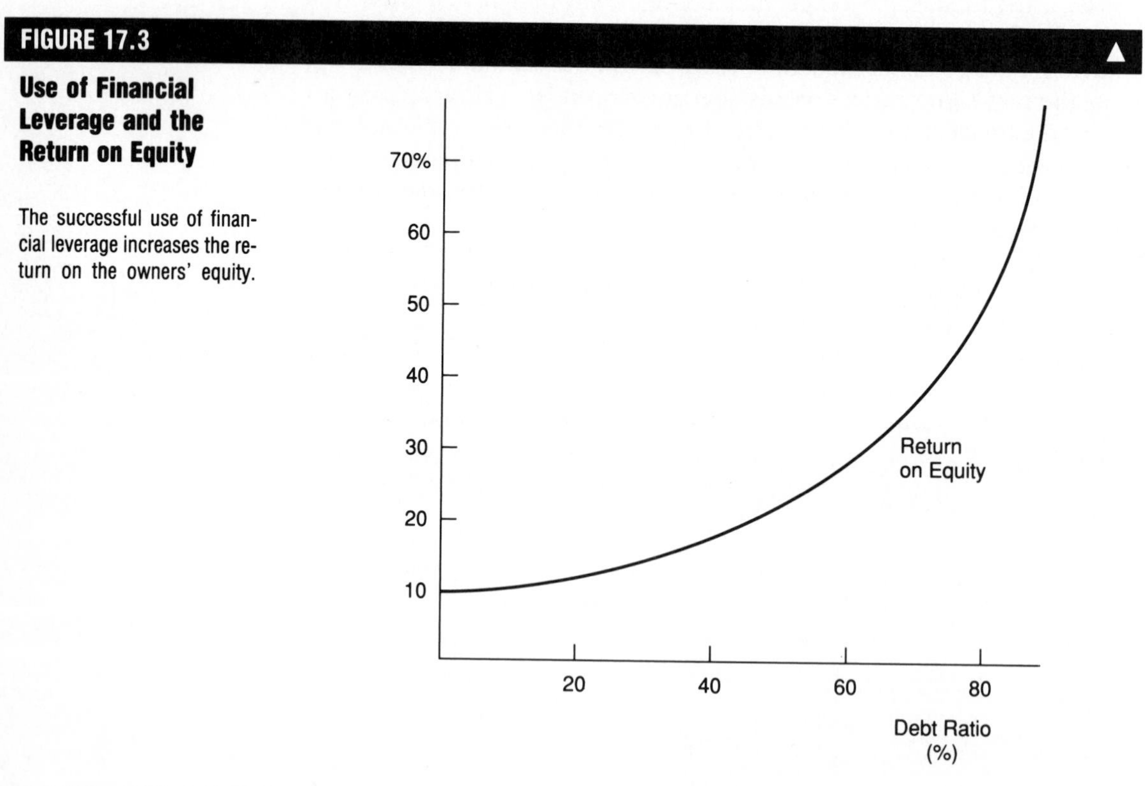

The use of debt causes the total net profit to decline from $12 to $10.80. What effect does this method of financing have on the owners' rate of return? It increases from 12 percent to 18 percent. How does this reduction in the net profit produce an increase in the owners' rate of return? The answer is that the owners invested only $60, and that $60 earned them $10.80. They made 18 percent on their money, whereas previously they had earned only 12 percent.

There are two sources of this additional return. First, the firm borrowed money and agreed to pay a fixed return of 5 percent. The firm, however, was able to earn more than 5 percent with the money, and this additional earning accrued to the owners of the firm. Second, the entire burden of the interest cost was not borne by the firm. The federal tax laws permit the deduction of interest as an expense before determining taxable income, and thus this interest expense is shared with the government. The greater the corporate income tax rate, the greater the portion of this interest expense borne by the government. In this case 40 percent, or $0.80, of the interest expense was borne by the government in lost tax revenues. If the corporate income tax rate were 50 percent, the government would lose $1.00 in taxes by permitting the deduction of the interest expense. These then are the two sources of the additional return to the owners: the additional money earned on the borrowed capital, and the tax dollars lost by the federal government.

As was seen in the above example, a firm's management may increase the owners' rate of return by the use of debt (i.e., the use of financial leverage). By increasing the proportion of the firm's assets that are financed by debt, management is able to increase the rate of return on the owners' equity. Exhibit 17.2 shows the effect of various levels of debt financing (as measured by the debt ratio) on (1) the resulting earnings for the firm, and (2) the rate of return on the investors' equity. The table was constructed using a 50 percent tax rate. The rate of interest is assumed to be 5 percent no matter what proportion of the firm's assets are financed by debt. This unrealistic assumption will be dropped later in the chapter. Figure 17.3 plots the material presented in Exhibit 17.2. From both the table and the figure it may be seen that as the debt ratio rises, the rate of return on the owners' equity not only rises but rises at an increasing rate. This dramatically indicates how the use of financial leverage may significantly increase the rate of return on a firm's equity.

FINANCIAL LEVERAGE AND RISK

Since the use of financial leverage increases the owners' rate of return, the question becomes: Why not use ever-increasing amounts of debt financing? The answer is that as the firm becomes more financially leveraged it becomes riskier. This increase in risk increases (1) the potential for fluctuations in the owners' returns, and (2) the interest rate that the creditors charge for the use of their money.

The fact that the use of financial leverage increases the potential risk to the owners may be seen by employing the simple example presented in the previous section. What happens to the rate of return on the equity if sales decline by 10 percent (from $100 to $90) and expenses remain the same? The income statements for the financially unleveraged and leveraged firms become as follows:

	Unleveraged Firm (0% Debt Ratio)	**Leveraged Firm (40% Debt Ratio)**
Sales	$90.00	$90.00
Expenses	80.00	80.00
Earnings before interest and taxes	$10.00	$10.00
Interest	—	2.00
Taxable income	$10.00	$ 8.00
Taxes (40% tax rate)	4.00	3.20
Net profit	$ 6.00	$ 4.80

The 10 percent decline in sales produces substantial declines in the earnings and the rates of return on the owners' investment in both cases. For the unleveraged firm the rate of return is now 6 percent ($6/$100); for the financially leveraged firm the rate of return plummets from 18 percent to 8 percent ($4.80/$60).

Why does the return decline more for the leveraged firm than for the unleveraged firm? The answer rests with the *fixed* interest payment. When the firm borrowed the capital, it agreed to make a fixed interest payment. This agreement is a legal obligation stipulating that the firm must pay or default on the loan. The fixed interest payment, which was a source of the increase in the owners' rate of return when sales were $100, becomes the cause of the larger decline in the owner's rate of return when the firm's sales decline. If the firm had been even more leveraged (i.e., if the debt ratio had been greater), the decline in the rate of return on the owners' investment would have been even larger. This suggests a general conclusion: The greater the proportion of a firm's assets that are financed by fixed obligations, the greater the potential fluctuation in the owners' rate of return. Small changes in revenue or costs will produce larger fluctuations in the firm's earnings.

Firms that use large amounts of financial leverage are viewed by creditors as being risky. Creditors may refuse to lend to a highly leveraged firm or do so only at higher rates of interest or more stringent loan

EXHIBIT 17.3

Relationship between Increased Interest Rates and the Rate of Return on the Investor's Equity (Tax Rate = 40 Percent)

The higher interest rates associated with the increased use of financial leverage will reduce the return on equity.

Debt Ratio	**0%**	**20**	**50**	**70**
A				
Earnings before interest and taxes	$20.00	20.00	20.00	20.00
Interest at 5 percent	NA	$ 1.00	2.50	3.50
Taxable income	$20.00	19.00	17.50	16.50
Taxes (40% rate)	$ 8.00	7.60	7.00	6.60
Net earnings	$12.00	11.40	10.50	9.90
Rate of return on investors' equity	12.00%	14.25	21.00	33.00
B				
Earnings before interest and taxes	$20.00	20.00	20.00	20.00
Interest rate	NA	6.00%	10.00	12.00
Interest	NA	$1.20	5.00	8.40
Taxable income	$20.00	18.80	15.00	11.60
Taxes (40% rate)	$ 8.00	7.52	6.00	4.64
Net earnings	$12.00	11.28	9.00	6.96
Rate of return on investor's equity	12.00%	14.10	18.00	23.20

conditions. As the interest rate increases, the owners' rate of return on their equity in the firm diminishes. This may be seen in the example presented in Exhibit 17.3, which illustrates what happens to the investors' rate of return as the interest rate rises. The first case (A) illustrates the rate of return if the interest rate is held constant as more debt is employed. The second case (B) assumes that interest rates rise as the debt ratio increases to compensate creditors for the increased risk. The bottom row in each case gives the rate of return on the owners' equity, and, as would be expected, the increased interest expense causes the owners' rate of return to diminish. This may be seen by comparing the bottom lines of both cases. However, even though the rate of return may diminish when the interest rate rises, it might still exceed the rate of return obtained when no debt was used, in which case financial leverage would still be favorable.

As long as the return on the assets financed by debt exceeds the after-tax **cost of debt** (i.e., the interest rate adjusted for the tax savings), financial leverage is favorable and will increase the return on the owners' investment. This after-tax cost of debt is determined by Equation 17.8:

Cost of debt
Interest rate paid adjusted for any income tax savings

$$k_d = i(1 - T) \tag{17.8}$$

The after-tax cost of debt (k_d) depends on the interest rate (i) and the firm's marginal tax rate (T). The larger the tax rate, the smaller the effective cost of debt, because the tax savings that result from deducting the interest expense from taxable income are larger. It is this after-tax cost of debt that is the true cost of using debt financing. While the interest rate paid for the use of borrowed funds obviously affects the cost of borrowing, it is after-tax cost of borrowing that determines if financial leverage is favorable.

The use of the effective cost of debt to determine if financial leverage is favorable may be illustrated with the first example presented in this chapter. When the firm did not use debt financing, it earned 12 percent on its assets after taxes. However, the effective cost of debt was only

$$0.05(1 - 0.4) = 0.03 = 3\%,$$

so financial leverage was favorable. As long as the firm could borrow at an effective cost of 3.0 percent and put those funds to work at 12 percent, financial leverage would be favorable.

Actually, in this illustration financial leverage would have been favorable if the interest rate had been 12, 15, or even 18 percent, because the effective cost of debt after adjusting for taxes would have been 7.2, 9, and 10.8 percent, respectively. It is only at 20 percent that financial leverage would have become unfavorable, for then the interest charges would have risen sufficiently to absorb every dollar earned on the borrowed money. If the firm had financed operations with $60 equity and $40 debt at 20 percent, it would have had the following income statement:

Sales	$100.00
Expenses	80.00
Earnings before interest and taxes	$ 20.00
Interest	8.00
Taxable income	$ 12.00
Taxes (40 percent)	4.80
Net earnings	$ 7.20

The rate of return on the equity is 12 percent ($7.20/$60), which is exactly the rate of return earned on the equity by the unleveraged firm.

Why can the interest rates be so high and financial leverage still be favorable? A major reason is the ability of the firm to deduct the interest expense before determining taxable income. Only when the after-tax cost of debt exceeds the rate of return earned on the firm's assets acquired by debt financing is financial leverage unfavorable. In the above example, the after-tax cost of debt must rise to 12 percent (i.e., 20 percent before-tax cost of debt) before financial leverage becomes unfavorable.

The ability to share the interest expense with the government encourages the use of debt financing. Corporations whose federal income tax rate is 34 percent share almost a third of their interest expense with the federal government. From the firm's viewpoint, $1.00 paid in interest to creditors reduces the firm's taxes by $0.34. The true interest cost of $1.00 interest expense is only $0.66, and thus the tax laws become a major incentive to use financial leverage.

FINANCIAL LEVERAGE THROUGH PREFERRED STOCK FINANCING

In the preceding sections we saw how financial leverage was achieved through the use of debt. Financial leverage may also be acquired through the use of preferred stock, for preferred stock has a fixed dividend that is similar to the fixed interest payment on borrowed money. The significant differences between debt and preferred stock financing are that the dividend on the preferred stock is neither a contractual obligation nor a tax-deductible expense, and that the company may not have to retire the preferred stock. The fact that the dividend is not a contractual obligation is the major advantage of preferred stock financing. Preferred stock is less risky for the firm than debt financing. If the firm is unable to meet the dividend payment, the owners of the preferred stock cannot force the firm to make the payment. In the case of debt, if the firm fails to pay the interest, the creditors can take the firm to court to force payment or force bankruptcy.

Although preferred stock financing is a less risky means to acquire financial leverage, another significant difference between it and debt financing argues strongly against the use of preferred stock. Since interest is a tax-deductible expense and the preferred dividends are not, the effective cost of debt financing is cheaper. If a firm borrows money at 12 percent, the true cost of the money is reduced as a result of the tax laws. If a firm issues preferred stock and pays a 12 percent dividend, the true cost to the firm is 12 percent. Since the cost of debt financing is shared with the government, firms tend to use debt instead of preferred stock as a means to obtain financial leverage.

The tax laws also reduce the amount of financial leverage that a firm may obtain with preferred stock. The difference in the rates of return to the common stockholder that result from the use of debt and preferred stock financing is illustrated in the following example. The firm issues $50 worth of common stock and needs an additional $50. It may issue either $50 of debt with a 5 percent interest rate or $50 of preferred stock with a 5 percent dividend. In both cases the firm acquires $50 and pays out $2.50 in either interest or dividends. However, the earnings available to the common stockholder are larger when debt is used instead of preferred stock. This is shown in the following income statements:

	Debt Financing	Preferred Stock Financing
Sales	$100.00	$100.00
Expenses	80.00	80.00
Earnings before interest and taxes	$ 20.00	$ 20.00
Interest	2.50	—
Taxable income	$ 17.50	$ 20.00
Taxes (50 percent)	8.75	10.00
Net earnings	$ 8.75	$ 10.00
Preferred dividends	—	2.50
Earnings available to common stock	$ 8.75	$ 7.50

When debt financing is used, the earnings available to the common stockholders are $8.75, while they are only $7.50 when the preferred stock is used. Thus, the rate of return on the common stockholders' investment is larger (17.5 percent versus 15 percent) when debt financing is used. The ability of the firm to share the interest expense with the federal government encourages the use of debt financing instead of preferred stock financing. The use of preferred stock financing has declined over time, and this decline is partially explained by the unfavorable tax treatment afforded preferred stock.

THE DEGREE OF FINANCIAL LEVERAGE

As was explained earlier in the chapter, operating leverage may be one means for management to increase the firm's profitability. Regardless of how the firm's assets are financed, the use of fixed costs instead of variable costs increases the firm's potential profitability. However, the use of fixed costs increases the volatility of the firm's operating income and thus increases risk.

Financial leverage is also a means to increase the return to the firm's owners. By using debt financing instead of equity financing, management may be able to magnify the return on the owners' funds invested in the firm. As with operating leverage, the use of financial leverage increases the volatility of the firm's net earnings and thus increases risk.

Degree of financial leverage ▲
Measure of the responsiveness of net earnings to changes in operating income (EBIT)

In the preceding sections, the use of debt financing was measured by the debt ratio (debt/total assets). This ratio measures the extent to which the firm uses financial leverage but does not indicate the volatility of the firm's earnings that results from the use of debt financing. This volatility may be measured by the **degree of financial leverage.** The degree of financial leverage, like the degree of operating leverage, is a measure of responsiveness. It measures the responsiveness of net earnings to changes in operating income at a given level of output (or revenues). While the degree of operating leverage is defined as the percentage change in operating income divided by the percentage change in output (or sales), the degree of financial leverage is the percentage change in net earnings divided by the percentage change in operating income. This relationship is expressed in Equation 17.9.

17.9
$$\text{Degree of financial leverage (DFL)} = \frac{\text{Percentage change in net earnings}}{\text{Percentage change in earnings before interest and taxes}}.$$

The larger the numerical value of the degree of financial leverage, the more responsive are net earnings to changes in operating income. If the numerical value is 2, that means a 10 percent change in the firm's operating income results in a 20 percent change in its net income. If the ratio were only 0.5, a 10 percent change in operating income would produce only a 5 percent change in the firm's net income.

The degree of financial leverage may be computed by using the formula presented in Equation 17.10:[5]

---

[5] Equation 17.10 may be derived as follows:

$$\text{Net earnings} = (\text{Operating income} - \text{Interest})(1 - \text{Tax rate})$$
$$E = (EBIT - I)(1 - t)$$

in which E is net earnings, $EBIT$ is operating income, I is interest, and t is the tax rate. At a given level of output (and the degree of financial leverage, like the degree of operating leverage, is computed at a given level of output), there is no change in interest, so change in earnings is

$$\Delta E = (\Delta EBIT)(1 - t).$$

The degree of financial leverage was defined as:

$$\frac{\text{Percentage change in net earnings}}{\text{Percentage change in EBIT}}.$$

Thus,

$$DFL = \frac{\frac{\Delta E}{E}}{\frac{\Delta EBIT}{EBIT}}$$
$$= \frac{\frac{(\Delta EBIT)(1 - t)}{(EBIT - I)(1 - t)}}{\frac{\Delta EBIT}{EBIT}}$$
$$= \left(\frac{(\cancel{\Delta EBIT})(\cancel{1 - t})}{(EBIT - I)(\cancel{1 - t})}\right)\left(\frac{EBIT}{\cancel{\Delta EBIT}}\right)$$
$$= \frac{EBIT}{EBIT - I}$$

17.10
$$DFL = \frac{\text{Operating income}}{\text{Operating income} - \text{Interest}} = \frac{EBIT}{EBIT - I}.$$

How this equation works may be illustrated by continuing the example used earlier in the chapter to demonstrate the degree of operating leverage. The firm had total revenues of $5,000, variable costs of $3,000, and fixed costs of $1,000. The operating income was $1,000 and the degree of operating leverage was 2. None of this information, however, considers how the firm financed its assets. It could have used 100 percent equity or a combination of debt and equity, in which case it employed financial leverage.

Consider the following two simple balance sheets. In case A the firm uses no debt financing, but in the second case one-third of its financing comes from borrowed funds.

A

Assets	$6,000	Liabilities	$ 0
		Equity	$6,000

B

Assets	$6,000	Liabilities	$2,000
		Equity	$4,000

If the interest rate is 10 percent and the income tax rate is 30 percent, the two income statements are as follows:

	A	B
Revenues	$5,000	$5,000
Expenses	4,000	4,000
Operating income	$1,000	$1,000
Interest	0	200
Before-tax income	$1,000	$ 800
Taxes	300	240
Net income	$ 700	$ 560

The degree of financial leverage at revenues of $5,000 in each case is

A

$$\frac{\$1{,}000}{\$1{,}000 - 0} = 1.$$

B

$$\frac{\$1{,}000}{\$1{,}000 - \$200} = 1.25.$$

These numbers imply that if the firm's operating income increases, there will be a larger increase in net income in case B (in which the firm used financial leverage), because a 10 percent increase in its operating income will produce a 12.5 percent increase in net income. For example, suppose operating income did rise by 10 percent, from $1,000 to $1,100. The net incomes of A and B become:

	A	B
Operating income	$1,100	$1,100
Interest	0	200
Before-tax income	$1,100	$ 900
Taxes	330	270
Net income	$ 770	$ 630

In case A the degree of financial leverage was 1, which indicates that a 10 percent increase in operating income would produce a 10 percent increase in net income. That is exactly what happened (i.e., net income rose from $700 to $770 for a 10 percent increase). However, in case B when the degree of financial leverage was 1.25, the 10 percent increase in operating income produced a 12.5 percent increase in net income. That increase in net income occurred because when operating income rose by 10 percent (from $1,000 to $1,100), income rose from $560 to $630, which is a 12.5 percent increase ($70/$560).

COMBINED FINANCIAL AND OPERATING LEVERAGE

Operating leverage refers to the use of fixed costs to alter operating income, and financial leverage refers to the use of borrowed funds to alter net income. The **total leverage** that a firm has depends on its combined use of operating leverage and financial leverage. Total leverage, then, is the product of the firm's degree of operating leverage and degree of financial leverage. This total leverage is given by Equation 17.11 as follows:

Total leverage ▲
Product of the degrees of operating leverage and of financial leverage

17.11
$$\text{Total leverage} = \text{Degree of operating leverage} \times \text{Degree of financial leverage}$$

This concept may be illustrated by continuing to use the example presented above. At total revenues of $5,000 the firm had a degree of operating leverage of 2 and a degree of financial leverage of 1.25. Thus, its combined leverage is

$$2 \times 1.25 = 2.5.$$

This means that a 10 percent increase in its revenues will produce a 25 percent increase in its net income. To verify this, consider the following income statements. In A the initial level of revenue ($5,000) is given. In B that level of output and revenue is increased by 10 percent to $5,500. The last line gives the net income.

	A	B
Total revenue ($5 times quantity of 1,000 in A and 1,100 in B)	$5,000	$5,500
Variable costs ($3 times quantity of 1,000 in A and 1,100 in B)	3,000	3,300
Fixed operating costs	1,000	1,000
Operating income	$1,000	$1,200
Interest expense	200	200
Before-tax income	$ 800	$1,000
Taxes	240	300
Net income	$ 560	$ 700

The combined leverage factor is 2.5, which suggests that a 10 percent increase in sales or operating revenues will produce a 25 percent increase in net income. Did net income increase by 25 percent after revenues rose 10 percent from $5,000 to $5,500? The answer is yes, because net income rose from $560 to $700, which is a 25 percent increase ($140/$560).

Firms may use either operating leverage or financial leverage, or both, to increase the return on their stockholders' investment in the firm. However, either form of leverage may increase the element of risk. The use of operating leverage increases business risk because the firm must now meet higher fixed costs to be profitable. The use of financial leverage increases financial risk because the firm must now meet the expenses (especially the interest payments) associated with debt financing. Some firms may use a substantial amount of operating leverage but very little financial leverage. For example, IBM has considerable investment in plant and equipment but only a modest amount of debt. Other firms may use a substantial amount of financial leverage but little operating leverage. Most insurance companies (e.g., Aetna) use a large amount of financial leverage, since their policies represent claims on them, but these firms may have little operating leverage.

It is generally not wise to use a large amount of both financial and operating leverage. Any firm that has a substantial amount of fixed equipment that has been financed with borrowed funds has both operating and financial leverage. The use of both sources of leverage will certainly increase the risk exposure of the firm. That is perhaps why airlines are considered among the riskiest of firms. Many airlines have used a substantial amount of debt to buy planes and have both financial and operating leverage. It is not surprising to find many airlines experiencing large swings in earnings from year to year, as their use of both operating and financial leverage increases the fluctuations in their net income.

LEVERAGE, RATIO ANALYSIS, AND STOCK VALUATION

The previous discussion indicated that the use of fixed factors of production (operating leverage) and debt financing (financial leverage) will lead to greater fluctuations in a firm's earnings and its return on equity. These fluctuations increase the investor's risk and may lead to a lower price for the stock.

How does the financial analyst perceive a firm's use of leverage? The answer for financial leverage is simple. The greater the debt ratio, the greater is the use of financial leverage. This relationship was illustrated in the explanation of financial leverage presented earlier. The answer for operating leverage is not as simple since there is no ratio that indicates what proportion of total costs are fixed costs.

Instead, the financial analyst must infer the use of operating leverage from other ratios. This may be done by measuring fixed assets relative to total assets and to revenues. Firms with large amounts of operating leverage tend to be those with substantial investment in fixed assets. Although the airline illustration used in this chapter is typical of firms with a large amount of operating leverage, there are many other firms with major investments in fixed assets. Electric utilities, phone companies, petroleum refiners, and steel mills also have substantial investment in plant and equipment. In 1989, Pacific Telesis's investment in plant and equipment exceeded $17 billion; Southern Company, a major utility headquartered in Atlanta, had utility plant and equipment valued at $18.6 billion on its balance sheet.

The importance of fixed assets to a firm's operations may be determined by computing the ratio of fixed assets to total assets (plant and equipment to total assets) or by computing the ratio of revenues to fixed assets (i.e., the fixed asset turnover discussed in the previous chapter). A high ratio of plant and equipment to total assets suggests a firm's primary costs are fixed. Low turnover of fixed assets suggests that a firm needs substantial investment in plant and equipment to generate sales, from which the analyst may infer that a firm has substantial operating leverage. Plant and equipment constituted over 80 percent of Pacific Telesis's total assets and over 90 percent of Southern's total assets. Their fixed asset turnover ratios were 0.56X and 0.40X, respectively. These ratios suggest that PacTel required about $2 invested in plant and equipment to generate $1 in revenues. For Southern the implication is that about $2.50 in fixed assets was necessary to generate $1 in revenues ($1/0.4). The obvious inference has to be that both firms have substantial operating leverage.

Leverage affects valuation by altering earnings (and hence dividends and the ability to grow) and risk. To the extent that the use of operating leverage is successful, operating income is increased. Although the successful use of financial leverage does not increase total net earnings, it does increase earnings per share and the return to the common stockholders. Successful use of leverage then could lead to higher stock prices through increased dividends and growth. However, the unsuccessful use of leverage will decrease operating income, earnings per share, and the return to equity. Lower earnings will decrease the firm's capacity to pay dividends and to finance growth and could lead to a lower stock price.

In addition, stock prices do not depend solely on dividends and potential growth, because the investor's required return also affects the value of a stock. The increased volatility of earnings will tend to increase the volatility of the firm's stock price. The beta coefficient, which measures the volatility of the return on the stock relative to the return on the market, should rise and cause investors to require a higher return to induce them to buy the stock.[6] Higher required returns will decrease the value of the stock. Thus, two counter-balancing forces are working simultaneously. The use of leverage may increase dividends and/or growth, which argues for a higher stock price, but the increase in risk argues for a lower stock price.[7]

SUMMARY

The break-even level of output is that level of production at which a firm's revenues cover its costs of production. Revenues depend on the number of units sold and their price. Total costs depend on fixed costs, which are independent of the level of production, and variable costs, which rise and fall with changes in the level of production. While break-even analysis does not identify the most profitable level of output, it is useful when management anticipates introducing a new product or substituting fixed for variable costs of production.

The degree of operating leverage is a measure of the responsiveness of operating income to changes in output. It brings to the foreground

---

[6] Beta was discussed in Chapter 8. For a discussion of the mathematical relationship between leverage and a firm's beta coefficient (which is beyond the scope of this text), see an and Jeffrey F. Jaffe, *Corporate Finance*, 2d ed. (Homewood, Ill.: Richard D. Irwin, Inc., 1988), pp. 470–471.

[7] One of the most important advanced theoretical concepts in finance is that the value of a firm is independent of its capital structure (i.e., its use of financial leverage). For a discussion of this proposition see Stephen A. Ross, Randolph W. Westerfield, and Jeffrey F. Jaffe, *Corporate Finance*, 2d ed. (Homewood, Ill.: Richard D. Irwin, Inc., 1988), pp. 385–410.

the importance of fixed costs relative to variable costs. Firms that have large fixed costs have a higher degree of operating leverage. These firms must achieve a higher level of sales to break even. Firms with costs that fluctuate with the level of output do not have a high degree of operating leverage; they may achieve profits at a lower level of production. However, once profitable levels of output are achieved, the firm with the higher degree of operating leverage will experience more rapid increases in operating income for given changes in production. This increased volatility of operating income increases the business risk associated with the firm.

All assets must be financed. There are two basic sources of finance: debt and equity. If a firm uses debt financing or preferred stock financing, it is financially leveraged. If the firm is then able to earn more with the funds acquired by issuing debt than it must pay in interest, the residual accrues to equity. Thus, by successfully using debt financing, the firm increases the earnings available to equity, and the owners' return on their investment is increased.

Although the successful use of debt financing increases the return on equity, it also increases financial risk. If the firm experiences a decline in sales or profit margins, it must still pay the interest and retire the principal. Failure to do so may result in bankruptcy. Thus, while the use of debt financing may increase the return on equity during periods of success and growth, the opposite may be true during periods of difficulty. Then the use of debt financing reduces the return on equity, as the firm must meet the fixed obligations of its debt financing.

The degree of financial leverage is a measure of the responsiveness of net income to changes in operating income. It brings to the foreground the importance of debt financing, for the degree of financial leverage measures fluctuations in net income associated with debt financing.

The degree of total leverage is the product of the degree of operating leverage and the degree of financial leverage. It measures the responsiveness of net income to changes in revenues or output. If a firm combines both operating and financial leverage (i.e., if it has substantial investment in plant and equipment financed primarily with borrowed funds), it will tend to experience large swings in its net income. This large amount of business risk and financial risk may increase investors' required rate of return and result in a decline in the value of the firm.

Review Questions

1. If the management of a firm is considering introducing a new product, how can break-even analysis be used to help make the decision? What will probably be the most difficult (and the most important) part of the analysis?
2. Why is the degree of operating leverage different for a bus company than for a retailer? For a given percentage change in sales, which firm may experience the greater change in operating income?

3. Your firm operates in a very stable environment. Sales forecasts can be made with reasonably good accuracy. Is that an argument for the use of more or the use of less operating leverage?
4. You are a risk-averse manager. A new employee suggests the substitution of new equipment to replace several workers. What additional information should you request of this employee?
5. In many businesspeople's minds, financial leverage is the name of the game. What is meant by this? What are the possible risks and rewards associated with using financial leverage?
6. What feature of preferred stock makes it a source of financial leverage? Since both debt and preferred stock are means to obtain leverage, why will a debt issue with a 10 percent yield achieve more leverage than an equal amount of preferred stock with a 10 percent dividend? If tax laws were changed to equalize the differences, would a firm find it more advantageous to use debt or preferred stock?
7. Financial leverage is associated with financial risk. As a firm becomes more financially leveraged, why does it become more risky? How will creditors seek to protect the funds they have lent? Why may the value of the firm's stock decline as the firm becomes more leveraged?
8. If a firm has a large amount of operating leverage, should the firm also use a substantial amount of debt financing?

Problems

1. Management believes it can sell a new product for \$8.50. The fixed costs of production are estimated to be \$6,000, and the variable costs are \$3.20 a unit.
   a. Complete the following table at the given levels of output and graph the relationships between quantity and fixed costs, quantity and variable costs, and quantity and total costs.

Quantity	Total Revenue	Variable Costs	Fixed Costs	Total Costs	Profits (Loss)
0					
500					
1,000					
1,500					
2,000					
2,500					
3,000					

   b. Determine the break-even level using the above table and illustrate it on the graph. Then use Equation 17.5 to confirm the break-even level found using the above table.
   c. What would happen to the total revenue schedule, the total cost sched-

ule, and the break-even level of output if management determined that fixed costs would be \$10,000 instead of \$6,000?

2. A firm has the following cost and revenue functions:

$$TR = PQ = \$4Q.$$
$$TC = FC + VC = \$3{,}000 + \$3Q.$$

   a. What is the break-even level of output?
   b. If the level of output is 5,000 units, what is the degree of operating leverage?
   c. If the output increases to 10,000 units, what happens to the degree of operating leverage?
   d. If the firm changes its costs so that the new cost schedule is $TC = \$5{,}000 + \$2.5Q$, what happens to (1) the break-even level of output and (2) the degree of operating leverage at 5,000 and 10,000 units of output?

3. A firm can produce a new product by either of two methods. With method A the fixed costs are \$100,000 and the variable costs are \$5 a unit. With method B the fixed costs are \$200,000 and the variable costs are \$4 a unit. The output sells for \$7 a unit. What is the break-even level of output for each method and which should the firm prefer if it anticipates rising sales?

4. The management of a successful firm wants to introduce a new product. The product will sell for \$4 a unit and can be produced by either of two scales of operation. In the first, total costs are

$$TC = \$3{,}000 + \$2.8Q,$$

while in the second scale of operation, total costs are

$$TC = \$5{,}000 + \$2.4Q.$$

   a. What is the break-even level of output for each scale of operation?
   b. What will be the firm's profits for each scale of operation if sales reach 5,000 units?
   c. One-half of the fixed costs are non-cash (i.e., depreciation). All other expenses are for cash. If sales are 2,000 units, will cash receipts cover cash expenses for each scale of operation?
   d. The anticipated levels of sales are

Year	Unit Sales
1	3,000
2	4,000
3	5,000
4	6,000

If the firm selects the scale of production with more operating leverage, what can it expect in years 1 and 2? On what grounds can it justify selecting this scale of operation? If sales reach only 5,000 a year, was the correct scale of operation chosen?

5. A firm has the following total revenue and total cost schedules:

$$TR = \$2Q.$$
$$TC = \$4{,}000 + \$1.5Q.$$

   a. What is the break-even level of output? What are the level of profits and the degree of operating leverage at sales of 9,000 units?
   b. As the result of a major technological breakthrough, the total cost schedule is changed to:

$$TC = \$6{,}000 + \$0.5Q.$$

   What is the break-even level of output? What are the level of profits and the degree of operating leverage at sales of 9,000 units?

6. The manufacturer of a product that has a variable cost of $2.50 per unit and total fixed costs of $125,000 wants to determine the level of output necessary to avoid losses.
   a. What level of sales is necessary to break even if the product is sold for $4.25? What will be the manufacturer's profit or loss on the sales of 100,000 units?
   b. If fixed costs rise to $175,000, what is the new level of sales necessary to break even?
   c. If variable costs decline to $2.25 per unit, what is the new level of sales necessary to break even?
   d. If fixed costs were to increase to $175,000, while variable costs declined to $2.25 per unit, what is the new break-even level of sales?
   e. (optional) If a major proportion of fixed costs were non-cash (e.g., depreciation), would failure to achieve the break-even level of sales imply that the firm cannot pay its current obligations as they come due? Suppose $100,000 of the above fixed costs of $125,000 were depreciation expense. What level of sales would be the cash break-even level of sales?

7. You are starting a new firm to make home videos and believe you can sell the tapes for $25 each. The operation will require several fixed costs, such as leased equipment, that will run $100,000 a year. Variable costs are expected to be $18 a unit.
   a. What will be the break-even level of output?
   b. What is the degree of operating leverage if 20,000 units are sold?
   c. Given the degree of operating leverage in (b), by how much should operating income rise if sales increase by 10 percent?
   d. Verify your answer in (c) by calculating operating income for sales of 20,000 units and for 22,000 units (i.e., a 10 percent increase in units sold). Did operating income rise by the percent you expected?

8. You are starting a new firm to make pumpkin-seed poppers and anticipate selling these appliances for $20 each. Fixed costs associated with the operation are $345,000 and the variable costs are $13 a unit.
   a. What is the level of output necessary to break even?

b. What is the degree of operating leverage at 60,000 units of output?
c. If sales *decline* from 60,000 units to 54,000 units (i.e., a 10 percent decline), by how much should operating income decline?
d. Confirm your answer to (c) by calculating operating income for sales of 60,000 and 54,000 units. Did operating income decline by the percentage you expected?

9. A firm needs $100 to start a business. It expects:

Sales	$200
Expenses	$185
Tax rate	33% of earnings

a. What is the profit the owners will receive if they put up the $100?
b. If the firm borrowed $50 of the initial $100 at 10 percent interest, what is the profit the owners will receive?
c. What is the rate of return on the investment in each case? Why is the rate of return to the owners in (b) larger than the rate of return in (a)?
d. If expenses rise to $194, what will be the rate of return on the owners' investment in (a) and (b)?
e. In which case will the rate of return fall more? Why?
f. What generalization can you draw from the above?

10. Firm A has $10,000 in assets entirely financed with equity. Firm B also has $10,000 in assets, but these assets are financed by $5,000 in debt (with a 10 percent rate of interest) and $5,000 in equity. Both firms sell 10,000 units of output at $2.50 per unit. The variable costs of production are $1, and fixed production costs are $12,000. (To ease the calculation, assume no income tax.)
a. What is the operating income (EBIT) for both firms?
b. What are the earnings after interest?
c. What are the degree of operating leverage, degree of financial leverage, and total leverage associated with each firm?
d. If sales increase by 10 percent to 11,000 units, by what percentage will each firm's earnings after interest increase? Verify your answer by determining the earnings before taxes and computing the percentage increase in these earnings from the answers you derived in part b.

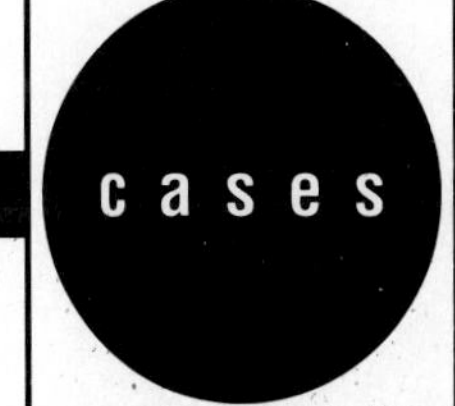

Using Break-Even Analysis to Justify an Investment

Joseph Galleher, who has produced several successful plays, is considering producing *The Hard Lesson,* a play concerning the adjustment to life after the death of a spouse. The serious nature of the play raised doubts in the backers who previously had financed Galleher's successful plays. Although the individuals with the funds to finance the play were well aware of the risks associated with such investments, they were also aware that the possibility existed for large returns if the play were made into a movie or used as the basis for a TV production. If successful, the backers would receive a residual or royalty that could generate cash flow for years into the future. For this reason, Galleher realized that the backers' primary concern was that the initial production break even. If he could convince them that the show would recoup its initial costs, the possibility of residuals would be sufficient to induce the individual investors to finance the play.

Play production involves certain costs that are fixed and others that are variable. For example, an estimated $250,000 is needed to stage the play. These funds would cover the cost of rehearsals, sets and costumes, initial advertising, and other expenses necessary to mount the production. Once *The Hard Lesson* opens, the actors will receive $20,000 a week, and the producer's fee is $4,000 a week plus 5 percent of gross receipts. The director will also receive a fee of 5 percent of the gross receipts, and the actors will have an incentive contract that pays them an additional 10 percent of the receipts. The author will receive a royalty of $5,000 per week, and it is estimated that weekly advertising expenses will run $12,000.

Galleher is considering two different theaters in which to stage the play. The first, with only 300 seats, has a reputation for housing quality productions of interesting works. It tends to draw an audience that will pay $40 a ticket, and the rent is $10,000 a month. The other theater has 1,300 seats, and since the building is larger its rent is $16,000 a month. However, the theater management has a policy of charging no more than $15 a ticket. In both cases the play would be performed five times a week.

While Galleher is concerned with making a profit, the fact that he will receive a weekly payment reduces his personal need for the show to earn a profit. In addition, since the backers are primarily concerned with not losing money and secondarily with the possibility of earning large residuals, the greatest financial emphasis is to avoid losses (i.e., to break even).

Case Problems

1. Excluding the initial production costs, calculate for each theater how many seats must be sold for each performance in order for the play to cover its weekly operating expenses.
2. If the play ran at 80 percent of capacity in the smaller theater and 70 percent of capacity in the larger theater, how long would it take to recoup the initial $250,000?

Suggested Readings

Berstein, Leopold A. *Analysis of Financial Statements,* rev. ed. Homewood, Ill.: Dow Jones-Irwin, 1984.

Chapter 8 in this book, written for individuals who use financial analysis, gives a succinct description of break-even analysis, its uses, assumptions, and limitations as seen from the perspective of an accountant.

Jaedicke, Robert K., and Alexander A. Robichek. "Cost-Volume-Profit Analysis under Conditions of Uncertainty." *The Accounting Review* (October 1964), pp. 917–926. Reprinted in *Financial Management Classics,* edited by C. D. Aby, Jr. and D. E. Vaugh, pp. 38–50. Santa Monica, Calif.: Goodyear Publishing Co., 1979.

This classic article adds risk analysis to break-even analysis.

Morris, James R. *The Dow Jones-Irwin Guide to Financial Modeling.* Homewood, Ill.: Irwin, 1987.

This book explains how financial models should be structured and used to bridge the gap between the computer expert with little background in finance and the financial analyst with little computer background.

Reinhardt, U. E. "Break-Even Analysis for Lockheed's TriStar: An Application of Financial Theory." *Journal of Finance* (September 1973), pp. 821–838.

This article presents an excellent (but difficult) case study of the use of break-even analysis.

appendix to chapter 17

The Relationship between the Degree of Operating Leverage and Break-Even Analysis

A simple way to illustrate the relationship between the degree of operating leverage and break-even analysis is to examine Figure 17A.1. This figure is divided into three graphs. The top graph reproduces the total costs and total revenues from Figure 17.1. The middle graph shows the relationship between output and operating income. In either component, at levels of output below Q_B the firm is operating at a loss. At Q_B level of output, the firm is breaking even. At levels of output above Q_B, the firm earns operating income. The profit or loss position of the firm that is illustrated by the middle graph is essentially no different from the material in the top graph. Thus, at Q_2 the fact that the firm is experiencing losses of "*ab*" may be read from either. At Q_1 the operating income of "*cd*" may also be read from either. For the purpose of showing the relationship between the degree of operating leverage and break-even analysis, the middle graph (the relationship between operating income and the level of output) will be used.

The degree of operating leverage was defined as the percentage change in operating income divided by the percentage change in revenue or output. This was expressed symbolically in Equation 17.6. The percentage change in operating

FIGURE 17A.1

Relationships between Output, Operating Income, and Operating Leverage

Operating leverage declines as output moves from the break-even level of output.

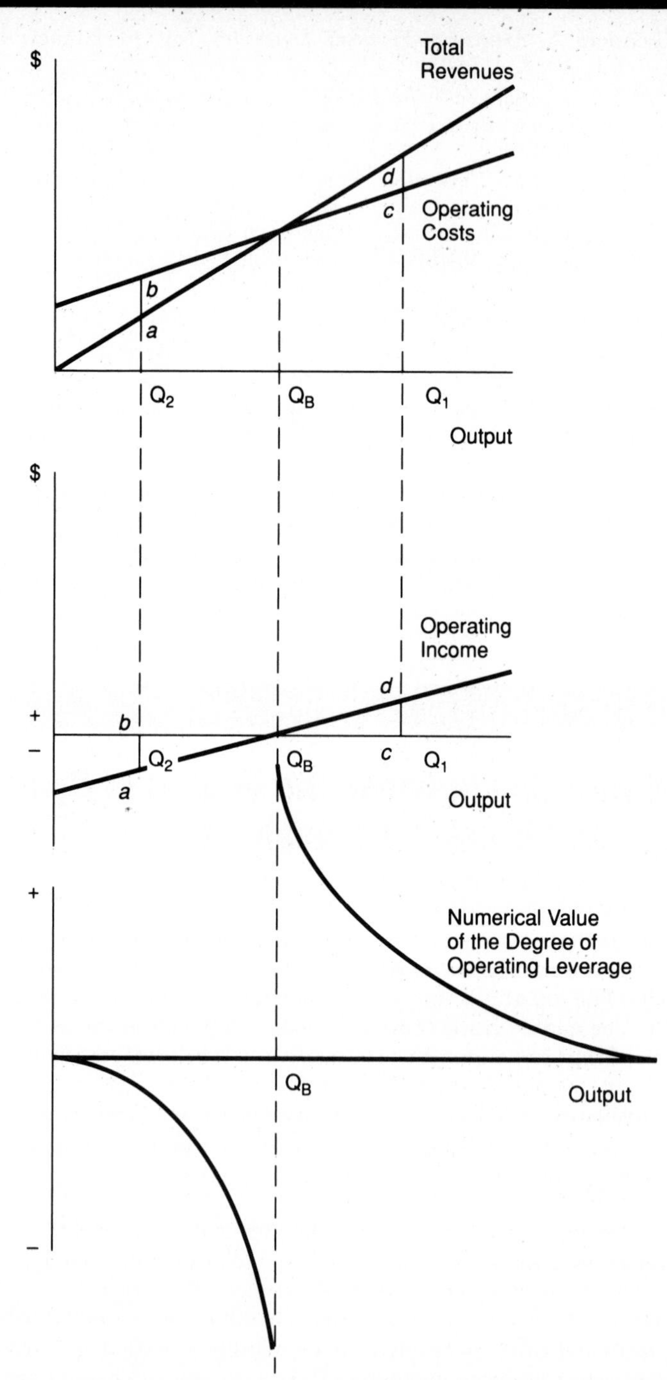

income was $\%\Delta EBIT$, and $\%\Delta Q$ represented the percentage change in output. These terms in Equation 17.6 may be rearranged as follows:

17A.1
$$\frac{\%\Delta EBIT}{\%\Delta Q} = \frac{\frac{\Delta EBIT}{EBIT}}{\frac{\Delta Q}{Q}} = \left(\frac{\Delta EBIT}{\Delta Q}\right)\left(\frac{Q}{EBIT}\right)$$

In this form the degree of operating leverage consists of two factors that are multiplied. The first component ($\Delta EBIT/\Delta Q$) is the slope of the total operating income line in Figure 17A.1. The second component ($Q/EBIT$) is the reciprocal of a point on that line. For example, point *d* represents a particular combination of output and operating income, such as 600 units of output and EBIT of $300. If the slope of the operating income line is equal to 2, then the degree of operating leverage at point Q_1 is

$$2 \times 600/300 = 4.$$

This indicates that if management increases the level of output by 10 percent, the level of operating income will rise by 40 percent. For example, an increase in output from 600 units to 660 units (a 10 percent increase) will produce an increase in operating income from $300 to $420 (a 40 percent increase).

Decomposing the degree of operating leverage into two component pieces helps reveal the relationship between the degree of operating leverage and break-even analysis. At the break-even level of output (Q_B in Figure 17A.1), the level of operating income is zero. When zero profit is substituted into the ratio $Q/EBIT$, the value of the ratio becomes infinite (or undefined). Thus, at zero operating income the degree of operating leverage is infinite, which tells management that a small percentage change in the level of output will produce a very large percentage change in operating income. This is exactly what management should expect. The percentage change in EBIT is very large because previously the firm was either operating at a loss or breaking even.

As the firm continues to increase output above Q_B, the degree of operating leverage falls. While the slope of the profit line ($\Delta EBIT/\Delta Q$) is not affected as output increases, the other component of the degree of operating leverage declines. The ratio of $Q/EBIT$ declines as the level of output and operating income rises. Thus, the degree of operating leverage falls as output increases. This is illustrated in the bottom graph in Figure 17A.1. As the level of output increases beyond Q_B, the numerical value of the degree of operating leverage declines and approaches zero. Further increases in the level of output still have an impact on operating income, but the impact diminishes as the firm reaches higher levels of output and sales.

The converse applies if the firm starts to operate at a loss. A small decline in output from the break-even level of output generates a large percentage decline in operating income. However, the percentage declines in operating income diminish with further reductions in output. That is, as the level of output decreases from Q_B, the negative numerical value of the degree of operating leverage rises and approaches zero. Further decreases in the level of output still have an impact on operating income, but the amount of the impact diminishes as the firm reaches lower levels of output and sales.

1

Planning: Forecasting and Budgeting

Learning Objectives

1. Differentiate between forecasting and budgeting.
2. Identify the assets and liabilities that spontaneously vary with the level of sales.
3. Illustrate the percent of sales method of forecasting.
4. Describe the use of estimated equations to forecast.
5. Construct a cash budget.
6. Explain the purpose of the cash budget.

In *Don Quixote,* Cervantes suggested that to be "forewarned" is to be "forearmed." To be forearmed is the purpose of planning. By constructing financial plans and budgets today, the financial manager is forewarned of future problems. Once problems are identified, the financial manager can take actions to solve (or at least alleviate) them before they become unmanageable.

This adjustment process was certainly evident in the oil drilling and oil service industries during the mid-1980s when the price of crude oil dramatically declined from about $30 a barrel to about $10. In McDermott's 1986 annual report, management said: "New business will continue to be scarce, and competition for the available market will be fierce. . . . We have every intention of surviving this difficult period." The forecasts led McDermott and other oil service firms to consolidate operations, reduce staff and lay off workers, and cut operation expenses. Three years later in 1989, management reported, "Although we have experienced weak markets and losses over the past several years . . . (we believe) that the long-term outlook for our markets is excellent." Reading between the lines suggests that the short-term picture for oil service firms was still weak but finally improving.

Compare the above remarks with comments by the management of Schering-Plough, a leading drug and pharmaceutical firm. In 1986, management forecasted continued growth, and three years later management persisted and once again forecasted growth. To help achieve this growth, management announced that spending on research and development (R&D) would reach $370 million during 1990. The forecasts and financial plans developed by the management of Schering-Plough obviously were perceptibly different than those developed by the management of McDermott.

Although planning applies to all facets of a firm's operations, it is particularly important for financial management. Since all assets must be financed, it is crucial for the health of a firm to forecast the anticipated level of assets in order to plan for their financing. In addition, the financial manager is concerned with the day-to-day timing of cash flows. Cash receipts and disbursements are rarely synchronized. When disbursements precede receipts, the cash must be obtained somewhere, or the firm will be unable to pay its bills. Budgets, especially the cash budget, are constructed to help solve this problem by determining in advance when the firm will need funds to pay its current obligations and when the firm will generate the cash to retire any short-term loans that covered cash deficiencies.

This chapter is concerned with financial planning and forecasting. Two techniques, the percent of sales forecasting method and regression analysis, are illustrated as means to predict the need for funds to finance the expansion of assets. The chapter concludes with a discussion of budgeting.

PLANNING

Planning is the process of establishing goals and identifying courses of action (strategies) to meet the goals. Planning is like a road map; it helps point out the roads (i.e., the alternative methods) to reach the destination (i.e., the goal). In finance, the goal of management is often stated as being the maximization of the value of the firm. The facets of the financial manager's job, such as the decision to acquire plant and equipment or how to finance the firm's assets, are means to obtain the desired goal of increasing the value of the firm.

The financial manager, however, does not work in a vacuum but must work within the framework of the firm. The management of a firm encompasses marketing, production, and administration as well as finance. The senior executives in charge of a firm's functional areas and operations develop a strategic plan. This is a general guide for the management of a firm and encompasses the development of new products through research and development, the expansion of current markets and the identification of new markets for existing products, the controlling of costs and operations, the expansion (or contraction) of plant and equipment required by changes in anticipated sales, and the financing of additional plant and equipment.

Financial management is one part of the strategic plan, as is planning for marketing and production. Financial decisions cannot be made without forethought. Financial planning is a process of anticipating future needs and establishing courses of action today to meet financial objectives in the future. Thus, financial management and planning are concerned with when funds will be needed and how much will be available from internally generated sources. The need for external sources raises questions such as, Should the firm use long- or short-term credit? What is the best combination of debt to equity financing?

Financial management is not limited to anticipating the future. An integral part of a financial manager's role involves monitoring financial conditions to take advantage of changes in the financial markets. In addition, a financial manager should periodically reevaluate financial plans and decisions to avoid repeating past errors and to improve future financial planning and decision making.

In a sense, virtually every chapter in this text is concerned with financial planning. For example, several earlier chapters considered the variety of debt instruments and stock. Chapter 22 puts these pieces together by discussing the optimal combination of debt and equity financing. This information is required before investments in plant and equipment (i.e., capital budgeting, discussed in Chapter 23) can be undertaken.

Several specific techniques are used in the planning process. For example, break-even analysis, which determines the level of output and sales necessary to avoid sustaining losses, was covered in the previous chapter. This type of analysis helps establish long-term plans, as the management will seek to reduce costs or increase revenues if it appears that the firm will operate at a loss. Break-even analysis, along with the capital budgeting techniques considered in Chapter 23, is a crucial component of long-term financial planning.

The topics in this chapter are more concerned with short-range planning. In the first, external financial requirements are determined by projecting assets and liabilities through the use of percent of sales method or regression analysis. Such analyses help determine if the firm will need external financing as sales expand or contract. An alternative means to determining if the firm will need external funds is the cash budget. While the former techniques stress short-term asset requirements, the cash budget highlights the flow of cash through the firm. It identifies whether the firm will generate cash (i.e., when receipts exceed disbursements) or whether the firm will lose cash (i.e., when disbursements exceed receipts). Such cash shortages will require short-term external funding.

FLUCTUATIONS IN ASSET REQUIREMENTS

Firms must have assets in order to operate. The amount and type of assets vary with each industry. Airlines and utilities have primarily fixed assets. Retailers must carry current assets such as inventory and accounts receivable. Other firms, especially those providing services, may have few assets. Other than space (which may be rented), the local barbershop or travel agency may operate with almost no assets.

Just as the amount and type of assets required for operations vary with each industry, the level of a firm's assets within an industry may also vary. For example, a firm that sells swimming pools will not want to stock a large supply of pools during the winter. Sales are obviously seasonal. Firms whose sales are primarily seasonal (or cyclical, such as homes or automobiles) will experience periodic increases and decreases in the level of assets needed for their operations.

These fluctuations are illustrated in Figure 18.1, which presents the levels of various assets over a period of time. Fixed assets (0A) are given and do not vary. Current assets have been divided into two groups: those that remain at a particular level (AB) and those that vary (BC). The firm may carry a minimum amount of inventory and may always have a certain amount of accounts receivable. In addition, the firm will carry current assets that vary over time. The level of inventory will fluctuate with anticipated changes in demand, which in turn will generate varying amounts of accounts receivable and cash. These fluctuations in the levels

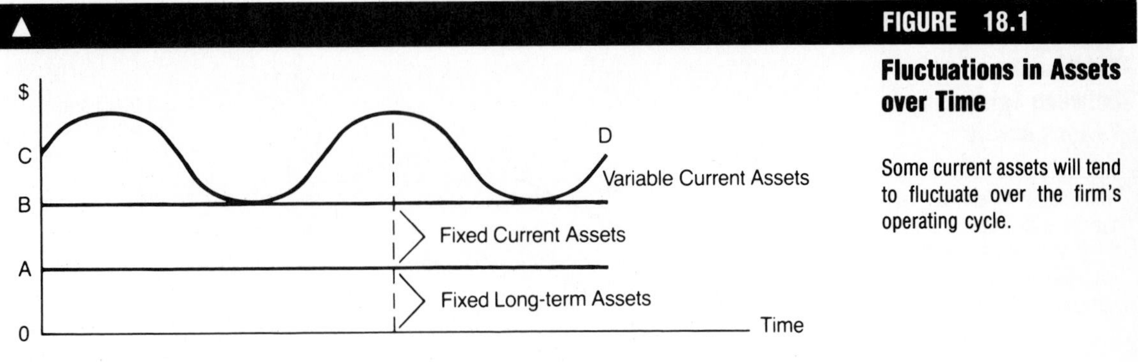

FIGURE 18.1

Fluctuations in Assets over Time

Some current assets will tend to fluctuate over the firm's operating cycle.

of inventory, accounts receivable, and cash are illustrated by CD in Figure 18.1.

The firm may also require additional assets as it expands. As the firm grows, some assets automatically expand with the level of sales. For example, the level of inventory expands to meet the higher volume of sales. Other assets, especially long-term assets such as plant and equipment, will not automatically expand with the level of output. At first the existing plant and equipment will be used more intensively. The number of shifts will be increased, or employees may work overtime. However, if the expansion of sales continues and appears to be permanent, management will expand the firm's investment in plant and equipment.

This difference is illustrated in Figure 18.2. The left-hand side illustrates those assets that increase with expanding output. This relationship is shown by the steadily increasing line *AA* that represents the level of these assets at each level of sales. The right-hand side illustrates those assets that are increased only after a higher level of sales has been achieved. From zero sales to sales of S_1, the level of plant and equipment remains constant. After the level of S_1 has been obtained, further increases in the level of output require expansion in the plant and equipment. The level of fixed assets rises from A_1 to A_2. This higher level of assets is maintained until sales rise from S_1 to S_2, when plant and equipment must be further expanded. The level of fixed assets then is increased to A_3.

In the discussion that follows, it is initially assumed that the firm can expand the level of production without having to increase capacity. Thus, only those assets that spontaneously fluctuate with the level of sales will be affected by an increase (or decrease) in sales. Two techniques (the percent of sales and regression analysis) that may be used to forecast the firm's need for financing are described. Such finance may be necessary to carry those assets (e.g., inventory and accounts receivable) that fluctuate with the level of sales. After these techniques have been explained, the assumption that the firm has excess capacity will be relaxed. Then,

FIGURE 18.2

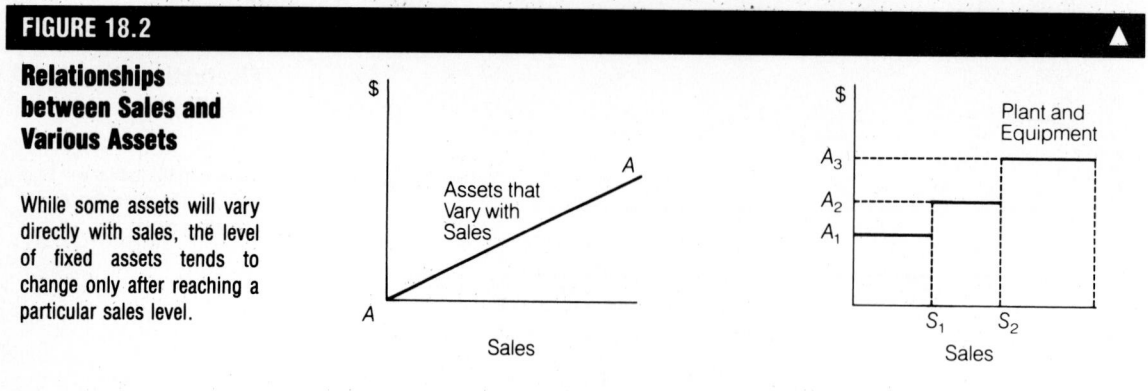

Relationships between Sales and Various Assets

While some assets will vary directly with sales, the level of fixed assets tends to change only after reaching a particular sales level.

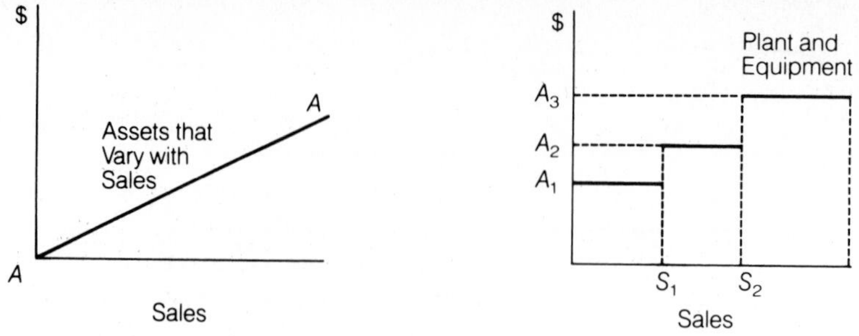

expanding the level of sales may require additional investment in plant and equipment, as well as increased inventory and accounts receivable. Since all increases in assets must be financed, the forecasts of the expansion in assets forewarn the financial manager of the firm's future needs for funds.

FORECASTING EXTERNAL FINANCIAL REQUIREMENTS: PERCENT OF SALES

Percent of sales ▲ Forecasting technique that assumes specific assets and liabilities will vary directly with the level of sales

The **percent of sales** technique for forecasting financial requirements isolates the assets and liabilities that change with the level of sales and expresses each as a percent of sales. These percentages are then used to forecast the level of each asset and liability. The forecasted increase in the level of assets must be financed and the increased level of liabilities will automatically finance some of the increase in assets. The difference between the increase in the assets and the liabilities must be financed by other means.

What assets vary with the level of sales? Consider a firm with the following balance sheet:

ASSETS		LIABILITIES AND EQUITY	
Cash	$ 100	Accounts payable	$ 200
Accounts receivable	300	Bank note	200
Inventory	300	Other current liabilities	100
Plant and equipment	500	Long-term debt	300
	$1,200	Equity	400
			$1,200

Several of the assets will vary with the firm's level of sales. A higher level of sales will require that the firm carry more inventory and will also increase the accounts receivable, as credit sales should expand if all sales increase. The level of cash may also rise with increased cash sales, and the firm will want to increase its level of cash holdings to meet the expanded liquidity needs, such as the payroll associated with higher sales volume.

While cash, inventory, and accounts receivable increase as sales rise, other assets do not automatically expand. For example, plant and equipment may not be increased but will be used at a higher level of capacity. If the level of sales rises sufficiently, more plant and equipment will need to be acquired, but no automatic increase in these fixed assets must occur as sales volume increases.

All the assets that increase with the higher level of sales must be financed. The funds to finance these assets must come from somewhere, and one source is any liability that also expands with the level of sales. If liabilities increase sufficiently, they will cover the expansion in assets, but if they do not, the firm will have to find additional financing to operate at the higher level of sales.

Accounts payable are the primary liabilities that increase with expanded sales. This expansion in accounts payable occurs because the firm's suppliers increase goods sold to the firm on credit, and other liabilities such as accrued wages and salaries automatically expand. These accounts payable are the primary sources of finance that spontaneously expand with an increase in the level of operations of the firm. The other short-term liabilities, such as notes payable and the current portion of long-term debt due this fiscal year, do not spontaneously expand with the level of sales and thus are not automatic sources of financing.

The previous balance sheet may illustrate how the percent of sales technique of forecasting works. After those assets and liabilities that spontaneously vary with the level of sales are identified, they are expressed as a percent of sales. Thus, if the firm has inventory of $300 and sales of $2,000, inventory is 15 percent of sales ($300/$2,000). The following exhibit expresses as various percentages of sales all of the assets and liabilities in the previous balance sheet that vary with the level of sales (assuming a level of sales of $2,000):

ASSETS		LIABILITIES	
Cash	5%	Accounts payable	10%
Accounts receivable	15%		
Inventory	15%		

The percent of sales for the assets and liabilities that do not automatically increase with the level of sales has not been determined. Thus, as may be seen from the exhibit, the ratio of all assets that vary with sales is 35 percent, and the ratio of liabilities is 10 percent.

Once the percentages have been determined and the anticipated level of sales has been forecasted, the anticipated level of sales is multiplied by each percentage to determine the anticipated level of each asset and liability necessary to sustain that level of sales. For example, if management anticipates that the level of sales will rise to \$2,400 (a 20 percent increase), the percent of sales technique will forecast the following level of assets and liabilities for each asset and liability that varies with sales:

ASSETS		LIABILITIES	
Cash	\$120	Accounts payable	\$240
Accounts receivable	360		
Inventory	360		

In this case the percent of sales forecasting method states that the level of inventory will rise to \$360 (\$2,400 × 0.15), the level of accounts receivable will be \$360 (\$2,400 × 0.15), and the level of cash will be \$120 (\$2,400 × 0.05). The automatic expansion in assets is \$140, which may be found by multiplying the increase in sales (\$400) by 35 percent, which is the sum of the ratios of all assets that vary with the level of sales.

Concurrently with the increase in assets, accounts payable will rise to \$240 (\$2,400 × 0.10). The total increase in assets is \$140, while the increase in liabilities is \$40. This \$40 increase in liabilities will finance only part of the increase in assets. Thus, \$100 (\$140 − \$40) of assets will require other sources of financing. Management may expect that the firm will operate at a profit, and these profits could be retained to finance the additional assets. But profits after taxes would have to be at least \$100 to finance the expansion in assets. If management cannot anticipate after-tax profits of \$100, an outside source of finance (such as a bank loan) will have to be found to finance the anticipated increase in assets necessitated by the increase in sales.

If management anticipates earning 5 percent on the total sales and retaining 60 percent of the earnings, the forecasted increase in equity is

$$(0.05)(\$2{,}400)(0.6) = \$72.$$

Given this increase in equity and the forecasted levels of the current assets and current liabilities, management may construct the following pro forma balance sheet.

ASSETS		LIABILITIES AND EQUITY	
Cash	\$ 120	Accounts payable	\$ 240
Accounts receivable	360	Bank note	200
Inventory	360	Other current liabilities	100
Plant and equipment	500	Long-term debt	300
	\$1,340	Equity	472
			\$1,312

The balance sheet entries include the forecasted entries (i.e., the assets and liabilities that spontaneously changed with the level of sales), the entries that did not change such as the long-term debt, and the new equity which is the old equity plus the earnings that are to be retained.

Immediately it is obvious that the balance sheet does not balance. The forecasted increase in the assets exceeds the forecasted increase in the liabilities and equity. Total assets exceed total liabilities plus equity by $28. To achieve the forecasted increase in assets, the firm will have to find $28 in additional funding. Without these additional sources, the expansion in assets cannot occur. However, this is a forecasted and not an actual balance sheet, so management now has the task (and presumably the time) to obtain the additional sources of finance.

Management has several options. Any increase in equity, any increases in liabilities, or any decrease in assets will help provide the needed financing. For example, the dividend policy may be changed to reduce dividends and increase the retention of earnings. Another possibility may be to seek an additional bank loan. A third option is to reduce the holdings of cash. In the above analysis, it was assumed that cash increased, and such an increase will require financing. If the firm can avoid the increase in cash and perhaps decrease its holdings of cash, the effect will be to reduce the firm's need for additional finance.

If management decides not to reduce dividends, not to reduce the firm's cash, but instead to increase borrowing from the bank by $28, the pro forma balance sheet becomes

ASSETS		LIABILITIES AND EQUITY	
Cash	$ 120	Accounts payable	$ 240
Accounts receivable	360	Bank note	228
Inventory	360	Other current liabilities	100
Plant and equipment	500	Long-term debt	300
	$1,340	Equity	472
			$1,340

The balance sheet now balances; the sum of the projected assets equals the sum of the projected liabilities plus equity.

The Percent of Sales Summarized as an Equation

The previous example illustrates the percent of sales technique of forecasting. Obviously, it is a very simple technique, for in effect it asserts that if an asset or liability is some percent of sales and sales expand by some percentage, then the assets and liabilities will also expand by the same percentage. This relationship is illustrated in Figure 18.3. The horizontal axis represents the level of sales, and the vertical axis shows

FIGURE 18.3

Relationship between Inventory and Sales

Inventory and other current assets such as receivables tend to change spontaneously with changes in the level of sales.

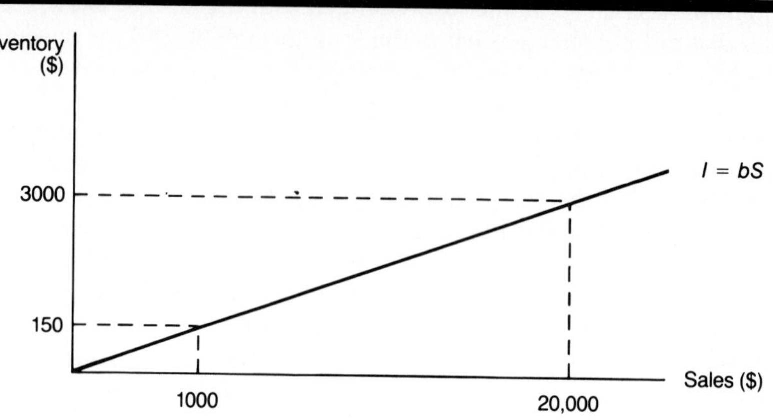

the level of inventory. (A similar graph may be drawn for any asset that varies with sales.)

The relationship between inventory and sales is summarized by the following equation:

18.1 $$I = bS.$$

I is inventory; S is the level of sales; and b is the percent of sales, which in this case is also the slope of the line. Once this percentage is known, it is easy to predict the level of inventory associated with any level of sales. Thus, if sales are \$1,000, inventory will be \$150 (\$1,000 × 0.15). If sales expand to \$20,000, inventory must expand to \$3,000 (\$20,000 × 0.15). By this method, all that is necessary to forecast the level of the asset is (1) the ratio of the current level of that asset to current sales and (2) the anticipated level of sales.

While Figure 18.3 summarizes the relationship between one current asset and sales, other similar graphs could be constructed showing the relationships between any assets or liabilities that vary with the level of sales. Such graphs, however, would be only modestly useful for forecasting the firm's need for funding. The financial manager may instead use a simple equation that summarizes (1) the assets and liabilities that vary with sales, (2) the profits the firm earns on its projected sales, and (3) the distribution of those earnings. The equation, summarizing the percent of sales forecasting method, is

$$\text{External Funding Requirements} = \left[\left(\frac{\text{Assets that vary with sales}}{\text{Sales}}\right) \times \text{Change in sales} - \left(\frac{\text{Liabilities that vary with sales}}{\text{Sales}}\right) \times \text{Change in sales}\right] - \text{Increase in retained earnings}$$

In symbolic form this equation for external funding requirements (EFR) is

18.2 $$EFR = \left[\frac{A}{S}(\Delta S) - \frac{L}{S}(\Delta S)\right] - (PS_1)R.$$

While this equation may look formidable, it is not. The equation states that the firm's requirements for outside financing equal the funds needed to finance those assets generated by the projected change (Δ) in sales (S) minus the funds generated by the change in sales and the increase in retained earnings. Both the assets and liabilities that vary with the level of sales are expressed as a percent of current sales (A/S and L/S, respectively). The new retained earnings depend on the profit margin of the firm's *projected sales* (PS_1) and the proportion of the earnings that are retained (R).

Suppose that a firm with sales of $10,000 has the following balance sheet:

ASSETS		LIABILITIES AND EQUITY	
Accounts receivable	$ 3,000	Accounts payable	$ 2,500
Inventory	2,000	Long-term debt	4,000
Plant and equipment	8,000	Equity	6,500
	$13,000		$13,000

Accounts receivable, inventory, and accounts payable all vary with sales; the other entries do not. If the firm expands sales from $10,000 to $12,000, these assets and liabilities will spontaneously increase. Accounts receivable and inventory are 50 percent of sales, while accounts payable are 25 percent of sales. Thus, the first part of the equation is

$$EFR = (0.5)(\$2{,}000) - (0.25)(\$2{,}000).$$

If the firm earns 5 percent on its total sales and distributes 30 percent of its earnings as dividends, it retains the remaining 70 percent. Thus, the retained earnings are

$$\text{Retained earnings} = (0.05)(\$12{,}000)(0.7).$$

The firm's need for external financing, then, is

$$\begin{aligned} EFR &= (0.5)(\$2{,}000) - (0.25)(\$2{,}000) - (0.05)(\$12{,}000)(0.70) \\ &= \$1{,}000 - \$500 - \$420 \\ &= \$80. \end{aligned}$$

The spontaneous increase in current assets will require $1,000. The spontaneous increase in liabilities generates only $500, and the firm retains only $420 of its earnings generated on its projected sales. Thus, the firm will need $80 of external financing to cover the anticipated increase in assets that will be a concomitant part of its sales expansion.

By this analysis the financial manager now knows that the firm will need more funds than will be generated by the spontaneous increase in liabilities and the retention of earnings. If the financial manager is reluctant to obtain this money outside of the firm, one possible internal source is to distribute fewer dividends (i.e., retain more earnings). It should be obvious that if the firm retains a larger percentage of its earnings, those retained earnings can finance more assets. In this case, if the firm retained all of its earnings, its need for outside funding would be

$$\begin{aligned} EFR &= (0.5)(\$2{,}000) - (0.25)(\$2{,}000) - (0.05)(\$12{,}000)(1) \\ &= \$1{,}000 - \$500 - \$600 \\ &= (\$100). \end{aligned}$$

The firm would have no need for outside finance to cover the expansion in assets spontaneously generated by the increase in sales. It would even have excess funds that could be invested elsewhere or be distributed as dividends.

The percent of sales forecasting method is one technique for predicting the firm's need for outside finance. Unfortunately, the method may produce biased and inaccurate estimates. If such estimates understate financial needs, finding additional credit rapidly may be difficult. If the technique overpredicts the financial needs, it may cause the firm to borrow more than is necessary and cause the firm to pay unnecessary interest expense.

The percent of sales method assumes that the current percentage will hold for all levels of sales. This assumption need not be true and is a potential source of bias. For example, the firm may be able to economize on inventory as it becomes larger. Thus, inventory as a percent of sales may decline as the level of sales rises. The converse may also be true as sales decline. The firm may continue to carry items even though sales have diminished, or there may be a lag after the decline in sales before the firm recognizes which items are moving slowly and ceases to carry them. Thus, inventory as a percent of sales may rise when the level of sales declines.

While the percent of sales technique of forecasting may produce biased estimates, it is still employed as a forecasting tool for two reasons. First, it is very simple and may be computed with ease. Second, if the change in sales is relatively small, the estimate may not be significantly biased. The larger the increase in sales, the greater the bias will be; but if management is concerned with only a small change in the level of sales, the percent of sales method of forecasting financial needs may be sufficient.

EXHIBIT 18.1

Five-Year Level of Inventory and Sales

Even though inventory may rise with increases in sales, inventory as a percent of sales may decline.

Year	Sales	Inventory	Inventory as a Percent of Sales
19X5	$2,000	$600	30%
19X4	1,700	530	31
19X3	1,400	500	36
19X2	1,200	470	39
19X1	1,000	400	40

FORECASTING EXTERNAL FINANCIAL REQUIREMENTS: REGRESSION ANALYSIS

One method by which to overcome this bias is to consider the relationship between the asset or liability and sales over several years. For example, Exhibit 18.1 depicts a firm's level of inventory and sales for the last five years. This information indicates that there is a positive relationship between the level of inventory and sales, but inventory as a percent of sales has declined. If this decline continues, the use of a percentage determined from only one year's observations will overpredict the necessary level of inventory.

This relationship between sales and inventory is plotted in Figure 18.4, which also indicates a positive trend, since the points are rising. Using the graph in this form, however, may be difficult. For example, it would be difficult to project the level of inventory if the level of sales were to rise to $2,500. This problem can be overcome if the points are expressed as an equation. The technique that summarizes the points in equation form is called **regression.**

Regression Statistical technique that estimates an equation summarizing a set of data

Figure 18.5 reproduces the points in Figure 18.4 but in addition passes a line through the points so that the relationship between inventory and sales is expressed by the following simple linear equation:

18.3 $$I = a + bS.$$

The vertical intercept, a, gives the level of inventory the firm carries even when it has only the minimal amount of sales. The rate at which the line rises is the slope, $\Delta I/\Delta S$, and this is represented by the symbol b. Regression analysis estimates numerical values for a and b, the intercept and the slope.

FIGURE 18.4

Trend in Inventory and Sales

The ratio of inventory to sales may vary as sales increase.

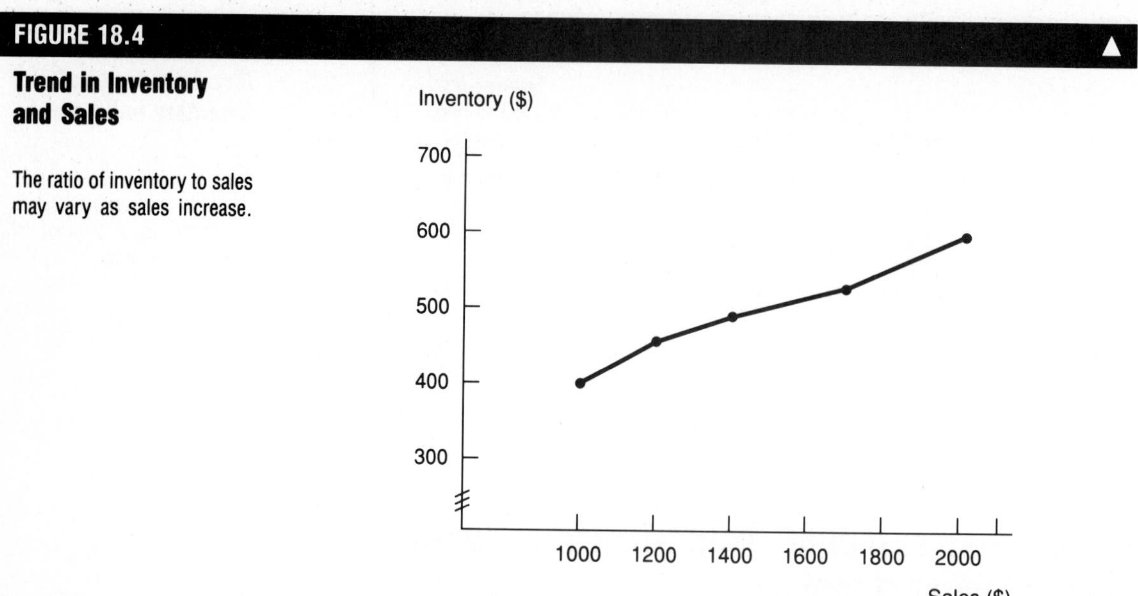

FIGURE 18.5

Trend in Inventory and Sales (Using Linear Regression Analysis)

A regression equation summarizes the relationship between sales and inventory.

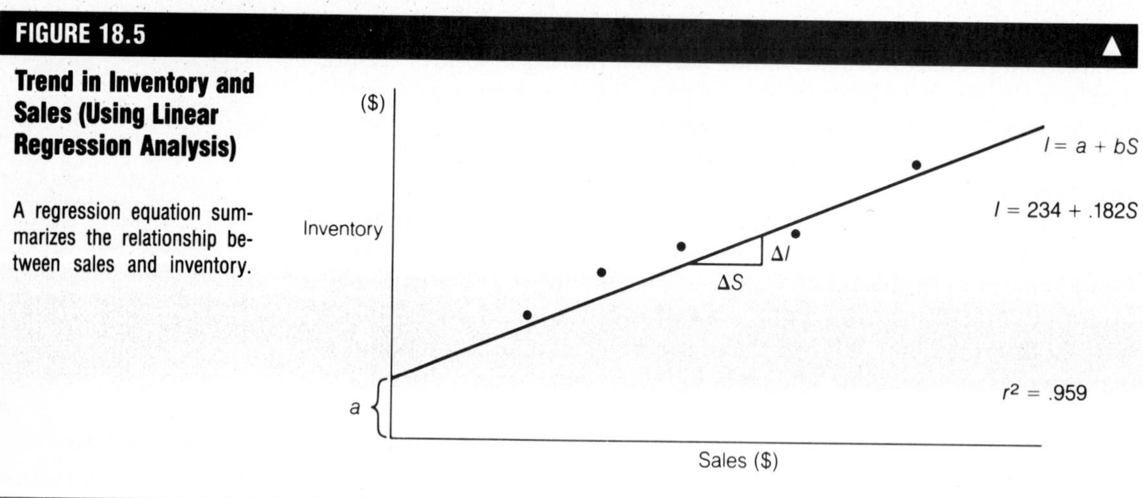

For this firm, regression analysis indicates that the equation for the relationship between inventory and sales is

$$\text{Inventory} = \$234.28 + 0.182 \text{ Sales}.$$

The $234.28 is the y-intercept and indicates the level of inventory if there were no sales. The 0.182 is the slope of the line and indicates that for every increase in sales of \$1,000, the level of inventory will rise by \$182.[1]

Once the equation has been formulated, it can then be used to forecast the level of inventory for any level of sales. For example, if sales are \$3,000, the equation estimates that the level of inventory will be \$780. This number is obtained from the equation by substituting \$3,000 for sales and solving for inventory:

$$\begin{aligned}\text{Inventory} &= \$234.28 + 0.182(\$3{,}000)\\ &= \$780.28.\end{aligned}$$

Figure 18.5 indicates that the relationship between sales and inventory is close, since the individual observations (i.e., the individual points) lie very close to the regression line. Such closeness indicates a high correlation between the independent variable (sales) and the dependent variable (inventory).

This correlation may be measured by the "correlation coefficient" or the "coefficient of determination." In statistics these are often symbolized as "r" or "r^2," respectively. As was explained in Chapter 8, in which regression analysis was used to estimate a stock's beta coefficient, the numerical value of the correlation coefficient ranges from +1.0 to −1.0. If the two variables move exactly together (i.e., if there is a perfect positive correlation between the independent and dependent variables), the numerical value of the correlation coefficient is 1.0. If the two variables

[1]Although regression is generally done through a computer program, it may be performed manually, in which case the slope and intercept are computed as follows:

X	Y	X^2	Y^2	XY
2,000	600	4,000,000	360,000	1,200,000
1,700	530	2,890,000	280,900	901,000
1,400	500	1,960,000	250,000	700,000
1,200	470	1,440,000	220,900	564,000
1,000	400	1,000,000	160,000	400,000
$\Sigma X = 7{,}300$	$\Sigma Y = 2{,}500$	$\Sigma X^2 = 11{,}290{,}000$	$\Sigma Y^2 = 1{,}271{,}800$	$\Sigma XY = 3{,}765{,}000$

n = number of observations (5).

$$\begin{aligned}\text{slope} = b &= \frac{n\Sigma XY - (\Sigma X)(\Sigma Y)}{n\Sigma X^2 - (\Sigma X)^2}\\ &= \frac{(5)(3{,}765{,}000) - (7{,}300)(2{,}500)}{(5)(11{,}290{,}000) - (7{,}300)(7{,}300)} = 0.182.\end{aligned}$$

$$\begin{aligned}\text{intercept} = a &= \frac{\Sigma Y}{n} - b\frac{\Sigma X}{n}\\ &= \frac{2{,}500}{5} - (0.182)\frac{7{,}300}{5} = 234.28.\end{aligned}$$

move exactly opposite of each other, the correlation coefficient equals −1.0. All other possible values lie between these two extremes. Numerical values near zero such as −0.12 or +0.19 indicate little relationship between the two variables.

The coefficient of determination is the square of the correlation coefficient and measures the proportion of the variation in the dependent variable explained by movement in the independent variable. Thus, if the correlation coefficient is 0.1, the coefficient of determination is 0.01 (0.1^2), which indicates that the movement in the independent variable explains very little of the movement in the dependent variable.

Computation of these two coefficients is part of statistics and need not concern us in this text.[2] The computer programs that estimate the regression equation routinely give the numerical values of the correlation coefficient and the coefficient of determination. The interpretation of the coefficients is potentially useful to the financial manager who is concerned with the accuracy of the estimated equation. The coefficient of determination (i.e., the r^2) given in Figure 18.5 is 0.959, which indicates a very close relationship between sales and inventory. The high r^2 should increase the financial manager's confidence in using the regression equation to forecast inventory as sales change.

Such a close correspondence between the variables need not occur, but regression analysis will still summarize the relationship. For example, consider the relationships between sales and inventory presented in Exhibit 18.2 and Figure 18.6. In case A, the individual observations relating sales and inventory are scattered throughout the graph, but the regression technique still estimates an equation summarizing the individual observations. The correlation is low, with an r^2 of only 0.216, so the quality of the equation as a forecasting tool is questionable.

The same conclusion concerning the forecasting ability of the estimated equation applies to case B. In this case, the individual observations for all levels of sales between $1,000 and $2,000 lie above the line. However, regression analysis still estimates an equation that summarizes the relationship between sales and inventory. While the quality of the equation is rather high ($r^2 = 0.813$), the forecasting ability of the estimated equation is suspect.

This example points out a possible problem with simple linear regression analysis. First, the actual relationship between the variables may not be a straight line. Case B in Figure 18.6 implies that the relationship between inventory and sales is curvilinear. The dots rise but appear to taper off as the level of sales increases. By visual inspection the true rela-

[2] How the correlation coefficient is determined may be found in an elementary text on statistics. See, for instance, George W. Summers, William S. Peters, and Charles P. Armstrong, *Basic Statistics in Business and Economics*, 4th ed. (Belmont, Calif.: Wadsworth, 1985), pp. 307–308 and 534–537.

EXHIBIT 18.2

Relationships between Sales and Inventory

Sales	Case A Inventory	Case B Inventory
$1,000	$400	$400
1,200	380	550
1,400	600	600
1,700	500	700
2,000	450	750

The relationship between inventory and sales may not be summarized by a simple, linear equation.

FIGURE 18.6

Relationships between Sales and Inventory

A simple linear regression may have little predictive capacity if the correlation is low or the relation is nonlinear.

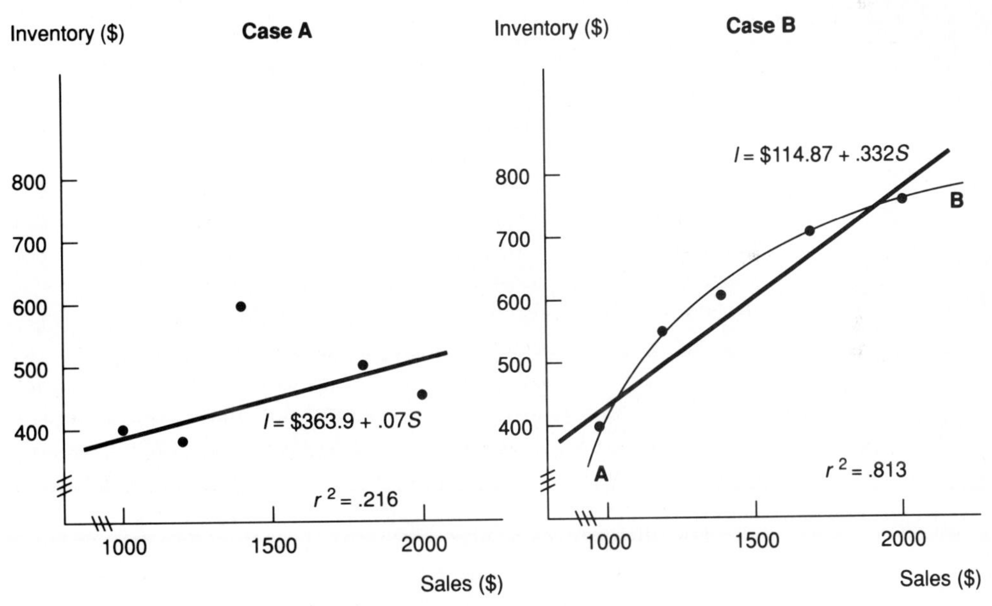

tionship between sales and inventory appears to be the curved line AB drawn through the points. An equation for this curved line should give more reliable forecasts than the simple straight line (linear) equation that was previously estimated.

Another potential source of difficulty with simple linear regression is the possibility of several variables affecting the dependent variable. For

EXHIBIT 18.3

Comparison of Percent of Sales and Regression Techniques of Forecasting

The forecasts using percent of sales and regression may differ.

Sales	Percent of Sales Forecast	Regression Analysis Forecast
	(Inventory = $0.30 Sales)	(Inventory = $234.28 + 0.182 Sales)
$1,500	$450	$507.28
2,000	600	598.28
2,500	750	689.28
3,000	900	780.28

example, the level of inventory may be affected not only by sales but also by the availability of the goods, the season of the year, or the cost of credit. That appears to be the situation in case A in Figure 18.6 because the relationship between inventory and sales is weak. Something other than sales must explain the level of inventory.

These problems with simple linear regression may be solved by using nonlinear regression analysis or multiple regression, which includes more than one independent variable. Both of these statistical techniques are covered in more advanced texts and will not be pursued here.

While nonlinear and multiple regression analysis will not be developed here, it is desirable to compare simple linear regression with the percent of sales technique for forecasting. The percent of sales is the simple case of regression analysis in which there is no intercept and the slope is determined by the origin and one observation. The percent of sales technique assumes that the present ratio of inventory to sales will remain constant, and it takes that ratio as the slope of the equation. On the basis of that assumption, the technique then projects the level of inventory. Regression analysis, however, does not make that assumption and formulates an equation using several observations that relate inventory and sales.

The differences in the predictive power of the two techniques are illustrated in Exhibit 18.3, which is based on the previous example. The first column gives the level of sales, and the second and third columns give the estimated levels of inventory. The second column uses the percent of sales method, which assumes that the ratio of inventory to sales is constant (30 percent). The third column uses the regression equation ($I = \$234.28 + 0.182S$), which was formulated on the basis of data for past levels of inventory and sales.

As may be seen in Exhibit 18.3, the higher the anticipated level of sales, the larger the estimated level of inventory. But the estimated level of inventory is larger for the percent of sales method than for the regression technique. The percent of sales technique may be overestimating the desired level of inventory. For example, if as the firm grows there are economies in inventory management, the level of inventory need not continue to grow at the same rate. Thus, the ratio of inventory to sales will decline. Under these circumstances, regression analysis gives a better estimate of the desired level of inventory and is the more accurate predictor.

FORECASTING EXTERNAL FINANCIAL REQUIREMENTS: CHANGES IN FIXED ASSETS

In the two previous sections it was assumed that as the firm expanded sales, only those assets that spontaneously changed with the level of sales varied. Such expansion of sales can only occur if the firm has excess capacity. In this section, it will be assumed that the firm will have to expand its fixed assets, as well as those assets that spontaneously change with the level of sales.

To ease the explanation, the example that was used for the percent of sales will be employed here. The firm in that illustration had the following balance sheet:

ASSETS		LIABILITIES AND EQUITY	
Cash	$ 100	Accounts payable	$ 200
Accounts receivable	300	Bank note	200
Inventory	300	Other current liabilities	100
Plant and equipment	500	Long-term debt	300
	$1,200	Equity	400
			$1,200

Sales were $2,000, which increased to $2,400. If the net profit margin on sales is 10 percent and the firm retains 40 percent of its earnings, the percent of sales method would forecast the following projected balance sheet entries:

ASSETS		LIABILITIES AND EQUITY	
Cash	$ 120	Accounts payable	$ 240
Accounts receivable	360	Bank note	200
Inventory	360	Other current liabilities	100
Plant and equipment	500	Long-term debt	300
	$1,340	Equity	496
			$1,336

Cash, accounts receivable, inventory, and accounts payable all increased because they spontaneously changed with the level of sales. Equity increased by $96 since the firm earned $240 on its sales ($2,400 × 0.1 = $240) and retained 40 percent of its earnings ($240 × 0.4). The other entries remained constant because it was assumed that they did not change with the level of sales.

In the example, assets increased by $140 while liabilities and equity increased by $136. The projected balance sheet, of course, does not balance; the difference (i.e., $4) equals the projected shortage of funds. The financial manager would have to plan for this $4 in additional finance to cover the projected expansion in assets. Since the required amount is so modest, it is safe to assume that finding the additional finance would not be a major problem.

Suppose, however, the expansion in sales also required an increase of $200 in fixed assets. The projected balance sheet would become:

ASSETS		LIABILITIES AND EQUITY	
Cash	$ 120	Accounts payable	$ 240
Accounts receivable	360	Bank note	200
Inventory	360	Other current liabilities	100
Plant and equipment	700	Long-term debt	300
	$1,540	Equity	496
			$1,336

The firm's need for finance is considerably larger (i.e., $204), since the expansion in sales cannot be achieved in this example without an expansion in plant and equipment.

What choices are available to the financial manager to raise the $204 required to balance the balance sheet? Actually, the financial manager has several options. First, the holdings of cash could be reduced to acquire another asset. Second, a larger proportion of the earnings could be retained instead of being distributed. Earnings that are retained, of course, could help finance the projected expansion in assets. Third, the firm could issue additional debt, such as bonds, or issue additional stock to raise the cash to acquire other assets.

Obviously, the financial manager has several possible courses of action. One of the questions that he or she will have to face is what combination of debt and equity financing is the most desirable to finance the expansion. As was previously explained, the use of debt financing may increase the return earned by the owners of the firm. However, the additional use of financial leverage also increases the risk associated with the firm, so determining which combination of debt and equity financing is best is obviously an important issue that must be addressed. That question, however, will be deferred until Chapter 22, which covers the firm's optimal capital structure. For the purposes of this discussion, assume

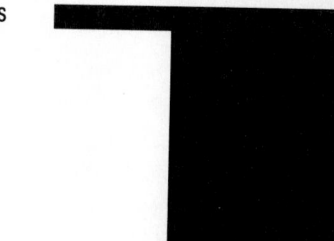

Quantitative Financial Analyst

■ Job Description: Build models; use computer-driven programs and statistical testing as applied to investment and financial decisions. Use forecasting, regression analysis, and multiple discriminate analysis to determine if and when the firm will need funds. ■ Job Requirements: Strong background in computer programming and statistical methods, in addition to knowledge of finance. Excellent oral and written skills are necessary to communicate both the rationale for the methods being used and the results of the analysis. An advanced degree in a technical area is desirable. ■ Characteristics: Quantitative financial analysis offers individuals with backgrounds in finance, statistics, computers, and business communications an excellent means to integrate various skills. Problems solved can be varied, crossing many facets of a firm's operations. The position is very visible, since the results of quantitative analysis can have a large impact on management decisions.

---

that the financial manager decides to (1) reduce the holdings of cash to $80, which releases $40, (2) distribute only 40 percent of earnings and thus retain $144 instead of $96, and (3) float additional debt to cover the remaining deficiency. After these changes occur, the projected balance sheet becomes:

ASSETS		LIABILITIES AND EQUITY	
Cash	$ 80	Accounts payable	$ 240
Accounts receivable	360	Bank note	200
Inventory	360	Other current liabilities	100
Plant and equipment	700	Long-term debt	416
	$1,500	Equity	544
			$1,500

Thus, the financial manager has provided for the expansion in accounts receivable, inventory, and plant and equipment through the spontaneous increase in accounts payable, a reduction in cash, the issuing of new long-term debt, and the retention of earnings.

THE CASH BUDGET

In the previous sections, forecasts of short-term assets and liabilities were used to determine the firm's need for finance resulting from an expansion in the firm's sales. The firm may also require cash to cover periods when receipts are insufficient to cover disbursements. Cash receipts are seldom synchronized with cash disbursements, and if disbursements temporarily exceed receipts, the shortage will have to be financed.

Cash budget ▲ Projected financial statement that enumerates cash receipts and disbursements for a period of time

To help determine when the firm will need external funds (e.g., a loan from a commercial bank) to cover cash disbursements, the financial manager may construct a **cash budget.** This is simply a table that enumerates all the firm's cash outlays and cash receipts. A cash budget is not synonymous with an income statement, which enumerates revenues and expenses. Some revenues may not be cash. For example, a credit sale generates revenues but the cash will not immediately be collected. The same applies to a purchase on credit. While such purchases may be expenses for the firm, the actual cash outlay occurs in the future. In addition, the firm may make some cash payments that are not expenses. For example, principal repayment requires an outlay of cash but is not an expense.

The term "budget" is often encountered in conjunction with financial planning and decision making. All budgets are estimates of anticipated receipts and disbursements for a period of time. Individual households as well as firms may construct such plans, and certainly the budget of the federal government is one of the most discussed documents that emanate from Washington. In each case these budgets are important planning devices, as their construction requires that financial managers anticipate when outlays will be made and receipts collected.

In addition to being planning devices, budgets may also be used as tools of control. Individual departments within the firm can have budgets that constrain their ability to spend or require that excess spending decisions be made by higher management. The budgets then act as a constraint on the firm's divisions and give management more internal control of the firm's operations. The budget may also be used as a tool to judge performance. Was the budget maintained? Which divisions within the firm overextended their budgets? By comparing the actual performance with the anticipated performance, management may be able to identify sources of financial problems.

The period of time for a budget is variable and depends on the nature of the firm and the purpose of the budget. Some budgets may be for short periods of time (e.g., six months). A firm with seasonal or fluctuating sales may develop a budget that covers the season. Other budgets may cover many years. For example, a public utility may have a budget for capital spending on plant and equipment that covers planned receipts and disbursements for five to ten years.

Budgets are particularly useful planning tools for short time periods. A cash budget may be constructed for a short period (e.g., three or six months) and then used to predict the short-term needs of the firm for cash. The cash budget helps the financial manager to determine not only that cash is needed but also *when* it is needed. This element of time is crucial, for the financial manager can contact sources of short-term credit in advance of the need for funds. Such early contact will indicate that management is aware of its financial needs, and this should increase the confidence of lenders in the firm's management. Such confidence may in turn result in more favorable terms, which reduce the cost of the funds.

While the cash budgets of firms in different industries will vary because the flows of cash differ, the desirability of good cash management applies to all firms. Emphasis on the management of cash has recently increased. This may in part be explained by the recent high yields on short-term assets. Also, the short-term money market is very well developed, for there are a variety of short-term assets (e.g., Treasury bills, certificates of deposit, commercial paper) in which excess funds may be put to work. Good management of cash is an important means to increase the profitability of the firm. The cash budget, which indicates when the firm will have excess cash and when it will need short-term credit, is an integral tool in planning the management of cash.

The cash budget is basically a table relating time, disbursements, and receipts. The units of time may be monthly, weekly, or even daily. For purposes of exposition, a monthly cash budget will be developed. The cash items are grouped into inflows (receipts) and outflows (disbursements). The difference between the inflows and the outflows is the summary that indicates to the financial manager whether to expect excess cash that needs to be invested or cash deficiencies that must be financed.

The construction of a simple cash budget for the fall season may be illustrated by the following example. The financial manager has determined the following anticipated levels of sales for the next seven months:

May	$15,000	August	50,000	November	10,000
June	20,000	September	40,000		
July	30,000	October	20,000		

Thirty percent of the sales are for cash, and 70 percent are on credit. Of the credit sales, 90 percent are paid after one month, and 10 percent are paid after two months. Thus, the financial manager expects that of the anticipated sales of $15,000 in May, $4,500 will be for cash ($15,000 × 0.3) and $10,500 will be on credit ($15,000 × 0.7). Of these credit sales, $9,450 will be collected after one month ($10,500 × 0.9), and $1,050 will be collected after two months ($10,500 × 0.1).

If the firm owns any other assets that will become cash during the time period, those assets must also be included in the cash budget. For example, if the firm owns a short-term asset (e.g., a U.S. Treasury bill) valued at $10,000 that will be due on June 1, it must be included in the cash budget. Since the purpose of the cash budget is to determine the excess or shortage of cash that the firm will experience, all cash items must be included in the budget. Non-cash expenses like depreciation are excluded.

EXHIBIT 18.4

Monthly Cash Budget (for a Firm's Fall Season)

The cash budget enumerates cash receipts and disbursements to indicate when the firm will need short-term financing.

		May	June	July
Part 1				
1	Anticipated sales	$15,000	$20,000	$30,000
2	Cash sales	4,500	6,000	9,000
3	Accounts collected (one-month lag)		9,450	12,600
4	Accounts collected (two-month lag)			1,050
5	Other cash receipts		10,000	
6	Total cash receipts	4,500	25,450	22,650
Part 2				
7	Variable cash disbursements	3,000	25,000	38,000
8	Fixed cash disbursements	3,000	3,000	3,000
9	Other cash disbursements			
10	Total cash disbursements	6,000	28,000	41,000
Part 3				
11	Cash gain (or loss) during the month (line 6 minus line 10)	(1,500)	(2,550)	(18,350)
12	Cash position at beginning of month	12,000	10,500	7,950
13	Cash position at end of month (line 12 plus line 11)	10,500	7,950	(10,400)
14	Less desired level of cash	(10,000)	(10,000)	(10,000)
15	Cumulative excess (or shortage) of cash (line 13 minus line 14)	500	(2,050)	(20,400)

In this case, the firm's sales are seasonal, so it will seek to build up inventory in anticipation of the seasonal business. As the inventory is produced, the firm must pay for labor and materials. The estimated disbursements for wages and materials for the season are

May	$ 3,000	August	30,000	November	3,000
June	25,000	September	10,000		
July	38,000	October	5,000		

These estimated disbursements indicate that the buildup in inventory occurs in June, July, and August. The sales, however, occur primarily in July, August, and September. There is a lag in sales after the buildup of inventory; thus there will be a drain on the firm's cash.

Besides the cash outlays that vary with the level of output, the firm has fixed disbursements that do not vary with the level of operations. These include interest and rent of $1,000 a month and administrative expenses of $2,000 a month for a total of $3,000 a month. The firm also has to make an estimated quarterly income tax payment in September of $2,500 and a payment of $1,000 on August 1 to retire part of a debt

August	September	October	November	December	January
$50,000	$40,000	$20,000	$10,000		
15,000	12,000	6,000	3,000		
18,900	31,500	25,200	12,600	6,300	
1,400	2,100	3,500	2,800	1,400	700
35,300	45,600	34,700	18,400		
30,000	10,000	5,000	3,000		
3,000	3,000	3,000	3,000		
1,000	2,500				
34,000	15,500	8,000	6,000		
1,300	30,100	26,700	12,400		
(10,400)	(9,100)	21,000	47,700		
(9,100)	21,000	47,700	60,100		
(10,000)	(10,000)	(10,000)	(10,000)		
(19,100)	11,000	37,700	50,100		

issue. Management likes to maintain a minimum cash balance of $10,000 as a safety valve in case of emergency. The firm's cash position at the beginning of May is $12,000, which exceeds the desired minimum level for the cash balance.

The financial manager now uses this information to obtain estimates of the monthly net increase or decrease in the firm's cash position. (The budget may be constructed on a weekly, monthly, or quarterly basis depending on the time available for its construction, the need for extreme accuracy, and the volatility of the entries.) The monthly cash budget is illustrated in Exhibit 18.4. The first part of the table presents the estimated cash that the firm receives monthly. The first line of the table gives the estimated sales, and the next three lines give the estimated cash generated by the sales. The second line enumerates the cash sales; the third line gives the collections that occur on the credit sales after one month; and the fourth line gives the credit collection that occurs two months after the sales. In the table the arrows show when May's credit sales yield cash receipts. The fifth line gives other sources of cash receipts (i.e., the short-term debt instrument that matures). The sum of lines two through five is the monthly cash receipts of the firm and is given in line six.

Financial Facts

The Cash Budget and Electronic Spreadsheets

Perhaps one of the most useful applications of an electronic spreadsheet, such as Lotus 123 or SuperCalc, is the cash budget. The financial manager can set up the spreadsheet to perform the calculations (e.g., the spreadsheet can be set up to do all the arithmetic in Exhibit 18.4). The various entries (called "cells") in the spreadsheet are the anticipated sales, the collections, other cash receipts, the disbursements, and the firm's beginning cash. Once the numbers are entered into the various cells, the cumulative cash balance or shortage can immediately be calculated. • While the initial calculations are obviously quicker, the main appeal of the spreadsheet is the financial manager's ability to alter one number and have the spreadsheet recalculate all the other numbers in the affected cells. Just contemplate the amount of arithmetic that would be necessary to recompute the spreadsheet in Exhibit 18.4 if the anticipated sales in June were $18,000 instead of $20,000. Total cash receipts in June would change; the cash gain (or loss) would change; the cash position at the end of the month would change; and the cumulative cash position at the end of the month would change. All these changes would require changes in the cumulative cash position for each of the subsequent months. With the advent of electronic spreadsheets, the financial manager can enter the new June sales and let the spreadsheet perform all the recalculations. • Since electronic spreadsheets release financial managers from having to perform these calculations, the individuals may use the spreadsheets to determine the impact of a change in one of the components on the entire cash budget. The financial manager may change (1) the desired level of cash, (2) when accounts receivable will be collected, or (3) the initial cash position; in each case, the spreadsheet is recalculated. The financial manager immediately becomes aware of the impact of the change on the firm's cumulative cash position. This flexibility gives management a major tool to analyze various "what if" situations, and this can lead to increased profitability through better planning for the firm's needs for short-term finance. •

The second part of the table enumerates the firm's monthly cash disbursements. Line seven gives the monthly disbursements that vary with the level of sales, while line eight gives the disbursements that do not vary with the level of sales (i.e., the interest, rent, and administrative disbursements). The ninth line gives other cash disbursements (i.e., the $2,500 tax payment and the $1,000 debt retirement payment). The sum of all the monthly cash payments is given in the tenth line.

The third part of the table summarizes the first two parts and indicates whether the firm has a net inflow or outflow of cash during the month. Thus, the cash budget establishes whether the firm has excess cash that it can use to purchase short-term income-earning assets (such as a certificate of deposit) or has insufficient cash, which requires that the firm find short-term financing. The eleventh line is the difference between lines six and ten; it gives the net inflow or outflow of cash during the month. The twelfth line gives the firm's cash position at the beginning of the month. The sum of the eleventh and twelfth lines equals the firm's cash position at the end of the month, which is given in line thirteen. The minimum desired level of cash is given in the fourteenth line. The difference between cash position at the end of the month and the desired minimum level of cash is given in the fifteenth line of the table. This is the most important line, for it indicates either that the firm will have excess cash generated by operations during the month or that it will have a cash deficiency.

How is the information contained in the cash budget interpreted? The process of interpretation may be illustrated by considering several months. For example, during the month of May the firm has a net loss of cash of $1,500 (line 11), but since the firm began the month with $12,000 in cash, it has enough to cover the anticipated cash loss and still maintain its desired level of cash holdings. This is indicated in line 15, which shows that there is excess cash of $500 over the desired cash balance level. In the month of June cash disbursements once again exceed receipts (by $2,550). The extent to which the cash expenditures exceed the receipts, however, is reduced by the receipt of the $10,000 payment on the short-term asset. Thus, it appears that the financial manager was previously aware of the firm's cash needs in June and July and purchased a short-term asset that matured in June. Even with this extra inflow of cash, the cash position at the end of the month drops to $7,950 (line 13), which is less than the desired level of cash balances by $2,050 (line 15). The financial manager would then have to decide either to let the cash position fall below the desired minimum or to borrow the $2,050 to maintain the desired minimum level of cash.

In July the difference between the cash outflows and cash receipts grows even larger. Anticipated cash payments exceed cash receipts by $18,350, before allowance is made for the desired minimum level of cash. When the actual cash outflow and the desired level of cash are added, the firm is short $20,400 (line 15), and this cash deficiency continues through August. Thus, the financial manager can anticipate that the firm will need $20,400 of short-term financing to cover the firm's cash needs for July. In August, cash receipts slightly exceed disbursements, so the shortage falls to $19,100. After August the firm's cash position improves dramatically as the cash from its credit sales flows into the firm. In September the firm will have generated a cash gain of $30,100. After September the firm's cash position continues to improve, and the cumulative excess cash grows to $50,100 by the end of November. Thus, the financial manager can anticipate having excess cash that can be used to purchase a short-term income-earning asset that matures when the cycle begins again.

If the financial manager decides to maintain the minimum cash balance and to borrow from the bank the funds necessary to cover the cash shortages, the firm will have a short-term bank loan outstanding in June, July, and August. The excess cash, cash shortage, and bank loan outstanding are illustrated in Figure 18.7. The top half shows the firm's ex-

FIGURE 18.7

Excess and Shortage of Cash and Borrowings to Cover the Cash Shortages (May–October)

The period of cash shortage (i.e., borrowings) is followed by a period of excess cash during which the firm may invest these funds in short-term assets.

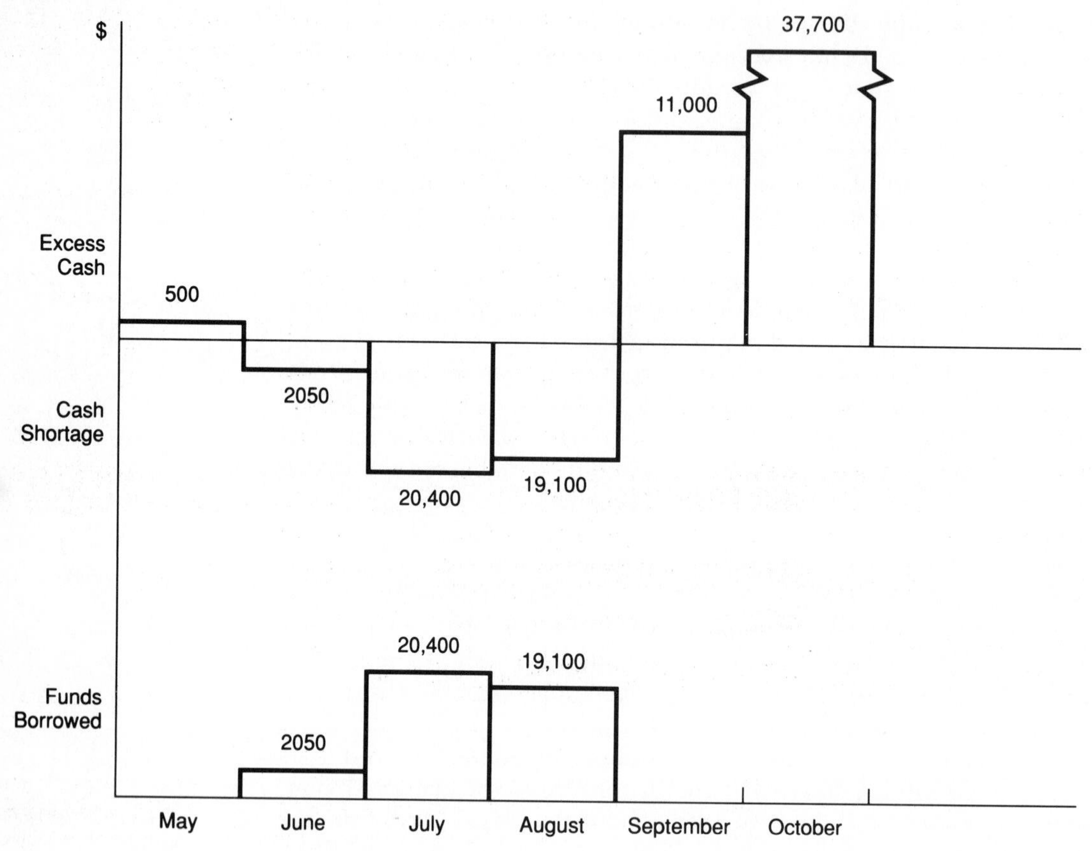

cess cash or shortage of cash. The bottom half gives the amount of the outstanding loan. This loan, of course, balances the cash shortages in June through August. Once the cash flows into the firm in September, the loan is repaid and no longer is outstanding.

The cash budget helps the financial manager to establish when the firm will need external financing. In the example, the financial manager can anticipate how much cash the firm will need in June, July, and August, and he or she also knows when the firm will generate sufficient cash

Director of Financial Planning and Analysis

■ Job Description: Responsible for the preparation of budgets, long-range financial plans, periodic forecasts, profit and loss statements, and periodic summaries of corporate spending and performance. ■ Job Requirements: This individual must have a strong background in finance with substantial knowledge of accounting, or he or she must be a C.P.A. with substantial knowledge of the techniques of financial analysis. An advanced degree (such as an M.A. in finance or an M.B.A.) plus several years of experience in various financial positions are required. ■ Characteristics: This high-level position reports to the vice-president of finance and may lead to the position of chief financial officer. Any student seeking to obtain such a position should combine course work in finance and accounting as an initial step toward achieving this goal.

---

to retire the short-term loan. Thus, the financial manager can approach the lender with estimates of (1) the firm's cash needs and (2) when the firm will be able to repay the loan. This information is particularly important for the lender, who is primarily concerned with earning interest and being repaid the principal. From the lender's viewpoint, a cash budget is more important than the firm's income statement, since it shows how the cash will be used and when repayments will be made. Such cash budgets should increase the lender's confidence in the borrower, as the budget shows the control management has over the firm's finances.

Preparing the cash budget will also permit the financial manager to shop around for terms. Since the financial manager is able to anticipate the firm's financial needs, he or she is able to arrange for the necessary financing in advance. Such planning should increase the bargaining position of the borrower and may result in more favorable credit terms.

SUMMARY

Management constructs strategic plans that establish general goals for a firm. The strategies designed to meet the goals are executed by the various executives responsible for a firm's operations, marketing, and finance. The plans and their execution need to be periodically evaluated to determine if the general goals are being achieved.

Financial plans must fit within the general strategic plan of a firm. These plans require forecasts of when a firm will need outside sources of finance. These forecasts can have a short- or long-term time horizon, but this chapter emphasizes forecasting a firm's short-term needs for finance. Such requirements arise when a firm must acquire assets for operations or cover shortages resulting from the non-synchronization of receipts and disbursements.

Some assets, such as accounts receivable and inventory, automatically expand with increases in a firm's sales. Other assets, such as plant and equipment, have to be increased after a firm reaches a certain level of sales. Once capacity is reached, further expansion will require additional investment in plant and equipment.

All assets have to be financed, so projecting a firm's level of assets is crucial to the financial health of a firm. One forecasting technique uses the percent of sales. It expresses all assets and liabilities that spontaneously change with the level of sales as a percent of sales. That percentage is then used to forecast the future level of these assets and liabilities as sales increase. A more sophisticated forecasting technique uses estimated equations (regression analysis) to estimate the level of assets and liabilities associated with various levels of sales.

Either technique may be used to construct a projected balance sheet that indicates a firm's estimated future assets, future liabilities, and future equity. If the estimated assets exceed the estimated liabilities plus equity, the financial manager must plan today to find the finance required by the forecast of the firm's future assets.

Budgeting is another tool for financial planning and control. The cash budget, which enumerates cash inflows and outflows, enables management to plan its short-term cash needs. By constructing such a budget, management is better able to plan its financial strategy, for the cash budget indicates both the timing and the amount of a firm's need for short-term financing.

Review Questions

1. Budgeting is a means by which management in a large firm may control operations. Is such budgeting also necessary in a small firm? What role can a cash budget play in a firm of any size?
2. A firm uses the percent of sales method of forecasting. Its inventory is 12 percent of sales, while accounts receivable are only 6 percent of sales. If sales double, what happens to the levels of inventory and accounts receivable? What assumption has been made by this technique of forecasting? Is this assumption more valid for small or large changes in sales?
3. What differentiates a cash budget from an income statement?
4. If a firm collects its receivables quickly, but delays paying its payables, what impact will that have on the cash budget?
5. Why is the use of regression less restrictive than the use of the percent of sales method of forecasting?

Problems

1. ABC, Inc., with sales of $1,000, has the following balance sheet:

ABC, Incorporated
Balance Sheet
as of 12/31/X0

ASSETS		LIABILITIES AND EQUITY	
Accounts receivable	$ 200	Trade accounts payable	$ 200
Inventory	400	Long-term debt	600
Plant	800	Equity	600
	$1,400		$1,400

It earns 10 percent on sales (after taxes) and pays no dividends.

a. Determine the balance sheet entries for sales of $1,500 using the percent of sales method of forecasting.
b. Will the firm need external financing to grow to sales of $1,500?
c. Construct the new balance sheet and use newly issued long-term debt to cover any financial deficiency.

2. A firm with sales of $100 million has the following balance sheet entries for those assets and liabilities that vary with sales:

Accounts receivable	$23,000,000
Inventory	31,000,000
Accounts payable	17,000,000
Accruals	10,000,000

a. Use the percent of sales technique to forecast new entries for this firm's balance sheet when sales rise to $110 million.
b. Will the firm need external financing if it earns 8 percent on sales after taxes and retains the earnings?
c. If the firm distributes $6 million of its earnings determined in (b) as cash dividends, will it need external financing? If so, how much?

3. CDE, Inc. has the following balance sheet:

CDE, Incorporated
Balance Sheet
as of 12/31/X0

ASSETS		LIABILITIES AND EQUITY	
Cash	$ 1,000	Accounts payable	$ 5,300
Accounts receivable	7,200	Bank note	3,200
Inventory	6,100		
Long-term assets	4,200	Equity	10,000
	$18,500		$18,500

It has estimated the following relationships between sales and the various assets and liabilities that vary with the level of sales:

Accounts receivable = \$3,310 + 0.35 Sales,
Inventory = \$2,264 + 0.28 Sales,
Accounts payable = \$1,329 + 0.22 Sales.

a. If the firm expects sales of \$20,000, what are the forecasted levels of the balance sheet items above?
b. Will the expansion in accounts payable cover the expansion in inventory and accounts receivable?
c. If the firm earns 12 percent on sales after taxes and retains all of these earnings, will it cover its estimated needs for short-term financing?
d. Construct a new balance sheet that incorporates the issuing of additional short-term debt to cover any needs for additional finance. (Assume cash remains \$1,000.)

4. A firm has the following monthly pattern of sales:

January	\$ 100
February	300
March	500
April	1,000
May	500
June	300

(Sixty percent of the sales are on credit and are collected after a month.)

The company pays wages each month that are 60 percent of sales and has fixed costs (e.g., rent) of \$100 a month. In March it receives \$200 from a bond that matures; in April and June it makes a tax payment of \$200. The firm seeks to maintain a cash balance of \$150 at all times. Construct a cash budget that indicates the firm's monthly needs for short-term financing. Its beginning cash position is \$150.

5. Mangement wants to know if there will be a need for short-term financing in February. Essential information is as follows:
a. Estimated sales for January and February are \$1 million and \$800,000, respectively.
b. Sixty percent of sales are for cash and 40 percent are credit sales that are collected the next month.
c. Cash disbursements that vary with sales are 40 percent of sales.
d. Fixed operating disbursements are \$300,000 a month.
e. Depreciation expense is \$50,000 a month.
f. A tax payment of \$100,000 is due in January.
g. A bond payment of \$300,000 is owed and will be due in February.
h. The cash balance at the beginning of January is \$12,000.
i. Management seeks a minimum cash balance of \$10,000.
j. December credit sales were \$100,000.

6. Firm X has the following balance sheet:

Firm X
Balance Sheet
as of 12/31/X1

ASSETS		LIABILITIES AND EQUITY	
Cash	$ 100	Accounts payable	$ 300
Accounts receivable	300	Long-term debt	800
Inventory	400		
Plant and equipment	700	Equity	400
	$1,500		$1,500

Currently sales are $4,000 with a net profit margin on sales of 15 percent. Management expects sales to increase to $5,000 and wants to determine if the firm will need external financing to cover this expansion. Construct a forecasted balance sheet for sales of $5,000 using the percent of sales technique of forecasting assets and liabilities that spontaneously vary with sales. If the firm needs additional finance, these funds may be acquired through a bank loan. If the firm has excess funds, they should be invested in marketable securities. (Assume that cash does *not increase* with the increase in sales and that the firm pays *no dividends*.)

7. A firm with sales of $10 million and a net profit margin of 7 percent in 19X0 is expecting sales to grow to $12 million and $14 million in 19X1 and 19X2, respectively. Management wants to know if additional funds will be necessary to finance this anticipated growth. Currently, the firm is not operating at full capacity and should be able to sustain a 25 percent increase in sales. However, further increases in sales will require $2 million in plant and equipment for every $5 million increase in sales. The firm's balance sheet is as follows:

ABD Corporation
Balance Sheet
as of 12/31/X0

ASSETS		LIABILITIES AND EQUITY	
Cash	$1,500,000	Accruals	$1,500,000
Accounts receivable	2,000,000	Accounts payable	1,000,000
Inventory	1,500,000	Notes payable	500,000
Plant and equipment	3,000,000	Long-term debt	3,000,000
		Equity	2,000,000
	$8,000,000		$8,000,000

Management has followed a policy of distributing at least 70 percent of earnings as dividends. Management believes that the percent of sales method of forecasting is sufficient to answer the question: "Will outside funding be necessary?" In order to use this technique, management has assumed that accounts receivable, inventory, accruals, and accounts payable will vary with the level of sales.

a. Prepare projected balance sheets for 19X1 and 19X2 that incorporate any necessary outside financing. Any short-term funds that are required should be obtained through a loan from the bank, and any excess short-term funds should be appropriately invested. Any long-term financing that is needed should be obtained through long-term debt and/or appropriate reductions in short-term assets.
b. If the firm did not distribute 70 percent of its earnings, could it sustain the expansion without issuing additional long-term debt?
c. If the percent of sales forecasts are replaced with the following regression equations:

$$\begin{aligned}\text{Accounts receivable} &= \$100{,}000 + 0.12\ \text{Sales},\\ \text{Inventory} &= \$250{,}000 + 0.15\ \text{Sales},\\ \text{Accruals} &= \$100{,}000 + 0.07\ \text{Sales},\\ \text{Accounts payable} &= \$250{,}000 + 0.08\ \text{Sales},\end{aligned}$$

what is the firm's need for outside funding (if any) in 19X2?
d. If the firm's creditors in part (c) required a current ratio of 2 : 1, would that affect the firm's financing in 19X1 and 19X2? If so, what additional actions could the firm take?

8. Firm X has the following balance sheet:

Firm X Balance Sheet
as of 12/31/XX

ASSETS		LIABILITIES AND EQUITY	
Cash	$ 3,500	Accounts payable	$ 14,500
Marketable securities	—	Bank loans	35,000
Accounts receivable	27,000	Bonds	21,500
Inventory	31,000	Common stock	10,000
Plant and equipment	80,000	Retained earnings	60,500
	$141,500		$141,500

Sales are $100,000 and the financial manager expects them to increase to $120,000 (20 percent). The profit margin on sales is 10 percent, and the firm distributes 30 percent of its earnings as cash dividends.

a. How much external finance will be required by the expansion according to the percent of sales forecasting technique?
b. If the firm needs external finance, the funds should be acquired by issuing new long-term debt. If the firm has excess funds, they should be held in marketable securities. Complete the following pro forma balance sheet for the new level of sales.

The Pro Forma Balance Sheet of Firm X as of 12/31/XX

ASSETS		LIABILITIES AND EQUITY	
Cash	$3,500	Accounts payable	$
Marketable securities		Bank loans	
Accounts receivable		Bonds	
Inventory		Common stock	
Plant and equipment	____	Retained earnings	____
	$		$

9. Given the information below, complete the cash budget:
   a. Collections occur one month after the sale.
   b. January's credit sales were $80,000.
   c. The firm has a certificate of deposit for $40,000 that matures in April.
   d. Salaries are $145,000 a month.
   e. The monthly mortgage payment is $25,000.
   f. Monthly depreciation is $20,000.
   g. Property tax of $35,000 is due in February.

	February	March	April
Sales	$150,000	$200,000	$250,000
Cash sales	30,000	20,000	60,000
Collections	—	—	—
Other receipts	—	—	—
Total cash receipts	—	—	—
Salaries	—	—	—
Other disbursements	—	—	—
Total cash disbursements	—	—	—
Net change during the month	—	—	—
Beginning cash	30,000	—	—
Ending cash	—	—	—
Required level of cash	10,000	10,000	10,000
Excess cash or (shortage)	—	—	—

10. A firm has the following balance sheet:

ASSETS		LIABILITIES AND EQUITY	
Cash	$ 3,200	Accruals	$ 4,900
Marketable securities	2,000	Accounts payable	17,050
Accounts receivable	17,130	Notes payable	7,000
Inventory	19,180		
		Long-term debt	22,000
		Common stock	20,000
Plant and equipment	41,000	Retained earnings	11,560
	$82,510		$82,510

Sales are currently $160,000, but management expects sales to rise to $200,000. The net profit margin is expected to be 10 percent, and the firm distributes 60 percent of its earnings as dividends.

Management is concerned about the firm's need for external funding to cover the expansion in assets required by the expansion in sales. To achieve sales of $200,000, management will have to *expand plant by $10,000* and expects to *increase its holdings of cash by $1,000*. However, the holding of marketable securities may be reduced to zero. Management has also determined the following relationships exist between various assets and liabilities that vary directly with sales:

Accounts receivable = $1,100 + 0.16 Sales,
Inventory = $2,500 + 0.18 Sales,
Accruals = $545 + 0.07 Sales,
Accounts payable = $1,900 + 0.21 Sales.

a. Will the firm need external finance, and if so, how much?
b. Construct a pro forma balance sheet indicating the forecasted new entries for sales of $200,000. If the firm has excess funds, they should be invested in marketable securities. If the firm needs funds, these should be covered by issuing new long-term debt.

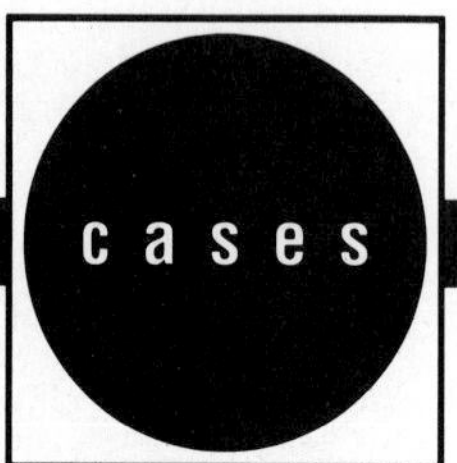

Forecasting the Impact of a Decline in Sales

Leonard Copland is the financial manager for a firm with the following balance sheet:

ASSETS		LIABILITIES AND EQUITY	
Cash	$ 1,000	Accounts payable	$16,000
Marketable securities	2,000	Accruals	4,100
Accounts receivable	14,130	Bank loan	5,000
Inventory	17,180	Long-term debt	12,000
Plant and equipment	31,000	Common stock	10,000
		Retained earnings	18,210
	$65,310		$65,310

Sales are currently $80,000, but Copland expects them to fall to $60,000, which will require a contraction of assets. Copland uses the percent of sales technique to forecast those assets and liabilities that vary directly with sales (i.e., accounts receivable, inventory, accounts payable, and accruals). Since the firm is contracting, Copland would like to retire the long-term debt; however, the terms of the issue do not permit a partial repayment. Copland would like to retain the short-term bank loan, but the bank will not renew the loan if the renewal results in the firm having a current ratio of less than 2:1. Since the firm is contracting, management would like to increase the marketable securities by $1,500 to meet emergencies. However, if the firm needs funds to retire debt, Copland is willing to liquidate all the marketable securities. Copland anticipates that the firm's historic profit margin on sales of 10 percent and the firm's policy of distributing 30 percent of earnings will be maintained.

To help forecast the firm's future financial position, fill in all the anticipated entries in the following balance sheet *prior* to any change in the firm's debt structure:

ASSETS		LIABILITIES AND EQUITY	
Cash	$	Accounts payable	$
Marketable securities		Accruals	
Accounts receivable		Bank loan	
Inventory		Long-term debt	
Plant and equipment		Common stock	
		Retained earnings	
	$		$

Then, construct a new pro forma balance sheet that incorporates all the anticipated changes with the assumption that the firm pays the dividend. If the firm has funds after the change in the debt structure, add them to cash.

ASSETS		LIABILITIES AND EQUITY	
Cash	$	Accounts payable	$
Marketable securities		Accruals	
Accounts receivable		Bank loan	
Inventory		Long-term debt	
Plant and equipment		Common stock	
		Retained earnings	
	$		$

Case Problems

1. Can the firm retain the short-term bank loan?
2. Can the firm retire the long-term debt?
3. If the firm distributed no dividends and retained all of its earnings, could the firm retire the long-term debt?

Suggested Readings

Most of the bibliographic material on financial planning is very technical, as various models and mathematical techniques are used for forecasting purposes. In order to comprehend much of this material, the student needs sufficient background in statistics and other quantitative techniques. For students who lack this background, the next step in their learning about forecasting is to tackle the chapters on forecasting in more advanced managerial finance textbooks. See, for instance:

Brigham, Eugene F., and Louis C. Gapenski. *Financial Management: Theory and Practice,* 6th ed. Hinsdale, Ill.: The Dryden Press, 1991, chapter 19.

Ross, Stephen A.; Randolph W. Westerfield; and Jeffrey F. Jaffe. *Corporate Finance,* 2d ed. Homewood, Ill.: Richard D. Irwin, Inc. 1990, chapter 25.

The student may also wish to consult:

Heckerman, Donald A. "Financial Modeling: A Powerful Tool for Planning and Decision Support." *Managerial Planning* (March–April 1982), pp. 21–25.

This brief article specifies the structured process by which a financial model is constructed and explains why such models play an increasingly important role in planning and decision making.

Parker, George G. C., and Edilberto L. Segura. "How To Get a Better Forecast." *Harvard Business Review* (March–April 1971), pp. 99–109. Reprinted in *Financial Management Classics,* edited by C. D. Aby, Jr. and D. E. Vaughn, pp. 50–65. Santa Monica, Calif.: Goodyear Publishing Co., 1979.

This article presents a straightforward explanation of regression analysis and its use for forecasting sales and earnings.

chapter

19

Management of Short-Term Assets

41 pages in chapter

Learning Objectives

1 Define working capital, net working capital, and working capital policy.

2 Isolate the risks and advantages of an aggressive working capital policy.

3 Explain how the operating cycle may lead to fluctuations in a firm's need for current assets.

4 Calculate the economic order quantity (EOQ) for an order of inventory.

5 Differentiate between LIFO and FIFO and their impact on a firm's taxes.

6 Enumerate the components of credit policy.

7 Explain the advantage offered by lockbox systems and electronic funds transfers.

8 List several alternative money market instruments and distinguish their features.

"Yesterday is a cancelled check; tomorrow is a promissory note; today is ready cash." This quote from Hubert Tinley expresses working capital management. The management of current assets seeks to increase the speed with which inventory and accounts receivable flow into cash. If once the cash is collected it is not immediately needed, it is invested in short-term income-earning securities, such as the commercial paper of creditworthy corporations or the short-term obligations of the federal government (i.e., Treasury bills), to earn interest income.

The amount of the short-term investments can be substantial. VF Corporation, maker of Vanity Fair intimate apparel, Lee and Wrangler jeans, and Jantzen sportswear, held at the end of 1990 $62,015,000 in cash and short-term investments. The Coca-Cola Company, one of the nation's leaders in soft drinks and juice-based beverages, had over $1,429,555,000 in cash and marketable securities, which accounted for 34.5 percent of the firm's total current assets. Other firms, however, may have very little cash. Ladd Furniture reported cash and money market deposits of only $259,000. This modest amount was less than 1 percent of the firm's total current assets.

This chapter and the one that follows consider the management of current assets and current liabilities. This chapter is devoted to the management of the firm's cash and other current assets; the subsequent chapter considers the sources of short-term funds. Current assets flow through the firm. Inventory is acquired and subsequently sold for cash or on credit. Accounts receivable are collected, and the cash is used to acquire other income-producing assets or to retire debt. The cycle is then repeated as the firm acquires new inventory for sale.

Since all assets must be financed—and the sources of finance are not free—the financial manager must establish the firm's optimal level of inventory and the firm's credit policy. Any excess cash must not be left idle. The management of short-term assets is a dynamic job that requires keeping up with day-to-day changes in the economic environment and the demand for the firm's products.

This chapter begins with a discussion of the firm's working capital policy, its operating cycle, and the choice between long-term and short-term financing. This is followed by a discussion of inventory management: the inventory cycle, the optimal order quantity, and inventory valuation. The next section considers the management of accounts receivable: the establishment of credit policy and the analysis of accounts receivable. Once these accounts are collected, the firm receives cash, so the chapter concludes with a discussion of cash management. This discussion includes policies for collecting cash more rapidly and the various short-term securities that may be acquired by the financial manager as temporary parking places for the firm's cash.

WORKING CAPITAL AND ITS MANAGEMENT

A firm's day-to-day operations are primarily centered around generating sales and managing current assets and current liabilities. Although the determination whether to invest in new plant and equipment or refund a bond issue is obviously important, such decisions may be made intermittently. Management, however, is continuously concerned with current assets and how they are financed. Managing inventory, selling the inventory, collecting accounts receivable, investing temporary excess cash, raising short-term funds, and meeting current obligations as they come due require decisions on a daily basis.

A firm's short-term assets (i.e., its current assets) are often referred to as its **working capital.** The difference between its current assets and current liabilities is its **net working capital.** The way a firm manages its short-term assets and short-term liabilities is its **working capital policy.** Management of working capital is exceedingly important to a firm's well-being. Most business failures can be related to the mismanagement of current assets and their financing. Excess investment in inventory, inability to collect accounts receivable or retire its own accounts payable, or excessive use of short-term finance can rapidly destroy a firm that previously generated earnings and appeared to be profitable.

Working capital ▲
Short-term assets; cash, cash-equivalents, accounts receivable, and inventory

Net working capital ▲
Difference between current assets and current liabilities

Working capital policy ▲
Management of short-term assets and liabilities

The two essential questions regarding working capital are: What should be the level of the various current assets? and, How should these assets be financed? The second question divides into two additional questions: Should management use sources of short-term or long-term finance? and, What specific sources should be used? The answers to these questions vary among industries and among firms within a given industry.

THE IMPACT OF THE OPERATING CYCLE ON WORKING CAPITAL POLICY

Working capital policy is affected by the operating cycle of the firm and by the fact that cash receipts and disbursements are rarely synchronized. The longer the operating cycle, the greater will be the firm's investment in current assets. Also, the less synchronization of receipts and disbursements, the greater will be the need for working capital.

EXHIBIT 19.1

The Operating Cycle The operating cycle takes raw materials, converts them into finished products, sells the finished goods, and collects the accounts receivable generated by credit sales.

January 1 →		January 10 →		January 20 →	
Firm buys raw materials ($100) from suppliers.		Workers convert raw materials into finished goods; workers are owed $50.		Goods are sold on credit for $190.	
Raw materials $100	Accounts payable $100	Finished goods $150	Accounts payable $100	Accounts receivable $190	Accounts payable $100
			Accrued wages 50		Accrued wages 50
					Retained earnings 40

In order to have the product to sell, the firm must have inventory. In many cases the inventory will have to be produced, so the firm acquires raw materials and employs labor to transform the raw materials into finished goods. The carrying of raw materials, goods-in-process, and finished goods requires a source of funds. Paying the firm's suppliers and the labor that processes the goods also requires funds. However, the finished goods will generate funds only after they are sold, and if the sales are on credit, funds will be obtained only after the accounts receivable are collected.

This process, the operating cycle, is illustrated in Exhibit 19.1, which presents a time line in which a firm acquires raw materials, processes them, sells its inventory, collects its credit sales, and pays its creditors. The whole process is compressed into a month, and the firm's balance sheet is given as each step in the operating cycle occurs. On January 1, the firm buys $100 worth of raw materials on credit from its suppliers. At that point in time, the firm has $100 in assets financed by $100 in accounts payable. On January 10, the firm's workers convert the raw materials into finished goods. This adds $50 to the value of the raw materials, and the firm owes accrued wages of $50. The firm now has $150 in assets financed by the accounts payable ($100) and the accrued wages ($50).

On January 20, the goods are sold on credit for $190. The firm's assets become the $190 accounts receivable, which are financed by the $100 in accounts payable, $50 in accrued wages, and $40 in retained earnings. On January 30, the accounts receivable are collected, so the firm now has $190 in cash. On January 31, all the liabilities are paid off,

January 30 ⟶

Accounts receivable are collected.

Cash	$190	Accounts payable	$100
		Accrued wages	50
		Retained earnings	40

January 31 ⟶

All liabilities are paid off.

Cash	$40	Accounts payable	$ 0
		Accrued wages	0
		Retained earnings	40

so the firm's cash declines to $40. The accounts payable and accrued wages cease, and the firm retains the $40 in earnings, which finances the $40 in cash. The operating cycle is complete. The goods have been produced and sold, and the accounts receivable have been collected. The firm now has cash and is ready to repeat the cycle.

For some firms, this process may occur over an extended period of time. Consider a building contract. A house takes several months to complete, during which time raw materials are converted into the finished product. This implies that the contractor may need a substantial amount of short-term financing during the construction process. However, once the house is sold, the builder may rapidly collect payment, as a commercial bank or savings and loan association issues a mortgage loan to the buyer, who in turn immediately pays the builder. For homebuilders, the need for working capital and short-term funds is primarily a need to finance construction—not to carry accounts receivable generated by the sale.

Firms in other industries may not have as great a need for working capital because their operating cycle differs or is shorter. Consider a public utility that generates electric power. This firm's primary assets are plant and equipment. It has little inventory, and its primary short-term assets are accounts receivable, which are continually being collected as customers pay their utility bills. An electric utility does not experience the same buildup of short-term assets as the building contractor. Instead, the utility bills some of its customers each day and receives payment each day. It needs fewer short-term sources of funds than many

Financial Facts

Deb Shops' Operating Cycle

A firm's operating cycle may be mirrored in its financial statements. Selected current assets and current liabilities of Deb Shops at two times during its fiscal year reveal some differences. • In January 1987, Deb Shops held only a modest amount of inventory ($14,214,833) and a substantial amount of cash ($28,893,901). Its trade accounts, which are a major source of short-term funds to carry inventory, were a modest $13,567,672. However, by the end of October 1987, Deb Shops had almost tripled its inventory ($40,247,522) in anticipation of the holiday season. Trade accounts had also increased to $21,881,091. If the firm has a successful season, its inventory and trade accounts should be substantially lower (and its $17,059,105 in cash and cash equivalents substantially higher) in January 1988. •

---

other firms because there is a virtual synchronization of payments and receipts.

A firm's working capital policy is also affected by the nature of its sales (especially if the sales are cyclical or seasonal), the firm's credit policy (i.e., its willingness to sell on credit), and management's willingness to bear risk. With cyclical or seasonal sales, sales are not evenly spread over a period of time. Management may increase the firm's investment in inventory in preparation for the period of increased sales, and the firm will need funds to carry the inventory. Once the inventory is sold, there may still be a need for financing if the sales are for credit. After these accounts receivable are collected, the firm may use the cash to retire the liabilities that financed the initial increase in inventory and the subsequent accounts receivable.

A firm's credit policy may also affect working capital. A lenient credit policy is designed to increase sales, so the firm may be able to move (i.e., sell) its inventory more rapidly. However, a lenient credit policy will generate more accounts receivable that the firm must carry, and may retard its collection of cash. Such a policy means that the firm must have sufficient sources of funds to carry the additional receivables.

Management's willingness to bear risk also affects working capital policy in several ways. A conservative management may carry more inventory to be certain that sales are not lost from lack of goods in stock or to protect against work stoppages. The increased inventory will require financing. Willingness to bear risk will also affect management's choice of funding for the firm's short-term assets. As is explained in the next section, the use of short-term instead of long-term funds to finance short-term assets increases the element of risk, because there are the additional risks associated with refunding the debt and changes in the cost of credit (i.e., changes in the rate of interest).

FINANCING AND WORKING CAPITAL POLICY

All assets must be financed. One of the most important tasks facing a financial manager is the choice of financing. Various sources of long-term financing were previously discussed (from the investor's perspective) in Chapter 9 (bonds), Chapters 10 and 11 (preferred and common stock), and Chapter 12 (convertible bonds and convertible preferred stock). The next chapter will consider specific sources of short-term finance, while this section covers the trade-off between sources of short-term and long-term finance and how that trade-off affects the risk associated with a firm's working capital policy.

Exhibit 19.1 illustrated that a firm's current assets vary through the operating cycle. As a firm's current assets rise, its sources of finance also must increase. In the illustration, the increase in assets was covered by increases in accounts payable and accrued wages. These are, of course, not the only possible sources, but a major principle of finance suggests that a financial manager should seek to match the sources of finance with their use.

Short-term sources of finance, such as a loan from a commercial bank, require frequent refunding; long-term debt and equity do not require frequent refunding, which makes them appropriate for financing long-term assets. The firm should not use short-term sources to finance long-term assets. Borrowing short-term funds and investing them in plant and equipment could prove to be a grave error. It may be years before the long-term assets generate funds; the short-term loans, however, must be repaid during the fiscal year. Unless this credit can be refunded (i.e., the funds borrowed from one source can be used to retire the debt from another source) or renewed, the firm will face a substantial problem meeting its short-term obligations as they come due.

While the firm should not use short-term finance to acquire long-term assets (i.e., it should use long-term sources), the firm may use either short- or long-term sources to acquire short-term assets. Short-term sources may be used to finance inventory and accounts receivable because as these assets are converted into cash, the funds may be used to repay the short-term loans. Long-term sources may be used to finance current assets since these sources do not have the problem of frequent refunding.

Since long-term sources may be used to finance both short-term and long-term assets, why does the financial manager use short-term sources?

The answer revolves around the cost and the risks associated with each source. The choice of long- versus short-term sources of funds is ultimately a question of the funds' impact on earnings and the risk associated with management's choices of finance. Generally, short-term sources are riskier because these obligations continually have to be refinanced. The firm is not pressed with the continual need to refinance or retire long-term sources. Hence, long-term sources are not as risky as short-term sources.

If the use of short-term sources increases risk, the question again arises, "Why do firms use this source?" There are both specific and general answers to that question. The specific answers will be developed in the next chapter, which covers short-term sources of finance. The general answer is that short-term sources are often less expensive than long-term sources. Short-term lenders are willing to accept lower interest rates for rapid repayment of principal. They trade some return for increased liquidity. This lower interest cost results in increased earnings for the firm using short-term rather than long-term debt financing.

The possible impact on the firm's earnings may be shown by the following illustration. Firm A has a balance sheet as follows:

Balance Sheet
as of 12/31/X0

ASSETS		LIABILITIES AND EQUITY	
Assets	$10,000	Debt	$6,000
		Equity	$4,000

The balance sheet does not specify the term of the debt. For illustrative purposes, we shall assume three cases: (1) one year at 8 percent, (2) five years at 10 percent, and (3) fifteen years at 12 percent. If sales are $4,000 and other expenses are $2,500, the profits earned by the firm in each case are

	1	2	3
Sales	$4,000	$4,000	$4,000
Expenses	2,500	2,500	2,500
Earnings before interest expense	1,500	1,500	1,500
Interest expense	480	600	720
Earnings after interest expense	$1,020	$ 900	$ 780

As one would expect, the higher interest cost associated with the long-term debt produces the lowest earnings, and the lowest interest cost associated with the short-term debt produces the highest earnings.

Now consider what happens to the firm's profits if after a year the short-term interest rate rises to 13 percent. The income statements now become:

	1	2	3
Sales	$4,000	$4,000	$4,000
Expenses	2,500	2,500	2,500
Earnings before interest expense	1,500	1,500	1,500
Interest expense	780	600	720
Earnings after interest expense	$ 720	$ 900	$ 780

If the firm had initially used short-term debt, its earnings would now be reduced because short-term debt is more expensive. The earnings that resulted from the use of intermediate-term and long-term debt (i.e., five and fifteen years, respectively) are not changed. Even if the cost of long-term debt is currently higher (e.g., 15 percent), the earnings of the firm are unaffected. This is because the firm borrowed in the past at 12 percent, and this rate is fixed for the term of the debt. The current cost of long-term debt only matters if the firm is currently issuing more long-term debt.

This example illustrates that the use of short-term instead of long-term debt may increase the firm's earnings now but reduce them in the future if short-term interest rates rise. The fact that short-term interest rates do fluctuate and can rise above long-term rates was previously illustrated in Figure 2.2, which plotted the yields on short-term Treasury bills and long-term Treasury bonds. As was illustrated in that figure, short-term rates can change significantly and rapidly.

Even though financing short-term assets with short-term finance is an aggressive working capital policy, the managements of some firms choose to follow it. This may be seen by comparing the current ratios of Burlington Coat Factory and Child World, which are 2.6 : 1 and 1.2 : 1, respectively. Both firms are specialty retailers, but Child World has the lower current ratio, which indicates it is financing a larger proportion of its current assets with current liabilities. Burlington Coat Factory is following a more conservative working capital policy in which it uses a larger proportion of long-term debt or equity to finance its current assets.

Large and rapid changes in the cost of short-term credit imply that the choice of short-term finance can affect both the earnings and the risk exposure of the firm. Managements of companies that are in cyclical industries (e.g., building and construction) may seek to have a more conservative working capital policy and use more long-term sources of finance. Managements of firms with stable revenues such as electric utilities may follow a less conservative working capital policy. They can afford the risk associated with having a larger proportion of current assets financed by current liabilities.

The next chapter and the remainder of this chapter are devoted to the individual current assets and current liabilities that are affected by working capital management. While Chapter 20 is concerned with short-term sources of finance, this chapter is devoted to current assets. Since revenues, and ultimately earnings, start with selling inventory or providing a service, the next section is devoted to the management of inventory. This is followed by discussions of accounts receivable and the investment of any temporary cash holdings.

THE INVENTORY CYCLE

A firm produces output to sell, or it buys items wholesale and retails the product. In either case the firm currently acquires inventory to sell in the future. This inventory must be paid for; it must be financed by either borrowed funds or equity. The more rapidly the firm turns over the inventory, the less finance is necessary to carry the inventory. (In Chapter 16 in the section on ratio analysis, one of the important ratios used to analyze the firm was the inventory turnover.) Rapid turnover indicates that the firm is able to sell the inventory quickly, and hence the firm ties up fewer of its funds in inventory. Rapid turnover, however, is not in itself desirable, for such turnover may result in the firm's not having inventory available when there are buyers. Being out of stock may result in the loss of sales and profits. While rapid inventory turnover will decrease the firm's financial needs, it may also result in lower profits for the firm.

The inventory cycle is illustrated by Figure 19.1. The firm initially purchases inventory (AB) and sells this inventory over time. As time passes, some inventory is sold, and the stock of inventory is drawn down. After a period of time (T_1), the inventory is sold and the stock is depleted. The firm then purchases new inventory (AB), and the cycle is repeated (T_1 to T_2).

In reality a firm would not let its inventory fall to zero before it restocked its shelves. Instead, it would seek to maintain a minimum level of inventory (i.e., a **safety stock**) to assure that some stock is always available for sale. Such a safety stock is illustrated in Figure 19.2. The minimum level of inventory (i.e., the safety stock) is OA. The inventory order is added to the safety stock, so that the firm has a maximum inventory of OB, which consists of the safety stock OA and the order AB. This total inventory is drawn down as sales are made. As the level of inventory approaches the safety stock, the firm reorders.

Safety stock ▲ Desired minimum level of inventory designed to protect against loss of sales due to being out of stock

The firm could avoid reordering the inventory by increasing its initial purchase. By doubling its initial purchase, the firm can double the

FIGURE 19.1

Simple Inventory Cycle

Inventory is drawn down, replenished, and the cycle is repeated.

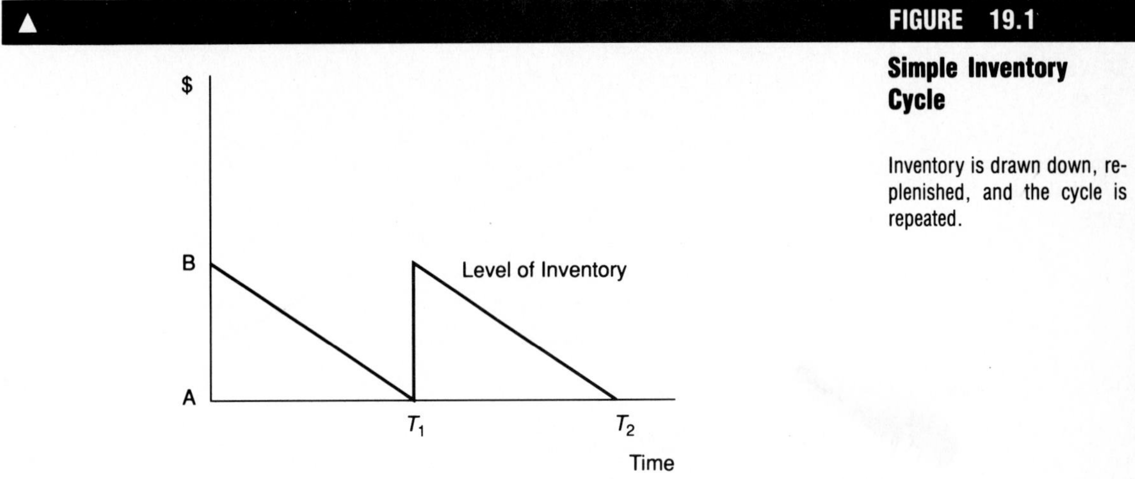

FIGURE 19.2

Simple Inventory Cycle Including a Safety Stock

A safety stock is often maintained to avoid lost sales from being out of inventory.

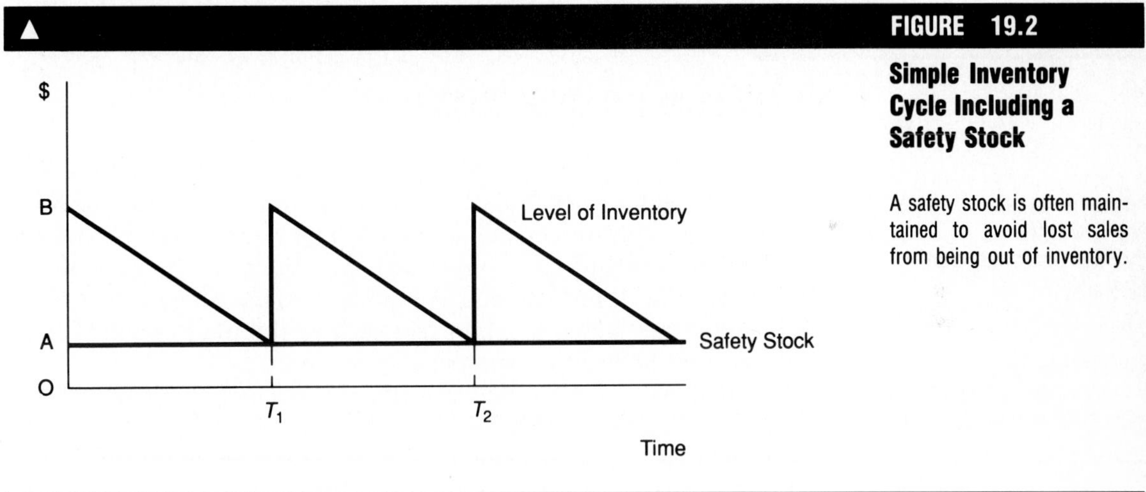

time before it has to reorder. This is illustrated by Figure 19.3, which reproduces Figure 19.2 and adds a larger inventory purchase (AC) that is twice AB. The inventory OC is sufficient to last to T_2 before the firm must repeat the procedure. Of course, the firm could avoid all inventory cycles if it had sufficient inventory. However, it costs money to carry the inventory; hence, management should determine the best level of inventory to purchase to reduce the carrying costs.

FIGURE 19.3

Longer Inventory Cycle

If the firm has more inventory, the length of the cycle is longer.

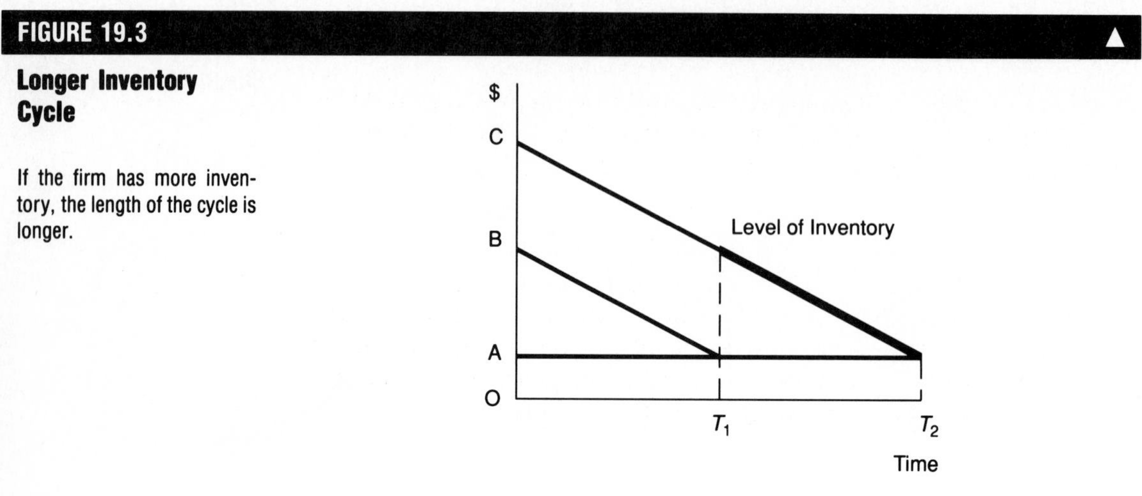

THE ECONOMIC ORDER QUANTITY

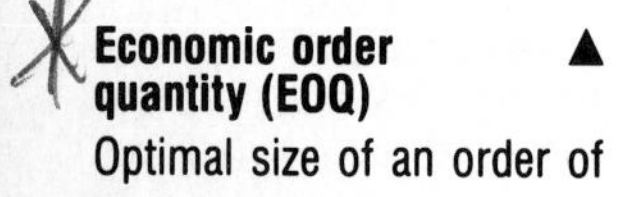

Economic order quantity (EOQ)
Optimal size of an order of inventory

The optimal size of an order of inventory is commonly called the **economic order quantity (EOQ),** which is the amount that minimizes the cost of carrying and processing inventory. This cost has several components, and minimizing one component may significantly increase another component. What are these components? First, there is the cost of placing the order, which includes fees such as shipping and brokerage and the cost to the firm of processing the order.

A second set of costs consists of those associated with carrying the inventory, including not only insurance, storage, and handling expenses but also the cost of the financing necessary to carry the inventory.

Inventory, like any other asset, must be financed, and this cost must be included to determine the economic order quantity. These carrying costs increase as the size of the inventory increases. Thus, these expenses will tend to offset the lower per-unit costs of larger orders. The job of management, then, is to balance the savings from larger orders with the increased carrying costs.

The total annual cost associated with inventory is the sum of ordering costs and carrying costs. Ordering cost (OC) is the product of (1) the number of orders and (2) the fixed cost per order (F). The number of orders depends on the number of units sold (S) and the size of each order (Q). The number of orders equals units sold divided by the size of each order. Thus, total ordering costs are

19.1
$$OC = \left(\frac{S}{Q}\right)F.$$

If annual sales are 10,000 units and the size of each inventory order is 1,000 units, the firm places 10 orders a year. If the cost of placing an order is $50, then total ordering costs are $500.

$$OC = \left(\frac{10{,}000}{1{,}000}\right)\$50 = \$500.$$

Carrying costs include such items as insurance, storage and warehouse expense, interest, and property tax on the inventory. Annual carrying costs (CC) are the product of average inventory ($Q/2$) and per-unit carrying costs (C). Total carrying cost is

19.2
$$CC = \left(\frac{Q}{2}\right)C.$$

If the firm orders 1,000 units of inventory and sells them evenly over the year, its average inventory is 500 units (1,000/2). If the per-unit carrying cost is $10, the annual carrying cost is $5,000.

$$CC = \left(\frac{1{,}000}{2}\right)\$10 = \$5{,}000.$$

Total inventory costs (TC) are the sum of the two components:

19.3
$$TC = OC + CC = \left(\frac{S}{Q}\right)F + \left(\frac{Q}{2}\right)C.$$

In this example, total inventory costs are

$$TC = \left(\frac{10{,}000}{1{,}000}\right)(\$50) + \left(\frac{1{,}000}{2}\right)(\$10) = \$5{,}500.$$

The relationships between inventory and ordering costs and inventory and carrying costs are presented in Exhibit 19.2. The first column presents the given level of sales, while the second and third columns give various possible levels of inventory and the number of inventory orders for the given level of sales. As the level of inventory is increased, the number of orders is reduced. The fourth column specifies the cost of placing an order. Column 5, which is the product of the number of orders and the cost per order (i.e., the product of columns 3 and 4), presents the total order costs associated with various levels of inventory. Notice how the total ordering costs decline with higher levels of inventory because the firm is placing fewer orders and thus is incurring fewer ordering costs.

EXHIBIT 19.2

Relationships between Inventory and Ordering Costs and Inventory and Carrying Costs

Order costs decline while carrying costs rise.

Total Sales (S = 10,000 units)	Inventory	Number of Orders	Cost per Order (F = $50)	Total Order Costs	Average Inventory	Per-Unit Carrying Costs (C = $10)	Total Carrying Costs	Total Costs
10,000	50	200	$50	$10,000	25	$10	$ 250	$10,250
10,000	100	100	50	5,000	50	10	500	5,500
10,000	200	50	50	2,500	100	10	1,000	3,500
10,000	300	34	50	1,700	150	10	1,500	3,200
→ 10,000	316	32	50	1,600	158	10	1,580	3,180←
10,000	400	25	50	1,250	200	10	2,000	3,250
10,000	500	20	50	1,000	250	10	2,500	3,500
10,000	600	17	50	850	300	10	3,000	3,850
10,000	800	13	50	650	400	10	4,000	4,650
10,000	1,000	10	50	500	500	10	5,000	5,500

The second part of Exhibit 19.2 presents in column 6 the average level of inventory (i.e., column 2 divided by two) and the per-unit carrying costs (column 7). The total carrying costs (column 8) are the product of columns 6 and 7. Notice how total carrying costs rise with the level of inventory. Higher levels of inventory inflict more costs on the firm in order to carry the inventory.

The sum of the total ordering costs (column 5) and the carrying costs (column 8) is the total cost associated with each level of inventory. That cost is presented in column 9. As may be seen in this column, total costs initially decline as the level of inventory is increased. However, the decline moderates, reaches a minimum point at 316 units, and then starts to increase. The level of inventory that minimizes the total cost of the inventory is the best quantity for the firm to order. That quantity is the economic order quantity.

The trade-off between ordering costs and carrying costs demonstrated in Exhibit 19.2 is illustrated in Figure 19.4. The horizontal axis measures the size of the inventory order while the vertical axis shows the total costs associated with those orders. Line AB shows total ordering costs, which decline as the size of each order increases. This decline occurs because the total number of orders is reduced. Line CD shows total

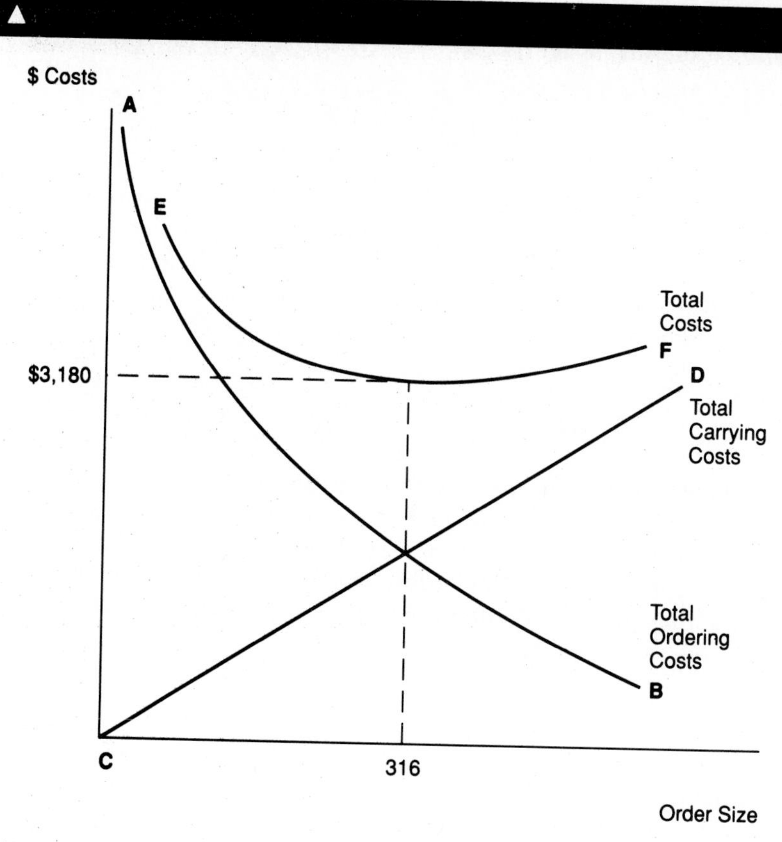

FIGURE 19.4

Determination of EOQ

The economic order quantity minimizes the sum of carrying costs and ordering costs.

carrying costs, which rise with increased order size. These increased costs are the result of the firm having more inventory. Line EF combines these two costs and illustrates the total costs associated with each level of inventory. It clearly demonstrates the initial decline in total costs, their minimum value ($3,180 at 316 units), and their subsequent increase as the level of inventory increases beyond 316 units. The financial manager must determine the quantity that minimizes the combined ordering costs and carrying costs, that is, the economic order quantity.

Mathematical models have been developed to help determine this economic order quantity. Perhaps the simplest model starts with Equation 19.3:

$$TC = OC + CC = \left(\frac{S}{Q}\right)F + \left(\frac{Q}{2}\right)C,$$

and then determines the order size which minimizes total costs. This is a calculus problem in which the first derivative with respect to ordering quantity is set equal to zero and solved. The resulting solution is referred to as the economic order quantity (EOQ) and is given in Equation 19.4.[1]

19.4
$$EOQ = \sqrt{\frac{2SF}{C}}$$

The example in Exhibit 19.2 may be used to illustrate how the formula works. A firm uses 10,000 units of an item each year, and it costs the firm $10 to carry each unit. The cost of an order is $50. When these values are substituted into Equation 19.4, the economic order quantity is determined as follows:

$$EOQ = \sqrt{\frac{2(10{,}000)(\$50)}{\$10}} = 316.$$

Thus, the most economical size order for this item is 316 units.

How this information is related to the inventory cycle is illustrated in Figure 19.5. In this illustration a safety stock of 50 units has been assumed. The initial order is 366 units, which is the sum of the safety stock (50) and the economic order quantity (316). Since annual sales are 10,000 units, sales per day are

$$\text{Sales per day} = 10{,}000/365 = 27.4.$$

If sales per day are approximately 28 units, the economic order quantity is sold in approximately 11 days.

$$\begin{aligned} \text{Duration of the EOQ} &= \text{EOQ/Daily sales.} \\ &= 316/28 = 11.3. \end{aligned}$$

This passage of time is shown in Figure 19.5 from day 0 to day 11, at

---

[1] Calculus is used to determine the EOQ. The calculation is as follows:

$$TC = (S)(F)(Q)^{-1} + (Q)(C)/2$$

Take the first derivative with respective to Q:

$$\frac{d(TC)}{d(Q)} = -(S)(F)(Q^{-2}) + C/2$$

Set the first derivative equal to zero and solve for Q:

$$\begin{aligned} (S)(F)(Q^{-2}) &= C/2 \\ C &= \frac{2(S)(F)}{Q^2} \\ Q^2 &= \frac{2(S)(F)}{C} \\ Q &= \sqrt{\frac{2(S)(F)}{C}} \end{aligned}$$

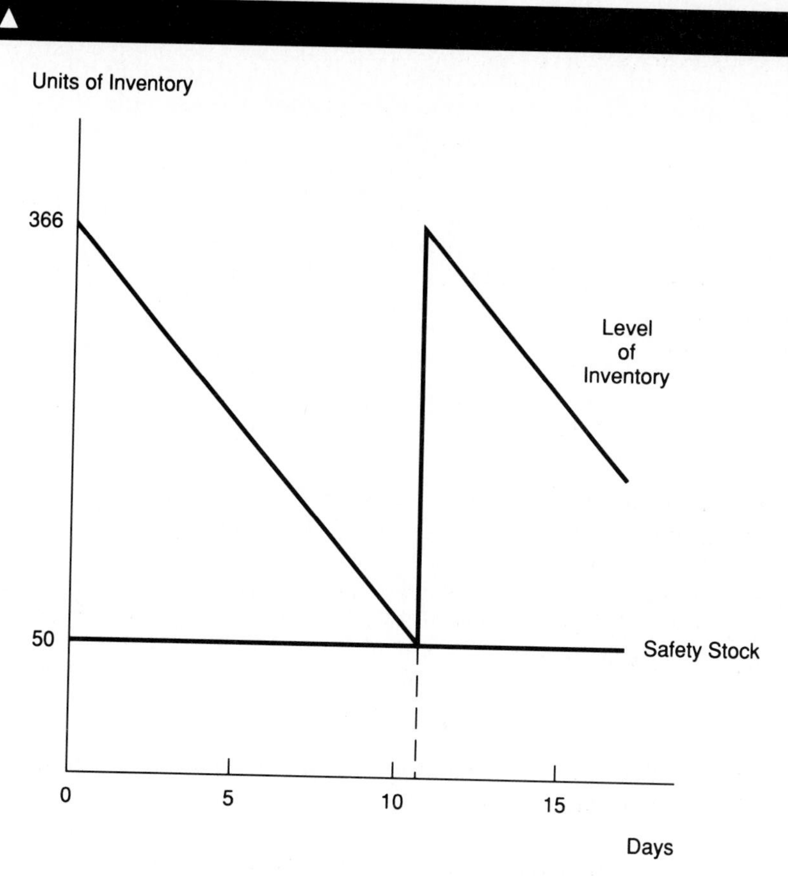

FIGURE 19.5

Inventory Cycle with EOQ

The EOQ is added to the safety stock to determine the maximum level of inventory. Inventory is drawn down over eleven days and then restored.

which time the level of inventory has declined to the safety stock and must be replenished. Then the cycle is repeated. The amount of inventory the firm should reorder once again is the EOQ, which remains 316 units unless the carrying costs or the ordering costs have changed.

When will management place an order for the 316 units? The answer depends on how long it takes to receive delivery. For example, if the firm expects shipment to take five days and the EOQ to last 11 days, then management must place an order six days after taking possession of the inventory to be certain to receive the next order. Of course, if the order is late, the firm will start to use its safety stock, so the possibility of late shipments is one reason for carrying a safety stock. If delivery is slow, the reorder point may be several weeks before the inventory is needed. If delivery requires 14 days, for example, the firm will have to place a second order before the first order is received, since the duration of the EOQ is 11 days. If delivery is rapid, however, the reorder may occur close to when shipment is needed. If the firm could receive shipment within a day, the reorder point would be only one day before the inventory is needed.

A change in any of the variables used to calculate the EOQ will, of course, affect the desired amount of each order. For example, if the cost of placing an order in the previous illustration increases from $50 to $100, the economic order quantity becomes:

$$\text{EOQ} = \sqrt{\frac{2(10{,}000)(100)}{10}} = 447.$$

The increase in the cost of processing the order raises the best reorder size from 316 to 447 units. If the carrying costs were to rise from $10 to $20, the EOQ would decline from 316 to 224:

$$\text{EOQ} = \sqrt{\frac{2(10{,}000)(50)}{20}} = 224.$$

It is important to note that these changes in costs do not produce proportionate changes in the economic order quantity. The doubling of the order cost does not double the economic order quantity and a doubling of the carrying cost does not result in halving the optimal order. There is more than one variable affecting the optimal order quantity. If one variable changes and the others are unaffected, there is no reason to assume that there will be a proportionate change in the economic order quantity. Hence, there is no simple proportionate relationship between one component of the costs and the EOQ.

Weaknesses in the EOQ

The EOQ model is a simple model for the determination of the optimal order quantity. It is based on several simplifying assumptions that rarely apply to all firms at all times. Of course, this criticism may apply to other models explained and illustrated in this text. Each model has a set of assumptions. However, of all the models presented in this text, the simple EOQ may have the least realistic assumptions. Thus, totally relying on the model is hard to justify.

A major assumption is that sales occur smoothly during the time period. This assumption permits the line representing the level of inventory in Figure 19.5 to decline at the same rate of 11.3 units a day. Sales, however, generally do vary over a period of time. Some sales are seasonal, and even non-seasonal sales may occur at different rates throughout the year. There are periods when sales are sluggish and inventory is drawn down at a slower rate. Even stable sales do not imply that the same amount is sold daily as suggested by the simple EOQ model.

Also, there may be variations in the level of economic activity that affect sales and hence affect the level of inventory. Periods of economic expansion tend to boost sales and reduce inventory, while recession has the opposite effect. The EOQ model uses sales, and unanticipated changes in the level of economic activity may generate unexpected changes in sales, in which case the model could give an incorrect optimal economic order quantity.

In addition, the simple EOQ model does not consider the possibility of quantity discounts and delays in processing orders. Of course, discounts for large purchases and delays in shipping may affect the level of inventory carried by the firm. Such considerations are excluded from the simple EOQ model. It is this lack of realism that is the primary source of criticism of the model.

However, even if the model were expanded and made more sophisticated, the basic concept that it illustrates would not be altered. The EOQ seeks to determine the size of the order that minimizes the total costs of carrying and processing inventory and as such brings to the foreground the importance of carrying and ordering costs. Failure to balance ordering and carrying costs will decrease the profitability of the firm.

If management overestimates the cost of ordering and underestimates carrying costs, the effect will be to order too much inventory. In tough economic times, carrying excess inventory may be more costly than losing potential sales. In the reverse situation, in which management underestimates the ordering cost and overestimates the carrying costs, a firm may lose sales but it will avoid the cost of carrying the inventory.

This avoidance of the cost of carrying may be crucial if sales do not materialize. The cost of short-term credit does change and can rise rapidly. One of the quickest means to place a firm in financial difficulty is to have excess inventory during a period of rising short-term rates. If management has followed an aggressive working capital policy, it may find itself with unsold inventory being financed with more expensive short-term credit.

A firm could avoid these problems if it could coordinate the receipts of inventory with its sales. Raw materials would arise "just in time" for the production process and the production process would be completed "just in time" for delivery. Inventory would consist only of goods-in-process for a manufacturer and would be virtually non-existent for a retailer.

A "just-in-time" inventory system seeks to achieve just that. Raw materials arrive only as needed and finished goods are immediately shipped. The concept was developed by Japanese industry but is also applied by U.S. firms. Just-in-time inventory management requires (1) very accurate sales forecasts that are updated often, (2) a flexible production schedule with tight deadlines, (3) reliable equipment and preventive maintenance programs (a breakdown in part of the process throws the tight schedules off), and (4) frequent communication with and cooperation from suppliers.

When successful, just-in-time inventory management erases the need for determining the economic order quantity. Just-in-time reduces the need for safety stocks and for capacity since facilities and labor are used more intensely, and increases the firm's ability to respond to changes in customers' demands. The system manufactures exactly what customers need when they need it, permitting customers to also institute just-in-time inventory management. Shipping costs tend to increase because the firm must make more (and smaller) shipments; however, increased supplier and buyer loyalty, the savings in inventory carrying costs, and the reduced need for plant and equipment result in increased earnings when just-in-time inventory management is successfully employed.

Maximum, Minimum, and Average Inventory

The EOQ gives the optimal order quantity for inventory; that, however, is not the same as the maximum inventory to be carried by a firm. Consider the firm in Figure 19.5 at the beginning of day 1. Its maximum is the EOQ (316) plus the safety stock (50). The minimum inventory at the end of day 11 is the safety stock, if sales occur as anticipated. Of course, the minimum possible inventory is 0 if the entire safety stock is sold before new inventory is received.

The average inventory depends on the EOQ and the safety stock. If sales occur evenly throughout the time period (approximately 28 units per day), the average inventory associated with the EOQ has to be the EOQ/2. The inventory at the beginning of day 1 is 316 units and at the end of day 11 is 0. The average of these two numbers is 158 ([316 + 0]/2). At the beginning of the second day, its inventory is 288 units because 28 were sold during the first day. At the end of the tenth day its inventory is 28 units. The average of these two numbers is 158 ([288 + 28]/2). By similar reasoning, it may be shown that the average inventory associated with the EOQ is always the EOQ/2, as long as sales occur evenly throughout the period.

The average inventory associated with the safety stock is the amount of safety stock. Consider the safety stock in Figure 19.5. At the beginning of day 1, the safety stock is 50 units. At the end of day 11, the safety stock is still 50 units. The average of these two numbers is obviously 50. As long as the safety stock is not drawn down, the average safety stock is 50 units.

Of course, the firm's average inventory is the sum of the two averages. Thus,

$$\text{Average inventory} = \text{EOQ}/2 + \text{Safety stock}.$$

The average inventory for the firm in Figure 19.5 is 208 units ([316/2] + 50), while the maximum and minimum levels of inventory are 366 and 50 units, respectively.

INVENTORY VALUATION

The preceding section considered the determination of the optimal order quantity, which was expressed in units of inventory. This section considers the valuation of that inventory. The inflation experienced during the 1970s and 1980s points out the effect that valuation of inventory has on a firm's earnings and income taxes. A firm purchases inventory at different times. During periods of fluctuating prices, the cost of the inventory will vary. The firm subsequently sells the inventory, and an important question arises. Which units of the inventory were sold? Were the first units of inventory the first to be sold, or were the last units of inventory the first units to be sold? During periods of fluctuating prices, such as the recent inflation, this is an important question that can affect the firm's profits and income taxes.

There are two prevalent means to value inventory. According to one method, the first units of inventory purchased are the first units sold. This system is called **first in, first out (FIFO).** In the second method the last units of inventory purchased are the first units sold. Under this system the newest inventory is sold first. This system is called **last in, first out (LIFO).** If the firm sold all of its inventory and carried none over from one year to another, or if prices did not fluctuate, the difference between the two methods would not be important. However, firms do carry inventory from one fiscal year to another; hence, it is important to establish which items of inventory are actually sold. This determination becomes even more important during periods of fluctuating prices because the cost of the inventory fluctuates. For example, during a period of inflation the cost of the inventory will probably increase during the year. Under this condition, the selection of the method of inventory valuation affects the determination of the firm's profits and income taxes.

First in, first out (FIFO) ▲
Method of inventory valuation in which the first inventory received is the first inventory sold

Last in, first out (LIFO) ▲
Method of inventory valuation in which the last inventory received is the first inventory sold

How this effect occurs may be illustrated by the following example. A firm purchases 100 units of inventory every two months. As a result of inflation the cost of the inventory increases during the year. The following schedule gives the dates of purchase and the cost of the inventory:

	Price per Unit	Total Cost of Inventory
January	$1.00	$100
March	1.04	104
May	1.06	106
July	1.08	108
September	1.11	111
November	1.15	115
		$644

During the year the firm purchased 600 units of inventory for a total cost of $644. During the period in which the firm was purchasing the inventory, it was also selling it for $1.30 a unit. Total sales were 500 units, for total revenues of $650. The firm thus ended the year with 100 units of inventory to sell during the next year. How much profit did the firm earn during this year? The answer will be influenced by the method of inventory valuation that is selected, because the cost of the inventory rose during the year.

If FIFO is used, the first inventory is sold first. The firm sold the 500 units of inventory acquired from January to September, and this inventory cost $529. If LIFO is used, the last inventory was sold first. The firm sold the 500 units acquired during March through November, and this inventory cost $544.

The effect on the firm's earnings of the choice of LIFO or FIFO is illustrated by the following simple income statements. The first statement is constructed using FIFO, and the second statement is constructed using LIFO.

	FIFO Income Statement	**LIFO Income Statement**
Sales	$650	$650
Cost of Goods Sold	529	544
Income	$121	$106

The profits of the firm are higher in the FIFO income statement because the cost of the goods sold is less. The use of the lower inventory valuation produces higher profits, and these higher profits will result in higher income taxes. In effect, the cost of the inventory acquired during the year has been understated, which creates the illusion of higher profits. If the firm had used LIFO to evaluate the inventory, profits would be less, and thus the taxes on its income would be less. During a period of inflation the use of LIFO may give a better indication of the firm's true profitability, because LIFO uses the higher cost of goods sold to determine profits. In fact, many firms have switched from FIFO to LIFO, and as a result their profits are lower. Frequently, management of publicly held corporations make special efforts to inform their stockholders that the lower earnings were the result of a change in inventory valuation and not a decrease in profitability.

The impact of the choice of LIFO over FIFO during a period of inflation is not limited to the effect on taxable income; the choice also affects the analysis of the firm's financial statements, especially inventory turnover. Since a firm sells its most expensive inventory first with LIFO, its year-end inventory (and thus its average inventory) is lower. Inventory turnover (i.e., sales divided by average inventory) is increased because the fraction's denominator is decreased.

Inventory valuation also affects profitability ratios. The choice of LIFO during a period of rising prices reduces any ratio that uses net income. For example, the return on sales and return on equity ratios both use net income. Since the choice of LIFO reduces profits during inflation, both of these ratios are reduced. Lower earnings also suggest that retained earnings will rise less (unless the firm reduces its dividend). This implies that the debt ratio or the ratio of debt to equity is also affected. The firm will appear to be using more financial leverage.

The financial analyst needs to be aware of the firm's choice of LIFO or FIFO in order to make consistent comparisons of a firm's financial statements over time or to compare a firm's financial statements with those of other firms. Obviously, if one set of financial statements is constructed using LIFO while another is constructed using FIFO, any comparisons may be misleading unless the analyst restates the financial statements to put them on a common footing.

MANAGEMENT OF ACCOUNTS RECEIVABLE

Accounts receivable arise through credit sales. Sales may be for cash or for credit. If the firm accepts credit, it is accepting a promise of payment in the future. The firm must determine its credit policy, and there are several factors management should consider when determining the firm's willingness to accept credit sales. As in all financial decisions, these factors involve the potential benefits versus the costs associated with the policy. The potential benefit of offering credit is increased sales, for credit is a competitive device to encourage sales. Many consumers use credit extensively and many firms, especially retailers, also buy on credit. Thus, to increase the level of sales, the firm may extend credit.

But credit involves costs. There are the obvious processing fees, for the firm must bill its credit customers and keep records. These processing costs have encouraged many firms to accept credit cards instead of directly billing customers. Cards such as MasterCard or VISA provide an alternative means by which firms can offer credit. The retailer accepts the card and lets the issuing agent process and collect the accounts receivable. The retailer, however, only collects some percentage of the credit sales, such as $0.98 on every $1.00, with the $0.02 going to the collecting agent. While this arrangement reduces the proceeds of the sale, it virtually eliminates the processing costs of credit.

Offering credit also involves the possibility of loss; not all credit sales are collected, as some purchasers will default. Of course, many accounts are of excellent quality, as is illustrated by the accounts receivable of utilities. These accounts are generally of high quality because the company can force payment by threatening to discontinue service. One method of increasing the safety of accounts receivable is to require the buyer to pledge the merchandise against the loan. In case of default the seller will repossess the goods, which may then be resold. However, the goods are now used, and the seller may be unable to sell them for the full value of the account receivable. In such a case the seller still has a claim on the buyer for the balance but may never be able to collect that claim.

While the ability to use merchandise as collateral to secure an account receivable will increase the quality of the account receivable, such use of merchandise for collateral is not practical for many goods and services. It is primarily limited to durable goods such as cars. When the account receivable is not secured, the probability of collecting the account is reduced and the risk of loss is increased. This risk of loss is a very important element in determining a firm's credit policy. Obviously, if the firm suffers considerable losses, it must protect itself in some way. The firm may grant credit sparingly or under extreme terms, such as very high interest rates, that encourage buyers to use cash. Also, the firm can seek to protect itself by charging more for its products, in which case all buyers share in the cost of the losses on the credit sales.

Credit Policy

Credit policy has three components: the selection of those customers who will be granted credit, the terms of credit, and the collection policy. While all three components are important, the firm faces legal constraints with regard to the granting of credit and the terms. For example, the firm may not discriminate in granting credit; it must be given to all who meet the standards. Furthermore, the firm may not discriminate in the terms offered. Once the firm establishes the terms, they apply to all.

To determine who will be granted credit, the firm establishes credit standards. These standards consider factors such as the capacity of the borrower to pay, the collateral the borrower may have to secure the loan, and the borrower's record of payment. The capacity to pay primarily depends on the borrower's income and other sources of cash. Individuals with higher levels of income have more capacity to meet credit payments and thus are better credit risks. However, income level is not the only consideration because the individual (or firm) may have other debt obligations. Thus, the lender will also consider the amount of debt the borrower already has outstanding. While it may seem that such information is unobtainable, such is not the case. The lender may ask for the information directly and not grant credit if such information is withheld. Even if the information is supplied by the borrower, it is wise to verify the information through various credit bureaus, which keep a substantial amount of financial information on individuals and firms. Such information may be purchased by firms who desire financial information concerning potential borrowers.

The Job Mart

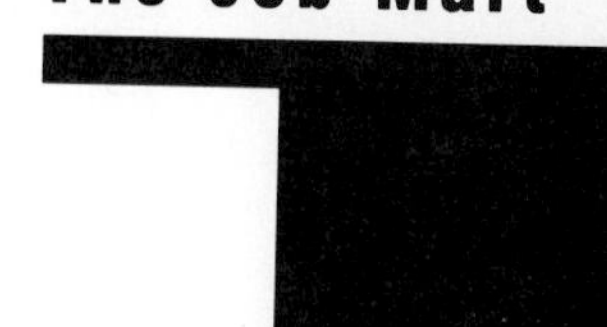

Credit Manager

■ Job Description: Responsible for the administration of credit and collection policies. Determine terms of credit and collection procedures. Increase profitability through the management of accounts receivable. ■ Job Requirements: Strong background in working capital management, especially in the analysis of financial statements to determine creditworthiness. Extensive analytical skills are required and an advanced degree in finance is desirable. ■ Characteristics: The credit manager is in a visible position that may report directly to the corporate controller, to the head of finance, or to marketing divisions of the firm. He or she must have excellent interpersonal skills, since the position involves contact with clients, customers, and sales and marketing staffs.

Collateral, of course, refers to specific assets that may be pledged to secure a loan. As was explained previously, collateral that is used to secure a loan reduces the risk of loss to the lender. However, not all assets make good collateral. For an asset to be good collateral, a market must exist for it. For this reason, marketable securities such as stocks and bonds make excellent collateral, for they may be readily sold. Real estate may also be excellent collateral, as it too may be sold. However, it may take an extended period of time to sell real estate, during which time the lender's funds are tied up in the bad loan. Since the marketability of assets differs, their usefulness as collateral varies. Creditors will only lend a fraction of the asset's value. The variation in assets' quality helps explain why creditors will lend varying amounts against specific assets. The more readily the asset may be sold near its assessed value, the more it can be used to secure the loan.

Actually, lenders do not want the collateral that is used to secure the loan. A bank makes its profits through lending; a retailer generates revenues through sales. Neither is in the business of selling assets seized for the nonpayment of debt. Thus, part of the role of collateral is psychological. The purpose is to encourage the borrower to meet the payments due. Failure to meet the payments may result in the borrower losing the pledged asset. Since the pledged asset is worth more than the amount of the loan, the borrower may suffer a substantial loss. It is this threat of loss that gives the use of collateral teeth and increases the likelihood that the borrower will meet the required payments.

In addition to the borrower's capacity to meet its debt obligations and the assets that are available to secure the loans, the lender will consider the borrower's past credit history. Does the borrower have a history of slow payment? Has the borrower ever declared bankruptcy? A good track record implies that the borrower is a safer risk. Once again this information may be obtained through credit-rating agencies and credit bureaus that maintain credit histories on individuals for the previous seven years (ten years in case of a previous bankruptcy). While such past histories do not assure the creditor will continue to be a good risk, they do differentiate borrowers with a good credit history from those who have been slow payers or who have defaulted in the past.

After establishing who will be granted credit, the firm must establish the terms. The terms of the loan include the time period for the loan, the discount (if any) for early payment, and the penalty for late payment. In the next chapter, the terms of trade credit are illustrated by 2/10, n30. In that case, the term is 30 days with a 2 percent discount for early payment. (These terms do not specify any penalty for failure to pay by the thirtieth day.) Often terms are n30 (or n60) with interest on the unpaid balance at 1.5 percent monthly (18 percent annually) after the initial 30 days have elapsed. Such terms let the borrower have the "free" use of credit for 30 days (60 days if the terms are n60). Of course, that means the lender is carrying the loan for the specified term and has built this cost of credit into the price of the goods sold to the borrower. Since the credit is already paid for, such terms encourage the borrower not to pay until the term of the loan has lapsed.

Actually, the lender may have little flexibility in the terms that are offered, since competition will tend to force firms to offer similar terms. However, while competition may determine the terms and legal constraints may restrict the selection of potential borrowers, the firm has more flexibility with regard to its collection policy. Such policy can range from sending a second billing or an overdue statement to harsher measures such as threats of legal action. Failure to collect forces the lender to (1) write off the loan as uncollectible, (2) take more drastic action, such as initiate legal action designed to force payments, or (3) sell the account to a collection agency. While drastic action may force payment, it may also result in the loss of goodwill. Buyers may feel threatened if the firm follows a stern collection policy. Of course, the lender may follow such a policy in a subtle way so that potential customers are not aware of the collection policy.

Like all assets, accounts receivable are a use of funds that must be financed. These funds should earn a return that exceeds their cost to the firm. While some of these accounts do earn interest, all accounts receivable must offer an implied return or benefit (e.g., increased profitable sales) to justify their use of funds. If credit sales do not yield this return, they decrease the profitability of the firm. Credit policy, then, is ultimately designed to assure that the extension of credit does increase the profitability of the firm.

Analyzing Accounts Receivable

Having granted credit, management needs to supervise and analyze the firm's accounts receivable. One technique for monitoring accounts receivable is to analyze their turnover. Turnover ratios such as annual sales/accounts receivable or the average collection period (i.e., days that sales are outstanding) were discussed in Chapter 16 on the analysis of financial statements. The faster the accounts receivable turn over, the faster they are collected and converted into cash. This cash may then be used to acquire other income-earning assets or to retire debt.

The potential for savings from increasing turnover of accounts receivable may be seen in the following example. The industry average turnover ratio is 6 (i.e., every two months). This particular firm has credit sales of $100,000,000 and accounts receivable of $25,000,000. Thus, its accounts receivable turn over four times a year (Credit sales/Accounts receivable = $100,000,000/$25,000,000 = 4). If this firm were able to match the industry average, what would be the amount of its accounts receivable? The answer is

$$6 = \frac{\$100{,}000{,}000}{X},$$

$$X = \$100{,}000{,}000/6 = \$16{,}666{,}667.$$

If the firm achieved a receivables turnover that was comparable to the industry average, its accounts receivable would decline from $25,000,000 to $16,666,667. That is a net reduction of $8,333,333 in accounts receivable. If funds cost 12 percent annually, the reduction in the accounts receivable would save the firm $1,000,000 a year in finance charges ($8,333,333 × 0.12 = $1,000,000). Obviously, in this case increasing the turnover of the accounts receivable increases the profitability of the firm.

Another tool used to analyze credit sales is to age the accounts. This is a simple technique that uses a table showing the length of time each account has been outstanding (i.e., unpaid) to determine the length of time in which various accounts are being converted into cash. How this technique works is illustrated by the following example. A firm has total accounts receivable of $1,100, which are composed of five customers. The amount of each account and the number of days outstanding are as follows:

Customer	Amount of the Account	Number of Days Outstanding
A	$300	45
B	100	70
C	200	20
D	200	35
E	300	15

From this information, the following table can be constructed:

Accounts	Aging Schedule (in Days) 0–30	31–60	61–90	More than 90
A	—	$300	—	—
B	—	—	$100	—
C	$200	—	—	—
D	—	200	—	—
E	300	—	—	—
	$500	$500	$100	$0
Percentage of total accounts receivable	45.5%	45.5%	9.1%	0%

This table clearly shows that $600 (i.e., 54.6%) of the accounts receivable has been outstanding for more than a month and that one account has not been paid for more than two months.

If the financial manager frequently ages the receivables, a pattern, or norm, will be established. Then, if the percentage of slow accounts increases, the financial manager has identified a problem and can take action either to force collection or to acknowledge the accounts to be bad and discontinue carrying them at the stated value on the firm's books. However, slow accounts are not necessarily bad and may eventually be collected. In many cases a firm's best or most important customers may be slow payers. This may be especially true if the buyer is larger than the seller and accounts for a major portion of the smaller firm's sales. Such a buyer has the power to ride the credit, and the small supplier may not press for payment because it fears loss of future sales.

The Decision to Grant Credit

The decision to grant credit is simply a comparison of the benefits from an increase in sales and presumably earnings versus the additional costs associated with granting the credit. These include (1) the cost of the additional goods sold, (2) the cost of credit checks, (3) collection and bad debt expenses, and (4) the cost of carrying the accounts receivable. Suppose a firm has sales of $100,000 without offering credit, but management believes that it can increase sales by 50 percent if the firm offers customers 30 days to pay. Should the firm make the offer?

The answer, of course, depends on the costs associated with the additional sales. To ease the illustration, make the following assumptions:

1. The cost of the additional goods sold is 60 percent of sales.
2. Credit checks and collection costs are $7,000.

3. Five percent of the new sales will be uncollectible.
4. In addition to new customers, all existing customers will take thirty days to pay, while previously they paid immediately.
5. The cost of borrowing the funds to carry the receivables is 10 percent.

Consider the following projected income statement that will result from offering customers credit for thirty days.

Additional sales		$50,000
Costs		
Cost of additional goods sold	$30,000	
Credit/collection costs	7,000	
Bad debt expense	2,500	
Carrying costs (interest)	1,250	
Total costs		40,750
Net increase in earnings		$ 9,250

The cost of the additional goods sold, the credit/collection costs, and the bad debt expenses were given. The carrying costs are figured as follows. Annual sales will be $150,000; all sales will be on credit; and all accounts receivable will be collected at the end of thirty days. Thus, accounts receivable will be $150,000/12 = $12,500. Since the cost of carrying the receivables is 10 percent, the interest expense is $1,250.

The analysis indicates a net increase of earnings of $9,250, which argues for granting the credit. However, several crucial assumptions were made. First, and most important, offering the credit was assumed to increase sales. If the firm's competitors also offer similar credit terms, the projected sales increase may not materialize. Second, the costs were assumed to be accurate. However, an increase in any of the costs obviously reduces the projected increase in earnings. Thus, increased collection expense, an increase in defaults (bad debt), or an increase in the rate of interest will reduce earnings. Third, the analysis assumed that payments will be made on the thirtieth day. If customers pay late, the accounts receivable will remain outstanding for a longer period of time and increase the carrying costs even if the rate of interest remains unchanged.

In summary, a firm's credit policy, like all economic decisions, involves a balancing of offsetting variables. By offering credit, a firm may increase sales and profits, but with these increased sales come increased costs. There are the cost of processing collections, the cost of financing the accounts, and the risk of loss. Like any investment decision, a firm's credit policy considers the potential benefits of offering credit versus the increased expenses. If these benefits exceed their present costs, the firm extends credit, for such a credit policy will enhance the value of the firm.

CASH MANAGEMENT

After inventory flows through the firm into sales, and when accounts receivable have been collected, the financial manager must decide what to do with the cash. Cash management is important because, as was explained earlier, the firm must have sufficient liquidity to meet its obligations as they come due. However, liquidity reduces profitability because cash itself earns nothing. The cash must be used to purchase an income-earning asset in order to increase profitability.

With the increase in short-term interest rates in the 1980s and the technological advances of the age of computers, cash management has increased in importance. The purpose of such management is to minimize the amount of cash held so that excess cash may be invested in income-earning assets, especially liquid, short-term financial assets such as Treasury bills or commercial paper.

A firm holds cash for two reasons: to make transactions and as a precaution. While individuals may also hold cash for the purpose of speculating on a decline in security prices, firms probably hold a minimal amount of cash or no cash at all for speculative purposes. Firms are not in business to speculate on changes in security prices but to make profits through the production and sale of goods and services.

The demand for money for transactions is the result of a lack of synchronization of receipts and disbursements. Money flows into the firm and the firm makes monetary payments, but there is no reason to anticipate that the cash inflows and the cash outflows will be synchronized. The firm may have to acquire and hold cash and subsequently pay it out as the bills come due. The firm will also maintain a cash balance for precautionary purposes. These cash holdings would be used to meet an emergency. (Such a safety stock of cash was previously discussed as part of the cash budget in Chapter 18.)

Cash Management Policies

Cash management policies revolve around (1) hastening collections and retarding disbursements and (2) investing excess short-term funds into income-earning assets, especially money market securities that offer yield plus safety of principal. Increasing the speed of collections is not to be confused with increased turnover of inventory or accounts receivable. The turnover of these assets depends on inventory control and credit policy. Cash management is concerned with the speed with which cash is processed, especially the speed with which checks clear.

The more rapidly checks that are payable to the firm clear, the sooner the firm has the use of the funds. Correspondingly, the slower the checks that the firm has distributed clear, the longer the firm has the use of the funds. If the firm can increase the time that it has the use of the funds, it increases its profitability. An extension of just one day can generate thousands of dollars in earned interest. For example, suppose a firm were to increase its cash holdings by $1 million a day. At 10 percent, such a holding generates $273.97 in interest daily ($1,000,000 × 0.10/365). That amounts to $100,000 annually and certainly justifies the salary of the individual who determines how the firm can generate the additional million in cash.

To generate this additional cash, the firm may establish a **lockbox** system of collections. When a firm bills a customer, the customer sends a check for payment. Checks take time to clear (this is the "float" discussed in Chapter 4 on the Federal Reserve System). The firm does not have the use of the funds until the check clears; thus, a system for decreasing the float (i.e., speeding up collections) will increase the cash that the firm has to use. A lockbox system is designed to do just that—increase the speed of collections.

Lockbox ▲
(system of collections) System designed to decrease the float (i.e., increase the speed of collecting checks) to obtain the use of the funds more quickly

A lockbox system is very simple. Instead of having a central billing location to which all payments are sent, the firm establishes several collection points throughout the country. The individual is instructed to remit payment to the specified address (i.e., the lockbox). A local bank then removes the checks and immediately processes them for payment. Notice that the bank processes the checks; the firm does not use its own staff, which would increase the time necessary to process the checks. At the end of each day, the bank sends by wire the funds that have cleared and are available for use to a central location, which is usually another bank in a financial center (or the firm's corporate headquarters). The funds are now available for the firm to use either to reduce its outstanding short-term debt (and thus reduce interest expense) or to invest in short-term securities.

Figure 19.6 illustrates how a lockbox system works. The top half of the exhibit shows the process by which a check clears through a centralized system. As may be seen in the exhibit, the check may spend several days in the mail arriving at its destination and several days being cleared as it works its way through the Federal Reserve's clearing mechanism. However, in the second half of the exhibit the firm uses a lockbox system. The check is sent to a location that requires less time in the mail. The location of the lockbox facilitates the collection of the funds, which are then sent to the centralized bank for the firm to use.

For such a lockbox system to be profitable, the firm must have a considerable volume of business. The banks that operate the lockboxes, process the checks, and wire the funds charge for this service. The firm obviously must earn a sufficient return on the additional funds generated by the system to justify the expenses associated with the lockboxes.

Electronic funds transfer ▲
Transfer of funds from one account to another through the use of computer terminals

Cash receipts may also be speeded up by the use of **electronic funds transfers.** Under such a system, funds are transferred electronically from one account to another through the use of computer terminals in-

FIGURE 19.6

Flows of Checks and Funds through a Lockbox or a Centralized Collection System

The regional collection of checks reduces the float so the firm has use of the funds faster.

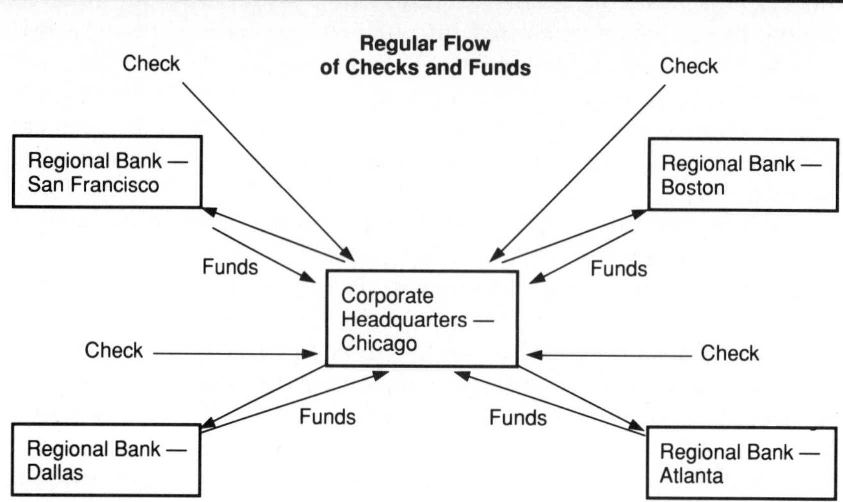

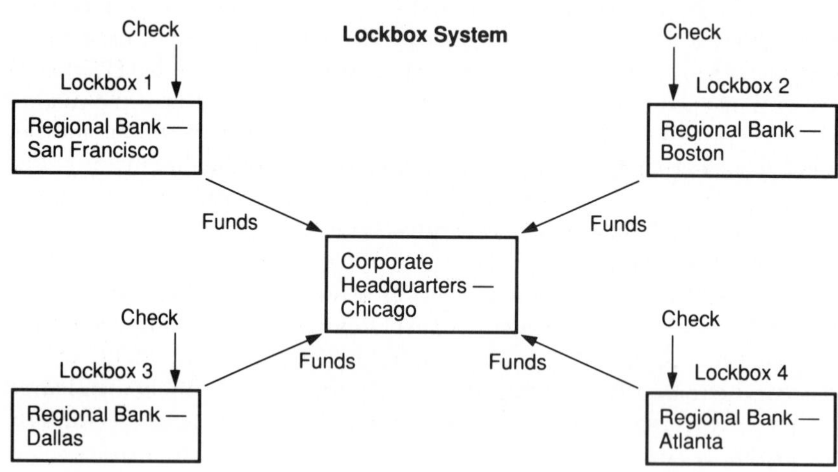

stead of checks. For example, an individual may make a purchase at a store, and payment is made through an immediate transfer of funds from the buyer's account at a commercial bank to the seller's account.

Wide acceptance of such systems may come in the future. However, even today many banks offer similar services to customers to facilitate payments. Funds may be automatically transferred from the customer's account to pay specific bills, such as utility bills. Also, many banks have a correspondent relationship with discount brokerage firms that permit the bank's customers to make payments to and receive payments from the brokerage firm without writing checks.

While such electronic funds transfers are in their infancy for individual consumers, some large corporations have electronic funds transfer systems. Such corporations deposit funds in accounts at several banks throughout the nation, because their operations are national. Each day the funds in the various banks are transferred electronically to one central bank. Since the funds are transferred electronically and not by check, they are immediately available for use. Thus, the corporation is able to transfer excess funds that might have been idle and immediately invest those funds to earn a return.

Management of disbursements is, of course, the exact opposite of collections. Except in those cases where immediate payment reduces interest charges (e.g., a commercial bank loan in which interest owed is determined daily), the intent is to retard payment so the firm may have the use of the money for a longer period of time. This may be achieved by making payments on Friday so they cannot possibly clear the bank until the next week or by remitting funds drawn on banks in another geographic location. The recipients of the checks will consider the funds received, even though the checks may take several days to clear. Of course, the banks may require that the checks actually clear before the depositor has the use of the money. In such cases, the firm disbursing the funds drawn on a distant bank is increasing its use of the cash at the expense of the recipient of the check.

An analysis of when checks clear may offer a means to increase the firm's funds. For example, suppose a firm distributes dividend checks totaling $1 million throughout the country. The financial manager knows that not all of those checks will immediately clear. Exhibit 19.3 presents an analysis of when the checks do clear. The first column presents the number of days the checks are outstanding, and the second and third columns present the daily amount and the cumulative amounts that have cleared. As may be seen in this exhibit, the firm needs only $700,000 to meet the checks that clear during the first four days. Thus, there is no need to have the entire $1 million in the bank when the disbursement is made. If $1 million were available now, the financial manager could invest this cash for a few days to earn interest. All he or she must be sure of is that there will be sufficient money available to cover the checks as they clear.

The financial manager's capacity to effectuate such a strategy is enhanced by two facts. First, since firms obtain lines of credit from commercial banks, these lines may be used to meet the checks should they clear more rapidly than anticipated. Second, the market for short-term investments is so sophisticated that the financial manager may invest excess funds for as short a period as one day. If the financial manager can determine that the cash will be available for an additional day, it may be invested for that short a time period and need not lie idle.

EXHIBIT 19.3

Speed with which Dividend Checks Clear

Number of Business Days for Checks to Clear	Amount	Cumulative Total
1	$250,000	$250,000
2	250,000	500,000
3	120,000	620,000
4	80,000	700,000
5	70,000	770,000
6	60,000	830,000
7	60,000	890,000
8	40,000	930,000
9	25,000	955,000
10	15,000	970,000
Checks still outstanding:	$ 30,000	

Money Market Instruments

There are a variety of short-term liquid assets that the financial manager may purchase with the firm's excess cash. As was explained in Chapter 2, these short-term securities are bought (and sold) in what is called the money market. This term differentiates short-term financial assets from long-term securities such as stocks and bonds, which are traded in what is sometimes referred to as the capital market.

While there are many different issuers of money market instruments and each instrument has its specific name, they have common characteristics. All money market instruments are short-term obligations that may be readily converted into cash. Of course, stocks and bonds may also be readily sold and converted into cash, but the investor runs the risk of loss of principal should the stock or bond be sold for a lower price than was paid to purchase it. Money market instruments offer liquidity; that is, they may be converted into cash with little or no risk of loss of principal. Thus, these instruments offer a safe haven for funds that would otherwise sit idle. Money market instruments are a means for both individual investors and financial managers of firms (or of governments and nonprofit operations such as churches) to earn interest on idle funds with a minimum possibility of loss of principal.

Money market instruments include:

- U.S. Treasury bills
- commercial paper
- negotiable certificates of deposit
- money market mutual funds

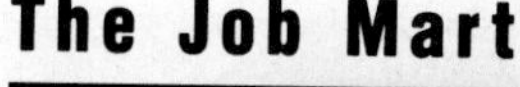

Certified Cash Manager (CCM)

■ Job Description: Assist in the planning, negotiation, and documentation of transactions in money market securities. Identify financing opportunities and increase profitability through better management of receipts and disbursements. ■ Job Requirements: A degree in finance with emphasis on cash management is required, along with a knowledge of payment and collection systems and bank compensation systems. The individual should be well-rounded and have a comprehensive knowledge of cash management. ■ Characteristics: CCM certification is appropriate for bankers, cash management consultants, and corporate, government, and institutional professionals who are responsible for cash management. Information on certification may be obtained from the National Corporate Cash Management Association, P.O. Box 7001, Newton, Connecticut 06470.

- repurchase agreements
- bankers' acceptances
- tax anticipation notes

Commercial paper will be covered in the next chapter; money market mutual funds were discussed before in Chapter 2. The subsequent discussion will be limited to those money market instruments that are not covered elsewhere.

U.S. Treasury bill ▲ Short-term security issued by the federal government

The safest short-term asset is the **U.S. Treasury bill.** Treasury bills are federal government debt. They are sold in denominations of $10,000 to $1 million, and mature in three to twelve months. Treasury bills pay no set amount of interest; instead they are sold at a discount. The Treasury continually auctions off these bills, and potential buyers bid for them, with the highest bidders obtaining the bills. Buyers bid a price such as $9,300 for a six-month $10,000 bill and subsequently earn $700 on an investment of $9,300, for the buyer receives $10,000 at maturity. This is a six-month yield of 7.5 percent (700/9,300); the annual simple rate of interest (i.e., non-compounded) is 15.0 percent. If the bid price had been higher, the interest cost to the Treasury (and the yield to the buyer) would have been lower.

Once Treasury bills have been auctioned, there is a secondary market for them. Bills are quoted daily in the financial press and many daily newspapers. For example, the quotes for January 4, 1991, given in *The Wall Street Journal,* are reproduced in Exhibit 19.4. These quotes indicate that for the bill maturing on April 18, 1991, buyers were willing to bid a price that yielded 6.46 percent. Sellers, however, were willing to offer

EXHIBIT 19.4

Yields on U.S. Treasury Bills (January 4, 1991)

Quotes on Treasury bills are expressed in terms of yields. Since the bid price is less than the ask price, the yield from the bid price is greater than the yield based on the ask price.

Feb 20	ci	10:00	10:03	− 9	8.07
Feb 20	bp	10:05	10:08	− 10	8.01
May 20	ci	9:31	10:02	− 9	8.01
May 20	bp	10:01	10:04	− 8	7.99
Aug 20	ci	9:26	9:29	− 9	8.00
Aug 20	bp	9:31	10:02	− 9	7.94

TREASURY BILLS

Maturity	Days to Mat.	Bid	Asked	Chg.	Ask Yld.
Jan 10 '91	2	6.99	6.89	+0.19	6.99
Jan 17 '91	9	6.64	6.62	+0.03	6.72
Jan 24 '91	16	6.67	6.61	+0.10	6.72
Jan 31 '91	23	5.84	5.82	+0.09	5.92
Feb 07 '91	30	5.99	5.97	+0.06	6.08
Feb 14 '91	37	6.29	6.27	+0.10	6.40
Feb 21 '91	44	6.41	6.39	+0.13	6.53
Feb 28 '91	51	6.42	6.40	+0.13	6.55
Mar 07 '91	58	6.47	6.45	+0.07	6.61
Mar 14 '91	65	6.52	6.50	+0.08	6.67
Mar 21 '91	72	6.49	6.47	+0.08	6.65
Mar 28 '91	79	6.48	6.46	+0.08	6.64
Apr 04 '91	86	6.53	6.51	+0.09	6.70
Apr 11 '91	93	6.52	6.50	+0.11	6.70
Apr 18 '91	100	6.46	6.44	+0.10	6.65
Apr 25 '91	107	6.56	6.54	+0.09	6.76
May 02 '91	114	6.52	6.50	+0.09	6.73
May 09 '91	121	6.51	6.49	+0.09	6.73
May 16 '91	128	6.51	6.49	+0.09	6.74
May 23 '91	135	6.50	6.48	+0.09	6.73
May 30 '91	142	6.48	6.46	+0.09	6.72
Jun 06 '91	149	6.43	6.41	+0.12	6.68
Jun 13 '91	156	6.48	6.46	+0.12	6.74
Jun 20 '91	163	6.47	6.45	+0.11	6.74
Jun 27 '91	170	6.43	6.41	+0.10	6.70
Jul 05 '91	178	6.51	6.49	+0.11	6.80
Aug 01 '91	205	6.49	6.47	+0.10	6.79
Aug 29 '91	233	6.49	6.47	+0.11	6.80
Sep 26 '91	261	6.44	6.42	+0.13	6.76
Oct 24 '91	289	6.49	6.47	+0.10	6.83
Nov 21 '91	317	6.47	6.45	+0.09	6.83
Dec 19 '91	345	6.42	6.40	+0.10	6.80

Source: The Wall Street Journal, *January 7, 1991, p. C18.*

the bills at a smaller discount (i.e., higher price) that yielded 6.44 percent. The 6.65 percent in the yield column gives the annualized yield on the bill based on the asking price.

Treasury bills may be bought not only through brokerage firms but also through commercial banks and the Federal Reserve. These may be purchases of new issues or purchases made through the secondary market. One-year bills are auctioned once a month. Three- and six-month bills are auctioned every Monday. If the buyer purchases the bills directly through the Federal Reserve, there are no commissions. Brokers and commercial banks do charge commissions, but the fees are modest.

Treasury bills are the best short-term investments offering liquidity and safety. The bills mature quickly, as the above quotes indicate, and there are many issues from which the investor may choose. Like all Treasury debt, the bills are safe, for there is no question that the federal government has the capacity to refund or retire the bills. Since bills are extremely liquid and safe short-term debt instruments, they are excellent short-term investments for firms and banks. For example, if a firm has to make a payment in four months and currently has the cash, the financial manager can purchase a Treasury bill that matures in four months. The financial manager will earn interest for the firm but assure the firm of having the funds to meet the payment.

In addition to U.S. Treasury bills, the firm may invest excess cash in commercial paper and negotiable certificates of deposit. Commercial paper is short-term unsecured promissory notes issued by corporations in denominations of $100,000 or greater. **Negotiable certificates of deposit,** also called jumbo CDs, are issued by commercial banks. They differ from the non-negotiable certificates sold by banks in three important ways. First, the negotiable CDs are issued in denominations of $100,000 and larger, with $1 million being the customary unit of sale. Second, the terms, including the rate of interest and the maturity date, are open to negotiation. Non-negotiable CDs come in smaller denominations (e.g., $1,000, $10,000) and are sold with predetermined maturity dates, such as six months or a year. Third, jumbo CDs may be bought and sold like other securities. There is no secondary market for non-negotiable CDs.

Negotiable certificate of deposit ▲
Certificates of deposit issued in amounts of $100,000 or more whose terms are individually negotiated between the bank and the lender and for which there exists a secondary market

The yields on Treasury bills, commercial paper, and negotiable certificates of deposit change daily with changes in conditions in the money markets. However, the yields on these three instruments are similar, with the yields on the Treasury bills being the lowest, since they are the safest of the three securities. The fact that the yields are similar and move together is illustrated in Figure 19.7, which shows the yields on six-month U.S. Treasury bills and six-month commercial paper for 1978–October 1990. The yield earned on the commercial paper is higher than the yield on the Treasury bills because the possibility of default exists. While such a default is rare, it has occurred (e.g., Penn Central defaulted on its commercial paper, and that default threw the firm into bankruptcy). Such risk does not apply to Treasury bills because the power to tax and to create money means the Treasury can always meet its interest and principal repayment obligations.

Another possible short-term investment is a **repurchase agreement** or **REPO.** If a firm needs short-term funds, it may sell an asset but agree to repurchase that asset at some specified time in the future at some specified price. For example, a commercial bank needing funds for a potentially profitable short-term investment may sell one of its assets, such as a U.S. Treasury bill, and agree to repurchase the bill in the future. The buyer of the bill remits funds to the bank, which then are used by the bank to acquire the desired short-term investment. To induce the buyer to purchase the bill, the bank agrees to repurchase the bill at a higher price. That is, if $1 million face amount of bills is sold for $957,000, the bank may agree to repurchase the bills after two weeks for $968,000. The seller thus earns $11,000 on the $957,000 invested for two weeks. Of course, the buyer could have purchased any U.S. Treasury bill on the open market with the intent to sell it after two weeks have elapsed, but then the buyer would not know the price that would be received in the future. By buying the repurchase agreement, the inves-

Repurchase agreement (REPO) ▲
Sale of a short-term security in which the seller agrees to buy back the security at a specified price

FIGURE 19.7

Yields on Six-Month Treasury Bills and Six-Month Commercial Paper (1978–October 1990)

The yield on commercial paper exceeds the yield on Treasury bills, but the rates move closely together.

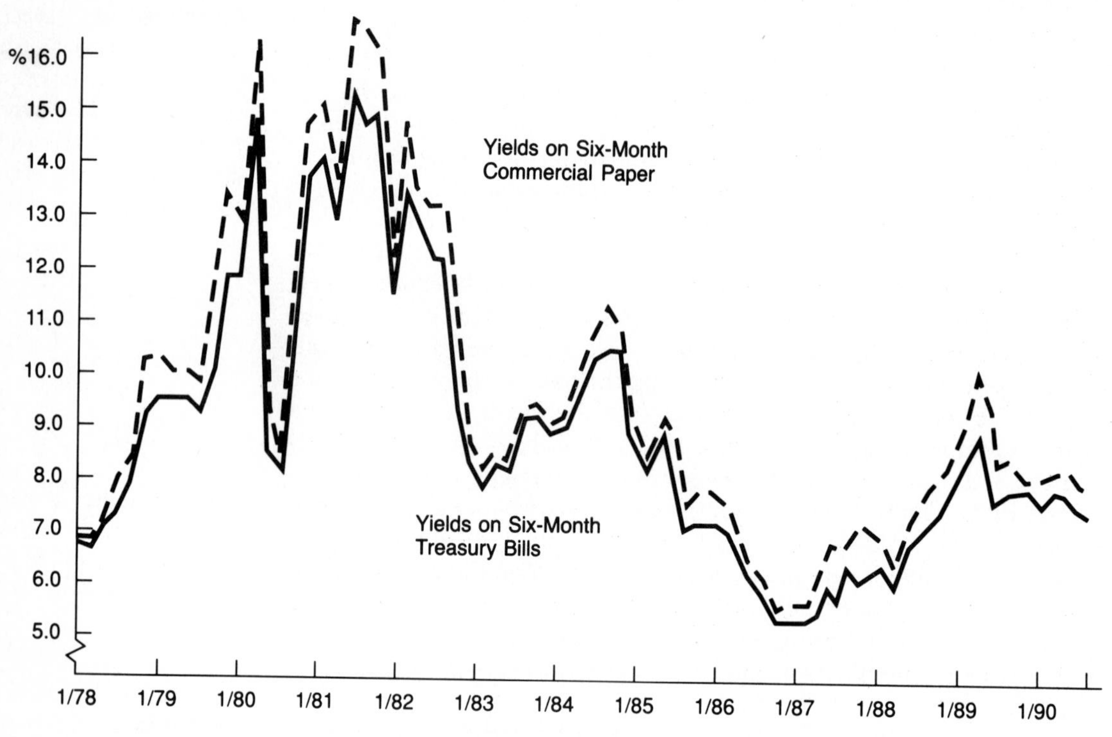

Source: Derived from Federal Reserve Bulletin, *various issues.*

tor knows exactly how much will be made on the investment and when the funds will be received. Thus, the uncertainty associated with the future price is removed.

The market for repurchase agreements, like the markets for commercial paper and other money market instruments, is exceedingly well developed. Since repurchase agreements are between two parties, the terms (especially the time when the security will be repurchased) can be constructed to the benefit of both parties. For example, if Harcourt Brace Jovanovich (HBJ) must make a royalty payment to its authors on July 1 and has the cash available on June 22, it can enter into a repurchase agreement that it will execute on July 1 when HBJ remits payments to its authors. Thus, HBJ is able to invest the funds for exactly the amount of time that they may have sat idle.

Bankers' acceptances are another possible investment that the financial manager can use to invest short-term funds. These acceptances arise through international trade. Suppose a firm ships goods abroad and receives a draft drawn on a specific bank that promises payment after two months. If the firm does not want to wait for payment, it can take the draft to a commercial bank for acceptance. Once the bank accepts the draft (and stamps it "accepted"), the draft may be sold. The buyer purchases the draft for a discount, which becomes the source of the return to the holder. Bankers' acceptances are considered to be good short-term investments because they are supported by two parties: the firm on which the draft is drawn *and* the bank that accepts the draft.

Bankers' acceptances ▲
Short-term promissory note guaranteed by a bank

Treasury bills, commercial paper, negotiable certificates of deposit, repurchase agreements, and bankers' acceptances do not exhaust all the possibilities available to the financial manager. The firm's excess cash may be invested in short-term debt issued by state and municipal governments. Such investments not only offer after-tax yields that are comparable to other money market instruments but also offer the advantage of tax-free interest income.

Tax anticipation notes are issued by states or municipalities to finance current operations before tax revenues are received. As the taxes are collected, the proceeds are used to retire the debt. Similar notes are issued in anticipation of revenues from future bond issues and other sources, such as revenue sharing from the federal government. While these anticipation notes do not offer the safety of Treasury bills, the interest is exempt from federal income taxation. Commercial banks and security dealers maintain secondary markets in them, so the notes may be liquidated should the firm need ready cash.

Tax anticipation notes ▲
Short-term government security secured by expected tax revenues

In addition to domestic short-term securities, the financial manager with temporary excess funds may invest in **Eurodollar certificates of deposit.** These are similar to domestic negotiable CDs except they are issued either by the branches of domestic banks located abroad or by foreign banks. Like domestic negotiable CDs, there is a secondary market in Eurodollar CDs, so they may be bought and sold. The center for trading is London, and most Eurodollar CDs are issued by commercial banks that have branches in London.

Eurodollar CDs ▲
Certificate of deposit issued abroad but denominated in dollars

For investors, the primary advantage of Eurodollar CDs is a small yield advantage over domestic CDs. This yield differential is the result of two factors. First, Eurodollar CDs are not as liquid as domestic CDs. Second, there is additional risk since the securities are issued in a foreign country. These factors suggest that Eurodollar CDs are marginally less attractive than domestic negotiable CDs and hence require a yield advantage to induce investors to purchase them.

THE CALCULATION OF YIELDS

Most short-term securities are illustrations of discounted securities. For example, Treasury bills and commercial paper are bought at a discount and the holder receives the face value at maturity. The difference between the purchase price and the maturity value is the source of interest. With repurchase agreements, the difference between the purchase price and the subsequent resale price is the source of interest.

The yield the investor earns on these securities (and the interest rate the borrower pays) depends on the interest earned, the amount invested, and how long the security is held. For example, an investor (e.g., a corporate cash manager) may buy a Treasury bill for \$9,691 with 180 days to maturity and hold the bill until it is redeemed for \$10,000. What is the yield on the investment? Although that seems like a simple question, the answer is not simple because the yield may be calculated in different ways. The word "yield" is ambiguous, because there is more than one yield. (A similar ambiguity occurred in the discussion of bonds, which considered the "current yield" and the "yield to maturity.")

The "discount" yield (y_d) is calculated as follows:

$$y_d = \frac{\text{Par value} - \text{Price}}{\text{Par value}} \times \frac{360}{\text{Number of days to maturity}}.$$

Thus, in the above illustration employing the Treasury bill, the discount yield is

$$y_d = \frac{\$10{,}000 - \$9{,}691}{\$10{,}000} \times \frac{360}{180} = 6.18\%.$$

The discount yield understates the true yield because it uses (1) the par value and not the amount the individual must invest and (2) a 360-day year.

An alternative method corrects these two problems. The calculation for the "simple" yield (y_s) is

$$y_s = \frac{\text{Interest earned}}{\text{Amount invested}} \times \frac{365}{\text{Number of days to maturity}}.$$

In this illustration, the simple yield is

$$\frac{\$309}{\$9{,}691} \times \frac{365}{180} = 6.47\%.$$

This rate is higher than the discount rate because it uses the amount invested (\$9,691) instead of the principal amount (\$10,000) in the denominator and 365 days instead of 360 days.

The simple yield, however, is not the true annualized rate when compounding is considered. In the previous example, the term of the investment is 180 days, so the investor can repeat the process twice a year. The annualized "compound" yield (i) is determined by the following equation:

$$\$9{,}691(1 + i)^n = \$10{,}000,$$

in which n is 180/365 or 0.49315. Rephrased, the question is: $9,691 grows to $10,000 in 0.49315 of a year at what rate? The solution for the compound interest rate the borrower is paying and the investor is earning is

$$\$9{,}691(1 + i)^{0.49315} = \$10{,}000$$
$$(1 + i)^{0.49315} = \$10{,}000/\$9{,}691 = 1.03188$$
$$i = (1.03188)^{2.0278} - 1 = 6.66\%.$$

Thus, the true, annualized compound yield is 6.66 percent.[2]

In this illustration, the difference between the true annualized rate and the simple rate is small (6.66 percent versus 6.47 percent). However, as the time period shortens (so the frequency of compounding increases) and the amount of the discount increases (so more interest is earned), the difference between the two calculations increases. Suppose the investor purchases a Treasury bill for $9,560 and sells it for $9,630 after thirty days. The simple rate is

$$\frac{\$70}{\$9{,}560} \times \frac{365}{30} = 8.91\%.$$

The true, annualized compounded interest rate is

$$\$9{,}560(1 + i)^{30/365} = \$9{,}630$$
$$\$9{,}560(1 + i)^{0.08219} = \$9{,}630$$
$$(1 + i)^{0.08219} = \$9{,}630/\$9{,}560 = 1.007322$$
$$i = 1.007322^{12.1669} - 1 = 9.28\%.$$

The difference between the simple rate and the true compounded rate is greater than in the previous example (9.28 percent versus 8.91 percent).

The discount rate and the simple rate may be easier to calculate, but they give a less accurate indication of the true annual yield being earned. Selecting among the various money market instruments with differences in prices, interest earned, and time horizons (and hence differences in compounding) requires that the cash manager determine the true yield on each security. Reliance on the discount rate or the simple rate may

---

[2] $(1.03188)^{2.0278}$ may be determined by using an electronic calculator with a y^x key. Enter 1.03188; press the y^x key; enter 2.0278, and press =.

lead to the selection of a security with a lower yield. The financial manager may select an alternative with a lower yield for a valid reason (e.g., selecting a Treasury bill over commercial paper because it is the less risky of the two alternatives). But that is considerably different than selecting one security over another based on inaccurate estimates of their respective yields.

SUMMARY

This chapter has been devoted to a firm's current assets. How these assets are managed and financed is a firm's working capital policy. In general, the cost of short-term funds is less than the cost of long-term funds. Thus, the use of short-term credit tends to increase a firm's profitability. However, sources of short-term finance are riskier because they must be retired or renewed within a year. The terms may become more onerous or the costs may increase when the firm seeks to refinance these short-term obligations.

Inventory is acquired and sold, generating accounts receivable or cash. To facilitate the flow of current assets through the firm, the financial manager analyzes the speed with which inventory and accounts receivable turn over, determines how much inventory to order and carry through use of the economic order quantity (EOQ) model, and selects LIFO or FIFO to determine the valuation and allocation of the cost of inventory when it is sold.

Inventory is sold either for cash or on credit. Increased sales may be generated by a more lenient credit policy. However, more credit sales will require that the firm carry more accounts receivable, which must be financed. The firm's credit policy is a crucial component of working capital management, as the credit policy determines who will be granted credit, the terms of the credit, and the enforcement of the terms. The financial manager faces a typical economic trade-off: additional sales through easier credit versus the increased cost of carrying the receivables. Once the credit policy has been established, the financial manager monitors the collection of accounts receivable through turnover ratios and aging schedules, which identify slow-paying accounts.

Increasing the turnover of inventory or accounts receivable will generate more cash, which may be used to acquire other income-earning assets or to retire debt. If there is a temporary lag between the receipt of the cash and its subsequent disbursement, the funds may be invested in money market securities, including U.S. Treasury bills, corporate commercial paper, repurchase agreements, negotiable certificates of deposit, bankers' acceptances, money market mutual funds, and tax anticipation notes. Money market securities are safe havens for funds that are invested for short periods of time. These securities offer the financial manager a means to increase profitability by earning money market rates of interest instead of holding non-interest-bearing cash.

Review Questions

1. What is working capital? What is the impact on net working capital of each of the following:
   a. the firm issues stock and holds the cash;
   b. cash is used to retire an account payable;
   c. a firm borrows from a commercial bank to acquire inventory;
   d. cash is used to retire an issue of bonds (long-term debt);
   e. cash is used to acquire inventory;
   f. equipment is sold for cash?
2. How will the following affect the amount of cash a firm has?
   a. an increase in the turnover of accounts receivable
   b. an increase in administrative expenses
   c. an increase in cash dividends
   d. an increase in the turnover of accounts payable
3. Why may an aggressive working capital policy increase a firm's profitability but also increase its risk exposure?
4. What are the costs associated with carrying inventory? Why might a firm have a safety stock? If inventory turns over rapidly, does that necessarily increase profits?
5. What does the EOQ model seek to establish? Do you think this is a realistic model for firms with seasonal sales?
6. During a period of inflation, why may the use of FIFO instead of LIFO result in higher taxes? Why, during a period of falling prices, will the use of FIFO instead of LIFO result in lower profits?
7. If a firm has a slow turnover of its accounts receivable, why may that reduce its profitability?
8. If a firm offers credit, why may collateral reduce the risk of loss? What features must this collateral have?
9. If a firm has excess liquidity, what are several possible short-term assets that it could acquire?
10. Both Treasury bills and commercial paper are sold at a discount. What does this mean? Can one suffer a loss by buying these debt instruments?

Problems

1. A firm needs $1 million in additional funds. These can be borrowed from a commercial bank with a loan at 10 percent for one year or from an insurance company at 12 percent for five years. The tax rate is 30 percent.

a. What will be the firm's earnings under each alternative if earnings before interest and taxes (EBIT) are $430,000?
b. If EBIT will remain $430,000 next year, what will be the firm's earnings under each alternative if short-term interest rates are 8 percent? If short-term interest rates are 14 percent?
c. Why do earnings tend to fluctuate more with the use of short-term debt than with long-term debt? If long-term debt had a variable interest rate that fluctuated with changes in interest rates, would the use of short-term debt still be riskier than long-term debt?

2. The following structure of interest rates is given:

Term of Loan	Interest Rate
1 year	7%
2 years	8%
5 years	10%
10 years	12%

Your firm needs $2,000 to finance its assets. Three possible combinations of sources of finance are listed below:

1)

Assets	$2,000	Liabilities $	0
		Equity	2,000

2)

Assets	$2,000	Liabilities $ 800 (a one-year loan)
		Equity 1,200

3)

Assets	$2,000	Liabilities $ 800 (a ten-year loan)
		Equity 1,200

a. The firm expects to generate revenues of $2,400 and have operating expenses of $2,080. If the firm's tax rate is 40 percent, what is the return of equity under each choice?
b. During the second year, sales decline to $2,100 while operating expenses decline to $1,900. The structure of interest rates becomes:

Term of Loan	Interest Rate
1 year	6%
2 years	7%
5 years	8%
10 years	10%

Given the three choices in the previous year, what is the return on equity for the firm during the *second* year?

c. What is the implication of using short-term instead of long-term debt during the two years?

3. a. What is the EOQ for a firm that sells 5,000 units when the cost of placing an order is $5 and the carrying costs are $3.50 per unit?
   b. How long will the EOQ last? How many orders are placed annually?
   c. As a result of lower interest rates, the financial manager determines the carrying costs are now $1.80 per unit. What are the new EOQ and annual number of orders?

4. A firm with annual sales of $1 million has the following balance sheet items that are financed with a bank loan costing 12 percent annually.

Inventory	$300,000
Accounts receivable	250,000

The industry averages for inventory turnover and the average collection period are 5 times and 45 days, respectively. How much in interest expense can the firm save if it achieves the industry averages for inventory turnover and the collection of accounts receivable? (Assume the previous year's inventory was also $300,000.)

5. A firm has the following accounts receivable:

Receivable	Amount Due	Days Outstanding
A	$1,000	35
B	2,500	42
C	1,500	57
D	3,500	29
E	1,200	48
F	3,100	52
G	1,700	39

The firm offers credit terms of net 30 days. Construct an aging schedule that shows the amount and percentage of total accounts receivable that are 0, 10, 20, and 30 days overdue.

6. A firm sells 100,000 units of inventory for $10 a unit. Inventory purchases and their costs were

Date	Inventory Purchased	Cost per Unit
1/2	30,000 units	$7.70
4/7	30,000	8.20
8/1	30,000	8.40
12/1	30,000	8.90

If the firm's income tax rate is 40 percent, how much will the firm save in taxes if it uses LIFO instead of FIFO for inventory valuation?

7. Management of a firm with annual sales of 5,000 units decides to establish the EOQ model for inventory management. The firm has two possible suppliers. Data concerning these suppliers are as follows:

Supplier A	Shipping costs $1,000 Per-unit carrying costs $74
Supplier B	Shipping costs $800 Per-unit carrying costs $80

a. What is the EOQ for each supplier?
b. If the firm establishes a safety stock of 100 units, what is the firm's average inventory for both suppliers?
c. What will be the firm's expected maximum and minimum inventory with each supplier?
d. If delivery takes eight days, what should be the firm's level of inventory when it places an order with supplier A?

8. Big Toy, Inc. annually sells 100,000 units of Big Blobs. Currently, inventory is financed through the use of commercial bank loans. Big Toy pays $12.20 per Big Blob. The cost of carrying this inventory is $3.20 per unit while the cost of placing an order involves expenses of $400 per order. Since Big Blobs are imported, delivery is generally twenty days but may be as long as thirty days. In order to manage inventory more efficiently, the management of Big Toy, Inc. has decided to use the EOQ model plus a safety stock to determine inventory levels.
   a. What is the economic order quantity?
   b. Today is January 1 and the current level of inventory is 10,000 units; when should the first order be placed based on the economic order quantity?
   c. Management always wants sufficient Big Blobs so that they never are out of stock. If management considers late deliveries to be the prime reason for being out of stock, what should be the safety stock?
   d. According to the above analysis, what are the maximum inventory, the minimum inventory, and the average inventory?
   e. If sales of Big Blobs double, will the average inventory also double?

9. Firm X has sales of $5,000,000; $3,000,000 are for cash, but two customers who generate sales of $2,000,000 pay after 30 days. Management believes that sales will increase by 20 percent if all customers have 30 days to pay. Should the firm change its credit policy given the following information?
   a. The cost of the additional goods sold is 70 percent of sales.
   b. Credit checks and collection costs will be $5,000.
   c. Three percent of the new sales will be uncollectible.
   d. The cost of borrowing the funds to carry the receivables is 12 percent.

cases

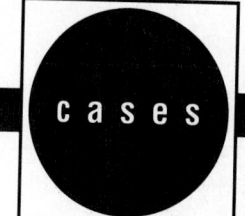

Using the Economic Order Quantity to Minimize Inventory Costs

Alexander and Charlene Weber operate a small retail store that serves a small, but wealthy, community. Most of the items carried tend to be high markup but slow moving goods. Since many of the goods are imported, there is often a substantial time lapse between when the goods are ordered and when they are received. No analysis is used to determine what is the best quantity to order. The Webers know that carrying excess inventory is expensive, because their commercial bank charges a substantial interest rate for the funds the Webers use to buy their inventory. Thus, they believe that better inventory management may increase profitability by reducing the amount of inventory they carry.

Sales are generally spread evenly throughout the year with a small increase during the Christmas season. The Webers recently read that a computer program would help them determine the best or optimal level of each order, so they purchased the program (a computerized model to calculate the economic order quantity). Since applying the model to all of the firm's inventory items seemed excessive, the Webers decided to first determine the economic order quantity (EOQ) of only three items. They would then use the EOQ of each item to determine what the average inventory should be, and use that information to determine how much could be saved in carrying costs. If there were a savings, then they could apply the model to more items carried in the store.

The annual sales of the three items (A, B, and C) is 120, 420, and 720 units, respectively. On the average, the Webers maintain four months' supply. The wholesale prices are $300, $128, and $85, for items A, B, and C, respectively. The Webers invest $36,000 in item A each year, and the average amount of inventory is 40 units ($12,000 invested). At an interest rate of 15 percent, the annual carrying cost of item A is $1,800, and the per-unit carrying cost is $15. The cost of placing an order, including shipping, is $150, $70, and $80 for items A, B, and C, respectively.

Case Problems

1. What is the annual amount invested in items B and C, and what are their per-unit carrying costs?
2. Based on the economic order quantity, what should be the average inventory of each item?

3. What is the potential savings in carrying costs if the firm adopts the average inventory associated with the EOQ?
4. If there is no potential savings in carrying costs, what does that imply about the ordering costs paid by the Webers?
5. Since the economic order quantity assumes no safety stock and the Webers want to carry inventory to cover five days' sales, what is the additional carrying cost (i.e., interest charges) necessary to sustain the safety stocks?

Suggested Readings

For texts devoted to working capital, obtain:

Gallinger, George W., and P. Basil Healey. *Liquidity Analysis and Management,* 2d ed. Reading, Mass.: Addison-Wesley Publishing Company, 1991.

Hampton, John J., and Cecilia L. Wagner. *Working Capital Management.* New York: John Wiley & Sons, 1989.

These texts emphasize a firm's everyday operations from a financial perspective. They cover such topics as analysis of cash flow, management of short-term assets, and international cash management.

Essentials of Cash Management, 2d ed. Newtown, Conn.: National Corporate Cash Management Association, 1985.

This is a book of readings covering collection systems, disbursement systems, methods for cash concentration, and the management of corporate liquidity. Each chapter includes a set of multiple choice questions that cover the material in the chapter and a suggested set of readings.

Other readings in current asset management include:

Altman, Edward I., ed. *Handbook of Corporate Finance.* New York: John Wiley & Sons, 1986.

Kallberg, Jarl G., and Kenneth L. Parkinson. *Current Asset Management.* New York: John Wiley & Sons, 1984.

These books include material on forecasting, automation, and the management of cash, accounts receivable, and inventory. Case studies and extensive bibliographies are also included.

chapter 20

Sources of Short-Term Funds

Learning Objectives

1. Differentiate the types of bank loans.
2. Explain compensating balances and how they affect the cost of a loan.
3. Distinguish between an installment loan and a mortgage loan.
4. Be able to determine the cost of trade credit.
5. List the advantages of accepting trade credit.
6. Distinguish among commercial paper, a bank loan, and trade credit.
7. Understand why commercial paper is a major source of credit for a small number of firms.
8. Explain how pledging or factoring accounts receivable can provide short-term finance.

Ralph Waldo Emerson said, "Pay every debt as if God wrote the bill." While short-term creditors are not God, they may possess a substantial amount of power over the firm. When a firm has financial difficulties, its problems generally arise when the firm is unable to meet its short-term obligations. Even if the firm has quality long-term assets, the inability to meet current obligations can cause the firm to fail. And such failure is not limited to firms. When the PTL (Praise the Lord) Club was racked by scandal during 1987, it too was forced into bankruptcy, for it was unable to meet its short-term obligations.

Few firms can exist without short-term funds. Even HRE Properties, a real estate firm that owns properties and leases them to others, has a few short-term obligations. (About $3.5 million of its $150.0 million in liabilities is short-term debt.) Virtually all the obligations of some firms are short-term. In its 1989 annual report, Salomon Inc., a large investment banker and securities dealer, reported assets of $118,250 million, of which 94.54 percent was financed with a variety of short-term debt obligations. That amounted to $111.8 billion in short-term debt!

Commercial banks are a major source of short-term financing for large and small firms, especially manufacturers, wholesalers, and retailers. Unless the firm is exceptionally risky, commercial banks may individually be the most important source of short-term funds. The first section of this chapter is devoted to the loans made by commercial banks. Special emphasis is placed on the terms of the loans and how they affect the true cost of the loan.

Many firms use their suppliers as a source of funds. Trade credit is spontaneous and is a major source of short-term finance for small firms, especially retailers. The text covers how this credit is created, the terms of the credit, and how the interest cost is figured.

Large, creditworthy firms have alternative sources of short-term finance. The third section of the chapter discusses commercial paper, which consists of unsecured promissory notes issued by corporations with excellent credit ratings. Since commercial paper is unsecured, its use is limited primarily to large firms. The terms, types, and interest cost of this paper are covered.

The last section of the chapter is devoted to other sources of short-term financing, including secured loans, warehouse financing, and factoring. There are significant differences in the terms and costs of short-term sources of financing, and not all of these sources will be available to every firm. The financial manager needs to know these terms and costs, for without this knowledge he or she will be unable to compare them. Such comparisons are, of course, necessary to select the source that best meets the firm's financial needs.

COMMERCIAL BANK LOANS

Commercial banks are concerned with liquidity; they want to make loans that are of a relatively short duration. Therefore, commercial banks are a primary source of short-term financing. Bank loans are used by virtually all types of firms, but the primary users of this type of loan are retailers and wholesalers. Firms that have large amounts of fixed assets do not use short-term bank financing to purchase the fixed assets, for such financing is inappropriate. Such long-term assets should be financed by long-term financing such as bonds or equity. Retailers and wholesalers, however, are primarily concerned with short-term assets, and bank loans are an appropriate means to finance these assets. The primary users of bank credit are small firms. While this does not mean that large firms do not use bank financing, the proportion of a firm's financing that is obtained from commercial banks declines as the size of the firm increases. Larger firms have the ability to obtain a larger variety or wider range of financing and thus do not have to rely so heavily on commercial banks.

A loan from a commercial bank is a package that is individually negotiated between the borrower and the bank. Since loans are individually negotiated, it is important for the potential borrower to maintain an excellent relationship with the banker. The negotiated package will include the size of the loan, the maturity date, the amount of the interest, any security requirements such as the pledging of specific assets of the firm or the subordination of other debt, and other limitations on the financial activity of the firm. Since the bank is lending its funds, it is generally in a position to demand financial constraints on the company. For example, the bank may demand that the firm maintain a minimum current ratio (such as 2 to 1), or the bank may place limitations on the ability of the firm to pay dividends.

Besides lending money, the bank may provide other services to the firm. For example, the bank's economists may be used for economic forecasts, or the bank may be a source of information on the financial condition of the borrower's credit customers. If the firm has foreign transactions, the bank can handle foreign exchange (i.e., foreign currency). These services may be advantageous to the firm and help justify borrowing from one bank rather than another.

Promissory note ▲
Document specifying the amount owed, the interest rate, the maturity date, and other features of a loan

The firm may borrow a specific amount of money or it may arrange for the right to borrow up to a specified amount. The former creates a promissory note while the latter is called a line of credit. A **promissory note** is an agreement between the borrower and the commercial bank for a specific amount of money for a specified time period. When the note is signed (i.e., executed), the bank credits the funds to the borrower's account with the bank. The note specifies the rate of interest, collateral requirements (if any), and the repayment schedule. Repayment either may be made in one lump payment or may be spread over time through a series of installment payments.

Line of credit ▲
Informal agreement in which a bank extends the right to borrow (at the option of the borrower) up to a specified amount

A **line of credit** is an informal (noncontractual) agreement that grants the firm an option to borrow up to a specified amount whenever the firm needs the funds. For example, the financial manager may arrange a line of credit for $500,000. If the firm requires $100,000 to finance inventory, the financial manager draws $100,000 from the line of credit. The firm now has a $100,000 loan outstanding but still can borrow an additional $400,000 if the funds are needed. The credit line thus offers the borrower the flexibility to use the credit only when it is needed. Under this type of agreement, the firm has a source of short-term financing but does not have to use the funds. Interest is paid only on the funds the firm actually borrows.

Revolving credit agreement ▲
Formal agreement in which the bank extends the right to borrow up to a specified amount within a specified time period

An alternative to the credit line is the **revolving credit agreement.** Revolving credit is similar to the line of credit in that the bank agrees to extend the firm credit up to a specified limit whenever the firm needs the funds. However, while the line of credit is an informal agreement, revolving credit is a formal, contractual obligation of the bank. The agreement has a time limit (generally a year to fifteen months), after which the terms are renegotiated. The bank charges a commitment fee for establishing revolving credit, which tends to be ¼ of a percent of the amount of credit granted by the bank. Thus, a revolving credit agreement for $10 million will require a payment of $25,000.

Fees charged by commercial banks for establishing revolving lines of credit may be paid either at the beginning or at the end of the loan period. If the fee is solely for establishing the credit, it is paid up front. If the fee is on the unused balance, the bank will not know the amount of the fee until after the period of the loan has elapsed. These differences may be seen by the following illustration of terms:

Bank A: $1,000,000 revolving credit for one year at 10 percent with a fee of ½ percent of the amount of the loan

Bank B: $1,000,000 revolving credit for one year at 10 percent with a fee of ½ percent on the unused balance of the loan

Bank C: $1,000,000 revolving credit for one year at 10 percent with a fee of ¼ percent of the amount of the loan and ¼ percent on the unused balance of the loan.

Bank A requires a payment of $5,000 when the credit is granted whether the loan is, or is not, used. If the creditor lacks the $5,000, the borrower may have to use the credit to cover this fee. Bank B requires a payment of $5,000 only if the loan is not used. Obviously, this payment cannot be made when the loan is granted. (The bank may determine the amount of this fee monthly instead of waiting until the end of the year.) Bank C initially charges $2,500, with the balance dependent upon the use of the revolving credit.

Revolving credit agreements are used primarily by large firms. The agreements are for many millions, and the bank usually farms out part of the loan so that a group of banks participate in the revolving term agreement. Revolving credit, like the line of credit, is used to finance short-term assets. However, the firm may also use revolving credit to finance the development of long-term assets. For example, the firm may draw on its revolving credit to pay for the construction of plant and equipment. After the plant is completed, the revolving credit is converted into an intermediate-term loan, or the firm may retire the outstanding balance on the revolving credit loan. This can be done through an issue of long-term bonds, new equity, or any other source of funds available to the borrower.

Cost of Commercial Bank Credit

The costs of the line of credit and revolving credit and their effective interest rates depend on the commitment fees charged, the interest paid, the amount borrowed, and how long the firm has the use of the funds. For example, a firm obtains revolving credit for $1,000,000 at 12 percent annually (i.e., 1 percent monthly) plus a commitment fee of ¾ percent on the *unused* balance. If the firm borrows the entire $1,000,000, the annual interest is $120,000. If the firm uses only $600,000 for the year, the interest cost will be $72,000 ($600,000 × 0.12) *plus* ¾ percent of the unused balance of $400,000 (i.e., $3,000). The total amount paid is $75,000 ($72,000 + $3,000) for the use of $600,000, so the effective interest cost of the loan is 12.5 percent ($75,000/$600,000). If the firm does not use the credit, it still must pay the $7,500 commitment fee, which is the cost of obtaining, but not using, the credit.

The cost of any type of bank loan varies with the quality of the borrower and the conditions of the loan. The bank's best customers (i.e., the best credit risks) are charged the **prime rate.** Other customers may be charged the prime plus a percentage, such as 2 percent. Thus, if the prime rate is 10.5 percent, the rate to other customers might be 12.5 percent. If the prime rate rises, the cost of other loans will also rise. Thus, any interest rate that is tied to the prime will vary as the prime rate varies.

Prime rate ▲
Interest rate charged by commercial banks on loans to their best customers

During periods of tight money, the prime rate can rise very rapidly to ration scarce credit. For example, the prime rate was 11.5 percent in July 1979, 15.5 percent in December 1979, and 20 percent in April 1980. The increase from 11.5 percent to 20 percent illustrates the potential volatility of the prime rate. These fluctuations are related to the demand for short-term funds and the supply of short-term credit. While the period July 1979 to April 1980 is unique, it does illustrate that short-term interest rates can significantly fluctuate during a limited period of time.

While commercial banks often quote a prime rate, some large corporate borrowers are able to negotiate loans at interest rates below the prime. Many commercial business loans made by the nation's largest banks are at a discount from the prime. This means that in effect there are two prime rates: the announced rate and the discounted rate, which is available to large corporate borrowers.

The effective cost of a commercial bank loan (or any loan) may not be the stated rate of interest. The effective cost is related to the interest paid, the amount of funds that the borrower can use, and the term of the loan. There are subtle ways in which the commercial bank can increase the effective cost of the loan by altering the amount that the borrower can use or by altering the length of time the loan is outstanding.

Equation 20.1 may be used to approximate the effective cost of a commercial bank loan (i_{CB}) that is paid off *with interest at maturity.*[1]

20.1
$$i_{CB} = \frac{\text{Interest paid}}{\begin{array}{c}\text{Proceeds of the loan}\\ \text{that the borrower}\\ \text{may use}\end{array}} \times \frac{12}{\begin{array}{c}\text{Number of months}\\ \text{that the firm has}\\ \text{use of the proceeds}\end{array}}.$$

How commercial banks increase the effective interest cost of a loan may be illustrated by several examples that use this equation. All of the subsequent examples will be based on the following simple loan: $1,000 at 6 percent for one year. The borrower has $1,000, and if the loan is retired at the end of the year and the borrower pays the $60 interest at that time, the cost of the loan is

$$\frac{\$60}{\$1{,}000} \times \frac{12}{12} = 6\%.$$

The borrower has the use of the $1,000 for the entire year and pays $60 for the use of the proceeds; thus the effective rate of interest is 6 percent.

The bank may require that the borrower pay the interest in advance; that is, the bank requires that the loan be discounted. The borrower receives not $1,000 but $940 ($1,000 − $60). In effect, the borrower is paying $60 for the use of $940, which increases the cost of the loan. Instead of an interest rate of 6 percent, the interest rate is

$$\frac{\$60}{\$940} \times \frac{12}{12} = 6.38\%.$$

[1]For non-annual compounding, see the discussions of trade credit and commercial paper later in this chapter.

By discounting the loan in advance the bank has caused the true cost of interest to rise from 6 percent to 6.38 percent.

A second method for affecting the cost of the loan is for the bank to require that the borrower maintain a **compensating balance.** A compensating balance is some proportion of the outstanding balance (such as 20 percent) that the bank requires the borrower to keep in an account in the bank. This compensating balance is not to be confused with any minimum balance that the bank may require to avoid service charges on the account. The compensating balance refers to the funds required on deposit by the loan. Funds used to meet the compensating balance may also serve to cover the minimum balance requirement and vice versa.

Compensating balance
Funds that a commercial bank requires be deposited as part of a loan agreement

The amount of the compensating balance and the account in which the funds are deposited are subject to negotiation. The net effect of this compensating balance, however, is to raise the interest cost of the loan. If the borrower must maintain a compensating balance of 20 percent, the cost is increased because the borrower has use of only 80 percent of the borrowed funds. The cost of the loan now becomes

$$\frac{\$60}{\$800} \times \frac{12}{12} = 7.5\%.$$

The borrower is in effect paying $60 for the use of $800, and the effective cost of the loan is 7.5 percent, which is considerably higher than the stated 6 percent interest rate.

If the firm needs the entire $1,000, it will have to borrow more than $1,000 to have that amount and cover the compensating balance. In this illustration, the financial manager will have to borrow $1,250. Then the firm will have the $1,000 to use plus the compensating balance of $250. The interest paid will be $75 ($1,250 × 0.6), so the effective cost of the loan is

$$\frac{\$75}{\$1{,}000} \times \frac{12}{12} = 7.5\%.$$

The amount of the loan necessary to cover the needed funds plus the compensating balance is given in Equation 20.2:

20.2
$$\text{The amount of the loan} = \frac{\text{Funds needed}}{1.0 - \text{Compensating balance requirement (as a decimal)}}.$$

The compensating balance requirement has the effect of reducing the denominator, which increases the amount borrowed. Thus, in this illustration, the amount of the loan with a 20 percent compensating balance is $1,000/(1.0 − 0.2) = $1,250.

Commitment fees paid up front have the same impact as the compensating balance. If the above firm had a commitment fee of ½ percent in addition to the compensating balance it would have to borrow \$1,257.86 (\$1,000/[1.0 − 0.2 − 0.005]) to meet the compensating balance and the commitment fee. The interest paid on \$1,257.86 is \$75.47 (\$1,257.86 × 0.06), so the effective interest rate to borrow \$1,000 is 7.547 percent:

$$\frac{\$75.47}{\$1{,}000} \times \frac{12}{12} = 7.547\%.$$

If the compensating balance is placed in a savings account or time deposit (and this is possible, for the loan is individually negotiated), the effective cost of the loan will not be 7.5%, because the borrower will earn interest on the funds in the savings account. In the example where \$1,000 is borrowed but a 20 percent compensating balance is required, if the borrower is permitted to place the funds in a savings account that pays 5 percent, the \$200 will earn \$10 in interest. The net interest that the borrower now pays for the loan is \$50, so the effective interest rate for the loan (assuming the firm does not borrow the compensating balance) is

$$\frac{\$50}{\$800} \times \frac{12}{12} = 6.25\%.$$

This effective cost is still greater than the stated 6 percent.

Another factor that affects the true interest cost of a loan subject to a compensating balance is the extent to which the borrower maintains funds in accounts at the bank. In Chapter 18 it was suggested that a firm will seek to maintain some amount of cash in a checking account to serve as a safety stock. This money may simultaneously serve as a compensating balance. Thus, if this borrower maintains a balance in a checking account of \$100, only an additional \$100 must be kept in the checking account to meet the 20 percent required compensating balance. In this case the borrower has the use of \$900 of the \$1,000 loan, and the effective interest rate becomes

$$\frac{\$60}{\$900} \times \frac{12}{12} = 6.67\%.$$

As these examples illustrate, the effect of the compensating balance on the cost of the loan is determined by various factors. These include the amount of funds that must be diverted from the loan to an account in the bank, the type of account, and the borrower's policy of maintaining funds in the account independent of the required compensating balance. However, the important question is always the same: Does the compensating balance increase the true cost of the loan? It is this effective cost that is important, and the financial manager should determine this cost in order to compare it with the costs of other sources of short-term credit.

Another way that the bank may increase the interest cost of a loan is to require that the loan be paid off in installments (i.e., be an **installment loan**). Instead of repaying the loan in one lump sum at the end of the loan's term, the borrower pays off the loan in equal installments. The monthly payments may be determined by adding the principal and the amount of interest and dividing by the number of pay periods. If the previous loan for $1,060 (i.e., $1,000 principal plus $60 interest) is paid off in equal monthly installments, the monthly installment is $88.33 [($1,000 + $60)/12].

Installment loan ▲
Loan retired in a series of equal payments

What is the effective interest rate being charged on this loan? Equation 20.1 cannot be used to determine the true rate of interest because the loan is being retired in installments instead of in one lump-sum final payment. Instead, Equation 20.3 is used to determine the effective rate of interest of an installment loan (i_{IL}).

20.3
$$i_{IL} = \frac{2md}{P(n + 1)}.$$

The definitions of the variables are

i_{IL} = the effective rate of interest
m = the number of periods in a year
d = the dollar amount of interest
P = the proceeds of the loan
n = the number of periods required for repayment

In this example the effective rate of interest is

$$i_{IL} = \frac{(2)(12)60}{1{,}000(12 + 1)} = \frac{1{,}440}{13{,}000} = 0.1108 = 11.08\%.$$

Even though the stated interest rate is 6 percent, the effective rate charged on the funds the borrower can use is 11.08 percent.

The fact that the borrower does not have the full use of $1,000 for a year may be seen in Exhibit 20.1, which presents the repayment schedule for the loan. The first and second columns present the pay period and the cumulative amount paid. Columns 3 and 4 give the amount of interest and the principal repayment. The last column shows the balance that the borrower owes (i.e., the amount the borrower still may use). The amount of interest is determined by using the effective rate on a monthly basis (i.e., 11.08%/12) times the balance owed in column 5. For example, at the end of six periods, the borrower has use of $514.33 and will pay $4.75 ($514.33 × 0.1108/12) in the next period for the use of $514.33 for one month.

It should be obvious from the repayment schedule that the true cost of the loan is not the stated 6 percent. After six pay periods the borrower

EXHIBIT 20.1

Repayment Schedule for $1,000 Installment Loan with 6% Interest and $88.33 Monthly Payment

The equal, monthly payments are divided into interest and principal repayment.

Number of Payment	Total Amount Paid	Interest Payment	Principal Repayment on $1,000	Balance Owed (Funds Available to Borrower)
1	$ 88.33	$9.23	$79.10	$920.90
2	176.66	8.50	79.83	841.07
3	264.96	7.76	80.57	760.50
4	353.32	7.02	81.31	679.19
5	441.65	6.29	82.04	597.15
6	529.98	5.51	82.82	514.33
7	618.31	4.75	83.58	430.75
8	706.64	3.96	84.37	346.38
9	794.97	3.20	85.13	261.25
10	883.30	2.41	85.92	175.33
11	971.63	1.62	86.71	88.62
12	1,059.96	0.82	87.51	1.11*

** This small balance is added to the last payment.*

has use of $514.33, but the $60 interest charge was determined on the $1,000 initially borrowed. Since the borrower does not have the use of $1,000 for a year, the true rate of interest must exceed 6 percent.

While installment loans are rarely used by firms of any substantial size, they are employed by consumers and small firms to finance purchases of durable goods (e.g., a car). Before truth-in-lending legislation (i.e., the Consumer Credit Protection Act of 1968), the lender would not necessarily inform the borrower of the effective interest rate of the loan. Instead, the interest would be stated as some percentage, such as 6 percent, but since the principal was being retired in installments, the effective cost was considerably higher. Truth-in-lending legislation has altered this practice, for now the lender is required to inform the borrower of not only the amount of interest that must be paid (which is called the finance charge) but also the effective rate of interest, the true cost of the debt.

Installment loans should not be confused with mortgage loans, illustrated in Exhibit 7.3. Both involve equal monthly payments. In the case of mortgages the amount of interest paid each month depends on the amount of principal that is still outstanding, but the total amount of interest does not depend on the total amount borrowed. Since the total amount of interest charged is determined from the outstanding principal, the effective cost of the loan can be determined from the stated interest rate.

The difference between an installment loan and a mortgage loan is not readily apparent by comparing Exhibit 20.1, the repayment schedule for the installment loan, and Exhibit 7.3, the repayment schedule for

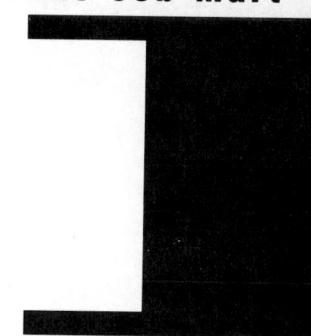

Credit Analyst

■ Job Description: Analyze and monitor the liquidity, debt service, and coverage of interest payments, cash flow, and industry trends that affect the creditworthiness of short-term borrowers. ■ Job Requirements: Bachelor's degree with knowledge of the analysis of financial statements and knowledge of credit rating services. The ability to write reports accurately and succinctly is also important. ■ Characteristics: This is an entry-level position; an individual may become a credit analyst after a modest period of training. The position may thus be viewed as a stepping-stone to a more advanced position, such as an investment analyst or portfolio manager.

---

the mortgage. The monthly payments are equal in both cases. The dollar amount of interest paid declines and the amount of principal retired monthly increases in both repayment schedules. The interest rate, which is paid on the balance of both the installment note and the mortgage, is a fixed percentage. Hence, the interest payment declines each month because the amount of principal declines. However, for the installment note, the *total* interest is not figured on the remaining balance of the loan but on the initial amount borrowed, while for the mortgage the *total* interest is determined from the balance owed. Thus, the effective interest rate for the installment loan is greater than the stated rate, while the stated and effective rates are equal for the mortgage.

In summary, commercial bank credit is a primary source of short-term financing. It is usually cheaper than alternative sources such as trade credit. The prime disadvantage of borrowing from a commercial bank is the extent to which the bank imposes restrictions on the firm. The bank is concerned with its liquidity and seeks to protect its investment. Therefore, it will demand those restrictions that it believes are necessary to insure repayment. These restrictions may be viewed by the borrower as excessive and thus may encourage the use of other sources of short-term financing.

TRADE CREDIT

Trade credit, which is credit granted by a firm's suppliers, is individually the most important source of short-term finance for small firms, especially retail establishments. It can be, however, a very expensive source, and the financial manager should be aware of the cost of this type of

Trade credit ▲
Credit extended by suppliers to their customers

credit. Trade credit arises when a supplier sells goods but does not demand immediate payment. Instead, the purchaser is permitted to choose between immediate payment or payment in the future. For immediate payment, or for payment within a short time period such as 10 days, the buyer may be given a discount, such as 2 percent off the purchase price. If the buyer does not remit during the first 10 days, payment in full must be made within a specified time period, such as 30 days. These terms are written 2/10, net 30, which means a 2 percent discount for payment within the first 10 days or the net (i.e., full) price within 30 days. These terms of trade have no mention of credit or interest payments and thus may not appear to be a source of short-term credit. But inventory must be financed, and goods acquired by trade agreements are no exception. When trade credit is used, the source of the finance is the supplier, who lets the buyer have the use of the goods before having to pay for them.

The fact that these trade agreements are a source of finance may be illustrated by T-accounts. A supplier sells $100 worth of goods to a retailer but does not receive immediate payment for the goods. Instead, the supplier accepts the retailer's promise to pay in the future. Excluding any profit or loss for the supplier, the effect on each firm's balance sheet is as follows:

SUPPLIER		RETAILER	
ASSETS	**LIABILITIES**	**ASSETS**	**LIABILITIES**
Accounts receivable ↑ $100		Inventory ↑ $100	Accounts payable ↑ $100
Inventory ↓ $100			

The supplier has accepted an account receivable for the output, and the retailer has received the goods, which are now part of inventory. The retailer does not immediately pay for the inventory but accepts a new liability, the account payable. This increase in liabilities finances the increase in inventory.

This type of arrangement may be very beneficial to a firm that must carry a large amount of inventory. As the firm expands its inventory, its suppliers expand their credit. The expansion of trade credit, then, is in response to the expansion in inventory and comes automatically without the need for the firm to seek credit elsewhere. If the firm is able to turn over the inventory rapidly, it may obtain cash quickly enough to pay the suppliers without having to use other sources of credit. For example, if the terms of trade credit are 2/10, net 30, the firm has the use of the goods for a month before payment is due. If the inventory turns over once a month, trade credit may be sufficient to cover the entire inventory. Of course, the firm is still paying the cost of the trade credit. If the firm is able to turn over the inventory only six times a year (i.e., every two months), trade credit will carry only one-half of the firm's inventory. Since the terms of trade are for one month and the inventory turns over every two months, the firm must find other sources of financing to cover the cost of maintaining the inventory for the second month.

The important question that the financial manager must consider is whether trade credit is the best source of finance for carrying the inventory. This is the question of the cost of trade credit versus the cost and availability of other sources of finance. The cost of the credit depends on the terms of the credit. If the terms are net thirty days (n30), the cost of the credit is nil. The supplier has built the cost of offering the credit into the price of the goods. Unless the financial manager can negotiate a discount for prompt payment, the firm should use the credit as extensively as possible, for there is no advantage to paying before the thirtieth day.

Cost of Trade Credit

If the terms are 2/10, net 30, trade credit is not free. It may appear that trade credit is free, for the supplier is permitting the buyer to use the goods for no explicit interest charge. That, however, is a misconception of what constitutes the *price* of the goods and the *interest charge.* In finance, the price of the product is considered to be the discounted price. The discounted price is the price that the buyer pays if cash is available and the buyer promptly pays for the goods. The net price, then, includes the purchase price plus a penalty for not paying the bill promptly. This penalty should be treated as the interest charge for the use of the goods. Thus, if an item costs $100 and is supplied under the terms 2/10, net 30, the price of goods is $98, and the firm has 10 days in which to pay it. If the firm does not or cannot meet that price within 10 days, it pays a finance charge (i.e., interest) of $2 for the use of the goods for the next 20 days. When expressed in those terms, the interest charge becomes evident.

How expensive trade credit really is may be seen when the interest cost (i_{TC}) is expressed in annual terms. This calculation may be approximated by Equation 20.4.

20.4

$$i_{TC} = \left(\frac{\text{Percentage discount}}{\text{100\% minus percentage discount}}\right) \text{times} \left(\frac{360}{\text{Payment period minus discount period}}\right)$$

The component parts of the equation are the percentage discount, the number of days for which the credit is extended (i.e., the payment period minus the discount period), and 360, which is the term that converts the cost to an annualized basis.[2] When the terms are substituted into this

[2]The use of 360 is a common convenience that has the effect of understating the interest rate.

equation, the cost of trade credit is determined. For 2/10, net 30, the cost of credit is

$$i_{TC} = \left(\frac{0.02}{1 - 0.02}\right)\left(\frac{360}{30 - 10}\right)$$
$$= 36.7\%.$$

On an annual basis 2/10, n30 costs approximately 36.7 percent, which is quite expensive compared with other sources of credit.[3]

Equation 20.4 may be used to illustrate the factors that affect the cost of trade credit. As may be seen from the equation, the cost of trade credit is related to (1) the amount of the discount and (2) the length of time for which the buyer has the use of the goods. An increase in the amount of the discount increases the cost of trade credit. An increase in the payment period reduces the cost of trade credit. Both of these statements may be explained with the aid of the equation.

An increase in the discount in effect reduces the price of the goods and increases the cost of carrying the goods on credit. If the discount were 3 percent instead of 2 percent (i.e., 3/10, net 30), then the firm would pay $97 for the goods during the first ten days and a $3 penalty for the use of the goods after the discount period. Using Equation 20.4, the cost of credit can be calculated as

$$i_{TC} = \left(\frac{0.03}{1 - 0.03}\right)\left(\frac{360}{30 - 10}\right)$$
$$= 55.7\%.$$

The cost of trade credit is now 55.7 percent, which is higher than the 36.7 percent cost of trade credit when the terms are 2/10, net 30. The increase in the discount then increases the cost of trade credit, for the penalty is larger (i.e., the interest charge is greater). Thus, if a supplier wants to induce prompt payment, one method is to increase the discount. This tells the buyer that credit is more expensive and should encourage the buyer to find credit elsewhere and pay the supplier promptly.

An increase in the payment period means that the buyer has the use of the goods longer, and thus the cost of trade credit is less. If the payment period is increased from 30 days to 60 days (i.e., 2/10, net 60), the cost of the trade credit becomes

$$i_{TC} = \left(\frac{0.02}{1 - 0.02}\right)\left(\frac{360}{60 - 10}\right)$$
$$= 14.7\%.$$

---

[3] 36.7 percent is a simple, non-compound rate of interest. As will be subsequently illustrated, the compound rate of interest is higher.

By lengthening the payment period from 30 to 60 days, the supplier has reduced the cost of trade credit from 36.7 percent to 14.7 percent. The cause of this reduction in cost is, of course, the fact that the buyer has the use of the goods for 30 additional days but does not have to pay a higher penalty for the longer time period. If a supplier wishes buyers to use trade credit, increasing the length of the payment period reduces the cost of trade credit and encourages its increased use.

The above equation may be used to compare the costs of different terms of trade credit. Such comparisons will permit management to select among the most advantageous terms of trade credit. Such selection is important if the firm has sufficient funds to pay some but not all of its suppliers promptly. If, for example, management faces the following terms of credit:

(a) 2/10, net 30

(b) 3/10, net 30

(c) 2/15, net 30,

it can determine that the cost of each is as follows:

$$\text{(a) } i_{TC} = \left(\frac{0.02}{1-0.02}\right)\left(\frac{360}{30-10}\right) = 36.7\%$$

$$\text{(b) } i_{TC} = \left(\frac{0.03}{1-0.03}\right)\left(\frac{360}{30-10}\right) = 55.7\%$$

$$\text{(c) } i_{TC} = \left(\frac{0.02}{1-0.02}\right)\left(\frac{360}{30-15}\right) = 49.0\%.$$

Thus, by determining the cost of each of the terms of trade credit, management knows that its scarce funds should be used to pay (b) first, because it is the most expensive of the three credit terms.

Actually, the above calculations understate the true annualized rates of interest, because they fail to consider the impact of compounding. If a supplier grants credit such as 2/10, n30 and collects the receivable after twenty days, the process may be repeated every twenty days. The supplier may compound the interest in excess of eighteen times annually.

To determine the true interest cost of trade credit, treat the credit as a discounted note and rephrase 2/10, n30 into the following question: \$98 at the beginning of the period (P_0) grows to \$100 at the end of the time period (P_n) of twenty days *at what rate* (i)? That is,

20.5

$$P_0(1+i)^{n/365} = P_n$$
$$\$98(1+i)^{n/365} = \$100,$$

in which n is the number of days in the credit period and i the true interest rate. If the terms of credit are 2/10, n30, then n is 20, and the equation to be solved is

$$98(1 + i)^{20/365} = \$100.$$

The solution is

$$(1 + i)^{0.05479} = \$100/\$98 = 1.0204$$
$$i = (1.0204)^{18.25} - 1 = 1.4456 - 1 = 44.56\%.$$

The effective rate of interest is 44.56 percent when the interest is compounded 18.25 times a year.[4]

This calculation for the determination of the compounded rate of interest when an amount (P_0) is borrowed for n days and the terminal value (P_n) includes the repayment of the principal plus the interest is stated in Equation 20.6.

20.6 $$i = (P_n/P_0)^{365/n} - 1.$$

Equation 20.6 may be used to determine the interest rate on any discounted loan in which the entire interest payment and principal repayment occur at the end of the term of the loan.

If a firm uses trade credit, when should it make payments? If a firm intends to pay the discount price and thereby not accept trade credit, the payment should be made as late as possible during the discount period. The price that the seller is charging includes the cost of supplying the goods during the discount period. Thus, the purchaser should seek to take advantage of this "free" use of the goods during the entire discount period, for the price paid includes this use of the goods. If the buyer is unable to make the payment by the end of the discount period, payment should be made at the end of the payment period. Once the discount period has passed, the buyer has to pay the cost of the trade credit. There is nothing to be gained by paying early. If early payment is made, the cost of trade credit is increased, for the buyer does not have the use of the credit for the entire period.

While the terms of trade credit set the cost of the credit, what affects these terms? Trade credit is very competitive, and suppliers are aware that the terms they offer may affect the sale of their products. By offering more generous terms, the supplier may be able to execute a sale. The terms of credit then become a means to differentiate one supplier from another. As each supplier tries to encourage sales by offering trade

---

[4] $(1.0204)^{18.25}$ may be determined by using an electronic calculator with a y^x key. Enter 1.0204; press the y^x key; enter 18.25; press =, and 1.4456 is derived.

credit, the terms of the various offers should be similar, for competition will force the suppliers to offer comparable terms.

If trade credit tends to be expensive, why is it used? There are several explanations. First, it is very convenient. By deferring payment until the end of the payment period, the buyer automatically receives the trade credit. Second, trade credit avoids several sources of financial interrogation. A public offering of securities is subject to the security laws, and a bank scrutinizes the financial condition of the borrower before a bank loan is granted. Trade credit, however, may automatically come from suppliers who do not require the buyer to be subjected to this financial analysis. Third, the buyer may lack an alternative source of credit. While bank credit is cheaper, it may not be available to risky small firms. Suppliers, however, need outlets for their goods, and offering trade credit may be a way to assure themselves of buyers for their goods. These suppliers are usually larger firms with established sources of credit. They are able to borrow at cheaper rates from their sources and in turn pass on the credit to the small retail firms. The sellers cannot exist without their markets. Trade credit may assure the existence of these markets by offering a source of finance to small firms that may lack alternative sources.

This section has covered the mechanics and cost of trade credit. In reality, however, trade credit may work differently. Buyers may stretch the terms of credit by either (1) remitting the discounted price after the payment period instead of the net price, or (2) "riding the credit" and paying after the payment period. This latter situation may occur if the buyer has not sold the inventory and does not have the funds to pay the supplier. Such practices, of course, reduce the cost of credit. When such practices occur, the suppliers then must decide whether to enforce the terms of the credit or be lenient and let the credit ride. In many cases the suppliers may not enforce the terms, for they need the retailers to purchase their goods. If the supplier's cost of credit is significantly lower than the cost of trade credit, the supplier may be able to afford to let the retailers ride the terms of credit. Such extensions of credit, however, cannot be indefinite. Eventually the supplier must decide how rapidly it wants to collect its accounts receivable. While suppliers may initially be lenient and not enforce the terms of trade, their cost of carrying the receivables will eventually force them to seek payment.

COMMERCIAL PAPER

Commercial paper consists of unsecured short-term promissory notes issued by corporations. The debt is issued in denominations of $100,000 or greater and usually matures in two to six months. It may have a maturity

Commercial paper ▲ Short-term unsecured promissory note issued by a corporation

date of only one day, but it never has a maturity date beyond nine months (270 days). Maturities of longer than 270 days must be registered with the SEC. By limiting commercial paper issues to less than 270 days, corporations avoid the expense of registering the issue with the SEC.

Since there are no specific assets backing commercial paper, only companies with exceptionally good credit ratings are able to issue this type of debt. The majority of firms are unable to sell commercial paper, and thus for them it cannot be a source of funds. Even though the paper is issued by large corporations with excellent credit ratings, there still is an occasional default. Perhaps the most celebrated example was the Penn Central Railroad. The firm had issued commercial paper and was thrown into bankruptcy when it was unable to retire the paper at the time of maturity. This failure to retire or refinance the paper inflicted large losses upon the buyers of the paper. And these losses then made it more difficult for other firms to sell their commercial paper.

Evidence of the quality of a firm's credit rating may be obtained through one of the credit rating services. These services and their respective ratings for commercial paper are

- Moody's Investor Service: Prime 1 (P-1), Prime 2 (P-2), and Prime 3 (P-3);
- Standard & Poor's Corporation: A-1, A-2, and A-3;
- Fitch Investors Service: F-1, F-2, and F-3.

P-1, A-1, and F-1 are the highest ratings, and these are obtained only by the best and safest firms.

Commercial paper is issued by a variety of firms, but the primary issuers are finance companies and large bank holding companies. These account for about three-fourths of all commercial paper sold. The rest is issued by manufacturers and utilities. Manufacturers may use it as a source of funds to meet seasonal needs, and utilities may issue commercial paper to help finance construction of plant and equipment. After the construction is completed, the firm sells new debt or equity, and the proceeds of the sale are used to retire the commercial paper. Thus, the commercial paper is often used as a temporary source of funds prior to the firm's obtaining more permanent financing.

Commercial paper has become a major source of funds, as can be seen from the substantial growth in the amount of paper outstanding. In 1975, $48 billion face amount of commercial paper was issued, but this amount grew to more than $533 billion in 1990. Part of this growth resulted from the Federal Reserve's tightening of credit. When commercial banks lack lending capacity, many firms substitute commercial paper for bank loans. Also, during this period there was a considerable growth in money market mutual funds, which invested heavily in commercial paper.

Firms may issue commercial paper and sell it directly to buyers. This is called *direct paper.* Direct sales require a sales staff or the service of an investment banker who is willing to place the paper. Such direct sales require sufficient volume of commercial paper to justify the sales expense. Direct paper constitutes the bulk of commercial paper issued. The remaining sales are made through dealers (*dealer paper*). These dealers generally charge ⅛ of one percent of the face amount for selling the paper (e.g., $1,250 for $1 million principal amount).

Commercial paper is purchased by banks, insurance companies, financial institutions, pension funds, trust departments, and companies that have excess liquidity and need a safe short-term investment. Individual investors rarely have a sufficient amount of money to participate in the market for commercial paper, especially when it is issued in large denominations such as $100,000. Of course, individuals may indirectly participate by purchasing shares of money market mutual funds, which in turn buy commercial paper.

For large corporations, commercial paper is a substitute for other types of short-term debt. It is usually cheaper than bank loans, for the interest cost is generally about 0.5 percent less than the prime rate. Unlike bank loans, commercial paper does not have restrictive convenants and may not have a compensating balance requirement. This is particularly true for paper with the highest credit ratings. However, the investment community frequently requires that the issuing firm have unused credit lines at a bank to support the paper. To get these credit lines, the firm may have to maintain a compensating balance of 10 to 20 percent of the line of credit. Thus, to sell commercial paper the firm must still bear the cost of the credit line, but other restrictions often required by banks are not placed on the firm.

Commercial paper does not pay a stated amount of interest. Instead the paper is sold for a discount. A $1 million 180-day note may be sold for $950,000. When the paper matures, the firm retires $1 million of debt and thus pays $50,000 for the use of $950,000 for six months. To figure the interest rate, Equation 20.1, which was used earlier to calculate the cost of a bank loan, may be rephrased and used to approximate the cost of commercial paper. In this example, the approximate cost of commercial paper (i_{CP}) is

20.7

$$i_{CP} = \frac{\text{Interest}}{\text{Proceeds used}} \times \frac{12}{\text{Number of months paper is outstanding}} = \frac{\$50{,}000}{\$950{,}000} \times \frac{12}{6} = 10.53\%.$$

If the paper had been for $940,000, the approximate cost would have risen to

$$i_{CP} = \frac{\$60{,}000}{\$940{,}000} \times \frac{12}{6} = 12.77\%,$$

because the firm now pays \$60,000 for the use of \$940,000, while in the previous example it paid \$50,000 for the use of \$950,000.

As with the cost of trade credit, this simple calculation is an oversimplification, because it does not consider the impact of compounding. This omission is readily corrected by rephrasing the problem as follows:

$$\$950{,}000(1 + i)^{n/365} = \$1{,}000{,}000$$

in which n is 180 days. So, the compounded interest rate is

$$(1 + i)^{180/365} = \$1{,}000{,}000/\$950{,}000 = 1.0526$$
$$i = (1.0526)^{2.0278} - 1 = 1.1124 - 1 = 11.24\%$$

when the six-month paper was sold for \$950,000, and

$$(1 + i)^{180/365} = \$1{,}000{,}000/\$940{,}000 = 1.0638$$
$$i = (1.0638)^{2.0278} - 1 = 1.1336 - 1 = 13.36\%$$

when the paper was sold for \$940,000.

In these illustrations, the compounded rates of interest are only slightly higher than the rates using the simple, approximation formula (11.24 percent versus 10.53 percent and 13.36 percent versus 12.77 percent). Compounding makes a difference, but the discrepancy is not as large as when comparing the true cost and the approximation of the cost of trade credit. Commercial paper with a term of 180 days compounds only twice a year while trade credit with a twenty-day credit period compounds eighteen times a year. Obviously, commercial paper with a shorter maturity (e.g., 30 days or less) compounds more frequently, and the impact of such compounding should be considered when determining the true cost of the paper.

Even after adjusting for compounding, the rate may still understate the true cost of the paper. If the firm pays a dealer a fee to sell the paper, the proceeds of the sale are reduced, which raises the cost. If the issuer must maintain a credit line with a commercial bank in order to sell the paper, the costs associated with the credit line also reduce the amount of cash the issuer can use from the sale of the paper. Once again, these expenses raise the cost of borrowing through the issuance of commercial paper.

SECURED LOANS

The last type of short-term debt to be considered in this chapter is secured loans. Inventory, accounts receivable, or any other sound short-term asset (e.g., government security) may be used to secure a short-term loan. This collateral then serves to protect the loan because the lender has a lien against the asset. This security should increase the availability of credit and reduce the interest cost of the loan to the borrower.

Secured loans are made by commercial banks and other financial institutions. These lenders make their profits through the lending process; they do not want to take title to the pledged assets. If they are forced to take the pledged asset, they can choose either to hold the asset or to liquidate it. Liquidation will rarely bring the face value of the asset; thus the lender will not grant a loan for the entire value of the pledged asset. Instead, the bank or finance company may lend some proportion, such as 70 percent of the asset's stated value. The borrower must have some equity in the asset that will be lost in case of default and seizure of the asset. This equity then is a margin of safety for the creditor. The amount that the creditor will lend against the pledged asset depends on the quality of the pledged asset, the ease with which the asset can be liquidated should the debtor default, the anticipated value, and the transaction costs of liquidation. A firm's short-term assets are not equally desirable for pledging against short-term loans. Inventory is less liquid than accounts receivable (especially raw materials and goods-in-process). Hence, creditors may be less willing to accept inventory than accounts receivable as collateral to secure short-term loans.

When inventory is pledged to secure a loan, one of three general types of agreement is used. In the first type of agreement, the lender receives a lien against all of the borrower's inventory. Such an agreement is frequently referred to as a blanket inventory lien because it covers all of the inventory. The second type of inventory loan is a trust receipt. The borrower holds specified inventory in trust for the lender. As these goods are sold, the borrower remits the proceeds to the lender to retire the loan.

The third type of loan secured by inventory involves a third party (in addition to the borrower and the lender). The pledged inventory is placed in a warehouse controlled by the third party, who is usually in the business of warehousing. When purchase orders for the merchandise are received, the borrower informs the lender of the pending sales. The lender instructs the warehouse to deliver the goods, and the proceeds of the sale are then used to repay the loan. Such warehouse financing obviously reduces the risk of loss to the creditor, because the creditor has effective control over the goods. The warehouse will only release the inventory on the instructions of the lender.

Just as warehouse financing is advantageous to lenders, it can also have advantages to borrowers. Manufacturers know that finished goods may not be sold as soon as they are available for sale. (If finished goods were sold that quickly, the need to finance them would be limited to the time required to convert the raw materials into finished goods.) Obviously, the goods have to be stored until they are sold and delivered. Unless the firm uses its own facilities, it will store the inventory at a warehouse and pay for the space. Thus, the warehouse may offer the manufacturer both space and the custodial service that facilitates financing the inventory.

When accounts receivable are used to help obtain short-term financing, the firm may either pledge the accounts to secure the loan or sell them outright for cash. When the accounts are pledged, the borrower retains them and, of course, must collect them. If an account cannot be collected, the firm still owes the bank or finance company the amount of the loan that was secured by the account.

The lender is aware that not all accounts receivable may be collected. If an account does not meet the lender's standards, it is not accepted as collateral for a loan. The lender realizes that if a buyer were to default on the receivable, the seller (i.e., the borrower and owner of the account receivable) might not be able to pay off the loan. By refusing to accept riskier accounts receivable as collateral, lenders protect themselves from the risk of loss.

Pledging short-term assets offers the firm a cost advantage over other sources of finance. The security for the loan reduces the cost of obtaining short-term financing from finance companies, and secured loans are much cheaper than trade credit. Secured credit from finance companies is generally more expensive than credit from commercial banks, but it has the advantage of avoiding the restrictions placed on the firm by commercial banks. While these restrictions may not have stated costs, the management of the firm may feel that there are implicit costs in the restrictions and thus may avoid bank credit when other sources of short-term financing exist. Bank credit can always be used in addition to this secured credit should the need arise.

FACTORING

Factoring
Selling of accounts receivable

If the firm does not want to retain and collect its accounts receivable, it may sell them. This process is called **factoring.** The sale of the accounts receivable is a source of funds, because a reduction in any asset is a cash inflow. Thus, factoring the accounts receivable is similar to pledging the accounts and borrowing from a commercial bank. In both cases, the firm receives cash. The question then becomes: What is the advantage offered by factoring?

Factoring offers one major advantage: The seller is no longer concerned with collecting the accounts receivable. The risk of collecting is transferred to the buyer (i.e, the factor).[5] However, there are two means by which the factor can control this transfer of risk. First, when the seller

[5]The factor can demand and may receive recourse if there is a default, in which case the risk is not transferred from the seller to the factor.

receives an order on credit, he or she may be required to have the sale approved by the factor. If the factor believes that the credit sale is a bad risk, approval may be denied (i.e., the factor may refuse to accept the account receivable). Thus, the seller will have to choose between carrying the account or refusing the credit sale. Second, the factor may either accept the receivable at a substantial discount or establish a large reserve that is not remitted until the account is collected. The larger the discount or the larger the reserve, the greater is the incentive not to factor the account receivable. The firm must then decide if its cash needs are sufficient to accept the discount or the reserve.

Factoring is often considered to be an expensive source of funds. This need not be the case if the financial manager compares the cost of factoring to 2/10, n30 from suppliers or to a commercial bank loan with a large compensating balance and other subtle terms that increase the cost of the loan. The cost of factoring depends on (1) the factor's commission, (2) the interest cost on the outstanding balance owed the factor, and (3) any reserve held by the factor. The commission cost is generally 2.5 percent of the price and covers the cost of credit checks and collections. The interest rate is generally related to other short-term interest rates. The reserve is similar to any reserve set up for the collection of loans. However, since the factor does not remit the amount of the reserve to the seller until the account is collected, the reserve both increases the cost of the source of funds to the seller and gives the factor a means to control his or her risk exposure.

How these elements affect the cost of factoring may be seen in the following illustration in which a firm makes a \$10,000 credit sale for n30 and the resulting account receivable is sold to a factor. The factor (1) charges a 2.5 percent commission, (2) charges the seller 10 percent interest on the balance owed the factor, and (3) establishes a \$1,000 reserve. What does the firm receive from the sale of the account? First, the factor takes out the \$250 commission (\$10,000 × 0.025). Second, since the account will be outstanding for a month, the factor takes out \$83.33 in interest (\$10,000 × 0.1 × 1/12). Third, the factor holds the \$1,000 reserve. So, the firm receives \$10,000 − (\$250 + \$83.33 + \$1,000), or \$8,666.67. If it is assumed that the reserve is returned at the end of the month, the firm has paid \$333.33 for the use of \$8,666.67 for one month, which is an interest cost (before considering compounding) of:

$$\frac{\$333.33}{\$8{,}666.67} \times \frac{12}{1} = 46.1\%.$$

If the reserve had been only \$200, the firm would have received \$9,466.67, and the interest cost would have been

$$\frac{\$333.33}{\$9{,}466.67} \times \frac{12}{1} = 42.3\%.$$

Thus, the smaller the reserve, the lower is the interest rate.

These interest costs are substantial, but they probably overstate the cost of factoring. Since the firm has passed the costs of credit checks and collections to the factor, it avoids these expenses. However, credit checks and collection costs are included in the above calculations, since they are embodied in the factor's commission. If the seller can obtain the same services for less than the $250 commission fee, then the factor is expensive. However, many sellers may not be able to perform these tasks as cheaply as the factor. In this case, the combined costs of credit checks, collection expenses, and the carrying of the accounts may be more expensive than selling the accounts to the factor.

SUMMARY

The management of a firm's current assets and liabilities is one of the most important facets of the financial manager's job. The firm must meet its current obligations as they come due or face bankruptcy. Short-term debt (current liabilities) is a major source of finance for current operations, but it is also a potential problem since it must be frequently retired or rolled over, increasing the firm's risk.

The major sources of short-term funds are loans from commercial banks, trade credit, commercial paper, secured loans, and factoring. Commercial banks may grant short- to intermediate-term loans called promissory notes, installment loans, and long-term mortgage loans. The banks may also grant lines of credit and revolving term credit agreements that may be converted into intermediate-term loans at maturity. Discounting loans in advance, requiring compensating balances, and charging commitment fees are methods banks use to increase the effective cost of the credit.

Many firms use trade credit, which is spontaneously generated through purchases of inventory. The seller grants the credit (an account receivable to the seller and an account payable for the borrower) to encourage the sale. Trade credit is a particularly important source of credit for small retailers who may lack other sources of short-term finance. The terms of credit (such as 2/10, net 30) establish the cost of this credit, but many firms attempt to ride their accounts payable, which reduces the cost of trade credit.

Large, creditworthy firms are able to issue commercial paper, which consists of unsecured promissory notes sold in large denominations through dealers or directly placed with buyers. Commercial paper is sold for a discount. At maturity the issuing firm pays the principal, so the cost of the paper to the issuing firm depends upon how long the security is outstanding and the difference between the discounted price and the principal amount.

Firms may also factor (i.e., sell) accounts receivable to raise cash, and they may pledge current assets, such as inventory or accounts receivable, as collateral for loans. These secured loans are for less than the value of the collateral, because the creditors do not want to take title to the collateral, and liquidation will rarely bring the face value of the asset. Without this reduction in risk, it is doubtful that the lenders would be willing to grant the short-term credit.

Since the terms of the various types of short-term credit differ, the financial manager must find a means to compare them. Such comparisons may be achieved by determining the effective interest rate of each source of credit. By analyzing how much the firm pays and how long the firm gets the use of the credit, the financial manager is able to express all the sources on a common basis. This process should determine which source is cheapest and facilitate the selection of the best source of short-term credit.

Summary of Equations

Commercial bank loan with interest and principal paid at the end of the time period (not compounded):

20.1

$$i_{CB} = \frac{\text{Interest paid}}{\begin{array}{c}\text{Proceeds of the loan that}\\ \text{the borrower may use}\end{array}} \times \frac{12}{\begin{array}{c}\text{Number of months that}\\ \text{the firm has the use}\\ \text{of the proceeds}\end{array}}$$

Installment loan:

20.3

$$i_{IL} = \frac{2md}{P(n + 1)}$$

Trade credit (not compounded):

20.4

$$i_{TC} = \frac{\text{Percentage discount}}{\begin{array}{c}\text{100\% minus percentage}\\ \text{discount}\end{array}} \times \frac{360}{\begin{array}{c}\text{Payment period minus}\\ \text{discount period}\end{array}}$$

When a short-term loan consists of an initial amount borrowed (P_0) for n days and a terminal payment consisting of interest and principal (P_n), the compounded annual rate of interest (i) is

20.6

$$i = (P_n/P_0)^{365/n} - 1$$

Commercial paper (not compounded):

20.7

$$i_{CP} = \frac{\text{Interest}}{\text{Proceeds used}} \times \frac{12}{\begin{array}{c}\text{Number of months}\\ \text{paper is outstanding}\end{array}}$$

Review Questions

1. Why is a line of credit or a revolving credit agreement a flexible source of short-term funds? What does it mean to say that the interest rate is not fixed but is a variable rate? If a firm has a revolving credit agreement but does not borrow any funds, must it pay any interest or fees associated with the agreement?
2. Why is trade credit a spontaneous source of funds? Who uses trade credit? What advantages does it offer?
3. If you were a supplier and your customers had a high rate of failure, would you increase or decrease the cash discount when stating the terms of trade credit? Would you lengthen or shorten the discount period or pay period?
4. If a firm needs to finance purchases of plant and equipment, should it use trade credit or a credit line with a commercial bank as the source of these funds?
5. Why do discounted loans and installment loans yield a true rate of interest on the principal that is greater than the rate of interest stated? To determine the true interest rate, what factors should be considered? What role does truth-in-lending legislation play in informing borrowers of the cost of a loan?
6. If the terms of credit are n30, what is the cost of the credit? Since all accounts receivable must be financed, who is supplying the funds when a firm uses trade credit?
7. What is the difference between a line of credit and a revolving credit agreement? Why does a compensating balance increase the cost of a bank loan?
8. Do all firms that borrow from commercial banks pay the prime rate?
9. How does an installment loan differ from a mortgage loan?
10. What is commercial paper and who issues it? If you had $5,000, could you buy commercial paper? Compared to many investments, purchasing commercial paper is relatively safe. Why?

Problems

1. Firm A borrows $1 million from a commercial bank. The bank charges an annual rate of 15 percent and requires a compensating balance of 10 percent of the value of the loan. What is the interest cost of the loan? (Assume the loan is outstanding for one year.)
2. Which of the following terms of trade credit is the more expensive?
   a. A 3 percent cash discount if paid on the fifteenth day with the bill due on the forty-fifth day (i.e., 3/15, net 45).
   b. A 2 percent cash discount if paid on the tenth day with the bill due on the thirtieth day (i.e., 2/10, net 30).
3. Trade credit may be stated as n60 plus 18 percent on the balance outstanding after two months. What is the cost of this credit?
4. If $1 million face amount of commercial paper (270-day paper) is sold for $965,000, what is the approximate annual rate of interest being paid? What is the effective compound rate?

5. A financial manager may sell $1 million of six-month commercial paper for $950,000 or borrow $1 million for six months from a commercial bank for 10 percent annually and a 5 percent compensating balance. Which set of terms is more expensive?

6. Bank A offers the following terms for a $10 million loan:
   - interest rate: 12 percent for one year on funds borrowed
   - compensating balance: 10 percent of the outstanding balance
   - commitment fee: 0.5 percent of the unused balance for the unused term of the loan

   Bank B offers the following terms for a $10 million loan:
   - interest rate: 12.6 percent for one year on funds borrowed
   - compensating balance: 7 percent of the outstanding balance
   - commitment fee: none

   a. Which terms are better if the firm intends to borrow the $10 million for the entire year?
   b. If the firm plans to use the funds for only three months, which terms are better?

7. A cash manager has $1,000,000 to invest and is considering two money market instruments that are sold at a discount. The first is a piece of commercial paper that is due in three months and currently sells for $974,000. The alternative investment is a three-month $1,000,000 Treasury bill that sells for $979,000. What are the approximate and effective yields offered by these two securities?

8. A commercial bank offers you a $200,000 annual line of credit with the following terms:
   - origination fee: $2,000 paid when the line is accepted
   - fee on unused balance of 1 percent paid at the end of the year
   - interest rate of 9 percent
   - compensating balance equal to 5 percent of the outstanding balance owed

   What is the effective cost of the loan

   a. if you expect to borrow the entire $200,000 for the year?
   b. if you expect to borrow the $200,000 for only three months?

9. What is the effective interest rate on a $5,000 installment loan for a car that is paid off in monthly installments over three years when the stated interest rate is 10 percent (i.e., total interest payment of $1,500 or $500 annually for three years)?

10. Little Store buys inventory using trade credit. The terms are stated as 2/10, n30, but Little Store rides the credit and generally pays on the fortieth day. Occasionally, payment is made as late as the fiftieth day. What is the approximate cost of the credit (a) if paid on time, (b) if paid on the fortieth day, and (c) if paid on the fiftieth day? What is the true, effective cost of credit in each case? Why does the cost change?

11. High Time's suppliers tend to offer generous terms of trade credit (2/30, n90), but High Time can also issue commercial paper, receive $0.978, and repay $1.00 at the end of sixty days. What are the effective interest rates offered by the two alternatives? What would be the impact if High Time's suppliers changed the terms to n30?

12. CD Inc. is a large distributor of compact discs. It carries a wide selection of discs that are purchased on credit. Its suppliers generally offer 1/10, n40. CD Inc. may also obtain credit from a local commercial bank at 10 percent plus a compensating balance of 20 percent, or it can issue commercial paper. Currently, 90-day paper is priced at $97,533 per $100,000. Management, however, is anticipating interest rates to rise and expects the following changes: (1) the terms of trade credit to change to 1/10, n30, (2) the bank rate to increase to 11 percent, and (3) the discount on the commercial paper to rise and the price to fall to $97,250.
    a. Which of the three alternatives is the cheapest source of finance if interest rates do not rise?
    b. If interest rates do rise, which of the three alternatives offers the cheapest credit?

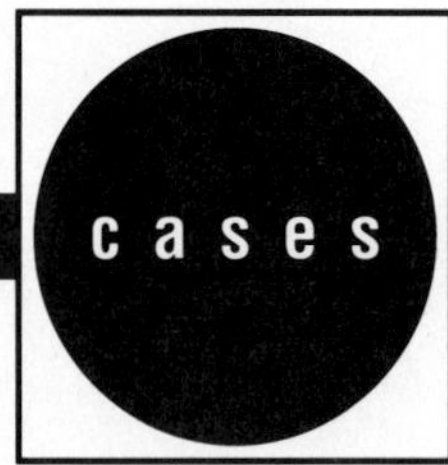

Determining the Cost of Short-Term Funds

Alaine Scarlatti is the financial manager of a moderately sized manufacturer of women's apparel. The firm has been exceptionally successful in the market for young women ages 25 to 40. It has seasonal needs for working capital, and its excellent credit rating has given it the enviable position of being able to consider a variety of possible sources. Ms. Scarlatti is planning the firm's short-term financing strategy for the next six months. She anticipates either one of two situations arising:

1. The firm will need $40,000,000 for six months.
2. The firm will need $40,000,000 for only three months.

Ms. Scarlatti, however, must plan for either situation since there is an equal likelihood that either will occur.

One possible source of short-term funds is commercial paper. She has been informed that the firm may issue $42,190,000 worth of commercial paper and receive $40,000,000. The paper will be due at the end of six months. A second possibility is to borrow from the First Bank of Town which offers a line of credit with an annual interest rate of 9.5 percent and a compensating balance requirement of 7 percent. A competing bank, the First Bank of City, offers revolving credit of $50,000,000 at 9 percent but with a fee on the unused balance of 0.5 percent paid at the end of the six months.

In order to help Ms. Scarlatti determine which of the three alternatives is the most attractive, answer the following questions.

Case Problems

1. How much will the firm have to borrow from each bank?
2. What is the interest rate on each of the alternatives if the money is borrowed for six months? (To ease the comparison, compute simple, non-compound rates of interest.)
3. If the firm generates $40,000,000 after three months and thus can pay off the loan, what is the rate of interest under each alternative?
4. If Ms. Scarlatti does select the commercial paper and the firm generates the $40,000,000 at the end of three months, she expects to be able to invest the money in a three-month Treasury bill that will earn $700,000. What impact will that have on the interest rate paid for the commercial paper?
5. Is the difference between a line of credit and a revolving credit agreement important to Ms. Scarlatti's decision?
6. Which alternative source of finance do you believe Ms. Scarlatti should accept?

Suggested Readings

Ballinger, George W., and P. Basil Healey. *Liquidity Analysis and Management,* 2d ed. Reading, Mass.: Addison-Wesley Publishing Company, 1991.

This is one of the few textbooks devoted to working capital. Its title is misleading in that the book covers not only the management of liquidity and short-term assets but also the management of accounts payable, off–balance sheet financing, factoring, hedging, signals of financial distress, and reorganization. The chapters have extensive reading lists; however, these tend to stress academic offerings over material written for practitioners.

Christie, George N., and Albert E. Bracuti. *Credit Management.* Lake Success, N.Y.: Credit Research Foundation, 1981.

This is a general reference on credit policy and its application.

Smith, Keith V. *Management of Working Capital,* 3d ed. St. Paul, Minn.: West Publishing, 1988.

This is a collection of individual readings on working capital and sources of short-term funds. The reader should be forewarned that some of this material is technical and requires an understanding of mathematics.

Standard & Poor's Corp. *Credit Overview.* Standard & Poor's Corp., 1982.

This book highlights the key areas of analysis used by Standard & Poor's to determine their credit ratings of short- and long-term debt instruments.

Stigum, Marcia. *The Money Market: Myth, Reality, and Practice,* rev. ed. Homewood, Ill.: Dow Jones-Irwin, 1983.

This comprehensive volume discusses in detail the major sources of short-term funds.

chapter

21

Intermediate-Term Debt and Leasing

Learning Objectives

1. Differentiate the features of intermediate-term notes from long-term bonds.
2. Calculate the repayment schedule of a term loan.
3. Differentiate operating and financial leases.
4. Explain the accounting for leases.
5. Determine if the firm should lease or buy a piece of equipment.
6. Illustrate the impact of leasing on the debt ratio used to analyze a firm's use of financial leverage.

"That which we call a rose by any other name would smell as sweet." This famous line, spoken by Juliet from her balcony, could be paraphrased by the financial manager as, "That which we call a debt by any other name would still be a debt." So it is with leasing. A lease is an obligation that resembles debt because a lease requires the firm to enter into certain obligations, such as lease payments. In 1990, The Limited reported that its long-term debt was $445.7 million but that its lease obligations would exceed $250 million annually for 1990 through 1994 and $1.2 billion after 1994.

Some firms own properties in order to lease them. Washington Real Estate Investment Trust, for example, owns shopping centers and rents the properties to retail stores, such as Dart Drug and Bradlee. These retail establishments are committed to lease payments that, unlike interest and debt repayments, are often tied to the level of sales. If the firm does well, the amount of the lease payment rises. Such lease contracts permit the owners of the properties to enjoy the success of those who rent the properties.

While the previous chapter considered short-term debt obligations, and Chapters 9 and 12 covered the variety of corporate bonds, this chapter will cover two alternatives to short-term debt and long-term bonds: intermediate-term debt and leasing. Since these two sources require the firm to enter into fixed, legal obligations, they are similar to other types of debt financing. The chapter describes the features and terms of intermediate-term debt and leases and covers what the financial manager should consider when selecting them over alternative sources of funds.

INTERMEDIATE-TERM DEBT

Intermediate-term debt ▲
Debt instrument with five to ten years to maturity

Term loan ▲
Loan obtained from a bank or insurance company for a period of five to ten years

While accountants classify all liabilities as either short-term (due in less than one year) or long-term (due in more than one year), debt can also be classified as short-term, intermediate-term, or long-term. **Intermediate-term debt** is outstanding for more than a year (and hence appears as long-term debt on the firm's balance sheet), but it matures quicker than long-term debt. While long-term bonds may mature twenty, twenty-five, or thirty years after being issued, most intermediate-term debt will mature in five to ten years.

Intermediate-term debt issued by corporations and sold to the general public may be referred to as "notes" to differentiate it from the bonds of the corporation, which are long-term debt. For example, in January 1991, Ford Capital, a finance subsidiary of Ford, issued $500 million of seven-year notes. Different terminology may be used when intermediate-term debt is obtained from a commercial bank or an insurance company. Such debt is often referred to as a **term loan.**

Notes and term loans are alternatives to long-term debt financing, and the characteristics of intermediate-term debt can be significantly different from those of long-term debt. Term loans are usually secured by equipment or real estate. Commercial banks, which make term loans of one to five years' duration, generally require that the loan be secured by equipment. Insurance companies, which tend to make term loans of from five to fifteen years, generally use real estate as collateral for the loan.

In addition to the collateral, term loans have restrictive covenants that are negotiated between the debtor and the creditor. Common restrictions include a minimum current ratio such as 2.5:1, or a minimum amount of net working capital (i.e., the difference between current assets and current liabilities must exceed some specified dollar amount). The creditors will also require periodic financial statements from the borrower and may require prior approval before the debtor can issue additional debt. While these restrictive covenants are commonly found in term loan agreements, they do not exhaust all the possibilities, as each loan is individually negotiated. Conditions in the credit markets and the relative strengths of the parties will obviously affect the terms that are ultimately agreed on.

Term loans are generally paid back in installments and hence are like the mortgage loans discussed in the previous chapter. The repayment schedules call for the payment of interest and the retirement of the principal. The way in which the payment is determined and the schedule of the reduction in a term loan are illustrated by the following example.

A firm wants a piece of equipment that costs $12,000 and has an expected life of five years. The firm arranges a term loan with a commercial bank. The conditions of the loan are

1. The firm must make a down payment of 20 percent of the cost of the equipment.
2. The firm must make five equal and annual payments that retire the loan and meet the interest that is due.
3. The rate of interest is 9 percent figured on the declining balance.
4. The equipment must be pledged to secure the loan and in case of default may be seized by the creditor to satisfy any outstanding balance on the loan.

The first condition establishes the amount that the bank is willing to loan. Notice that the bank is not willing to lend the entire amount and instead requires that the borrower have some funds invested in the equipment. In this case the borrower must put up $2,400 (0.20 × $12,000) and the bank will finance the balance, $9,600. Terms 2 and 3 establish the rate of interest and the means of payment. The fourth term designates the equipment as collateral against the loan and gives the bank the right to take the equipment and sell it to recoup the bank's funds should the debtor default.

The repayment schedule is determined as follows. The borrower must make equal annual payments so that the $9,600 lent by the bank earns 9 percent annually and the loan is retired in five years. This is an-

EXHIBIT 21.1

Repayment Schedule for a $9,600 Term Loan at 9 Percent for Five Years

The annual interest payment declines as the balance owed is reduced, and the principal repayment increases with each payment.

Year	Payment	Interest	Principal Retirement	Balance Owed on Loan
1	$2,467.87	$864.00	$1,603.87	$7,996.13
2	2,467.87	719.65	1,748.22	6,247.91
3	2,467.87	562.31	1,905.56	4,342.35
4	2,467.87	390.81	2,077.06	2,265.29
5	2,467.87	203.87	2,264.00	1.29*

** The $1.29 results from rounding off and would be added to the last payment.*

other illustration of the time value of money. The equation necessary to solve this problem (i.e., to determine the annual payments) is

$$\$9{,}600 = \frac{X}{(1+0.09)^1} + \frac{X}{(1+0.09)^2} + \frac{X}{(1+0.09)^3} + \frac{X}{(1+0.09)^4} + \frac{X}{(1+0.09)^5}.$$

This is an example of an annuity, so the problem collapses to:

$$\begin{aligned} \$9{,}600 &= X(\text{PVAIF } 9\%, 5Y) \\ \$9{,}600 &= X(3.890) \\ X &= \$9{,}600/3.890 = \$2{,}467.87. \end{aligned}$$

Thus, $2,467.87 is the annual payment that will retire this loan and pay 9 percent on the declining balance.

The actual payment schedule and the division of the payment into interest payment and principal reduction are given in Exhibit 21.1. This table is essentially the same as the mortgage loan amortization schedule illustrated in Exhibit 7.3 in Chapter 7. In both examples, the amount of the interest declines with each payment as the outstanding balance on the loan is reduced. Conversely, the amount of the principal repayment rises with each payment as the interest required by the lower principal is reduced.

Generally, the depreciation of the equipment and the resulting cash flow will cover the required loan payments. In this case, the annual depreciation expense would be $2,400 ($12,000/5) if straight-line depreciation is used. The cash flow generated by this $2,400 depreciation expense is approximately equal to the $2,467.87 payment required by the loan. (Of course, in many cases accelerated depreciation would be used so that the initial depreciation expense would be increased.) By matching the repayment schedule with the cash flow generated through depreciation, the firm enhances its capacity to service the debt. If the re-

EXHIBIT 21.2

Repayment Schedule for a $9,600 Term Loan at 9 Percent with Equal Principal Repayments

In this repayment schedule, the amount of the annual repayment is fixed.

Year	Principal Repayment	Interest	Balance of Loan	Total Payment
1	$1,920	$864.00	$7,680	$2,784.00
2	1,920	691.20	5,760	2,611.20
3	1,920	518.40	3,840	2,438.40
4	1,920	345.60	1,920	2,265.60
5	1,920	172.80	0	2,092.80

payment schedule is faster than the depreciation expense, the firm will have to use other sources of cash to retire the debt.

Since each loan is individually negotiated between the borrower and the lender, a variety of possible terms exist. One possibility is for the lender to require equal principal repayments with interest being computed on the remaining balance for each period. The repayment schedule under these terms for the $9,600 term loan presented above is given in Exhibit 21.2. In this case, the principal is retired in five equal installments of $1,920 ($9,600/5 = $1,920), which is given in the second column. The amount of interest (column 3) depends on the balance owed (column 4). Thus, the payment in the second year is the sum of the principal repayment ($1,920) plus the interest on the balance owed at the end of the first year ($691.20), for a total payment of $2,611.20 (column 5).

Other possible terms include no principal repayment until the loan is due at the end of the fifth year. In this case, the firm would annually remit the $864 interest payment, and at the end of the fifth year make the last interest payment plus the principal repayment (i.e., $864 + $9,600 = $10,464). The lender could combine the two previous illustrations and annually require a partial principal repayment (e.g., $1,000) with the balance of $4,600 ($9,600 − $5,000) paid at the end of the term of the loan. Such a lump repayment at the end of a loan is referred to as **balloon payment.**

Balloon payment
Large, single payment to retire a debt obligation at maturity

Although firms obtain most of their intermediate-term credit from banks and other financial institutions, intermediate-term securities may also be sold to the general public. These intermediate-term notes may differ from the term loans obtained from commercial banks and insurance companies. Notes sold to the general public might not be collateralized while term loans usually are, and the notes frequently do not have a compulsory repayment schedule. Such notes are really more similar to long-term bonds than to term loans. However, these notes may have specific features that make them attractive to investors. For example, the intermediate term (e.g., ten years) may make these notes attractive to investors who do not want to make investments for a longer term (e.g., twenty years). In addition, intermediate-term notes frequently cannot be called and refunded before maturity. Since the notes lack a call feature, the investor knows that the firm cannot force the buyer to give up the security should interest rates fall. Since many long-term bonds can be called and refunded if long-term interest rates fall, this non-callability of intermediate-term notes assures investors of their interest income (if no default) for the duration of the notes.

LEASING

The second alternative to long-term debt is leasing. Leasing is essentially renting, and the two terms are often interchanged. Since many lease contracts are for more than one year, lease financing is considered to be an alternative to long-term debt. However, since leases may be for less than ten years, leasing is also a source of intermediate-term financing.

Lessee ▲
Firm that rents (i.e., leases) property or equipment for its own use

Lessor ▲
Firm that owns property or equipment and rents it (i.e., leases the equipment) to other firms or individuals (i.e., the lessees)

Lease ▲
Renting (as opposed to owning) property or equipment; the contract between the lessee and the lessor

Operating lease ▲
Lease for the use and maintenance of equipment in which the term is less than the expected life of the asset

Financial lease ▲
Lease in which the term is equal to the expected life of the asset

A lease contract is for the use of an asset such as plant or equipment. Firms want the use of the asset. They perform the capital budgeting techniques discussed in Chapter 23 to determine which investments are profitable. After deciding which investments to make, they must decide how to finance the asset. Notice that it is the use of the asset that the firm desires and not necessarily title to the asset. Leasing permits the firm (the **lessee**) to use the asset without acquiring title, which is retained by the owner (the **lessor**). In return, the lessee enters into a contract (the **lease**) to make specified payments for the use of the asset.

Leases take one of two forms. An **operating lease** provides the lessee with both the use of the asset and a maintenance contract. The cost of servicing the equipment is built into the lease. The contract may be canceled after proper notice if the lessee should desire to change equipment. This type of lease is primarily used for renting equipment, especially computers, cars, and trucks. The length of the lease is usually less than the expected life of the asset but the lease may be renewed. Since the lease is not for the life of the asset, the lessor anticipates either having the lease renewed or selling the asset at the lease's expiration.

A **financial lease,** which may also be referred to as a capital lease, differs from an operating lease in several significant ways. These contracts are not cancelable and do not include a service clause. The duration of a financial lease is the expected life of the asset. The lease payments cover the cost of the asset and earn a set return for the lessor. Thus, a financial lease is similar to debt financing. If the firm had issued bonds to obtain the funds to acquire the asset, the payments to the bondholders would cover the cost of the equipment plus their set return (i.e., the rate of interest). Of course, if debt had been used, the firm would own the asset, while with leasing it does not acquire title. This difference may be important if at the end of the asset's life there is salvage value that accrues to the asset's owner.

While there are two classes of leases, there are three types of lease agreements. From the viewpoint of the lessee the type of lease agreement is immaterial; the firm still acquires the use of the asset. The type of lease has an impact only on the lessor. The first type of lease agreement is the **direct lease.** The lessor owns the asset and directly leases it to the lessee. Direct leases are offered by manufacturers who build the asset, such as IBM, as well as by finance companies and leasing companies that acquire assets with the intent to lease them to prospective users.

Direct lease ▲ Lease agreement in which the owner (the lessor) directly leases the asset to the user (the lessee)

The second type of lease is a **sale and leaseback.** Under this type of agreement, the firm that owns the asset sells it to the lessor and then leases it back. The selling firm immediately receives cash from the lessor that can be put to other uses but still retains the use of the asset. The lessee, however, relinquishes title to the asset and thus loses any salvage value that the asset might have. And, of course, the firm must now make the lease payments.

Sale and leaseback ▲ Financial agreement in which a firm sells an asset such as a building for cash and subsequently rents (i.e., leases) that asset

The third type of lease is a **leveraged lease.** Since the lessor owns the asset, that firm must have the funds to acquire it. In a leveraged lease the lessor borrows part of the funds necessary to acquire the asset. For example, a finance company may borrow from a commercial bank so that it may acquire an asset that it in turn leases to the ultimate users of the asset. If financial leverage is favorable, the lessor will increase the return on its funds invested in the asset.

Leveraged lease ▲ Lease agreement in which the lessor acquires an asset (which it subsequently leases) through the use of debt financing

Lease or Purchase

The question of whether it is better to buy or to lease depends on several crucial variables. These include the firm's tax bracket, the terms of the lease, the asset's salvage value, and the cost of obtaining funds to buy the asset. While this introductory text cannot fully develop this topic, the following example will provide some of the essential information necessary to make the choice.

A firm decides to acquire equipment that costs $5,000. The equipment has an expected life of five years, after which the equipment will be sold for an expected salvage value of $500. Depreciation will be straight-line (to ease the calculation; normally the firm would use accelerated depreciation if possible).[1] Maintenance is expected to be $200 annually, and the firm's marginal tax rate is 40 percent.

---

[1] As was explained in Chapter 15, depreciation expense starts after six months have lapsed. This half-year convention is ignored to simplify the illustration.

Financial Facts

The Deductibility of Lease Payments

The ability to deduct lease payments is obviously crucial to the analysis of leasing versus owning. If a firm owns, both interest and depreciation are tax deductible. If lease payments were not deductible expenses, the attractiveness of leasing would virtually vanish. • The IRS has established rules that determine if lease payments can be deducted. While the purpose of these rules is not to stifle leasing, the IRS is concerned that lease arrangements are not set up solely to avoid taxes. To assure that the lease payments are deductible, firms often consult lawyers and accountants to obtain an opinion on the deductibility of the lease payments prior to entering into the lease agreement. The IRS rules include the following: • 1. The lessee does not have the option to buy the asset for less than its fair market value. Such a bargain sale would represent equity in the asset and equity is not deductible. • 2. Options to renew must reflect the market value of the asset at the time of renewal. If the option were for a lower amount, once again the lessee would have an implied equity position in the asset. • 3. The lease cannot be a subterfuge to avoid paying taxes. For example, if the lessor offers low payments and does not earn a positive return on the lease, and the lessee deducts the lease payments, there is no income tax paid by the lessor, and the lessee's taxes are reduced. The lease payment must be sufficient to generate the lessor a reasonable rate of return on the asset. Also, the lease payments cannot be structured in such a way as to avoid income taxes. For example, if the initial lease payments were high followed by a period of low payments, that would suggest the purpose of the lease is to avoid income taxes by the lessee. If the IRS makes that determination, the lease payments are not tax deductible. • 4. The term of the lease must be less than 30 years. If the term exceeds 30 years, the IRS considers the transaction to be a sale (i.e., the lessee has in effect purchased the asset). While such a long time period applies to few assets, it would apply to real estate, whose life could easily extend beyond 30 years. •

Suppose the firm borrows $5,000 to buy the equipment, and the terms of the loan require the firm to retire $1,000 of the debt annually and pay 10 percent on the declining balance. The cash outflows from borrowing and buying for each year are as follows:

Year	1	2	3	4	5
Principal repayment	$1,000	1,000	1,000	1,000	1,000
Interest	$500	400	300	200	100
Maintenance	$200	200	200	200	200
Depreciation	$1,000	1,000	1,000	1,000	1,000
Tax deductible expenses	$1,700	1,600	1,500	1,400	1,300
Tax savings	($680)	(640)	(600)	(560)	(520)
Sale of asset (after tax)					(300)
Cash outflows	$1,020	960	900	840	480

To determine the cash outflow, the financial manager must determine the tax saving. The sum of interest, maintenance, and depreciation expenses (i.e., \$500 + \$200 + \$1,000 in year 1) is tax deductible. These expenses reduce taxes, which reduces the cash outflow associated with owning the asset. The financial manager also identifies the actual cash outflow. This is the sum of the principal repayment, interest, and maintenance minus the tax saving (i.e., \$1,000 + \$500 + \$200 − \$680 = \$1,020 in year 1). The tax saving is presented in parentheses to indicate the reduction in the cash outflow.

Each year follows the same general pattern except the last year, the year in which the asset is sold. The sale is a cash inflow and hence reduces the cash outflow in that year. If the asset is sold for more than its book value, the cash inflow is reduced by the taxes generated by the sale. (If the asset were sold for less than its book value, the sale would reduce taxes.) In this illustration, the asset is completely depreciated so its book value is \$0. All of the sale is taxable income, so the firm only nets \$300 after paying taxes of \$200 on the \$500 sale.

Alternatively, the firm could lease the equipment from a lessor who wants a 10 percent return. To determine the annual lease payments, the lessor answers the following question: How much must I charge each year such that my \$5,000 invested in the equipment will yield 10 percent? That is,

$$\$5{,}000 = \frac{X}{(1 + 0.1)^1} + \ldots + \frac{X}{(1 + 0.1)^5}$$
$$\$5{,}000 = X(\text{PVAIF}).$$

This problem is another example of an annuity. In order to solve the equation it is necessary to determine the interest factor for the present value of an annuity for five years at 10 percent. That interest factor is 3.791, so the equation becomes

$$\$5{,}000 = 3.791X,$$
$$X = \$5{,}000/3.791 = \$1{,}319.$$

For the lessor to earn 10 percent, the annual lease payment should be \$1,319.

If the lessor does charge \$1,319 annually, the lessee's annual cash outflows will be

Year	1	2	3	4	5
Lease payment	\$1,319.00	1,319.00	1,319.00	1,319.00	1,319.00
Tax savings	(\$527.60)	(527.60)	(527.60)	(527.60)	(527.60)
Cash outflow	\$791.40	791.40	791.40	791.40	791.40

As may be seen by comparing the two projections, the cash outflows differ under leasing and owning. Leasing produces a constant $791.40 outflow each year, while owning results in varying cash outflows.

Which alternative is better? That depends on the time value of money. Which alternative produces the *lower* present value of the cash outflows? If the firm uses 12 percent to judge alternatives, the two cash outflows are discounted back at 12 percent.[2] The present value of the cost of owning (i.e., the present value of the cash outflows associated with owning) is

$$\begin{aligned}\text{Present value of cost of owning} &= \frac{\$1{,}020}{(1+0.12)^1} + \frac{\$960}{(1+0.12)^2} + \frac{\$900}{(1+0.12)^3} \\ &\quad + \frac{\$840}{(1+0.12)^4} + \frac{\$480}{(1+0.12)^5} \\ &= \$1{,}020(0.893) + \$960(0.797) + \$900(0.712) \\ &\quad + \$840(0.636) + \$480(0.567) \\ &= \$911 + \$765 + \$641 + \$534 + \$272 \\ &= \$3{,}123\end{aligned}$$

The present value of the cost of leasing (i.e., the present value of the cash outflows associated with leasing) is

$$\begin{aligned}\text{Present value of cost of leasing} &= \frac{\$791.40}{(1+0.12)^1} + \ldots + \frac{\$791.40}{(1+0.12)^5} \\ &= \$791.40(3.605) \\ &= \$2{,}853\end{aligned}$$

Since the present value of the cash outflows associated with leasing is less than the present value of the cash outflows associated with borrowing and owning, leasing is preferred.

While this illustration argues for leasing, there are several critical variables in the illustration. The first is the expected residual or salvage value. If the anticipated salvage value were higher, that would argue against leasing. The owner of the equipment receives the salvage value, and this present value is lost if the firm leases. The smaller the expected salvage, the stronger is the argument for leasing. Second, the owner pays the maintenance and the lessee does not. However, if the lease contract does not include maintenance, the lessee will also have to pay that expense, and maintenance is a cash outflow. Third, the present value of the cash outflows depends in part on the choice of the discount rate. The discount rate used in lease/buy decisions is subject to considerable debate

[2] For a discussion of the determination of the firm's cost of capital used to discount investments, see Chapter 22.

in the finance literature.[3] If a lower discount rate had been used in the illustration, the present value of the cash outflows generated by borrowing and buying may have been less than the present value of the cash outflows generated by leasing. This may occur because the lower rate would increase the present value of the salvage value in year 5.[4]

Accounting for Leases

Prior to changes in accounting standards, one of the prime reasons for using leasing as a source of funds was that the lease would not appear on the firm's balance sheet. While the lease would be mentioned in the footnotes, the fact that it did not appear on the balance sheet tended to understate the firm's use of financial leverage. This important distinction between the use of debt, which must appear on the balance sheet, and leasing, which would not appear on the balance sheet, is illustrated by the following example. Both firms initially have the same assets, liabilities, and equity:

FIRM A BALANCE SHEET AS OF 12/31/X0

Assets	$10,000	Debt	$5,000
		Equity	5,000

FIRM B BALANCE SHEET AS OF 12/31/X0

Assets	$10,000	Debt	$5,000
		Equity	5,000

Both firms acquire a $5,000 piece of equipment. Firm A purchases the equipment and sells bonds to acquire the funds to pay for it. Firm B leases the equipment. After these transactions, their respective balance sheets become:

FIRM A BALANCE SHEET AS OF 1/31/X1

Assets	$10,000	Debt	$5,000
Equipment	5,000	Bonds	5,000
		Equity	5,000

FIRM B BALANCE SHEET AS OF 1/31/X1

Assets	$10,000	Debt	$5,000
		Equity	5,000

Both firms have the use of the equipment, but Firm A has more debt outstanding. Firm A appears to be riskier because its debt ratio is now higher. In reality, however, it is no riskier than Firm B, for Firm B also

[3] See the Bower article in the suggested readings at the end of this chapter for a discussion of this debate.

[4] For a discussion of the impact of different discount rates, see the discussion of mutually exclusive investments in Chapter 23.

has a new contractual obligation, the lease. Since the lease does not appear on the balance sheet, Firm B appears to be less risky.

The use of leases to obtain such "off the balance sheet" financing is in many cases no longer possible. The Financial Accounting Standards Board ruled that if the lease gives the lessee substantially all the benefits and risks of ownership, the lease must be capitalized and included on the firm's balance sheet. The lease must be included if it meets *any* of the following conditions:

1. the lease transfers ownership of the asset at the end of the lease,
2. the lease permits the lessee to buy the asset below its value at the expiration of the lease,
3. the length of the lease is more than 75 percent of the asset's estimated life,
4. the present value of the lease payments exceeds 90 percent of the fair market value of the property to the lessor.

The first two conditions obviously give the lessee the benefits and risk of ownership. In the first condition, ownership is transferred and in the second condition the lessee has the option to buy the asset at a bargain price. While the lessee does not have to exercise the option and buy the asset, the important consideration is the existence of the option.

The third and fourth conditions require some explanation. Consider the illustration presented earlier in which the financial manager had to choose between either the lease or borrowing and buying. In the illustration, the analysis indicated that leasing is the better alternative. So, will the lease have to be capitalized? The answer is yes because it meets the third condition. The life of the asset is five years and the lease is for five years, so the length of the lease exceeds 75 percent of the estimated life of the asset.

The fourth condition would require calculating the present value of the lease payments. In the illustration, that is the present value of the \$1,319 lease payments. Of course, the present value of the lease payments depends upon the discount rate. This rate has to be the lower of (1) the rate used by the lessor to establish the lease payments or (2) the interest rate the lessee would pay to borrow the funds to purchase the assets. In the illustration, the lessor used 10 percent and the lessee used 12 percent, so 10 percent must be the discount rate. When the lease payments are discounted at 10 percent, the present value is

$$\$1{,}319(3.791) = \$5{,}000.$$

The present value of the lease payments is greater than 90 percent of the cost of the investment; hence, the lease must be capitalized.

Many leases do not meet any of the above criteria for capitalizing a lease. If an employee rents a car for a week, that is certainly an operating lease, and it will not be capitalized. But if the car is rented for several years, the terms of the lease may meet one of the criteria and hence must be capitalized. If management wants to avoid having to capitalize the lease, then the terms must be structured in such a way as to avoid all of the criteria. The lease payments will still have to be reported in a footnote to the firm's financial statements, but it need not be reported on the balance sheet.

The inclusion of the lease would have the following impact on the balance sheet of Firm B if the lease were capitalized:

FIRM B
BALANCE SHEET
AS OF 1/31/X1

Assets	$10,000	Debt	$5,000
Assets under capital lease	5,000	Capital leases	5,000
		Equity	5,000

This revised balance sheet for Firm B brings to the foreground the fact that a financial lease is an alternative to debt financing. Both Firms A and B have $15,000 in assets and $5,000 in equity. The remaining sources of funds are either debt or the capitalized lease. The debt ratio for both firms then is $10,000/$15,000 = 67 percent. Now the balance sheets indicate that Firm A and Firm B are equally financially leveraged.

Arguments for Leasing

Since many leases can no longer be hidden, the advantages of leasing are hard to isolate. For example, it may be argued that the use of lease financing avoids the restrictive covenants associated with debt financing, which are designed to protect the lender. However, lessors will also take steps to protect themselves. If they believe that the lessee is a poor credit risk, they will not grant the lease or will charge higher rentals to protect themselves.

A second argument offered in favor of leasing is that the firm obtains the use of the asset without using any of its own funds. The lessor puts up 100 percent of the funds to acquire the asset. But certainly the lessor would not lease the asset to the lessee if the latter did not have an equity base, and the use of the lease should reduce the borrowing capacity of the lessee.

A third argument in favor of leasing is that the lessee avoids the risk of obsolescence. The gist of this argument is that if a firm buys equipment that becomes obsolete through technological change, that firm is left with outmoded equipment, which puts it at a competitive disadvantage. If this firm had leased the equipment, it could choose to cancel the lease (if that option were available) or not renew the lease when it expired. Obtaining the use of the asset through leasing instead of purchasing makes replacing the obsolete equipment easier.

This line of reasoning has led some advocates of leasing to assert that leasing shifts the risk of loss from the lessee to the lessor. However, the lessor will certainly seek to charge a rental fee that compensates for this risk. In effect, the lessee pays the lessor to bear the risk. Of course, if the lessor does not anticipate the obsolescence, the lessee may be able to shift the risk. However, many firms that are lessors are also manufacturers of or specialists in a particular type of equipment (e.g., computers or trucks). Presumably, they should know the risk of obsolescence and charge accordingly. Failure on their part to protect themselves from this risk of loss would soon result in their being out of business.

While leasing may not be a means to (1) hide the use of debt financing, (2) avoid having equity in an investment, or (3) shift the risk of obsolescence, it is still a viable means to obtain the use of an asset. The primary argument for leasing revolves around the tax positions of the lessor and the lessee. The terms of the lease may be structured to generate savings for both parties. For example, if a firm is in the highest income bracket, it may seek to own rather than lease its assets. Accelerated depreciation of these assets generates a tax shelter, and the firm then becomes a lessor. To induce others to lease the assets, the lessor may offer attractive terms that potential users could not obtain by borrowing and purchasing. In such cases, the lessor's tax benefits may be partially transferred to the lessee, and both parties benefit.

In addition to possible tax savings, leasing may offer flexibility. Manufacturers may offer leases to potential users of their product. Many firms such as IBM and Xerox lease their computers and copiers to users in addition to selling them. Lease terms are structured to the benefit of both parties. This may be particularly true if the lessee needs the use of the asset for a time period that is less than the life of the asset. For example, virtually all retail space is leased. Sears, The Limited, and Kmart do not own the shopping malls in which they locate their stores. If these retailers seek to move, they don't have to sell the buildings. Although they will have to meet the terms of the leases and they run the risk of higher payments when the leases are renewed, these retailers find flexibility in leasing that may not be possible in owning the buildings.

Coverage of Lease Payments

The lessor will charge a fee that is sufficient to cover the cost of the asset and to earn a return. In setting that fee, the lessor must consider both the riskiness of the asset and the creditworthiness of the lessee. One means to ascertain the ability of a firm to service its lease payments is to construct a coverage ratio similar to the times-interest-earned ratio dis-

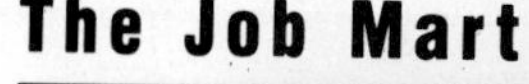

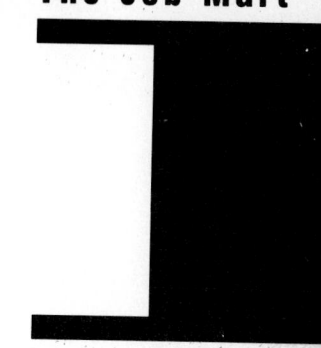

Lease Administrator

■ Job Description: Perform lease versus buy analysis; prepare capital budgets and negotiate lease terms. ■ Job Requirements: Knowledge of sources of funds (especially debt financing), taxation, and estimation of cash flow. The lease administrator (as lessor) must have excellent communication skills and sales experience, since he or she is selling the use of the equipment instead of the equipment itself. ■ Characteristics: A person may also work as a lease administrator for the firm that is doing the leasing; in this case, the lease administrator (as lessee) performs the same financial analysis as the lessor. While selling skills are not as important, excellent communication and negotiation skills are crucial to avoid entering into a financially harmful contract.

---

cussed in Chapter 16. That ratio indicated the capacity of a firm to service its debt. Such a coverage ratio for lease payments is

$$\text{Coverage of lease payments} = \frac{\text{EBIT} + \text{Lease payments}}{\text{Lease payments}}.$$

The numerator presents what is available to service the lease. Notice that the amount available includes earnings before interest and taxes plus the amount of the lease payments. Since lease payments are subtracted to obtain earnings before interest and taxes, these payments must be added back to EBIT to obtain the earnings available to meet the lease payments. Obviously, the greater the amount available to meet the payments (i.e., the greater the numerical value of the ratio), the safer the lease payments should be. If a firm's coverage ratio is low, the lessor may choose not to enter into the contract or may decide to increase the cost of the lease to cover the additional risk of default on the terms of the lease agreement.

If the firm has both debt and lease obligations, the coverage ratio may be adjusted to indicate coverage of both interest and lease payments.

$$\text{Coverage of lease payments} = \frac{\text{EBIT} + \text{Lease payments}}{\text{Interest} + \text{Lease payments}}.$$

This ratio may be preferred, because it indicates the extent to which the firm has sufficient earnings to cover all of its fixed charges. The lessor should definitely prefer this coverage ratio if the debt obligations are senior to the lease obligations, because the lessee would be required to pay the interest expense prior to making the lease payments, and the firm would have to have sufficient funds to cover both in order for the lessor to be paid.

SUMMARY

This chapter has briefly considered two sources of financing—intermediate-term debt and leasing—that are alternatives to short-term debt and long-term bonds. Intermediate-term debt is generally outstanding for five to ten years. While it may be similar to other forms of long-term debt, its shorter maturity and the fact that it is often secured by collateral differentiates it from long-term bonds. The repayment schedule of intermediate-term debt is generally paired with the anticipated cash flow that is generated by the acquired asset.

Leasing is similar to renting. The firm (the lessee) acquires the use of the asset without actually owning it. In return, it must make periodic payments to the owner (the lessor) for the use of the asset. Leases may be classified as operating leases or financial leases. The latter type of lease is very similar to purchasing the asset with debt financing; the present value of the lease payments (and the value of the asset) must be capitalized and included on the lessee's balance sheet.

The cash inflows and outflows generated by leasing may differ from the cash flows generated through borrowing and purchasing the asset. The financial manager needs to determine and compare the present value of the cost of owning and the cost of leasing to determine which is cheaper. Taxation, the timing of interest payments or lease payments, depreciation schedules, and estimates of the asset's salvage value will affect these present values and affect the decision to either lease or purchase.

Review Questions

1. What differentiates short-term, intermediate-term, and long-term debt? How may the repayment schedule for an intermediate-term loan be determined? What assets may secure a term loan?
2. What impact will each of the following have on the annual payment required by an intermediate-term loan?
   a. an increase in the interest rate
   b. an increase in the term from five to seven years
   c. an increase in the balloon payment
3. What is the difference between an operating lease and a financial lease? If an employee takes a business trip and rents a car at the airport, is that an example of an operating or financial lease?
4. Why is a financial lease similar to a long-term bond? What is the implication of a financial lease for the firm's use of financial leverage? Does this lease appear on the firm's balance sheet?
5. Many manufacturers will lease their products instead of selling them. Such leases often include maintenance contracts. Are these leases financial or operating leases? Does the lessee avoid the risk of obsolescence?

6. In the analysis of the lease versus purchase decision, why may the residual or salvage value individually be the riskiest, but the most important, determinant?

7. The lease versus purchase analysis stresses cash inflows and outflows. What impact does each of the following have on the estimates of cash flows and do they argue for leasing or owning?
   a. depreciation is spread over more years
   b. the residual value is increased
   c. the lease payments occur at the beginning instead of at the end of the year
   d. estimated maintenance is increased

8. If an asset's estimated life is five years and the firm enters into a lease agreement that covers four years, does the lease have to be capitalized?

Problems

1. A five-year $100,000 term loan has an interest rate of 9 percent on the declining balance. What are the equal annual payments required to pay interest and principal on the loan? Construct a table showing the declining balance owed after each payment.

2. What are the repayment schedules for each of the following five-year, 10 percent $10,000 term loans:
   a. equal annual payments that amortize (retire) the principal and pay the interest owed on the declining balance;
   b. equal annual principal repayment, with interest calculated on the remaining balance owed;
   c. no principal repayment until after five years, with interest paid annually on the balance owed; and
   d. $1,000 annual principal repayment, with the balance paid at the end of five years and annual interest paid on the balance owed?

3. A firm wants the use of a machine that costs $100,000. The firm may borrow the funds through a loan that will be retired in four annual payments. Each payment retires $25,000 of the loan and covers the interest on the balance outstanding at the annual rate of 12 percent. If the firm finances the purchase of the equipment with this loan, it will depreciate the equipment at the rate of $20,000 a year for four years, at which time the equipment will have a residual value of $20,000. Maintenance will be $2,500 a year. The firm could lease the equipment for four years for an annual lease payment of $26,342. Currently, the firm is in the 40 percent income tax bracket.
   a. Determine the firm's cash outflows under borrowing and purchasing the equipment and under leasing.
   b. If the firm uses a 14 percent cost of funds to analyze decisions that involve payments over more than a year, should management lease the equipment or borrow and purchase it?

4. A lessor acquires equipment for $83,250 and plans to lease it for a period of five years. If the equipment has no estimated residual value, what must be the annual lease charge for the lessor to earn 12 percent on the investment?

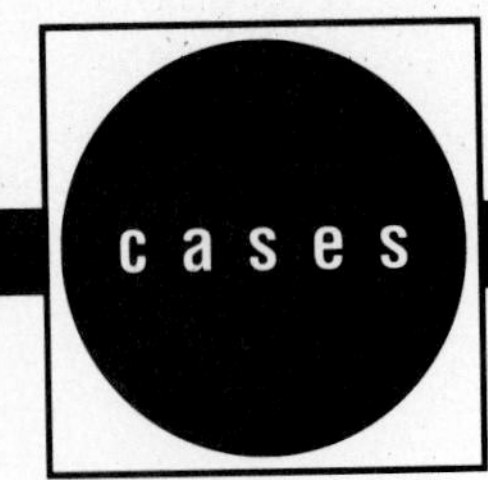

Comparing Leasing to Purchasing an Asset

Clara Schuman, the financial manager for Flex-Tronics, has decided to acquire a new asset that costs $100,000. However, she has not determined the best method of financing the acquisition. Essentially, her choices are to lease the equipment or to borrow the funds and purchase the equipment. The asset has an economic life of five years and will be depreciated according to the schedule presented later. Ms. Schuman does not anticipate using the asset for five years, but plans to sell it at the end of the fourth year or beginning of the fifth year for its book value of $14,000.

If she borrows the $100,000, the five-year loan will (1) have an interest rate of 10 percent, (2) be retired in equal, annual payments with interest being determined on the declining balance, and (3) be secured by the equipment. The firm may pay off the balance owed at any time without any prepayment penalty. Any sale of the asset will require the loan to be paid off immediately with transfer of title to the asset. Owning will also require an estimated maintenance expense of $3,500 a year.

The terms of the lease are as follows: (1) The lease payment will be $35,000 a year. (2) The lessor will grant the lease for four years with an option to renew the lease for an additional year at $35,000. (3) The lease payment includes maintenance, and the lessor has agreed to accept payment at the end of each year instead of at the beginning of each year, as is customary with most leases.

The firm is in the 30 percent income tax bracket; any taxable expense that reduces taxable income by $1.00 reduces income taxes by $0.30. To help determine which alternative is to be preferred, Ms. Schuman completes the following schedules:

Cost of Leasing:

Year	Lease Payment	Tax Savings	After-Tax Cash Outflow	Present Value of Outflow
1	$35,000			
2	35,000			
3	35,000			
4	35,000			
5				

Sum of present value of cash outflows:

Cost of Owning (Part I):

Year	Mortgage Payment	Interest	Principal Repayment	Maintenance	Depreciation
1					$21,000
2					25,000
3					21,000
4					19,000
5					14,000

Cost of Owning (Part II):

	Tax Deductible Expenses	Tax Savings	After-Tax Cash Outflow	Present Value of Outflow
1				
2				
3				
4				
5				
		Sum of present value of cash outflows:		

Ms. Schuman realizes that the alternative with the lower present value is the better alternative.

Case Problems

1. Based on this analysis, should she select leasing or borrowing and owning?
2. How does the sale of the asset at the end of the fourth year fit into the analysis?
3. What impact would this sale have if the anticipated price were less than $14,000?

Suggested Readings

The basics of lease financing (e.g., tax implications, accounting for leases, cancelable leases, and the impact of inflation) are covered in the following concise book:

Bierman, Harold, Jr. *The Lease Versus Buy Decision.* Englewood Cliffs, N.J.: Prentice-Hall, 1982.

In addition to the bibliography given in Bierman's book, the reader may consult any of the following articles that are devoted to specific aspects of the lease-versus-buy decision.

For a discussion of which of several techniques should be used to evaluate leveraged leases, see:

Athanasopoulos, Peter J., and Peter W. Bacon. "The Evaluation of Leveraged Leases." *Financial Management* (Spring 1980), pp. 76–80.

One of the major issues in leasing is the proper discount factor. For a discussion of this issue, see:

Bower, Richard S. "Issues in Lease Financing." *Financial Management* (Winter 1973), pp. 25–34. Reprinted in *Issues in Financial Management,* 2d ed., edited by E. F. Brigham and R. E. Johnson, pp. 229–244. Hinsdale, Ill.: The Dryden Press, 1980.

Carson, Roger L. "Leasing, Asset Lines, and Uncertainty: A Practitioner's Comments." *Financial Management* (Summer 1987), pp. 13–16.

Surveys of lease practice include:

Ang, James, and Pamela Peterson. "The Leasing Puzzle." *Journal of Finance* (September 1984), pp. 1055–1065.

O'Brien, T. J., and B. H. Nunnally, Jr. "A Survey of Corporate Leasing Analysis." *Financial Management* (Summer 1983), pp. 30–39.

The impact of leasing on the firm's ability to borrow is covered in:

Bayless, Marc E., and J. David Diltz. "An Empirical Study of Debt Displacement Effects of Leasing." *Financial Management* (Winter 1986), pp. 53–60.

Cost of Capital

2

Learning Objectives

1. Identify the components of a firm's capital structure.
2. Explain why the cost of capital is an opportunity cost concept.
3. Differentiate the factors that affect the costs of debt, preferred stock, and common stock.
4. Compute the cost of capital and determine the optimal capital structure.
5. Distinguish between the average cost of funds and the marginal cost of funds.
6. Determine the relationship between the optimal capital structure and the value of the firm's stock.

"The human species is composed of two distinct races, the men who borrow and the men who lend." According to this quote from Charles Lamb, individuals are either borrowers or lenders. But many individuals do both, as they borrow funds and use their own money to acquire income-earning assets. Very few firms operate without using both debt and equity financing, so a fundamental question arises: What is the best combination of these sources of finance? What is the firm's optimal capital structure?

Lenders and stockholders are not altruistic; creditors demand interest payments, and stockholders seek a return through dividends and price appreciation. What combination of debt and equity financing generates these returns and minimizes the firm's cost of capital? Coca-Cola has traditionally been a very conservatively managed firm. In 1980, total debt financed less than 10 percent of Coke's total assets, and long-term debt was less than 6.0 percent of equity. By 1990, total debt financed 24 percent of Coke's assets, and long-term debt rose to 16 percent of equity. Even these numbers are conservative, but they also indicate that management decided that Coke's capital structure permitted the increased use of financial leverage. Management also announced that in an effort to increase shareholder wealth, part of the increased debt financing would be used to repurchase shares in order to decrease the equity base and increase earnings per share.

This chapter is concerned with the determination of the cost of capital and the firm's optimal capital structure; the following chapter uses this cost of capital to select among various competing uses for the firm's capital. This chapter starts with the costs of the various components in the firm's capital structure. This is followed by a discussion of the weighted cost of capital and the determination of the optimal capital structure. Once this capital structure has been determined, it should be maintained as it generates the lowest cost of funds.

Maintaining the optimal capital structure does not mean the cost of capital is fixed. The cost of additional finance may rise even though the optimal capital structure is maintained, so it is necessary to differentiate between the average cost of capital and the cost of additional funds, which is the marginal cost of capital. The chapter ends by tieing the cost of capital to the value of the firm's stock and showing how the excess use of financial leverage will lead to a higher cost of capital and lower valuation of the stock.

COMPONENTS OF THE COST OF CAPITAL

As was previously explained in Chapter 17, the use of financial leverage may increase the rate of return on stockholders' equity, but may also increase the risk associated with the firm. This suggests a question: What is the best combination of debt and equity financing? This best combination of the firm's sources of finance is its **optimal capital structure.** The optimal capital structure takes advantage of financial leverage without unduly increasing financial risks. In effect, it minimizes the overall cost of finance to the firm.

Optimal capital structure ▲
Combination of debt and equity financing that minimizes the average cost of capital

To determine the optimal capital structure, the financial manager must first establish the cost of each source of finance and then determine which combination of these sources minimizes the overall cost. This minimum cost of capital is extremely important, because the financial manager must be able to judge investment opportunities. The selection of investments requires knowledge of the firm's cost of capital, since an investment must earn a return sufficient to cover the cost of the funds used to acquire the asset. Thus, the determination of the firm's cost of capital is necessary for the correct application of the capital budgeting techniques that are explained in Chapter 23.

This section is devoted to the determination of the costs of the components of the firm's capital structure. After these costs have been determined, the financial manager constructs a weighted average of the various costs. By varying the mix of sources of capital and recomputing the weighted averages, the optimal capital structure is determined.

Cost of Debt

The cost of debt is related to the interest rate, the corporate income tax rate, and risk. As was previously explained in the discussion of financial leverage, the income tax laws permit the deduction of interest before computing taxable income. The interest expense is shared with the federal government, so that the effective cost of debt financing is reduced. The amount of this sharing depends on the firm's marginal income tax rate. For many incorporated businesses, the tax on additional income is 34 percent, which reduces the cost of debt by nearly one-third. For example, if a firm has a marginal tax rate of 34 percent (T), and issues bonds that pay 8 percent (i), the effective cost of debt (k_d) using Equation 17.8 is

$$\begin{aligned} k_d &= i(1 - T) \\ &= 0.08(1 - 0.34) = 0.0528 = 5.28\%. \end{aligned}$$

Notice that the effective cost of debt is the cost at which new debt may be issued; it is not the cost at which debt was issued in the past. If a firm has debt that was issued ten years ago with a fixed interest rate below the current interest rate, it is the current interest rate that is used to determine the firm's current cost of capital. When the older debt was issued, the previous rate was used to determine the firm's cost of capital at that time. Current cost is the interest rate that the firm must presently pay to borrow the money, adjusted for the tax deduction.

The cost of debt is affected by any flotation costs associated with issuing new securities and by the term of the debt. Flotation costs reduce the proceeds of the sale of the securities and increase the interest cost per dollar borrowed. The larger the flotation costs, the greater the effective interest rate will be.

As was previously explained, short-term debt generally carries a lower yield (lower interest cost) than long-term debt. Thus, if the firm issues long-term debt, the interest expense will probably be higher than if the firm had used short-term financing. However, by using long-term debt, the firm avoids the problem of rolling over or refunding short-term debt, thus avoiding the risk associated with refinancing short-term debt.

The cost of debt also depends on the riskiness of the firm. The risk is related to the nature of the business (i.e., business risk) and to the use of financial leverage (i.e., financial risk). The more the firm uses debt financing, the greater will be the potential for it to fail to meet its debt obligations. This increase in the risk of default means that as the firm's use of financial leverage increases, the interest rate on borrowed money will increase. This is illustrated by the line k_d in Figure 22.1. Initially, the cost of debt may be stable, as the firm uses more financial leverage without significantly increasing risk for the creditors. Eventually, as the debt increases, the cost of debt starts to rise, because creditors demand more interest to compensate them for the increased risk of loss.

Cost of Preferred Stock

As was explained in Chapter 11, the price or value of preferred stock depends on the dividend and the yield required to induce investors to buy the shares. The valuation equation given was

$$P_p = \frac{D_p}{k_p}.$$

P_p was the price of the preferred stock, D_p was the dividend paid by the preferred stock, and k_p was the return required by investors necessary to induce them to buy the stock. This equation may be rearranged to isolate the yield or the firm's cost of preferred stock:

22.1

$$P_p \times k_p = D_p,$$
$$k_p = \frac{D_p}{P_p}.$$

FIGURE 22.1

Cost of Debt

The cost of debt rises as the firm becomes more financially leveraged.

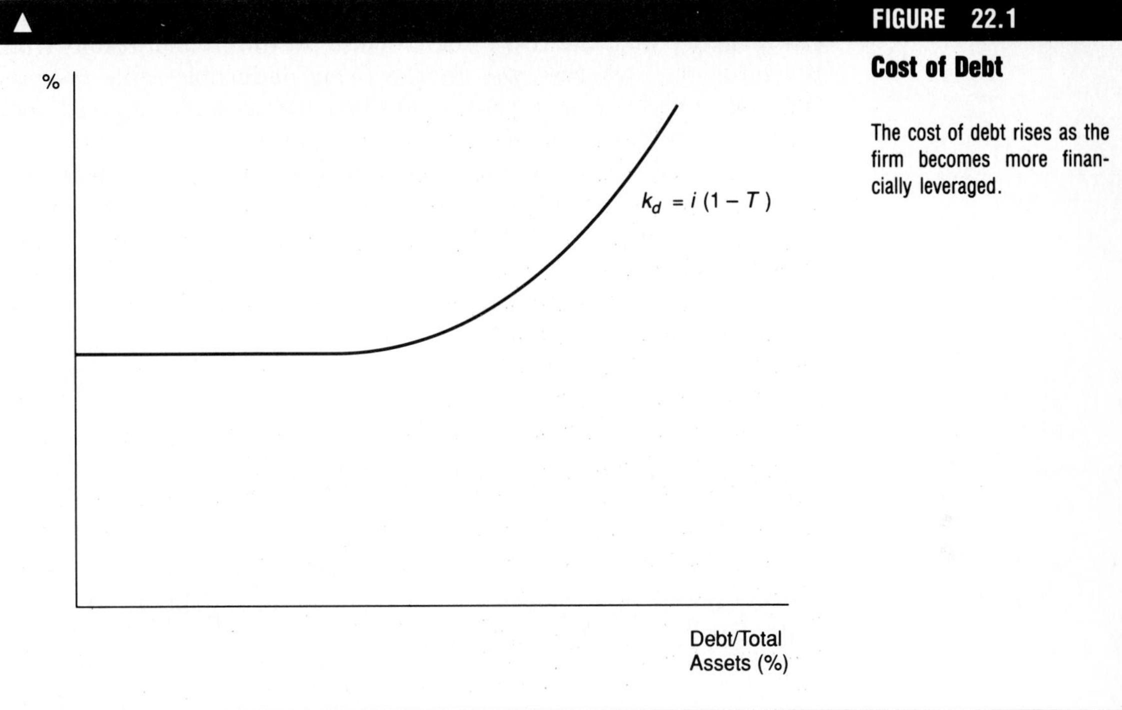

As may be seen from this equation, the cost to the firm of the preferred stock depends on its dividend and the price that investors are willing to pay for the stock. If the preferred stock pays $1.00 dividend and sells for $12.00, the cost of the preferred stock to the firm is

$$k_p = \frac{\$1.00}{\$12.00} = 0.0833 = 8.33\%.$$

The 8.33 percent is the cost of the funds if the firm currently uses preferred stock financing.

For a new issue of preferred stock, the company should use the net price after selling the stock, which deducts the expense of selling the shares. For example, if this firm issued new preferred shares and had to pay an underwriting fee of 7 percent, it would net only $11.16 [$12.00 (1 − 0.07)] per share. Thus, the cost of preferred stock financing would be

$$k_p = \frac{\$1.00}{\$11.16} = 8.96\%.$$

The cost of selling new shares to the public raises the cost of preferred stock. In this case, the cost increased by over half a percentage point.

From the viewpoint of the firm, the cost of preferred stock is significantly higher than the cost of debt. This cost differential results from federal income tax laws; the interest is tax deductible while the preferred dividend payments are not. The increased cost of preferred stock as a means to obtain financial leverage argues for the use of debt securities instead. In recent years, there has been relatively little preferred stock financing (unless the preferred stock was issued as part of a merger or is convertible into the common stock of the company). While the preferred stock does not legally bind the firm to pay dividends and meet other indenture agreements, its additional cost overshadows these advantages.

Cost of Common Stock

The cost of common stock is the return required by investors to buy and hold the firm's common stock (required return was discussed previously in Chapters 7 and 11). This cost of common equity is an opportunity cost: it is the return that investors could earn on comparable, alternative uses for their money. This cost applies both to existing shares and to new shares being issued by the firm.

Unfortunately, since the cost of common stock is an opportunity cost, there is no identifiable expense such as interest that the financial manager may use to determine the cost of these funds. However, the financial manager knows that the cost of common stock must exceed the cost of debt. There is no tax advantage associated with equity, because dividends are paid in after-tax dollars (i.e., dividends are not tax deductible), while interest is paid in before-tax dollars (i.e., interest is a tax deductible expense). In addition, common stock represents ownership and, therefore, is a riskier security than the firm's debt obligations. Although the firm is legally obligated to pay interest and meet the terms of indentures of its debt agreements, there is no legal obligation for the firm to pay dividends.

Since equity is riskier than debt to the investor, one means to estimate the cost of equity is to start with the interest rate paid to the holder of debt and add a risk premium. In this specification the cost of equity is

22.2 $$k_e = i + \text{Risk premium},$$

in which k_e is the cost of equity and i is the interest rate being paid on new issues of debt (i.e., the current rate of interest unadjusted for the tax advantage). The risk premium associated with the common stock is then added to the interest rate. Although the financial manager knows the interest rate, the amount of the risk premium is not known. Quantifying the amount of this premium could be considered making an educated guess at best or, if you are a cynic, a matter of conjecture.

An alternative approach to the determination of the cost of equity is the capital asset pricing model (CAPM) presented in Chapter 8 and used in Chapter 11 to value common stock. In the CAPM, the required return on equity was expressed in Equation 8.3 as:

$$k_e = r_f + (r_m - r_f)\text{beta}$$

In this specification, the cost of equity depends on the risk-free rate of interest (r_f) plus a risk premium. The risk premium depends on (1) the difference between the return on the market as a whole (r_m) and the risk-free rate and (2) the firm's beta coefficient, which measures the systematic risk associated with the firm.

Since this required return is the return necessary to induce investors to buy the stock, it may be viewed as the firm's cost of equity. Notice that to make the CAPM operational, the financial manager needs estimates of the risk-free rate, the return on the market, and the beta coefficient. Thus, the financial manager encounters the same general problems making the CAPM operational as the individual investor faces using the model as a tool for the valuation of common stock. However, the approach is theoretically superior to using the interest rate on the firm's bonds and adding on a risk premium, as it more precisely specifies the risk premium associated with investing in the stock.

A third approach defines the cost of equity in terms of investors' expected return on the stock; that is, the expected dividend yield plus expected growth (i.e., capital gains). In Chapter 11, this rate of return (r) was specified in Equation 11.7 as

$$r = \text{Dividend yield} + \text{Growth rate}$$

$$r = \frac{D_0(1 + g)}{P} + g.$$

As with the CAPM approach, the financial manager has to make this model operational. Although the current dividend and the price of the stock are known, estimates must be made of the future capital gains. This is, of course, the same problem facing the investor who seeks to use the common stock valuation model presented in Equation 11.6 (the dividend-growth model) in Chapter 11.

While the three approaches appear to be different, they are essentially the same. The interest rate plus risk premium method and the CAPM method are very similar. However, the CAPM specifies more clearly the risk premium in terms of the return on a risk-free security, the return on the market, and the systematic risk associated with the individual firm.

The CAPM method and rate of return method are virtually identical if it is assumed that financial markets are in equilibrium. If that assumption holds, the required return found using the CAPM would also be the investors' rate of return determined by using the expected dividend yield plus the expected capital gain. For example, if the expected return exceeded the required return, investors would drive up the price of the stock, causing the expected return to fall. If the expected return were less than the required return, the opposite would occur. Investors would seek to sell the shares, which would drive down their price and increase the yield. These changes will cease when the market is in equilibrium and the required return is equal to the expected rate of return.

The same argument may be expressed in terms of a stock's valuation and its price. The CAPM was used in the dividend-growth model to determine the value of the stock. If the price of the stock is less than the valuation, investors bid up the price. If the price exceeds the valuation, investors seek to sell, which drives down the price. The incentive for stock prices to cease changing occurs when the price and the valuation are equal. Thus, if the equity markets are in equilibrium, a stock's price must equal its valuation, and the required rate of return equals the expected rate of return.

If the equity markets are in equilibrium, the stock's price may be substituted for its value in the dividend-growth model (i.e., $V = P$):

$$P = \frac{D_0(1 + g)}{k_e - g}$$

By rearranging terms, the required return is

$$k_e - g = \frac{D_0(1 + g)}{P}$$

22.3 $$k_e = \frac{D_0(1 + g)}{P} + g.$$

In this form, the required rate of return is the sum of the dividend yield plus the capital gain. This is identical to the investor's rate of return and may be used as the cost of common equity.

Equation 22.3 expresses the cost of equity under the assumption that the firm does not have to issue new shares (i.e., the cost of equity is the cost of retained earnings). If the firm were to issue additional shares, it would not receive the market price of the stock because it would have to pay the flotation costs associated with selling new stock. To adjust for this expense, the flotation costs (F) must be subtracted from the price of the stock to obtain the net proceeds to the firm. This cost of new shares (k_{ne}) is expressed in Equation 22.4:

22.4 $$k_{ne} = \frac{D_0(1 + g)}{P - F} + g.$$

Obviously, the greater the flotation costs, the smaller will be the amount obtained from the sale of each new share, and the greater will be the cost of the stock.

The following example illustrates how the above model of the cost of common stock is used. A firm's earnings are growing annually at the rate of 7 percent. The common stock is currently paying \$0.935 a share, and this dividend will grow annually at 7 percent so that the year's dividends will be \$1 [i.e., $D_0(1 + g) = \$1$]. If the common stock is selling for \$25, the firm's cost of common stock is

$$k_e = \frac{\$0.935(1 + 0.07)}{\$25} + 0.07$$
$$= 0.04 + 0.07 = 0.11 = 11\%.$$

This tells management that investors currently require an 11 percent return on their investment in the stock. That return consists of a 4 percent dividend yield and the 7 percent growth. Failure on the part of management to achieve this return for the common stockholders will result in a decline in the price of the common stock.

If the firm has exhausted its retained earnings and must issue new stock, the cost of common stock must rise to cover the flotation costs. If these costs are \$1 a share (4 percent of the price of the stock), the firm nets \$24 per share, and the cost of equity is

$$k_{ne} = \frac{\$0.935(1 + 0.07)}{\$25 - \$1} + 0.07$$
$$= 0.0417 + 0.07 = 11.17\%$$

The cost of equity is now higher. The firm must earn 11.17 percent in order to cover the flotation costs and investors' required return.[1]

As this discussion indicates, the cost of common equity may be viewed from the standpoint of the investor or of the firm. The investors' required return is the cost of equity to the firm, since this return must be met for investors to commit their funds to the firm. Failure to meet this cost will result in a lower value of the stock as investors seek to move their funds to alternative investments. The lower stock price will increase the difficulty of raising a given amount of money through a new issue of stock. The lower stock price will also hurt the firm's employees, whose compensation is tied to the value of the stock.

In addition to the dividend amount and the potential for growth, the value of the firm also depends on risk. Increased risk will increase the required return; equity funds become more expensive, and the firm

---

[1] Flotation costs are a cash outflow that occurs when the securities are issued. This expense is capitalized on the balance sheet as an asset that is depreciated or "amortized" over the lifetime of the security (e.g., the flotation costs associated with a ten-year bond issue are written off over ten years). The depreciation generates a cash inflow that recaptures the flotation costs. Although writing off the capitalized asset restores the initial cash outflow, the timings of the outflows and of the inflows differ. The outflow occurs first, which raises the cost of a new issue of securities.

FIGURE 22.2

Cost of Equity

As the firm uses more debt and becomes more financially leveraged, the cost of equity rises.

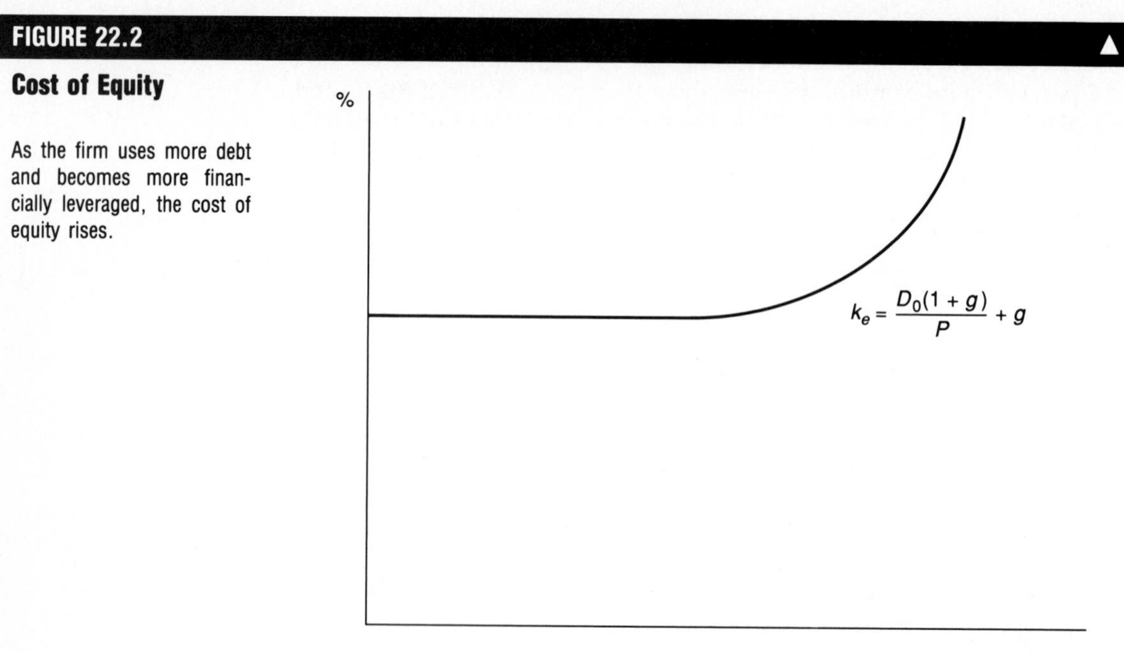

will have to earn a higher return on its investments to compensate equity investors for the additional risk.

Risk partially depends on the nature of the business (i.e., business risk) and partially on how management finances the firm's operations (i.e., financial risk). The relationship between financial risk and the cost of equity is illustrated in Figure 22.2, which relates the cost of equity (k_e) to the firm's use of financial leverage. The same relationship between the cost of debt and the firm's use of financial leverage was previously illustrated in Figure 22.1. In both cases, the cost of equity and the cost of debt may be initially stable, but ultimately both of these costs start to rise as the firm becomes more financially leveraged and hence more risky.

COST OF CAPITAL: A WEIGHTED AVERAGE

Cost of capital ▲
Weighted average of the costs of a firm's sources of finance

The **cost of capital** to the firm is a weighted average of the costs of debt, preferred stock, and common stock. The weights depend on the proportion of the firm's assets financed by each source of finance. Management seeks to determine the optimal combination of the various sources that minimizes the weighted average cost of funds and maximizes the value of the owners' investment in the firm.

Determining the firm's optimal capital structure requires understanding how the weighted average cost of funds is derived. Since this section develops the weighted average, it is assumed that the best combination (i.e., the weights) is known. After the discussion of the weighted cost of capital, the determination of the optimal capital structure will be covered.

Management has calculated that the current cost of each type of financing is as follows:

Cost of debt	5.28%
Cost of preferred stock	8.96
Cost of common stock (retained earnings)	11.00

The proportion (i.e., the weights) of the firm's assets financed by each type of financing is

Debt	40%
Preferred stock	10
Common stock (retained earnings)	50

To find the cost of capital, multiply the proportion of each component of the optimal capital structure by its respective costs and add the results. For this firm that yields:

	Cost	×	Weight	=	Weighted Cost
Debt	5.28%	×	0.40	=	2.112%
Preferred stock	8.96	×	0.10	=	0.896
Common stock	11.00	×	0.50	=	5.500
	Cost of capital			=	8.508%

The process of determining the cost of funds is generalized in Equation 22.5.

22.5 $$k = w_1 k_d + w_2 k_p + w_3 k_e.$$

The equation states that the cost of capital (k) is a weighted average in which the costs of debt (k_d), preferred stock (k_p), and equity (k_e) are weighted by the extent to which they are used (i.e., w_1, w_2, and w_3, respectively). These weights, along with the cost of each source, then determine the overall cost of funds. In the above illustration, the cost of capital is

$$k = (0.4)5.28 + (0.1)8.96 + (0.5)11.00 = 0.08508 = 8.508\%.$$

For this firm the weighted average cost of capital is 8.508 percent. The firm must earn at least 8.508 percent on its investments to justify using its sources of finance. It is this 8.508 percent cost of capital that will be used in the subsequent chapter to determine whether a firm should make a particular investment in plant and equipment (i.e., the cost of capital will be the discount factor used in capital budgeting).

If a firm does earn 8.508 cents after taxes on the investment of a dollar, then the firm has 2.112 cents to pay the interest, 0.896 cent to pay the dividends on the preferred stock, and 5.5 cents to pay dividends on the common stock or to reinvest in the company so that it may grow. The 8.508 cents covers the cost of each individual component of the firm's cost of capital.

If the company earns more than 8.508 percent, it is able to pay its debt expense and the preferred stock dividends, and it will have more than is necessary to meet the expected return of the common stockholders. For example, if the firm earns 10 percent (i.e., 10 cents), 2.112 cents are paid to creditors and 0.896 cent goes to the preferred stockholders. That leaves 6.992 cents for the common stockholders, which exceed the 5.5 cents required as a return on common stock. The firm may increase its dividends or increase its growth rate by reinvesting the earnings. Either way, investors will bid up the price of the stock. Since the return on an investment in the stock exceeded investors' required rate of return, the value of this firm is increased.

THE OPTIMAL CAPITAL STRUCTURE

The previous section illustrated the determination of the firm's weighted cost of capital. In that illustration, the cost of debt was less than the cost of equity because debt is less risky to the investor and the borrower may deduct interest payments before determining taxable income. If debt costs less than equity, couldn't management reduce the firm's cost of capital by substituting cheaper debt for more expensive equity? The answer is both yes and no. As management initially substitutes cheaper debt, the cost of capital does decline. However, as debt finances a larger proportion of the firm's assets and the firm becomes more financially leveraged, the costs of both debt and equity rise. What management needs to determine is the optimal combination of debt and equity financing that minimizes the firm's cost of capital. Once determined, management should seek to maintain that particular combination of debt and equity financing.

The process of determining the optimal capital structure is illustrated in Exhibit 22.1. The first column in the table presents the proportion of debt financing. The second and third columns give the cost of debt and the cost of equity, respectively. (To ease the calculation, it is as-

EXHIBIT 22.1

Determination of the Optimal Capital Structure

The cost of capital initially declines, reaches a minimum (the optimal capital structure), and then rises.

Proportion of Debt Financing	Cost of Debt	Cost of Equity	Weighted Cost
0%	4%	10.0%	10.00%
10	4	10.0	09.40
20	4	10.0	08.80
30	4	10.0	08.20
40	4	10.5	07.90
50	5	11.5	08.25
60	6	13.0	08.80
70	8	15.0	10.10
80	10	18.0	11.60
90	15	22.0	15.70

sumed that this firm has no preferred stock.) The cost of debt is less than the cost of equity, and both are constant over a considerable range of debt ratios. The costs of both debt and equity start to rise as the firm becomes more financially leveraged. The fourth column presents the weighted average cost of capital, which incorporates the cost of debt and the cost of equity, weighted by the proportion of assets financed by each.

If the firm is entirely financed by equity, the weighted average cost of capital is the cost of equity. When the firm begins to use some debt and substitutes the cheaper debt financing for equity financing, the weighted average cost of capital is reduced. As the use of debt increases, the weighted average cost of capital initially declines.

However, this decline does not continue indefinitely as the firm substitutes additional cheaper debt. Eventually, both the cost of debt and the cost of equity begin to increase, because creditors and investors believe that more financial leverage increases the riskiness of the firm. At first, the increases in the cost of debt and the cost of equity may be insufficient to stop the decline in the weighted cost of capital. But as the costs of debt and equity continue to increase, the average cost of capital reaches a minimum and then starts to increase. In the table, this optimal capital structure occurs at 40 percent debt (i.e., 40 percent debt financing to 60 percent equity financing). As additional debt is used, the costs of both debt and equity rise sufficiently to cause the cost of capital to increase.

This determination of the optimal capital structure is also illustrated by Figure 22.3, which plots the cost of debt (k_d), the cost of equity (k_e), and the weighted average cost of capital (k) given in Exhibit 22.1. As is readily seen in the graph, when the use of debt increases, the weighted average cost of capital initially declines, reaches a minimum at debt of 40 percent (D_1 = 40% and k_1 = 7.9%), and then starts to increase.

Financial Facts

AT&T's Use of Debt Financing

AT&T is an excellent illustration of a firm moving towards its optimal capital structure. Prior to divestiture in 1984, AT&T was the nation's largest telephone company. Telephone operations require a large investment in plant and equipment. To meet its needs for funds, AT&T sold to the general public many issues of bonds and common stock. The company had an excellent credit rating and was always able to market new issues of securities. However, AT&T could not issue bonds and exclude issuing new stock, because such a strategy would increase the use of financial leverage and risk. Issuing only debt would result in a higher cost of capital. • Even though excessive use of debt financing will increase a firm's cost of capital, AT&T did issue a substantial amount of debt. During the decade 1965–1975, AT&T's debt ratio rose from 31 percent to more than 50 percent. At that time management became very concerned about the increased use of debt financing. In particular, the management of AT&T did not want to lose the firm's excellent credit rating. If the firm's rating were lowered, future debt issues would require higher interest rates, which could reduce profitability and lead to higher telephone rates. • To reduce the need for debt financing, AT&T placed more emphasis on internally generated funds and new equity financing. Besides selling new stock to the general public, AT&T used increased retention of earnings, a revised dividend reinvestment plan, and employee stock plans to raise additional equity funds. When divestiture occurred in 1984, the debt ratio had been reduced to 42.5 percent. • Since divestiture, management has continued to improve AT&T's debt ratio. Since the firm is no longer a regulated utility but a competitive communications firm, its prices are not set by regulatory commissions. Thus, the risk exposure of its creditors and stockholders has been increased. To offset this increased business risk, AT&T's management has decided to reduce the risk associated with the firm's financing. In AT&T's *1989 Annual Report,* management stated that the debt ratio had continued to decline to 38.7 percent. •

The optimal capital structure is reached at the minimum point on the weighted average cost of capital structure. The financial manager should acquire this combination of financing because it involves the lowest cost of funds.

This minimum cost of capital should be used to judge potential investments; it will be employed in the capital budgeting techniques discussed in the next chapter. As the firm expands and makes additional investments in plant and equipment, it must also expand its sources of financing. These additional sources should maintain the firm's optimal capital structure. Additional (or marginal) investments are financed by additional (or marginal) funds. As long as the optimal capital structure is maintained, additional funds should cost the same as the weighted average (i.e., the weighted marginal cost of funds is equal to the firm's average cost of capital). Of course, if the additional investments increase the riskiness of the firm or the flotation costs associated with issuing new securities rise, then the cost of the additional funds will increase. In that case, which is discussed in the next section, the cost of the marginal funds will exceed the firm's weighted average cost of capital.

FIGURE 22.3

Cost of Capital

As the firm uses more debt financing, the cost of capital initially declines. It reaches a minimum (the optimal capital structure) and then starts to rise as the firm becomes excessively leveraged.

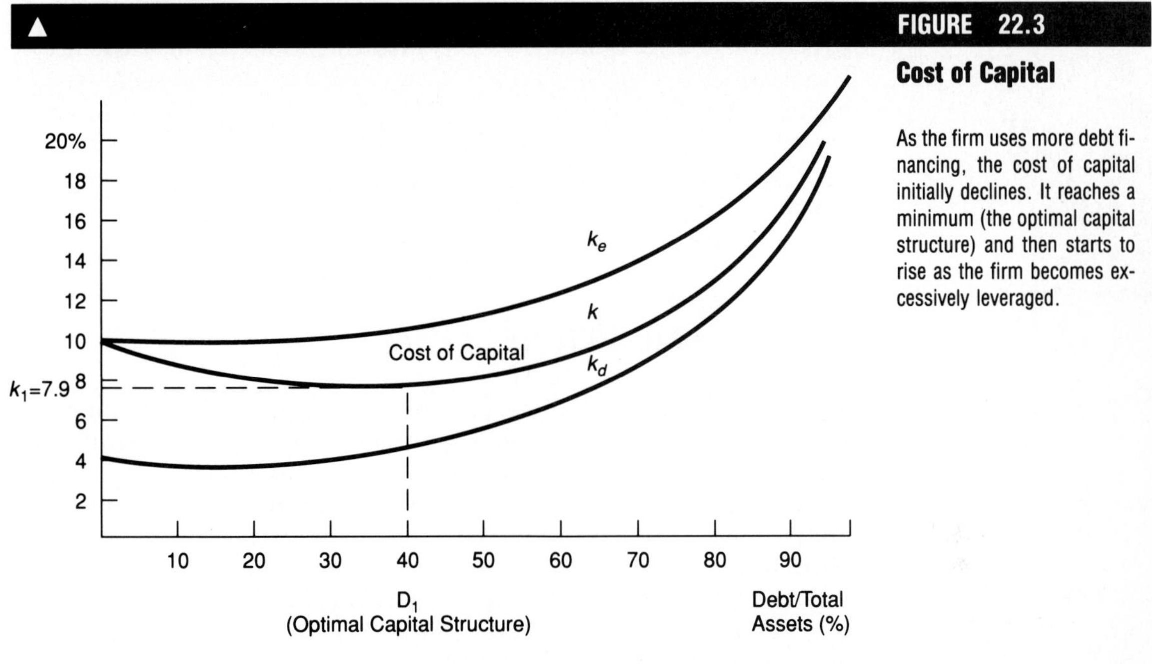

For many firms, the optimal capital structure is a range of debt financing. In the example presented in Exhibit 22.1 and Figure 22.3, the weighted average cost of capital does not vary significantly for debt financing ranging from 30 to 50 percent. This indicates that the effect of debt financing in lowering the firm's cost of capital is achieved when 30 percent of the firm's assets are debt financed. Additional use of debt, however, does not start to increase the cost of capital until more than 50 percent of the assets are debt financed. Thus, the optimal capital structure is a range of debt-to-equity financing and not just a specific combination of debt to equity.

The fact that the optimal capital structure is a range and not a specific combination is important from a practical viewpoint. New issues of debt or common stock are made infrequently, and when debt or stock is issued, the dollar amount of the issue may be substantial. A firm will not bother to issue new securities for a trivial amount of money because of the cost of issuing them. Thus, when new securities are issued, the proportions may be significantly altered. If the optimal capital structure were not a range, every new issue of securities would alter the firm's cost of capital. Since the optimal debt structure is a range, a firm has flexibility in issuing new securities and may tailor the security issues to market conditions. For example, if management anticipates that interest rates will increase in the future, it may choose to issue debt now and use equity financing at some future date. This flexibility in the type of securities issued is in part the result of the fact that the optimal capital structure is a range of debt-to-equity financing. But even the existence of a range does not mean (1) that a firm can always use the same type of financing, or (2) that it is not important for a firm to seek the optimal capital structure. Finding the optimal capital structure, like finding the most profitable level of output, is required if management wants to maximize the value of the firm.

THE MARGINAL COST OF CAPITAL

Marginal cost of capital ▲
Cost of additional sources of finance

Once the optimal capital stucture has been determined, the financial manager should seek to maintain it. Preserving the optimal capital structure, however, does not necessarily mean that the cost of capital is constant. The cost of additional funds (i.e., the **marginal cost of capital**) can rise. If the cost of debt or the cost of equity increases as the firm uses more debt and equity financing, the marginal cost of capital will rise, even though the optimal capital structure is preserved. For example, the cost of common stock depends on whether the firm is using retained earnings or issuing new shares. New shares cost more than retained earnings because of flotation costs. The marginal cost of capital will increase when new shares are issued even though the optimal combination of debt and equity financing is preserved.

Consider the illustration in Exhibit 22.1, in which the optimal cost of capital was 7.9 percent with 40 percent debt and 60 percent equity. That cost consisted of the 4 percent after-tax cost of debt and the 10.5 percent cost of equity. This cost of equity is the cost of retained earnings because these equity funds are used before the firm would issue new (and more expensive) common stock.

Suppose, however, the firm has additional investment opportunities that would require more than its retained earnings. It could borrow all of the necessary funds, which would increase the firm's use of financial leverage. Such a course of action would be undesirable because the firm would no longer be maintaining its optimal capital structure. To maintain the optimal capital structure, the firm will have to issue additional shares (and pay the associated flotation costs) and simultaneously borrow some additional funds if it wants to make these investments. The firm must borrow 40 percent of the additional funds and issue new shares to cover the remaining 60 percent of the additional financing. The impact of the increase in the cost of equity due to the flotation costs is to increase the cost of capital, even though the proportion of debt to equity is maintained.

To illustrate this increase in the cost of capital, suppose the 10.5 percent cost of equity consisted of the following dividend yield and growth rate:

$$k_e = \frac{\$0.95(1 + 0.055)}{\$20} + 0.055$$

$$k_e = \frac{\$1.00}{\$20} + 0.055 = 0.05 + 0.055 = 10.5\%$$

Once retained earnings are exhausted, the firm will have to issue new shares with a flotation cost of $1.00 per share, so the firm nets $19 per share. The cost of these new shares is

$$k_{ne} = \frac{\$0.95(1 + 0.055)}{\$20 - \$1} + 0.055$$

$$k_{ne} = \frac{\$1.00}{\$19} + 0.055 = 0.0526 + 0.055 = 10.76\%$$

The cost of the common stock rises from 10.5 percent to 10.76 percent and the firm's cost of capital rises to

$$k = (0.4)(4\%) + (0.6)(10.76\%) = 8.056\%.$$

The cost of capital has risen from 7.9 percent to 8.056 percent even though management is maintaining the optimal capital structure of 40 percent debt and 60 percent equity.

Which of these two costs (7.9 percent and 8.056 percent) does the firm use when making investment decisions? The answer depends on how many investment opportunities the firm has. If the firm has insufficient opportunities to consume its retained earnings, the cost of capital is 7.9 percent. However, after the retained earnings are exhausted and new shares must be sold, the firm's cost of capital rises to 8.056 percent. Then, 8.056 percent should be used to judge additional investment opportunities because that is the firm's cost of capital.

The following example will illustrate this process of making additional investments and maintaining the optimal capital structure as the cost of finance changes. Currently, the firm desires to make six $1,000,000 investments. (Remember, the techniques for selecting investments will be discussed in the subsequent chapter. In reality, the determination of the cost of capital and the decision to make long-term investments are tied together, but only one piece of the puzzle can be discussed at a time!) The firm has $10,000,000 in assets financed 40 percent with debt and 60 percent with equity. This optimal capital structure was determined earlier and has a cost of capital of 10.5 percent. The information used to determine that cost of capital was

1. an after-tax cost of debt of 4 percent,
2. a current dividend of $0.95 which will rise to $1.00 during the year,
3. a stock price of $20,
4. a growth rate of 5.5 percent.

During the period when the desired investments are to be made, the firm will generate retained earnings of $1,200,000. In addition, the firm's creditors have informed management that if the firm borrows more than $2,000,000, the rate of interest will have to be increased, even if the firm maintains its capital structure. The impact of this increase will raise the after-tax cost of debt to 5 percent. What will be the marginal cost of each additional dollar to the firm?

This is the most complicated question posed in this chapter. Management knows the optimal capital structure is 40 percent debt and that this structure should be retained. Thus, for every additional $400,000 of borrowed funds, the firm must have $600,000 in new equity. Thus, the $1,200,000 in new retained earnings will support $800,000 in additional borrowed capital for a total of $2,000,000 in new finance. The cost of these funds is

$$k = (.4)(4\%) + (.6)(10.5\%) = 7.9\%.$$

Thus, the cost of the first $2,000,000 in additional funds (i.e., the marginal cost) is 7.9%. $2,000,000, however, will not cover all the investment opportunities.

Since an additional $4,000,000 is needed to make all the desired investments, the financial manager decides to issue $2,400,000 in additional stock (i.e., 0.6 × $4,000,000). $2,400,000 in additional stock will support $1,600,000 in additional debt and still maintain the 40 percent debt financing. What will be the cost of the additional funds? If the after-tax cost of debt remains 4 percent and the cost of new shares is 10.76 percent, the firm's cost of capital is

$$k = (.4)(4\%) + (.6)(10.76\%) = 8.056\%.$$

However, does the after-tax cost of debt remain at 4 percent? The answer is yes only for the first $2,000,000; above that, additional debt has an after-tax cost of 5 percent. The financial manager anticipated borrowing $800,000 to be used in conjunction with the $1,200,000 in retained earnings and $1,600,000 to be used with the $2,400,000 raised through the issuing of new shares. That is a total of $2,400,000. Only the first $2,000,000 will have an after-tax cost of 4 percent. The last $400,000 will cost 5 percent. Once again, the cost of capital changes even though the optimal combination of debt and equity financing is maintained. The cost of capital now rises to

$$k = (.4)(5\%) + (.6)(10.76\%) = 8.456\%.$$

These different costs of capital are illustrated in Figure 22.4, which presents the firm's marginal cost of capital. As additional funds are needed, the marginal cost of capital rises. The first increase occurs at $2,000,000, when the firm runs out of retained earnings. The second increment occurs at $5,000,000, when the firm runs out of borrowing capacity with the lower after-tax cost of debt.

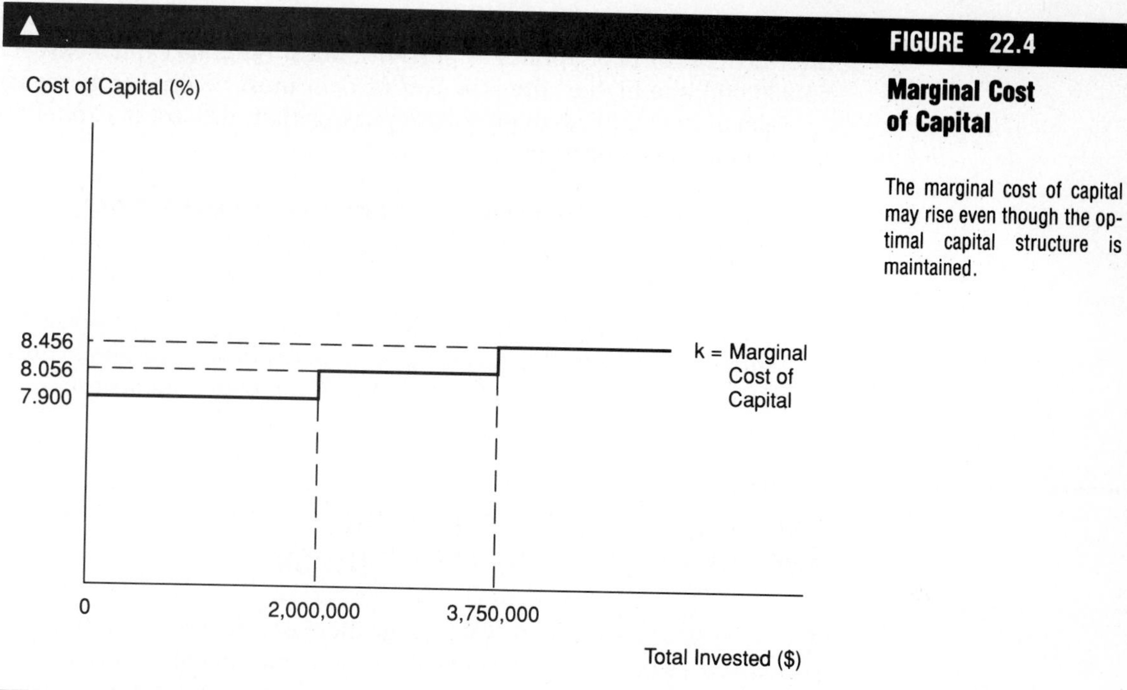

FIGURE 22.4

Marginal Cost of Capital

The marginal cost of capital may rise even though the optimal capital structure is maintained.

How are these amounts ($2,000,000 and $5,000,000) determined? These breaks in the marginal cost of capital schedule may be determined by the following equation:

22.6
$$\text{Break-point} = \frac{\text{Amount of funds available at a given cost}}{\text{Proportion of that component in the capital structure}}$$

For example, there were $1,200,000 of available retained earnings, and equity constituted 60 percent of the capital structure. Thus, the break-point for the retained earnings is

$$\text{Break-point (retained earnings)} = \frac{\$1{,}200{,}000}{.6} = \$2{,}000{,}000.$$

Thus, the cost of capital of the first $2,000,000 uses the lower cost of retained earnings (10.5 percent) in the calculation. Once $2,000,000 is exceeded, the higher cost of new stock (10.76 percent) must be used.

The same logic applies to the cost of debt. The break-point for debt is

$$\text{Break-point (cheaper debt)} = \frac{\$2{,}000{,}000}{.4} = \$5{,}000{,}000.$$

As long as the total funds raised are less than \$5,000,000, the lower after-tax cost of debt applies (4 percent), but if the total capital exceeds \$5,000,000, the higher after-tax cost of debt must be used (5 percent).

When these individual pieces are put together, the cost of capital for different amounts of funds is

$$\begin{aligned} \$0 - \$2{,}000{,}000&: (.4)(4\%) + (.6)(10.5\%) = 7.9\% \\ \$2{,}000{,}001 - \$5{,}000{,}000&: (.4)(4\%) + (.6)(10.76\%) = 8.056\% \\ \text{above } \$5{,}000{,}000&: (.4)(5\%) + (.6)(10.76\%) = 8.456\% \end{aligned}$$

This is, of course, the schedule of the marginal costs of funds presented in Figure 22.4, which illustrates the increments in the marginal cost of capital and at what level of additional funds these increments occur.

THE OPTIMAL CAPITAL STRUCTURE AND THE VALUE OF THE FIRM'S STOCK

The successful use of financial leverage increases the return on the firm's equity and increases earnings per share. Earnings per share increase because as the firm uses more debt financing and becomes more financially leveraged, it issues relatively fewer shares. Thus, earnings are spread over fewer shares, which increases per-share earnings. Does this increased use of debt and higher per-share earnings lead to a higher stock price? What is the relationship between the optimal capital structure and the price of the stock?

These are important and difficult questions that are developed more fully in advanced texts on finance. The following discussion can, at best, only indicate the relationship among the components of the cost of capital, the optimal capital structure, and stock valuation.

Since the goal of management is to maximize the value of the firm's stock, the optimal capital structure is that combination of debt and equity financing that maximizes the value of the stock. The financial manager substitutes debt for equity as long as this substitution increases per-share earnings without unduly increasing the risk associated with debt financing. The increase in per-share earnings, when coupled with only a moderate addition to risk, should increase the value of the stock. However, if the firm continues to substitute debt for equity and use more financial leverage, the element of risk will increase sufficiently to offset the advantage of higher per-share earnings. The net effect is to cause the value of the shares to fall.

This trade-off is illustrated in Exhibit 22.2. The firm needs \$1,000, so the financial manager considers the impact of borrowing the funds. In part I, the first row presents the amount of debt to be issued in incre-

EXHIBIT 22.2

Determination of the Optimal Capital Structure Using Market Value of Stock

The value of the stock rises as the cost of capital declines. This value is maximized when the cost of capital is minimized.

I.							
Amount of debt	$ 0	$100	$200	$300	$400	$500	$600
Cost of debt	10%	10%	10%	11%	12%	14%	16%
Cost of equity	15%	15%	15.5%	16.6%	17.8%	19.4%	21.5%
Number of shares outstanding	10	9	8	7	6	5	4
II.							
Earnings before interest & taxes	$250	$250	$250	$250	$250	$250	$250
Interest	$ —	$ 10	$ 20	$ 33.0	$ 48.0	$ 70	$ 96.0
Earnings before taxes	$250	$240	$230	$217.0	$202.0	$180	$154.0
Tax (at 40%)	$100	$ 96	$ 92	$ 86.8	$ 80.8	$ 72	$ 61.6
Net income	$150	$144	$138.00	$130.20	$121.20	$108.00	$ 92.40
Earnings per share	$ 15	$ 16	$ 17.25	$ 18.60	$ 20.20	$ 21.60	$ 23.10
III.							
Value of a share	$100	$106.67	$111.29	$112.05	$113.48	$111.34	$107.44
IV.							
Cost of capital	15%	14.1%	13.6%	13.6%	13.56% ↑	13.9%	14.36%

ments of $100. The second line presents the before-tax cost of the debt, and the third line gives the cost of equity. As the firm becomes more financially leveraged, the before-tax cost of debt and the cost of equity rise. The fourth line indicates that as the firm uses more debt financing, the number of shares outstanding is reduced (fewer shares will have to be issued to raise the necessary capital).

Part II presents a simple income statement for the firm as it uses more debt. Operating income ($250) is the same regardless of the choice of financing. As more debt is used (and as the rate of interest charged rises), interest expense rises, reducing taxable earnings and, correspondingly, reducing taxes. The lower taxes do not completely offset the higher interest payments, so net income declines. Earnings per share, however, rise because the smaller earnings are spread over a fewer number of shares.

Parts III and IV present the value of the stock and the cost of capital at the various combinations of debt and equity financing. Initially, the use of financial leverage increases the value of the stock. These values are derived using the dividend-growth model:

$$V = \frac{D_0(1 + g)}{k_e - g}$$

To simplify the illustration, it is assumed that all earnings are distributed. Therefore, the value of the stock is

$$V = \frac{D_0(1 + g)}{k_e - g} = \frac{\text{Earnings per share}}{k_e}$$

when $g = 0$. Thus, when per-share earnings are \$17.25 (at \$200 debt), the value of the stock is \$17.25/0.155 = \$111.29.

As may be seen in part III, the value of the stock initially rises because the firm is successfully employing financial leverage. However, as the firm becomes more financially leveraged, the increased risk starts to offset the advantage of financial leverage. The value of the stock reaches a maximum and then starts to decline.

The combination of debt and equity financing that maximizes the value of the stock also is the firm's optimal capital structure. This is illustrated in part IV, which presents the cost of capital. In this illustration, the minimum cost of capital occurs when the firm seeks to use \$400 in debt so that 40 percent of its assets are financed with debt and 60 percent with equity. At that capital structure, the minimum cost of capital is

$$\begin{aligned} k &= w_d(k_d)(1 - T) + w_e(k_e) \\ &= (.4)(.12)(1 - .4) + (.6)(.178) = 13.56\%. \end{aligned}$$

Exhibit 22.2 presents the same concept that was illustrated in Exhibit 22.1 but ties together the maximization of the value of the stock with the minimization of the firm's cost of funds. The combination of debt and equity financing that minimizes the cost of capital will also maximize the value of the stock. This statement has intuitive appeal. If the financial manager is able to minimize the firm's cost of funds, that should benefit the firm's owners. If the financial manager is not minimizing the cost of capital, the firm will not be as attractive to investors, and the value or the equity will be reduced. Thus, the maximizing the value of the firm requires minimizing the cost of capital.

COST OF CAPITAL REVIEW AND PROBLEM AREAS

No topic in this text is more important than the determination of a firm's cost of funds and its optimal capital structure. As the previous discussion indicated, it is a complex procedure that in reality is difficult to apply. The following discussion reiterates some of the problem areas and reveals others that until now have been swept under the carpet.

First, to determine the cost of capital, the financial manager must know all the component costs. As was previously mentioned, the estimation of the cost of equity requires information (e.g., the future growth rate in dividends, the firm's beta coefficient, the appropriate risk-free rate, the expected return on the market) that is not readily observable. An inaccurate measure of the cost of equity leads to an inaccurate estimate of the cost of capital.

Second, the financial manager needs to know how the market will value the shares after the financing decision is made. This is, of course, impossible to know with certainty. Obviously, the financial manager makes the financing decision in anticipation of the market treating the shares in a particular way, but conditions change and the anticipated correct financial structure in one environment may not be correct in a different environment. The large use of debt financing leverage during the leveraged buyout period of the late 1980s generated lower stock prices for some firms during the early 1990s. Hindsight is perfect, but financial decisions must be made with foresight.

Third, the discussion examined the optimal capital structure in terms of maximizing the value of a firm's stock. That may be acceptable for publicly held firms, but the vast majority of businesses are not publicly held. Even though most privately held firms are small, the determination of their cost of capital remains important. As is explained in the next chapter, this determination is a critical part of the decision to invest in plant and equipment. However, the financial managers of small firms cannot know for certain the current value of their firm's equity or the impact their decisions will have on that value.

Fourth, depreciation was excluded from the above discussion. Depreciation expense may generate cash that may be used in a variety of ways, such as restoring the asset that is being depreciated, investing in an alternative investment, or returning capital to its sources (i.e., retiring debt or equity). Many competing uses exist for the cash generated through depreciation charges, and the financial manager needs an estimate of the cost of depreciation-generated funds in order to help determine the best use of these funds.

Fifth, there is a notable theory in finance that contends a firm's capital structure may be irrelevant. This conclusion is derived from several important assumptions, one of which is that if a firm uses too little financial leverage, investors can substitute their own leverage for the firm's. Consider a firm with no debt financing. Investors can borrow money to buy the stock (i.e., buy the stock on margin). In such a case, the stockholders are substituting their own leverage for the firm's use of financial leverage. If the firm uses a large amount of financial leverage, the stockholders can then hold portfolios of cash and the stock, which reduces the impact of the firm's large use of financial leverage. By having stockholders alter their portfolios to offset a firm's use of financial leverage, one can reason that an optimal capital structure is irrelevant. What is important is the operating income the firm generates, and not how that income is divided between creditors in the form of interest payments and owners in the form of dividends and capital gains.[2]

If the firm's capital structure is irrelevant, it is possible for a firm to have no equity. Consider the following simplified balance sheet for Joy Technologies as of the end of its 1990 fiscal year:

ASSETS (IN THOUSANDS)		LIABILITIES AND EQUITY (IN THOUSANDS)	
Current assets	$313,160	Current liabilities	$169,628
Plant and equipment	122,400	Long-term debt	393,037
Other assets	145,335	Other liabilities	31,152
Total assets	$580,895	Total liabilities	$593,817
		Preferred stock	52,027
		Common stock	22,705
		Retained earnings	(79,574)
		Other adjustments	(8,080)
		Total equity	(12,922)
		Total liabilities and equity	$580,895

As is immediately apparent, total liabilities exceed total assets ($593,817 in liabilities to $580,895 in assets). Liabilities can only exceed assets if equity is negative. If Joy Technologies ceased operations and the assets were sold for their values on the balance sheet, there would not be sufficient funds to retire all the debt. Nothing would be left for the stockholders; there is no equity.

How can such a balance sheet occur? One possible explanation is that the firm has consistently operated at a loss. The accumulated retained earnings will be negative, and if the negative retained earnings are sufficiently large, it will exceed the positive numbers in the other equity accounts, so that total equity will be negative. Another possible explanation is that leveraged buyouts and recapitalizations may result in negative equity. In 1988, the management of Joy issued a substantial amount of debt and executed a leveraged buyout by repurchasing most of the outstanding stock. The repurchase price exceeded the book value

[2] For a discussion of this proposition and the theory that dividend policy is irrelevant, see the latest edition of an advanced text on corporate finance, such as Eugene Brigham and Louis Gapenski, *Financial Management: Theory and Practice,* 6th ed. (Hinsdale, Ill.: The Dryden Press, 1991), pp. 446–462, or Stephen A. Ross, Randolph W. Westerfield, and Jeffrey F. Jaffe, *Corporate Finance,* 2d ed. (Homewood, Ill.: Richard D. Irwin, Inc., 1990), pp. 385–388 and 392–400.

of the stock, which erased the amounts in the equity accounts. In effect, Joy Technologies became a highly leveraged, privately held firm.

The heavy use of debt financing during the late 1980s and the issuing of various types of high-yield securities and "junk bonds" to finance takeovers and recapitalizations led to some firms' having large amounts of debt relative to equity. As the Joy Technologies balance sheet indicates, a leveraged buyout can result in total debt exceeding total assets, so the firm has negative equity. Such capital structures are consistent with the concept that a firm's capital structure is irrelevant. What is important is the ability of the firm to generate cash flow to service its sources of finance and not the division of the sources into debt and equity.

The managements of many firms that issued substantial amounts of debt during the 1980s found that operations could not generate the cash flow needed to service the debt. While some have defaulted on their debt obligations (e.g., Interco, Southland, and TWA), others have not. Even though these firms have not defaulted, many are in financial difficulty. However, the existence of financial problems does not mean that these firms will fail. Instead, some have sold assets and others have issued stock to raise funds to retire debt and reduce the use of financial leverage. Interestingly, reduction in financial leverage by firms that issued excessive amounts of debt during the 1980s may occur in the 1990s.

Many highly leveraged firms are currently seeking to reduce outstanding debt, which suggests that their financial managers believe there is an optimal combination of debt and equity financing. This chapter emphasized how management lowers a firm's weighted average cost of funds by substituting cheaper debt for more expensive equity. However, as the firm becomes more financially leveraged, it becomes riskier, and the cost of capital rises. Management thus seeks to determine the best combination of debt and equity financing that takes advantage of financial leverage without unduly increasing risk. Such an optimal capital structure must include both debt and equity financing.

SUMMARY

All assets must be financed; although there may be a variety of instruments, there are ultimately only two sources: debt and equity. If the firm uses debt financing or preferred stock financing, it is financially leveraged. If the firm uses financial leverage, it increases risk, which may increase the cost of the components of the firm's capital structure.

One component, the cost of debt, depends on the interest rate that must be paid and the tax savings associated with the deductibility of interest payments. Another component, the cost of preferred stock, depends on the dividend that is paid and the proceeds from the sale of the preferred stock. A third component, the cost of common equity, depends on whether the firm is using retained earnings or issuing new shares of stock. New equity is more expensive because of the flotation costs associated with the sale of the new shares.

The cost of common equity is an opportunity cost concept: it is the return necessary to induce investors to own the stock. This cost may be determined by adding a risk premium to the interest rate paid creditors such as bondholders. An alternative approach to determine the cost of common stock is to use the capital asset pricing model, which incorporates the return on a risk-free security, the return on the market as a whole, and the systematic risk associated with the stock. A third approach uses the expected dividend yield and capital gain to determine the cost of common stock.

A weighted average of the component costs is computed to determine the firm's cost of capital. This cost of capital is calculated for various capital structures in order to determine the best or optimal capital structure. That structure takes advantage of financial leverage without unduly increasing risk, so the cost of capital is minimized. This minimization of the cost of capital will also increase the value of the common stock and help meet one of the financial manager's goals: the maximization of the value of the firm's equity.

Review Questions

1. What impact does a firm's tax rate have on the cost of debt? Will lower federal income tax rates encourage the use of equity or debt financing?
2. Why will a firm tend to prefer to issue debt instead of preferred stock in order to obtain financial leverage?
3. What impact will each of the following have on a firm's cost of equity?
   a. an increase in flotation costs
   b. a decrease in the firm's beta
   c. a decrease in interest rates
   d. the firm's increased use of operating leverage
4. What happens to a firm's cost of capital as it initially substitutes debt for equity?
5. Why would you expect the cost of common stock to exceed the cost of preferred stock and the cost of preferred stock to exceed the cost of debt?
6. Why may the marginal cost of capital exceed the firm's weighted average cost of capital?
7. If a firm reduced its dividend payments and retained a larger proportion of its earnings, what would happen to the firm's marginal cost of capital?
8. If a firm achieves its optimal capital structure, what does that imply about the value of its common stock?

Problems

1. A firm's current balance sheet is as follows:

Assets	$100	Debt	$10
		Equity	$90

a. What is the firm's weighted average cost of capital at various combinations of debt and equity, given the following information?

Debt/ Assets	Cost of Debt	Cost of Equity	Cost of Capital
0%	8%	12%	
10	8	12	
20	8	12	
30	8	13	?
40	9	14	
50	10	15	
60	12	16	

b. Construct a pro forma balance sheet that indicates the firm's optimal capital structure. Compare this balance sheet with the firm's current balance sheet. What course of action should the firm take?

Assets	$100	Debt	$?
		Equity	$?

c. As a firm initially substitutes debt for equity financing, what happens to the cost of capital, and why?

d. If a firm uses too much debt financing, why does the cost of capital rise?

2. The financial manager of a firm determines the following schedules of cost of debt and cost of equity for various combinations of debt financing:

Debt/Assets	Cost of Debt	Cost of Equity
0%	4%	8%
10	4	8
20	4	8
30	5	8
40	6	10
50	8	12
60	10	14
70	12	16

a. Find the optimal capital structure (i.e., optimal combination of debt and equity financing).
b. Why does the cost of capital initially decline as the firm substitutes debt for equity financing?
c. Why will the cost of funds eventually rise as the firm becomes more financially leveraged?
d. Why is debt financing more common than financing with preferred stock?
e. If interest were not a tax deductible expense, what effect would that have on the firm's cost of capital? Why?

3. a. Given the following, determine the firm's optimal capital structure:

Debt/Assets	Cost of Debt	Cost of Equity
0%	8%	12%
10	8	12
20	8	12
30	9	12
40	9	13
50	10	15
60	12	17

b. If the firm were using 60 percent debt and 40 percent equity, what would that tell you about the firm's use of financial leverage?
c. What two reasons explain why debt is cheaper than equity?
d. If the firm were using 30 percent debt and 70 percent equity and earned a return of 11.7 percent on an investment, would this mean that stockholders will receive less than their required return of 12 percent? What return will stockholders receive?

4. A firm has the following capital structure that it believes to be optimal:

Assets	$10,000	Debt	$3,000
		Preferred stock	1,000
		Common stock	6,000

The current rate of interest is 10 percent. The firm's federal income tax rate is 40 percent, and its stock sells for $40 a share. The firm pays a $2 per share cash dividend that is expected to grow annually at 7 percent. Preferred stock pays a $10 per share annual dividend and currently sells for $90 a share.

a. What is the cost of debt?
b. What is the cost of preferred stock?
c. What is the cost of common stock?
d. What is the firm's weighted average cost of capital?

cases

Calculating the Cost of Capital while Maintaining the Optimal Capital Structure

Hector Albeniz was recently promoted to the position of Vice-President of Finance. His first assignment is to determine the firm's cost of finance, which is necessary to judge long-term investments. This is an important assignment since the firm is anticipating substantial growth, which will require considerable investments in additional plant and equipment. Overestimating the cost of funds could lead to the rejection of profitable investments. Even worse, if the cost is underestimated, the firm could acquire assets that are unprofitable.

Over a period of many years, management has adopted a conservative policy of never permitting debt to exceed 30 percent of total financing. Even if the firm could sustain more financial leverage, Albeniz realizes that management would not use additional debt financing if the debt ratio were to exceed 30 percent. If the firm needs equity financing to make desirable long-term investments and simultaneously maintain its conservative capital structure, management is, however, willing to consider reducing the dividend to \$1 or issuing additional shares.

Albeniz estimates that the firm will earn \$10,000,000 during the year. Forty percent of the earnings will be distributed as cash dividends, and the firm will have retained earnings of \$6,000,000 to invest in plant and equipment. Currently, the price of the stock is \$50 a share, the dividend is \$2, and the expected growth rate is 10 percent. That yields a cost of equity (retained earnings) of

$$k_e = \frac{\$2}{\$50} + 0.10 = 14\%.$$

Management believes that even if the dividend were reduced to \$1, the price of the stock would not decline as long as excellent investment choices were made, in which case increased growth would compensate for the lower dividend. Albeniz has ascertained from the firm's investment bankers that additional shares can readily be sold, but that there would be a flotation cost of \$2 a share. The firm would net \$48 for each share sold, in which case the cost of equity (new shares) becomes:

$$k_{ne} = \frac{\$2}{(\$50 - \$2)} + 0.10 = 14.17\%.$$

Currently, the rate of interest on the firm's long-term debt is 10 percent and the firm's income tax rate is 32 percent. Up to $2,400,000 face amount in new debt can be issued at the going rate. If the firm were to issue more than $2,400,000, the interest would rise to 11 percent.

Albeniz knows that management wants to know the cost of raising additional finance in increments of $3,000,000, consisting of $900,000 in debt and $2,100,000 of equity (i.e., 30 percent debt and 70 percent equity). Thus, Albeniz must construct a marginal cost of capital schedule, but he decides to present two versions. The first version assumes that the dividend is maintained so that retained earnings will be $6,000,000. In the second version, it is assumed that the dividend is reduced so that retained earnings are increased to $8,000,000. To construct the schedules, Albeniz accepts management's belief that the change in dividend policy will have no impact on the cost of equity.

Case Problems

1. Develop the two marginal cost of capital schedules.
2. What would be the impact on the second schedule if the price of the stock declined as a result of the lower dividend?
3. If the firm's income tax rate rises, what impact would that have on the marginal cost of capital schedule?
4. If the firm needs $12,000,000 in increments of $3,000,000, what is the cost of these funds if it retains $6,000,000?

Suggested Readings

Financial leverage and the cost of capital are among the most controversial topics in finance. There is a considerable amount of material on measuring the cost of capital and the impact of leverage on the valuation of a firm. Much of this material is very theoretical, and the empirical work on these topics requires knowledge of statistics. A good starting point is an advanced text on financial management. See in particular:

Brigham, Eugene F., and Louis C. Gapenski. *Financial Management: Theory and Practice.* 6th ed. Hinsdale, Ill.: The Dryden Press, 1991, chapter 8.

Ross, Stephen A.; Randolph W. Westerfield; and Jeffrey F. Jaffe. *Corporate Finance.* 2d ed. Homewood, Ill.: Richard D. Irwin, Inc., 1990, chapters 14 and 15.

The actual techniques used by firms to determine their capital structures have been surveyed in:

Gitman, Lawrence J., and Vincent A. Mercurio. "Cost of Capital Techniques Used by Major U.S. Firms: Survey and Analysis of Fortune's 1000." *Financial Management* (Winter 1982), pp. 21–29.

Recent research on capital structure is summarized in:

Smith, Clifford. "Raising Capital: Theory and Evidence." *Midland Corporate Finance Journal* (Spring 1986).

chapter 23

Capital Budgeting

31 pages in chapter

Learning Objectives

1. Determine an investment's payback period, net present value, and internal rate of return.
2. Distinguish between an investment's profit and cash flows.
3. Compare net present value and internal rate of return.
4. Describe the reinvestment assumption employed by net present value and internal rate of return.
5. Define mutually exclusive investments.
6. Adjust capital budgeting techniques for risk.
7. Apply discounted cash flows techniques to various long-term investment decisions.

According to Henry David Thoreau, "goodness is the only investment that never fails." Unfortunately, many financial managers know from experience that some investments do fail. But in the view of Sir William Gilbert and Sir Arthur Sullivan, "nothing venture, nothing win." This is, of course, the dilemma facing financial managers. They must seek profitable long-term ventures to assure the firm's long-term survival, but they simultaneously run the risk of failure.

Virtually every firm invests in long-term assets to generate future sales and growth in earnings. During 1989, Exxon committed $4.4 billion to additional plant and equipment. United Telecom, one of the largest telephone networks with sales of $4.3 billion, invested $1.4 billion in telephone plant and equipment during 1989. Even tiny Clifton Forge–Waynesboro Telephone with sales of only $20 million increased its investment in telephone plant and equipment by $4.1 million.

The managements of each of these firms had to decide which long-term investments to make. This selection process is referred to as capital budgeting. Capital budgeting seeks to answer such questions as: (1) Should an old machine be replaced with a new machine? (2) Should the level of operation of the firm be expanded by purchasing new plant and equipment? or (3) Which of two competing new machines should the firm purchase? These decisions are crucial to the life and profitability of the firm. Failure to make profitable investments will certainly reduce the value of the firm. Since capital budgeting techniques aid in this decision-making process, they are crucial to increasing the wealth of the firm and its stockholders.

This chapter is concerned with these techniques. Capital budgeting is a complicated topic, one to which an entire text could be devoted. The treatment in this chapter will only indicate the essence of the subject; at best, it lays the groundwork for the student to pursue the subject in more advanced courses. Even if you do not intend to pursue the study of finance, the chapter will give you a basis for understanding the concept. Since many firms use capital budgeting, all students of business need an understanding of its purposes and techniques.

Three methods for selecting among competing uses of long-term capital are covered in this chapter: (1) payback period, (2) internal rate of return, and (3) net present value. All three methods aid in the decision to purchase a fixed asset *now*, but the benefits from the investment occur to the firm *in the future*. Understanding this time element is very important. All capital budgeting techniques require a forecast of the anticipated cash flow (i.e., profits plus depreciation).

The availability of good forecasts and reliable data is as crucial for capital budgeting as the correct application of the techniques.

After describing and illustrating each technique, the chapter explores using net present value and internal rate of return to choose between mutually exclusive investments. While net present value and internal rate of return often result in the same rankings for investments, the possibility of differing rankings does exist. The chapter briefly discusses what may cause the conflicts and how they may be resolved.

The next section of the chapter introduces risk into capital budgeting and suggests means to adjust for differences in risk. The chapter ends with applications of net present value to the decision to replace equipment before it is worn out and the decision to refund a bond issue prior to maturity.

VALUATION AND LONG-TERM INVESTMENT DECISIONS

Chapter 9 discussed the determination of a bond's present value and its yield to maturity. Chapter 11 discussed the determination of a stock's value and its return. In both cases, the process required estimating future cash flows (e.g., interest or dividend payments), which were discounted back to the present. For bonds this rate was the yield on debt, and for common stock this rate was the investor's required rate of return.

An investment in long-term assets such as plant and equipment is conceptually no different than an investment in a financial asset. Such long-term investments in physical assets require the financial manager to identify and estimate future cash flows and either discount them back to their present value or compute the investment's rate of return. The process of determining the value of an investment in plant and equipment or its return and selecting among various long-term investments is referred to as **capital budgeting.**

Capital budgeting ▲
The process of selecting long-term investments

Many types of long-term investment decisions fall under the heading, "capital budgeting." Some are obvious, such as investing in research and development (R and D) to develop new products, or acquiring new plant and equipment to expand output to enter new markets for existing products. Capital budgeting techniques may also apply to the decision to replace existing plant and equipment prior to the end of their anticipated lives or the decision to refund a bond issue prior to maturity. In some cases, such as the acquisition of an office building or a corporate headquarters or the purchase of environmental or safety equipment, long-term investment decisions must be made even though no specific product may be generated by or identified with the investment.

Occasionally, long-term investment decisions are beyond the control of the financial manager. The maintenance of equipment necessary to produce a profitable product, the installation of pollution control equipment required by environmental legislation, or meeting new safety standards will require mandatory investments by the firm. The choice is not whether to make the investment but which of the competing means should be employed.

Some long-term investments rapidly generate profitable returns. At the other extreme are investments in R and D, which require years to develop and even then may never generate a profit. For example, a firm may make a large expenditure on research for the development of a cure for AIDS but never succeed. If it does develop a cure, it may achieve a commercial success only if other firms do not develop a comparable or superior product.

All investments involve costs. In some cases, the costs may be readily identifiable. When Hertz acquires new cars, their cost is obviously known. Other costs associated with the investment may not be so readily identifiable. Will Hertz have to invest in additional storage and maintenance facilities? Will it have to open additional rental outlets? Will it have to hire more employees and invest in their training? These costs associated with the new cars could be substantial and convert what on the surface appears to be a profitable and wise investment into a money-losing proposition.

In addition to identifying and quantifying the costs, the financial manager must estimate the investment's cash flow. For investments that are similar to existing products, such estimates may be relatively easy. New products, however, or proposals to enter new markets will require estimates of sales and expenses that are not readily available. These estimates may be susceptible to built-in biases. If management desires to enter a new field, it may make overly optimistic estimates of future cash flows. The history of business is replete with illustrations of firms entering new markets, taking a beating, and retreating. RCA started to manufacture computers in direct competition with IBM, and Midway Airlines entered the Philadelphia market in direct competition with USAir. Both decisions were probably made after much discussion and analysis of anticipated cash flows. Both failed.

Cash flow was previously defined as earnings plus non-cash expenses, of which depreciation is generally the most important. Other examples of non-cash expenses include the depletion of natural resources such as oil reserves. Notice that the emphasis is not on accounting earnings. As was explained in the sections on accounting in Chapter 16 on the analysis of financial statements, earnings are not synonymous with cash. Depreciation expense, the deferral of income taxes from the current accounting period to another, or changes in current assets (i.e., changes in net working capital) such as an increase (or decrease) in accounts receivable or inventory affect cash flows. It is the investment's impact on these cash flows that is important for the decision to invest in a long-term asset.

Consider the following situation, in which the financial manager must decide whether to acquire new equipment that costs $50,000 and requires an outlay of $5,000 to install. To make the decision, the financial manager must determine the cash flow generated by the investment. The $5,000 installation charge is a current cash outflow that will be recaptured over the same five years that the equipment will be depreciated. Estimated annual operating earnings generated by the equipment are $17,200 before the annual depreciation expense. In addition, the firm's investment in inventory will rise by $2,000 and its accounts receivable will increase by $3,000. These increases in inventory and accounts receivable require additional working capital. In the fifth year the inventory and accounts receivable will be restored to their current levels (i.e., before the investment in the equipment). At that time the equipment will be removed at a cost of $4,500 to be paid in cash. If the income tax rate is 20 percent, what are (1) the accounting earnings and (2) the cash flow generated by the investment?

The answer to these two questions for years 1, 2–4, and 5 are as follows:

	Year 1	**Years 2–4**	**Year 5**
Determination of earnings:			
Earnings before depreciation and taxes	$17,200	$17,200	$17,200
Depreciation	10,000	10,000	10,000
Depreciation of installation expense	1,000	1,000	1,000
Removal expense	0	0	4,500
Taxable income	6,200	6,200	1,700
Taxes (20%)	1,240	1,240	340
Net income	$ 4,960	$ 4,960	$ 1,360
Determination of cash flows:			
Net income	$ 4,960	$ 4,960	$ 1,360
Depreciation	10,000	10,000	10,000
Depreciation of installation expense	1,000	1,000	1,000
Change in working capital	(5,000)	0	5,000
Cash flow	$10,960	$15,960	$17,360

The earnings are $4,960 per year in years 1 through 4 and $1,360 in year 5, but the cash flows are $10,960 in year 1, $15,960 per year in years

2 through 4, and $17,360 in year 5. How can the earnings and cash flows be so different?

In each year, operating income was reduced by the depreciation of both the equipment and installation expense, which had been capitalized.[1] (In reality, the installation expense would be added to the cost of the equipment to determine the depreciable base and that amount would be spread over the time period. This presentation, however, helps illustrate that depreciation is not limited to the cost of the equipment but also covers other costs associated with putting the equipment into use, such as commissions and installation expenses.) These expenses are non-cash expenses that reduce income for tax purposes. Notice also that there is a removal expense in year 5. Since that occurs at the end of the investment's life, it is not depreciated; it is expensed, which reduces taxable income in the fifth year. It is possible for the opposite to occur: the equipment is sold and cash is received. (If the sale is for more than the asset's book value, the sale also increases taxable income and taxes.)

The net income in years 1 through 5 does not represent cash. Cash flow is determined by adding back the non-cash expenses and making any other adjustments that generate or consume cash. In each year, the $11,000 in non-cash expenses are added back to net income. (Remember that the cash outflow occurred when the equipment was purchased and the installation costs were paid.) Adding back non-cash expenses increases the cash flow generated by the investment. Conversely, in year 1, the investment requires an increase in inventory and accounts receivable. These increases are cash outflows that reduce the investment's cash flow in year 1. However, when inventory and accounts receivable are reduced in year 5 to their former levels, cash is released and contributes to the investment's cash flow in year 5.

The difference between net income and the cash flow generated by the investment is immediately obvious from a comparison of the two bottom lines. An investment of $55,000 ($50,000 to buy the equipment plus $5,000 in installation expense) generates $4,960 in profits in years 1 through 4 and only $1,360 in year 5. That does not appear to be an attractive investment—$55,000 to generate less than $5,000 in profits for each of the five years. However, the same investment generated $10,960 in cash in year 1, $15,960 in years 2 through 4, and $17,360 in year 5. The firm more than earns back the initial $55,000 cash outlay. From this perspective, the investment looks perceptibly more attractive.

However, just because the investment now looks more attractive is not justification to make it. Instead, the financial manager should apply

---

[1]To simplify the illustration, the requirement that depreciation not start until after six months have passed (the "half-year" convention) is ignored.

one or more of the subsequent methods of capital budgeting to determine if the investment constitutes a wise use of the firm's scarce resource, its capital.

PAYBACK PERIOD

The **payback period** determines how long it takes for an investment's cash flow to recoup the cost of the investment. For example, in the previous illustration, the investment in equipment required an initial cash outlay of $55,000. The cash flow of $10,960 in year 1 and $15,960 in years 2 through 4 recouped the initial cash outflow in slightly less than four years. If four years are an acceptable period of time to recover the initial cost (and the determination of what is an acceptable time period is arbitrary), the investment is made.

Payback period ▲
Period of time necessary to recoup the cost of an investment

The payback period may also be used to rank alternative investment opportunities. The more rapidly the initial money is returned, the more desirable the investment. If three $1,000 investments have the following cash flows:

A	B	C
$250	$333	$400
250	333	100
250	333	400
250	333	100
250	333	400

Investment B would be preferred since it recoups the $1,000 in three years while the other investments take four years.

Obviously, the payback method is a very simple means to rank alternatives and select investment projects. There are many flaws in the technique, but it is better to use the payback method than to make long-term investment decisions without using any capital budgeting techniques. The inability to predict accurately the future suggests that placing emphasis on the near future may be a desirable, or at least pragmatic, means to select among investment alternatives.

The criticisms of the payback method illustrate why other capital budgeting techniques are superior. The weaknesses criticized include (1) the cost of capital (or interest factor) is omitted, (2) the timing of the cash flow is ignored, and (3) cash flows after the payback period are disregarded. Each of these weaknesses will be discussed briefly. How these limitations may be overcome will be subsequently examined in the sections on the net present value and internal rate of return methods of capital budgeting.

Neglecting to consider the cost of capital means that alternative uses of the money are ignored. The firm must raise funds to acquire an investment, and these funds have a cost, the cost of capital. The suppliers of the capital could invest their money elsewhere. An investment should earn, or at least be expected to earn, a return sufficient to compensate investors for the use of their capital. Since the payback period is only concerned with recouping the investment's cost, it says nothing about the investment's return.

This weakness is compounded when the other weaknesses are considered. Consider the following cash flows of $1,000 investments:

A	B	C
$100	$400	$200
200	300	200
300	200	200
400	100	200
0	0	200
0	0	200

The payback method's inability to differentiate the timing of the cash flows means that, if strictly applied, the method cannot distinguish between Investment A's and Investment B's cash flows. Both have payback periods of four years. Of course, B is superior (by common sense), since the cash flow in the early years is greater, which provides money that can be reinvested profitably elsewhere.

The third limitation is that payback does not consider cash flows received after the payback period. The failure to consider cash flows after the payback period will result in selecting investments A and B before C. Once again, common sense indicates that C is superior. A and B only recoup the $1,000 cost. They offer no profit. An investment must generate cash flow after the payback period to be profitable, and even then the investment might not be the most profitable when the return offered by an alternative investment is considered.

In summary, the payback method places the emphasis on the quick return of the cost of an investment. It is not concerned with the profitability of the investment or the time value of the money. Many investments, however, have very long payback periods. For example, pharmaceuticals may require years of research and testing. While this payback period is long, the product may be very profitable once marketed. Power plants operate for years, and the payback on a college education is also very long. Investments in research, plants, or education are discouraged by the payback method of capital budgeting. It biases the investment decision in favor of short-term investments.

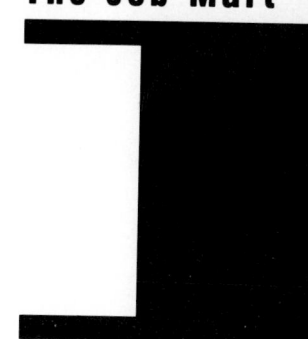

Manager of Capital Budgets

■ Job Description: Administer long-term investments in plant and equipment. Analyze projections of cash flow, determine cost of funds, participate in the lease versus buy decision, negotiate with lenders, lessors, and suppliers, and prepare budgets and financial statements. ■ Job Requirements: Strong background in accounting and use of capital budgeting techniques. An M.B.A. degree is often required. Technical skills include the ability to use information systems, spreadsheets, and other computer-driven programs. ■ Characteristics: The allocation of scarce resources among competing long-term investment alternatives cuts across many divisions within a firm. The individual needs strong interpersonal skills, along with the ability to listen to proposals and reduce them to the essentials needed for applying capital budgeting techniques. The ability to delegate specific tasks and to integrate the pieces of the analysis is also crucial to success.

While the payback method is consistently criticized, it is frequently used. The reasons for this use are (1) it is readily understood, (2) it is extremely easy to apply, and (3) it avoids making projections into the more distant future. The more uncertain the future, the stronger may be the case for use of the payback method. In the minds of many businesspeople, dollars received in the distant future are worth very little today, for the future is very uncertain. Thus, while the payback method has little support on theoretical grounds, it has support on pragmatic grounds. It is easy to perform and places the emphasis on the immediate return of the cost of the investment. The small businessperson may simply lack the time, knowledge, or capacity to do more sophisticated types of capital budgeting.

INTRODUCTION TO DISCOUNTED CASH FLOWS METHODS OF CAPITAL BUDGETING

The most widely used alternatives to the payback method, net present value (NPV) and internal rate of return, are discounted cash flows techniques. The phrase "discounted cash flows" means that future cash flows are brought back to the present; that is, "discounted." Both methods overcome the weaknesses associated with the payback method, for both techniques explicitly use the time value of money and all the cash flows generated by an investment. Both techniques recognize that (1) investment decisions are made in the present, (2) the cash flows are generated in the future, and (3) the cash flows must be compared to the investment's present cost or the cost of funds required to make the investment.

Such comparisons are necessary if the financial manager seeks to increase the value of the firm. If the return on an investment is less than the firm's cost of capital, that investment will reduce the value of the firm. Selecting investments by using net present value or internal rate of return should increase the value of the firm. Using these techniques will preclude making investments that do not cover the firm's cost of capital. Only investments that are equal to or better than the firm's alternative uses for the capital will be made.

Net present value (NPV) ▲
Present value of an investment's cash flows minus the cost of the investment

Internal rate of return (IRR) ▲
Rate of return that equates the present value of an investment's cash flows with the cost of making the investment

Net present value and internal rate of return use the same essential information but process it in a different way. **Net present value (NPV)** discounts future cash flows at the firm's cost of capital to determine the present value of the investment. This present value is then compared to the present cost of making the investment. **Internal rate of return (IRR)** determines the return that equates the present value of the cash flows and the present cost of the investment. This return is then compared to the cost of capital necessary to make the investment.

While the two techniques are similar, there is one essential difference: the treatment of the discount factor that each employs. This difference may be important if the two techniques give conflicting signals as to which investments should be selected. While this conflict may not occur, the possibility does exist and will be illustrated in the section devoted to selecting between mutually exclusive investments.

The initial discussion, however, will be devoted to explaining and illustrating net present value and internal rate of return. Several symbols will be used:

- C: the cost of making the investment in the present
- $R_1, R_2, \ldots R_n$: the cash flows generated by the investment in years one, two, and on through the last year (n)
- n: the number of years in which the investment generates cash flow
- PV: the present value of the investment's cash flows
- NPV: the net present value (i.e., PV minus C)
- k: the firm's cost of capital
- r: the investment's internal rate of return

Generally, the cash flows and number of years are estimated; in very few investments will these payments be known with certainty. Initially, the discussion will avoid the question of risk; no adjustment is made for riskier investments. Also realize that the cash flows in the last year (year n) may be increased if the firm is able to sell the asset for some residual amount or may be reduced if there is a cost to have the asset removed.

NET PRESENT VALUE

The net present value technique of capital budgeting determines the present value of the cash flows from an investment and subtracts from this present value the cost of the investment. The difference is the net present value. This technique is illustrated by the following example. A firm may be considering an investment that costs $1,000 and has the following estimated cash flows:

uses of all of your cash flows

Year	Cash Flow
1	$300
2	400
3	500
4	400

The firm is now faced with the question of whether it should make this investment. To answer this question, the firm needs to know the present value of the cash flows. To determine the present value, the firm must know the cost of funds used to acquire the asset (i.e., the cost of capital). If the cost of capital is 8 percent, the present value of the investment is the sum of the present value of each of the cash flows. The following illustrates the process of determining the present value of this investment:

Year	Cash Flow ×	Interest Factor =	Present Value
1	$300	0.926	$ 277.80
2	400	0.857	342.80
3	500	0.794	397.00
4	400	0.735	294.00
			Σ = $1,311.60

The individual present values are summed to obtain the present value of the investment. In this case, the present value is $1,311.60. The present cost of making this investment is $1,000. The net present value of this investment, then, is $311.60 ($1,311.60 − $1,000). The net present value is positive, which indicates that the investment is profitable and will increase the value of the firm. Therefore, the investment should be made.

This technique is applied to all of the firm's investment opportunities to determine their net present values. Suppose the firm is considering the following investments in addition to the one previously discussed:

	Cash Flow			
Investment	**Year 1**	**2**	**3**	**4**
B	$295	$295	$295	$295
C	330	330	330	330
D	250	150	330	450
E	357	357	357	357

The firm must determine the net present value of each of these investments before deciding if it should make any or all of them. The general procedure used for Investment A is repeated for each investment. Investments B, C, and E are annuities, and the present value of an annuity table may be used instead of the present value of a dollar table (which will reduce the amount of arithmetic). Investment D, however, is not an annuity; hence the present value of a dollar table must be used.

For Investment B the present value is

$$\$295(3.312) = \$977,$$

where 3.312 is the interest factor for the present value of an annuity at 8 percent for four years. The net present value of Investment B is

$$\$977 - \$1,000 = (\$23).$$

The net present value of this investment is negative, which means that the firm should not make the investment.

The net present values of Investments C, D, and E are $93, ($48), and $182, respectively. (The student should verify these results as a means to test his or her ability to compute an investment's net present value.) These results give the following ranking of all five investments:

Investment	Net Present Value
A	$312
E	182
C	93
B	(23)
D	(48)

The firm should make Investments A, E, and C (for a total outlay of $3,000) because their net present values are positive. The firm should reject Investments B and D because their net present values are negative. Notice that the firm accepts *all* investments whose net present values are positive.

The net present value technique of capital budgeting may be stated in more formal terms. First, determine the present value (PV) by discounting the cash flow (R) generated each year ($R_1, R_2, \ldots R_n$) by the firm's cost of capital (k). Thus, the present value of an investment is

23.1 $$PV = \frac{R_1}{(1 + k)^1} + \frac{R_2}{(1 + k)^2} + \ldots + \frac{R_n}{(1 + k)^n}$$

Second, determine the net present value (NPV) of the investment by subtracting the cost (C) of the investment from the present value of the investment. That is,

23.2 $$NPV = PV - C.$$

If the net present value is positive, the investment should be undertaken by the firm. If the net present value is negative, the firm should not make the investment. The acceptance and rejection criteria for the net present value method of capital budgeting are summarized as follows:

Accept the investment if
$PV - C = NPV \geq 0.$
Reject the investment if
$PV - C = NPV < 0.$

INTERNAL RATE OF RETURN

The internal rate of return method of capital budgeting determines the rate of return that equates the present value of the cash flows and the present cost of the investment. This particular rate of return is called the "internal rate of return" because it is a rate (i.e., a percentage) that is unique (internal) to that investment. In effect, the internal rate of return method sets up the following equation:

23.3 $$\text{Present cost} = \begin{matrix}\text{Present value} \\ \text{of the cash flows}\end{matrix}$$

The method may be illustrated by the same examples used to illustrate the net present value approach. The information for Investment A is substituted into the equation for determining present value. That is,

$$\$1{,}000 = \frac{\$300}{(1 + r)^1} + \frac{\$400}{(1 + r)^2} + \frac{\$500}{(1 + r)^3} + \frac{\$400}{(1 + r)^4}$$

Then the equation is solved for the unknown r, the internal rate of return. While the equation may appear to be formidable, it may be solved with ease by computers.

The equation may also be solved by trial and error. This is done by selecting a rate of return and solving the equation. If the chosen r does not equate the two sides of the equation, another r is selected until one is found that does equate both sides of the equation. For example, if a rate of return of 10 percent is used in the equation to determine the present value of the cash flows, the present value of the investment is found to be

$$\begin{aligned}\$1{,}251.80 = {} & (\$300)(0.909) + (\$400)(0.826) + (\$500)(0.751) + \\ & (\$400)(0.683)\end{aligned}$$

This present value is larger than the cost of the investment. The selected rate of return is too low; hence, the internal rate of return must be greater. The cash flow must be discounted at a higher rate to equate the present value and the present cost of the investment.

If a rate of return of 24 percent is selected, the present value becomes

$$\begin{aligned}\$933.00 = {} & (\$300)(0.806) + (\$400)(0.650) + (\$500)(0.524) + \\ & (\$400)(0.423)\end{aligned}$$

This present value is less than the cost of the investment. The selected rate of return is too high; thus, the internal rate of return must be lower. By continuing this process, the internal rate of return (which equates the present value of the cash flows and the cost of the investment) may be found. In this case, that internal rate of return is approximately 20 percent, since at that rate of return the present value of this investment is \$1,009.80, which is approximately equal to the cost of the investment (\$1,000).[2]

$$\begin{aligned}\$1{,}000 &\approx \frac{\$300}{(1 + 0.2)^1} + \frac{\$400}{(1 + 0.2)^2} + \frac{\$500}{(1 + 0.2)^3} + \frac{\$400}{(1 + 0.2)^4} \\ &= \$300(0.833) + \$400(0.694) + \$500(0.579) + \$400(0.482) \\ &= \$249.90 + \$277.60 + \$289.50 + \$192.80 \\ &= \$1{,}009.80.\end{aligned}$$

Should the firm make this investment? The answer is yes, because the return on the investment exceeds the firm's cost of capital. This invest-

[2]The use of the word "approximately" is the result of interest factor tables being insufficiently detailed. It is not possible in this text to present tables covering 6.4 percent or 5 years and 3 months. Financial managers, of course, need calculations of the IRR to be more precise. Such precision will require, at a minimum, the use of an electronic calculator that computes the internal rate of return. The use of a computer program such as *PROFIT+* determines the internal rate of return in this illustration to be 20.5 percent.

ment's internal rate of return of 20 percent is greater than the 8 percent cost of capital. Thus, the investment should be made.

As with the net present value technique, the firm calculates the internal rate of return for each possible investment (i.e., for Investments B, C, D, and E). The interest factor that equates the present value of the cash flows with the present cost of the investment must be determined. For Investment B that is

$$\$1{,}000 = \frac{\$295}{(1 + r)^1} + \frac{\$295}{(1 + r)^2} + \frac{\$295}{(1 + r)^3} + \frac{\$295}{(1 + r)^4}.$$

Investment B is an annuity, so this calculation is easy:

$1,000 = $295 times the interest factor for the present value of an annuity for four years.

Solving for the interest factor (IF) gives

$$\$1{,}000 = \$295IF$$
$$IF = \$1{,}000/\$295 = 3.389.$$

Then, 3.389 must be found in the interest table for the present value of an annuity for four years (i.e., $n = 4$). This yields an internal rate of return of approximately 7 percent.

The internal rates of return for Investments C, D, and E are computed in the same manner. Their respective internal rates of return are 12, 6, and 16 percent. (The student should try to duplicate these results to test his or her ability to compute each investment's internal rate of return.) Given these internal rates of return, the ranking of the five investments is

Investment	Internal Rate of Return
A	20%
E	16
C	12
B	7
D	6

The firm should make Investments A, E, and C because their internal rates of return exceed the firm's cost of capital but should reject Investments B and D because their internal rates of return are less than the firm's cost of capital (i.e., less than 8 percent). The total cost of these investments is $3,000, and once again notice that the firm makes *all* investments whose internal rates of return exceed the firm's cost of capital. Like the net present value method of capital budgeting, the internal rate of return assumes that the firm has the funds or can obtain the funds necessary to make all of the acceptable investments.

The internal rate of return method of capital budgeting may be summarized in symbolic terms. The internal rate of return is that value, r, that equates

23.4 $$C = \frac{R_1}{(1 + r)^1} + \ldots + \frac{R_n}{(1 + r)^n}$$

and the criteria for accepting an investment are

$$\text{if } r \geq k \text{, accept the investment,}$$
$$\text{if } r < k \text{, reject the investment.}$$

Hurdle rate ▲
Return necessary to justify making an investment often set higher than the firm's cost of capital

While the above are the acceptance criteria, many firms that use the internal rate of return approach do not accept all investments with an internal rate of return greater than the cost of capital. Instead, they establish a higher rate of return (or **hurdle rate**) that is used as the acceptance criterion for selecting investments. For example, if the cost of capital is 10 percent, the firm may make all investments with an internal rate of return in excess of 15 percent. Such a hurdle rate helps the firm provide for risk because it excludes the investments with the lowest anticipated internal rates of return.

NET PRESENT VALUE AND INTERNAL RATE OF RETURN COMPARED

The internal rate of return and net present value methods of capital budgeting are very similar. Both methods use all the cash flows generated by an investment, and both consider the timing of those cash flows. Both methods also explicitly incorporate the time value of money into the analysis. When the two methods are compared,

(Net present value)

$$NPV = \frac{R_1}{(1 + k)^1} + \ldots + \frac{R_n}{(1 + k)^n} - C,$$

(Internal rate of return)

$$C = \frac{R_1}{(1 + r)^1} + \ldots + \frac{R_n}{(1 + r)^n},$$

the primary difference is the discount factor. The net present value approach uses the firm's cost of capital to discount the cash flows. The internal rate of return method determines the rate of return that equates the present value of the cash flows and the present cost of the investment. The use of different discount factors results in different statements of the acceptance criteria. For the net present value approach, an investment must yield a net present value equal to or greater than zero to be accepted. For the internal rate of return method, the investment's internal rate of return must be equal to or exceed the firm's cost of capital to be accepted.

While the obvious difference between the two techniques is the discount factor and the resulting difference in the statement of the acceptance criteria, the different discount factors have an important and subtle assumption. That assumption involves the reinvestment rate. The net present value technique assumes that funds earned in years one, two, and so on are *reinvested at the firm's cost of capital.* The internal rate of return assumes that the funds earned in years one, two, and so on are *reinvested at the investment's internal rate of return.*

Consider the investment used earlier in the chapter to illustrate both techniques. It had the following cash flows:

Year	Cash Flow
1	$300
2	400
3	500
4	400

When the cost of capital was 8 percent, the net present value of the investment was determined to be $311.60. The reinvestment assumption requires that the $300 received in year one be invested for the next three years at 8 percent. The $400 received in year two will be reinvested for the next two years at 8 percent, and the $500 received in year three will be reinvested for one year at 8 percent. If these funds are not reinvested at 8 percent, the net present value will not be $311.60. If the reinvestment rate is higher, the net present value will exceed $311.60; if the reinvestment rate is lower, the net present value will be lower than $311.60.

When the internal rate of return technique was applied to the above cash flows, the return was calculated to be approximately 20 percent. The reinvestment assumption requires that all the cash flows be invested at that rate. Thus, the $300 received in the first year must be reinvested at 20 percent for the next three years, and the same reinvestment rate is required for each of the subsequent cash flows. If these reinvested funds earn less than 20 percent, the true internal rate of return is less than 20 percent. If these reinvested funds earn more than 20 percent, the internal rate of return is greater than 20 percent.

In many investment decisions, the actual reinvestment rate is not important. It would not be important in the above illustration if that were the only investment considered by the financial manager. However, when the financial manager must rank investments and select among competing investments (as will be required in the next section of this chapter), the realized reinvestment rate may be crucial to the decision-making process.

If the financial manager cannot determine the rate at which the funds will be reinvested, then there is a strong argument for preferring the net present value technique over the internal rate of return. The assumption that the cash flows will be reinvested at the firm's cost of capital is a more conservative assumption. Consider the above illustration. The net present value technique assumed the $300 received in the first year would be reinvested at 8 percent, while the internal rate of return required a reinvestment rate of 20 percent. Certainly, it should be easier to reinvest the funds at the lower rate. Furthermore, if no such investment can be found, the cash flow may always be used to reduce the firm's capital. The $300 cash generated during the first year, for example, could be used to retire some of the debt and equity issued to make the investment. Since these funds cost 8 percent, their retirement means the financial manager is able to save this cost even if he or she is unable to earn more elsewhere.

RANKING INVESTMENT OPPORTUNITIES

In the preceding section, the decision of whether or not to purchase an asset depended on the investment's net present value or its internal rate of return. The firm made all investments whose net present value was positive or whose internal rate of return exceeded the firm's cost of capital. Since the firm made all investments that met these criteria, there was no need to rank investments as to which were the most preferred. However, there are circumstances in which the firm will need to rank investments and choose among the alternatives.

Mutually exclusive investments ▲
Two investments for which the acceptance of one automatically excludes the acceptance of the other

The need to rank investments will occur when the investments are mutually exclusive. **Mutually exclusive investments** occur when selecting one alternative automatically excludes another possible investment. For example, when land is used for one type of building, it cannot be used for a different type of structure. Mutually exclusive investments also occur if a number of investments achieve similar results. Once one of the alternative investments is selected, the others are excluded. Students are well aware of this type of problem. If you select one class at period A, all other classes at that period are excluded. Or, if you select one section of a finance course, all other sections are excluded. These choices are mutually exclusive.

Once mutually exclusive investments exist, it is necessary to rank investment proposals in order to make the most profitable investments first. In some cases such ranking may pose no problem. Consider the following hypothetical investment proposals. Each costs $1,000 and has a net present value and internal rate of return as listed:

Investment	Net Present Value	Internal Rate of Return (Cost of Capital = 6%)
A	$22	19%
B	43	37
C	5	9
D	6	10

A and B are mutually exclusive, and C and D are mutually exclusive. Therefore, B is selected and A is excluded, and D is selected over C. Both the net present value and internal rate of return techniques select B over A and D over C. Notice also that Investment D is made but that A is not, even though A has a higher net present value than D. This occurs because the acceptance of B automatically excludes A. The acceptance of D is immaterial to the acceptance of A, because A's acceptance depends on its net present value relative to B and not to any other investment.

In the above example, both the net present value and internal rate of return techniques selected B over A and D over C. The question becomes, Do the two techniques always produce the same rankings? The answer is no. There are two situations in which the rankings may diverge: the timings of the cash flows differ or the costs of the investments differ. These disparities are, of course, immaterial if the investments are independent. The firm may select (or reject) any of the investments. But these differences may be crucial if the firm must select between Investments A and B when net present value favors A while internal rate of return favors B. The financial manager, in effect, must favor one of the two methods of capital budgeting for determining which of the two long-term investments to make.

Differences in the Timing of Cash Flows

Consider the following two mutually exclusive investments. Each investment costs $10,000, but the cash flows occur in different time periods.

	Cash Flows	
Year	A	B
1	$12,400	—
2	—	—
3	—	$15,609

The cash flow of Investment A is earned quickly, while Investment B has a higher dollar cash flow but takes longer to earn those funds. Since the two investments are mutually exclusive, the firm must choose between the two alternatives. This requires that the financial manager rank the two investments.

The determination of the net present value and internal rate of return for each investment is easy. If the firm's cost of capital is 10 percent, the net present value of each investment is

$$NPV_A = \frac{\$12{,}400}{(1 + 0.1)} - \$10{,}000 = \$12{,}400(0.909) - \$10{,}000$$
$$= \$11{,}272 - \$10{,}000 = \$1{,}272.$$
$$NPV_B = \frac{\$15{,}609}{(1 + 0.1)^3} - \$10{,}000 = \$15{,}609(0.751) - \$10{,}000$$
$$= \$11{,}722 - \$10{,}000 = \$1{,}722.$$

The internal rate of return for each investment is

$$\$10{,}000 = \frac{\$12{,}400}{(1 + r_A)} \quad \text{and} \quad \$10{,}000 = \frac{\$15{,}609}{(1 + r_B)^3}.$$

Solving for r_A for Investment A yields: \$12,400 IF = \$10,000.

$$IF = \frac{10{,}000}{12{,}400} = 0.8065 \quad \text{and} \quad r_A = 24\%.$$

Solving for r_B for Investment B yields: \$15,609 IF = \$10,000.

$$IF = \frac{10{,}000}{15{,}609} = 0.6407 \quad \text{and} \quad r_B = 16\%.$$

A summary of these results is

	Investment A	**Investment B**
Net present value	\$1,272	\$1,722
Internal rate of return	24%	16%

Immediately, one sees that the financial manager faces a quandary. Investment A has the higher internal rate of return, while Investment B has the higher net present value. Which investment is preferable? Unfortunately, the net present value and internal rate of return methods for capital budgeting are giving conflicting answers. If the investments were not mutually exclusive, the firm would make both investments and the conflicting rankings would not matter. However, in this case the investments are mutually exclusive, and the firm must choose between the two alternatives. The question then becomes how to resolve the conflicting signals.

The reconciliation is built around the answer to a second question: What will the firm do with the cash flow generated by Investment A in year one (i.e., what is the reinvestment rate)? Certainly the firm will not let these funds sit but will invest them in year two in an investment with an anticipated return. If the firm selects Investment B, it receives the funds in year three and thus cannot reinvest them in years one and two. The choice between Investment A and Investment B depends on what the firm can do with the cash flow generated in year one by Investment A. In effect, the firm must consider a third investment that starts in year two and is purchased with the funds generated by Investment A.

Suppose the firm could reinvest the $12,400 at 14 percent for the next two years. The question becomes, What is the terminal value of the investment? That is, What is the future value of Investment A if the reinvested funds grow annually at 14 percent for two years? The answer is

$$\$12{,}400(1 + 0.14)^2 = \$12{,}400(1.300) = \$16{,}120,$$

where 1.300 is the interest factor for the compound value of a dollar at 14 percent for two years. If the $12,400 is reinvested at 14 percent for two years, the terminal value of Investment A is $16,120, which is greater than the final value of Investment B (i.e., the $15,609). Thus, the conflicting signals from the net present value and internal rate of return methods can be resolved. The firm should make Investment A because its terminal value ($16,120) exceeds the terminal value ($15,609) of Investment B.

In the above illustration, the conflict was resolved in favor of Investment A. This, however, need not have been the case. Suppose the firm could have invested the $12,400 received in year one at only 12 percent instead of 14 percent. Would the firm still have selected Investment A? The answer is no, because at 12 percent the $12,400 would grow to only

$$\$12{,}400(1 + 0.12)^2 = \$12{,}400(1.254) = \$15{,}549.60.$$

The terminal value of Investment A when the cash flow is reinvested at 12 percent is $15,549.60, which is smaller than Investment B's terminal value ($15,609). Thus, Investment B would have been selected.

As these illustrations demonstrate, reconciling the conflict between the net present value and the internal rate of return depends on what the firm can do with the cash flows that it earns in the early years of an investment's life. If the firm has alternatives that offer relatively high returns, the choice will be the investment with the higher initial cash flows even though it may have the lower net present value. The lower net present value is offset by the returns earned when the cash flows are reinvested at profitable rates. The converse is true when the initial cash flows

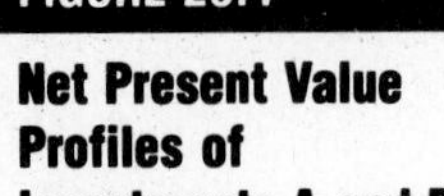

FIGURE 23.1

Net Present Value Profiles of Investments A and B

Net present value profiles of Investments A and B indicate that at low costs of capital (i.e., less than 12.2 percent) Investment B is preferred. This preference contradicts the IRR technique, which selects A over B.

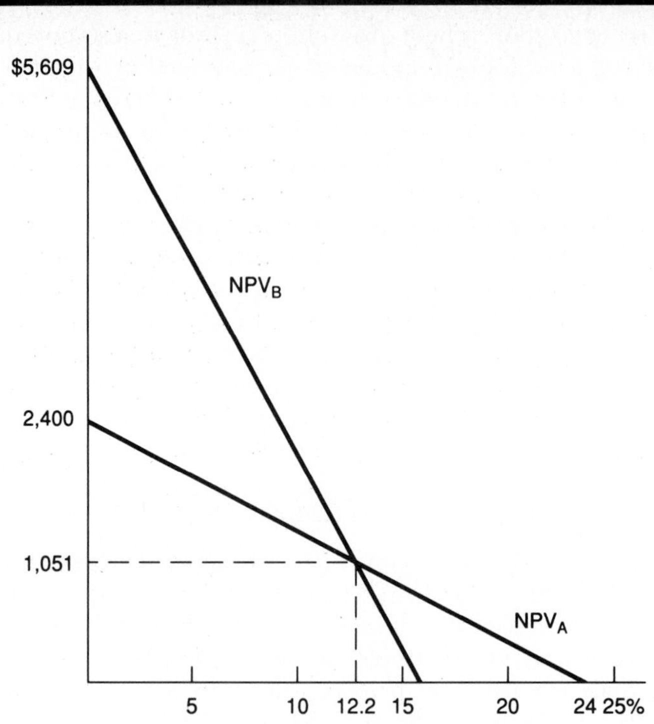

are reinvested at less profitable rates. Then, the funds earned through reinvesting are not sufficient to justify making the investment with the lower net present value, and thus the conflict is resolved in favor of the investment with the higher net present value but longer time horizon.

This general conclusion is illustrated in Figure 23.1, which presents a profile of the net present value of both investments at various costs of capital. If the discount factor is zero percent, then the net present values of Investments A and B are $2,400 and $5,609, respectively. As the discount factors rise, the net present values fall. If the discount factors are sufficiently high, the net present values fall to zero. This occurs at 24 percent for Investment A and 16 percent for Investment B. (These discount factors are, of course, each investment's internal rate of return. Since the internal rate of return equates the cost of an investment with the present value of its cash flows, the net present value must equal zero.)

It should be noted that the net present value of Investment B exceeds the net present value of Investment A as long as the discount factor is less than 12.2 percent.[3] When the discount factor is less than 12.2 percent, the net present value method selects Investment B. However, if the discount factor exceeds 12.2 percent, Investment A's net present value is higher; therefore, Investment A would be preferred. Thus, as long as the discount factor (i.e., the firm's cost of capital) exceeds 12.2 percent, the net present value and the internal rate of return give the same ranking: A is preferred to B. However, if the cost of capital is less than 12.2 percent, the two techniques produce a contradictory ranking that raises the reinvestment question. If the reinvestment rate is less than 12.2 percent, Investment B is to be preferred; the funds earned through the reinvestment of Investment A's earlier cash flows do not offset Investment B's higher net present value.

Differences in Cost

The previous section showed that differences in the timing of cash flows may lead to conflicting rankings of investments by net present value and internal rate of return. The same problem may arise if there is a difference in the cost of two mutually exclusive investments. Consider the following mutually exclusive investments:

	Investment	
	A	**B**
Cost	$1,000	$600
Cash flow year 1	$1,150	$700
Cost of capital: 10 percent		

All the cash flow occurs in year one but the costs of the investments differ. (In the previous illustration the cash flows occurred in different years and the costs of the investments were equal.) The net present values of the two investments are

[3] The two discount factors are equal when

$$\frac{\$12{,}400}{(1+r)} = \frac{\$15{,}609}{(1+r)^3},$$

$$\frac{(1+r)^3}{(1+r)} = \frac{\$15{,}609}{\$12{,}400},$$

$$(1+r)^2 = 1.2588,$$

$$1+r = \sqrt{1.2588},$$

$$r = 1.122 - 1,$$

$$r = 12.2\%.$$

$$NPV_A = \$1{,}150(0.909) - \$1{,}000 = \$45.35$$
$$NPV_B = \$700(0.909) - \$600 = \$36.30.$$

The internal rate of return for A is

$$\$1{,}000 = \$1{,}150/(1 + r_A)$$
$$1 + r_A = \$1{,}150/\$1{,}000 = 1.15$$
$$r_A = 1.15 - 1 = 0.15 = 15\%.$$

The internal rate of return for B is

$$\$600 = \$700/(1 + r_B)$$
$$1 + r_B = \$700/\$600 = 1.167$$
$$r_B = 1.167 - 1 = 0.167 = 16.7\%.$$

Obviously, there is a conflict. The net present value of A exceeds the net present value of B. Their internal rates of return are reversed; B's is higher than A's.

The cause of the problem is the differences in amounts invested. Investment A costs more and that additional money earns 15 percent. These earnings contribute to the investment's net present value, so it exceeds the net present value of B, even though B earns a higher rate of return on the smaller amount invested.

The conflict may be resolved by asking what the firm can do with the money it saves by selecting B instead of A. Certainly, the $400 not spent by selecting B will not sit idle. If the funds were to sit idle, the financial manager should select Investment A and earn 15 percent on the entire $1,000, which is preferable to earning 16.5 percent on $600 and 0 percent on $400. However, the $400 can always be returned to the firm's creditors and stockholders and save the firm 10 percent, the cost of capital. Therefore, the worst alternative, return, is not 0 percent; it is the cost of capital.

If the firm earns 10 percent on $400 and 16.7 percent on $600, the return on $1,000 is a weighted average:

$$(0.4)(10) + (0.6)(16.7) = 14.02\%.$$

Obviously, 14.02 percent is inferior to the 15 percent internal rate of return on Investment A, which uses the entire $1,000. If the firm earns 13 percent on $400 and 16.7 percent on $600, the return on $1,000 is

$$(0.4)(13) + (0.6)(16.7) = 15.22\%,$$

in which case combining Investment B with the additional investment is superior to investing the entire amount in Investment A.

The same conclusion may be seen by using net present value. The net present value of Investment B is added to the net present value of the additional investment. For example, if the $400 is invested at 10 percent, the cash flow at the end of the first year is $440 (the return of the $400 invested plus 10 percent). The net present value of Investment B plus the additional $400 investment is

$$\begin{aligned} NPV &= \$700(0.909) + \$440(0.909) - (\$600 + \$400) \\ &= \$1{,}036 - \$1{,}000 = \$36, \end{aligned}$$

which is obviously inferior to the $45 offered by Investment A.

If, however, the $400 were invested at 13 percent (i.e., the cash flow at the end of the year is $452), the net present value of Investment B plus the additional $400 is

$$\begin{aligned} NPV &= \$700(0.909) + \$452(0.909) - (\$600 + \$400) \\ &= \$1{,}047 - \$1{,}000 = \$47. \end{aligned}$$

Investment B is now the preferred choice, because its net present value when combined with the net present value of the additional investment is higher than the net present value of all the funds invested in A.

As the above examples illustrate, the net present value and internal rate of return approaches to capital budgeting are superior to the payback method but are not free from possible problems. Although in many cases these problems will not arise, they may if the financial manager must select among alternative investments, all of which may be acceptable by themselves. Is there any reason to prefer one technique over the other? The answer is yes. Many individuals prefer the internal rate of return because it may be easier to interpret. Rates of return are frequently used in finance (e.g., the yield to maturity is an illustration of a rate of return) and many comparisons use percentages (e.g., the return on assets or equity is expressed as a percentage). This has led many financial managers to be more comfortable with the internal rate of return than with the absolute numbers generated by net present value. However, net present value is the more conservative technique and hence should be preferred.

This conservatism is the result of the reinvestment assumption discussed above. If an investment generates cash flow, the worst case for reinvesting the cash is to return it to the firm's sources of finance. The cost of these funds is the firm's cost of capital, so if the financial manager retires some of these sources, he or she is at least meeting the firm's alternative use for the cash. Since net present value assumes that all cash flows are reinvested at the firm's cost of capital, there is no reason to believe that this assumption will not be met. If the financial manager is able to find even better alternative uses for the cash flow, then such reinvestment should increase the value of the firm.

Such may not be the case when the internal rate of return is used, since that technique assumes that the cash flows are reinvested at the internal rate of return. Of course, it may be possible to reinvest the cash flows at a higher rate and realize a higher return which would, of course, increase the value of the firm. But if the cash flow is invested at a lower rate, the true realized return will not be the internal rate of return. If failure to consider the reinvestment rate were to lead to incorrect investment decisions (as was previously illustrated when choosing between mutually exclusive investments), the technique could result in a reduction in the value of the firm.

THE INTRODUCTION OF RISK INTO CAPITAL BUDGETING

In the previous discussion of net present value and internal rate of return, the same cost of capital was used to analyze each investment. This implicitly assumes that the risk associated with each investment is the same. Such is not the case; some investments are riskier than others, and some investments may be very risky by themselves but are not particularly risky when taken in a portfolio context. These investments may actually reduce the firm's risk exposure.

These differences in risk should be part of the analysis when applying capital budgeting techniques. Failure to consider risk may lead to accepting high-risk investments because they may have a higher internal rate of return while rejecting low-risk projects with lower internal rates of return. Once risk is incorporated into the capital budgeting techniques, high-risk/high-return investments may be less attractive than low-risk/low-return alternatives.

The incorporation of the analysis of risk is similar to the inclusion of risk in determining the cost of common stock discussed in the previous chapter. In that discussion, a risk premium was added to find the cost of equity. The question then became how to determine the risk premium. The same concepts apply to capital budgeting; that is, knowing that the cost of capital should be adjusted, and knowing how to make the adjustment.

One possible method requires a qualitative judgment on the part of the financial manager. The cost of capital is the required return rate to be used for investments of average risk. Thus, if the firm is expanding known products into new markets that are comparable to its existing markets, then the use of the cost of capital may be justified. However, if the financial manager is seeking to determine the net present value of developing a new product, that may be considered riskier than the typical investment made by the firm, and a risk premium should be added to the cost of capital. If the investment is less risky than the typical investment, the rate used may be less than the cost of capital. Thus, the financial manager may start with the cost of capital (e.g., 12 percent) and add a premium of 2 percent for riskier investments and subtract 2 percent for less risky investments. Extremely risky investments may command an even larger risk premium.

This approach does present a major problem. How is risk to be measured and how much of a risk premium should be added? One means to measure risk discussed in Chapter 8 was the dispersion around an expected value. If two investments have the same expected cash flows, the investment with the larger variability in the cash flows would be riskier. This variability could be measured by the standard deviation around the expected cash flows in the same way that the dispersion around an investment's return was used to measure risk from the individual investor's perspective. This method, however, does not tell the financial manager how large a risk premium should be added to the firm's cost of capital. The amount of the risk premium remains a judgment call by the financial manager.

An alternate means to measure risk is to use the beta coefficients also discussed in Chapter 8. In that chapter, beta coefficients were used to indicate the volatility of a stock's return relative to the volatility of the market's return. Beta coefficients were then used in Chapter 11 as the required rate of return in the valuation of common stock. The same concept may be applied to adjust for risk in capital budgeting. The risk-adjusted required return for an investment (k_a) is

$$k_a = r_f + (k - r_F)\beta,$$

where k is the firm's cost of capital for the typical or average investment made by the firm, r_f is the risk-free rate, and β is the beta coefficient associated with the investment. If the risk-free rate is 9 percent and the firm's cost of capital is 15 percent, the general equation for the risk-adjusted required return is

$$k_a = 0.09 + (0.15 - 0.09)\beta.$$

If an investment has an estimated beta of 1.2, it is riskier than the typical investment made by the firm. The adjusted required rate of return is

$$k_a = 0.09 + (0.15 - 0.09)1.2 = 0.162 = 16.2\%,$$

which exceeds the firm's cost of capital. If an investment has a beta of 0.7, it is less risky than the firm's typical investment. Its adjusted required return is

$$k_a = 0.09 + (0.15 - 0.09)0.7 = 0.132 = 13.2\%.$$

This return is less than the firm's cost of capital, because this particular investment is less risky than the average investment made by the firm.

Although the above discussion suggests means to incorporate risk into the capital budgeting process, making these propositions operational may be quite difficult. The inclusion of risk will increase the accuracy of capital budgeting only if the estimates of risk are accurate. Consider a drug firm whose investment in research may take years to develop and to receive government approval to market a new product. How can the firm estimate the beta for such an investment? In Chapter 11, betas were used to value a stock and hence help determine if an investment in the security should be made. The estimation of the stock's beta was relatively easy. The historical returns on the stock and the market are known. The biggest problems to estimate the beta and subsequently employ it were (1) determining which measure of the market to use and (2) after estimating the beta, assuming that the historical beta was an accurate measure of the current beta. While these are important problems, they pale when compared to the problem of estimating a beta for a non-existent product that may result from a firm's investment in research and development.

Thus, the problem for the financial manager is not the inclusion of risk into capital budgeting but the accuracy of its measurement. In some cases this measurement may be highly subjective, so the selection of investments will also be subjective. Accurate data are obviously crucial to capital budgeting decisions. Obviously, estimating an investment's future cash flows is no easy task, so it should hardly be any surprise that the measurement of the investment's risk will be an exceedingly difficult task.

ADDITIONAL APPLICATIONS

In the prior discussion, net present value and internal rate of return were used to aid in the decision to make new investments in plant and equipment. Capital budgeting techniques may also be used to help determine if equipment should be replaced or whether long-term debt (i.e., bonds) should be refunded prior to maturity. These decisions are conceptually no different from investing in new plant and hence may be analyzed in terms of their impact on the firm's cash flows.

The Replacement Decision

Equipment has a finite life and must be replaced. This need for replacement is obvious once the equipment is worn out. However, new equipment may be developed that offers the firm savings before the old equipment needs to be replaced. This raises the question of whether the firm should retain the old, less productive equipment or replace it with the new, cost-saving equipment. This replacement decision, like the decision of whether or not to invest in new plant and equipment, should be made by using capital budgeting techniques. The new equipment must have a positive net present value to justify replacing the old equipment.

The following factors influence this net present value: (1) the potential savings from the new equipment; (2) the cost of the new equipment; (3) the firm's income tax rate; (4) the salvage value or price for which the old equipment may be sold; (5) the depreciation on the new and old equipment; and (6) the firm's cost of capital. To make the replacement decision, the firm must determine the net present value of the new equipment in light of these factors. Some of the factors produce cash inflows for the firm, while others result in cash outflows. For example, purchasing the new equipment will result in a cash outflow, but the savings from the new equipment will increase the firm's cash inflows. The question basically reduces to: Does the present value of these cash inflows exceed the present value of the cash outflows? If it does, the replacement should be made; if it doesn't, the replacement should not be made.

First, the firm must determine all the cash inflows. The potential savings from the new equipment are a cash inflow, for the new equipment will increase the profits for the firm. The depreciation on the new equipment is a cash inflow, because this non-cash expense will produce cash flow in the future. The salvage value, or price at which the old equipment may be sold, is a cash inflow, for when the old equipment is sold, the firm will receive payment. Thus, the primary cash inflows are (1) the potential savings, (2) depreciation charges on the new equipment, and (3) any salvage value on the old equipment. Next, the firm must determine the cash outflows, such as the purchase price of the new equipment. The depreciation on the old equipment that will be *lost* when it is replaced is also treated as a cash outflow. Finally, the firm must consider its corporate income tax rate, which will affect the cash flows by reducing the firm's profits.

How the replacement decision should be made may be illustrated by a simple example. A firm has an opportunity to replace an old machine with a new machine that costs $1,000 and will save the firm $150 a year. The old machine still operates and may be sold for its book value of $500. Both the old and new machines have anticipated lives of five years and are depreciated on a straight-line basis. Thus, the depreciation on the new equipment will be $200 a year ($1,000/5), while the depreciation on the old equipment is $100 a year ($500/5). The firm's income tax rate is 40 percent, and its cost of capital is 9 percent.

The decision to replace the old equipment depends on the net present value of the cash inflows. To determine these inflows, consider the following income statements:

	Present Equipment	New Equipment	Net Change
Sales	$1,000	$1,000	$ —
Expenses	700	550	(150)
Depreciation	100	200	100
Profits before taxes	200	250	50
Taxes (40% tax rate)	80	100	20
Net profits	$ 120	$ 150	$ 30
Cash flow (profits plus depreciation)	$ 220	$ 350	$130

The first column presents income and cash flow generated by the current equipment, while the second column gives the income and cash flow that would result from selling the old equipment and replacing it with the new, cost-saving equipment. The third column gives the change in columns one and two that results from the replacement of the existing equipment.

Replacing the old equipment results in an increase in profits and an increase in depreciation expense. Since the depreciation expense is a non-cash expense that recoups the cost of the investment, it is added back to profits to obtain the cash flow generated by the investment. The question now becomes: Is this $130 increase in cash flow an acceptable use of that portion of the firm's resources that would be spent on the new equipment? In other words, is the present value of this cash flow greater than the cost of the investment?

The cost of the investment is the amount that the firm spends to acquire the new equipment. In this case, the new equipment costs $1,000, but the firm is able to sell the old equipment for $500, so the net cash outlay to replace the old equipment is reduced to $500. The decision as to whether to replace the existing equipment thus depends on the present value of increased cash flows and the present value of the $500 cash outflow required to make the investment. The net present value of the investment is

$$\begin{aligned} NPV &= \sum_{1}^{5} \frac{\$130}{(1 + 0.09)^n} - \$500 \\ &= \$130(3.890) - \$500 \\ &= \$505.70 - \$500 = \$5.70. \end{aligned}$$

Since the net present value of the investment is $5.70, the replacement should be made. The firm should replace the old equipment, because the present value of the new cash flows exceeds the cost of the investment.

While this example is very simple, it does give the basic mechanics of the replacement decision. The mechanics become more complex as other factors are considered, such as a tax loss or gain on the old equipment, or differences in the expected lives of the new and old equipment. However, the basic concept and approach are not altered by adding additional factors. The basic approach still remains to determine the net present values of the cash inflows and outflows. As long as the present value of the cash inflows exceeds the present value of the cash outflows, the firm should replace the old equipment with new equipment, for this replacement is profitable and will increase the value of the firm.

The Refunding Decision

The refunding decision is very similar to the replacement decision. The firm seeks to replace an old issue of debt with a new issue. Once again, if the present value of the cash inflows from the refunding exceed the present value of the cash outflows, the investment (i.e., the refunding) should be made.

Consider the following situation. A firm has an outstanding ten-year $1,000,000 bond with a 12 percent coupon with a call penalty of one year's interest. Currently, the firm could issue a new bond with a 10 percent coupon and use the proceeds to retire the existing bond. Should the firm refund the more costly bond? The first impulse may be, of course, to refund the bond. There is an obvious annual savings of $20,000 in interest.

Unfortunately, the answer is not that simple, because there are other factors to consider. If the existing bond is called prior to maturity, the firm must pay the call penalty, which requires a current cash outflow of $120,000. This cost is a tax-deductible expense, so part of the burden of the call penalty is shared with the federal government. If the firm's income tax rate is 40 percent, the $120,000 reduces income taxes by $48,000, so the net cash outflow is reduced to $72,000.

In addition to the call penalty, there will be a cost to issue new bonds (e.g., $10,000). While this flotation cost requires a current cash outflow, this cost is capitalized and recaptured over the lifetime of the bond through amortization expense. The impact of amortization is the same as depreciation on the firm's cash flows. Amortization is a non-cash expense that recaptures the cost of an intangible asset, such as the capitalized cost of the bond issue. Thus, in this illustration, the $10,000 cost is amortized at the rate of $1,000 each year.

The total cash outflows to retire the bond are $1,000,000 to retire the bond, $72,000 (after tax) to pay the penalty, and $10,000 to issue the new bond, for a total cash outflow of $1,082,000. The cash inflows from the refunding include the annual saving in $20,000 interest, but this savings increases taxes by $8,000, so the firm nets only $12,000 annually in interest savings. The other cash inflows are the $1,000 non-cash amortization of the flotation costs and the $1,000,000 cash from issuing the new debt.

The cash inflow from the new debt cancels the cash outflow from the old debt, so the analysis is reduced to a comparison of the present value of the annual $13,000 cash inflows (the after-tax interest savings plus the amortization) and the initial $82,000 cash outflow (the interest penalty plus the flotation expense). If the firm's cost of capital is 12 percent, the present value of the cash inflow is

$$\$13{,}000(5.650) = \$73{,}450,$$

so the net present value is

$$\$73{,}450 - \$82{,}000 = (\$8{,}550).$$

The net present value is negative, so the firm should not refund the bond.

This answer may be surprising, but consider the following alternative. The firm has $82,000 and uses the money to buy an annuity that yields 12 percent each year for the next 10 years. How much will the firm receive each year? The answer is

$$\frac{\$82{,}000}{5.650} = \$14{,}513.27,$$

where 5.650 is the interest factor for the present value of an ordinary annuity. This answer suggests that the financial manager could use the $82,000 necessary to refund the bond to instead purchase the annuity and receive $14,513.27 for the next ten years. That is better than generating $13,000 a year through the refunding, so the implication is obvious. Pay the old higher rate of interest and purchase the annuity. It is the better use of the $82,000.

SUMMARY

Firms make long-term investment decisions, such as whether or not to expand plant and equipment. The process of selecting these investments is called capital budgeting. This chapter covered three methods for selecting long-term investments: the payback method, the net present value, and the internal rate of return.

The payback method determines how long it takes the cash flow to recapture the cost of an investment; those investments with the fastest payback are selected. The net present value (NPV) technique determines the present value of an investment's cash flows and subtracts the cost to determine the net present value. If the net present value is positive, the investment is selected. If the financial manager must rank competing investments, those investments with the highest net present value are selected first.

The internal rate of return (IRR) determines the discount factor that equates the present value of an investment's cash flows with the cost of the investment. If this factor, called the internal rate of return, exceeds the firm's cost of capital, the investment should be made. If the financial manager must rank competing investments, those investments with the highest internal rates of return are selected first.

The rankings determined by the net present value and the internal rate of return may conflict. Such conflicts can occur when there are differences in the costs of the investments or differences in the timing of their cash flows. Reconciliation of the conflicts may be achieved by analyzing the reinvestment rates. If the financial manager must choose between the net present value and the internal rate of return techniques, the net present value is to be preferred since it makes the more conservative assumption concerning the reinvestment of cash flow (i.e., the cash flows are reinvested at the firm's cost of capital).

Risk analysis may be incorporated into capital budgeting by adjusting the cost of capital. For investments that are more risky than the firm's typical investment, a risk premium is added to the cost of capital. For less risky investments, the financial manager reduces the cost of capital. One method for determining the amount by which the cost of capital is adjusted is the use of beta coefficients. These measure the volatility of an investment's return relative to the volatility of the return on a firm's typical investment.

In addition to determining if a firm should invest in new plant and equipment, capital budgeting techniques may be used to determine if existing plant and equipment should be replaced or if an existing bond issue should be retired. The present value of the cash inflows generated by the change is compared to the cash outflow required by the investments. If the present value of the inflows is greater, the investment in the new equipment is made or the existing bond is refunded.

Review Questions

1. What impact will each of the following have on an investment's net present value?
   a. an increase in interest rates
   b. an increase in current assets required as part of making the investment
   c. an increase in the estimated price at which the equipment may be sold
   d. an increase in investors' required return on equity
2. What impact will each of the following have on an investment's internal rate of return?
   a. a decrease in the firm's cost of capital

b. an increase in the cost to acquire the investment
c. a switch from straight-line to accelerated depreciation

3. What is the difference between an investment in plant and equipment and an investment in securities? Why does an investment's value rise when interest rates fall?

4. The net present values of two investments are positive, but the investments are mutually exclusive. Should you make both investments? If the investments' internal rates of return were equal, would that affect your previous answer?

5. Why may it be advantageous for a firm to replace equipment before it wears out or to retire a bond issue prior to its maturity? What factors will influence these decisions?

6. If an investment's estimated internal rate of return is 16 percent but the firm will not be able to reinvest the investment's cash flow at that rate, what does that imply about the rate of return the firm will earn?

7. Two investments are mutually exclusive and the IRR of Investment A exceeds the IRR of B but the NPV of B exceeds the NPV of A. Why does the internal rate of return technique tend to favor the investment with the quicker payback?

Problems

The use of *PROFIT+* (or any comparable set of computer programs) will greatly facilitate the calculation of net present value and internal rate of return. However, the computer cannot answer the questions posed by some of the problems in this section. Thus, while capital budgeting is one of the best topics to illustrate the use of personal computers, it is also one of the best to illustrate their limitations and the need for the individual to interpret and apply the results of the computer's output.

1. The cost of capital for a firm is 10 percent. The firm has two possible investments with the following cash flows:

	A	B
Year 1	$300	$200
2	200	200
3	100	200

a. Each investment costs $480. Which investment(s) should the firm make according to net present value?
b. What is the internal rate of return for the two investments? Which investment(s) should the firm make? Is this the same answer you obtained in (a)?
c. If the cost of capital rises to 14 percent, which investment(s) should the firm make?

2. A firm has the following investment alternatives:

	Cash Flows		
	A	**B**	**C**
Year 1	$1,100	$3,600	—
2	1,100	—	—
3	1,100	—	$4,562

Each investment costs $3,000; Investments B and C are mutually exclusive, and the firm's cost of capital is 8 percent.

a. What is the net present value of each investment?
b. According to the net present values, which investment(s) should the firm make? Why?
c. What is the internal rate of return on each investment?
d. According to the internal rates of return, which investment(s) should the firm make? Why?
e. According to both the net present values and the internal rates of return, which investments should the firm make?
f. If the firm could reinvest the $3,600 earned in year one from Investment B at 10 percent, what effect would that information have on your answer to (e)?
g. If the firm could reinvest the $3,600 earned in year one from Investment B at 14 percent, what effect would that information have on your answer to (e)?
h. If the firm's cost of capital had been 10 percent, what would be Investment A's internal rate of return?
i. The payback method of capital budgeting selects which investment? Why?

3. A firm's cost of capital is 12 percent. The firm has three investments to choose among; the cash flows of each are as follows:

	Cash Flows		
	A	**B**	**C**
Year 1	$395	—	$1,241
2	395	—	—
3	395	—	—
4	—	$1,749	—

Each investment requires a $1,000 cash outlay, and Investments B and C are mutually exclusive.

a. Which investment(s) should the firm make according to the net present values? Why?

b. Which investment(s) should the firm make according to the internal rates of return? Why?

c. If all funds are reinvested at 15 percent, which investment(s) should the firm make? Would your answer be different if the reinvestment rate were 12 percent?

4. A firm owns a piece of land that it wants to develop. One alternative is a production plant that will cost $10,000,000 and generate annual cash flows of $950,000 for 18 years. A second alternative is a research center that will cost $12,000,000. Such a facility could be very profitable, but research projects take years, so the estimated cash flow of $1,300,000 annually for 20 years will not start until five years have passed.

   a. If the firm's cost of capital is 12 percent, what is the net present value of each project? Which investment(s) should be made?

   b. Which investment is riskier? If the firm uses a cost of capital of 14 percent to judge riskier projects, does that alter the decision in (a)?

5. An investment with total costs of $10,000 will generate total revenues of $11,000 for one year. Management thinks that since the investment is profitable, it should be made. Do you agree? What additional information would you want? If funds cost 12 percent, what would be your advice to management?

6. An investor purchases a bond for $949. The bond pays $60 a year for three years and then matures (i.e., it is redeemed for $1,000). What is the internal rate of return on that investment? In Chapter 9, what was this return called?

7. A record company determines the following cash outflows must be made before a tape is produced and released for sale:

Artist advance	$100,000
Production expense	250,000
Overhead costs	150,000
Distribution and advertising	125,000

   The expected life of the record is eight years, with cash flows annually of $200,000 for the first four years and $100,000 annually for the next four years. If the firm's cost of capital is 12 percent, should the firm produce the tape?

8. A dog lover determines that breeding requires a $2,000 investment (e.g., equipment and a quality dam and sire). Each puppy may be sold for $400, but after various expenses (e.g., vet bills), the breeder can anticipate earning about $150 per dog. It is anticipated that each litter will produce four surviving puppies and the life of the bitch is one litter a year for five years.

   a. If the breeder's cost of funds is 12 percent, what is the net present value of the investment?

   b. What is the internal rate of return on the breeding operation?

   c. Should the dog lover make this investment on economic grounds?

9. (This problem combines material from Chapters 22 and 23.) The financial manager has determined the following schedules for the cost of funds:

Debt Ratio	Cost of Debt	Cost of Equity
0%	5%	13%
10	5	13
20	5	13
30	5	13
40	5	14
50	6	15
60	8	16

a. Determine the firm's optimal capital structure.

b. Construct a simple pro forma balance sheet that shows the firm's optimal combination of debt and equity for its current level of assets.

Assets	$500	Debt	$
		Equity	
			$500

c. An investment costs $400 and offers annual cash flows of $133 for five years. Should the firm make the investment?

d. If the firm makes this additional investment, how should its balance sheet appear?

Assets	$	Debt	$
		Equity	

e. If the firm is operating with its optimal capital structure and a $400 asset yields 20.0 percent, what return will the stockholders earn on their investment in the asset?

10. Investments S and L cost $1,000 each, are mutually exclusive, and have the following cash flows. The firm's cost of capital is 10 percent.

	Cash Flows	
	S	L
Year 1	$1,300	$386
2	—	386
3	—	386
4	—	386

a. According to the net present value method of capital budgeting, which investment(s) should the firm make?
b. According to the internal rate of return method of capital budgeting, which investment(s) should the firm make?
c. If S is chosen, the $1,300 can be reinvested and earn 12 percent. Does this information alter your conclusions concerning investing in S and L? To answer, assume that L's cash flows can be reinvested at its internal rate of return. Would your answer be different if L's cash flows were reinvested at the cost of capital (i.e., 10 percent)?

11. A firm has the following investment alternatives. Each one lasts a year.

Investment	**A**	**B**	**C**
Cash flow	$1,150	560	600
Cash outflow	$1,000	500	500

The firm's cost of capital is 7 percent. A and B are mutually exclusive, and B and C are mutually exclusive.

a. What is the net present value of Investment A? Investment B? Investment C?
b. What is the internal rate of return on Investment A? Investment B? Investment C?
c. Which investment(s) should the firm make? Why?
d. If the firm had unlimited sources of funds, which investment(s) should it make? Why?
e. If there were another alternative, Investment D, with an internal rate of return of 6 percent, would that alter your answer to (d)? Why?
f. If the firm's cost of capital rose to 10 percent, what effect would that have on Investment A's internal rate of return?

12. A lessor, whose cost of capital is 10 percent, may acquire equipment for $113,479 and lease it for a period of five years.

a. If the lessor charges $36,290 annually to rent the equipment, what are the net present value and the internal rate of return on the investment? Should the lessor acquire the equipment?
b. If the equipment has no estimated residual value, what must be the minimum annual lease charge for the lessor to earn the required 10 percent on the investment?
c. If the lessor can sell the equipment at the end of the fifth year for $10,000 and receive annual lease payments of $36,290, what are the net present value and the internal rate of return on the investment? What is the impact of the residual?
d. If the $10,000 residual resulted in the lessor charging only $34,290 for the rental payments, what is the impact on the investment's net present value?

cases

Choosing Between Long-Term Investment Alternatives

William Still is faced with a dilemma. His firm needs additional storage and production facilities and essentially has two choices. The first is to remodel the existing building and to expand on to vacant land next to the plant. This is the least costly alternative since the building exists and the vacant land is owned. The facility will cost an estimated $25,000,000 and should generate annual cash flow of approximately $6,500,000 for ten years after which it will have to be replaced because the current building will need substantial repairs. However, the building may be sold at that time for its book value, $5,000,000.

The second alternative is to build a new facility. This will cost more and require changes in the firm's working capital. In addition, the plant cannot possibly be put into operation for three years while the first alternative could be ready in less than a year. The new plant does, however, offer a major advantage. Its expected life is at least 20 years and perhaps could last 25 years without major repairs. Thus, the decision to build the new plant avoids a major decision after 10 years which will be necessary if the first alternative is chosen.

The estimated cost of the new plant is $64,000,000 plus an increase in current assets of $6,000,000 is expected to result from the larger operation. The estimated cash flow, starting after three years, is $10,000,000 annually for 20 years at which time the plant may be sold for its book value, $20,000,000. If the plant operates for another five years, the estimated cash flow drops to $8,000,000 for the last five years since repairs will increase. After 25 years it may be sold for its book value, $12,000,000.

Still has to report to the firm's chief operating officer, Vaughan Williams. He knows that Williams has a bias for investments with a short duration, but Still intuitively believes that the new plant is the better alternative. Intuition, however, is insufficient to justify this type of investment; an analysis of each alternative's net present value and internal rate of return is required.

Still decided to determine the net present value for the alternatives: (1) the expansion of existing facilities, (2a) the new facility assuming cash flows for 20 years, and (2b) the new facility assuming cash flows for 25 years. To facilitate the calculations, he assumed that (1) all cash flows occur at the end of each year, (2) all cash outflows occur immediately, and (3) the increase in working capital is permanent. The firm uses a cost of capital of 9 percent to evaluate typical investments and 10 to 12 percent to judge riskier investments. Still thought the expansion was comparable to the firm's average investment but that the new plant was riskier. He decided to use 10 percent for alternative 2a and 12 percent for alternative 2b.

Case Problems

1. What is the net present value of each investment?
2. Would the IRR of alternative 2a exceed the cost of capital?
3. What is the conclusion that may be drawn from this analysis?
4. What is your reaction to Still's using two discount factors to analyze the second alternatives?
5. Are the sale prices for the new plant important to the final decision?

Suggested Readings

Bierman, Harold, Jr., and Seymour Smidt. *The Capital Budgeting Decision.* 7th ed. New York: Macmillan, 1988.

Seitz, Neil E. *Capital Budgeting and Long-Term Financing Decisions.* Hinsdale, Ill.: The Dryden Press, 1990.

These are texts designed for undergraduate courses in capital budgeting. They develop the material presented in this and the previous chapter.

Doenger, R. Conrad. "The 'Reinvestment Problem' in a Practical Perspective." *Financial Management* (Spring 1972), pp. 85–91. Reprinted in *Financial Management Classics,* edited by C. D. Aby, Jr. and D. E. Vaughn, pp. 207–213. Santa Monica, Calif.: Goodyear Publishing Co., 1979.

This article develops the text material on mutually exclusive investments and capital rationing through a discussion of the rate at which an investment's early cash flows are reinvested.

Gitman, Lawrence J., and John R. Forrester, Jr. "A Survey of Capital Budgeting Techniques Used by Major U.S. Firms." *Financial Management* (Fall 1977), pp. 66–71.

This survey found that large corporations are increasingly using sophisticated capital budgeting techniques.

Oblak, David J., and Roy J. Helm, Jr. "Survey and Analysis of Capital Budgeting Methods Used by Multinationals." *Financial Management* (Winter 1980), pp. 37–41.

This survey found that multinational firms primarily use internal rates of return and payback for selecting investments.

chapter

24

Mergers and Bankruptcy

21 pages in chapter

Learning Objectives

1 Identify the types of and reasons for mergers.
2 Differentiate the means of payment in a merger.
3 Enumerate the terms of a merger agreement.
4 Distinguish between pooling and purchase methods of accounting.
5 Explain how management may fight a hostile takeover attempt.
6 Identify the causes of bankruptcy.
7 Determine the order of payment in a bankruptcy liquidation.
8 Explain why creditors may accept reorganization instead of liquidation.

The twentieth-century novelist John Phillips Marquand suggested in *The Late George Apley* that "marriage . . . is a damnably serious business, particularly around Boston." Mergers are also damnably serious business, even outside Boston. Hardly a business day passes without reference in the financial press to a merger or takeover. For example, the February 5, 1991, issue of *The Wall Street Journal* had several articles on mergers and acquisitions. Coldwell Banker, the real estate arm of Sears, announced that it would acquire Schlott Realtors. Pirelli proposed to merge with Continental AG to form one of the largest tire firms in the world, and Barold announced that it would acquire Diamant Boart Stratabit S.A. That's a total of three merger articles in one day, and early 1991 was a slow economic period during which merger activity significantly declined from its high levels of the late 1980s.

While some firms succeed, others fail. According to Rudyard Kipling, "We have forty million reasons for failure, but not a single excuse." The same February 5th issue of *The Wall Street Journal* reported that Hills Department Stores had filed for bankruptcy. This action was the result of Hills's being unable to reach a restructuring agreement that was acceptable to its creditors, who were owed over $900 million and who had not received their December interest payment. Inability to meet such payments in a timely fashion is often a reason, if not an excuse, for failure.

Mergers and bankruptcies are involved topics. Many schools of business devote entire courses to each. This chapter can only touch on some of the financial topics concerning mergers and bankruptcy. The section on mergers stresses types of mergers, their causes, and the different methods used by accountants to combine the assets and liabilities of the firms involved in the merger. The section on bankruptcy and reorganization is primarily concerned with the causes of bankruptcy and explains why creditors may be willing to accept a reorganization instead of a liquidation of the bankrupt firm.

MERGERS

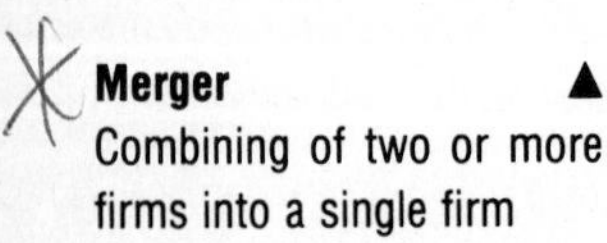

Merger ▲
Combining of two or more firms into a single firm

Firms may expand by external as well as by internal growth. Firms grow internally by retaining earnings and using their cash flow to replace and expand plant and equipment. Firms expand externally by purchasing or merging with another existing firm. This section covers **mergers,** the combining of two firms into a single firm, and will briefly consider the causes of external growth and different types of mergers.[1] The subse-

[1]The term "merger" is often used to imply two firms mutually agreeing to join together into one firm. The term "acquisition" is often used to imply one firm taking over another firm.

quent sections will discuss how the combination of two firms may be accomplished, how the balance sheets of the two firms are combined, hostile takeovers, and leveraged buyouts.

Reasons for Mergers

There are several reasons for external growth. First, if a firm seeks to enter an industry, there are considerable start-up costs. The firm must plan for the entry and contract for the plant and equipment. This process may be not only expensive but also time consuming. The span of time from the decision to enter a new field to the actual production and sales of the output may be many years. Purchasing an existing firm will significantly reduce the time necessary to enter the industry and may reduce the cost of entry. Second, entry into a new industry has risk and is uncertain of success. While management will not enter a new line of business unless it anticipates earning profits, success is not assured. For example, RCA entered the computer industry to compete with IBM and Digital Equipment. Even though RCA had previously been a leader in electronics, it failed to compete successfully with the established computer firms and suffered one of the largest losses ever incurred by a corporation. By purchasing or merging with an existing, profitable firm, this uncertainty and risk of loss are reduced. Third, when a firm enters a new industry, it increases the number of firms within the industry. This increases the element of competition and may reduce the level of profits for all firms in the industry. Such an increase in competition might not occur if the entering firm purchases or merges with an existing firm.

Possible Impact on Earnings

Mergers may be a means for a firm to increase its per-share earnings. Consider the following information concerning two firms:

	Firm A	Firm B
Net income	$1,000,000	$2,000,000
Number of shares outstanding	500,000	500,000
Earnings per share (EPS)	$2	$4
Price per share	$14	$40
Price earnings ratio (price divided by EPS)	7.0	10.0

Firm B offers to exchange its stock for the stock of Firm A at the rate of one share of A for 0.45 share of B. These terms may be very attractive to the stockholders of A since 0.45 of B is worth $18 (i.e., 0.45 × $40), which is greater than the current market price of $14 for a share of A.

If the stockholders accept the offer and the two firms merge, Firm B will issue 225,000 of its shares (i.e., 0.45 × 500,000) for the 500,000 shares of A. The effect of this transaction on the per-share earnings of B is

Net income	$3,000,000
Number of shares outstanding	725,000
Earnings per share	$4.14

As a result of this merger, B's per-share earnings are increased from $4 to $4.14.

What effect will this increase have on the stock's price? This question is impossible to answer before the merger, because no one knows for certain how the market will value the new, larger firm. If B's price earnings ratio remains 10, the price of the stock will rise to $41.40. If the market views the combination of A and B to be a stronger firm than B by itself, the price should rise above $41.40. However, if the market believes that the acquisition of A by B will be detrimental to B, the price of B's stock will fall.

Presumably, management will follow the course of action that will maximize the value of the shares. The takeover of A by B does increase the value of A's stock. Unless management can arrange better terms elsewhere, accepting the offer may be in the stockholders' best interests (but not necessarily the best interests of management). The decision of B's management to make the offer need not result in a higher value for B's stock. As with all investment decisions, the realized results will not be known until after the investment (in this case the merger) is completed.

Not all mergers lead to an immediate increase in earnings per share. Instead, there may be a decrease in per-share earnings as the firm that takes over another firm issues new stock, which dilutes the existing stockholders' position. Earnings per share may also be reduced if the firm has to issue substantial debt to finance the takeover, since this debt will require interest payments that may reduce the firm's net earnings. If the additional interest expense is substantial, the increase in operating income from the merger may be insufficient to offset the interest expense. Thus, net income could decline even though the firm issues no additional stock to finance a takeover.

Such a decline in earnings was forecasted by the management of GTE Corporation when it sought to purchase Contel. GTE offered 1.27 of its shares for each share of Contel. At a price of $28 per GTE share, the value of the merger was $5.5 billion for Contel's 160 million shares. The increase in GTE shares issued in exchange for the Contel shares resulted in lower earnings per share. Management, however, anticipated that the rate of growth in earnings would increase. Thus, while there would be an initial decline in per-share earnings, future earnings would rise more rapidly as a result of the merger.

Synergy

In addition to increased potential for growth or increased per-share earnings, mergers may be justified on the grounds that the combined firm is stronger than the two individual firms. This is called **synergy.** Synergy may occur when two firms with different but complementary strengths are merged so that the resulting firm is stronger than the sum of its parts. For example, if one firm has a strong marketing department while another firm has excellent product facilities but lacks marketing skills, a merger of the two may produce a firm that is stronger than the individual firms were previously. Combining the marketing proficiency and the production capabilities may result in synergy. Synergy has been frequently used to justify mergers. Firms with low profitability have been taken over on the grounds that the management of the company doing the takeover could "turn around" the unprofitable firm. While it may be impossible to verify that such synergy existed, it is an intuitively appealing explanation (or perhaps rationalization) for such takeovers.

Synergy ▲
Combining of two firms so that the combined firm is stronger than both firms were individually

Types of Mergers

Mergers may be classified into three types: horizontal, vertical, and conglomerate. Mergers of two firms within the same industry (i.e., those which produce the same products) are **horizontal mergers.** Thus, the merger of Texaco and Getty Oil is an example of a horizontal merger. **Vertical mergers** involve the merging of two firms in different aspects of the same industry, especially when one of the firms is a supplier for the other firm. If an automobile manufacturer merged with a producer of automobile parts, that would be a vertical merger. Another example is the merger of a steel mill with an ore producer. Since steel mills buy iron ore to produce steel, the producer of the ore is one of the steel mill's suppliers. If a steel mill merged with a metal fabricator, that also would be a vertical merger because the steel mill sells its product to the fabricator. Many mergers are vertical mergers, since firms seek to assure themselves of supplies of raw materials by merging with firms that are suppliers of these materials. During the energy crisis, firms that were dependent on sources of fuel would purchase fuel suppliers.

Horizontal merger ▲
Merger of two firms in the same industry

Vertical merger ▲
Combination of a firm with a supplier or distributor

There are also mergers between firms with diverse product lines. These conglomerations are called **conglomerate mergers,** and in some cases there is no apparent relationship between the two firms. Many firms that currently have diverse product lines grew through such mergers.

Conglomerate merger ▲
Merger between two firms in different industries

Synergy has been an important rationale for conglomerate mergers, for the surviving firm was presumed to be stronger and able to achieve greater growth than the individual firms could achieve by themselves. Conglomerate firms would frequently seek as merger candidates firms whose earnings growth had been inferior and whose stock prices were low relative to the firms' earnings or book value. The conglomerate's management would assert that the merger would significantly benefit both firms, making them stronger through synergistic effects. The conglomerate's managerial talent and financial skill could be applied to the merger candidate's problems, turn the firm around, and thereby achieve greater profitability. This greater profitability should then lead to higher stock prices. The lure of higher stock prices induced the stockholders and managements of many firms to agree to these mergers.

Some conglomerate mergers produced (at least in the short run) phenomenal results. Through such mergers some companies were able to increase in size from small corporations to large industrial giants whose earnings growth and increase in stock prices were spectacular. Perhaps the most famous example is Ling Temco Vought (LTV), which grew in seven years from a modest manufacturer of electronic products with sales of $154 million to a firm with sales of $2.7 billion in such varied fields as food, electronics, aerospace, steel, and computer software. Such an increase in sales is an annual growth rate in excess of 100 percent, or, in other words, sales more than doubled each year! During the same period its earnings grew from a loss of more than $7 million to profits of more than $24 million, and the price of the stock also rose rapidly, from $20 a share to a high of $169.50.

Unfortunately for investors, LTV's amazing growth was not sustained. The growth in sales and earnings could not be maintained. The price of the stock fell precipitously and eventually the firm went bankrupt. Obviously, many investors suffered significant losses of their investments in LTV, not realizing that the company could not possibly maintain its rapid growth rate for any extended period of time. The period of super growth had to come to an end. Perhaps what surprised investors was the severity of the decline in earnings and stock prices once the rapid growth ceased.

The decline in earnings of LTV (and many conglomerates) can be explained in part by the method used to finance growth. LTV is an excellent example of the risk associated with financial leverage, for the growth was primarily financed by debt. During the period of rapid growth, LTV's debt expanded from $69.6 million to $1.28 billion. This debt had the effect of increasing the growth in earnings as long as financial leverage was favorable. However, when sales lagged and profit margins fell, this debt required the continued payment of fixed interest charges. Thus, LTV's earnings per share declined more rapidly than the earnings of less financially leveraged firms when the economy experienced a period of recession.

The failure of some conglomerate firms has led to the dismantling of many; Paramount Communications is perhaps the best illustration. During the 1960s and 1970s, Paramount Communications (then called Gulf & Western) grew into a large and diverse industrial firm with operations in financial services (Associates Corp.), publishing (Simon and Schuster, Prentice Hall), film and TV production (Paramount), natural resources (New Jersey Zinc), and consumer products including food and agricultural products. In addition, Gulf & Western held a large portfolio of common stocks of other firms, so that by 1980 it was one of the best illustrations of a conglomerate firm.

With the death of its founder and the resulting new management, the firm changed direction. Management sold Gulf & Western's stock portfolio, divested entire divisions, and streamlined the operation into a firm primarily concerned with entertainment. Gulf & Western's name was changed to Paramount Communications, which, ironically, was one of the firms Gulf & Western took over during its period of merger activity. As of 1990, Paramount was one of the most successful producers of TV shows ("Cheers") and movies (the *Indiana Jones* series, *Star Trek,* and the *Godfather* series) and had become rumored to be a major takeover candidate for Japanese firms seeking entry into the lucrative American entertainment market.

EXECUTING THE MERGER

External growth through a merger is an investment and should be treated in the same way as other investment decisions. The capital budgeting techniques discussed in Chapter 23 should be applied to prospective mergers. These techniques will help identify possible merger candidates and establish the terms of a merger that are acceptable to the acquiring firm.

The terms of a merger are extremely important. They include the following: (1) the price paid for the acquired firm; (2) the relationship between the acquired firm's previous management and the acquiring firm's management; (3) relationships among divisions of the two firms; and (4) the relationship between the new management and labor unions affected by the merger. In some cases, the managements of the acquiring firm and the firm to be acquired are compatible and able to establish mutually acceptable terms. However, if the two firms are not on friendly terms, the acquiring firm may seek to gain control from the other firm's management. This may be done through a cash offer for the firm's stock at a price sufficiently high to induce the current stockholders to sell their shares. Once the acquiring firm gains control, it may replace the old management and merge the two companies.

After the price has been established, the means of payment must be determined. The acquiring firm has basically the following three choices: (1) pay in cash; (2) issue a specified amount of debt in trade for the acquired firm's stock; or (3) issue a specified amount of stock in trade for the acquired firm's stock. These three choices are significantly different from each other from the viewpoints of both the buyer and the seller.

If the firm pays cash, it is trading one asset for the acquired firm's stock. It receives the firm's assets and liabilities, but no new shares are issued, and its current stockholders' ownership is not diluted. Payment with cash means that the firm must either have the cash or a ready source of funds. From the viewpoint of the sellers the prime advantage is the receipt of money, which the sellers may use as they desire. However, since this is a cash sale of their stock, the sale is subject to capital gains tax if the stockholders sell their shares for a profit.

If the firm issues debt to pay for the acquisition, it conserves its cash but increases its use of financial leverage. This obliges the firm to meet the terms of the indenture, to pay the interest, and to retire the debt. There is no dilution of its current stockholders' position, however, for no new shares are issued (unless the debt is convertible into the firm's stock). From the viewpoint of the sellers, the flow of interest income and the obligation of the acquiring firm to meet the terms of the indenture may be important advantages. Since the sellers have agreed to accept debt instead of cash, they may be able to negotiate a higher price for the shares to compensate them for accepting payment that is spread over several years.[2] There is, however, a major disadvantage in accepting debt instead of cash. The Internal Revenue Service treats the acceptance of debt as being no different from a cash sale. For tax purposes capital gains are realized, and the sellers must pay capital gains taxes if they have made a profit on the transaction. This tax payment may be a real burden if the sellers have insufficient cash to meet their required tax obligation.

If the acquiring firm issues stock as payment, its current stockholders' position may be diluted. This dilution depends on the earnings of the acquired company and the number of shares issued. However, no additional debt is issued that requires interest payments and eventual retirement. The sellers receive equity (i.e., stock) in the acquiring firm and can sell these shares or retain them. The shares may appreciate in value if the firm flourishes and grows, but there is no assurance that the firm will prosper, and the firm is not obligated to pay dividends. Should the

[2] Another possibility would be a higher interest rate on the debt the stockholders receive for their stock.

The Job Mart

Acquisitions Specialist

■ Job Description: Identify firms that are candidates for possible acquisitions and mergers. Participate in merger negotiations with sellers and with the banks and financial institutions that are providing the financing. Seek buyers for the divisions being sold. ■ Job Requirements: Strong knowledge of accounting and valuation techniques and the ability to perceive strengths not indicated by financial statements. Knowledge of security laws and excellent negotiation skills are also important. ■ Characteristics: Individuals specializing in mergers and acquisitions have visible positions in which they must work well under pressure and be able to make judgments rapidly. Individuals need to be able to assess the risk associated with any acquisition and its financing.

---

value of the stock decline, the sellers might not realize the purchase price of the shares.

There is a major tax advantage in accepting stock as payment instead of cash or debt. The Internal Revenue Service does not treat the swapping of stock in a merger as a realized sale. The seller, who receives the new shares, has the cost basis of the old shares transferred to the new shares and does not recognize any gains or losses for the purpose of capital gains taxes. Those investors who want cash or who do not want to invest in the combined firm may sell their stock and pay any applicable capital gains taxes. Other investors, however, may continue to hold the new stock and not pay any capital gains taxes until the stock is sold in the future. This tax advantage strongly argues for accomplishing mergers through stock swaps, for stockholders may more readily accept the terms of the merger since profits are not subject to capital gains taxes unless the stock is sold.

The firm taking over a second firm may offer to swap convertible preferred stock instead of common stock or debt. Since the preferred is convertible into the common stock of the company doing the takeover, such a transaction is considered a swap of "like" securities and is not subject to capital gains taxation. In addition, the value of the convertible security will rise if the surviving firm prospers and its stock price increases. The dividend on this preferred may also be higher than would be paid to the holders of the firm's common stock. Thus, the preferred stockholders can receive a larger flow of income that is more comparable to the flow of interest paid by a bond but that does not have the tax consequences associated with swapping their stock for a debt instrument. This tax advantage is probably the primary reason that convertible preferred stock is frequently issued in a merger. The stockholders can earn more income, have potential for capital gains through the conversion feature, and defer any applicable capital gains taxes until the shares are sold.

POOLING AND PURCHASING

Purchase accounting ▲ Method of accounting for a merger in which one firm is considered to have bought the other firm

Pooling ▲ Method of accounting for a merger that combines the merging firms' balance sheets

There are two ways of accounting for mergers. In one case, **purchasing accounting,** the surviving firm is considered to have purchased the other firm. In the other case, **pooling,** the two firms are consolidated and their assets and liabilities are pooled, even though the resulting firm may retain the name of only one of the firms. While the difference between the two is a complex topic in accounting and beyond the scope of this text, the following discussion will give an indication of the differences between the two accounting methods.

Two firms (A and B) have the following simple balance sheets:

Firm A
Balance Sheet as of 12/31/XX

ASSETS		LIABILITIES AND EQUITY	
Current assets	$2,000	Current liabilites	$1,000
Fixed assets	3,000	Long-term debt	3,000
		Equity	1,000
	$5,000		$5,000

Firm B
Balance Sheet as of 12/31/XX

ASSETS		LIABILITIES AND EQUITY	
Current assets	$ 3,000	Current liabilities	$ 1,000
Fixed assets	7,000	Long-term debt	3,000
		Equity	6,000
	$10,000		$10,000

Firm B offers its stock to the owners of Firm A in trade for their stock in Firm A, and this offer is accepted. If the merger is treated as a consolidation, and the assets and liabilities are pooled, the two balance sheets are combined. The balance sheets are added horizontally. Thus, the new firm (Firm C) has the following balance sheet:

Firm C
Balance Sheet as of 12/31/XX

ASSETS		LIABILITIES AND EQUITY	
Current assets	$ 5,000	Current liabilities	$ 2,000
Fixed assets	10,000	Long-term debt	6,000
		Equity	7,000
	$15,000		$15,000

This new balance sheet is created by adding both firms' current assets, fixed assets, current liabilities, long-term debt, and equity. All the similar items on the two balance sheets have been combined on the new consolidated balance sheet.

In the case of a purchase, one firm actually buys the other firm. Payment may be made in cash, or the firm may issue stock or debt in trade for the stock of the acquired firm. The important consideration is not the means of payment, however, but the price relative to the book value of the assets and equity of the acquired firm. For example, if Firm B borrows $1,000 and buys the stock of A for $1,000, then Firm B acquires $5,000 in assets, $4,000 in liabilities, and $1,000 in equity. When the balance sheets are consolidated, Firm B's new balance sheet is

Firm B
Balance Sheet as of 12/31/XX

ASSETS			LIABILITIES AND EQUITY		
Current assets	$2,000		Current liabilities	$1,000	
	3,000			1,000	
		$ 5,000			$ 2,000
Fixed assets	$3,000		Long-term debt	$3,000	
	7,000			4,000	
		10,000			7,000
			Equity		6,000
		$15,000			$15,000

Although Firm B acquires $5,000 in assets, it also has assumed $4,000 of A's debt. Thus, the net assets acquired are worth only $1,000, which is what Firm B paid for them. It also should be noted that these assets were financed by the issuing of $1,000 in long-term debt.

If Firm B had issued $4,000 of long-term debt and bought the stock of A, Firm B would be paying $4,000 for net assets worth only $1,000. In this case, there is a discrepancy of $3,000 that must be accounted for. The difference between the purchase price of the assets and the book value of the net assets is called **goodwill.** Goodwill is added to the assets of the acquiring firm so that the new balance sheet for Firm B is

Goodwill ▲
Accounting entry (intangible asset) that arises when the cost of an asset exceeds its book value

Firm B
Balance Sheet as of 12/31/XX

ASSETS			LIABILITIES AND EQUITY		
Current assets	$2,000		Current liabilities	$1,000	
	3,000			1,000	
		$ 5,000			$ 2,000
Fixed assets	$3,000		Long-term debt	$3,000	
	7,000			7,000	
		10,000			10,000
Goodwill		$ 3,000	Equity		6,000
		$18,000			$18,000

The effect of the purchase has been to create $3,000 in goodwill on Firm B's balance sheet.

The creation of goodwill leads to serious tax consequences. Generally accepted accounting principles (GAAP) require that goodwill be amortized, which is the allocation of the cost of the asset over a period of time. Amortization is like depreciation. Both are non-cash expenses that allocate the cost of an asset over time, and both reduce the firm's income. However, the Internal Revenue Service requires that goodwill arising from a merger be amortized *after taxes.* Thus, goodwill creates an expense that reduces earnings but does not reduce the firm's taxes.

Obviously, a firm would prefer to use pooling instead of purchasing as the means to account for the merger, since goodwill cannot arise when pooling is used. Pooling is permitted, however, under very restrictive circumstances. Only mergers that are effectuated through a stock swap are eligible. Thus, swaps of debt for equity and outright purchases of stock for cash cannot result in the use of pooling by the surviving firm. In these cases, the purchase method of accounting for the merger must be used, which leads to the creation of goodwill on many firms' balance sheets.

THE HOSTILE TAKEOVER

Not all business combinations are the result of the managements of two firms willingly merging their operations. In many cases, one firm seeks to acquire another whose management prefers to remain independent. This leads to a hostile takeover attempt. The managements of the two firms square off in a fight for control: The acquiring firm fights to gain control, while the other firm battles to retain control.

Often the scenario of such battles follows a distinct pattern. In this discussion, the firm initiating the takeover is called Suitor, and the target firm is called Takeover. Suitor may initially take a position in Takeover's stock. While this purchase is unannounced, an increase in the volume of trading in a given stock is often an indication that someone is accumulating a position in the shares. Once Suitor has accumulated 5 percent of Takeover's stock, Suitor is required to file with the SEC Form 13-D, which discloses the position. For this reason, Suitor may cease accumulating the stock prior to acquiring 5 percent. On the other hand, Suitor may file the required document and continue to accumulate the shares.

If Suitor desires to pursue the acquisition, it may announce an offer to buy the remaining shares at a specified price. That is, Suitor makes a "tender offer" for the shares that it does not already own. The price is almost inevitably above the current market price to induce current stockholders to sell. This immediately puts the stock "in play" as the market awaits the reaction from Takeover's management.

The reaction is almost always negative. Takeover's board of directors meets to consider the offer to buy the firm, but the answer is generally that the price is "inadequate."[3] Suitor may respond by threatening to take the offer to Takeover's stockholders and seek their approval for the sale of the company. Since most stockholders vote by proxy and not in person, this scenario produces the "proxy fight," in which current management and Suitor each fight for the votes (i.e., the proxies) of Takeover's stockholders. The procedure can be costly to both sides, so some alternative course of action usually develops.

For example, Suitor may fight the claim that the price is inadequate by raising the offer. This puts immense pressure on Takeover's management and the board of directors to accept the sweetened offer. If they refuse and the offer is withdrawn, the price of the stock will probably return to its pre-takeover level. Stockholders will obviously sustain a loss and may sue management and the board of directors for failure to perform their financial responsibilities to stockholders.

Another possibility is that Takeover will find a different buyer. Once Suitor makes the offer and the stock is in play, an alternative buyer may surface, which could lead to a bidding war. The alternative buyer, White Knight, may strike a deal with Takeover's management, which accepts the offer to sell the company to White Knight. Although the price may not exceed Suitor's sweetened offer, it should be comparable. A higher price, of course, ends the possibility of legal action against management since the firm is sold to the highest bidder (assuming that Suitor does not further increase its offer).

If this scenario occurs, Takeover's management positions are often retained. Suitor also fares well. Since it initially took a position prior to making its offer, it has stock acquired for a price that may be considerably below the price paid by White Knight. Even if White Knight does not emerge or eventually withdraws, Suitor's initial purchases usually cost less than its subsequent purchase of the remainder of Takeover's shares.

In the previous illustration, White Knight "saved" Takeover's management; however, if White Knight does not emerge, there is still the possibility that Takeover will fend off the unsolicited and unwanted offer to buy the firm. Takeover's management may offer to repurchase the shares already acquired by Suitor. This offer may even exceed the going market price, in which case Takeover pays "greenmail" to induce Suitor to cease the hostile offer. The terms of the sale may include a stipulation in which Suitor agrees not to purchase stock in the company for a period of time (e.g., five years). In other cases, the terms may permit Suitor to

---

[3]There is an obvious potential conflict of interest. Takeover's board of directors and management have fiduciary responsibility to the firm's stockholders. Fighting the takeover attempt, however, may be motivated by a desire to protect the board's position and the manager's salaries, perks, and other benefits—not to benefit stockholders.

Financial Facts

Fending Off Hostile Takeovers

How can management reduce the likelihood of a takeover? One means that many publicly held firms have adopted is the rights offering. Such a strategy is designed to make the takeover more expensive, which reduces the firm's attractiveness to possible buyers. The strategy cannot be used to erase the possibility of a takeover. That would obviously be beneficial to existing management at the expense of the firm's stockholders. • How the strategy works may be illustrated by the plan established in 1990 by El Paso Electric. A right was attached to each share of El Paso common stock that grants the shareholder the right to buy an additional share for $25. These rights trade with the stock and may be exercised only if (1) 15 percent or more of the stock is acquired by an individual or another firm or (2) an offer to buy the company is made. • These terms will certainly increase the cost of a takeover if the price of El Paso stock exceeds $25 a share. For example, suppose El Paso stock is trading for $29 and another firm offers to buy the stock for $33. Immediately the rights may be exercised. Each current stockholder may buy an additional share at $25 for each share held. The firm seeking control of El Paso would have to purchase two shares instead of one. Although this will not preclude a takeover attempt, it obviously raises the cost. • Since this additional cost generates cash for the existing stockholders, it can be argued that they are the beneficiaries of the rights offering. But the strategy does reduce the probability of an outsider seeking to buy the firm. Thus, the rights also protect existing management from a hostile takeover that would, in all probability, result in management's losing its job. •

---

hold a position for "investment purposes" but forbid the purchase of additional shares (a "stand still agreement"). Suitor's management then may hold the shares, a strategy it will find acceptable if the managers believe that Takeover's stock is undervalued and the price will rise in the future.

To discourage an unwanted offer, Takeover's management may take actions in anticipation of and prior to an attempted hostile takeover. (See, for example, the Financial Facts: "Fending Off Hostile Takeovers.") Management may break up the firm and spin off pieces to its stockholders. In 1989, Ethyl Corporation distributed Tredegar to its stockholders. This course of action could be motivated by several reasons. First, the parent desires to rid itself of a division that is not doing well and hence is hurting the parent's financial position. Second, the parent desires to divest itself of a profitable division that no longer fits into its long-term goals. Third, the parent desires to remove a division that other firms may want. The other firms will no longer consider taking over the parent as a separate entity. When the last possibility is the motivating factor, the spin-off (or any sale of a division) may be referred to as a "scorched earth" policy designed to protect the parent from a hostile takeover attempt.

Other strategies used to fend off takeovers include the recapitalization and the leveraged buyout. Leveraged buyouts may be motivated by other considerations and are covered in the next section. In a recapitalization, management borrows a substantial amount of money and uses it to repurchase stock or pay a large cash dividend. For example, in 1987, GenCorp borrowed $1.3 billion and used the money plus other internally generated funds to repurchase 54 percent of its outstanding stock at $130 a share. The effect of this repurchase was to completely change GenCorp's financial structure. Long-term debt rose from $200 million to over $1.4 billion and equity declined from $1.1 billion to a *negative* $360 million.

A variation of this strategy was employed by Harcourt, Brace, Jovanovich (HBJ), which borrowed $2.5 billion and used the money to distribute a one-time cash dividend of $40 a share. While this action did not reduce the number of shares, it certainly changed the firm's capital structure. In effect, HBJ substituted a substantial amount of debt for equity, as the dividend distribution wiped out HBJ's retained earnings.

These actions were taken by GenCorp and HBJ in response to hostile takeover offers. In both cases, the large reduction in equity coupled with the large amount of new debt thwarted the takeover. In a sense, the recapitalization is a variation on the scorched earth strategy because incurring the new debt thwarts the takeover by destroying at least part of the firm. While both managements obviously anticipated that the surviving firm would be viable, that is not a certainty. After these recapitalizations, managements of both GenCorp and HBJ have been forced to sell off divisions and streamline operations in an attempt to restore the financial viability of their respective firms. As of January 1991, GenCorp had significantly reduced debt and increased equity, but total debt still constituted over 85 percent of total financing. HBJ, however, was still sustaining losses from the burden of the interest expense, and its long-term viability remained in doubt. At the beginning of 1991, its stock was selling for less than $1, and the debt issued to finance the recapitalization sold for a significant discount from face value.

LEVERAGED BUYOUTS

During the 1980s, several firms were sold not to other firms but to their managers and/or other private investors. In some cases, these sales were in response to hostile takeover offers. Instead of accepting an offer to sell the company, management itself bought the company (i.e., bought out the existing stockholders). After the purchase was completed, the firm was no longer publicly held but became a private corporation owned by a few individuals.

Few investors have sufficient funds to buy all of the firm's publicly held shares. To finance these purchases, the buyers borrow the funds from commercial banks and pledge the assets of the firm to secure the loans. In effect, the investors are using the firm's borrowing capacity

Financial Facts

E-II Holdings and Pac-Man

The takeover in 1986 of Beatrice Companies was one of the largest leveraged buyouts: $6.2 billion. Soon after completing the purchase, management started to restructure the firm. Several divisions were sold in order to raise funds to retire some of the large debt issued to finance the purchase of Beatrice. Then, a hodgepodge of consumer products, such as Samsonite luggage, Stiffel lamps, and Louver drapes and blinds, were put together and sold back to the general public. The new company's name: E-II Holdings. • E-II Holdings illustrates the new financial restructuring/takeover game. The sale of E-II to the public not only raised funds to help pay off debt but also raised a substantial amount of money to continue the process, that is to acquire additional companies. However, when E-II Holdings sought to make a major acquisition, the unexpected happened. E-II offered to purchase American Brands, but the firm resisted by using the "Pac-Man" defense. This defense is named after the video game in which the character seeks to gobble up its opponents before it is eaten. American Brands counteroffered to buy the shares of E-II Holdings. While this defense is rarely used to fend off an unwanted takeover attempt, it succeeded in this case. E-II Holdings did not acquire American Brands but was itself acquired by its target, and American Brands maintained its independence. •

(and not their own) to buy the company. The buyers have to invest only a modest amount of the total purchase price, since the bank finances the balance. The loans are subsequently repaid with funds generated by the firm's assets.

Leveraged buyout ▲ Acquisition (i.e., purchase) of a firm through the use of debt financing

Such **leveraged buyouts** have become an important strategy for avoiding an unwanted takeover. For example, Cone Mills, a major manufacturer of denim, received an unwanted offer to purchase the firm from Western Pacific Industries. Instead of seeking a merger partner to buy Cone Mills as a means of avoiding the takeover, management chose a leveraged buyout. It offered the stockholders $70 a share, which was higher than the offer by Western Pacific Industries. The total cost was $465.3 million. The primary source of funds to finance this purchase came from ten commercial banks that put up $420 million. These loans, which accounted for more than 90 percent of the total purchase price, were secured by the company's assets. By such a leveraged buyout, Cone Mills's management avoided the takeover and maintained their control of the firm.

Not all leveraged buyouts were the results of hostile takeover attempts. Some firms used the leveraged buyout as a means to dispose of unwanted divisions. For example, Mobil sold its Montgomery Ward division to its managers in a leveraged buyout. Mobil received cash for the sale. The managers of Montgomery Ward retained their positions and became the owners of the firm. If they successfully manage the independent company, they could earn a substantial return on their investment in the firm.

All leveraged buyouts result in the creation of substantial amounts of debt, virtually all of which would be classified as high yield "junk bonds." At the beginning of 1991, a large number of firms had already defaulted on their junk bonds, so that investors who had financed the leveraged buyouts sustained large losses. However, not all leveraged buyouts will fail, and it is safe to assume that some of the successful ones will issue and sell stock back to the general public in the future. For example, it would not be surprising to learn that the managers and owners of Montgomery Ward intended to take the firm public and sell some, if not all, of their stock in Ward. It is through such sales that the individuals who managed these highly leveraged firms will realize the potential large returns that, in part, motivated the initial buyout.

BANKRUPTCY AND REORGANIZATION

While some firms are able to achieve growth, others are not so fortunate. Actually, many firms fail every year, but most of these are relatively small firms. Failures by large companies are rare, but these failures can be spectacular, and they may receive a significant amount of publicity. The Southland (Seven-Eleven) and Campeau (Federated Department Stores) collapses certainly received more publicity than the failure of many small operations, and they probably received more publicity than the success of Xerox, Johnson and Johnson, or IBM.

The cause of failure is usually the same for large and small firms—poor management. This cause, however, can cover a broad spectrum of errors, from failure to perceive changes in the industry or economy to fraud and embezzlement. One of the most frequent types of mismanagement is financial. Many companies fail because they are too heavily financially leveraged (i.e., have too much debt relative to equity) or because management did insufficient financial planning, lacked financial control, or, in the case of leveraged buyouts, made overly optimistic forecasts of future cash flows.

A firm must meet financial claims as they come due and meet the terms of its debt obligations. If the company fails to meet these financial claims, it is insolvent, and the debt goes into default. An insolvent firm need not be bankrupt. **Bankruptcy** is a legal procedure for the reorganization or liquidation of a firm that cannot meet its obligations.

Bankruptcy ▲
Legal proceeding for the liquidation or reorganization of an insolvent firm

If a firm cannot meet its obligations, creditors must decide on a course of action. Creditors will act in the manner that they believe is in their own best interest. They may not press for payment or liquidation of the firm, for forcing payment through bankruptcy court proceedings may be expensive and perhaps futile. Thus, the creditors of many financially troubled firms have accepted a restructuring of debt instead of pressing for payment through court action.

In many cases, the insolvent firm will itself solicit a voluntary reorganization with its creditors. Such voluntary reorganizations seek to restructure the firm's obligations. For example, creditors may extend the maturity of the debt or waive some of the restrictive covenants. Long-term debt obligations may be converted into equity in a new, reorganized firm. Why would creditors be willing to agree voluntarily to such changes? The question really is: Are the creditors better off with the firm operating or closed? If the creditors seek to have the firm liquidated, they probably will not receive the full value of their claims but may instead receive a mere fraction of what they are owed. If they permit the firm to continue to operate, profitable operations may be established and the creditors may receive the full value of what they are owed. Since these profits cannot occur until some time in the future, the creditors are faced with a typical financial question: Which is greater, the present liquidation value of their claims or the present value of the future claims if the firm is permitted to continue to operate?

How individual creditors answer this question will depend in part on their positions in the pecking order in which claims are met. Not all claims are equal. Some are subordinate to others and the superior claims are paid first. If the firm is liquidated, the order of payment is

1. the cost of the liquidation (i.e., court expenses)
2. unpaid labor expenses
3. taxes
4. secured debt
5. unsecured debt
6. preferred stock
7. common stock

This list points out the tenuous position of the unsecured debt, preferred stock, and common stock. Even the secured creditors may prefer reorganization if the firm's assets have deteriorated in value or if they have to be sold at bargain basement prices through a forced liquidation, for they may receive only a fraction of their claims. These creditors realize that they may profit through a voluntary reorganization that avoids formal bankruptcy proceedings, and thus they agree to accept reorganization.

If the firm is unable to work out an arrangement with its creditors, it may be forced into bankruptcy. Bankruptcy is as much a legal as a financial question. The firm may seek bankruptcy voluntarily, in which case the court protects the firm from its creditors while the firm and the creditors work out a reorganization. The firm may be involuntarily thrown into bankruptcy by a creditor seeking payment. The court appoints a trustee for the debtor's property who will continue to operate the business, examine the debtor's books for fraud, and initiate a plan for reorganization. The emphasis is usually on reorganization and not

EXHIBIT 24.1

A reorganization may result in bondholders receiving new bonds and stock in the reorganized firm.

Itel Reorganization Distribution

	Reorganization Distribution				
Old Obligation	**Cash**	**New 14% Bond, $1,000 Face, Due 1998**	**New 10% Bond, $1,000 Face, Due 2002**	**New Shares of Preferred Stock**	**Shares of New Common Stock**
$1,000 bond, 10½%, of 1998	$471	$162	$145	1.3	13.9
$1,000 bond, 9¾%, of 1990	$563	$196	$175	1.6	16.8
$1,000 bond, 10½%, of 1993	$593	$206	$185	1.6	17.6
$1,000 subordinate bond, 9⅝%, of 1998	$155	—	$119	—	12.4
$1,000 general unsecured claims	$434	$144	$129	1.1	12.4
100 shares of preferred stock	—	—	—	—	38.7
100 shares of common stock	—	—	—	—	8.7

on liquidation, but liquidation may be the final result. The final plan for reorganization must be acceptable to two-thirds of the creditors. The court will accept the plan if it believes that the plan meets the statutory requirements of being feasible, fair, and equitable. Once the plan has been accepted, the firm is released from bankruptcy.

The process of reorganization can be seen by the bankruptcy and subsequent reorganization of Itel Corporation. Itel owns boxcars and other equipment that it leases. To acquire its assets, Itel issued a substantial amount of long-term debt. When a recession occurred and many of its assets were not leased, the firm found itself in financial difficulty. Since Itel was not receiving lease payments, it was unable to meet its debt obligations, and the firm was forced to file for bankruptcy. The court suspended interest payments and other claims by creditors. Subsequently, a reorganization plan was completed and accepted by Itel's creditors.

Major components of the reorganization plan are given in Exhibit 24.1. As may be seen in the exhibit, the creditors received payment in cash, new bonds, preferred stock, and common stock. For example, the holders of the $1,000 10½% bond due in 1998 received $471 in cash, $307 face amount of new debt securities, 1.3 shares of new preferred stock, and 13.9 shares of new common stock in the reorganized firm. The old common stockholders, however, received only 8.7 new shares for every 100 shares. In effect, the creditors have become the new stockholders of the reorganized firm. If Itel returns to profitability, these new stockholders may prosper and recoup the amount they initially lent to the firm prior to the bankruptcy.

Some creditors fare very well in reorganizations. For example, Interstate Stores went bankrupt in 1978. The creditors, which were owed more than $168 million, received stock in a subsidiary that was spun off from Interstate. The terms were one share for every $10 of principal plus one share for every $10 of accrued and unpaid interest. The subsidiary was Toys R Us. An Interstate creditor received 100 shares of Toys R Us for every $1,000 of claims on Interstate. Within six years, that stock in Toys R Us was worth over $17,000! While Toys R Us is obviously an exceptional example, it does illustrate why creditors may accept reorganization instead of liquidation. Some firms do successfully bounce back from bankruptcy and generate substantial profits for those investors and creditors willing to accept the risk associated with the reorganization.

PREPACKAGED BANKRUPTCIES

The leveraged buyout binge of the late 1980s resulted in many firms with substantial amounts of debt. Some of these firms found that the burden of the debt exceeded their capacity to service it. Prior to default, management would attempt to work out a restructuring that altered the terms and that ended, or at least deferred, the threat of bankruptcy.

Obtaining concessions from bondholders is a formidable task, especially with a large issue that is held by many investors. The indentures of these issues often specify that a large proportion of the bondholders (e.g., 90 percent) must agree to accept the change in the terms for it to be effective. Thus, a small proportion of the bondholders may refuse to agree in an effort to obtain a better settlement. In 1990, Southland (Seven-Eleven) tried unsuccessfully to reach an agreement with its bondholders in an effort to avoid bankruptcy. Although a majority of the bondholders did accept the terms of the reorganization, a minority was able to block the proposed reorganization.

Prepackaged bankruptcy ▲
Reorganization plan accepted by the firm and a majority of its creditors prior to the firm filing for bankruptcy

Failure to win approval often means that the firm will default and either seek protection by entering bankruptcy or be forced into bankruptcy by the creditors. Since bankruptcy proceedings can take years to work out a reorganization plan and win court approval, the managements of several firms have developed a new strategy called the **prepackaged bankruptcy.** The idea is deceptively simple: devise a reorganization plan and obtain approval of at least 50 percent of the creditors holding at least two-thirds of the debt. File this plan with the bankruptcy court, and if the court accepts the plan, it can impose the terms on the dissenting minority of creditors. Once the plan has been imposed, the firm emerges from bankruptcy. The whole process can take six months, while a normal bankruptcy proceeding can last for years.

While a prepackaged bankruptcy sounds simple, there are risks. Militant creditors may seek to fight the plan in court. The disclosure of information may be insufficient or some detail of the agreement may not meet a facet of the bankruptcy standards, either of which results in the plan being voided. If the plan is thrown out, then management and creditors must start again, and all the expenses associated with developing and filing the prepackaged plan are lost.

The initial prepackaged bankruptcy filing by Republic Health was successful but that does not mean that future ones will be equally successful if reluctant creditors learn how to better fight the technique. By the end of 1990, several firms including Southland, Trump's Taj Mahal, and Vestron (producer of several movies and distributor of movie videos) had filed prepackaged bankruptcies designed to reorganize the companies without extended bankruptcy proceedings.

Since each filing is judged on its own merits, it is impossible to anticipate how each plan will be received, and whether or not the prepackaged bankruptcy will become the preferred means of reorganizing a firm in financial difficulty. However, the Southland reorganization plan was confirmed by the bankruptcy court in less than five months. The speed with which this reorganization was achieved should encourage the future use of the prepackaged bankruptcy strategy.

PREDICTING CORPORATE BANKRUPTCY

Bankruptcy does not occur overnight. It usually happens after a period of financial deterioration. Johns-Manville declared bankruptcy after extended litigation concerning its liability for asbestos contamination. Pan Am, Southland, Lionel, and many other firms that went bankrupt experienced a period of financial decline. The ultimate cause of failure may be declining profit margins, mismanagement of working capital, excess use of financial leverage, declining demand for the firm's product, or a variety of other factors. These factors occur over a period of time. Bankruptcy rarely happens rapidly. Of course, there is always an exception. For example, when there was a massive recall of canned vichyssoise soup by Bon Vivant, the company never recovered from the recall. However, it is rare that bankruptcy is caused by this type of random event. Instead, it is the steady deterioration of management, especially financial management, that is the major cause of failure.

Since a deteriorating financial condition occurs over a period of time, studying a firm's financial statements is one means to forecast failure. This is illustrated in Exhibit 24.2, which presents selected financial information for Heck's Inc., a chain of discount department stores that went bankrupt in 1987, and for Hills Department Stores that went bankrupt in 1991. While Heck's experienced only a modest decline in reve-

EXHIBIT 24.2

Selected Financial Information by Year

Heck's deteriorating financial position and the large amount of debt financing used by Hills suggest weakening financial condition.

	1986	1985	1984	1983
Hecks				
Earnings per share	($2.05)	($0.86)	($0.55)	$1.03
Current ratio	1.4:1	1.7:1	1.9:1	2.3:1
Debt ratio	70.0%	70.0	65.6	55.0
Return on equity	NA	NA	NA	8.4%

	1990	1989	1988
Hills Department Stores			
Earnings per share	$0.15	$0.60	$1.26
Current ratio	1.1:1	1.1:1	1.0:1
Debt ratio	96.1%	88.3	94.0
Return on equity	21.1%	107.5%	NA

nues prior to bankruptcy, there was a substantial decline in earnings. The current ratio and debt ratio clearly indicate the deteriorating financial position of the firm.

The ratios for Hills do not show a deterioration but instead a failure to improve. The high debt ratio means that the firm was using a substantial amount of financial leverage. The equity base was so small that Hills earned more than its equity in 1989 (i.e., its return on equity exceeded 100 percent). However, earnings per share declined in 1990, and neither the debt ratio nor the current ratio improved from 1988 through 1990. This failure to improve suggests the firm would have difficulty if sales and profit margins deteriorated. Such declines started in 1990, and the firm declared bankruptcy in 1991.

It should be pointed out that the financial analyst cannot conclude in either of these examples that the firms will, in fact, go bankrupt. The ratios only indicate financial weakness that could lead to bankruptcy, but their failures should not be a surprise. Certainly Heck's deteriorating financial position and Hills's failure to reduce its use of financial leverage were obvious to any individual who computed the ratios and analyzed the firms' financial statements.

SUMMARY

This chapter has considered mergers and bankruptcy. Both topics may be very complex, and the business student could devote considerably more time to each of these subjects than is possible in an introductory survey.

Mergers may be justified on the grounds of increased per-share earnings, increased potential for growth, and synergy, and they may be horizontal, vertical, or conglomerate. The surviving firm may purchase another firm for cash, through a swap of stock, or through a swap of debt. Stock swaps offer the advantage that any capital gains taxes owed by the selling stockholders are deferred until these stockholders sell their newly acquired stock. Mergers may be accounted for through a pooling of both firms' balance sheets or as a purchase. An increase in hostile takeovers has led to more leveraged buyouts, in which a firm's management uses the firm's borrowing capacity to buy out the shares held by the general public. The leveraged buyout, then, becomes a means to avoid the takeover.

The blame for business failure ultimately rests with management. However, its cause is often financial mismanagement. When a firm is unable to meet its financial obligations, it may voluntarily seek the protection of the court from its creditors, or these creditors may take the firm to court to force payment. Bankruptcy courts tend to encourage the reorganization of the firm into a viable operation instead of its liquidation. Creditors often accept such reorganizations because they realize that selling the firm's assets may raise only a modest amount of funds. In such cases, the creditors will probably be better off accepting claims on the reorganized firm, for if it returns to financial health, they may receive a larger return on their initial claims.

There is a basic similarity between mergers and bankruptcy. Earlier, it was suggested that management will make investment decisions that maximize the value of the firm. The decision to merge or to reorganize affects the value of the firm. In each case, the potential benefits are weighted by the cost of the investment. Management should seek mergers when such action will increase the value of the firm. This may be achieved by purchasing undervalued firms or firms that offer to increase the capacity of the surviving firm to grow more rapidly. Creditors and courts may view business failure in the same light, since a successfully reorganized firm may be more beneficial to both owners and creditors than the forced sale of its assets.

Review Questions

1. How would each of the following mergers be classified?
   a. Chrysler and Honda
   b. Ethyl (a maker of gasoline additives) and Exxon
   c. MGM and U.S. Steel
2. What is synergy? Does it explain why some firms merge?
3. What is the tax implication of accepting stock instead of cash when you tender (i.e., sell) your stock in a merger?

4. How may management fight an unsolicited or hostile takeover?
5. What is the difference between a voluntary and an involuntary bankruptcy? When AutoTrain was unable to secure a loan to obtain funds to pay off creditors, what course of action would you expect its management (or creditors) to take?
6. Why did the leveraged buyouts of the 1980s result in many bankruptcies?
7. Penn Central went bankrupt but was not liquidated. The rail operations are now run by Conrail. The remaining operations of Penn Central were reorganized into a new firm in which the creditors became major stockholders. Why were these creditors willing to accept this reorganization?

Problems

1. a. Two firms with the following balance sheets merge through a stock swap. What will be the new balance sheet of Firm AB if "pooling" is used to account for the merger?

A

Cash	$ 100	Accounts payable	$ 500
Accounts receivable	1,000	Equity	4,500
Inventory	3,900		

B

Accounts receivable	$ 500	Accounts payable	$ 300
Plant and equipment	2,500	Long-term debt	1,700
		Equity	1,000

b. If Firm A issues stock worth $5,000 to acquire Firm B and treats the merger as a purchase, will goodwill arise? What are the implications of goodwill for a firm's earnings and taxes?

2. Given the following information:

	Firm A	Firm B
Price of stock	$50	$25
Earnings per share	$5.00	$1.00
Number of shares outstanding	1,000,000	200,000

a. What will be the earnings per share if A swaps 0.6 of a share for 1 share of B?
b. What will be the price of A's stock if its P/E ratio is unaffected by the merger and subsequent change in earnings per share?
c. What will be the stock's price if the P/E ratio increases to 12? Why might the P/E ratio increase?

3. A firm has the following balance sheet:

ASSETS		LIABILITIES AND EQUITY	
Cash	$ 1,000	Bank loan (secured by inventory)	$ 3,000
Accounts receivable	10,000	Accounts payable	11,000
Inventory	9,000	Taxes due	2,000
Plant and equipment	13,000	Mortgage (on plant and equipment)	10,000
		Debentures	8,000
		Preferred stock	2,000
		Common stock	3,000
		Retained earnings	(6,000)
	$33,000		$33,000

a. If the firm has not defaulted on any loan, is it in bankruptcy proceedings?
b. If the bank loan is due tomorrow, can the firm make the payment?
c. If the firm were forced into bankruptcy and the assets were liquidated at the value carried on the books, would the holders of the mortgage loan receive the amount owed? What will the stockholders receive?

Suggested Readings

MERGERS

A simple method for evaluating mergers is presented in:

Rappaport, Alfred. "Strategic Analysis for More Profitable Acquisitions." *Harvard Business Review* (July–August 1979), pp. 99–110.

Other easily read articles on mergers include:

Cohen, M. F. "Takeover Bids." *Financial Analysts Journal* (January–February 1970), pp. 26–29 and 100–103.

This article describes how management can resist takeover attempts.

Hester, Richard M. "How to Sell Your Company." *Harvard Business Review* (October 1968), pp. 71–77.

While most material on mergers is written from the buyer's viewpoint, this article discusses mergers and acquisitions from the viewpoint of the seller.

For descriptions of acquisitions and mergers (i.e., accounting for, income taxation of), joint ventures, and divestitures, see:

Chastian, Clark E. *Corporate Asset Management.* New York: Quorum Books, 1987.

Diamond, Stephen C., ed. *Leveraged Buyouts.* Homewood, Ill.: Dow Jones-Irwin, 1985.

BANKRUPTCY AND BUSINESS FAILURE

Altman, Edward I. "Financial Ratios, Discriminant Analysis, and the Prediction of Corporate Bankruptcy." *Journal of Finance* (September 1968), pp. 589–609. Reprinted in *Issues in Managerial Finance,* 2d ed., edited by E. F. Brigham and R. E. Johnson, pp. 44–48. Hinsdale, Ill.: The Dryden Press, 1980.

While this classic article may be difficult to read, it does illustrate how financial ratios may be combined with statistical techniques to aid in the prediction of corporate bankruptcy.

Beaver, William H. "Market Prices, Financial Ratios, and the Prediction of Failure." *Journal of Accounting Research* (Autumn 1968), pp. 179–92.

While this article is simpler than the Altman work, Beaver also uses ratios to signal increased probability of failure.

Collins, Robert A. "An Empirical Comparison of Bankruptcy Prediction Models." *Financial Management* (Summer 1980), pp. 52–57.

This brief article compares the efficacy of models designed to forecast bankruptcy.

"How to Figure Who's Going Bankrupt." *Dunn's Review* (October 1975), pp. 63–65 and 107–108.

This article presents a layman's explanation of Altman's work and other techniques used to predict bankruptcy.

More general material on bankruptcies include:

Herzog, Richard B. *Bankruptcy: A Concise Guide for Creditors and Debtors.* New York: ARCO, 1983.

Platt, Harlan D. *Why Companies Fail: Strategies for Detecting, Avoiding and Profiting from Bankruptcies.* Lexington, Mass.: Lexington Books, 1985.

chapter 25

Overview of Corporate Financial Management

Review Objectives

1 Reexamine the role of the financial manager.

2 Restate the criterion for judging a firm's performance.

3 Explain the possible impact that monetary and fiscal policy may have on a firm.

4 Contemplate why you read this text and ask yourself the following:

- **a** Was my conception of finance too narrow?
- **b** Do I understand why financial management is crucial for the successful management of a firm?
- **c** Do I realize how the study of finance will help me make personal financial decisions?

The very famous saying, "They cannot see the forest for the trees," applies to this (and many) textbooks. Topics are individually discussed and developed in each chapter, but these concepts are not independent of each other. They are part of a larger picture. A textbook is like a mural. You study one facet of a discipline at a time, but the pieces ultimately fit together.

Financial institutions, investments, and corporate finance are not independent of each other. The financial manager constructs financial plans and budgets, makes long-term investment decisions, determines how the firm's current assets will be managed, and obtains the financing necessary to acquire the assets.

FIGURE 25.1

The Composition of Finance

The components of finance—financial institutions, investments, and business finance—overlap and are interdependent.

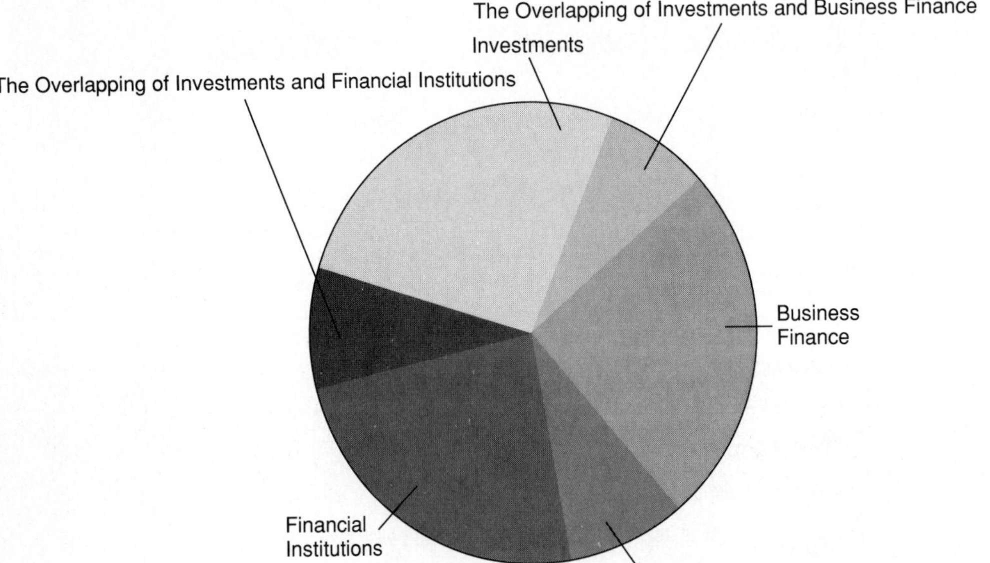

None of these decisions can be made in a vacuum. For example, the firm can obtain assets only if savers (be they individuals, governments, or other firms) are willing to invest the funds in the firm. Certainly one of the primary purposes of financial institutions is to facilitate the transfer of money from those with excess funds to those in need of the funds. This interdependence of corporate finance, investments, and financial institutions was symbolized in Figure 1.1 in Chapter 1 by the pie chart with the overlapping sections, which is reproduced here as Figure 25.1.

Just as corporate finance is not an independent world unto itself, a firm's financial decision making is not independent of other necessary business decisions, such as marketing, location, or management structure. While the financial manager integrates the facets of finance, the firm's management must integrate financial decision making with the other functional areas of business administration. Finance is obviously a crucial component of any firm's decision-making process, but financial decisions must fit into the firm's overall strategy.

Ultimately, management's (and the financial manager's) performance must be judged. In finance, the criterion used to judge performance is the value of the firm. Management should take those actions that increase this value. Even decisions involving nonfinancial aspects of a firm's operations are judged by their impact on the value of the firm. A course of action should not be taken if it is not in the best interest of the owners of the firm (i.e., if the action reduces the value of the firm).

In the modern corporate world many firms are owned by investors (i.e., stockholders) who do not in reality participate in management decisions. Management is employed by these stockholders, and it is the value of these owners' investments that management should seek to maximize. It is the effect on this value that is the ultimate test of the financial manager's performance. Successful financial management will lead to an increase in the value placed on the firm. The tools, concepts, and facts presented in this text are a means to achieve this goal.

THE ROLE OF THE FINANCIAL MANAGER

The role of the financial manager has been described in the preceding chapters. It is a complex job that must be performed by someone in the firm. For sole proprietorships, the job will probably fall into the hands of the sole proprietor, the owner. Along with other roles, such as manager, salesperson, purchaser, and bookkeeper, the owner will have to perform the many roles of the financial manager. With so many varied duties that must be performed, is it any wonder that many small firms fail? Large corporations may have staffs reporting to a vice-president in charge of finance to perform the financial manager's job, but even the existence of these staffs does not guarantee that the job will be adequately performed.

What is a restatement of the financial manager's job? First, the financial manager must assure that the firm has sufficient liquidity to meet its financial obligations as they come due. Perhaps this is individually the most important facet of the financial manager's job, for the firm must survive day to day. If the firm cannot meet these current cash needs, it will have no future. Thus, it is crucial that the financial manager ensure that the firm has cash coming in to meet its bills as they come due. Of course, increased liquidity costs the firm profits, for liquid assets (i.e., cash and demand deposits) do not earn any income. The financial manager must seek a balance between sufficient liquidity and the investment of excess short-term funds in income-earning assets. Thus, successful cash management requires not only knowledge of the firm's liquidity needs but also knowledge of the money market and the various short-term money market instruments in which excess cash may be invested.

The financial manager has a variety of tools available to help forecast the level of sales and the assets necessary to achieve the anticipated level of sales. The percent of sales technique of forecasting, regression analysis, and the cash budget may be used to plan the firm's cash needs by permitting the financial manager to plan the firm's sales and expenses and its anticipated level of assets and liabilities. Such planning permits the financial manager to know when cash will be coming in and when the firm will have to seek outside sources of short-term financing.

Besides these planning tools, the financial manager may use a variety of ratios to analyze the firm's performance and financial condition. These ratios may be used not only to identify trends but also to compare the firm with other firms in the industry. Each ratio may be classified into one of five groups. Liquidity ratios give an indication of the firm's ability to meet its obligations as they come due. Activity ratios show how rapidly assets flow through the firm. Leverage ratios indicate the extent to which debt is used to finance the firm, and profitability ratios rate the firm's performance. Coverage ratios indicate ability to make, "cover," specific expenses such as interest or lease payments. However, some ratios will give similar information and may be redundant. Thus, the financial manager (or any user of ratio analysis) should select those ratios most pertinent to the situation being analyzed.

Besides assuring that the firm has sufficient liquidity and that excess cash is invested in income-earning assets, the financial manager plays a role in managing all assets. First, investments must be chosen from the many alternative uses of the firm's resources. Obviously, the firm cannot make every possible investment but must select among the alternatives. There are several methods of capital budgeting, ranging from the simple payback method to net present value and internal rate of return approaches. These latter techniques can be made very complex, as an investment is analyzed under different hypotheses concerning risk and possible outcomes. Even after the decision to acquire a particular long-term asset has been made, these assets must still be managed and eventually must be replaced.

Investments are made in the present, but the returns accrue in the future. The future is not certain; the financial manager works in a world of uncertainty and risk. There is the risk associated with the nature of the business. For example, some industries require substantial amounts of fixed assets (i.e., they have a high degree of operating leverage). These firms will feel a greater effect from fluctuations in the industry's sales and are inherently more risky than firms in industries that require fewer fixed assets. Also, the speed with which technological change occurs and the rapid manner in which consumers alter their preferences make some businesses more risky. For example, many a small firm in the computer field found itself in serious difficulty as newer and more advanced equipment made its products or services obsolete.

A second source of risk pertains to a firm's financing. All assets must be financed, and there are two sources of financing: the owners' funds or creditors' funds. When a firm (or anyone) uses creditors' funds, it is financially leveraged. The prime advantage to the firm of borrowing funds is the potential to make the creditors' funds generate sufficient revenue not only to pay the interest charges but also to generate additional funds that accrue to the owner. By borrowing funds and successfully using financial leverage, the firm increases its return on equity. The use of borrowed funds commits the firm to several legal obligations that vary with such factors as the amount of the loan, the length of time the loan is outstanding, and the creditworthiness of the borrower. Every loan is an individual package of terms, and each loan may have some subtle clause that differentiates it from other loans. If the firm fails to meet these terms, the creditors can take the firm to court to enforce the obligations. Such legal obligations may increase the element of risk. Thus, the financing of a firm influences not only the potential return to the owner but also the degree of risk.

One important role of the financial manager is to determine the firm's optimal combination of debt and equity financing. This optimal capital structure takes advantage of debt financing but does not unduly increase the element of financial risk. By determining the optimal capital structure, the financial manager minimizes the cost of capital, the criterion by which all potential investments must be judged. A firm's cost of capital is a measure of what the funds could earn if placed in alternative investments; hence, the firm must earn at least its cost of capital to justify using these funds. The cost of capital is thus one of the most important elements in capital budgeting.

To determine the optimal capital structure, the financial manager must know the varied sources of financing and their respective costs. A

Financial Facts

Financial Theory and the Nobel Memorial Prize in Economic Science

In 1990, the Nobel prize in economics was awarded to Harry Markowitz, William Sharpe, and Merton Miller for their contributions to the theory of finance. The awarding of the economics prize to academicians whose primary research is in finance highlights the importance that finance and financial decision making play in an advanced economy. • Markowitz developed the concepts of diversification and efficient portfolios. Sharpe's contributions grew from the work of Markowitz and led to the development of the capital asset pricing model and beta as the crucial measure of risk. While today it may seem intuitively obvious that investors will make riskier investments only if they anticipate a higher return, the specification of the relationship between risk and return and making the model operational were major contributions that currently permeate both the theory and practice of finance. • Merton Miller, along with Franco Modigliani who won the Nobel prize in economics in 1985, advanced the theory of the cost of capital. Modigliani and Miller demonstrated that in perfect capital markets, the earning capacity of a firm's assets and not how the assets are financed determines the value of a firm. Taken to its logical conclusion, their theory indicates there is no optimal capital structure. If there is an optimal capital structure, it depends on factors such as taxes (e.g., the deductibility of interest expense), rigidities in the capital markets (e.g., firms and investors cannot borrow at the same rate of interest), and certain costs (e.g., the costs associated with bankruptcy). If these real world considerations did not exist, then no optimal capital structure would exist. This startling conclusion became the theoretical underpinning that justified the debt explosion, leveraged buyouts, and takeovers of the 1980s. •

---

firm may borrow from commercial banks, insurance companies, trade creditors, and the general public. Securities may be privately placed with financial institutions, sold to the general public through investment bankers, or sold to current owners. The financial manager must be aware of all the potential sources of finance and know when the utilization of a particular source is the best alternative for raising funds.

To some extent the nature of the assets being financed influences the type of financing. In general, long-term assets should be financed only with long-term debt or equity. Such permanent sources of finance are more suitable than short-term sources because the latter must continually be refinanced. The use of short-term debt to finance long-term assets may subject the firm to liquidity problems if the firm has to sell the assets to meet its debt obligations. While it is desirable that a firm match the type of financing with the asset being financed, the very nature of some businesses violates this important financial principle. Perhaps the most striking example of this violation is the banking industry, which receives the majority of its funds by borrowing short-term (from depositors) and then lending the funds, sometimes in the form of long-term loans. Of course, commercial banks seek to protect themselves by stressing short-term and quality loans, but sometimes they do violate the principle of matching the assets and the types of sources used to finance the assets.

THE IMPACT OF COMPETITION

No firm operates in a vacuum. All firms compete among each other for markets for their products. In many cases this competition is obvious. Exxon, Mobil, and Arco, all large oil refiners, compete for the sale of gasoline and other petroleum products. Major book publishers such as The Dryden Press produce textbooks such as this one which must compete against texts published by McGraw Hill and Prentice Hall. As competition intensifies, profit margins are squeezed and firms become less profitable.

Competition is not limited to markets for products but extends to sources of finance. Since all firms must have funds, they must compete for the available supply of debt and equity capital. As this competition intensifies, interest rates and the cost of equity rise to ration the available supply. This higher cost of capital reduces the attractiveness of some of the firm's possible investments, and the profitability of those that the firm does make is reduced by the higher cost of finance.

While competition has always played a major role in a free market economy, today it is even more intense since many markets are not national, but global, in scope. Competition is not limited to domestic firms but extends to firms from many nations. GM and Ford not only have to compete with Chrysler but also have to compete with Japanese, German, British, and other European automobile manufacturers such as Honda, Nissan, Toyota, Volkswagen, BMW, and Volvo.

While U.S. firms have for years made investments abroad, foreign firms are now investing in the United States. For example, several foreign car manufacturers (e.g., Toyota and Honda) not only import automobiles but have also built manufacturing operations in the United States. GM and Ford are forced to compete with these foreign firms for buyers of their cars and for the skilled labor to design, build, and market their products.

Rising foreign economies with their emerging global firms imply that, unless trade barriers are increased (which is possible), the competition facing American firms will become more fierce. All firms will have to innovate, invest in research and development, and remain abreast of technological change in order to maintain their competitive position.

Foreign firms also compete for financing. Securities issued by firms such as Honda or Sony trade in the U.S. security markets in competition with the securities issued by Ford and CBS. Capital will flow where returns are greatest for a given level of risk. Once again, unless barriers are established, money will flow across national borders. If potential returns from foreign nations' securities rise, investors in the United States will not invest in domestic firms but will invest in foreign firms. This certainly has happened in the past when foreign investors purchased securities issued in the United States. The reverse will certainly occur if investors perceive opportunites to be greater in Europe or Asia.

This flow of funds will interlock the economies of virtually all nations. A nation's supply of money and credit, domestic interest rates, and the value of its currency cannot be independent of investment opportunities and events in other countries. Without artificial barriers, isolation in today's global markets for goods and services and for financing will be virtually impossible.

THE IMPACT OF FISCAL AND MONETARY POLICY ON FINANCIAL DECISION MAKING

Besides the forces of competition, the firm is affected by national economic policy. This policy emanates from two sources: the fiscal policy of the federal government, and the monetary policy of the Federal Reserve. Fiscal policy concerns federal expenditures and taxation, and management of the national debt. Federal government expenditures may affect the firm directly if it is a government supplier or indirectly through the federal government's effect on other firms and households. Federal taxation at both the corporate and individual levels affects virtually every firm. All taxes are a transfer of resources from the private sector to the public sector. Changes in taxation alter the resources that firms and households have to use.

Monetary policy is concerned with changes in the supply of money and the capacity of banks to lend. It primarily affects firms by altering the cost of funds and the availability of credit. To the extent that monetary policy affects aggregate spending, it will also alter the demand for a particular firm's output. This policy is implemented by the Federal Reserve, the nation's central bank. While the Federal Reserve is owned by private interests (i.e., the member banks), it operates as a quasi-governmental organization. It is independent of both its owners and the federal government but pursues economic goals, such as price stability, that are national in scope. To carry out its goals, the Federal Reserve has several tools of monetary policy. Of the various tools, the three most important are the reserve requirement, the discount rate, and open market operations. These tools are used to affect the reserves of banks, which in turn alters their ability to lend.

By far the most important of these tools is open market operations. The Federal Reserve may continuously and in any desired volume purchase or sell U.S. government securities. By buying these securities, the Federal Reserve is able to expand the money supply and the lending capacity of banks, thereby increasing the supply of money in the nation.

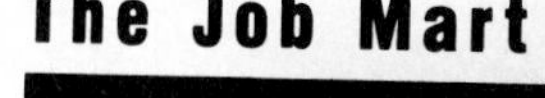

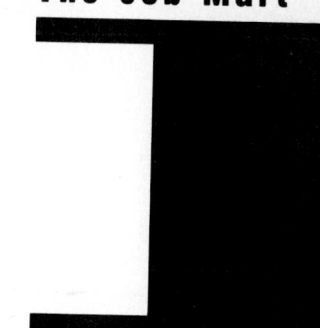

Instructor in Training Program

■ Job Description: Instruct employees, especially support staff, in the fundamentals of finance to enhance their ability to use computer-driven finance programs and to service financial officers. Help individuals pass tests required for certification and licensing, such as the examinations required to become a stockbroker or a certified financial planner (CFP). ■ Job Requirements: Knowledge of the areas of finance being taught and the ability to present financial concepts clearly and engagingly. ■ Characteristics: Instruction combines specialized knowledge with business communication and interpersonal skills. The abilities to listen to and answer questions, to think on one's feet, and to determine the needs of the audience increase the individual's chances of success.

The opposite effect occurs when the Federal Reserve sells securities; this absorbs the banks' reserves and decreases the supply of money.

While the effect of monetary policy is to alter the available supply of money and the cost of capital of all firms, the impact is felt more by firms in particular industries. For example, utilities need large amounts of capital to finance expansion of plant and equipment. Tight money and higher costs of capital significantly increase the expense associated with financing these investments. Of all industries, perhaps the hardest hit by tight credit is construction. Buildings are primarily financed by mortgage loans, and a reduction in the supply of credit means a reduction in available mortgage money. Even if potential buyers are willing to pay higher interest charges, their inability to secure financing results in a reduction in the demand for the industry's product.

The financial manager needs to be aware of this economic environment. Fiscal and monetary policies can have a major impact on the firm's financial health by altering both the cash flow from investments and the cost of funds. To some extent the financial manager may be able to anticipate particular actions by the federal government and the Federal Reserve and take steps to insulate the firm from the effects. For example, the cost of finance does vary over time, and the firm may seek to obtain funds during periods of lower interest rates. The firm may issue long-term debt securities and invest the money in short-term assets such as Treasury bills. The bills can then be converted into cash as funds are needed. Thus, if the financial manager anticipates future increases in the cost of credit, it may be desirable to issue long-term securities now, for such an action will lock in lower interest charges.

The financial manager may anticipate some policy actions emanating from Washington but cannot foresee all policy changes that may be forthcoming. Some changes in policy may be swift and abrupt. For example, on August 15, 1971, the sudden and unexpected change in President Nixon's stand, from favoring moderate fiscal and monetary restraint to a wage-price freeze for the purpose of fighting inflation, vividly illustrates how rapidly government policy may change. Many firms found themselves with frozen higher costs but were unable to raise prices to maintain profit margins. If these firms had anticipated such a change in policy, they might have been able to raise prices prior to the wage-price freeze. Of course, the sudden change in policy was designed to freeze all prices; since it would have been ineffective had the change been widely anticipated, it is not surprising that financial managers were unable to anticipate the policy change.

While financial managers may be unable to insulate their firms from the effects of national economic policy, they certainly will react to this policy. Of course, much of this policy is designed to induce particular behavior. For example, accelerated depreciation is designed to induce spending on capital equipment by increasing the cash flow from the investment. High interest rates are designed to discourage investment spending by increasing the cost of capital. Financial managers will incorporate these policy changes into the analyses they perform and respond accordingly. If a financial manager fails to react to changes in national economic policy, this may significantly hurt the firm and reduce its value in the marketplace. Financial managers must work within the constraints of national economic policy and should be well informed on current economic issues and how they affect their particular firms.

THE PURPOSE OF THE BOOK RESTATED

The student who has read the preceding chapters must be amazed by the complexity of the world of finance. But every firm and every individual makes financial decisions. The role of the financial manager is not limited to firms; individuals also may use similar information and techniques in everyday financial decision making.

For many students, an introductory course may be their only academic exposure to the discipline of finance. Many of these students may have to work and communicate with financial specialists. They need at least an elementary knowledge of finance. It is for these students that this text was designed, for the text briefly covered many facets and analytical tools used in the world of finance. No attempt was made to be exhaustive or to develop theoretical concepts fully.

Of course, reading this text is only a beginning. The text has served as an introduction to the world of finance, and a good introduction lays the foundation for further study. Students desiring specialization in finance will encounter this material again at greater depth and at a higher level of sophistication in more advanced courses.

While many students may not continue in finance, it is hoped that this text has whetted the appetite of some nonfinance students to do further work within the discipline. In many businesspeople's minds, finance is *the* crucial element for a successful business operation, and poor financial management is frequently a major cause of business failure. Thus, even for the nonspecialist, additional knowledge of finance may be extremely helpful for a successful career in business. This is well acknowledged, for example, by the accounting profession, for finance is part of the CMA certification, and financial topics and techniques appear on the CPA examination. Even people who work in the public sector or with nonprofit organizations make financial decisions. Knowledge of the world of finance is useful for virtually every type of career.

Finally, finance is a crucial component of one's private life. Financial leverage is frequently used by individuals as they borrow funds to finance purchases ranging from consumer goods to homes. Households must manage their cash in order to have money to pay bills as they come due. Many individuals are able to save and must decide on the form in which to hold their savings; they must design the portfolio of assets that best matches their financial needs and goals. To function in modern society requires a great deal of knowledge and understanding of the world of finance.

Review Questions

1. In finance, what is the specific goal of management?
2. What is the difference between business risk and financial risk? Why should the financial manager be concerned with determining the firm's optimal capital structure?
3. Day-to-day financial decisions are concerned with the management of short-term assets and short-term liabilities. Why is this management of working capital so important? How may the firm's liquidity position be monitored? Why may liquidity reduce profitability?
4. How may economic policy affect financial decision making? Why may anticipating changes in economic policy be crucial to a firm's success?
5. Many firms fail because of poor financial management. Now that you have completed this text, could you explain why the previous statement is true?

Suggested Readings

Now that you have completed this introductory text in finance, you may wish to pursue the topic at greater length and depth. One possible approach is to tackle a more sophisticated textbook in financial management. Two possibilities are:

Brigham, Eugene F. and Louis C. Gapenski. *Financial Management: Theory and Practice,* 6th ed. Hinsdale, Ill.: The Dryden Press, 1991.

Ross, Stephen A.; Randolph W. Westerfield; and Jeffrey F. Jaffe. *Corporate Finance,* 2d ed. Homewood, Ill.: Richard D. Irwin, Inc., 1990.

A second approach is to sample the literature on finance. This may be facilitated by using a book of readings that brings several articles together in a convenient package. Two possibilities include:

Kolb, Robert W., ed. *The Corporate Finance Reader.* Miami, Fla.: Kolb Publishing Company, 1991.

Kolb, Robert W., ed. *The Investments Finance Reader.* Miami, Fla.: Kolb Publishing Company, 1991.

The corporate reader includes material on capital structure, leveraged buyouts, bankruptcy, and changes in corporate financial policy. The investments reader includes material on globalization of financial markets, junk bonds, efficient financial markets, and options. Both readers are designed to supplement undergraduate courses in financial management and investments.

If you are interested in pursuing the study of investments and personal finance, you may prefer to read:

Amling, Frederick, and William G. Droms. *The Dow Jones-Irwin Guide to Personal Financial Planning.* Homewood, Ill.: Dow Jones-Irwin, 1982.

Radcliffe, Robert C. *Investments—Concepts, Analysis, and Strategy,* 3d ed. Glenview, Ill.: Scott, Foresman, 1990.

The Radcliffe text is a thorough and rigorous treatment of investments, while the Amling-Droms book is a reworking of a personal finance textbook into a trade book that is readily accessible to the layman.

***Financial markets change swiftly. Any student of business and finance should develop the habit of reading professional publications, especially* The Wall Street Journal, Business Week, Fortune, *and* Forbes.**

Such readings will certainly help you keep abreast of the events that affect financial decision making.

Financial planning has become an important career. For material on insurance, investments, and financial planning for retirement consult:

Crowe, Robert M. *Fundamentals of Financial Planning.* Bryn Mawr, Pa.: The American College, 1990.

appendix

A

Interest Factors for the Future Value of One Dollar: FVIF = $(1 + i)^n$

Time period (e.g., year)	1%	2%	3%	4%	5%	6%	7%	8%	9%	10%	12%	14%	15%	16%	18%	20%
1	1.010	1.020	1.030	1.040	1.050	1.060	1.070	1.080	1.090	1.100	1.120	1.140	1.150	1.160	1.180	1.200
2	1.020	1.040	1.061	1.082	1.102	1.124	1.145	1.166	1.188	1.210	1.254	1.300	1.322	1.346	1.392	1.440
3	1.030	1.061	1.093	1.125	1.158	1.191	1.225	1.260	1.295	1.331	1.405	1.482	1.521	1.561	1.643	1.728
4	1.041	1.082	1.126	1.170	1.216	1.262	1.311	1.360	1.412	1.464	1.574	1.689	1.749	1.811	1.939	2.074
5	1.051	1.104	1.159	1.217	1.276	1.338	1.403	1.469	1.539	1.611	1.762	1.925	2.011	2.100	2.288	2.488
6	1.062	1.126	1.194	1.265	1.340	1.419	1.501	1.587	1.677	1.772	1.974	2.195	2.313	2.436	2.697	2.986
7	1.072	1.149	1.230	1.316	1.407	1.504	1.606	1.714	1.828	1.949	2.211	2.502	2.660	2.826	3.186	3.583
8	1.083	1.172	1.267	1.369	1.477	1.594	1.718	1.851	1.993	2.144	2.476	2.853	3.059	3.278	3.759	4.300
9	1.094	1.195	1.305	1.423	1.551	1.689	1.838	1.999	2.172	2.358	2.773	3.252	3.518	3.803	4.436	5.160
10	1.105	1.219	1.344	1.480	1.629	1.791	1.967	2.159	2.367	2.594	3.106	3.707	4.046	4.411	5.234	6.192
11	1.116	1.243	1.384	1.539	1.710	1.898	2.105	2.332	2.580	2.853	3.479	4.226	4.652	5.117	6.176	7.430
12	1.127	1.268	1.426	1.601	1.796	2.012	2.252	2.518	2.813	3.138	3.896	4.818	5.350	5.936	7.287	8.916
13	1.138	1.294	1.469	1.665	1.886	2.133	2.410	2.720	3.066	3.452	4.363	5.492	6.153	6.886	8.599	10.699
14	1.149	1.319	1.513	1.732	1.980	2.261	2.579	2.937	3.342	3.797	4.887	6.261	7.076	7.988	10.147	12.839
15	1.161	1.346	1.558	1.801	2.079	2.397	2.759	3.172	3.642	4.177	5.474	7.138	8.137	9.266	11.973	15.407
16	1.173	1.373	1.605	1.873	2.183	2.540	2.952	3.426	3.970	4.595	6.130	8.137	9.358	10.748	14.129	18.488
17	1.184	1.400	1.653	1.948	2.292	2.693	3.159	3.700	4.328	5.054	6.866	9.276	10.761	12.468	16.672	22.186
18	1.196	1.428	1.702	2.026	2.407	2.854	3.380	3.996	4.717	5.560	7.690	10.575	12.375	14.463	19.673	26.623
19	1.208	1.457	1.754	2.107	2.527	3.026	3.617	4.316	5.142	6.116	8.613	12.056	14.232	16.777	23.214	31.948
20	1.220	1.486	1.806	2.191	2.653	3.207	3.870	4.661	5.604	6.728	9.646	13.743	16.367	19.461	27.393	38.337
25	1.282	1.641	2.094	2.666	3.386	4.292	5.427	6.848	8.623	10.835	17.000	26.462	32.919	40.874	62.688	95.396
30	1.348	1.811	2.427	3.243	4.322	5.743	7.612	10.063	13.268	17.449	29.960	50.950	66.212	85.850	143.370	237.370

appendix

B

Interest Factors for the Present Value of One Dollar: PVIF = $1/(1 + i)^n$

Time period (e.g., year)	1%	2%	3%	4%	5%	6%	7%	8%	9%	10%	12%	14%	15%	16%	18%	20%	24%	28%	32%	36%	40%	50%	60%	70%	80%	90%
1	.990	.980	.971	.962	.952	.943	.935	.926	.917	.909	.893	.877	.870	.862	.847	.833	.806	.781	.758	.735	.714	.667	.625	.588	.555	.526
2	.980	.961	.943	.925	.907	.890	.873	.857	.842	.826	.797	.769	.756	.743	.718	.694	.650	.610	.574	.541	.510	.444	.391	.346	.309	.277
3	.971	.942	.915	.889	.864	.840	.816	.794	.772	.751	.712	.675	.658	.641	.609	.579	.524	.477	.435	.398	.364	.296	.244	.204	.171	.146
4	.961	.924	.889	.855	.823	.792	.763	.735	.708	.683	.636	.592	.572	.552	.516	.482	.423	.373	.329	.292	.260	.198	.153	.120	.095	.077
5	.951	.906	.863	.822	.784	.747	.713	.681	.650	.621	.567	.519	.497	.476	.437	.402	.341	.291	.250	.215	.186	.132	.095	.070	.053	.040
6	.942	.888	.838	.790	.746	.705	.666	.630	.596	.564	.507	.456	.432	.410	.370	.335	.275	.227	.189	.158	.133	.088	.060	.041	.029	.021
7	.933	.871	.813	.760	.711	.665	.623	.583	.547	.513	.452	.400	.376	.354	.314	.279	.222	.178	.143	.116	.095	.059	.037	.024	.016	.011
8	.923	.853	.789	.731	.677	.627	.582	.540	.502	.467	.404	.351	.327	.305	.266	.233	.179	.139	.108	.085	.068	.039	.023	.014	.009	.006
9	.914	.837	.766	.703	.645	.592	.544	.500	.460	.424	.361	.308	.284	.263	.226	.194	.144	.108	.082	.063	.048	.026	.015	.008	.005	.003
10	.905	.820	.744	.676	.614	.558	.508	.463	.422	.386	.322	.270	.247	.227	.191	.162	.116	.085	.062	.046	.035	.017	.009	.005	.003	.002
11	.896	.804	.722	.650	.585	.527	.475	.429	.388	.350	.287	.237	.215	.195	.162	.135	.094	.066	.047	.034	.025	.012	.006	.003	.002	.001
12	.887	.788	.701	.625	.557	.497	.444	.397	.356	.319	.257	.208	.187	.168	.137	.112	.076	.052	.036	.025	.018	.008	.004	.002	.001	.001
13	.879	.773	.681	.601	.530	.469	.415	.368	.326	.290	.229	.182	.163	.145	.116	.093	.061	.040	.027	.018	.013	.005	.002	.001	.001	.000
14	.870	.758	.661	.577	.505	.442	.388	.340	.299	.263	.205	.160	.141	.125	.099	.078	.049	.032	.021	.014	.009	.003	.001	.001	.000	.000
15	.861	.743	.642	.555	.481	.417	.362	.315	.275	.239	.183	.140	.123	.108	.084	.065	.040	.025	.016	.010	.006	.002	.001	.000	.000	.000
16	.853	.728	.623	.534	.458	.394	.339	.292	.252	.218	.163	.123	.107	.093	.071	.054	.032	.019	.012	.007	.005	.002	.001	.000	.000	
17	.844	.714	.605	.513	.436	.371	.317	.270	.231	.198	.146	.108	.093	.080	.060	.045	.026	.015	.009	.005	.003	.001	.000	.000		
18	.836	.700	.587	.494	.416	.350	.296	.250	.212	.180	.130	.095	.081	.069	.051	.038	.021	.012	.007	.004	.002	.001	.000	.000		
19	.828	.686	.570	.475	.396	.331	.276	.232	.194	.164	.116	.083	.070	.060	.043	.031	.017	.009	.005	.003	.002	.000	.000			
20	.820	.673	.554	.456	.377	.312	.258	.215	.178	.149	.104	.073	.061	.051	.037	.026	.014	.007	.004	.002	.001	.000	.000			
25	.780	.610	.478	.375	.295	.233	.184	.146	.116	.092	.059	.038	.030	.024	.016	.010	.005	.002	.001	.000	.000					
30	.742	.552	.412	.308	.231	.174	.131	.099	.075	.057	.033	.020	.015	.012	.007	.004	.002	.001	.000	.000						

appendix

Interest Factors for the Future Value of an Annuity of One Dollar: $FVAIF = \frac{(1 + i)^n - 1}{i}$

Time period (e.g., year)	1%	2%	3%	4%	5%	6%	7%	8%	9%	10%	12%	14%	16%	20%
1	1.000	1.000	1.000	1.000	1.000	1.000	1.000	1.000	1.000	1.000	1.000	1.000	1.000	1.000
2	2.010	2.020	2.030	2.040	2.050	2.060	2.070	2.080	2.090	2.100	2.120	2.140	2.160	2.200
3	3.030	3.060	3.091	3.122	3.152	3.184	3.215	3.246	3.278	3.310	3.374	3.440	3.506	3.640
4	4.060	4.122	4.184	4.246	4.310	4.375	4.440	4.506	4.573	4.641	4.770	4.921	5.067	5.368
5	5.101	5.204	5.309	5.416	5.526	5.637	5.751	5.867	5.985	6.105	6.353	6.610	6.877	7.442
6	6.152	6.308	6.468	6.633	6.802	6.975	7.153	7.336	7.523	7.716	8.115	8.536	8.978	9.930
7	7.214	7.434	7.662	7.898	8.142	8.394	8.654	8.923	9.200	9.487	10.089	10.730	11.413	12.915
8	8.286	8.583	8.892	9.214	9.549	9.897	10.260	10.637	11.028	11.436	12.300	13.233	14.240	16.499
9	9.369	9.755	10.159	10.583	11.027	11.491	11.978	12.488	13.021	13.579	14.776	16.085	17.518	20.798
10	10.462	10.950	11.464	12.006	12.578	13.181	13.816	14.487	15.193	15.937	17.549	19.337	21.321	25.958
11	11.567	12.169	12.808	13.486	14.207	14.972	15.784	16.645	17.560	18.531	20.655	23.044	25.732	32.150
12	12.683	13.412	14.192	15.026	15.917	16.870	17.888	18.977	20.141	21.384	24.138	27.271	30.850	39.580
13	13.809	14.680	15.618	16.627	17.713	18.882	20.141	21.495	22.953	24.523	28.029	32.089	36.786	48.496
14	14.947	15.974	17.086	18.292	19.599	21.051	22.550	24.215	26.019	27.975	32.393	37.581	43.672	59.195
15	16.097	17.293	18.599	20.024	21.579	23.276	25.129	27.152	29.361	31.772	37.280	43.842	51.659	72.035
16	17.258	18.639	20.157	21.825	23.657	25.673	27.888	30.324	33.003	35.950	42.753	50.980	60.925	87.442
17	18.430	20.012	21.762	23.698	25.840	28.213	30.840	33.750	36.974	40.545	48.884	59.118	71.673	105.93
18	19.615	21.412	23.414	25.645	28.132	30.906	33.999	37.450	41.301	45.599	55.750	68.934	84.140	128.11
19	20.811	22.841	25.117	27.671	30.539	33.760	37.379	41.446	46.018	51.159	63.440	78.969	98.603	154.74
20	22.019	24.297	26.870	29.778	33.066	36.786	40.995	45.762	51.160	57.275	72.052	91.025	115.37	186.68
25	28.243	32.030	36.459	41.646	47.727	54.865	63.249	73.106	84.701	98.347	133.33	181.87	249.21	471.98
30	34.785	40.568	47.575	56.085	66.439	79.058	94.461	113.283	136.308	164.494	241.333	356.787	530.310	1181.8

appendix

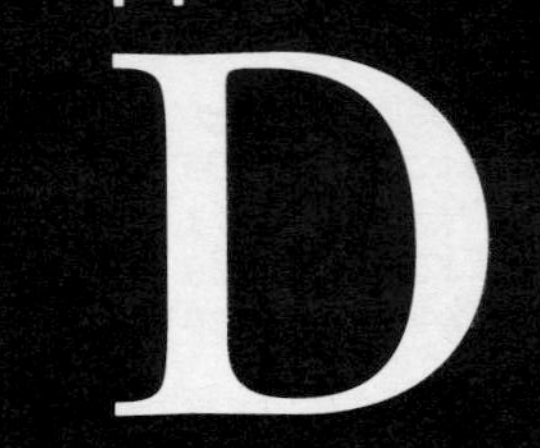

Interest Factors for the Present Value of an Annuity of One Dollar: PVAIF = $\frac{1 - \frac{1}{(1+i)^n}}{i}$

Time period (e.g., year)	1%	2%	3%	4%	5%	6%	7%	8%	9%	10%	12%	14%	16%	18%	20%	24%	28%	32%	36%
1	0.990	0.980	0.971	0.962	0.952	0.943	0.935	0.926	0.917	0.909	0.893	0.877	0.862	0.847	0.833	0.806	0.781	0.758	0.735
2	1.970	1.942	1.913	1.886	1.859	1.833	1.808	1.783	1.759	1.736	1.690	1.647	1.605	1.566	1.528	1.457	1.392	1.332	1.276
3	2.941	2.884	2.829	2.775	2.723	2.673	2.624	2.577	2.531	2.487	2.402	2.322	2.246	2.174	2.106	1.981	1.868	1.766	1.674
4	3.902	3.808	3.717	3.630	3.546	3.465	3.387	3.312	3.240	3.170	3.037	2.914	2.798	2.690	2.589	2.404	2.241	2.096	1.966
5	4.853	4.713	4.580	4.452	4.329	4.212	4.100	3.993	3.890	3.791	3.605	3.433	3.274	3.127	2.991	2.745	2.532	2.345	2.181
6	5.795	5.601	5.417	5.242	5.076	4.917	4.766	4.623	4.486	4.355	4.111	3.889	3.685	3.498	3.326	3.020	2.759	2.534	2.399
7	6.728	6.472	6.230	6.002	5.786	5.582	5.389	5.206	5.033	4.868	4.574	4.288	4.039	3.812	3.605	3.242	2.937	2.678	2.455
8	7.652	7.325	7.020	6.733	6.463	6.210	5.971	5.747	5.535	5.335	4.968	4.639	4.344	4.078	3.837	3.421	3.076	2.786	2.540
9	8.566	8.162	7.786	7.435	7.108	6.802	6.515	6.247	5.985	5.759	5.328	4.946	4.607	4.303	4.031	3.566	3.184	2.868	2.603
10	9.471	8.983	8.530	8.111	7.722	7.360	7.024	6.710	6.418	6.145	5.650	5.216	4.833	4.494	4.193	3.682	3.269	2.930	2.650
11	10.368	9.787	9.253	8.760	8.306	7.887	7.499	7.139	6.805	6.495	5.988	5.453	5.029	4.656	4.327	3.776	3.335	2.978	2.683
12	11.255	10.575	9.954	9.385	8.863	8.384	7.943	7.536	7.161	6.814	6.194	5.660	5.197	4.793	4.439	3.851	3.387	3.013	2.708
13	12.134	11.348	10.635	9.986	9.394	8.853	8.358	7.904	7.487	7.103	6.424	5.842	5.342	4.910	4.533	3.912	3.427	3.040	2.727
14	13.004	12.106	11.296	10.563	9.899	9.295	8.745	8.244	7.786	7.367	6.628	6.002	5.468	5.008	4.611	3.962	3.459	3.061	2.740
15	13.865	12.849	11.938	11.118	10.380	9.712	9.108	8.559	8.060	7.606	6.811	6.142	5.575	5.092	4.675	4.001	3.483	3.076	2.750
16	14.718	13.578	12.561	11.652	10.838	10.106	9.447	8.851	8.312	7.824	6.974	6.265	5.669	5.162	4.730	4.003	3.503	3.088	2.758
17	15.562	14.292	13.166	12.166	11.274	10.477	9.763	9.122	8.544	8.022	7.120	6.373	5.749	5.222	4.775	4.059	3.518	3.097	2.763
18	16.398	14.992	13.754	12.659	11.690	10.828	10.059	9.372	8.756	8.201	7.250	6.467	5.818	5.273	4.812	4.080	3.529	3.104	2.767
19	17.226	15.678	14.324	13.134	12.085	11.158	10.336	9.604	8.950	8.365	7.366	6.550	5.877	5.316	4.844	4.097	3.539	3.109	2.770
20	18.046	16.351	14.877	13.590	12.462	11.470	10.594	9.818	9.128	8.514	7.469	6.623	5.929	5.353	4.870	4.110	3.546	3.113	2.772
25	22.023	19.523	17.413	15.622	14.094	12.783	11.654	10.675	9.823	9.077	7.843	6.873	6.097	5.467	4.948	4.147	3.564	3.122	2.776
30	25.808	22.397	19.600	17.292	15.373	13.765	12.409	11.258	10.274	9.427	8.055	7.003	6.177	5.517	4.979	4.160	3.569	3.124	2.778

appendix

E

Answers to Selected Problems

Chapter 5

1. \$1/1.25 = 0.8 pounds
2. Balance on current account (\$1.7)
   Balance on capital account (\$16.5)
4. a. payment in terms of the current price: \$1,600,000
   b. payment in terms of the futures price: \$1,560,000
   c. loss = (\$250,000)
   d. \$40,000

Chapter 6

1. margin = 25%; return = 100%
2. margin = 75%; return = (33%)
3. collateral = \$53; return = (17%)

4. b. $396
   d. (39.2%)

Chapter 7

These answers assume the use of the interest tables. Since the tables use discrete numbers, some answers can only be approximated. Exact answers may be derived through the use of electronic calculator programs.

1. a. $1,967
2. a. $68,643
   b. $109,658
3. total accumulated: $126,498
   annual withdrawals: $11,941
5. $114,700
6. PVA: $4,029
   PVB: $3,731
7. b. $503,150
8. a. $26.76
   b. $35.24 (The increase in interest more than doubles since $15.24 is more than two times $6.76.)
9. b. $144,104
10. 15%
11. $6,000
12. At 6% select the $900; at 14% select $150 for five years.
13. approximately 4 years
14. $32,036
17. $16,274
18. 12%
19. $31,273

Chapter 7 Appendix

1. Bob: $91,524
   Betty: $98,846
2. Investment B: $6,253

Chapter 8

1. 5.75%
3. a. 13%
   b. 15.18%
4. a. average return A: 18%
   average return B: 18%
   b. standard deviation A: ±8.4%
   standard deviation A: ±2.55%
5. realized return: 3.25%

Chapter 9

The bond valuation answers assume annual compounding.

1. a. $1,171
   b. $1,076
   e. current yields: 10.25% and 11.15%
   yields to maturity: 10% and 10%
2. XY: $596
   AB: $1,341
3. a. 7.2%
   b. approximately 10%
   c. $810.50
4. b. $856
   d. $1,126
5. a. Bond A: $1,000
   Bond B: $629
6. $204
7. a. $1,000
   d. $467,639.36

Chapter 10

1. a. cash: $26,000,000
   retained earnings: $60,000,000
   common stock: no change
   b. cash: no change
   retained earnings: $56,000,000
   common stock: 2,100,000 shares outstanding
   $105,000,000 value of common stock
   paid-in capital: $11,000,000

3. earnings per share: $2.10
   total equity: no change
   long-term debt: no change
   paid-in capital: no change
   shares outstanding: 2,000,000
   earnings: $4,200,000 (no change)
4. times-interest-earned (for preferred stock in 19X1): 5.0X
5. a. new price: $18
   b. new price: $49.09

Chapter 11

1. a. $40
   b. $48.96
3. b. loss: $167
   loss: $113
4. a. $26.50
   b. $39.75
   c. $30.29
   d. $23.33
   e. $23.92
5. a. $15.29 < $23
6. a. 13.6%
   c. $29.04
   e. $36.89
7. b. stock A: 16.8%
   stock B: 12.6%
8. value of stock A: $4
   value of stock B: $9.45
9. a. required return: 13.4%
   value: $61.93

Chapter 12

1. a. 4.8%
   b. $864
   c. $38.52
   d. $176
   e. $817.40
   f. $222.60

2. a. $552.14
   b. 40 shares
   c. $1,200
   d. $1,200
   f. $1,040
3. a. $11.22

Chapter 13

1. a. $2,500
   b. $29,400
   c. 11.8%
   d. (12%)
   e. (100%)
2. intrinsic value $30 option: $5
   time premium: $2½
   loss on $30 option: ($6½)
3. a. intrinsic value: $1
      time premium: $3
   b. value of the warrant if stock is $20: $0
      value of the warrant if stock is $25: $0
      value of the warrant if stock is $30: $5
      value of the warrant if stock is $40: $15
   c. return on stock: 73.1%
      return on option: 400%
4. a. $1
   b. $4
   c. declines
   d. $5
   e. no limit
   f. $1
   g. ($1)
   h. ($5)
   i. $5
6. b. $3
   c. $2
7. b. At price of the stock = $40, writer makes $3.

Chapter 14

1. a. NAV = $7.68
3. 42.0%
4. 19.96%

Chapter 15

1. a. $280
   b. $280
   c. $280
3. straight-line: $10,000 annually except years 1 and 11
   accelerated (10-year schedule):
   year 1: $4,000
   year 2: $14,000
   year 3: $12,000
4. year 2: net earnings: $7,500
   cash flow: $9,500

Chapter 16

1. Income statement:

Sales	$1,000,000
Cost of goods sold	600,000
Other expenses	100,000
EBIT	300,000
Interest	80,000
EBT	220,000
Taxes	100,000
Net earnings	$ 120,000
Earnings per share	$1.20

Balance Sheet:

Assets	
cash	$ 50,000
accounts receivable	250,000
inventory	300,000
plant and equipment	400,000
Total assets	$1,000,000
Liabilities	
accounts payable	$ 200,000
other current liabilities	50,000
long-term debt	300,000
Equity	450,000
Liabilities & equity	$1,000,000

2. earnings per share: $2.48
5. current ratio: 1.84 : 1
   quick ratio: 0.92 : 1
6. 95 days (assumes 365-day year)
7. debt/net worth: 1.5
   debt ratio: 60%
8. $75,000 decline
9. times-interest-earned issue C: 0.7
10. $3,167,137
11. operating profit margin–A: 15%
    net profit margin–A: 9%
    return on assets–A: 18%
    return on equity–A: 22.5%
12. return on total equity: 11.7%
    return on common equity: 12.2%
14. Summary for 19X0

current ratio	3.9 : 1
quick ratio	0.5 : 1
average collection period	1 day
inventory turnover (Sales/Inventory)	4.0
operating profit margin	9.9%
net profit margin	5.1%
return on assets	14.7%
return on equity	20.9%
debt ratio	29.8%
times-interest-earned	10.3X

Chapter 17

1. a. profit at 2,000: $4,600
   c. 1,887 units
2. a. 3,000 units
   b. 2.5
   c. 1.43
   d. break-even level: 3,333 units
      degree of operating leverage at 5,000 units: 3
      degree of operating leverage at 10,000 units: 1.5
4. a. break-even levels of output: 2,500 and 3,125
   b. $3,000 in both cases
   c. cash generated $900 and $700, respectively
6. a. break-even level: 71,429
      earnings: $50,000

b. 100,000 units
c. 62,500 units
d. 87,500 units

7\. d. Earnings rise from $40,000 to $54,000 for a 35 percent increase

9\. a. net earnings: $10
b. net earnings: $6.67
c. return on equity: 10% and 13.34%

10\. c. degree of financial leverage firm B: 1.2
d. B's income rises from $2,500 to $4,000

Chapter 18

1.	a.	accounts receivable	$300
		inventory	$600
		trade accounts payable	$300
	b.	external funds needed: $50	
	c.	accounts receivable	$300
		inventory	600
		plant	800
		total assets	$1,700
		trade accounts	300
		long-term debt	650
		equity	750
		total liabilities and equity	$1,700
3.	a.	accounts receivable:	$10,310
		inventory:	7,864
		accounts payable:	5,729
	b.	forecasted expansion in accounts receivable:	$3,110
		inventory:	1,764
		accounts payable:	429
	c.	earnings to be retained: $2,400	

4\. excess cash (shortage):

January	($120)
February	($220)
March	($40)
April	($240)
May	$160
June	$100

5\. shortage in cash:

January	($98,000)
February	($138,000)

7. a. balance sheet entries for 19X1:

accounts receivable	$2,400,000
inventory	1,800,000
accruals	1,800,000
accounts payable	1,200,000
retained earnings (increase in)	252,000

excess funds generated: $52,000

c. balance sheet entries for 19X1:

accounts receivable	$1,540,000
inventory	2,050,000
accruals	940,000
accounts payable	1,210,000
retained earnings (increase in)	252,000

external funds needed: $188,000

8. external funds required: $300
9. cash shortage in February ($75,000)
   cash shortage in March ($105,000)
   excess cash in April $5,000

Chapter 19

1. a. earnings with bank loan: $231,000
      earnings with insurance company loan: $217,000
   b. earnings year 2, bank loan: $203,000
      earnings year 2, insurance company loan: $217,000
2. a. return on equity–alternative a: 9.6%
      return on equity–alternative b: 13.2%
      return on equity–alternative c: 11.2%
   b. return on equity–alternative a: 6.0%
      return on equity–alternative b: 7.6%
      return on equity–alternative c: 5.2%
3. a. 120 units
   b. duration of EOQ: 9 days
      41–42 orders a year
4. $27,204
5. not overdue: 24.1%
   20–30 days overdue: 31.7%
6. tax saving: $9,600
7. a. supplier A: 368 units
      supplier B: 316 units
   b. average inventory supplier A: 284

c. maximum inventory supplier A: 468
   minimum inventory supplier A: 100
d. 212 units

8. a. 5,000 units
   b. approximately January 16
   c. maximum safety stock: 2,740 units
   d. maximum inventory: 7,740
      minimum inventory: 2,740
      average inventory: 5,240
   e. EOQ: 7,071 units
      average inventory: 9,016 units
9. additional sales: $1,000,000
   total costs: $775,000

Chapter 20

1. 16.67%
2. a. 37.1% (true cost = 44.1%)
   b. 36.7% (true cost = 43.8%)
3. 0%
4. 4.8%
5. Both cost 10.53%.
6. a. bank A: 13.3%
      bank B: 13.5%
   b. bank A: 15.0%
      bank B: 13.5%
7. commercial paper: 10.68%
   Treasury bill: 8.58%
8. a. 9.57%
9. 19.46%

Chapter 21

1. annual payment: $25,706.94
   answers for year 2:
   interest payment: $7,496.38
   principal repayment: $18,210.56
   balance owed: $65,082.50

2. a. annual payment: \$2,637.83
   answers for year 3:
   interest payment: \$656.06
   principal repayment: \$1,981.77
   balance owed: \$4,578.79
   b. annual payment: \$2,000
   answers for year 3:
   interest payment: \$600
   principal repayment: \$2,000
   balance owed: \$4,000
   c. answers for year 3:
   interest payment: \$1,000
   principal repayment: \$0
   balance owed: \$10,000
   d. answers for year 3:
   interest payment: \$800
   principal repayment: \$1,000
   balance owed: \$7,000
3. cash outflows owning: year 1 \$25,700
   year 2 \$23,900
   cash outflows leasing: year 1 \$15,805
   year 2 \$15,805
4. \$23,093

Chapter 22

1. a. cost of capital at 40% debt: 12.0%
   b. debt \$20; equity \$80
2. a. cost of capital at 20% debt: 7.2%
3. d. stockholders earn 12.86%
4. a. 6%
   b. 11.1%
   c. 12.35%
   d. 10.32%

Chapter 23

1. a. NPVA: \$33
   NPVB: \$17
   b. IRRA: approximately 14% (14.7%)
   IRRB: 12%

2. a. NPVA: ($166)
   c. IRRB: 20%
   f. $4,356
3. a. NPVA: ($51)
   b. IRRB: 15%
   c. at 15%: $1,887
5. NPV: ($177)
6. 8%
9. a. 40% debt
   cost of capital: 10.4%
10. a. NPVS: $181.70
    c. terminal value S: $1,827
    terminal value L: $2,072
12. IRR: 18%

Chapter 24

1. a. total assets: $8,000
   accounts payable: $800
2. a. shares issued: 120,000
   EPS: $4.64
   b. $46.64
3. c. $0

Index